gale
encyclopedia of
e-commerce

gale encyclopedia of e-commerce

Volume 1
A–I

Jane A. Malonis, Editor

Foreword by Dr. Paula J. Haynes

GALE GROUP

THOMSON LEARNING ™

*Detroit • New York • San Diego • San Francisco
Boston • New Haven, Conn. • Waterville, Maine
London • Munich*

Staff

Editorial: Jane A. Malonis, *Senior Editor.* Erin Braun, *Managing Editor, Business Content.*
Jacqueline K. Mueckenheim, *Managing Editor, Business Product.* Paul Lewon, *Technical Training Specialist.*

Product Design: Cynthia Baldwin, Michelle DiMercurio, *Senior Art Directors.*

Composition and Electronic Prepress: Mary Beth Trimper, *Manager.* Evi Seoud, *Assistant Manager.*
Rhonda Williams, *Buyer.*

Library of Congress Cataloging-in-Publication Data

Gale encyclopedia of E-commerce / Jane A. Malonis, editor.
　　　　p. cm.
Includes bibliographical references and index.
　　ISBN 0-7876-5660-7 (set : hardcover) — ISBN 0-7876-5748-4 (vol. 1) —ISBN
0-7876-5749-2 (vol. 2)
　　1. Electronic commerce—Encyclopedias. I. Malonis, Jane A.
　　HF5548.32 .G35 2002
　　381'.1—dc21

2001055543

ISBN 0-7876-5660-7 (set), ISBN 0-7876-5748-4 (Vol. 1), ISBN 0-7876-5749-2 (Vol. 2)

CONTENTS

This first edition of the *Gale Encyclopedia of E-Commerce (GEE)* presents a comprehensive look at the topics and terms, companies, people, events, and legislation most relevant to the e-commerce industry. Designed for e-enterpreneurs and students performing industry research, as well as for individuals simply interested in understanding the industry more fully, *GEE* is an all-encompassing source of the information most critical to understanding the e-commerce industry.

Through over 470 essays, readers will encounter a wide array of information on the terminology, players, people, and laws in the industry, including:

- Advanced Encryption Standard (AES)
- Advertising, Online
- Auction Sites
- Banking, Online
- Jeff Bezos
- Business-to-Business (B2B) E-Commerce
- Business-to-Consumer (B2C) E-Commerce
- Cyberstrategy
- Digital Cash
- E-tailing
- David Filo
- Global E-Commerce (Africa, Asia, Australia, Central and South America, Europe, and North America)
- Internet Tax Freedom Act
- Novell Inc.

- Pierre Omidyar
- Shipping and Shipment Tracking
- Travelocity.com
- Web Site, Design and Set-up of
- Yahoo! Inc.

GEE's essays offer a unique starting point for individuals seeking comprehensive information that can't be adequately conveyed through brief dictionary-like definitions. Put into context, the topics covered in these volumes are of both current and enduring interest.

ADDITIONAL FEATURES
1. Contents are arranged alphabetically from A to Z across two volumes
2. One enhanced multi-tiered Master Index simplifies accessibility
3. Cross-references abound to help readers locate information
4. "Chronology and Timeline" of the events critical in shaping the industry
5. "Further Reading" section at the end of each essay provides source suggestions for further study, including URLs

Composed by business writers, under the guidance of an expert advisory panel, *GEE* represents a substantial contribution to general business reference. Students, scholars, and business practitioners alike will find a wealth of information in these new volumes.

INTERNET BEGINNINGS

It was breaking news—an earthquake had rocked the San Francisco Bay area, just as many commuters crowded the roads, bridges, and mass transit for home. My best friend and her husband were two of those commuters. Were they injured, trapped, maybe worse? You could not get an open phone line to that part of the West Coast for days. Too many people, just like me, were trying to find out if friends and family were alright. My friend worked in one of the many computer-related businesses in the Bay area and we often e-mailed each other. So that's what I did: in the midst of all the chaos in the San Francisco area, I e-mailed her asking if her family was OK. They were, she let me know quickly. Our computers and e-mail let us accomplish something while other ways of communicating were not available. She had ended her message to me with the words "BITNET rules!"

"Wait a minute," you say, "BITNET? And wasn't that earthquake in 1989? No one's computer was saying 'you've got mail' then!" The answer is both 'yes' and 'no.' In 1989, computers were not a common part of most households. Desktop computers could be found in most businesses, but not on every desk. BITNET (Because It's Time Network) was a network that linked IBM mainframe computers together beginning in 1981. Earlier, the Internet (Interconnected Network) had been launched on a small scale when computers at three universities in the United States were linked in 1969. Driving the development of computer networks were the needs to communi-cate quickly and to be able to respond to information effectively.

Exchanging text messages was the main focus of these fledgling networks, with most users connected to the military or to academic institutions. The sending of text, or communicating through what became termed "e-mail," dominated the use of the Internet for its first twenty years. This new way of sending messages seemed surprisingly efficient. Answering machines and voice mail were not yet common. Use of e-mail reduced the frustration of "phone tag." Instead of trying to time phone calls based on differences in time zones, users could send and receive messages on their individual schedules. But for most of us during that period, e-mail was something we had not even heard about.

BROWSERS SHIFT INTERNET FOCUS

For years, most of the digital information flowing through computer networks had been text. That was about to change. In 1989, a new approach was introduced. Instead of requiring you to remember specific, and often awkward, text commands, this new approach let you select highlighted words (hypertext) and then click-linked you easily to other people, places, and information. This was the World Wide Web, which uses the Internet to link sites (or Web pages) locally and remotely. The tool that made the Web feasible for most of us was called a "browser." Browser software let us move more easily and quickly through the content the Web offered. Instead of figuratively rummaging about in our grandmother's attic with only one forty-watt bulb for illumination, we suddenly had lots of 100-watt bulbs for every nook and cranny. We were no longer limited to text, but pictures, moving and still, and audio were now possible. "Ah," we thought, "they've made it easier for us to use." And so they had. The official terminology for this tool was a "graphical user interface (GUI) that provided transparent technology for the user."

BUSINESS USE OF THE INTERNET

The next change involved the way the Internet computer network was funded. U.S. government funding had launched the original network, so commercial use had been restricted. Independent commercial networks began to grow so that by the early 1990s it was possible to send messages across the country without passing through the government funded Internet backbone. In 1994, the U.S. government eliminated its subsidy for the Internet, removing the commercial restrictions that funding had previously imposed.

The need to communicate quickly and effectively is critical to a commercial organization. The Internet represented a tool with enormous potential for these entities. People within organizations could swiftly and easily get in touch with one another. A firm with a Web site could let any potential customer, anywhere in the world, see who they were and what they had to offer. An alternative way to do business had begun. The ability to complete transactions using the Internet (e-commerce) would become essential in many organizations' operations.

Business use drove much of the growth of the Internet and the Web through the 1990s. In the early part of the decade, most of us did not have a computer at home. We may have had one at work, however. The workplace had been home for computers for many years. In the 1970s businesses began using networked computers to exchange information (electronic data interchange or EDI) and to perform financial transactions (electronic funds transfer or EFT). E-commerce, or the completion of transactions online, was inherent in these early business activities. Business had been using a form of e-commerce for nearly two decades by 1990. The idea of using the emerging global Internet for transactions didn't seem to be so different. How would their customers feel?

Businesses often have other businesses as their customers. Many business customers felt great about the possibilities of e-commerce and the Internet. However, using the Internet in their daily operations would require firms to invest in technology and training. These requirements may have seemed a major obstacle to small- and medium-sized organizations. Larger companies, with greater resources, often had spearheaded the use of technology in their operations. Such companies frequently had entire departments devoted to training personnel to deal with their technology. Before the Internet, only these large companies could afford private computer networks. The speed and efficiency of EDI and EFT were limited to these companies. Though small- and medium-sized firms were concerned about learning to use the technology, they also realized that any sized business could use the Internet to exchange information within their own company and with other businesses. The size of your company was not the limiting factor in being able to incorporate digital technologies that could enhance your operations. The Internet represented a new opportunity for these businesses.

HOUSEHOLD USERS AND E-COMMERCE

Household customers didn't have twenty years of familiarity with the idea of exchanging information digitally. What could the Internet offer that would make the idea of e-commerce from home seem like something perfectly reasonable instead of bringing to mind a scene from a science fiction novel? Maybe it began when we realized we were already performing digital transactions every time we used our credit cards, or when we stopped by an ATM to get cash. More of us bought home computers and Internet Service Providers (ISPs) began offering easier and faster ways to connect our computers online. Our first usage may have been e-mails to family and friends. They may have told us about Web sites that we would find interesting. There is a certain fascination with being able to explore an area filled with things that are both familiar and new. Like the boxes and trunks in our grandmother's attic, the Internet seemed filled with possibilities, both great and trivial. After our initial exploration through the area, we often started being more practical. In a sense, we brought the items we could use every day down from the attic, "bookmarking" or storing sites in our "favorites" folder. On these and other sites we began to check out businesses and products that interested us. We could do this according to our own schedules, whether it was the middle of the day or the middle of the night. Instead of being limited to the choices we might find listed in our local telephone directory, it was possible to browse choices from other areas, from anywhere in the world. We began to purchase online. E-commerce had arrived in our homes.

SECURITY AND E-COMMERCE TRANSACTIONS

Whether we are making purchases for our businesses or our households, this final step raises one of the major issues of using the Internet for completing transactions: security. When companies operated their own much smaller networks security issues seemed important, but manageable. A network increases in value to its users with the number of connections. If you and I can only talk to one another, that has a certain value. If we can each talk to anyone in the world, at any time, that network of connections would be far more valuable. However, as networks become more extensive, security issues also increase in size and number.

When we use a credit card for purchases in a store, account information is transmitted (often online) for our financial institution's payment approval. Similar actions must also take place with e-commerce transactions, with all of the account and approval information sent through the network of computers that make up the Internet. Access to that information should be limited only to the persons and organizations directly involved: the transaction should be secure. Whether between businesses and other business customers, or our own households, the use of e-commerce means such security issues must be addressed. "Well," you might say, "I never buy anything online, so this problem doesn't affect me." Perhaps. Remember that the organizations we deal with in person are likely to use the Internet to place orders with their suppliers, or to get approval on our credit card purchases. When only large companies with proprietary networks were exchanging digital information, security and privacy issues certainly existed. Now, organizations of all sizes and types use the Internet as a tool to exchange digital information. A garden ornament store in Maine increases its order of moose-shaped vegetable markers. A southern state's Web site allows citizens to renew their driver's licenses online. A catalog merchandiser out of Wyoming reduces its unsold inventory by offering items in online auction sites. Even if we are not a direct party to any of these transactions, they may affect our household's choices and decisions. Security and privacy in digital transactions are important, whether or not we are directly engaged in online buying.

When only a few of us have a problem, it may take some time to come up with possible solutions. However, when a great many of us share a similar problem, the speed and extent of the search for answers increases rapidly. Consequently, several solutions to e-commerce security concerns have been adopted. We learn we may need special software at home to provide a "firewall." The precautions of user names and passwords may be needed to access confidential information. When we, or companies, need to exchange confidential information such as credit-card numbers or payment authorization codes, we will enter into a secure area of a Web site. Just as signs mark the checkout area of a store, the transaction area of a Web site will also be clearly designated. Your browser will likely open a small window letting you know when you are entering or leaving these secure areas. Think of those times that you needed to access your safe deposit box at your bank. You would go to a certain location in the bank to make the request, bringing your personal safe-deposit box key with you. Bank personnel would use both your key and a bank key to open your box. Use of the two keys helped provide secure access to the box. Secure areas of Web sites also involve special requirements for access. Information you send from a secure site is coded, or encrypted, with a special key required to decode the message. We at our computers at home or work do not have to create or understand complicated codes to use these security procedures. This technology is also transparent—easy for us to use.

BALANCING PRIVACY AND PERSONALIZATION

Privacy is perhaps a more complicated matter. For a secure transaction, it will be necessary to verify that you are who you say you are. It may be a prank when someone orders a pizza to be delivered to a fictitious address. On a thousand-fold scale it would not seem to be a prank at all, but something much more serious. We also like being treated as individuals, not just as numbers. We may prefer our browser to look a certain way, or open with a focus on the news categories we are most interested in. We may be pleased when the travel site we use welcomes us by name each time we log on. The convenience of being able to access our financial information online may now be essential to us. All of these things require personalization. To receive the degree of individual treatment we want, we cannot remain anonymous. Privacy must also be balanced against our desire for personalized treatment.

UNDERSTANDING THE ROLE OF E-COMMERCE

Still think e-commerce doesn't have much to do with you? Have you ever bought anything? Well, e-commerce may have entered into any of those purchases. The pervasive role of e-commerce and the Internet in our daily lives is reflected in many of the terms and phrases we hear every day. Some of the language of e-commerce uses metaphors for things we already know and understand. "Surfing" can now be done "on the Web." A "cookie" is what allows you to check your bank account balance online. The phrase "you've got mail" may herald a message from a family member, your boss, or a company. The e-mail you check may include "spam" or, in a more unfortunate instance, a "computer virus." Other aspects of e-commerce are dominated by less familiar sounding acronyms such as HTML, B2B, URL, and ASP.

Your goal may be to gain a passing acquaintance with this new language of business. Or, you may wish to deepen your understanding of the fundamental shifts that changing technology has caused in business and society. The *Gale Encyclopedia of* *E-Commerce* allows a wide variety of readers to achieve their goals. In addition to the key terms and ideas described and discussed in these pages, we also meet many of the people who created the ideas and technologies involved in e-commerce. It is clear we are not at the end, but in the midst of the changes that e-commerce brings to the world of business. The essays in these volumes offer us a chance to better understand the impact of e-commerce, both now and in the future.

Dr. Paula J. Haynes
George Lester Nation Centennial Professorship of
Entrepreneurship
College of Business Administration
University of Tennessee, Chattanooga

PREFACE

Welcome to the first edition of the *Gale Encyclopedia of E-Commerce (GEE)*. Published in recognition of today's rapidly evolving business landscape, these volumes offer readers solid explanations of relevant concepts, issues, and terms, as well as profiles of pioneering companies, organizations, and individuals seen at the forefront of the e-commerce revolution. Readers new to the world of electronic business will find a wealth of basic information designed to answer their immediate questions and light their research path. Those already versed in the specifics of the New Economy will find in *GEE's* essays useful background that lends richer context to their daily e-business interactions.

GEE includes coverage of topics both far-ranging and finely focused. Into the former category might fall an overview of online business models, a general discussion of advertising in cyberspace, or a broad view of global internet security concerns. Within the latter category, readers can expect to find guidance on the ins and outs of designing a "storefront" or relaunching a Web site, the definitions of terms like "disintermediation" and "Weblining," or Timothy Berners-Lee's take on the state of his brainchild, the World Wide Web. Among the people covered in GEE are true pioneers (think Bill Gates, Gordon Moore, Robert Noyce, and Dr. Nicholas Negroponte) and, of course, many of the youthful visionaries who have made their way into the spotlight over the last few years.

GEE's coverage of firms that have in some way significantly impacted, or been crucially impacted by, the online revolution is not intended to be all-encompassing, but rather, our intention is to provide in these pages a strong sampling of companies that, as a whole, help to tell the story—sometimes in colorful and dramatic ways—of the internet's influence on business practice and business culture. Mega-mergers, flash-in-the-pans, established bricks-and-mortars, and heroic survivors are all represented here. During the Gold Rush days of the 1800s, you didn't necessarily have to be a gold miner to benefit from the shiny substance unearthed from the ground. And so it is today; you don't have to be a computer manufacturer in order to reap the rewards, and to suffer the risks, of taking part in the internet economy. You just have to log-on, and go where you want the Web to take you. We invite you to open these volumes, and step into the dynamic and compelling world of e-commerce.

USER'S GUIDE

GEE has been designed for ease of use. Comprised of two volumes, the essays are arranged alphabetically from A to Z by topic title throughout the set, and all essay titles are listed in full for easy perusal within the Table of Contents.

Included at the end of most essays are two special features: "Further Reading" sections, designed to reference quoted source material and to point readers toward suggested sources for further study, and "See Also" references, which refer the reader to essays of closely related interest elsewhere within *GEE*.

At the back of the second volume is a list of suggested Books for Additional Reading, and the Master Index, a tiered, cumulative listing of thousands of citations with their corresponding volume and page numbers. The Master Index contains, specifically, alphabetical references to the following as mentioned within GEE essays: important or unusual terms; names of companies, institutions, organizations, and associations; specific legislation; relevant court cases; key events; and names of prominent or historically important individuals.

ACKNOWLEDGMENTS

The editors gratefully acknowledge the wise counsel and helpful suggestions of our advisors.

David P. Bianco, M.B.A., M.A.
Business author, editor, and consultant specializing in advertising, marketing, and public relations.

Marilyn M. Helms, D.B.A., CFPIM, CIRM
Professor and Sesquicentennial Endowed Chair
Division of Business and Technology
Dalton State College
Dalton, Georgia

Special thanks to foreword writer Dr. Paula J. Haynes, holder of the George Lester Nation Centennial Professorship of Entrepreneurship in the Marketing Department of the College of Business Administration at the University of Tennessee, Chattanooga. Dr. Haynes has served as a consultant to a variety of for profit and not-for-profit organizations on quality program implementation, market analysis, and survey procedures. Her current research interests focus on the entrepreneurial process and the impact of the internet on marketing activities.

A significant debt of gratitude is owed to our contributing writers, listed here in alphabetical order: David P. Bianco, Gerald E. Brennan, Paul R. Greenland, Allison Jones, Tom Rajt, and AnnaMarie L. Sheldon.

COMMENTS AND SUGGESTIONS

Comments and suggestions regarding the *Gale Encyclopedia of E-Commerce* are invited and encouraged. Please contact:

Managing Editor, Business Product
Gale Group
27500 Drake Rd.
Farmington Hills, MI 48331-3535
Telephone: 800-347-GALE
BusinessProducts@gale.com

1904 The Fleming valve, the first vacuum tube, is patented by Sir John A. Fleming.

1905 Albert Einstein publishes the theory of relativity.

1915 The first transcontinental call, between San Francisco and New York, is placed by researchers working at AT&T.

1920 Czech author Karel Capek coins the word, "robot."

1924 The Computing-Tabulating-Recording Company is renamed International Business Machines (IBM).

1934 Federal legislation is passed in the form of the Communications Act in an attempt to begin regulation of the telephone industry.

1939 The first digital computer prototype is created at Iowa State College by Clifford Berry and John Atanasoff. Hewlett-Packard is founded.

1941 Regular television broadcasting begins.

1947 Walter Brattain, John Bardeen, and William Shockley invent the first point-contact transistor at Bell Labs.

1948 Bell Labs unveils the transistor to the U.S. military and to the public at large.

1951 The UNIVAC 1, considered the first commercial computer, is sold to the U.S. Census Bureau by the Eckert and Mauchly Computer Co.

1956 Shockley, Bardeen, and Brattain win the Nobel Prize for their work on the transistor. IBM researchers unveil the first hard-disk drive.

1958 The U.S. Dept. of Defense creates the Advanced Research Projects Agency (ARPA). The first integrated circuit or "silicon chip" is invented.

1962 Dr. J.C.R. Licklider defines the concept of global networking in a pioneering thesis at MIT, "On-Line Man Computer Communications."

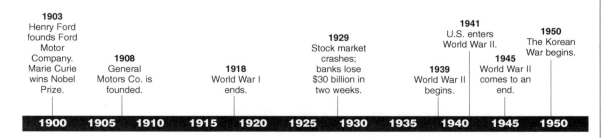

1903 Henry Ford founds Ford Motor Company. Marie Curie wins Nobel Prize.

1908 General Motors Co. is founded.

1918 World War I ends.

1929 Stock market crashes; banks lose $30 billion in two weeks.

1939 World War II begins.

1941 U.S. enters World War II.

1945 World War II comes to an end.

1950 The Korean War begins.

1900 1905 1910 1915 1920 1925 1930 1935 1940 1945 1950

1965 Moore's Law is espoused for the first time by Gordon Moore.

1968 Robert Noyce and Gordon Moore form the Intel Corp.

1969 ARPAnet is created.

1970 Glass fiber, precursor to the development of fiber optics, is created at Corning Glass.

1971 Intel creates the first microprocessor.

1972 The concept of electronic mail is introduced, as is the concept of open-architecture networking.

1974 Barcoded products appear in U.S. stores and cashiers begin using scanners.

1975 Bill Gates and Paul Allen form a partnership, naming their new business Microsoft.

1976 Steve Jobs and Steve Wozniak found Apple Computer Co. Cray Research, Inc. unveils the Cray-1, a supercomputer with revolutionary speed capabilities.

1981 IBM introduces its personal computer.

1982 The TCP/IP protocol is developed.

1983 Microsoft Word is unveiled, as is the Windows operating system. Time magazine chooses the PC as its 1982 "Man of the Year."

1984 Apple Computer Co. introduces the Macintosh.

1985 The National Science Foundation establishes NSFNET, an enhanced version of ARPAnet.

1986 Microsoft Corp. conducts its IPO.

1989 BITNET is born.

1990 Microsoft Corp. revenues exceed $1 billion. ARPAnet is decommissioned and shut down.

1991 The World Wide Web comes into existence as the National Science Foundation's decree that prevents commercial use of the Internet dissolves.

1993 Graphics-based Web browser Mosaic is released. The U.S. Justice Dept. begins its antitrust investigation into Microsoft Corp.

1994 The World Wide Web Consortium (W3C) is established.

1995 Amazon.com goes online for the first time. The National Science Foundation's financial support of the Internet is terminated.

2000 Technology stocks plummet in value as the dot-com shakeout takes hold. Internet startups are hit hard and many fold or merge.

2001 Time Warner and America Online (AOL) finalize their mega-merger.

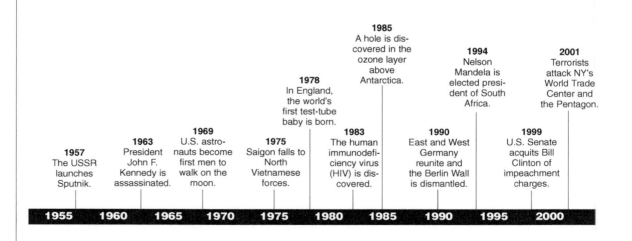

1985 A hole is discovered in the ozone layer above Antarctica.

1994 Nelson Mandela is elected president of South Africa.

2001 Terrorists attack NY's World Trade Center and the Pentagon.

1978 In England, the world's first test-tube baby is born.

1957 The USSR launches Sputnik.

1963 President John F. Kennedy is assassinated.

1969 U.S. astronauts become first men to walk on the moon.

1975 Saigon falls to North Vietnamese forces.

1983 The human immunodeficiency virus (HIV) is discovered.

1990 East and West Germany reunite and the Berlin Wall is dismantled.

1999 U.S. Senate acquits Bill Clinton of impeachment charges.

1955 **1960** **1965** **1970** **1975** **1980** **1985** **1990** **1995** **2000**

gale
encyclopedia of
e-commerce

A

ACQUIRING BANK

Acquiring banks, also known as merchant banks, act as middlemen in the online transaction route. They are the link between online merchants and credit-card-issuing banks, and play a vital role in coordinating the relationship and data flow between them. When a customer agrees to an online purchase and enters his or her credit card information, it travels first to the merchant, who sends it along to the acquiring bank. The acquirer processes the transaction information, coordinates and updates its accounts, and then relays the sales data directly to the issuing bank, which actually authorizes the sale in accordance with the customer's account. The authorization then is submitted back to the acquirer, who informs the merchant that the sale has been approved.

Acquiring banks operating in the e-commerce world have not gone without criticism. The most common complaints leveled at acquirers are that they spend too little time and money on customer service, and that they are reluctant to process payments for companies trying to establish new and unproven online storefronts. Acquirers defend themselves on the latter charge, claiming such scrutiny is necessary for protecting themselves from risky investments. Acquirers attributed the claim of poor customer service to rapid expansion, during which current accounts were neglected at the expense of broadening customer bases. Such neglect can damage merchants' online sales efforts. For example, Zona Research found that one-third of customers who encounter a delay in online transactions, usually defined as more than eight seconds, simply abandon the purchase, and only seven percent of those move on to another Web site. Acquirers were thus urged to keep up their customer service and infrastructure in order to facilitate the high-speed Internet culture customers expect.

Credit card fraud was another particularly troublesome issue for e-commerce acquiring banks in the early 2000s. Acquirers had to concern themselves with protecting their issuing-bank clients from losses stemming from online fraud, as one facet of nurturing their customers' comfort level in working with online merchants. Sectors of the e-commerce market deemed risky, such as Internet gambling and online pornography, caused a great many headaches because customers in these sectors were more likely to generate charge-backs and fraud, as well as other account hassles. Some acquirers simply dumped such industry sectors from their portfolios. Meanwhile, credit card companies increasingly put extra restrictions on the latitude acquiring banks could extend to such customers. Acquirers with a high proportion of their business concentrated in risky sectors could see decreased revenue stability.

Acquiring banks also faced increasing competition from online services offering one-stop e-commerce solutions. In order to defend and expand their market share in the online world, merchant banks sought to add value by offering bundled services. They thus began augmenting traditional acquiring activities with a broader array of financial services, such as streamlined account management and advanced tools for transaction authorization, routing, and settling.

FURTHER READING:

''Acquirers Letting Down Internet Retailers.'' *Electronic Payments International.* January 31, 2000.

Hisey, Pete. "At War Over Merchant Risk." *Credit Card Management*. July, 2000.

Nelson, Kristi. "Acquirers to Offer Electronic Check Acceptance Service." *Bank Systems & Technology*. December 2000.

"The Scramble for International Acquiring." *Electronic Payments International*. September 30, 1999.

SEE ALSO: Authorizaton and Authorization Code; Card-Issuing Bank; Charge-back; Electronic Payment; Interchange and Interchange Fee; Internet Payment Provider

ADAMS, RICHARD L.

Richard L. Adams, Jr. is the founder of UUnet Technologies, the first commercial Internet Service Provider (ISP) and one of the largest Internet traffic carriers in the world. Among other things, Adams's accomplishments at the helm of UUnet include the invention of Serial Line Internet Protocol (SLIP), technology that allows personal computers to connect to the Internet via modems.

With a master's degree in computer science from Purdue University, Adams launched his career as a programmer for San Diego, California-based Science Application International Corp. He left there in 1982 to accept a position as a data-gathering specialist with the Center for Seismic Studies, an outfit hired by the U.S. Department of Defense to develop technology for nuclear testing violation detection. It was there that Adams first encountered ARPAnet, precursor to the Internet. After hearing several individuals express their interest in using ARPAnet despite its high cost, Adams began toying with the idea of creating a nonprofit enterprise to offer moderately priced access to the fledgling network. He presented his plan to the Usenix Association, a Unix software users group to which he belonged, and secured $250,000 in funding.

In 1987 Adams formally established UUnet. Although the ISP initially offered services only to research institutes and universities, it wasn't long before Adams began expanding operations. The launch of AlterNet in 1990 marked UUnet's first foray into commercial service, as well as its conversion to a for-profit company. The firm's new focus on the corporate sector paid off a few years later when it landed the contract to carry Internet traffic for the Microsoft Network, beating out competitors like AT&T Corp. and MCI Communications Corp.

Adams took UUnet public in 1995, in one of the largest technology public offerings to date, and a year later agreed to a $2 billion buyout offer from MFS Communications, which was acquired by WorldCom shortly thereafter. Although he remained chairman and chief technology officer for a while, Adams eventually resigned and pursued other ventures.

As a subsidiary of WorldCom, UUnet remained one of the largest ISPs in the world. Its global pipeline—more commonly referred to as an Internet "backbone"—carries more than 2,500 points of presence (areas with local phone line access) in North and South America, Europe, Asia, and Australia. The firm also offers virtual private networks, World Wide Web hosting, security, and other e-commerce services to its roughly 70,000 corporate clients.

FURTHER READING:

"Fortune Visits 25 Cool Companies." *Fortune*. July 10, 1995.

Swisher, Kara. "Anticipating the Internet: Good Timing, Good Deal-Making and Good Luck Turned Rick Adams' UUNet Into a Star." *The Washington Post*. May 6, 1996.

UUNET. "About UUNET." Ashburn, VA: UUNET, 2001.

"UUNet Technologies." *Jobcircle*. March 7, 2001. Available from www.jobcircle.com/career/profiles/104.html.

"Web Crawlers." *Forbes*. October 9, 2000.

"Web Masters." *Forbes.com*. October 11, 1999. Available from www.forbes.com.

SEE ALSO: Connectivity, Internet; Internet; Internet Access, Tracking Growth of; Internet and WWW, History of the; Internet Service Providers (ISPs)

ADHOCRACY

An adhocracy is an organization that lacks structure—the complete opposite of a bureaucracy. This form of organization is common among advertising agencies and other creativity-based companies. Start-ups often opt for such a structure as well because of its tendency to foster a team atmosphere. Characteristics of an adhocracy-type firm include taking risks and being flexible as new projects arise.

Not surprisingly, one e-company even chose to use the term as its name. Adhocracy LLC is an Internet-based marketing communications company consisting of advertising, communications, and Web professionals who work in a tele-computing atmosphere. The firm's creative teams provide advertising, Web design, direct mail, ideation (sometimes described simply as the development of ideas), cyber-commerce, and market strategy services to mid-level businesses. It supports clients via offices in Los Angeles, New York City, Philadelphia, Detroit, and Washington, D.C.

Adhocracy got its start in the 1990s when an ad hoc group of advertising professionals began to work on freelance projects together. The group noticed a strong demand within mid-sized companies for marketing communication services. This demand led President Brooks Richey to develop an organization that utilized the skills of top-level advertising and communications professionals to offer marketing services.

One of the services offered by Adhocracy is the creation of cyber-commerce sites. Roper Starch Worldwide polled 30 nations and found the United States to have the largest proportion of e-commerce consumers and the fastest-growing number of Internet users. To take advantage of these statistics, businesses continue to look for ways to promote their product or service online. Adhocracy provides its services to businesses seeking online growth and works with them to develop secure online cyber-stores which enable Web surfers to browse and shop on the site and make online purchases.

The firm also provides Web design using both HTML and flash-based Web content, including streaming audio and video programming. It develops and creates Internet advertising programs and other marketing strategies that allow for maximum exposure on the Internet. Additionally, the company's team of professionals offers ideation (brainstorming) and other marketing services.

FURTHER READING:

Adhocracy LLC. ''Welcome to Adhocracy.com.'' Adhocracy LLC, 2001. Available from www.adhocracy.com.

''Adhocracy.'' *Encyclopedia of the New Economy.* Waltham, MA: Terra Lycos, 2001. Available from www.hotwired.lycos.com/special/ene.

''Facts and Figures.'' The Internet Economy Indicators, 2001. Available from www.internetindicators.com/factfigure.html.

Tovey, Roberta. ''Best Firms More Alike Than Different—Around the Globe.'' *Insights From MSI.* 2000. Available from www.msi.org.

ADOBE SYSTEMS INC.

EARLY HISTORY: WARNOCK AND GESCHKE

Adobe Systems Inc. was founded in 1982 by research John Warnock and Charles Geschke. Less than two decades later, with annual sales exceeding $1 billion, Adobe held the third-place spot among the largest PC software companies in the United States. The firm emerged in the mid-1980s as a major force in desktop publishing and in the late-1990s as a leader in Web authoring tools and other Internet publishing technology.

Adobe's founders met at Xerox Corp. While earning his doctorate degree in electrical engineering at the University of Utah, Warnock—who would be named one of the ''Ten Revolutionaries of Computing'' in 1998 by *Computer Reseller News*—had worked for IBM Corp., as well as a handful of other technology companies. In 1980, he accepted a graphics research position at Xerox's new graphics and imaging lab, which was headed up by Geschke. Together, Warnock and Geschke created the PostScript computer language, which conveyed to printers how electronic characters, lines, and digital images appear on paper. Dissatisfied with Xerox's limited interest in the new product, Warnock and Geschke decided to resign and establish a new company, Adobe Systems, as a vehicle for selling PostScript. Their printer language would soon fuel the desktop publishing industry's explosive growth, as well as the surging popularity of laser printers.

Adobe's first big break came when Geschke and Warnock convinced Apple Computer Inc. to use PostScript with its LaserWriter printer. As part of the deal, Apple purchased a 19-percent stake in Adobe. The first printer using the PostScript language was made available for sale in 1985. Texas Instruments Inc. began using PostScript in its IBM-compatible PCs in 1986. That year, Adobe conducted its initial public offering (IPO).

In 1987, Adobe launched its Illustrator design software program and expanded overseas by establishing Adobe Systems Europe. Soon thereafter, the company increased its international operations by founding a sales unit in the Pacific Rim. The acquisition of BluePoint Technologies, Nonlinear Technologies, and OCR Systems in the early 1990s marked the beginning of an expansion period. Along with seeking growth through acquisition, Adobe had already started licensing its PostScript software to printer manufacturers. In 1993, the firm also unveiled Acrobat, a software program that allowed users to create and view documents that included text, graphics, and even photos, regardless of whether they worked on a Macintosh or PC. Acrobat's portable document format (PDF) not only allowed for the transfer of files between incompatible systems, it also greatly simplified the electronic distribution of all sorts of documents.

MAJOR ACQUISITIONS

Adobe wanted to secure a desktop publishing application for its PostScript printing language. In 1994, it approached Aldus Corp., maker of PageMaker, the leading desktop publishing program for both Macintosh and Windows operating systems. A $450 million merger completed later that year secured Adobe's position as a leading PC software manufacturer among giants like Microsoft, Novell, and Lotus. The deal also positioned Adobe as a market leader in design and illustration software, image editing, and electronic document technology—areas that would prove essential to its emergence as a leader in Web publishing.

Adobe's second major acquisition—the $31.5 million purchase of Frame Technology Corp., maker of the Unix-based FrameMaker desktop publishing program—proved ill fated. Adobe was unfamiliar with Frame's enterprise market, and the unit began to lose money soon after the transaction was completed in 1995. Consequently, Adobe's stock price plunged more than 50 percent to $33 per share in July of 1996, compared to a high of approximately $74 per share earlier that year.

FOCUS ON INTERNET PUBLISHING

Depending on its recent acquisition of Web tools manufacturer Ceneca Communications to prove fruitful, Adobe shifted focus in 1996 to Internet publishing and converted the popular PDF into a Web format. Sales neared the $1 billion mark in 1997. Recessionary economic conditions in Japan undercut earnings in 1998, spurring Adobe to lay off roughly 10 percent of its management staff and place more of an emphasis on creating new products, particularly those that would help secure the firm's position as a key player in Web authoring tools. More than $207 million— roughly one-quarter of sales—was earmarked for research and development. The firm also hunted for strategic acquisitions like GoLive Systems Inc., a maker of Web development and design tools that it purchased early in 1999. The GoLive technology allowed Adobe to later launch its award-winning Live-Motion program, a graphics and animation manipulation software package for both novice and expert Web page designers.

Believing that electronic books, particularly educational and professional publications, would become a key online market, Adobe began developing software for displaying such books. It also sought ways to protect authors, publishers, and other parties from the illegal distribution of copyrighted material—a major issue for book vendors considering a move into electronic commerce. In 1999, the firm unveiled PDF Merchant, which allows publishers to prevent individuals from downloading PDF files until they have purchased the right to do so. Once payment has been received, the document in question is sent directly to the recipient's hard drive. Web Buy, an Acrobat "plug-in" program, is attached to the document to thwart unauthorized distribution by prompting the recipient of such a file for payment prior to allowing access.

Adding to its e-books holdings, Adobe purchased display software manufacturer Glassbook Inc. in August of 2000. Adobe Content Server, a program that allows book merchants to sell e-books in a secure format online, was launched the following year in conjunction with the Adobe Acrobat e-Book Reader, a product based upon the Glassbook Reader. Along with granting users electronic access to books, with both text and graphics in PDF, the new software also offers searching, marking, annotating, and other interactive capabilities.

By 2001, Internet publishing products accounted for more than 50 percent of Adobe's revenues. More importantly, Adobe's presence on the Internet was prolific. In the October 2000 issue of *Forbes* Elizabeth Corcoran wrote, ''Pull up the Bridgestone/ Firestone Web site to learn about defective tires and it tells you to use Adobe's free Acrobat Reader to see a graphical interpretation of the hieroglyphics on your tires' sidewalls. On ESPN's extreme sports site teethgritting images have been tweaked with Adobe tools. At Barnes & Noble on the Web you will find e-books viewable with readers from Microsoft and Adobe.'' In fact, says Corcoran, more than 90 percent of all Web sites make use of Adobe's Photoshop software, while nearly three-fourths of all Web pages are designed with Adobe Illustrator.

Seeing the development of strategic alliances as essential to remaining at the forefront of Internet publishing technology, Adobe continually seeks to establish relationships with other key players. For example, in the second half of 2000 Adobe integrated its Go-Live software with WebTrends Corp.'s Web tracking technology. This allowed clients creating Web sites with GoLive the ability to monitor things like site traffic. At roughly the same time, the firm reached a similar technology integration agreement with e-commerce software and services provider Allaire Corp. Future plans include the creation of Adobe Studio—a Web site that allows Adobe software users to share technology and ideas, as well as to post and find jobs—and the development of technology that allows electronic documents to be published on cell phones, palm pilots, and other mobile devices.

FURTHER READING:

''Adobe and Allaire Join to Simplify Development of E-Business; ColdFusion Extension for GoLive is First of Many Joint Development Efforts.'' *Canadian Corporate News.* August 28, 2000.

''Adobe and WebTrends Form Alliance to Provide E-Business Intelligence for Adobe Web Applications.'' *Canadian Corporate News.* August 29, 2000.

Boeri, Robert J. and Martin Hensel. ''Ecommerce Dilemma: Controlling What You Sell.'' *EMedia Magazine.* September 2000.

Collett, Stacy. ''Adobe's Stock Price Gets Better with Age; Aggressive Plan Credited for Record Stock Price.'' *Computerworld.* August 30, 1999.

Corcoran, Elizabeth. ''Go Forth and Publish.'' *Forbes*. October 2, 2000.

Crouch, Cameron. ''Seybold: Adobe Unveils Secure PDF.'' *Network World*. September 6, 1999.

DeLong, Bradford J. ''Why the Valley is Here to Stay.'' *Fortune*. May 29, 2000.

Hane, Paula J. ''Adobe Introduces Two New eBook Products.'' *Information Today*. March, 2001.

Ricadela, Aaron. ''Adobe Sets Its Sights on Mobility.'' *InformationWeek*. November 6, 2000.

Sheldon, AnnaMarie L. ''Adobe Systems and Aldus.'' In *Cases in Corporate Acquisitions, Buyouts, Mergers, & Takeovers*. Farmington Hills, MI: Gale Group, 1999.

Wintrob, Suzanne. ''Analyst Confident Adobe Will Rebound.'' *Computing Canada*. February 1, 1996.

SEE ALSO: E-books; Electronic Publishing

ADVANCED ENCRYPTION STANDARD (AES)

The Advanced Encryption Standard (AES) is the U.S. government-sponsored, data-coding, algorithmic system designed to protect electronic information on hardware and software from security breaches. By providing a basic framework for coding and scrambling sensitive information, AES facilitates easy electronic data sharing and protection across a wide variety of platforms as well as across borders.

The predecessor to AES, the Data Encryption Standard (DES), was adopted in 1977. By the mid-1990s, DES had begun to show its age. As new, more intensive security needs arose as a result of the proliferation of the Internet and home computers, the National Institute of Standards and Technology (NIST), an agency of the United States Department of Commerce, announced in 1997 its plans to develop the Advanced Encryption Standard. When DES's five-year review came up in 1998, NIST reported that the 56-bit-key encryption was no longer capable of withstanding the kinds of attacks that would now threaten electronic data in the Internet world.

In short order, over a dozen groups were working on contenders for the new encryption standard, and NIST called for cryptographers all around the world to put the contestant algorithms to vigorous tests by applying various kinds of attacks. The contestants were judged on their performance in a number of areas, including speed, versatility (the encryption is to work across a variety of platforms, such as smart cards, satellite communications, and ATM networks, in addition to online information exchange), the

amount of chip and memory space they consume, flexibility, and, of course, the strength of their security. In addition, the algorithms were to work with both hardware and software applications; DES, a product of its age, was geared more specifically toward hardware.

In October 2000, after three years spent wading through the various algorithms, the Department of Commerce finally declared the Rijndael system the winner. Developed by Joan Daemen of Proton World International and Vincent Rijmen of Katholieke Universiteit Leuven (Catholic University of Leuven) in Belgium, Rijndael is both much stronger and more flexible than its DES predecessor. While DES maintained an encryption key length of only 56 bits, the new AES was designed to support 128-, 192-, and 256-bit keys. Built on algebraic constructs, Rijndael undergoes a complex series of steps and operations to define, scramble, redefine, and mathematically encode data.

The AES specifications demanded that any standard adopted be available free of royalties anywhere in the world. The choosing of a Belgian model signaled the NIST's commitment to the internationalization of AES. (DES, by contrast, was developed under the purview of the U.S. National Security Agency.)

While federal computer systems will be the first to integrate AES upon final Commerce Department approval, expected sometime in 2001, the private sector, particularly financial services and similar industries, will certainly adopt the new encryption algorithm to safeguard the increasing number of online transactions.

FURTHER READING:

Harrison, Ann. ''Advanced Encryption Standard.'' *Computerworld*. May 29, 2000.

———. ''Feds Propose New Encryption Standard.'' *Computerworld*. October 9, 2000.

Hulme, George V. ''Commerce Department Picks Rijndael Encryption Formula.'' *InformationWeek*. October 16, 2000.

Landau, Susan. ''Designing Cryptography for the New Century.'' *Communications of the Association for Computing Machinery*. May 2000.

Loshin, Pete. ''Cryptographic Turning Points.'' *Computerworld*. August 28, 2000.

SEE ALSO: Computer Security; Cryptography, Public and Private Key; Data Encryption Standard (DES); Encryption

ADVERTISING, ONLINE

Although the Internet economy experienced a general slowdown in 2000, there was a record number of online ad impressions—more than 172 billion—in the fourth quarter of that year, according to a report by AdRelevance, a subsidiary of Jupiter Media Metrix. Online ad impressions in December 2000 rose 21 percent over November to reach more than 65 billion ads viewed. The report predicted that Internet users in the United States would view 610 ad impressions per day in 2001. By 2005 the number was projected to reach 950 per day.

What is the purpose of online advertising? According to a Myers Report cited in the February 28, 2001 issue of *eMarketer,* some 85 percent of advertising and marketing companies in the United States believed the most important aspect of online advertising was to drive traffic to Web sites. The other principal reason cited for using online advertising was brand building and related opportunities for branding and sponsorship.

The same report also asked ad agency executives and marketers what obstacles prevented them from increasing their expenditures for online advertising. The major obstacles cited included budget limitations, low click-through rates, high cost-per-impression (CPM), inadequate research, difficulties in measuring return-on-investment (ROI), and a lack of faith in the Web's branding abilities. Other reasons given for not spending more on online advertising included lack of measurement standards, low conversion rates, market fragmentation, and bandwidth limitations.

BANNER ADS DOMINATE ONLINE ADVERTISING FORMATS

Although still the dominant format in the year 2000, banner ads were in decline and losing favor. One problem had to do with click-through rates, a measure that advertisers used to help determine return-on-investment (ROI). Since many Internet users go to Web sites to perform specific tasks, it's not surprising that they often ignore unrelated messages. By mid-2000, click-through rates had fallen to .3 percent, with business-to-business advertisers reporting average click-through rates around .5 percent.

The key to successful banner advertising is proper targeting, which ensures that ads appear in contexts relevant to the target audience. Banner performance also can be enhanced by purchasing larger banners; this might involve purchasing what is called the "skyscraper" unit, which runs down the right-hand side of a Web page, in addition to the standard banner centered at the top of a page.

Advertisers who are focused on ROI typically use banner ads to drive traffic to their Web sites. Another strategy involves using banner ads for brand building. The practice of using banners for brand building recognizes that driving traffic may not necessarily be the best measurement of a banner's effectiveness. Click-through rates do not measure offline actions that people may take as a result of seeing a banner ad, nor do they measure visits to Web sites that may take place later as a result of seeing an ad.

Effective use of banner ads also is dependent on profiling techniques. The pioneering Internet advertising agency DoubleClick Inc. introduced its proprietary DART (Dynamic Advertising Reporting and Tracking) software technology in 1996. DART enabled the company to determine within 15 milliseconds which banner ad should be presented to the current user, based on pre-selected criteria. In order for DART to match ads to target audiences so quickly, it uses the controversial "cookie" technology that creates a user profile and monitors an Internet browser's movements through Web sites in DoubleClick's media network. Using this technology DoubleClick created a database of user profiles that enabled it to better target banner ads to users who visited Web sites in the DoubleClick network. Similar technology is used by other online ad networks such as 24/7 Media and Engage.

As the technology for profiling Internet users improves, targeting and banner performance will become stronger. Technology advances also are expected to enhance the performance of other Web marketing techniques, including opt-in e-mail, sponsorships, Webcasting, and rich media advertisements. Rich media ads cover a wide range of formats. The more widely used and accepted rich media formats include HTML pull-down menus and forms, Java and JavaScript, Audio, Enliven (by @Home Network), Flash (by Macromedia), Jump Page, RealAudio (by RealNetworks), Shockwave (by Macromedia), Video, and VRML.

According to a report commissioned by the Interactive Advertising Bureau (IAB), banner ads accounted for 47 percent of online ad revenue in 2000, but only 40 percent for the fourth quarter, confirming the decline in revenue from banner advertising. Sponsorships accounted for 28 percent of online ad revenue for the year and 31 percent for the fourth quarter. Other types of online advertising cited in the report included classified ads, which accounted for seven percent of online ad revenue for the year and 10 percent for the fourth quarter; referrals, which accounted for four percent of online ad revenue for the year and five percent for the fourth quarter; interstitials, which accounted for four percent of online ad revenue for the year and five percent for the fourth quarter; e-mail advertising, which accounted for three percent of online ad revenue for the year and four percent for the fourth quarter; and rich media, which accounted for two percent of online ad revenue for the year and for the fourth quarter. Keyword searches accounted for one percent of online ad revenue for the year and two percent for the fourth quarter.

AD NETWORKS OFFER REACH, CONVENIENCE FOR ADVERTISERS

The first Internet advertising network was created in 1996 by the newly formed Internet ad agency DoubleClick Inc. The DoubleClick Network began as a group of about 30 Web sites that the firm represented to advertisers. It was a model that other Internet advertising agencies would emulate. Over the course of its first five years DoubleClick expanded the network of Web sites it represented, segmented it to match the needs of Internet advertisers, and reorganized it to reflect changing market conditions. By April 2001 the DoubleClick Network represented nearly 1,500 Web publishers worldwide. It consisted of 16 different networks. Advertisers could purchase ad space on any individual country network, as well as in categories such as automotive, business, commerce, entertainment, technology, travel, and women and health. The company's premium network was called the Double-Click Select Network. Consisting of high-profile, high-traffic sites, DoubleClick claimed its Select Network reached 48 percent of the U.S. Internet audience.

Other smaller networks compete with DoubleClick. They include the 24/7 Network, operated by Internet ad agency 24/7 Media. The 24/7 Network is a global advertising network represented in 24 countries. It includes high profile, high-traffic Web sites that 24/7 Media represents to advertisers, including more than 400 Web sites in the United States, 80 in Canada, more than 250 in Europe, and more than 30 in Latin America. Through an agreement with China-dotcom Corp., 24/7 Media represents more than 500 major Web sites in Asia. The 24/7 Network is organized into topical channels representing such areas as automotive, business/financial, career, college, entertainment, music, news/information, search engines, sports, and more.

Engage Inc. is a multi-channel marketing company that also operates a global interactive media network. Its integrated network of more than 4,700 Web sites reaches more than half of the U.S. Internet market, according to the company. Engage is a majority-owned subsidiary of CMGI Inc.

ValueClick Inc. employs a different type of model for its network of Web sites. With its cost-per-click (CPC) model, ValueClick only receives payment from an advertiser—and in turn pays a publisher of a Web site—when an Internet user clicks on the advertiser's banner ad. At the end of 2000 ValueClick's network consisted of more than 20,000 small and medium-sized independent Web sites that had agreed to sell their advertising inventory to ValueClick on a non-exclusive basis. According to Jupiter Media Metrix, the ValueClick network reached more than 30 percent of the U.S. Internet population in early 2001, and it delivered more than 40 million ads daily. Through a strategic investment transaction completed in February 2000, DoubleClick owns about 30 percent of ValueClick. In exchange, ValueClick is allowed to use DoubleClick's ad serving technology, known as DART.

ONLINE ADVERTISING REVENUE

Online advertising revenue has increased steadily from 1996, when the Internet Advertising Bureau (IAB) began compiling its *Advertising Revenue Report,* through 2000. According to IAB reports, which were conducted independently by the New Media Group of PricewaterhouseCoopers, online advertising revenue grew from $906.5 million in 1997 to $1.92 billion in 1998. In 1999 the IAB report noted that quarterly online advertising revenue exceeded $1 billion for the first time in the third quarter.

Having changed its name to the Interactive Advertising Bureau, the IAB reported in April 2001 that year 2000 online advertising revenue reached $8.2 billion in the United States. Fourth quarter ad revenue increased by nine percent sequentially over the third quarter, but the percentage increase was markedly lower than historical levels. That reflected the overall slowdown in ad revenue in the second half of 2000 across all media sectors, as well as a higher revenue base. The report also noted that advertisers were being more selective in reaching the online audience of more than 140 million users. There was a higher concentration of ad spending in the top sites; high-profile, high-traffic Web sites were gaining ad revenue at the expense of smaller sites.

According to AdRelevance, in December 2000 the top two advertising sites on the Internet were Yahoo! and the Microsoft Network (MSN). MSN brought in the most advertising revenue that month with $180 million, while Yahoo! was second at $118 million. In terms of number of ads served, Yahoo! took the top spot with 7.6 billion ad impressions in December, while MSN had 6.3 billion ad impressions. It was the difference in advertising clients that gave MSN the top spot in terms of revenue. MSN's clients spent an average of $486,000 each on advertising there, while Yahoo!'s advertising clients spent an average of $105,000.

ONLINE ADVERTISING STRATEGIES

Two principal advertising strategies are used in online advertising: building brand recognition and direct response. Advertisers may focus on one or the other or combine the two strategies. Online retailer Amazon.com, for example, focused on building brand recognition during much of 2000, and then switched its emphasis to direct response ads in the middle of the all-important holiday shopping season. An ad designed to build brand recognition might say, ''Buy Books and CDs at Amazon.com'' and allow the user to click through to the company's Web site. On the other hand, a direct response ad typically would extend a special offer, such as free shipping.

ONLINE ADVERTISERS

According to a IAB report, consumer-related advertisers accounted for 31 percent of online advertising in 2000, followed by computing (18 percent), financial services (14 percent), business services (nine percent), and media (eight percent). According to AdRelevance, Amazon.com was the most advertised company on the Internet for eight out of nine weeks during the 2000 holiday shopping season. The company employed a combination of brand recognition and direct marketing advertisements in its campaign. Before the holiday season, 270 million of the company's 275.3 million ad impressions were branding impressions, while only 5.3 million were direct marketing impressions. By the end of November, Amazon.com had begun to place more emphasis on direct marketing impressions in an effort to achieve immediate results. During the last week of November, Amazon.com ran 320 million branding impressions and approximately 212 direct marketing impressions. Seven of the company's top 10 holiday ads offered free shipping. Each direct marketing ad had 4 million impressions, while each branding ad had 750,000 impressions.

Amazon.com advertised on more than 100 Web sites, but it made an effort to dominate on the top sites. The top five sites it advertised on were MSN, AOL, Netscape, Juno, and Excite. Amazon.com was the number one advertiser on four of those sites and third on Excite behind the Home Shopping Network and First USA. AdRelevance reported that Amazon.com spent the most on Internet advertising in December 2000 with its $61.8 million budget. It led all advertisers with nearly 3 billion ad impressions. Amazon.com spent 42 percent of its ad budget in December on MSN. Other major advertisers in December 2000 included Barnesandnoble.com at a distant second with $23.8 million, Classmates.com with $19.3 million, First USA with $11.2 million, and eBay at number five with $11.1 million spent on online advertising. The ad spending figures include all Internet banner and button advertising, excluding house ads and sponsorships. The most heavily advertised company, Amazon.com purchased 6.1 billion impressions in the fourth quarter of 2000. The other top five advertisers during the quarter were Microsoft (4.1 billion ad impressions), MSN (3.2 billion impressions), America Online (2.6 billion impressions), and Netscape (1.6 billion impressions).

Advertisers also like to advertise on their own Web sites. A study by AdRelevance found that 28 percent of U.S. Web sites used self-promotional advertising. In the entertainment and society sectors, some 30 percent of ad inventories were used for self-promotional online ads.

Although there were cutbacks in online ad spending in the second half of 2000, dot-coms continued to spend more as a group than traditional brick-and-mortar companies. According to AdRelevance, Internet companies of all sizes purchased 769 million ad impressions on average during the fourth quarter of 2000, more than twice as many per firm than traditional companies. Mid-sized Internet companies purchased an average of 454 million impressions per company, roughly four times as many as mid-sized traditional companies. Another report issued by AdRelevance in November 2000 indicated that traditional companies were beginning to show more confidence in the Internet as an advertising medium. The fact that half of AdRelevance's ''Hot 100'' online advertisers were traditional, non-Internet based companies suggested that online advertising was becoming a bigger part of those companies' overall marketing strategy.

WIRELESS ADVERTISING

Although advertising opportunities on wireless devices are limited by small screens, text-only capabilities, and the potential to annoy consumers, marketers have found ways to exploit this opportunity. According to a study published in the *eMarketer Newsletter,* wireless advertising was projected to grow slowly through 2002 due to technological hurdles. However, it was then expected take off in 2003 through 2005.

The top three markets for wireless advertising were Europe, Asia/Pacific, and North America. In Europe, for example, expenditures on wireless advertising were projected to grow from $2 million in 2000 to $443 million in 2002, accelerate to $1.5 billion in 2003 and then reach nearly $6 billion in 2005. Expenditures in Asia/Pacific were projected to reach $4.7 billion by 2005, and in North America expenditures were projected to increase from $363 million in 2002 to $4.6 billion in 2005.

Wireless advertising can take many forms. Brand building and awareness messages can accompany other content, such as news or stock quotes. Wireless devices can be used to notify users of sales or other timely offers. Discounts or coupons that users can redeem through their mobile device can be offered. In addition, traditional telemarketing pitches can be delivered to cell phones.

Other forms of wireless advertising include e-mail messages that allow mobile users to buy an item by clicking on an advertisement. Links also can be embedded in advertisements that enable users to click through to an e-tailer's Web site. Finally, direct response ads can be sent to wireless devices that allow users to call the marketer with one click.

Wireless ads can be part of a ''push'' strategy or a ''pull'' strategy. Ads that users download as part of other content rely on the user to ''pull'' them to their device. Other types of wireless ads can be sent to mobile devices at unexpected times as part of a ''push'' strategy.

Wireless advertising offers advertisers the possibility of delivering ads based on the user's location. While current technology only allows wireless operators to roughly estimate a user's location, that is expected to change. As part of a Federal Communications Commission (FCC) initiative, mobile operators will be required to be able to trace users to within 400 feet of their location. While the initiative was designed for emergency calls, it potentially could benefit marketers.

One big question affecting the viability of wireless advertising is how receptive consumers will be to the ads. Unsolicited wireless ads that are pushed at the user have the greatest potential for alienating consumers. Such annoyance can be alleviated to some extent by using opt-in models, whereby the consumer has to agree to accept commercial messages on his or her wireless device. Another problem affecting wireless advertising concerns how wireless time is billed. Most wireless users are billed by minutes of use, so that an ad sent to a wireless device would cost the consumer in terms of time used. To overcome this, wireless advertisers must be prepared to compensate users for every ad received.

OUTLOOK FOR ONLINE ADVERTISING

Although revenue from online advertising has consistently grown more than predicted, the online advertising industry faces many challenges. Operators of online ad networks like DoubleClick and 24/7 have yet to turn a profit. Low click-through rates and the difficulty of measuring ROI for advertising dollars are symptomatic of a larger problem: the lack of standards for measuring online ads. The IAB has made the development of such standards a top priority, and one the industry must address in 2001. Without them, ad-

vertisers and their agencies will be reluctant to commit to online advertising as part of their marketing mix. Other problems facing the online advertising industry include the general slowing of the Internet economy, the dot-com shakeout of 2000, and tighter budgets at the surviving dot-com companies.

In spite of these obstacles, a report from Forrester Research predicted that the amount traditional U.S. companies will spend on digital marketing campaigns, which include online advertising, promotions, and e-mail marketing, will increase from $11 billion in 2000 to $63 billion in 2005. Spending on online advertising alone was projected to increase to $42 billion worldwide by the end of 2005. Among nearly 60 vendors surveyed for part of its report, Forrester found that the amount spent on online marketing per company would double by 2003.

FURTHER READING:

Callahan, Sean. ''Banner Believers Endure Season of Disenchantment.'' *B to B.* October 23, 2000.

Engage Inc. Company Information. April 23, 2001. Available from www.engage.com/company/.

Enos, Lori. ''Amazon Ranked as Net Ad Champ.'' *E-Commerce Times.* December 14, 2000. Available from www.ecommercetimes.com.

Fineberg, Seth. ''Dot-com Sea Change Forces Ad Networks to Rethink Strategies.'' *Advertising Age.* September 25, 2000.

Frook, John Evan. ''U.S. Firms Dominate Worldwide Ad Networks.'' *B to B.* November 20, 2000.

Gimenez, Sylvia. ''eValuating Online Advertising.'' *eMarketer.* February 28, 2001. Available from www.emarketer.com.

———. ''These Ads Are on the House.'' *eMarketer.* March 2, 2001. Available from www.emarketer.com.

''Interactive Advertising Bureau (IAB) Reports $8.2 Billion Online Ad Revenue in the United States for Year 2000.'' April 23, 2001. Interactive Advertising Bureau. Available from www.iab.net/news/content/revenue.html.

Jackson, Jonathan. ''Advertising Unplugged.'' *eMarketer.* April 5, 2001. Available from www.emarketer.com.

Mahoney, Michael. ''Established Firms Drive Net Ad Spending.'' *E-Commerce Times.* November 21, 2000. Available from www.ecommercetimes.com.

Riedman, Patricia. ''Ad Networks Face Troubles as Stocks Fall.'' *Advertising Age.* December 4, 2000.

Saliba, Clare. ''Report: Digital Advertising Set for Rebound.'' *E-Commerce Times.* January 26, 2001. Available from www.ecommercetimes.com.

———. ''Study: Online Ads Soar 21 Percent.'' *E-Commerce Times.* January 23, 2001. Available from www.ecommercetimes.com.

SEE ALSO: Banner Ads; DoubleClick Inc.; Microsoft Network (MSN); 24/7 Media Inc.

AFFILIATE MODEL

The affiliate (or click-through) model is a popular e-commerce relationship in which an online merchant agrees to pay an affiliate in exchange for providing an advertisement and link to the merchant's site. Each sale generated as a result of a customer "clicking through" from an affiliate to the merchant results in a small commission for the affiliate. The deal provides a stream of cash to affiliates and brings the merchant, which owns the affiliate network, a host of new traffic, cutting customer-acquisition costs and allowing it to target its desired audience.

Forbes magazine reported that affiliate deals generated annual retail sales of about $5 billion, or roughly 13 percent of all Web-based retail commerce, in the late 1990s and early 2000s. However, all affiliates were not equal. In 1999, Jupiter Communications reported that only 15 percent of all affiliates accounted for 85 percent of affiliate-generated sales. The retailer with the largest stable of affiliates, at 430,000, was e-commerce giant Amazon.com, whose affiliates generated annual sales of about $200 million.

Retailers may run their affiliate networks in-house or farm them out to third-party services that manage the networks, issue regular checks to affiliates, and address technical problems. The sales commission paid to affiliates generally falls between five and seven percent, according to *Forbes*. However, depending on the type of arrangement, the size of the firms, and the click-through rates, commissions often reach as high as 15 percent. The most common format for routing visitors to a merchant was the ubiquitous banner advertisement—electronic "billboards" that sprawl across Web pages. These provide merchants with virtual storefronts all over the Web, rather than only on their own sites.

Amazon.com largely pioneered the affiliate model in 1996, when it began recruiting thousands of smaller Web sites to help generate new traffic to its online store. Amazon.com and other companies found willing partners among smaller e-businesses, content-based Web sites, and Web portals. Indeed, for several years banner ads were the lifeblood of most major Web portals, and many content sites depended heavily on click-through banners as well. By offering to route users to a merchant's Web site to spend money, affiliates stand to draw revenue by hopping on the coattails of the retailer's sales. However, a danger lurks in directing visitors away to another site, perhaps never to return. In that case, if the visitor chooses not to purchase anything from the retailer, the affiliate has potentially sent away its visitor, perhaps never to return.

By 2001, the click-through model's future was cloudy at best, amidst a growing consensus that banner ads simply don't work well. Although banner ads constituted about 50 percent of all Web-based advertising revenue, the click-through rate had fallen to a paltry 0.3 percent; direct-mail response rates, never viewed as particularly strong, were nonetheless estimated at up to 1.4 percent by comparison, according to *Business Week*. While online advertising revenues grew more than 100 percent annually in the late 1990s, Merril Lynch & Co. expected the 2001 growth rate to plummet to just 17 percent, totaling $9.7 billion. The timing couldn't have been worse, as the steep plummeting of click-through rates coincided with a drying e-commerce revenue stream. Sites that depended on affiliate deals were thus increasingly seeking out alternative sources of funding or courting acquisition by leveraged firms.

FURTHER READING:

Andrews, Kelly J. "Art.com for the Masses." *Target Marketing*. October 1999.

Blankenhorn, Dana. "New Twists and Terms for Affiliates." *B to B*. July 31, 2000.

Green, Heather, and Ben Elgin. "Do e-Ads Have a Future?" *Business Week*. January 22, 2001.

Schoenberger, Chana R. "Don't Go There." *Forbes*. October 2, 2000.

Tedeschi, Bob. "To Cut Costs of Finding Consumers on the Internet, Online Merchants Pay Other Web Sites for Customer Referrals." *New York Times*. May 22, 1999.

SEE ALSO: Advertising, Online; Amazon.com; Banner Ads; Marketing, Internet

AGGREGATORS

The Internet is a vast sea of electronic information. However, to be of any value that information must be combined in ways that end-users find meaningful and useful, or in ways that bring buyers and sellers together in new ways. Aggregators, of which there are several kinds, play an important role in making this happen.

Web aggregators combine information—including sports scores; weather forecasts; articles from different newspapers, magazines, and trade journals; financial information; and even applications—and either display it for all to see or sell it to other companies through syndication for use on Web sites or corporate intranets. The format in which aggregators deliver information can vary, and may include full text, HTML (hyper-text markup language) links to headlines, rich media (pictures, video, and sound) and formats for wireless devices like mobile phones or personal digital assistants.

Companies need information of this kind to make their Web sites interesting. By providing added value, visitors are likely to visit a site more often and stay longer when they do. By contracting with only one or two aggregators, companies can conveniently and cost-effectively obtain information from hundreds of different sources. Jupiter Communications has estimated that online content licensing revenues will climb from $126 million in 1998 to $1.5 billion by 2004, according to *Searcher.*

Another type of aggregator brings large groups of buyers and sellers together in an online marketplace. In the early 2000s, one such example was Chemdex, an aggregator in the life sciences industry. Its customers were technicians who often searched for chemical compounds and antibodies in different paper catalogs. By allowing them to easily search for more than one million items from different vendors at one Web site, and in several different ways, Chemdex saved its customers time and money.

A variation of this kind of aggregation involved small business owners and consumers joining together to get better rates on things like long-distance telephone service. Group purchasing enabled all of the individuals to get better rates than they could have obtained separately. One business-to-business aggregator, Demandline.com, combined similar requests for services—including retirement plans and Web hosting—from small business owners and used a reverse auction approach to obtain rates normally reserved for larger corporations.

Aggregators are as varied as the information they aggregate, or the environments in which they operate. Because there's money to be made by introducing buyers to products and information, aggregators will likely remain key components of the e-commerce environment.

FURTHER READING:

Alexander, Steve. ''Aggregators.'' *Computerworld,* September 4, 2000.

Andrews, Whit. ''Courting Retailers: Metasearchers Increasingly Cozy Up to e-Commerce Sites?'' *Internet World,* January 15, 2000.

Charski, Mindy. ''Content Syndicators' New Aim: Bucks.'' *Interactive Week,* February 21, 2001.

''Content Aggregator.'' *Tech Encyclopedia,* February 20, 2001. Available from www.techweb.com/encyclopedia.

DeMocker, Judy. ''B-To-B Aggregators: Vertical Domination.'' *Planet IT,* February 22, 2001. Available from www.planetit.com.

Funke, Susan. ''New Web Site Content Options From New Content Aggregators.'' *Searcher,* July/August 2000.

Van Winkle, William. ''Strength in Numbers.'' *Home Office Computing,* September 2000.

SEE ALSO: Content Provider

ALLEN, PAUL

In 2000, *Forbes* ranked Paul Allen as the third-wealthiest person in the United States, with an estimated net worth of $36 billion. Allen was born in Seattle, Washington, on January 21, 1953, and attended Lakeside High School there, where he was friends with Bill Gates. Gates and Allen co-founded Microsoft in 1975, after Allen left his job as a programmer at Boston-based Honeywell. Allen served as Microsoft's head of research and new product development. According to his Web page (www.paulallen.com), Allen helped to engineer many of Microsoft's most successful products, including MS-DOS, Word, Windows, and the Microsoft Mouse.

Allen left Microsoft in 1983 to battle Hodgkin's disease, a battle he apparently won. In 1985 he founded his own software company, Asymetrix (subsequently renamed Click2learn.com), and in 1986 established Vulcan Northwest Inc. and Vulcan Ventures. Today, Vulcan Northwest manages Allen's personal and professional endeavors, including the Paul G. Allen Charitable Foundations, Vulcan Ventures Inc., First & Goal Inc., Experience Music Project, Entertainment Properties Inc., and others. Vulcan Ventures is Allen's investment capital firm, through which he has invested in nearly 150 companies, many of which are involved in high technology, e-commerce, media, and entertainment.

Allen's other interests include sports and music. He plays in a rock band called Grown Men. His interest in the life and music of Jimi Hendrix led him to create the Experience Music Project in Seattle, which opened its doors in 2000. Following his passion for sports, Allen purchased the Portland Trail Blazers professional basketball team in 1988, and in 1997 exercised his option to buy the Seattle Seahawks professional football team. In 2000 he acquired *The Sporting News,* which had been publishing sports news for 114 years, from the Times Mirror Co.

INVESTMENTS IN MEDIA AND E-COMMERCE

Allen's investments have been guided by his vision of a ''wired world,'' in which people are empowered by their connection to information and allowed to personalize it. According to Allen's Web site, "When you combine [a microprocessor] with a communication channel, you get the possibility of personalized information, a quantum leap in value for the user."

Allen's interest in media and entertainment is reflected in his investments in companies like Ticketmaster, in which he acquired a majority interest in 1993, and Dreamworks SKG, for which he provided $500 million in venture capital in 1995. In 1998 Allen became interested in broadband technology and especially in cable TV companies. Broadband offered an alternative to telephone lines and satellites for the delivery of high-speed Internet services. In 1998 and 1999 he spent an estimated $24.5 billion to acquire companies involved in cable television, wireless modems, Web portals, and more. After acquiring two major cable systems, Marcus Cable of Dallas for $2.8 billion and Charter Communications of St. Louis for $4.5 billion, Allen combined the two and spent an additional $10 billion to acquire 12 more cable companies. When Charter Communications went public in November 1999, its initial public offering (IPO) raised more than $3.2 billion. At the time, Charter Communications was the fourth largest multi-system operator (MSO) in the United States with 6.2 million customers.

In terms of Allen's investment portfolio, his $4.6 billion stake in Charter is second only to his Microsoft holdings. Other major investments include $1.65 billion invested in 2000 in RCN Corp., an over-builder slated to build out high-speed Internet access to 1.3 million homes. As of mid-2000 Allen also had invested $419 million in Internet portal Go2Net for a 30.3-percent interest; $409 million (a 41.6-percent interest) in Metricom, which operates the Richochet mobile data service for wireless Internet access; and $263 million in USA Networks, the parent company of Ticketmaster. In 2000 Allen helped to launch Digeo Broadband Inc., a company that planned to create next-generation content for interactive television and computers.

In 2000, Allen sold 58 million shares of his Microsoft holdings, worth more than $7 billion, and resigned from the company's board of directors. He retained some 200 million shares, worth about $12.5 billion at October 2000 prices. The press speculated that Allen's connections with Microsoft were hindering his investment strategy. His moves left him free to invest in Microsoft's competitors, such as Transmeta, a new company that included Linux innovator Linus Torvalds on its payroll. Linux is the operating system that poses the most direct threat to Microsoft Windows' market share.

Allen also invests in social and political causes. For example, he has donated $3.4 million to help Washington State conservationists purchase 50,000 acres of forest. Additionally, in 1997 Allen established the Paul G. Allen Forest Protection Foundation.

SLOWDOWN LED TO CUTBACKS, 2000-2001

Following the slowdown of the Internet economy and the dot-com shakeout of 2000, Vulcan Ventures cut back on some of its investments. Among the companies affected were pop.com, the Internet entertainment site set up by Dreamworks SKG, which folded in spite of $50 million in financing from Vulcan. Priceline.com's grocery affiliate, WebHouse Club, also folded in October 2000 after announcing it was unable to raise enough capital for the coming year to complete its business plan. Still, Allen provided Priceline.com with $64 million in funding in August 2000, just before its stock collapsed. Following due diligence, Allen also decided not to participate in a $300 million private placement for online brokerage Datek Online. Vulcan also withdrew from a $25 million investment in Island, an alternative trading network in which Datek owned a majority interest. On the other hand, Vulcan invested $7.5 million in financial news site TheStreet.com, taking a five-percent interest in the company.

Other failing dot-coms in which Vulcan has invested include software distributor Beyond.com, Stamps.com, Drugstore.com, and ValueAmerica. Early in 2000, Allen closed Interval Research, a think tank and research laboratory in Palo Alto, California, that he had established in 1992. Like other venture capitalists, Vulcan Ventures has tightened its investment criteria in response to the dot-com shakeout and faltering Internet economy of 2000. Notably, Vulcan is looking to invest in established, operating companies rather than pure start-ups. According to Allen's Web site, the strategy of Vulcan Ventures is to, "invest in established, operating businesses that are involved in the Wired World technologies. We are not interested in pure start-ups at this time. We do, however, consider new ventures being planned by established companies."

FURTHER READING:

Alsop, Stewart. "What's a New Economy without Research?" *Fortune*. May 15, 2000.

Baker, M. Sharon. "Allen's Interactive-Television Empire Gears Up." *Business Journal-Portland*. May 19, 2000.

Donohue, Steve. "Allen Answers ITV Queries." *Multichannel News*. December 4, 2000.

Jones, Tim. "St. Louis-Based Sports Magazine Finds New Owner." *Knight-Ridder/Tribune Business News*. February 16, 2000.

Kirkpatrick, David. "Are You Experienced?" *Fortune*. July 24, 2000.

———"Why We're Betting Billions on TV." *Fortune.* May 15, 2000.

Mermigas, Diane. "Digeo Rollout Brings 'Wired World' Closer." *Electronic Media.* July 10, 2000.

Moltzen, Edward F. "Eighteen: Paul Allen, the Money Man." *Computer Reseller News.* November 13, 2000.

"Net Leader Finds Reason to Retreat." *Internet World.* December 1, 2000.

"Paul Allen Leaves Microsoft Board." *Computer Weekly.* October 5, 2000.

"The Paul Allen Story." April 30, 2001. Available from www.paulallen.com.

Stross, Randall E. "This Keg's On Me, Fellas." *U.S. News & World Report.* November 13, 2000.

"Top Five." *Forbes.* October 9, 2000.

SEE ALSO: Broadband Technology; Gates, William (Bill); Microsoft Corp.; Microsoft Windows

ALTAVISTA CO.

AltaVista—the name means "the view from above"—is a Web portal that offers Web pages, shopping, news, live audio and video, and community resources including e-mail. The site is run by AltaVista Co., a majority-owned operating company of Palo Alto, California-based CMGI Inc. AltaVista is perhaps best known for its search technology. It provided the first full-text search service in the world when it was created in 1995 at the Palo Alto research laboratory of Digital Equipment Corporation (DEC). DEC's engineers devised a plan to store every word of every page on the entire Internet in a searchable index, and then utilize DEC's new Alpha 8400 computers to extract relevant information from this body of knowledge.

AltaVista has been awarded more search-related patents than any other company. The 2001 version of AltaVista Search is available in 25 languages with eight distinct search dimensions. Other innovations credited to AltaVista include the first-ever multilingual search capacity on the Internet and the first search technology to support Chinese, Japanese, and Korean languages. AltaVista created Babel Fish, the first machine translation service on the Web. AltaVista also created advanced and multimedia search centers that let users search the Web for photos, videos, and music through its index of more than 30 million multimedia objects.

HISTORY

When DEC was absorbed into Compaq Computer Corporation in 1998, AltaVista became a division of Compaq. Instead of selling off AltaVista, Compaq invested more money in it. By the end of 1998 AltaVista had a user base of 12 million people and 32 million page views per day. With its core strength of extraordinary search technology that generated results faster than most other search engines, AltaVista's goal was to become one of the top five sites within three years. Its principal competitors at that time were Yahoo!, Excite, and Lycos. AltaVista was generating about $50 million a year in revenue, primarily from banner ads on its site.

In early 1999 Compaq spun AltaVista off into an independent company. Rod Schrock, senior vice president of Compaq's Consumer Product Group, was named president and CEO of AltaVista Co. In January 1999, he announced: "We're going to design e-commerce into the very fabric of AltaVista." AltaVista got a boost from Microsoft Corp., a longtime partner of Compaq, with the addition of Microsoft's HotMail e-mail service. Microsoft also said it would provide future instant messaging technology to AltaVista and that AltaVista would replace Inktomi Corp. as the search engine for the Microsoft Network (MSN).

Compaq added shopping capabilities to AltaVista in early 1999 with the $211 million acquisition of Shopping.com, an online retailer that offered more than 2 million products over the Internet. Compaq also acquired Zip2 Corp., a company that specialized in providing directory and database services for newspapers. Zip2 Corp. had 160 media partners—newspapers for whom Zip2 put their content and advertising into an online, searchable format. AltaVista planned to combine Zip2's directory and database features with the e-commerce capabilities of Shopping.com and to give local merchants access to the features of Shopping.com through the Web sites of their local newspapers. The *Houston Chronicle's* Houston4U.com Web site was showcased as an example of how AltaVista's local portals would work.

ALTAVISTA SOLD TO CMGI INC. IN 1999

With Compaq experiencing financial difficulties following its acquisition of DEC, AltaVista was sold to CMGI Inc. in mid-1999 for $2.3 billion. CMGI gained an 83-percent interest in AltaVista, with Compaq retaining 17 percent of the company. As part of the deal Compaq received 19 million shares of CMGI stock, a $220 million three-year note, seats on the boards of directors of AltaVista and CMGI, and an interest in the 40 Internet companies operated by CMGI. At the time of the sale, AltaVista was ranked 15th among the most popular Internet sites and had fewer than 10 million separate visitors each month.

In the months following the sale, AltaVista announced a global branding campaign. Initially budgeted for $50 million, some $120 million was spent on the campaign by June 2000. The campaign coincided with the launch of an upgraded and redesigned AltaVista Network, which included features from Shopping.com and local content from Zip2 Corp. Around this time AltaVista also announced it would offer free Internet access to subscribers who were willing to view ads and provide information about themselves. In a month of testing, the free Internet service gained 45,000 users, and by October 1999 there were 500,000 subscribers to the free service. AltaVista also introduced a free ''microportal'' service, which gave users continual access to their own range of favorite Web sites through a window on their computer desktop.

Following the sale to CMGI, AltaVista cancelled plans to incorporate previously announced services from Microsoft into its portal, including HotMail and instant messaging. Instead, e-mail service bureau Critical Path was tapped to provide e-mail for the new AltaVista portal to be launched later in the year (CMGI was a minority owner of Critical Path). For instant messaging, AltaVista selected the PowWow instant messaging service developed by Tribal Voice.

Gearing up for the 1999 holiday shopping season, AltaVista introduced a major redesign to its Web site at the end of October 1999. Among the major changes was a simplification of its Internet searching technology, which included using subject categories to help users narrow their searches. Another major change involved the site's shopping features. The newly designed AltaVista site would rely less on Shopping.com, which had experienced a high level of complaints about late delivery of merchandise, and add a number of online stores. Other new features included product reviews and comparative shopping.

At the end of November 1999, AltaVista acquired Raging Bull Inc., an online investor chat forum and financial site partially owned by CMGI. Raging Bull was known for developing an online community for nonprofessional stock pickers and was the second most popular online investor forum behind Yahoo!'s stock market and finance section. The addition of Raging Bull was expected to build traffic at AltaVista and serve as the model for other online forums devoted to a wide range of subjects.

The changes AltaVista made to its site started to result in higher traffic. According to Media Metrix, AltaVista was the eleventh-most-visited site in November 1999, up from 15th earlier in the year. In its December 1999 filing for an AltaVista IPO (initial public offering), CMGI claimed that AltaVista was the fifth-most-popular Internet search engine. However, changing market conditions in 2000 would prevent AltaVista from going public, and the IPO was later withdrawn. Other developments at the end of 1999 included the launch of an AltaVista site in the United Kingdom, a European advertising campaign, and local rollouts in France, Italy, and Germany. AltaVista planned to expand its European presence to 18 countries in 2000.

NEW INITIATIVES TO INCREASE TRAFFIC IN 2000

AltaVista launched its AltaVista Affiliate Network in early 2000 and quickly gained 1,600 applications for membership in the program. Under the program, AltaVista would let Web sites of any size or scope offer AltaVista services such as search, stock quotes, or language translation free of charge. AltaVista also would pay affiliated sites three cents for every click-through to an AltaVista Web page. AltaVista planned to distribute the HTML code to allow Web sites to feature an AltaVista search box and other services on their sites. For January 2000 AltaVista moved up to the ninth-most-visited site on the Internet with 13.4 million visitors, up from 12th in December 1999, according to Media Metrix.

AltaVista's strategy for growth was focused on three principal areas: searching, e-commerce, and financial information services. In February 2000 the company introduced three multimedia search centers that allowed users to search for more than 3 million MP3, video, and image files. Through partnerships with CDnow Inc., EMusic.com Inc., and Riffage.com Inc., AltaVista was able to offer more than 1 million downloadable MP3 audio files. Through additional partnerships with ABC News Internet Ventures, Merrill Lynch & Co., and Entertainment Boulevard Inc.'s Vidnet site, AltaVista expanded its coverage of breaking news and financial and entertainment news.

AltaVista also continued to build its presence in Europe. It was able to boast that more than half of its search requests came from outside of the United States. In March AltaVista began offering free Internet access in the United Kingdom. The company noted that high telephone charges for time spent online were hindering Internet usage in the United Kingdom. However, problems with British Telecom resulted in a suspension of AltaVista's free Internet access in the U.K. by August 2000.

Financially, AltaVista had not reported a profit since its inception, but it hoped to report positive cash flow by December 2000. After canceling plans for its IPO in April 2000, the company laid off about six percent of its workforce by eliminating 50 positions. It already had cut about 60 other jobs since fall 1999. For the six months ending January 31, 2000, AltaVista reported an operating loss of $542.9 million, due in part to acquisitions and the addition of new features to its Web site.

REFOCUSED ON BEING A SEARCH PORTAL, 2000-2001

In the second half of 2000 AltaVista began to reposition itself as a search portal and focus on unveiling more powerful search technologies. The company introduced a new Advanced Search Center that would take up to 800 characters and allow Boolean searches. In September AltaVista cut an additional 225 employees, reducing its workforce by about 25 percent. In October CEO Rod Schrock stepped down, leaving the company to be run by President Greg Memo and Chief Financial Officer Ken Barber. In addition, AltaVista's free Internet service was terminated in the United States. In February 2001 AltaVista sold Raging Bull to competitor Terra Lycos.

For 2001 AltaVista appeared to be fully refocused on its core strength of search engine technology. In addition to offering advanced search capabilities at its Web site, AltaVista was pursuing the enterprise search market by licensing its search software to businesses. In an effort to make its search results more relevant to individuals, AltaVista partnered with Moreover, a specialty search company, to make news available within 15 minutes for searching. As part of their partnership, the two companies planned to approach corporate portals with a proposal to sub-index their corporate information to enable employees to search internal documents.

FURTHER READING:

"AltaVista Announcement Sparks UK Internet Access Price War." *Internet Business News.* March 2000.

AltaVista Co. "AltaVista Company Background." April 30, 2001. Available from doc.altavista.com.

"AltaVista Going Public." *San Francisco Business Times.* December 24, 1999.

"AltaVista Offloads Raging Bull." *New Media Age.* February 1, 2001.

Andrews, Whit. "In Redesign, AltaVista Is Returning to Its Roots." *Internet World.* October 19, 1998.

Corcoran, Elizabeth. "Compaq Plans to Spin Off AltaVista." *The Washington Post.* January 27, 1999.

King, Julia. "AltaVista: Free Net Access." *Computerworld.* August 16, 1999.

Mack, Jennifer. "AltaVista to Seed Web with Code." *PC Week.* February 7, 2000.

Morneau, Jill. "AltaVista Yanks Plug on Free Internet Service." *TechWeb.* December 6, 2000.

Schwartz, John. "CMGI Buys AltaVista from Ailing Compaq." *The Washington Post.* June 30, 1999.

Tucker, Henry. "AltaVista Quits Portal Business." *PC Magazine (UK).* December 2000.

Williamson, Debra Aho. "AltaVista Paints 'Smarter' Pose to Focus Brand." *Advertising Age.* March 13, 2000.

Zimmerman, Christine. "All the News That's Fit to Index." *InternetWeek.* March 26, 2001.

SEE ALSO: CMGI; Compaq Computer Corp.; Digital Equipment Corp.; Portals, Web

AMAZON.COM

Although Amazon.com built its reputation as an online bookstore, the Seattle-based company has pursued a strategy of offering a wide assortment of products, which it promotes as "Earth's Biggest Selection." An early 2001 version of the company's home page offered links to several categories, among them books, electronics, toys, video, music, health and beauty, wireless phones, camera and photo, computer and video games, software, tools and hardware, lawn and patio, cars, auctions, and gifts.

Amazon.com went online in July 1995 and quickly set the standard for other e-tailers. The company changed the way people buy books by staying open 24 hours a day, seven days a week. It also developed its own user-friendly ordering system and provided reviews and other information about the books it sold that no traditional bookstore could match. Amazon.com's head start on other booksellers helped it to dominate the online book market. Barnes and Noble, the largest traditional book retailer, had a market value of $2 billion in 1998, compared to $5.8 billion for Amazon.com.

Amazon.com was founded by Jeff Bezos. Bezos determined that books, videos, computer software and hardware, and CDs would be the easiest products to sell online. They were items that a customer did not necessarily need to see or handle before ordering, and they were easy to pack and ship. Without the physical space limitations of a bricks-and-mortar store, Bezos realized that an online store could offer a wider selection of those items.

In the beginning, Amazon.com was aided by the established wholesale network for books that already existed. The company didn't need a big inventory to start with. One reason Amazon.com chose Seattle, Washington, as its base was that it would be near the world's largest book wholesaler, which was based in Oregon. Seattle also offered a well-educated employment pool. Amazon.com added a warehouse in Delaware in 1997, but the company began in Bezos's garage and then moved its shipping operation into a 20-by-20-foot space. After nearly two years in this small space, the company finally began using a large warehouse in Seattle. In 1998 Amazon.com began selling CDs and computer games in addition to its selection of 3 million books.

THE FIRST E-HOLIDAY SHOPPING SEASON, 1998

The fourth quarter of 1998 was the first holiday shopping season in the United States that had substantial retail sales over the Internet. The Boston Consulting Group estimated that American consumers spent about $4 billion buying goods and services online during the fourth quarter of 1998, and nearly $10 billion throughout the year. While that amounted to less than one percent of all U.S. retail sales, e-commerce sales more than tripled from 1997. The same report estimated that more than 8 million U.S. households made an online purchase during 1998.

In the fourth quarter of 1998 America Online (AOL) was the Internet's most popular shopping mall, but Amazon.com was the number one e-tailer. It sold a variety of books, CDs, videos, and gifts, including a selection of 185 toys. It also spent heavily on marketing and advertising—$29 on average to acquire a new customer, which is one reason the company had yet to turn a profit.

EXPANSION INTO NEW MARKETS, 1999

In June 1999 Amazon.com formed an alliance with auction house Sotheby's Holdings Inc. to launch a joint auction site specializing in art, antiques, and collectibles. Amazon.com agreed to invest $45 million in Sotheby's. Amazon planned to host the site as part of its growing auction page, which offered 20 different categories of auctions. All of the property would be offered by Sotheby's and other dealers. In addition, the authenticity and condition of each item would be guaranteed. The site also planned to conduct online auctions in conjunction with live auctions from Sotheby's in New York. The site (www.sothebys. amazon.com) launched in November 1999.

By mid-1999, Amazon.com was valued at $22 billion, according to *Newsweek*. In two years its customer base had grown from 2 million to 11 million. Not only was Amazon the dominant bookseller, it had become the biggest music retailer on the Internet. The company also sold toys and consumer electronics. However, although Amazon was a flagship for e-commerce, it had yet to turn a profit. The company explained that revenue was being used to build the business, and that they eventually planned to offer anything and everything online.

For the 1999 holiday shopping season, Amazon.com added four new stores to its site: home improvement, software, video games, and gift ideas. It was part of the firm's strategy to offer a large selection of items across multiple product lines. Amazon.com had introduced online auctions in spring 1999, followed by its zShops marketplace, which let customers sell their own items for a set price or by auction.

NEW PARTNERS HELP TO INCREASE REVENUE

During 2000 Amazon.com entered into new partnerships designed to increase the firm's revenue and make it profitable. Amazon.com had spent heavily to attract customers. Now it was entering into agreements with other dot-coms to give them access to its base of 16 million customers in exchange for a fee and an ownership interest. The agreements also were part of Amazon.com's strategy to offer the widest possible assortment of products through its Web site. Each agreement would add to Amazon.com's operating income, offsetting a projected loss of $41.7 million for 2001.

In January 2001 Amazon.com invested an additional $30 million in Drugstore.com, increasing its ownership interest in the dot-com to 28 percent. In return, Amazon.com would receive $105 million over three years to display Drugstore.com prominently on its Web site by giving the site its own category tab on Amazon.com's home page. Amazon.com also invested an undisclosed amount for a five-percent interest in Greenlight.com, which sold cars online. Greenlight.com agreed to pay Amazon.com $82.5 million over five years for promoting its site to Amazon.com customers.

Other partnerships involved such dot-coms as Ashford.com, a seller of luxury goods; NextCard, which was creating a co-branded MasterCard and Visa credit card; and Gear.com, which sold sporting goods at a discount. During the year additional links were added to Pets.com and Homegrocer.com. As the year progressed, the Internet economy weakened and several dot-coms reorganized or went out of business. One casualty was Living.com, which had promised to pay Amazon.com $145 million over five years to be its home-furnishings partner. That revenue stream was lost when Living.com closed up in August 2000. Weakening support for dot-coms also caused Amazon.com to rearrange its terms with several other partners who were part of the Amazon Commerce Network, including Greenlight.com and Drugstore.com, again reducing the company's revenue.

Although management's strategy was aimed at achieving certain operating income levels rather than revenue growth, Amazon.com continued to lose money during 2000. For the second quarter ending June 30, Amazon.com reported a loss of $115.7 million on revenue of $578 million. Customer accounts rose by 2.5 million during the quarter to reach a total of 22.5 million customers. Repeat orders made up 78 percent of Amazon.com's total, up from 70 percent a year earlier. The company also noted that its book and video sales had finally become profitable. Its electronics division posted the biggest gain during the quarter, while its U.S. book, music, and DVD sales totaled $385.28 million, with a profit of $10.06 million. The company also announced it expected to end the year with about $1 billion in cash. Investors expressed concern about Amazon.com's rising debt load, which increased from $1.5 billion at the end of 1999 to $2.1 billion at the end of June. Servicing its debt cost Amazon.com an estimated $150 million annually.

Through its agreement with Greenlight.com, Amazon.com added cars to its product offerings in August 2000. The new link presented information on automobiles and trucks in the standard Amazon.com format. They were listed on Amazon.com's new ventures section, which included all of Amazon.com's non-media products. Amazon.com was able to offer new car and truck sales in 27 metro markets through affiliated dealers, including three of the top dealership networks.

After less than a year online, Amazon.com's co-branded auction site with Sotheby's auction house was closed in October 2000. The listings from Sothebys.amazon.com were consolidated on Sothebys.com, the auction house's primary Web site. The reason given for the consolidation was the need to achieve a larger scale and offer customers a much deeper selection in a single site. The consolidation also made it easier for Sothebys.com's 5,000 associates to conduct business online.

Amazon.com also expanded internationally during 2000, opening sites in France and Japan in addition to its existing sites in Germany and the United Kingdom. The Japanese-language site was launched in November 2000 and focused on books. Japan already was Amazon.com's largest export market, with nearly 200,000 Japanese customers ordering $34 million in products each year from the company's U.S.-based site. The Japanese site was supported by a corporate office in Tokyo, a distribution center in Ichikawa, and a customer service center in Sapporo, Hokkaido. Although Japanese publishing regulations prevented the e-tailer from offering large discounts on Japanese-language books, it could continue to discount its English-language titles up to 30 percent. For the rest of 2000 the Japanese site offered free shipping as an incentive.

A November 2000 report compiled by Forrester Research revealed a tight three-way race among online booksellers. For the first time, Borders.com passed Amazon.com as the top online bookseller, with Barnesandnoble.com a close third. Forrester's PowerRankings of major U.S. e-commerce sites, which were based on consumer surveys followed by its own online shopping tests, gave Borders.com a 66.83 rating, compared to 66.76 for Amazon.com and 65.46 for Barnesandnoble.com. The results demonstrated that while Amazon.com was focused on branching out into other product lines, Borders.com and Barnesandnoble.com were working hard to sell books over the Internet. In the Forrester survey, Borders was tops in the categories of transaction efficiency, cost, and delivery/returns, while Barnesandnoble.com led in ease of use and customer service. Subsequently, in April 2001 Borders announced its exit from online retailing and turned over the operation of Borders.com to Amazon.com, for which Amazon.com received a one-time payment and a percentage of revenue from sales.

A December 2000 report by Jupiter Media Metrix revealed the strength of Amazon.com's international appeal. It was the most visited e-tailer in Australia, Canada, the United Kingdom, and the United States. In addition, Amazon.com was among the top five online retailers in Brazil, Denmark, France, and Japan. In the United Kingdom the company actually ranked first and second, with its U.K. site attracting 1.75 million unique visitors in November, while its U.S. site attracted 993,000 visitors. The U.S. site reported 1.22 million visitors during November from Canada and 461,000 from Australia.

AMAZON.COM DOMINATED THE HOLIDAY SHOPPING SEASON, 2000

According to AdRelevance, Amazon.com was the most advertised company on the Internet for eight out of nine weeks during the 2000 holiday shopping season. Its $61.8 million ad budget for December led the pack in Internet advertising, with nearly 3 billion ad impressions. Barnesandnoble.com was a distant second with $23.8 million spent on Internet advertising in December. Amazon.com advertised on more than 100 Web sites, but it made an effort to dominate on the top sites. The top five sites it advertised on were MSN, AOL, Netscape, Juno, and Excite, where it was the number one advertiser on four of those sites and the number three advertiser on Excite.

Amazon.com employed brand recognition as well as direct marketing advertisements in its campaign. Before the holiday season, only 5.3 million of the company's 275.3 million ad impressions were direct marketing impressions. By the end of November, Amazon.com had begun to place more emphasis on direct marketing impressions. During the last week of November, Amazon.com ran 320 million branding impressions, compared to 212.8 direct marketing impressions, in an effort to achieve immediate results. Each direct marketing ad had 4 million impressions, while each branding ad had 750,000 impressions.

Perhaps Amazon.com's most important partnership of 2000 was its online joint venture with Toys 'R' Us, which had been struggling to develop its own online strategy. For the 2000 holiday shopping season, Amazon.com and bricks-and-mortar retailer Toys 'R' Us joined forces to create Toysrus.com. The alliance was announced in August 2000, with the newly created Toysrus.com to select and purchase the toys using its parent company's clout, while Amazon.com would run the store on its Web site, ship the products, and handle customer service. The venture played to the strengths of both companies, and it paid off in a big way for the 2000 holiday shopping season. According to a report by Nielsen/NetRatings, the joint site was the number one online shopping site during the holiday season with 123 million visitors. Coming in second with 21.12 million shopping visits during the season was rival eToys, followed by Dell.com with 21 million visitors, Barnesandnoble.com with 20.25 million visits, CDNow.com with 20 million, and Walmart.com with 18 million.

FOCUSED ON PROFITABILITY, 2001

Amazon.com continued to outpace its online competition in January 2001, registering 2.3 million projected buyers according to a report from PC Data—nearly double the number for January 2000. Although Amazon.com beat Wall Street's estimates for the fourth quarter of 2000, the company announced at the end of January that it would lay off 1,300 workers, or 15 percent of its workforce. Other cost-cutting measures included closing a distribution center in Georgia and a customer service center in Seattle. The company also lowered revenue estimates for 2001, mainly due to the slowdown of the overall economy toward the end of 2000. Amazon.com projected that sales would grow from 20 to 30 percent in 2001 to $3.3 to $3.6 billion. Still, the company maintained that it would reach operating profitability by the end of 2001, and that it would have about $900 million in cash and marketable securities at the end of the year.

FURTHER READING:

"All Boxed In." *Time.* September 4, 2000.

"Amazon in New E-tail Deals." *Puget Sound Business Journal.* January 28, 2000.

Dembeck, Chet. "Amazon and Sotheby's Launch Upscale Auction Site." *E-Commerce Times.* November 19, 1999. Available from www.ecommercetimes.com.

"Double Play." *Business Week.* October 23, 2000.

Enos, Lori. "Amazon Ranked as Net Ad Champ." *E-Commerce Times.* December 14, 2000. Available from www.ecommercetimes.com.

"Inside the First e-Christmas." *Fortune.* February 1, 1999.

Macaluso, Nora. "Amazon and Toys 'R' Us Take E-Holiday Prize." *E-Commerce Times.* January 2, 2001. Available from www.ecommercetimes.com.

Rabinovitz, Jonathan. "Santa Monica, Calif.-Based Internet Entrepreneur Sells Toys." *Knight-Ridder/Tribune Business News.* October 25, 1998.

Reid, Calvin. "Amazon.com in Pact to Take Over Borders.com." *Publishers Weekly.* April 16, 2001.

Saliba, Clare. "Report: Amazon Smashed E-tail Competition in January." *E-Commerce Times.* February 14, 2001. Available from www.ecommercetimes.com.

"We Have Lift-off." *The Economist (US).* February 3, 2001.

"Wired for the Bottom Line." *Newsweek.* September 20, 1999.

SEE ALSO: Barnesandnoble.com; Bezos, Jeff; Business-to-Consumer (B2C) E-Commerce

AMERICAN NATIONAL STANDARDS INSTITUTE (ANSI)

A private, non-profit organization that works to coordinate voluntary standards, the American National Standards Institute (ANSI) is the hub of all standards-related policy decisions in the United States. It is the primary U.S. body that coordinates the efforts of industry, consumer, and governmental standards developers, and is the sole organization that accredits other U.S. standards organizations. With offices in New York City and headquarters in Washington, D.C., ANSI's mission is to boost the competitiveness of U.S. business and the American quality of life by ensuring the U.S. voluntary standardization system is well coordinated and promoted. Therefore, ANSI sees to it that U.S. businesses and industries maintain an adequate performance level for products, services, and processes, ideally keeping in mind the range of affected interests.

ANSI has played an important role in U.S. commerce for many years. It was founded in 1918 by a coalition of five engineering societies and three government agencies. The organization generates funding through its membership, which is comprised of nearly 1,000 private and public sector members, including individual companies, organizations, governmental agencies, institutions, and international organizations.

Mainly a service to the U.S. private sector and its position in the global economy, ANSI also works closely with governmental organizations. ANSI often coordinates its efforts with the National Institute of Standards and Technology (NIST), an agency of the U.S. Department of Commerce's technology administration. A key area of activity is conformity assessment. Through its accreditation process, ANSI oversees the moves made by manufacturers and others to incorporate voluntary standards. ANSI confers the "American National Standard" (ANS) designation upon those organizations that meet its basic guidelines of due process, openness, balance, and consensus in setting and meeting the organization's voluntary standards.

ANSI does not, however, actually write or implement standards. Rather, the organization acts as a consensus-generating facilitator between various groups devoted to developing standards specific to their areas of concern. In this way, ANSI eschews a top-down approach to standards development, leaving the various sectors with autonomy in creating standards appropriate to the conditions they face. ANSI simply seeks to ease the standards into use with an eye toward a holistic look at U.S. competitiveness and quality-of-life issues.

ANSI ON THE WORLD STAGE

ANSI is the U.S. affiliate of the International Organization for Standardization (ISO), of which it is a founding member and one of the five permanent members of the governing ISO Council. ANSI also is a member of the International Accreditation Forum (IAF) and the International Electrotechnical Committee (IEC). Additionally, ANSI champions the adoption of U.S.-based standards on the international scene, and when appropriate, aims to incorporate international standards in the United States.

There is a perpetual tension surrounding the nationalistic character of standards, whereby individual nations insist on autonomy in setting their own standards. Conversely, the internationalization of standards carries some of the same complications to the next level. Nations sometimes disagree when another tries to impose its standards as the global ones, thereby attaining a state of hegemony and other advantages. In the late 1990s, European organizations increasingly introduced new standards that some in the United States feared would undermine U.S. competitiveness in the global marketplace. ANSI and related organizations thus recognized the need to produce a more systematic and responsive U.S. standardization environment.

Facing the emergence of relatively clear European standards and their influence on global commerce, in September 2000 ANSI presented a proposed ''National Standards Strategy for the United States'' to the U.S. House Science Committee's Subcommittee on Technology. Stemming from a 1998 standards summit co-hosted by ANSI and NIST, which gathered government, industry, and consumer groups, the proposal marked the end of two years of cooperative efforts. With the dramatic increase in global trade, foreign competition, and the growing concern with protecting health, safety, and the environment, we ''can't assume that U.S. technology and practice will automatically be adopted everywhere,'' the proposal stated, noting that ''emerging economies with the potential for explosive growth are looking to ISO and IEC for standards'' rather than to the United States.

While renewing support for the established U.S. standards-writing principles—which cherish open participation by all interested parties and easy access to the status and progress of standards writing—ANSI called for a 12-step program to be undertaken in the United States. Its purpose was to give the nation a unified voice and a quick, fair, and workable standards-writing and implementation process for competing in the global marketplace. The steps involved included integrating several elements into the writing process. Among these were the environmental, health, and safety concerns of affected parties; a greater awareness and consideration of consumer concerns; and coordinated efforts with industries in other countries. In December 2000, ANSI and NIST signed a memorandum of understanding (MoU) that aimed to further the National Standards Strategy by increasing communication between the two organizations and private and public interests in the United States. Moreover, the MoU shored up the recognition of ANSI as the sole international representative of U.S. standards interests.

The voluntary nature of U.S. standards is one impediment to the systematic adoption of standards throughout an industry, country, or across the globe, despite ANSI's efforts to broaden the application of voluntary standards. Moreover, the wave of downsizing in the U.S. economy in the 1990s often eliminated the layers of workers devoted to the technical aspects of applying standards. The National Standards Strategy was designed to address and overcome these difficulties.

ANSI AND THE INTERNET

Before e-commerce, ANSI already was involved in standardizing processes for computers. For instance, the well-known C programming language was approved by the ANSI committee, thereby ensuring that most C compilers were compatible with each other, regardless of the vendor. Additionally, ANSI established a range of standards for both electronic and electrical components and interactions, and set the standards for a range of communications protocols, including those for fiber-optic data transmission.

As the Internet opened up in the early 1990s and e-commerce became an increasingly important social and economic phenomenon, ANSI again kicked into high gear to coordinate the virtually wide-open move to develop protocols and standards. With the Internet and e-commerce speeding the pace of development and change, there grew increasing calls for a speeding of the standards-setting process. For instance, developments in the methods of online payments are crucial to the development and expansion of e-commerce, and it's crucial that the speed and security of such payments keep pace with the speed of the Internet in general. In that spirit, ANSI oversaw the development of uniform standards for electronic signatures, which facilitate the employment of e-checks for online payment. These standards set guidelines for the generation, verification, and security of electronic signatures.

In the early 2000s, the ANSI-accredited ASC X12 Committee focused on pan-industrial business standards for Extensible Markup Language (XML), a hypertext meta-language allowing for the definition of Web-based information, design, and communication. The committee based its standards-writing on the Electronic Business XML (ebXML) initiative, which is designed to facilitate the business-to-business e-commerce market. The standards aim to coordinate a set of business ''objects,'' valid across national boundaries, which define elements of online transactions.

ANSI also oversaw the many different groups dedicated to developing standards for storage-area networks (SANs). Often, the major manufacturers in a given industry will proceed with the development of a de facto standard before ANSI even gets involved. However, according to *Computer Technology Review,* such ANSI-less standards are much more difficult to establish when dealing with many vendors that provide very similar products that must work in an open network environment, as is the case with SANs. As a result, ANSI took the initiative in working with SAN companies and organizations at a fairly early stage in the standards-development process.

In the late 1990s, ANSI joined 24 other standards organizations worldwide in calling for the development of international e-commerce standards, mainly to protect consumers. These proposals included measures to ensure the reliability of merchants and to safeguard privacy and the security of financial information. At the ISO's Committee on Consumer Policy (COPOLCO) meeting in May 2000, COPOLCO presented evidence that consumers, for lack of confidence in these areas, often were hesitant to engage in online commerce. Thus, the development of such standards was of great concern to consumers and businesses alike. The lack of standardization in an area with such rich opportunities provided business groups with a vital stake in contributing to and facilitating an e-commerce standardization process.

The result of the COPOLCO meeting was the creation of the E-Commerce Consumer Standards Solutions Forum, which centers worldwide discussion on the implementation of international standards for the online marketplace. The ultimate goal was increased consumer acceptance of and involvement in e-commerce, aided by multilateral governmental agreements, domestic regulations, standards created and implemented through the normal domestic and international channels, consumer education and outreach, and other approaches.

FURTHER READING:

''Implementation of the U.S. National Standards Strategy and Coordinated Efforts in International Standardization Play Key Roles in Revised MoU Between ANSI and NIST.'' Washington, D.C.: American National Standards Institute, February 2001. Available from web.ansi.org.

''An Introduction to ANSI.'' Washington, D.C.: American National Standards Institute, 2000. Available from www.ansi.org/.

''ISO COPOLCO and the Euro Commission Establish On-line Forums for E-Commerce Discussions.'' Washington, D.C.: American National Standards Institute, August 2000. Available from web.ansi.org.

Lyford, Richard. ''Developing Standards for Storage Area Networks.'' *Computer Technology Review.* October 1999.

Murphy, Patricia A. ''Building An Internet Payments Platform.'' *Bank Technology News.* September 2000.

Nailen, Richard L. ''As the World Turns, Standards Writing Gets More Complex.'' *Electrical Apparatus.* December 2000.

Zuckerman, Amy. ''Hot Global Standards and Testing Trends.'' *World Trade.* October 2000.

AMERITRADE HOLDING CORP.

Ameritrade Holding Corp. offers online discount brokerage services through five subsidiaries, each of which has its own strategy and target market. Ameritrade Inc. (www.ameritrade.com) is the company's principal retail broker-dealer. It combines discount brokerage fees with trading over the Internet and only charges an $8 brokerage fee for each Internet equity market order. Ameritrade also provides a relatively high level of service and offers a number of investment tools, including free real-time quotes, customizable charts, market summaries, and research tools like company profiles and earnings estimates. It also makes current financial information from Reuters, PR Newswire, and Business Wire available to its customers. Another service of Ameritrade provides free market reports and individual stock alerts that can be delivered via e-mail, alphanumeric pager, and e-mail enabled mobile phone. Ameritrade customers also can request assistance from a customer service representative or technical support person via e-mail or phone.

Another subsidiary, Accutrade Inc. (www.accutrade.com), provides a higher level of service for customers who are willing to pay for it, including personal service from a discount broker. Freetrade.com (www.freetrade.com) was introduced in May 2000 for experienced investors who require little in the way of personalized service. Freetrade charges no commission on Internet market orders and only $5 for stop-

and-limit orders and odd lots. Freetrade's limited service includes buying and selling equities, as well as short sells and buys and option orders. However, it does not trade in mutual funds or over-the-counter, pink sheet, or bulletin board orders. All communication with Freetrade must be done by e-mail, and funding of accounts must be done by wire. Freetrade does not accept account transfers, and there are no personnel assigned to open mail or answer the telephone. To qualify for a Freetrade account an investor must have at least two years of experience as a customer of a discount broker and two years of experience as an Internet user. A deposit of $5,000 is required to activate an account at Freetrade. Freetrade expected to generate revenue through interest income, from payments by market makers and specialists based on order flow, and from advertising on its Web site.

Two other subsidiaries, AmeriVest Inc. and Ameritrade Institutional Services Inc. (AIS), enable the company to provide discount online brokerage services to customers of other financial institutions or service providers. AmeriVest provides wholesale brokerage services to financial institutions such as banks, savings and loans, credit unions, and their customers. AIS was introduced in late 2000 to provide brokerage services to financial planners and investment advisors and their customers. Another subsidiary, Advanced Clearing, provides clearing services to Ameritrade Holdings' subsidiaries, as well as to independent broker-dealers and others.

Ameritrade Holding also operates a financial portal, OnMoney.com, which was launched in late 1999. OnMoney.com offers personal financial management services that enable customers to view and manage their various personal financial accounts, including checking and savings accounts, credit cards, reward programs, and investments—all on one statement and without having to transfer any account balances. When Ameritrade Holding acquired Financial Passport Inc. in July 2000, OnMoney.com was able to expand the services it offered to include financial planning and a wide range of other financial products and services. At the OnMoney.com Web site visitors can link to deals on mortgages, discount brokers, banks, auto insurance, life insurance, bill payment services, auto loans, financial planners, and more. The site also features links to up-to-date financial news.

ONE OF THE FIRST DISCOUNT BROKERAGE FIRMS

Ameritrade Holding Corp. has a long history as a discount brokerage firm that goes back to May 1975, when the Securities and Exchange Commission (SEC) deregulated the brokerage industry and made negotiated commissions available to individual inves-

tors. Around this time J. Joe Ricketts and his partners became associated with the company, then known as First Omaha Securities, which had been established in 1971 as a local investment-banking firm in Omaha, Nebraska. First Omaha Securities became one of the first firms to offer negotiated commissions, later known as discount brokerage, in 1975.

First Omaha Securities later became First National Brokerage Services Inc., and then Accutrade Inc. In 1987 TransTerra Co. was established as the holding company for AmeriTrade Clearing (later known as Advanced Clearing), a clearing broker established by the company in 1983, and the company's discount brokerages. During the 1980s and 1990s Accutrade developed its customer-oriented business strategy by offering multiple means of access to trading. In 1988 the company was the first to offer trading by touch-tone phone. In 1995 customers were able to trade over a portable communications device. In 1996 the company launched Accutrade for Windows, the first online investing system that allowed individuals to engage in program and basket trading.

In 1994 the company launched Ceres Securities Inc., a deep discount brokerage. In 1995 it acquired K. Aufhauser & Co. Inc., which had the first Internet trading site launched in August 1994. In 1995 it also acquired All American Brokers Inc., and in 1996 launched eBroker, an Internet-only broker, as a division of All American Brokers. In November 1996 the parent company TransTerra was renamed Ameritrade Holding Corp.

AMERITRADE INC. LAUNCHED IN 1997

Ameritrade Holding Corp. had its initial public offering (IPO) on March 3, 1997, with shares opening at $15 per share. During the year the company established marketing alliances with America Online, The Microsoft Network, The Motley Fool, Yahoo!, the Quicken.com Channel, and Infoseek's Personal Finance Channel. In October 1997 Ameritrade Inc. was launched, incorporating the most popular features of Aufhauser, Ceres, and eBroker into one firm and offering breakthrough pricing of $8 per Internet trade. It also was during 1997 that Ameritrade Holding began developing OnMoney, its Internet-based financial services mall.

By mid-1997 Internet trading had grown to about 25 percent of the firm's brokerage activity, or about 25,000 trades per month. Following the consolidation of Aufhauser, Ceres, and eBroker into Ameritrade Inc., the company launched a $20 million national advertising campaign focusing on the Ameritrade's online trading fee of $8. For fiscal 1997, ending September 26, Ameritrade Holding reported net income of $13.8 million on net revenue of $77.2 million (subsequently restated to $95.7 million).

Heavy advertising expenditures helped to increase the number of new accounts at Ameritrade and boost revenue, but they also resulted in much higher quarterly losses. For the first quarter of fiscal 1998 the company reported a loss of $11.2 million on revenue of $25.7 million, while customer accounts increased by 50 percent to 147,000. The company handled an average of 10,600 trades a day during the quarter. Ameritrade justified its strategy of pursuing market share by noting that online accounts were relatively cheap to acquire through advertising and marketing. In mid-1998 Ameritrade expanded its relationship with America Online by committing to pay $25 million over two years for a prominent spot on America Online's finance page. After reporting losses for the first two quarters of fiscal 1998, Ameritrade had a profitable third quarter as it began earning revenue from newly acquired customer accounts.

Ameritrade's average number of online trades was 21,400 by mid-1998. Market turbulence later in the year resulted in a one-day record of 35,000 trades for the company. In some cases the high volume of trading resulted in temporary shutdowns of Ameritrade's service, something Chairman and CEO J. Joe Ricketts termed "a multi-million dollar fiasco." Installing new software was one of the problems facing the company. The other was the possibility of declining stock prices and the lower trading volumes that might result. For fiscal 1998 Ameritrade reported revenue of $134.9 million (later restated to $164.2 million). The company barely broke even, with net income of $210,438. For the year it spent $40 million on advertising, and the number of accounts more than tripled to 306,000. Other developments during the year included the introduction of electronic trade confirmations by e-mail and Internet-delivered stock quotes.

GROWTH AND EXPANSION, 1999

Ameritrade Holding grew and expanded during fiscal 1999 as revenue increased to $315.2 million. The profitable company had net income of $11.5 million, and the number of accounts rose to 560,000. During the year the company expanded its facilities by opening a customer service center in Fort Worth, Texas, and a technology development center in Maryland. It acquired the online brokerage firm, The R.J. Forbes Group Inc. The company also partnered with banks in Germany and France to offer customers the ability to buy and sell the stocks of major French, German, and European companies. In September Ameritrade began offering extended hours trading.

Ameritrade continued to spend heavily to attract new customers. It launched OnMoney.com, its financial portal, with a $50 million advertising campaign

in 1999. The company said it planned to spend $200 million on advertising in fiscal 2000, up from about $60 million in fiscal 1999. *Business Week,* which ranked Ameritrade Holding Corp. 30th on its list of best performing information technology companies, noted that Ameritrade was facing increased competition. There were some 140 companies offering Internet trading in mid-1999, up from only 24 two years before. By the end of calendar year 1999 Ameritrade averaged 81,000 trades a day, an increase of 142 percent over the previous year's levels. The number of accounts rose from 354,000 at the end of calendar 1998 to 686,000 at the end of calendar 1999.

REVENUE MORE THAN DOUBLED IN FISCAL 2000

Ameritrade's revenue more than doubled in fiscal 2000, reaching $654.4 million. However, heavy advertising and marketing expenses resulted in a net loss of $13.6 million for the year. In the first quarter alone the company spent nearly $60 million on advertising in an effort to build market share. Trading volume averaged a record 173,000 trades a day in March 2000, but then declined throughout the rest of the year. Also contributing to Ameritrade's losses was its financial services portal, OnMoney.com. After spending $90 million on the portal, Ameritrade only realized revenue of $602,000 from OnMoney.com during fiscal 2000.

New products and services introduced during 2000 included the Ameritrade Online Investor Index, a daily index that reported the top 10 stocks traded that day by Ameritrade's customers. The index also reported whether customers were net buyers or sellers. Through separate marketing agreements with Sprint PCS, AT&T Wireless Services, and Nextel Communications, Ameritrade began offering wireless access to customer account information and allowed customers to place trades and get real-time quotes over their wireless devices. Through a strategic alliance with NetB@nk, Ameritrade applicants were able to apply for a NetB@nk account without having to enter any additional information. In addition, NetB@nk customers gained access to Ameritrade's brokerage services. Another strategic alliance between Ameritrade and MBNA America Bank, N.A., resulted in MBNA's credit card services being provided to Ameritrade's customers, with Ameritrade offering its brokerage services to MBNA customers. Finally, a partnership with 1stUp.com Corp. of San Francisco gave Ameritrade's customers free unlimited Internet access.

BEAR MARKET DAMPENED REVENUE OUTLOOK, 2000-2001

A slumping stock market and lower trading volume by its customers caused Ameritrade to report a $23 million loss for the quarter ending December 31, 2000. Unfavorable market conditions held through the next quarter, causing Ameritrade to cut its revenue outlook for fiscal 2001 to between $470 million and $600 million, down from earlier projections of $570 million to $650 million. Trading volume for Ameritrade's customers averaged 131,000 a day in January and 114,000 in February. In March 2001 the company hired Joseph Moglia as its new CEO. Moglia was formerly a senior vice president at Merrill Lynch & Co. Ricketts would remain as Ameritrade's chairman. With the company projecting a fiscal 2001 loss of $43.7 million, Ameritrade was taking steps to cut costs and remain financially healthy. In January the company laid off 9 percent of its workforce, and a debt-repurchase program was expected to cut interest expenses.

FURTHER READING:

Accutrade Inc. ''Company Information.'' March 19, 2001. Available from www.accutrade.com.

Ameritrade Inc. ''Company Information.'' March 19, 2001. Available from www.ameritrade.com/.

''Ameritrade's Credit Rating Gets Boosted to Junk Status.'' *Knight-Ridder/Tribune Business News.* February 23, 2001.

Freetrade.com. ''Company Information.'' March 19, 2001. Available from www.freetrade.com/.

Fugazy, Danielle. ''Ameritrade Plans Advertising Blitz as It Continues to Lose Money.'' *Web Finance.* February 14, 2000.

———. ''Online Brokerages Face Challenge of Bear Market as Indexes Wobble.'' *Web Finance.* January 22, 2001.

''Omaha, Neb., Online Stock Brokerage Surpasses Earnings Expectations.'' *Knight-Ridder/Tribune Business News.* July 26, 2000.

OnMoney.com. ''Financial Planning, Personal Finance, and Financial Information from OnMoney.com.'' March 19, 2001. Available from www.onmoney.com.

Petrecca, Laura, and Mercedes M. Cardona. ''DDB Wins Ameritrade's OnMoney.'' *Advertising Age.* June 21, 1999.

''Where No-Frills Net Trades Are Sacred.'' *Business Week.* June 28, 1999.

SEE ALSO: Charles Schwab & Co., Inc.; Datek Online Brokerage Services LLC; Day Trading; Electronic Communications Networks (ECNs); E*Trade Group, Inc.; Ricketts, Joseph; Volatility

ANALOG

Information can be presented in one of two formats, analog or digital. The main difference between the two involves continuity. Analog information is representative of the way events or phenomena unfold in the real world. Mechanical wristwatches are an excellent example because the hands of a watch display every possible point in time as they unfold, including the very smallest fractional units, in a smooth, continuous, uninterrupted fashion. Other examples of analog devices are thermometers and speedometers, the measurements on which correspond directly to conditions in the real world. By comparison, digital devices are only able to display information in finite units (10 degrees versus, for example, 10.0625 degrees).

Although the majority of computers are digital machines, meaning that they process information in a binary format of zeroes and ones (0, 1, 10, 11, 100, 111, and so on), analog computers do exist. They are used for simulating real-world systems in the fields of hydraulics, electronics, nuclear power, and so forth. Through the use of a component called an operational amplifier, these devices create complicated mathematical expressions that companies and scientists use to make more informed decisions.

In the Edge Foundation Inc.'s *The Third Culture,* Freeman Dyson, professor of physics at Princeton University's Institute for Advanced Study, explained that two mathematicians at the University of Minnesota by the names of Ian Richards and Marian Pour-El ''proved a theorem twenty years ago that says, in a mathematically precise way, that analog computers are more powerful than digital computers. They give examples of numbers that are proved to be noncomputable with digital computers but are computable with a simple kind of analog computer.''

FURTHER READING:

''Digital and Analog Information.'' *The PC Guide.* May 9, 2001. Available from www.pcguide.com.

Massey, Howard. ''Analog Vs. Digital.'' The International Association of Electronic Keyboard Manufacturers. May 12, 2001.

''The Mathematics of Computing.'' *The PC Guide.* May 9, 2001. Available from www.pcguide.com.

''Question of the Day.'' *How Stuff Works.* May 12, 2001. Available from www.howstuffworks.com.

SEE ALSO: Digital

ANDREESSEN, MARC

Marc Andreessen is a well-known and influential figure in the world of electronic business. In *E-Commerce Times,* Mitchell Levy, chair of ECM-sym.com, described Andreessen as ''Probably the most significant person I can think of'' in terms of e-commerce. Andreessen made his mark by developing breakthrough Internet browser software, first with Mosaic and then with Netscape Navigator, and co-founded Netscape Communications Corp. with Jim Clark. After Netscape was acquired by America Online and Sun Microsystems, Andreessen served as AOL's chief technology officer for about six months. He left AOL in September 1999, and the following month announced the formation of Loudcloud Inc., a new e-commerce services company that builds complicated Web sites and infrastructure and provides a range of support services.

Andreessen was born in Iowa in 1972 and grew up with his parents in the small town of New Lisbon, Wisconsin. He took an early interest in computers and wrote his first computer program on a computer at school when he was in the sixth grade. The next year his parents bought him his own computer, a TRS-80 from Radio Shack. Marc taught himself BASIC, a programming language known for its simplicity, so he could create video games for his new computer.

DEVELOPED FIRST POPULAR WEB BROWSER

After graduating from high school, Andreessen attended the University of Illinois at Champaign-Urbana. It was while working at the university's National Center for Supercomputing Applications (NCSA) that he became interested in the Internet. At the NCSA he worked with master programmer Eric Bina to develop an interface for the World Wide Web that would integrate text, graphics, and sound. In 1993 the NCSA team completed an interface called Mosaic and made it available for free over the Internet. More than 2 million copies of the browser were downloaded in the first year, and Mosaic was responsible for a ten-thousand fold increase in Web users over a period of two years.

Andreessen graduated from college in 1993 and took a job with California-based Enterprise Integration Technologies, which made Internet security enhancement products. However, one day he received an e-mail message from Jim Clark, a former associate professor of computer science at Stanford University. Clark was something of an entrepreneur, having founded Silicon Graphics Inc. He was interested in

setting up a new company to work on Mosaic and improve it. Andreessen agreed to meet with Clark, and the two decided to combine Andreessen's technical know-how with Clark's business expertise to launch their own company in 1994.

CO-FOUNDED NETSCAPE COMMUNICATIONS CORP.

At first the new company was called Mosaic Communications Corp. However, the NCSA, which held the copyright to Mosaic software, objected and the company was renamed Netscape Communications Corp. Andreessen, then 22 years old, became Netscape's vice president of technology. His job was to make the Web browser Mosaic faster and more interactive. He persuaded several NCSA team members to join him at Netscape, and soon the company released its new browser. While the development team wanted to call it Mozilla, short for Mosaic Killer, the company's marketing executives insisted on calling it Netscape Navigator.

Like Mosaic before it, Netscape Navigator was distributed for free on the Internet and quickly became very popular. The development of a downloadable browser and its introduction in October 1994 removed a significant technological hurdle for people seeking to go online; *E-Commerce Times* considered it one of the 10 key moments in the making of e-commerce. It was Netscape's browser that established the now-well-known brand name, prompting computer users to try other Netscape products. Soon, the company was profitable, and on August 9, 1995, made its initial public offering (IPO). One the first day of the IPO, Netscape's shares opened at $7 and closed at $29 after reaching a high of $36. In one day, Andreessen, who had worked at NSCA for $6.85 an hour, achieved a net worth of more than $50 million. By the end of 1995 his shares were worth $171 million.

For some time, Netscape enjoyed little or no competition for its browser. It was clear, however, by 1997 that Netscape was losing market share to Microsoft, which had introduced a competing browser— Internet Explorer 2.0— in 1995, followed by Explorer 3.0 in 1996. Andreessen, as Netscape's executive vice president in charge of product development, oversaw a staff of 1,000 tasked with staying ahead of the software giant. The most serious blow to Netscape's market position occurred when Microsoft brought out Internet Explorer 4.0 in September 1997 and bundled it with its Windows operating system. Netscape began to lose money, and by April 1998 Microsoft had captured some 40 percent of the browser market, while Netscape's share had shrunk from around 80 percent to 60 percent.

Andreessen refocused Netscape toward enterprise software for corporate intranets and electronic commerce in an effort to develop new sources of revenue. Before the year was over, however, America Online and Sun Microsystems announced they would jointly acquire Netscape's assets for $4.2 billion. Sun took over Netscape's intellectual property and the continuing development of its products, while America Online got Netscape's popular Web portal NetCenter and other assets. After the acquisition was completed in 1999, Andreessen became AOL's chief technology officer and worked from an office at AOL's headquarters in Virginia. Andreessen soon got restless, and he resigned in September 1999.

CO-FOUNDED LOUDCLOUD INC.

The next month Andreessen announced the formation of a new company called Loudcloud Inc. which would provide technology, infrastructure, and services to Internet companies and e-commerce Web sites. The company was co-founded by Andreessen, who would serve as chairman, and Ben Horowitz, who became president and CEO. Loudcloud officially opened for business in February 2000 with seven customers and $68 million in venture capital financing. By mid-2000 Andreessen had raised another $120 million in capital. In March 2001 Loudcloud went public, selling 25 million sharees, and raising $150 million through its IPO in an investment climate unfavorable to Internet-based start-ups. In the interval since Netscape's IPO—the first for an Internet company—some 420 dot-coms and Web companies had raised funds through IPOs. With Internet companies out of favor with investors, Loudcloud's may have been the last IPO for an e-commerce company for some time. As noted by business educator John H. Freeman, in *Business Week,* "There's no question the whole mind-set of businesses and investors has changed. An era has ended. Loudcloud confirms it."

FURTHER READING:

Byron, Christopher. "Netscape Founder Offers a New Cash-Burning Dot-Com." *Los Angeles Business Journal.* February 26, 2001.

Chandrasekaran, Rajiv. "Netscape's Boy Wonder Looks Beyond the Browser." *Washington Post.* March 25, 1997.

Elmer-DeWitt, Philip. "How the Internet Was Tamed." *Time.* September 26, 1994.

Hazlewood, Sara. "Andreessen: AOL's New Evangelist." *The Business Journal.* April 2, 1999.

Henry, Shannon. "Andreessen to Start New Firm." *The Washington Post.* October 27, 1999.

Herhold, Scott. "Netscape Co-Founder to Launch Start-Up as Talent Exodus Continues." *Knight-Ridder/Tribune Business News.* October 26, 1999.

Hill, Jonathan. "Marc Andreessen and Ben Horowitz." *Internet World.* October 15, 2000.

Holzinger, Albert G. "Netscape's Founder Points, and It Clicks." *Nation's Business.* January 1996.

Kaplan, David A. "Nothing but Net." *Newsweek.* December 25, 1995.

"The Last Days of Net Mania." *Business Week.* April 16, 2001.

Nash, Kim S. "Hey! Don't Call It a Browser." *Computerworld.* October 21, 1996.

"A New Electronic Messiah." *The Economist (US).* August 15, 1995.

"A Pioneer Once More." *Business Week.* February 28, 2000.

Sliwa, Carol. "Andreessen Targets Web Outsource Model." *Computerworld.* September 25, 2000.

"Spinning a Golden Web." *People Weekly.* September 11, 1995.

Tetzeli, Rick. "What It's Really Like to Be Marc Andreessen." *Fortune.* December 9, 1996.

Tetzeli, Rick, and David Kirkpatrick. "Marc Andreessen: 'The Concept of Being Always on Is a Very Powerful One.'" *Fortune.* October 9, 2000.

SEE ALSO: Clark, Jim; Initial Public Offering (IPO); Loudcloud; Netscape Communications Corp.

ANGEL INVESTORS

Angel investors are a vital component of the venture capital industry. Known for making a splash in the e-commerce world of the late 1990s and early 2000s, they have emerged as a hugely successful economic force, attracting droves of well-leveraged individuals and groups looking for the early investment that can spawn an industry powerhouse. The decade-long U.S. economic expansion produced ever more wealthy individuals willing and able to invest in risky new business ventures. As the dot-com mania picked up speed, more of these new ventures turned angel investing into one of the most glamorous sectors of finance.

In a sense, angel investing has been around as long as business itself. Traditionally, before an entrepreneur even created a sound or semi-promising business plan or prototype to attract seed money from institutional investors, he or she would seek initial start-up funds from a wealthy patron. Angels provide entrepreneurs with the early-stage seed money needed to get on their feet, while venture capital (VC) funds tend to steer their money toward firms that are in the later stages of early development, closer to an initial public offering (IPO). In addition, angels put their own money into companies, unlike venture capitalist firms, which pool funds and invest them in a manner similar to mutual funds.

Risk is an inherent component for angels. Besides backing entrepreneurs that are not yet attractive enough even for VC funds, angels also eschew other investment safeguards, such as Federal Deposit Insurance Corp. (FDIC)-insured accounts. With excess money at their disposal, angels more or less take a chance when handing checks over to entrepreneurs, albeit not without an often-heavy hand in guiding the development process. And even in the fairy-tale dot-com boom of the late 1990s and early 2000s, the risk was very real; roughly nine out of ten angel investments proved to be washouts. However, the high yield of winners makes the field what it is. Thus, angels tend to approach their investments as though they were buying lottery tickets; it takes only one success to hit it big, and that one easily pays for all the others.

Different angels have different styles. While some bring in lawyers to negotiate deals and demand a great deal of say in company development, others are more relaxed and hands-off. Some specialize in greasing the wheels between entrepreneurs, banks, and investors, while other angels concentrate almost exclusively on seeking out new entrepreneurs, giving little attention to how things progress. Hands-off angels work on the idea that one big winner will pay for the less-sound investments. There also are those philanthropic angels who, with money to spare, throw it behind valuable and socially redeemable projects out of altruistic motives.

According to *Fortune*, an angel or small group of angels provides between $100,000 and $1 million in exchange for up to 30 percent of a company. While such deals tend to be private, *Fortune* reported that angels poured at least $40 billion into roughly 50,000 start-ups a year in the late 1990s. According to some estimates, this amounted to 30 or 40 times the level of investment provided by institutional venture capitalists. According to the Center for Venture Research at the University of New Hampshire, about 400,000 active (at least one deal a year) angels were in operation in 2000, representing 60-percent growth since 1997, while the entire field of angels numbered about 3 million.

With the millionaire population of the United States doubling between 1994 and 1999, a whole new league of players was eligible to play the angel investing game. The tremendous boom in angel investing in the late 1990s was primarily attributable to the avalanche of dot-com initial public offerings (IPOs) that seemed to flout all traditional market logic. In other words, earnings, fundamentals, and other typical variables of valuation, took a back seat to the fact that the words "dot-com" were appended to a company's name. Additionally, a symbiotic relationship existed between the strong economy and the proliferation of angels. Edward G. Boehne, former president of the Philadelphia Federal Reserve Bank, said that angels are "a big part of the extensive infrastructure that's developed to finance and support entrepreneurs." According to Boehne, Angels helped to spur a wave of entrepreneurship that was largely responsible for sustaining a long period of economic growth and expansion, which exceeded the expectations of many.

Among analysts, however, there was widespread consensus that the tech boom and the lure of fantastic returns created a glut of angel investors. For this reason, they felt the field was unlikely to sustain the astronomical growth rate of the late 1990s. With tech and dot-com stocks finally returning to financial reality in 2000 and 2001, high-stakes angel investing appeared less fashionable and less feasible. But no one expected the practice to completely go away. In fact, angel investing was taking even firmer root in U.S. culture. Some 150 formal angel clubs were established throughout the country by 2001, mostly in the late 1990s and early 2000s, at which local and regional elites could share information and turn angel investing into a potent and coherent economic force. Such investors typically pay between $25,000 and $100,000 to join these exclusive pools.

FURTHER READING:

Bruner, Richard. "Angel Investors." *ENEWS*. November 27, 2000.

Colkin, Eileen. "Pennies From Heaven Keep On Falling." *InformationWeek*. January 29, 2000.

Darrow, Barbara. "Touched By An Angel." *Computer Reseller News*. April 17, 2000.

Fox, Loren. "Another Face for Venture Capitalism." *Upside*. October 1999.

Gordon, Joanne. "Wings." *Forbes*. October 30, 2000.

Helyar, John. "The Venture Capitalist Next Door." *Fortune*. November 13, 2000.

Van Osnabrugge, Mark, and Robert J. Robinson. *Angel Investing: Matching Startup Funds with Startup Companies*. San Francisco: Jossey-Bass, 2000.

SEE ALSO: Financing, Securing; Start-ups, Dot-com; Volatility

AOL TIME WARNER INC.

AOL Time Warner Inc., formed by the merger of America Online, Inc. and Time Warner Inc., is a major media conglomerate that combines the power of the Internet with highly recognized information and entertainment brands. According to the combined companies' first annual report, released in early 2001, AOL Time Warner reached more than 130 million subscribers, 266 million Web users, 268 million magazine readers, 1.4 billion monthly prime-time television viewers, and 50 million monthly home video viewers. Altogether, AOL Time Warner estimated that it touched consumers more than 2.5 billion times each month.

When America Online, Inc. and Time Warner Inc. completed their merger on January 11, 2001, they created the first—and largest—Internet-powered media and communications company. Following the merger, America Online and Time Warner each became wholly-owned subsidiaries of AOL Time Warner. The firm's numerous businesses and brands were organized into seven fundamental areas:

AMERICA ONLINE. The world's leader in consumer-oriented interactive services, Web brands, Internet technologies, and electronic commerce services, AOL's operations include the AOL service, which had more than 28 million members as of March 31, 2001, and the CompuServe service, which had about 3 million members. Also included among AOL's operations are Netscape; local brands such as Digital City, AOL Moviefone, and MapQuest; AOL messaging services, including AOL Instant Messenger; and AOL's music properties, such as Spinner.com, Winamp, and SHOUTcast.

Other AOL operations have been organized under ''AOL Anywhere'' services, including AOLTV, an interactive television service; the AOL Mobile Communicator service, which offered wireless access to e-mail and instant messaging using pager-sized two-way wireless devices; and the AOL-byPhone service. The company's ''AOL Anywhere'' strategy was designed to offer key features and content of the AOL service through multiple platforms and devices, including mobile phones, pagers, and other handheld devices.

Finally, through its strategic alliance with Sun Microsystems, Inc., AOL is involved with the development of electronic commerce and enterprise solutions under the brand iPlanet E-Commerce Solutions, developed and marketed through the Sun-Netscape alliance.

CABLE TV AND INTERNET ACCESS. As of December 30, 2000, Time Warner Cable served some 12.8 million subscribers through cable systems that it either owned or managed. Approximately 92 percent of its cable systems had been upgraded to deliver more channels and provide two-way transmission capability, the key to offering high-speed Internet access and other interactive services via the cable line. These upgrades permit roll-out of such advanced services as digital and high-definition television (HDTV) programming, video-on-demand, telephony, and other services. As of March 31, 2001, Time Warner Cable had launched its high-speed Internet service, Road Runner, in 36 of its 39 field divisions.

FILMED ENTERTAINMENT. The company's filmed entertainment businesses comprise several well-known brands, including Warner Bros. Pictures, New Line Cinema Corporation, Warner Home Video, and Warner Bros. Television. Also included with AOL Time Warner's film unit are the Turner classic film and animation libraries.

NETWORKS. AOL Time Warner's networks include domestic and international basic cable networks, pay-television programming services, a broadcast television network, and sports franchises. The principal cable networks and sports franchises are owned by Turner Broadcasting System, Inc., a wholly-owned subsidiary of AOL Time Warner. They include TBS Superstation, TNT, Cartoon Network, Turner Classic Movies, and the CNN network. Turner Broadcasting also operates the CNN family of Internet destinations and other large advertiser-supported online sites. AOL Time Warner's pay television programming services include HBO and Cinemax. The WB Television Network is the company's sole broadcast television network. In sports, a source of programming and merchandising content for the firm, it owns professional teams in baseball (Atlanta Braves), basketball (Atlanta Hawks), and hockey (Atlanta Thrashers).

MUSIC. AOL Time Warner's worldwide recorded music and music publishing businesses are conducted under the umbrella name Warner Music Group (WMG). Principal U.S.-based record labels include Warner Bros. Records Inc., Atlantic Recording Corporation, Elektra Entertainment Group Inc., and London-Sire Records Inc., and their affiliated labels, as well as WEA Inc. companies. WMG's music publishing companies, Warner/Chappell, own or control the rights to more than 1 million musical compositions.

PUBLISHING. Time Inc., a wholly-owned subsidiary, is AOL Time Warner's largest concern in the publishing business. As of March 1, 2001, Time Inc. published 64 magazines, including *Time, Sports Illustrated, Fortune, Money, Entertainment Weekly,* and *In Style.* During 2000 Time Inc. acquired Times Mirror Magazines, whose titles included *Golf, Ski, Skiing, Popular Science, Field and Stream,* and *Yachting.* In addition to those mainstays, the company also has recently launched new periodicals like *Real Simple,* a lifestyle magazine, and *eCompany Now,* a business magazine and Web site focused on electronic commerce. Time Inc.'s trade-book publishing operations are conducted primarily by Time Warner Trade Publishing Inc. through its two major publishing houses, Warner Books and Little, Brown. During 2000 Time Warner Trade Publishing had 27 titles on the *New York Times* best-seller lists.

HISTORY OF AMERICA ONLINE

America Online's roots go back to 1985, when Steve Case and Jim Kimsey founded Quantum Computer Services. Quantum provided online services for users of Commodore computers, then a popular brand of home computers. Two years later Quantum began providing online services for Apple Computer, Inc.'s operating system and developing software for both the Macintosh and the Apple II. After that Quantum grew quickly and was soon providing online services and related software for other companies, including Tandy Corporation and computer industry-leader IBM.

Quantum's costs were high, and it quickly ran through its capital. In 1991 Quantum was renamed American Online (AOL), with Case taking Kimsey's place as CEO and Kimsey becoming chairman of the company. AOL held its initial public offering in March 1992 and raised $66 million, with shares initially selling for $1.64.

At that time, the two leaders in providing online services were Prodigy and CompuServe. Case focused on achieving market dominance and pursued a strategy that included forming alliances with companies that would benefit AOL. He dropped membership prices below that of the major competitors and shipped out huge quantities of software diskettes to potential customers, offering them a free trial period using the AOL service. These marketing efforts paid off in rapid membership growth for AOL, and by the end of 1993 the company had more than 600,000 subscribers.

AOL was the subject of two takeover attempts in 1993, one from Microsoft cofounder Paul Allen, the other from Microsoft head Bill Gates. Allen, who had already left Microsoft, acquired a 24.9 percent interest in AOL and attempted to secure a seat on its board of directors. Both takeover attempts were thwarted by Case and AOL, eventually prompting Microsoft to develop its own online service, the Microsoft Network.

Key acquisitions in late 1994 helped AOL provide its subscribers with access to the World Wide Web, a part of the Internet that was quickly becoming popular because of its open platform and ease of use via graphical browsers like Netscape. Until this time AOL was essentially a closed network that offered subscribers access only to its own content providers, vendors, and other AOL subscribers. Content agreements with the New York Times, Time, NBC, and others had expanded AOL's content, but it was an essential part of the company's strategy to become a gateway to the Internet. This strategy was facilitated by the acquisition of Advanced Network Services, Inc., which built fiber optic networks to support Internet access. This was followed by the acquisition of BookLink Technologies and the Global Network Navigator, which enabled AOL customers to browse the Internet using graphic browsing software from BookLink. Later, in 1996, AOL would reach agreements with Netscape and Microsoft, who were competing heavily in the browser market, to use their browsers.

AOL began to grow more rapidly as it added new content providers and gave its subscribers greater access to the public Internet. In March 1995 AOL's subscriber base reached 2 million, and by August 1996 the company had 6 million subscribers. In October 1996 AOL introduced flat-rate service for a monthly fee of $19.95. In 1996 Bob Pittman, founder of MTV and considered a successful brand-builder, was hired to improve AOL's customer service and strengthen AOL's brand among consumers. After Pittman reduced AOL's subscriber growth to a sustainable level and improved the company's customer service reputation, he was promoted to president and chief operating officer. Case gave up his title of president and remained chairman and CEO.

By 1997 AOL had 9 million subscribers. During the year it gained 2.6 million CompuServe subscribers, which it continued to operate as a separate business. After WorldCom had acquired CompuServe from H&R Block, WorldCom traded CompuServe's subscriber base to AOL in exchange for AOL's network integration division.

AOL's stock rose 600 percent in 1998 and even more in 1999. This infusion of market capital gave it the power to make more and bigger acquisitions. In November 1998 AOL announced it would acquire Netscape Communications Corp. for $4.2 billion in stock, about 10 percent of AOL's market value. Included in the acquisition were the Web browser Netscape Navigator and Netscape's Web portal, Netcenter. A third party to the acquisition was Sun Microsystems, which agreed to pay $350 million over three years to license Netscape's software, while AOL agreed to purchase $500 million worth of servers from Sun. The Sun-Netscape alliance adopted the brand iPlanet to market the next generation of Netscape Web and application servers. During 2000 AOL recast Netscape Netcenter as a business professional's portal, and in fall 2000 AOL unveiled its new Netscape Netbusiness service, which was designed to help small businesses build Web-based storefronts and engage in business-to-business e-commerce.

In January 2000 AOL announced its bid to acquire Time Warner Inc. for approximately $165 billion in stock, with the exact value to be determined by the stock prices of both firms after the acquisition was finalized. As of June 30, 2000, the end of AOL's fiscal 2000, AOL had 23.2 million subscribers, plus 2.8 million CompuServe subscribers. By that point

AOL alone had four major lines of business: the Interactive Services Group, the Interactive Properties Group, the AOL International Group, and the Netscape Enterprise Group.

THE AOL TIME WARNER MERGER

When AOL announced its intention to acquire Time Warner, AOL's stock was near its all-time high. In the month following the announcement AOL's stock lost about 30 percent of its value. The announcement caused Time Warner's stock to rise nearly 50 percent before settling back some 20 percent off its peak.

In addition to requiring the shareholders' approval at both companies, the merger had to pass regulatory approval from the European Union, the U.S. Federal Trade Commission (FTC), and the U.S. Federal Communications Commission (FCC). While the merger was being reviewed, both companies undertook actions that would appease regulators. Both promised they would not block other Internet service providers or content providers from using their distribution system. In March 2000 AOL announced it would pay up to $8.25 billion to buy out German media conglomerate Bertelsmann AG's interest in AOL Europe and AOL Australia, a move to allay fears that Bertelsmann and AOL Time Warner would pool their interests to undermine other competitors. Bertelsmann, whose holdings included book publishers and record labels, was considered a competitor to Time Warner, particularly in the music business.

Several companies that were opposed to the merger joined together to lobby U.S. regulators to impose strict limits on the proposed company's business practices. Leading the group was the Walt Disney Co., which benefited from the keyword shortcut of ''Disney'' on the AOL service and also ran its Disney Channel over several Time Warner cable franchises. Disney proposed that regulators split AOL Time Warner into two companies, one for handling content and the other for handling distribution. Four consumer groups led by the Consumers Union filed a 120-page letter with the FCC expressing concerns about the concentration of power in television and Internet content and their distribution through telephone lines and broadband cable. In May 2000 the National Association of Broadcasters went on record with the FCC opposing the merger and asked the FCC to require that AOL Time Warner not discriminate against properties they didn't own. SBC Communications Inc. also joined the opposition to the merger, expressing concern about AOL Time Warner's interlocking business relationships with competing telephone carriers such as AT&T-Media One and Bell Atlantic-GTE (later reconfigured as Verizon).

Following a lengthy FCC hearing in July, Time Warner announced an agreement in August with Juno Online Services Inc. that gave the Internet service provider (ISP) access to Time Warner's cable subscribers. The agreement was Time Warner's first with an unaffiliated ISP and allowed Juno to offer its services to cable subscribers. As part of the deal the two companies would split the Internet access subscription revenue from the service.

The AOL Time Warner merger was also being scrutinized in Europe by the European Commission (EC), the antitrust regulatory body of the European Union (EU). Following a hearing in early September, AOL and Time Warner issued a list of concessions designed to win approval from the EC. The concessions focused on the EC's primary concern about discrimination in the delivery of online music. In general, the EC, like U.S. regulatory agencies, was concerned that AOL Time Warner would discriminate against competitors seeking access to its content and Internet services. To satisfy the EC, Time Warner agreed to call off its planned merger with British music company EMI Group PLC. Within a week the EC approved the AOL Time Warner merger.

Meanwhile, the U.S. House of Representatives was holding hearings on the proposed merger, and the FCC said it would wait until the FTC issued its ruling first. By November it was clear that the FTC wanted proof in the form of a cable-access agreement with a rival ISP before it would approve the merger. In November Time Warner and Earthlink, the second largest ISP in the United States, reached such an agreement. Under the agreement, Earthlink would be allowed to offer its service over Time Warner's high-speed cable lines starting in the second half of 2001.

The FTC gave its approval to the merger on December 14, 2000. Focusing on Time Warner's vast cable television network, the FTC required that Time Warner open its cable lines to ISPs that competed with AOL, in effect turning Time Warner's privately owned system into a kind of public channel for Internet access, much in the way telephone systems were treated under the telecommunications regulatory reforms of the middle and late 1990s. In addition to the agreement with Earthlink, AOL Time Warner was required to make deals with two other competing ISPs within 90 days of making AOL available to Time Warner subscribers in large markets. Such deals would also require the approval of the FTC. The FTC requirements were to remain in effect for five years.

FCC approval, with some additional conditions, quickly followed in January 2001. The value of the merger was estimated at approximately $110 billion, with AOL's stock trading at about half of its value at the time the merger was originally announced. The new company began business with about 88,500 employees.

Prominent figures from both companies were chosen for the executive team, but some favor was given to the acquirer, AOL. Steve Case became chairman of the new company, while Time Warner's chairman Gerald Levin was named CEO. Ted Turner was named vice chairman; however, within a year he was forced out of that role in a board reshuffling.

The executives put in charge of integrating the two companies included Kenneth Novack, AOL's vice chairman; Bob Pittman, AOL's president; Richard Parsons, Time Warner's president; and Richard Bressler, Time Warner Digital Media CEO. While AOL Time Warner's new headquarters would be located in New York City, Case and many other AOL executives would remain at the AOL campus in Dulles, Virginia. Board meetings would alternate between the two locations.

For the future, the company's management announced four priorities:

- to transform the consumer experience and reinvent the way people communicate, do business, inform, educate, and entertain themselves

- to become a truly global company

- to foster an entrepreneurial culture and function as one company

- to act in the public interest and make a difference, both locally and globally, in the communities where AOL Time Warner operates.

FURTHER READING:

Green, Heather, and Catherine Yang. ''Not So Odd a Couple After All.'' *Business Week,* December 21, 1998.

Gunther, Marc. ''Understanding AOL's Grand United Theory of the Media Cosmos.'' *Fortune,* January 8, 2001.

Halonen, Doug. ''Kennard FCC's Last Act—AOL Merger OK'd.'' *Electronic Media,* January 15, 2001.

McConnell, Bill. ''Taking on Goliath.'' *Broadcasting & Cable,* June 19, 2000.

Sager, Ira. ''A New Cyber Order.'' *Business Week,* December 7, 1998.

Sandberg, Jared. ''Net Gain.'' *Newsweek,* December 7, 1998.

Sliwa, Carol, and Stefanie McCann. ''A Big Yahoo for AOL.'' *Computerworld,* December 7, 1998.

Sullivan, John, and Michael Robuck. ''AOL and Time Warner.'' *Boardwatch Magazine,* February 2001.

Swisher, Kara. *AOL.com: How Steve Case Beat Bill Gates, Nailed the Netheads & Made Millions in the War for the Web.* New York: Crown Publishing, 1999.

SEE ALSO: Case, Stephen; Netscape Communications Corp.; Sun Microsystems, Inc.

APPLE COMPUTER INC.

Apple Computer is best known for its Macintosh personal computers (PCs), including the colorful iMac desktop and iBook laptop, which are designed to facilitate easy access to the Internet. Although the firm's new product releases in the late 1990s garnered media attention and boosted sales, Apple's share of the worldwide PC market had dwindled to less than three percent by 2001.

EARLY HISTORY

Stephen G. Wozniak and Steven P. Jobs founded Apple Computer Co. in April of 1976. The partners launched operations by making and selling a computer circuit board, dubbed the Apple I. The machine had no keyboard, case, sound, or graphics. Computer retailing chain Byte Shop ordered 50 Apple I units a month later, and Jobs used his parents' garage as a temporary manufacturing site. Mike Markkula, a former marketing executive for both Intel Corp. and Fairchild Semiconductor, paid $250,000 for a 33-percent stake in Apple and helped Jobs to create a long-term business plan. In 1977, the firm unveiled the Apple II—the first PC to offer color graphics capacity. The new machine also included a keyboard, power supply, case, and 4KB of standard memory. That year, the company's sales reached $1 million.

Apple's earliest venture into online technology came in 1978 when it began offering Apple II users a telephone-based connection service to Dow Jones. Just two years after its inception, the company became one of the fastest growing companies in the United States. Sales grew tenfold and the firm's dealer network grew to include roughly 300 distributors. Employees were required to give up their typewriters in favor of PCs in 1979. The firm also released the Apple II Plus, which offered 48KB of memory, and the first Apple printer, known as the Silentype. In an effort to tap into the school market, Apple established the Apple Education Foundation. Sales of the Apple II jumped 40 percent, reaching 35,000 units, and the company's employees totaled 250.

In 1980, Apple released the Apple III, its most advanced machine to date. Boasting a new operating system, a built-in disk controller, and four peripheral slots, the Apple III was priced at $3,495—nearly double the price of its predecessors. To bolster international sales, Apple constructed a manufacturing plant in Ireland and a European support center in the Netherlands. EDUNET, an online network serving professionals in higher education and research fields, adopted the Apple II as its network access PC. Apple also established Apple Seed, a computer program designed to promote computer literacy among elementary and high school students. That year, the firm conducted its initial public offering (IPO), selling 4.6 million shares at $22 apiece. The IPO was the largest in U.S. corporate history since Ford Motor Co. first listed its shares in 1956. At that time, employees exceeded 1,000. With a dealer network of 800 distributors in the United States and Canada, and an another 1,000 distributors overseas, Apple had the farthest reach of any major player in the computer industry.

In 1981, Apple established offices in both France and England. Of the firm's 40 new product releases that year, the most notable were the Apple Language Card, which increased the compatibility of Apple II machines with programs written in languages such as Pascal and Fortran; the IEEE-488 interface card, which allowed Apple II units to work with more than 1,400 scientific and technical instruments; and Profile, a 5MB hard disk. In 1982, Apple became the first PC company to attain sales of $1 billion. Competition intensified as more than 100 companies started manufacturing PCs. Apple unveiled its dot matrix printer that year. In 1983, Apple introduced the Apple IIe and Apple III Plus PCs; the ImageWriter printer and other peripheral devices; and AppleWorks, a suite of products including word processing, spreadsheet, and database software. The firm was ranked 411 on the *Fortune* 500 list. To further entrench itself in schools, Apple launched the ''Kids Can't Wait'' program, through which it gave 10,000 computers to schools in California.

ADVENT OF THE MACINTOSH

Apple shipped its blockbuster Macintosh machine in 1984, after first advertising it on television during the Super Bowl. Initial versions of the Macintosh retailed for $2,495, while the more powerful Macintosh 512KB was priced at $3,195. That year, the firm established the Apple University Consortium, which included 24 major colleges and universities that collectively agreed to use the Macintosh for educational programs and to spend $61 million over a three-year period. Other product releases included 300- and 1200-baud modems, the Scribe printer, and the Apple IIc. Shortly after roughly 2,000 dealers ordered 52,000 Apple II machines at a conference titled ''Apple II Forever,'' Apple stopped making the Apple III machine due to continued engineering glitches. By the year's end, more than 400,000 Apple IIc machines had been sold.

The LaserWriter printer—priced at roughly $7,000—made its debut in 1985, as did the AppleTalk Personal Network. Northern Telecom and Apple began working together to connect Macintosh computers via telephone lines. An inventory glut prompted the firm to shut down manufacturing plants for one week. The firm also permanently closed three of its six plants and laid off 20 percent of its work force, or roughly 1,200 employees. As a result, Apple posted its first-ever quarterly loss, and Jobs resigned to start a new computer venture. The AppleLink telecommunications network went online that year, connecting Apple employees, dealers, and suppliers to Apple information libraries, as well as to each other via e-mail. Apple also created the Education Advisory Council, allowing leaders in education to take part in the development of Apple's school programs and related products.

By 1986, more than 200,000 AppleTalk local area computer networks were in place. Internationally, Apple had extended its reach to 80 countries. Earnings rebounded, growing 151 percent to reach a record high. The following year, new product releases included desktop communications products, such as the AppleTalk PC Card and the AppleShare file server, as well as an updated version of Apple IIe and the next generation of Macintosh PCs. Apple also founded Claris, an independent software manufacturer.

The late 1980s were marked by a series of strategic alliances with other leading technology firms. For example, Digital Equipment Corp. and Apple began working together to integrate Macintosh personal computers and AppleTalk networks with VAX systems. In 1988, Apple shipped a Unix-based version of Macintosh II. Apple and Quantum Computer Services created AppleLink-Personal Edition, an online communication and information service designed specifically for Apple II computer owners. The firm also worked with Texas Instruments to integrate Macintosh II with Texas Instruments' Explorer Lisp coprocessor board. The joint venture with Texas Instrument proved to be one of Apple's largest value-added reseller agreements for the Macintosh line. That year, Apple filed suit against Microsoft Corp. for allegedly using the ''look and feel'' of the Macintosh operating system as the basis for its increasingly popular Windows platform. Apple's lawyers requested that Microsoft either pay royalties or simply stop selling Windows. Net income exceeded $400 million on revenues of roughly $4 billion.

In 1989, Apple released several new networking and communication products designed to enhance the communication capabilities of Apple machines. For example, the IIGS System Software 5.0 was the first 16-bit operating system for an Apple PC that operated over the AppleTalk network system. Sales climbed to $5.28 billion. In response to intense competition, Apple reduced its prices in 1990 and introduced a series of low-cost Macintosh PCs. The following year, it shipped several low-cost printers. Apple also asked the Federal Communications Commission (FCC) to allow computers to send and receive information over radio waves. The FCC granted permission for this type of electronic communication, and the decision fostered the development of a new class of data communications known as Data Personal Communications Services.

In 1991, in an effort to steal market share back from Microsoft, IBM and Apple forged an alliance to develop a new operating system that would make computers easier to use and also increase compatibility between IBM and Apple machines. By then, roughly 90 percent of worldwide PCs used Microsoft's Windows platform, and Apple had broadened its litigation against Microsoft. However, a judge ruled in favor of Microsoft in 1992 after deciding that the appearance of the Macintosh operating system was not protected by Apple's copyrights. Apple appealed the decision, but the Supreme Court refused to hear Apple's case.

In 1993, Apple ranked as the world's second-largest PC maker, behind Microsoft. Sales exceeded $7 million, and employees totaled roughly 15,000. The following year, the firm unveiled its PowerPC microprocessor. In the mid-1990s, sales began to slow and inventory mounted, prompting Apple to cut its prices by up to 25 percent. As Microsoft continued to gain market share, many firms stopped developing new software for the Macintosh. Units shipped fell from 4.6 million in 1995 to 3.7 million in 1996 as market share decreased to 5.2 percent, compared to 10 percent in the late 1980s. Management shakeups also plagued the firm. Market share tumbled to 3.2 percent in 1997, and Apple posted a $1.1 billion loss. The firm then purchased NeXT Software Inc. from original Apple founder Steve Jobs, who agreed to serve as an advisor to Apple. Shortly thereafter, Jobs was reinstated as Apple's CEO.

INTERNET STRATEGY

The iMac, a PC designed to make Internet access as straightforward as possible, was launched in 1998. Available in a variety of bright colors, the iMac housed its monitor and hard drive in a single unit. The new machine's popularity boosted the performance of Apple, which earned $309 million in its first profitable year since 1995. According to a March 1999 article in *Microprocessor Report,* the iMac's "box-to-Internet" approach did two things for Apple. "It rekindled the public's love for Apple, and it delivered the most approachable, friendly personal computer yet." In 1999, Apple released a laptop version of the iMac called the iBook.

The iMac was a key component of Jobs's strategy to gain Internet dominance by offering an easy-to-

use machine along with a series of free Internet services known as iTools. These iTools included 20MB of online storage space, content filters for parents, e-mail and greeting card services, and a World Wide Web site rating system called iReview. In additional to the new machines and free services, Apple also released a new operating system, Mac OS X, in 2001. As stated by Charles Haddad in *BusinessWeek Online,* "Based on Unix, OS X has supercharged Internet and networking capabilities. It could be the thread that ties together all the other pieces of Jobs's plan." However, deteriorating PC sales and a weak North American economy began to undercut sales and earnings at Apple in 2001. The firm's lackluster performance, along with its steadily dwindling market share, led many analysts to question Apple's future performance.

FURTHER READING:

"Apple Computer Inc." In *Notable Corporate Chronologies.* Farmington Hills, MI: Gale Group, 1999.

"Apple Stronger, Not Out of the Woods." *Microprocessor Report.* March 29, 1999.

Bethoney, Herb. "Rumors of Apple's Death are Greatly..." *eWeek.* April 23, 2001.

Deutschman, Alan. "Despite Recent Stock Slip, Jobs Isn't Finished With Apple." *Computer Reseller News.* October 16, 2000.

Haddad, Charles. "Steve Jobs's New Lesson Plan." *BusinessWeek Online.* March 28, 2001. Available from www.businessweek.com.

Schlender, Brent. "Steve Jobs: The Graying Prince of a Shrinking Kingdom." *Fortune.* May 14, 2001.

"Steve Jobs' Apple Gets Way Cooler." *Fortune.* January 24, 2000.

SEE ALSO: Jobs, Stephen; Microsoft Corp.; Microsoft Windows; Wozniak, Stephen

APPLICATION SERVICE PROVIDER (ASP)

An application service provider (ASP) is a company that delivers and manages software applications and computer services from a remote data center to multiple users. Companies typically access these applications and services over the Internet, through a virtual private network (VPN), or through dedicated lease lines. A wide range of both applications and communications and infrastructure capabilities are available from ASPs. Among the most commonly used are enterprise applications, including enterprise resource planning (ERP), customer relationship management (CRM), supply management, human resources, and financial management. Software companies such as Microsoft Corp. and Corel Corp. are developing ASP versions of their productivity applications. When it comes to information technology (IT) and network infrastructure, ASPs can deliver network services, complex mission-critical hosting, software and hardware provisioning, infrastructure integration and support services, business continuity services, network management and administration services, and managed VPNs. ASPs also deliver network-based access to processing power and remote data storage facilities.

ASPs have evolved from simply hosting Web services to building and managing e-commerce and platforms. They handle e-commerce issues such as security, registration, and payments, and also provide Internet-based technologies. ASPs can provide communications platforms for messaging, voicemail, IP fax, and hosted collaboration platforms, as well as portals that offer such services as free Web e-mail, contact management, and calendaring.

By hosting these services for other businesses, ASPs enable smaller businesses to benefit from high-priced software packages and systems without having to purchase them. Larger companies tend to use ASPs for outsourcing, while smaller businesses with low budgets use them to gain access to high-end enterprise computing that would be too expensive to purchase. Whatever the size of the client company, using ASPs allows businesses to focus their resources on their core competencies rather than on their information systems (IS) and information technology.

ASPs offer several benefits to both small and large companies. These include a quick launch for new e-commerce, supply chain, and CRM applications. Client companies have to spend less on buying, maintaining, and upgrading software and hardware to run basic applications. They also are free from the need to devote personnel and other resources to keeping up with rapid technological change. ASPs not only provide seamless and inexpensive upgrades, they apply their experience to the best IT practices in order to achieve high levels of availability, security, backup, disaster recovery, and shadowing. ASPs also allow for easy upscaling and downscaling as business volumes change. Finally, ASPs—which typically operate on one-to-three-year contracts with service level agreements (SLAs)—provide predictable costs to client companies. With an ASP, payments are amortized over time so companies don't have to make large capital expenditures on software and hardware.

Of course, there are tradeoffs when using an ASP. Among the factors to consider are the loss of hands-on control, the lack of a software license, and a contractual commitment lasting from one to three years. Successful ASPs must deliver on application reliability and availability. A survey by information technology industry magazine *CIO* found that guaranteed reliability and availability was the number one factor in evaluating ASPs. The second-most-important factor was faster implementation than could be achieved in-house. Another important factor in deciding whether or not to use an ASP was the ability to avoid IS staffing problems. Being free from having to devote resources to hiring and training IS employees was rated as a significant benefit in deciding whether to outsource applications to an ASP.

GROWING MARKET FOR ASPS

According to the Gartner Group, companies spent $2.7 billion on ASPs in 2000. That figure is expected to increase to anywhere from $16 billion to $22.7 billion by 2003. Application hosting has been driven by several converging technologies including the growth of the Internet, which permitted the linking of computers to a mostly IP standards-based server network; access to larger amounts of communications bandwidth, which made it easier to reliably send and retrieve large amounts of complex data; and a widely embraced user interface in the form of Web browsers.

The ASP Industry Consortium was formed in May 1999 by 25 leading technology companies. Founding companies included AT&T Corp., Cisco Systems Inc., Compaq Computer Corp., GTE Corp., IBM Corp., Sun Microsystems Inc., and UUNET Technologies. The consortium has grown to more than 700 companies and includes ASP companies, software and hardware companies, network service providers, ISPs, and others.

According to the ASP Industry Consortium, there were some 300 ASPs in business at the end of 2000, and that number has grown considerably. In addition to calling themselves ASPs, some also were known as managed (or management) service providers (MSPs), network service providers (NSPs), net-sourcers, total service providers (TSPs), and software rental companies. A full-service provider (FSP)—also known as a total service provider—is an ASP that offers a wide range of Web-based information technology services, such as planning and creating a Web presence, software applications, and Web hosting and maintenance. Business service providers (BSPs) are similar to ASPs in that they provide customers with application packages over networks. However, BSPs differ from ASPs in that they tend to tailor software packages to a customer's needs and offer back-office solutions for processes like payroll and bookkeeping. A management service provider (MSP) provides the personnel to manage and administer IT services for other companies, thus saving clients the need to have their own administrative personnel.

FURTHER READING:

ASP Industry Consortium. ''Glossary.'' June 6, 2001. Available from www.aspindustry.org.

''ASPs: Setting Off a Sea of Change.'' *CIO.* October 1, 2000.

Bolding, Jeb. ''ASP Adoption Malaise.'' *NetworkWorldFusion.* February 21, 2001. Available from www.nwfusion.com.

''Compelling Numbers Point to Accelerating ASP Use.'' *CIO.* October 1, 2000.

Cooper, Cathy. ''Global ASP Deal Is Sealed.'' *Computer Weekly.* May 11, 2000.

Semilof, Margie. ''ASP Group Boosts Its Membership.'' *Computer Reseller News.* July 5, 1999.

''The Value of Opting for an ASP.'' *CIO.* October 1, 2000.

SEE ALSO: Hosting Services; Internet Service Provider (ISP); Management Service Provider (MSP); Scalability; Software

ARCHIPELAGO HOLDINGS LLC

Archipelago Holdings operates Archipelago LLC, one of the four original electronic communications networks (ECNs) approved by the Securities and Exchange Commission (SEC) to serve as a new breed of institutional stock broker—one that matches stock buyers and sellers more quickly than traditional brokers by using an Internet-based electronic platform. Rather than attempting to secure profits like a conventional trader—by selling stocks at a higher price than it paid, which involves waiting for a favorable spread—Archipelago simply matches buyers with sellers, executes transactions immediately, and charges a small commission, much lower than typical processing fees, for each trade it completes. Like most other ECNs, Archipelago also displays the prices and sizes of public stock orders, although it does so for free, unlike its bigger competitors Instinet Corp. and Island ECN. At the end of the twentieth century, Archipelago agreed to merge with Pacific Stock Exchange into a new electronic stock exchange that would compete with NASDAQ and the New York Stock Exchange (NYSE). That deal was pending SEC approval in early 2001, though by autumn of the year analysts were skeptical of the outlook for future consolidation among big ECNs, citing a lack of overlap between their strong market niches.

Archipelago got its start in November of 1994 when Wall Street broker Gerald D. Putnam established TerraNova Trading LLC, a day trading firm, in Chicago, Illinois. Putnam met Stuart Townsend, founder of stock trading industry software manufacturer Townsend Analytics Ltd., and the two eventually began discussing the viability of an electronic communications network. Motivated by new SEC regulations in place that encouraged the development of ECNs, TerraNova launched Archipelago as an Internet-based equities trading service in January of 1997.

It was no accident that the firm's founding coincided with SEC-mandated revisions to the order handling protocol required by brokers and traders. The modifications came in response to a trading scandal in which the SEC accused the leading Wall Street players and NASDAQ dealers of price fixing. While the ensuing class-action suit was settled out of court for roughly $1 billion, the changes in order handling ''opened the door to ECNs by requiring limit orders be displayed on the NASDAQ system and that the best prices be matched by market makers,'' according to Ian Celarier in an *Investment Dealers' Digest* article. In short, the new rules gave NASDAQ market access to ECNs like Archipelago who were approved by the SEC to display quotes on NASDAQ terminals. However, beyond simply displaying quotes, ECNs also were able to make public their own prices, which were sometimes more attractive than NASDAQ listings.

By mid-1998 Archipelago had secured nearly 4,000 subscribers, most of whom were institutional. While individual investors were not able to buy or sell stock via the ECN, they could work through a trading firm willing to place orders with Archipelago. In 1999, Instinet Corp., E-Trade Group Inc., and investment bankers Goldman Sachs & Co. and J.P. Morgan spent a combined total of more than $100 million to buy roughly 66 percent of Archipelago, which was valued at $300 million and employed 21 professionals. Growth continued when subsidiary Archipelago Investment LLC expanded the company internationally for the first time by investing $3.6 million in London's Tradepoint Stock Exchange.

In August of 1999, another of the firm's subsidiaries, Archipelago Securities Exchange LLC, submitted a request to the SEC for permission to operate as a full-scale national stock exchange. Becoming a stock exchange would move Archipelago out of the jurisdiction of the National Association of Securities, the owner and operator of competitor NASDAQ, and allow the firm to regulate itself under the direct authority of the SEC. It also would allow Archipelago to levy transaction charges for listing new stocks, to market statistics and other trading information, and to trade NYSE stocks. Access to NYSE stocks would open a lucrative door for Archipelago whose trading, like all other ECNs, was restricted mainly to NASDAQ. At the time, most ECNs made money by completing mass quantities of trades. Therefore, gaining access to the high-activity stocks of the NYSE was viewed by many as crucial to Archipelago's long-term success. The request garnered a great deal of attention because the SEC had not considered such an application since the 1970s.

Archipelago moved to New York in January of 2000 and leased a facility there to hold more of the computers it uses to electronically match stock buyers and sellers. At that time, the firm conducted roughly one percent of all NASDAQ trading market transactions, compared to the 11 percent processed by competitors Instinet and Island. Because its trading activity was so much lower than its rivals, Archipelago had developed software that routinely channeled a large portion of its trading through other exchanges and ECNs to secure premium prices for clients. The technology, known as SmartBook, is based on an algorithm that searches several internal and external prices. If external prices are better, the program then looks at information regarding the external participants before determining who receives an order. Although the firm initially developed this process as a means of getting around its lack of customers, the willingness and ability to use other sources to secure the best deal for its clients later emerged as a feature that distinguished Archipelago from other ECNs.

Determined to realize its goal of becoming an exchange, in March of 2000 Archipelago agreed to merge with the Pacific Stock Exchange and form the first completely electronic stock exchange to trade NYSE stocks. Although the two firms finalized the terms of their deal in July, its completion remained subject to approval by the SEC. A month later, Archipelago saw another major barrier dissolve when it gained access to the Intermarket Trading System, "a computer system that links the nation's exchanges and that is jealously guarded by those who use it, against those who want access to it," according to *Investment Dealers' Digest* writer Heike Wipperfurth.

Archipelago's battle to become an exchange reflects a much larger clash between ECNs in general and Wall Street in particular. As of 2001, they processed more than one-third of all NASDAQ transactions, and their success represented lost business for traditional brokerages and trading houses. In 2000, the SEC launched a one-year investigation of what the major Wall Street players refer to as fragmentation in the marketplace, which they assert makes it more difficult for smaller investors to get the best price. One proposed solution is the creation of a Central Limit Order Book (CLOB) through which all orders would be processed on a first-come-first-served basis. In contrast, ECNs argue that what Wall Street calls market fragmentation simply is competition. They argue that a CLOB would undercut a key factor in the success of ECNs: the ability to execute orders quickly.

Like many Wall Street giants, NASDAQ also is determined to win back market share from the ECNs.

In 2000 it began working on Super Montage, a voluntary centralized order book for national stock that would display stock buy and sell prices on a single system and allow traders to complete deals electronically. While the impact this will have on ECNs remains to be seen, one thing is certain: by using the Internet as a platform for matching stock buyers and sellers, electronic communications networks like Archipelago have permanently altered the stock trading industry.

FURTHER READING:

"Archipelago Becomes First ECN to Trade Listed Stocks Through Nasdaq Intermarket Link." *PR Newswire.* August 8, 2000.

Archipelago Holdings LLC. "History." Chicago: Archipelago Holdings LLC, 2001. Available from www.tradearca.com.

Celarier, Ian S. "The ECN Dilemma: Blasting Fragmentation, Wall Street Calls for a Centralized Market Structure That Threatens the Upstarts." *Investment Dealers Digest.* March 6, 2000.

Ceron, Gaston F. "Tales of the Tape: ECNs Face a Fork in the Road." *Dow Jones News Service.* March 8, 2001.

"Going Electronic." *Futures.* May 2000.

Goldstein, Matthew. "SMARTMONEY.COM: The Next Generation Stock Exchange?" *Dow Jones News Service.* January 26, 2000.

Murphy, Chris. "BIZ MODEL: ARCHIPELAGO—Sure This Network Offers Fast Trading. But Can It Really Stand Up to Nasdaq?" *InformationWeek.* June 26, 2000.

Schroeder, Mary. "Meridien Report: ECNs Not Likely to Consolidate." *Securities Industry News.* August 6, 2001.

"The Un-Brokers." *Forbes.* December 11, 2000.

SEE ALSO: Ameritrade Holding Corp.; Day Trading; Electronic Communications Networks (ECNs); E*Trade Group Inc.; Instinet Corp.; Island ECN, Inc.; Nasdaq Stock Market; Volatility

ARPANET

Considered the predecessor of the Internet, ARPAnet was established by the Advanced Research Projects Agency (ARPA) in 1969 for two main reasons: to allow for the transfer of data between various institutes of research, and to answer the call of the U.S. Department of Defense for a technology that would provide messaging capabilities to the government in the event of nuclear war. Seven years earlier, ARPA hired Dr. J.C.R. Licklider to oversee how best to use emerging computer technology. Licklider is credited as being one of the first individuals to begin looking beyond the mathematical uses of computer technology and see its potential for facilitating communication between institutions and between individuals.

ARPA began formally moving forward on its plan to create a Wide Area Network (WAN) in 1967. After deciding to use Interface Message Processors (IMPs) to connect host computers via telephone lines, ARPA began looking for a contractor able to create the underlying network needed to connect the IMPs. Bolt Beranek and Newman, the Cambridge, Massachusetts-based research and development outfit that Licklider left when he began working for ARPA, successfully bid on the project. The final piece of technology needed—the protocol, or set of standards that would actually allow the host sites to communicate with one another—was developed internally by the Network Working Group.

The first three organizations connected by ARPAnet were the University of California at Los Angeles (UCLA), the Stanford Research Institute, and the University of Utah. Via ARPAnet's Network Control Protocol (NCP), users were able to access and use both computers and printers in other locations and transport files back and forth between computers. Ironically, one of the most important developments in ARPAnet technology, a more sophisticated network code known as Transmission Control Protocol/Internet Protocol (TCP/IP), also established the groundwork for what would one day supercede ARPAnet. TCP/IP replaced NCP in 1983, allowing ARPAnet to be connected with a variety of other networks that had since been launched. This group of networks evolved into what later became known simply as the Internet.

Several other key technologies emerged from various efforts to tweak ARPAnet. For example, e-mail capabilities, first introduced by Ray Tomlinson, were added to ARPAnet in 1971. Online discussion groups sprang up a short while later from address lists of e-mail users with common interests. Although the U.S. Department of Defense disbanded ARPAnet in 1990, its effects on online communications in the late 20th and early 21st centuries were immeasurable.

FURTHER READING:

Hauben, Michael. "History of ARPANET." 2001. Available from www.dei.isep.ipp.

Martin, Richard. "Present at the Creation: An Oral History of the Internet." *PreText Magazine,* March 1998. Available from www.pretext.com.

National Museum of American History. "Birth of the Internet: ARPANET: General Overview." Washington, D.C.: Smithsonian Institution. 2001. Available from smithsonian.yahoo.com/arpanet2.html.

SEE ALSO: History of the Internet and WWW

AT&T CORP.

AT&T Corp. is the world's leading long-distance telephone service provider and also one of the top telecommunications services providers. As competition among long-distance firms intensified throughout the 1980s and 1990s, AT&T struggled to find new markets in which it could succeed. Efforts to convert cable television lines into integrated Internet, local phone, and entertainment networks were sharply criticized by analysts in 2000. Late that year, CEO Michael Armstrong announced plans to split the telecommunications giant into four separate companies. AT&T Wireless is the third-largest wireless firm in the United States, behind Verizon Wireless and Cingular Wireless. AT&T Broadband is comprised of AT&T's cable holdings, which sells local phone, Internet, and cable television services via cable telephony lines to roughly 400,000 customers. AT&T Consumer houses the firm's traditional long-distance services and the WorldNet dial-up Internet service. All other AT&T operations are housed in AT&T Business, the largest of the four units.

EARLY HISTORY

Alexander Graham Bell and two partners created the Bell Telephone Co. in 1877 with plans to begin marketing the newly-invented telephone. Bell Telephone licensee New Haven District Telephone Co. developed the world's first telephone exchange and issued the world's first telephone directory one year later. To handle the licensing of various patents, Bell Telephone founded the New England Telephone Co. In 1879, Bell Telephone merged with New Haven District Telephone to form the National Bell Telephone Co., which reorganized as the American Bell Telephone Company in 1880, after acquiring various holdings from Western Union. A year later, American Bell acquired Western Union's telegraph equipment supplier, Western Electric Manufacturing Co. As a result of the purchase, American Bell became the sole manufacturer of Western Union equipment. The firm diversified into long-distance telephone operations with the formation of American Telephone and Telegraph Co. (AT&T) in 1885. American Bell hoped its new subsidiary would be able to create a widespread national telephone network before several of its patents expired in 1893.

Shortly after its inception, AT&T began building its first long-distance telephone line, which would connect New York City to Philadelphia, Pennsylvania. In 1888, after several blizzards in the northeastern U.S. destroyed long-distance lines, AT&T began looking into underground cable options. Two years later, American Bell began upgrading its one-wire circuits to two-wire circuits to allow for long-distance transmissions. Within two years, these two-wire, or metallic, circuits connected roughly 12 percent of American Bell's 240,000 customers. When Bell's original telephone patent expired in 1893, several competitors emerged, prompting lawsuits by AT&T, which strove to retain its monopoly in the long-distance market. Busy with this litigation, AT&T eventually lost substantial market share to rivals in the West and Midwest.

AT&T's network comprised more than 2.2 million telephones in 1905. Although that number rose to more than 3 million in 1907, the firm struggled with public relations problems, low employee morale, and mounting debt. These problems prompted management to begin taking over competitors, rather than engaging in litigation against them. The firm also started cutting prices, discounted bond prices in an effort to generate fresh capital, and bolstered its research and development arm. In 1913, faced with charges of unlawful conspiracy to monopolize the long-distance market in the Northwest, AT&T agreed to sell previously purchased Western Union assets and to allow competing local telephone service providers to use its long-distance lines.

During World War I, AT&T supplied phone service to the U.S. military. The firm also put in place a communications system of radios, telephones, and telegraph lines in France for use by American forces. In 1918, President Wilson nationalized the U.S. phone network, promising that rates would fall under public control. However, expenses related to wartime activities prompted AT&T to raise prices, and U.S. citizens began calling for the government to release control of the phone system. By then, AT&T operated a network of roughly 10 million telephones. Mounting public pressure prompted the government to privatize AT&T in 1919. Two years later, AT&T linked Key West, Florida, and Havana, Cuba, via its first submarine cable. After the government began allowing telephone company mergers in the early 1920s, AT&T launched an expansion effort that was fueled by several acquisitions. AT&T spun off its research and development arm as Bell Telephone Laboratories in 1925. The new firm was funded by both AT&T and Western Electric.

In 1934, the U.S. government created the Federal Communications Commission (FCC) to regulate the interstate telephone industry. The FCC launched an investigation of AT&T's competitive practices the following year. By then, the firm controlled 83 percent of U.S. phones and 98 percent of long-distance cables. Officials also were concerned about its Western Electric subsidiary, which held a 90-percent share

of the nation's telephone equipment market. With assets of $5 billion, AT&T was the largest company in the United States.

World War II granted AT&T a reprieve from the antitrust investigation. However, the FCC did force the firm to cut prices then. By the war's end, long-distance telephone calls had started to take the place of letter writing in American society as the most common means of communication. The FCC's investigation heated up again in 1949, prompting the U.S. Attorney General to file suit against AT&T for violating antitrust laws. Although the attorney general's recommendation included separating AT&T and Western Electric, the two firms managed to remain united by agreeing to several limitations. For example, AT&T was restricted to providing common carrier service, while Western Electric was limited to supplying equipment to AT&T and fulfilling government contracts. The complex litigation was formally resolved in 1956.

AT&T, the British Post Office, and the Canadian Overseas Telecommunications Corp. put in place the first transatlantic telephone cable in 1955. Two years later, AT&T and Western Electric landed a contract to build an early warning radar system for the U.S. military. AT&T also created a new subsidiary, named Bellcom, to manufacture communications equipment for the U.S. space program. The firm launched a $2.6 billion infrastructure overhaul in 1960. Developments during the early part of the decade included the first wide area telephone service, which allowed customers to pay a flat fee for unlimited long-distance calls; Centrex, which allowed offices to maintain their own automatic switching exchange; and Telstar, AT&T's first satellite. The firm also created Comsat to oversee its U.S. satellite communications operations and began offering touch-tone service for the first time. By mid-decade, AT&T had established the seven-digit phone number as standard throughout North America. The installation of electronic switching equipment allowed for an increased volume of calls. Employees totaled roughly 1 million.

AT&T's legal battles continued in the mid-1970s when both Microwave Communications Inc. (MCI) and the U.S. Department of Justice filed two suits against the telephone giant, alleging both monopoly and conspiracy to monopolize the telecommunications industry. Six years later, a jury found AT&T guilty in the MCI suit and ordered AT&T to pay damages of $1.8 billion. A jury eventually reduced those damages to $37.8 million in an appeal. In 1982, AT&T and the U.S. Department of Justice settled their landmark antitrust suit when AT&T agreed to sell off its regional operating companies, which would become unregulated, competing businesses. As part of the agreement, AT&T created American Bell

Inc. as a separate, unregulated subsidiary to sell equipment and services. AT&T was allowed to once again pursue non-telecommunications ventures, a freedom that would enable it to enter the computer market.

Plans for the breakup of AT&T were formalized in 1983, and the firm began spinning off BellSouth, Bell Atlantic, NYNEX, American Information Technologies, Southwestern Bell, U.S. West, and Pacific Telesis as regional phone service providers. Although AT&T retained control of its long-distance services, it was no longer protected from competition. Once the divestitures were completed, AT&T reorganized its remaining operations into two units; its communications unit managed the long-distance network, and its technologies unit manufactured and sold telecommunications equipment.

Within a year of its reorganization, AT&T had started pursuing markets across the globe in anticipation of increased domestic competition. Along with establishing a regional headquarters in Brussels, Belgium, for operations in Europe, the Middle East, and Africa, AT&T also began forging joint ventures with overseas companies. Its share of the U.S. long-distance market fell in 1987 to 76 percent, compared to 91 percent just four years earlier. AT&T laid off 16,000 workers and took a one-time $6.7 billion network modernization charge, which resulted in a $1.7 billion loss in 1988.

When government regulators allowed AT&T to match the lower long-distance rates of competitors MCI Communications Corp. and Sprint Corp. in 1989, profits rebounded to $2.7 billion, their highest point since the 1984 spin-offs. In 1991, AT&T diversified into computers for the first time when it bought NCR Corp. for $7.4 billion, becoming the fourth-largest U.S. and seventh-largest worldwide computer maker. The firm entered the cellular telephony market in 1993 by paying $12.6 billion for McCaw Cellular. The NCR unit was renamed AT&T Global Information Solutions in 1994.

MOVE TO CABLE AND INTERNET MARKETS

To promote its image as a leading technology developer and content provider, AT&T launched a Web site, with various online services, in 1995. The Telecommunications Act of 1996, which essentially deregulated the U.S. telecommunications industry, allowed local and long-distance phone companies, Internet firms, and cable businesses to begin competing in each other's markets. AT&T took advantage of the legislation almost immediately, launching WorldNet, an Internet Service Provider (ISP), in March. By November, WorldNet had secured roughly 425,000 sub-

scribers. Other leading telecommunications firms began announcing billion dollar mergers. While consolidation in the industry already had been happening on a limited basis prior to February of 1996, the act opened up unprecedented cross-market penetration opportunities. To prepare itself for such deals, AT&T split into three separate entities in December. The firm retained its communications operations; consolidated the Bell Laboratories equipment manufacturing operations into a new public company, called Lucent Technology; and spun off its struggling computer operations, which had lost roughly $4 billion over the past five years.

In 1997, AT&T added two electronic catalogs—one for residential customers and one for small business clients—to its Web site. Plans to allow e-commerce transactions to take place on the site were launched by the newly formed AT&T Interactive Group. The firm also began marketing its first virtual private network (VPN) service to corporations in December. Earlier in the year, C. Michael Armstrong had replaced Robert Allen as CEO. Wanting to reduce his firm's reliance on the increasingly competitive long-distance market, particularly since attempts to penetrate the computer market had failed, Armstrong orchestrated the $11.3 billion purchase of Teleport Communications Group—a local phone service for businesses owned by cable operators Tele-Communications Inc. (TCI), Cox Enterprises, and Comcast—in 1998. That year, in a deal valued at $10 billion, AT&T and British Telecommunications PLC agreed to merge their international operations to form WorldPartners.

Believing that local telephone, cable, and Internet services would converge into one giant industry in the near future, AT&T also began eyeing cable and Internet firms. Almost immediately after taking over as CEO, Armstrong had approached TCI, attracted to its broadband Internet services and cable operations. After watching several deals unfold—the $10.8 billion purchase of Continental Cablevision, the third largest U.S. cable operator, by regional telephone operator U.S. West Inc.; the $16 billion purchase of Pacific Telesis by SBC Communications to form the second-largest phone company in North America; the $25.6 million joining of Bell Atlantic Corp. and Nynex Corp.; and the $37 billion merger of WorldCom Inc. and MCI Communications Corp.—AT&T and TCI decided to act. They announced a $48 million merger agreement in June of 1998 and received Justice Department approval in January of 1999. When the $59 billion deal closed in March, AT&T changed TCI's name to AT&T Broadband & Internet Services. The firm then began working on upgrading TCI's infrastructure to allow for integrated local telephone, cable television, and broadband Internet services.

AT&T became the largest U.S. cable carrier when it paid $58 billion for MediaOne Group Inc. in the middle of the year. However, stock prices began to plummet when several analysts criticized the firm for underestimating the cost and complexity of transforming cable networks into local telephone and Internet pipelines. According to a February 2001 article in *Multichannel News,* "In its struggle to transform itself into an Internet and wireless communications leader, AT&T slowly began to implode. Almost $20 billion of its revenues were still generated from its long-distance business, slowly depleting the company's deep pockets, which funded the ongoing makeover. Meanwhile, AT&T's stocks continued to reach new lows."

Early in 2001, AT&T sold 574,000 cable subscribers to Charter Communications for $1.79 billion and 840,000 subscribers to Mediacom Communications Corp. for $2.2 billion. AT&T and British Telecommunications revealed plans to shut down Concert, a joint venture they had established in January of 2000 to provide high-speed Internet and phone services to multinational corporations. In May, AT&T agreed to purchase bankrupt Internet Service Provider (ISP) NorthPoint Communications Inc., including its Digital Subscriber Line (DSL) services. Although the firm's WorldNet ISP had grown rapidly to 1.1 million subscribers by mid-1998, its growth in 1999 and 2000 had been stagnant. AT&T hoped to bolster its performance with the launch of DSL services by the end of 2001. In June, the firm announced its intent to begin acting as an ISP in Thailand. According to Armstrong, who insists that AT&T's diversification into cable telephony will pay off for the firm, despite the dire predictions of analysts, the four-way split of AT&T's operations will be finalized by the middle of 2002.

FURTHER READING:

"AT&T Corp." In *Notable Corporate Chronologies.* Farmington Hills, MI: Gale Research, 1999.

Davis, Stephania H. "Interact With Us: AT&T Enhances its Online Offering." *Telephony.* November 24, 1997.

Higgins, John M. "AT&T for Sale?" *Broadcasting & Cable.* December 4, 2000.

Kastre, Michael. "The Inevitable Demise of 'Ma Bell.'" *Multichannel News.* February 26, 2001.

Mehta, Stephanie N. "Great Ball of Wire! CEO Mike Armstrong's Latest Plan to Save AT&T Splits into Four Parts." *Fortune.* November 13, 2000.

Mermigas, Diane. "The Wheels Are Turning at AT&T." *Electronic Media.* March 5, 2001.

"Q&A with AT&T's Mike Armstrong: You Damn Betcha it's for Shareholders." *BusinessWeek Online.* October 27, 2000. Available from www.businessweek.com.

Wooley, Scott. "Mike Strikes Back." *Forbes.* December 13, 1999.

SEE ALSO: Broadband Technology; Connectivity, Internet; Lucent Technologies Inc.; Mergers and Acquisitions

ATTENTION ECONOMY

The attention economy is a buzz term that was used in the late 1990s and early 2000s to describe the economic period that followed, in succession, the agricultural economy, the industrial economy, and the information economy. On the heels of the information economy, according to proponents of the attention-economy concept, human attention has become the scarcest resource amidst the swirl of information constantly bombarding consumers. The proliferation of communication media—television, radio, telephone, print, wireless communications, and the Internet—and their expanding and overlapping reach, creates a situation in which audiences are easily distracted. In order to gain and hold consumers' attention in such an environment, marketers must offer messages that audiences find meaningful and significant. Thus, products and services must be sold and marketed not just on their merits of utility, cost savings, and enjoyment, but with a thick layer of symbolic packaging and narratives that confer meaning in order to capture consumers' attention and money. In short, the attention economy privileges and emphasizes context over content.

On a less abstract level, the attention economy describes a state in which, on a Web site, the content, product, or service being offered is important but hardly sufficient. Rather, as a way of getting visitors to stay at a site and spend money, the site must feature an attractive image and user interface designed to augment the feelings and images the merchant wants them to harbor.

A central characteristic of the attention economy, according to Esther Dyson—a prominent commentator on Internet matters and the woman who coined the phrase—is the relative end of economic scarcity and general fulfillment of human needs. In the attention economy, she contends, consumers generally are free of want for life's necessities and comforts. This sets the stage for one of the primary challenges that e-commerce merchants face in their marketing strategies. Essentially, what marketers compete for is the attention of otherwise fulfilled customers.

Amidst an increasingly sophisticated advertising and entertainment culture, along with perpetual connectivity to media and a vast wealth of information at people's fingertips, the race to capture, hold, and channel people's attention has begun. Individual businesses and the greater economy count attention among the scarcest resources. Thus, attention has become a nexus of competition and strategy. Firms have begun to develop new ways of measuring and testing attention in order to harness it for economically beneficial ends. Meanwhile, the public's already fragmented attention continues to be divided into ever more potential revenue streams.

FURTHER READING:

Davenport, Thomas H., and John C. Beck. ''Getting the Attention You Need.'' *Harvard Business Review.* September/October 2000.

———. *The Attention Economy: Understanding the New Currency of Business.* Cambridge: Harvard Business School Press, 2001.

Howard, Henry. ''Capturing 'Attention.''' *Home Textiles Today.* February 2000.

Roberts, Kevin. ''Brand Identity 2000: Redefining the World.'' *Advertising Age.* November 29, 1999.

Sviokla, John. ''The Attention Economy.'' *Industry Standard.* March 6, 2000.

SEE
ALSO: Cyberculture

AUCTION SITES

Online auctions have proven very popular with consumers and businesses alike. They offer many benefits to both buyers and sellers. Online auctions offer buyers the promise of lower prices for merchandise and collectibles. Yet, spirited bidding for desirable items may drive up prices beyond what they would have been in a fixed price environment. Online auctions have virtually unlimited geographic reach, bringing together buyers and sellers from almost anywhere in the world. While not yet fully realized, online auctions have the potential to revolutionize pricing by replacing sticker (or fixed) prices, with a dynamic pricing model whereby merchandise is priced according to what the market will bear.

Initially, collectibles were the dominant type of merchandise sold at online auctions. While collectibles remained a popular category, merchandise such as office supplies, computers, and heavy machinery became more prevalent during 2000. High-ticket items for consumers have not been as successful at auction as once hoped. In April 1999 eBay, the leading auction site, acquired Butterfield & Butterfield, a 134-year-old U.S. auction house that specialized in fine art auctions. As a result eBay launched eBay Great Collections in October 1999, offering authenti-

cated art items priced between $250 and $10,000. At its launch, eBay Great Collections had signed up 80 art dealers to provide items for auction. In March 2001 a high-priced auction on eBay of early photographs of Marilyn Monroe failed to result in a sale when bids fell short of the seller's reserve price. However, the same sale saw items in the $15,000 to $20,000 range sell through bids that were placed over eBay's art and collectibles site, eBay Premier.

In mid-1999 Amazon.com formed an alliance with auction house Sotheby's Holdings Inc. to launch a joint auction site specializing in art, antiques, and collectibles. All of the items were offered by Sotheby's and other affiliated art dealers at Amazon.com's auction site, and the authenticity and condition of each item was guaranteed. The site launched in November 1999, but it closed after less than a year in October 2000. Sothebys.com continued to offer fine art auctions, as did other major art auction houses.

Online auction sites also can offer unusual items that would be difficult, if not impossible, to find elsewhere. Their wide geographic reach is especially useful to collectors, who would have difficulty hooking up with sellers in different parts of the world without the Internet. Sometimes, controversial items are offered for sale. In September 1999 a human kidney was offered for auction on eBay. Bidding reached more than $5.7 million before eBay blocked the sale as illegal.

AUCTIONS BUILD TRAFFIC

Because of their popularity with consumers, online auctions are seen as a way for Web sites to increase traffic. Online auctions have a certain ''game'' quality for consumers, who often approach them as a winning or losing proposition. Online auctions typically stretch out over several days or even weeks and end at a specific time. Consumers may employ automated bidding software to find desired items and place bids at appropriate times. They often develop a bidding strategy to increase their chances of getting the items they want at a reasonable price. One strategy known as ''sniping'' involves placing a winning bid at the last possible second, just before the auction expires.

Forrester Research estimated that online auction sales reached $1.4 billion in 1998 and projected they would increase to $19 billion by 2003. Consumer-to-consumer online auctions accounted for $3 billion in sales in 1999, according to *E-Commerce Times.* eBay is the leading auction site on the Internet and as of November 2000 it was the tenth-most-visited Internet site. At that time some $12 million worth of daily merchandise was sold at auction on eBay. Yahoo! Auctions sold about $500,000 a day, and Amazon.com's auctions sold about $200,000 per day.

The 2000 holiday shopping season saw a surge of visitors to online auction sites. According to Media Metrix, eBay had 2.6 million average daily unique visitors, compared to 1.6 million for Amazon.com, for the week ending December 3, 2000. That represented an 89-percent increase over the same week in 1999 for eBay. Daily visits to online auction sites in general were up 62 percent over the previous year during the holiday season.

BUSINESS-TO-CONSUMER AUCTIONS

Businesses also sell goods and services through auction sites. Small businesses use auction sites such as eBay, Yahoo! Auctions, and Auction World not only to sell merchandise, but also to build their brand and reputation. Online auctions also give businesses an outlet for selling excess inventory that would have remained in their warehouse. Other uses that businesses find for auction sites include test marketing new products to see if they will sell. Occasionally, bidders will drive up the price of item to a level well above what was expected.

Most auction sites post feedback on how well sellers perform. While positive feedback can enhance a seller's reputation, a few negative comments from a small number of buyers have the potential to tarnish a seller's name. In order to ensure positive feedback, sellers must devote more resources to providing high levels of customer service. Auction shoppers tend to be value-oriented and have high expectations for service.

Businesses that use auction sites to list their merchandise must also be prepared to devote time to posting their listings, answering a large volume of e-mail, and managing functions such as billing, shipping, and payment collection. Some of the larger auction sites provide tools to help with some of these chores, and there are even businesses that specialize in providing auction management services to small businesses in the form of Web-based tools. AuctionWatch.com promotes itself as ''The Complete Auction Management Solution'' and offers a range of services for buyers and sellers.

Selling items to the highest bidder without running a credit check on them leaves sellers open to the risk of non-payment. As a result some of the top auction sites offer an escrow service, where a third party holds the buyer's payment until the product is shipped and received. Escrow services were designed primarily to protect buyers from receiving shoddy or inaccurately described merchandise, but they also offer a measure of protection to sellers as well. At Amazon.com's auctions, bidders pay using their credit card, and Amazon.com handles the financial aspects of the auction transaction.

Businesses that want to sell at auction have several options. First, they can list their items at the major auction sites. They also can utilize more specialized auction sites that are devoted to business-oriented items. For a bigger fee, businesses can use the services of an auction portal, such as FairMarket Auction Place, which places auction items by category on several other Web sites.

AUCTION FRAUD

A report released by the Federal Bureau of Investigation (FBI) in March 2001 ranked online auction fraud as the number one scam on the Internet. Internet auction fraud was the cause of 64 percent of complaints filed with the U.S. government's Internet Fraud Complaint Center (IFCC). By comparison, credit and debit card fraud accounted for only five percent of the complaints. Among the practices included by the IFCC as Internet auction fraud were non-delivery of items, misrepresentation of items' value, stealing of goods from an online merchant through the involvement of a third party (triangulation), adding extra charges once bidding was completed (fee stacking), the sale of black-market goods, multiple bidding by the same buyer under different accounts or aliases, and false bidding by the seller (shill bidding).

In October 2000 the U.S. Federal Trade Commission (FTC) also reported that online auction fraud topped its list of ''Top Ten Dot Cons,'' based on complaints it received through its Consumer Sentinel database. The FTC said that the number of reported cases of online auction fraud rose from 100 in 1997 to 10,000 in 1999. The FTC's guide to Internet auctions provides information about protecting against online auction fraud.

FURTHER READING:

Centeno, Cerelle. ''Going Once, Going Twice: eAuction Fraud in the U.S.'' *eMarketer Newsletter.* May 30, 2001. Available from www.emarketer.com.

Dembeck, Chet. ''Amazon and Sotheby's Launch Upscale Auction Site.'' *E-Commerce Times.* November 19, 1999. Available from www.ecommercetimes.com.

Enos, Lori. ''Online Auctions Top FBI Net Fraud List.'' *E-Commerce Times.* March 7, 2001. Available from www.ecommercetimes.com.

Frey, Bruce. *Online Auctions! I Didn't Know You Could Do That.* Alameda, CA: Sybex, 2000.

''Going, Going, Gone.'' *Business Week.* April 12, 1999.

Goldsborough, Reid. ''Internet Auctions Examined.'' *Link-Up.* November 2000.

Gonzalez, Julio. ''The Dark Side of Net Auctions.'' *E-Commerce Times.* December 18, 2000. Available from www.ecommercetimes.com.

Hunt, Justin. ''You've Got to be Bidding.'' *Internet Magazine.* December 1999.

O'Loughlin, Luanne, et al. *Online Auctions: The Internet Guide for Bargain Hunters & Collectors.* New York: McGraw-Hill, 2000.

"Online Auctions Are Taking Off." *InfoWorld.* February 8, 1999.

Saliba, Clare. "Study: Auction Fraud Still Top Cybercrime." *E-Commerce Times.* January 10, 2001. Available from www.ecommercetimes.com.

Vallone, Julie. "Going Once, Going Twice." *Entrepreneur.* February 2000.

SEE ALSO: Amazon.com; eBay; Fraud, Internet; Yahoo!

AUTHENTICATION

When consumers attempt to withdraw money from a bank, rent movies from a video store, write checks, or obtain passports for international travel, they are required to provide one or more forms of identification that authenticate who they are or prove their identity. These situations usually involve face-to-face encounters with other people in the physical world. E-commerce occurs on the Internet, where a general atmosphere of anonymity pervades. In general, it is possible to do a wide variety of things online without divulging one's identity. However, when it comes to engaging in financial transactions and building trust between buyers and sellers, the issue of authentication is just as important online as it is offline. Put simply, parties engaging in transactions and attempting to access closed systems must be able to prove that they are indeed who they say they are.

Security is a cornerstone of e-commerce, as it helps alleviate fears consumers and businesses may have about conducting transactions online. According to *e-tailing,* authentication is one of five requirements necessary for secure e-commerce. It must occur prior to authorization, which allows entry and access to a system, and fulfills three critical functions: it ensures confidentiality, maintains data integrity, and provides non-repudiation (making it difficult for entities to deny involvement in electronic transactions).

A wide variety of methods, used alone or in combination, are employed to authenticate online entities of businesses or individuals. User names and passwords are perhaps the most basic means of authenticating users. In this scenario, someone gaining access to privileged information, such as bank-account data or credit-card information, is required to enter a user name, which is normally not secret, as well as a secret password consisting of varying character combinations of letters or numbers. Personal identification

numbers (PINs), digital certificates, biometrics, and RSA SecurID tokens were other common methods by which users were authenticated in the early 2000s. Biometrics, an emerging technology, involved a range of equipment—including voice recognition software, retina scanners, fingerprint readers, and cameras—that identified unique physical characteristics. Such devices could be installed on both laptops and desktop computers. As described in *Information Security,* "SecurID tokens are essentially one-time passwords for user authentication and can be used to authenticate to a Windows domain. The time-synchronized SecurID card has an LCD screen that shows a string of numbers that changes every minute." Along with a PIN number, such numeric strings are used together when users attempt to gain access to certain systems.

FURTHER READING:

Andress, Mandy. "Reach Out and ID Someone." *Information Security,* April, 2001. Available from www.infosecuritymag.com.

Dembeck, Chet. "Equifax Trumpets Online Shopper ID Method." *E-Commerce Times,* July 14, 2001. Available from www.ecommercetimes.com.

Saliba, Clare. "EU Signs Off on E-Signature Initiative." *E-Commerce Times,* August 1, 2001. Available from www.ecommercetimes.com.

SEE ALSO: Biometrics; Computer Security; Digital Certificate; Digital Signature

AUTHORIZATION AND AUTHORIZATION CODE

Credit cards are the main method consumers use to pay for goods and services when engaged in e-commerce transactions. In general, businesses and consumers obtain credit cards by applying for varying lines of credit from one of the many card-issuing banks located throughout the world. Although the process of using a credit card may appear to be simple to an end-user, many steps are actually involved when a transaction takes place. These steps involve several different entities including merchants, the acquiring banks that handle credit card transactions for them, acquiring processors, card-issuing banks, and cardholders.

Authorization is the process by which card-issuing banks ultimately verify to merchants that cardholders have enough credit to cover purchases. This process often is handled by acquiring processors, which act on behalf of merchants' acquiring banks. Authorization is a very important step in a credit-card transaction because it determines whether or not a purchase will be allowed. If a cardholder's attempt to use their credit card is denied because of insufficient credit or any other reason, the acquiring processor returns a denial code to the merchant. If the credit card usage is allowed, the merchant receives an authorization code. These codes correspond specifically to each transaction. Authorization codes cause card-issuing banks to hold funds (which are immediately deducted from the cardholder's credit limit) until they are actually received at a later time (usually the end of the business day) by the merchant.

FURTHER READING:

"Glossary of E-Commerce Terms." *E-com Publishing,* June 4, 2001. Available from www.ecompublishing.com.

Klemow, Jason. "Credit Card Transactions Via the Internet." *TMA Journal,* January/February 1999.

Wilson, Dr. Ralph F. "Unraveling the Mysteries of Merchant Credit Card Accounts for Web Commerce." *Web Commerce Today,* August 15, 1997. Available from www.wilsonweb.com.

SEE   Acquiring Bank; Card-Issuing Bank; Merchant Model;
ALSO: Transaction Issues

AWARDS, WEB

The evolution of Web sites from bland depositories of information to sophisticated and user-friendly entities of conscious design carried with it a growing tendency to recognize the achievements of intelligent, artistic, and useful Web design practices with awards. There were countless Web awards created by the early 2000s, ranging from the relatively anonymous to the highly prestigious. Awards were sponsored by established organizations and followed by pundits and Web aficionados alike. In addition, many magazines—both hardcopy and online—issued awards for excellent Web achievements in fields of interest to their readers. Lastly, awards cater to different audiences. Some are devoted mainly to popular recognition by average users, while others recognize technical excellence as judged by professional peers. Accordingly, then, some Web awards are highly sought after by Web designers, while others are essentially giveaways of which the recipients may not even be aware.

Awards Scoop categorized Web awards into six types.

- First, elite awards were the most highly prized, and were the most competitive, since the prestige generally carried other benefits, such as increased user traffic at the site.

- The second category covered awards based on professional recognition. While these were also relatively serious awards, they were not as hotly contested since the audience for them was more insular than for elite awards.

- Third, promotional Web awards were those that Web sites sponsored in part to have the winners somehow promote the award-granting site or entity by placing a mark of the award—and perhaps a link to the presenter's site—on their winning Web sites.

- Fourth, popular awards based on the votes of average users were often significant, but not as hotly contested, since they tend to be less prominent and their criteria highly subjective.

- The fifth category included what *Awards Scoop* called the "everybody wins" awards, which are mainly presented as a way to draw traffic to the presenter's own site. Such awards tend to be very loosely distributed, and thus the standards for winning are rather low.

- Finally, noncompetitive awards were issued usually to children or amateurs primarily to encourage them to continue in their development efforts.

THE GROWTH OF WEB AWARDS

According to Mic Miller's "A History of Web Awards" in *Awards Scoop,* Web awards had their genesis in 1994 with the Best of the Web Awards program established by Brandon Plewe of the State University of New York at Buffalo. The winners were announced in May of that year at the First International Conference on the World Wide Web in Geneva, Switzerland. The winners were chosen by popular vote, and the awards' intention was to highlight the possibilities of the World Wide Web, which was at the time just beginning to hit critical mass. Thus, the Best of the Web Awards were simultaneously a recognition of emerging aesthetic and usability standards and a vast promotional effort to spread use of the Web by promoting sophisticated design standards.

Following the Best of the Web Awards, a spate of other awards sprang up in the mid-1990s, usually presenting digital badges or medals to Web sites judged excellent by the awards' criteria. Soon, Web designers shifted their design strategies from attempting to impress their loosely affiliated peers in the design community to chasing after specific awards recognized by large swaths of the Web population. In this way, Web awards contributed to the development of widely-recognized design standards. By 1995, awards began to be institutionalized. Rather than prominent individuals, awards were thus distributed by established organizations, particularly universities. Among the first of these was the University of Michigan's Cool Central, which issued new awards constantly, featuring ''sites of the day'' and other honors based on the opinions of established and respected judges from around the world.

Through the mid- and late 1990s, the Web grew exponentially, and it seemed like just about everyone was setting up their own Web site. At the same time, design standards evolved and tools grew more sophisticated, upping the ante for Web awards and pushing them into different niches. However, as awards proliferated, they were often used largely as a gimmick to draw more traffic to the presenter's sites. The dearth of Web awards thus threatened to dilute the meaning of awards altogether. To separate the wheat from the chaff, the Award Sites! Web site was established in 1997 by David Bancroft as a way of judging the awards themselves and creating a degree of critical distinction between them. Similar programs followed, and by the 2000s a handful of Web awards had emerged as the most highly respected and sought-after on the Web.

THE WEBBY AWARDS

Perhaps most widely known were the Webby Awards, presented by the International Academy of Digital Arts and Sciences (IADAS). Based in San Francisco, the International Academy was founded two years after the Webbies began, sprouting from the original awards' judging academy, and its members were generally recognized leaders in fields related to electronic media. The Webbies is the annual ceremony, designed to mimic music's Grammies or Hollywood's Oscars, at which the academy bestows awards on sites in various categories and for various criteria of excellence. (Unlike those awards ceremonies, however, the Webby Awards limit acceptance speeches to five words or less.) In general, the Webbies aim to honor those sites that are most likely to make Web surfers want to visit and provide the best overall browsing experience.

In 2001, the Webbies covered 27 categories, including commerce, community, education, activism, government and law, humor, news, sports, and ''weird.'' On top of category awards, the Webbies recognize excellence in technical and artistic achievement, as well as outstanding individual contributions and achievements. The IADAS selects all nominees, but for each category two awards are bestowed: the Webby (presented by the academy) and the People's Voice Award (voted by the online public). The Webbies draw celebrity power, as well. The 2001 ceremony—featuring performance art, film, video, and animation—was hosted by ABC television journalist Sam Donaldson.

THE GOLDEN WEB AWARDS

The Golden Web Awards were prestigious within the Web design community, as they were based on peer recognition. Presented by the International Association of Web Masters and Designers (IAWMD), the Golden Web Awards recognized intelligent and innovative Web design practices from the Web master's viewpoint. The IAWMD, in addition to the Awards, provided a forum for members and students to exchange information and ideas related to Web design and maintenance, aiming to promote awareness of and education about Web practices via international networking and recognition.

Unlike the Webby Awards, which are marked with an elaborate ceremony, the Golden Web Awards are presented throughout the year. Web sites are submitted for awards by designers and users to the IAWMD, members of which evaluate the nominations on the basis of design, originality, and content. In addition, the IAWMD sponsors the Junior Web Awards specifically for students aged 13 to 17 to hone their skills by competing with other students worldwide for recognition.

MÉDAILLE D'OR FOR WEB SITE EXCELLENCE

Another prominent Web award was the Médaille d'Or Award for Web Site Excellence, based in the United Kingdom. Médaille d'Or, as an organization, was developed specifically for the purpose of recognizing achievements in Web design and the presentation of its award. Médaille d'Or judges look for a variety of characteristics, such as

- the initial impression of the site

- the extent to which it grabs one's attention and maintains it

- whether the site downloads reasonably quickly

- whether it is regularly updated

- whether there is a smooth and intuitive navigation scheme

- general attractiveness

- whether the subject matter is intriguing and whether the presentation is appropriate to the subject.

Not being part of a professional organization nor based on peer review, the Médaille d'Or Award, its popularity notwithstanding, is admittedly more subjective than some of its rival awards. Winners of the Médaille d'Or receive, appropriately enough, a digital gold medal to display on their Web sites to advertise the recognition the site has achieved.

FURTHER READING:

''International Association of Web Masters and Designers: Golden Web Awards.'' Wellington, FL: International Association of Web Masters and Designers, September, 2001. Available from www.goldenwebawards.com.

''Médaille d'Or Award—Main Site.'' United Kingdom: Médaille d'Or, 2001. Available from www.arachnid.co.uk.

Miller, Mic. ''A History of Web Awards.'' *Awards Scoop,* 2001. Available from www.awardsscoop.org.

———. ''Types of Web Awards.'' *Awards Scoop,* 2001. Available from www.awardsscoop.org.

''The Webby Awards.'' San Francisco, CA: The Webby Awards, 2001. Available from www.webbyawards.com.

''World Best Websites: Website Excellence Awards—Best of the Web.'' Melbourne, Australia: WorldBest.Com, 2001. Available from www.worldbestwebsites.com.

SEE
ALSO: Web Site Basics; Web Site Design and Set-up; Web Site Usability Issues

B

BALLMER, STEVE

When Steve Ballmer assumed the CEO position at Microsoft Corp., he filled the shoes of Bill Gates— the world's richest man and most famous software mogul. He took over at the start of 2000, in the thick of the government's antitrust lawsuit against the company. A longtime friend and number-two man to Bill Gates, Ballmer was tapped as CEO to smooth over Microsoft's transition to a post-litigation phase by streamlining the company's internal bureaucracy and freeing Gates to concentrate on a future vision for the company, a vision which Ballmer would be charged with implementing.

Ballmer and Gates first met when the two were classmates at Harvard University. While Gates famously dropped out to start Microsoft, Ballmer stayed on to graduate, before accepting a job at Procter & Gamble. After Gates lured him to Microsoft, where he started in the sales department in 1980, Ballmer spent many years managing the company's relationship with high-tech giant IBM and overseeing the development of the Windows operating system, which would become the company's premier product and cash cow. In 1998, Gates named Ballmer president of the company, and his appointment to CEO followed less than two years later.

One of Ballmer's responsibilities was overhauling Microsoft's image in the face of its contentious legal difficulties. During this challenging period, Ballmer was insistent about the company's innocence. Additionally, Ballmer announced the next phase in Microsoft's technological evolution, that of transforming Windows products into a fundamentally new kind of operating system that will be spread throughout the Internet and all machines connected to it.

Notorious for his bombastic and hard-headed management style, along with an easygoing and affable personal demeanor—features that distinguished him from Gates—Ballmer was widely viewed as the logical and perfect choice to succeed Gates amidst the company's late-1990s difficulties. Meanwhile, managing the ambitions and difficulties of Bill Gates has paid off handsomely; in 2000, *Forbes* listed Ballmer as the 12th-richest man in the world.

FURTHER READING:

Bank, David. "How Steve Ballmer is Already Remaking Microsoft." *Wall Street Journal.* January 17, 2000.

Ignatius, David. "A Kinder, Gentler Microsoft?" *Washington Post.* May 7, 2000.

Markoff, John. "Microsoft's Chief Settles into His Best Friend's Old Job." *New York Times.* January 15, 2000.

Rooney, Paula. "Steve Ballmer: Citizen Microsoft." *Computer Reseller News.* November 13, 2000.

Schlender, Brent. "The $100 Billion Friendship." *Fortune.* October 25, 1999.

SEE ALSO: Allen, Paul; Gates, William (Bill); Microsoft Corp.; Microsoft Network (MSN); Microsoft Windows

BANDWIDTH

Bandwidth is the amount of data that moves along transmission lines or circuits at a given speed.

For example, the time it takes a personal computer to load a word-processing program is dependent upon bandwidth, as is the load time for a World Wide Web page. Transmission speed is expressed either in bits-per-second (bps) for digital devices such as modems, or cycles-per-second, more commonly known as hertz (Hz), for analog devices such as microprocessors.

When bandwidth is inadequate for the function being performed, the slowdown that occurs is called a bottleneck. Bottlenecks can reduce either the transmission speed of data between components of a computer or within both local area and wide area networks. To circumvent this problem, personal computer manufacturers have developed machines with much faster busses—the circuits that actually carry data throughout a computer—such as the 40 mHz VL-bus and the 66 mHz AGP. Similarly, increased Internet traffic, and the more sophisticated graphical applications available on the World Wide Web, have prompted networking technology firms to develop devices like Gigabit Ethernet, Fast Token Rings, and T1 lines as a means of offering increased bandwidth rates to businesses and other institutions, as well as to individuals.

FURTHER READING:

''Bandwidth.'' In *Ecommerce Webopedia*. Darien, CT: Internet.com, 2001. Available from e-comm.webopedia.com.

''Bandwidth.'' In *NetLingo*. NetLingo Inc., 2001. Available from www.netlingo.com.

''Bandwidth.'' In *Techencyclopedia*. Point Pleasant, PA: Computer Language Co., 2001. Available from www.techweb.com/encyclopedia.

SEE ALSO: Bandwidth Management; Connectivity, Internet; Microprocessor

---

BANDWIDTH MANAGEMENT

Bandwidth management refers to the process of optimizing the bandwidth that carries traffic over networks. Bandwidth—the amount of data transferred over a communication channel in a specific amount of time—can be controlled by bandwidth management tools, which often are referred to as traffic or packet shapers. These tools enable network managers to control communications by allowing high-priority traffic to utilize more bandwidth than something given a lower priority status. Business-critical applications, including e-commerce transactions, are dependent upon successful bandwidth management.

The need for bandwidth management has significantly increased since the mid-1990s as more information is transferred over the Internet in increasingly diverse formats. Key factors that led to its development include

- the growing number of new users added to networks

- the popularity of streaming media applications, which allow users to listen to radio stations or view video clips via the Internet

- the development of peer-to-peer Web sites, such as Napster, that allow file-swapping over the Internet

- and the rise of e-commerce applications.

As online traffic and the demand for media-rich and e-business applications grows, a network without successful bandwidth management tools in place can experience severe bottlenecks or slowdowns.

Controlling bandwidth is important for Internet service providers (ISPs), application service providers (ASPs), hosting service providers (HSPs), and other networked enterprises. ISPs, for example, can pinpoint how much bandwidth a member is using for billing purposes to ensure an adequate amount of bandwidth is allocated for such transactions. For ASPs and HSPs, bandwidth management can ensure that critical software applications and solution-based operations have network resources available. Wide-area networks, intranets, and extranets use bandwidth management to control network traffic and ensure that business-critical applications have the necessary resources.

BANDWIDTH MANAGEMENT TOOLS

Instead of adding additional bandwidth to networks to solve bottleneck problems—a short-term solution that is rather costly—network managers use bandwidth management tools or packet and traffic shapers to control bandwidth allocation. These tools identify and prioritize packets that carry information through networks. For instance, when university networks experienced problems in the late 1990s and early 2000s as students began using campus resources to share music via Napster, network administrators avoided purchasing more bandwidth or restricting access to their sites by using tools that would slow access to sites like Napster and give priority to academic requests on the network.

These tools also enable network managers to identify network traffic patterns, establish priorities, optimize application performance, and allocate resources. PacketShaper, a popular tool developed by bandwidth management technology pioneer Packeteer Inc., is able to optimize bandwidth by categorizing network traffic based on application, protocol, subnet, and URL, allowing managers to prioritize requests on the network. PacketShaper also analyzes networks to determine efficiency and bandwidth allocation; enables managers to look at system reports and statistics; and allows them to control traffic and optimize critical application performance. For example, PacketShaper gives online businesses the ability to allocate more bandwidth to e-commerce transaction traffic than to less important applications.

Other popular tools on the market in 2001 included Intel's NetStructure 7340 Traffic Shaper and the Packeteer PacketShaper/ISP. These tools allow ISPs to prioritize and optimize network bandwidth by controlling levels and limiting server bandwidth. The Intel NetStructure 7370 Application Shaper is another management system that enables ASPs and HSPs to control the quality of application services and monitor resources. Allot Communication also offers a Virtual Bandwidth Manager (VMB), which allows corporate networks to remotely control bandwidth by accessing a VMB unit at a service provider office.

As the number of Internet users continues to increase and demand for media-rich and peer-to-peer applications rises, bandwidth management will continue to play a role in network management. However, finding a management solution is not always an easy task. While there are many tools on the market, the continual evolution of technology, including e-commerce applications, can make network management a tough chore. In a February 2001 *Communicate* article, Packeteer Director of Market Development Greg Dalvell explained that "emerging multimedia applications delivering streaming video or audio content on a peer-to-peer basis threaten to consume vast amounts of Internet bandwidth at the expense of less hungry but more critical tasks." The same article also indicates that "the e-business issue is compounding the problems by effectively extending networks beyond internal firewalls, making performance and availability even harder to gauge." As a result, network managers continue to look for and utilize solutions that optimize bandwidth in order to avoid bottlenecks and ensure that enough resources are allocated to business-critical applications.

FURTHER READING:

"Bandwidth Management." In *Techencyclopedia*. Point Pleasant, PA: Computer Language Co., 2001. Available from www.techweb.com/encyclopedia.

Barnes, Cecily. "Schools, Businesses Restrain Bandwidth Hogs." *CNET News*. February 15, 2001. Available from news.cnet.com.

Hunter, Philip. "The Perennial Problem." *Communicate*. February 2001.

Jude, Michael, and Nancy Meachim. "Bandwidth Management and the Profit Thing." *Network World ASP Newsletter*. May 17, 2000. Available from www.nwfusion.com.

Liebmann, Lenny. "Bandwidth Management Evolves." *Planet IT News*. August 9, 2000. Available from www.planetid.com.

Packeteer Inc. "Packeteer's PacketShaper." Cupertino, CA: Packeteer Inc. 2001. Available from www.packeteer.com.

Spangler, Todd. "Bandwidth Tools Branch Out." *Interactive Week*. October 25, 1998. Available from www.zdnet.com.

SEE ALSO: Application Service Provider (ASP); Bandwidth; Broadband Technology; Internet Service Provider (ISP); Multimedia; Streaming Media

BANKING, ONLINE

When the clicks-and-bricks euphoria hit in the late 1990s, many banks began to view Web-based banking as a strategic imperative. The attraction of banks to online banking are fairly obvious: diminished transaction costs, easier integration of services, interactive marketing capabilities, and other benefits that boost customer lists and profit margins. Additionally, Web banking services allow institutions to bundle more services into single packages, thereby luring customers and minimizing overhead.

A mergers-and-acquisitions wave swept the financial industries in the mid- and late 1990s, greatly expanding banks' customer bases. Following this, banks looked to the Web as a way of maintaining their customers and building loyalty. A number of different factors are causing bankers to shift more of their business to the virtual realm. Among these are electronic billing; the validity of e-signatures, approved by Congress in 2000; account aggregation (whereby a customer's entire range of financial relationships are coalesced on a single Web site); and the move in the wake of the Financial Services Modernization Act to create one-stop shopping for financial services. A report by New York-based eMarketer Inc. estimated that about 86 percent of all banks, credit unions, and savings institutions would offer online transactional sites by 2003.

Online banking encompasses both the Web-based operations of established brick-and-mortar banks as well as Internet-only banks. The latter offer several perks, including higher interest rates on checking accounts, higher yields on certificates of deposit, and electronic billing free of charge. However, Web-only banks suffer from several drawbacks, such as the inability to provide local business loans and other regionally-based services, a lack of ATM machines, and sketchy viability in the minds of consumers.

THE EVOLUTION OF ONLINE BANKING

While prototypic PC banking systems were first developed in the 1980s, the online banking industry of the early 2000s originated with Microsoft Corp.'s home banking network, introduced in 1994. By 1997, some 4.2 million U.S. households did their banking on the Internet. For several years, online banking was synonymous with PC banking, but this reduction is no longer adequate because Internet-based financial transactions are increasingly used with cell phones and other wireless devices. Indeed, ever more gadgets are expected to be outfitted with Internet and smart-card capabilities, moving toward perpetual connectivity for consumers.

Wireless banking provides all the benefits of online banking without the PC. Wireless bankers can use cell phones and similar handheld devices to do their banking anywhere, at any time. In 2001, wireless banking was more common than PC banking in Europe and Asia. Some analysts expected the same to be true in the United States within a matter of years. Some argued that wireless technology could be the stimulus needed to take online banking from a niche activity to a mass-market staple.

Leading U.S. banks lag behind their European and Asian-Pacific counterparts in offering wireless services to their customers. According to Meridien Research, less than 30 percent of the top banks in the United States provided such service in 2001, compared with about 80 percent of Asian-pacific leaders and 70 percent of European banking majors.

LUKEWARM CUSTOMER RESPONSE

Framingham, Massachusetts-based International Data Corp. (IDC), a leading research firm, found that while nearly 50 percent of U.S. households were online in 2000, only 10 percent were active in any online banking. Estimates for the future showed only modest growth; by 2004, IDC expected about 22 percent of U.S. households to bank over the Internet.

Online banking is fraught with difficulties. Leading this list in the early 2000s was consumer confidence to protect financial information from potential hackers and cyber thieves. Mainspring Inc. of Cambridge, Massachusetts conducted a survey of 209 defectors from online banking and found that nearly one-third did so out of concern for security. Those fears were given weight when, in September 2000, Western Union Financial Services was the victim of a high profile hacking in which nearly 16,000 accounts were compromised. Online banking also was hampered by customer service problems. To their dismay, banks found that simply getting their systems online was only the tip of the iceberg; the process ne-cessitates significant investments in new forms of customer service. For instance, online customers expect return emails rapidly, in a matter of hours. Thus, systems and personnel need to be in place to make such a quick turnaround on a customer's inquiry. Other key reasons for customer hesitance included basic connection problems with logging on to the banking network, and a lack of clear advantages in banking online versus through traditional channels.

Online churn, whereby customers allow their accounts to lapse, was another problem for online bankers who not only sought to maintain online customers, but to keep them active so their online efforts would pay off. Efforts toward increasing the user-friendliness of online banking, including more easily navigable Web sites, improved inquiry-response times, and other measures seemed to finally pay off in 2000 as churn rates fell to 9.8 percent in the second quarter, compared with 49.2 percent in the same period the year before, according to CyberDialogue, a New York-based research firm.

The eMarketer report, compiling and analyzing data from Forrester Research, Grant Thornton, Tower Group, and several other leading banking sources, found that despite the lackluster performance of Internet banking, most banks (especially those with assets exceeding $100 million) intended to create or augment their Web banking operations, often as a defensive posture. Thus, while frustration and complications abound, online banking was firmly established as part of the financial services paradigm in the early 2000s.

FURTHER READING:

Bielski, Lauren. "Online Banking Yet to Deliver." *ABA Banking Journal.* September, 2000.

Condon, Mark. "The Shape of Things to Come." *Credit Union Magazine.* January, 2001.

Engen, John R. "Banking on the Run." *Banking Strategies.* July/August, 2000.

Hamlet, Clay. "Community Banks Go Online." *ABA Banking Journal.* March, 2000.

Hernandez, Jr., Louis. "The Boom Beneath the Bust: Internet Strategies to Win—Banks Need to Know How to Maneuver Within Cyberspace." *Banking Wire.* October 4, 2001.

Monahan, Julie. "In the Out Door." *Banking Strategies.* November/December 2000.

Robinson, Teri. "Internet Banking: Still Not a Perfect Marriage." *InformationWeek.* April 17, 2000.

Salkever, Alex. "Online Banking: The Nightmare." *Business Week.* October 9, 2000.

Skousen, Mark. "Online Banking's Goodies." *Forbes.* June 12, 2000.

SEE ALSO: Churn; Digital Certificate; Digital Certificate Authority; Electronic Payment; International Data Corp. (IDC); Merchant Bank; Online Payment Options and Services; Recurring Payment Transactions

BANNER ADS

Ever since their debut on the HotWired site in October 1994, banner ads have been the dominant format for online advertising. They also have been a disappointment for advertisers and Web site publishers alike. They have been blamed, perhaps unfairly, for everything from the high rate of failure of content-based Web sites (which are dependent on advertising revenue) to creating a one-inch wasteland on computer screens.

Banner ads come in a variety of sizes and are measured in pixels. The most popular size in 2000 was the 468-by-60 size, which was used more than six times as often as the next most popular size, 125-by-125, according to the 2000 *Engage Adknowledge Online Advertising Report.* In February 2001 the Interactive Advertising Bureau (IAB) released a new set of recommended guidelines for banner ad sizes, but it remained to be seen whether these would be adopted by the industry. In general, the newly recommended sizes were larger and would require more computer memory.

While banner ads were the dominant online advertising format in 2000, they fell out of favor with advertisers as click-through rates declined. According to a report commissioned by the IAB, banner ads accounted for 47 percent of online ad revenue in 2000, but only 40 percent for the fourth quarter, confirming the decline in revenue from banner advertising. By mid-2000, click-through rates had fallen to .3 percent, with business-to-business advertisers reporting average click-through rates around .5 percent. In other words, only three to five of every 1,000 impressions resulted in a click-through on a banner ad. In an environment where there were too many ad pages and too few advertisers, the cost of advertising online fell dramatically and an estimated 75 percent of the Internet advertising inventory remained unsold.

Some of the potential benefits of banner ads resulted in criticism of the banner ad format. While they had the potential to be the most targeted and most measurable of all advertising media, online advertising in practice often was poorly targeted and not measurable. For example, click-through rates may be used to measure an ad's effectiveness in terms of making a sale or generating some other type of consumer action, but they cannot be used to measure how effectively a banner ad builds brand awareness.

WHAT ARE BANNER ADS SUPPOSED TO DO?

Banner ads serve three basic functions. Their purpose is to build brand awareness, sell something, and drive traffic to an advertiser's Web site. While the latter two functions are measurable and can be tracked, the first is not measurable, leaving proponents of banner advertising some wiggle room when critics point to declining click-through rates. In order for advertisers to make effective use of banner ads, they need to establish goals for their ad campaigns and determine whether they want to build brand awareness, sell something, or drive traffic to their Web sites.

Advertisers may purchase advertising space for their banner ads on individual Web sites, but most advertisers work through an ad agency or network. Networks such as DoubleClick Inc., 24/7 Media, and Engage represent groups of Web sites and sell advertising on them in addition to offering other services to advertisers. Advertisers are charged for banner advertising using one of two models. Under the CPM (cost per thousand impressions) model, rates are based on the number of viewers. Because advertisers demanded a model that was more action-based, the CPA (cost per action) model was developed, whereby advertisers are charged only when a click-through is made on their banner ad.

Another option is to join an affiliate network, such as Commission Junction (www.cj.com) or LinkShare (www.linkshare.com). Through affiliate programs, Web sites select banner ads they believe are appropriate to display on their site. The affiliate network then keeps track of click-throughs and pays the Web site a commission on each click-through instance.

TARGETING AND TRACKING

Banner ads have the potential to offer unlimited targeting, tracking, and measurability. Tracking and measuring the performance of banner ads allow advertisers to analyze and select the best performing ads for each placement. This makes it possible to replace poorly performing ads quickly and efficiently. Targeted banner advertising means serving the appropriate ad to a specific type of user based on a user profile. Targeting is typically based on past behavior, whereby banner ads are served onscreen based on the viewer's previous actions. This may involve knowing what Web pages the viewer has visited recently, as well as whether or not they made a purchase, signed a registration form, or took other similar actions. Tracking such behavior is somewhat controversial and opposed by privacy advocates. Some marketers defend such practices, arguing the information is used in aggregate form only and not revealed on an individual basis.

While banner ads may be targeted based on an overall profile of a Web site's typical visitors, more effective targeting relies on creating a user profile. Using software technology such as the Dynamic Advertising Reporting and Tracking (DART) program, introduced by Internet advertising agency DoubleClick Inc. in 1996, it is possible to quickly determine which banner ad to present to the current user. DART and other proprietary systems used by advertising networks match ads to target audiences through the use of the controversial "cookie" technology.

Cookies obtain information about a user's hardware and software, as well as their Internet connections and are used to create a user profile without obtaining the user's permission. This raises concerns among privacy advocates that the technology will be used to obtain confidential information against the wishes of individual users. Another profiling issue involves combining online and offline information to create even more comprehensive user profiles that might include individual names, addresses, and telephone numbers. Again, marketers attempt to address these concerns by not releasing information on individuals and only using the data in aggregate form. As the technology for creating user profiles improves, it is expected that banner ads will realize their full targeting potential and their performance will improve.

FURTHER READING:

"Banner-Ad Blues." *The Economist (US).* February 24, 2001.

"Banner Standards." Banner Ad Museum. June 16, 2001. Available from www.banneradmuseum.com.

Callahan, Sean. "Banner Believers Endure Season of Disenchantment." *B to B.* October 23, 2000.

Claburn, Thomas. "The Banner Ad is Dead. (OK, Not Really)." *Ziff Davis Smart Business for the New Economy.* March 1, 2001.

"Company Information." Engage Inc. April 23, 2001. Available from www.engage.com.

Macklin, Ben. "Can Broadband Save the Banner Ad?" *eMarketer Newsletter.* May 8, 2001. Available from www.emarketer.com.

Randall, Neil. "Profiting: Adding an Affiliate Program Links Site Content to Product Sales." *PC Magazine.* February 20, 2001.

Schwartz, Matthew. "Online Ads Enter the Next Generation." *B to B.* March 5, 2001.

Vlahos, Christopher J. "The Internet Banner Ad Now Exists in Survival Mode." *Business First—Columbus.* April 27, 2001.

SEE ALSO: Advertising, Online; Affiliate Model; DoubleClick Inc.; Marketing, Internet; Privacy: Issues, Policies, Statements; 24/7 Media Inc.

BARBOUR, JOHN

Scotland native John Barbour took over Toysrus.com in August of 1999 when Robert Moog, the original CEO of the fledgling e-commerce venture, resigned after a mere five weeks at the helm. Barbour had worked for nine years as a marketing executive at Hasbro when he was tapped for the job at Toys 'R' Us. Prior to that, Barbour served as a marketing vice president for Universal Matchbox Group, based in the United Kingdom. Earlier in his career, he also completed stints in the sales and marketing departments of General Mills, M&M Mars, and Procter & Gamble.

Toys "R" Us officially launched its e-commerce site in April of 1999 with $80 million in capital. Difficulties emerged almost immediately when Benchmark Capital backed out of its agreement to front the dot-com venture an additional $10 million. Moog's sudden resignation dealt the giant toy retailer another blow. By the time Barbour joined the fray, he was left with a mere four months to not only get a new site up and running, but also to prepare for the approaching holiday crunch. To entice customers to try the site, Barbour and his management team developed promotions such as free delivery and a $10 coupon for merchandise bought online.

Unfortunately, the marketing efforts worked a bit too well. In what was eventually regarded by some industry analysts as a classic example of both the potential and pitfall of e-commerce ventures, traffic on the site grew 10 times beyond projected numbers. Despite increasing its servers fourfold, Toysrus.com soon realized it would be unable to meet the unprecedented demand. Hoping to salvage the company's reputation, Barbour spearheaded a plan to send customers whose deliveries were late a $100 gift certificate. When the dust settled, Toysrus.com began looking at ways to increase its capacity and better prepare for spikes in growth. The firm adopted ColdFusion, a program that tripled each server's capacity, and hired an outside Internet consultant to examine the site's technology and recommend improvements.

Barbour also began looking for strategic alliances. In August of 2000, Toysrus.com joined forces with Amazon.com to build a Web site that coupled the inventory of Toys 'R' Us with the e-commerce savvy of Amazon. Holiday sales for Toysrus.com grew more than threefold, and as Molly Prior reported in *DSN Retailing Today,* "the pundits can't help but wonder if the marriage of a pure-player to a bricks-and-clicks category leader is the wave of the future for Internet retailing."

FURTHER READING:

Cirillo, Rich. "Toyrsrus.com Learns E-Biz Lessons the Hard Way." *VARbusiness.* January 10, 2000.

Corral, Cecile B. "New Toysrus.com CEO Looks to the Future." *Discount Stores News.* August 23, 1999.

"Misadventures in E-retailing." *Promo.* August 2000.

Prior, Molly. "Amazon, TRU Web Site Proves Successful Online Model." *DSN Retailing Today.* January 22, 2001.

Radolf, Michael. "Barbour Takes Toys 'R' Us Online." *Brandweek.* September 6, 1999.

Sliwa, Carole. "Holiday Lessons." *Computerworld.* July 10, 2000.

SEE ALSO: Business-to-Consumer (B2C) E-Commerce

BARKSDALE, JIM

Jim Barksdale is best known for his role in Netscape Communications Corp.'s battle with Microsoft Corp. for the Internet browser market. He joined Netscape as a seasoned executive, having served as vice president and chief operating officer (COO) of Federal Express Corp. from 1984 to 1991; president and COO of McCaw Cellular between 1992 and 1994; and chief executive officer (CEO) of AT&T Wireless Services after McCaw merged with AT&T Corp. Netscape founders Jim Clark and Mark Andreessen offered him a board seat at their fledgling Internet browser firm in October of 1994. Three months later, Barksdale agreed to run Netscape, taking on the roles of both president and CEO.

One of Barksdale's first tasks at the helm of Netscape was taking the upstart public in what would amount to one of the most lucrative initial public offerings (IPO) in history. Less than a year later, Netscape's Navigator had secured roughly 80 percent of the Internet browser market. Although Microsoft's competing browser, Internet Explorer, entered the market soon after Navigator made its debut, its wasn't until Microsoft launched Windows 95, which included a free version of the Internet Explorer browser, that Netscape began to feel the pinch. The move by Microsoft was the first of many in the highly publicized "browser wars" between Microsoft and Netscape.

In an attempt to strengthen Netscape's position, Barksdale launched a plan that included selling Navigator rather than giving it away—a move some analysts criticized for allowing Microsoft to gain an even stronger foothold—and changing the firm's focus to enterprise markets. This shift in focus grew out of what *Chief Executive* columnist C.J. Prince called Barksdale's vigilance. Prince pointed out that, rather than bask in Netscape's early success, Barksdale "began using it immediately to shore up business on the server side, selling Netscape's commerce, mail, and intranet server applications to big corporate customers." However, despite his foresight, Barksdale's plan flopped because Netscape simply couldn't match the support and services offered by its much larger competitors.

Barksdale laid off 12 percent of Netscape's employees in 1997 after fourth-quarter performance failed to meet expectations. By then, Microsoft had commandeered almost half of Netscape's browser market share. Although the U.S. Department of Justice had responded to Barksdale's earlier allegations that Microsoft was violating anti-compete laws by ordering Microsoft to offer a version of Windows 95 unbundled from Internet Explorer, the decision was later overturned. While this was not the outcome Barksdale had hoped for, the litigation had serious long-term consequences for Microsoft. Eventually, the case over the browser wars turned into a full-blown investigation of alleged monopolist practices by Microsoft, culminating in a 2000 ruling that the computing behemoth be split into two companies. An appeal was pending in early 2001.

Dissatisfied with Netscape's performance, Barksdale decided to decline his salary in 1997 and again in 1998. It wasn't until mid-1998 that the firm again seemed to find its niche. According to *Newsweek* writer Brad Stone, Barksdale was able keep his firm afloat because he "ultimately guided Netscape into the lucrative e-commerce software and Web-portal markets." Although some pundits believe Barksdale waited too long to develop it, Netscape's Netcenter—which acts as a portal for services offered both by Netscape and its clients—became one of the leading full-service Web sites.

In November of 1998, Netscape agreed to be purchased by America Online (AOL) for roughly $4.2 billion. Stock prices soared on news of the deal, and by its completion in March of 1999 the price tag exceeded $10 billion. Barksdale stepped down, $700 million richer, and founded the Barksdale Group, a venture capital company that funds e-commerce startups.

FURTHER READING:

Blackmon, Douglas A. "Launching Barksdale, Version 4.0." *The Wall Street Journal.* September 7, 1999.

Gallagher, Sean. "Netscape Changing Course." *InformationWeek.* June 15, 1998.

Hamm, Steve. "Jim Barksdale, Internet Angel." *Business Week.* May 10, 1999.

Karpinski, Richard. "Netscape's Legacy—Upstart Energized Network Biz Model." *InternetWeek.* November 30, 1998.

Mitchell, Russ. "Finally, the Trial is About to Begin." *U.S. News & World Report.* October 19, 1998.

Prince, C.J. "Barksdale's Byte." *Chief Executive.* December, 1997.

Stone, Brad. "Barksdale Kicks Back." *Newsweek.* April 19, 1999.

Taft, Darryl K. "The Men Who Took Down Microsoft." *Computer Reseller News.* June 26, 2000.

SEE ALSO: Andreessen, Marc; AOL Time Warner Inc.; Microsoft Corp.; Microsoft Windows; Netscape Communications Corp.

BARNESANDNOBLE.COM

Before the onset of online bookselling and the rise of Amazon.com, Barnes & Noble Inc. was the undisputed leader in bookselling. The giant chain had the most brick-and-mortar stores and the largest market share. Its U.S. bookselling subsidiaries included the flagship Barnes & Noble Booksellers, as well as B. Dalton Booksellers, Doubleday Book Shops, and Scribner's Bookstores. The company also owned an interest in Canadian bookseller Chapters, and Calendar Club, which operated internationally.

Barnes & Noble entered the world of online bookselling in March 1997 as the exclusive bookseller on America Online (AOL). Two months later the company set up its own Web site for online purchases, barnesandnoble.com. Sales at barnesandnoble.com doubled in each of 1997's first three quarters, and reached $11.9 million that year. In addition to being the exclusive bookseller on AOL, the online bookseller also reached an agreement with Microsoft to be the exclusive bookseller on three of its Web sites: MSNBC, Microsoft Investor, and Expedia. All of the Microsoft Web sites attracted millions of visitors daily. By the end of 1998 barnesandnoble.com was the exclusive English language bookseller on Microsoft's MSN.com and its global network of Web portals.

REORGANIZED WITH NEW INVESTOR, 1998

Barnesandnoble.com was reorganized in 1998 when German media conglomerate Bertelsmann AG agreed to invest $200 million in the online bookseller for a fifty percent interest. Barnesandnoble.com became a limited liability company (LLC) in order to operate online retail bookselling operations. As a result of Bertelsmann's investment, the bookseller postponed its planned initial public offering (IPO) until 1999. For 1998 barnesandnoble.com reported sales of $61.8 million and a net loss of $83.1 million.

Toward the end of 1998 barnesandnoble.com upgraded and redesigned its Web site, offering a wider range of products and services. It added electronic greeting cards through an agreement with Blue Mountain Arts. Rare and out-of-print books were offered through the Advanced Book Exchange, which had a network of some 3,600 book dealers. Also added to the Web site were enhanced search capabilities that allowed users to find related magazine and newspaper articles after searching for a book. Through an agreement with Northern Lights Technology, the articles could then be purchased electronically.

WENT PUBLIC IN 1999

In March of 1999, together with Bertelsmann, Barnes & Noble announced it would spin off barnesandnoble.com as a public company, selling 15 to 20 percent of the company's stock to the public. In May 1999 barnesandnoble.com went public with an initial stock price of $18 per share. The IPO was popular with investors and raised $421 million, more than double what the company expected. Some 25 million shares were sold, closing at $22.94 at the end of the first day, an increase of 27 percent. Following the IPO, Barnes & Noble and Bertelsmann each owned about 41 percent of barnesandnoble.com, with the public holding the remaining 18 percent. Around this time the online bookseller also shortened its Web site address, or URL, from www.barnesandnoble.com to www.bn.com.

For 1999 barnesandnoble.com's overall revenue was $202.5 million (though later restated to $193.7 million), an increase of 211 percent over 1998. International sales doubled to more than $12 million. In 1999 book sales accounted for 93 percent of the online bookseller's revenue, compared to 98 percent in 1998. During the year the company rolled out its music store, which sold CDs and DVDs. It also formed an electronic greeting card service and launched a prints and poster gallery. In November 1999 barnesandnoble.com acquired the rights to the domain name www.books.com from Cendant Corp. It already owned the www.book.com URL and said that users going to books.com or book.com would simply be redirected to the www.bn.com site.

Other marketing initiatives for 1999 included increasing the discount of *New York Times* bestsellers from 40 percent to 50 percent. The company also opened two new distribution centers. Pursuing a strategy to increase sales and its customer base, barnesandnoble.com reported a loss of $102.4 million in 1999 (later restated to $48.2 million), due in large part to the company's marketing expenses and costs associated with the new distribution centers.

Barnesandnoble.com also had to deal with a patent infringement suit raised by rival online bookseller Amazon.com. Amazon.com had received a patent on its technology for streamlining the purchase process, which it called 1-Click. Its suit claimed that barnes andnoble.com's Express Checkout system violated its patent. When a federal judge issued an injunction against barnesandnoble.com to stop using the technology until the suit was settled, the company had to introduce a new online ordering technology to its Web site. While the suit had yet to be settled by mid-2001, the injunction was lifted in February 2001.

NEW INITIATIVES, 2000-2001

In the first quarter of 2000 barnesandnoble.com acquired a 32-percent interest in eNews.com for $26.4 million in cash and $12.8 million in stock. As a result of the investment, eNews.com became the exclusive seller of magazines at www.bn.com with an offering of some 1,000 different magazine subscriptions. Barnesandnoble.com and parent company Barnes & Noblesubsequently acquired a majority interest in eNews in April 2001.

In February 2000 the company launched an Internet radio service called bnRadio, which allowed customers to listen to more than 25,000 full-length songs as well as three-to-five-minute selections from audiobooks. In mid-2000 barnesandnoble.com launched an Internet television service, Barnes & NobleTV. Its first programs were three-minute films called bookVideos. In fall 2000 a daily author interview series debuted on the Internet service. Another initiative included the debut of Barnes & Noble University, a free online education resource that offered courses in a wide range of subjects through www.bn.com. Around this time the online bookseller added a video store that offered tens of thousands of video titles in both DVD and VHS formats from the All-Movie Guide database. Titles were listed in 16 major genres and 800 subcategories, and the database included more than 65,000 cast and crew filmographies, reviews, as well as ratings and recommendations. The Video Interview Gallery allowed customers to view clips of major film stars.

In September 2000 barnesandnoble.com replaced Amazon.com as the featured bookseller on the popular Internet portal Yahoo!. Two months later, barnesandnoble.com completed its acquisition of Fatbrain.com, a transaction that *Publishers Weekly* called "the largest example so far of consolidation among online book retailers." Fatbrain was the third-largest online bookseller and specialized in professional and technical titles for the corporate market. In addition to online bookselling, Fatbrain was involved in digital publishing ventures through its subsidiary MightyWords, and in providing Web-based information management services, including document delivery, to large corporations. Following the acquisition,

which was valued at $64 million, Fatbrain's operations were integrated into barnesandnoble.com. In April 2001 barnesandnoble.com and MightyWords began selling articles that could be purchased, downloaded, and printed instantly through a new barnesandnoble.com Articles for Download store.

Other initiatives planned for 2001 included the launch of Barnes & Noble Digital, an electronic publishing imprint that would publish a variety of titles in e-book editions and sell them through bn.com. Barnesandnoble.com and parent company Barnes & Noble also planned more joint programs to leverage the parent company's more than 550 brick-and-mortar bookstores. The joint initiatives included installing Internet service counters at Barnes & Noble superstores and the creation of a Barnes & Noble loyalty program. In addition, customers who made purchases through barnesandnoble.com would be able to return items to Barnes & Noble stores for credit.

For the year 2000, barnesandnoble.com reported sales of $320.1 million, an increase of 65 percent over 1999, and a net loss of $65.4 million. The company's strategy for 2001 was to reach profitability in 2002 and to focus on cost cutting. In February 2001 the online bookseller laid off 350 workers, or 16 percent of its workforce. On the positive side, the company had a strong balance sheet and no outstanding debt, and sales for 2001 were projected to increase another 40 percent.

FURTHER READING:

"Barnesandnoble.com Breaks into the Film Business." *Book.* January, 2001.

"Bertelsmann AG." *Brandweek.* October 12, 1998.

Duvall, Mel. "Amazon Files Against B&N." *Inter@ctive Week.* October 25, 1999.

"How Barnes & Noble Misread the Web." *Business Week.* February 7, 2000.

Milliot, Jim. "B&N.com Grabs Majority Stake in enews." *Publishers Weekly.* April 16, 2001.

———. "Books Accounted for 93 Percent of B&N.com Sales in 1999." *Publishers Weekly.* April 17, 2000.

Murphy, Chris. "Barnesandnoble.com Seeks to Close Book on Losses." *InformationWeek.* February 14, 2000.

Nawotka, Edward. "B&N.com Replaces Amazon as Featured Bookseller on Yahoo!." *Publishers Weekly.* September 25, 2000.

Reid, Calvin. "B&N.com Launches E-Book Imprint." *Publishers Weekly.* January 8, 2001.

———. "B&N.com, Microsoft in Multimillion-Dollar Deal." *Publishers Weekly.* December 14, 1998.

Solomon, Melissa. "Retailer Launches Free Online Radio Station." *Computerworld.* March 6, 2000.

Woollacott, Matthew. "Patent Lawsuit: 'One-Click' Dispute Rages on in Court." *InfoWorld.* February 19, 2001.

SEE ALSO: Amazon.com; Bertelsmann AG; Business-to-Consumer (B2C) E-commerce; E-books; E-tailing

BASIC

BASIC stands for Beginner's All-Purpose Symbolic Instruction Code, a computer programming language known for its simplicity. Many college students are first taught BASIC before moving on to more complex languages like Fortran and C++. Thomas Kurtz, professor of mathematics at Dartmouth College, and John G. Kemeny, chairman of the mathematics department there, developed BASIC, which is one of the easiest high-level programming languages to learn. They created it so that students could write programs for the General Electric, or GE-225—a mainframe, timesharing computer system.

BASIC was first developed as a compiled language, one which is translated into machine language prior to execution. However, because BASIC was never copyrighted or patented, all sorts of variations cropped up, including versions that were interpreted, or translated into statements that executed individually. In the mid-1970s, Harvard student Bill Gates and Honeywell employee Paul Allen used an interpreted version of BASIC when they created a language for Altair, the world's first personal computer (PC). When Gates and Allen moved back to Seattle, the former grade school classmates began customizing BASIC for use with other platforms. Their efforts eventually led to the founding of Microsoft Corp.

Other early PC developers also preferred interpreted versions of BASIC, mainly because such versions allowed more computer memory to remain free. Computer manufacturers like IBM, Hewlett-Packard, and Digital Equipment Corp. used interpreted versions of BASIC in the read-only memory (ROM) of their machines. By the mid-1980s, technology companies including RadioShack Corp., Apple Computer Inc., and Intel Corp. had written their own versions of BASIC. In fact, hundreds of versions of the language were in existence. Although the American National Standards Institute (ANSI) started working on a standardized version of BASIC in 1974, it wasn't until Thomas Kurtz became chairman of ANSI in 1984 that work toward this end began in earnest. ANSI began circulating Standard BASIC in 1988.

Variations of BASIC are still widely used by companies such as Microsoft. For example, Visual BASIC, created in 1992, is an object-oriented language designed specifically for Microsoft Windows applications. Another Microsoft invention, QBASIC, acts as an interpreter between BASIC and both the DOS and Windows platforms. It replaced GW-BASIC, the interpreter used solely with the DOS operating system. However, computer companies are not the only ones that can tweak BASIC to meet their needs. Because the language is so easy to learn, several word processing and spreadsheet programs allow users to write simple programs or macros in BASIC to automate certain tasks.

FURTHER READING:

"BASIC." In *Ecommerce Webopedia*. Darien, CT: Internet.com, 2001. Available from www.e-comm.webopedia.com.

"BASIC—Beginner's All-Purpose Symbolic Instruction Code." In *Jones Telecommunications & Multimedia Encyclopedia*. Engelwood, CO: Jones International, 1999. Available from www.digitalcentury.com.

"BASIC." In *Techencyclopedia*. Point Pleasant, PA: Computer Language Co., 2001. Available from www.techweb.com.

Hudson, Daniel P. "A Brief History of the Development of BASIC." Available from www.phys.uu.nl/~bergmann/history.html.

"Interpreter." In *Ecommerce Webopedia*. Darien, CT: Internet.com, 2001. Available from e-comm.webopedia.com.

SEE ALSO: Programming Language

BBBONLINE INC.

BBBOnLine Inc. serves as the Better Business Bureau of the Web. Since its inception in the summer of 1996, it has operated as a subsidiary of the Council of Better Business Bureaus. Browsers visiting BBBOnLine can search for information on specific companies, view consumer guides, file complaints, and ask for assistance with dispute resolution. This advocate for fair and ethical online business practices also helps consumers to locate member businesses. It accomplishes this by offering two Web site seals to companies that are willing to make public their status with the Better Business Bureau.

Web sites with the BBBOnLine Reliability Seal—introduced in April 1997—are operated by companies that hold current membership with their local business bureau, meet certain truth in advertising standards, and adhere to a set of customer service policies similar to those required for brick and mortar businesses affiliated with the Better Business Bureau. By clicking on the seal, online shoppers are able to view a company's record with the Better Business Bureau, as well as information about location and ownership. By March of 2001, the reliability seal had been issued to 9,480 companies including eToys, CDNow, eBay, and Travelocity.

The BBBOnLine Privacy Seal, created in March 1999, is issued to businesses that meet certain criteria with regard to how they gather, process, and protect the personal information of online customers. To qualify for the seal, a site must disclose in its privacy statement what information is being gathered, where it may be used in the future, and whether or not a customer has any control over that use. Prior to issuing the seal, BBBOnLine also reviews the site in question to determine if its security measures are sufficient. Within two years of its inception, the privacy seal had been granted to nearly 800 firms including AT&T Corp., Hewlett-Packard, New York Times Co., and Dun & Bradstreet Corp.

BBBOnLine also issues its Kid's Privacy Seal to qualified online businesses targeting children under the age of 13. Companies must complete the necessary steps for obtaining a regular privacy seal. Additionally, they must meet the criteria established by the Children's Online Privacy Protection Act, along with standards set forth by the Council of Better Business Bureaus' Children's Advertising Review Unit (CARU), the Online Privacy Alliance, and the Children's Online Privacy Protection Act of 1998. These requirements include obtaining permission from parents before their children disclose certain personal information or communicate with other users, using clear language to issue notices or cautions, gathering only information deemed absolutely necessary, and monitoring links to other sites.

Along with helping consumers in their dealings with online businesses, BBBOnLine also helps businesses regulate themselves. In October of 2000, BBBOnLine established the Code of Online Business Practices to offer guidance to companies engaged in e-commerce. This code covers five major issues:

- satisfying customers by responding to queries and addressing concerns promptly

- using both advertising and the technology driving the advertising for honest and accurate dissemination of information

- readily disclosing information about the merchandise or services being sold, as well as the online transaction itself

- protecting the personal information of customers and honoring their requests to be taken off mailing lists

- and following the CARU Self-Regulatory Guidelines for Children's Advertising when marketing products or services to children under 13 years of age.

Sites displaying the reliability seal must begin following the code by September of 2001.

FURTHER READING:

BBBOnLine Inc. ''About BBBOnLine.'' Arlington, VA: BBBOnLine Inc., 2001. Available from bbbonline.org.

Bennefield, Robin M. ''BBB Online: A Seal with Teeth.'' *U.S. News & World Report.* March 3, 1997.

Enos, Lori. ''Consumer Watchdog Unveils Net Conduct Code.'' *E-Commerce Times.* October 25, 2000. Available from www.ecommercetimes.com.

SEE ALSO: Authentication; Computer Fraud and Abuse Act of 1986; Digital Certificate; Fraud, Internet; Privacy: Issues, Policies, Statements; Secure Electronic Transactions (SEC)

BERNERS-LEE, TIMOTHY

Tim Berners-Lee is founder and director of the World Wide Web Consortium (W3C). His greatest invention draws numerous comparisons to Gutenberg's printing press because it brings information and tools, formerly reserved for a select few, to the masses. Sitting at a tiny cubicle in a physics laboratory in Switzerland, the reclusive, soft-spoken Berners-Lee gave birth to the World Wide Web and helped transform the economic, cultural, and social realms of the modern world. Moreover, he insists that the Web is still a child. ''The glorified television channel you see today,'' Berners-Lee proclaims, ''is just part of the plan.''

Born in London in 1955, Timothy J. Berners-Lee is the son of two mathematicians who worked on the first commercially sold computers. A physicist by training, he did his pioneering work at the Centre Europen de Recherche Nucleaire (European Laboratory for Particle Physics, or CERN), the Geneva-based physics laboratory, as a contract programmer. His proposal to develop an interactive, universal interface for use on the Internet—the project that would become the World Wide Web—was twice rejected at CERN until he put the lab's 10,000-name phone book into his programming language as a prototype to show the Web's possibilities. His prototype, designed to function in a ''brain-like way'' but also to track and connect all the random associations that are often buried in the brain, was called Enquire Within Upon Everything. In just two months, he gave the Pentagon-funded, technical-user-oriented communications program known as the Internet a human face, ready for global use. Bypassing the need for large centralized registries, he developed uniform resource locators (URLs), as well as hypertext transfer protocol (HTTP) for transferring data to and from any connected computer. He also designed the lingua franca of the

Web: Hypertext Markup Language (HTML). Thus, the World Wide Web was born in 1991, at which point he simply gave it all away for free, only promoting its wider use.

In 1994 Berners-Lee left CERN for a position at the Laboratory for Computer Science at the Massachusetts Institute of Technology (MIT), where he founded the World Wide Web Consortium, a loose-knit collection of Web, hardware, and software firms as well as other interested parties. The W3C's primary mission simply was to oversee the Web's development (although it is not a governing body), and in large part the consortium worked to stave off proprietary battles over standards and protocols. The W3C and Berners-Lee were both instrumental in the fight to keep the Web free and nonproprietary.

Berners-Lee continued to push the Web's development forward, particularly through his pioneering work on Extensible Markup Language (XML), a meta-language that focuses on the conceptual meaning of Web content, rather than simply on page formatting. XML allows for two-way communication between Web servers so as to facilitate more comprehensive treatment of content and transactions. According to Berners-Lee, XML would be the driving force in creating the next step in the Web's evolution—the Semantic Web.

Broadly, the Semantic Web is Berners-Lee's vision for a system that will perform the more mundane tasks of human interactions and transactions, leaving the actual thinking to humans. With dramatically enhanced ability to define objects in cyberspace, the XML-driven Semantic Web promises vastly more powerful and accurate search engines that will make the Web more navigable and a less dizzying mess of information. True to its name, the Semantic Web is intended to make reading and interpreting Web content easier for computers by increasing their recognition of context and their ability to make logical inferences. It also is supposed to allow more direct communication between machines and will free individuals to concentrate on more involved and creative thinking. This is a crucial step in the development of what Berners-Lee sees as the development of cells within a global brain.

While Berners-Lee may not himself show much interest in capitalizing on the profit-making potential of the Web, his invention nonetheless radically transformed traditional business models and helped to redefine the relationship between business and customer. E-commerce is only one small element of his concern, however. Pushing openness and decentralization of knowledge and resources, his vision of the Web is of an all-encompassing democratic force for global civilization, in which business issues are dominated by their social implications. While his claim that the Web will serve as the vehicle for the next stage of human civilization may at first sound grandiose, few seem ready to dismiss the possibility.

FURTHER READING:

Berners-Lee, Tim, and Mark Fischetti. *Weaving the Web: The Original Design and Ultimate Destiny of the World Wide Web by Its Inventor.* San Francisco: HarperCollins, 1999.

Lee, Mike. "Top 10 Most Influential People: No. 1—Tim Berners-Lee." *Network Computing.* October 2, 2000.

Luh, James C. "Tim Berners-Lee." *Internet World.* January 1, 2000.

Owens, Ross. "E-business Innovators: Tim Berners-Lee; XML." *InfoWorld.* October 9, 2000.

Port, Otis. "How the Net Was Born—and Where It's Headed." *Business Week.* November 1, 1999.

Quittner, Joshua, and Frederic Golden. "Network Designer: Tim Berners-Lee." *Time.* March 29, 1999.

Reinbach, Andrew. "Sidestepping Bureaucracy in the Web's Next Iteration." *U.S. Banker.* February 2000.

Reiss, Spencer. "St. Tim of the Web." *Forbes.* November 15, 1999.

Woolnough, Roisin. "Meet the Man Who Invented the Web." *Computer Weekly.* November 30, 2000.

SEE ALSO: HTML (Hypertext Markup Language); Internet and WWW, History of the; World Wide Web Consortium (W3C); XML (Extensible Markup Language)

BERTELSMANN AG

German publishing giant Bertelsmann AG is the world's third-largest media company, behind AOL Time Warner and Walt Disney. Book publishing operations include Random House, Bantam Books, Dell Publishing, Crown Publishing, Ballantine Publishing, Knopf Publishing, Doubleday, and Broadway Books. The firm's entertainment arm, known simply as BMG, oversees all Bertelsmann music, television, and radio holdings, including the RCA/Ariola and Arista record labels. Other non-book publishing segments include Bertelsmann Industrie, which handles printing for the company; magazine and newspaper publisher Gruner+Jahr; and Bertelsmann Book, which markets Bertelsmann's consumer book clubs. In June of 2000, Bertelsmann folded its growing group of e-commerce activities—including its wireless, cable, and broadband operations, as well as BarnesandNoble.com and BOL.com—into a new unit called Bertelsmann eCommerce Group. Its agreement later that year to join forces with music file swapping site Napster—part of Bertelsmann's plan to become the world's leading content provider on the Internet—garnered global attention.

EARLY HISTORY

Carl Bertelsmann began working as a bookbinder in his hometown of Gutersloh, Germany, in 1819. The bookbinder's initial work consisted of printing and binding hymnals for nearby churches. In 1835, Bertelsmann incorporated his business as C. Bertelsmann Verlag. Bertelsmann died in 1850, leaving his son Heinrich a sizable inheritance and control of the family business. *Missionsharfe* (Missionary Harp) was first published in 1853 and became Bertelsmann's first bestseller with a circulation of more than 2 million copies. The firm's early success encouraged Heinrich to began expanding beyond religious books to publish historical works and even novels.

Friederike Bertelsmann, Heinrich's daughter, married Johannes Mohn in 1881. Because Heinrich had no male heirs, the Mohn family inherited the business upon his death in 1887. In an effort to increase production at a minimal cost, Mohn expanded Bertelsmann's internal printing operations.

The firm nearly went under twice in the first half of the twentieth century—once due to skyrocketing inflation in Germany and another time thanks to World War II. Allied forces bombed Gutersloh in 1945, destroying most of Bertelsmann's 400 printers, typesetters, and publishers there. Reinhard Mohn, grandson of Johannes Mohn, set about rebuilding the company almost immediately. In 1950, to counter a marked drop in book purchasing by Germans, Mohn launched Bertelsmann Lesering, a book club that granted bargains and other perks to members. To boost membership numbers quickly, Mohn also marketed Lesering to retail booksellers in West Germany by offering those who chose to become members a set number of free books each year.

The rapid success of Bertelsmann Lesering—which amassed 1 million members in less than four years—set the stage for additional growth. Bertelsmann bought a small portion of Gruner+Jahr, a publishing company based in Hamburg in 1969, and 10 years later upped its stake to nearly 75 percent. Bertelsmann also entered the American book publishing arena by purchasing a controlling stake in thriving U.S. paperback publisher Bantam Books. The company also ventured outside of book publishing for the first time by acquiring the Arista record label from Columbia Pictures.

GLOBAL GROWTH AND DIVERSIFICATION

A string of acquisitions during the 1980s vaulted Bertelsmann to a leadership position among global media and communication companies. For example, Bantam became a wholly owned subsidiary of Bertelsmann in 1981. The firm also added to its U.S. holdings with the $475 million purchase of Doubleday, a leading U.S. book publisher, in 1986. The deal gave Bertelsmann control of the well-known Dell paperbacks line, along with various book clubs and retail stores. To supplement its growing music holdings, Bertelsmann bought 75 percent of RCA's record division for $330 million, instantly becoming the world's third largest recording company. *Fortune* magazine ranked Bertelsmann as the world's largest publishing company in 1991.

Further diversification came in 1993 when Bertelsmann and TeleCommunications Inc. (TCI) forged a joint venture to establish a cable television channel for music and video distribution in the United States. The 1995 purchase of a minority stake in America Online (AOL) marked Bertelsmann's first Internet venture. The $50 million investment turned into a $5 billion windfall and established the groundwork for Bertelsmann's future alliances with AOL and its later move into the e-commerce arena.

Late in 1997, Advance Publications Inc. began negotiating its sale of Random House with Bertelsmann. At the time, the $1.4 billion deal was the largest in industry history. It was finalized in July of the following year, leaving Bertelsmann with control of nearly one-third of all hardcover bestsellers and half of the leading paperback books in the United States.

FOCUS ON E-COMMERCE

Although Bertelsmann had dabbled in various online ventures in the mid-1990s, it wasn't until a few years later that a concrete e-commerce plan emerged. In 1998, the firm paid roughly $200 million for a 50-percent stake in BarnesandNoble.com to shore up its position in the U.S. online book industry and launched its own retail book site, BOL.com, to compete with Amazon.com in Europe. After deciding to focus more closely on its Internet ventures, the firm sold off the pay television business it had previously acquired and made plans to establish its own high-speed Internet service provider (ISP) operation.

By 2000, Bertelsmann was pumping more than $13 billion into its Internet operations. In May of that year, the firm played a role in the creation of Terra Lycos, formed when Spain's Terra Networks paid $12.5 billion for Lycos, one of the largest U.S.-based World Wide Web gateways. Bertelsmann agreed to spend roughly $1 billion on advertising and other Internet services from Terra Lycos over the next five years in exchange for access to the 50 million customers already using either Terra Networks or Lycos. The next month, Bertelsmann merged its increasingly diverse e-commerce operations into a single entity known as Bertelsmann eCommerce Group. The firm lured Adreas Schmidt away from its European partnership with AOL, known as AOL Europe, to head up the new unit and, according to a June 2000 article in *The Economist,* charged him with the task of pushing ''everything in the Bertelsmann stable—from books and magazine to television programs and compact discs—into customers' laps via the Internet.''

After honing its Internet focus to selling online content rather than services, Bertelsmann divested several peripheral holdings including MediaWays, a German ISP it had previously acquired, to Spain's Telefonica for $1.6 billion. Bertelsmann then bought online music retailer CDNOW and, in perhaps its most daring move to date, joined forces with music indexing site Napster in October of 2000. The latter move happened despite widespread controversy over alleged copyright infringement regarding the technology that allows Napster users to exchange songs for free. One of the plaintiffs in the copyright infringement suit against Napster, Bertelsmann agreed to drop its charges when Napster begins charging users for file sharing capabilities. To help speed the development of this fee-based service, Bertelsmann extended Napster roughly $50 million in credit.

Continuing its efforts to become the world's leading Internet content provider, Bertelsmann upped its stake in RTL Group, the largest television firm in Europe, from 30 percent to 67 percent in February of 2001. According to *BusinessWeek Online,* Bertelsmann ''is girding itself for the day when Internet users routinely could trade their favorite episodes of *Benny Hill* as easily as Napsterites now swap tracks by Eminen. To fund the purchase, privately owned Bertelsmann made an unprecedented move by swapping a chunk of its own shares, leaving RTL's parent, Groupe Bruxelles Lambert, holding a 25 percent stake in Bertelsmann. Whether or not Bertelsmann achieves its lofty e-commerce goals remains to be seen. However, it willingness to sell off a large block of shares, as well as its pursuit of alliances with upstart ventures like Napster, certainly are indicative of the importance the media giant is placing on this segment of its business.

FURTHER READING:

Bertelsmann AG. ''Bertelsmann Chronicles.'' Gutersloh, Germany: Bertelsmann AG, 2000. Available from www.bertelsmann.com.

''Bertelsmann AG.'' In *Notable Corporate Chronologies.* Farmington Hills, MI: Gale Group, 1999.

''Bertelsmann Completes Acquisition of CDNOW.'' *PR Newswire.* September 1, 2000.

''Bertelsmann—Under e-construction.'' *The Economist.* June 10, 2000.

Christman, Ed. ''BMG Owner Investing in Book Net Site.'' *Billboard.* October 17, 1998.

Ewing, Jack. ''Bertelsmann: Building a Video Napster.'' *BusinessWeek Online.* February 5, 2001. Available from www.businessweek.com.

Gibney, Frank. ''Middlehoff's Vision: The Bertelsmann Boss Pulls Off a Shocking Deal with Renegade Napster. And He's Just Warming Up.'' *Time International.* November 13, 2000.

Kesgin, Tayfun and Howell Llewellyn, et al. ''Bertelsmann in Online Alliance.'' *Billboard.* May 27, 2000.

Kontzer, Tony. ''BMG's Man on the Move—Andreas Schmidt Plays a Part in the Music Industry's Digital Awakening.'' *InformationWeek.* January 1, 2001.

''The Man Who Would Be Cool—Face Value: Thomas Middlehoff, Napster's Music-Industry Ally.'' *The Economist.* March 10, 2001.

SEE ALSO: AOL Time Warner Inc.; E-books; Electronic Publishing

BEYOND.COM

Beyond.com designs, builds, and manages e-stores for companies like Symantec Corp. and Inprise/Borland, which have established name brands. The firm sets itself apart from other e-commerce service providers by offering back-end services, such as product distribution, along with more traditional Web page design services. Thanks to its eStore 3.0 system, Beyond.com can construct an online store in less than four weeks. The firm also sells software online to government agencies and, on a lesser scale, to individuals. In September of 2000, Deloitte and Touche ranked Beyond.com as tenth on its Silicon Valley Technology Fast 50 list, which evaluates the fastest growing technology firms in California's Silicon Valley based on revenue growth.

Founded in 1994 by former Egghead executive William McKiernan, Beyond.com was first known as Software.net. After running his upstart firm for roughly four years, McKiernan convinced Mark Breier to leave his post as director of marketing at Amazon.com to head up operations at Beyond.com. By 1999, the online software retailer was selling 45,000 software titles—nearly 5,600 of which could be downloaded via the Internet—to governmental entities, businesses, and individual consumers. At that point, customers exceeded the 1 million mark and annual sales topped $37 million, roughly 50 percent of which came from software downloads. Despite its status as the world's largest online software vendor, Beyond.com lost nearly as much money as it made.

Recognizing that competition was only going to become more fierce in the online retail software market, Breier and his management team opted early in

2000 to shift Beyond.com's focus to the business-to-business (B2B) market by offering e-commerce services such as constructing and operating e-stores for other companies. The firm had already built both an online store for McAfee and an international online store for Symantec in 1999. Believing this new aim was beyond the scope of his expertise, Breier relinquished control of daily operations to C. Richard Neely Jr., who served as Interim CEO until the firm hired Ron Smith in June of 2000.

Less than two years after its shift to e-commerce services, Beyond.com had pulled together a suite of extensive e-commerce services offered via the firm's eStores. Services included the actual construction and management of e-stores, from customer screening to order fulfillment, and eStores clients could also opt for eMarketing Solutions, which included tactics for increasing and retaining site traffic such as eMail, eNewsletter, eBanner, eCoupon, ePartners, eChannels, and BeDirect Mail. Although Beyond.com had yet to achieve profitability in mid-2001, many consider the firm to be an e-commerce services pioneer.

FURTHER READING:

Berman, Phyllis. "Hat Trick." *Forbes.* May 3, 1999.

"Beyond.com Launches eStores in Germany and France for McAfee.com, Expanding Physical Product Distribution Capabilities." *Business Wire.* March 1, 2001.

"Beyond.com Named Silicon Valley's Tenth Fastest Growing Company by Deloitte & Touche." Santa Clara, CA: Beyond.com, 2000. Available from www.beyond.com.

Campbell, Scott, and David Jastrow. "E-commerce Pioneer Goes Beyond Software Sales." *Computer Reseller News.* June 12, 2000.

"Ronald S. Smith—Beyond.com." *The Wall Street Transcript.* September 4, 2000. Available from www.twst.com.

SEE   E-commerce Solutions; E-tailing; Storefront Builders;
ALSO: Web Site Design and Set-up

BEZOS, JEFF

Jeff Bezos is the founder and CEO of Amazon.com, the world's largest online retailer of books, CDs, electronics, and more. Although the site experienced explosive growth from the time it was founded in 1995 through the end of the 1990s, analysts in late 1999 began to question the firm's likelihood of achieving profitability. As a result, stock prices plummeted and Bezos found himself having to defend his business model. Some analysts believe Amazon may become profitable in 2002, depending on the direction in which Bezos steers his firm. Although Amazon is best known for selling books online, its ability to assist other companies wishing to engage in e-tailing may well be its eventual focus.

LAUNCHING AMAZON.COM

After graduating from Princeton University with degrees in electrical engineering and computer science, Jeff Bezos began working on Wall Street. Banker's Trust hired him to develop electronic fund management systems. Eventually, he left there to begin working for hedge fund firm D.E. Shaw & Co., where he became the youngest senior vice president. Despite his success, the 30-year-old Bezos left his job at Shaw in 1994 to pursue his dream of creating an Internet retailer. He moved to Seattle, Washington, and began working on a business plan that would allow him to capitalize on what many analysts were predicting to be explosive growth in Internet use. After researching 20 different products he believed could be sold via the Internet, including magazines, CDs, and computer software, Bezos settled on books, guessing that this sizable market, with its wide range of purchase choices, would be well served by electronic searching and organizing capabilities. Books also were relatively inexpensive, and Bezos concluded that consumers would be more likely to make their first purchase online if the risk was minimal. In addition, the small size of most books made for easier distribution. Bezos liked the fact that market share was distributed among many leading publishers. In fact, industry leader Barnes & Noble held less than 12 percent of the $25 billion book retailing market. He believed this market fragmentation left room for fledgling companies.

Bezos decided to set up shop in Seattle, where he would be close to the warehouse of Ingram, a leading U.S. book distributor, as well as to a large pool of technology professionals. He hired four employees and began working in the garage of his new home to build the software that would operate his online site. Although he initially planned to call his new business Cadabra, Bezos eventually settled on Amazon, believing the name of the largest river in the world conveyed Amazon's potential to reach vast numbers of customers. In July of 1995, Bezos launched Amazon.com, a World Wide Web site that offered books at low prices and allowed visitors to search for books by author, title, subject, or keyword. Once a customer placed an order, Amazon requested the title or titles from the appropriate publisher, who shipped them to Bezos' home. At first, Bezos packaged the orders himself and took them to the post office. Typically, customers received their books within five days of placing an order. Books were shipped to all 50 states and 45 countries throughout the world.

In October, three months after its inception, Amazon achieved its first 100-order day. Shortly thereafter, the site became so busy that the beep heard at the office each time a customer completed an order was turned off because its tone became continual. Throughout Amazon's first year, Bezos worked to continually update the site to increase its user friendliness and customer service options. Many of these options also were designed to garner repeat business for Amazon. For example, customers could choose to sign up for e-mail messages that would let them know when their favorite author released a new title.

GROWING AMAZON.COM

During Amazon's second year of operation, Bezos began to look for ways to increase the firm's growth. One of his first moves was to create the "associates" program in July of 1996. This program allowed individual Web site owners and operators to offer links to Amazon from their sites. The associates then received a commission any time a visitor clicked on those links and bought books. To help fund future acquisitions, Bezos secured $10 million in capital from Kleiner Perkins Caufield & Byer in exchange for a minority stake in Amazon and a seat on the board. Advertising efforts included banner bars on some of the most heavily trafficked Web sites, as well more traditional plugs in print sources likely to be perused by book lovers. By the end of 1996, Amazon employed 110 people and its book database had grown to include more than more than 1 million titles. According to Bezos, the breadth of its offerings was key to the site's success, along with the fact that most books were discounted between 10 to 30 percent.

In May of 1997, although it had not earned a profit, Amazon went public, listing its shares for $18 apiece on NASDAQ. In less than a year those shares were worth nearly $100, and Bezos was on his way to becoming a billionaire. Bezos planned to use some of the funds from the offering to enhance Amazon's distribution arm. In October, Amazon became the Internet's first retail operation with one million customers. To commemorate this milestone, Bezos himself personally delivered the site's one-millionth order to a customer's home in Japan. The firm's name recognition was bolstered further when Vice President Al Gore spent a day answering customer service calls. Bezos forged alliances with America Online Inc. and Yahoo Inc., both of which resulted in Amazon's promotion on these high-traffic sites. Growing 20 to 30 percent each month, sales at Amazon neared the $150 million mark, and book offerings grew to roughly 2.5 million. Amazon's success left traditional book retailers scrambling to retain customers. Many chains began staying open later, offering entertainment, hosting book clubs, selling coffee and pastries, and even

opening up their own retail Web sites, which Barnes & Noble did in May of 1997. According to the September 1997 issue of *Chain Store Age Executive,* book retailing had been permanently altered. "Bezos redefined book and information merchandising and distribution. He has changed the way some customers shop and purchase books, and continues to challenge the definition of the traditional book store."

The associates program reached 30,000 members in 1998. Bezos then oversaw the launch of Amazon.com Advantage, a program designed to promote the sales of independent authors and publishers. In April, the firm expanded internationally and also diversified into online video sales when it acquired the United Kingdom's Internet Movie Database. Two months later, after Bezos decided to expand Amazon's product line with CDs, he unveiled Amazon Music, which offered more than 125,000 music titles online. International growth continued with the purchase of Bookpages Ltd., an online bookseller based in the United Kingdom, and ABC Telebook Inc., based in Germany. Both firms eventually were folded into international sites such as Amazon.co.uk and Amazon.co.de. In December of 1998, more than 1 million new customers shopped online at Amazon for holiday gifts. Customers exceeded 6.2 million, securing Amazon's position as the number three U.S. bookseller, behind Barnes & Noble and Borders.

In March of 1999, Amazon launched Amazon Auctions, an online auction house that allows businesses to market products to consumers and consumers to market products to each other. A month later, the site began allowing visitors to create and send free electronic greeting cards. In June, Amazon secured its 10 millionth customer. Expanding his site's offerings even further, Bezos created Amazon Toys and Amazon Electronics. He also launched Amazon zShops, which permitted manufacturers to offer products for sale on Amazon. Bezos conducted a $1.25 billion bond offering to fund an acquisition spree that included stakes in drugstore.com, HomeGrocer.com, Pets.com, Gear.com, and della.com. This move later proved costly as several of the smaller dot-com businesses went bankrupt and Amazon was left with nearly $2 billion in debt.

Eventually, Bezos divided Amazon's offerings into virtual stores that focused on merchandise like software, video games, gifts, and hardware. Customers also were able to sign up for a wish list service. By the end of 1999, Bezos had overseen nine acquisitions and the opening of seven new stores. Amazon had shipped 20 million items to 150 countries across the globe. Bezos was elected "Person of the Year" by *Time* magazine. According to *United Press International,* Bezos earned the award because his "vision of the online retailing universe was so complete, his

Amazon.com site so elegant and appealing that it became from day one the point of reference for anyone who had anything to sell online.''

DEFENDING AMAZON.COM

January of 2000 marked the first cutback in Amazon's history when president and chief operating officer Joseph Galli, a Black & Decker executive hired by Bezos in June of 1999, laid off 150 employees, or roughly two percent of Amazon's workforce. Galli also hired several new managers, determined to tighten the firm's spending practices and budgeting procedures. In April, Amazon.com began selling lawn and patio furniture, as well as health and beauty aids, on its site and also launched Amazon Kitchen, offering kitchen products to customers for the first time. In one of its first moves to offer e-commerce services to other companies, Amazon agreed to work with Wineshopper.com, a California-based Internet upstart seeking to become the leading online wine retailer. In June, Lehman Brothers convertible analyst Ravi Suria released a report critiquing Amazon's financial state. As a result, share prices fell by 19 percent. While Amazon's sales had experienced incredible growth in the late 1990s, investors were becoming increasingly concerned by the firm's failure to earn a profit, its $2 billion debt which cost about $125 million in interest each year, and emerging competition from the likes of Wal-Mart and other major retailers who were opening their own online stores. In 1997, Amazon had lost $27.6 million on sales of $147.8 million. In 1998, it lost $125 million. Although sales reached $1.6 billion in 1999, losses continued to mount, reaching $720 million.

To make matters worse, Galli resigned suddenly to take on the CEO role at VerticalNet, an online business-to-business portal. Stock prices fell to $45 per share as investor confidence faltered. By August, stock prices had plummeted to $28 per share, decreasing 14 percent after the firm's announcement of poor second quarter results. Nevertheless, Amazon continued to operate as the leading online shopping site in the world, serving 17 million people in 160 countries. To bolster its image, the firm began touting its offerings as the ''Earth's Biggest Selection'' of products, including books, e-cards, online auctions, CDs, videos, DVDs, toys and games, housewares, and electronics. With only 24 percent of sales coming from international operations, Bezos began working to expand the firm's international base. He also changed the firm's focus from pursuing growth at all costs, a philosophy Bezos had dubbed ''Get Big Fast,'' to cutting costs wherever possible, building on the corporate overhaul started by Galli.

Forbes writer Katrina Brooker explained that the success of Bezos's efforts became evident in the third quarter of 2000, when losses of 25 cents per share beat Wall Street predictions of 33 cents per share, and operating losses were nearly halved, decreasing from 22 percent of sales to just 11 percent. Even more important was the fact that the division housing books, music, and video—Amazon's core businesses—netted $25 million on $400 million in revenues. However, despite evidence that Bezos was taking Amazon toward profitability, by the end of 2000 stock remained down roughly 80 percent from its high. Losses for the year totaled $1.4 billion on sales of $2.76 billion.

Determined to quiet his naysayers, Bezos laid off another 1,300 employees early in 2001, or roughly 15 percent of Amazon's total workforce. He also announced his intent to shut down a service center in Seattle and a warehouse in Georgia. Growth projections were trimmed from 40 percent to roughly 25 percent. While most analysts agree that Amazon.com will likely earn a profit and remain a key force in e-tailing, they remain divided over what level of success the firm will achieve. Those bullish on Amazon's future point to deals like the August 2000 alliance with Toysrus.com, which resulted in a Web site that coupled the inventory of Toys 'R' Us with the e-commerce savvy of Amazon. According to the terms of the agreement, Amazon gets not only a fee for allowing the toy giant to use its software, but also a commission on each toy sold on the site. Toys ''R'' Us benefited as well. Once the new site was in place, holiday sales for Toysrus.com grew more than threefold.

According to Molly Prior in *DSN Retailing Today,* ''the pundits can't help but wonder if the marriage of a pure-player to a bricks-and-clicks category leader is the wave of the future for Internet retailing.'' However, Amazon's critics point out that despite deals like this and Bezos's cost cutting measures, the firm still spends much more money than it earns, and projected profit margins are no higher than those of traditional retailers. As the giant e-tailer works to find its niche in the ever-changing world of e-commerce, Wall Street likely will continue to watch Bezos, who owns 32 percent of Amazon, very closely.

FURTHER READING:

''Amazon Paddles Along.'' *Chain Store Age Executive.* March, 2001.

''Amazon.com Chief Honored By Time.'' *United Press International.* December 20, 1999.

''An Amazonian Survival Strategy: The E-Tailer is Long on Web Savvy, Short on Profits.'' *Newsweek.* April 9, 2001.

Appelbaum, Alec. ''Amazon's Juggling Act.'' *Money.* March 1, 2001.

''Bottom Line Bites Amazon.'' *Puget Sound Business Journal.* February 2, 2001.

Brooker, Katrina. ''Beautiful Dreamer.'' *Fortune*. December 18, 2000.

Eads, Stephani. ''Will Jeff Bezos Be the Next Tim Koogle?'' *BusinessWeek Online*. March 12, 2001. Available from www.businessweek.com.

''From Zero to 10 Million in Less Than Four Years: Amazon.com to Pass E-Commerce Milestone Today.'' *PR Newswire*. June 7, 1999.

Hazleton, Lesley. ''Jeff Bezos: How He Built a Billion-Dollar Net Worth Before His Company Even Turned a Profit.'' *Success*. July, 1998.

Hof, Robert D. ''Jeff Bezos.'' *BusinessWeek Online*. May 15, 2000. Available from www.businessweek.com.

Martin, Michael H. ''The Next Big Thing: A Bookstore?'' *Fortune*. December 9, 1996.

Prior, Molly. ''Amazon, TRU Web Site Proves Successful Online Model.'' *DSN Retailing Today*. January 22, 2001.

Scally, Robert. ''The Force That's Altering E-tail, One Category at a Time.'' *DSN Retailing Today*. May 8, 2000.

Schaff, William. ''Insight Into Technology Investing—Amazon's Profit Potential is Growing, But it Still isn't a Sure Bet.'' *InformationWeek*. April 16, 2001.

Zaczkiewicz, Arthur. ''Jeff Bezos Amazon.Com; A Wall Street Veteran is Taking the Internet to the Bank.'' *HFN: The Weekly Newspaper for the Home Furnishing Network*. November 27, 2000.

SEE ALSO: Amazon.com

BIOMETRICS

Biometrics is a field of security and identification technology based on the measurement of unique physical characteristics such as fingerprints, retinal patterns, and facial structure. To verify an individual's identity, biometric devices scan certain characteristics and compare them with a stored entry in a computer database. While the technology goes back years and has been used in highly sensitive institutions such as defense and nuclear facilities, the proliferation of electronic data exchange generated new demand for biometric applications that can secure electronically stored data and online transactions.

HOW BIOMETRICS WORKS

Usually, biometric systems require two forms of input for identity verification. Typically, these include the biometric input along with a personal identification number (PIN). Upon receiving the PIN, the computer accesses its stored database and locates the biometric template for that individual. The computer scans the two biological features looking for differences and, if it produces an exact match, verifies the individual's identity and grants access. In a simple identification system, on the other hand, the computer receives no cues from PINs or access cards, and scans its entire database of biometric templates looking for a match. As a result, these systems must be more powerful.

TYPES OF BIOMETRIC SYSTEMS

FINGERPRINTS. Fingerprint-based biometric systems scan the dimensions, patterns, and topography of fingers, thumbs, and palms. The most common biometric in forensic and governmental databases, fingerprints contain up to 60 possibilities for minute variation, and extremely large and increasingly integrated networks of these stored databases already exist. The largest of these is the Federal Bureau of Investigation's (FBI) Automated Fingerprint Identification System, with more than 630 million fingerprint images.

FACIAL RECOGNITION. Facial recognition systems vary according to the features they measure. Some look at the shadow patterns under a set lighting pattern, while others scan heat patterns or thermal images using an infrared camera that illuminates the eyes and cheekbones. These systems are powerful enough to scope out the minutest differences in facial patterns, even between identical twins. The hardware for facial recognition systems is relatively inexpensive, and is increasingly installed in computer monitors.

EYE SCANS. There are two main features of the eye that are targeted by biometric systems: the retina and the iris. Each contains more points of identification than a fingerprint. Retina scanners trace the pattern of blood cells behind the retina by quickly flashing an infrared light into the eye. Iris scanners create a unique biological bar code by scanning the eye's distinctive color patterns. Eye scans tend to occupy less space in a computer and thus operate relatively quickly, although some users are squeamish about having beams of light shot into their eyes.

VOICE VERIFICATION. Although voices can sound similar and can be consciously altered, the topography of the mouth, teeth, and vocal cords produces distinct pitch, cadence, tone, and dynamics that give away would-be impersonators. Widely used in phone-based identification systems, voice-verification biometrics also is used with personal computers.

HAND GEOMETRY. Hand-geometry biometric systems take two infrared photographs—one from the side and one from above—of an individual's hand. These images measure up to 90 different characteristics, such as height, width, thickness, finger shape, and joint positions and compare them with stored data.

KEYSTROKE DYNAMICS. A biometric system that is tailor-made for personal computers, keystroke-dynamic biometrics measures unique patterns in the way an individual uses a keyboard—such as speed, force, the variation of force on different parts of the keyboard, and multiple-key functions—and exploits them as a means of identification.

FEARS OF MISUSE AND LOSS OF PRIVACY

With the increasing demand for and applications of biometric devices comes serious ethical and legal questions and concerns. Chief among these considerations is privacy. The storing of such intimate biological detail in large networks sparks fear of serious privacy invasion, as well as possibilities for severe misuse. Such fears have hampered the biometric industry's movements into new markets, particularly in the United States where concern for privacy is markedly high. Just how far a business or government has the right to look into the identities of individuals in the name of security was a matter that was just beginning to draw serious attention from government, industry, and various organizations in the early 2000s. The European Union initiated the Data Protection Directive, which called for the implementation of international privacy standards, geared particularly toward electronic information and online transactions. Meanwhile, the U.S. government appointed privacy advocate Peter Swire to facilitate the development of federal privacy policies for e-commerce, databases, and information technology under the Office of Management and Budget's Office of Information and Regulatory Affairs. Swire also was to lead in the drafting of an Electronic Bill of Rights.

THE BIOMETRICS MARKET

As biometric technologies have grown more sophisticated and affordable, they have found ever more markets to penetrate. Governmental applications remained the most common at the end of the 20th century, as governments sought to safeguard their sensitive computer networks. But the private sector was adopting the technology at an accelerating rate. Total industry sales were expected to jump from $100 million in 2000 to $600 million by 2006, according to the International Biometrics Industry Association (IBIA), while the International Biometric Group forecast sales of $600 million as early as 2003.

An area that drew intense demand for tight security using biometric devices was online and networked finance, including automatic teller machines (ATMs), electronic record keeping, and e-commerce. As e-commerce grows, so will the number of PCs and handheld computing devices with embedded biometrics system and smart-card readers. Indeed, Compaq, Hewlett-Packard, NEC Technologies, DataStrip, and IBM built such security systems into their newer models in the late 1990s and early 2000s. Some machines came outfitted complete with barcode readers and fingerprint readers along with smart-card slots.

Biometrics manufacturers may find their gold mine in the expansion of e-commerce. Smart cards, outfitted with embedded microprocessor chips that can store biometric data as well as personal identification numbers and other pieces of identification, can only be read by a smart card reader. Industry analysts expect them to prove more secure and reliable for making online purchases, accessing bank accounts, and entering secured networks. While the European Smart Card Industry Association (ESCIA) of Brussels, Belgium, reported that only a fraction of the 1.4 billion smart card shipments in 1999 were in the United States, Frost & Sullivan expected U.S. shipments to skyrocket from 14.4 million in 1999 to 114.7 million in 2006. Moreover, the ESCIA predicted that about 30 percent of all online transactions would be based on smart cards by 2005. With more powerful encryption technologies for encoding the sensitive information embedded in smart cards, consumers were expected to feel more at ease making such transactions with biometrics devices online.

FURTHER READING:

Bankston, Karen. ''Biometrics: Toys or Tools?'' *Credit Union Management.* January, 2001.

''Biometric Keys to Networks, PCs Finally Come Alive.'' *Security.* September 1, 2000.

''Biometrics, Smart Cards On the Rise.'' *Information Security.* June, 2000.

''An Evolving Biometrics Market.'' *ID World.* November, 1999.

Hammel, Benjamin. ''Are Digital Certificates Secure?'' *Communications News.* December 15, 2000.

McGarr, Michael S. ''Tuning in Biometrics to Reduce E-commerce Risk.'' *Electronic Commerce World.* February, 2000.

''The Measure of Man.'' *The Economist.* September 9, 2000.

O'Shea, Timothy, and Mike Lee. ''Biometric Authentication Management—Biometric Authentication Systems Are Being Integrated into Desktop Systems.'' *Network Computing.* December 27, 1999.

Pepe, Michele. ''Buzz About Biometrics.'' *Computer Reseller News.* November 27, 2000.

SEE   Authentication; Computer Ethics; Computer Security;
ALSO: Privacy: Issues, Policies, Statements

BIONOMICS

Bionomics is a field of economic thought. It breaks from previous economic philosophy by situating economics as an extension of biology and ecology. Proponents of bionomics, such as its founder Michael Rothschild, reject what they describe as the idea of the economy as a mechanistic process, and instead view the economy as an "evolving ecosystem." Adherents interpret all actors and elements in an economy as organisms acting naturally and organically in a complex web of relationships, some cooperative and some competitive.

Bionomics takes as its metaphor the natural evolutionary process in which actors seek to survive in a complex and changing environment, working toward ever-greater levels of complexity and efficiency. Thus, bionomics interprets economic phenomena as autonomous; the economy essentially runs itself. In his book *Bionomics: The Economy as Ecosystem,* Rothschild insists that all the technological information available in modern books, on the Internet, in journals, and in people's brains forms the basis of modern life in the same manner in which DNA constitutes the basis of biological life. This concept applies only to capitalism, which is viewed as a natural and spontaneous system, as opposed to socialism, which proponents of bionomics view as a belief system.

As a result, bionomics has more or less fixed and determined ideas about economic policy. Basically, it suggests that governments should do as little as possible to interfere with what it interprets as a natural, organic process. Thus, bionomics looks down on governmental regulations, re-distributive tax schemes, and other measures to plan, control, or fix the economy. Markets are viewed as the optimal means to achieve economic efficiency and societal improvement.

Critics view bionomics as an elaborate apologia for right-wing politics, and as replicating some of the uglier manifestations of social Darwinism beneath a guise of ecological and biological science. Some, such as economist Paul Krugman of the Massachusetts Institute of Technology, go so far as to accuse bionomics of failing to grasp either traditional economics or natural evolution. And while bionomics criticizes governmental action for impeding rather than nurturing technological development, debunkers point out that nearly all high-tech industries in which the United States is competitive—including biotechnology, computers, the Internet, and electronics—were heavily subsidized, protected, and developed directly and indirectly through governmental intervention. Despite such criticism, bionomics won strong support from powerful groups and individuals, including the libertarian think tank The Cato Institute and former Speaker of the House Newt Gingrich.

FURTHER READING:

Borsook, Paulina. *Cyberselfish: A Critical Romp Through the Terribly Libertarian Culture of High-Tech.* New York: Public Affairs, 2000.

Kakutani, Michiko. "Silicon Valley Views the Economy as a Rain Forest." *New York Times.* July 25, 2000.

Krugman, Paul. "New-Age Market Theory is Bio-Babble: Pseudo-Economics Meets Pseudo Evolution." *Ottawa Citizen.* November 1, 1997.

Prime, Eugenie. "The Spider, the Fly, and the Internet." *Econtent.* June/July 2000.

Rothschild, Michael. *Bionomics: The Economy as Ecosystem.* New York: Henry Holt, 1990.

"Welcome to the Bionomics Institute." San Rafael, CA: The Bionomics Institute, 2001. Available from www.bionomics.org.

BITNET

Ira Fuchs and Greydon Freeman founded the Because It's Time Network (BITNET) on May 5, 1981. Used mainly in academia, BITNET quickly became one of the world's largest networks, eventually connecting more than 500 U.S. and 1,400 international universities and research institutions by allowing for the electronic transfer of messages and files. Although BITNET itself had become obsolete by the mid-1990s, its development was important to the growth and popularity of the Internet and, in particular, e-mail.

As director of the City University of New York's (CUNY) computing center, Fuchs recognized that liberal arts scholars would benefit from a messaging network similar to ARPAnet, a U.S. Department of Defense network that had been used by mathematics and physics researchers since its inception in 1969. Fuchs began discussing his idea with Freeman, one of the heads of technology development at Yale. Recognizing that most campuses already were equipped with the remote spooling communications system (RSCS) built into IBM computers, Fuchs and Freeman began researching ways to use RSCS to allow messages and files to pass back and forth between universities. The network structure they came up with—which simply required a mainframe system, a modem, and a phone line—was based on NJE, a communications protocol developed and used by IBM.

In March of 1981, Fuchs and Freeman established a group of computing center directors from several universities in the northeastern United States. The organization began operating as the managerial board for BITNET, which was formally launched when CUNY and Yale were connected less than two months later. More than 150 campuses were linked via BITNET over the next three years. BITNET networks soon emerged in Europe as the European Academic and Research Network, in Asia as Asia Net, and in Canada as NetNorth. Much of the international expansion was funded by IBM, as was the construction of a central office known as BITNET Network Information Center.

Several new supplemental technologies sprang up for BITNET, the most long-lasting of which was LISTSERV, developed by Eric Thomas in 1986. Mailing list software that served as both a list manager and a file server, LISTSERV allowed BITNET users to send email messages to a single list address with multiple recipients. Messages sent to a LISTSERV address were then automatically routed to everyone on the mailing list. Eventually, LISTSERV evolved into well-known commercial mailing list server software, sold by L-Soft International, that was compatible with other platforms like Unix.

The rising popularity of the Internet, along with the emergence of Transmission Control Protocol/Internet Protocol (TCP/IP) technology as an Internet standard, prompted BITNET's managerial board to merge BITNET with CSnet, a struggling TCP/IP network, in 1991. The newly merged entity, known as the Corporation for Research and Educational Networking (CREN) created BITNET II, which relies on TCP/IP for message and file transfers. Although it is used by some academic institutions today, BITNET II never achieved the popularity of the original BITNET network, which was officially halted by CREN in 1996.

FURTHER READING:

Center for Research and Educational Networking. ''BITNET Overview.'' Washington: BITNET Network Information Center, 1992. Available from www.nethistory.dumbentia.com.

Fox, Barbara. ''Making the Internet Work for Princeton.'' *U.S. 1 Newspaper.* November 27, 1996. Available from www.princeton.edu/fuchs.

Grier, David Alan, and Mary Campbell. ''A Social History of Bitnet and Listserv, 1985-1991.&lrquo; In *IEEE Annals of the History of Computing.* Washington: Institute of Electrical and Electronic Engineers, 2000. Available from www.computer.org/annals/articles.bitnet.

Indiana University Knowledge Base. ''What Was BITNET and What Happened to It?'' Bloomington, IN: Indiana University, 1998. Available from www.kb.indiana.edu/data/aaso.

SEE ALSO: ARPAnet; Connectivity, Internet; Internet and WWW, History of the

BIZRATE.COM

Just five after its inception, BizRate.com grew to become one of the Internet's busiest retail hubs, second only to Amazon.com. Monthly traffic rates at the end of 2000 reached an average of 6.5 million different visitors, and in early 2001 that number jumped to more than 7 million. Along with allowing shoppers to search for items they would like to purchase and then offering direct links to the e-stores that sell the merchandise, BizRate.com also rates online businesses for consumers. Before making a purchase, shoppers can see how past customers rated their experience with an e-business. Rating criteria, which users can rank in terms of importance to them, include customer support, live phone support, on-time delivery, site performance, order ease, product information, product pricing, order tracking, and privacy policy. Shoppers can search within one of nineteen product categories—such as apparel, books and magazines, computer hardware, computer software, DVD and videos, electronics, flowers and garden, office supplies, and pet and hobbies—or search the entire marketplace. Consumer Reports Online, Microsoft Network, Alta Vista, CNET, and other online information providers list BizRate ratings on their sites.

COMPANY HISTORY

BizRate was founded in June of 1996 by 27-year-old Farhad Mohit. While earning his master's degree in entrepreneurial management at the Wharton School, Mohit gained his first in-depth experience with the World Wide Web by creating an online site for the school's journal. It was then that he came up with the idea for BizRate, which he believed would address some of the major concerns many consumers have with online purchasing. As stated in a January 2000 article in *Computer Weekly,* ''however professional and enticing an online store may look, it could be run by a company with little financial backing or less-than-honest intentions.'' To help customers find reputable and reliable places to shop in the rapidly growing and increasingly diverse Web marketplace, Mohit wanted to build a site that would give consumers objective information about an e-store before they actually made a purchase.

He wrote a business plan for the venture as his thesis, and enlisted the help of fellow student Henri Asseily to develop the technology. Using $260,000 borrowed from family and friends, including marketing professor Dave Reibstein, Mohit and Asseily began creating the site. Over the next two years, they also worked on securing additional financial backing.

The largest chunk came when Mission Ventures, based in San Diego, California, contributed $4.5 million in April of 1998. Chuck Davis was brought in as CEO in December of 1998. He previously had worked as president of Internet gateway Go.com, owned by Walt Disney Co. While Davis focused on day-to-day managerial issues, Mohit continued to work on developing strategy. When BizRate was officially up and running, Mohit offered things like product discounts, a $50,000 sweepstakes, and a $50 instant-win offer to draw people to the site. He also differentiated the site from competitors like Gomez.com by using data from actual shoppers to create ratings rather than hiring a staff to do that.

BizRate gets its information from customers who shop at the site of a participating e-business, which is labeled with a ''BizRate Customer Certified'' seal. Once a shopper completes a purchase from a site participating in BizRate's ranking program, a BizRate questionnaire appears on the screen. Each time a questionnaire is completed, BizRate adds the data to the existing information about the e-store, so overall ratings may change over time. BizRate visitors can view these ratings and base shopping choices on them, while the e-businesses themselves can use the information to improve their performance. Online retailers can purchase monthly data reports specific to their e-store for $20,000 per year.

In the fall of 1999, the firm repositioned itself as a shopping portal by offering direct links to those retailers who were willing to participate in the ranking system and give BizRate a portion of the sales—ranging from one percent to 20 percent—that originate at its site. Within a year, more than 50 percent of BizRate's revenues came from these commissions. The firm also made money by licensing its data to sites like Consumer Reports Online.

The firm published *The Best of Online Shopping 2001* in November of 2000 to help holiday shoppers who were still leery about making online purchases. As quoted in the November 2000 issue of *Business Wire,* BizRate CEO Chuck Davis stated, ''The real question on every consumer's mind this holiday season isn't the financial future of dot-coms—it is whether Internet retailers will be able to provide compelling gift ideas and deliver on service.'' Davis believes that the book, along with his firm's rating system, will help to boost shoppers' confidence about online purchasing, a goal that was of particular importance to many online retailers after a few e-commerce fiascos during the 1999 holiday season left shoppers shaken. For example, Toysrus.com's inability to meet an unexpected spike in online orders left many customers empty-handed on Christmas Day, without the toys they had purchased from the site.

At the end of 2000, BizRate launched its C3 Marketplace, which included features like improved search capabilities covering more than 1,500 e-tailers, a discount area that showcases special deals on certain products, a listing of the best-selling items on the Web, standardized check-out procedures, and a gift idea center. The C3 Marketplace also let customers opt, for the first time, to allow BizRate to save their password and other personal details such as address and credit card information for future purchases. A seller's auction allows merchants to request their e-store appear at a specified place within the search results of certain product categories. For example, Flowers.com might request that their site appear first anytime a BizRate.com visitor searches the Flower and Garden category for roses. Unlike its competitors, BizRate doesn't charge e-tailers for each placement they receive. Rather, fees are based on how many users actually visit a site. Therefore, Flowers.com would not be charged each time its site appeared first within specified search results. Rather, its fees would vary based upon the amount of traffic it received from the placement.

Most analysts recognize the value of BizRate's rating system for both consumers and merchants in the relatively new world of e-commerce. However, some critics argue that BizRate's rating system will become obsolete as online shoppers who become increasingly familiar with the Web will likely return to their favorite sites to do business. Mohit counters this by pointing out that new businesses, particularly traditional brick-and-mortar companies, continue to open e-stores and overhaul existing sites. Instead of relying solely on a growing base of new sites to rate in order to justify its potential for continued success, BizRate also is developing new technology to bolster its presence as one of the Internet's top shopping hubs. Hoping to give online shoppers another reason to visit its site, the firm began working in 2001 on a system that will allow customers to keep track of their online spending by listing all completed purchases in a single account.

FURTHER READING:

''About BizRate.com.'' Los Angeles, CA: BizRate.com, 2001. Available from www.bizrate.com.

''BizRate.com Becomes Second to Amazon as the Most Popular Retail Site on the Web.'' *Business Wire.* February 15, 2001.

''BizRate.com Launches an A-Z Online Shopping Guide Book in Time for Holiday 2000.'' *Business Wire.* November 15, 2000.

''BizRate.com Solves e-Commerce Woes with Launch of New C3 Marketplace.'' *Business Wire.* October 17, 2000.

Mcnamara, Paul. ''BizRate.com Founder Farhad Mohit Eyes Every Aspect of His Business the Same Way Comic Steve Martin's Cop Character on 'Let's Get Small' Looked at a Shrunken Motorist: We're Gonna Have to Measure You.'' *Network World.* February 5, 2001.

''Siteseeing.'' *Computer Weekly.* January 13, 2000.

Smith, Geoffrey. ''There's Good Reason for the Buzz about BizRate.'' *Businessweek Online.* November 26, 1999. Available from www.businessweek.com.

Weintraub, Arlene. ''E-Commerce Crusader.'' *Businessweek Online.* June 5, 2000. Available from www.businessweek.com.

SEE ALSO: Amazon.com; Business-to-Consumer (B2C) E-Commerce; E-tailing

BLOOMBERG, MICHAEL

Michael R. Bloomberg runs Bloomberg L.P., one of the world's largest financial information, news, and media companies. Considered an industry mogul by most accounts, Bloomberg is best known for parlaying his financial information services upstart into a billion dollar media giant that competes with the likes of Dow Jones, Knight-Ridder, and Reuters. Despite Bloomberg's initial reluctance to compete on the Internet—a medium he viewed as targeting a much more general audience than the one his company served—his firm's Web site, launched in 1995, became one of the most frequently visited financial information sites on the Internet. In 2001, Bloomberg resigned as chairman of his firm, and ran successfully for the office of mayor of New York City. His term was expected to begin in 2002.

A native of Boston, Massachusetts, Bloomberg graduated from John Hopkins University in 1964 and from Harvard Business School two years later. He spent many of the early years of his career working in equity trading and sales for securities trader Salomon Brothers Inc., where he eventually achieved general partner status and headed up the development of an in-house computerized financial system. Salomon Brothers fired Bloomberg in October of 1981. After pocketing millions of dollars by selling off his Salomon Brothers stock, Bloomberg considered founding his own company.

Five months later, he established Innovative Market Systems (IMS) and put together a team of computer programmers to develop something he believed Wall Street sorely needed: a computerized information system that would grant subscribers, mainly Wall Street firms, access to real-time securities market data via a desktop terminal. In 1983, Bloomberg and his partners unveiled the first such machine to Merrill Lynch, which agreed to order 20 terminals and pay $30 million for a 30-percent stake in the fledgling information provider. Bloomberg's timing proved fortuitous. Ready for electronic access to the kinds of financial information Bloomberg was peddling, other major firms began signing up for the terminals. Bloomberg changed his company's name to Bloomberg L.P. in 1986.

Perhaps Bloomberg's keenest move in growing his company was convincing the *New York Times* to publish Bloomberg Business News articles with the Bloomberg byline in exchange for providing the newspaper with a free terminal. By 1992, Bloomberg had secured a similar deal with every major newspaper, virtually guaranteeing his firm's name recognition among financial news readers.

By the end of the 1990s, Bloomberg was publishing magazines and producing radio and television shows. The company also was operating a Web site with live broadcasts and an electronic trading vehicle, and making its information available over mobile devices like pagers. By placing real-time financial data at the fingertips of securities investors, Bloomberg not only launched a successful business, he also played an instrumental role in the industry's increasing reliance on online mediums. His firm's success in the twenty-first century, according to several analysts, depends on how Bloomberg handles competition from two fronts: the deluge of financial information increasingly made available for free on the Internet (a medium Bloomberg discounts as too unreliable to become a major threat) and the cheaper versions of Bloomberg-like information provided by competitors Reuters and Bridge Information Systems.

FURTHER READING:

''Bloomberg Anticipates No Threat from Internet.'' *AsiaPulse News.* June 29, 2000.

''Bloomberg Steps Down.'' *United Press International.* March 6, 2001.

''Bloomberg Timeline.'' New York: Bloomberg L.P., 2001. Available from www.bloomberg.com/corp/press/timeline.

Dolan, Kerry A. ''Bloomberg for Sale?'' *Forbes.* September 18, 2000.

Spiro, Leah Nathans. ''In Search of Michael Bloomberg.'' *BusinessWeek Online.* May 5, 1997. Available from www.businessweek.com/1997.

SEE ALSO: Bloomberg L.P.; Bloomberg U.S. Internet Index

BLOOMBERG L.P.

Bloomberg L.P. is among the world's leading financial information, news, and media companies. Along with selling real-time financial data to banks, investment firms, government agencies, and other institutions, the firm operates 79 news bureaus throughout the world, publishes magazines, produces radio and television shows, and manages one of the Internet's most frequently visited financial information sites, which averaged roughly 200 million page views per month in 2000. Customers included the 250,000 financial professionals who leased Bloomberg terminals, 8 million radio listeners, 200 million television viewers, and 350 million newspaper and magazine readers.

EARLY HISTORY

When Harvard Business School graduate Michael Bloomberg was fired from Salomon Brothers Inc. in October of 1981, he began to explore the idea of establishing his own business. Bloomberg had worked in equity trading and sales for Salomon Brothers, where he eventually was named general partner. Bloomberg also spearheaded efforts to create an in-house computerized financial system there. It was while working for the securities trader that Bloomberg first saw the need among Wall Street firms for a more sophisticated method of gathering and analyzing information.

In March of 1982, Bloomberg sold off his Salomon Brothers stock and used the fresh capital to create Innovative Market Systems (IMS). He hired a team of computer programmers to begin developing an electronic information system that would grant users access to real-time securities market data via a desktop terminal. In December of that year, Merrill Lynch became IMS's first customer by ordering twenty terminals on the condition that IMS not market the machines to any Merrill Lynch competitors for five years. Impressed by the technology's potential, Merrill Lynch also bought a thirty-percent stake in IMS for $30 million.

IMS launched the Portable Bloomberg machine in 1984. By pointing out that increased sales would up the value of Merrill Lynch's stock in IMS, Bloomberg convinced Merrill Lynch to lift the five-year sales restriction, freeing IMS to begin widespread marketing of its terminals at a price of $1,500 per month for a single terminal, and $1,000 per month for additional machines. IMS focused on marketing its technology to pension funds, central banks, mutual funds, insurers, and other ''buy side'' firms. Bloomberg changed his company's name to Bloomberg L.P. in 1986 and increased its user base by selling terminals to securities underwriters, trading firms, and other ''sell side'' firms for the first time.

International expansion efforts heated up in 1987 when the firm opened offices in both London and Tokyo. Global growth continued in 1989 with the launch of an office in Sydney, Australia. An office in Singapore opened in 1990. Bloomberg moved into Germany in 1992 by establishing a unit in Frankfurt and established a Hong Kong office in 1993. Eventually, the company established units in Brazil and India, and by the end of the 1990s, its customers spanned more than 100 countries.

Technological developments throughout these years also fueled the firm's growth. For example, a new securities trading feature allowed the firm to launch the Bloomberg Trading System in 1988—an electronic bond trading system that made the company a player in the electronic commerce arena before the term e-commerce had even been coined. The firm also launched the Bloomberg Traveler, which allowed subscribers to access Bloomberg information from remote locations. The 10,000th Bloomberg terminal was installed in 1990. Enhancements such as color monitors and video training materials, as well as e-mail and multimedia capabilities, came in the early 1990s.

GROWTH VIA NEW MEDIA OUTLETS

In 1991, the firm diversified into a new industry when Bloomberg hired former *Wall Street Journal* writer Matthew Winkler as the editor-in-chief of Bloomberg's Business News, a Washington, D.C.-based upstart news service that would cover the financial aspects of politics, business, general news, and sports. The news service eventually allowed Bloomberg to complete with the likes of Bridge Information, Dow Jones, Knight-Ridder, Reuters, and other news wires that served the world's largest newspapers and magazines.

That year, in what many would later call one of his most astute maneuvers, Bloomberg convinced the *New York Times* to publish Bloomberg Business News articles with the Bloomberg byline in exchange for providing the newspaper with a free terminal. It wasn't until January 1, 1999 that Bloomberg began charging a monthly fee for the terminals it had been giving away for free to newspapers and magazines. By 1992, Bloomberg had secured a similar deal with every major newspaper in the United States, essentially guaranteeing name recognition among financial news readers for his company.

Bloomberg began capitalizing on that name recognition almost immediately by venturing into other types of media. It acquired radio station WNEW, based in New York City, for $13.5 million, and changed its call letters to WBBR, which stood for Bloomberg Business Radio. The company also began publishing the *Bloomberg Magazine,* and in 1994, launched a new Sunday insert magazine called *Bloomberg Personal.* That publication's initial circulation of roughly 6 million marked it as the magazine industry's largest launch to date.

The company moved into television when it aired its first episode of the Bloomberg Forum, a television show that consisted of interviews with corporate executives. In January of 1994, Bloomberg Information Television, a 24-hour financial news service produced by Maryland Public Television and distributed by DirecTV, made its debut. In 1995, to allow subscribers to access the television service from their terminals, Bloomberg began wiring each terminal for compatibility with DirecTV satellite dishes. Bloomberg Information Television was launched in Europe that year. By then, Bloomberg Business News had expanded to include more than 330 reporters in 56 bureaus, and the firm had installed its 50,000th terminal.

Bloomberg Press began publishing works from its two imprints, Bloomberg Personal Bookshelf, aimed at consumers, and Bloomberg Professional Library, targeting financial professionals, in 1996. Bloomberg Business News was renamed Bloomberg News in 1997, when it began including more general coverage. That year, Bloomberg and WEFA reached a licensing agreement that granted Bloomberg permission to post WEFA's Country Profile and Country Monitor reports—including detailed economic and political news from more than 100 countries—on its terminals. The firm launched two new print magazines, *Wealth Manager* and *On Investing,* in 1999.

BECOMING AN "OPEN" SYSTEM

In the mid-1990s, Bloomberg stood apart from its competitors by being the only market data provider that required customers to lease one of its terminals to gain access to its information. Rivals like Bridge Information, Dow Jones, and Reuters all allowed subscribers to use their own PCs to link into a digital data feed, from which they could dump selected information into applications like spreadsheets, databases, and word processors for customization. Even more importantly, users could integrate data from a variety of sources for any purpose short of publishing it themselves. Despite the obvious benefits of such a system to clients, Bloomberg gave in to market pressures to offer a more "open" system rather slowly. In 1995, the firm began allowing subscribers to access its data from any PC, but restricted the actual download of raw data so that users could do little more than dump numbers into spreadsheet software. The price of the data was the same as the terminal itself—roughly $1,140 per month. This package, known as the Open Bloomberg, required that data be transferred via a Bloomberg server to desktops using either Unix or Windows NT. It also required subscribers to use a Bloomberg keyboard, which had built-in audio capabilities and color-coded keys.

In 1996, the firm's Bloomberg Data License opened things up a bit further. The license gave subscribers access to a raw data feed and allowed them to select the data they wanted, which varied in price depending on the amount and type chosen. However, Bloomberg's analytic features, which many analysts believe are its most valuable commodity, could not be downloaded. Eventually, the firm also introduced technology, called ActiveX, that allowed subscribers to customize the information displayed on their Bloomberg boxes.

Despite being criticized for maintaining a more "closed" system than its competitors, Bloomberg received praise for its proprietary machines, which were considered among the most comprehensive in the industry. Rodger Shaw, a writer for *America's Community Banker* claimed Bloomberg's technology was "like the Internet, with none of the 'signing on' and 'looking up' complications." Bloomberg terminals use high-speed telephone lines that allow users to access real-time market price information about securities. They also offer comprehensive information about the securities themselves; detailed historical information about prices, including comparisons of prices spreads over several months or several years; and extensive financial information on corporations, including documents filed with the Securities and Exchange Commission. Thanks to Bloomberg's extensive news wires, the terminals display financial news as it breaks. Analytic features allow the machines to examine a bond's past performance and project its future potential, as well as to assess things like how a bond purchase will fit into a specific portfolio. Subscribers also can use their "Bloombergs" for video conferencing, e-mailing, trip planning, employee recruiting, and even personal tasks like reading horoscopes and gift hunting.

IMPACT OF THE INTERNET

Although Bloomberg believed that the financial information increasingly made available for free on the Internet was too unreliable and served too broad an audience to pose any real threat to his service, the firm launched its own Web site at the end of 1995. Due in large part to the Bloomberg name recognition, it quickly became one of the world's most heavily trafficked Internet sites. As with its traditional service, Bloomberg offers a wide-ranging combination of both financial data and news and general news on its site. However, the highly condensed data targets a mass market and does not compete with Bloomberg's fee-based service. According to Bloomberg himself in a *AsiaPulse News* article dated June 29, 2000, "The Internet is not fast and reliable enough for professionals. It is for the man on the street.&rquo;

Unlike most of its competitors, Bloomberg is not racing to use the Internet as a commerce vehicle. In fact, the company's electronic trading developments in the late twentieth century—which included the Bloomberg Trade Book, an electronic commerce network for equity securities launched in December of

1996, and an electronic trading network for fixed-income securities established in February of 2000—are not made available on the Internet at all. Rather, their access is limited solely to Bloomberg subscribers.

However, Bloomberg hasn't completely divorced itself from Internet-based deals. In December of 1997, it conducted its first Webcast (a live broadcast via the Web) of the Bloomberg Forum. Early in 1998, the firm moved into interactive television products and also inked a content agreement with America Online, which began hosting live Bloomberg news feeds. LendingTree Inc. and Bloomberg launched an online consumer loan center in 1999. That year, Bloomberg Television and RespondTV formed a joint venture to develop an interactive television feature allowing viewers to obtain stock quotes on demand. Bloomberg also added to its Web site a new section called the Entrepreneur Network, featuring programs, services, and information for small business owners. In 2000, small business site Inc.com began adding articles to various sections of the Entrepreneur Network, covering such small business topics as financing options, management issues, marketing efforts, tax strategies, and e-business solutions. Bloomberg also agreed to link its site to MoneyZone.com, which agreed to provide various interactive features to Bloomberg's Loan Center and Entrepreneur Network. That year, an agreement with the Real Estate Exchange Network (REXnetwork) resulted in the addition of a real estate section to Bloomberg.com that allowed users to post real estate listings on Bloomberg's site, as well as on all REXnetwork sites. The firm also added a searchable news archive to Bloomberg.com.

Analysts remain uncertain about whether or not Bloomberg's insistence on charging high prices for what he believes is exceptional information and unmatched analytics will continue to pay off for the firm. By placing real-time financial data at the fingertips of securities investors for the first time, Bloomberg did more than just launch a highly successful business. He also played an instrumental role in the industry's increasing use of online platforms. One online platform in particular—the Internet—is poised to cause a major shift in Bloomberg's strategy, according to some analysts, as increasingly sophisticated financial information continues to make its way to the Web for free. Bloomberg also is facing competition from rivals Reuters and Bridge Information Systems, which offer similar information at much cheaper prices.

FUTURE PLANS

In December of 2000, the firm decided to focus its efforts on increasing its end-to-end securities pro-

cessing capabilities from order placement to transaction completion. According to *InformationWeek* writer Anthony Guerra, Bloomberg is looking to "position itself as the company that can guide its clients onto the smooth path of straight-through processing by doing nothing more than turning on a terminal that might already be on their desks." To do so, Bloomberg will need to open its platform to such an extent that it can process orders from all types of systems. This focus represents a substantial shift for Bloomberg in that it targets a broader base of trading clients than ever before. If the shift is successful, it should improve Bloomberg's bottom line. After all, if the firm can convince clients to use its terminals for securities processing, they likely will need more of Bloomberg's machines.

FURTHER READING:

Berman, Dennis. "What's Hot in the Newsrooms: Bloomberg's 'Free Lunch' is Over." *BusinessWeek Online.* October 12, 1998. Available from www.businessweek.com.

"Bloomberg Anticipates No Threat from Internet." *AsiaPulse News.* June 29, 2000.

"Bloomberg L.P." In *Notable Corporate Chronologies.* Farmington Hills, MI: Gale Group, 1999.

"Bloomberg Timeline." New York: Bloomberg L.P., 2001. Available from www.bloomberg.com.

Dolan, Kerry A. "Bloomberg for Sale?" *Forbes.* September 18, 2000.

Guerra, Anthony. "Bloomberg Aims to Simplify Straight-Through Processing." *InformationWeek.* December 18, 2000.

Harding, James, and Peter Thal Larsen. "Companies & Finance the Americas: Hot Debate Over Bloomberg's Future is Political Issue." *Financial Times.* March 13, 2001.

Kover, Amy. "Why the Net Could Be Bad News for Bloomberg." *Fortune.* October 12, 1998.

Moukheiber, Zina. "Open—a Little: In an Age of Open Systems, Mike Bloomberg Only Reluctantly Separated His Data from His Terminals. Is He Resisting a Tidal Wave?" *Forbes.* December 16, 1996.

O'Leary, Mick. "Bloomberg Empire Takes On the Web." *InformationToday.* November 1, 1998.

Shay, Rodger. "Have Your Own Bloomberg." *America's Community Banker.* August, 1996.

SEE ALSO: Bloomberg, Michael; Bloomberg U.S. Internet Index

BLOOMBERG U.S. INTERNET INDEX

The Bloomberg U.S. Internet Index is a stock market benchmark for the dot-com contingent. It is owned and operated by Bloomberg L.P., a leading business publisher with scores of products relating to business news, statistics, and analysis. Among the nearly 300 companies tracked by the index are Web retailers of all varieties, Web-based advertising firms, content providers, Internet software vendors, Web portals, networking equipment companies, and other Internet-based service providers. The index weighs companies by their market capitalization, with the minimum capitalization set at $250 million, and includes those companies whose initial public offerings (IPOs) meet or exceed that total. Among the major companies tracked by the index are Yahoo!, AOL, E*TRADE, eBay, Priceline.com, and Amazon.com.

As e-commerce grew in the mid-1990s and the slate of new dot-com startups began turning investors into millionaires, interest grew in the specific tracking of Internet-based companies' stock market performance. Bloomberg began tracking these stocks in its own index on December 31, 1998, at which point the index totaled 100 firms. The index's short history more or less told the story behind the dot-com economy. Skyrocketing more than 250 percent in its first year, it far outpaced the growth of other major benchmarks such as the Standard & Poor's 500. However, the dot-com shakeout and larger tech-market bust in spring of 2000 that sank the NASDAQ index took the Bloomberg U.S. Internet Index with it. By the end of 2000, the index had fallen from its peak of $2.9 trillion to $1.2 trillion. Those investors anxious to see how dot-com mania and panic will sort itself out will doubtless have their eyes affixed to Bloomberg's index.

FURTHER READING:

''Bloomberg.com Financial Markets Commodities News.'' New York: Bloomberg L.P., 2001. Available from: www.bloomberg.com.

''Charting e-Business.'' *Globaltechnology.com.* September 26, 2000. Available from www.globetechnology.com/archive.

Mitchell, Ian. ''Have Dotcoms Had Their Day?'' *Computer Weekly.* November 16, 2000.

SEE   Bloomberg, Michael; Bloomberg L.P.; Volatility
ALSO:

BLUELIGHT.COM LLC

BlueLight.com was established in 1999 as part of Kmart Corp.'s efforts to gain an Internet presence. The venture, majority owned by Kmart and funded by SOFTBANK Venture Capital, Martha Stewart Living Omnimedia, and Yahoo!, originally operated as an Internet Service Provider (ISP). However, in just two years BlueLight grew into an online discount shopping destination, as well as a leading ISP with nearly 7 million subscribers.

By the end of the 1990s, Kmart stood as the third-largest discount retailer in the United States behind Wal-Mart Stores Inc. and Sears, Roebuck & Co. However, a lack of innovative marketing tactics and slowing sales had left the 100-year-old company scrambling to hold onto its market share. Believing the Internet might prove to be a lucrative growth vehicle, Kmart management began to formulate an e-business plan aimed at bolstering the company's image and boosting sales.

In May of 1998, the Kmart launched its Web site as Kmart.com. The company's first attempt at creating an online presence failed, as it neither improved the firm's faltering image nor increased revenues. Run by an inexperienced in-house staff, the site was a far cry from what Kmart executives had envisioned. Consequently, Kmart sought out investment capital firm SOFTBANK and put plans in motion to create a new e-business strategy. While discouraged by Kmart's suffering brand image, SOFTBANK was impressed with its customer reach. According to a November 2000 *Fortune* article, 85 percent of the U.S. population lived within 15 minutes of a Kmart store, 4 million people visited a Kmart store each day, and more than 70 million Kmart advertising circulars were mailed out each week. Seeing Kmart's expansive customer base as a significant growth advantage, SOFTBANK agreed to fund the floundering retailer's Internet venture. Kmart immediately hired an experienced executive staff, including CEO Mark H. Goldstein, founder of Impulse! Buy Network, and Chief Web Officer Brian Sugar, the former head of e-commerce at clothing retailer J.Crew.

Goldstein laid out a three-part business plan that included getting Kmart shoppers online, creating a successful online shopping destination, and increasing both online and in-store sales. The first goal of Goldstein's plan—getting Kmart shoppers to use the Internet—proved to be the backbone of Kmart's e-business strategy. The firm's lackluster Web site was replaced with a new venture entitled BlueLight.com, which was launched in December of 1999 as an independent ISP.

The name BlueLight.com was chosen to reflect the infamous ''BlueLight Specials'' started by Kmart in the 1960s. The venture began operation as a free ISP with headquarters in San Francisco. Realizing that many Kmart shoppers did not have Internet access, the company sought to boost its online presence by first enticing customers to start using the Web by way of BlueLight's free service. Kmart also marketed the ISP in its stores by offering shoppers CD-ROMs that contained BlueLight.com software. The ISP was powered by Spinway Inc., a virtual ISP that leased telephone lines and equipment. Via Spinway, Blue-Light's free ISP service was available to 96 percent of the U.S. population, which was the largest ISP coverage available to U.S. Web surfers.

BlueLight.com experienced overwhelming success in its first months of operation. By March of 2000, it had secured 1 million customers and was on its way to becoming the fastest-growing ISP in the United States. According to the company, 40 percent of its customers were first-time Internet users and did not have Web access before signing up for BlueLight services. To continue encouraging its shoppers to get online, Kmart also sold branded personal computers, made by LG Electronics, that came equipped with BlueLight software and sold for approximately $700 in its stores.

As the number of Web surfers visiting Blue-Light.com continued to grow at a rapid clip, the firm began preparing for its official launch as an online shopping destination. BlueLight formed several key partnerships to boost its product offerings. For example, Global Sports Inc. teamed up with the firm to offer sporting goods on the site. A deal also was formed with CoolSavings.com Inc. that allowed Blue-Light shoppers to receive special discounts and coupons for BlueLight merchandise by visiting the CoolSavings.com Web site. By the time BlueLight's e-commerce capabilities were fully operational, shoppers could find nearly 220,000 items available for purchase on the site. According to a 2000 Media Metrix study, BlueLight.com was the top home furnishings Web site in June, securing the highest number of unique visitors to its Web site and beating out competitors J.C. Penney and Sears. By August, it had signed on 3 million free ISP customers, reaching that milestone more quickly than any other paid or free ISP.

That month, BlueLight also secured another round of financing from Kmart and SOFTBANK. The $80 million cash infusion was used for increased Web development. In September, BlueLight had secured 4 million customers and launched its free ISP service in Spanish. To promote the new service, the firm distributed more than 55,000 CD-ROMs at Major League Soccer games in the United States and also hosted "Get to Know the Internet" classes in Kmart's top Hispanic stores. In addition, the BlueLight.com Web site was revamped to increase ease of use and customer services. Its product count increased to 250,000 items. However, two months later BlueLight experienced its first major stumbling block when Spinway announced that it was going out of business. As a result, BlueLight was forced to buy certain Spinway assets to keep its 5.2 million customers online during the holiday season.

By March of 2001, BlueLight had signed on nearly 7 million members. However, converting these subscribers into BlueLight shoppers proved much more difficult. To encourage online purchases, Blue-Light began charging $9.95 a month for 100 hours of Internet service. However, subscribers who spent more than $100 in a single order received a free month for every $50 spent. Free service was still offered to those who spent less than 12 hours a month online. Kmart also installed Internet shopping kiosks in 1,100 of its stores in April 2001, allowing Kmart shoppers to purchase out-of-stock merchandise and items that were not available in the company's stores. According to Goldstein in a 2001 *Direct Marketing* article, "the BlueLight.com online shopping kiosk is a major cornerstone in our e-selling strategy. Working with Kmart, we are developing multi-channel programs that answer the consumer's needs and wants— no matter where they are, no matter what they are looking for."

In 2000, Kmart increased its control over Blue-Light when the slowing economy began wreaking havoc among those in the dot-com industry. In May of 2001, the firm was forced to begin restructuring efforts aimed at making BlueLight more profitable. Jobs were cut, and BlueLight began relying more heavily on its majority owner. Analysts began to speculate that Kmart was considering a full purchase of the Internet start-up, as marketing and merchandising responsibility shifted to the retailer. At the same time, Goldstein announced his departure as CEO of Blue-Light, staying on as an Internet advisor for Kmart. BlueLight and Kmart executives continued working together to boost revenues, improve overall operations, and help secure future growth for both Kmart and BlueLight.com.

The future of BlueLight.com is uncertain as of January 2002, as Kmart Corp. has filed for bankruptcy.

FURTHER READING:

Blakey, Elizabeth. "Is BlueLight.com a Model or Muddle?" *E-Commerce Times.* December 18, 2000. Available from www.ecommercetimes.com.

"BlueLight.com CEO Resigns." *DSN Retailing Today.* June 4, 2001.

"BlueLight Takes on Spinway." *San Francisco Business Times.* December 8, 2000.

Davis, Jessica. "Net Prophet: BlueLight Special Lesson." *InfoWorld.* June 4, 2001.

Enos, Lori. "BlueLight Cutting Jobs in Reorganization Under Kmart." *E-Commerce Times.* May 24, 2001. Available from www.ecommercetimes.com.

"Kmart Installs 3,500 Shopping Kiosks in Stores Nationwide." *Direct Marketing.* April 2001.

Koudsi, Suzanne. "Attention Kmart Bashers: The Folks at BlueLight Are Turning The Troubled Retailer Into an Online Force." *Fortune.* November 13, 2000.

Lee, Louise. "Going for Gold at BlueLight." *BusinessWeek Online.* November 20, 2000. Available from www.businessweek.com.

Thau, Barbara. "Kmart Puts the Spotlight on BlueLight Site." *HFN—The Weekly Newspaper for the Home Furnishing Network.* October 23, 2000.

Vance, Ashlee. "BlueLight May Cut Some Users Off Free Access." *Network World.* December 18, 2000.

Wasserman, Todd. "BlueLight, Green Light." *Brandweek.* October 2, 2000.

SEE ALSO: Business-to-Consumer (B2C) E-commerce; Kiosks

BOOLEAN OPERATOR

When individuals use search engines to find information on the Internet, the Boolean Operators "AND," "OR," and "NOT" are often used to maximize the relevancy and effectiveness of their search. By entering them in the form of a search query, these operators specify the parameters of a search. For example, someone searching for information about surfing in California might enter the following query to target their search: "Surfing AND California". By using the "AND" operator, the search will only include results that contain the words California and surfing, not results that include only one of the two terms. If the individual were interested in results about California, surfing, or California and surfing, the following query could be used: Surfing OR California. Finally, if someone wanted information about surfing, but specifically *not* about surfing in California, the NOT operator could be used as follows: Surfing NOT California.

Boolean operators are a fundamental component of a kind of algebra called Boolean Logic. Named after 19th century English mathematician George Boole, Boolean Logic boils down all values to one of two states: true or false. This closely mirrors the binary approach digital computers use to interpret and process information, whereby commands are converted to sequences of either zeroes or ones. The millions of transistors found on a computer's microprocessor are always in one of two states (on or off). These two states, which are represented by ones and zeroes, respectively, correspond to Boolean Logic.

FURTHER READING:

"Boolean." *CNET.com,.* May 29, 2001. Available from www.cnet.com/Resources/Info/Glossary.

"Boolean Expression." *Ecomm Webopedia,* May 25, 2001. Available from www.e-comm.webopedia.com.

"Boolean Logic." *Ecomm Webopedia,* May 25, 2001. Available from www.e-comm.webopedia.com.

"Boolean Logic." *Tech Encyclopedia,.* May 25, 2001. Available from www.techweb.com.

Morton, Douglas. "Refresher Course: Boolean AND (searching OR retrieval)." *Online,* January, 1993.

BRAND BUILDING

The key to a successful brand lies in delivering value to the customer. Brands offer customers a promise, a set of values that will motivate them. Brands are positioned to echo the brand promise. This requires understanding customer needs. It is also important for companies to deliver a brand that reflects what customers thought they were promised. Brands are built around successful products, not the other way around. Sometimes this insight has been lost on e-businesses, in particular, which have spent millions of dollars on e-brand building programs, motivated by speed, by the need to be first in order to capture "eyeballs." Along the way, some e-business companies neglected to develop products that lived up to the brand images they wished to project.

There are many benefits to having a recognized brand. A strong brand is regarded as an important strategic asset that can enable a company to build stronger relationships with its customers and give it a measure of strategic control. A strong brand cuts through clutter in a fragmented marketplace and keeps a firm's products from becoming commodities. A strong brand name can affect investment decisions and a firm's market capitalization. A strong brand, then, has come to be regarded as an asset to be managed like any other corporate asset.

Brand building is multi-dimensional. A strong brand is the result of a long-term, cumulative effort. It involves more than advertising, although most marketing executives believe that traditional advertising is the best way to reach a broad audience, according to a Mercer Management Consulting survey as reported in *Advertising Age.* Brand building also includes investments in areas such as customer service, product development, and enhancing the customer experience.

Companies need to determine what is important to their customers and recognize that different customers have different preferences. Companies learn what is important by listening to their customers. Gathering information from their customers enables them to learn what their customers' needs are. They can then build and position their brand to offer the promise of satisfying those needs. Factors such as low price, high quality, broad selection, and personal service figure into customer preferences and brand building. One group of online customers may prefer high quality, a reputable brand, and the lowest possible price. Another group may prefer speed, convenience, and a high level of functionality and interactivity when shopping online.

USING THE WEB FOR BRAND BUILDING

Brands originally came into existence to identify the creator of a product or service and create some type of competitive advantage. The Internet has the potential of helping companies use their brands to create new sources of competitive advantage through content richness, interactivity, and targeting. Internet-related investments in brand building include using the Web as a way to manage customer relationships and cross-sell. Customer service has always been a key element in building a brand. In e-commerce, the Internet has raised the importance of customer service and accelerated the time frame in which companies have to provide superior service to their customers. Having a Web site up and running accelerates how a company's brand is interpreted. The nature of the Web site experience thus becomes an important part of building the firm's brand. It gives the company an opportunity to build on its strengths.

For companies with an existing brand, Web sites are an extension of their brand franchise. Web sites can tap into demand by offering product information that differentiates a firm's products from its competition. Customers may gather information on the products at the Web site and then take the information to the firm's brick-and-mortar store. Building a brand requires an integrated set of messages across all media, including the Internet. Companies need to achieve a high degree of integration among all point of contact with customers, including call centers, Web sites, and stores. By giving value to the customer when they are online, the firm enhances its brand image and the brand becomes part of the value proposition.

BUILDING A BRAND THROUGH ADVERTISING

Banner ads can be successful brand-building tools. To measure the effectiveness of banner ads as brand-building tools, though, requires more than a glance at click-through rates. To study the effect of banner ads on brand awareness, market researchers use a control-exposed methodology, which compares responses from a group that has been exposed to a banner ad with those of a control group that has not seen the ad. According to *InformationWeek,* ongoing research has shown that banner ads can be an effec-tive brand-building tool. Companies such as Johnson & Johnson advertise on the Web, but they do not expect the ads to result in online sales. Rather, they are creating a brand awareness that they expect will translate into sales at the store. That is, the banner ad creates a relationship with the consumer that may result in sales at the counter.

Banner ads have been compared to billboard advertising. The advertiser has the consumer's attention for only a few seconds. During that time, the ad must capture the consumer's attention and leave a lasting impression through the use of compelling visuals that are memorable but not confusing.

Brand building must also exploit the synergies between Web advertising and traditional print and broadcast advertising. This is an area marketers continue to explore. A large media company such as Walt Disney Co., which owns ABC-TV and ESPN among other media properties, can exploit the synergy between ABC-TV and ABC.com, for example. Ads or messages placed on a television show direct viewers to a Web site where additional information can be obtained. In the case of ABC's hit TV quiz show, *Who Want to Be a Millionaire?,* viewers can go to the Internet to play the game. While there, they pick up brand awareness and have the opportunity to enter a sweepstakes.

BUILDING A NEW BRAND

New e-commerce companies that want to build their brands typically begin with an ad campaign to build brand awareness and market share. Oftentimes, that proves expensive, and funds may run out before the brand is established and the enterprise can sustain itself. In the crowded field of online brokerage firms, E*Trade and Ameritrade spent heavily to establish their brands. In 1997-98 Ameritrade Inc. spent $20 million on a national advertising campaign that focused on the company's $8 online trading fee. While heavy advertising expenditures built awareness and helped increase the number of new accounts, Ameritrade sustained higher quarterly losses as a result of its marketing expenditures. Apparently the company was satisfied with this approach, however, as in 1999 it spent another $50 million on advertising to launch OnMoney.com, its financial portal.

E*Trade's large expenditures on advertising to build its brand resulted in it being the fourth most recognized e-commerce brand in 1999, behind Amazon.com, eBay, and Priceline.com., according to the Internet Brand Study by Opinion Research Corp. In 2001 the company used its Super Bowl ad to position itself as a brand that could still be trusted amidst the failure of so many dot-com companies in 2000. The ad served to remind people that E*Trade was not going to go away like many other dot-coms.

A smaller start-up brokerage, Web Street Inc., spent $10 million in six months on cable TV and newspaper ads to make its name better known. MarchFirst, a newly named electronic commerce and information technology (IT) consulting firm formed by the merger of Whittman Hart Inc. and USWeb/CKS, launched an $18 million ad campaign to gain recognition for its new name. According to *Crain's Chicago Business,* the ads more than tripled the number of visitors to the MarchFirst Web site. That firm later became one of the higher-profile casualties in the dot-com shakeout.

Priceline.com appeared more successful at using advertising to reach a mass audience and build its brand. Its aggressive radio and newspaper advertising strategy (begun in 1998 and later expanded to include television) featured the actor William Shatner as a spokesperson. The company's ads resulted in name recognition for Priceline.com among at least a quarter of the U.S. adult population, or some 50 million people, according to a study by Opinion Research Corp., which listed the top five Internet ''megabrands'' as America Online, Netscape, Yahoo!, Amazon.com, and Priceline.com.

Once a company's brand and its market share have been established, it will typically cut back on brand-building advertising expenditures. After studies showed that Egghead.com's brand was fairly well established, for example, the company slashed advertising and marketing expenditures by 65 percent year-to-year in the fourth quarter of 2000. Replacing online advertising at Egghead.com were telemarketing, direct marketing, and more marketing to the firm's customer base. As with so many of the dot-coms, it was difficult to say whether this strategy succeeded; by the second half of 2001 Egghead had filed for bankruptcy.

MORE THAN BRAND AWARENESS

Critics of large advertising expenditures for brand building point out that awareness is only one aspect of creating a strong brand. More significant to a brand's strength is the underlying business and how it relates to its customers. Brands simply cannot be invented overnight. A strong brand is the result of creating a promise to consumers—one that is clear and memorable—and then creating a history of fulfilling that promise. Once awareness is achieved, companies must focus their brand-building efforts on conveying what the company does rather than what it represents.

Before the dot-com shakeout of 2000, many dot-com brand managers mistakenly believed that brand awareness would of itself create enough momentum to lead to brand loyalty. As an example, the domain name Business.com was sold for $7.5 million, with the buyers reportedly believing that the name itself would constitute the bulk of the company's brand building. Other dot-coms, such as Computer.com, believed that an expensive one-shot Super Bowl ad would build its brand overnight. For the 2000 Super Bowl, some 17 dot-coms placed ads, compared to only three in 2001.

That thinking has been replaced by the realization that brand-building is a long-term process that needs to be established on a solid customer relationship based on service and community. The most successful online brands have created online communities; they include Yahoo!, America Online, and eBay.

AFFILIATE PROGRAMS AND CO-BRANDING

Start-up and relatively unknown online companies can use affiliate relationships to build awareness of their brand as well as to attract new customers. When barnesandnoble.com became the featured bookseller on America Online, its brand awareness rose significantly in the online community. In mid-1998 Ameritrade expanded its relationship with America Online by committing to pay $25 million over two years for a prominent spot on America Online's finance page, thereby strengthening its brand name among AOL's subscriber base. 1-800-Flowers.com, which has been in business for 24 years, told the *New York Times* that its partnership with AOL was its most productive; the company also had productive marketing agreements with MSN.com and Yahoo!.

Co-branding with an established brick-and-mortar company is another way that online retailers can gain the benefits of a strong brand. Virtual retailers without their own brand identity can co-brand with traditional merchants to gain credibility and trust and drive traffic to their Web sites. Flooz.com, for example, used its merchant partners—including Martha Stewart and Tower Records—in its advertising to help strengthen its brand name, build trust and confidence, and explain the benefits of its Web site.

MARKETING BRAND-NAME PRODUCTS ON THE INTERNET

The Internet has opened new possibilities for traditional advertisers of established brand-name products. The Web has given marketers new ways to communicate with their customers and to establish deeper relationships with them. General Mills, for example, brought Betty Crocker to the Web in 1997, well after competitors like Kraft, Nabisco, and Pillsbury had their Web sites up and running. General Mills entered into a multiyear alliance with America Online to produce online and offline marketing programs, including contests. The alliance with AOL enabled General Mills to reach a key audience segment: women at home with children. Another Web-based initiative for General Mills involved creating a Web site where consumers could create their own cereals. The company also planned to improve the Betty Crocker Web site by adding more interactivity and thus build stronger relationships with its customers.

Companies with strong brands are using the Web to acquire new customers. Consumer goods manufacturer Procter & Gamble created a new beauty products company, Reflect.com, to market on the Web. The concept behind Reflect.com, which launched in September 1999, was to provide customized beauty products for women, based on answers they provided to a list of questions. To be a successful brand, Reflect.com had to provide a good Web site experience for women and a high level of service. Emphasizing personalization and customization, Reflect.com soon distinguished itself from typical e-commerce sites that sold off-the-shelf beauty products.

STILL SEEKING THE FAST LANE

In spite of the lessons inherent in the dot-com shakeout, startup online companies still continued to seek instant brand recognition. One company, X10.com, went from being a relatively unknown seller of home networking and security devices, to a leader in Internet traffic. Following a massive pop-up advertising campaign, X10.com went from 8.4 million visitors in March 2001 to 28 million in May 2001. That put it in Jupiter Media Metrix's top five, ahead of such e-commerce giants as Amazon.com and eBay. Critics pointed out that most of X10.com's traffic was not voluntary; traffic counts were based on the number of people who viewed the pop-up browser window that featured the X10 ad, even if they closed it immediately. It remained to be seen if X10 could convert those visitors to customers and whether it could establish its brand by offering a sufficient level of service and community to its visitors.

FURTHER READING:

Berger, Warren. "After Ads That Shouted, Dot-Com Survivors Try Quieter, Cheaper Spots." *New York Times,* February 28, 2001.

Elliott, Stuart. "Betty Crocker: Can She Cook in Cyberspace?" *New York Times,* December 13, 2000.

Gilbert, Jennifer. "Running on Empty." *Advertising Age,* November 6, 2000.

Greenberg, Paul A. "Keep the Faith, Net Advertisers!" *E-Commerce Times,* January 15, 2001. Available from www.ecommercetimes.com.

Moon, Michael. *Firebrands!: Building Brand Loyalty in the Internet Age.* New York: McGraw-Hill Professional Book Group, 2000.

Pierce, Andrew, and Eric Almquist. "Brand Building May Face a Test." *Advertising Age,* April 9, 2001.

Regan, Keith. "What Makes a Good Online Brand Name?" *E-Commerce Times,* May 4, 2001. Available from www.ecommercetimes.com.

———. "The X10 Question: Traffic without Dollars?" *E-Commerce Times,* June 14, 2001. Available from www.ecommercetimes.com.

Strahler, Steven R. "Going to the Next Level." *Crain's Chicago Business,* September 18, 2000.

Sweeney, Terry. "Advertisers Seek More Bang for Their Web Bucks." *InformationWeek,* October 2, 2000.

"When E-Brands Fail: Building New Brand Value with Old Brand Tricks." *Chief Executive (U.S.),* May 2001.

SEE ALSO: Advertising, Online; Affiliate Model; Banner Ads; Marketing, Internet; Promoting the Web Site

BROADBAND TECHNOLOGY

Broadband technology refers to a high-speed, higher bandwidth connection to the Internet than is offered by a standard telephone line. The greater bandwidth of a broadband connection allows for more data to be transmitted at higher speeds than a conventional telephone line. While the definition of broadband data transmission rates vary, 144 Kbps (thousands of bits per second) represents a minimum broadband transmission rate, compared to 56 Kbps for a telephone modem. Unlike telephone line connections to the Internet, which typically involve dialing in to use the service, broadband connections are always on.

Broadband technology includes cable modem and digital subscriber line (DSL) connections to the Internet as well as a number of alternative technologies. DSL technology uses ordinary copper telephone lines to deliver a high-bandwidth connection to the Internet, with typical data transmission speeds ranging from 512 Kbps to 1.5 Mbps (millions of bits per second). However, DSL service requires a certain proximity to the DSL provider's central office, and DSL providers must set up many such offices to serve a large area. If a DSL subscriber was more than 20,000 feet from the central office of the DSL provider, then the service was typically unavailable.

Cable modems are the most popular broadband connection among consumers. To provide high-speed Internet access over cable lines, cable system operators have had to upgrade their systems and replace old one-way lines with lines that can handle two-way traffic. Alternative broadband technologies, mostly used by businesses, include leased lines, frame relay, fiber optics, asynchronous transfer mode (ATM), T1 and T3 lines, and integrated services digital network (ISDN). High-speed Internet access is also available through satellite services, although the number of subscribers remains small in comparison to cable modem and DSL subscribers.

According to a mid-2001 survey of consumer households from Kinetic Strategies, there were 7.6 million broadband subscribers in the United States and 1.7 million in Canada. Taken together, that represented 8.2 percent of all North American households. Among broadband subscribers, 70 percent or 6.4 million households connected to the Internet through a cable modem, while 2.9 million had DSL connections. In separate statistics, according to the Yankee Group, about 10 percent of U.S. households, or 5.4 million, had a broadband Internet connection at the end of 2000.

A mid-2001 report from Strategy Analytics predicted that by the end of 2001, 14.1 percent of all North American households would have a high-speed Internet connection. By 2005, the study predicted that 53 percent of North American households would have a broadband connection to the Internet. In Europe, by contrast, Strategy Analytics found that only 3.3 percent of all European households would have a high-speed Internet connection at the end of 2001. Within Europe, the rate of penetration varied significantly by country, with Sweden having the highest penetration at 9.4 percent, compared to the lowest rate in England of just 0.9 percent. Other countries surveyed included

- the Netherlands, with 6.1 percent of all households having a broadband connection

- Germany (4.8 percent)

- Spain (3.6 percent)

- France (2.0 percent)

- and Italy (1.1 percent).

The percentage of households having a broadband Internet connection in 2004 was projected to increase dramatically in European countries, led by

- Sweden with 37.3 percent

- the Netherlands (33.9 percent)

- Germany (27.4 percent)

- France (22.6 percent)

- Spain (21.9 percent)

- the United Kingdom (19.5 percent)

- and Italy (10.6 percent).

While broadband offers consumers many benefits, it appeared that its higher costs, relative to dial-up services, were hindering the rate of broadband adoption among consumers. In addition, there was no "killer application" to drive demand for broadband, particularly in the wake of Napster's demise as a free music-trading network. In other words, broadband to date offered no new abilities that dial-up users didn't already have, only the ability to do existing tasks faster and perhaps more reliably when large files were involved. Benefits such as being able to view streaming media better or download Web pages faster were often not enough to make consumers dissatisfied with a simple telephone line connection to the Internet. As of mid-2001, most U.S. broadband services to consumers were priced at more than $40 per month.

WHAT DO BROADBAND CONSUMERS WANT?

Studies indicate that speed is the primary motivation for having a broadband connection. As of mid-2001, broadband users tended to surf the Internet more and make more online purchases than narrowband users, but otherwise their usage patterns were the same. A secondary reason for having a broadband connection was that it freed up the telephone line, while a third factor was that the connection was always on.

There is conflicting data as to whether or not broadband users are interested in enhanced and premium services, and whether they are prepared to pay for them. In general, fairly large segments of online users have some interest in premium services, but only a minority say they are willing to pay extra for them. A mid-2001 broadband study by Strategy Analytics found that while 60 percent of all U.S. households with broadband connections expressed a "general interest" in value-added services offered only with a high-speed Internet connection, that percentage dropped to 25 percent if there was a $5 to $10 monthly fee involved. Furthermore, only 16 percent of all U.S. broadband households were interested in the services if additional hardware and/or software had to be leased or purchased.

A mid-2001 study by BroadJump provided additional details. Similar to the other research, the BroadJump study showed that anywhere from 50 percent to almost 70 percent of broadband users expressed a general interest in certain applications and services, including virus protection, firewalls, streaming audio, and Internet telephony. When it came to paying for these benefits, though, the number interested dropped considerably:

- virus protection (28 percent willing to pay)

- firewall (26 percent)

- Internet telephony (20 percent)

- software rental (19 percent)

- video on demand (19 percent)

- instant messaging (16 percent)

- streaming audio (15 percent)

- and online gaming (12 percent).

Conversion rates from ''general interest'' to ''willing to pay'' were highest for software rental (75 percent conversion rate), followed by video on demand (60 percent), video conferencing (45 percent), firewall (42 percent), virus protection (41 percent), and Internet telephony (40 percent). Although video on demand had a high conversion rate, the BroadJump study revealed that users would prefer to view the videos on TV rather than on their computer. From the study it appeared that premium entertainment content was less important to U.S. broadband users than utility services.

BROADBAND FOR BUSINESSES

Broadband connections offer several benefits to business enterprises. The benefits include time savings, an ''always on'' connection to the Internet, and freed up telephone lines. Broadband facilitates greater information flow and communication within the organization as well as with clients and suppliers. It also enables companies to use rich media, such as streaming video and audio, to communicate with employees, while video conferencing can save on travel expenses.

According to a mid-2001 study on Internet connectivity by Insight Research, only 11 percent of small and medium-sized business enterprises (SMEs) had broadband connectivity. While DSL offered businesses a cheap alternative to leased T1 and T3 lines and provided more dedicated bandwidth than ISDN, DSL's distance limitations excluded many companies that weren't within its reach. For many DSL providers, it was not economically viable to add the extra equipment to central offices located outside of major metropolitan areas, thus leaving many areas without an affordable broadband alternative.

Several forecasts indicated that businesses would adopt broadband connections much faster than consumers in the early 2000s. Insight Research predicted that some 50 percent of U.S. small and medium-size businesses would have a broadband connection by 2005, while a study of businesses of all sizes by Jupiter Media Metrix forecast that nearly 100 percent of U.S. businesses would have a broadband connection by 2005. Globally, the number of broadband business connections to the Internet was projected to grow from about 5 million lines in 2000 to more than 16 million lines in 2004, based on a study by Ovum. In North America, the number of businesses with broadband connections was projected to grow from just over 1 million in 2000 to nearly 4 million in 2004.

FURTHER READING:

Centeno, Cerelle. ''High-Speed Homes in North America.'' *eMarketer Newsletter,* June 5, 2001. Available from www.emarketer.com.

————. ''Living Without Broadband, and Happily So.'' *eMarketer Newsletter,* May 28, 2001. Available from www.emarketer.com.

————. ''No-Frills Broadband Junkies in North America.'' *eMarketer Newsletter,* June 13, 2001. Available from www.emarketer.com.

Henderson, Rick. ''Guide to the State of Broadband Service in Los Angeles.'' *Los Angeles Business Journal,* January 17, 2000.

Macklin, Ben. ''Broadband for Small Business.'' *eMarketer Newsletter,* June 12, 2001. Available from www.emarketer.com.

————. ''Give Broadband Users What They Want.'' *eMarketer Newsletter,* June 5, 2001. Available from www.emarketer.com.

SEE ALSO: Bandwidth Management; Connectivity, Internet

BROKERAGE MODEL

Whether a company sells products or services to consumers, other businesses, or both, there are many different ways to approach the marketplace and make a profit. Business models, of which the brokerage model is simply one, are used to describe how companies go about this process. They spell out the main ways in which companies make profits by identifying a company's role during commerce and describing how products, information, and other important elements are structured. Just as there are many different industries and types of companies, there are many different kinds of business models. While some are simple, others are very complex. Even within the same industry, companies may rely on business models that are very different from one another, and some companies may use a combination of several different models.

General business models by themselves do not necessarily map out a company's specific strategy for success. Strategic marketing plans, which are a specialized type of business model, are used for that purpose. They identify the specific situation a company finds itself in within a particular marketplace, the differentials that set a company apart from its competitors, the marketing tactics used to accomplish strategic objectives, and so on.

Business models involve different levels in what are known as supply/value chains. Value chains outline the activities involved in creating value from the supply side of economics—where raw materials are used to manufacture a product—to the demand side when finished products or components are marketed and shipped to re-sellers or end-users. Companies review and analyze different steps in value chains to create optimal and effective business models.

Some long-established business models used in the physical world have been adopted on the Internet with varying degrees of success. Among these are mail-order models, advertising models, free-trial models, subscription models, and direct marketing models. Other business models are native to the Internet and e-commerce and focus heavily on the movement of electronic information. These include digital delivery models, information barter models, and freeware models.

Every business model has its own inherent strengths and weaknesses. Just as is the case in the physical world, online business models vary in their suitability for different enterprises. Business models themselves are not enough to guarantee success in the physical or online worlds. As Jeffrey F. Rayport explains, ''Every e-commerce business is either viable or not viable. They hardly qualify for the paint-by-number prescriptions that business people seem to expect. Business models themselves do not offer solutions; rather, how each business is run determines its success. So the success of e-commerce businesses will hinge largely on the art of management even as it is enabled by the science of technology.''

THE BROKERAGE MODEL

One Internet business model is the brokerage model. At the heart of this model are third parties known as brokers, who bring sellers and buyers of products and services together to engage in transactions. Normally, the broker charges a fee to at least one party involved in a transaction. While many brokers are involved in connecting consumers with retailers, they also may connect businesses with other businesses or consumers with other consumers. A wide variety of different scenarios or business configurations fall under the banner of a brokerage model. These include everything from Web sites posting simple online classified ads and Internet shopping malls (Web sites that sell products from a variety of different companies) to online marketplaces, online auctions, aggregators, and shopping bots.

Some brokers simply focus on fulfillment between buyers and sellers. Travel agents like Travelocity.com are one example of this approach. According to the company, Travelocity.com was the third largest e-commerce site in the early 2000s. Along with a large database of information on different travel destinations, Travelocity.com was able to provide reserva-

tions ''for 95 percent of all airline seats sold, more than 49,000 hotels, more than 50 car rental companies and more than 5,000 vacation and cruise packages.''

Online marketplaces are example of brokers with a business-to-business focus. These entities bring large groups of commercial buyers and sellers together online. In the early 2000s, third-party companies like Commerce One Inc. and Ariba Inc. offered software and services that were used to operate different online marketplaces. Numerous other companies provided similar kinds of services and applications. Online marketplaces existed for many different industries, ranging from the food and beverage industries to consumer packaged goods and interior design. The costs for participating in an online marketplace varied. In some cases, participating companies (suppliers, purchasers, or both) were required to purchase special software from a third party. Third parties also levied different charges for making transactions, joining the network, updating catalogs of available products, and so on.

Aggregators are brokers that bring business owners or consumers together to get better rates on things like long-distance telephone service. The key concept is group purchasing, which enables individual businesses or consumers to get better rates than they could obtain on their own. In the early 2000s, a business-to-business aggregator called Demandline.com combined similar requests for core business services like retirement plans and Web site hosting from small business owners and used a reverse auction approach to obtain rates normally reserved for larger corporations. Demandline.com received small commissions from service providers and did not charge its customers (those bidding for services) any fees.

Metamediaries are another kind of broker. These entities, which include online shopping malls, not only bring interested parties together, they also provide different services related to the actual transaction, such as billing or order tracking. HotDispatch was one such broker. It provided services involving technical communities (groups of technical professionals with specific interests). These professionals used HotDispatch to market and purchase knowledge services, including bids for different technical projects, software, and even questions and answers. According to the company, members of this service were able to ''post a question or project and assign a dollar value for either the resolution of the question, or the compensation fees associated with the outsourced project. Once the question or project is posted, it is visible to members in all of the technical communities that subscribe to the service.''

Intelligent agents such as shopping bots are essentially software programs that operate unattended on the Internet. Consumers use them to search for product and pricing information on the Web. Each shopping bot operates differently, depending on the business model used by its operator. In one scenario, shopping bots direct users to retailers who, by subscribing for a fee, are part of a closed system. Shopping.Yahoo and Shop@AOL were examples of this model in the early 2000s. Open systems are a more common arrangement and involve agents that include the entire Web in their searches. Shopping bots were very popular with consumers in the 1990s and early 2000s. International Data Corp. revealed that about 4 million shoppers took advantage of the technology in October 2000 alone. However, shopping bots weren't popular with some companies because of their ability to initiate bidding wars and eat away profits in the process.

In addition to searching for durable goods, electronics, and other items, consumers also were expected to use bots more frequently in the area of personal finance. In *Bank Systems & Technology*, Andersen Consulting reported that personal financial bots (PFBs) would reshape this industry by becoming ''virtual financial intermediaries'' that carry out transactions and searches for financial products via ATMs, wireless phones, and televisions. While this concept had not been widely adopted in the early 2000s, it posed a possible threat to the umbrella model used by many traditional banks, in which several products and services—including loans, credit cards, and insurance—were offered to customers by one provider.

FURTHER READING:

''About Demandline.com.'' Demandline.com, Inc. April 27, 2001. Available from www.demandline.com.

Bambury, Paul. ''A Taxonomy of Internet Commerce.'' *First-Monday*. 1998. Available from www.firstmonday.

Baumohl, Bernard. ''Can You Really Trust Those Bots?'' *Time*. December 11, 2000.

Gove, Alex. ''Bot and Sold.'' *Red Herring Magazine*. August, 1999. Available from www.redherring.com.

McDowell, Dagen. ''Dear Dagen: Business Models Explained.'' *TheStreet.com*. September 13, 1999. Available from www.thestreet.com.

Pallmann, David. *Programming Bots, Spiders, and Intelligent Agents in Microsoft Visual C++*. Redmond, Washington: Microsoft Press. 1999.

Rappa, Michael. ''Business Models On The Web.'' April 9, 2001. Available from www.academic.uofs.edu.

Rayport, Jeffrey F. ''The Truth About Internet Business Models.'' *Strategy & Business*. Third Quarter, 1999. Available from www.strategy-business.com.

Schneider, Ivan. ''R2-D2 Meets 401(k).'' *Bank Systems & Technology*. November, 2000.

Schwartz, Ephraim. ''Web Bots Enhance Self-Service Experience.'' *InfoWorld*. February 7, 2000.

Timmers, Paul. ''Business Models for Electronic Markets.'' *Electronic Markets*. April, 1998. Available from www.electronicmarkets.org.

Van Winkle, William. ''Strength in Numbers.'' *Home Office Computing*. September, 2000.

SEE ALSO: Aggregators

BUFFETT, WARREN

An extremely high-profile investor with rare job qualifications in the late 1990s—expansive patience and discomfort with technology, despite his close friendship with Microsoft mogul Bill Gates—Warren Buffett's investment success in the final decades of the 20th century knew no peer or rival. Worth about $30 billion, Buffett is one of the world's richest men, second in the United States only to Gates, and one of the very few of his class to attain such fortune solely on the strength of stock investments. The chairman of Omaha, Nebraska-based Berkshire Hathaway, Buffett has been known to refer to his annual stockholders' meeting as a ''Woodstock weekend for capitalists.'' Accordingly, the event draws investors from around the world who flock to hear his sermon. Buffett's awe-inspiring success and cult-like status spawned a potpourri of investment-related Web sites, magazine stories, and books, many offering advice on how to ''invest like Warren Buffett.'' The fawning, sometimes almost worshipful attitude of some of Buffett's followers earned him the affectionate nickname, the ''Sage of Omaha.''

A standard story within the investment world perhaps best illustrates the reasoning behind the Buffett legend: if one invested just $10,000 into Berkshire Hathaway in 1965, when Buffett first assumed control, by the end of the century one would have turned that initial investment into $50 million. By way of comparison, if the same investor had sunk that $10,000 into the Standard & Poor's 500 stock index in 1965, by the end of 1999 it would have been worth less than $500,000. Thus it's easy to see why so much of the investment world strains to hear every word and scrutinize every move of Warren Buffett.

Equally famous as his astronomical investment success was his notorious sourness toward the new economy and dot-com mania. Buffett and his legions of followers are well known for eschewing the trendy and faddish in stock investment. Buffett in large part built his reputation by attracting like-minded investors, who were in it for the long term rather than for quick speculative profits. His method ignores macroeconomic trends and Wall-Street tips and wisdom, focusing instead on companies that boast significant market share and growth potential, but with low earnings and depressed valuation. In short, he looks for solid, strong companies that will put together sound earnings over the long term. The naysayers who view this strategy as quaint, or as a fossil of a bygone age in an era of tip- and rumor-based day trading, more often than not end up coming to see his moves as conventional market wisdom.

While his favored established firms' stocks tumbled in the late 1990s, the dot-com mania swept the markets, producing a surge of new investment hotshots and poking holes in the aura of mystique that surrounded the Buffett legend. By 2000, however, dot-coms were in trouble, and once gain Buffett came out ahead of the pack. The question of whether or when the Internet players will build themselves into the kind of companies that Buffett, or the thousands upon thousands of would-be Buffetts, would choose as their investment vehicles remains to be seen.

THE SAGE'S STORY

Born in Omaha in 1933, Warren Edward Buffett showed a very early affinity for remembering and calculating numbers. According to a profile in the online magazine *Salon,* the young Buffett was marking the board at his father's brokerage and purchasing his first stock at age 11. Within three years, Buffett used his paper route savings to dive into real estate, purchasing 40 acres of farmland and leasing it to a tenant farmer.

He came across the highly regarded investment tome *The Intelligent Investor,* by Benjamin Graham, as a senior at the University of Nebraska, and was strongly influenced by the investment principles therein. Graham was a famous skeptic of Wall Street trends, encouraging so-called value investors to seek out "cigar butts"—those firms that Wall Street had all but abandoned but which could still be lit up for a few good puffs of stock activity. Buffett's first investment success came in 1951, when he threw $10,282 into the auto insurance firm Geico. Just a year later, he pulled out for $15,259. In 1952, the 21-year-old Buffett began offering his own classes on investing, selling his course via an advertisement in a local Omaha newspaper.

After a few years working and studying with Graham, Buffett began to feel constrained by the former's strict rules of value investment. Instead of picking up nearly lifeless companies cheaply, Buffett began to experiment with buying stocks of still vigorous but undervalued companies. In 1956 Buffett began an investment partnership on the seed money provided by himself, his sister, his neighbor, and his lawyer. The following year, a local couple who had attended his class invested $100,000 into the partnership. Buffett's earliest believers, known as the Berkshire Bunch, amassed enormous fortunes over the years by putting money behind the young investment guru's ideas. In Omaha alone, according to *Forbes,* more than 30 families accumulated at least $100 million in Berkshire Hathaway stock.

In 1962, Buffett began purchasing shares of Berkshire Hathaway, a struggling textile manufacturer in New Bedford, Massachusetts. Three years later he controlled the entire company. Berkshire's book value per share registered nearly 25 percent compound annual gains through the rest of the century, according to Credit Suisse First Boston Corp. By the end of the 1960s, finding good bargains few and far between, Buffett dissolved the investment partnership, returning his investors' money. From this point, he concentrated on Berkshire, which at first functioned primarily as a textile company with a small investment operation. Before long, however, investments were Berkshire's bread and butter and Buffett returned to his practice of picking up depressed companies. There were many such firms by the early and mid-1970s, after the 1960s stock rally gave out and inflation set in, making cheap stocks plentiful.

Buffett's bold moves and foresight helped him weather the tough economic climate of the late 1970s, and despite the tremendous market crash in 1987, Berkshire finished that year in much better shape than the year before. His head-scratching investments in companies such as Coca-Cola proved ingenious, with their brand-name recognition and untapped international potential. By 1993, Berkshire's $8.3 billion placed it at the very top of the *Forbes* 100 list.

Once viewed basically as an investment fund, acquisitions of insurance firms, such as Geico and General Reinsurance, through the 1990s transformed Berkshire Hathaway primarily into an insurance company in which the investment portfolio happened to be managed by one of the world's most famous investors. By the end of the 1990s, insurance accounted for more than 70 percent of Berkshire's revenues. Buffett came to believe that his company's greatest strength lay in purchasing companies outright rather than simply picking established stocks at the right stages of their valuations.

Buffett's attraction to the insurance industry was fairly logical. Since policyholders pay their premiums up front, while the firms pay out claims later, the company can be used as a strong investment catalyst. With a constant stream of revenue coming in, the insurers have a gap of time in which they have a good deal of money to invest before the claims are actually paid. This was Berkshire's strength, using the premium money to invest in Buffett's favored brands of undervalued stock.

His methods of investing and strategizing were extremely out of fashion and against the grain in the dot-com explosion of the late 1990s. The year 1999 saw Buffett's first down year in a decade, with Berkshire's per-share book value under-performing the S&P 500 index for the first time in 20 years. At the time, the judgmental pronounced his insistence on investing in firmly established, proven businesses out of date for the much-heralded, dot-com-heavy new economy. In 2000, however, Buffett appeared to have the last laugh, as reality weighed down the dot-com mania and the high-tech stock bubble burst. Buffett's portfolio, meanwhile, bounced back as investors ran to established companies, and once again pundits and analysts were praising the far-sighted wisdom of Buffett.

Buffett is a committed stickler for rigorous balance-sheet scrutiny, teasing out the elements that will produce long-term profitability. While he eyes technology stocks with a degree of skepticism, Internet stocks, at least as of the early 2000s, were almost completely off the menu for Buffett. Given his commitment to balance sheets and sound predictability, it's not difficult to ascertain why. Buffett refuses to throw money into a company unless he actually can visualize the company's numbers a decade or so down the road. With regards to the Internet, Buffett admits his vision is extremely cloudy at best.

FURTHER READING:

Atlas, Riva. "Warren Buffetted." *Institutional Investor.* January, 2000.

Bary, Andrew. "What's Wrong, Warren?" *Barron's.* December 27, 1999.

"For the Buffett Faithful, Time Paid Off." *Forbes.* October 12, 1998.

Kadleck, Daniel. "Berkshire's Buffett-ing." *Time.* October 25, 1999.

Kanter, Larry. "Salon Brilliant Careers: Warren Buffett." *Salon.com.* August 31, 1999. Available from www.salon.com/people.

Kover, Amy. "Warren Buffett: Revivalist." *Fortune.* May 29, 2000.

Lenzer, Robert. "The Berkshire Bunch." *Forbes.* October 12, 1998.

SEE ALSO: Gates, William (Bill); Volatility

BUNDLING

Bundling is the process of combining multiple products or services and selling them as a single package. Most major telecommunications and computer technology firms bundle at least some of their products and services. In some cases, both products and services are bundled together. For example, Internet service providers sometimes offer personal computers free to customers who are willing to sign up for two or more years of service. E-commerce site builders bundle page design software and online traffic monitoring tools with e-marketing services. Online content providers like the *Wall Street Journal Online* offer subscriptions that not only include access to an online version of a publication, but also accounts with other online publications, the ability to retrieve archived articles, real-time stock quotes, stock tracking services, and more.

For years, personal computer manufacturers have sold their machines with several software programs already loaded onto the hard drive, and leading word processing programs like Microsoft Word and WordPerfect have come bundled with spreadsheet, database, and presentation software. The Telecommunications Act of 1996 deregulated the communications industry in the United States, allowing broadcasting, cable, wireless, and telephone industries to compete in one another's markets for the first time and opening up a host of new bundling opportunities. Cable television companies began bundling their traditional cable service with Internet access, as did telephone companies. For example, using digital subscriber line (DSL) technology, which offers a much faster connection speed than traditional modems, in late 2000 Sprint began offering a bundle of local and long-distance telephone services that also included five e-mail addresses, a data line, and six megabytes of Web space.

A particularly noteworthy example of bundling is Microsoft's inclusion of its Internet Explorer browser with its Windows 95 operating system in the mid-1990s. The move allowed the firm to compete with browser rival Netscape, but some critics believe it worked a bit too well. It resulted in an antitrust investigation conducted by the U.S. Department of Justice that eventually made its way to court. A judge ruled that Microsoft must offer a version of Windows 95 unbundled from Internet Explorer, although that verdict was later overturned on appeal. The litigation sparked by the bundling continued, however, until 2000 when Microsoft was found guilty of monopolistic practices and ordered to split into two companies, a ruling that also was appealed.

FURTHER READING:

Arnst, Catherine. "The Coming Telescramble: Deregulation is Launching a $1 Trillion Digital Free-for-All." *Business Week.* April 8, 1996.

Buckman, Rebecca. "Looking Through Microsoft's Window." *The Wall Street Journal.* May 1, 2000.

Dix, John. "The Future is Bundles, Even for DSL." *Network World*. October 23, 2000.

Hamilton, David P. "With Free PCs, You Get What You Pay For." *The Wall Street Journal*. April 4, 1999.

Schwartz, Evan I. "Turning Surfers Into Subscribers." *Mediaweek*. October 30, 2000.

SEE ALSO: Microsoft Corp.

BUSINESS-TO-BUSINESS (B2B) E-COMMERCE

Internet-based business-to-business (B2B) e-commerce is conducted through industry-sponsored marketplaces and through private exchanges set up by large companies for their suppliers and customers. Of course, companies also sell to business customers through their own Web sites.

In the early 2000s, industry-sponsored marketplaces (ISMs) accounted for only a small percentage of B2B transactions. The main reason, according a survey of 25 ISMs published in the industry periodical *B to B*, is that ISMs have had problems convincing buyers and sellers to use them. For one thing, companies are reluctant to acquire customized designs through marketplaces because they don't want to reveal proprietary information on an site that is shared by competitors. These companies fear they will give away too much information about their competitive strategies simply by taking part in such a marketplace. ISMs also do not necessarily level the playing field for small companies against larger competitors. As a result, companies use such marketplaces mainly to purchase commodity goods, manage their supply chains, and conduct indirect procurement transactions not related to their core business.

Business-to-business (B2B) e-commerce is significantly different from business-to-consumer (B2C) e-commerce. While B2C merchants sell on a first-come, first-served basis, most B2B commerce is done through negotiated contracts that allow the seller to anticipate and plan for how much the buyer will purchase. In some cases B2B is not so much a matter of generating revenue as it is a matter of making connections with business partners.

B2B E-COMMERCE QUANTIFIED

A March 2001 study by the Gartner Group reported that $433 billion was spent worldwide on B2B e-commerce in 2000, reflecting a 189 percent increase over the $145 billion spent online in 1999. The study noted that online B2B marketplaces accounted for only a small percentage of B2B Internet commerce in 2000. Looking ahead, Gartner predicted that B2B e-commerce would reach $919 billion in 2001 and $1.9 trillion in 2002, estimates that took into account the general economic downturn that was taking place.

A U.S. Census Bureau survey of U.S. manufacturers found that, for all of 1999, the most frequently used electronic networks for accepting orders were electronic data interchange (EDI), which more than half of the manufacturers used, and the Internet, which about one-third of the manufactures used to accept orders. However, the value of EDI-based orders accounted for 67 percent of electronic sales in 1999, while the value of Internet-based orders only accounted for 5 percent. The findings reflect the fact that manufacturers have been conducting business electronically using EDI systems for several years.

In terms of procurement, the same survey, conducted in June 2000, revealed that the Internet was used most frequently to make electronic purchases. Still, the value of EDI-based purchases accounted for 65 percent of electronic purchases, and the Internet only 14 percent. Overall, e-commerce activity accounted for 12 percent of all sales among U.S. manufacturers in 1999.

B2B is far and away the largest sector of e-commerce. Comparing B2B with B2C e-commerce, the U.S. Department of Commerce reported that B2B online sales accounted for 90 percent of all online transactions during 1999. Still, the study noted that less than one percent of all U.S. transactions in 1999 were conducted over the Internet. It attributed the high percentage of B2B e-commerce sales to the long-standing use of proprietary networks, such as EDI, in the B2B sector. The manufacturing industry was the leader in e-commerce, with $485 billion or 12 percent of its total shipments resulting from electronic sales. Merchant wholesalers were second, with $134 billion in electronic sales, or 5 percent of their total sales. Drugs and pharmaceuticals accounted for 75 percent of all e-commerce merchant wholesale deals.

B2B e-commerce requires a significant investment in infrastructure. ActivMedia Research predicted in May 2001 that sales of B2B software would reach $10 billion by 2004, as B2B Web sites invested heavily in marketing, infrastructure, and e-procurement. The research firm also noted that the percentage of B2B Web sites that had been in business for less than a year grew from 32 percent in 2000 to 38 percent in the first part of 2001, a finding that suggested that more new initiatives were being launched despite the relatively austere conditions facing many Internet businesses. Separately, an April 2001 study by Jupiter Media Metrix predicted that spending on infrastructure technology for private B2B trading networks would grow from $230 million in 2000 to $37 billion in 2005. Through 2003 the study projected that spending on private networks would grow 300 percent a year, compared to 95 percent a year for public networks.

B2B E-COMMERCE IN EARLY ADOPTER STAGE

Although companies have been doing business electronically for many years using proprietary EDI systems, B2B commerce over the Internet remained in the early adopter stage at the start of the 2000s. The notion of an early adopter comes from a popular marketing theory which holds that buyers of a new product enter the market in several stages, starting with the early adopters who set the trends and ending with so-called laggards who purchase only after the vast majority has already bought. If B2B is still attracting mainly the early crowd, it suggests great potential for growth, as do the figures from the Census Bureau and private firms. However, another part of the theory suggests there is a gap, sometimes called a chasm, that must be bridged between the early adopters and the early majority buyers; many products are believed to fail after doing well among early buyers but failing to catch on in the wider market. Whether B2B Internet commerce crosses the chasm remains to be seen.

The economic slowdown that began in 2000 was expected to dampen the development of B2B e-commerce and decelerate the migration from proprietary EDI systems to the Internet. All this came on top of the reality that corporate decision-makers were slow to adopt the benefits of B2B e-commerce, even though the technology was available. Some believe part of the problem has been that adopting B2B e-commerce could be challenging to the existing corporate culture. Additional barriers, ranging from a shortage of technology resources to competitive strategies, are discussed below.

Often a prerequisite to certain types of B2B e-commerce is compatibility between a company's computer systems and the online exchanges or marketplaces where it seeks to conduct e-commerce. A survey by Computer Sciences Corp. found that in late 2000, less than 15 percent of North American businesses' Web sites had the ability to conduct business online. Other estimates of enterprises able to transact business online ranged up to 20 percent.

There are several reasons why businesses have remained on the sidelines of e-commerce. Small and mid-size suppliers appear to be waiting to see what kind of e-commerce initiatives their larger trading partners will undertake. Suppliers are faced with a choice of building their own Web site, selling over a public exchange, or joining the private exchanges of multiple trading partners. They may feel there is not enough demand from their customers to sell online. Also, many businesses do not have the internal information technology (IT) resources to enter into e-commerce. E-commerce operations typically require significant deployment costs and integration work, much more than simply offering a hosted Web site.

Surveys have suggested that first-generation B2B e-commerce Web sites were difficult for customers to use. Problems included too many Web pages to click through, distracting and unhelpful content, difficulty signing up for online service, and difficulty researching products. Next-generation B2B Web sites are expected to be more customer-friendly. They will incorporate such elements as personalization software that will reduce the number of click-throughs required. Other features will facilitate customer self-service, letting them check such things as inventory status on potential orders and track order shipping. Next-generation sites will reflect customer service as business's top priority, with companies leveraging the Internet to better serve their customers.

A May 2001 study by Jupiter Media Metrix also noted the slow adoption among businesses of online marketplaces. Since it is expensive for suppliers to move online, there must be more of an incentive than to simply meet the few buyers already online. Suppliers were urged to research and study the top buyers, implement buyer training programs, move existing buyers online, and attract new business through the exchange. Critics have pointed out that the slow growth of online B2B marketplaces is due in part to a heavy reliance on generating transactions. As part of its study of online B2B marketplaces, Jupiter Media Metrix recommended focusing on strengthening the quality of buyer-seller relationships, with new efficiencies to follow.

The Jupiter Media Metrix study also suggested that suppliers would be in a better position to become ''preferred vendors'' if they offered more value-added services online, including collaborative product design and supply chain inventory. Buyers wanted suppliers to provide services that would help simplify routine contact.

In May 2001 Accenture, a large consulting firm, released a study of B2B buyers that categorized them into five types:

1) Traditionalists (28 percent), who were principally brand sensitive but also valued customer service and good prices

2) eService Seekers (23 percent), for whom customer service was the most important

3) Price Sensitives (21 percent), for whom value lay in the price

4) eSkeptics (17 percent), who valued brand above all

5) and eVanguard (17 percent), who were comparison buyers.

The study aimed to help sellers understand online B2B buyers and help them market to companies that were or could be potentially involved in online buying.

In April 2001 *InfoWorld* reported that ''fizzling interest in public [B2B] exchanges, coupled with the general slowdown, is forcing e-business vendors to refocus their development energies.'' The IT periodical noted that B2B technology vendors were shifting their focus away from building public supplier marketplaces to integration technologies and getting suppliers' content online. While some businesses began to question the value of public B2B marketplaces, claiming they would lose their competitive advantage by participating in a public exchange, private exchanges and highly focused public exchanges were being developed. One example of a specialty public exchange was eScout.com, which worked with regional banks to help small businesses make online purchases. Trade Matrix Network was a series of private exchanges that focused on vertical industries and offered a range of services, including financial settlement, collaboration, catalog management, and fulfillment and logistics.

Analysts highlight several key factors for private and public exchanges to survive and achieve success. For private exchanges, they include focusing on direct procurement, serving specialty markets, and offering extra services. Keys for public exchanges include focusing on specific business needs, providing economies of scale, providing scalable technology, and building a community.

CUSTOMER SERVICE

Poor customer service has a negative effect on B2B e-commerce, according to a May 2001 study by Jupiter Media Metrix. In terms of responding to e-mail inquiries, the study found that only 41 percent of B2B companies responded to customer e-mails within six hours, and only half of those responses were deemed satisfactory. Approximately 64 percent answered e-mail inquiries within 24 hours, and 29 percent said they never responded. As a result, there was a lack of confidence in e-mail as a customer service channel.

B2B Web sites also need to make it easier for potential customers to find what they want quickly. Remarkably, Jupiter Media Metrix found that only two percent of B2B Web sites had search engines. Most employed static ''frequently asked questions'' links, which were often cumbersome to use. The research also showed that 70 percent of Web users would not return to a site if they could not find the information they were looking for.

PUBLIC MARKETPLACES AND PRIVATE EXCHANGES

Industry sponsored marketplaces (ISMs) and consortia-led exchanges were only beginning to roll out their technologies in mid-2001 for their potential users to evaluate. Covisint, an e-marketplace backed by the major auto makers General Motors, Ford Motor Co., and DaimlerChrysler, was first announced in February 2000. As of mid-2001, the online auto marketplace still was not fully operational, illustrating the difficulties of integrating supply chains online.

The retail industry is served by several trading exchanges, including GlobalNetXchange (GNX), Worldwide Retail Exchange (WWRE), and Transora. WWRE was formed in early 2000 by a group of retailers including the Gap, Target, Walgreen, Best Buy, and Albertson's, among others. To help ensure the cooperation of companies that were competitors, the exchange set up collaborative teams with representatives from different retailers.

GNX was also formed in early 2000. Its founding companies included Sears, Roebuck & Co., Carrefour, and Oracle. While GNX's equity partners promised a purchase volume of $260 billion through the exchange, a year after GNX was founded only 5 percent of that amount had been used. In 2001 GNX was close to offering member retailers collaborative planning, forecasting, and replenishment (CPFR) services.

Transora is a consortia-led exchange serving packaged goods manufacturers and the retail industry. It began with 57 original investors, including companies such as Coca-Cola and Procter & Gamble. As of 2001 it was putting together a services package for potential users to consider. Among the components offered by Transora were online catalogs, auctions, and procurement. It also offered a collaborative planning, forecasting, and replenishment (CPFR) solution, which enabled retailers and consumer product manufacturers to share information. Transora's objective was to sign up large manufacturers, selected primarily from its group of original investors. The next step after that would be to present packaged subscription offerings to retailers. As more retailers completed their own internal integration, they would gain experience running some of their e-commerce activity through consortia-led systems.

In February 2001 Transora and GNX announced plans to form a megahub that would allow companies to collaborate with multiple trading partners through a single exchange. The site planned to operate as a transmissions application provider, translating EDI into versions of the platform-independent Extensible Markup Language (XML), thus facilitating the migration from proprietary EDI systems to Internet-based commerce and furthering collaboration among trading partners.

One exchange serving the consumer electronics industry is e2open, which was established in 2000 by IBM, Lucent Technologies, and other international computer manufacturers. The marketplace is for computer, electronics, and telecommunications companies to buy and sell goods and services. The exchange also provides the participating companies with an opportunity for collaboration on product design and supply chain visibility.

Exostar is an Internet-based marketplace that serves the aerospace and defense community. Founding companies were BAE Systems, Boeing, Lockheed Martin, Raytheon, and Rolls-Royce. The participation of major manufacturers has attracted thousands of suppliers to register with the exchange. As of mid-2001 Exostar was planning to offer a range of products and services. Its long-term goal was to provide a measure of standardization to e-commerce in the aerospace industry.

Private exchanges are created by companies for their suppliers. They may be set up with multiple tiers: e.g., first-tier suppliers, second-tier suppliers, etc. All first-tier suppliers might be expected to join the exchange or risk losing business. The cost of building a private trading exchange platform could cost a Fortune 500 company anywhere from $50 million to $100 million, according to AMR Research. The estimated cost would include not just a supply chain hub, but also all of the external enterprise systems that would link a very large company to its supply chain partners, its customers, and other key trading partners.

Another technology firm, Idapta, estimated that it would cost from $5 million to $125 million to build an industry-wide exchange, depending on the complexity of the products to be traded. Other expenditures to consider include integration costs, which Jupiter Media Metrix projected could cost a consortia-led trading exchange from $50 million to $100 million. Forrester Research estimated that individual companies could spend between $5.4 million and $22.9 million to integrate with online exchanges.

Large companies typically look to exchanges for procurement. Sales efforts that are conducted through their own Web sites can be directed at customers or to distributors and dealers. Thus, while Ford Motor Co. participates in Covisint for procurement, it has established FordDirect.com to provide an extranet for its dealers and distributors. Boeing Company has run its online procurement and supply chain management activities through Exostar. For its customers, Boeing established MyBoeingFleet.com, which allows airplane owners and maintenance workers to purchase replacement parts online and provides them with extensive information about Boeing's products.

Typically, large companies will sell through multiple online channels. Office-supply retailer Staples, for example, operated three different portals for its business customers.

On the procurement side, some organizations are using reverse auctions to let buyers, contractors, and service providers bid down prices. Benefits include reducing the bidding process from several months to a matter of days, being able to reach a broader audience of suppliers, and enabling sellers to tailor their bids to the bidding process. In a reverse auction, the buyer requesting services or goods sets an initial price. Matching engines and marketplaces can be used to make the reverse auction known to a wider audience. Unlike a sealed bid process, a reverse auction keeps the industry posted of the prices while the bidding is in progress. This enables suppliers to submit additional bids at lower prices and tailor their bids to the bidding process. In this situation, suppliers need to know the lowest they could possibly go on a particular deal and still make money. Small companies can utilize reverse auctions to learn about the negotiation process and see a much larger array of suppliers. In some cases reverse auctions can become a reverse pricing tool that helps companies determine their own pricing as well as that of their competitors. Software company Egghead.com, for example, provides instant responses for larger-quantity product requests by using NexTag's pricing engine in its online Volume Pricing Center.

BuyUSA is a marketplace launched in 2001 by the U.S. Department of Commerce to help primarily small and mid-size U.S. businesses find international buyers and distributors for their products. The site allows businesses outside the United States to view product catalogs and obtain background information on U.S. companies. Other privately run e-marketplaces designed to facilitate international trade include GlobalSources.com and VLINX.com.

Recognizing that 28 million small U.S. businesses represent a lucrative market, Internet portals serving consumers have added B2B features. Yahoo! Small Business debuted in August 1998 and provides content, services, and commerce opportunities. In March 2000 the portal launched Yahoo! Business to Business Marketplace, which allows businesses to search for products and services across industries. In January 2001 it created three Yahoo! Industry Marketplaces for IT hardware, IT software, and electronics. AOL Time Warner went after the small business market through its subsidiary Netscape, which introduced its small business portal Netbusiness in September 2000. Microsoft's entry was bCentral, a small business portal that was launched in October 1999 and has since grown to offer a range of technologies and services.

B2B E-COMMERCE OUTLOOK

Internet-based B2B e-commerce remained in the early adopter stage as of mid-2001. Public marketplaces continue to evolve and find new ways to appeal to corporate sales directors and purchasing agents. They are adding services that would enable suppliers and buyers to collaborate more closely on product development, inventory control, and other areas. To survive and prosper they need to overcome the limited functionality associated with earlier versions and make it easier for suppliers to integrate their computer systems to work with the marketplace. As more large companies develop private exchanges for their supply chains, many suppliers will be forced to invest in their own IT infrastructure and develop the capability to conduct business online.

FURTHER READING:

Butler, Steve. ''Charting the Course for eBusiness.'' *E-Commerce Times,* June 29, 2001. Available from www.ecommercetimes.com.

Centeno, Cerelle. ''Marketing B2B: Back-to-Basics.'' *E-Commerce Times,* May 11, 2001. Available from www.ecommercetimes.com.

Enos, Lori. ''The Biggest Myths about B2B.'' *E-Commerce Times,* June 22 and 25, 2001. Available from www.ecommercetimes.com.

Grygo, Eugene, et al. ''B-to-B Players Retrench.'' *InfoWorld,* April 9, 2001.

Mahoney, Michael. ''Dell B2B Marketplace Unplugged.'' *E-Commerce Times,* February 7, 2001. Available from www.ecommercetimes.com.

Ott, Karalynn. ''Special Report: Consumer Portals Step up B-to-B Features.'' *B to B,* April 2, 2001.

Regan, Keith. ''Boring Old B2B Steals E-Tail's Thunder.'' *E-Commerce Times,* March 9, 2001. Available from www.ecommercetimes.com.

———. ''Study: Customer Service Lapses Hurt B2B.'' *E-Commerce Times,* May 16, 2001. Available from www.ecommercetimes.com.

''Retail Exchanges Have Only Tapped Tip of the Iceberg.'' *DSN Retailing Today,* June 18, 2001.

Saliba, Clare. ''Study: B2B Exchanges Need to Supply More Services.'' *E-Commerce Times,* May 24, 2001. Available from www.ecommercetimes.com.

Sanborn, Stephanie. ''Reverse Auctions Make a Bid for Business.'' *InfoWorld,* March 19, 2001.

Tedeschi, Bob. ''Why Purchasing Agents Turned out to Be Hard to Herd.'' *New York Times,* February 28, 2001.

SEE ALSO: Business-to-Consumer (B2C) E-Commerce; Covisint; Electronic Data Interchange (EDI); Vortals

---

BUSINESS-TO-CONSUMER (B2C) E-COMMERCE

Business-to-consumer (B2C) e-commerce has woven itself into the fabric of business and consumer relations. Major strategic alliances have been formed among e-commerce giants. Television advertisements for e-commerce Web sites are plentiful, and consumers and the business community generally seem to accept that B2C e-commerce is here to stay.

Even as the United States weathered a general economic slowdown in the early 2000s, online spending continued to grow, with consumers spending more on average with each online purchase. Meanwhile, stocks of leading e-tailers began to level off after losing much of their value in 2000. There was a general sense that the worst was over, and certainly long-term prospects looked good for B2C e-commerce.

GROWTH AND GROWING PAINS

Swift growth has been perhaps the most celebrated feature of e-commerce. According to the U.S. Census Bureau, online shopping grew from $7.7 billion in 1998 to $17.3 billion in 1999 to $28 billion in 2000. Those figures are lower than other estimates of online consumer spending because the Census Bureau typically does not include online travel services, financial brokers or dealers, or ticket sales agencies in its totals.

The 1998 holiday season represented the first ''e-tail Christmas'' for U.S. consumers. Online consumers spent an estimated $4 billion during the fourth quarter of 1998 for goods and services, including travel, and nearly $10 billion for the year, according to the Boston Consulting Group. For the first time, online retailer Amazon.com surpassed $1 billion in annual sales as a result of the 1998 holiday shopping season. Internet portal America Online generated $1.2 billion in sales in the 10-week holiday season alone.

The next year marked an even greater success for online retailers, with big gains over the previous year. Jupiter Communications (now Jupiter Media Metrix) estimated total holiday Internet sales at $7 billion, while PC Data Online reported online holiday sales of $5 billion. Other estimates of 1999 holiday sales online varied from $8 billion to $13 billion, but all agreed that the 1999 holidays posted a large gain over the 1998 holiday shopping season.

One of the biggest problems online shoppers have faced, particularly during a holiday rush, is late delivery of merchandise. In December 1999 the U.S. Federal Trade Commission (FTC) received numerous complaints about prominent e-tailers failing to deliver merchandise by promised delivery dates. As a result, seven top e-tailers, including Macys.com, Toys-rus.com, and CDNow, were fined a total of $1.5 million. The FTC found that those e-tailers violated the agency's mail-and-telephone order rule that required an order to be shipped within 30 days. If delivery could not be made on time, the customer should've been told and given the option of agreeing to a new shipping date or canceling the order. In 2000 the FTC issued a delivery warning to more than 100 e-tailers reminding them of their obligation regarding shipment dates, consumer notification, and refunds.

A holiday season field-test of e-tailers conducted by Resource Marketing of Columbus, Ohio, reported in *Fortune* magazine, found it was easy to find and order products, but the service component was flawed. The company noted that shoppers could not even place an order 25 percent of the time; 20 percent of the packages arrived late or never; and 36 percent of the sites had busy or unhelpful customer service phone numbers. Another study released by Datamonitor estimated that poor customer service cost e-tailers $11 billion in lost sales during 2000, including incomplete purchases that could have been salvaged if better service were provided.

FALLING STOCKS, FULFILLMENT FOIBLES

During 2000 the stock prices of many top online retailers fell dramatically as the stock markets in general, and technology firms in particular, suffered a broad and protracted sell-off amid investor concerns about future growth and general economic conditions. The E-Commerce Times Stock Index fell 82 percent from the end of 1999 through the end of 2000. The year 2000, as a result, was also the year of the dot-com shakeout, with many e-tailers going out of business. An estimated 150 dot-coms folded during the year, including Boo.com, Toysmart.com, Petstore.com, Living.com, Pop.com, WebHouse Club, Eve.com, Pets.com, MotherNature.com, and Garden.com. While the downturn was devastating for many of the companies involved, not to mention their long-term shareholders, lower stock prices made it easier for large offline companies to acquire online retailers during 2000. German media conglomerate Bertelsmann AG, for example, acquired the struggling online retailer CDNow.

B2C e-commerce was also tarnished in 2000 by a rash of denial-of-service attacks on prominent Web sites and service outages caused by high levels of customer traffic. The attacks, believed to be orchestrated by individual hackers, forced well-known consumer destinations like Amazon.com offline for hours at a time and caused them to lose sales due to the downtime. Out-of-stock merchandise and late shipping continued to be problematic and, in e-commerce jargon, signaled a problem of scalability for some e-tailers who couldn't handle peak volume. In fact, some believed the biggest challenge to B2C e-commerce was order fulfillment, as consumers grew frustrated with out-of-stock merchandise, high shipping costs, and late deliveries of products ordered over the Web. For e-tailers, meanwhile, high shipping and fulfillment costs often resulted in negative operating margins. Successful B2C firms were those that focused on operational excellence and pleasing customers. Many in the business believed fulfillment was handled most economically by outsourcing it, not by attempting to fulfill orders in-house.

UNDERLYING STRENGTH

Despite difficulties, during 2000 online shopping continued to rise. Growth was attributed to new shoppers as well as to more spending by established customers. During the year online retailing received greater support from offline retailers who wanted to add new distribution channels and shore up their revenues. Strong ties to established brands in 2000 helped the growth of "bricks and clicks," further integrating traditional retailing with online channels.

In 2000 approximately 64 million Internet users participated in some form of online shopping-related activity, and 24 million households purchased at least one item online, according to a report from eMarketer. According to the U.S. Census Bureau, the third quarter of 2000 saw a 15.3 percent increase in online sales over the previous quarter. Total Internet sales reached $6.37 billion in the quarter, but online purchases made up only 0.78 percent of all retail sales, up from 0.68 percent in the second quarter. The categories of online retailers with the strongest growth in the quarter were mail-order firms, automobile companies, and online bookstores. Mail-order companies and traditional retailers showed faster growth in the quarter than pure-play e-tailers. Their strong performance was attributed to having infrastructures in place, such as distribution, customer relation, and billing systems, as well as having recognizable brands. Consumers also appeared more comfortable making online purchases: repeated Internet use and knowing other people who bought online were reducing concerns about security and Internet fraud.

For the 2000 holiday season, online shoppers spent an estimated $10.7 billion, according to a study by Goldman Sachs and PC Data Online. That included $878 million spent online in the week after Christmas. The report found that online sales during December increased 60 percent over the previous year, and online sales for the 2000 holiday season more than doubled from the $5.2 billion spent during the 1999 holiday season. A study by Media Metrix (now Jupiter Media Metrix) found that traffic to e-tail Web sites during the 2000 holidays increased by more than 30 percent over 1999 levels, with online retailers reporting an average of 34.2 million unique visits each week. Other estimates of online spending for the 2000 holidays ranged from $10.8 billion to $12.5 billion.

Estimates of the amount spent online during all of 2000 varied considerably. In January 2001 ActivMedia Research reported that online shopping in 2000 reached $56 billion, with sales during the holiday season of about $9 billion. That compared to an estimated $3.5- to $4.5 billion spent during the 1999 holiday season. Factors contributing to the surge in online holiday spending included better order processing systems and more effective marketing promotions. Some 57 percent of all consumer-oriented Web sites had e-commerce capabilities, while an additional 36 percent provided pre-sale information and post-sale support without actually taking orders. The research firm projected that online B2C sales would reach $1.1 trillion by 2010.

The U.S. Census Bureau reported that online shoppers in the United States spent $28 billion in 2000, an increase of 62 percent over the $17.3 billion spent in 1999. The Census Bureau said that online shoppers spent $7.8 billion on airline tickets in 2000, followed by $5.1 billion on personal computers and $2.1 billion on hotel rooms. The Bureau's figures did not include online travel services, financial brokers and dealers, or ticket sales agencies. The study was prepared for the Census Bureau by Jupiter Media Metrix, which projected that total e-commerce sales would reach $213 billion by 2005.

A 2001 report by the Boston Consulting Group found that 68 million Internet users in the United States—representing 55 percent of all Internet users—purchased something online in 2000, up from 53 million in 1999. Some 70 percent of Internet shoppers reported problems with Web sites taking too long to load, followed by 20 percent having trouble getting a site to accept their credit card. About 11 percent reported a problem of not receiving merchandise that was ordered and paid for.

ONLINE SPENDING GROWTH CONTINUED IN 2001

Consumers spent a reported $3.4 billion online in February 2001, according to the National Retail Federation and Forrester Research. That represented a 13.3 percent increase over January, when consumers spent $3 billion online. Those figures compared to $2.8 billion for January 2000 and $2.4 billion for February 2000.

In March 2001 online consumer spending reached $3.5 billion, according to Nielsen/NetRatings

and Harris Interactive. The report, based on a survey of 39,000 Internet users, found that more than 81 percent of all adults with Web access had purchased something online since being connected to the Internet. The Nielsen-Harris study found that online travel and apparel accounted for more than half of online spending growth. A similar report from Forrester Research and Greenfield Online agreed on the total level of spending in March 2001, but reported a much lower dollar value of apparel purchases than those estimated by Nielsen and Harris. Both studies agreed that apparel was the most popular small-ticket item purchased online, however.

For the first quarter of 2001, the U.S. Census Bureau reported that e-commerce sales reached $7 billion, excluding online travel services, financial brokers and dealers, or ticket sales agencies. E-commerce sales represented 0.91 percent of total retail sales for the quarter, according to the Census Bureau.

In May 2001 the Boston Consulting Group predicted that online retail sales in North America would grow from $44.5 billion in 2000 to more than $65 billion in 2001. BCG, together with online retail trade association Shop.org, found that the three strongest online retail segments in 2000 were computer hardware and software, books, and travel reservations. The travel segment included air, lodging, car, cruise, and tour reservations. For 2000 travel generated $13.8 billion in online sales, followed by computer hardware and software at $8.2 billion, then books with $1.9 billion in online sales. As a percentage of overall retailing, online sales were projected to increase from 1.7 percent in 2000 to 2.5 percent by the end of 2001, according to the study.

BUSINESS MODELS SEEK PROFITABILITY

B2C e-commerce is conducted essentially via three business models.

- Pure-play online retailers, such as Amazon.com, sell only over the Internet. They do not sell offline and do not have traditional brick-and-mortar stores that consumers can visit.

- A second type of online retailer includes companies that have traditional stores or sell offline through catalogs or mail-order, but that also have a presence on the Web. These are known as "bricks-and-clicks" because they sell to consumers both through an offline channel and an online storefront.

- A third category consists of portals, such as America Online, where goods and services from several online retailers are offered to consumers.

PURE PLAYERS

Most pure-play e-tailers had little concern for profits when they first launched. They focused on acquiring market share, spending to gain new customers, and building their brands. They succeeded in driving traffic to their Web sites, but their margins were not enough to achieve profitability. As a result, many pure-play e-tailers went out of business in the wake of the dot-com shakeout of 2000. Others faced cash shortages and needed to raise funds to cover their cash-burn rate and lack of profitability.

In early 2001 some of the leading pure-play e-tailers, such as Amazon.com and Buy.com, took steps to become profitable by the end of the year. Amazon.com cut its work force by 15 percent, laying off 13,000 employees. Buy.com announced plans to focus on higher-margin products, such as technology and consumer electronics products, instead of its entertainment offerings.

BRICKS-AND-CLICKS

By mid-2001 many considered the brick-and-click formula the leading model for success in online retailing. A study by McKinsey & Co. revealed that more than 75 percent of the best-performing e-tailers were online cousins of traditional retailers. Bricks-and-clicks had the benefit of existing brands, established marketing and distribution arrangements, and an installed information technology base. The study found that e-tailers that sold clothing and apparel did the best in terms of gaining revenue from customers, with an average 21 percent operating margin. In fact, it was the only e-tail category with an average positive operating margin. In other categories, such as electronics, books, and gifts, the average operating margin was negative, with only the leading players making money on every sale.

Bricks-and-clicks also had the ability to bring the Internet into their traditional stores. In-store kiosks with Web access allowed consumers to research potential purchases online, then find the merchandise they wanted in the store. Brick-and-click bookseller Barnes & Noble took steps in 2001 to more fully integrate its online bookselling with its stores. For example, the company allowed customers who purchased books online the convenience of being able to return them to a Barnes & Noble bookstore.

PORTALS

Portals such as Yahoo! and America Online (AOL) have evolved from being large directories that helped people find places on the Internet to places that offered their own content and services. Leading portals such as Yahoo!, AOL, AltaVista, and MSN all offer shopping areas for consumers. In June 2000 the top portal shopping site was Yahoo! Shopping, which attracted 5.8 million unique home-based visitors, or nearly 7 percent of all Internet users. AOL's Shopping Channel had more than 3.4 million unique visitors that month. AltaVista's shopping area attracted 2.6 million unique visitors, while MSN's shopping sections had 1.2 million unique visitors.

Portal shopping areas provide added value to new and experienced online shoppers alike. They offer specialized search engines and many give consumers the opportunity to comparison shop across several sites. The storefront business model made popular by Yahoo! Shopping has also succeeded in attracting more small businesses. These online storefronts enable small businesses to maintain an online presence with minimal expense, and they benefit from the traffic attracted to the major portals.

A January 2001 study by the Yankee Group found that B2C e-commerce at portals and online malls grew at a faster rate than for stand-alone e-tailers during the 2000 holiday season. AOL reported an 84 percent increase in holiday sales over its 1999 holiday sales of $2.5 billion, while Yahoo! and Lycos reported that their holiday sales doubled over the previous year. Stand-alone e-tailers, on the other hand, reported an average growth rate of 40 percent. Another Yankee Group study found that 57 percent of online consumers began their shopping trip at a portal or portal-based mall during the 2000 holiday season.

KEYS TO PROFITABILITY

As e-tailers seek to achieve profitability by cutting costs and spending less to gain customers, the ability to generate positive gross margins becomes the number one factor in e-tail success. Another critical factor is driving traffic to the Web site, but that needs to be combined with a high conversion rate. That is, it is important to have not only sustained visitor traffic, but also to be able to convert 10 to 15 percent of the visitors into buyers. According to a December 2000 study by the Yankee Group, the average conversion rate for e-tailers was only 1 percent.

Successful e-tailers must also provide consumers with products they want and be able to convince them that the Web is the place to buy them. Successful e-tailers must be able to provide consumers with a positive Web experience, make it easy to find products and information about products, and ease any fears or concerns that consumers may have.

FURTHER READING:

Cuneo, Alice Z. "Retailers Stress Bricks over Clicks." *Advertising Age,* September 25, 2000.

Davis, Jessica, and Dan Neel. ''Pure-Play E-Tailers Retrench.'' *InfoWorld,* February 5, 2001.

Enos, Lori, and Elizabeth Blakey. ''Portals Turn Eyeballs into E-Commerce.'' *E-Commerce Times,* July 20, 2000. Available from www.ecommercetimes.com.

Hampton, Jennifer M. ''U.S. Fines E-tailers $1.5M for Late Holiday Deliveries.'' *E-Commerce Times,* July 27, 2000. Available from www.ecommercetimes.com.

''Inside the First E-Christmas.'' *Fortune,* February 1, 1999.

Jerome, Marty. ''E-Commerce.'' *Ziff Davis Smart Business for the New Economy,* December 1, 2000.

Mahoney, Michael. ''Report: Brick-and-Clicks Now E-tail Model.'' *E-Commerce Times,* December 20, 2000. Available from www.ecommercetimes.com.

———. ''Report: North American E-Commerce to Grow 46 Percent in 2001.'' *E-Commerce Times,* May 3, 2001. Available from www.ecommercetimes.com.

Saliba, Clare. ''New Data Confirms $10B+ E-Holiday.'' *E-Commerce Times,* January 17, 2001. Available from www.ecommercetimes.com.

Schulz, Rick. ''Retailers Bring the Internet Inside to Compete Effectively.'' *DM News,* January 15, 2001.

''The Straight Dope on Web Retailers.'' *Fortune,* February 21, 2000.

———. ''The Making of E-Commerce: 10 Key Moments.'' *E-Commerce Times,* August 22, 2000. Available from www.ecommercetimes.com.

SEE ALSO: Business-to-Business (B2B) E-commerce; Business Models

BUSINESS MODELS

The advent of e-commerce in the mid-1990s brought with it many new ways of doing business. Some were viable and others were not. While the number of ways to conduct business electronically is vast, only a handful of business models—methods by which businesses generate revenue—proved worthy enough to survive the dot-com fallout of 2000. Several variations exist within each model, and many firms attempt to meld models to increase profitability.

MERCHANT MODEL

Perhaps the most well-known e-commerce business model, Internet-based merchandising is what comes to mind for many when the subject of e-commerce is raised. One of the most successful online merchants using this model, Amazon.com, began operating as a business-to-consumer (B2C) Internet company by selling books online from a database that exceeded one-million titles by the end of 1996. Amazon's wide selection, along with its practice of discounting books by 10 to 30 percent, were key factors in its success. The firm developed one-click shopping technology, which allowed returning shoppers to purchase an item with a single click. Although the site experienced meteoric growth from its inception in 1995 to the end of the decade, analysts in late 1999 began to question whether or not Amazon.com would ever attain profitability. Consequently, the company's stock prices plunged and founder Jeff Bezos was forced to defend the viability of his business model. The world's largest online retailer, with vast offerings that include books, CDs, and electronics, Amazon began to offer business-to-business (B2B) services in 2000 by selling the technology it had developed and employed so successfully. For example, it helped Toysrus.com strengthen its Internet infrastructure after the toy retailer found itself unable to keep pace with holiday orders in 1999.

Unlike Amazon, catalog clothing company Landsend.com was run by a traditional brick-and-mortar parent, Lands' End Inc. Landsend.com began selling 100 items on the Internet in 1995. The firm decided to move into Internet sales after examining the demographics of typical Lands' End shoppers. Many Lands' End shoppers owned PCs, and they were twice as likely to have online access as the rest of the population. Also, they typically were between 35 and 54 years of age, college educated, employed in a professional or managerial position, and earned an average household income of $60,000. Within three years, sales from Landsend.com had reached $18 million, and the online venture had achieved consistent profitability. The firm added technology to its site that allowed shoppers to build their own outfits; create three-dimensional models of their body shape to see which articles of clothing were best suited to that shape; and establish personalized accounts that would store billing and shipping information to streamline future online purchases.

In 1999, Landsend.com launched Lands' End Live, an innovative live customer service program that offered online shoppers real-time personal assistance 24 hours a day, seven days a week. By then, Landsend.com had evolved into the leading online apparel site. Its success prompted the firm to expand its business model and begin offering Web site development services to firms like the Saturn division of General Motors Corp. and RadioShack. In 2001, online sales totaled $218 million, accounting for roughly 16 percent of the total revenues secured by Lands' End Inc.

By targeting more lucrative clients, both Amazon.com and Landsend.com followed a pattern typical of Internet retailers after the dot-com shakeup. According to Daniel Levine, columnist for the *Sacramento Business Journal,* "For surviving business-to-consumer companies, that approach represents a shift to business-to-business and to selling the technology they developed as a service to businesses."

ADVERTISING MODEL

This model relies on advertising to make money. To attract users to its site, leading Web portal Yahoo! offers things like free e-mail, extensive content, and travel services. The firm got its start in early 1995 when founders Jerry Yang and David Filo put together a simple list of favorite Web sites. The firm's lucrative initial public offering in April 1996 allowed it to launch an acquisition spree that eventually would exceed $10 billion. In September of 1997, Yahoo! bought a news delivery service, as well as technology that allowed it to add people-searching and e-mail to its free online services. Purchases in the following year allowed Yahoo! users to play games and shop. The firm paid $4 billion for Geocities and $5.7 billion for video services provider Broadcast.com in 1999. This aggressive growth strategy reflected management's belief that more features, services, and content would attract more visitors and advertising dollars.

Unlike many other dot-com startups, Yahoo! actually was able to parlay advertising dollars into profitability. This partially was due to the technology the firm developed for monitoring each visitor's online activity, selecting the advertisements displayed to each visitor, and tracking the hits received by each ad. Eventually, Yahoo! proved too reliant on other dot-com upstarts for advertising revenue. When these fledgling ventures were forced to curtail spending, Yahoo! began looking to traditional brick-and-mortar companies. However, many of these firms also were cutting costs, and quite often the dollars earmarked for online advertising were the most vulnerable to cuts. Eventually, the firm recognized that it needed to reduce its reliance on advertising, which accounted for roughly 85 percent of sales in 2000. Yahoo! altered its business model when it began offering fee-based services like online bill paying to consumers, and fee-based services like e-store management to corporate clients.

INFORMATION MODEL

Several online ventures focus on the sale of information. For example, the *Wall Street Journal Online,* one user of this model, offers a subscription that includes access to articles, detailed company information, and real-time stock quotes for a monthly fee. *Consumer Reports Online* offers access to its product ratings and reports for a fee as well. To draw more readers, both offer a limited amount of free content and charge a subscription for access to premium content. Quite often, sites like these also rely on advertising to make money.

BROKERAGE MODEL

Like Amazon, eBay is another pure-play Internet company, meaning that it conducts business solely on the Internet. However, instead of using the retailing model employed by Amazon, the firm uses a brokerage format that brings sellers and buyers together. The world's largest online auction site, eBay was founded by Pierre Omidyar in 1995 as Auction Web, a site that allowed sellers to list descriptions of items for sale, require a minimum bid, and set an auction's length between three and 10 days. When the auction expired, the highest bidder was able to purchase the object for the bid price, providing the minimum had been met. The buyer and seller were responsible for handling payment and delivery.

As site traffic grew, Auction Web began charging a small fee, basing it on the final price of each object sold. Because the auctioning process was automated, overhead costs were kept to a minimum and the site achieved profitability quickly. A feedback forum, which allowed buyers and sellers to rate one another, was put into place in 1996. Auction Web changed its name to eBay the following year. Despite competition from the Internet leaders like Yahoo! and Amazon.com in the late 1990s, eBay continued to thrive, mainly because it had developed the online auction business model first and had secured an extensive base of buyers and sellers.

Auction site Covisint functions as a B2B marketplace for the worldwide automobile industry. Launched in November of 2000, Covisint was first conceptualized in late 1999 by industry leaders Ford Motor Co., General Motors, and DaimlerChrysler to streamline the purchasing and production processes of automobile making in an effort to cut costs. The automakers envisioned an online marketplace that would improve new parts development processes by enhancing communication between automakers and suppliers; cut the time needed for vehicle development; and grant dealers more inventory control by helping them to stock what consumers want and maintain fewer cars on their lots. In mid-2001, Covisint functioned mainly as a procurement vehicle, making its money by charging fees for each transaction.

According to a July 2001 article in *PC Magazine,* eBay and Covisint stood out among the many online marketplaces that failed soon after they launched. It explained: "The Web-based business-to-business marketplace assumed that automating transactions would be enough to bring buyers and sellers together online.'' According to the article, successful implementation of this business model also requires a high volume of buyers and sellers, as is the case with eBay, or a strong incentive to join, which in Covisint's case stems from the ability of the large automotive buyers to ask smaller suppliers to participate the marketplace.

Another type of online brokerage model is the reverse auction. Using reverse auction technology, Priceline.com allows users to name the price they are willing to pay for airline tickets, hotel rooms, automobile rentals, mortgages, new cars, and long-distance telephone calls. Customers who submit a price are obligated to complete the purchase if a seller matches that price. Priceline makes its money via any spread between the price it pays for tickets, rooms, etc. and the price consumers are willing to pay. The firm achieved profitability in July of 2001, roughly six years after it was founded, lending credibility to the frequently criticized business model.

MySimon.com is an online brokerage that locates the lowest prices on a wide range of products and services for consumers and allows them to link directly to merchants to complete purchases. Known as a shopping bot, mysimon.com uses virtual learning agent software to search the inventory of more than 2,000 e-tailers. Search results may be sorted by price, merchant ratings, and other criteria. Shoppers who reach a decision about which item they wish to purchase begin the transaction by clicking the ''Buy'' button located beside each product. They are then routed to the Web site selling the item, where they can complete their purchase. Shoppers can use mysimon.com for free; the site makes money via online advertising and by charging merchants who wish to boost their visibility by paying a fee to add a bolder typeface to their listing.

ONLINE SERVICES MODEL

At the core of online service providers like Earthlink, MCI WorldCom, and America Online Inc. (AOL) is a subscription-based model; revenues are generated by charging users a monthly fee for Internet access and e-mail service. Quite often, these firms also generate revenues by doing things like selling advertising space on their sites. For example, AOL founder and CEO Steven Case developed a successful business model that allowed his firm to make money in a variety of ways, such as charging subscription fees, selling online advertising, and developing e-commerce deals with online retailers.

In May of 1985, Case launched AOL as Quantum Computer Services Inc., a modem-based online service offered to Commodore personal computer (PC) users. Within two years, the service had been expanded to include owners of PCs made by Tandy Corp. and other companies. Profitability came in 1987, and by the end of the decade the young firm had made online services available to owners of IBM-compatible PCs and Macintosh machines. Believing a mass market existed for interactive online services and content, Case began working on a nationwide online network for PC owners called America Online. Officially launched in 1989, AOL included games, e-mail, and real-time chat capabilities. The firm used aggressive marketing tactics, like giving AOL software away for free, to grow its subscriber base.

Realizing that additional content would draw more subscribers to the site, AOL orchestrated licensing deals with media firms like Knight-Ridder and CNN. To counter predictions that the World Wide Web would render online services like AOL obsolete, the firm created a gateway, AOL.com, to offer subscribers a link to the Internet from AOL. A pivotal cross-marketing deal with Microsoft, signed in 1995, resulted in Microsoft including AOL software on its Windows 95 platform. By 1996, AOL was a leading online services provider. Robert Pittman, hired that year as president and chief operating officer, was charged with the task of developing AOL's e-commerce strategy. Pittman began forging agreements with online retailers, such as Amazon.com, who wanted to sell their merchandise on AOL. With a membership of more than 10 million subscribers by 1997, AOL also found itself well positioned to sell advertising on its site.

To grow both its subscriber base and its services, AOL completed two key acquisitions in 1998: rival CompuServe Inc. and instant messaging firm ICQ. The following year, AOL bought browser firm Netscape Communications, and in 1999 the firm extended its services to wireless consumers via AOL Mobile Messenger. In perhaps its boldest move to date, in 2001 AOL took part in one of the largest mergers in media industry history—a $183 billion union with Time Warner Inc. to form AOL Time Warner Inc. The marriage of an online services provider with a major media player created a ''new media business model,'' according to an April 2001 article in *Electronic Media,* which explained: ''AOL Time Warner is dependent upon subscriber growth and advertiser partnerships and its ability to leverage those relationships while selling its content to its own and other outlets.'' AOL Time Warner's ability to develop this new business model will likely have a significant impact on future business models in both e-commerce and media industries.

FURTHER READING:

Elkind, Peter. ''The Hype is Big, Really Big, at Priceline.'' *Fortune.* September 6, 1999.

Levine, Daniel S. "Survey Tells Tale of Dot-Com Survivors Gaining New Lives." *Sacramento Business Journal.* June 15, 2001.

Mermigas, Diane. "AOL Time Warner's New Formula." *Electronic Media.* April 23, 2001.

Rappa, Michael. "Business Models on the Web." 2001. Available from www.digitalenterprise.org/models.

Roberts-Witt, Sarah L. "Lessons From the Year of Living Dangerously." *PC Magazine.* July 1, 2001.

Sweat, Jeff. "Well-Tailored E-Commerce." *InformationWeek.* April 16, 2001.

"We Have Lift-Off; Amazon, Yahoo! and eBay Grow Up." *The Economist.* February 3, 2001.

Wilson, Tim. "210 'Dotbombs' Don't Spoil the Whole Bunch." *InternetWeek.* January 15, 2001.

SEE ALSO: Affiliate Model; Brokerage Model; Community Model; Infomediary Model; Manufacturer Model; Merchant Model; Subscription Model; Utility Model

BUSINESS PLAN

A business plan is a document written by an individual or group of individuals interested in launching a new business. Along with helping to determine whether or not an idea can be transformed into a functional company, a business plan is also used to secure capital and recruit executives. During the dot-com mania of the late 1990s, several analysts began to criticize the many Internet-based ventures operating without a formal business plan, as well as the business investors pouring funding into these upstarts.

A March 2000 study of 300 e-commerce businesses in California revealed that most had launched operations with no business plan in place. Those who did develop e-business plans tended to produce documents much less exhaustive than their traditional counterparts. This lack of planning began to backfire for a variety of reasons. When the Internet revolution took off, many existing brick and mortar businesses built World Wide Web sites without figuring out who it was they were targeting; as a result, traffic remained minimal and those who did visit such sites complained of poor design and limited customer service. In some cases, companies that began selling directly to consumers via the Web alienated their traditional retailers. For example, Macy's and J.C. Penney threatened to stop selling Levi brand clothing in their stores after Levi Strauss began selling its merchandise via the Web; as a result, Levi Strauss abandoned its e-commerce efforts.

In 2000, the highly publicized bursting of the dot-com bubble prompted venture capitalists to begin scrutinizing business plans, particularly those for Internet-related ventures, more closely. As a result, the business plans developed for Internet-based businesses began to resemble those created for more traditional ventures, in terms of both length and level of detail. Rather than favoring condensed 15-page plans, lenders began paying attention to more thorough documents, which numbered 25 pages or more. Although business plans continue to vary in format and style, they typically include the following information, regardless of industry.

TARGET MARKET

Most business plans cover both the existing size and the anticipated growth rate of the market they are targeting. For example, a business plan for an online discount travel service might point out that travel is the most successful segment of the online industry, and that despite the rapid demise of many dot-com businesses, analysts continue to forecast substantial growth in online travel bookings, particularly as a weak North American economy prompts travelers to search for discounted options. Business plans also quite often include descriptions of potential customers, including their gender, age, level of education, marital status, how they make purchases, and the reasons behind those purchases. When clothing retailer Lands' End began creating a business plan for Landsend.com, the firm knew that a large portion of its customer base owned a personal computer and was twice as likely to have online access than the rest of the population. A typical Lands' End shopper was between the ages of 35 and 54, with an average household income of $60,000. Nearly 88 percent had earned a college degree, and two-thirds were employed in a professional or managerial position.

Discussions of target market also provide information on the history of the market, as well as various trends within the market. While e-commerce entrepreneurs planning to target an emerging market might be unable to produce historical data, they might be able to make comparisons with related markets. Although Amazon.com founder Jeff Bezos was unable to analyze the online consumer book industry—which for all practical purposes did not exist prior to Amazon's launch—while creating his business plan, he was able to examine the traditional book industry. In fact, it was only after researching 20 different products that he believed could be sold via the Internet—including magazines, CDs, and computer software—that Bezos settled on books, guessing that this sizable market, with its wide range of purchase choices, would be well served by the electronic searching and organizing capabilities of the Web.

PRODUCTS AND SERVICES OFFERED

Along with describing exactly what it is a company will sell, business plans also explain why these products or services are more likely to sell than similar offerings by competitors. For example, travel discounter Hotwire.com could have justified in its business plan the superiority of its services to those offered by rival Priceline.com, a name-your-own-price travel service, by pointing out key differences. Online shoppers who purchase airline tickets on Hotwire.com know their dates of travel, their estimated number of layovers, and the exact purchase price before they actually complete a transaction. They also know they are getting the lowest fare possible among those listed on Hotwire. In comparison, shoppers on Priceline.com are required to commit to a purchase—if the price they request is available—before knowing the exact travel dates or approximate number of layovers. Priceline also does not alert the consumer if a price lower than the one requested is available.

MARKETING TACTICS

An explanation of how customers will be made aware of your products and services is another key feature of most business plans. Often discussed are advertising mediums—including print, television, and the Internet—as well as pricing strategies, major promotions, and any guarantees or warranties that might be used to attract customers. Priceline.com could have included in its business plan mention of its intent to use celebrity William Shattner in a flurry of television advertisements designed make Priceline a household name. Similarly, America Online's decision to give its software away for free in an effort to attract a wide base of customers is an example of the type of activity that might be included in this section of a business plan.

DISTRIBUTION

Business plans describe the channels through which customers will obtain products and services, including retail stores, catalogs, and Web sites. In the case of Amazon.com, the ease of distribution was a key concern for Bezos, who believed the small size of most books would facilitate easy shipping. Another of his decisions related to distribution was location. Liking its proximity to the warehouse of Ingram, a leading U.S. book distributor, Bezos chose Seattle, Washington, as his base of operations. According to Bezos' plans, upon receipt of an order, he could request the title or titles be shipped to his home, where he would package the order and take it to the post office. Using this process, customers would receive their books within five days of placing an order, and

Bezos could ship books to all 50 states and 45 countries throughout the world, an incredibly broad market for an upstart.

COMPETITION

Analysis of competition is an essential component of most business plans. This section tends to cover the strengths and weaknesses of rivals and includes information about their market share, profitability, and pricing strategies. Prior to choosing books as Amazon's initial focus, Bezos analyzed his competition and realized that market share was distributed among many leading book publishers. In fact, industry leader Barnes & Noble held less than 12 percent of the $25 billion book retailing market. This market fragmentation, Bezos believed, left room for upstarts. He also planned to gain a competitive advantage over traditional book retailers by offering a wider selection and undercutting prices by 10 to 30 percent. Successful brick and mortar firms drawing up business plans for new online ventures might also include a discussion of how their established customer base and distribution outlets affords them an advantage over rivals only operating online.

TRADEMARKS AND LICENSES

The steps a business has taken or will take to gain protections like trademarks and licenses are also relevant to many business plans. In the case of businesses engaged or planning to engage in e-commerce, domain name registration plans may also be included.

PRODUCTION

Information about how a business will obtain what it is selling, whether it be by manufacturing it or simply purchasing it wholesale, is also important to a business plan. A discussion of production processes can cover anything from the cost and construction of needed facilities to the availability of qualified labor. Quite often, the location of a company's headquarters is based on proximity to things like needed supplies and labor pools. Many Internet-based ventures landed in California, particularly Silicon Valley, because business owners planned to tap into the technologically savvy talent base there.

MANAGEMENT

According to a June 2000 article in *BusinessWeek Online*, a survey of venture capitalists completed by Centurion Consulting revealed common problems with business plans. ''The No. 1 problem they identified was the lack of a management team,&rquo; stated Barbara Lewis, co-owner of the business plan consultancy. ''Understandably, it's hard for a new entrepreneur without the contacts or the ability to get contacts to come up with a high-powered management team. But at least they should try to find an advisory board that will help them find management-team members.'' Resumes of any managers or board members recruited by the time the plan is completed can be included, as well as discussion of how it is they can help the business succeed. The section might also include a listing of the desired qualifications for positions that remain vacant, an explanation of how candidates will be recruited, and an organizational chart that details chain of command and the roles that will be played by various executives.

NECESSARY FINANCING

Most business plans also set forth how much capital is needed to sustain operations for five years. According to an April 2000 issue of *Tampa Bay Business Journal*, ''Most new businesses stumble and fail somewhere during the first and fifth year. One of the biggest stumbling blocks is not having the cash when you need it to grow your business. The better you anticipate your need for capital the less it's likely to cost. That's why its important to have a business plan.'' Along with the dollar amount needed, most business plans detail plans for securing the needed funding, such as selling off a portion of the company to private investors or conducting an IPO.

FINANCIAL PROJECTIONS

Many analysts argue that this section is the most consequential portion of a business plan, particularly in terms of securing funding. In short, lenders and investors want to know what kind of revenues a business will generate and how soon it will be profitable. While many dot-com investors in the late 1990s appeared willing to wait several years for profitability, an October 2001 article in *Inc.* stated ''the business plan that impresses investors today is a very different beast from the one that pulled in the dough two short years ago; the path to profitability has to be both clear and short—a year to 18 months.'' Detailed profit and loss statements, balance sheets, and cash flow projections for the first five years of operations are usually included in an appendix.

EXECUTIVE SUMMARY

Although it appears at the beginning of a business plan, most business plan experts recommend that entrepreneurs write the two- or three-page executive summary, perhaps an even more important business plan component than the financial projections, last. The executive summary gives readers a thumbnail sketch of the contents of the entire plan. It briefly describes the type of business detailed in the plan, as well as what need it is that the business is meeting. The more concise and compelling the executive summary, the more likely readers will be to continue examining the remainder of the plan.

FURTHER READING:

Barker, Emily. ''The Bullet-Proof Business Plan.'' *Inc.* October 1, 2001.

Belgum, Deborah. ''Study Finds Few E-Commerce Firms Have Real Business Plan.'' *Los Angeles Business Journal.* March 6, 2000, 4.

Hawk, Ken. ''10 Weeks to a Business Plan.'' *Catalog Age.* July 1997, 189.

Klein, Karen E. ''Building Your Business Plan: Where to Begin, Part 1.'' *BusinessWeek Online.* June 20, 2000. Available from www.businessweek.com.

———. ''Building Your Business Plan: Where to Begin, Part 2.'' *BusinessWeek Online.* June 22, 2000. Available from www.businessweek.com.

Regan, Keith. ''New Rules for Writing an E-Business Plan.'' *E-Commerce Times.* October 30, 2001. Available from www.ecommercetimes.com.

Simon, Geoffrey. ''Anticipate Cash Needs Through Business Plan Development.'' *Tampa Bay Business Journal.* April 14, 2000.

SEE
ALSO: Financing, Securing

BUY.COM INC.

Buy.com's tagline says it all: ''The Internet Superstore—Low Prices on Top Brands.'' Launched in November 1998, Buy.com claimed to offer the lowest prices on the Web for a wide range of consumer goods, which it offered through specialty stores devoted to such categories as computers, software, office products, wireless products, electronics, books, videos, games, music, and sports. The company's prices were so low, in fact, that Buy.com's business model was not designed to make money on its margins the way traditional retailers have done, but to generate a profit by selling advertising on its Web site. By selling merchandise at, near, or even below cost, Buy.com hoped to attract enough eyeballs to make consumer goods manufacturers want to advertise on its Web site. It was a revolutionary business model, and one that founder Scott Blum hoped would make Buy.com the fastest-growing company in U.S. history.

INITIAL REACTIONS WERE SKEPTICAL

Barely two months after the Buy.com Web site was launched, *Fortune* magazine described it as a ''seemingly crazy new model'' and compared it to a Web site selling dollars for 85 cents. If Buy.com proved to be successful, the magazine argued, it would demonstrate that it was possible to build a brand completely on price. It also would have revolutionary implications for Internet retailing.

Buy.com originally was BuyComp.com, a discount seller of computer products founded in October 1996 by Scott Blum. BuyComp.com was selling about $1 million worth of computer products a day when it changed its name to Buy.com in November 1998. The name change reflected the wider range of products the company would sell. With $60 million in venture capital financing from Japanese software distributor Softbank, Buy.com was able to acquire SpeedServe, the Internet division of Ingram Entertainment that sold videos, DVDs, books, and computer games. Almost immediately the company launched a consumer advertising campaign that included national TV spots and print advertising. Buy.com offered videos and DVDs through a new sub-site of Buy.com called BuyVideos.com, thereby establishing a pattern it would follow of creating specialty stores for new product lines. To prepare for the addition of new specialty stores, Buy.com purchased the rights to more than 2,000 domain names beginning with the word ''buy.''

If Buy.com's business model was to work, the company had to offer the lowest prices on the Internet. To accomplish this Blum spent more than a year perfecting search agents that would automatically scan the Web for the lowest prices on products he was selling. The company also did not carry any inventory, instead having wholesalers ship products directly to Buy.com's customers. The company got off to a fast start. For 1998 it posted sales of $125 million, beating a 15-year-old record held by Compaq Computer Corp. for a company in its first year. By February 1999 it was selling about $2 million worth of merchandise a day, and for 1999 it reported total revenue of nearly $600 million.

EXPANSION, CUSTOMER COMPLAINTS MARKED FIRST YEAR

During 1999 Buy.com added an online music store that featured every title on the Billboard 200 for $9.95, excluding two-CD and box sets. In mid-1999 Buy.com redesigned its Web site to allow customers to buy products from its different specialty stores with one shopping cart. Specialty stores in operation included buycomp.com for computer hardware and software, buyvideos.com, buygames.com, and buybooks.com.

While Buy.com was hoping to gain customer loyalty on the basis of price, it was falling short in the area of customer service, according to some complaints. Protest sites with names like BoycottBuy.com began to appear, criticizing the company's customer service. A survey by ResellerRatings.com that was published in *Sm@rt Reseller* reported that more than 60 percent of online shoppers felt the company's sales staff was not knowledgeable and easy to deal with. More than 80 percent said exchanges were not handled professionally, and only about half said they would recommend Buy.com to a friend.

One area of consumer concern was the company's billing practices. Buy.com would book orders and bill the customer's credit card even if the item ordered was not in stock at its distributor, Ingram Micro. If the order went unfilled, then Buy.com would credit the customer's account—in some cases days or even weeks after the order was placed. When Buy.com's advertised price for a Hitachi monitor was mistakenly listed $400 below the company's intended price, it refused to deliver the monitors at the incorrect price. That resulted in a class action lawsuit on behalf of customers who ordered the monitor, and the initial ruling in the case went against Buy.com.

All of this was especially troubling to Buy.com's new CEO, Gregory Hawkins, who joined the company from Ingram Micro. To smooth things over, Hawkins invited a group of unhappy customers to the firm's Orange County headquarters in Aliso Viejo, California, and promised to hire customer service representatives to improve the firm's customer transactions. Before the end of the year, founder Scott Blum resigned as chairman and director, although he remained the company's largest shareholder with a 48-percent interest. Hawkins became chairman, CEO, and president.

Buy.com continued to advertise heavily in 1999 to build its brand. It took a TV spot in the Super Bowl and was expected to spend $25 million on advertising in the fourth quarter. When Nike Inc. ended its seven-year sponsorship of the Professional Golf Association's developmental tour, Buy.com signed a five-year deal to sponsor the tour starting in 2000.

IPO RAISED $182 MILLION IN 2000

Buy.com's initial public offering (IPO) took place in February 2000. The company sold 14 million shares at $13 each, raising approximately $182 million. Investors quickly bid the price up to $35 on the first day of trading before closing at $25.12 a share. Investor interest appeared to be unaffected by Buy.com's failure to turn a profit. Although revenue for 1999 increased nearly fourfold to $296.8 million, the company's loss for the year was $130.2 million, compared to a loss of $17.8 million in 1998.

As part of its sponsorship agreement with the PGA Tour, Buy.com made a heavy investment. It issued 1,125,000 shares to the tour, and made a cash payment of $8.5 million from the IPO. This was in addition to $6.4 million paid to the PGA Tour in 1999 and a $17 million letter of credit issued as security for payment of the sponsorship fee.

Buy.com expanded in several ways in 2000 with varying degrees of success. Through an alliance with United Airlines it opened a full service airline ticket booking service called buytravel.com. The site offered discounted fares and rates from United, fares from about 500 other airlines, and other travel-related services including hotels and car rentals. Buytravel.com operated from February to November 2000 before it was shut down. Other specialty stores that opened during 2000 included a new business superstore offering more than 55,000 office products, and a new sports store powered by Global Sports that offered activewear and sporting goods. In April 2000 Buy.com launched its License Online Program, which offered software licenses on the entire line of Microsoft licensing products. The program was later expanded to include software from Symantec, Computer Associates, Executive Software, and Trend Micro.

The company expanded internationally by opening Web sites in the United Kingdom and Australia. Both sites were accessible from Buy.com's home page. However, Australian operations were discontinued in November 2000, and the company's operations in the United Kingdom were sold to Britain's department store group, John Lewis Partnership, in March 2001.

Buy.com added wireless phones, service, and accessories to its product mix with the mid-2000 acquisition of online retailer Telstreet.com for about $8 million in stock. In October 2000 Buy.com opened its Wireless Store, which enabled customers to compare mobile phones and plans. The site also offered cellular phones and accessories, cellular plans, Web-enabled phones, and FRS radios. Among the wireless companies represented at the store were Ericsson, Nokia, Motorola, Mitsubishi, AT&T, Nextel, and Verizon. In the second half of 2000 Buy.com began offering wireless access to its Web site through agreements with Sprint PCS and AT&T Wireless, and Web-enabled mobile phone users could access and shop the Buy.com Web site.

WEAK HOLIDAY SALES LED TO CUTBACKS AND REFOCUS

As early as mid-2000 some analysts—notably investment banker Goldman, Sachs & Co.; financial magazine *Barron's;* and the stock market Web site TheStreet.com—thought Buy.com was in danger of running low on capital by the end of the year or in early 2001. Although the company raised its prices slightly at the beginning of the year and reported a positive gross margin of 4.3 percent in the first quarter, it still reported a net loss of $66.4 million for the first half of 2000 on revenue of $400.8 million. Its third quarter net loss amounted to $21.4 million on revenue of $190.2 million. By November Merrill Lynch & Co. issued a warning on Buy.com that the company was funding its operations from a dwindling supply of cash. That was followed by a report in *The Orange County Register* that Buy.com had enough working capital to last another year, even if it lost $30 million a quarter. The company's stock was trading around $2 a share in late November.

Buy.com had taken steps during 2000 to improve its customer service for the holiday season. In December Forrester Research ranked Buy.com the top e-tailer in its PowerRankings, which were based on a survey of 20,000 online customers. The rating was based on customer service, low prices, free shipping promotions, and quick e-mail responses. In terms of buyers, *PC Magazine* ranked Buy.com third among Web retailers for September 2000 with 428,000 buyers, behind Amazon.com and ticketmaster.com. Buy.com had every reason to be optimistic about the 2000 holiday shopping season, but competition from brick-and-mortar retailers and their Web sites reduced Buy.com's Web traffic by 10.8 percent in the first week of December and by 16.5 percent in the second week, compared to the same weeks of the previous year.

As a result, Buy.com's fourth quarter revenue was $196.7 million, about $23 million less than estimates. Fully expecting to be in business for the 2001 holiday season, Buy.com announced it would focus on delivering positive operating cash flow by the fourth quarter of 2001. It planned to refocus its resources on its core product categories: computer hardware and software, consumer electronics, wireless products, plus a general clearance category. It closed its sports store in March. Buy.com also planned to focus its efforts on the U.S. market and announced it would discontinue its Canadian store operations effective February 2, 2001. The company's British operations were sold to the John Lewis Partnership in March. Layoffs of 150 employees, together with other cost-cutting measures, were expected to reduce the company's annual operating expenses by $70 million.

Meanwhile, the company entered 2001 with a new management team. Chairman and CEO Gregory Hawkins and chief financial officer (CFO) Mitch Hill resigned in February 2001. Donald Kendall, former chairman and CEO of PepsiCo and a Buy.com board member, was appointed chairman. James Roszak was named interim CEO, and Robert Price joined the firm from PairGain Technologies as CFO.

FURTHER READING:

''Buy.com IPO a Hit.'' *Publishers Weekly.* February 14, 2000.

Chen, Christine Y. ''All I Want for Christmas is a Pulse.'' *Fortune.* November 27, 2000.

''The Everything Website.'' *Fortune.* December 7, 1998.

Foster, Ed. ''Dubious Marketing Ploys at Buy.com Expose the Seamy Side of E-Commerce.'' *InfoWorld.* May 3, 1999.

Gurley, J. William. ''The Lowest Prices on Earth.'' *Fortune.* January 11, 1999.

''I-Way Bumps.'' *Business Week.* May 15, 2000.

Milliot, Jim. ''Buy.com Hopes to Net $138 Million in Public Offering.'' *Publishers Weekly.* November 8, 1999.

Nee, Eric. ''Meet Mister Buy (Everything).com.'' *Fortune.* March 29, 1999.

Panettieri, Joseph C. ''Customer Boycott Bites Buy.com.'' *Sm@rt Reseller.* April 5, 1999.

Sacirbey, Omar. ''Buy.com Signals E-Tailings Long Farewell?'' *The IPO Reporter.* February 7, 2000.

''Top 10 Web Retailers.'' *PC Magazine.* December 5, 2000.

Vogelstein, Fred. ''Whoa! Has Buy.com Got a Deal for You!'' *U.S. News & World Report.* February 15, 1999.

SEE ALSO: Business-to-Consumer (B2C) E-commerce

C

C (PROGRAMMING LANGUAGE)

C is a high-level programming language that is used to develop many kinds of software, including applications that are used during e-commerce. High-level programming languages are much closer to human language than machine language, through which computer hardware accepts commands. High-level languages eventually get translated to machine language, which is numeric (consisting mainly of zeros and ones). C allows programmers to manipulate the main elements—bytes, bits, and addresses—that influence the way a computer functions.

Although it is a high-level language, C is capable of controlling the computer on which it operates at a low level, much like assembly language—a form of computer language that resides between machine languages and high-level languages. This enables programs written in C to perform in a very stable manner. Its mix of high- and low-level capabilities make C ideal for a wide variety of different uses. Additionally, compared to other programming languages C enables programs to be written in smaller formats that require less memory. Finally, perhaps one of the most popular features of C is its portability—a characteristic that lies at the heart of its creation.

C was created in 1972 by Ken Thompson and Dennis Ritchie, researchers at AT&T's Bell Labs in Murray Hill, New Jersey who also invented the UNIX operating system (a program used to operate computer systems). After creating UNIX, the two programmers needed to enable it for use on many different kinds of computers. Improving upon a language called B that Thompson had developed, they created C to accomplish this task. By doing so, they created the first portable operating system, and UNIX became the first major program to be written in the C language. According to *C Programming* by Augie Hansen, C went through a long period of development before it was released in Brian Kernighan and Dennis Ritchie's 1978 book *The C Programming Language.* Later, the American National Standards Institute (ANSI) developed a standardized version of the language to make it more acceptable for international use.

In the early 2000s, an enhanced version of C called C++ was widely used by programmers for just about every kind of program imaginable, especially on Windows and Macintosh systems. Developed at Bell Labs by Bjarne Stroustrup, C++ was effective for creating games, interpreters, spreadsheets, word processors, project managers, and more. In addition to the features of C, C++ contained many improvements, and it supported object-oriented programming (OOP)—techniques that allow programmers to increase efficiency and reduce complexity.

FURTHER READING:

Appleman, Daniel. *How Computer Programming Works,* Berkeley: Apress. 2000.

"C." *Ecommerce Webopedia,* March 27, 2001. Available from www.e-comm.webopedia.com.

"C." *Techencyclopedia,* March 7, 2001. Available from www.techweb.com/encyclopedia.

Computer Languages. Alexandria, Virginia: Time-Life Books. 1986.

Hansen, Augie. *C Programming.* New York: Addison-Wesley Publishing Publishing Co., Inc. 1989.

"The Origins of C and C++." *Cyberdiem*, January 30, 2001. Available from www.cyberdiem.com/vin/learn.html.

SEE ALSO: BASIC; COBOL; FORTRAN; Programming Language; UNIX

CAHNERS BUSINESS INFORMATION

Cahners Business Information published more than 150 magazines and 140 Web sites. It emerged as the world's leading provider of business-to-business information in the late 1990s with a subscriber base of more than 7 million. Having evolved from a consumer magazine publisher to a leading business-to-business publisher, Cahners's new focus was on operating online portals including e-INSITE, Variety.com, Buildingteam.com, and Manufacturing Marketplace. Its divisions, Cahners In-Stat Group and Cahners Research, also offered specialized directories, databases, business lists, market research, newsletters, conferences, and seminars.

The creation of Cahners Business Information stemmed from a series of acquisitions made by Reed Elsevier Inc. Founded in the late 1940s by Norman Cahners, the company began as a single magazine and grew into a business-to-business publishing and trade show company by the 1960s. Reed International purchased the firm in 1976, and Cahners grew steadily under its parent by acquiring the bibliographic directories of R.R. Bowker and many medical and consumer magazines. The firm also operated the Reed trade show division.

One of Reed's key purchases, The Travel Group, was established in the mid-1960s by Ziff Davis and included the operations of the *Hotel & Travel Index,* a guide used by travel agents across the globe. Reed International bought the group in 1989 from Rupert Murdoch and formed the Reed Travel Group. In 1993, Reed International merged with the Dutch publishing firm Elsevier, forming publishing giant Reed Elsevier. Two years later, Cahners sold its consumer magazines to focus on its operations in the business, professional, and medical markets.

In 1997, Reed Elsevier purchased the Chilton Business Group from ABC Inc. Chilton, whose early history dated back to 1904, was operating as a large business-to-business publisher with three major divisions including US Trade Magazines, Professional Exposition Management Co. (PEMCO), and Chilton Research Services. The acquisition was the final link in Reed's plan to create the largest business-to-business publisher in the world. In 1998, Reed formed Cahners Business Information, which included Cahners Publishing Co., Chilton Business Group, and Reed Travel Group.

Shortly after the formation of the new firm, Cahners's management began divesting certain magazine interests and started focusing on beefing up its operations in the electronic marketplace. In late 1998, Cahners formed a partnership with Microsoft's online travel service, Expedia.com, to create the largest Internet-based hotel database. Early the next year, the company continued to restructure operations as part of its Internet strategy. Supermarketworld.com was launched as Cahners's first Web-only magazine. It offered news and information on the retail grocery industry. By this time, the firm had established such Web sites as the Manufacturing Marketplace, a leading business-to-business Internet site for manufacturing and engineering professionals; e-inSITE, an Internet resource for the electronic original manufacture market; and Buildingteam.com, an Internet resource catering to the design and construction industry. Cahners also partnered with PartMiner, a company that would provide the technology needed to make online purchases on the e-inSITE Web site.

Cahners's transition from a traditional publishing firm to a technologically advanced business-to-business unit was not necessarily a smooth ride. The company, while divesting operations not related to its core industries, was forced to cut jobs by nearly 500 in 1999 alone. Operating profits also declined by 40 percent that year. In February 2000, Marc Teren took over as CEO of Cahners after Bruce Barnet's sudden resignation. Under new leadership, the firm bounced back and focused its Internet strategy primarily on creating vertical portals (Web sites that provided Web content), information, and purchasing capabilities for the electronics, manufacturing, construction, and publishing industries. As part of this strategy, the firm acquired the construction information firm CMD Group. Cahners also partnered with u.Bid.com to launch a live auction site for construction equipment, and also teamed up with Aspect Development Inc., a company that would enable its Manufacturing Marketplace site to handle purchasing transactions. In June 2000, Cahners announced plans to acquire eLogic Corp., a Web developer and application service provider. Management planned to utilize the firm's expertise to construct and maintain its Web sites.

Cahners continued to focus on expanding its business-to-business outreach and created an Internet division, Cahners Digital, to oversee its growth in the Internet arena. According to Teren, creating the division would increase the firm's speed to market and expand its impact in these markets. Through its development of vertical portals and its increased presence on the Web, Cahners had secured a leading position among business-to-business information providers. The company had made a significant impact in the electronic media industry in just two short years—

more than 67 percent of U.S. managerial and professional laborers utilized Cahners's information services.

FURTHER READING:

"A Brief History of Cahners Business Information." New York: Cahners Business Information, 2001. Available from www.cahners.com.

Callahan, Sean. "Cahners's CEO Exits Company Amid Restructuring." *B to B.* October 1, 1999.

Callahan, Sean. "Cahners Rethinks Web Plans." *B to B.* March 27, 2000.

———. "Cahners Revs Up Net Operations." *B to B.* April 10, 2000.

———. "Deals Pump Up Cahners's Internet Presence." *B to B.* June 19, 2000.

Russell, Anne M. "Cahners: The Fast-Moving Company." *Folio.* December, 1998.

SEE ALSO: Auction Sites; Business-to-Business (B2B) E-Commerce; Electronic Publishing

CALL CENTER SERVICES

Call center services have changed dramatically over the past 10 years due in part to increased business taking place on the Internet. Historically, a consumer contacted a call center via a telephone number and was able to talk to a customer service representative to obtain product or service information, register a complaint, and discuss other service-related issues. E-commerce-driven technology, however, has changed how call centers interact with customers and has broadened the services that a call center can provide.

Modern, Web-enabled call centers have adapted to the increased amount of business taking place on the Web by offering consumers both telephone and online service contacts. Many companies have begun to link their call centers to their Web sites in order to provide advanced customer service options. These centers have added e-mail; instant chat, which enables consumers to exchange text messages in real time with service representatives; and other Web-based services such as interactive voice response (IVR), a service that allows consumers to actually speak to service representatives over the Web via PC microphones. Some call centers even offer video services, which enable online customers to see the representative with whom they are in contact. By integrating their Web site with call center services, companies expect to improve customer service, which can increase online sales and eventually cut call center costs.

Many companies that sell their merchandise online find that some consumers, frustrated with the lack of service available online, abandon their order midway through the process. By offering advanced call center services on their Web sites, firms hope to turn those lost sales into completed transactions. The April 2001 edition of *Informationweek.com* reported that 70 percent of call center managers surveyed believed a Web-based call center strategy was critical to their companies, and 26 percent of those surveyed had integrated Web-based call center services into their current operations. The article also stated that "companies should prepare for communications from customers by way of chat, collaboration, e-mail, and Web-based self service," to increase dramatically over the next several years. In fact, according to International Data Corp., the demand for Web-enabled call center services is expected to have an annual growth rate of 20.5 percent through 2003.

Like most traditional brick-and-mortar businesses that shift to Web-based operations, call centers that integrate Web services into their current operations face problems associated with the change. The integration itself, along with problems of staffing and training as well as maintaining quality control, and the cost associated with upgrading current business structures, are all major issues facing a company that wishes to begin offering Web-based services. Companies that offer solutions for Web-based call center services include WorldCom, AT&T Corp., and Qwest Communications. WorldCom, for example, offers network-based call center services that alleviate the high cost of reorganizing a company's infrastructure. By utilizing their call center services—voice, e-mail, fax, and Web-based chat—firms can take advantage of WorldCom's network without having to establish one of their own. When a customer contacts a call center that subscribes to WorldCom's services, either by telephone or by clicking on a link from the specific company's Web site, the request is first sent to a WorldCom network server and then routed to a specific call center that can handle the request.

According to IBM.com, the shift from its traditional call center services to Web-enabled services has been well received. Customers who used Web call-back—a feature that allows consumers to click a specific button on a Web site to request that a customer service representative call them back—and Web chat have spent twice as much money as those using traditional call center services such as an 800 number. These new services have enabled IBM.com customers to get quick answers to questions about products and services. The company's response time for Web call-back and Web chat was two minutes, and e-mail requests typically were handled within four hours.

As the number of online shoppers continues to increase, call centers will continue to integrate Web-based services along with more traditional services. According to the aforementioned *Informationweek.com* article, "the ability of Web-enabled call centers to enhance customer service and to close sales more quickly isn't only appealing, it can be crucial to the bottom line. Call center agents who use e-mail, instant chat, and Web collaboration to interact with customers are able to more quickly and completely handle questions and resolve problems."

FURTHER READING:

Wallace, Bob. "The Modern Call Center." *Informationweek.com News.* April 9, 2001. Available from www.informationweek.com.

————. "WorldCom Bets the Future on its Web Center Service." *Informationweek.com News.* April 9, 2001. Available from www.informationweek.com/832/call_side.htm.

Wilde, Candee. "Web-Enabled Call Center Services Promise to Let Service Providers Put on Quite a Show—Assuming They Don't Drop the Ball." *CMP Media.* June 26, 2000. Available from www.teledotcom.com/.

SEE ALSO: Customer Relationship Management (CRM)

CANION, (JOSEPH) ROD

Joseph Rod Canion is the co-founder of Compaq Computer Corp., one of the largest personal computer (PC) makers in the world. Canion played an instrumental role in the launch of the world's first portable IBM-compatible PC in 1983. He also is credited with parlaying Compaq from a PC upstart into a firm largely responsible for wresting control of PC standards from IBM Corp.

Canion earned a master's degree in electrical engineering from the University of Houston. Eventually, he began working as an engineer for Texas Instruments. In October of 1981, he and partners James Harris and William H. Mutro approached venture capitalists with their plans to build a disk drive for IBM's new PC. When funding appeared imminent, Canion and his partners left their management positions with Texas Instruments. However, the anticipated financial backing fell through, and Canion began examining other options. According to *Computer Reseller News* writer Craig Zarley, "On Jan. 9, 1982, the idea that would change the PC industry forever came to him. He decided to make a better portable PC than the Osborne. But more importantly, it had to run IBM software, a concept of adhering to industry standards that would become Compaq's hallmark."

The idea garnered roughly $1.5 million in venture capital, allowing Canion, Harris, and Mutro to create Compaq Computer. In June, after a prototype of the portable PC had been completed, Compaq secured an additional $8.5 million in funding. The machine hit the market in January of 1983, and sales that year of $111 million set a record for highest first year revenues in U.S. corporate history. Also that year, Canion took his firm public, securing $67 million in fresh capital.

Compaq's early success was due in large part to its ability to bring new products to market in roughly six to nine months, must faster than the industry average of 12 to 18 eighteen months. In July of 1984, Canion oversaw the release of Compaq's first desktop PC, the Deskpro. Sales that year reached $329 million. Microprocessor giant Intel Corp. agreed in 1986 to partner with Compaq to develop its new microprocessor, shortly after IBM revealed its intent to postpone the use of Intel's 386 chip in its PCs. Compaq's Deskpro 386, launched in September, was roughly three times faster than IBM's fastest machines. That year, Compaq became the youngest firm to join the *Fortune* 500. Sales in 1987 eclipsed the $1 billion mark for the first time.

During the late 1980s, Canion was instrumental in Compaq's involvement with the group of PC makers who championed the Extended Industry Standard Architecture (EISA), which undermined IBM Corp.'s effort to put in place its own private set of standards. As the new millennium arrived, he began to steer Compaq toward the server market, believing that PCs would play a pivotal role in the burgeoning networking industry. In 1992, Compaq's board of directors decided that Canion might not be the best person to lead the firm's foray into enterprise computing. Chairman Ben Rosen replaced Canion with Eckhard Pfeiffer that year. Eventually, Canion went on to create consultancy Insource Technologies Corp. From May of 1999 to November of 2000, he served as co-CEO of Tricord Systems Inc. Canion was inducted into the Texas Business Hall of Fame in 2001.

FURTHER READING:

"Compaq Co-Founder, Rod Canion, Named to 2001 Texas Business Hall of Fame." *Business Wire.* September 26, 2001.

Deckmyn, Dominique. "Canion Responds to the Lure of a Start-Up; Compaq Co-founder is Coming out of Semiretirement to Help Reshape Tricord." *Computerworld.* May 24, 1999.

Zarley, Craig. "Rod Canion." *Compuer Reseller News.* November 16, 1997.

SEE ALSO: Compaq Computer Corp.; IBM Inc.; Intel Corp.

CANNIBALIZATION

Cannibalization refers to the business process whereby engaging in one activity or practice necessarily eats into another activity or practice. Cannibalization can take place within a firm, between businesses, or across industries. Cannibalization became a crucial concern as e-commerce flourished in the late 1990s and early 2000s, since the efforts to cash in on the new commercial medium often sacrificed other business practices and sales channels. At the end of 1999, Jupiter Communications predicted that by 2002 only about six percent of all online expenditures would derive from incremental sales, while the remaining 94 percent would proceed through traditional channels, indicating a high degree of cannibalization.

Channel cannibalization involves the devouring of one avenue for generating sales, such as a particular sales outlet or distribution chain, in the name of moving to an Internet-based direct relationship between companies and consumers. With fewer actual stores and physical distribution channels, companies transforming themselves into dot-com players have had to walk the fine line between over-cannibalizing their established distribution channels, thus losing business altogether, and losing their market share by a laggardly shift to the Internet. In addition, many of these established distribution channels are deeply rooted and highly valued by the companies in question, and may be of intrinsic necessity to their success, which raises the stakes of their cannibalization in the pursuit to get online.

The extent to which cannibalization has occurred, and the nature of its effects, varies considerably by industry. Some industries are built on infrastructures that are more conducive to the process of cannibalization than others. In the banking industry, for instance, Deloitte Consulting encouraged not just a basic online operation to supplement regular banking operations, but a more radical infrastructure transformation incorporating the emerging e-business model, even at the risk of cannibalizing existing operations. Online publishers face a similar dilemma. In the rush to set up their online content, magazine and newsletter publishers are faced with a number of questions. To what extent does the online content serve to simply give away our subscription-based content? How do we avoid cannibalizing our subscription revenues while maintaining a Web site with enough content to make it worth visiting? How can the Web site be used to keep revenues flowing and build brand recognition? Some publishers offer only selected content, while others offer their online content via subscription. Additionally, others put their content online for free but offer special bundled content bonuses just to subscribers.

According to the July 2000 issue of *Bank Technology News*, 35 percent of finance professionals in an Arthur Andersen survey felt that a primary effect of cannibalization would be the decline of traditional channels:

- 19 percent cited an affect on middlemen
- 13 percent expected an increase in direct marketing
- 12 percent stated that cannibalization would lead to more price competitiveness
- 11 percent thought that all existing channels would be affected
- 8 percent pointed to inter-industry conflict
- 7 percent thought it would lead to an overhaul of market strategy
- 6 percent expected greater labor mobility
- and 5 percent thought that retail banking operations would be affected.

Despite the harshness of the term, cannibalization is sometimes viewed as a good, or at least necessary, business practice. In these cases, the implementation of new operations or new business channels at the expense of existing ones is deemed an acceptable means of gaining a foothold in changing market conditions. This was particularly true in the relatively rapid transformation from a strictly bricks-and-mortar world to the modern day clicks-and-bricks economy. Getting products and business operations online often was viewed as an absolute market necessity in the late 1990s and early 2000s. Because of this, many companies deliberately cannibalized their existing operations and channels in order to establish an online presence. The alternative was to be completely squeezed out of the game by more Internet-savvy competitors.

Planned cannibalization, however, must be carefully considered and delicately executed. Eating away at existing operations may be a necessary step for restructuring. However, if not mediated the results can quickly devolve into internal chaos that can bring a company's productivity and earnings tumbling. Even where cannibalization is viewed as an advisable strategy, analysts agree that over the long run, businesses and industries would do well to limit the degree of attendant cannibalization, as it inevitably involves suboptimal efficiency and lower profits.

FURTHER READING:

Christman, Ed. ''Retail 'Cannibalization' By Net Sales Seen.'' *Billboard*. August 21, 1999.

Cuneo, Alice Z. ''Cannibalization is the Buzzword and the Consumer is King, But the Day-to-Day Pressure to Cut Costs Will Squeeze Store Chains.'' *Advertising Age*. September 20, 1999.

Dean, Bill. ''Cannibalization? Don't Bet on It.'' *Marketing News.* June 26, 2000.

''Fear of Cannibals.'' *Bank Technology News.* July, 2000.

Lehmann, R. J. ''Is Your Web Site Stealing Your Readers.'' *Folio.* September 15, 2000.

———. ''Learn e-Business—or Risk e-Limination.'' *Business Week.* March 22, 1999.

''Ready, Set—Innovate.'' *Community Banker.* February, 2000.

SEE
ALSO: Channel Conflict/Harmony; Channel Transparency

CARD-ISSUING BANK

Card-issuing banks issue credit cards to consumers. When a consumer uses a credit card to purchase a product or service, an acquiring bank, also known as a merchant bank, obtains approval from the card-issuing bank at the time of the transaction. A merchant is a business—or in terms of e-commerce, a Web site—that accepts credit or debit cards in exchange for goods or services. Merchants must establish a relationship with an acquiring bank in order to process transactions and obtain cash from credit card purchases. A merchant also must utilize online credit card processing software in order to accept credit or debit cards as a method of payment on the World Wide Web.

A basic credit card transaction begins when a consumer selects goods or services on a merchant's Web site and begins filling out a merchant commerce application. Because of consumer fears about the risks associated with online credit card use, most merchants utilize secure electronic transaction (SET) specifications that support credit card payments over the Web. Once a commerce application is complete, the merchant sends it to the acquiring bank by way of real-time online processing software, which allows for real-time transactions. A real-time transaction is one that either is accepted or declined immediately after the commerce application is completed. Once the acquiring bank receives the commerce application, it then sends a request for credit card authorization to the acquiring processor—a company that provides credit card processing, billing, reporting, and settlement services. The acquiring processor sends the request to the card-issuing bank, which either issues an approval or denial code and sends a message back to the acquiring bank. The acquiring processor then sends the code to the merchant. This entire process usually takes 10 to 15 seconds.

A consumer's credit card is not charged at the time of purchase. However, the card-issuing bank does put a hold on the card for the transaction amount. A merchant's batch—all of the credit card transactions that took place during a specific timeframe—typically are settled at the end of the business day. The consumer's credit card is charged and the acquiring bank receives the funds, in a transaction known as an interchange, from the card-issuing bank. Those funds are then placed into the merchant's bank account.

In the past, credit card transactions took place either in a retail outlet or by mail or telephone order. However, e-commerce has led to a growing number of transactions that take place on the Web. Card-issuing banks will, no doubt, continue to play an important role in this process.

FURTHER READING:

''Glossary of E-Commerce Terms.'' E-com Publishing Pty. Ltd. Samford, Australia: E-com Publishing Pty. Ltd., 2001. Available from www.ecompublishing.com/glossary.

SEE
ALSO: Acquiring Bank; Authorizaton and Authorization Code; Charge-back; Electronic Payment; Interchange and Interchange Fee

CARPENTER, CANDICE

Candice Carpenter is co-founder and chairman of iVillage Inc., the largest online service for women and one of the largest content sites on the World Wide Web, with traffic rates of more than 5 million users monthly. The network, geared toward women between the ages of 25 and 54, offers 18 different channels: astrology, babies, beauty, books, computing, diet and fitness, food, games, health, home and garden, Lamaze, money, news and issues, parenting, pets, relationships, shopping, and work. Among other things, visitors are able to communicate with online experts on a wide range of topics, join discussion and support groups, post messages, provide links to their own Web sites, enter contests, and shop. Membership is free, as the company makes its money via advertising and sponsorships, as well as from products it sells online.

After earning a bachelor's degree in biology from Stanford University, Carpenter went on to attain a master's degree from Harvard Business School in 1983. She launched her career at American Express Co., where she eventually was appointed vice president of the financial firm's consumer marketing division. Between 1989 and 1993, Carpenter served as president of Time Warner's Time Life Video and Television. In 1994, she convinced QVC Inc. Chairman Barry Diller to create a home shopping channel that offered more high-end merchandise. Diller agreed, and appointed Carpenter president of the new Q2 shopping channel, a venture that eventually flopped.

When America Online (AOL) hired Carpenter as a consultant in 1995, she had already been entertaining ideas about how the Internet could serve as a resource for women. The result of her vision, iVillage.com, was launched in June of 1995 with Carpenter at the helm as CEO. AOL backed the new venture with a $2 million investment.

Carpenter spent the next few years broadening iVillage's content base and developing e-commerce alliances with companies that sold products specifically for women. She added the additional role of co-chairperson to her duties at iVillage in December of 1998, and took her company public four months later. As with the initial public offerings of many dot-com upstarts, the newly public firm saw its share prices skyrocket on the first day of trading. However, the high was short-lived as shareholders began grumbling when iVillage had not yet achieved profitability by the middle of the following year. In August of 2000, Carpenter handed managerial control of the firm to president Doug McCormick. As chairperson, she continues to work on honing iVillage's strategy and steering its scaled down expansion efforts.

FURTHER READING:

Brookman, Faye. ''An i Toward Profitability; iVillage Inc.'' *Crain's New York Business.* November 27, 2000.

————. ''Millionaires of Silicon Alley: Candice Carpenter.'' *Crain's New York Business.* November 29, 1999.

iVillage Inc. ''Corporate Profile.'' New York: iVillage Inc., 2000. Available from www.corporate- ir.net.

SEE ALSO: AOL Time Warner Inc.; iVillage.com; Women and the Internet

CARSDIRECT.COM

In mid-2001, CarsDirect.com was one of the few surviving online direct auto buying services and a brand leader in the industry. It acquired competitor Greenlight.com at the end of January 2001, while other sites—including Microsoft CarPoint's Drive-Off.com subsidiary and CarOrder.com of Austin, Texas—were shutting down. Nevertheless, CarsDirect.com CEO Robert Brisco was confident that the company would survive, eventually go public, and even achieve profitability.

SUCCESSFUL TEST LED TO NATIONAL MAY 1999 LAUNCH

CarsDirect.com was created at the Internet incubator Idealab, which also developed such Internet companies as eToys.com and GoTo.com. Co-founders were Bill Gross, founder of Idealab, and Scott Painter, who became CarsDirect.com's CEO. At the time CarsDirect.com was founded in Culver City, California, in late 1998, it was a bold step to try and sell autos and trucks directly to consumers through a Web site. Existing auto buying services, such as Autoweb.com and Autobytel.com, did not sell cars themselves. Rather, they referred prospective buyers to brick-and-mortar dealers, who paid them for the referrals.

CarsDirect.com began selling vehicles over the Internet through a test program launched in December 1998. Loan and lease financing for customers was provided by Bank One Corp., which partnered with CarsDirect.com to form CD1 Financial.com, an Internet auto lending and leasing company. The outlook for online car-buying services was favorable, according to Forrester Research, whose report noted that 2 million people researched their new car purchases online in 1998. Forrester projected that 17,000 people would buy their cars online in 1999, a figure that was projected to increase to 470,000 households by 2003, representing $12 billion in online sales.

CarsDirect.com's test proved successful. It sold 277 cars in April 1999, and in May the company launched its national Web site. It had received about $30 million in financing from several sources, including Idealab, which held a 40 percent stake in the company, and Michael Dell's venture capital firm MSD Capital LP. In the two months following its official launch, CarsDirect.com sold more than $1.5 million worth of vehicles a day, making it the fastest growing company developed by Idealab. It obtained vehicles from a network of 1,200 dealers.

To purchase a vehicle, prospective customers would use a series of pull-down menus at the company's Web site to select their cars and choose their options. In the final step, customers chose a method of financing their purchase. As the *Los Angeles Business Journal* noted, ''CarsDirect is the only company through which a customer can make a complete purchase on the Web'' of an automobile or truck. Later in the year, Gomez Advisors Inc., which ranked Web retailers, named CarsDirect.com the best overall automotive resource for online customers among the more than 100 automotive Web sites that offered some type of shopping help.

AIMED TO BE A BRAND LEADER

Five months after its national launch, CarsDirect.com began building its brand with a $20 million advertising campaign for the fourth quarter of 1999. The company hoped the campaign would help boost sales from more than 1,000 cars a month to more than 2,500 by the end of the year. According to Media Metrix, CarsDirect.com received 215,000 unique visitors in August 1999. Comparatively, referral site Autoweb.com received 731,000 visitors and Autobytel.com received 1.1 million. By November the company was selling more than 1,400 vehicles a month. As part of its brand-building efforts, CarsDirect.com announced a three-year deal to sponsor a NASCAR Winston Cup race at the Las Vegas Motor Speedway.

Also in the fourth quarter, CarsDirect.com named Robert Brisco as its new CEO, with former CEO and co-founder Scott Painter moving to vice chairman. Brisco was 36 years old when he joined CarsDirect.com. He formerly was president of the theme park and entertainment complex Universal Studios Hollywood and CityWalk. At one time, Brisco also worked as an advertising and marketing executive at the *Los Angeles Times.* He joined CarsDirect.com just after the company had raised $280 million in its mezzanine round of financing, an amount considered one of the largest private equity placements ever secured by an Internet company. Brisco planned to use the new investment capital to improve customer service and build the firm's brand. He told the *Los Angeles Business Journal,* ''We want to make this the best retail experience consumers have ever had.'' Brisco also announced plans to expand the company's network of 1,700 dealer partners.

SURVIVED DOT.COM SHAKEOUT OF 2000

By the time Brisco took over as CEO, CarsDirect.com had figured out how to price its vehicles without losing money on every sale. Initially, its policy was to price vehicles at invoice plus one percent. That resulted in under-pricing by about $1,500 per vehicle. CarsDirect then changed its policy to make deals at market prices. The company found that some high-demand vehicles could be sold at a much larger premium over invoice, while other vehicles could be sold below invoice price. By the end of 1999 the company was breaking even on its vehicle sales. It expected much of its revenue would come from the finance, leasing, insurance, and warranty products it could sell along with each vehicle. Dealers would participate by earning incremental income and handling trade-ins.

In early 2000 CarsDirect.com began offering extended service contracts, which added $800 to $900 to the cost of a vehicle. The company also improved its Web site by adding live online customer service technology that helped shoppers fill out forms and complete the purchase process. In March 2000 CarsDirect forged an alliance with competitor Autoweb.com in an effort to capture a larger share of online automotive buyers. The two companies planned to jointly develop a direct new car buying service on Autoweb.com which would enable consumers to receive a fixed price on vehicles and conduct the entire purchase process online.

CarsDirect.com, as well as the entire online auto business, suffered through several speed bumps in 2000, some more serious than others. At least two consumer-based studies offered negative assessments of the online auto business. They included one by CNW Marketing/Research, which showed that eight different Web sites, including CarsDirect.com, routinely published inaccurate pricing information. An evaluation of five sites by *Consumer Reports* found that in many cases potential customers did not receive requested price quotes within two days. Oftentimes, the quotes were for vehicles other than those consumers requested. Meanwhile, established brick-and-mortar dealers were lobbying state legislatures to further restrict online auto sales, which already were prohibited in 11 states. Additional opposition was coming from the Big Three automakers, which warned their dealers not to sell cars to online brokers. For its part, CarsDirect.com noted that it was not a broker, did not intend to buy dealerships, and was not violating any dealer franchise agreements with the automakers.

CarsDirect.com planned to go public in 2000 and filed for an initial public offering (IPO) in May 2000. It planned to raise $175.2 million through its IPO. However, as the market for Internet IPOs shriveled during the year, CarsDirect.com scrapped its IPO plans in December. It was one of 27 companies that withdrew their registration statements for IPOs. Although CarsDirect.com lost $144 million in the previous 15 months, the company announced it had developed plans to be a profitable, long-term player. As a private company, it had raised more than $300 million in private equity financing since its inception. That included a mid-2000 investment from the Penske Automotive Group, which bought a 10-percent interest in CarsDirect.com for $17 million. As a result, all 117 Penske-owned dealerships would display their inventory on CarsDirect.com's Web site. By this time CarsDirect.com had 2,500 licensed franchised dealers in its network. Following the investment by Penske, Roger Penske replaced Scott Painter on CarsDirect.com's board of directors, and Painter subsequently left the company to start a new company called Direct Ventures.

The end of 2000 and early 2001 saw an industry downturn for online auto sales. CarsDirect.com reduced its workforce by 12 percent in November, laying off about 90 of its 750 employees. On February

15, 2001, Microsoft CarPoint shut down its Drive-Off.com subsidiary. The direct selling segment of the online auto business further consolidated in February 2001 when CarsDirect.com acquired competitor Greenlight.com, which enjoyed exclusive arrangements with Amazon.com and Autotrader.com. Following the acquisition, CarsDirect.com CEO Robert Brisco noted three immediate benefits. First, CarsDirect.com experienced a 25-percent increase in sales and traffic, much of which came from Greenlight.com's relationships with Amazon.com and Autotrader.com. Second, the acquisition brought in three more top dealer groups to the company's network of dealer partners, giving CarsDirect.com four of the top six automotive dealership groups in the United States. Finally, CarsDirect.com gained customer relationship management (CRM) technology in the acquisition. As a result of the acquisition of Greenlight.com, CarsDirect.com became the exclusive automotive partner of Amazon.com and had a ''car tab'' on its site. The company also gained direct mail access to Amazon.com's huge customer base of 29 million people, representing one in 10 U.S. households.

By 2001 CarsDirect.com had increased the size of its affiliated dealer network to nearly 3,000 dealers. Brisco noted that the industry was in the midst of a shakeout, where only the strongest, best-capitalized companies would survive. He predicted that there would be another year or two of industry consolidation. Meanwhile, CarsDirect.com would offer consumers the largest multi-brand automotive shopping experience in the marketplace.

FURTHER READING:

CarsDirect.com. ''The Company.'' March 30, 2001. Available from www.carsdirect.com.

Couretas, John. ''CarsDirect Tops Online Buying List from Gomez.'' *Automotive News.* September 20, 1999.

''Dot-Coms to Dot-Bombs.'' *Automotive News.* January 22, 2001.

Edgerton, Jerry. ''Cars: Smart Strategies for Shopping Online.'' *Money.* October 15, 2000.

Gordon, Maynard M. ''Battle Lines Forming in the Wild World of the Automotive Websites.'' *Ward's Dealer Business.* June, 2000.

Harris, Donna. ''Greenlight.com CEO Steps Down; CarsDirect.com Founder Leaves.'' *Automotive News.* August 14, 2000.

Sieroty, Chris. ''Wheeling through Cyberspace.'' *Los Angeles Business Journal.* February 19, 2001.

Smith, Jennifer. ''Brisco Has Plans for Investment Money at CarsDirect.com.'' *Los Angeles Business Journal.* November 22, 1999.

Taub, Daniel. ''Firm Proves People Are Ready to Buy Cars on the Web.'' *Los Angeles Business Journal.* August 23, 1999.

Wang, Andy. ''CarsDirect Closes Near-Record Equity Placement.'' *E-Commerce Times.* November 16, 1999. Available from www.ecommercetimes.com.

SEE ALSO: Greenlight.com; Business-to-Consumer (B2C) E-commerce

CASE, STEPHEN M.

Stephen Case is chairman of media colossus AOL Time Warner Inc. Credited with making the Internet accessible to the general public, Case oversaw America Online's growth from a small online service into the world's number one Internet access provider, with 28 million members. One of the first profitable Internet ventures, America Online also was the first Internet-based company to be listed in the *Fortune* 500. Case developed a business model that allowed his firm to make money in a variety of ways, include charging subscription fees, selling online advertising, and developing e-commerce deals with online retailers. Prior to its 2001 merger with Time Warner, employees at AOL, where Case served as chairman and CEO, totaled 14,000 and revenues had reached nearly $7 billion.

A native of Hawaii, Case earned his undergraduate degree in political science at Williams College. He launched his career as a marketing manager at Procter & Gamble, where he developed brands of different health and beauty products. In the early 1980s, he joined Pizza Hut and began developing new types of pizza for the chain. Well before personal computers became commonplace in American homes, Case went online, using a service known as the Source, along with his Kaypro personal computer and a 300-baud modem. He began working in the marketing department of Control Video, which ran an online service for Atari users, in 1983.

When Control Video went bankrupt, the 26-year-old Case and partner Jim Kimsey secured $2 million in financial backing for a new venture. In May of 1985, the pair established Quantum Computer Services Inc. in conjunction with Commodore International Ltd. At first, Quantum offered Q-Link, its modem-based online service, to Commodore personal computer (PC) users only. Owners of PCs made by Tandy Corp. and other companies were able to link to the service starting in 1987. That year, the firm achieved profitability for the first time on total sales of $9 million. Case made online services available to owners of IBM-compatible PCs in 1988 and unveiled a version compatible with Macintosh machines the following year. Enticed by the potential of a mass market for interactive online services and content, Case put together a nationwide online network for PC owners called America Online (AOL) and eventually convinced his partners to change the firm's name to

America Online Inc. When the service was officially launched in 1989, it included games, e-mail, and real-time chat capabilities.

Case was named president of AOL in 1990. One of his first moves was to orchestrate a reorganization that entailed consolidating operations to focus on IBM-compatible and Macintosh computer markets and upping the firm's subscribers base via intense marketing efforts, like giving AOL software away for free, and partnerships with media firms. For example, to strengthen its position in the Midwest, AOL forged an alliance with Tribune Co., publisher of the *Chicago Tribune,* to develop an online information service consisting mainly of local news for residents of Chicago and surrounding areas. As part of the deal, Tribune paid $5 million for a minority stake in AOL. Case took his firm public in 1992 and was appointed chairman and CEO the next year.

After convincing his board to turn down a buyout offer from Microsoft in 1993, Case forged content deals with media firms like Knight-Ridder and CNN. He also steered AOL's development of a version of its online service for the Windows platform. In response to predictions that the World Wide Web would render online services like AOL obsolete, Case decided in 1994 to develop a gateway, AOL.com, to offer subscribers a link to the Internet from AOL. That year, the number of AOL members exceeded 1 million for the first time.

Case took his firm international for the first time in 1995 with service in Germany. Subscribers grew to 3 million. He entered Canada, France, and the United Kingdom the following year and also oversaw a landmark deal with Microsoft in which AOL agreed to include Microsoft's Internet Explorer browser in its software, and Microsoft agreed to include AOL software on its Windows 95 platform. Determined to position his firm as the leader in online services, Case reached similar cross marketing deals with AT&T, Apple, Sun Microsystems, Hewlett-Packard, and Netscape Communications. In October of 1996, AOL hired Robert Pittman as president and chief operating officer. Case put him in charge of AOL's e-commerce strategy, and Pittman began securing agreements from online retailing giants like Amazon.com to sell their merchandise on AOL. With revenues of more than $1 billion, AOL entered Japan in 1997. Membership grew to more than 10 million subscribers that year. According to Case, the reason for AOL's success was its simplicity. In an October 1996 *Forbes* article he stated, ''If you want to reach a mainstream audience, you have to make it more plug and play. One-stop shopping. One disk to install. One price to pay. One customer service number to call.''

AOL's meteoric rise to dominance certainly wasn't glitch-free, however. For example, the firm became the target of a class-action lawsuit regarding its billing practices in the mid-1990s. Also, a technical snafu in 1996 shut the service down for 19 hours. When the firm launched a $19.95 per month flat fee program, with no limits on usage, it was ill-prepared for the crush of increased traffic it received. Users trying to get online became increasingly frustrated by busy signals, and eventually representatives from 36 state attorneys general offices met to address the issue. In an effort to counter the negative publicity, Case put in place a $350 million expansion program that included upping AOL's system capacity and hiring 600 new customer service representatives. The firm also agreed to give refunds to U.S. customers who frequently were unable to access their accounts.

Despite being lambasted for AOL's troubles, Case stuck to his strategy of offering a user-friendly, comprehensive online service to an increasing number of subscribers. With the technical snags behind him, Case oversaw two major acquisitions in 1998: instant messaging firm ICQ and rival CompuServe Inc. In 1999, AOL added Netscape Communications to its growing list of holdings. Case's tenacity served him well. According to *BusinessWeek Online* writer Catherine Yang in September 1999, ''more than any other leader in e-business, the 41-year-old chairman of America Online Inc. is responsible for bringing the Internet revolution to the masses.''

The following year, AOL began offering online access to wireless consumers with AOL Mobile Messenger, after recognizing that an increasing number of Web surfers were using things like cell phones and broadband technology, rather than PCs, to access the Internet. AOL also purchased MapQuest.com Inc. In 2001, Case made a bold move designed to cement AOL's future position as a leading Internet player. He orchestrated one of the largest mergers in media industry history—the $183 billion union of AOL and Time Warner Inc. to form AOL Time Warner Inc. Case accepted the post of chairman of the newly merged firm and began focusing his efforts on honing AOL Time Warner's strategy. The impact this merger will have on both firms, as well as on the Internet and media industry, remains to be seen.

FURTHER READING:

''America Online Inc.'' In *Notable Corporate Chronologies.* Farmington Hills, MI: Gale Group, 1999.

''At the Epicenter of the Revolution.'' *BusinessWeek Online.* September 16, 1999. Available from www.businessweek.com.

Byrne, John A. ''Commentary: Is This Baby Built for Cyberspace?'' *BusinessWeek Online.* January 24, 2000. Available from www.businessweek.com.

''Executive Biography: Stephen M. Case.'' New York: AOL Time Warner Inc., 2000. Available from www.aoltimewarner.com.

Gilbert, Jennifer. ''Steve Case.'' *Advertising Age.* April 17, 2000.

Koprowski, Gene. ''AOL CEO Steve Case.'' *Forbes*. October 17, 1996.

Simons, John. ''Steve Case Wants to Get America Online.'' *U.S. News & World Report*. March 25, 1996.

''A Theory of Case.'' *The Economist*. January 15, 2000.

''Timeline.'' New York: AOL Time Warner Inc., 2000. Available from www.aoltimewarner.com/about/timeline.

Vogelstein, Fred. ''The Talented Mr. Case.'' *U.S. News & World Report*. January 24, 2000.

Yang, Catherine. ''America Online: Often Down, Never Out.'' *BusinessWeek Online*. July 20, 1998. Available from www.businessweek.com/1998/29/b3587058.htm.

———. ''Stephen M. Case.'' *BusinessWeek Online*. September 27, 1999. Available from www.businessweek.com.

———. ''Steve Case.'' *BusinessWeek Online*. May 15, 2000. Available from www.businessweek.com.

SEE ALSO: AOL Time Warner Inc.; Internet Access, Tracking Growth of; Internet Service Provider (ISP)

CASIO COMPUTER CO. LTD.

Casio Computer Co. Ltd., headquartered in Tokyo, Japan, is one of the world's leading developers of consumer electronic devices like calculators and watches. The firm also makes digital cameras, business organizers, and pagers. One of its most popular products, the Cassiopeia Pocket PC, is the leading handheld computer using the Windows CE platform. In the late 1990s, Casio began focusing on developing wireless Internet, personal computer, and telecommunications products.

EARLY HISTORY

In April of 1946, engineer Tadao Kashio and his three younger brothers began developing a fully electric calculator. More than a decade later, in June of 1957, the Kashio brothers began selling the 14-A all-electric compact calculator. They incorporated their company under the name Casio Computer Co. Ltd. In 1965, the firm introduced the 001, one of the world's first desktop calculators with memory functions. Although they were becoming smaller in size, calculators were still beyond the financial reach of most consumers, so Casio began working on a more affordable device. In August of 1972, the company unveiled the first personal calculator, the Casio Mini. By that time, the firm's factory in Kofu had begun to mass-produce electronic calculators, and was the first Japanese plant to do so. The firm also had expanded internationally by marketing its products in the United States and Germany.

Using similar digital technology, Casio turned its attention to watches in the early 1970s. As a result, the world's first electronic wristwatch, the Casiotron, was developed in November of 1974. It was able to digitally display not only time, but also date. International expansion continued in 1975 when the firm launched operations in London. Casio Taiwan Ltd. was established three years later. An electronic cash register came in 1976, followed by a wristwatch with a liquid crystal display (LCD) in 1978, an office computer in 1979, and an electronic music synthesizer, known as Casiotone 201, in 1980. Three years later, Casio introduced pocket LCD televisions and calculators the size of credit cards. With increased competition undercutting prices, and thus profits, Casio devoted more resources to research and development efforts in 1985. The following year, the firm unveiled an office computer based on Unix. North American operations were bolstered with a new office in Canada. Units also opened in Hong Kong, South Korea, and Tokyo in 1987, and a new series of automated data-processing machines were shipped. By the end of the 1980s, Casio was the world's largest calculator manufacturer in terms of market share, and calculators accounted for roughly 42 percent of revenues.

In the early 1990s Casio sought to expand existing markets by developing new technology, which allowed for further diversification within those markets. For example, the company began expanding its reach in musical markets by creating sound devices for use in live performances. It also developed a digital piano with a CD player. In 1991, the firm founded Casio Electronic Devices to begin marketing its component products, including miniaturized electronic circuitry and LCDs. Casio also purchased a majority stake in Asahi Corp., a communications equipment and electrical appliances manufacturer. Additional product releases at that time included printers, word processors, and a lightweight LCD television.

FOCUS ON WIRELESS COMMUNICATIONS

Casio was a fairly early player in the personal communications services (PCS) market. In March of 1994, the firm shipped its first paging device, which offered alphanumeric messaging capabilities. A year later, it introduced the Casio PhoneMate LT-70 video telephone and an FM teletext receiver. Casio became the world's first mass producer of digital cameras in 1995 when it shipped the QV-10 digital camera with an LCD monitor. In 1996, Casio unveiled the Cassiopeia, a Windows CE-based handheld computer system with 2MB of RAM, audio capabilities, and limited versions of popular word processing, spreadsheet and scheduling programs. The Cassiopeia also boasted e-mail capabilities via Microsoft Exchange and was able to accommodate wireless data transfer.

Casio entered the U.S. pager market in 1997 after announcing an intent to increase its focus on telecommunications products. The following year, the firm established Casio Soft Inc. to develop and market additional Windows CE applications for its U.S. customers. In January of 2000, America Online and Casio agreed to develop software that would allow AOL subscribers to use their Cassiopeia handheld computer for checking, sending, and receiving e-mail. According to a January 2000 *Business Wire* article, the deal was part of Casio's attempt to "target the mobile needs that arise for personal computers, the Internet, and the rapid growth of mobile telecommunications markets." In keeping with this strategy, the firm worked with FotoNation Inc. to develop a digital camera from which users could upload pictures directly to the Zing.com Web site.

It was at this time that Casio began seriously targeting the corporate sector with its Pocket PC. In June of 2000, Casio and Sybase Inc.'s iAnywhere Solutions unit forged a joint venture to make mobile e-business products and market them on a global scale. Specifically, Casio began using the SQL Anywhere Studio—along with mobile integration and database technology—on its corporate Pocket PCs. Early in 2001, to set its product apart from competitors like Palm and address security concerns about giving corporate intranet access to wireless devices, the firm connected its Cassiopeia E-707 Pocket PC to a packet communications service that only allows authorized users to access corporate networks.

FURTHER READING:

"Casio Aims for Corporate Niche with Wireless Handheld." *Bloomberg News.* December 12, 2000. Available from news.cnet.com/news.

"Casio and American Online Announce Agreement to Deliver AOL E-Mail Via Casio's Pocket PCs." *Business Wire.* January 6, 2000.

Casio Computer Co. Ltd. "Company Information." Tokyo: Casio Computer Co. Ltd., 2001. Available from world.casio.com/.

"Casio Computer Co. Ltd." In *Notable Corporate Chronologies.* Farmington Hills, MI: Gale Group, 1999.

"Casio & Sybase Inc. to Provide Mobile E-Business Solutions." *Software Industry Report.* June 19, 2000.

"Casio, Zing.com and FotoNation to Announce the First Internet Camera End-to-End Solution." *Business Wire.* January 6, 2000.

SEE ALSO: Personal Digital Assistant (PDA)

CDNOW INC.

Since October of 2000, CDNow Inc. has operated as a division of the Bertelsmann eCommerce Group, a unit of German media behemoth Bertelsmann AG. A leading online music retailer, CDNow sells more than 50,000 items including CDs, VHS and DVD movies, and digital music downloads. Along with making purchases, the site's roughly 700,000 daily visitors can download free music from a database of 650,000 samples; peruse album reviews, music industry news, and related content; and view video clips of interviews with various musicians. CDNow had approximately 4 million customers in the early 2000s.

RAPID GROWTH AS A DOT-COM STARTUP

After having difficulty locating information about various musicians in the retail music stores he frequented, Jason Olim dreamed up the idea of selling CDs on a Web site that also would house a database of the information typically found in a music encyclopedia. Jason recruited his twin brother Matthew, a Columbia University astrophysics student, to write the code for the site. In August of 1994, with $20,000 in capital, the partners launched CDNow from their parents' basement in Fort Washington, Pennsylvania. Visitors to the virtual store could search its database for any CD or artist and make a purchase with a credit card. To facilitate order fulfillment, Olim forged agreements with several warehouses, which shipped purchases directly to customers.

Within a year, sales at CDNow had reached $2 million. RealAudio sound samples were added to the site in 1996, allowing visitors to listen to various song samples from a CD before making a purchase. By 1997, roughly 500 new titles were being added to CDNow's database every week. That year, revenues jumped to $6.3 million. Advertising efforts in 1997 included links from leading online search site Yahoo!, live promotions on the Howard Stern radio show, and spots in leading magazines. Content offerings were enhanced with music reviews from "Rolling Stone," *Spin,* and other leading music magazines, as well as articles submitted by freelance writers. CDNow's e-mod (encoded music for online delivery) technology allowed the firm to legally transmit copyrighted music via the Web, although it did not actually begin selling music online until two years later. By the end of its third full year of operation, CDNow had become the leading music retailer on the Internet, with sales of $17.4 million and a market share of roughly 33 percent.

The Olim brothers took their firm public in 1998, selling shares for $16 each. They also launched My CDNow, allowing visitors to customize their shopping experience based on their musical preferences, and ShopperConnection, which linked their site to other top e-tailers. The purchase of superSonic-BOOM, the first online music retailer to allow shoppers to purchase customized CDs, allowed CDNow to create its Custom Shop and begin selling customized CDs. In December of 1999, CDNow began selling music downloads for the first time. The initial 13,000 tracks for sale, available in Liquid Audio format, included works by Tony Bennett, Johnny Cash, Frank Sinatra, and Beck. The firm also began selling VHS and DVD movies for the first time via a new virtual Video Shop. Sales in 1999 grew to $147 million. However, like most dot-com startups, CDNow found profitability elusive, losing $119 million that year.

IMPACT OF INCREASED COMPETITION AND DOT-COM FALLOUT

Despite CDNow's rapid growth, competition from the likes of Amazon.com and barnesandnoble.com began taking its toll on the firm in 2000. That year, Amazon surpassed CDNow in music sales. CDNow found it difficult to compete with Amazon's massive customer base and customer service savvy. A survey completed by Forrester Research Inc. ranked CDNow fourth—behind Amazon, barnesandnoble.com, and buy.com—on its list of the best music Web sites, citing poor customer service, unreliable delivery, and technology glitches as common problems faced by users of CDNow. However, the survey complimented CDNow on its buyers' guides, which helped users to select merchandise.

A merger deal with club-based music and video seller Columbia House, announced in July of 1999, fell through in March of 2000. This prompted speculation that the dot-com fallout and CDNow's resulting stock price plunge had soured the deal. Others pointed to CDNow's $30 million debt and lack of profitability—it had lost roughly $200 million since its inception—as reasons for the nixed plans, which caused share prices to tumble 28 percent. Columbia House co-owners Sony Corp. and Time Warner Inc. still invested $51 million in CDNow. However, reports that the firm might run out of cash by September pushed stock to a record low of $3.50. According to a March 2000 issue of *Billboard* magazine, after the demise of the merger deal, CDNow was perceived as "struggling to keep pace with market leader Amazon.com and as scrambling to find a partner with deep pockets before it runs out of money."

To cuts costs, CDNow slashed its advertising expenditures and closed its London office. The firm also began diversifying its revenue stream by increasing sales of ads, such as banner bars, buttons, and sponsorships, on its site. Customer retention programs, including reward and incentive schemes, were put in place. According to a June 2000 article in *Brandweek,* the changes were designed to "make the beleaguered music e-tailer a more attractive package for potential investors or partners." CDNow's efforts paid off in July, when international media giant Bertelsmann agreed to purchase the firm for roughly $117 million, or $3 per share.

Bertelsmann's e-commerce efforts had been formally launched in 1998, when the firm bought half of barnesandnoble.com for $200 million and created its own online retail book site to take on Amazon.com in Europe. By the time it began considering a takeover of CDNow, Bertelsmann had funneled roughly $13 billion into its Internet operations. For example, it had involved itself in the founding of Terra Lycos, created when Spain-based Terra Networks bought Lycos, a leading U.S.-based World Wide Web portal, for $12.5 billion. Bertelsmann secured itself access to the 50 million customers already using either Terra Networks or Lycos. CDNow's founders believed that Bertelsmann's market reach would allow their firm to better compete with Amazon.

In October, Bertelsmann merged CDNow into its newly formed Bertelsmann eCommerce Group, headed by former AOL Europe executive Adreas Schmidt. Jason Olim was named chairman of CDNow, which began operating as a wholly owned subsidiary of Bertelsmann. Believing that CDNow had built a viable brand, Schmidt maintained the CDNow name and planned to use the site mainly as a music hub for Bertelsmann's existing online music operations, such as its GetMusic site, a joint venture with Seagram Co.'s Universal Music Group. With access to Bertelsmann's deeper pockets, CDNow continued to grow in the months following its takeover. For example, the firm began offering wireless access to its site in late 2000 via deals with ViaFone Inc. and Sprint PCS. CDNow also saw its video sales double by early 2001 after expanding its video offerings to more than 70,000 titles and adding content such as film reviews and best seller lists to its Video Shop.

FURTHER READING:

"Bertelsmann to Acquire CDNow." *Direct Marketing.* October 2000.

"CDNow." *Inc.* January 1, 2001.

"CDNow Achieves Milestone of One Million Daily Visits; Reports Record-Breaking Number of Visits to the Site Within 24-Hour Period." *PR Newswire.* December 8, 1999.

"CDNow's Movie Sales More Than Double in One Year Since Launch of New Store." *PR Newswire.* February 26, 2001.

"CDNow To Sell Track Downloads." *Billboard.* December 11, 1999.

Garrity, Brian, and Don Jeffrey. ''What Now for Col. House, CDNow?'' *Billboard.* March 25, 2000.

Gillen, Marilyn A. ''Bertelsmann Gains Web Hub with Purchase of CDNow.'' *Billboard.* July 29, 2000.

Mack, Ann M. ''CDNow Shifts Strategy from Spending to Selling.'' *Brandweek.* June 12, 2000.

Nelson, Randolf. ''CDNow Takes a Leading Role in Mobile Commerce.'' *InformationWeek.* November 6, 2000.

''New Forrester Powerrankings Find Amazon.com Number One on the Online Music Charts.'' *Business Wire.* May 8, 2000.

SEE ALSO: Amazon.com; Bertelsmann AG; Terra Lycos Inc.

CHANGE, MANAGING

Traditional brick-and-mortar enterprises are finding it necessary to adopt some sort of e-business strategy as the Internet continues to become a powerful venue for exchanging information as well as for buying and selling products and services. According to Forrester Research, business-to-business e-commerce alone is predicted to generate $1.3 trillion by 2003. Managing the changes that go along with integrating traditional business strategies and e-business plans, however, can often be a multi-faceted and challenging task. Nevertheless, the ultimate goal for many enterprises embarking on an e-business mission is to become a holistic Internet-enabled entity. This entity is one that has fully integrated its e-commerce initiatives into its corporate vision.

Whether simply creating a company Web site or developing a plan to provide products and services via the Internet, an enterprise entering the e-business world is faced with several major issues. Developing an e-business vision and strategy, training employees, adapting to new technology, integrating the new e-business strategy into current operations, and handling new customer relationships, are all important steps in managing change.

MANAGING THE DEVELOPMENT OF AN E-BUSINESS STRATEGY

The shift from a traditional brick-and-mortar enterprise to a click-and-mortar entity typically begins with the formation of the e-business strategy itself, which is often a time consuming and labor intensive process. Many steps are involved in creating an effective business approach, and many levels of management are typically involved. The enterprise must first decide on the common goals it wishes to achieve by implementing an e-business plan. Management should decide why it is going online and what benefits the Internet can provide. It must decide if it is going to target existing customers or try to attract new ones. The enterprise also needs to select target markets and advertising methods, decide what it will be promoting online, identify competitors, and be in tune with conditions in its selected markets.

While these steps are no doubt important, managing the change that goes along with creating a new business strategy is often difficult, and even overlooked. According to a study done by Deloitte and Touche in 2000, 70 percent of online retailers surveyed did not have an e-commerce strategy. Many simply had established a Web site to test demand for their product or service on the Internet. The study did find that those who took the time to develop a strategy were outpacing their competition. According to a January 2000 *E-Commerce Times* article, ''these e-tail leaders have developed a strategy that integrates their Web efforts with other channels. Their e-business effort is designed to win market share and mind share with innovative value-added service—not just to get a presence on the Web.''

MANAGING STAFFING ISSUES

In order to successfully manage an e-business strategy, the enterprise must also have an employee base that is open to change. These employees must be adaptable to new technology and able to learn new skills. Major decisions management must make include deciding whether or not to use existing staff, hire new information technology (IT) employees, create new departments, or outsource e-business-related tasks. These employees, as well as the enterprise as a whole, must also learn how to interact with customers, suppliers, and colleagues, by utilizing new communication methods—Web chat or e-mail, for example—that will stem from the new e-business model.

Staffing issues can also be a major snag in implementing an e-business strategy. According the previously mentioned Deloitte and Touche study, nearly 50 percent of retailers surveyed in 2000 did not have a specified leader heading up their e-business initiatives. The study also reported that many executives believed they lacked sufficient staffing levels to support the business that the Internet could generate. Another study done by Andersen Consulting and the Economist Intelligence Unit in July 2000 also found issues concerning employee and enterprise adaptation. According to the report, e-commerce business plans were updated often, which required knowledgeable manpower. The report also predicted that by 2005, over half of e-business initiatives will have a planning life span of less than 12 months. In order to manage quickly evolving e-business development, enterprises need to have employees in place who can work effectively in a fast-paced, changing environment.

The Andersen study also found that financial executives must be will to adapt to new roles and responsibilities as e-business initiatives are set in place—these initiatives often necessitate different accounting methods than traditionally used in the past. Adopting an e-business strategy not only affects accounting executives, but other officers and executive managers as well. Those in key roles must adapt as their positions and job descriptions evolve due to the development of e-business initiatives that affect their area of expertise. Advertising and marketing executives, IT executives, and other key players must manage change effectively in order to keep the strategy in place.

MANAGING INTEGRATION AND NEW CUSTOMER RELATIONSHIPS

An effectively integrated e-business plan has the potential to increase profits, secure a competitive position in a market, and help establish strong relationships with customers. Integrating the e-business plan into existing operations, however, can be a major task. Along with traditional business operations, management is faced with setting financial budgets and allocating resources for e-business initiatives. The enterprise must also manage the increased business generated by entering the world of e-commerce and make sure staffing and systems levels are adequate to ensure quality customer service. Communication across departments is also crucial and management needs to be able to measure success and return on investment (ROI) in its e-business initiatives.

Providing high levels of customer service is also key to successfully integrating an e-business strategy. As the number of shoppers on the Web continues to increase, enterprises need to offer services on their Web sites that parallel a brick-and-mortar experience. Many stores that now have purchasing capabilities on their sites allow shoppers to buy an item online and return in a physical store, if they so choose. Many offer price comparisons. Dell Computer, for example, allows a consumer to build a computer online and track the machine's assembly and shipping status. Amazon.com, recognized as a leader in Web customer service, utilizes software that analyzes customer purchases to make suggestions on music and books in which a consumer might be interested. As Web consumers continue to demand high levels of customer service, enterprises that begin to offer products and services online must have adequate staffing levels in

place to manage customer relations and to ensure that these products and services are issued in a timely manner.

Three companies that have successfully managed e-commerce business initiatives are Victoria's Secret, Eddie Bauer, and Cheap Tickets. Victoria's Secret, its online venture operating as a separate business entity, has integrated its catalog, Web site, and retail outlets effectively and has recorded profits from its initiatives. In 1999, the firm used the Internet to promote its fashion show, which was broadcast to over 10 million Web surfers by way of streaming video. By using cutting-edge marketing as well as integrating product data, inventory, and demographics of online shoppers, Victoria's Secret has increased customer transactions on its Web site. Eddie Bauer launched its Web site in 1996, and has also succeeded in recording a profit for its online ventures by integrating customer and inventory information. As a March 2001 *E-Commerce Times* article stated, ''in order for e-tailers to thrive in the new e-commerce environment, companies must integrate their customer and inventory information across all channels and view every customer interaction as an opportunity to learn.'' Eddie Bauer has been successful with this integration by utilizing software that captures crucial customer information such as size and preference. The software then searches the inventory to come up with purchase suggestions tailored to customer as they shop online. Cheap Tickets, a travel ticket firm, has also managed its e-commerce ventures well. According to the company, its Internet bookings, which grew by 78 percent in 2000, accounted for more gross booking than any of its other distribution methods. Its Internet business was expected to continue to grow faster than any of its other divisions.

While many companies successfully integrate their e-business initiatives, there are enterprises that do falter. Toys 'R' Us Inc., for example, suffered many problems during the 1999 holiday season and was unable to deliver its products in time for Christmas. Many of the toy retailer's online customers were left scrambling to find substitute gifts at the last minute. At the time, the firm was utilizing its traditional distribution channel for its online sales and found itself ill-prepared to handle an unexpected spike online ordering. A class action law suit eventually brought against the firm alleged that Toys 'R' Us deceived its customers by stating it could deliver products on time when it knew this task was impossible. Toysrus.com also came under fire when claims surfaced that it was selling customers' private information to marketing firms.

The company did, however, facilitate a turnaround for the 2000 holiday season. It revamped its distribution methods and partnered with Amazon.com. Under the terms of the ten-year deal, Toys

'R' Us was able to utilize Amazon's experience in e-business by operating its Web site under the Amazon.com platform. Sales increased dramatically. In fact, the company secured holiday revenues of $124 million, a 218 percent increase over the previous year.

Most enterprises realize the importance of not only having a presence on the Web, but also of having an effective business plan that supports its e-business initiatives. Operating a company Web site that enables consumers to find information on products and services, as well as purchase those items, can be beneficial on many levels. A sound e-business strategy has the potential to increase sales, reach markets that traditional brick-and-mortar platforms are unable to access, and reduce operating costs. E-business can also provide an increased level of customer service and a faster exchange of information between the consumer and the enterprise. According to the Gartner Group, "enterprises that have implemented e-commerce as part of a business strategy have been more successful in reducing business cycle times, improving cash flow, reducing inventories, decreasing administrative costs, and opening new markets and distribution channels." While managing the change that goes along with ever-changing e-business initiatives can be difficult, successful management of these initiatives has the potential to pay off in the long run.

FURTHER READING:

E-Business Systems Integration Center. "E-Business Strategy." Falls Church, VA: E-Business Systems Integration Center, 2000. Available from www.sic.nvgc.vt.edu/Thompson.

Enos, Lori. "Study: CFOs Not Ready for E-Commerce." *E-Commerce Times.* July 26, 2000. Available from www.ecommercetimes.com.

Hof, Robert D. "What Every CEO Needs to Know About Electronic Business." *BusinessWeek Online.* March 10, 1999. Available from www.businessweek.com/1999.

Intel Corp. "E-Business Going Forward." Santa Clara, CA: Intel Corp., 2001. Available from www.intel.com/eBusiness/products.

Mahoney, Michael. "Special Study: Look Who's Making Money Online, Part II." *E-Commerce Times.* March 29, 2001. Available from www.ecommercetimes.com.

Speigel, Robert. "Report: 70 Percent of Retailers Lack E-Commerce Strategy." *E-Commerce Times.* January 26, 2000. Available from www.ecommercetimes.com.

Weisman, Jon. "Toysrus.com Rebounds After 1999 Stumble." *E-Commerce Times.* January 5 2001. Available from www.ecommercetimes.com

SEE ALSO: Shakeout, Dot-com; Integration

Channel conflict refers to a situation in which business partners clash in some of their operations, such as distribution networks, in such a manner that it causes stress to the relationship, effectively turning them into both competitors and partners simultaneously. In the Internet-driven business world, channel conflict is a well-known phenomenon. As the online medium has forced separate players closer together, it has resulted in many of them stepping on each other's toes.

Also called disintermediation, channel conflict is a problem that many in the e-commerce world aggressively took on as a consequence of devising an online strategy. In the process, the chain of business relationships became scrambled and confusing. Drastically lower transaction costs and higher margins for merchants make Internet-based direct customer sales irresistible. While companies fret over alienating their resellers, they risk losing valuable time and market share to aggressive competitors that move to become online distribution fixtures. These simple economics lay at the heart of channel conflict. Forrester Research, a Cambridge, Massachusetts-based market research firm, found that 66 percent of the consumer goods manufacturers it surveyed listed channel conflict as the chief barrier to online sales. However, the fact of channel conflict appears to be inevitable as more companies set up shop online. Companies have thus begun turning to strategies that will enable them to manage channel conflict and eventually turn it into an advantage.

Along with the advent of e-commerce, many merchants moved their distribution outlets online to reach customers directly and save on transaction costs. This caused powerful distributor networks, which often enjoyed extremely valuable relationship with the merchants, to take offense at the abandonment of their businesses. For example, manufacturers who have established brand name recognition and loyalty may want to reap greater returns on their sales by bypassing retailers, with whom they may have built lasting relationships that contributed greatly to both parties' success. Meanwhile, distributors—perhaps the most endangered victims of disintermediation—are increasingly challenged to prove they add immediate value and justify their margins. According to *InformationWeek,* one method was for distributors to forego the assumption of ownership over inventory and instead charge manufacturers a transaction fee, while assuming order-management and other value-added duties. Meanwhile, a whole new crop of distributors rose up to encroach on the e-commerce distribution channels, marketing themselves as e-commerce services that handle logistics and other tasks specifically for dot-coms.

In old-fashioned, linear distribution networks, channel conflict would arise when manufacturers and distributors established sales and distribution channels to the same group of customers. The proliferation of the Internet greatly exacerbated this problem, as individual companies sought to derive greater value from their sales by going directly to customers. By the end of the 20th century, however, channel conflict included all the areas of tension in which partners in one area of business were competitors in other areas, using the same channels of operation. While partnerships in the early stages of business are good, particularly for companies trying to turn themselves into e-merchants, eventually the collaboration can give rise to channel conflict, as each partner pulls in the direction it finds most relevant and attempts to play those channels to its strengths. What makes channel conflict in e-commerce so potentially devastating is that the Internet allows for extremely comprehensive, often seamless cooperation between partners. Thus, the roots of channel conflict run that much deeper.

More important than what the firm values in these cases is what the customer values in each segment of business. If customers have come to appreciate, expect, and depend upon a certain type of service and presentation they received through an experienced retailer, a manufacturer may be shooting itself in the foot by trying to sell direct to customers over the Web. No matter how important the drive to establish an online presence and an Internet-based distribution scheme, the ultimate goal is to turn channel conflict into channel harmony.

Channel harmony creates a synergy out of the conflict. For example, an online store might seek to take advantage of the fact that it has a physical storefront, and vice versa. Separate manufacturers and retailers are learning to create symbiotic relationships that include the Web as a distribution channel. The trick is to establish creative frameworks in which both manufacturers and retailers can keep a hand in and enhance the overall efficiency and profitability of the process. Thus, distribution channels are moving away from traditional linear models and toward more collaborative agreements. Channel harmony refers to the complementary environment in which a customer's use of one channel has a ripple effect throughout the organization or partnership.

FURTHER READING:

Chen, Ben, and Lara Kass. ''Avoid the Supply Chain Squeeze.'' *e-Business Advisor*. July, 2000.

Cohen, Andy. ''When Channel Conflict is Good.'' *Sales and Marketing Management*. April, 2000.

Gilbert, Alorie, and Beth Bacheldor. ''The Big Squeeze.'' *InformationWeek*. March 27, 2000.

Greenberg, Paul A. ''Manufacturers Beset by E-Commerce 'Channel Conflict.''' *E-Commerce Times*. January 7, 2000. Available from www.ecommercetimes.com.

Kador, John. ''Love-Hate Business Relationships.'' *Electronic Business*. October, 2000.

La Monica, Martin. ''Rutting an End to Channel Conflict.'' *InfoWorld*. January 22, 2001.

Zetlin, Minda. ''Channel Conflicts.'' *Computerworld*. September 25, 2000.

SEE ALSO: Cannibalization; Channel Transparency; Disintermediation

CHANNEL TRANSPARENCY

Channel transparency refers to the flexibility and versatility of sales channels within a business. Channel transparency is a major goal of businesses struggling to remain competitive. This is attributable to several factors, including: the rise of e-commerce; the increasingly complex web of relationships between manufacturers, retailers, and distributors; and the variety of physical and virtual channels firms maintain with their customers and partners. Customers more and more seek quick, easy, and cheap means of finding, purchasing, and receiving products and services using the Web. Channel transparency makes the avenues for each of these tasks nearly interchangeable. Additionally, it eliminates conflict within and between firms associated with utilizing new channels to reach customers in ways that subtract from, rather than add to, business operations and profit margins.

Therefore, channel transparency creates the opportunity for customers to conduct research through one channel, make their purchase through another channel, and receive customer service through yet another channel, where each channel supports the others and is quickly and easily navigable. In e-commerce, channel transparency refers specifically to the resolution of the conflict between traditional and Web-based sales channels, where channel conflict is transformed into a seamless click-and-mortar operation.

Frequently the drive toward channel transparency involves a great deal of coordination between firms. Simply setting up online operations in pursuit of reduced transaction costs can lead to dangerous channel conflict. In the automobile business, for example, dealerships felt threatened by automakers' moves to sell cars directly to customers over the World Wide Web, thereby cutting dealers out of the process. Dealers raised so much opposition that manufacturers like Ford initially were forced to back down from their e-commerce plans. Companies seeking to resolve channel conflict and create channel transparency need to consider their relationships with distributors and customers. In large part, this entails understanding just what customers want and value in their dealings with companies. If customers have come to develop a taste for the particular brand of service offered by retailers, manufacturers would do well to preserve their relationship with those retailers rather than eye the bottom line of perceived boosted profit margins.

A strategy for channel transparency, then, would seek to bundle and augment the different sales channels to create a more desirable experience for the consumer. For example, a physical storefront can offer online services with the purchase of a product, while an online storefront can coordinate customer service at a retail outlet near the customer. In all cases, the parties are encouraged to play to their strengths, but without the disintermediation of their business partners. Retailers' sales and service expertise becomes an even more valuable commodity, while the manufacturers still sit at the heart of the process by maintaining control over the products themselves.

In addition, channel transparency achieves a greater synchronicity between online and offline operations. This means purchasing and service processes are similar to customers whether they are at a storefront, talking to a call center, ordering from a catalog via mail, or sitting at a personal computer. Thus, an order purchased online could be returned to a retail store before sending for a replacement product in a catalog.

However, this can be harder than it sounds. Often the creation of channel transparency involves going deep into a company's infrastructure and updating or overhauling entire systems in order to create a single system that can harmonize operations and partner relationships to achieve transparency. This investment, in fact, is one of the chief obstacles click-and-mortar companies face in striving for channel transparency. Nonetheless, the pressure to create a seamless, integrated relationship with customers across all channels was growing, forcing more and more firms to take such measures, no matter how initially problematic it may seem.

FURTHER READING:

"e-Biz on the Fast Track." *eWeek*. November 13, 2000.

Gibson, Stan. "Say it Again: Channel Transparency." *eWeek*. September 4, 2000.

Hollen, Cynthia. "The New Channel Dynamic: Age-Old Partnership Endures." *e-Commerce Times*. June 9, 1999. Available from www.ecommercetimes.com.

Paul, Lauren Gibbons, and Lisa Vaas. "Click or Brick? Your Pick." *eWeek*. November 13, 2000.

SEE ALSO: Channel Conflict/Harmony; Disintermediation

CHARGE-BACK

Credit cards are essential components of e-commerce. Although there are other ways to make payments on the Internet, the majority of e-commerce sites receive payment for goods and services via credit card. When consumers are dissatisfied with a transaction in which a credit card was used, or if their card was stolen and used illegally, it is possible for a charge-back to occur. In this event, the seller or merchant is billed back for the costs involved.

Merchants who deal with consumers face-to-face use a variety of steps to ensure a cardholder's legitimacy, including verification of the person's signature. When these precautions are taken, the bank that issued the credit card normally is responsible for any charge-backs due to fraud. However, when transactions take place without an actual card being presented to the merchant, as in e-commerce, the merchant is liable for fraud-related charge-backs.

With this in mind, online fraud is a major concern for companies engaging in e-commerce. According to an April 2001 report issued by the Worldwide E-Commerce Fraud Prevention Network, half of the businesses in the United States saw online fraud as a major problem. Because prosecuting offenders is very difficult, more than 30 percent of those surveyed listed it as the most significant threat. *Planet IT* revealed that Web merchants suffered higher charge-back rates than traditional offline retailers because malicious individuals had around-the-clock opportunities to attempt fraudulent purchases using various technologies.

In the early 2000s, companies like Home Depot, Wal-Mart, and Nike used real-time payment and risk management technologies from companies like CyberSource to reduce their risk. To decrease the incidence of online fraud at Nike.com, Nike used CyberSource's Internet Fraud Screen Service that relied on 150 different factors to evaluate the risk of fraud in transactions before they were processed. Measures like these were unfortunate but necessary, not only to prevent losses for companies, but to prevent higher charges for consumers as well.

FURTHER READING:

Miller, Keith. "Chargeback Control In The E-Shoplifting Age." *Planet IT*, June 17, 1999. Available from www.planetit.com/docs.

''Nike Significantly Reduces Credit Card Fraud From Its Internet Storefront.'' *CyberSource,* May 30, 2001. Available from www.cybersource.com/solutions.

Obie, Delilah. ''The Mechanics of Credit Card Chargebacks.'' *Workz.com,* August 21, 2000. Available from www.workz.com.

Reardon, Marguerite. ''CyberSource Helps Detect Consumer Fraud Online.'' *Informationweek,* March 6, 2000.

''Worldwide E-Commerce Fraud Prevention Network: U.S. Firms Concerned About Online Fraud.'' Nua Internet Surveys. April 10, 2001. Available from www.nua.ie/surveys.

SEE ALSO: Acquiring Bank; Electronic Payment; Fraud, Internet; Recurring Payment Transactions; Transaction Issues

CHARLES SCHWAB CORP.

Although it wasn't the first company to offer securities trading over the Internet, Charles Schwab & Co. Inc.—the principal operating subsidiary of the Charles Schwab Corp.—was the leading online brokerage firm at the end of the 20th century. More than 3.3 million of the company's 6.6 million active accounts were online accounts, representing nearly half of the company's client assets.

LEADING DISCOUNT BROKER OFFERED INTERNET TRADING IN 1996

When Schwab began offering securities trading over the Internet in April 1996, it was the leading discount brokerage firm in the United States. The firm's brokers were paid salaries rather than commissions, and customers paid fixed fees rather than commissions when they bought and sold stocks and other securities. Schwab's first online trading venture was called e.Schwab and was set up as a separate business unit with its own dedicated personnel. Under the company's two-tier pricing system, customers could make trades for a fixed fee of $29.95, but only if they traded online. In addition, they were limited to one phone call per month to a broker or customer representative. Customers who wanted a higher level of service had to pay a higher fee that was still less than that charged by the full-service brokerages.

Although Schwab pioneered the bare-bones discount brokerage and was for many years little more than an order-taker for independent investors, the company had begun offering some level of service to its customers by 1996. Catering to the wave of baby boomers who were planning for their retirement, Schwab employees were now willing to discuss investment objectives with their clients and suggest investment strategies to reach those goals. An impor-

tant part of the company's customer service initiative was the expansion of its branch network, which made it convenient for customers to come in and talk with a Schwab broker. Schwab also offered 24-hour staffing at its customer service call centers. As long as Schwab was able to distinguish itself from other discount brokerages on the basis of customer service, it wouldn't compete solely on the basis of price. Its $29.95 online charge was not the lowest in the industry, nor was its minimum regular commission of $39.00

By the end of 1997 online trading accounted for $81 billion in client assets for Schwab, but the company realized its two-tier pricing system was creating a long-term problem. The company's traditional customers were resentful that they weren't getting the lower fees, while the company's online customers didn't like the lack of service. As a result, in January 1998 Schwab took the bold step of offering the $29.95 flat fee to everyone, along with access to whatever help and information the company could provide. Although the decision meant an immediate $150 million loss of earnings, it also resulted in increased trading volume and the addition of more new accounts. For 1998 Schwab's client assets increased by 40 percent, new accounts rose by 20 percent, and net income rose 30 percent to $348.5 million. Total revenue reached $2.16 billion.

Once the pricing issue was settled, Schwab was more committed than ever to improving customer service. By 1999 Schwab's Web site was offering extensive research, including analyst reports, company reports, insider-trading reports, industry research, live CEO interviews, and a stock screening service. Most of the services were offered free to investors, although the stock screening tool was free only to those with $100,000 in assets or who made at least 12 trades per year. In addition to providing research and analytical tools, Schwab began offering e-mail alerts that would tell investors when a stock or mutual fund reached a pre-set high or low. Later in the year, wireless e-mail alerts to pagers and cell phones were offered and the company introduced after-hours trading. In mid-1999 Schwab Chief Information Officer Dawn Lepore told *Business Week* that the company's Web site was receiving 76 million hits a day. The company's customer service strategy was paying off. Schwab had captured 42 percent of all assets invested in online trading accounts, and it added 1.3 million Internet accounts between January 1998 and June 1999.

As part of its strategy to attract new customers over the Internet, Schwab teamed up with Internet portal Excite Inc. (which eventually became Excite@ home) to create MySchwab, a personalized Web page service that was available to customers and non-customers alike. Using the co-branded MySchwab site, individuals could create their own personalized Web page with their favorite links and receive customized investment information, including lists of stocks to watch, access to breaking news stories, general business and technology news, and access to popular content such as sports, travel, and shopping. Schwab hoped that MySchwab would attract many non-customers and allow them to sample the company's products and services.

SCHWAB CONTINUED TO REDEFINE ITSELF, 2000-2001

In February 2000 Schwab announced it would acquire CyBerCorp. Inc., a closely held electronic trading technology and brokerage firm based in Austin, Texas, for about $488 million. The acquisition was designed to enhance services offered to very active traders. CyBerCorp., which would operate as a subsidiary, allowed traders to scan multiple electronic communications networks, market makers, and market specialists for the best prices and then place orders. The company also provided customers with streaming quotes and news. To further attract very active traders, Schwab announced it would reduce fees to $19.95 per trade once a customer made more than 30 trades in a quarter. The fee would be further reduced to $14.95 per trade once a customer exceeded 60 trades in a quarter. Analysts noted that the new fee structure, along with the acquisition of CyBerCorp., made Schwab more appealing to day traders.

Schwab's largest acquisition of the year was U.S. Trust Corp., which Schwab acquired in June 2000 in a stock swap valued at $2.7 billion. The two companies would each retain their separate brand identities. U.S. Trust Corp. offered personalized asset management services, primarily to wealthy clients. Its minimum account balance was $400,000. The acquisition was notable in several respects, one being that it required the approval of the Federal Reserve Board. In order to complete the transaction Schwab had to apply to the Federal Reserve Board to become a bank holding company, and then convert to a financial holding company. It was the first financial conglomerate created under the Gramm-Leach-Bliley Act, which eased restrictions on the combination of securities firms, banks, and insurers. The combined companies would have client assets totaling $913 billion and net revenue of $4.5 billion. By August 2000 Schwab's client assets surpassed $1 trillion, then fell to $961 billion in September and $944 billion in October.

A significant segment of Schwab's client assets consisted of advisor-managed accounts, which accounted for $243 billion of Schwab's $944 billion in client assets in October 2000. Some 6,000 independent investment advisors used Schwab for trading and custody of their clients' investments. The acquisition of U.S. Trust enabled Schwab to further promote the use of its services by independent investment advisors by offering them access to U.S. Trust's administrative trustee services. In addition, Schwab gave them access to U.S. Trust research and Webcasts with U.S. Trust analysts. Later in the year Schwab acquired Chicago Investment Analytics Inc., which produced software to select securities based on quantitative analysis. Following the acquisition Schwab made Chicago Investment Analytics' investment tools available to the independent investment advisors who used Schwab for trading and custody. An annual fee of $8,000 was required to become part of Schwab's program for independent investment advisors.

Throughout 2000 Schwab continued to automate as many processes as possible to reduce costs. For investment advisors, Schwab gave them access to external markets, not only through CyBerCorp.'s systems and high-speed connectivity, but also through an extranet that provided access to resources that enabled them to automate many paper-based functions. At its Web site Schwab introduced features that allowed customers to automate processes such as funds transfers and password changes, which previously required a phone call or visit to a branch office. Schwab estimated that bringing these functions online saved at least $50 million a year in costs, and that its Web site was handling the equivalent volume of three or four call centers. Even as Schwab automated more functions and encouraged its customers to use its Web site, the company continued to expand its branch office network. Some 50 new branch offices were opened between June 1999 and June 2000, for a total of 356 offices. A company spokesperson told *InternetWeek,* "We do 88 percent of our trades online, but 70 percent of our accounts are opened at a branch office."

BEAR MARKET LED TO CUTBACKS, 2001

Schwab had doubled its workforce to 25,500 full-time employees during the bull market surge from 1998 through the end of 2000. When stocks tumbled in February 2001, the company announced plans to cut 11 to 13 percent of its workforce in the second quarter, including 2,000 to 2,300 employees who would be laid off and another 600 to 900 who would leave through attrition. In February 2001, Schwab's clients lost a combined $83.4 billion as the total value of client assets dropped to $845 billion. The average account balance sank to $111,000 from a peak of about $137,400 in August 2000. Trading volume was down about one-third from the same month the previous year.

While Schwab remains the leading online brokerage firm with an estimated 22 percent of all Internet trades, investors perceive it as a well-diversified financial services firm. Its branch office network makes it a "click-and-mortar" type of company, and the acquisition of U.S. Trust helped to diversify its revenue sources. As a result, the company is not as dependent on online trading for its continued success as other pure-play online brokerages.

FURTHER READING:

Anderson, Amy L. "Schwab Offers Trust, Custody Services for Advisors." *American Banker.* December 1, 2000.

"Capital Briefs: Schwab Deal to Buy U.S. Trust Wins Federal Reserve Approval." *American Banker.* May 2, 2000.

Gorham, John. "Charles Schwab, Version 4.0." *Forbes.* January 8, 2001.

"Schwab, Going Upscale, Steps on Some Toes." *Business Week.* December 11, 2000.

"Schwab-U.S. Trust Merger Completed." *San Francisco Business Times.* June 9, 2000.

Schwartz, Jeffrey. "Schwab Reaps Benefits of Early Net Investments." *InternetWeek.* June 12, 2000.

SEE   Ameritrade Holding Corp.; Datek Online Brokerage
ALSO: Services LLC; E*Trade Group Inc.

CHILDREN AND THE INTERNET

More than any other group, children have been a center of controversy on the Internet. American youth access the Internet for school, communication, shopping, and recreation. Children's relationship with the Internet has attracted the attention of Internet providers, marketers, advertisers, teachers, lawmakers, and public interest groups. The Internet's role in education, the online collection of children's personal information, and the nature of the material available on the Web, raise a host of controversial issues, including freedom of access to information, regulation of Web site content, and invasion of children's privacy, along with broader issues of social equality, education, and the regulation of business.

CHILDREN, DEMOGRAPHICS, AND THE INTERNET

Nearly two-thirds of all children use the Internet, each logging on for at least seven hours per week. In 2002, according to Jupiter Research, almost 50 percent of Americans aged 13 to 17 will access the Web, as will approximately 22 million children between the ages of eight and 12. An AOL survey of 10,000 parents reported that 25 percent of their children were using computers by age two, and 90 percent were by age six.

The under-21 crowd constitutes the most rapidly burgeoning segment of the Internet population. Those born after 1983, the so-called Generation Y, represent 21 percent of the total U.S. population. They form America's first wired generation, at ease with computer technology and online information. As they come of age and enter the workforce, they will exert a profound influence on the business, consumer, and social habits of the nation. Hard on their heels is an even more Internet savvy group, children under 12, the Internet's second generation. Microsoft Chairman Bill Gates dubbed them "Generation I" because they represent the first truly Internet-immersed Americans.

However, not all American children enjoyed equal online opportunities. Only 58 percent of schools where a third or more of the students qualify for government subsidized school meals were connected to the Internet at the end of the 1990s, according to the National Center of Education Statistics. In comparison, that rate increased to 78 percent of schools where only a tenth of the students were eligible for meal subsidies. While the U.S. Department of Education reported that nearly every American child had some Internet access at school, studies suggested that children in lower income families and minority households had less access overall.

MARKETING TO CHILDREN ONLINE

Jupiter Research reported that 67 percent of teens and 37 percent of children between the ages of five and 12 purchased or researched products on the Internet. American youth aged five and older were expected to spend roughly $1.3 billion online for consumer goods by 2003. According to Forrester Research, children's online spending constitutes a market worth $37 billion. As a result, it was a market that businesses increasingly coveted.

The Internet has accelerated "age compression," and American children have more sophisticated consumer tastes than those of past generations. Trends are communicated almost instantaneously across the Net. Half of American children grow up in dual-income families, and another fourth in single-parent households. Thus, they experience more independence than ever before. This independence often encompasses autonomy when it comes to shopping.

Since advertisers believe brand preferences are set by age 12, merchandisers are anxiously probing this market and devising new methods to tap its potential. Specialized market research firms have emerged that conduct information gathering via online focus groups, surveys, and chat sessions. By 2001, online research was expected to constitute 20 percent of the $4 billion spent each year on U.S. market research overall. Online market researchers often pay children for their participation, either in cash, gift points, or certificates. Additionally, some companies integrate purchasing options into all areas of their Web sites. Others notify registered members by e-mail of special, Internet-only sales promotions. Many advertisers seek visibility on well-known children's sites, such as Disney.

In the past, children's lack of credit cards impeded their online shopping. However, credit-card issuers increased solicitations to young people through the 1990s, mailing out 3.2 billion card offers at the turn of the millennium. Nearly seven out of 10 college students possess their own cards, and issuers are reaching for even younger customers. Some Internet vendors offer Web-only debit cards to teens, good for purchases at an affiliated-Web site.

Online marketing targeted at children has stirred parental concerns, especially about the saturation that can be achieved by a constant bombardment of ads. Parents worry about their inability to supervise children's online purchases, about children's fiscal responsibility, and about marketer's aggressive invasion of children's privacy. In response to such concerns, marketers have focused on generating ways to allay parental fears. Sites such as DoughNET, RocketCash, and iCanBuy offered ''digital wallets'' funded by a specified cash amount that draws, much like debit cards, on a savings account to prevent children from overspending. Other sites permit parents to stipulate where kids can shop.

Companies argue that the Net provides an opportunity for children to learn about financial responsibility. Even insurance companies have Web sites designed for young people. FleetBoston Financial Corp. claimed that 2,500 schools and 400,000 students accessed its FleetKids site, aimed at kindergarteners through sixth-graders. The site teaches financial skills through games such as the BuyLo/SellHi stock market game and Front Yard Fortunes, in which children build their own businesses.

ONLINE PORNOGRAPHY

Children's ever-increasing Net access, much of it unsupervised, has generated concerns beyond those about target marketing. Many parents worry about children's exposure to inappropriate Web site content, such as excessive violence and pornography. Suggested methods for combating this problem include creating special domain names, such as.xxx to indicate sexually explicit sites, and others to specify content acceptable for children—similar to the rating system used for movies. However, the Internet Corporation for Assigned Names and Numbers (ICANN) has rejected this option because of the inability to adequately enforce such an arrangement.

In addition to accessing online pornography, children also may serve as its subjects. Sites featuring

illegal child pornography prompted the creation of Condemned.org, an activist group dedicated to eradicating such sites, whether by hacking into child pornography servers or prosecuting them through standard legal channels. Internet users can report U.S. child pornography sites and the servers carrying them via an online template, and the information is then forwarded to the FBI. The FBI and U.S. Customs Service cooperate with foreign governments on international investigations of child pornography sites. However, servers located in countries that lack treaties with the U.S. are often difficult to shut down.

PRIVACY

Many marketers use the Internet to compile market research profiles of pre-adult Net surfers. They may elicit sought-after information with the promise of some of form of compensation. A study by the Annenberg Public Policy Center found that two-thirds of children polled would supply the names of their favorite stores when offered a ''great free gift,'' while 40 percent would volunteer details concerning family cars, their allowances, and family political opinions. Thus, children serve as sources of information about not only their own, but also their family members' purchasing and lifestyle habits. Concerns over such practices center on the fact that children are far less guarded than adults. Hence, the possibility for abusing minors' privacy runs high.

Proponents of greater safeguards for children's online privacy argue that personal information gathered online aids marketers in further targeting a highly vulnerable audience. Marketers use the information to tailor online ads to children and their families, and frequently flood children with unsolicited messages. Some of those concerned also question whether Web sites adequately monitor the parties to whom they supply child-data. Children may expose themselves to dangers when they post personal information on bulletin boards or access chat rooms. An FBI and Department of Justice study determined that child predators utilize such online information.

The Federal Trade Commission (FTC) investigated the privacy issues connected to children's Internet use in 1996. It concluded that children form ''a large and powerful segment'' of online consumers actively targeted by commercial Web sites. In 1998 the FTC published its findings in *Privacy Online: A Report to Congress*. The report characterized industry self-regulation as ineffective and called for legislation to protect children's online privacy. The FTC based its recommendations on a survey of 1,402 Web sites, 212 of which were children's sites. While most sites collected children's personal data, only a few informed their users this was being done. Most lacked comprehensive privacy policies. Fewer than one in ten facilitated parental control over site use and less than 25 percent suggested that children ask parental permission before supplying personal data online.

CHILDREN'S ONLINE PRIVACY PROTECTION ACT IN 1999 (COPPA)

The FTC's findings led the U.S. Congress to pass the Children's Online Privacy Protection Act in 1999. The act mandated that the FTC produce rules to govern the online compilation and use of personal information from children under 13. Web site operators must provide notice and obtain "verifiable parental consent" before they can gather or disclose information from children. Web sites must alert parents about their policies concerning children's personal data, and site operators must remedy situations when a child's information has been disclosed. If a parent requests it, the operator is required to describe the personal information collected from the child. COPPA restricts enticing children to disclose personal information through contests or prizes. However, it does not provide parents or children a private right of action. It also shields Web sites from liability if they can demonstrate a good faith effort to remedy prior disclosure of a child's personal information. Under the FTC's rule, businesses may implement self-regulatory "safe harbor" programs by submitting guidelines to the FTC for approval. Many smaller Internet businesses protested COPPA, stating that compliance costs would be impossible to manage. They argued that parental compliance forms would discourage traffic to lesser-known sites and many children would access teen or adult-oriented sites to circumvent parental compliance altogether.

INDUSTRY SELF-REGULATION AND FILTERING SOFTWARE

Congressional legislation wasn't the only vehicle to regulate children's Internet interactions. The industry voluntarily launched several self-regulatory practices concerning children. In 1998, the Online Privacy Alliance (OPA), a coalition of industry groups, was formed to tackle Web-related privacy concerns. Among its measures were proposed online privacy guidelines governing the online collection of personal data, and guidelines protecting children's privacy.

TRUSTe, a nonprofit organization, certifies that its members have disclosed their online information-collection practices. In return, members display a seal verifying program participation. The Better Business Bureau Online sponsors a similar effort. Members must inform users of their collection practices, supply data security, submit to periodic monitoring, and use encryption for the receipt and transfer of sensitive information. Skeptics counter that industry self-regulation doesn't guarantee compliance or enforcement of programs. Moreover, few Web providers participate in seal programs.

Filtering software was another protective measure Web sites could use to safeguard children. Such software shields children from objectionable Web sites and protects children's privacy by screening incoming and outgoing text. Specific terms prompt outgoing screening and block sensitive information from being sent to the provider. Among software available was Cybersitter, NetNanny, CyberPatrol, and Specs for Kids.

Adults also can access the Internet from "filtered ISPs," which invoke blocking criteria at the server level. Safe sites offer access to pre-approved pages suitable for young children. Finally, adults can access several Web sites that monitor the appropriateness of other Web sites for their children.

E-LEARNING

The Internet's role in American elementary and secondary education was far from settled in the early 2000s. Proponents argued that the technology would make education more relevant to children by better preparing them for the modern workplace and by capitalizing on a form of technology that children already access for pleasure. As of 2000, nearly 95 percent of public schools supplied Internet access to their students, a 60-percent increase since 1994. However, less than two percent of the $360 billion annual public education budget was earmarked for technology.

Teacher preparation constituted another obstacle to enhanced utilization of the Internet. The National Education Association estimated that only one-third of teachers possess the knowledge to use technology effectively. However, school technology spending has increased, and most major technology firms are poised to take advantage of this. IBM, Intel, and Microsoft all launched initiatives aimed at teacher training. Many start-ups have appeared to fill the vacuum as well, drawing about $1 billion in venture capital in 1999 and 2000, according to Merrill Lynch & Co.

Commercial initiatives include the Virtual High School of Concord, Massachusetts, America's largest Web-based school, which offers Net courses. For each course a teacher contributes online, his or her school can enroll up to 20 students. AP courses are also available for purchase, delivered via distance learning to schools that can't afford to set up their own offerings. Applications include student-designed course-related Web pages, parent-teacher communication via e-mail, and homework on the Internet. The Internet also allows teachers to collaborate with colleagues across the nation to develop lesson plans and share teaching strategies.

Some warn that, due to budget limitations, schools will rely on online advertising to foot the bill. For example, ZapMe! Corp. provided schools with computer labs and Internet access free of charge in exchange for permission to run ads on the school computers. Additionally, the New York City Board of Education voted to create a school Internet portal funded through online ad sales and e-commerce site licensing.

LIBRARIES

Libraries face particular challenges concerning children's access to the Internet. Though voters and the courts have favored a lack of restrictions in the interests of intellectual freedom, many groups call for mandatory filtering of the Internet in schools and public libraries. Some libraries require parental agreement forms before granting children Internet access. Others mandate that youngsters be accompanied by a parent when using computers. Still others install filtering software on computers utilized by children.

Although they serve as protective measures, strategies such as filtering also carry disadvantages. Though ''objectionable'' terms can be blocked, filters may prevent students from conducting research on legitimate topics such as medical advances or disease. A student, for example, might not be able to conduct online searches regarding AIDS transmission or breast cancer, if such filtering were in place.

AN UNRESOLVED FUTURE

While the myriad issues surrounding children and the Internet create a complex web of conflicting interests, ethical complications, and social and economic implications, the Internet is here to stay, and kids are becoming increasingly sophisticated about incorporating it into their daily lives.

FURTHER READING:

Anderson, Pat. ''Child's Play.'' *Marketing Week.* September 9, 1999.

Anthony, Barbara, and Thomas Cohn. ''Putting Parents Back in Charge of Kids' Privacy.'' *Computerworld.* May 15, 2000.

Chen, Christine Y. ''Chasing the Net Generation.'' *Fortune.* September 4, 2000.

Cheng, Kipp. ''Wee Web.'' *Brandweek.* May 3, 1999.

Chilik Wollenberg, Yvonne. ''Do You Know What Your Kids are Saying About You Online.'' *Medical Economics.* October 23, 2000.

Chordas, Lori. ''A New Generation in the Cross Hairs.'' *Best's Review.* February, 2001.

Crockett, Roger O. ''Forget the Mall. Kids Shop the Net.'' *Business Week.* July 26, 1999.

Hertzell, Dorothy. ''Don't Talk to Strangers: An Analysis of Government and Industry Efforts to Protect a Child's Privacy Online.'' *Federal Communications Law Journal.* March, 2000.

Holton, Lisa. ''The Surfer in the Family.'' *American Demographics.* April, 2000.

Jezzard, Helen. ''Is the Internet Beyond Control?'' *Information World Review.* June 2000.

Kwak, Mary. ''Fair Play?'' *Inc.* March 14, 2000.

Leonard, Bill. ''After Generations X and Y Comes Generation I.'' *HRMagazine.* January, 2000.

Long, Tim. ''On the Road to a Safe Net for Kids.'' *Computer Reseller News.* August 14, 2000.

Marmer Solomon, Charlene. ''Ready or Not, Here Comes the Net Kids.'' *Workforce.* February, 2000.

Martens, Ellin. ''A Laptop for Every Kid.'' *Time.* May 1, 2000.

Minkel, Walter. ''Dealing with the Filtering Stigma.'' *Library Journal.* Spring, 2000.

———. ''Young Children and the Web: A Boolean Match, of Not?'' *Library Journal.* January, 2000.

Pepe, Michele. ''Safety Net for Young Surfers.'' *Computer Reseller News.* December 6, 1999.

Radcliff, Deborah. ''Vigilante Group Targets Child Pornography Sites.'' *Computerworld.* January 17, 2000.

Rogers, Michael, and Norman Oder. ''School Net Logs Case Hits Snag.'' *Library Journal.* January, 2001.

Ross, Sid. ''Clicks for Kids.'' *Adweek.* January 8, 2001.

Symonds, William C. ''Wired Schools.'' *Business Week.* September 25, 2001.

SEE
ALSO: Digital Divide; Higher Education, E-Commerce and; Global E-Commerce Regulation; Legal Issues; Privacy: Issues, Policies, Statements; Profiling

CHURN

An increasingly pressing concern among e-commerce businesses of all types, churn refers to the inability of firms to maintain a consistent, longtime, loyal relationship with their customers. More specifically, churn is the turnover of a customer base as customers allow their accounts to lapse or switch to competitors' online products and services. Churn is usually quantified as the percentage rate at which customers are lost. It is one of the chief obstacles to companies' efforts to realize profits from their extensive investments in establishing and maintaining an online presence.

Churn is particularly problematic for firms for several reasons. First, the inability to maintain customer loyalty makes for poor public relations. More immediately, customer churn simply is expensive. Customer acquisition and account set-up and maintenance all cost money, and the higher the level of churn, the lower a firm's overall profit margin is likely to be.

Broadly speaking, the remedy for churn is "stickiness." Sticky services are those designed to hook a customer, who will find the service too valuable to easily give up. Firms implement strategies such as greater personalization of services, bundled services, or other perks to create this stickiness whereby customers are induced to build loyalty to the company. Differentiation is another tactic. In their efforts to simply get Web sites up and running, firms often fail to take the time to create an online presence that distinguishes itself from those of others, thus making it very easy for customers to switch without feeling any negative impact.

Online banks were among the hardest hit by customer churn. The New York-based research firm CyberDialogue reported churn rates for Web banking as high as 49.2 percent in mid-1999. Efforts to create stickiness seemed to pay off, however, as Cyber-Dialogue estimated a drop to just 9.8 percent a year later. While this represents a vast improvement, that figure was still exceptionally high. Essentially, the dilemma of online churn has intensified customer outreach programs. In order to assure the most valuable online experience and avoid churn, firms need to familiarize themselves with exactly what their customers want, expect, and value, and then tailor their services toward those ends.

FURTHER READING:

Kreitter, Dana. "Controlling ISP Churn: Borrowing from the Telco Model." *Telecommunications.* November, 2000.

Monahan, Julie. "In the Out Door." *Banking Strategies.* November/December 2000.

Schneiderman, Carla. "Managing Churn at the Core." *Telecommunications.* July, 2000.

Verton, Dan. "Churn." *Computerworld.* February 5, 2001.

SEE ALSO: Loyalty

CISCO SYSTEMS INC.

With 34,000 employees, Cisco Systems was the world's largest manufacturer of routers and switches in the early 2000s. Both form an integral part of the networking technology used to connect users to the Internet. Roughly 80 percent of the firm's revenues stem from transactions completed on Cisco's Web site, which is considered to be one of the most successful business-to-business sites in the world. Although sales in 2001 grew 17.8 percent to $22.2 billion, Cisco posted a loss of more than $1 billion. Management blamed this on a steep drop in orders—fueled by cuts in spending, particularly in the telecommunications sector—which left the firm with high levels of inventory.

EARLY HISTORY

Two Stanford University computer scientists—Leonard Bosack and Sandra Lerner—established Cisco Systems in December of 1984. The new company began marketing the internetworking technology Bosack had developed while at Stanford to universities, research centers, and government agencies. The following year, Stanford asked Cisco for $11 million in licensing fees, arguing that Stanford held rights to Bosack's technology since it had been developed at the University. Stanford accepted a settlement of $150,000 and free products and support services in 1986. That year, Cisco became one of the first networking technology firms to develop a router, a device linking a number of local area networks (LANs), compatible with Transmission Control Protocol/Internet Protocol (TCP/IP).

Sales reached $1.5 million in 1987, and Cisco began marketing its networking products to businesses with offices in a wide range of locations. To fund future growth, Cisco conducted its initial public offering (IPO) in 1990. Sales that year grew to $70 million and more than doubled in 1991 to $183 million. Pacific Bell began purchasing the bulk of its routers from Cisco in 1992. New product developments that year included integrated services digital routers, as well as upgrades to fiber distributed data interface (FDDI) and token ring technologies. International expansion was launched via an original equipment manufacturer (OEM) agreement with British Telecom, and Cisco also started to market its routers to U.S. long-distance providers. After revenues surged to $340 million, *Forbes* ranked Cisco number two on its list of the fastest growing companies in the United States.

When the development of asynchronous transfer mode (ATM) technologies threatened to render router technology obsolete in 1993, Cisco developed routers that could assist ATM transmissions. International expansion continued with the establishment of Cisco Systems HK Ltd. in Hong Kong and new units in Europe, Japan, and Australia. AT&T Corp. and Strata-Com agreed to work with Cisco to foster compatibility among rival protocols.

GROWTH VIA ACQUISITION

Cisco launched an acquisition spree in 1993, paying $100 million for Crescendo Communications, creator of copper distributed data interface technology. Setting the stage for how future acquisitions would be integrated into existing operations, Cisco retained Crescendo head Mario Mazzola and all of his employees. Eventually, Crescendo served as the foundation for a unit of Cisco that brought in roughly one-third of total revenues. Success with this purchase prompted Cisco to continue paying for companies with products and services in high growth areas, rather than spending money on research and development to create its own products. In essence, Cisco started looking for a startup to purchase any time management determined that a rival had gotten a considerable jump start in an area the firm wanted to pursue.

Cisco paid $91 million for LAN technology developer Newport Systems Solutions in 1994. In October, the firm beat out IBM Corp. with a $204 million bid for Ethernet switch maker Kalpana Inc. When Kalpana executive Mimi Gigoux criticized Cisco's integration efforts, the firm appointed her an integration specialist. She eventually headed up a team of 11 employees dedicated to making the integration process for Cisco's many acquisitions as smooth as possible. Eventually, Kalpana's team was responsible for reducing the turnover rate of employees gained via takeovers to roughly two percent, compared to an average rate throughout the networking industry of 20 percent.

Also in 1994, the firm released its newest networking technology, dubbed CiscoFusion, which eventually included an ATM interface processor and Catalyst FDDI-to-Ethernet LAN switching technologies. By then, Cisco held a 57-percent share of the worldwide multiple protocol networking market, and its routers had started being used to power the Internet. Sales exceeded $1 billion for the first time. Although shareholders protested a proposed $348 million takeover of Ethernet switch maker Grand Junction Networks Inc., and expressed their support of internal research and development rather than continued purchases, Cisco continued to seek growth via acquisitions. It completed the takeover of Grand Junction networks the following year. In fact, it was these aggressive acquisition tactics that were later credited for Cisco's astronomical growth well into the late 1990s.

U.S. Robotics and Cisco inked a technology sharing alliance in 1995. By the following year, Cisco's routers were considered an integral part of the Internet. Making its largest purchase to date, Cisco paid roughly $4 billion for Stratacom Inc. in 1996. The firm also paid $100 million for Nashoba Networks, a maker of token-ring network hubs; $79 mil-

lion for NetSys Technology Inc., a networking technology vendor; and $220 million for Granite Systems, a manufacturer of gigabit Ethernet technologies. As a result, Cisco ended up owning plants manufacturing three rival Ethernet switching systems. Although Cisco's Internet-related activities thrived, the anticipated threat of emerging low-cost routers prompted the firm to continue its efforts to grow via acquisition.

CONDUCTING BUSINESS VIA THE INTERNET

The 1997 purchases of Ardent Communications Corp. and Global Internet Software Group elevated Cisco to the number one spot among worldwide networking equipment makers, with an 80-percent share of the Internet router market. That year, the firm sold nearly $1 billion worth of networking equipment via its Web site, one of the earliest business-to-business sites to prove successful. By 1998, Internet sales accounted for more than 40 percent of Cisco's $3.6 billion in annual revenues, which grew 44 percent from the previous year (earnings jumped 55 percent over the same time period). According to a March 1998 article in *InternetWeek,* Cisco's Web site went well beyond simply allowing clients to place orders and make payments. It explained: ''The site provides online documentation, order updates, design tools and help-desk support. Cisco delivers the tools to cut the time required for negotiating contracts, determining pricing, calculating lead times, checking on status and verifying shipment dates.'' In December, the firm established its Internet Business Solutions Group after clients began asking Cisco for helping with setting up their own Internet-based business ventures.

Also in 1998, Cisco attained a market capitalization of $100 billion, setting a record for reaching that milestone less than nine years after completing an IPO. Microsoft Corp., which had set the previous record, took 11 years to reach the $100 billion mark. Acquisitions that year included American Internet Corp., Pipelinks Inc., Clarity Wireless Corp., and NetSpeed Inc., a converter of traditional phone lines into digital subscriber lines (DSL). Qwest Communications International Inc. joined forces with Cisco in 1999 to create one of the largest Internet-based networks in the United States. In doing so, roughly 80 percent of Quest's transmissions began using Cisco lines.

With a 50-percent share of the $21 billion networking devices industry, Cisco boasted sales and earnings far above those of competitors 3Com Corp., Bay Networks, and Cabletron. Looking for new growth areas, the firm decided to diversify into the $250 billion telephone equipment industry and compete with the likes of Lucent Technologies Inc. and Nortel Networks. The first step in this strategy called for the acquisition of three fiber-optics developers. In August of 1999, Cisco bought Monterey Networks Inc. for $500 million in stock, gaining access to the high-speed optical internetworking technology Monterey used to process traffic at a network hub. Three months later, Cisco superceded its $4 billion Stratacom purchase with the $7 billion acquisition of Cerent Corp., a manufacturer of fiber-optic network equipment serving metropolitan areas. In December, Cisco paid $2 billion for the optical systems unit of Italy's Pirelli SpA. Cisco hoped to use Pirelli's dense wave division multiplexing (DWDM) technology to transmit data between network hubs and end users in metropolitan areas.

Since its acquisition spree began in 1993, Cisco had spent nearly $19 billion on 42 companies by the beginning of 2000. Spending continued that year, when Cisco paid $5.7 billion in stock for ArrowPoint Communications Inc., a maker of network switches, and completed 19 additional purchases. By then, Internet sales accounted for roughly 80 percent of Cisco's total revenues. The firm's continued success selling its technology via the Web fueled the growth of its Internet Business Solutions Group, whose clients included Lands' End, The Gap, and WalMart. According to the unit's managing director, Mohsen Moazami, as quoted in *Chain Store Age Executive,* "We're not only selling a lot online. We're profitable. We have a networked supply chain where forecasting accuracy has increased, and inventories have decreased. Cisco has very credible business practices— not only when it comes to selling online, but deep into the back end of fulfillment, manufacturing and materials sourcing. A lot of retailers want to see how we do it. They're looking for the secret sauce." Cisco served as a model of e-business efficiency. Its accounting practices were so automated that the firm was able to operate with several hundred less accountants than other firms its size. Merely four auditors handled Cisco's travel and expense reports, compared to the roughly 40 auditors employed by comparable firms. Also, more than 90 percent of customer service requests were taken care of on the firm's Web site. Productivity gains in 1999 allowed Cisco to save $825 million, and savings the following year reached $1.35 billion. In April of 2000, Cisco achieved a market capitalization of $550 billion, usurping both Microsoft and General Electric as the world's most highly valued company.

Despite its continued success, Cisco also found itself vulnerable to competition from smaller, more nimble rivals. The firm saw its market share for Internet-only traffic routers, known as "core" routers, fall from 80 percent in 2000 to 69 percent in 2001, due mainly to competition from Juniper Network, which developed an Internet traffic router in 1996 that was faster than any of Cisco's offerings. Hoping to speed its diversification efforts, in 2000 Cisco funneled considerable resources into developing its recently acquired telecommunications equipment operations. To sell its innovative IP-based telecommunications products, the firm tended to rely on the upstarts that had emerged in the telecommunications industry since 1996. According to a May 2001 article in *Fortune,* "deregulation in the U.S. telecommunications industry, enacted in 1996, coupled with a robust stock market and the boom of the Internet, prompted the creation of hundreds of new companies, all eager to build new networks and swipe business from established players like the Bell telephone companies, AT&T and WorldCom." As a result, the telecommunications market began growing at nearly twice its average rate. By mid-2000, startups accounted for half of Cisco's telecommunications revenues.

When the U.S. economy buckled later in the year, many of these young businesses began to slow spending, and in several cases they simply declared bankruptcy. Consequently, Cisco saw a large portion of its orders dissolve virtually overnight. To make matters worse, the firm had spent the last several months beefing up its inventory in an effort to fill customer orders more quickly. As a result, Cisco announced its intent to take a one-time $2.5 billion charge to write off its inventory glut. The company also cut roughly 8,000 jobs in March 2001, which amounted to nearly 17 percent of its workforce. Acquisitions ground to a near halt as Cisco executives pondered how to best prepare the firm for an anticipated economic rebound. Looking to the future, several analysts believed the firm would make a major strategic shift by paring down non-core operations and increasing internal research and development efforts.

FURTHER READING:

"Cisco Fractures Its Own Fairy Tale." *Fortune.* May 14, 2001.

"Cisco Systems Inc." In *Notable Corporate Chronologies.* Farmington Hills, MI: Gale Group, 1999.

Goldblatt, Henry. "Cisco's Secrets." *Fortune.* November 8, 1999.

Hardy, Quentin. "Cisco Kidding?" *Forbes.* May 14, 2001. Available from www.forbes.com.

Moazami, Mohsen. "The Web's Largest Store." *Chain Store Age Executive.* August, 2000.

Nee, Eric. "Cisco: How It Aims to Keep Right on Growing." *Fortune.* February 2, 2001.

Rodriguez, Karen. "Cisco Keeps Growing and Growing." *The Business Journal.* March 17, 2000.

Walsh, Brian. "Best Site for Business-to-Business Commerce." *InternetWeek.* March 9, 1998.

Yang, Dori J. "Cisco's Spectacular Slide from Stardom." *U.S. News & World Report.* April 16, 2001.

SEE
ALSO: Business-to-Business (B2B) E-Commerce; Hardware;
Internet Infrastructure

CLARK, JAMES (JIM) H.

James H. (Jim) Clark is best known as the co-founder of Netscape Communications Corp., the upstart World Wide Web browser firm that battled Microsoft Corp.'s Internet Explorer and eventually merged with America Online (AOL). Clark also founded two other billion-dollar ventures. Long before his days at Netscape, Clark created Silicon Graphics, the pioneer of three-dimensional computer graphics technology. Clark's third brainchild, Healtheon Corp., which eventually merged with WebMD to form Healtheon/WebMD, grew into a leading health industry Web site offering health information to consumers, as well as electronic transaction processing for medical facilities and physician groups.

While a computer science professor at Stanford University in the late 1970s, Clark developed the Geometry Engine, a three-dimensional graphics chip. In 1981, he resigned from his position at Stanford to start his own business for developing and marketing the chip. Clark formally established Silicon Graphics a year later. The new firm launched the first three-dimensional terminal, called the IRIS 1000, in 1983. Clark chose IRIS as the terminal's name to reflect his technology's focus on appealing to the sense of sight. In 1984, Clark developed IRIS 1400, the industry's first three-dimensional workstation, which sold for $75,000. Recognizing his limitations as a manager, Clark appointed Edward McCracken, a former executive at Hewlett-Packard, as president of Silicon Graphics.

Clark incorporated his company in 1986. By then, the firm was the leading maker of high-end three-dimensional workstations, which it marketed mainly to technical and scientific organizations. Believing diversification was key to the company's success, McCracken decided to place Silicon Graphics in direct competition with industry leaders like Sun Microsystems by manufacturing less expensive workstations. In 1987, Clark and his engineers added reduced instruction set computing (RISC) chips to the company's terminals. The Personal IRIS, the first personal graphics workstation to hit the market, was shipped in 1988, as was the IRIS POWER Series of compatible multiprocessing workstations. To generate capital for new product development, Clark divested 20 percent of Silicon Graphics' stock to Control Data for roughly $68.5 million. He also licensed the IRIS Graphic Library to IBM Corp. in an attempt to entice software vendors to develop programs that would run on Silicon Graphics workstations.

By the early 1990s, Silicon Graphics had made its way to the *Fortune 500,* and sales had reached $550 million. Software programs available for Silicon Graphics workstations totaled more than 1,400. Increasing tension with McCracken prompted Clark to leave his firm in 1994. He considered investing his earnings into an interactive television venture. However, after meeting 22-year-old Marc Andreessen—who had developed the Mosaic graphic user interface (GUI) program for World Wide Web browsing with a group of fellow University of Illinois students—Clark decided to turn his attention to the Internet. Clark and Andreessen agreed to launch Mosaic Corp. in April of 1994 with $3 million of Clark's money and additional venture capital from investor John Doerr. A few months later, Clark agreed to change the firm's name to Netscape when the University of Illinois claimed they had rights to the name Mosaic, since the technology was developed when Andreessen had worked there.

In October of 1994, Clark and Andreessen offered AT&T executive Jim Barksdale a seat on Netscape's board. Three months later, they talked him into running Netscape. Although the firm wasn't yet profitable, Clark convinced Andreessen and Barksdale into taking the firm public in 1995 in what amounted to one of the most lucrative initial public offerings (IPO) in industry history. Many analysts consider Clark and Andreessen's launch of Navigator, Netscape's free Web browser, as crucial to the advent of the Internet revolution. According to Charlotte Dunlap in *Computer Reseller News,* "Clark helped launch the Internet craze by commercializing the government-based network's first GUI." Less than a year after Netscape's IPO, Navigator was serving roughly 80 percent of the Web's browser market. That success was short-lived, however, thanks to Microsoft's launch of its Internet Explorer browser.

Clark continued to work for Netscape as it battled Microsoft in what became known as the "browser wars." By 1997, Microsoft's Internet Explorer, sold along with the Windows 95 operating system, had reduced Netscape's browser market share by nearly 50 percent. When Netscape filed a complaint alleging that Microsoft's strategy of bundling Explorer with Windows 95 was anti-competitive, the U.S. Department of Justice ruled that Microsoft must offer a version of Windows 95 unbundled from Internet Explorer. Although that decision was later overturned in an appeal, the litigation sparked a wide reaching investigation of Microsoft's alleged monopolist tactics. In 2000, the computer industry giant was found guilty and ordered to split into two companies, a verdict which Microsoft immediately appealed.

In 1996, before Netscape was even two years old, Clark already had set his sights set on a new enterprise. To help streamline what he saw as a bloated and highly inefficient healthcare industry, he launched Healtheon Corp. The firm's first product, an Internet-based system that automated enrollment in health plans for insurance companies and large employers, flopped. Clark found himself having to work hard to reassure his investors that Healtheon was still a lucrative idea. Recognizing that he needed someone with experience in marketing computer services, Clark also brought in a new CEO, Mike Long, in 1997. Long shifted Healtheon's focus to physician groups, believing that they would be more likely to embrace new technology than giant insurers.

According to *Fortune* columnist Julie Creswell, it was Microsoft that helped to finally spark Healtheon's growth. ''When Healtheon learned that Microsoft was on the verge of investing $100 million in an Atlanta online health startup called WebMD, Clark and Long foresaw a battle they wanted to avoid. Instead of fighting Microsoft, they made a deal valued at $6.5 billion to merge Healtheon and WebMD.'' The deal with WebMD proved to be lucrative. Consumers already were using the site to gather reputable medical information. While Healtheon could continue to devise ways to automate information processing procedures for healthcare providers, WebMD would be able to take advantage of the advertising potential a growing base of online visitors offered. Although his goal of revolutionizing the American healthcare system proved too broad, at least for the immediate future, Clark eventually was able to put together a leading heathcare Web site serving both physician groups and consumers.

Clark's involvement with Netscape essentially ended in November of 1998, when AOL agreed to pay roughly $4.2 billion for Netscape. When news of deal became public, stock prices skyrocketed. By the time AOL completed its acquisition in March of 1999, the value of the deal had reached $10 billion. Clark invested some of his windfall into yet another venture, myCFO Inc., an Internet-based financial management services firm catering to the wealthy. He continues to serve as chairman of Healtheon/WebMD and CEO and chairman of myCFO.

FURTHER READING:

Creswell, Julie. ''What the Heck is Healtheon?'' *Fortune.* February 21, 2000.

Dunlap, Charlotte. ''5 Biggest Investors: Jim Clark—The Man With the Midas Touch—Integral to the Launch of Three Billion-Dollar Start-up Companies.'' *Computer Reseller News.* September 20, 1999.

Hof, Robert D. ''No Satisfaction in Silicon Valley.'' *BusinessWeek Online.* November 8, 1999. Available from www.businessweek.com.

''Know Thyself.'' *The Economist.* October 30, 1999.

Sherrid, Pamela. ''Jim Clark's Hat Trick.&rquo; *U.S. News & World Report.* October 5, 1998.

''Silicon Graphics Inc.'' In *Notable Corporate Chronologies.* Farmington Hills, MI: Gale Group, 1999.

Taft, Darryl K. ''The Men Who Took Down Microsoft.'' *Computer Reseller News.* June 26, 2000.

SEE ALSO: Andreessen, Marc; AOL Time Warner Inc.; Barksdale, Jim; Microsoft Corp.; Netscape Communications Corp.

CMGI INC.

CMGI Inc., with origins dating back to 1968, rose to be a leader among Internet holding firms under the direction of David Wetherell. With the 1995 creation of @Ventures, one of the first Internet-only venture capital firms, CMGI operated as an incubator—a firm that invests in business start-ups with the intent of spinning them off or operating the start-ups themselves. By 2001, the company's arsenal included 65 majority-owned and venture investment companies, including AltaVista Co. and uBid.com. CMGI also had forged strategic partnerships with the likes of Compaq Computer Corp., BellSouth, Microsoft Corp., Pacific Century CyberWorks, and Sumitomo Corp. However, the downturn in the dot-com industry forced CMGI to restructure operations by cutting investments and selling off unprofitable businesses.

EARLY HISTORY

CMGI began operation in 1968 as the College Marketing Group (CMG). The company's focus was the sale of educational publishing products and, eventually, the mailing lists it had compiled. Software expert Wetherell bought the firm in 1986 and transformed it into a database management business. In 1989, CMG purchased a printing and direct mail company, which it renamed SalesLink.

Wetherell took the firm public in 1994 under the name CMG Information Services Inc.—the firm officially adopted the name CMGI Inc. in 1998—and sold 1.2 million shares. At the time of the initial public offering (IPO), the company had started focusing on investing in and developing Internet-based firms. Its first business venture, entitled Book Link Technologies, was launched with a $900,000 investment. It was one of the first commercial World Wide Web browsers that allowed users to search and purchase textbooks. The venture was sold to America Online (AOL) that year for $30 million in stock.

MAJOR INVESTMENTS, PARTNERSHIPS, AND IPOS

Using the proceeds from the Book Link sale, CMGI formed @Ventures, the first venture capital firm concentrated solely on Internet-based firms. @Ventures began investing in companies building Web communities; providing Web tools for online advertisers and direct marketers; offering content-related services; and those offering e-commerce and infrastructure services. Via the @Ventures subsidiary, CMGI purchased the commercial rights of search engine Lycos and took it public in 1996. It also invested in GeoCities Inc., ThingWorld.com, Silknet Software, Premiere Technology, and Vicinity Corp. That same year, CMGI created its first majority-owned companies, Engage Technologies and Navisite. Engage was involved in providing Internet marketing solutions, while NaviSite operated as an application service provider (ASP).

CMGI continued to grow in 1997, keeping pace with the booming dot-com industry. The firm struck key partnerships with Intel Corp. and Microsoft, securing large investments from both firms. The following year, CMGI formed a partnership with Sumitomo Corp., which smoothed its entrance into the Japanese market. Meanwhile, @Ventures continued to invest, adding Ventro Corp., Speech Machines, Reel.com, PlanetAll, Softway Systems, and KOZ.com to its holdings. CMGI also launched Planet Direct, a content provider whose name eventually was changed to MyWay.com, and online advertising network Adsmart.

Along with making key investments and creating new firms, CMGI also was gaining recognition by selling off properties and initiating successful public offerings. In 1998, the firm sold PlanetAll to Amazon.com and Reel.com to Hollywood Entertainment, a move that made CMGI the largest shareholder of the entertainment firm. GeoCities went public that year, and in 1999 Yahoo! bought it for $3.9 billion in stock. CMGI conducted several IPOs in 1999, including Critical Path, Silknet Software, and Ventro Corp., as well as its own NaviSite and Engage units.

In March, the firm sold off its CMGI Direct arm, exiting the direct marketing industry it had been involved in since its inception. At the same time, CMGI announced plans to launch a new majority-owned Internet broadcasting company called iCAST. The firm also began to develop CMGI Solutions, a majority-owned enterprise business solutions provider. Acquisitions during the year included Internet traffic verification firm I/PRO; Internet marketing and management services company Adknowledge; Internet advertising firm Adforce, and Web-based advertising network Flycast. However, the largest deal of 1999 was the purchase of an 83-percent stake in search engine AltaVista from Compaq Computer Corp. As part of the deal, Compaq gained a 16.4-percent interest in CMGI, making it the firm's largest outside shareholder.

As CMGI entered the new millennium, it was intent on continuing its growth. It purchased uBid.com, continued investing in emerging Internet-based firms through its @Ventures arm, and formed a strategic alliance with Pacific Century CyberWorks, which allowed it to penetrate the Asian market. The firm also formed CMGion to operate as a Web content distributor. However, the aggressive growth strategy CMGI had employed during the late 1990s was stifled in the second half of 2000. While the company had been posting substantial revenue gains, its profits had been faltering since 1999, along with its stock price. According to a December 2000 *InternetWeek* article, "the venture cap company bought up Internet businesses willy-nilly during the delirious days of hyperinflated dotcom stock prices, but has since failed to figure out a way to make its many companies work together for profits." Like many in the dot-com industry, CMGI was forced to restructure. In an effort to cut costs and improve efficiency, it consolidated its 17 operating companies into six different business units including search and portals, infrastructure and enabling technologies, Internet professional services, e-business and fulfillment, interactive marketing, and venture capital.

In November of 2000, CMGI divested both iCAST and 1stUP.com, marking its exit from the entertainment portal market. CMGI also called off a planned IPO for AltaVista. By December, stock was hovering around $9.50 per share, after trading at $163.50 at the start of the year. Over the course of one year, CMGI had lost 96.6 percent of its market value.

CMGI's restructuring continued into 2001, and the firm announced that its @Ventures business was going to pare back new investments. CMGI also closed down its AdForce business in June 2001, along with exiting the online payment industry by selling off its ExchangePath subsidiary. Management believed the firm would succeed by remaining focused on its core business units.

FURTHER READING:

Chidi, George A. "CMGI Chief Tries to Reassure Investors." *Network World.* December 21, 2000.

"Company History." Andover, MA: CMGI Inc., 2001. Available from www.cmgi.com.

Conhaim, Wallys W. "CMGI: Profile of a Holding Company." *Link-Up.* May/June, 1999.

Hillebrand, Mary. "CMGI Deals Brings Compaq Many New Partners." *E-Commerce Times.* August 19, 1999. Available from www.ecommercetimes.com.

Lewis, David. "CMGI Ventures Into the Red." *InternetWeek.* December 18, 2000.

Macaluso, Nora. "CMGI Sheds Two Dot-Coms." *E-Commerce Times.* November 14, 2000. Available from www.ecommercetimes.com.

Saunders, Christopher. "CMGI Closes AdForce." *Internet-News.* June 12, 2001. Available from www.internetnews.com.

SEE ALSO: AltaVista Co.; Angel Investors; Incubators, E-Commerce; Financing, Securing; Wetherell, David

CNET NETWORKS INC.

CNET Networks Inc. is a leading provider of technology and e-commerce news and information across several media, including the Internet, television, radio, and print. Its target audiences include both consumers and businesses, and the company has created online marketplaces for technology and consumer products. Its subsidiary, CNET Data Services (CDS), plays a central role in providing information that drives computer and electronics sales and distribution channels. CDS licenses access to its multilingual product database to online computer retailers, resellers, and e-commerce companies. At the end of 2000 CDS had some 135 licensing agreements in place with companies that included Dell Computers, Hewlett-Packard, Ingram Micro, and Yahoo!. The CDS database included information on more than 600,000 different products.

CNET Networks has an Internet presence in more than 25 countries. Its Internet operations include flagship Web site CNET.com, which provides technology news and product reviews. According to *B to B,* CNET.com had 20 million unique monthly visitors during the first quarter of 2001, nearly 80 percent of whom were influential at all stages of their company's buying process. More than 95 percent of CNET.com visitors planned to purchase hardware or software during the next 12 months.

Following the acquisition of Ziff-Davis Inc. and ZDNet in October 2000, CNET Networks gained control of ZDNet.com, another flagship Web site that provides information on technology products and services. In January 2000 CNET Networks acquired the comparative shopper mySimon (www.mysimon.com). The company also operates dozens of other Web sites under a range of sub-brands and has two news sites, news.com and zdnn.com, that focus on breaking news in the technology industry.

CNET Networks also is active in television, radio, and print. Its television programming, News.com, can be seen on CNBC on Saturday and Sunday afternoons. CNET Radio, which can be heard in San Francisco, was formed in January 2000 through a partnership with radio station owner AMFM Inc. and was the first all-tech radio format in the United States. A live audio feed of CNET Radio can be heard on the Internet at www.cnetradio.com. The company's magazine, *Computer Shopper,* has a circulation exceeding 500,000.

CNET Networks also disseminates technology news and information through electronic newsletters. It gained some newsletters through the acquisition of Ziff-Davis, which helped to increase its number of newsletters from 61 in the first quarter of 2000 to 150 in the first quarter of 2001. The company boasted some 10 million opt-in subscribers to its newsletters.

According to an interview with CNET Networks' chairman and CEO Shelby Bonnie in *B to B,* about 66 percent of CNET Networks' revenue comes from advertising (online, print, and broadcast). Other revenue streams include lead generation (21 percent); channel services, including license and subscription fees (5 percent); and international revenue (8 percent).

FOUNDED IN 1992 BY HALSEY MINOR

CNET Inc. was founded in San Francisco in 1992 by Halsey Minor, 27, who led the company as its chairman and CEO until 2000. In March 2000 CNET's vice chairman Shelby Bonnie succeeded Minor as CEO, with Minor remaining as chairman. In 2001 Bonnie became chairman and CEO, with Minor becoming chairman emeritus. As a managing director of venture capital firm Tiger Management in 1992, Bonnie was the first major investor in CNET. In 1993 he became the company's third employee and was its chief financial officer and chief operating officer. Prior to founding CNET, Minor was an investment banker and publisher.

By 1994 the company was attempting to launch a new cable network, C\NET: The Computer Network. It planned to start with a single show called "C\NET Central" that would run for several hours over a weekend. The start-up cable network received a significant investment from Microsoft co-founder Paul Allen in 1994, and in 1995 USA Networks became a minority investor. At the time a competing computer channel, Jones Computer Network, reached 1.5 million homes, and Microsoft was planning to launch the PC Channel in association with cable operator Tele-Communications Inc. (TCI). USA Networks agreed to show C\NET programming on its USA and Sci-Fi cable channels.

The president of C\NET Networks was Kevin Wendle, who was an original member of the Fox Broadcasting team and an Emmy Award-winning producer. In 1995 the network was developing two shows in addition to "C\NET Central." One was to be called "The Web" and focus on the Internet, while the other would consist of multimedia software and product reviews. The company also began developing a Web site that would be a leading source of information about computer technology and digital media. By mid-1995 C\NET Online had more than 43,000 registered users. Its lead advertisers were Hewlett-Packard, IBM, and MCI. The demand for online advertising was such that CNET created a separate department to provide data to potential advertisers. Within four months the number of employees working on the Web site increased from six to more than 85.

In 1996 CNET and E!Entertainment Television formed a joint venture called E!Online, which began as a Web site providing entertainment news. However, the venture was short-lived. In 1997 E!Entertainment Television bought out CNET's 50-percent interest in E!Online for $10 million.

The national exposure that resulted from the weekly airing of "C\NET Central" on the USA and Sci-Fi channels helped toboost traffic at CNET's Web sites. The company's flagship Web site was CNET Online (www.cnet.com), which was getting 9 million hits a day in mid-1996. It offered technology news, game reviews, technical support, bulletin boards, and product reviews, as well as an online radio component that delivered audio. Visitors to CNET Online also could view C\NET Central's studio. In addition to CNET Online, the company also operated Shareware.com, an archive of more than 170,000 free software titles, and Search.com, a Web site that gathered search engine programs that indexed Web sites.

DEVELOPED NEW ONLINE PROPERTIES, 1996-1999

CNET went public in 1996. Later in the year the company added more Web sites and scaled back plans to operate a 24-hour cable channel, deciding instead to stick with limited cable TV programming and to focus on the Internet. CNET's newly launched Web sites included News.com, a source of technology news; Download.com, a library of software demo titles; and BuyDirect.com, a site that allowed registering, purchasing, and downloading software. TV programming included three additional shows: "TV.com," which featured presidential son Ron Reagan as a correspondent; "The Web," in which young hosts discussed cool Web sites; and "The New Edge," which looked at how technology was affecting our daily lives.

In 1997 CNET launched Snap! Online, a combined online service, directory, and tutorial. Challenging America Online, which then had 12 million subscribers, Snap! included a comprehensive CD-ROM tutorial for first-time Internet users. The free service also organized Internet content into channels for news, sports, entertainment, and other topics. In 1998 Snap! attracted a $5.9 million investment from NBC, which had an option to acquire a 60-percent interest in the Web portal for an additional $38 million.

In mid-1998 CNET launched a comparative shopping site for computer and technology products called Shopper.com. The site maintained a database of 100,000 products and 1 million prices. It had 62 participating computer retailers who listed their products on Shopper.com and then paid a fee based on a "pay-per-click" advertising model.

For 1998 CNET's revenue increased by 69 percent over 1997, from $33.6 million to $56.4 million. Net income for 1998 was $2.6 million (later reclassified to $3 million), compared to a net loss of $24.7 million in 1997. The company's Web sites were generating 8.2 million page views a day at the end of the year, and analysts forecast that CNET's multiple revenue streams would enable it to sustain its profitability for the next several years.

CNET continued to develop its e-commerce strategy in 1999 with the acquisition of NetVentures Inc. and its ShopBuilder (www.shopbuilder.com) online store creation system for $12 million. It planned to help resellers of unbranded computer systems, or "white boxes," build their own online stores and benefit from CNET's marketing clout. In August 1999 CNET began a store-hosting service for small-to-mid-sized merchants at www.store.com.

In early 1999 CNET began providing online computer buyer guides to America Online. Around this time CNET reorganized its Web sites into an efficient e-commerce platform. Shopper.com, News.com, Builder.com, and Computers.com were reconfigured into 10 content areas. The company's main page, www.cnet.com, focused on searching and included archived articles, editors' picks, the Snap portal, searches from Inktomi, and links to retailers. In May 1999 CNET strengthened its search engine capabilities by acquiring Sumo Inc., an Internet Service directory, for $29 million in stock. In a separate deal with RealNetworks, Snap.com would be used as a search tool to locate video and audio content online by users of RealPlayer G2 and on all RealNetwork sites. Later in 1999 CNET acquired Internet search firm SavvySearch Ltd. for $22 million.

CNET stepped up its branding efforts in 1999 as well. The company started out the year with an advertising budget for a national branding campaign estimated at $40-$45 million. Then, putting growth before profits, CEO Halsey Minor announced in mid-1999 he would spend $100 million on advertising to build CNET's brand and make it synonymous with technology. The new national branding campaign featured the tagline: "CNET: The source for computers and technology."

ACQUISITIONS AND MERGERS, 2000

CNET continued to be active in broadcast media in 1999 and 2000. In fall 1999 CNET News.com debuted on CNBC, and the company launched the CNET Investor Channel. In January 2000 CNET formed an alliance with AMFM Inc. to create CNET Radio, the first U.S. all-tech radio format. That same month CNET spent $700 million to acquire comparative shopper mySimon.com. In March the company changed its name from CNET Inc. to CNET Networks Inc.

In July the merger of two major technology portals, CNET and ZDNet, was announced, with CNET acquiring Ziff-Davis Inc. With 16.6 million unduplicated users, CNET Networks became the eighth-largest Internet property, according to Media Metrix. The sale of Ziff-Davis Inc. and ZDNet to CNET was completed in October for approximately $1.6 billion. Earlier in the year Ziff-Davis Inc., ZDNet's parent company, had sold its Ziff-Davis Publishing business, which included computer magazines *PC Magazine, PC Computing,* and *PC Week.* Also not included in the sale to CNET was ZDTV, which had been sold to Paul Allen's Vulcan Ventures. In addition to the Web portal ZDNet.com, CNET gained *Computer Shopper* magazine, the SmartPlanet online service, and an equity stake in Red Herring Communications. Japanese software giant Softbank Corp., which owned 50 percent of Ziff-Davis, would have a 17-percent interest in the new company.

As a result of its acquisition activity, CNET reported revenue of $264 million for 2000, compared to $112.3 million for 1999. However, acquisition costs and interest expense resulted in a net loss of $484 million, compared to net income of $416.9 in 1999. For 2001, the company appeared committed to making more acquisitions. In April it acquired a 90-percent interest in the technology industry research firm TechRepublic Inc. from the Gartner Group for $23 million.

FURTHER READING:

Andrews, Whit. "NBC Buys into CNET's Web Hub, Snap." *Internet World.* June 15, 1998.

Atwood, Brett. "C Net Sets Sights on Cable-TV Market." *Billboard.* April 6, 1996.

Chandrasekaran, Rajiv. "Free New Service Aims to Make Direct Internet Access Easy as AOL." *The Washington Post.* September 23, 1997.

"CNET: Can Tech Guru Handle Wine, Too?" *Business Week.* October 30, 2000.

"CNET Goes for Broke." *Business Week.* July 12, 1999.

"CNet's Paper Chase." *Forbes.* June 3, 1996.

"CNET: Revenge of the Preppies." *Fortune.* June 21, 1999.

"CNET Spins a Wider Web." *Business Week.* March 27, 2000.

"Halsey Minor's Major Plans." *Business Week.* July 26, 1999.

Henry, Shannon. "AOL to Offer Advice, Sell New PCs Online." *The Washington Post.* February 10, 1999.

Steinert-Threlkeld, Tom. "Electronoclast: If You Can't Beat 'Em." *Inter@ctive Week.* July 24, 2000.

Strauss, Robert. "Networked TV: Cable Shows Take the Lead in Connecting Viewers to Computers." *The Washington Post.* February 12, 1997.

"Tech Sites Merge as Net Eats Computer Publishing." *Communications Today.* July 20, 2000.

SEE ALSO: MySimon.com; Ziff-Davis, Inc.

COBOL

COBOL (COmputer Business Oriented Language), is a programming language used in many different business applications, both on mainframe computers and desktop systems. It is one of the first high-level computer languages, meaning that it is much closer to human language than the machine language through which computer hardware accepts commands. High-level languages eventually get translated to a primary, numeric machine language consisting of zeros and ones.

COBOL has several strengths. One is the language's ability to process data. It is especially valuable when simple processes—such as calculating percentages or performing basic addition and subtraction—must be applied to large amounts of information. Another one of COBOL's strengths is its simplicity. Because it is very readable and easy to understand, it's difficult to hide malicious or destructive computer code within COBOL, and easy to spot and correct programming errors. Finally, COBOL is capable of running on many different kinds of computers, which makes it attractive.

COBOL was released in April of 1959. Shortly after the introduction of FORTRAN—another high-level programming language used mainly for engineering programs—users from academia and the manufacturing sector convened at the University of Pennsylvania to discuss the need for a standardized business language that could be used on a wide variety of computers. A developmental process followed, involving representatives from leading corporations and the U.S. Department of Defense. After several political struggles, COBOL eventually emerged. After its initial release, COBOL was updated several times. The first update occurred in 1962, which included improvements like a report-writing feature that made the language especially popular.

In the early 2000s, COBOL was a frequently discussed topic in e-commerce circles. Many companies sought to allow customers to access data on mainframe computers running COBOL programs. Finding ways to enable COBOL to interface with hypertext markup language, which is used to create pages on the World Wide Web, became important.

Another issue involved security. Because COBOL is so simple, it is very secure by design. The language also can include time-tested security controls. By combining COBOL with, or translating it to, more complicated languages like Java, Pearl, C, and C++, and using less-secure operating systems, the possibility for compromised security existed. As explained in *Computerworld,* such "efforts could, by virtue of this added complexity, inadvertently allow unauthorized viewing of the converted data or glimpses into previously protected areas of the mainframe itself."

FURTHER READING:

Computer Languages. Alexandria, VA: Time-Life Books. 1986.

Copeland, Lee. "Webifying Mainframe Apps: Lessons from the Field." *Computerworld,* January 3, 2000.

Glass, Robert. "COBOL—a Contradiction and an Enigma." *Communications of the ACM,* September, 1997.

Radcliff, Deborah. "Moving COBOL to the Web—Safely." *Computerworld,* May 1, 2000.

SEE ALSO: C; FORTRAN; Programming Language; UNIX

COMMERCE ONE INC.

Commerce One builds business-to-business (B2B) e-commerce exchanges that allow companies to do business via the World Wide Web or other electronic platforms. The idea behind these exchanges, or marketplaces, is to cut costs for all parties involved by creating a single place where buyers, sellers, distributors, and suppliers can complete commerce transactions. Commerce One exchanges, based on the firm's Market Site Portal software, offer auction capabilities, which let clients collect offers for their merchandise to get the best possible prices. Similarly, reverse auctions allow businesses to solicit competitive bids for products and services they are looking to purchase. Commerce One's BuySite procurement software suite is geared more toward creating private supply chain sites for individual companies. This technology also allows buyers to view various supplier catalogs online and complete secure transactions electronically.

Founded in 1994 as DistriVision Development Corp. by Tom Gonzales and his son, the firm first fo-

cused on selling office automation software to banks. By the time Mark Hoffman, co-founder of Sybase Inc., was named president and CEO of DistriVision in 1996, it had also moved into multimedia catalog development. Hoffman secured more than $7 million in financial backing and brought in new managers, some from Sybase, to steer DistriVision's transformation into Commerce One the next year, creating a firm that sold products and services that facilitate B2B electronic commerce. According to *InternetWeek* writer Judith Mottl, Hoffman's "idea was to use DistriVision's supply-chain software to move the procurement process to the Web, linking buyers and sellers to a circle of exchanges and marketplaces that would automate, simplify, and speed business-to-business transactions."

The firm went public in 1999. It experienced intense growth that year, reaching sales of $33 million, compared to $2 million the previous year. Employees grew from roughly 500 to 1,300 over the same time period. Lending credibility to the upstart was its ability to sign on customers like automobile maker General Motors, which ended up holding a 20-percent stake in Commerce One, and Atlanta, Georgia-based telecommunications firm BellSouth. Commerce One also was busy forging partnerships with firms like Microsoft. In fact, Commerce One was one of the few e-commerce upstarts to use Microsoft's Windows operating system, rather than Unix, as its main platform. Because Microsoft was looking for ways to extend its reach into electronic commerce, Commerce One's decision to use Windows was of particular importance to the software giant.

By mid-2000, the firm was working on developing more than 100 commerce exchanges for its clients. Faced with increased competition from rivals Oracle Corp. and Ariba Inc., Commerce One continued to develop new technology and forge deals that would increase the comprehensiveness of its suite of products. For example, the firm formed a licensing joint venture with Germany's SAP AG, a leading developer of software applications that allow enterprises to manage their resources electronically. In September, Commerce One unveiled an upgrade to its auction software that expanded the number of languages and currencies it supported and allowed related items to be grouped together for an auction that accepts bids for the entire grouping, as well as for individual items. In 2001, Commerce One paid $78 million in stock for business network management software maker Exterprise Inc.

Commerce One makes its money by licensing its software, levying service and network charges, and retaining a stake (typically 50 percent) in the exchanges it creates. Market Site Portals cost anywhere from $500,000 to more than $2 million, depending on the amount of work involved in putting catalogs on-line, creating search engines, training employees, and so on. Once the site is up and running, the company or companies operating the exchange charge those who use the site—suppliers, distributors, sellers, and buyers—a fee for each transaction completed. Commerce One gets a portion of each of these fees. For these fees to amount to profits for Commerce One, suppliers must be willing to complete a high number of transactions at these sites. Therefore, in an effort to promote B2B marketplace use across the globe, the company also requires its Market Site Portal clients to join the Global Trading Web, which by mid-2000 linked 58 B2B online marketplaces.

One of Commerce One's largest exchange projects is Covisint, the online marketplace for the worldwide automotive industry launched in November of 2000 by Ford Motor Co., General Motors, and DaimlerChrysler. In December of 2000, Ford and GM each ended up with a seven-percent stake in Commerce One, and Commerce One received a two-percent stake in Covisint. Critics of the B2B exchange model point out that the exchange, like many others, has yet to return on promises of significant savings. However, the auto industry, like many other markets, continues to invest in the technology, believing that the potential benefits are too great to ignore.

FURTHER READING:

Bull, Katherine. "Mark Hoffman: Changing the Face of the Digital Exchange Industry—Commerce One CEO Believes Digital Exchange Growth Depends on Supplying Both Software and Services." *InfoWorld.* July 3, 2000.

Farmer, Melanie Austria. "Covisint Founders Take $1.26 Billion Stake in Commerce One." *CNET News.com.* December 12, 2000. Available from news.cnet.com/news.

Greene, Jay. "Microsoft's Little Bro." *BusinessWeek Online.* December 11, 2000. Available from www.businessweek.com.

Kerstetter, Jim. "Mark Hoffman." *BusinessWeek Online.* May 15, 2000. Available from www.businessweek.com.

Meisner, Jeff. "Ariba, Commerce One Battling It Out for No. 1 Spot in B2B." *The Business Journal.* October 13, 2000.

Mottl, Judith N. "Commerce One Rides Internet Wave—Supply Chain Software Provider Benefits from Growing Demand for Internet Exchanges." *InternetWeek.* May 15, 2000.

Mulqueen, John T. "E-Commerce Made Easy." *CommunicationsWeek.* April 14, 1997.

"Q&A with Commerce One's Mark Hoffman." *BusinessWeek Online.* December 11, 2000. Available from www.businessweek.com.

SEE ALSO: Business-to-Business (B2B) E-commerce; Covisint; Platforms

COMMODITIZATION

Commoditization is the dilution of a market sector's internal differentiation and competitive nuances in favor of a mass market where price alone determines consumer behavior. The industry's mode of competition thus moves away from innovation of the underlying, commoditized product and toward alternative methods of building value.

As industries mature, barriers to market entry gradually erode, competition intensifies, and the market becomes saturated, forcing prices downward. In the eye of the consumer, there is increasing parity among a market sector's products and services, and building customer loyalty becomes all the more challenging. As the proliferation of products within a market sector reaches the commoditization point, the perceived distinction between brands and varieties vanishes altogether, and customers base their purchasing decisions solely on price. This in turn leads to a pricing war that wreaks havoc on profit margins. To combat commoditization, firms generally seek out new operating models, bundle services to add value, or diversify or specialize their product to capture a niche market within a broader market. If all else fails, firms may simply cut realized or potential losses by exiting the market.

The Internet's relationship to commoditization is something of a paradox. On one hand, the Internet provided a vehicle in which firms could escape commoditization of their products and services by opening new areas of competition. Firms shifted their business plans, often very rapidly, to quickly capitalize on the possibilities afforded by the Internet in fear of losing market share to rivals that were quicker to adapt. The avalanche that ensued, however, created another form of commoditization. Many firms simply established their online presence with too little attention to how to successfully integrate the Web into their existing operations, or how to distinguish their online storefronts from those of others. This process was greatly accelerated by the emergence of the World Wide Web as a medium of commerce, making transactions, comparison shopping, and bidding quick and effortless.

In the sort of mass merchandising that regularly takes place as industries mature and begin to consolidate through mergers and acquisitions, products and services grow more removed from the level of the customer, particularly in services, where the personal touch provided by local companies is replaced by larger national or multinational outfits. Meanwhile, personal dealings with customers are streamlined and mechanized in order to boost customer rolls and margins. This brings about a different sort of commoditization that requires careful remediation. Once again, the Web is a double-edged sword in this case. On one hand, it furthers this process since customer service is thoroughly mechanized and removed from the face-to-face medium. This dramatically decreases the firm's transaction costs and offers convenience to the customer. For those reasons, the Web has been vigorously embraced by firms across many industries. However, it also tends to erode any sense of personal connection to the firm.

A thoroughly commoditized market within the Internet spectrum was telecommunications bandwidth for high-speed Internet access. In this sector, commoditization was not so much fought as it was incorporated. The telecommunications industry established the Bandwidth Trading Organization to coordinate the trading of bandwidth in a manner similar to energy commodities. Such trading would facilitate the implementation of sophisticated financial tools that could manage market risk and generate stronger returns, much as is done in other financial markets.

There is no formula for combatting commoditization; how it is dealt with largely depends on the nature of the industry and the mode of competition therein. Commoditization is less likely to infect markets that require more capital investment to enter, such as heavy manufacturing. But even those industries are affected by burgeoning online business-to-business marketplaces. The capital investment required to enter into the modern information technology and computer software industries, meanwhile, is relatively small. As technology develops, it gets smaller all the time. Companies can distinguish themselves and stay a step ahead of industry commoditization by augmenting their brick-and-mortar operations with their online operations, rather than allowing online storefronts to eat into existing sales channels. The latter often was the case in the 1990s and early 2000s. One way or another, commoditization was a fact of life in the Internet economy, and how firms adjust will largely determine whether they have a place in it.

FURTHER READING:

Colvin, Goeffrey. ''You Could Soon Be Selling Soybeans.'' *Fortune.* November 13, 2000, 80.

King, Julia. ''Businesses Weigh Pros and Cons of Web Marketplaces.'' *Computerworld.* March 13, 2000, 28.

———. ''Dodging the Commodity Bullet.'' *Telephony.* January 19, 2001, 42.

Schmerken, Ivy. ''The Challenge: Coping With Commoditization.'' *Wall Street & Technology.* January 2001, 54.

Surowiecki, James. ''The Commoditization Conundrum.'' *Slate.* January 29, 1998. Available from: slate.msn.com/MotleyFool/98-01-29.

Vincent, Lynn. ''The Brand That Binds.'' *Bank Marketing.* November 2000, 24.

SEE ALSO: Channel Conflict/Harmony; Channel Transparency

COMMUNICATION PROTOCOLS

In order for e-commerce to take place, computers must be able to communicate with one another. To do so, they must use a language format and rules that each understands. Protocols, which can reside either in software or hardware, are the means by which this occurs. Protocols ensure that each device understands exactly how information will be sent and received. They define the format in which data will be communicated; whether it will be transmitted in a steady stream or at irregular intervals; the speed in which it will be sent, usually in bauds per second (BPS); whether data will be transmitted between two devices at the same time (full duplex) or alternately in turns (half duplex); whether data will be compressed, or reduced into a smaller format during transmission. Protocols also provide a means of ensuring that data sent from one device arrives intact on the receiving end. There are many different kinds of protocols that focus on communication. One of the most important Internet communication protocols, TCP/IP, is described below.

OPEN SYSTEMS INTERCONNECT MODEL

The Open Systems Interconnect Model (OSI), created by the International Standards Organization in 1974, provides a solid framework for understanding how communication protocols work. As its name suggests, OSI is a model, not a type of computer program or an actual device. The model was designed so that many different kinds of computer systems could exchange data in a seamless, universal way. Many companies design their products to follow the OSI model when communicating.

The OSI Model divides computer networks into seven different layers (the physical, data link, network, transport, session, presentation, and application layers). Each layer plays a different role in the transmission of information. Many different kinds of protocols can be involved at each layer, and individual protocols can be involved in more than one layer of the model. For example, TCP/IP plays a role on levels seven, four, and three. The first four layers of the OSI Model ensure that data sent from one machine arrives intact on the receiving end.

The *physical layer* resides at the bottom of the OSI Model. It deals exclusively with the transmission and reception of electronic or mechanical signals (which contain bits of information) between two mediums. This level includes the actual cables and hardware involved in the communication process.

When data is sent over a local area network (LAN)—a network of computers and servers in a specific area, such as within a company—it is often done so in packets or chunks known as frames, which conform to the type of network involved. At the *data link layer,* bits of information are changed into frames, such as Ethernet frames. Ethernets are one very common type of way of accessing LANs with PCs and Macintosh computers.

At the *network layer,* the most efficient pathway is determined for the transmission of information between a sender and receiver. This involves different points on the networks involved, which are called nodes. At this level, data from one network is relayed to other networks via devices called routers.

Unlike the first three levels of the OSI Model, which are concerned with the movement of information from one node to another, the *transport layer* is responsible for determining the overall integrity of a message. In other words, this level determines that data sent arrives intact on the receiving end. This level also ensures data is received in a timely way, and in the correct order or sequence. End-to-end communication between the sending and receiving sources is possible at this level. From the transport layer on, the focus is on how information moves between processes or programs, instead of nodes or points on a network.

The *session layer* is where communication links between two network stations originate, are managed, and terminated. The timing, direction (one-way or two-way), and flow of a connection are managed at this level. According to *Tech Encyclopedia,* this layer is sometimes unused, or the steps at this level often occur at the transport layer.

The translation of data—encryption, decryption, and presentation—is determined at the *presentation layer.* This layer is responsible for taking data from many different systems and putting it into a format that can be read by computers on a network. Like the session layer, the presentation layer is not always used by all protocols.

Finally, the *application layer* involves the management of interactions between users and programs, or between two programs. At this level, files are opened, closed, transferred, and written; and e-mail messages are sent.

TCP/IP

There are scores of different communication protocols. Those that work behind the scenes as people engage in e-commerce are used on the Internet—a network of many computer networks, that includes millions of different computer systems. In order for networks to share data, the Internet relies on a collection of protocols often referred to as the TCP/IP model. Short for Transmission Control Protocol/Internet Protocol, there are many different TCP/IP protocols. Roughly 30 of them are among the most widely used and important protocols on the Internet. They are used when information is transmitted between a host computer (one containing information) and the remote users who obtain information from them. The TCP/IP model can be compared to the OSI model. However, beyond physical networks, it relies upon only four layers to send and receive information (the data link, network, transport, and application layers).

Among the most recognizable TCP/IP protocols are Hypertext Markup Language (HTML), used for creating documents that can be linked together with hypertext; Hypertext Transfer Protocol (HTTP), used by computers to transfer hypertext documents and other chunks of information over the Internet; Domain Name System (DNS), which ties the name of computers or networks to specific addresses; File Transfer Protocol (FTP), used for transferring files between computer systems; Point-to-Point Protocol (PPP), which allows a host computer to link directly with a network; and World Wide Web (WWW), which allows users to graphically view a system of hypertext documents, or Web pages.

FURTHER READING:

''Communications Protocol.'' *Ecommerce Webopedia.* 2001. Available from e-comm.webopedia.com.

''Communications Protocol.'' *Tech Encyclopedia.* 2001. Available from www.techweb.com/encyclopedia.

Loshin, Pete. *TCP/IP Clearly Explained.* San Diego: Academic Press. 1997.

Naugle, Matthew. *Network Protocols.* New York: McGraw Hill, 1999.

''OSI Model.'' *Tech Encyclopedia.* March 29, 2001. Available from www.techweb.com/encyclopedia.

Spurgeon, Charles E. *Ethernet: The Definitive Guide.* Sebastopol, California: O'Reilly and Associates. 1995. Available from www.ots.utexas.edu/ethernet.

SEE ALSO: HTML (Hypertext Markup Language); Three Protocols, The

COMMUNITY MODEL

The community model is a method of developing an online presence in which several individuals or groups are encouraged to join and participate in ongoing interaction designed around a common purpose. Web communities, or virtual communities, were not only a way for like-minded people to come together online, they also were an increasingly important element of business plans. The late 1990s and early 2000s saw the cropping up of countless new Web communities facilitating one-to-one, one-to-many, many-to-one, and many-to-many lines of communication and cooperation.

Communities utilize electronic tools such as forums, chat rooms, e-mail lists, message boards, and other interactive Internet mechanisms, which are usually tailored to the particular community. Ideally, such communities are as interactive as possible, creating the greatest level of synthesis between their various offerings. Thus, the discussions that take place in the forums can be linked to content elsewhere on a Web site, while the company or community host can generate new content based on discussions that take place between community members.

Broadly, the community model comes in two basic varieties: those centered on relationships and those centered on tasks. The former typically are informal, grassroots-oriented communities that revolve around shared interests, ideas, topics, and goals. In these communities, the development of relationships is the primary goal. To maximize member involvement, community sites must offer maximum degrees of interactivity and personalization. For example, GeoCities offers space and tools for members to set up their own Web sites and establish virtual communities within the broader GeoCities community. Task-centered communities generally are more structured and impersonal. The relationships established or augmented online are a means to a mutual end, such as enhanced profits. More specifically, Web communities are established between business partners, between businesses and their customers, between different groups of customers, within companies, and between individuals and groups devoted to particular topics.

In business-to-business (B2B) relationships, the community model provides all community members with the ability to share and check electronic invoices, communicate and exchange funds on secured networks, and resolve problems quickly and openly. Internet communities offer exceptionally streamlined workflow processes between and within companies, where the functionality of key tasks is integrated and synthesized. This necessitates less personnel, paperwork, and software, and boosts efficiency, thereby minimizing operating costs and enhancing profit margins.

Web communities allow companies to use the Web to open up new channels for customer support and outreach, advertising, sales, ordering, distribution, and communication. In the field of customer service, the online community is often viewed as a vital step in creating consistent and seamless service across all kinds of media, mirroring the call center as a vehicle for quick service but going beyond it in the level of interactivity. For instance, companies may encourage their users to access the Web to receive customer support in an online forum, in which they can seek advice from a company expert and interact with other customers. In this way, customers are encouraged to become part of a coherent community tied to the company, thereby creating added value and boosting customer loyalty. This built-in source of customer feedback can be extremely valuable, allowing companies to take proactive measures to improve products and customer service. It also enables firms to further personalize their sites and build customer profiles that can be utilized for later advertising and product development. In addition, companies can take advantage of such features to monitor their customers' needs and values, and modify their products and services accordingly. Finally, such arrangements can lighten the burden on company support staff, as customers are encouraged to get and offer help to other customers.

Communities were increasingly popular within companies in the early 2000s. Linking employees to each other and to managers, intra-business Web communities facilitate communication within and across departments and divisions, enhance coordination of strategies starting from the bottom up (rather than mandating them from the top down), and provide a forum for training programs, employee grievances, conflict resolution, and socializing. Furthermore, as *Sloan Management Review* pointed out, intra-firm online communities are an excellent way to encourage and foster voluntary employee participation and initiative, which are crucial concerns among employers.

The infrastructure of an online community consists of hardware, software, design elements, and an interface. All of these characteristics, analysts point out, are best tailored to the specific needs of the community; no one formula is appropriate for every community. Ultimately, communities must revolve around their members, not their features. While the tools available for Web communities are often highly attractive, hosts must keep in mind that the tools must fit the community, not the other way around, or the purpose of the model is lost. In general, a community must grow organically from the genuine needs and desires of the members themselves, and will gradually take shape over time as the community grows.

FURTHER READING:

Brenner, Ev. ''Virtual Communities in the Business World.'' *Information Today*. December 2000.

Chaudhury, Abhijit, Debasish N. Mallick, and H. Raghav Rao. "Web Channels in e-Commerce." *Communications of the Association for Computing Machinery.* January, 2001.

Marks, Andrew. "E-maintenance Management." *Chain Store Age.* May, 2000.

Philbin, Tamara. "Old-Line to Online." *Association Management.* December 2000.

Williams, Ruth L., and Joseph Cothrel. "Four Smart Ways to Run Online Communities." *Sloan Management Review.* Summer, 2000.

Wonnacott, Laura. "To Create a Community, Look to a Good Platform and Examine the Needs of Your Customers." *InfoWorld.* April 3, 2000.

SEE ALSO: Business Models; Channel Conflict/Harmony; Channel Transparency; Virtual Communities

COMPAQ COMPUTER CORP.

Compaq Computer Corp. is one of the largest personal computer (PC) manufacturers in the world. Among diversified computer companies like IBM and Hewlett-Packard, Compaq ranks third. Its products include desktop PCs, notebook computers, the Alpha operating system and Alpha chips, handheld computers, monitors, networking and communications equipment, parallel-processing computers, printers, servers and server software, storage products, and workstations. Compaq also offers consulting, outsourcing, project management, system design, system integration, and e-business services. After facing struggles in the late 1990s—involving troubles integrating its $8.45 billion purchase of Digital Equipment Corp. and being slow to upgrade its product delivery system to take advantage of Internet-based technology—the firm began retooling itself. Its "Everything to the Internet" initiative, launched by CEO Michael Capellas in 2000, reflects Compaq's new focus.

RAPID GROWTH AS A PERSONAL COMPUTER MANUFACTURER

Joseph R. Canion, James Harris, and William H. Murto left their management positions with Texas Instruments in 1982 to found a PC manufacturing business. The new firm, named Compaq Computer, was partly funded by high technology venture capitalist Sevin-Rosen Partners. An initial public offering the next year secured $67 million in additional capital. Sales totaled $111.2 million, a record for first full-year sales of a U.S. business.

A major component of the fledgling company's early success was its ability to bring new products to market in roughly six to nine months, must faster than the timeframe by which much larger competitors like IBM Corp. operated. In fact, the industry average for turning a concept into a product on the shelves was 12-18 months. Annual revenues in 1984 reached $329 million. Nearly 150,000 Compaq PCs were shipped that year, and the firm established sales units in France, Germany, and the United Kingdom.

In 1985, Intel agreed to form a joint venture with Compaq to develop a new microprocessor. The resulting Deskpro 386 topped the speed of IBM's fastest PC threefold. Less than four years after its inception, Compaq set another record by becoming the youngest firm to ever join the *Fortune* 500. International expansion continued with the establishment of a printed circuit board assembly facility in Singapore and a manufacturing plant in Scotland. As the 1980s came to a close, Compaq found itself the second-largest maker of PCs for European businesses.

Standard & Poor's Composite Index of 500 included Compaq in 1988. Compaq's SLT/286 laptop computer, shipped that year, was an overnight success, and the firm unveiled the Compaq LTE, its first notebook PC, in 1989. Growth continued with the purchase of the Stirling, Scotland-based Wang facility, which soon would house service operations. Compaq's efforts to enhance the speed and ability of its machines to handle complex applications led it to develop the Extended Industry Standard Architecture (EISA), which the firm began using in its servers by the turn of the decade.

Geographic expansion efforts extended to Latin America in the late 1980s. International operations were securing more than 50 percent of annual revenues by 1990. That year, new units were established in Austria, Finland, and Hong Kong. Compaq also reached licensed dealer agreements in Argentina, Germany, Hungary, Mexico, Trinidad, and Yugoslavia. The firm made its first inroads into the Asian PC market, particularly in Japan, in 1991.

Although new product development in the early 1990s continued with the launch of Deskpro/M computers and EDS, the industry's first worldwide systems-integration product, the firm struggled with organizational and managerial issues. As a result, Compaq initiated a restructuring that included laying off 14 percent of its employees and consolidating its operations into two product groupings: the Personal Computer Division, which accounted for 90 percent of sales, and the Systems Division. When Compaq posted a loss of $70 million in 1991, company co-founder Canion was ousted as CEO and succeeded by an executive vice president, Eckhard Pfeiffer. During the management shakeup, the last remaining company founder, Harris, also left Compaq.

Although layoffs continued, for the most part Compaq considered its reorganization complete and introduced 16 new products. Throughout the early and mid-1990s, the firm began scattered efforts to move into new markets, including developing its first printer products and inking a video conferencing joint venture agreement with PictureTel. Completing its largest deal to date, Compaq acquired Tandem Computers Inc. in 1997 for $4 billion. Tandem's server technology allowed Compaq to better meet the needs of its business clients, who were seeking more fully integrated products from PC makers, and also set the stage for future e-commerce ventures. A year later, Compaq topped the Tandem deal by paying $8.45 billion for Digital Equipment Corp., gaining access to that company's computer services and data storage operations.

TRANSITION TO A DIVERSIFIED COMPUTER COMPANY

The Digital Equipment acquisition vaulted Compaq to the ranks of industry giants like IBM and Hewlett-Packard Co. Revenues jumped from roughly $25 billion in 1997 to $31 billion in 1998. More importantly, sales from computer services operations grew from $462 million to $3.7 billion over the same time period, reflecting Compaq's decreasing reliance on the increasingly competitive PC market. The deal also marked Compaq's first real Internet undertaking as it gave the company control of Internet search engine Alta Vista.

Although it didn't unveil an actual e-commerce plan until mid-1999, rather late in comparison to most competitors, Compaq did begin an e-commerce push in 1998. The firm reached an agreement to integrate its Proliant server with Microsoft's Site Server Commerce, Raptor Systems Inc.'s Firewall, and Inex Corp.'s merchant software to form various e-commerce "bundles." Compaq's Tandem unit also launched iTP security software.

When problems surfaced regarding the integration of Digital Equipment with Compaq—mainly culture clashes and an inventory glut—surfaced in 1999, the board replaced Pfeiffer with Chief Information and Operations Officer Michael Capellas in April. Recognizing that the sales and distribution model that had served the PC maker well was no longer serving the more diverse operations of Compaq, Capellas began developing a new focus for the firm with an eye toward the Internet. He reorganized the firm into three separate business units. Enterprise Solutions and Services offers e-commerce services, as well as business critical application servers, industry standard servers, and storage devices for very large systems. The two remaining units, Commercial Personal Computer Group and Consumer Group, oversee PC development for their respective markets, a key focus of both

being Internet access. Flint Brenton was named vice-president of a newly formed e-commerce unit in August.

Several products emerged after the restructuring, the most popular being the iPAQ pocket PC, shipped in April of 2000. The handheld unit allows users to connect to the Internet or to a corporate network using wireless technology. Compaq also began working with CMGI on a business-to-employee Web-based marketplace called Freeup that will build Web sites for groups of employees such as information technology workers.

To further promote its new "Everything to the Internet" focus, in October of 2000 the firm launched a $300 million marketing program that "points to Compaq's latest technology, such as its Proliant servers and storage systems, and a new generation of wireless local-area network devices, such as the handheld iPaq computers. Those products are at the forefront of Compaq's efforts to be both at the heart of the Internet's infrastructure and at the edge of the growing wireless Web," stated the Houston Chronicle's Tom Fowler.

In 2000, PCs brought in less than half of Compaq's sales, which totaled roughly $42 billion. While the firm had succeeded in diversifying its operations, in 2001 analysts remained uncertain about what impact Compaq's decision to compete in so many different markets—including all sizes and shapes of PCs, networking devices, and e-commerce products and services—would eventually have on its bottom line. Talks began in spring of 2001 to discuss the acquisition of Compaq, by Hewlett-Packard, for $24 billion. As of late 2001 that deal was still pending.

FURTHER READING:

Abreu, Elinor Mills. "Compaq Appoints E-Commerce Unit Head." *Network World.* August 6, 1999.

Adams, Cindy A. "Compaq Computer Righting its Course After Troubled Waters." *Houston Business Journal.* June 9, 2000.

"Compaq Computer Corp." In *Notable Corporate Chronologies.* Farmington Hills, MI: Gale Group, 1999.

Fowler, Tom. "Compaq Reboots, Reclaims Image as Innovator." *Houston Chronicle.* October 2, 2000.

Kerstetter, Jim. "Compaq Issues E-Com Initiatives." *PC Week.* March 23, 1998.

Musthaler, Linda. "With a New CEO in Place, It's Back to Business at Compaq." *Network World.* August 6, 1999.

Nee, Eric. "Refocusing Compaq." *Fortune.* March 5, 2001.

Webb, Dave. "Compaq Arriving Late at E-Commerce Table." *Computing Canada.* April 23, 1999.

SEE ALSO: Dell Computer; Digital Equipment Corp.; Gateway, Inc.; Hardware; Hewlett-Packard Co.; IBM Inc.; Intel Corp.

COMPETITION

The concept of competition is well known in the fields of economics. In everyday usage, it also connotes a kind of positive, creative energy that fuels our markets. As mainstream use of the Internet grew exponentially through the 1990s, so did competition among the industry's many players. Hordes of upstart companies that became known as dot-coms emerged. They competed aggressively with one another, and with traditional industry leaders, to gain dominance in market niches such as online discount travel services and online product evaluation services. Competition was particularly intense in the online services sector between America Online (AOL) and rivals like Compuserve and Prodigy, and in the personal computer (PC) industry as players like Dell Computer Corp. used the Internet to challenge the dominance of larger competitors.

AOL made one of its first competitive moves in the early 1990s. Launching an intense branding program, which included giving AOL software away for free, the company also began growing its content via alliances with news firms like Tribune Co., Knight-Ridder, and CNN. By the mid-1990s, rivals CompuServe and Prodigy had begun to eat into AOL's market share. To boost subscriber rates, AOL forged an important agreement with Microsoft Corp. in 1996. As a result, AOL agreed to include Microsoft's Internet Explorer browser in its software, and Microsoft agreed to include AOL software on its Windows 95 platform. AOL sought similar alliances with AT&T Corp., Apple Computers, Sun Microsystems, Hewlett-Packard Co., and Netscape Communications. The firm also continued to hone its services to make them as easy to use as possible. According to AOL CEO Steven Case, as quoted in the October 1996 issue of *Forbes*, "If you want to reach a mainstream audience, you have to make it more plug and play. One-stop shopping. One disk to install. One price to pay. One customer service number to call." AOL set its competition back even further in September of 1997 when it purchased the consumer online service of CompuServe Corp. The acquisition boosted AOL's subscriber base to more than 10 million, placing major rivals such as Microsoft Network, AT&T WorldNet, and Prodigy at a distant second place.

Like AOL, Dell Computer Corp. also proved successful in its efforts to outperform competitors. When the firm was founded in April of 1984, it used a direct sales model rather than going through traditional retail outlets. As a result, Dell's machines were less expensive than those of other PC vendors, such as IBM Corp. and Compaq Computer Corp. In addition, the firm began offering on-site setup, mainte-

nance, and repair services for its products in 1987. When Japanese PC firms began lowering their prices, Dell hired a former IBM Corp. executive to oversee the firm's efforts to manufacture machines higher in quality than those of their Asian rivals. Along with focusing on improved technology, the firm also continued to develop its customer service practices. All employees were required to attend a six-week training program to learn how to answer questions, resolve complaints, take orders, and help clients select the best options for their computing needs. Weekly staff meetings included discussions about how to best resolve customer complaints. Dell's efforts, along with its leading ranking on J.D. Powers & Associates' first customer satisfaction survey regarding PC makers, moved the firm from 22nd place to sixth place among the largest U.S. PC manufacturers.

Dell was unique among PC makers in the early 1990s because it actually gained from the economic recession of the time, as those shopping for PCs began to seek less expensive options. However, at the same time the firm found itself facing competition from upstart direct sales vendors, such as Gateway 2000, which eventually usurped Dell as the top U.S. direct seller of PCs. One of Dell's most important moves in its quest for PC market share was to begin selling its PCs and related equipment on the Internet in 1996. Customers were able to place their orders on Dell's Web site as easily as they had done via the telephone. In 1997, roughly one-third of the orders Dell received were being placed on the Internet. More importantly, the majority of these online customers were new to Dell.

When PC prices began falling in the late 1990s, Dell found its Internet savvy even more important. As stated in a *BusinessWeek Online* article, "Thanks to efficiencies created, in part, by Dell's Web-based supply chain, the company can remain profitable even while it launches a bloody PC price war." In 2001, Dell unseated competitor Compaq Computer as the worldwide leader in PC sales.

FURTHER READING:

Jacobs, April. "Businesses Warm to Internet PC Sales." *Computerworld*. December 29, 1997.

Koprowski, Gene. "AOL CEO Steve Case." *Forbes*. October 17, 1996.

Mulqueen, John T. "Dell's Aiming to Take Corps to the Web." *InternetWeek*. December 22, 1997.

Shook, David. "The Winner of the PC Price Wars: Dell." *BusinessWeek Online*. May 1, 2001. Available from www.businessweek.com.

Simons, John. "Steve Case Wants to Get America Online." *U.S. News & World Report*. March 25, 1996.

Vogelstein, Fred. "The Talented Mr. Case." *U.S. News & World Report*. January 24, 2000.

SEE ALSO: AOL Time Warner Inc.; Apple Computer Inc.; AT&T Corp.; Compaq Computer Corp.; Competitive Advantage; Co-opetition; Dell Computer; Differentiation; Hewlett-Packard Co.; Microsoft Corp.; Netscape Communications Corp.; Sun Microsystems

COMPETITIVE ADVANTAGE

Competitive advantage has to do with a company's ability to outdo competitors, either by improving upon what competitors are currently doing or by doing something completely different in a way that proves successful. Being able to implement an e-commerce plan that improves sales or cuts costs might give one retailer a competitive advantage over another. At the same time, being the first to come up with a new e-commerce business model, or a unique twist on an existing model, might also allow an upstart to gain an early competitive advantage.

According to Dena Waggoner, in the Encyclopedia of Management, "The strongest competitive advantage is a strategy that cannot be imitated by other companies. Competitive advantage can also be viewed as any activity that creates superior value above its rivals."

A prime example of an upstart gaining an early competitive advantage by being first-to-market with a new business model is eBay.com, the world's largest online auction site, with more than 22 million registered users and roughly 8,000 product categories. Although rivals like Yahoo! and Amazon.com attempted to gain market share from eBay by launching their own auction sites, eBay's ability to gain critical mass gave it the competitive edge it needed to stave off its rivals. Despite Amazon's attempt to lure customers with guarantees of product quality and Yahoo!'s offering of commission-free auctions, eBay attracted more sellers than any other auction site simply because it had the most buyers.

Dell Computer Corp. was able to use the Internet to trim costs and boost sales, both of which were becoming increasingly difficult to do in the nearly saturated personal computer (PC) market of the late 1990s. Hoping to gain a competitive advantage, the firm started to sell PCs via the Internet in 1996. It became possible for customers who previously had placed custom orders via the telephone to place them on Dell's Web site. Customers could select configuration options, get price quotes, and order both single and multiple systems. The site also allowed purchasers to view their order status, and it offered support services to Dell owners. Within a year, Dell was selling roughly $1 million worth of computers a day via

the Internet. Even more importantly, nearly 80 percent of the online clients were new to Dell. With the more automated Web-based PC purchasing process, Dell found itself able to handle the growing sales volume without having to drastically increase staff. Cost savings also were achieved as the firm's phone bill began shrinking. Dell's business model, which allowed for easy tracking of customer purchases, also allowed the firm to keep inventory at a minimum. In 2001, Dell usurped Compaq Computer Corp. as the world's largest PC maker.

FURTHER READING:

Govidarajan, Vijay. "Strategic Innovation: A Conceptual Roadmap." *Business Horizons.* July, 2001.

Melendez, Tony. "It's Too Late for 'Wait and See' Approach in E-commerce Arena." *Houston Business Journal.* October 6, 2000.

Waggoner, Dena. "Competitive Advantage," in Helms, Marilyn, *Encyclopedia of Management, 4th Ed.* Farmington Hills, MI: Gale Group, 2000.

SEE ALSO: Business Models; Business Plan; Dell Computer Corp.; Differentiation; eBay

COMPUTER CRIME

According to the U.S. Uniform Crime Reporting Statistics, by 2000 more than 300 million users around the globe accessed the World Wide Web. Of those, at least 1 million were engaged in illegal Internet activities (computer crime or "cyber-crime"). Cyber-crimes include Internet-related forgery, embezzlement, fraud, vandalism, and the disposal of stolen goods. The potential threat to the overall development of e-commerce was serious—so much so that online security expenditures were expected to double to $30 billion in 2004.

The Computer Crime and Security Survey, issued by the Computer Security Institute (CSI) and the FBI, reported that 85 percent of the 538 firms and governmental institutions surveyed found security breaches in 2000. Sixty-five percent admitted that such breaches had caused financial losses. The 186 respondents willing to quantify their losses claimed they totaled $378 million, a 42-percent increase from 1999 and the highest amount recorded since the surveys began in 1995. Seventy percent cited their Internet connections as the source of security problems.

Perhaps 80 percent of all computer-related crimes result from insider attacks, sometimes perpetrated by recently laid-off employees with still-active computer accounts. Fraud and forensic experts reported that organized crime and terrorist groups recruit telecommunications workers to use telephone networks to commit fraud, piracy, and money laundering.

DEFINITIONS

Computer crime includes traditional criminal acts committed with a computer, as well as new offenses that lack any parallels with non-computer crimes. The diversity of offenses renders any narrow definition unworkable. The U.S. Department of Justice (DOJ) broadly defines computer crimes as ''any violations of criminal law that involve a knowledge of computer technology for their perpetration, investigation, or prosecution.'' Accurate statistics on the extent of this phenomenon have proven to be elusive because of the difficulty in adequately defining computer crimes. The statistics also are untrustworthy due to victims' failure to report incidents. The aggregate annual losses to businesses and governments are estimated to be in the billions of dollars.

Some of the most notorious computer crimes have involved computer viruses, such as the Melissa virus that appeared on the Internet in March 1999 and infected systems in the United States and Europe, and the February 2000 distributed denial of service (DDS) attacks on several leading commercial Web sites including Yahoo!, E*Trade, Amazon.com, and eBay.

Cyber-crimes are frequently grouped into three categories. The first are those in which the computer comprises the ''object'' of a crime and in which the perpetrator targets the computer itself. This includes theft of computer processor time and computerized services. The second category involves those in which the computer forms the ''subject'' of a crime, either as the physical site of the offense or as the source of some form of loss or damage. This category includes viruses and related attacks. Finally, the third category includes those in which the computer serves as the ''instrument'' used to commit traditional crimes in cyberspace. This encompasses offenses like cyber-fraud, online harassment, and child pornography.

Though teenage hackers and underage, e-fraud perpetrators have captured headlines, no ''typical'' cyber-criminal exists. Perpetrators also commit cyber-crimes for a variety of reasons. Motives range from a desire to showcase technical expertise, to exposing vulnerabilities in computer security systems, retaliating against former employers, or sabotaging government computer systems.

TYPES OF COMPUTER CRIMES

Distributed denial of service attacks rank among the most widely reported cyber-crimes. They first ap-

peared in mid-1999 and are relatively easy to perpetrate. Many of the tools required to carry them off are freely available online. Often, DDS attack networks consist of hundreds of compromised systems. The attacker inaugurates the attack sequence from one or more consoles, and it can affect thousands of systems worldwide.

Virus programs infect computer files by inserting copies of themselves into those files; they are spread from host to host when users transmit infected files by e-mail, over the Internet, across a company's network, or by disk. The Melissa Virus interrupted e-mail service around the world when it was posted to an Internet newsgroup on March 26, 1999, affecting perhaps 100,000 users and one-fifth of all U.S. businesses. Related problems include worms, which can travel within a computer or network without a user transmitting files; trojan horses, which are disguised as innocuous files but which, once activated, can steal users' login names and passwords, thus facilitating identity theft; and logic bombs, programs activated by a specific event.

Two reports issued by the CIA's National Intelligence Council and the Center for Strategic and International Studies in December 2000 predicted that, during the first two decades of the 21st century, Internet-enabled terrorists would launch attacks on the United States with computer viruses and logic bombs in an attempt to destroy America's private-sector infrastructure. The reports also envisioned a future cyber-arms race, for which the United States would need to develop a ''cyber-arsenal.''

The Internet facilitates terrorism by permitting virtually anonymous communication among terrorists—transmissions that are very difficult to track and intercept. The targets of cyber-terrorists could include air-traffic systems and stock exchanges. Hackers even have successfully broken into governmental systems and launched denial-of-service attacks, such as the 2000 hacker penetration of a printer at the U.S. Navy's Space and Naval Warfare Center that resulted in the transmission of potentially sensitive information to a server in Russia. In 1994, hackers breached the Air Force's main command and control research center. The following year, the Pentagon reported 250,000 attacks on its computers, with 65 percent resulting in computer network entry.

Other widely publicized computer crimes involved online fraud, such as stock scams and securities fraud via the Internet. The Securities and Exchange Commission (SEC), which receives about 300 complaints a day concerning online scams, devotes one-fourth of its enforcement staff to computer-related offenses. Theft of online content also is common. A Software & Information Industry Association study maintained that one-third of all business software applications in use in 1999 were pirated copies. And the Internet has made the distribution of information obtained in identity thefts, such as a person's name or social security number, much quicker and easier. The dissemination of child pornography online also has garnered widespread public and law-enforcement attention. Other offenses, such as stalking victims via the Internet, have only recently begun to be addressed.

ANTI-CYBER-CRIME LEGISLATION

Approximately 40 federal statutes govern the prosecution of computer-related crimes. Among the most prominent are the Copyright Act, the National Stolen Property Act, mail and wire fraud statutes, the Electronic Communications Privacy Act, the Communications Decency Act of 1996, the Child Pornography Prevention Act, and the Child Pornography Prevention Act of 1996.

Congress recognized computer-related crimes as discrete federal offenses with the 1984 passage of the Counterfeit Access Device and Computer Fraud and Abuse Law, which was revised four times in the following decade. This law narrowly protected classified U.S. defense and foreign relations information, files of financial institutions and consumer reporting agencies, and access to governmental computers.

Congress enacted another major anti-cyber-crime law in 1996, the National Information Infrastructure Protection Act (NIIPA). NIIPA broadened the scope of protection offered by the Computer Fraud and Abuse Law by covering all computers attached to the Internet and, therefore all computers used in interstate commerce. It also criminalized all unauthorized access of computer files in order to transmit classified government information; intentional access of U.S. department or agency non-public computers without permission; and accessing protected computers, without or beyond authorization, to defraud and obtain something of value.

The Copyright Act covers computer-related copyright infractions, such as software piracy. The act provides criminal remedies for any intentional infringement of a copyright perpetrated for commercial advantage or private financial gain. Given the ease and anonymity of nearly identical reproductions made of online intellectual property, such as software, digitized text, and audio and visual files—and the ability to disseminate those copies worldwide—many see copyright as an increasingly costly cyber-crime offense. Traditional exceptions to copyright privileges, such as "fair use" and the "right of first sale," may be eroded under evolving copyright protection laws in cyberspace. Digital intellectual property rights also are regulated by the No Electronic Theft Act of 1996, which criminalizes the electronic reproduction and dissemination of copyrighted material.

The National Stolen Property Act (NSPA) has been extended to cover the fraudulent transfer of funds online, as well as the theft of tangible hardware. The courts have determined that federal mail and wire fraud statutes, which outlaw the use of interstate wire communications or the mail to defraud persons of money or property, also can apply to computer-aided theft. However, the case law on this point is still evolving.

One of the most controversial areas of cyber law, the extent of online privacy protection, was addressed in the Electronic Communications Privacy Act of 1986 (ECPA). ECPA has been utilized to prosecute computer hacking, since it strengthens the privacy rights of computer users and permits law enforcement to use electronic surveillance when investigating computer crimes. ECPA also has been used in cases of the theft of encrypted, satellite-transmitted television broadcasts.

The problem of online child pornography spawned several laws intended to block the online transmission of pornographic material to minors. Congress passed the Communications Decency Act of 1996 (CDA, also Title V of the Telecommunications Act of 1996), which prohibited the transmission of "indecent," "patently offensive," and "obscene" material to minors over the Internet. However, the Supreme Court invalidated certain sections of the DCA in Reno v. American Civil Liberties Union, stating that they infringed the First Amendment protection of free speech.

In response, Congress passed the Child Online Protection Act, which penalized any commercial Web site that allowed children to access content that was "harmful to minors." By summer 2001, this act was challenged on First Amendment grounds in a U.S. circuit court. The Internet's role in the production and dissemination of child pornography also is addressed by the Child Pornography Prevention Act of 1996 (CPPA), intended to criminalize the production, distribution, and reception of computer-generated, sexual images of children. The CPPA has survived constitutional challenges in court.

Despite the plethora of anti-cyber-crime laws, few cases have been adjudicated under them. This is due to the reluctance of victims to lodge suits, the difficulty of gathering evidence and identifying perpetrators in cyberspace, the desire of many victims to pursue matters privately, and the fact that many such incidents were prosecuted under state, rather than federal, laws. Prosecution of cyber-crime raises several difficult constitutional dilemmas. Among these are Fourth Amendment concerns about the legality of the search and seizure of computer records and software, First Amendment concerns about freedom of speech, and general questions about the extent of citizens' online privacy.

Since 1978, the states also have addressed cyber-crimes in their own legislation, with Arizona and Florida being the first to do so. Every state has some such legislation on the books. The states have taken the lead in specifically addressing some forms of cyber-crime, such as online harassment. However, the expansion of state computer crime legislation also generates conflicts between federal and state authorities regarding cyber-crime prosecution.

ENFORCEMENT AGENCIES

Despite the relative infrequency of cyber-crime prosecutions to date, the U.S. government has backed numerous initiatives to encourage and invigorate prosecution efforts. In 1995, the Federal Bureau of Investigation (FBI) launched its ''Innocent Images'' probe to track down online child pornography. By March of 1999, the effort had resulted in more than 200 convictions. The FBI also hosts computer crime teams in its 56 field offices and organized the Infrastructure Protection and Computer Intrusion Squad (ICPIS) in Washington D.C., which constitutes a national investigative body and resource on cyber-crime. The FBI's InfraGard program fosters cooperation between federal law enforcement officials and the private sector. InfraGard maintains a secure Web site so businesses can alert law enforcement agencies about suspicious network activity or attacks.

The DOJ addresses computer crime through its Computer Crime and Intellectual Property Section (CCIPS), founded in 1991. Among other duties, CCIPS enforces the NET Act and collaborates with assistant U.S. attorneys around the country to target cyber-crimes. Other sections of the DOJ's Criminal Division target e-crime within their areas of particular concern, such as fraud, child exploitation and obscenity, and terrorism and violent crime.

The Electronic Crimes Task Force (ECTF) forms a central clearinghouse dedicated to computer-related crimes for all local, state, and national law enforcement. Based in New York City, it is headed by the U.S. Secret Service and cooperates with selected partners from private industry. ECTF has successfully cracked large drug cartels, organized crime groups, and individual hackers. The ECTF also generated the precedent for e-mail wiretapping when it arrested 44 members of the John Gotti Jr. crime group for telecommunications fraud.

The DOJ, FBI, Department of Defense, and members of business also cooperate in the National Infrastructure Protection Center (NIPC), created in 1998 to aid in the enforcement of existing anti-cyber-crime laws and to foster cooperation among public- and private-sector prosecution efforts. The NIPC focuses on identifying viruses, issuing warnings, and locating cyber-criminals.

Another government and industry collaboration is the Computer Emergency Response Team (CERT) Coordination Center, dedicated to detecting, disseminating information about, and disabling computer viruses. CERT, part of the Software Engineering Institute (SEI), a publicly and privately funded research and development center, was founded in 1988. CERT has combated more than 17,000 different viruses.

The September 11, 2001 terrorist attacks on the World Trade Center and the Pentagon threw into high relief the vulnerability of the United States to terrorist incursions. In response, the Bush administration authorized the creation of a new, cabinet-level National Homeland Security Agency (NHSA), which had been originally proposed in a series of recommendations by the U.S. Commission on National Security in January 2001. NHSA's responsibilities would include coordinating government and private sector efforts to protect the nation's critical infrastructure from cyber and physical attacks. Additional measures under discussion were the expansion of enforcement authority to investigate money laundering, control borders, detain immigrants, and to wiretap phones and screen e-mails without a warrant. Authorities also could use techniques such as data-mining programs to locate terrorists in cyberspace. Such efforts will build on the emerging field of computer forensics, which dissects storage media to find evidence via specialized software and techniques. One such tool is an IP filter, which uses fuzzy logic to track down e-mail addresses and URLs associated with Internet use.

INTERNATIONAL COMPUTER CRIME

Since the Internet is not limited by geography, crimes committed in cyberspace can easily achieve global dimensions. Systems can be accessed from anywhere in the world, and locating perpetrators is difficult. Many computer fraud and embezzlement schemes target international financial networks. Organized crime groups can utilize information technology to evade identification and carry out drug trafficking and money laundering on a global scale. Questions of jurisdiction and apprehension become much more complicated in international cyberspace.

Estimates place annual business losses to cyber crime at roughly $1.5 billion. Many hackers are based in countries far from those they affect. For example, the author of the Love Bug virus that affected the United States was located in the Philippines. Many authorities suspect that organized ''cyber-crime gangs'' frequently originate in developing countries, such as the former Soviet republics where computer-crime laws are lax and enforcement is haphazard.

Individual countries vary widely in the legal approaches they have taken to regulating the Internet.

Some strictly observant Islamic nations have tried to contain the dissemination of information online, which they view as containing messages potentially harmful to their populaces. Germany has tried to restrict Web sites containing Neo-Nazi content. China installed firewalls to prevent its citizens from accessing unauthorized sites, and Burma bans Internet access completely.

Britain has led in the passage of legislation designed to combat "cyber-terrorism." In February 2000 it passed the British Terrorism Act, which includes in its ban on terrorist groups those who disrupt hospitals or power supplies by hacking into computer systems. A revision of the Regulation of Investigatory Powers Act gives police broad access to e-mail and other online communications.

The Council of Europe's proposed cyber-crime treaty, the initial draft of which was released in April 2000, generated the most controversy of any international cyber legislation proposed to date. It spans a broad spectrum of cyber-crimes from copyright infringement to online terrorism. The treaty seeks to harmonize European criminal laws regarding data interception, interference, and online fraud. Any member nation's enforcement authorities would be granted online entry to any other state in order to pursue a cyber-crime investigation. Governments also could also employ new powers on wiretapping, real-time collection of traffic data, and the search and seizure of digital information. Opponents worry that the treaty ignores individual civil liberties and intellectual property rights. Many U.S. business and governmental officials also oppose adoption of the treaty in its proposed form.

Finally, the global interconnection of computer systems fostered a push for international cooperation to combat computer-related crimes. In 1998 Britain, Canada, France, Germany, Italy, Japan, Russia, and the United States agreed to coordinate efforts to investigate and prosecute cyber-crimes. Among the solutions under debate was an international treaty to standardize domestic cyber-crime laws. Thorny topics include the extent to which governments should allow the free movement of data encryption, which protects the electronic information from compromise but also can be used by criminals to shield their activities. Increased government surveillance of online communications is criticized by privacy advocates and members of various ethnic and racial groups, who feel that it constitutes a form of illegal profiling. The regulation of content, which might suppress hate speech or child pornography, faces obstacles from proponents of free expression.

FURTHER READING:

Brooke Paul. "DDoS: Internet Weapons of Mass Destruction." *Network Computing.* January 8, 2001.

Chen, Christine; and Greg Lindsay. "Viruses, Attacks, and Sabotage: It's a Computer Crime Wave." *Fortune.* May 15, 2000.

Chin, Woo Siew. "Insight into Cyber Terrorism." *New Straits Times.* October 3, 2001.

"Cybercrime: Community Accession to an International Convention." *European Report.* March 21, 2001.

Fletcher, Charlie. "ID Thievery is On the Rise." *Catalog Age.* June 2000.

Gantz, John. "Take a Bite Out of Crime on the Web." *Computerworld.* February 19, 2001.

Gittlen, Sandra. "World Organizations Urge Sharing of Security Info." *Network World.* October 23, 2000.

Godwin, Mike. "Save the Children." *American Lawyer.* August, 2001.

Grosso, Andrew. "The Promise and Problems of the No Electronic Theft Act." *Communications of the ACM.* February, 2000.

Munro, Neil. "Cybercrime Treaty on Trial." *National Journal.* March 10, 2001.

Neeley, DeQuendre. "Justice Department Report Arouses Concerns." *Security Management.* May, 2000.

Nicholson, Laura; Tom Shebar; and Meredith Weinberg. "Computer Crimes." *American Criminal Law Review.* Spring 2000.

Oreskovic, Alexei. "FBI Warns of Digital-Crime Wave from Eastern Europe." *Industry Standard.* March 11, 2001.

Radcliff, Deborah. "A Case of Cyberstalking." *Network World.* May 29, 2000.

———. "Crime in the 21st Century: The New Field of Computer Forensics." *InfoWorld.* December 14, 1998.

Rapaport, Richard. "Cyberwars: The Feds Strike Back." *Forbes.* August 23, 1999.

Shrimsely, Robert. "'Cybercrime' Covered by Extended Law on Terrorism." *Financial Times.* February 20, 2001.

Spiegel, Peter. "U.S. Cybercops Face Global Challenge as World Gets Wired Up." *Financial Times.* October 25, 2000.

Thibodeau, Patrick. "European Cybertreaty Raising Concerns." *Computerworld.* December 11, 2000.

Verton, Dan. "FBI Completes Cybercrime Program Rollout." *Computerworld.* January 15, 2001.

———. "National Security Threatened by Internet, Studies Say." *Computerworld.* January 1, 2001.

SEE ALSO: Children and the Internet; Computer Fraud and Abuse Act of 1986; Computer Security; Data Mining; Fraud, Internet; Intellectual Property; Legal Issues; National Information Infrastructure Protection Act of 1996; National Infrastructure Protection Center; Privacy: Issues, Policies, Statements; Safe Harbor Privacy Framework; Viruses; Worms

COMPUTER ETHICS

Computer ethics refers to the ways in which ethical traditions and norms are tested, applied, stretched, negotiated, and broken in the realm of computer technology. As computers brought about dramatically enhanced power of communication and data manipulation, new ethical questions and controversies were forced to the forefront of contemporary ethics debates. While ethics is concerned with codes of behavior, the arena of computer technology has created many uncertainties that make the establishment of such clear codes an often daunting task.

The more dramatic abuses of computer technology, such as major Internet hackings of company Web sites and online theft of credit card numbers, achieve a high profile. While there are few uncertainties about such cases, these are only the most visible examples of far more prevalent phenomena. Most cases are more subtle, frequent, and tied to the everyday workings of ordinary, law-abiding citizens. There are few clear rules to govern ethical computer behavior, and novel situations arise with great frequency, which can prove dangerous when these fields and practices are mixed with business and sensitive information.

The sheer scope of computer usage, spanning nearly every part of daily life and work, from medical records and communications to payment schedules and national defense systems, makes the untangling of ethical considerations all the more important, as unchecked ethical violations in one area can have severe repercussions throughout a wider system. On the personal level, individuals may run into ethical difficulties in considering what other activities they are facilitating by performing their particular functions via computer. Unfortunately, the speed of computer innovation has usually far outpaced the development of ethical norms to guide the application of new technologies.

The sheer volume of data available to individuals and organizations heightens the concern over computer ethics. No firm, for instance, can forego the opportunity to take advantage of the wealth of data and data manipulation afforded by modern information technology and telecommunications. The competitive nature of the economy provides an incentive to beat competitors to certain advantageous practices so as to capitalize on those advantages. The trick, then, is for organizations to devise ethical principles that allow for the greatest level of innovation and competitive strategy while remaining within the bounds of acceptable societal ethics, thereby maintaining the stability of the system from which they hope to benefit. Likewise, businesses need to coordinate codes of ethics to avoid having their own information systems compromised and putting themselves at a disadvantage.

Regarding the Internet itself, the ethical conundrum centers on several basic questions. Will this medium have negative effects on society? What preventive measures can and should be taken to protect against these negative effects? In what ways will these preventive measures give rise to even more ethical considerations? Ultimately, how does society balance potential benefits with potentially damaging effects?

E-commerce, in particular, creates a host of new ethical considerations, particularly in the area of marketing. The level of personal information and detail that can be accumulated about an individual—thanks to the conversion of integrated databases, polling and purchasing data, and other computer-based data—poses rather serious questions about an individual's rights to personal information in the digital spectrum. The easy collection and exchange of personal consumption patterns and interests over the Internet, while highly desirable to many firms, makes civil libertarians queasy. More broadly, those concerned with computer ethics ask to what extent information perceived as a public good ought to be transformed into a marketable commodity.

Of course, computer activity that is legal isn't necessarily ethical. For example, the invasion of employee privacy via the monitoring of computer-based communications and other computer activity, while generally held to be legal, nonetheless poses serious ethical dilemmas. In addition, computers and related technology greatly depersonalize information and communication and allow for enhanced anonymity, which in turn can lead to diminished barriers to unethical behavior.

Information technology and computer professionals began seriously considering the long-term effects of computer ethics in the late 1980s and early 1990s. They recognized the need to organize professionally through such bodies as the Association for Computing Machinery and the Institute of Electrical and Electronics Engineers to devise professional codes of conduct. However, the increasing proliferation of powerful computers in the hands of nonprofessionals widens the scope of potential problems.

Public interest groups such as the Computer Ethics Institute have made attempts to draw out basic guidelines for ethical computer behavior applicable throughout society. In that spirit, the institute formulated the ''Ten Commandments of Computer Ethics,'' a list of basic dos and don'ts for computer use. Several professional associations have attempted to devise computer ethics codes. The code devised by the Association for Computing Machinery, for instance, included specific instructions that it is ''the responsibility of professionals to maintain the privacy and integrity of data describing individuals,'' and that clear definitions for the retention and storage of such information and the enforcement thereof must be implemented for the protection of individual privacy.

COMPUTER ETHICS IN THE WORKPLACE

The bulk of the scholarly literature on computer ethics focuses on ethical issues in the workplace. Companies and organizations are continually confronted with ethical challenges and violations that require resolution either through clarifying internal policy, internal disciplining and enforcement, or litigation, depending on the nature and severity of the violation. But in addition to the obvious financial vulnerabilities of unethical computer use—such as compromised financial data, employee theft, and a battered public image—the organization's attempts to solve the problems internally can rack up significant costs as well.

While there certainly are no shortage of cases of willfully malicious acts of unethical computer behavior, most ethical lapses simply result from a lack of certainty on the part of the user and lack of policy clarity on the part of the organization. More broadly, since ethics are challenged repeatedly as technological innovations open new possibilities, society as a whole often is uncertain about the proper ethical behavior in given situations. In relatively young fields like information technology, the determination of appropriate behavior can be a particularly acute problem.

A major study in *Journal of Business Ethics* on the individual's determination of ethical computer behavior found that judgments are reached through a complex mix of individual experience, consideration of co-workers' behavior, and company expectations. Surveying more than 300 members of the Association of Information Technology Professionals (AITP), the study compared individuals' personal judgments of ethical behaviors with their assumptions about the judgments of their co-workers and their organizations. Interestingly, there were broad differences across these categories, reflecting a lack of clarity, both within firms and through the economy more broadly, of ethical computer behavior.

One major challenge for organizations, then, is to facilitate harmony between personal ethical norms, peers' ethical norms, and organizational norms, and eliminate confusion between them. Eliminating incongruence between different layers of expectations and ethical norms is pivotal to minimizing what ethical scholars call ''moral stress,'' which results from the lack of certainty over what constitutes ethical, appropriate behavior.

Although data are mixed, numerous studies in the field of computer ethics support the hypothesis that a written and clearly transmitted code of ethics is a strong influence on employee behavior when an ethical decision is involved. A survey of non-management employees at *Fortune* 500 companies by the *Journal of Business Ethics* found that 97 percent of employees felt their management should clarify and communicate what constitutes ethical computer use for employees, while nearly two-thirds reported that codes of computer ethics were widely known in their companies. Only one-fourth of respondents reported that they knew of direct evidence of computer abuse in their organizations, while 55 percent weren't aware of any computer abuse within the company.

There is a legislative history to the enforcement of ethical behavior in the business world and incentive for companies to implement and enforce their own codes of ethics. For instance, the Foreign Corrupt Practices Act of 1977 was designed to rein in questionable practices, and their consequences, among corporations. Meanwhile, the 1991 Federal Sentencing Guidelines held companies responsible for the acts of their employees, adding that as part of the remedy for violations a company is required to spell out what actions the company is taking to ensure that the offending practices will not occur in the future. Picking up on such outside pressure for codification, many companies began to move proactively to devise specific computer-related codes of ethics. Raising awareness of specific responsibilities can greatly eliminate the eventual resort to lawsuits and other costly and time-consuming measures of remediation.

PRIVACY

Aside from obvious criminal activities, subtler forms of computer activity can pose ethical problems. For instance, the use of company computer equipment by employees for personal activities has been vigorously debated, but no clear answers have been formulated that can apply in all organizations. Most employees that use computers maintain an e-mail account and regularly check their mail at work. Generally, this is essential since internal company communications often are transmitted via e-mail. However, employees also may receive personal e-mail at the same account and spend their time at work using the company computer to send and receive personal messages.

New technologies not only allowed for the monitoring of e-mail communications, but other Internet activity such as listservs, chat rooms, and even Web browsing. While companies may well wish to make sure their employees are using their time for company purposes, the monitoring of Web traffic strikes many as an ethical lapse, particularly since the reasoning behind visiting a Web site cannot be determined simply by knowing that an individual went there. This problem extended far beyond the company setting. Fears over governmental or private monitoring of individuals' activities on the Internet opens up an entire range of serious ethical concerns. Because the context of a certain kind of communication or site visitation may be unknown to outside monitors, there is a significant possibility of misunderstanding, misinterpretation, and misuse of such acquired data.

The conflict between personal privacy and company surveillance of e-mail communications and other computer activity was one of the most widely publicized computer-ethical controversies in the late 1990s and early 2000s. While companies argue that the monitoring of their own systems to ensure their appropriate use and the beneficial use of company time is necessary to maintain competitiveness, the moral right to personal privacy was continually asserted.

COMPUTER ETHICS AS EDUCATION

In addition to representing a pressing business and social concern, computer ethics increasingly was seen as an important area of study. Many universities have added computer ethics to their curricula, a measure that is now required for a computer science department to earn certification by the Computer Accreditation Board. Even elementary and secondary school students were exposed to computer-ethics lessons in the early 2000s. The generation that was raised with powerful computers and the Internet was a prime consideration for those concerned with the ethical use of such technology. According to the *Boston Globe,* more than half of the 47,000 elementary and middle school students surveyed in 2000 reported that they did not consider computer hacking to be a crime.

To get to these youngsters early, before unethical behavior becomes a habit, the U.S. Department of Justice partnered with the Information Technology Association of America, a technology trade group, to form the Cybercitizen Partnership. The partnership involved a nationwide campaign to build awareness of computer ethics by providing resources to schools and parents. It was hoped that by reaching students of all ages with the need to develop ethical codes of computer use, future disasters stemming from the misuse of tomorrow's even more powerful technologies could be averted.

FURTHER READING:

Bush, Victoria D.; Beverly T. Venable; and Alan J. Bush. "Ethics and Marketing on the Internet: Practitioners' Perceptions of Societal, Industry, and Company Concerns." *Journal of Business Ethics.* February, 2000.

Forester, Tom, and Perry Morrison. *Computer Ethics: Cautionary Tales and Ethical Dilemmas in Computing.* Cambridge, MA: MIT Press, 1993.

Goldsborough, Reid. "Computers and Ethics." *Link-up.* January/February, 2000.

Hilton, Timothy. "Information Systems Ethics: A Practitioner Survey." *Journal of Business Ethics.* December, 2000.

Kreie, Jennifer; and Timothy Paul Cronan. "Making Ethical Decisions." *Communications of the Association for Computing Machinery.* December, 2000.

Miller, Seumas; and John Weckert. "Privacy, the Workplace, and the Internet." *Journal of Business Ethics.* December, 2000.

Pierce, Margaret Anne; and John W. Henry. "Judgments About Computer Ethics: Do Individual, Co-worker, and Company Judgments Differ? Do Company Codes Make a Difference." *Journal of Business Ethics.* December, 2000.

Pliagas, Linda. "Learning IT Right from Wrong." *InfoWorld.* October 2, 2000.

Schroeder, Daniel. "Virtues and Voices." *Network World.* December 11, 2000.

Taylor, Paul. "Balancing the Benefits and Dangers." *Financial Times.* July 7, 1999.

Weinstein, Bob. "Right and Wrong on the Net: In New Frontier, Educators See Need to Teach Ethics to the Young." *Boston Globe.* January 14, 2001.

SEE ALSO: Computer Crime; Computer Ethics Institute; Computer Fraud and Abuse Act of 1986; Fraud, Internet; Hacking; Misinformation Online; Privacy: Issues, Policies, Statements

COMPUTER ETHICS INSTITUTE

The Computer Ethics Institute (CEI) is the most prominent organization dedicated toward the promotion of ethical computer use in the United States. Its primary function is to study, publicize, and coordinate the intersection of information technology innovations, business interests, regulations and other public policies, and ethics. The organization was founded in 1985 by the Brookings Institution, IBM, the Washington Consulting Group, and the Washington Theological Consortium, and was originally known as the Coalition for Computer Ethics. In 1992, the coalition changed its name and incorporated as a research, education, and policy study group.

CEI includes among its ranks members of the various computer science and information technology professions, corporate representatives, industry organizations, and academic and public policy groups. Thus, CEI positions itself as a forum in which diverse interests can pool their knowledge and resources to identify and remedy ethical difficulties that arise along with the development and proliferation of advanced computer technology.

One of the organization's hallmarks is its "Ten Commandments for Computer Ethics":

1) Thou shalt not use a computer to harm other people.

2) Thou shalt not interfere with other people's computer work.

3) Thou shalt not snoop around in other people's files.

4) Thou shalt not use a computer to steal.

5) Thou shalt not use a computer to bear false witness.

6) Thou shalt not use or copy software for which you have not paid.

7) Thou shalt not use other people's computer resources without authorization.

8) Thou shalt not appropriate other people's intellectual output.

9) Thou shalt think about the social consequences of the program you write.

10) Thou shalt use a computer in ways that show consideration and respect.

Recognizing that not all legal computing activity is in fact ethical, the CEI drew up the list of ethical commandments in part to elicit conversation about computer ethics, and it has since become a widely cited general code for computer ethics in the United States.

FURTHER READING:

Brookings Institution. "What is the Computer Ethics Institute?" Washington, D.C.: The Brookings Institution, 1998. Available from www.brook.edu/its/cei.

Goldsborough, Reid. "Computers and Ethics." *Link-up*. January/February, 2000.

SEE Computer Ethics
ALSO:

COMPUTER FRAUD AND ABUSE ACT OF 1986

The Computer Fraud and Abuse Act of 1986 is the primary federal legislation aimed at curtailing computer crime. It especially applies to interstate crimes that fall under federal jurisdiction. The act was designed to strengthen, expand, and clarify the intentionally narrow Computer Fraud and Abuse Act of 1984. It safeguards sensitive data harbored by government agencies and related organizations, covering nuclear systems, financial institutions, and medical records.

The act forbids interference with any federal-interest computer system or any system that spans across state lines. Obviously, the act assumed greater importance as the Internet, World Wide Web, and e-commerce grew in prominence. The law prohibits the unauthorized access of any computer system and the obtainment of classified government information. More specifically, it specifies three categories of unclassified information: information belonging to a financial institution, credit card issuer, or consumer reporting agency; information from a department or agency of the United States; and information from any computer deemed "protected," or used exclusively by a financial institution, the U.S. government, or used in interstate or foreign commerce or communication. In addition, the act aims to safeguard computer system integrity with specific prohibitions against computer vandalism. This includes the transmission of a virus or similar code intended to cause damage to a computer or system; unauthorized access that causes damage recklessly; or unauthorized access of a computer from which damage results, but where malicious intent may not be present.

For purposes of prosecution, the law focuses its attention on the actual damage done to computer systems and the specific economic losses stemming from an act of computer fraud or abuse. For instance, while possession of a code for a computer virus cannot be prosecuted under the law, the loading of such a virus onto a network would be criminal under the Computer Fraud and Abuse Act. Violators are prosecuted for knowingly or recklessly damaging such systems, and can be punished with prison sentences as long as 20 years and fines reaching as high as $250,000. Prosecutors under the law, however, often face the difficult challenge of proving that the defendant knowingly inflicted the damage, thereby establishing intent.

FURTHER READING:

Cantos, Lisa, Chambers, Chad, Fine, Lorin, and Randi Singer. "Internet Security Legislation Introduced in the Senate." *Journal of Proprietary Rights*. May, 2000.

Conley, John M., and Robert M. Bryan. "A Survey of Computer Crime Legislation in the United States." *Information & Communications Technology Law*. March, 1999.

Montana, John C. "Viruses and the Law: Why the Law is Ineffective." *Information Management Journal*. October, 2000.

SEE Computer Crime; Fraud, Internet
ALSO:

COMPUTER SECURITY

Computer security encompasses a wide range of technological issues. Computer security professionals work to combat hacking, which includes illegally accessing, manipulating, or destroying private information contained in computer networks. Computer security efforts typically involve the use of a combination of passwords, data encryption applications, virus detectors, and firewalls (hardware or software products that filter all information passed between a private intranet and other intranets or the Internet). Along with preventing hacking, computer security systems also offer detection programs, which allow network managers to determine if a security breach has happened and pinpoint the effects of the breach.

HISTORY OF COMPUTER SECURITY PROBLEMS

The issue of computer security first arose in the 1970s as individuals began to break into telephone systems. As technology advanced, computer systems became targets as well. The Federal Bureau of Investigation (FBI) made one of its first arrests related to computer hacking in the early 1980s. A group of hackers known as the 414s, named after their area code in Milwaukee, Wisconsin, were indicted for attacking 60 different computer systems including the Los Alamos National Laboratory and the Memorial Sloan-Kettering Cancer Center. Computer security breaches like these became increasingly commonplace throughout the 1980s, prompting the passage of the Computer Fraud and Abuse Act. The new legislation allowed more stringent punishments to be levied against individuals caught illegally abusing computer systems. Later in the decade, a 25-year-old hacker named Kevin Mitnick began tapping into the e-mail system used by computer security managers at both Digital Equipment Corp. and MCI Communications Corp. As a result, Mitnick was arrested and sentenced to one year in jail. Although a multitude of other hackers were brought to justice, many continued to operate, including one who successfully pilfered $70 million from the First National Bank of Chicago. Eventually, the Computer Emergency Response Team was established by the U.S. government to research the increasing number of computer security breaches.

Along with growth in hacking activity came the spread of computer viruses. Three of the most well known viruses—Cascade, Friday the 13th, and Stoned—all originated in 1987. When computer companies like IBM Corp. and Symantec Corp. began researching ways to detect and remove viruses from computers, as well as ways to prevent infection in the first place, virus writers began developing more elusive viruses. By 1991, more than 1,000 viruses had been discovered by computer security experts.

Computer security gaps were exposed at many major corporations and governmental bodies—

including AT&T Corp., Griffith Air Force Base, NASA, and the Korean Atomic Research Institute—during the early 1990s. For example, an attack on AT&T's network caused the firm's long-distance service to temporarily shut down. During 1995, computers at the U.S. Department of Defense were attacked roughly 250,000 times. A study conducted by the Computer Security Institute that year determined that one in every five Web sites had been hacked. Also that year, Mitnick was arrested for computer fraud and once again sentenced to serve jail time. His offense that time included stealing software, product plans, and data from Motorola Inc., Sun Microsystems Inc., NEC Corp., and Novell Inc., costing the firms a combined total of nearly $80 million. Later in the 1990s, the Web sites of several federal agencies, including the U.S. Department of Justice, the U.S. Air Force, NASA, and the CIA, were defaced by hackers. In addition, the U.S. Bureau of Labor Statistics received a deluge of bogus requests for information. In 1998, the U.S. Department of Justice created the National Infrastructure Protection Center, charging it with task of safeguarding domestic technology, telecommunications, and transportation systems from hackers.

As the amount of commerce handled via the Internet grew, so did the number of malicious attacks. Hacking in 2000 increased 79 percent over 1999 figures, according to a report released by the FBI's Computer Emergency Response Team (CERT). Even leading Web sites such as Yahoo!, America Online, eBay, and Amazon.com were exposed as vulnerable, costing the firms millions of dollars and undermining the already tenuous confidence online shoppers had in the security levels of these sites. Eventually, one of the key perpetrators in many of these attacks, a 16-year-old Canadian boy operating under the name Mafiaboy, was arrested, and authorities discovered he also had broken into the computer networks at Harvard and Yale Universities. While on parole, Mafiaboy was prohibited from using the Internet or shopping at stores that sold computers; only when supervised by a teacher at school, could he use a computer.

TYPES OF COMPUTER SECURITY PROBLEMS

As the need for high levels of computer security became increasingly apparent to business owners, many began to earmark additional dollars for security technology and for staff to oversee security measures. By then, the most popular form of attack was the denial of service (DOS), which simply overloads a network system until it crashes. For example, a DOS attack on online auction giant eBay in February 2000, which involved sending the site a barrage of fake requests for Web pages, caused eBay's system to crash. Similarly, CERT's Web site was shut down for two days after a myriad of fake information requests overloaded its system. A DOS known as a worm began gaining significant media attention in 2001. In July of that year, the worm entitled Code Red began attacking Microsoft Internet Information Server systems. Code Red infected servers running Windows NT 4, Windows 2000, Windows XP, and IIS 4.0, and it replaced Web site content with the phrase ''Welcome to www.worm.com! Hacked by Chinese!'' The damage caused by the Code Red worm was estimated at $1.2 billion. As Alex Salkever stated in a May 2001 *BusinessWeek Online* article, these types of attacks are commonplace. ''According to a study released last week by scientists at the University of California-San Diego's supercomputing facility, more than 4,000 DOS attacks happen each week. The most sophisticated and serious last for days as dozens, hundreds, even thousands, of hijacked 'zombie' computers pour forth an unceasing barrage of Web-page requests, all unbeknownst to the machines' owners.''

Mail bombs behave in the same manner. However, they target a network's mail server with the goal of shutting down e-mail service by overloading the system. Hackers targeting networks may also attempt to gain access to secure areas containing sensitive data, such as credit card numbers or social security numbers. A security breach of this type can cause serious damage to a business or institution since data files can be not only copied, but also deleted. AOL became victim to this type of attack in the late 1990s when teenagers from Wichita, Kansas, successfully hacked AOL's network and used the credit card numbers they found there to purchase video games.

Other types of attacks on computers include viruses and Trojan horses. A virus is a program designed to affix itself to something within a computer, such as a file or boot sector, and begin reproducing itself. A file virus, like the Friday the 13th virus that originated in the late 1980s, attaches itself to an executable file—one that controls applications—and begins overwriting parts of the file. Roughly two-thirds of all virus attacks involve boot sector viruses, which are harder to detect than file viruses because they make no discernible impact on a system until they actually attack. Boot sector viruses are quite often designed to overwrite an entire hard drive. A virus also might be designed to use all of a computer's resources and prompt it to crash. Two of the most popular transmission methods for viruses are floppy disks and e-mail. For example, the ''I LOVE YOU'' and the ''Love Bug'' viruses that appeared in May of 2000 were circulated via e-mail. The resulting damage to individuals, companies, and institutions was judged to be nearly $10 billion. Like viruses, logic bombs attack computer files and hard drives. Quite often, hackers

use a Trojan horse to gain initial access to computers. Trojan horses are disguised as harmless programs, but once executed might release a virus or even a worm.

COMPUTER SECURITY PROGRAMS

The first major computer security program was developed late in the 1970s, when three Massachusetts Institute of Technology (MIT) graduates created RSA encryption technology. The data-scrambling program eventually was used in leading computer platforms such as Microsoft Windows, and well-known software applications like Quicken and Lotus Notes. Computer security primarily remained a governmental concern throughout the 1970s and 1980s. The rise of corporate networks, along with the growth of e-commerce, prompted more widespread concern about computer security in the 1990s.

Companies using computers began linking them together via networks in the 1980s, and many of those networks were then linked to the Internet in the 1990s. Companies with many geographically dispersed offices were able to use the Internet to link networks. Similarly, those with employees on the road could grant off-site workers access to the intranet. In fact, according to *PC Week* writer Jamie Lewis, one of the Internet's most important benefits to businesses was its ability to ''simplify the often expensive and complex tasks of giving remote users access to corporate networks and of linking remote sites.'' The fact that one of the largest problems hindering that task was security encouraged the development of virtual private network (VPN) technology, which combined ''tunneling, authentication, and encryption technologies to create private sessions over the public Internet.''

Another major boon of the Internet revolution, the rise of e-commerce, also brought with it major security headaches. To make a purchase online, shoppers were normally required to input their credit card numbers. Eventually, even tax returns became something consumers could transmit via the Internet. To protect this sensitive data, companies began seeking sophisticated security systems. Most online merchants began using data encryption programs, such as Secure Sockets Layer (SSL), Secure Electronic Transactions (SET), and Data Encryption Standard (DES) to protect personal information transmitted over the Web.

The most popular method of computer protection among home computer users is anti-virus software. Companies including Symantec Corp. and Network Associates offer anti-virus applications that scan every file on a disk or on a computer's hard drive for infected material, alerting users if corrupted files are found. To keep pace with a the continual development of new viruses, many computer security software firms allow users to periodically download from their Web sites software upgrades which recognize newer viruses. Firewalls, once mainly used for computer networks, also have become popular with home users, particularly those who use cable modems and digital subscriber lines for uninterrupted online connections.

Other software options—mainly used to protect larger computer systems—include Intrusion Detection Systems (IDS), content filtering software, sandboxing software, and behavior analysis software. IDS is considered one of the best protection methods for large networks. With an IDS in place, system administrators can monitor network requests and detect large-scale malicious attacks. Content filtering software is advanced anti-virus software that reads compressed files and allows IT managers to set specific filtering parameters to block threatening e-mail. Sandboxing software protects against malicious codes by creating an isolated space within a computer where suspicious code can run, before it has a chance to interact with the main operating system. Still in its infancy in 2001, behavior analysis software protects computer systems by monitoring entire networks and checking every command of all operations.

Because many malicious hackers eye security systems not as a deterrent but as a mere obstacle to overcome, the numbers of computer security breaches may continue to rise. However, as long as hacking attacks persist, both individuals and businesses will continue to invest in programs and software designed to protect systems from unwanted intruders. In fact, while many computer industry experts believe that avoiding all hacking activity is nearly impossible, Datamonitor predicts that spending related to computer security will grow from $10.6 billion in 2001 to $22.3 billion in 2004.

FURTHER READING:

Blakey, Elizabeth. "Commit a Cybercrime? You're Hired!" E-Commerce Times. July 17, 2000. Available from www.ecommercetimes.com.

Costello, Sam. "'Code Red' Raises Disclosure Flags." InfoWorld. July 20, 2001.

Enos, Lori. "'Mafiaboy' Denies New Hacking Charges." E-Commerce Times. August 4, 2000. Available from www.ecommercetimes.com.

Hesseldahl, Arik. "Profiting From the Worm." Forbes.com. July 31, 2001. Available from www.forbes.com.

Lewis, Jamie. "VPNs: Fulfilling the Internet's Promise." PC Week. June 1, 1998.

Mandeville, David. "Hackers, Crackers, and Trojan Horses." CNN In-Depth Reports. March 29, 1999. Available from www.cnn.com/TECH/specials.

McCartney, Laton. "A Safety Net." Industry Week. April 21, 1997.

Morgan, Lisa. "Intrusion Detection Systems." InternetWeek. January 8, 2001. Available from www.internetweek.com.

Phillips, Ken. "Security Begins at Home." PC Week. August 5, 1996.

Salkever, Alex. "Patches Don't Make a Security Blanket." BusinessWeek Online. August 7, 2001. Available from www.businessweek.com.

———. "Scared of 'Zombies'? You Should Be." BusinessWeek Online. May 30, 2001. Available from www.businessweek.com.

Tinnirello, Paul C. "Internet Security: Are We Scared Yet?" PC Week. November 4, 1996.

Trigaux, Robert. "A History of Hacking." St. Petersburg Times. 2000. Available from www.sptimes.com.

Vamosi, Robert. "Alternative Protection Against Malicious Code." ZDNet., May 21, 2001. Available from www.zdnet.com.

SEE ALSO: Computer Crime; Cryptography, Public and Private Key; Data Encryption Standard (DES); Encryption; Hacking; Secure Electronic Transaction (SET); Viruses; Worms

COMPUWARE CORP.

Compuware Corp. makes and sells software that allows clients to test and debug corporate mainframe systems. It also offers a suite of system management tools, which have become increasingly important to companies conducting business electronically. Compuware's services, which bring in nearly half the firm's revenues, include systems integration and capacity testing. Compuware also operates three digital development centers (DDCs), which offer Web site design and creation and related e-business services. One of the firm's goals is to offer comprehensive e-commerce services and solutions to its clients.

EARLY HISTORY

Along with partners Thomas Thewes and Allen Cutting, Peter Karmanos Jr. founded Compuware Corp. in 1973. Based in Southfield, Michigan, the company offered professional data processing, computer installation help, and a team of programming consultants willing to take on short-term projects. Compuware operated on the premise that its technical services allowed clients to spend more time running their business, rather than dealing with technology concerns. Four years later, the firm unveiled its first software product, Abend-AID. The fault diagnosis tool made the jobs of programmers easier by examining corporate mainframe systems for errors and offering suggestions for alterations. Abend-AID's success prompted the firm to establish a separate software division.

In 1978, Compuware established an office in the northeastern United States. A year later, the company developed an interactive analysis and debugging software program called MBX Xpediter/TSO, which eventually won an International Computer Program (ICP) award. Sales exceeded $1 million in 1983. That year, Compuware shipped File-AID, a data management software line for IBM and IBM-compatible mainframe computers. The firm created its first automated testing tool, MVS PLAYBACK, in 1986. The following year, Abend-AID received an ICP award, and Compuware expanded internationally for the first time by purchasing European distributors. By the end of the decade, sales had grown to roughly $100 million. Software brought in 65 percent of that total, while services accounted for 30 percent.

In an attempt to shore up its position in the interactive analysis and debugging industry, Compuware acquired Centura Software in 1990. The firm created its first personal computer (PC) software product in 1991 by developing a PC version of File-AID. However, most of Compuware's new products continued to focus on improving the performance of large corporate mainframes. Other product releases included database manager DBA-XPERT and Pathvu/2, an interactive analysis and debugging program for the OS/2 platform. The purchase of XA Systems Corp. gave Compuware access to a business-critical application testing and management software program. In 1992, the firm completed its initial public offering.

International growth continued early in the decade with the creation of Tokyo-based Compuware Japan Corp. and Compuware Corporation Do Brasil. Compuware upped the number of its software product lines to nearly 30 with the acquisition of Landmark Systems Corp.'s Eyewitness software. Compuware also bought EcoSystems Software Inc., including its client/server network management software. According to the firm's corporate history, the acquisition was a pivotal one because it allowed Compuware to offer ''the most comprehensive suite of end-to-end applications and e-commerce performance management tools available.''

MOVE INTO E-COMMERCE SOFTWARE AND SERVICES

In the mid-1990s, Compuware acquired Uniface Holding B.V., a client/server software producer based in the Netherlands, and CoroNet, a management systems software maker based in Los Altos, California. Compuware then renamed CoroNet's software EcoSCOPE and merged it into its EcoSystems software line to increase the comprehensiveness of its network management tools, including those related to e-business. The firm continued its plan of growth via

acquisition with the 1996 purchase of London-based automated software testing products and services provider Direct Technology Ltd. and the 1997 purchase of NuMega Technologies Inc., one of the world's largest manufacturers of error detection and debugging software for Windows and Java systems.

Because mainframe computers—what Compuware's software attempted to debug and enhance—were losing ground to Internet-based networks, the firm shifted gears in the late 1990s. It devised a plan to spend a few years preparing firms for the Y2K transition and then retain many of those same firms by offering them e-commerce services and solutions once the transition was complete. In 1997, to position itself as an authority on the impending Y2K transition, Compuware published *Millennium,* a newsletter about the effects the year 2000 could have on the computer industry. Sales exceeded $1 billion for the first time that year. *Millennium* was published online in 1998.

To augment its growing base of e-commerce holdings, Compuware purchased CACI Products Co. in 1999. The firm integrated CACI's application capacity planning tools into its EcoSystems suite, allowing clients to better manage the performance of their e-commerce applications. Although Compuware was ultimately successful in its efforts to become a leading Y2K consultant for companies operating mainframe systems, it soon found that it had overestimated the number of clients who would be looking to move into e-commerce early in 2000, and underestimated the amount of time it would take to train its Y2K specialists to function as e-commerce consultants. As a result, the firm failed to meet earnings forecasts for the first time in several quarters, and stock prices tumbled by roughly 80 percent in 2000.

Despite the difficulties Compuware experienced as it worked toward becoming a full-scale e-commerce service provider, it continued to expand into other ventures. For example, in 1998 Oakwood Healthcare Inc. and Compuware established a joint venture called CareTech Solutions Inc. to offer technical application services to healthcare providers. The firm also continued to add to its software offerings. The acquisition of Programart Corp. marked Compuware's first foray into application performance management (APM) software. In 1999, the company moved into the western and southeastern regions of the United States when it bought Data Processing Resources Corp.

In 2000, Compuware turned two of its acquisitions—Montreal-based Nomex Inc., a provider of Web design and development services, and Kansas City-based Internet consulting services provider BlairLake Inc.—into digital development centers (DDCs). The DDCs were designed to offer full-scale e-commerce services to clients wishing to undertake e-business ventures. A third DDC was soon opened in Farmington Hills, Michigan, at the firm's headquarters complex. The purchase of Optima, an e-business performance measuring software developer, further increased Compuware's e-commerce holdings.

Network Computing magazine named Compuware's Application Expert 2.1 as the recipient of its Editor's Choice Award in 2001. The firm developed the product in response to growing demand by e-business operators, particularly those with increasing traffic, for tools that would allow them to manage their Web sites' performance. Compuware's Application Expert helps clients to pinpoint problems and their causes and also recommends solutions. Also in 2001, the firm unveiled a version of its Abend-AID program designed specifically for e-business applications and upgraded its EcoPredictor to include the ability to use simulation to predict potential network bottlenecks. Research has indicated that online customers who wait more than eight seconds for a page to begin loading will likely go to another site. Compuware's products, which work to address these crucial performance issues for e-businesses, seem to bode well for the firm's future as an e-commerce software developer and service provider.

FURTHER READING:

"Compuware Acquires E-Commerce Services Company." *PR Newswire.* May 10, 2000.

"Compuware Acquires Web Development Services Company." *PR Newswire.* February 15, 2000.

Compuware Corp. "Corporate History." Farmington Hills, MI: Compuware Corp. Available from www.compuware.com.

"Compuware Corp." In *Notable Corporate Chronologies.* Farmington Hills, MI: Gale Group, 1999.

"Compuware Extends Fault Management to E-Business Applications." *PR Newswire.* January 5, 2001.

"Compuware Lauded for E-Business Application." *Graphic Arts Monthly.* January, 2000.

Kahn, Jeremy. "Growth Elixirs May Be Risky: There Are Lots of Ways to Make a Business Sprout. Some of Them Can Be Positively Suicidal. Just Look at What Happened to Four of the Fastest-Growing Companies on Last Year's List." *Fortune.* September 4, 2000.

Macvittie, Lori. "Web Performance Monitoring is Critical to E-Business—Performance Monitoring Tools Will Help You Get to the Bottom of Those Nagging Problems." *InformationWeek.* November 13, 2000.

Mcconnell, John. "Better Monitoring Tools Good for E-Biz." *InternetWeek.* April 3, 2000.

Zeichick, Alan. "Network Crystal Ball—EcoPredictor Forecasts Effects of WAN Traffic Growth." *InternetWeek.* March 19, 2001.

SEE ALSO: Business-to-Business (B2B) E-Commerce; E-Commerce Solutions; Software

CONNECTIVITY, INTERNET

The term "Internet connectivity" refers to the way people are hooked up to the Internet, and may include dial-up telephone lines, always-on broadband connections, and wireless devices. Among these, wireless access to the Internet is the newest and, as of the early 2000s, had only reached a small group of users. Broadband connections, including DSL (digital subscriber line), ADSL (asymmetrical DSL), and cable modems, were becoming more widespread, but still represented a small percentage of Internet users. A study by Nielsen/NetRatings covering the year 2000 found that more than 85 percent of home-based users connected to the Internet with ordinary telephone modems ranging from 28.8 Kbps (thousands of bits per second) to 56 Kbps. Only 6.4 percent had high-speed Internet access, while 8.3 percent were still using 14.4 Kbps telephone modems.

Since the early days of the Internet, connectivity for the typical user has improved markedly by offering greater speeds for data transmission and wider bandwidth to accommodate special services such as audio and video. In the consumer market, the first improvements were made in dial-up telephone connections, with modems increasing in speed from 14.4 Kbps to 56 Kbps. With the growth in popularity of the World Wide Web and its ever expanding stock of multimedia content, the need for more bandwidth and higher transmission speeds created new demand in households and small businesses for broadband alternatives, which until that time were common only in large corporations, universities, and government agencies.

BROADBAND CONNECTIVITY

Although broadband technology offered high-speed Internet access, consumers were initially slow to adopt it. While the greater bandwidth of a broadband connection allowed for more data to be transmitted at higher speeds than a conventional telephone line, most consumers were unwilling to pay $40 or more a month for broadband services that would enable them to view streaming media better or download Web pages faster. A mid-2001 report from Strategy Analytics predicted that by the end of 2001, 14.1 percent of all North American households would have a high-speed Internet connection, up from the 6 to 8 percent other studies reported for the end of 2000.

By 2005, Strategy Analytics predicted the broadband user base would swell to 53 percent of North American households.

Broadband includes cable modem and DSL connections as well as alternative broadband technologies. Unlike telephone line connections to the Internet, which typically involve dialing up, broadband connections are always on. DSL uses ordinary copper telephone lines to deliver a high-bandwidth connection to the Internet, with typical data transmission speeds ranging from 512 Kbps to 1.544 Mbps (millions of bits per second). However, DSL service requires a certain proximity to the DSL provider's central office, and DSL providers must set up several such offices to serve a large area. Cable modems are the most popular broadband connection among consumers. To provide high-speed Internet access over cable lines, cable system operators have had to upgrade their systems and replace old one-way lines with lines that can handle two-way traffic. Alternative broadband technologies, mostly used by businesses, include leased lines, frame relay, fiber optics, asynchronous transfer mode (ATM), T1 and T3 lines, and ISDN (integrated services digital network). High-speed Internet access is also available through satellite services, although the number of subscribers remains small in comparison to cable modem and DSL subscribers.

WIRELESS CONNECTIVITY

Wireless connectivity to the Internet was still in its infancy in the early 2000s, awaiting the development of new protocols, specifications, and next-generation technologies. While most personal computers could access virtually any Web site, wireless devices could not because wireless systems used a different method of encoding Web content. When several major online brokerage firms began offering wireless trading in 2000, the biggest barrier was that the brokers were not compatible with all types of devices and service providers. The preferred method of wireless access to online brokerages appeared to be through Web-enabled cell phones. In some cases brokers were able to negotiate with national cell phone providers such as Verizon Wireless, AT&T, or Sprint PCS to obtain a position on their Web-phone menus. Otherwise, customers would have to key in their broker's Web address on the phone's small keypad.

Mobile phones, pagers, and personal digital assistants (PDAs) all offer limited wireless access to the Internet. But most of these do not offer the complete set of features users have on their PCs. Typically, wireless devices are used to retrieve e-mail and obtain a range of news, sports, stocks, weather, and local information. Cell phones enabled for Wireless Application Protocol (WAP), for instance, are used to retrieve e-mail as well as information from selected Web sites. For the most part, however, mainstream devices' small screens make it difficult, if not impossible, to surf the Internet and fill out the forms necessary to shop online. Device manufacturers have responded with innovations designed to make the wireless Internet experience easier. For example, Palm, maker of popular PDAs and related devices, introduced the M105 PDA, which included pre-installed Internet connectivity software that enabled users to check e-mail and surf the wireless Web through a compatible mobile phone.

Wireless connectivity to the Internet represented a small fraction of home-based Internet users in the United States and other countries at the end of 2000. According to a study by the Nomura Research Institute and reported by *eMarketer,* 2 percent of users who accessed the Internet from home in the United States had a wireless connection, compared to 92.1 percent having a landline connection. According to another study by Connecticut-based research firm Robert Francis Group, data accounted for less than 2 percent of mobile wireless traffic in early 2001. With wireless access to the Internet still in the early adopter stage, projections of future growth varied widely. A February 2001 eWireless Report from *eMarketer* found that estimates of wireless Internet users by 2004 ranged from 17 million to 161 million. One reason for such discrepancies was that there was not a large enough base of users to project from.

Wireless high-speed Internet access in public places began expanding in 2001. Public wireless access, designed for locations such as airport terminals, sports arenas, shopping malls, coffee shops, and convention floors, requires a base station that include a small transceiver and a broadband connection. An article in the *New York Times* predicted that there would be wireless access points installed in 5,000 Starbucks stores sometime in 2002.

These access points are able to transmit and receive data wirelessly using a technology standard called 802.11 for Windows and AirPort for Apple computers. Computers with an AirPort or 802.11 card installed have a ready, high-speed wireless Internet connection without any additional plug-ins. Users need to be within a few hundred feet or so of an access point to tap into a wireless network. Users can then send e-mail or visit Web sites. Most access points are expected to be commercial in nature, charging a monthly or one-time fee.

Barriers to roaming wireless access from a laptop computer have included the lack of a single standard and competition among providers. Competing standards meant that users might need to have two or three wireless standards to stay connected while traveling.

Until roaming agreements were in place among competing providers, users might find that one provider's service was available in some airports but not in others.

CONNECTING OVER ELECTRICAL POWER LINES

Electrical power lines offer the possibility of high-speed Internet access. With such access, households and buildings with multiple users would be able to access the Internet through power sockets. In the first quarter of 2001, Germany's biggest power utility, RWE, announced it would offer PowerNet—high-speed Internet access over electrical power lines—to some 20,000 customers by the end of the year in association with Swiss partner Ascom. The announcement came just after German electronics and engineering company Siemens said it would withdraw from the development of power line access.

With transmission speeds of up to two megabits per second, an electrical power line connection can process e-mail at rates 30 times faster than an ISDN connection. MP3 music files can be downloaded in less than 20 seconds over a power line connection. The increased bandwidth of a power line connection enables it to handle a higher volume of Internet traffic as well as more complex services, such as data, video, and audio, and even 3-D shopping.

Power line access faces several technological and regulatory hurdles before it becomes a reality. German officials had not yet given regulatory approval to Internet access over power lines. Technological hurdles are complicated by electrical transformers and other equipment. In developing countries, where electricity is more widespread than telephone connections, Internet access over electrical power lines could result in much greater Internet usage. In developed nations, Internet access over electrical power lines could provide a new revenue stream to electrical utility companies.

However, as of mid-2001 both Nortel and Siemens had abandoned the electrical power line market. One factor affecting their decision may have been that power lines are considered a ''noisy'' medium with fewer capabilities than copper loops, wireless, and cable systems. Siemens, for its part, planned on focusing its efforts on traditional broadband access over telephone lines.

INTERNET2

The future of Internet connectivity may be revealed in Internet2, an experimental high-speed network launched in the mid-1990s. The speed with which data, audio, and video can be transmitted over Internet2 boggles the imagination. A comparison of how long it would take to download a DVD version of a typical 2-hour movie showed that it would take approximately 171 hours over a 56K modem, 74 hours over an ISDN line, 25 hours with a DSL or cable modem connection, 6.4 hours with a T1 line, and only 30 seconds over Internet2.

Internet2 has been in development since 1996 and is supported by a nonprofit consortium of 185 universities and research institutions. By 2001 the initial phase of the ultra-fast, high-bandwidth network was in place. Although still only in the demonstration phase, Internet2 transmission speeds are expressed in gigabits, or billions of bits per second (Gbps). The backbone of the system was provided by Qwest Communications, which offered access to 10,000 miles of its advanced fiber-optic network. Nortel Networks and Cisco Systems provided computer and networking equipment, and each of the consortium members committed to installing fiber-optic hookups to the system.

With the backbone in place, the Internet2 consortium planned next to test its reliability, develop middleware to provide interoperability between the network and specific applications, and to expand access to thousands of educational institutions and to other parts of the world, including Central and South America and the Caribbean. One of the applications already demonstrated on Internet2 was interactive medicine, in which a physician in Washington, D.C., directed surgery taking place in Columbus, Ohio. In another application, symphony musicians in Atlanta and Miami were able to practice together in real time over Internet2. Within five years, consortium leaders predicted that Internet2 would impact Internet access from the home.

FURTHER READING:

Carter, Adrienne. ''Wireless Trading, Version 1.0.'' *Money,* October 1, 2000.

Centeno, Cerelle. ''High-Speed Homes in North America.'' *eMarketer,* June 5, 2001. Available from www.emarketer.com.

———. ''No-Frills Broadband Junkies in North America.'' *eMarketer,* June 13, 2001. Available from www.emarketer.com.

———. ''Picking up the Connection Pace.'' *eMarketer,* February 13, 2001. Available from www.emarketer.com.

———. ''Worldwide Internet Access.'' *eMarketer,* January 2, 2001. Available from www.emarketer.com.

Fleishman, Glenn. ''The Web, Without Wires, Wherever.'' *New York Times,* February 22, 2001.

Lyman, Jay. ''Shocking Concept: Internet over Electrical Lines.'' *E-Commerce Times,* March 27, 2001. Available from www.ecommercetimes.com.

''New eMarketer Report Reveals Discrepant Numbers among Wireless Researchers.'' *eMarketer,* February 28, 2001. Available from www.emarketer.com.

Pepe, Michele. "Forging the Wireless Pipeline." *Computer Reseller News,* March 5, 2001.

Pogue, David. "The Promise of Wireless." *The New York Times,* February 15, 2001.

Roberts-Witt, Sarah L. "Wireless Net Access: Over the Horizon, a Market Beckons." *Internet World,* February 21, 2001. Available from www.internetworld.com.

Wendland, Mike. "Speedy Internet2 Makes Wildest Dreams Tame." *Detroit Free Press,* May 10, 2001.

SEE ALSO: Bandwidth; Bandwidth Management; Broadband Technology; Personal Digital Assistant (PDA)

CONTENT PROVIDER

Content providers are generally perceived to be Web sites that supply different types of online information—including news, entertainment, traffic reports, and job listings—that is regularly updated. The first content providers were entities such as America Online (AOL), which provided content to users for a subscription fee. More recently, however, many providers offer some or all of their information services free of charge. Unlike e-commerce sites, whose user traffic ideally generates sales, content providers tend to derive revenue from sources such as banner ads and other forms of advertising and syndication. Some content providers purchase and aggregate industry-specific information from sources such as Lexis-Nexis. Many news content providers, such as Dow Jones, Hoover's, and Lexis-Nexis, also furnish archival content for users.

Among the most important controversies to surface in conjunction with the online distribution of copyrighted content (particularly e-books, music, and streaming media) is "digital rights management" (DRM), which pits the "fair use" of content (for example, for educational purposes) against the financial rights of the content's creators and purveyors. The federal Digital Millennium Copyright Act (DMCA) of 1998, which critics argue goes too far in protecting content providers, prohibits the "manufacturing, importing or offering to the public, providing or otherwise trafficking" in unlawful circumvention devices. Special software to prevent unauthorized duplication encrypts the content so that users can view or listen to it free of charge, but only duplicate or download it for a fee. Other means to record content usage also were under development in the early 2000s.

The most common business model for online content providers, the click-through model, faces an uncertain future. While the bulk of content providers derived a substantial proportion of their revenues from banner advertisements, the utility of those ads was increasingly questioned in the early 2000s, as click-through rates plummeted and firms realized the ads were too often ignored. Future growth areas for content providers include mobile phone operations, where providers can supply users with relevant information connected to location-based services such as malls, restaurants, and entertainment venues. Many content providers expect that customers will readily adjust to paying per-usage fees for such content, since they already do so for cellular phone service. Other content providers, such as those that show movies on their own Web sites, are looking beyond the Internet to furnish content to offline media venues such as cable TV networks.

FURTHER READING:

Agnew, Marion. "Syndicators Spin Out More News for Web Sites: Online Content Providers Offer Information from a Variety of Sources." *InformationWeek.* February 26, 2001.

Albiniak, Paige. "Do Not Pass Go." *Broadcasting & Cable.* November 6, 2000.

Cholewka, Kathleen. "Opting into the Wireless Web." *Sales and Marketing Management.* January, 2001.

"Content Provider." NetLingo: The Internet Language Dictionary, 2000. Available from www.netlingo.com.

Freeman, Laurie. "Web Syndication Catching On." *Advertisement Age.* January 22, 2001.

SEE ALSO: Affiliate Model; Aggregators

CONVERGENCE

In the field of e-commerce and information technology, convergence typically refers to media convergence, and especially to the combination of television, telecommunications, and the personal computer into a single box that would deliver high-speed Internet access, traditional television programming, and interactive services. However, as of mid-2001, interactive television (iTV) was more vision than reality. Major providers included WebTV, owned by Microsoft since 1997 and re-branded in April 2001 as MSNTV; and AOLTV, which launched in October 2000 following tests in select markets. WebTV quickly gained some 1.1 million subscribers, and then found it difficult to acquire more customers. AOLTV had to convince AOL subscribers it was worth an additional $14.95 a month, while non-subscribers had to pay $24.95 a month for access to AOLTV. Short of iTV, some TV shows—including *Who Wants to Be a Millionaire?*—offered some measure of interactivity by directing viewers to their Web sites.

Proponents of convergence expected it to develop between 2000 and 2005. Convergence at a technological level will enable voice, video, and data to be transmitted to consumers through a single pipeline. The pipeline may be wired, such as cable or DSL, or it may be wireless. Instead of accessing the Internet from a single box, however, consumers will be able to access high-speed networks from a variety of access points, including PCs, TVs, mobile phones, mobile devices, public kiosks, and home appliances. Technological convergence also is expected to result in further convergence at the business level. The merger of AOL and Time Warner to form AOL Time Warner was expected to help accelerate the convergence of traditional and Internet media. Other telecommunications, cable, Internet, and traditional media companies also would join forces, either through mergers or strategic alliances, to form fewer and larger organizations.

CONSUMERS SLOW TO ACCEPT MEDIA CONVERGENCE

Convergence has been an industry-driven rather than a consumer-driven phenomenon. Companies such as Microsoft and AOL Time Warner have invested heavily in developing iTV platforms. Consumers, on the other hand, have been less than enthusiastic. That reflects the fact that convergence is not simply a technological issue; it also is a matter of culture, lifestyle, and economics.

Televisions and personal computers represent different types of experiences in most consumers' lives. TV is visual with a strong sound component and emphasizes entertainment and news. Watching TV is a passive rather than an interactive experience, except for changing channels. TVs are easy to operate and require virtually no special training or education. Personal computers, on the other hand, tend to be more text-oriented and are highly interactive. They can be difficult to use and require some form of education or special training. They are used with more of a purpose in mind, and their content is geared more toward business and educational uses than entertainment.

Despite these differences, consumers appear to be integrating the personal computer into their home life. A study by the Gartner Group found that more than 44 million people used a personal computer and a television in the same room in 2000, compared to only 26 million in 1999. The study predicted that the number would grow to more than 50 million people by the end of 2001.

OBSTACLES TO CONVERGENCE

While cultural, lifestyle, and economic considerations may have slowed consumer acceptance, convergence had some technological obstacles to overcome before iTV became more widespread. Interactive applications can be offered by any type of TV operator, such as cable, satellite, or terrestrial broadcast. However, iTV also requires a return path, which may be cable, DSL, dial-up, or wireless. With so many different delivery networks, interactive platforms are expected to remain fragmented for many years to come. By the early 2000s, a single standard had yet to be developed.

Another obstacle involved the high cost of cable TV, both in term of the large investment required by providers and the subscription cost to consumers. Since iTV requires broadband technology to deliver interactive services, its penetration in the consumer market is dependent on broadband availability and acceptance. With limited broadband deployment, nearly half of all U.S. television households in late 2000 were without access to the high-speed service required for many iTV applications. As a result, the convergence represented by iTV was only available in select markets.

CONVERGENCE IN OTHER AREAS

Convergence is also taking place in other areas of commerce and technology. An auto industry conference called ''Convergence 2000'' promoted the convergence of technology and automobiles, including in-car navigation systems, entertainment systems, and always-on Internet connections. Convergence has become more of a reality in the financial services market, as banking, investing, and insurance were consolidated under one roof at some financial institutions.

FURTHER READING:

Berger, Robin. ''TV and Web Can Already Get Together.'' *Electronic Media.* January 22, 2001.

''The Big iTV Five.'' *Variety.* January 15, 2001.

Cheng, Kipp. ''AOL-Time Warner Deal Hastens Convergence.'' *Mediaweek.* January 17, 2000.

''Convergence.'' *Whatis?.com* July 25, 2001. Available from whatis.techtarget.com.

Gilman, Brian. ''I Want My ITV!'' *eMarketer.* June 5, 2000. Available from www.emarketer.com.

———. ''Is ITV Ready for Prime Time?'' *eMarketer.* October 16, 2000. Available from www.emarketer.com.

Greenberg, Daniel. ''AOLTV: Tuning in to Channel Zero.'' *The Washington Post.* December 8, 2000.

Jenkins, Henry. ''Convergence? I Diverge.'' *Technology Review.* June, 2001.

Macklin, Ben. ''The Broadband-iTV Blend.'' *eMarketer.* April 3, 2001. Available from www.emarketer.com.

SEE   Broadband Technology; Connectivity, Internet; Home
ALSO: Networking

CO-OPETITION

Co-opetition, a term combining the words ''co-operation'' and ''competition,'' refers to the arrangement between competing firms to cooperate on specific projects or in certain areas of business for mutual benefit, even while remaining competitors in general. The players enter into the agreement with the expectation that the isolated cooperation will lead to greater overall returns for each firm. The term was first coined in the early 1990s by Raymond J. Noorda, the founder of Novell Corp., and gradually achieved prominence, particularly in the dot-com economy.

A number of factors contributed to the rise of co-opetition in the late 1990s and early 2000s, including the accelerating breakthroughs in information and communication technologies and the development of internal and external networks by most major companies. The layers of interconnectedness, channel conflict, and novelty involved in e-commerce pushed the term co-opetition to the forefront of business strategy. For example, bitter rivals Microsoft Corp. and IBM entered into an arrangement whereby Microsoft agreed to supply its Windows NT operating systems to IBM for use in the latter's personal computers and workstations. Each firm recognized that greater overall margins would result from the temporary alliance. Although such arrangements have existed for ages, they have acquired new meaning and exceptional prominence in the virtual e-marketplace.

When the rush of information technology met e-commerce, co-opetition grew dramatically. This often occurred in complex webs of interconnecting relationships between several firms that operated in similar areas, and competed and cooperated with each other simultaneously. On the Internet, companies entering the new e-commerce arena from different angles and with different strategies often saw that creating strategic alliances to forge new online markets, and sharing sales channels and information in certain e-market areas, was a mutually beneficial strategy. Conversely, in the bricks-and-mortar world, they would necessarily remain rivals. As e-commerce upstarts emerged to challenge and, in some cases, out-compete established brick-and-mortar firms in their fields, as Amazon.com did to established book retailers, the entire nature of marketing and logistics began to rapidly change. New competitive strategies were needed to transform companies into viable e-merchants. Co-opetition was seen as one such strategy.

Co-opetition creates something of a paradox because it brings together both common and conflicting interests under one arrangement. The separation of these two kinds of interests is crucial if the goals of the co-opetitive strategy are to be reached. A chief concern of partners in a co-opetitive arrangement, for instance, is secrecy. Usually, such relationships call for a degree of information exchange and mutual access to potentially sensitive data. In these cases, the participating companies must walk a fine line to negotiate between their competing objectives. On one hand, a degree of openness and mutual trust is necessary if the arrangement is to bear the desired fruit. On the other hand, neither company wishes to give more to the other firm than the arrangement calls for, and neither wants to end the deal in a relatively weakened competitive position. Thus, the management of information flow between firms engaging in co-opetition is among the most difficult tasks companies face, and requires shrewd but diplomatic execution. The negotiation of these possible sources of conflicts has given rise to game-theoretical models of resolution.

Despite these difficulties, co-opetition was on the rise in the early 2000s. The reduction of transaction costs and other savings, not to mention the increasing expectation among customers of an online storefront, created an atmosphere where the creation of an online marketplace outweighed the potential losses of doing business with one's competitors. Though co-opetition clearly is a complex undertaking, the advantages it offers frequently are too enticing to ignore.

FURTHER READING:

Bengtsson, Maria, and Soren Kock. '''Coopetition' in Business Networks—to Cooperate and Compete Simultaneously.'' *Industrial Marketing Management.* September, 2000.

James, Keith. ''Sometimes, it Pays to Sleep with the Enemy.'' *Business Times* (Singapore). March 16, 1999.

Loebecke, Claudia, Van Fenema, Paul C., and Philip Powell. ''Co-opetition and Knowledge Transfer.'' *Database for Advances in Information Systems.* Spring 1999.

Manring, Audrey Y. ''Net Markets Gather B-to-B Momentum.'' *Informationweek.* November 20, 2000.

SEE   Competition; Noorda, Raymond J.
ALSO:

COVISINT

Launched in November of 2000, Covisint is an online marketplace for the worldwide automotive industry. Originally conceptualized in late 1999 by industry leaders Ford Motor Co., General Motors, and

DaimlerChrysler, the business-to-business (B2B) site has yet to live up to expectations that it will achieve significant savings by streamlining the purchasing and production processes of automobile making. In its first five months of operations Covisint had secured only 40 of the 30,000 manufacturers that supply parts to the world's largest automakers. With roughly 250 online catalogs, the site mainly functioned as a procurement and auction vehicle in early 2001. Design professionals also were able to use the site as a platform for collaborating with other automotive engineers.

The idea for Covisint grew out of a rivalry between Ford's Auto-Xchange and GM's Trade xchange, both launched in November of 1999. Realizing that a combined B2B exchange would likely be much more lucrative, Ford and GM executives began holding private meetings in early 2000 to discuss such an undertaking. A universal online automotive marketplace could improve the process of new parts development by facilitating better communication between automakers and suppliers. It also had the potential to speed vehicle development times and give dealers better control over inventory by allowing them to stock what customers want and maintain fewer numbers of cars on their lots. Intrigued by what appeared to be the potential to create one of the world's largest B2B exchanges, and by the possibility of a blockbuster dot-com initial public offering (IPO), Ford and GM approached DaimlerChrysler, who signed on as a third partner just weeks later. They announced their plan to create a joint site on February 25, 2000. France's Renault S.A. and Japan's Nissan agreed to join the partnership in April of that year.

It soon became clear that the creation of such an Internet portal would not be easy. For starters, Covisint's head executives, used to competing with one another, found it difficult to reach agreements on anything. Along with managerial clashes, the firm's technology experts—Commerce One and Oracle—also were intense rivals. To make matters worse, in March of 2000 the Federal Trade Commission (FTC), concerned about the possible anti-competitive repercussions the exchange could have on the supply industry, launched a six-month investigation of the venture. Although the FTC eventually granted its approval to Covisint, it did so after the dot-com stock meltdown, undermining Covisint's hope of cashing in on an IPO.

Despite these setbacks, as well as being unable to find a CEO to run the exchange, plans for Covisint continued to move forward. According to *Forbes* writer Meredith Robyn, ''The automakers persevere because the potential gains are riveting. A car has 5,000 parts on average, and the auto industry has one of the world's most complex and antediluvian supply chains. A car giant processes one million invoices a

year, at \$150 a piece. Covisint cuts that to \$15 a piece.''

Covisint's 350 employees are divided into three functional groups. The customer development division, managed by former Ford Motor purchasing executive Alice Miles, handles sales and marketing. The business development division, led by former General Motors executive Enrico Digirolamo, oversees finance, purchasing, human resources, and external relationships with other firms. The product development division, headed up by Peter Weiss, the former B2B exchange activities director of Daimler-Chrysler, is in charge of developing the actual technology that drives the site. To mediate technology disagreements between Commerce One and Oracle, Covisint attempted contract consultants, but many found the challenge too daunting to accept. One that did take on the task, Chicago-based Diamond Cluster International, eventually resigned.

Despite their differences, Commerce One and Oracle did begin working on uploading parts catalog information to the site. Commerce One also added traditional auction functionality, which allows suppliers to put their wares up for sale and get the best possible prices for them, as well as reverse auction functionality which lets automotive makers solicit competitive bids for products and services they need to purchase. Early in 2001, auction and catalog sales accounted for 90 percent of Covisint's revenues, mainly because those were the only functions offered by the site. In March, Supply Solution Inc. agreed to allow Covisint to be the sole provider of its i-Supply Service, which grants part-makers real-time access to information regarding the inventory of the automotive factories it supplies. Covisint hoped the i-Supply acquisition would boost its users as roughly 750 suppliers already used the technology.

Analysts remain split over the likelihood that Covisint will attain its goal of becoming the world's largest B2B exchange and help to shave hundreds of dollars off the production costs of each automobile. Working in the new venture's favor are the deep pockets of its founding companies. Although Covisint still lacked a CEO as of spring 2001, unlike most upstart Internet businesses, it had easy access to enough capital to create a highly sophisticated site regardless of traffic levels.

FURTHER READING:

''Company Information.'' Southfield, MI: Covisint LLC, 2001. Available from www.covisint.com/info/about.

Frook, John E. ''Update—Covisint One Year Later: Who's in the Driver's Seat? After a Quick Start, Big 3 Auto Parts Hub Sputters Along.'' *B to B*. March 19, 2001.

Kisiel, Ralph. ''Software Could Help Covisint into Fast Lane.'' *Automotive News*. March 26, 2001.

Konicki, Steve. "Steering Around the Wreckage." *Information-Week.* April 9, 2001.

Lauer, Stephane. "Speeding Custom-Tailored Cars Down the Info Highway." *BusinessWeek Online.* October 10, 2000. Available from www.businessweek.com/technology.

Meredith, Robyn. "Harder than the Hype." *Forbes.* April 16, 2001.

Milligan, Brian. "What Is Covisint?" *Purchasing.* March 8, 2001.

Moozakis, Chuck. "Auto Trading Exchange Still Stuck in Low Gear." *InternetWeek.* April 2, 2001.

Welch, David. "E-Marketplace: Covisint." *BusinessWeek Online.* June 5, 2000. Available from www.businessweek.com.

SEE ALSO: Business-to-Business (B2B) E-commerce; Commerce One; Initial Public Offering (IPO); Supply Chain Management; Vortals

CRYPTOGRAPHY, PUBLIC AND PRIVATE KEY

Cryptography—called "crypto" by its practitioners—is the study of codes and ciphers and their use to protect information. Cryptography has existed, in one form or another, since the ancient Greeks began toying with methods for encoding with mathematics. In the modern period, cryptography was utilized mainly in wartime to protect sensitive military information, and in the high-stakes and secretive world of diplomacy and spying.

For years, computer-based cryptography was almost exclusively used by the United States National Security Agency (NSA) for coding and decoding sensitive information and messages during the Cold War. For many years after private-sector computer scientists began working on cryptography, the government fought such efforts out of concern for national security. Cryptographers, however, were wary of government monopolization of the technology, which raised fears of a "big brother" capable of snooping into the private lives and communications of its citizens.

This door was opened in 1975 by Massachusetts Institute of Technology graduate Whitfield Diffie and Stanford University professor Martin Hellman. The two were searching for a way to share encrypted messages between two people who didn't know each other, and thus couldn't have devised their own scrambling formula beforehand. The Diffie-Hellman algorithm that resulted was the birth of contemporary public-key cryptography, the dominant cryptographic infrastructure used on the Internet.

Cryptography assumed a whole new significance with the development of e-commerce in the mid-1990s. Perhaps the biggest roadblocks to e-commerce were consumer fears over privacy and the security of their financial and personal information. Because of this, cryptography was of central importance to the growth of the Internet economy.

Encryption is the scrambling of text-based messages into unrecognizable code via a complex mathematical algorithm. Only those with the correct "key" are able to encrypt or decrypt such a message in a given cryptographic system. The key is a set of specific parameters, based on the algorithmic encryption formula, that act to lock and unlock the coded information. The formula typically consists of a long string of bits, sometimes more than 200 digits long. The more digits involved and the more complicated the algorithmic equation used to generate the code, the more difficult the hacker's job in breaking it.

The two basic infrastructures used in cryptographic systems are public-key and private-key. While early computer systems used private-key cryptography almost exclusively, by the late 1990s and early 2000s the tide was shifting in favor of public-key cryptography. The dominant encryption standards were testament to the sea of change. The 25-year-old Data Encryption Standard (DES), a private-key algorithm developed by the NSA, was being phased out due to its lack of flexibility and a level of security that could no longer withstand sophisticated modern attacks, not to mention the limited use of private-key systems in e-commerce. In its place, the public-key Advanced Encryption Standard (AES) was preparing for international launch in the early 2000s.

PRIVATE-KEY CRYPTOGRAPHY

Private-key, or symmetric, encryption systems employ a single common key, possessed by those on both sides of the transaction, to both lock and unlock a message. Private keys are generally smaller, meaning they contain less bits of information, and as a result compute more quickly than do public keys. However, that also means they are more vulnerable to attack than are public keys.

Because private-key cryptography involves a series of one-to-one transactions, the concern over secrecy is paramount. For example, if a firm maintained a private-key infrastructure with several thousand clients, the company would need to ensure the secrecy of several thousand separate keys, and the opportunity for compromised security escalates. Thus private-key encryption can pose difficulties, especially over large networks of individuals, simply because key management can become a headache that costs a good deal of time and effort to manage.

PUBLIC-KEY CRYPTOGRAPHY

Public-key, or asymmetric, cryptography involves two separate keys: both a private key maintained by a single entity and a public key available to any user over a network. A central authority, such as an online bank, broadcasts its public key, enabling any client to send encrypted messages to that destination. Only that original authority, however, can decrypt the communications using its private key, thereby securing the information from hackers and other unauthorized onlookers. Because the usage of these keys is spread over such a wide network of people, they typically contain a greater number of information bits to make the code more difficult to crack.

Because of its simple availability to large numbers of people, public-key encryption was considered the favored infrastructure for e-commerce in the early 2000s. Digital signature technology, for instance, relies on the public-key infrastructure. The 1999 passage of the Electronic Signatures in Global & National Commerce Act opened the floodgates for public-key cryptography as never before by creating legal parity between handwritten signatures and digital signatures. In turn, this was a major boon to a whole range of new and established forms of e-commerce, particularly in the financial services industries. The leading public-key encryption scheme used in e-commerce was Secure Sockets Layer (SSL), developed by Netscape but long supported by both Netscape and Microsoft browsers.

The primary vehicle by which transactions and messages are encrypted using public-key cryptography is the digital certificate. Digital certificates are issued by a central authority and contain the user's name and e-mail address, an expiration date, and the authority's name. Digital certificates are stored on the user's computer or, increasingly, on a smart card or a central server accessible over the Internet.

The complexity of the public-key infrastructure stems from the management of a hierarchy of different certificate authorities and central servers, along with the level of individual customization involved in using a digital certificate on a personal computer or smart card. But once a public-key infrastructure is in place and a sound key management system has been implemented, the rewards can be astounding, particularly for those e-commerce firms engaged in the transfer of massive amounts of sensitive information, as in online banking. In business-to-business operations, public-key cryptography also can lead to efficiency gains. With the security afforded by digital certificates, companies can allow each other mutual access to internal company network infrastructures, greatly streamlining the transaction processes between business partners.

THE CRYPTOGRAPHIC OUTLOOK

The Gartner Group estimated that by 2003 up to 80 percent of large businesses would test at least one public-key infrastructure, according to *Information-Week*. Meanwhile, the search for ever-more impenetrable encryption systems was certain to intensify. The U.S. Department of Energy's Los Alamos National Laboratory was home to a program dedicated to the development of quantum cryptography, which incorporates the laws of quantum physics into traditional cryptographic methods to design the most powerful encryption systems yet, overcoming the flaws and cracks in public-key encryption systems. Quantum cryptographic codes are built on a series of photons, each with their own individual and varying properties that render them analogous to computer language's ones and zeroes. Essentially, the development of such technologies and the increasing sophistication of hackers and code-breaking systems has set off a virtual arms race between those using cryptography to enhance security and those using cryptography to compromise security.

FURTHER READING:

Arden, Michelle, and Bradley Palmer. ''Enabling Secure Applications With a Public-Key Infrastructure.'' *Security*. May, 1999.

Crowe, David. ''Cutting-Edge Security.'' *Wireless Review*. January 1, 2001.

Fratto, Mike. ''Top 10 Technologies: Cryptography—Lock and Key for a Safer Net.'' *Network Computing*. October 16, 2000.

Harrison, Ann. ''Basically Uncrackable.'' *Computerworld*. January 19, 2000.

Kerstetter, Jim. ''Web Encrytpers.'' *Business Week*. February 19, 2001.

Levitt, Jason. ''In Keys We Trust.'' *InformationWeek*. June 14, 1999.

Levy, Stephen. ''Crypto.'' *Newsweek*. January 15, 2001.

Rothman, Mike. ''Public-Key Encryption for Dummies.'' *Network World*. May 17, 1999.

Schultz, Kieth. ''Network Infrastructure: SSL In the Driver's Seat.'' *Internetweek*. November 13, 2001.

SEE ALSO: Advanced Encryption Standard (AES); Computer Security; Data Encryption Standard (DES); Digital Certificate; Digital Certificate Authority; Digital Signature; Digital Signature Legislation; Encryption

CUBAN, MARK

Mark Cuban, the co-founder of Dallas-based firm broadcast.com and owner of the National Basketball Association's Dallas Mavericks, was among the most high-profile, outspoken, and wealthiest dot.com moguls of the late 1990s and early 2000s. Broadcast.com built its fortune by taking established media outlets online and streaming their signals over the Internet on the broadcast.com Web site in exchange for promotion on the firm's television or radio stations. Cuban positioned his company as adding value to traditional media outlets by offering them an online presence. Despite its success and its leadership in the online streaming media market, broadcast.com was one of the many dot-com sensations that failed to turn a profit despite its sizeable splash.

Although broadcast.com remained in the red, Cuban struck it rich when his former partner Yahoo! Inc. purchased the company in 1999 for $5.7 billion. However, although streaming media was the field in which broadcast.com earned its reputation, it wasn't the thrust of the company's revenue. About 70 percent of the firm's revenue came from its online conferences and assorted business services.

A Pittsburgh native born in 1958, Cuban's background in computers was modest, to say the least. He took only one computer course at Indiana University, where he majored in business, and failed because of poor typing skills, according to a profile in *Broadcasting & Cable*. Nonetheless, after graduation in 1981 he found a job with Mellon Bank as a computer systems integrator in Pittsburgh. After moving to Dallas, Cuban was fired from a job as a computer software salesman despite strong sales skills, because, according to Cuban, he wasn't interested in sweeping floors. However, Cuban felt his experience was strong enough to start his own firm, a computer networking outfit called MicroSolutions, which proved a modest success; he sold the firm to CompuServe for $3 million after seven years.

Streaming media and Cuban's love of basketball first merged in 1995 when he and his friend Tony Wagner affixed a phone line to a personal computer in order to watch the Indiana Hoosiers. They shopped their idea around on the message boards at America Online and were impressed by the level of influence. Inspired, they decided to launch a new firm called AudioNet to connect users to their favorite hometown sports teams over the Internet.

In 1998, they renamed the firm broadcast.com and took it public. The clients rolled in; at the time of the sale to Yahoo!, broadcast.com reached more than 60 million U.S. Internet users with its streaming media packages. While Wagner left the new partnership within a year after Yahoo!'s takeover, Cuban maintained two percent of Yahoo!'s shares. Cuban's main pursuit, however, was to live up the life he'd earned as a hotshot dot-com entrepreneur. He purchased the Dallas Mavericks for $280 million and

made himself one of the NBA's most visible and outspoken owners.

A prolific speaker, Cuban spent a great deal of time traveling the country extolling the glories and the necessities of entering the Internet business, and insisting that the online medium was destined to consume commerce as we know it. Cuban was among the strongest proponents of utilizing streaming media, urging broadcasters to junk their old business models that emphasized their channels or frequencies as identity markers, and instead embrace a model that highlighted "parallel programming" on the TV or radio and the Web at the same time. With technology and bandwidth becoming cheaper, competition in broadcasting was bound to explode, Cuban insisted, and traditional broadcasters could use their tremendous access to content to sell themselves in the emerging medium.

Thoroughly steeped in the high-speed competitive atmosphere of e-commerce, in 1999 Cuban told *Broadcasting & Cable* that "Business is like a game and the stock price and the money is the scorecard. The whole idea is to win." By any measure, Cuban had his share of victory. In 1999, *Forbes* ranked Cuban seventh on its list of the richest people in America involved in the Internet, with a net worth of $1.2 billion.

FURTHER READING:

Doyle, T.C. "The Cuban Story: From Neighborhood VAR to Internet Czar." *VAR Business*. October 25, 1999.

Gallagher, Leigh. "Take Back Your Poils." *Forbes*. October 9, 2000.

Kindley, Mark. "Mark Cuban: A Success Story You Can Relate To." *VAR Business*. October 25, 1999.

Newcomb, Peter, and Erika Brown. "The Forbes 400: Web Masters." *Forbes*. October 11, 1999.

Rathburn, Elizabeth A. "Crusader for Convergence." *Broadcasting & Cable*. October 18, 1999.

———. "Cuban: Embrace the Web." *Broadcasting & Cable*. October 4, 1999.

SEE ALSO: Streaming Media; Yahoo!

CUSTOMER RELATIONSHIP MANAGEMENT (CRM)

Customer relationship management (CRM) refers to the type of enterprise software that is designed to improve a company's interaction with its customers and thereby increase revenue from sales. In addition to offering the potential to increase revenue, CRM can also reduce the cost of supporting customers. CRM has the ability to move any transaction to the lowest cost channel possible and still satisfy customer needs.

CRM can provide a complete view of all customer relationships, taking into account all points of customer contact and the different media through which customers interface with the enterprise. CRM systems give companies the ability to track customer interaction across a range of channels, from e-mail to call centers. CRM can also provide the customer data required to conduct personalized marketing campaigns. Elements of such personalized marketing campaigns might include offers tailored to an individual visiting a company's Web site, dynamically served-up Web pages for different users, and personalized e-mail offers and announcements.

CRM helps companies learn as much as they can about their customers. Armed with this knowledge, companies can anticipate their customers' needs and keep them satisfied, resulting in higher revenues and lower costs. Data generated by CRM systems can be shared throughout an enterprise, allowing all departments or business units to coordinate their marketing efforts, including product development, advertising and promotion, and customer service.

CRM covers a range of products and vendors. It is often fragmented, with no single package delivering complete functionality, according to *Bank Systems & Technology* magazine. Among the technologies included in a CRM environment are sales force automation (SFA), customer analytics, real-time marketing solutions, customer behavior modeling, and real-time decision-making. CRM technology is designed to allow the customer to view, access, and interact with the complete set of services offered by the enterprise.

Different components of CRM relate to the different goals of customer acquisition, customer retention, and improved customer value. SFA and marketing applications are designed to help a company acquire more customers and convert prospects into customers. Data warehousing and analytical tools, along with customer service applications for call center and contact center management, help companies retain customers through improved communications and customer relations. CRM applications that can help improve customer value include marketing automation and campaign management software for cross-selling and up-selling. Data warehousing and analytical tools are also available to improve customer value.

CRM COMPONENTS AND VENDORS

Antecedents to today's Web-based CRM solutions include packaged contact management software, which was introduced in 1990. Around that time companies began to adopt formal telemarketing programs and develop multilevel customer service solutions. By 1997 the CRM marketplace was beginning to flour-

ish, and from 1997 to 2000 and beyond the market for front-office solutions focused on customers grew explosively. In 1999 the first packaged sales force automation (SFA) solutions became available, and custom CRM solutions appeared. PeopleSoft, a prominent developer of human resources applications and other integrated application suites for large enterprises, entered the CRM marketplace in 1999 with the acquisition of Vantive and became a leading CRM provider. Oracle, SAP, and Siebel emerged with other major product offerings. Since 1999 customer interaction with companies over the Web has grown, fueling the growth of Web-based CRM solutions.

CRM packages have several components and can be quite complex. Some CRM vendors, such as Oracle, have offered entry-level components, such as sales force automation (SFA) and customer service, for free as Web-delivered services. These free services are designed to get potential customers started on what would eventually become a more complex CRM package.

E-mail is one CRM tool that can be used to improve customer service and conduct personalized marketing campaigns. A 2001 study by AMR Research found that e-mail response management applications ranked second among leading CRM deployments in the United States, behind contact centers and ahead of Web-based self-service and sales force automation. Opportunities for CRM e-mail include newsletters, new product announcements, promotional discount offers, and traditional direct marketing campaigns, among others. E-mail can also be used to handle transactions, provide order confirmations, send personalized ''thank you'' messages, notify customers of shipping status, and more.

According to *eMarketer,* most consumers expect to receive a response to their e-mail inquiries within six hours. Most companies were not responding that fast, however, with only 38 percent providing a response within six hours. About one-third took three days or longer to respond, and 24 percent did not respond to e-mail inquiries at all.

An April 2001 research report published in *InfoWorld* identified 19 leading CRM vendors. The magazine surveyed 500 readers associated with acquiring CRM software and services and who worked for companies with 100 or more employees. The survey found that preferred vendors were those that offered both CRM and non-CRM applications, with the leading CRM vendors identified as Oracle, PeopleSoft, and Siebel Systems. Other well-known CRM vendors included E.piphany, Broadvision, SAS Institute, and Wheelhouse. The study categorized the principal CRM applications as sales force automation, marketing automation, and call or service centers.

In addition to providing CRM solutions, vendors may also offer outsourced applications and hosting services. In some cases, solutions are industry-based, especially in highly competitive industries such as financial services, travel, and retail.

MARKET FOR CRM

A mid-2001 report from *eMarketer* noted that businesses spent $3.9 billion on CRM software in 2000 and projected that they would spend $10.4 billion in 2001. *eMarketer* also estimated that for every dollar spent on CRM software, an additional $3 was spent implementing it. An earlier study from AMR Research and reported by *eMarketer* put worldwide CRM software revenue at $5.4 billion for 2000 and projected $7.9 billion in revenue for 2001, $11.5 billion for 2002, and $16.8 billion for 2003. The same study pegged revenue from worldwide CRM services at $67.4 billion in 2001, $74.4 billion in 2002, $97.8 billion in 2003, and $125.2 billion in 2004. According to a study by Ovum, in 2000 companies in North America spent $1.18 billion on e-commerce CRM, compared to just $100 million in Europe and only $30 million in Asia.

According to a mid-2001 study by Jupiter Media Metrix, three-fourths of all U.S. businesses were planning to increase CRM infrastructure spending by 25 to 50 percent in 2001. The number of online customers needing service was projected to increase from 33 million in 2001 to 67 million by 2005, thus making the investments a necessity. Jupiter, which hosts a national CRM forum called ''Connecting with Customers,'' warned companies against implementing a Web-only CRM system, or they would fail to build a consistent customer experience across all channels.

A March 2001 study of chief information officers (CIOs) from investment brokerage Morgan Stanley Dean Witter suggested that CRM was the most popular enterprise software application for 2001. The study found that customer service applications were the least likely of 33 possible IT spending categories to be cut during an economic downturn. For the same period in early 2001, leading CRM solutions providers such as Siebel Systems reported significant revenue increases over the previous year, with a great share of sales, sometimes the majority, coming from new customers.

A mid-2001 study by Forrester Research reported in *InfoWorld* found that 45 percent of the Global 3500 firms surveyed were considering CRM projects, and that 37 percent had CRM installations completed or in progress. The study also found that a typical firm would spend $15 million to $30 million per year on software and services to improve communications with customers.

CRM COSTS AND DEPLOYMENT

At the end of 2000 many companies were still in the early stages of deploying CRM systems. A late 2000 survey of more than 1,500 global companies by the Data Warehousing Institute found that only 7 percent of the respondents had achieved full deployment of their CRM systems. Some 38 percent were in the planning phase of their CRM programs, while 9 percent said they had no plans to implement a CRM solution. The early adopters of CRM were typically large companies with sales of more than $10 billion and were in highly competitive industries such as financial services or telecommunications. According to *eMarketer,* the Data Warehousing Institute study put the average budget for CRM projects at $4.1 million, a figure that was somewhat high because of the large size of the companies involved. Two-thirds of the respondents said they were spending less than $1 million on CRM deployment, while half were spending less than $500,000. The results suggested that many companies were taking an incremental approach to deploying their CRM solutions.

An online survey of chief technology officers (CTOs) conducted in mid-2001 by *InfoWorld* asked them how they would implement CRM. Some 60 percent said they would integrate a packaged software solution with their existing Web infrastructure, while 27 percent said they would integrate an outsourced CRM application from an external provider with their existing Web infrastructure. Only 7 percent said they would create a custom, in-house application, while another 3 percent planned to outsource CRM functions along with all of their Web operations. *InfoWorld* reported that worldwide revenue from CRM outsourcing would increase from $32 billion in 2000 to more than $66 billion in 2004, according to IDC estimates from May 2001.

According to a late 2000 study by the Gartner Group, CRM software made up less than one-third the cost of a CRM system. The highest costs were associated with related services, including consulting, integration, and maintenance. RealMarket Research estimated that for every $1 spent on CRM software, $2 to $5 was spent on consulting and implementation costs.

CRM MUST MEET HIGHER CONSUMER EXPECTATIONS

Consumer expectations for customer service have been heightened as a result of e-commerce. When companies opened themselves on the Internet to 24/7 access, customers gained much more visibility into companies and their products, services, policies, pricing, and business processes. Customers began to desire a much smoother, more seamless, transparent experience in dealing with companies, according to customer service expert Patricia Seybold, as quoted in *eMarketer.* Customers also wanted, and took, more control over the information that companies had about them. Customer concerns led to their taking more control of their profile information and their transaction histories. Customers were suspicious that companies were using that information to segment them in order to offer them different levels of service based on which segment they were in. Some companies began following the lead of the airlines and car rental companies by telling customers what segment they were in and letting them know what level of service they could expect.

Customer service can be expensive. *eMarketer*'s CRM report found that online self-service costs businesses only three cents per customer, while live help costs $5 per customer. The goal for companies is to make their online self-help capabilities so good that customers come to prefer them to interacting with a live customer service representative. Cisco Systems, for example, designed an online customer service wizard that prompts customers, helps them get their complaint logged, but along the way also offers suggestions for fixing the problem. In this way, customers are able to troubleshoot their own problem and find a solution.

EVALUATING CRM PERFORMANCE

CRM is more than a matter of having the right technology. It requires the support of a well-developed business plan. Perhaps the biggest cause of CRM project failures is not the technology, but the lack of a clear-cut business plan that includes a method for measuring the success of a CRM solution. A mid-2001 study by Jupiter Media Metrix looked at how companies measure the success of their CRM programs. Jupiter found that 63 percent use customer satisfaction metrics as a measure of their return on investment (ROI), while 33 percent used cost savings as a yardstick.

Jupiter Media Metrix also noted in mid-2001 that many Global 2000 companies were guilty of redundant spending, due to conflicting corporate goals and separate business units. The research firm estimated that such redundancy would cost Global 2000 companies between $3 billion and $4 billion over the next two years. To solve this problem, Jupiter recommended that companies adopt a company-wide customer culture.

An April 2001 *InfoWorld* survey asked respondents to identify what they wanted from CRM. Some 80 percent said they needed CRM to keep pace with customer demands, while more than 78 percent said they wanted to provide service across all communication channels. Three-fourths said they wanted CRM to improve customer retention. Thus, customer satisfaction was the principal goal for CRM as reported by respondents, followed by handling customer interactions more effectively and integrating systems and information. Financial goals, such as increasing sales revenue, appeared to be less significant and were cited as an objective by only 53 percent of the respondents. Survey respondents also expected CRM solutions to enable them to build a customer database or data warehouse, meet growing capacity demands, integrate activities of customers across channels, link front-office and back-office systems, improve customer profiling, allow for cross-selling and up-selling of products and services, and better coordinate various marketing and sales campaigns.

With companies eager to purchase CRM solutions, more software vendors began jumping on the CRM bandwagon. The marketplace became cluttered with software vendors, including some who defined CRM in a way that suited their interests rather than those of their clients. As a result, nearly 60 percent of CRM projects were not meeting user expectations, according to a mid-2001 study by the Gartner Group. *B to B* magazine reported that 55 percent of CRM projects were not expected to deliver any measurable ROI. The magazine noted that a typical CRM installation for a mid-size company, including software, consulting fees, and company labor costs, would cost between $250,000 and $500,000.

CRM HORIZONS

CRM has evolved from its customer service roots to include marketing and other applications. It has come to be used to manage relationships with suppliers, partners, and other non-employees. Other emerging features of CRM include real-time queuing and routing of customers based on their profiles. More valuable customers can be routed to a customer representative more quickly under such a system.

In the future, CRM will incorporate features such a voice-over Internet protocol, live chat, and other Web enabled tools to enhance the customer's experience. As of early 2001, *B to B* magazine reported that IBM was experimenting with creating virtual people—complete with photorealistic, digital human faces—that could interact with customers in real time. New technologies will result in expanding the boundaries of CRM to enable companies to engage in one-to-one marketing and provide customers with deeper, more meaningful, and lasting relationships.

FURTHER READING:

Apicella, Mario. ''Are You Being Served?'' *InfoWorld,* July 16, 2001.

Berkowitz, David. "Putting Customers First with Patricia Seybold." *eMarketer,* May 18, 2001. Available from www.emarketer.com.

Butler, Steve. "Budgeting for Customer Relationship Management." *eMarketer,* April 30, 2001. Available from www.emarketer.com.

Chiem, Phat X. "Special Report: Revolution Gives Way to Evolution." *B to B,* February 19, 2001.

Clark, Philip B. "The ROI of CRM." *B to B,* June 11, 2001.

Conlin, Robert, and Clare Saliba. "Report: Customer Service Spending to Buck Economic Downturn." *E-Commerce Times,* June 26, 2001. Available from www.ecommercetimes.com.

"The CRM Report." *eMarketer,* April, 2001. Available from www.emarketer.com.

"Customer Relationship Management." *InfoWorld,* April 16, 2001.

Jackson, Jonathan. "Giving Good eMail Service." *eMarketer,* May 14, 2001. Available from www.emarketer.com.

Leon, Mark. "CRM." *InfoWorld,* July 16, 2001.

Schmerken, Ivy, et al. "Technology Makes Convergence a Reality." *Bank Systems & Technology,* May 2001.

Seybold, Patricia. *The Customer Revolution,* New York: Crown Publishing Group, 2001.

SEE ALSO: Business-to-Consumer (B2C) E-Commerce; Mass Customization

CYBERCULTURE: SOCIETY, CULTURE, AND THE INTERNET

Few technologies in human history rival the Internet in its speed of adoption and range of impact. The Internet's spread has been compared to the advent of the printing press, which, like the Internet, greatly enhanced the availability of information and the rate of its reproduction. Many have commented on the Internet's ability to transform business and the broader economy, but perhaps an equally profound change is being felt throughout society and culture, where the Internet and the World Wide Web are transforming how people live and interact. The Internet's influence generates a range of reactions from different people, ranging from idealism to cynicism, but however it is received, there's no denying that it has led to dramatic shifts in such areas as interpersonal interaction, work culture, relations to time, expectations of speed and convenience, networking between individuals and groups, and even use of language.

The word "cyberculture" is used in a variety of ways, often referring to certain cultural products and practices born of computer and Internet technologies, but also to specific subcultures that champion computer-related hobbies, art, and language. In the 1970s, cyberculture was the exclusive domain of a handful of technology experts, including mathematicians, computer scientists, digital enthusiasts, and academics, devoted to exchanging and promoting ideas related to the growing fields of computers and electronics. These early cybercultures sometimes advanced a view of the future guided by the progressive and beneficial hand of technological change. But following the commercialization of the Internet and the World Wide Web in the mid-1990s, cyberculture took on a new life, and computer and information technologies took the dynamics of culture and social relations in dramatically new directions.

HOW WE LIVE

The Internet touches many parts of life in advanced industrial societies. Everything from shopping, paying bills, and playing the stock market to news gathering, family interaction, romantic courtships, and play all take place in cyberspace, whereas before the mid-1990s all these activities existed more commonly in the physical world. The Internet profoundly influences what and how children learn, the vocabulary employed in daily conversation, the way people coordinate their schedules and work habits, and perceptions of distance and time. With the ability to jump from China to Brazil to Los Angeles within a minute and with e-mail offering lightning-fast communication, the Web has taken the advancements of the telephone several steps further toward bridging physical distances between people, not to mention time. For that matter, the Internet is a 24-hour-a-day operation, and thus consumers are no longer confined by store hours to go shopping.

Some say the explosion of information technologies changes the dynamics between business, social, and ethical issues. According to this view, as individuals gain access to greater and greater quantities of information, the social and ethical ramifications of business practices will become widely known. This openness, the argument goes, will pressure business strategists to take controversial social issues into account to avoid jeopardizing their sales or, at the least, to avoid missing valuable business opportunities.

Internet and cyberculture enthusiasts come from all shades of political persuasion. Conservatives applaud the Internet's subversion of state functions such as taxation and regulatory interference with the free activity of commercial interests. Liberals applaud the Internet's capacities to network disenfranchised groups and coordinate efforts toward greater social equality. But if cyberculture has been hailed by politicos of all stripes, it is also criticized by as broad a spectrum. Social conservatives railed against the excessive openness of the Internet and its attendant capacity to spread materials and ideas they find indecent or morally or socially unacceptable, while left-leaning advocates warned against the excessive commercialization of the Internet and its tendency to transform social needs and relationships into personalized consumer needs, fracturing social solidarity. Thus, it is safe to say that arguments for and against Internet practices aren't drawn along clear political lines.

THE E-GENERATION GAP

Cyberculture of the 1990s and early 2000s was in a transitional stage, shaped and inhabited largely by those with a foot in both the pre-Internet era and the Digital Age. Children growing up in this period, however, will never know an era when the Internet wasn't an entirely natural component of life, when it was seen as a transformation from the life they knew. As a result, cyberculture's shape is likely to change rapidly as younger generations come of age. Parents may fret over the skills and experiences their children miss out on by being wrapped up in cyberculture, but in all likelihood the Internet will be entwined more and more with daily activities and the distinctions between cybercultures and the dominant cultures will blur.

Don Tapscott, in his book *Growing Up Digital,* reported that at the end of the 1990s two-thirds of what he called the "Net Generation" used personal computers either at home or in school. According to Tapscott, such children are less concerned about the technology itself, which increasingly is simply part of the background, as about the technology's functionality in their daily lives. In this way, children growing up in highly developed areas of the world in the early 2000s were fundamentally different from their parents, for whom such computer technology was a revolution occurring in their lifetimes, sharply separating, thanks to its speed and impact, the life they knew before the Internet and the one that exists today. This generational dynamic, according to Tapscott, speaking to *Communication World* in December 1999, was "about to—like a tidal wave—sweep across all of our institutions."

THE INTERNET AND WORK CULTURE

The Internet has greatly changed the nature of work in connected segments of the world. For instance, work increasingly is performed outside of the traditional work place—a central office or factory—and more often in homes and other remote locations. The most cybercultured companies, moreover, more or less do away with the physical models of work, and are little more than interconnecting networks rather than physical, hierarchical organizations. Telecom-

muting allows workers to adjust their schedules to their own convenience and perform work in the comfort of their home offices. Critics point out, however, that this isn't always the liberating force that proponents chalk it up to be. Telecommuting may indeed allow greater flexibility and some convenience, but it also signals work's encroachment into the personal lives of workers. By blurring the line between work time and personal time, critics contend, the Internet and business cyberculture foster a model of living in which employees are, in a sense, always "on call," potentially eroding the quality of personal time.

The cyberculture of business presents particular problems for established firms looking to remain competitive by adopting e-commerce. At the most basic level, embracing the Internet's technologies, not to mention its culture, can be disorienting if it subverts established traditions. The process of foregoing old supply chains for the efficiencies of the Internet must be carefully negotiated to avoid disintermediation, or losing business by being cut out of a supply chain altogether. Meanwhile, the internal culture of a firm, less easily quantified with statistics and difficult to transform with a new technology, may clash with the style of interactivity fostered by the Internet. Intranets largely undo direct top-down lines of communication in favor of a more complex web of interaction between individuals and departments, workers and managers. The Internet also fosters a greater dispersal of information among company members than was normal in traditional company models, where managers were more likely to monopolize information and coordinate plans in a traditional hierarchy. With e-mail lists and electronic message boards available, employees may view such managerial behavior as alienating. Finally, cyberculture in the business world encourages the practice of thinking outside of existing paradigms, and thus businesses hoping to build a strong Internet presence need to encourage innovation and novel ideas among all their employees.

CYBERPERSONALITIES IN VIRTUAL COMMUNITIES

The anonymity afforded by the World Wide Web is another crucial element of cyberculture. Individuals routinely create screen names and, in some cases, online personalities that may or may not diverge from the ones they project in the physical world. Again, this feature could be either a blessing or a curse. On the one hand, the anonymity offers space for individuals who may feel ostracized or isolated to access information and take part in communities that may be practically off limits in the physical world. On the other hand, critics note that the anonymity simply fosters a culture of mischief in which individuals may indulge in social behaviors online that are unacceptable in the ordinary world, perhaps even illegal or subversive activities.

Paul Soriano of the Internet Society pointed out that "the virtual communities of the cyberworld will not cure the acute crisis of identity that the world is suffering." Despite the emergence of virtual communities and the anonymous nature of Internet communications, the myriad ethnic, religious, national, sexual, and ideological divisions of the world are unlikely to disappear as a result of cyberculture and internetworking. Rather, these online communities are likely to find their way into the broader cultural matrix as yet another strand in a complex social fabric.

Some commentators, such as David Holmes in his book *Virtual Politics: Identity & Community in Cyberspace,* warn that individuals run the risk of losing all sense of identity and community the more they are submerged in cyberspace, with its dissolution of time and space and excessive simulation of reality. Still others see little that is so completely revolutionary in the kind of transformations wrought by the Internet. Christopher Barnatt, for instance, writing in *Human Relations,* noted that "[a]cross human history, mental activities have invariably come to dominate and 'displace' activities of the body." Moreover, Barnatt argued, blaming the Internet for eroding traditional communities is somewhat akin to the blaming the automobile for eroding the community structures that preceded the rise of "suburban fantasylands accessible only to those with the technology of an automobile." Barnatt likened complaints about the Internet's effect on community to wanting "to protect one hyperreality from the encroachment of another that merely accelerates forward the same sociotechnical agenda."

THE INTERNET: DOES IT UNITE OR DIVIDE?

Cyberculture is heralded for breaking down borders and barriers, not just between nations but also between groups and individuals separated by physical space or by political and social conditions. As a result, some would hold that the Internet fosters a more complex tapestry of relations than ever existed in the physical world.

However, skeptics warned that the Internet wasn't eliminating borders as much as shifting their definition and location. Instead of physical borders separating one people from another, these critics contend, the Internet establishes a border between those use it and those who do not or cannot go online. This "digital divide" was of increasing concern to social activists and policy planners, and to businesses as well, who see the divide as a stopgap to their future marketing strategies. This rift grows as cyberculture drifts away from being a specialized domain for technology experts and toward a force driving social change, economic relations, political policy, and cultural life. If cyberculture increasingly sets the agenda in the dominant culture, those on the "wrong" side of the digital divide will inevitably find themselves more and more isolated and alienated from the societies in which they live.

For regions outside the United States, the cultural implications of the Internet carry another important question: how will the U.S.-dominated Internet affect the sovereignty and integrity of local and regional cultures? The Internet was developed in the United States, as were the bulk of the technologies that support it, U.S. firms constituted by far the largest share of online businesses in the early 2000s, and English was the Internet's dominant language. Thus, to a great extent the models of Internet activities sprang from U.S. paradigms, which many non-U.S. interests eyed with some skepticism. Such fears were often tied to broader concerns about globalization, an economic and cultural force many saw as the sweep of American culture and businesses over the rest of the world. On the other hand, those who see the Internet as a leveling force point out that such technologies, far from steamrolling cultures and local sovereignty, actually provide a level playing field and thus a greater degree of autonomy and competitive leverage to non-U.S. cultures than they would enjoy in the global economy absent Internet technology.

FURTHER READING:

Barnatt, Christopher. "Apple Pie Thinking for the Wired Age?" *Human Relations,* April, 1999.

Braillard, Pierre. "Communication Technology and Cultural Identity." *Intermedia,* November, 2000.

Bournellis, Cynthia. "Cyberculture-Focus On Human Needs." *Electronic News,* July 20, 1998.

Doran, G. David. "Future Tech." *Entrepreneur,* May, 1999.

Gerstner, John. "Don Tapscott: Digital Dad." *Communication World,* December, 1999.

Heresniak, E.J. "Buffalo Hunters: Extinction of Traditional Way of Life Due to the Advent of Technological Processes," *Across the Board,* October, 1998.

Holmes, David, ed. *Virtual Politics: Identity & Community in Cyberspace.* 1997, London: Sage, 1997.

"The PC is a Cruel Mistress: How Computers Affect Quality of Life." *Canadian Business,* September 18, 2000.

"The Race for Cyberspace: Inequality of Information Technology Resources Among Countries." *Asian Review of Business and Technology,* March, 1998.

Rodriguez, Juan. "Speed, Time, and Cyberculture." *The Gazette* (Montreal), February 13, 2000.

Wilder, Clinton. "The Wilder Side: Learn to Work the 'Off' Switch." *Informationweek,* September 18, 2000.

SEE Community Model; Digital Divide; Virtual
ALSO: Communities

CYBERSPACE

Cyberspace refers to the online world that is formed by computer systems and networks. The word was coined by author William Gibson in his science fiction novel *Neuromancer*. It originated in the mid-1980s to define the virtual world that exists due to the advent of the Internet, which in its earliest form was a community that shared ideas and information.

Increasing interest in cyberspace has given way to a plethora of new ideas and related jargon. The term cyber is used as a prefix with increasing regularity. Cybergeography, for instance, is known as the study of the spatial nature of computer communications networks, or the geography of cyberspace. Cyberpsychology, the study of the psychological impact of cyberspace, also is becoming popular as the number of World Wide Web surfers increases.

One of the most significant additions to cyberspace has been e-commerce. With technological advances, the business world has been able to apply traditional brick-and-mortar ideas to the realm of cyberspace. Advocates of the early days of the Internet feel that e-commerce has had a negative effect on the integrity of cyberspace, while others argue that the growth of e-commerce in cyberspace is crucial to economic development. Originally used as a forum for exchanging information and ideas, cyberspace has become a virtual marketplace where a Web surfer can trade stocks, buy just about anything, take care of banking needs, and even apply for home loans.

The rising popularity of e-commerce has made it nearly impossible to go online and enter cyberspace without encountering a barrage of advertising and commerce information. For instance, when the search engine Yahoo! was first introduced, no shopping links appeared on its home page. By the early 2000s, this had changed. Web surfers using the site to search for information saw a list of online stores pop up, offering products related to their search. From November to mid-December 2000, online spending more than doubled over the same time period in the previous year, reaching $8.7 billion. These numbers are predicted to increase dramatically in coming years.

To protect the growing numbers of online consumers and merchants, e-commerce legislation known as cyberlaw has emerged. Similar to laws in the real world, cyberlaw deals with topics such as the protection of copyrights, business transactions, electronic payment systems, and privacy. This type legislation continues to develop in response to the evolution of cyberspace, commercial and otherwise.

FURTHER READING:

Barham, Richard. ''Quest for Harmony in Cyberspace.'' *The Banker*. August, 2000.

Colin, Robert, and Lori Enos. ''Report: 85 Percent of Net Surfers Shop Online.'' *E-Commerce Times*. May 31, 2000. Available from www.ecommercetimes.com/perl/printer/3440/.

Cyber-Geography Research. ''Welcome to Cyber-Geography Research.'' London, England: Cyber-Geography Research, Centre for Advanced Spatial Research, 2001. Available from www.cybergeography.org.

Enos, Lori. ''Study: E-Holiday Spending Doubled.'' *E-Commerce Times*. December 27, 2000. Available from www.ecommercetimes.com/perl/printer/6306.

Regan, Keith. ''These Are the Web's Good Old Days.'' *E-Commerce Times*. June 2, 2000. Available www.ecommercetimes.com.

SEE Cyberculture: Society, Culture, and the Internet; History of the Internet and World Wide Web (WWW);
ALSO: Virtual Communities

CYBERSQUATTING

The bane of companies, organizations, brand names, and celebrities, cybersquatting is the practice of registering the name of a company, trademark, brand, or person as a domain name for a Web site in hopes of misleading users to one's own site by using a well-known name. The top-level domain (TLD), the highest level of the Uniform Resource Locator (URL) such as *sitename.com* or *sitename.org*, is the portion of the Web address that companies covet most. Companies generally prefer the URL that will be easiest to remember and thus more recognizable to the visitor. Cybersquatters attempt to beat the company, individual, or organization to the punch in registering that domain. Failing that, squatters may try closely related alternatives, such as adding a hyphen or a single letter to the domain name to lure inattentive users. At times cybersquatters have registered these names in hopes of selling them back to their namesakes at a handsome profit, but U.S. court rulings and new laws have curtailed these activities.

Businesses fear that cybersquatting exploits and erodes their brand identities. The domain-name registration system doesn't prevent users from selecting a registered trademark as a domain name. In essence, if a particular name or variation of a name hasn't been registered already, almost anyone can register it for a small fee. Given the ease of acquiring names, the strategy of cybersquatters is to route traffic to their sites from unsuspecting followers of another brand or identity, thereby generating an audience for themselves. The most malicious form of cybersquatting happens when squatters take a certain brand or identity and associate it with negative or offensive materials, for example, routing a children-related domain name to a pornographic Web site.

Cybersquatters may have a variety of intentions. The most common goal is to hold the domain hostage, so to speak, and name a ransom price at which the squatter hopes to sell it to the company, trademark holder, organization, or individual. Cybersquatters also simply try to garner visitors to their Web sites by exploiting a popular name, either to expand the audience for their own message or product or to boost their advertising revenue.

Relief from cybersquatting came with the Anti-Cybersquatting Consumer Protection Act (ACPA), passed in 1999, which was designed specifically to curtail the registration of domain names that use others' trademarks or trade names. The law covers unregistered trademarks and individual names as well. ACPA applies to all TLDs, covering the three most common suffixes, known as generic top-level domain names (gTLDs), *.com,.net,* and *.org,* as well as all country-code top-level domain names (ccTLDs), such as *.ca* for Canada and *.fr* for France. Prior to ACPA, victims of cybersquatting had little recourse, and many ended up paying the exorbitant fees demanded by squatters to purchase their own names. Because cybersquatters can be prosecuted under ACPA, it has generally made cybersquatting less profitable, though it has hardly stamped out the practice.

The Internet Corporation for Assigned Names and Numbers (ICANN) is the official body charged with monitoring the allocation of domain names. In December 1999 ICANN unveiled a standard procedure for settling name disputes, the Uniform Domain Name Dispute Resolution Policy (UDRP). ICANN's procedure determines the plausibility of the cybersquatting claims using three tests. First, it verifies that the domain name is identical or confusingly similar to the trademark. Then, it determines whether the domain name owner maintains a legitimate interest in the name. Finally, ICANN judges whether or not the domain owner acted in bad faith.

In addition to litigation, individuals, firms, and organizations have a number of strategies at their disposal to combat cybersquatting. The most common is to simply register, as quickly as possible, other similar domain names, such as those with and without hyphens or with commonly used initials. Many companies and individuals have even gone so far as to register or purchase the domain names of possible ''gripe sites,'' also known as cyberbashers. Famously, during the 2000 U.S. presidential campaign the Web site www.GeorgeBushsucks.com routed curious visitors to the official George W. Bush campaign site. Chase Manhattan and other large companies engaged in similar preemptive strikes against cyberbashers and squatters.

However, since there can be dozens of possible domain-name variations that could fall victim to cybersquatting, the defense against cybersquatters may come down to a cost-benefit analysis. That is, the concerned entity must decide how many different names it should register in order to protect its identity, and determine at what point it begins to find diminishing returns. Most importantly, though, such strategies must be implemented quickly. Speed is the name of the game in cybersquatting, as cybersquatters are practiced in getting to domain names first.

FURTHER READING:

Brown, Marc E. ''Don't Pay Off a Cybersquatter.'' *Electronic Business,* March, 2000.

Copeland, Lee. ''Cyberbashers Proliferate.'' *Computerworld,* February 21, 2000.

''ICANN Call It What I Want.'' *Economist,* September 9, 2000, 74.

Lesser, Lori E. '''Cybersquatting' Law Aids in Pirate Prosecutions.'' *Journal of Property Rights,* January, 2000.

Plave, Lee J. ''Franchisors Brandish Pair of Powerful Weapons in the War on Cybersquatters.'' *Franchising World,* September/October, 2000.

Railo, Matt J. ''Protecting Brands Online: Practical Considerations in the Fight Against Cybersquatting.'' *Intellectual Property & Technology Law Journal,* December 2000.

SEE ALSO: Domain Name; ICANN; Uniform Resource Locator (URL)

D

Highly sensitive digital information is often the target of computer hackers, international spies, and criminals. In order to protect such information, in 1977 the National Security Agency (NSA) and the National Bureau of Standards (NBS) adopted the Data Encryption Standard (DES) to protect sensitive, un-classified, non-military digital information from un-authorized access. Encryption is the intentional scrambling or masking of digital data to protect it from compromise.

DES utilized symmetric-key (or private-key) en-cryption, in which the sender and receiver of a mes-sage share a single, common key that is used to encrypt and decrypt the message. The key is a string of digits that has been generated by a complex mathe-matical algorithm, or formula. Private-key encryption differs from public-key encryption, which utilizes two keys—a public key to encrypt messages and a private key to decrypt them. Private-key systems are simpler and faster, but their main drawback is that both parties must somehow exchange the key in a secure manner. Public-key encryption avoids this problem because the public key can be distributed in a non-secure way, and the private key is never transmitted. In the former case, secrecy is shared between only two users, whereas in the latter, the public key is a more or less an ''open secret.'' Thus, public-key encryption re-quires many more bits to rival private-key systems' level of protection.

Though the NSA usually supervises develop-ment of governmental encryption systems, its hesita-tion over creating such a system for public use led to an open call for the system's design. Ultimately IBM produced a 56-bit key algorithm that became DES. Controversy arose over the extent to which DES-encrypted products could be exported outside the United States, since federal regulations govern export of encrypted items. Security considerations led the U.S. government to limit the export of encryption sys-tems to those of 40 bits or less. Since DES employed 56 bits, most products incorporating DES could not be exported, despite a report on national encryption policy issued by the National Research Council in 1996 that called for a relaxation of export regulations.

DES underwent its most serious challenge in 1998, and failed. The Electronic Frontier Foundation constructed a custom-designed machine, which broke open a DES-encrypted code in 56 hours. Subsequent tests, conducted on 100,000 PCs networked with the EFF machine, reduced the time required to 22 hours. This procedure resulted in the lifting of the U.S. re-strictions on exporting DES-encrypted products.

DES's efficacy under continuous surveillance and was reassessed every five years after its inception. The 1998 EFF crack-through concluded that DES' Achilles heel was its short key length. It was recom-mended that DES should be replaced by Triple DES, a modified version employing 112- or 168-bit keys. DES's versatility also was limited because it worked only in hardware, and the explosion of the Internet and e-commerce led to much greater use and versatili-ty of software than could have been anticipated by DES's designers.

As DES's vulnerabilities became apparent, the National Institute of Standards and Technology (NIST) opened an international competition in 1997 to find a permanent replacement for DES. To be christened the Advanced Encryption Standard (AES), the replacement would be operable into the 21st century. NIST recommended a minimum key length of 128 bits, and sought to guarantee that encrypted files would continue to be secure even after AES was eventually phased out. In addition, the algorithm had to implement public-key cryptography and work with key sizes of 128, 192, and 256 bits. Flexibility also was a premium concern of AES' designers. AES had to function with eight-bit processors, smart cards, ATM networks, high-definition TVs, voice-recognition systems, and satellite communications. Finally, it had to be available internationally on a non-exclusive, royalty-free basis.

Ultimately, DES was testament to the pace of technological change in the late 20th century. It was considered to be adequately powerful and impenetrable in its day. However, the cracks in DES widened into gaping holes as cryptographic and computer technology developed, and as the Internet and other networked systems heightened the need for flexible and durable encryption.

FURTHER READING:

Anthes, Gary H., and Patrick Thibodeau. ''IT & the Feds: The Five Years.'' *Computerworld*. June 14, 1999, 52.

Harrison, Ann. ''Advanced Encryption Standard.'' *Computerworld*. May 29, 2000, 57.

———. ''Cryptographers Urge Review of Standard.'' *Computerworld*. August 23, 1999, 4.

———. ''Encryption Standard Finals.'' *Computerworld*. August 16, 1999, 6.

———. ''Feds Propose New Encryption Standard.'' *Computerworld*. October 9, 2000, 14.

Hulme, Geroge V. ''Commerce Department Picks Rijndael Encryption Formula.'' *InformationWeek*. October 16, 2000.

Landau, Susan. ''Designing Cryptography for the New Century.'' *Communications of the ACM*. May 2000.

Loshin, Pete. ''Cryptographic Turning Points.'' *Computerworld*. August 28, 2000.

Messmer, Ellen. ''Crypto Proposal Faces Long Journey.'' *Network World*. October 16, 2000.

Yasin, Rutrell. ''U.S. Picks AES Encryption Spec: Belgian Formula Seen Overcoming DES's Vulnerability to Hackers and Hardware Requirements.'' *Internetweek*. October 9, 2000.

SEE ALSO: Advanced Encryption Standard; Cryptography, Public and Private Key; Digital Certificate; Digital Signature; Encryption; Hacking

DATA INTEGRITY

Information is what gives power to the Web and e-commerce. In a matter of minutes, consumers are able to research, compare, and purchase products and services online. This availability of information has created more discriminating consumers and has put increased pressure on retailers to offer competitive prices. Understandably, the accuracy or integrity of data is very important during e-commerce.

SOURCES OF FAULTY DATA

The integrity of data can be compromised in a variety of ways, including malicious proprietors, human mistakes, and technical error. Unfortunately, like accurate information, faulty, inaccurate, or misleading information also travels freely on the Internet and consumers and companies alike have been negatively affected by it.

Fraudulent business schemes account for a significant amount of erroneous information on the Web. In this scenario, sellers often make faulty or exaggerated claims about products and services that sometimes do not exist. According to Nua Internet Surveys, a study by the Worldwide E-Commerce Fraud Prevention Network found that 50 percent of businesses in the United States saw online fraud as a significant problem. Ten percent of those companies ranked online fraud as their ''most significant problem.'' Among those surveyed, half had experienced losses between $1,000 and $10,000, and 19 percent in excess of $100,000. Online auctions were among the leading areas of e-commerce fraud in the early 2000s. Nua Internet Surveys reported that the U.S. Internet Fraud Complaint Center (IFCC) registered more than 20,000 complaints in its first six months of existence. Sixty-four percent of the complaints involved auction fraud.

In addition to information that is simply unreliable or inaccurate, the integrity of data can be compromised in other ways, including technical errors that happen during data transmission. Along with the growth of e-commerce came an increasing reliance on software programs that automate tasks involving databases of customer information. This opens the door for computers to accidentally execute tasks that affect thousands or tens of thousands of people at a time. Before the advent of e-commerce, mistakes usually involved a handful of customers, or at least could be caught in time to avert a major disaster. Although consulting firms, software developers, and leading companies all devote resources to this problem in their own ways, technical error was still a major concern in the early 2000s and no one solution existed that ensured the integrity of information during all Internet transactions.

A more simple source of technical errors, which some e-commerce developers were dealing with in a variety of ways, involved limitations of Web technology. Traditionally, Web servers (the computers or software responsible for maintaining and storing Web sites) break off connections with clients (individuals using Web browsers like Microsoft's Internet Explorer) after a Web page has been downloaded to their screen. This means that when consumers view a Web page, it may become outdated in a matter of seconds. Products that were available when the consumer initially downloaded the Web page may become unavailable several seconds later.

Errors were also attributed to online shopping carts—the technology that keeps track of items consumers are interested in until they are done shopping on a Web site. For example, if someone removes an item from their shopping cart before checkout because they don't want it and then clicks on their browser's ''back&rquo; button to revisit a Web page they just saw, it is possible that the unwanted item will be added back to their cart. Other similar sorts of mistakes can happen with online shopping carts.

Human mistakes as well are sources of compromised data. In October 2000, Buy.com agreed to a $575,000 class-action settlement when, due to a human data-entry error, it mistakenly priced a computer monitor at $164.50 instead of $564.50. Buy.com honored the price for the monitors it had in stock. However, when it refused to fulfill all of the orders it received, consumers sued. Around the same time, consumers threatened to sue Egghead.com for a similar blunder. The retailer mistakenly priced a $335 computer component at $34.85. Before the mistake was noticed, Egghead.com had received thousands of orders, which it cancelled.

CONSEQUENCES OF FAULTY DATA

The consequences of bad data are real. *Chain Store Age Executive with Shopping Center Age,* revealed how a lack of data integrity can cost companies money, explaining: ''At the most fundamental level data error attacks those things that affect revenue, costs, and ultimately, customer loyalty. Unanticipated out-of-stocks equal lost sales. Excess safety stock requires higher investment and more markdowns. Inaccurate inventory data demands that resources be allocated to determine the availability or shortages of items. Data error also feeds invalid information to the inventory replenishment system, driving poor merchandise planning and purchasing decisions, resulting in more obsolete and excess inventory.''

The *Chicago Tribune* listed several serious data errors that serve as examples of the kinds of things

that can happen when large volumes of information is digitized, stored, and transferred. Among them were a credit reporting company that accidentally labeled 1,400 residents of an Eastern town as having bad credit and a health insurance company that accidentally sent out $60 million worth of duplicate checks after its new computer system malfunctioned. Finally, *Legal Assistant Today* described how an engineer at PairGain Technologies Inc. created a false Web page announcing that it was about to be acquired by an Israeli telecommunications firm. The page's design was similar to that of a popular news service, and it falsely motivated investors, causing the company's stock to increase by 31 percent.

ENSURING DATA INTEGRITY

Although there is no universal way to ensure the integrity of data and technical errors are bound to occur from time to time, consumers and companies alike are able to take measures to protect themselves. Common sense and critical evaluation were essential first lines of defense for both parties. For consumers, measures could be taken to verify the identity of a Web site's owner. Secure certificates issued by companies like VeriSign and CyberTrust were means of doing this in the early 2000s. Additionally, consumers were able to limit their transactions to those companies providing encryption methods, whereby information was scrambled between the sender and receiver.

Companies engaging in e-commerce had several methods of ensuring the integrity of data. Simple measures involved limiting the number of parties responsible for posting data to their Web sites and building in extra layers for fact checking. Special software programs for detecting and correcting errors were likewise available.

Companies also developed elaborate data management strategies that involved reviewing the ways data was collected, stored, updated, and used. General Motors was completing a customer data quality project in late 1999 that involved ''capturing customer information from multiple sources in a standard, error-proof way, then merging it with detailed demographic and lifestyle information,'' according to *Informationweek.* Over time, some companies find themselves with a large number of different databases across the organization. A data management strategy might involve consolidating this information in one secure place and identifying the best ways to integrate it with different processes and systems.

FURTHER READING:

''Auction Sites Generate Most Complaints.'' NUA Internet Surveys. March 8, 2001. Available from www.nua.ie/surveys.

Bloomberg, Jason. ''Shopping Carts and Data Integrity.'' *EarthWeb,* April 27, 1999. Available from www.webdeveloper.earthweb.com.

''Data Integrity.'' *Ecommerce Webopedia,* May 3, 2001. Available from e-comm.webopedia.com.

Fitzpatrick, Michele. ''The Fight for Data Integrity.'' *Chicago Tribune,* July 7, 2000. Available from www.chicagotribune.com.

Goldsborough, Reid. ''Information on the Net Often Needs Checking.'' *RN,* May, 1999.

Kendis, Randall. ''Data Integrity—Who Cares?'' *Chain Store Age Executive with Shopping Center Age,* April, 1998.

''Pricing Error May Prove Costly for Egghead.com.'' Nua Internet Surveys. October 18, 2000. Available from www.nua.ie.

Rosencrance, Linda. ''Buy.com Settles Pricing Lawsuit.'' *Computerworld,* October 19, 2000. Available from www.pcworld.com.

Tyburski, Genie. ''Honest Mistakes, Deceptive Facts.'' *Legal Assistant Today,* March/April, 2000.

Wallace, Bob. ''Data Quality Moves to the Forefront.'' *Informationweek,* September 20, 1999.

''Worldwide E-Commerce Fraud Prevention Network: U.S. Firms Concerned About Online Fraud.'' NuaInternet Surveys. April 10, 2001. Available from www.nua.ie.

SEE ALSO: Data Warehousing; Database Management; Digital Certificate; Encryption; Fraud, Internet; Misinformation Online

DATA MINING

In the Information Age, it's not how much information is maintained but how it is managed, manipulated, and exploited that can make or break a firm. Data mining is the practice of ferreting out useful knowledge from the wealth of information stored in computer systems, databases, communications records, financial and sales data, and other sources. A staple in the so-called Information Economy, data mining has evolved into a standard—and often requisite—business practice, and is often as valuable to firms as their underlying products or services. With competition heating up and making use of the mountains of new information technologies, those most able to exploit data mining to derive insights for use in a business model or strategy are often those with a competitive edge.

Data mining combines expertise in data analysis with sophisticated pattern-searching software to crunch diverse mountains of data and churn out information designed to capture market share and boost profit margins. As the sheer wealth of information available escalated through the 1990s and early 2000s, such techniques assumed paramount importance. The focus of data mining is on organizing data and identifying patterns that translate into new understandings and viable predictions. Companies thus try to use data mining to discover relationships between data and phenomena that ordinary operations and routine analysis would otherwise overlook, and thereby identify squandered opportunity, redundancy, and waste.

Data mining combines features of various disciplines, particularly computer science, database management, and statistics, to map low-level data into more advanced and meaningful forms. In its truest form, data mining is part of the broader knowledge discovery from data (KDD) process, although the terms are often used interchangeably. KDD refers to the entire process of data warehousing, organization, cleansing, analysis, and interpretation. Colloquially, however, data mining stands for this entire process of deriving useful knowledge, using computational systems, from massive amounts of data.

Data-mining software systems are generally based on a combination of mathematical algorithms designed to seek out and organize information by variables and relationships. For instance, one common algorithm is called recursive partitioning regression (RPR). RPR processes all the variables chosen for a particular set of data and parses them for their explanatory power, that is, for the degree to which they account for variations in the data. In sifting through customer profiles, for example, the algorithm would isolate information such as personal incomes, education levels, sex, and so on.

The data-mining process is divided into three stages: data preparation, data processing, and data analysis. In the first stage, the data to be mined is selected and cleared of superfluous elements in order to streamline mining. In the second stage, the data is run through the algorithms at the heart of data mining, and characteristics and variables are identified and categorized, thereby transforming the data into broader, more meaningful pieces of information. In the final stage, the extracted information is analyzed for useful knowledge that can be applied to a business strategy.

Data-mining software was first developed in the late 1960s and 1970s as a way of tracking consumer-purchasing habits. Over the years, the application of data mining extended beyond retail to encompass larger-scale business practices, and was combined with advances in database management, artificial intelligence, computers, and telecommunications to constitute extremely powerful tools for knowledge extraction.

Traditionally, data mining was used primarily for categorized information; in other words, techniques and tools were designed to find relationships and patterns in masses of data that were already segmented into different categories via structured databases, such as a customer's age and residence. Later techniques greatly expanded the power of data mining by allowing for mining of unstructured text documents, such as e-mails, customer requests, and Web pages. In this way, data mining applies structure to loosely organized data, and highlights valuable information that might otherwise be missed. Moreover, this allows for the relevant extraction of information from documents that were assembled for any purpose, rather than specifically for the issue at hand, thereby increasing the efficiency of data flow and preventing the waste of potentially valuable information. This technique, known as text mining, creates a database of words that can be categorized and a sophisticated search engine to seek out those words and related alternatives.

Many times the first step toward data mining is building a data warehouse, or a vast electronic database to contain and organize the wealth of information collected. Without a data warehouse, companies lack the infrastructure to mine useful knowledge out of the data available. Like word processing programs and computer operating systems, data mining has grown more user-friendly and graphics-based as its application has spreads throughout society to less technically inclined users. Software programs increasingly feature visualization techniques to dramatize specified data, relationships, and patterns.

Data mining has become a crucial component of customer management. The most common form of data mining begins with the accumulation of various kinds of customer profiles. These can take the form of simple names and addresses derived from other firms' customer lists and used for purposes of mass mailing, or they can constitute more sophisticated and comprehensive reports on consumer tastes and buying habits. Over time, firms amass great quantities of customer profiles through their own sales and through arrangements with other firms, and apply data-mining techniques to sift through them for clues as to how to adjust their strategies.

Whether to attract, service, or maintain customers, businesses position data mining at the cornerstone of customer relations. Using advanced data mining techniques, companies can determine what level of spending can be expected from a particular customer, the range of his or her tastes, the customer's likeliness to churn, and a range of other information useful for customer relations. In these ways, companies are better able to assess the value of its individual customers, and adjust its resources accordingly. More broadly, they can derive comprehensive information on demographic patterns, like distinctions in purchasing patterns between age groups, income levels, and ethnic backgrounds, to discover additional retention and cross-selling possibilities. In this way they can seg-

ment their customer bases into specialized marketing focuses. By shifting outreach, advertising, and service resources to effectively capitalize on their diverse clientele, firms can realize cost savings, better conversion rates, and higher margins.

In the e-commerce world, data mining carries an additional range of benefits. In particular, as e-commerce merchants worked to create the maximum amount of value out of what the Web has to offer, they moved to personalize products and services. The extraction of personal information allowed by data mining greatly facilitated this process. By plugging data-mining analysis into customer-service databases and their Web applications, companies can tailor products and services to accord with individual customers' habits and preferences, thereby maximizing value.

Companies use such technology to mine data from within their own ranks as well. Company computer systems and intranets were increasingly searched as a method of retrieving information on key subjects that may have passed between employees at an earlier date, via email transmissions, word processor files, and Web page searches. In addition to harnessing the knowledge buried in these communications, sifting software can also be used to evaluate employees' strengths and weaknesses over a period of time for a comprehensive assessment of the employee's performance. However, while such techniques are attractive to companies, they make privacy advocates nervous with their implications for the retrieval of personal communications and their possible review out of context.

The software industry responsible for data-mining programs was enjoying solid sales growth, which was expected to remain brisk in the early 2000s. The market research firm International Data Corp. estimated that the market for analytic application software would grow from $1.9 billion worldwide in 1999 to $5.2 billion in 2003, while specifically data mining applications from $343 million in 1999 to $1.4 billion in 2004.

Meanwhile, more and more of the world's leading businesses were implementing data mining into their core operations in one way or another. Companies may perform data mining and analysis internally or outsource the job to the growing number of data mining solutions providers. Forrester Research reported that the percentage of Fortune 1,000 firms that planned to incorporate data mining into their marketing strategies grew from 18 percent in 1999 to 52 percent in 2001. Forrester's findings also indicated that the most successful applications of data mining were realized by those firms that most thoroughly embedded data mining into their daily operations.

FURTHER READING:

Cahlink, George. "Data Mining Taps the Trends." *Government Executive,* October, 2000.

Drew, James H., D.R. Mani, Andrew L. Betz, and Piew Datta. "Targeting Customers with Statistical and Data-Mining Techniques." *Journal of Service Research,* February, 2001.

Fielden, Tim. "Text-Mining Promises to Cull Answers from Random Text." *InfoWorld,* October 16, 2001.

Le Beau, Christina. "Mountains to Mine." *American Demographics,* August, 2000.

Lesser, Eric, David Mundel, and Charles Wiecha. "Managing Customer Knowledge." *Journal of Business Strategy,* November/December, 2000.

Liddy, Elizabeth D. "Text Mining." *Bulletin of the American Society for Information Science,* October/November, 2000.

Masi, C.G. "Data Mining Can Tame Mountains of Information." *Research & Development,* November, 2000.

Murphy, Victoria. "You've Got Expertise." *Forbes,* February 5, 2001.

Ruquest, Mark E. "Planning is Key to Exploiting Technical Data." *National Underwriter,* November 27, 2000.

Sullivan, Tom. "Picture This: Data Analysis Becomes More Graphic." *InfoWorld,* October 16, 2000.

SEE ALSO: Customer Relationship Management (CRM); Database Management

DATA WAREHOUSING

Data warehousing refers to the organization and assembly of data created from day-to-day business operations. Data warehousing enables a user to retrieve data from online transaction processing (OLTP) and online analytical processing (OLAP), and allows for the storage of that data in a format that can be read and analyzed. The integrated information, which is stored in a data warehouse, can be analyzed and queried to help management make more informed business decisions.

The idea of data warehousing dates back to the early 1980s. At that time, a popular system that utilized the concept of data warehousing was the relational database, which was run on minicomputers and used for OLTP functions. Quite often, relational database systems operated networks such as automated teller machines. As technology continued to advance, several key factors—including changing business trends, the evolution of the global economy, enterprise resource planning (ERP), business process reengineering (BPR), increased focus on customer needs, and the rise of e-business—led to the development of data warehouses in the 1990s.

Run on powerful client/server networks, not only can data warehouses read OLTP, they are equipped to translate OLAP as well. The development of data warehousing enabled companies to gather several types of information concerning business transactions, as well as important analytical data. In *Contract Professional Magazine,* Pam Derringer wrote that as a knowledge tool, "data warehousing restructures massive volumes of unorganized data into new formats that can be queried for answers to individual questions or sliced and diced for analytical trend reports."

Two important types of information in data warehousing are operational and informational data. Operational data—the data businesses use on a day-to-day basis—is stored, retrieved, and updated by an OLTP system. This type of data normally is stored in a relational database. Informational data is operational data that has been manipulated and summarized, and is what makes up a data warehouse. In the process of data warehousing, informational data is created from operational data and systems by using transformation or propagation tools. This process is necessary to ensure that the information can be retrieved in an easy and time-efficient manner. Multidimensional analysis, or OLAP, is the desired result of data warehousing. It allows a user to analyze large amounts of data regarding things like sales, products, time periods, and geographies. The multidimensional data structure, or data warehouse, allows for the storing and analyzing of such data.

Another component to data warehousing is metadata, which is made up of technical data and business data. Technical data is used by system administrators and contains information about the data warehouse itself. Business data, on the other hand, is what an analyst might be searching for in order to forecast sales or predict trends. Data mining tools are then used to interpret data and find patterns within the information. For example, a retail company might use data warehousing and data mining to find relationships in purchasing patterns and to gather information about its customers.

Implementing a data warehouse structure within a company can be a costly and time-intensive process. These barriers have led to the development of data marts—smaller versions of data warehouses that are more specialized to serve a specific department and/or cover a specific topic. Traditional data warehouses are measured in gigabytes and terabytes, whereas the more compact data marts are measured in megabytes. Smaller companies, with more limited budgets, often opt for this type of data structure.

With the rise of e-commerce, data warehousing is becoming a key business component in the operation of both brick-and-mortar companies as well as dot-com ventures. The evolution of customer relationship management (CRM), the increasing popularity of the Internet, and the formation of online marketplaces and business-to-consumer companies such as Amazon.com and other e-tailers, have increased the demand for data warehousing solutions. While implementing data warehousing can be very costly, a study conducted by International Data Corp. concluded that firms utilizing data warehouse systems saw an average return on investment of nearly 400 percent over three years. Each year, as the billions of dollars spent online for products and services increases, businesses are turning to advanced data management solutions to analyze information, make forecasts, look for trends, identify shopper characteristics, and control inventory. This has increased the demand for data warehousing and, therefore, increased competition between solution-based companies. According to *DM Review,* the top ten business intelligence vendors—those offering e-business, CRM, and data warehousing solutions—at the advent of the twenty-first century were SAS, NCR Corp., Oracle Corp., Computer Associates, Cognos Corp., MicroStrategy Inc., Microsoft Corp., IBM, Informix Business Solutions, and Hyperion.

FURTHER READING:

"2000 DM Review 100 Numerical Ranking." *DM Review.* November 2001. Available from www.dmreview.com/awards/top100/2000.

"Data Warehousing Concepts for AS/400." Armonk, NY: IBM Corp., 2000. Available from www-1.ibm.com.htm.

Derringer, Pam. "Data Warehousing: The Next Boom?" *Contract Professional Magazine.* 2000. Available from www.freeagent.com.

Eckerson, Wayne W. "Ten Rules for Building an Intelligent Business for the E-World." Seattle, WA: The Data Warehousing Institute, 2000. Available from www.dw-institute.com/resourceguide2000.

Moye, Joe, and Dave Upton. "Data Warehousing 101." *Strategic Finance.* February, 2001.

Schroeck, Michael. "Data Warehousing: The Past 10 Years Have Been Quite a Ride." *DM Review.* February, 2001. Available from www.dmreview.com.

SEE ALSO: Data Mining; Database Management; Information Management Systems

DATABASE MANAGEMENT

Database management refers to the process of storing and manipulating the information housed in a database. Databases can be as simple as the electronic address books used by individuals to keep track of e-mail recipients or as complex as electronic library systems or online flight reservation systems. Typically, some sort of query system allows users to gain access to specific information in a database. For example, electronic library systems often are designed to accept queries such as "a = author name," "t = title," and "s = subject." Therefore, the query "title = War and Peace" would retrieve all database entries which contained "War and Peace" in the title field. The tools used to actually manage databases are grouped together into database management systems (DBMSs). Several types of DBMSs exist, including those designed for personal computers (PCs), as well as those running on large mainframe systems.

HISTORY OF DATABASE MANAGEMENT

Although various rudimentary DBMSs had been in use prior to IBM Corp.'s release of Information Management System (IMS) in 1966, IMS was the first commercially available DBMS. IMS was considered a hierarchical database, in which standardized data records were organized within other standardized data records, creating a hierarchy of information about a single entry. In the late 1960s, firms like Honeywell Corp. and General Electric Corp. developed DBMSs based on a network data model, but the next major database management breakthrough came in 1970 when a research scientist at IBM first outlined his theory for relational databases. Six years later, IBM completed a prototype for a relational DBMS.

In 1977, computer programmers Larry Ellison and Robert Miner co-founded Oracle Systems Corp. Their combined experience designing specialized database programs for governmental organizations landed the partners a $50,000 contract from the Central Intelligence Agency (CIA) to develop a customized database program. While working on the CIA project, Ellison and Miner became interested in IBM's efforts to develop a relational database, which involved Structured Query Language (SQL). Recognizing that SQL would allow computer users to retrieve data from a variety of sources and sensing that SQL would become a database industry standard, Ellison and Miner began working on developing a program similar to the relational DBMS being developed by IBM. In 1978, Oracle released its own relational DBMS, the world's first relational database management system (RDBMS) using SQL. Oracle began shipping its RDBMS the following year, nearly two years before IBM shipped its first version of DB2, which would become a leading RDBMS competing with the database management applications of industry giants like Microsoft Corp. and Oracle. Relational databases eventually outpaced all other database types, mainly because they allowed for highly complex queries and could support various tools which enhanced their usefulness.

In 1983, Oracle developed the first portable RDBMS, which allowed firms to run their DBMS on various machines including mainframes, workstations, and personal computers. Soon thereafter, the firm also launched a distributed DBMS, based on SQL-Star software, which granted users the same kind of access to data stored on a network they would have if the data were housed in a single computer. By the end of the decade, Oracle had grown into the world's leading enterprise DBMS provider with more than $100 million in sales.

It wasn't long before DBMSs were developed for use on individual PCs. In 1993, Microsoft Corp. created an application called Access. The program competed with FileMaker Inc.'s FileMaker Pro, a database application initially designed for Macintosh machines.

IMPACT OF THE INTERNET ON DATABASE MANAGEMENT TECHNOLOGY

As stated by Uche Ogbuji in a July 2001 study of various DBMSs, "The database community is one of the oldest in the computer world, and it is almost as famous as the application programming community for the diversity of its ideas and the sharpness of the debates between its gurus. Lately events have conspired to expose these concerns to a wider audience. For instance, the seemingly inexhaustible march of the Web revolution has exposed more and more developers to database issues because of the desire for ever more dynamic Web sites." In fact, the rise of the Internet prompted the development of many new database management system features. These were designed to enable clients to take advantage of Internet-based opportunities such as e-commerce, which emerged in the late 1990s.

Database management giants like Oracle had begun tailoring their products to the Internet in the mid-1990s. For example, the firm's Web-enabled Oracle Express Server 6.0, launched in 1996, offered online data analysis functionality on both the Internet and corporate intranets. Oracle began to restructure itself around its Internet operations in 1998 when it released Oracle 8i, a version of its flagship database management product that allowed firms to manage all of their database functions on the Web. Oracle continued to develop new Internet-based technology in 2000. In May, the firm launched its E-Business Suite, as well as the Oracle 9i DBMS, which included an application server allowing users to run e-commerce applications related to their databases. The new product also offered file and document management, e-mail, Web server, and message queuing features.

By then, both Microsoft and IBM had begun to pay more attention to the DBMS market, recognizing its importance to the increasingly Web-based information technology industry. Microsoft began discussing plans to upgrade its SQL Server to support extensible markup language (XML), the language used to create Web documents, in 1997. According to an October 2000 article in *InformationWeek,* "XML is one of the primary areas that all the major database vendors have scrambled to embrace. Why is XML so important? XML facilitates communications between systems that normally don't speak the same language. Because of its self-describing nature, XML provides a way to pass information between dissimilar systems with some level of confidence that it will be properly interpreted on the other end. Direct XML support in the database means there is no need for any other tool to translate data from an external provider into something that can be used immediately." As a result, XML support, which included the ability to store, manage, index and search XML documents, was seen as increasingly necessary for DBMSs. Microsoft also wanted to be able to back up, restore, and reproduce XML applications. However, several delays kept the firm from offering these features until the release of SQL Server 2000 in mid-2000, well after both Oracle and IBM had added XML support to their databases.

Despite its delayed release, the new product boosted the firm's database management sales by roughly 45 percent, allowing it to gain crucial market share points. Microsoft also revealed its intent to include scale clustering—which would offer the increased processing and storage capabilities needed for e-commerce applications—in its 2001 release of SQL Server. During 2000, Microsoft increased its DBMS market share from 13.1 percent to 14.9 percent, while industry leader Oracle increased its share from 31.4 percent to 33.8 percent. Third place IBM gained less than one percent, growing its share from 29.9 percent to 30.1 percent.

IBM had upgraded its DB2 system in 1999 with features designed to facilitate e-business. Late in the year, the firm made the DB2 XML Extender, which added XML support to DB2, available for free to DB2 customers via a download. IBM shipped version 7.1 of DB2 in October of 2000. Designed to facilitate e-business operations, DB2 7.1 included a Net Search Extender tool, which offered high-speed Internet index searching and data warehousing capabilities. Early in 2001, IBM paid $1 billion for rival Informix Corp., which had begun adding XML support to its Internet Foundation DBMS in October of 1999. Along with bolstering IBM's database management offerings, gaining access to the 100,000 Informix clients also boosted IBM's market share. Many analysts predict that the rivalry between IBM, Oracle, and Microsoft will only intensify as each firm scrambles to added increased functionality to its line of DBMS products.

FURTHER READING:

Ferrill, Paul. "Databases That Focus on the Net." *Information-Week.* October 9, 2000.

"IBM vs. Oracle: It Could Get Bloody." *BusinessWeek Online.* May 28, 2001. Available from www.businessweek.com.

Korzeniowski, Paul. "Microsoft Delivers Knockout Punch." *VARbusiness.* October 1, 2001.

Ogbuji, Uche. "Choosing a Database Management System." July 2001. Available from www-106.ibm.com.

Ricadela, Aaron and Rick Whiting. "Microsoft Introduces SQL Server 2000." *InformationWeek.* December 20, 1999.

Seben, Larry. "Big 3 Square Off in Database Wars." *CRMDaily.com.* May 23, 2001. Available from www.CRMDaily.com.

SEE ALSO: Data Mining; Data Warehousing; Ellison, Lawrence J. (Larry); IBM Inc.; Information Management Systems; Microsoft Corp.; Oracle Corp.

DATEK ONLINE BROKERAGE SERVICES LLC

Datek Online was launched in June 1996 as an online trading firm. Founded by Jeffrey Citron and Peter Stern, the firm quickly grew to become one of the online trading industry's largest, with more than 640,000 customer accounts and nearly 100,000 trades per day. Among its products and services are online equity trading, option trading, mutual funds, IRAs, real-time quotes, level II quotes, extended-hours trading, margin trading, payment for order flow, Datek Direct, and decimalized trading. The company operates as a division of Datek Online Holdings Corp., which also acts as a parent company for iClearing LLC, BigThink, and Watcher Technologies LLC.

Jeffrey Citron's career in the trading industry began after he graduated from high school in 1988 and went to work for what was then called Datek Securities Corp. That same year, the NASDAQ introduced the Small Order Execution System (SOES), which forced market makers—firms that continually buy and sell particular stocks at listed prices—to execute electronically placed orders of up to 500 shares at whatever price was posted. Citron, originally hired as an office boy, manipulated the computer system at the New Jersey-based firm, enabling it to spot when a posted price was different from actual market value. Traders at Datek began to reap the financial rewards of catching market makers off guard by taking advantage of the posted listings that had not been updated. While many Datek traders eventually were fined and banned from the brokerage industry for unethical business practices, Citron's career in the electronic trading industry with Datek was just beginning.

In 1995, the technological entrepreneur teamed up with Peter Stern to take advantage of the burgeoning online trading industry. The twosome created Datek Online as a division of Datek Securities. Competing with the likes of E*Trade Group and Lombard Brokerage Inc., the company began enticing day traders with a low commission fee of $9.99 per trade. Soon after its inception, Citron and Stern teamed up with Levine to develop the Island Electronic Communications Network (ECN), a private financial trading technology platform that enabled Datek to offer fast order execution time. Island ECN operated as a separate entity from Datek, and its popularity grew throughout the industry. By 2001, the trading system served more than 500 subscribers and executed one out of every six trades on the NASDAQ.

Along with the creation of the Island ECN, Datek made key contributions to the development of online trading. Considered a pioneer in the industry, Datek was the first online brokerage to offer free real-time streaming quotes. It also was among the first to offer real-time account portfolio updates and account balance information to its customers. Additionally, the firm's execution speed was considered to be among the best, and the company backed it with a 60-second guarantee that ensured orders would be placed in a timely fashion. If the order took more than one minute, the commission fee was waived.

As the popularity of online trading continued to grow, Datek remained focused on introducing innovative concepts in an attempt to lure new customers. In July 1999, the firm became the first to offer extended-hours trading sessions. This enabled members to trade NASDAQ securities from 8 a.m. to 8 p.m. In July 2000, Datek also became the first online firm to offer decimal-based trading, a dramatic change from the traditional fractional system. This new cost-effective method of trading allowed customers to buy and sell stocks using one-cent increments. Datek Direct also launched in 2000 and was the first browser-based product that enabled investors to select the market maker or ECN of their choice, including the Island system. This new product gave investors more control over their orders.

Datek's innovative approach to online trading also led to top industry recognition. The company was ranked number one for frequent traders and new investors by *Money Magazine* in June 2000. That same year it was named one of the "Best of the Web" by *Forbes,* rated number one for the third year in a row in the Online Broker Survey 2000 by *TheStreet.com,* and named the top online broker by *PC Computing.* Stern and Levine also received industry recognition and were named two of the top 10 financial technology innovators of the decade by *Wall Street and Technology.*

While Datek Online quickly became one of the top players in the online trading industry, its parent company experienced some turbulence along the way. In 1995, Datek Securities cancelled an IPO due to a Securities and Exchange Commission (SEC) investigation into its trading operations. The company's questionable image, dating back to the SOES scandal and controversy over Citron's involvement, led to a corporate restructuring in 1998 when holding company Datek Online Holdings Corp. was formed. In 1999, Citron relinquished his CEO and chairman position and Edward J. Nicoll took over. Citron left the firm in hopes that his departure would brighten Datek's somewhat tarnished image.

In a move to strengthen its online trading arm, Datek Online Holdings Corp. announced a $700 million private equity investment by Bain Capital, TA Associates, and Silver Lake Partners in December 2000. As part of the deal, the holding firm gained control of all voting shares held by the original founders of Datek Online, and Island ECN was spun off as an independent firm. Steve Pagliuca of Bain Capital stated in a December 2000 company press release that, as a result of the deal, "Datek has the technology and the resources to build on its current position as a leader in the online investment field and to elevate the standards for serving retail investors."

The NASDAQ experienced the largest one-year drop in its history in 2000, and many Dow Jones Industrial Average stocks posted losses. While the market remained unstable into 2001, Datek pledged to continue developing innovative products and services that would keep its online trading customers informed of market conditions. As part of its plan, Datek announced a strategic partnership with MarketWatch.com, a leading Internet provider of financial news and information. The March 2001 deal enabled Datek customers to access CBS MarketWatch.com's financial news and real-time headlines via Datek's News Center.

FURTHER READING:

"About Datek." Iselin, NJ: Datek Online Holdings Corp., 2001. Available from datek.com.

Barnett, Megan. "Valuation Issues Stall ECN Deal." *The Industry Standard.* October 8, 1999. Available from www.thestandard.com.

"Datek Online Holdings Completes Strategic Transaction." *PR Newswire.* December 18, 2000.

"Datek Online Launches Financial News and Tools Content From MarketWatch.com." *PR Newswire.* March 20, 2001.

Deck, Stewart, L. "The Exchanging of the Guard." *Computerworld.* October 7, 1996.

"Edward J. Nicoll Named Chairman and CEO of Datek Online." *PR Newswire.* October 6, 1999.

Weisul, Kimberly. "Upstart Datek Starts Looking Conventional." *Investment Dealers' Digest.* February 9, 1998.

SEE ALSO: Day Trading; Electronic Communications Networks (ECNs); E*Trade Group Inc.; Island ECN

DAY TRADING

As one of the new economy's most popular pastimes, day trading generated intense emotions from supporters and detractors alike, and the practice was the source of much controversy. Sometimes referred to with derision as "recreational trading," day trading is a form of stock market activity in which investors, known as day traders, make blitzkrieg runs on several stocks for the purpose of generating very quick gains, but without an eye toward long-term returns. The logic behind day trading holds that the rapid buying and selling of securities in response to very incremental movements can generate quick profits that result in tremendous savings over time.

The practice is premised on the idea of that markets aren't completely efficient. Therefore, small profits can be made by trading in expectation of tiny, incremental movements in stock. Day traders move in to capitalize on the market's corrections. Repeated often enough, these small transactions can escalate into hefty profits by the end of a day's trading, at which point day traders generally liquidate their entire portfolios. Since companies may issue announcements and company news after a day's trading has closed, day traders don't generally want to hold onto stocks overnight, since their line of work entails making split-second buy and sell orders before others can beat them to it.

Day trading requires a nose for minute stock movements, keen trend-spotting skills, and a ready mouse-click. However, professional day traders also rely on tools like sophisticated analysis software and charting programs and a steady stream of financial news. Many online financial portals and content sites feature real-time stock quotes, and some provide charting and chart-customization services. Some electronic trading systems are capable of performing what are known as basket trades, in which several hundred securities are bought and sold in a single transaction. These systems were tailor-made for the day-trading world, in which traders frequently buy and sell thousands of stocks in a single day, and were particularly useful for the big, end-of-the-day liquidations.

DAY TRADING'S ROLLER-COASTER RIDE

Day trading, in its present form, got its start in the early 1990s, according to *Institutional Investor,* when a New Yorker named Harvey Houtkin began monitoring the delays between breaking news events and the adjustment of prices by certain dealers. Using the Nasdaq's Small Order Execution System, Houtkin made a name for himself by exploiting those delays to make a profit. By doing so, he opened the floodgates to hordes of new independent traders making connections to exchanges. In addition, these activities engendered the momentum that would evolve into the e-brokerage boom and the emergence of new trading media like electronic communications networks (ECNs).

Day trading made a splash in the late 1990s as the U.S. bull market seemed to defy gravity and news accounts lauded the new economy. Additionally, the Internet opened new lines of business and gave birth to the dot-com stock craze while also lowering the costs of trading. All of these factors enticed new entrants into the field of stock trading. In order to compete with the traditional Nasdaq market makers without paying hefty, profit-reducing fees, day traders began to create their own electronic trading networks, such as Island ECN, to provide a space for buyers and sellers to trade and share real-time market information. As day trading grew more mainstream, the major online trading houses increasingly assumed the capabilities of the larger brokerages. They developed the technological means to simultaneously scan several securities markets, locate the best prices on given securities, and then purchase them instantaneously.

The day-trading binge was cradled by the can't-miss buzz surrounding dot-com stocks in the late 1990s. Paradoxically, this was a buzz that day trading helped to sustain. The most sensational stories told of middle-level office workers making millions by trading on their lunch breaks, or quitting their jobs to trade full time and retire at age 30.

In all, however, the hype surrounding day trading tended to inflate individuals' expectations, often to drastic effects. While there was, indeed, no shortage of success stories, they were in fact an unrepresentative sample. The North American Securities Administrators Association (NASAA) reported in 1999 that 77 percent of all day traders wound up losing money, while the average profit of the winners was a mere $22,000 over a period of eight months. This was a far cry from the instant-success stories in which mechanics were able to retire after a few months' trading. The dizziness of the cultural phenomenon reached its most harrowing moment in July 1999, when a distraught day trader, having lost some $100,000, murdered his wife and children before wandering into two Atlanta day-trading offices—at which he had placed orders—with a gun, killing nine workers and himself. This horrifying event greatly exacerbated the growing backlash against day trading.

Day trading emerged as a fear among employers as well. With more and more workers secluded in offices or cubicles with their own computers and Internet access, the temptation to engage in day trading on company time was a source of growing concern. To stave off such slacking, companies resorted to installing Universal Resource Locator (URL)-filtering software on company machines, designed to lock employees out of selected sites or domain names.

Day trading eventually became nearly synonymous with the high-stakes excesses of the glorified bull market, while emerging as one of the primary forces driving the market's wild volatility in the late 1990s and early 2000s. On the other hand, it also was indicative of the wider democratization of the once exclusive world of Wall Street trading, and enhanced the market populism that became such a central part of U.S. culture in this period. In 2000, the NASAA reported that a whopping 7.5 million Americans maintained 7.5 million online brokerage accounts, while the Electronic Traders Association estimated between 5,000 and 10,000 investors placed orders through specialty day-trading houses.

Following the dot-com and tech-market bust in spring 2000, day trading was widely seen as a passing fad, and in large part the novelty was just that. But day trading never went away completely and by 2001 the practice was not only still alive but, by some estimates, healthier than ever, according to *Fortune*. While the field underwent a shakeout similar to that of the dot-com economy, meaning that the casual part-timers were largely forced out of the field, the ranks of professional day traders stabilized at about 50,000 nationwide. Bear Stearns reported that, while the market registered a 37-percent decline in 2000 in the volume of trading by occasional day traders—those making 15 to 40 transactions annually—day trading as a whole increased its volume by 55 percent.

As of 2001, the future of some major online brokerages looked murky. This especially was true for those firms, such as Ameritrade and E*Trade, for which occasional trading constituted the cornerstone of their business. Such firms poured vast sums into marketing in the early 2000s in efforts to maintain the footholds they'd acquired, and were likewise seeking to branch out in order to stay afloat, diversifying away from an increasingly risky market.

Day trading washed up on European shores several years after it dominated American business headlines. However, with it came the lessons of the American phenomenon. As a result, day trading was expected to take hold more slowly and more subtly than it had in the United States.

THE IMPACT OF DAY TRADING

Day trading brought mounds of new money into the market. Moreover, this was money managed not by the traditional blue-chip investors or fund managers, but those looking to enter and exit a market quickly with only a short-term gain in mind. As a result, day trading was largely responsible for the wild day-to-day fluctuations in stock markets, particularly the Nasdaq, in the late 1990s and early 2000s. In effect, day trading altered the traditional theories about how markets work by dramatically boosting the degree of market volatility and transforming perceptions of risk exposure.

Among professional money managers, day trading was widely perceived as a form of gambling engaged in by uninformed amateurs. Still, this didn't always lead to calls for the abandonment of the practice. Gregory J. Millman, writing in the investment journal *Barron's,* compared day traders to a swarm of maggots, insisting that, while they may be loathsome, day traders do a good job of eating away at the market's ''diseased tissue,'' those ''inefficiencies that slow and sicken markets.''

Such statements, though harboring much of the animosity still felt by traditional investment analysts, nevertheless reflect the general sentiment prevailing in the early 2000s that day-trading's existence was more or less accepted. Whatever one's feelings about the practice, day trading grew into such a force that, by the 2000s, investors of all stripes had little choice but to take day trading seriously, as its effects couldn't be denied. More positively, it was a growing source of income.

FURTHER READING:

Dunlap, Charlotte. ''The 1999 Top 25 Executives: The Day Trader.'' *Computer Reseller News.* November 15, 1999.

Futrelle, David. ''Let Us Now Praise the Day Traders.'' *Money.* October 1999.

Granitsas, Alkman. ''Risky Business.'' *Far Eastern Economic Review.* April 13, 2000.

Maiello, Michael. ''Day Trading Eldorado.'' *Forbes.* June 12, 2000.

McEachern, Cristina. ''Will Day Trading Face Scrutiny?'' *Wall Street & Technology.* October 1999.

McNamee, Mike. ''How to Build Your Own Trading Desk.'' *Business Week.* May 22, 2000.

Millman, Gregory J. ''The Dawn of European Day Trading.'' *Institutional Investor.* December 2000.

———. ''Maggot Therapy.'' *Barron's.* January 31, 2000.

Nathans Spiro, Leah. ''Day Trading is a Sucker's Game.'' *Business Week.* August 16, 1999.

Schack, Justin. ''The Next Leap in Trading Technology.'' *Institutional Investor.* June 2000.

Schwartz, Nelson D. ''Can't Keep a Good Day Trader Down.'' *Fortune.* February 19, 2001.

———. ''Meet the New Market Makers.'' *Fortune,* February 21, 2000.

SEE ALSO: Ameritrade Holding Corp.; Electronic Communications Networks (ECNs); E*Trade Group Inc.; New Economy; Volatility

DELL, MICHAEL

Michael S. Dell is the founder, CEO, and chairman of Dell Computer Corp., the largest personal computer (PC) vendor in the world and also the leading commercial seller of PCs via the Internet. Dell has served his firm—which boasted sales in excess of $32 billion and employed more than 38,000 individuals in early 2001—as CEO since its inception in 1984. His stint is the lengthiest of any CEO at a leading American computer firm. While PCs, half of which are sold on the Internet, account for roughly 55 percent of sales, Dell has worked to move his firm into the more lucrative Internet-based server and storage markets since the late 1990s. He retains a 12-percent stake in the company.

While a student at the University of Texas, Dell began selling IBM compatible computers from his dorm room. He bought parts at wholesale prices, constructed the machines on his own, and sold them to bargain PC shoppers. The success of his venture prompted Dell to quit school in April of 1984 and establish his own business, Dell Computer Corp., with $1,000 in capital. Dell advertised his low-cost custom built PCs in computer magazines, targeting savvy PCs users. Customers were able to call an 800 number to places orders, and Dell shipped completed PCs directly to customers. What set Dell's firm apart from competitors was his practice of direct selling. The elimination of middlemen allowed Dell to price his computers well below market prices.

To facilitate his firm's rapid growth, Dell hired investment banking executive E. Lee Walker as president in 1986. The following year, he launched an expansion of manufacturing facilities and developed a national customer support center. Dell also began offering on-site services for Dell products. International expansion was initiated by the creation of an office in the United Kingdom. The firm also published a catalog for the first time and expanded its sales force. In 1988 Dell completed a reorganization that was designed to facilitate improved customer service. New PC launches included 100, 200, and 310 models. That year, Dell took his company public, offering 3.5 million shares at $8.50 each. Dell's firm also began offering leasing options to customers and furthered international expansion by establishing units in Canada and West Germany. In 1989, Dell became one of the first firms to license the UNIX trademark from

AT&T Corp. The firm also began selling several new Epson dot matrix printer models and opened a unit in France. Record sales were marred by a 64-percent plunge in earnings, which Dell blamed on higher costs and an inventory glut.

Early in the 1990s, Dell intensified international expansion, overseeing the establishment of various operations in Ireland, Italy, Sweden, Poland, the Czech Republic, Belgium, Finland, Spain, Norway, Luxembourg, the Netherlands, and Mexico. Dell was the first personal computer manufacturer to offer applications software installation as a free standard service option. Copycat competitor Gateway 2000 usurped Dell as the top direct seller of PCs in the U.S. in 1992. To express his determination to reduce expenses at his firm, Dell reduced his pay by five percent.

Sales exceeded $2 billion in the mid-1990s. By then, Dell had grown into the world's sixth-largest desktop PC maker and seventh-largest notebook PC maker. The firm's success was due in large part to its ability to use the Internet to take and fill customers orders quickly and inexpensively. According to a May 2001 *BusinessWeek Online* article, "Michael Dell was e-business before e-business was cool. During the boom in technology spending, he used the Internet to reach out to customers and sell $50 million worth of computers a day." Dell's business model, which allowed for easy tracking of customer purchases, also allowed the firm to keep inventory at a minimum.

Wanting to reduce his company's reliance on PCs—which were being discounted by many rivals—Dell pushed his firm into the server market in 1996. Within two years, servers accounted for 16 percent of the company's $12 billion revenue, and within three years, Dell was second only to Compaq Computer Corp. in U.S. server sales. In 1999, when competitors began cutting PC prices further, Dell responded with its first PC under $1,000. That year, *Business Week* listed Dell among its top 25 managers for the third consecutive year. Stock grew roughly 140 percent, a rate it had maintained for the past four years.

As the PC market slowed in 2000, Dell began working to reposition his firm as a provider of Internet technology, focusing on servers and storage systems similar to those offered by Sun Microsystems Inc. The firm also began offering various Internet services such as Web hosting and wireless access to the Internet. Sales growth slowed nearly 10 percent to 38.5 percent, and stock prices began to falter, prompting Dell to reduce his bonus by 36 percent. Despite these troubles, Dell dethroned Compaq Computer as the leader in PC sales in April of 2001. That year, *Chief Executive* magazine named Dell CEO of the Year, adding to his list of previous awards, which included *PC* magazine's Man of the Year and *Inc.* magazine's Entrepreneur of the Year.

FURTHER READING:

"Can Michael Dell Escape the Box?" *Fortune*. October 16, 2000.

"Dell Computer Corp." In *Notable Corporate Chronologies*. Farmington Hills, MI: Gale Group, 1999.

"Michael Dell." *BusinessWeek Online*. May 14, 2001. Available from www.businessweek.com.

"Michael S. Dell." Round Rock, TX: Dell Computer Corp., 2001. Available from www.dell.com.

"A Revolution of One—Face Value: Michael Dell, A Lone Revolutionary." *The Economist*. April 14, 2001.

Shook, David. "The Winner of the PC Price Wars: Dell." *BusinessWeek Online*. May 1, 2001. Available from www.businessweek.com.

SEE ALSO: Dell Computer

DELL COMPUTER CORP.

Dell Computer Corp. is the largest personal computer (PC) vendor in the world, a position it has held since April 2001 when it usurped Compaq Computer Corp. The firm also is the leading seller of PCs via the Internet, a medium that accounts for more than half of Dell's PC sales. In 2000, total revenues reached roughly $32 billion, and employees exceeded 38,000. Although PCs account for roughly 55 percent of Dell's total annual sales, a late-1990s push into the Internet-based server and storage markets has started to pay off for the firm, which now is second only to Compaq in U.S. server sales. *Fortune* magazine ranked Dell 10th on its list of "Most Admired Companies" in 2001.

EARLY HISTORY

University of Texas freshman Michael S. Dell began selling IBM-compatible computers from his dorm room in 1984. Using parts he purchased at wholesale prices, Dell built the machines to closely resemble IBM models and then sold them to PC users looking to avoid the prices typically charged by computer retailers. Realizing that the $80,000 per month he brought in could easily be transformed into a full-fledged business, Dell left school and founded Dell Computer Corp. in April of 1984. Believing that more experienced computer users would likely recognize the value his custom-built machines offered, Dell began placing advertisements in computer magazines. Customers used an 800 number to places orders that Dell would ship via mail upon completion. Dell used no middleman, and the firm's direct sales model allowed it to price machines significantly lower than competing PC vendors.

Dell quickly found itself a leader in mail order PC sales. Revenues of $6 million in 1985 ballooned to nearly $40 million the following year. Realizing that he needed help managing the company's growth, Dell recruited several marketing managers from competitor Tandy Corp., as well as investment banker E. Lee Walker to serve as president. Dell himself served as CEO. In 1987, Dell began expanding its manufacturing facilities. The firm also created a national customer support center and started offering on-site setup, maintenance, and repair services for Dell products. An office in the United Kingdom marked the firm's initial foray into international sales. Dell also published its first catalog.

The firm's new marketing team began peddling Dell products to larger businesses. It also expanded Dell's sales force and increased advertising expenditures. Believing his firm was moving too far away from its initial direct selling model, Dell began criticizing his marketing executives for spending too much on advertising and using traditional marketing tactics. By the end of 1987, most of the executives from Tandy had either been asked to leave or had left on their own. Dell reorganized to improve its customer services in 1988. The firm also launched three new PC models, opened an office in Canada, began offering a leasing option, and increased its emphasis on targeting larger clients, such as governmental entities, corporations, and educational institutions. That year, Dell completed its initial public offering, selling shares for $8.50 each.

To better compete with Japanese PC firms that were lowering their prices, Dell began working to upgrade its machines. To this end, Dell hired former IBM Corp. engineer Glenn Henry in 1989, charging him with the task of overseeing product development. The firm also became one of the first to create file servers that used the Unix platform, and began working to incorporate Intel Corp.'s 486 microprocessor into its computers as soon as the chip was released. Dell also began selling several new dot matrix printers manufactured by Epson. Corporations accounted for 40 percent of the firm's 1990 revenues, which reached $546 million. Despite twofold sales growth, profits plunged by 64 percent, which Dell blamed on the higher research and development costs and a surplus inventory of memory chips. The firm began using retail outlets for the first time that year after reaching a sales agreement with Soft Warehouse Inc., the leading U.S. computer retailer. International growth continued with the construction of a manufacturing plant in Ireland and offices in France, Italy, and Sweden.

INTENSE GROWTH

Believing that its selling model was as important to the company's success as the products it sold, Dell devoted considerable resources to training its customer service staff, requiring all employees to complete a six-week training program—which covered how to answer questions, resolve complaints, take orders, and help clients select the best options for their computing needs—before allowing them to answer the phones. Customer complaints were aired in weekly staff meetings, which focused on how to best resolve issues. These efforts paid off in 1990 when J.D. Powers & Associates ranked Dell number one in its first customer satisfaction survey regarding PC makers. That year, the firm moved into the sixth place spot among the largest U.S. PC manufacturers, compared to 22nd in 1989.

In 1991, Dell unveiled its first notebook PC, hoping to become a major player in the burgeoning market. International growth continued at a rapid pace. Subsidiaries were established in Belgium, Finland, Luxembourg, Norway, and Spain; a customer support center was set up in the Netherlands; sales offices opened in Ireland and Belgium; and a direct marketing and on-site service program launched in Mexico. To enhance its industry leading customer service practices, Dell became the first PC maker to install applications software free for its clients.

Unlike many of its competitors, Dell actually benefited from the recessionary economic conditions of the early 1990s. Although corporate and consumer belt tightening was not severe enough to prevent PC users from making purchases, it did prompt many PC shoppers to seek discounted options for the first time. Consequently, Dell's customer base continued to swell. However, with the firm's success came increased competition from companies tying to imitate its direct sales model. Once such copycat rival, Gateway 2000, replaced Dell as the leading U.S. PC direct seller in 1992. That year, Dell implemented a program that reduced onsite service call response time to less than four hours. The firm also created its Professional Services Capabilities Unit, which facilitated communication among Dell's systems integrators, network integrators, and consultants across the globe. Subsidiaries opened in Poland, the Czech Republic, and Switzerland. Dell and Pertech Computer Ltd. of New Delhi agreed to jointly market systems throughout India. Sales grew to $890 million, and in 1992 Dell was listed as a *Fortune* 500 company for the first time.

By the end of 1993, Dell had become the world's fifth-largest PC maker with sales of more than $2 billion. A new service program allowed clients to choose the level of service they wanted from Dell. Technical problems with Dell's notebook PCs prompted the firm to shelve a new notebook line and take a $20 million hit. The firm deviated from its direct sales model when it agreed to let Sam's Club sell Dell Precision

PCs at its 200 retail outlets in the United States. However, within a year it had abandoned all efforts to sell its computers in warehouse clubs and superstores such as Soft Warehouse, limiting its focus once again to mail-order sales. To counter the deep discounting tactics of Compaq Computer Corp., Dell launched Dimensions by Dell, a new series of low-cost PCs. Competitors like Compaq found it difficult to compete with Dell because the direct seller's operating costs were only 18 percent, roughly half those of a traditional PC seller. Dell was able to achieve these operating costs in large part because it operated with a minimal inventory. Customers told Dell exactly what machine they wanted before Dell made it, eliminating the guesswork faced by PC makers who were selling their machines through retail outlets. In 1995, Dell's share of the worldwide PC market reached three percent.

IMPACT OF THE INTERNET

Dell's direct sales model was ideally suited to a medium like the Internet. Dell began selling its PCs and related equipment via the World Wide Web in 1996. Via a process similar to the one used when they called Dell on the phone, customers were able to place their order on Dell's Web site. The firm's Internet store allowed users to choose configuration options, solicit price quotes, and place orders for single or multiple systems. The site also allowed purchasers to view their order status and offered support services to Dell owners. Within a year, Dell was selling roughly $1 million worth of computers a day via the Internet, and nearly 80 percent of the online clients were new to Dell. Because the Web helped to automate the PC purchasing process, Dell found itself able to handle the growing sales volume without having to drastically increase staff. Cost savings also were achieved as the firm's phone bill began shrinking.

By the end of 1997, nearly one-third of the orders received by Dell were being placed on the Internet. Because most of these orders were coming from individual consumers and small businesses, Dell began investigating ways to lure its larger clients to place orders online. The firm decided to create customized Web pages, known as Premiere Pages, for these customers. Along with housing information such as the system configurations already used by the firm and any discounts Dell might offer the firm, the pages also allowed users to request service and track orders electronically. For example, Detroit Edison Co. began buying Dell computers online to reduce the amount of time its employees spent on technology procurement, to eliminate paperwork, and to speed delivery.

According to the May 14, 2001 issue of *BusinessWeek Online,* "Michael Dell was e-business be-fore e-business was cool. During the boom in technology spending, he used the Internet to reach out to customers and sell $50 million worth of computers a day." However, the Internet served as more than just a powerful sales medium for Dell in the late 1990s. The growing number of Internet users also fueled the server market, which Dell had started targeting in 1996, hoping to lessen its dependence on decreasingly expensive PCs. The following year, Dell also diversified into workstations. By 1998, servers were bringing in 16 percent of the Dell's total sales, which topped $12 billion. One year later, Dell was second only to Compaq Computer Corp. in U.S. server sales. That year, when competitors once again began cutting PC prices, Dell responded with its first PC under $1,000. Sales nearly doubled to $25.3 billion, and stock prices surged roughly 140 percent for the fourth consecutive year.

As the PC industry continued to decelerate in 2000, Dell started repositioning itself as an Internet technology provider, increasing its focus on servers and also moving into the storage systems market. The firm also started selling a variety of Internet services such as wireless access to the Internet and Web hosting. Sales growth for the year totaled 38.5 percent, down nearly 10 percent from the previous year, and stock prices began dropping. According to *BusinessWeek Online,* Dell's Internet savvy helped the firm to weather the storm. "Thanks to efficiencies created, in part, by Dell's Web-based supply chain, the company can remain profitable even while it launches a bloody PC price war." Because Dell had spent most of 2000 linking its suppliers to its online ordering system, suppliers only sent additional merchandise when Dell needed it. As a result, inventory was cut to one-third the amount stored by many competitors, and Dell saved roughly $50 million. In April of 2001, Dell moved ahead of Compaq Computer to become the world leader in PC sales.

Despite Dell's success in the PC price wars, several analysts criticize the firm, pointing out that more than half of Dell's sales still came from the deteriorating PC market. Furthermore, the firm's efforts in 2000 to develop an Internet PC called WebPC had dissolved when the firm realized it wouldn't be able to develop the technology without charging a relatively high price for it. In the past, Dell had been known more as a marketer of technology developed by other firms than a technology developer itself. The firm's attempt to develop a machine for the relatively new Internet appliance market marked a shift in direction for Dell. According to the October 2000 issue of *Fortune,* "Another way of explaining the troubles with WebPC is to say that Dell lost focus on being a market taker and tried instead to be a market maker. But as the company moves toward its third decade, it seems fair to ask if market taking will be enough." To maintain its second-place position in the server market and increase its sixth-place spot in the storage industry, Dell will find itself face to face with the likes of Sun Microsystems Inc., IBM, and EMC—all of which are known for their strength in developing new technology. However, those bullish on Dell's future cite the firm's past ability to use its direct sales model in new markets as an indication that it will likely succeed, despite formidable competition.

FURTHER READING:

Brown, Eryn. "First: Could the Very Best PC Maker Be Dell Computer?" *Fortune.* April 14, 1997.

"Can Michael Dell Escape the Box?" *Fortune.* October 16, 2000.

"Dell Computer Corp." In *Notable Corporate Chronologies.* Farmington Hills, MI: Gale Group, 1999.

DiCarlo, Lisa. "Dell Expands Net Plans." *PC Week.* April 28, 1997.

Gibbs, Lisa. "Is Dell's Ride Over?" *Money.* November 1, 2000.

Jacobs, April. "Businesses Warm to Internet PC Sales." *Computerworld.* December 29, 1997.

Lewis, Scott M. "Dell Computer Corp." In *International Directory of Company Histories.* Vol. 9. Detroit, MI: St. James Press, 1994.

"Michael Dell." *BusinessWeek Online.* May 14, 2001. Available from www.businessweek.com.

"Michael Dell's Plan for the Rest of the Decade." *Fortune.* June 9, 1997.

Mulqueen, John T. "Dell's Aiming to Take Corps to the Web." *InternetWeek.* December 22, 1997.

————. "Round Two for Dell's Web Site." *InternetWeek.* December 15, 1997.

Popovich, Ken, and Mary Jo Foley. "Dell Remains Committed to Pricing Strategy." *eWeek.* April 9, 2001.

"A Revolution of One; Face Value: Michael Dell, A Lone Revolutionary." *The Economist.* April 14, 2001.

Shook, David. "The Winner of the PC Price Wars: Dell." *BusinessWeek Online.* May 1, 2001. Available from www.businessweek.com.

SEE ALSO: Compaq Computer Corp.; Dell, Michael; Disintermediation; Gateway, Inc.; Hardware; IBM Inc.; Sun Microsystems; Supply Chain Management

DENIAL-OF-SERVICE ATTACK

Hackers have been known to place programs onto networked computers that create high volumes of dubious requests or messages, resulting in an interruption of network service. This practice is called a denial-of-service (DOS) attack. When more than one networked computer is used to flood a network with phony traffic, the practice is called a distributed denial-of-service attack (DDOS). There are different types of DOS attacks, including teardrop attacks, infrastructure attacks, buffer overflow attacks, smurf attacks, and those caused by computer viruses.

Depending on their type, DOS attacks work in different ways. For example, infrastructure attacks involve situations where service is impaired from a physical, real-world assault on cabling or other equipment used for network operations. Smurf attacks involve a utility called pinging. Normally, this utility is used to verify the existence and operation of a host computer (such as a Web server used to host a Web site). A signal is sent to the host, and a reply requested. Smurf attacks involve hackers spoofing, or using a phony reply address (the target for the DOS attack), and requesting that the reply be broadcast to multiple points within the target's network, causing a spike in dubious traffic. Regardless of the means, the ultimate objective of most DOS attacks is to prevent networks from working properly by overloading them with more traffic than they were designed to handle.

Although they can happen accidentally, DOS attacks normally are caused intentionally. *Network World* revealed that most attacks are targeted at different kinds of servers (such as Web servers or e-mail servers). As many as 20 percent of attacks are made on machines with broadband Internet connections, and a smaller number involve routers, which relay information on the Internet as it is sent from one location to another. Much like computer viruses, the consequences of DOS attacks are real, resulting in lost revenue for companies, frustrated consumers and companies who want to purchase goods and services, and sometimes damaged computer files. To make matters worse, tracking down attackers can be very difficult.

Unfortunately, DOS attacks were a routine occurrence in the early 2000s. In the span of only two months, several leading Web sites were attacked in early 2001. That January, Microsoft announced that a DOS attack aimed at the routers directing traffic to its Web sites caused an interruption in service. Additionally, an attack sidelined the Web site of security vendor Network Associates for approximately 90 minutes. In February, a Canadian hacker calling himself Mafiaboy was caught after attacking several sites, including Amazon.com, Charles Schwab, Yahoo, CNN, e*Trade, and eBay.

In mid-2001 there no were no proven ways to stop DOS attacks from happening. However, several organizations developed or offered solutions that were able to provide varying degrees of relief. These partial solutions ranged in price from $20,000 to as much as $55,000, and were useful to entities like Internet service providers (ISPs) and those hosting Web sites. They worked in different ways, and most had not achieved widespread use. Captus Networks offered equipment that detected traffic surges and held them back while it attempted to differentiate between legitimate and bogus messages. Captus's solution also was able to check spoofed addresses used in smurf attacks and either deny illegitimate traffic or send it to another location for investigative analysis.

Mazu Networks, a company with ties to the Massachusetts Institute of Technology (MIT), developed similar technology that, according to *Network World,* could "identify traffic characteristics of distributed denial-of-service attacks and communicate that information to the ISPs, Web-hosting centers or Web server owner via a private network or dial-up. The devices will be able to take active response measures, such as filtering and tracing the attack, and gathering forensics." In addition to Mazu, other companies with ties to universities, including Arbor (University of Michigan), Lancope (Georgia Institute of Technology), and Asta (University of California at San Diego and the University of Washington) were trying to tackle the pervasive threat posed by DOS attackers. Moreover, in November 2000 an industry group was created to work toward a solution and develop cooperation between ISPs, who play central roles in the attacks. DOS attacks were an especially pressing issue because the possibility that companies and ISPs would be held liable for their consequences was very real.

FURTHER READING:

"Denial of Service." *Whatis.com,* May 16, 2001. Available from whatis.techtarget.com.

Messmer, Ellen. "Start-ups Go on Attack vs. Denial-of-Srvice Threat." *Network World,* June 18, 2001.

———. "Start-ups Vie to Defeat DoS Attacks." *Network World,* February 5, 2001.

SEE ALSO: Computer Crime; Computer Security; Hacking; Viruses; Worms

DIFFERENTIATION

In terms of e-commerce, differentiation is, simply, how one company sets its e-commerce products and services apart from those offered by competitors. In some cases, the differentiation might be in name recognition. In a world filled with Internet startups, the familiarity of a name like Hewlett-Packard or Microsoft could be an important distinction to some

customers looking to purchase e-commerce technology and services. Pricing, product functionality, and the comprehensiveness of services also are common areas where Internet-based businesses look to differentiate from competitors.

BizRate.com, one of the Internet's busiest retail centers, successfully differentiated itself from other online business ranking sites via the method it uses to gather the information that makes up its ratings. Unlike rivals such as Gomez.com, BizRate uses data from actual shoppers to create ratings, rather than hiring a staff for that purpose. The site was created in June of 1996 by 27-year-old Farhad Mohit, who wanted to help online shoppers find trustworthy merchants in the rapidly expanding Internet marketplace. Mohit envisioned a site that would allow consumers to peruse objective information about an online store before they actually purchased merchandise from it.

At the BizRate site, potential shoppers can see how previous shoppers rated their experience with an online merchant. The rating criteria cover everything from customer support, live phone support, order tracking, and on-time delivery to site performance, ordering procedure, product information, pricing, and privacy policy. BizRate also acts as a shopping hub. Rather than going to individual sites, shoppers can use BizRate to search for a product they want, either by searching the entire site or by searching one of nineteen product categories including apparel, books and magazines, computer hardware, computer software, DVD and videos, electronics, flowers and garden, office supplies, and pet and hobbies. Shoppers who identify a product they wish to purchase may link directly to the vendor selling the product. Once the transaction is complete, shoppers are presented with a BizRate ranking screen, which solicits information that is immediately dumped into BizRate's rankings database. If Bizrate's traffic rates are any indication—roughly 7 million different visitors were frequenting the site each month by 2001—Mohit has successfully differentiated his business from competitors.

The Dow Jones Internet Index (DJII) is an example of an e-commerce venture that used name recognition to differentiate itself from a host of rivals. Since its early 1999 launch by Dow Jones and Co., DJII has gauged the stock performance of Internet companies based in the United States. Dow Jones established the DJII in response to the intense Internet stock trading that started to occur in the mid-1990s. Highly successful initial public offerings (IPOs) by firms like Netscape and Yahoo! sparked the trading frenzy,and in 1999 an unprecedented 240 Internet-based firms conducted their IPOs. According to Dow Jones Indexes Managing Director Michael A. Petronella in *Information Today,* "Internet stocks have rapidly become among the most volatile, popular sectors of the equities market. This has led to the need for an Internet benchmark that can be the standard Internet stock measurement tool for all investors.'' Many firms agreed with Dow Jones, prompting the launch of several competing indexes, such as the Business 2.0 Internet, USA Today Internet 100, Internet.com's Isdex, and the Inter@ctive Week @Net Internet index.

Along with its recognized and respected name, Dow Jones believed that a set of tangible inclusion standards would help to differentiate DJII from rivals. Therefore, the companies listed on DJII must secure at least half of their annual revenues from the Internet. Also, the firms must be valued at $100 million for a period of three months, must have operated as a public company for at least three months, and their stock prices must average a minimum of $10 per share.

Sapient Corp. offers a third example of differentiation. The firm offers Internet integration services to governmental entities and to firms like iwon.com, Janus, Nabisco, Staples, United Airlines, and Wal-Mart. Sapient was founded in 1991 by Jerry Greenberg and Stuart Moore, who decided to create a client-server integration services firm like no other. Like many other client-server integration consultants, Sapient helped clients determine how networking technology could streamline operations. However, the firm went several steps further than most rivals by also building, implementing, and supporting whatever technology they decided to use. Another point of differentiation came with the contracts Sapient offered clients—at the time, they were the only technology consultancy willing to commit to prices and deadlines before a project began. Also, employee pay was tied to customer satisfaction.

The firm's differentiation strategy paid off throughout the 1990s as sales and earnings grew consistently. An IPO in April of 1996 raised $33 million and allowed Sapient to make acquisitions that shifted its focus to e-business integration services. Eventually, the firm offered a comprehensive suite of e-commerce services that included the planning and creation of online stores. With sales exceeding $500 million in 2000, Sapient became the first pure-play Internet integration services firm added to Standard & Poor's 500 stock index, a fact which earned it further distinction from its rivals.

FURTHER READING:

''BizRate.com Becomes Second to Amazon as the Most Popular Retail Site on the Web.'' *Business Wire.* February 15, 2001.

Colkin, Ellen. ''Net Stocks Tracked.'' *InformationWeek.* February 22, 1999.

''Dow Jones Indexes Launches Internet Index.'' *Information Today.* April 1999.

''Dow Jones Internet and Technology Sector Indexes Become Now Tradable Through New Exchange-Traded Funds; Total Assets Linked to Dow Jones Internet Indexes Top $240 Billion.'' *Business Wire.* May 18, 2000.

Futrelle, David. ''The Internet Index Mania: There Are Many Benchmarks, but Few Measure Anything Meaningful.'' *Money.* November 1, 1999.

McNamara, Paul. ''BizRate.com Founder Farhad Mohit Eyes Every Aspect of His Business the Same Way Comic Steve Martin's Cop Character on 'Let's Get Small' Looked at a Shrunken Motorist: We're Gonna Have to Measure You.'' *Network World.* February 5, 2001.

Mulqueen, John T. ''Young Company Flourishes.'' *CommunicationsWeek.* June 17, 1996.

Rosa, Jerry. ''Eleven—Jerry Greenberg—The Stalwart.'' *Computer Reseller News.* November 13, 2000.

''Sapient Corp.'' *Advertising Age.* June 19, 2000.

''Siteseeing.'' *Computer Weekly.* January 13, 2000.

Smith, Geoffrey. ''There's Good Reason for the Buzz About BizRate.'' *BusinessWeek Online.* November 26, 1999. Available from www.businessweek.com.

Weintraub, Arlene. ''E-Commerce Crusader.'' *Businessweek Online.* June 5, 2000. Available from www.businessweek.com.

Whitford, David. ''The Two-Headed Manager: Sapient Co-CEOs Jerry Greenberg and Stuart Moore Have (Almost) Nothing in Common. That Helps Explain Why Their Relationship Works.'' *Fortune.* January 24, 2000.

SEE ALSO: Business Models; Competition; Competitive Advantage

DIGITAL

In the field of computing, information can be conveyed in digital or analog formats. Continuity is the differentiating factor between the two. For example, digital devices are only able to display information in finite units (10 degrees versus 10.0625 degrees), while analog devices display information that corresponds more precisely to real world phenomena. Digital watches display time in measured increments while analog watches show time unfold continuously through the circular movement of mechanical hands.

Although analog computers are used for simulating real-word conditions in a variety of fields, including nuclear power and electronics, the majority of computers, including those used for e-commerce, are digital machines. They process information in a binary format of zeroes and ones (0, 1, 10, 11, 100, 111, and so on). Accordingly, while the software programs used during e-commerce—including Web browsers and database programs—are written in high-level programming languages like C++ and Java that closely resemble human grammar, they eventually are converted to commands consisting of ones and zeroes that a computer's hardware can accept and understand. Digital computers function through four essential components: an input-output device; a control unit; main memory; and an arithmetic-logic unit.

The difference between analog and digital information can be shown in the audio recording process. Analog devices record sound waves directly onto magnetic tape, whereas digital devices take the same wave, convert it to a sequence of ones and zeroes, and store it for future use. When played back, the numbers are converted into electronic signals resembling the original sound wave. Digital information, including computer software programs, word processing documents, digital audio, and digital video, can be duplicated an infinite number of times without a loss in quality or integrity; the numeric expressions of zeroes and ones remain the same throughout time. In comparison, the quality of analog information, such as songs recorded on magnetic tape, deteriorates with successive generations as copies are made.

FURTHER READING:

''Digital.'' *Ecommerce Webopedia,* May 9, 2001. Available from e-comm.webopedia.com/TERM/d/digital.html.

''Digital.'' *Techencyclopedia,* May 9, 2001. Available from www.techweb.com/encyclopedia.

''Digital and Analog Information.'' *The PC Guide,* May 9, 2001. Available from www.pcguide.com/intro/works.

''Digital computer.'' *Encyclopedia Britannica,* May 12, 2001. Available from www.britannica.com/eb.

Massey, Howard. ''Analog Vs. Digital.'' The International Association of Electronic Keyboard Manufacturers. May 12, 2001.

''The Mathematics of Computing.'' *The PC Guide,* May 9, 2001. Available from www.pcguide.com/intro/works.

SEE ALSO: Analog

DIGITAL CASH

Digital cash, or electronic money, consists of encrypted data that serves as an electronic substitute for regular hard currency. It can exist in the form of a cash Internet transaction or as monetary value stored on a smart card. Descended from the electronic money used in bank transactions, currency exchanges, credit cards, and automatic tellers, by the 21st century digital currency was evolving rapidly.

A HISTORY OF DIGITAL CASH

In a sense, digital cash has been around for years in the form of the automated clearinghouse (ACH), automated teller machines (ATMs), point-of-sale debit cards, and credit card networks. Even coded subway and phone cards function as a type of electronic cash. In 1996, the U.S. government initiated a campaign to create a universal, all-electronic payment system to decrease the nearly 70 billion paper checks Americans write each year. The effort was instigated by the Financial Services Technology Consortium (FSTC), which was composed of members of the banking and information technology industries. In 1998, the U.S. Treasury Department sponsored a pilot program to test the workability of paying participating federal contractors with e-checks. More than $2.5 million was paid out during the test period. By 2000, the program was transferred to CommerceNet, a consortium of 500 e-commerce developers and users, which intended to launch it worldwide.

A 1999 study by Deloitte Consulting projected that Internet revenues would top $1.1 trillion by 2002. Businesses could save about $18.3 billion annually, or roughly 72 percent of associated costs, by developing efficient and secure online billing and payment strategies. But many of the first versions of e-money—including CyberCoins and CyberCash, which appeared in the early 1990s—eventually folded. They often worked like online gift certificates, whereby consumers bought a certain amount of digital cash and then redeemed it at participating online vendors. These versions failed to win consumer acceptance because of doubts about their validity, the limited venues where the cash could be spent, and the need to install special software just to use the products.

The second generation of e-cash appeared in the late 1990s. Related to technologies such as electronic checks (e-checks) and embedded-chip smart cards, digital cash systems transferred monetary amounts over the Internet on open networks and utilized public-key cryptography to protect the content of the messages being relayed over the system. Later developments in digital cash permitted users to transfer cash via e-mail once they established an online account with a provider permitting payment at online vendor sites. Customers therefore avoided usage fees and merchants avoided the one- to two-percent transaction costs associated with credit-card transactions. This e-cash didn't require software downloads, and some versions also allowed cash withdrawals at ATMs.

USES OF DIGITAL CASH

Credit card payments account for more than 90 percent of all Web site purchases, compared to only 25 percent of offline sales. Digital cash may not displace credit cards for large online purchases, but for small purchases it has overwhelming advantages including extremely low transaction costs. Among the transactions that digital cash may facilitate are small-volume sales by marketers, such as publishers or music sites, which sell individual books or songs on-line. Some e-cash services authorize "micro-payment" arrangements permitting shoppers to rack up a series of small purchases before charging the total to a credit card. Other systems deduct small amounts, from one-tenth of a cent to $10, from an account as purchases are completed. Still other arrangements enable registered users to e-mail dollars to each other or transfer amounts via wireless and hand-held devices.

RISKS AND LIMITATIONS

Digital cash systems pose unique risks for both online merchants and consumers, including questions about security, the ability to safeguard users' privacy, susceptibility to counterfeiting, and suitability as a medium for online fraud. All of these generate fears among e-commerce merchants over increased legal liability. While traditional monetary systems combat fraud by using closed networks that block unauthorized access to the system, the open networks along which e-cash payments are transmitted often lack adequate safeguards against fraudulent access. Therefore, they must utilize elaborate encryption methods to code the information in such a way that only authorized parties can read it. Furthermore, a new security apparatus and infrastructure must be devised to protect payment instruction transfers. A new public key infrastructure, which can be fairly expensive to implement, is required to diminish fraud risks.

Operational disruptions can generate serious hazards for e-cash systems. Even natural phenomena jeopardize e-cash operations. In 1993, a heavy snow-storm caused the roof-collapse of an Electronic Data Systems (EDS) facility that processed ATM transactions, interfering with 5,000 ATMs across the United Sstaes. Since digital cash is networked, difficulties with the Internet's physical networks, associated hardware, or software can compromise the system's efficiency and reliability. Computer viruses, damage to a centralized switching facility, or even software updates can all pose threats.

While digital cash renders online purchases more convenient for users, it poses risks for them as well. Foremost is a lack of anonymity. Unlike regular money, most e-cash systems track users' purchases, thus failing to protect their privacy. Concerns that anonymous e-money could encourage tax evasion and money laundering have led to demands that digital cash be traceable. The issuer's integrity also raises problems. The collapse of a branded network bank could free it of all liability for the e-cash it issued.

Finally, digital cash complicates the world's central banks' ability to formulate monetary policies and manage national monetary supplies. According to a 2000 *Survey of Electronic Monetary Developments* in 68 countries, conducted by the Swiss Bank for International Settlements, digital money works best in selected areas, such as public transportation, telecommunications, and potentially coin-free venues. E-cash easily crosses international borders, since any bank can issue digital cash and anyone can use it. E-money also can cheapen foreign exchange transactions, facilitating the shift from weak currencies to stronger ones and thereby impeding a country's effective management of its monetary policy.

The achievement of widespread, worldwide adoption will take time for digital cash. For this to take place, it must match old-fashioned, hard currency for liquidity, anonymity, reliability, and universal acceptability. The versions of e-money that come closest to mimicking the advantages of traditional currency seem the most likely to succeed in the long run.

FURTHER READING:

Bielski, Lauren. "New Wave of e-Money Options Hits the Web." *ABA Banking Journal.* August, 2000.

"E-Cash 2.0." *Economist.* February 19, 2000.

"Follow the e-Money." *Foreign Policy.* September/October 2000.

Kuykendall, Lavonne. "The Online Challengers." *Credit Card Management.* November, 1999.

"Leaders: Cash Remains King." *Economist.* February 19, 2000.

McAndrews, James. "E-Money and Payment System Risks." *Contemporary Economic Policy.* July, 1999.

Mitchell, Lori. "E-Cash Aims to Ease Security—and Privacy-Concerned Shoppers." *InfoWorld.* August, 2000.

Nocera, Joseph. "Easy Money." *Money.* August, 2000.

Ridgway, Nicole. "Down to the Wire." *Forbes.* November 13, 2000.

SEE ALSO: Cryptography, Public and Private Key; Digital Wallet Technology; Fraud, Internet; Micro-payments; Privacy: Issues, Policies, Statements

DIGITAL CERTIFICATE

Digital certificates are digitally encrypted storage vehicles for transporting personal information, especially digital signatures, over the Internet. They are appended as attachments to electronic communications in order to verify the identity of the sender and provide the tools necessary for the recipient to encode a response. The thrust of the technology is to provide individuals engaging in online transactions with authentic digital credentials for use over the Internet, and to secure those credentials in the transaction over multiple servers.

The appeal of digital certificates in e-commerce is obvious. They greatly enhance the security and speed of online transactions, making the Internet's instantaneous sales and communications possibilities more viable. In the early 2000s, digital certificates were a primary means for the advancement of Web-based commerce. They validate the user at the point of purchase, streamlining the transaction process by eliminating the need for third-party validation. The information contained in the certificate includes the user's name and e-mail address, expiration data, a serial number, and the name of the certificate authority that issued the certificate.

Certificates are granted upon successful application to a certificate authority, and are sent via electronic communication, usually e-mail. Issuers generally devise a certification practice statement to clarify the conditions upon which the authority authenticates the individual. Upon receiving the certificate, the user has the information verified by a notary, after which the certificate can be used officially for electronic transactions, acting as a legally binding electronic signature. Public-key infrastructure encryption methods are used to electronically mask signatures during transmission, simultaneously providing the recipient with a method for decrypting the signature and encrypting a reply.

Digital certificates were developed by Salt Lake City-based Zions First National Bank in conjunction with the American Bankers Association. The organizations launched a pilot program with the U. S. Social Security Administration in the late 1990s in which hundreds of companies filed their Social Security reports online using digital certificates. The tremendous success of the program opened the door for wider interest and application. In summer 2000, President Bill Clinton signed into law, using a digital certificate, the Electronic Signatures in Global & National Commerce Act. This legislation heralded a turning point, particularly for online banking, which had been forestalled by concerns over the security and authentication of online financial transactions. By making these digital signatures legally binding and secure, Web-based banking was expected to finally begin fulfilling its tremendous promise.

The early 2000s witnessed a flurry of new technologies aimed at facilitating the wider application and integration of digital certificates, such as Web forms designed to accept certificates. Other developments included storage space for digital certificates in secure central directories. Traditionally, digital certif-icates requiring desktop software didn't transfer easily between different kinds of computers or browsers. The process for utilizing digital certificates across different operating systems or browsers was cumbersome, generally involving a separate cryptography tool kit installed on a desktop. Downloading and storing certificates allows users to access their certificates from any remote location via the Internet. Security vendors such as RSA Security, Arcot Systems, Entrust Technologies, and VeriSign all rolled out versions of remote Web-based certificate storage and access in the early 2000s, according to *Internetweek*.

Digital certificates generally are stored as files on personal computer Web browsers and are protected by personal identification numbers (PINs), thereby verifying that communications come from particular users. However, some imperfections are implicit. For instance, a digital certificate essentially authenticates the computer, and not the individual using it. While users of digital certificates typically safeguard their machines with layers of personal verification for use, in addition to the PIN, certificates stored on computers are nonetheless susceptible to hackers. One highly touted solution to this difficulty was the augmenting of digital certificates with biometric technology, which verifies identity via personal characteristics such as fingerprints, retina, or voice.

Alternatively, certificates can be embedded on smart cards or similar devices. The latter method was becoming more common as computers were manufactured with built-in smart-card readers. This method affords the additional benefit of allowing users to employ the digital certificate both at their computer and, once the infrastructure is widely in place, in physical-world settings like automatic teller machines (ATMs) for credit and debit transactions.

FURTHER READING:

Bielski, Lauren. ''Digital Certificates Get Mobilized by 'E-Sign Act.''' *ABA Banking Journal.* September, 2000.

Connolly, P. J. ''Digital Certificates are Gaining Ground in Business.'' *InfoWorld.* October 16, 2000.

Hammell, Benjamin. ''Are Digital Certificates Secure?'' *Communications News.* December, 2000.

Harrison, Ann. ''Digital Certificates.'' *Computerworld.* August 14, 2000.

Koller, Mike, and Rutrell Yasin. ''Security Gets Some Legs: Digital ID Systems No Longer Hold Users Captive to a Single Browser, PC or Location.'' *Internetweek.* December 11, 2000.

O'Donnell, Anthony. ''Security on the Internet: Who Goes There?'' *Insurance & Technology.* January, 2001.

Streeter, Bill. ''Will Banks Have a Role in e-Commerce? It's a 'Cert'ainty.'' *ABA Banking Journal.* September, 2000.

SEE
ALSO: Banking, Online; Biometrics; Cryptography, Public
and Private Key; Digital Certificate Authority; Digital
Signature; Digital Signature Legislation; Encryption

DIGITAL CERTIFICATE AUTHORITY

Certificate authorities were at the hub of many e-commerce developments in the early 2000s. One of the greatest impediments to the widespread adoption of online commerce was the fear among many consumers and businesses of the security risks involved in sending financial or other information over the Internet. Certificate authorities hoped to alleviate such fears by acting as guarantors of the authenticity and security of online transactions. To accomplish this, they issued digital certificates, or encrypted electronic packages carrying information that authenticates its sender.

Digital certificates employ a public-key infrastructure. A public code, or key, can be used by anyone to encrypt a message to a given authority. However, only that authority can decrypt the message using its private key. Only the combination of the private key and the public key can authenticate a user's identity or a transaction using a digital certificate. Digital certificates, in turn, were the primary vehicles for digital signatures, which were set to play an enormous role in the e-commerce world of the 2000s. Certificate authorities maintain the private key, and therefore serve as the trusted agents behind these encrypted transactions. Certificates then carry an authority's stamp of approval wherever they travel, and recipients refer to that authority as the mark of trust to ensure that the given information is secure and the identity of the sender is sound. The authority legally binds an individual, or at least an individual computer, to a particular public key, and certifies that the certificate holder is officially recognized by a trusted third party.

Certificate authorities generally are run by corporations for their internal and external communications and transactions, or by commercial certificate authorities. For example, VeriSign, based in Mountain View, California, was a commercial authority that dominated the industry in the late 1990s and early 2000s. Certificate authorities determine the conditions of a certificate contract, including the duration of its activity, the breadth of privileges it affords, and the obligations of the certificate holder.

Certificates usually are issued for one year, although the duration can vary widely. Most authorities are wary of issuing certificates for longer periods because of concerns over long-term security in light of developing technology, the aversion to risk stemming from the trust of individual holders, and the desire to reap continued income from issuing new certificates. Certificates also can be revoked before their expiration date using a certificate revocation list (CRL)—a list digitally signed and issued by the certificate authority that signals to recipients of digital certificates that a given user is no longer validated by the authority.

The certificate authority relationship extends beyond the one-to-many relationship between the authority and its certificate holders. Within a public-key infrastructure, certificate authorities are organized hierarchically, so that each authority lower in the hierarchy maintains a parent authority to verify its public key. This relationship becomes particularly crucial in business-to-business Internet transactions, in which companies need to share secured information using digital certificates for verification. In such cases, the coordination and interoperability between certificate authorities is important to facilitate smooth interaction. The management of multiple certificates creates headaches and uses up valuable resources for a company. Thus, creating authority hierarchies in which certificate validity is smooth throughout various levels was considered an optimal business solution.

Moreover, authorities provide a mechanism for built-in fraud control, in that companies and individuals can trace the path of certificate authorities through which a transaction moved to determine where any mischief may have taken place. Upon discovering abuse of the certificate, the authority can immediately revoke the offending user's certificate. However, since certificate authorities are the trustees of signature security on the Internet, ensuring their own physical, personnel, and network security is a premium concern.

In the early 2000s, certificate authority models still had a number of wrinkles to be ironed out. In fact, one of the biggest obstacles to the public-key infrastructure was the lack of interoperability between certificate authorities and their certificates. As long as hierarchies remained incompatible over a tremendously wide network, the use of digital certificates for e-commerce was expected to be limited. The tremendous cost of establishing a public-key infrastructure, which can run as high as $1 million, prevented most companies from becoming in-house certificate authorities. Thus, these companies opted to outsource the management of their digital certificates to commercial authorities, which tailored the certificates to the companies' needs.

However, certificate authorities had a great deal of incentive to work with businesses and each other to create a seamless, compatible system. When digital signatures were officially recognized as legally binding by the passage of the Electronic Signatures in Global and National Commerce Act in 2000, the function of certificate authorities in the e-commerce world was taken up a few levels. As more and more transactions were readied to take place over the Internet, including Web-based banking, the secure validation of such transactions was among the remaining barriers to the floodgates of e-commerce, and certificate authorities held the keys to those gates.

FURTHER READING:

Andress, Mandy. "Multivendor PKI the Key to Smooth e-Business Communications." *InfoWorld.* May 29, 2000.

Bradner, Scott. "Are You Usefully Certifiable?" *Network World.* August 16, 1999.

Harrison, Ann. "Digital Certificates." *Computerworld.* August 14, 2000.

Hurley, Hanna. "Certificate Authorities Move In-House." *Telephony.* September 13, 1999.

Jackson Higgins, Kelly. "Outsourcing PKI is an Option to Building One." *Informationweek.* November 6, 2000.

Poynter, Ian. "In Pursuit of Validation." *Network World.* February 26, 2001.

SEE ALSO: Cryptography; Digital Certificate; Digital Signature; Digital Signature Legislation; Encryption, Public and Private Key

DIGITAL DIVIDE

In the beginning, the Internet, and particularly the World Wide Web, was extolled as a powerful force toward the democratization of information and, ultimately, of politics and economics. This was the idealistic vision of the Web's founder, Tim Berners-Lee. By placing such a wealth of information and opportunity at individuals' fingertips, the Web, according to its most ardent supporters, was to act as the great societal leveler. While some aspects of that vision may have leaked through, most observers note that the technology has taken a very different course, and has led to what is popularly known as the digital divide.

Both inside the United States and on the global level, the gulf between those individuals, families, organizations, and businesses that enjoy access to the Internet and those that do not constitutes the digital divide. The seeming ubiquity of the Internet in U.S. culture in the early 2000s seemed to gloss over the lingering digital divide. Indeed, amidst the hype surrounding the New Economy, it became difficult for many Americans to recognize that the majority of the

world's population had yet to make a phone call, much less log on to the Internet. And while the cost of personal computers and Internet software and access has inched downward since the mid-1990s, the digital divide persisted in various forms and with various implications.

MAPPING THE DIGITAL DIVIDE

Discussion of a gap between the Internet haves and have-nots formally began with the publication of "Falling Through the Net," a report issued by the National Telecommunications and Information Administration (NTIA) of the U.S. Department of Commerce in 1995. At first associated primarily with racial disparities, the general tenor of the discourse gradually broadened to include a wider array and matrix of social indicators, particularly those related to class. New York-based Jupiter Communications found the greatest disparity in Internet usage to be along income—rather than racial—lines. While wealth distribution is very strongly correlated to race and ethnicity in the United States, analysis of the digital divide by the early 2000s tended to consider a more holistic analysis of inequalities.

The digital divide, according to some observers, isn't a qualitatively new phenomenon; rather, it is the extension of age-old inequalities and social discrepancies into the Information Age. Some sociologists viewed the digital divide as a modern extension of chronic unemployment and lack of access to basic social services. With financial transactions; social, political, and economic news; and, increasingly, the pace of social life moving at Internet speed, the digital divide carries the possibility of exacerbating the deep economic divisions existing in U.S. society.

The U.S. Department of Commerce in late 2000 reported that 12.7 percent of Americans earning less than $15,000 per year had access to the Internet in their homes, compared with 77.7 percent of those making more than $75,000 a year. The *Journal of Housing and Community Development* noted that racial divisions intersected with income levels; 23 percent of African-Americans and Hispanics combined maintained home Internet access, while 46 percent of Caucasians were connected at home. Significantly, however, those low-income households that did have access to the Internet were relatively likely to use it to their economic advantage. For instance, those earning less than $15,000 were the most likely—at about 25 percent—to use the Web for employment searches.

The evolution of the digital divide was a mixed bag. Between 1998 and 2000, according to the Department of Commerce, African-American Internet access rose from 11.2 percent to 23.5 percent; while Hispanic access jumped similarly jumped from 12.6

percent to 23.6 percent. While this doubling of access for these groups was an important gain, it still represented a significant gap between these groups and white Americans. Over the longer term, the problem was even more acute. Between 1984 and 1998, according to the U.S. Census Bureau, the percentage gap in computer ownership between the highest and lowest income groups expanded from 20 percent to 64 percent.

The digital divide in the United States also encompassed a geographical disparity, primarily between the urban and suburban populations on the one hand and rural inhabitants on the other. According to *Journalism and Mass Communication Quarterly,* nonmetropolitan residents had a lot to gain from digital technologies since they stand to mitigate some of the disadvantages of geographical isolation, such as their relatively great distance from markets. Despite the universal-access provisions of the Telecommunications Act of 1996, however, access to high-speed networks was extremely limited in most rural areas at the start of the 2000s, particularly because Internet service providers (ISPs) can realize greater returns on their investments in densely populated metropolitan regions.

A study by *Journalism and Mass Communication Quarterly* concluded that, despite the more optimistic predictions of the Internet as a great societal equalizer and force for democratization, the innovations and advantages wrought by digital and information technology were likely to remain closely bound to other social indicators, such as income and education levels, race and ethnicity, and age.

In a global economy driven by knowledge and information in which the Internet is the increasingly dominant medium of interaction, Internet speed, access, use, and fluency are staples of the ability to successfully compete. With competition increasingly based on quick, information-based innovation, companies that failed to incorporate the Internet into their core operations risked placing themselves at a severe competitive disadvantage.

The tension between addressing the digital divide on the one hand and taking advantage of what the Internet had to offer on the other sometimes lead to difficult situations. Many companies, in the interest of creating value and attracting customers via their Web sites, began offering special Web-only deals, which prompted some analysts, concerned with widening the digital divide, to cry foul. At the heart of the Information Age in Silicon Valley, meanwhile, the point was drawn out by the fact that, according to *Computerworld,* Latinos and African-Americans were underrepresented in information-technology companies by about 50 percent. The potential implications for those on the ''wrong'' side of the digital divide can

be serious, according to some analysts. As cultural and economic life grows more and more bound to the Internet and digital technology, those outside of the loop may grow increasingly isolated from the mainstream of society, creating or exacerbating serious rifts that can rupture tranquility.

In addition to the technical and economic aspects of the digital divide, some analysts have pointed to the deepening psychological and ideological components, whereby individuals not on the cusp of the New Economy and technological innovations find themselves frustrated and remote from the endless barrage of media coverage that so popularized Internet culture. Stories of dot.com millionaires, breakthrough digital technologies, and the wonders of the New Economy, such observers note, may have intensified the already existing divide between the Net-savvy and the Net-illiterate.

Still others look at the digital divide as a marketing problem stemming from varying cultural attitudes toward technology. According to *MC Technology Marketing Intelligence,* the divide has as much to do with the degree to which groups perceive technology as a central component in their lives as to levels of access along the lines of social indicators. These perceptions feed and are fed by the nature of marketing campaigns, which tend to gravitate toward those groups that have consistently been the ''tech-haves'' rather than the ''tech-have-nots.'' Some companies, therefore, began to make a concerted effort to tap the traditionally underserved markets. Gateway, for example, launched an extensive campaign to build brand loyalty in the growing Hispanic community, pitching itself as a manufacturer of affordable computers catering to Hispanics.

Whatever the precise explanations and implications, the issue was taken seriously enough in political circles to warrant close attention. President Bill Clinton launched a crusade to close the digital divide in December 1999, and featured the problem in his State of the Union address a month later. The Clinton Administration was particularly concerned with the effects of the digital divide in the nation's school systems. If high standards of learning were to be increasingly associated with access to the Internet, then deep disparities in Internet access in schools imposed fundamental inequities upon children. By the end of the 20th century, over 90 percent of U.S. schools were wired for the Internet, though the extent of the access still varied considerably. Meanwhile, *America's Network* in 2001 listed the digital divide as the most pressing problem faced by the Federal Communications Commission under President George W. Bush.

There were, however, some holdouts when it came to addressing the digital divide. Indeed, some refused to accept that there was a problem at all, insisting that market forces had lowered the prices of digital technology and Internet access to the point that just about everyone could log on to the Internet if they so desired. According to such observers, the remedy lay not in any governmental policies or public investments but in the further unleashing of market forces. The Consumer Electronics Association, for example, held that digital technology was on its way to overwhelming market penetration, and that there wasn't a genuine crisis but a situation more likely born of the political realm.

ADDRESSING THE DIVIDE

An issue generating extremely mixed feelings was the level of responsibility companies feel, or should feel, in remediating the digital divide. According to an *InformationWeek* survey of 500 information-technology and business professionals, direct business involvement in addressing the digital divide was far from standard. While 77 percent of the respondents registered personal concern with the digital divide, only one-third reported that their companies maintained programs to enhance computer access in their communities. There were pragmatic reasons why companies might choose to help bridge the divide. For instance, running or sponsoring educational programs in conjunction with local schools or training institutes can provide a source of income and help nurture strong links between the company and the community. Moreover, offering space for learning computer skills can contribute to the supply of skilled computer workers.

Access, however, was only part of the problem, and bringing the Internet to traditionally underserved areas still left several stones unturned. Once access is available, the task of developing technological "fluency" begins. For example, fluency with the Internet involves not only the ability to surf the Web and download files, but the knowledge of how to create a successful Web site and develop grass-roots communication networks. As a result, technological education will be just as important as reading and writing in a world connected via the Internet and where cyberspace coexists on a par with physical-world interaction. A popular approach among policy makers, including the Clinton Administration, in the late 1990s and early 2000s was the creation of community technology centers, at which individuals of all ages can attend courses and use on-site computer resources for training, research, and personal use.

There were disagreements, of course, as to just what lay in store for the digital divide. While the U.S. Commerce Department expected the gap between ethnic groups to widen by 2005, Jupiter Communications predicted that in this category the divide would narrow. Jupiter held that by the middle of the decade, household income would be the leading indicator in assessing the digital divide, reporting that only 21 percent of households earning less than $15,000 would be online, while 78 percent of households bringing in at least $75,000 would enjoy Internet access. Jupiter expected the ethnic and racial gaps to remain, but in extremely diminished form, with 64-percent access for African Americans, 68 percent for Hispanics, 84 percent for Asian Americans, and 76 percent for Caucasians.

THE GLOBAL DIVIDE

The global dynamics of Internet access were expected to undergo some drastic changes through the first decade of the 21st century. While the United States and other western countries led the way in access at the start of the decade, by 2010 the two largest Internet user communities were likely to be China and India, as Internet availability begins to catch up to those countries' populations.

In booming Internet markets, such as Asia, internal disparities play a significant role as well. The Asian Development Bank (ADB), in its report *Asian Development Outlook 2000,* cautioned against the long-term effects of the limited and uneven development of information technology in the region, noting that, absent the adequate physical and network infrastructure, underdeveloped countries and communities of Asia risked being left even further behind their more developed neighbors when the Internet-based economy really takes hold. Among some key figures highlighting the regional divide, as reported in *Asian Business,* were the telephone and computer penetration rates in the Philippines, at only 3.7 percent and 1.5 percent, respectively. By way of comparison, the significantly more developed Hong Kong boasted telephone and computer penetration rates of 55.8 percent and 25.4 percent, respectively. Moreover, only 5 percent of public-school students and teachers in the Philippines enjoyed Internet access.

The report concluded that Asian countries should implement policies that encourage the development of a modern telecommunications infrastructure and eliminate regulations that inhibit private investment for such projects. A broad telecommunications and information-technology policy forum was conducted by the Southeast Asian Nations (Asean) eAsean Task Force, which formed in 1999. Meanwhile, the ADB insisted, as important as the technological infrastructure is the development of educational infrastructure and human resources so that the mass of the population can contribute to and take advantage of the blooming Internet culture.

In other regions, such as the Middle East, Africa, and Latin America, overall penetration was even lower, and the institutional and infrastructural barriers to bridging the digital divide were generally higher. Precarious political systems and little tradition of a strong, modern industrial and information economy made the building of Internet-ready populations and infrastructures exceptionally difficult to negotiate, though many countries had made important moves in that direction. Some leading companies from more developed nations, moreover, have viewed the Internet development of those regions as a potentially beneficial undertaking, and have initiated donation programs to send computer equipment to and wire schools and community centers in those countries. For example, IBM maintained programs aimed at not only delivering equipment but also at providing hands-on technical training in such countries as Brazil, Mexico, and Vietnam.

Only about 5 percent of the world's population was online as of 2000, and many observers saw this discrepancy as the tip of a much more ominous iceberg. With half the Earth's inhabitants living on less than $2 a day, activists, philanthropic organizations, and, increasingly, businesses and policy makers saw the growing disparities highlighted by the digital divide as the fuel for explosive global instability and potential upheaval that could have severe human and economic costs. President Joaquim Alberto Chissano of Mozambique, for instance, pointed out that the number of Internet hosts in New York City exceeded those in all of Africa. Recognizing such dangers, the Group of Seven (G-7) wealthiest industrialized nations, at their 2000 summit in Okinawa, placed the digital divide on their planning agenda for the first time. At Davos, Switzerland that same year, the World Economic Forum assumed a positive stance, pointing to the digital divide as a ''digital opportunity,'' whereby the remediation of the divide could be a springboard for more systematic reparation of societal inequalities. And, according to the *Far Eastern Economic Review,* major technology companies such as Microsoft and Hewlett-Packard, recognizing the emerging difficulties posed by the digital divide, sponsored an international conference addressing digital inequality.

Among political and business leaders gathered at the United Nations State of the World Forum in 2000, there was an emerging consensus that governments must stress education and technological infrastructure in their national strategies in order to ward off at least the worst excesses of the digital divide. In many countries, the problems to surmount are far more deeply based, including the uprooting of entrenched gender and ethnic discrimination and the quelling of political unrest. But most leaders agreed that the basic issues behind the digital divide were very real and a pressing issue of fundamental social and economic equality that needed to be addressed.

FURTHER READING:

Albrecht, Karl, and Ronald Gunn. ''Digital Backlash.'' *Training & Development,* November 2000.

Armstrong, Anne A. ''Missing the Boat.'' *Government Executive,* August 2000.

Blanks Hindman, Douglas. ''The Rural-Urban Digital Divide.'' *Journalism and Mass Communications Quarterly,* Autumn 2000.

Chanda, Nayan. ''Asian Innovation Awards: The Digital Divide.'' *Far Eastern Economic Review,* October 19, 2000.

Chon, Kilnam. ''The Future of the Internet Digital Divide.'' *Communications of the ACM,* March 2001.

''Damning the Digital Divide.'' *America's Network,* October 1, 2000.

''The Digital Divide.'' *CMA Management,* July/August 2000.

Ebenkamp, Becky. ''Divide and Culture.'' *Brandweek,* January 29, 2001.

Fattah, Hassan. ''The Digital Divide—Politics of a Real Problem?'' *MC Technology Marketing Intelligence,* September 2000.

Foley, Kathleen. ''Deeds, Not Words, Will Fix the Digital Divide.'' *InformationWeek,* March 26, 2001.

Gomolski, Barb. ''Web Users Get Special Deals: Is It the Digital Divide or Just Good Business Sense?'' *InfoWorld,* February 26, 2001.

Hecht, Ben. ''Bridging the Digital Divide.'' *Journal of Housing and Community Development,* March/April 2001.

Hoffman, Thomas. ''Leaders: Education Key to Bridging Digital Divide.'' *Computerworld,* September 11, 2000.

Kim, Michael C., and Dennis A. Steckler. ''Leaping the Digital Divide.'' *Best's Review,* February 2001.

Lach, Jennifer. ''Crossing the Digital Divide.'' *American Demographics,* June 2000.

Lipke, David J. ''Dead End Ahead?'' *American Demographics,* August 2000.

Melymuka, Kathleen. ''Dabbling at Diversity.'' *Computerworld,* December 11, 2000.

Rombel, Adam. ''The Global Digital Divide.'' *Global Finance,* December 2000.

Wallman, Kathleen M. H. ''Counting Down the Top Ten.'' *America's Network,* March 1, 2001.

SEE   Children and the Internet; Cyberculture; Digital Econ-
ALSO: omy 2000 Report

DIGITAL ECONOMY 2000 REPORT

In June 2000, the U.S. government issued the *Digital Economy 2000* report, a follow-up to its previous *Emerging Digital Economy* reports published in 1998 and 1999. The report was based on research conducted by the Council of Economic Advisors (CEA), the Congressional Budget Office (CBO), the Federal Reserve, and outside economists. It announced that information technology (IT) industries were responsible for at least 50 percent of increased U.S. productivity rates, which grew at an annual rate of 1.4 percent from 1973 to 1995, and 2.8 percent thereafter. Although IT industries only accounted for an 8.3-percent share of the U.S. economy by 2000, they generated roughly 30 percent of overall U.S. economic growth. Electronic commerce (e-commerce) led growth throughout the new digital economy.

Digital Economy 2000 identified several significant IT-related business and economic trends. In general, businesses turned ever more frequently to the Internet to boost efficiency by shifting supply networks and sales online and relying on networked systems to streamline internal procedures. The resulting improvement in productivity led to lower inflation and higher real wages. However, the report indicated that this still was an emerging trend.

The number of workers in the software and computer services industries rose from 850,000 in 1992 to 1.6 million in 1998. By 1998, there were 7.4 million workers in IT-related positions nationwide, or about six percent of the total U.S. workforce. Hiring of the most highly skilled employees, such as systems analysts, programmers, and computer scientists, rose by nearly 80 percent to about 1 million positions during the same period. IT salaries averaged $58,000 a year, 85 percent higher than the average for the private sector.

IT industries invested heavily in new research and development (R&D). Their investments accounted for 37 percent of all American R&D spending from 1995 to 1998. In 1998 alone, IT-industry investment for R&D totaled $44.8 billion, or about one-third of company-funded R&D.

Worldwide, approximately 304 million people had Internet access by 2000, a nearly 80-percent increase from the previous year. In contrast, only 3 million people around the globe had similar access in 1994. Most of the growth occurred outside of the United States and Canada, which for the first time totaled less than half of those with online access. However, the number of American Web users still rose by 40 percent. In most other areas of the world, Internet access at least doubled. Access in Africa showed a 136-percent increase; Asia and the Pacific, 155 percent; Europe, 108 percent; the Middle East, 111 percent; and South America, 102 percent.

Dramatic decreases in the price of IT-related technology fueled phenomenal growth in Internet expansion and use. From 1995 to 1999, computer prices

declined at a rate of 26 percent annually, rapidly making computer technology available to a widening percentage of the population. The report also identified falling IT prices as being directly responsible for lowering the U.S. inflation rate by an average of 0.5 percentage points per year.

Other studies corroborate *Digital Economy 2000's* findings. For example, a study of 3,000 IT industries conducted by the University of Texas-Austin, which was funded by Cisco Systems and issued on the same day as *Digital Economy 2000,* stated that the number of U.S. workers in Internet-related jobs doubled in 1999 to 2.5 million. At the same time, IT industry revenues grew by 62 percent to reach $524 billion in 1999, up from $322 billion the previous year.

Not of all *Digital Economy 2000's* conclusions were positive, however. As the report pointed out, a majority of Americans still lacked online connections at home. Those "on the wrong side of the digital divide," such as people in low-income jobs, those with a lower level of education, and members of minority groups, were falling further behind in reaping the benefits of the digital economy. Ironically, the runaway success of the New Economy also has created hardship in California's Silicon Valley, the epicenter of the IT universe. Astronomical increases in the cost of living there placed great hardships on many who lived and worked in the area, where many service-related employees earned an average $23,000 in 1999.

Not all IT-related industries benefited equally from the expanding digital economy. Outside of the IT industry itself, productivity increases were only discernible in goods-producing industries. But IT-intensive industries in the services sector actually witnessed a decline in productivity. In this sector, from 1990 to 1997 labor productivity fell by 0.3 percent. In contract, non-IT-related service sectors enjoyed an increase of 1.3 percent in productivity. Furthermore, when scrutinizing productivity at the level of individual firms, the study located no automatic correlation between investment in IT and growth in productivity. Such increases occurred only when major organizational transformations were implemented in tandem with IT investment. Thus, it appeared that decentralization emerged as an essential component in correlating IT spending and increased productivity.

The study also identified a very brief payback period for computer hardware investment in the United States. Thus, the high returns on IT investment did not constitute an unmixed blessing. Such returns must be high if they are to pay off, since hardware depreciation occurs so quickly.

It also is questionable whether the optimistic picture drawn for the digital economy can be realized fully outside the United States, since many of the conditions responsible for IT-related gains are specific to the United States. These include a large-scale IT supply industry targeted on high-value business, and favorable economies of scale. In addition, American business functions in a flexible investment environment that is amenable to risk-taking. Other parts of the globe, where more conservative and cautious approaches to business operations prevail, may be less favorably positioned to take advantage of the new information technologies.

Digital Economy 2000 concluded that "the U.S. economy has crossed into a new period of higher, sustainable economic growth and higher, sustainable productivity gains." Based on such conclusions, many economists adjusted their long-term economic growth forecasts upward, projecting a 3.1-percent annual growth rate for the first decade of the 21st century, instead of their earlier predictions of 2.5 percent. However, with the volatility of the stock market and the uncertain economic climate at the turn of the millennium, it remains to be seen whether *Digital Economy 2000's* forecasts will prove correct.

FURTHER READING:

Haskins, Walaika. "Super Economy." *PC Magazine.* August 1, 2000.

Mason, Paul. "'Boom is IT-Driven' Say US Economists." *Computer Weekly.* June 15, 2000.

Seipel, Tracy. "Digital Economy Emerges." *Motley Fool.* June 5, 2000. Available from http://www.fool.com.

Strassmann, Paul. "Fuzzy Math in D.C." *Computerworld.* Jan 8, 2001.

U.S. Department of Commerce. "Background for Digital Economy 2000 Report." Washington, D.C.: GPO, 2000.

———. *Digital Economy 2000.* Washington, D.C.: GPO, June 2000.

SEE ALSO: Digital Divide

DIGITAL EQUIPMENT CORP.

Digital Equipment Corp. was a leading developer of microprocessors, semiconductors, and other high-tech equipment in the 1970s and 1980s. Its breakthrough Alpha microprocessor, introduced in 1992, went on to power such well-known World Wide Web portals as Alta Vista and Lycos, although Lycos eventually switched to Microsoft's Wintel platform. Despite its technological breakthroughs, Digital struggled in the early 1990s to keep pace with competitors more adept at things like cutting costs and modifying sales strategies to take advantage of new industry trends. Eventually, the firm was taken over by Compaq Computer Corp. Digital's Alpha server line continues to serve many Unix-based systems.

EARLY HISTORY

Two engineers from the Massachusetts Institute of Technology (MIT), Kenneth Olsen and Harlan Anderson, joined forces in 1957 to establish Digital Equipment Corp. in Maynard, Massachusetts. The new computer technology firm launched a computer systems module the following year. In 1960, Olsen and Anderson developed the PDP-1 computer, the smallest and most interactive computer on the market at that time. They founded DECUS, the Digital Equipment Computer Users Society, in 1961. It became the world's largest computer society for a single manufacturer's products.

International expansion began in 1963, when offices were established in Munich, Germany, and Ottawa, Ontario. Digital then launched the PDP-5, the world's first minicomputer; and the PDP-1 operating system, which was the first system to make use of timesharing technology. In 1964, units opened in both Australia and the United Kingdom. The PDP-6, a 36-bit computer, shipped that year, and the world's first mass-produced minicomputer, the PDP-8, shipped in 1965. Olsen and Anderson took Digital public in 1966.

The late 1960s brought increased international growth. A manufacturing plant was established in Puerto Rico; a Japanese headquarters office opened in Tokyo; and a European headquarters office opened in Switzerland. In 1970, a new plant in Massachusetts began manufacturing peripheral and metal products. Product launches during the first half of the decade included the PDP-11/20, a 16-bit computer; MPS, the firm's first microprocessor; and the LSI-11, the firm's first 16-bit microcomputer. By 1975, Digital had sold more than 50,000 computer systems. The firm unveiled the DECSYSTEM-20, a 36-bit timesharing system, in 1976. The following year, Digital developed its first VAX computer, the VAX-11/780. Sales exceeded $1 billion for the first time in 1977, and employees totaled 36,000.

Digital made its first foray into retail sales in 1978 by establishing a store in New Hampshire. Computer systems sold reached the 100,000 mark. Two years later the firm launched its second VAX system, the VAX-11/750, which was the world's first Large Scale Integration (LSI) 32-bit minicomputer. Intel Corp. and Xerox Corp. began working with Digital on developing a local network, known as Ethernet. Sales exceeded $3 billion. The firm diversified into personal computers by launching DECmate II, Rainbow

100, Professional 325, and Professional 350 in 1982. International growth continued via a joint venture agreement between Brazil's Elebra Computadores and Digital. In 1984, Digital bought Trilogy Technology Corp. Late in the decade, the firm began forging strategic alliances with other industry leaders. As a result, Cray Research Inc., the world's top supercomputer maker, agreed to develop products compatible with Digital products, as did Apple Computer Inc. More than 50 percent of total annual sales came from international operations.

The firm expanded into Eastern Europe in 1990, with the establishment of Digital (Hungary) Ltd., in Budapest. That year, more than 20 new computers, peripherals, and software applications were introduced. Digital added to its holdings the financial services arm of London-based Data Logic Ltd., a leading manufacturer of UNIX-based software for brokerage houses. In 1991, Asea Brown Boveri Inc. (ABB) and Digital forged a joint venture known as EA Information Systems Inc. The venture focused on furthering the three-dimensional plant design work started in ABB's engineering automation software division. Microsoft Corp. agreed to use Digital's new PATH-WORKS software to allow Microsoft Windows users to retrieve and trade data on local area networks. Similarly, Intel Corp. and Digital agreed to work together on several software projects in 1992. Acquisitions included the information systems unit of Philips Electronics, BASYS Automation Systems, and leading PC software and accessories distributor 800-SOFTWARE. That year, Digital launched its RISC-based Alpha chip, the fastest such chip in the industry. Both Microsoft and Olivetti agreed to work with Digital to develop a platform to best utilize the new microprocessor.

ATTEMPT AT RESTRUCTURING

Despite the firm's cutting-edge technology, Digital found itself losing ground to competitors like Sun Microsystems and Silicon Graphics. According to an April 1997 article in *Marketing Computers,* "Digital couldn't compete in the cost-controlled, channel dependent environment of the 1990s with its archaic sale structure." After four consecutive years of losses, the firm announced a reorganization in 1994. Digital's workforce was slashed 21 percent the following year, and net income rebounded to $122 million as direct sales tactics were replaced with reselling agreements. In 1996, Digital, Microsoft Corp., and MCI Communications Corp. began working together to develop e-mail, groupware business communications, and other services to manage the corporate data networks known as intranets.

Intel Corp. agreed to pay $700 million for the semiconductor manufacturing operations of Digital in

1997. Per the terms of the deal, Digital retained intellectual property rights to the Alpha chip, as well as the right to continue developing it. According to Digital Chairman Robert Palmer, as quoted in a November 1997 issue of *InfoWorld,* the divestiture allowed Digital to "refocus on its core mission of building Internet business solutions based on high-performance platforms and services." To this end, the firm continued refining its Alpha chip, and in 1998 released the 21264 Alpha, the first microprocessor to operate at a speed faster than one gigahertz. Digital also sold its network products operations to Cabletron Systems Inc. for roughly $430 million.

TAKEOVER BY COMPAQ COMPUTER CORP.

Although Compaq had first considered buying Digital in 1995, it wasn't until three years later that the personal computer manufacturer and marketer made an offer. Some analysts believed it was Digital's 1997 decision to refocus on Internet technology and services, after making two major divestitures, that caught Compaq's eye in 1998. Others attributed Compaq's renewed interest to the extensive service division Digital had amassed over the years while developing new technology for corporate buyers. Digital's wide range of products and services—including its Alpha architecture, Digital Unix operating system, and 23,000 service employees—would allow Compaq to compete with the likes of IBM Corp.

In June 1998, Compaq finally acquired Digital, completing the largest merger to date in the computer industry. Compaq discontinued Digital's personal computer line and sought to move beyond making and selling personal computers by offering increased computer services to clients. By 2001, service made up more than 20 percent of Compaq's total revenues. In large part, this was due to the 23,000 service employees the firm had inherited from Digital. That year, Compaq announced its intent to stop making the Alpha chip in favor of Intel's Itanium chip, and the intellectual property rights of Alpha were transferred to Intel.

FURTHER READING:

Barker, Robert. "Missed the Boat on DEC? So Did Fidelity—Big Time." *BusinessWeek Online.* February 6, 1998. Available from www.businessweekonline.com.

Bilodeau, Anne. "Digital is Weaned from Direct Sales, and Finds it Likes the Freedom." *Marketing Computers.* April 1997.

Emigh, Jacqueline. "Digital Crashes 1 Gigahertz Speed Barrier." *Computing Canada.* February 23, 1998.

Pendery, David. "Internet Business Key to Digital's Future." *InfoWorld.* November 10, 1997.

Popovich, Ken. ''Compaq Turns on New Services Initiative.'' *eWeek.* July 16, 2001.

Ristelhueber, Robert. ''A Slimmer, More Attractive Digital.'' *Electronic Business.* February 1998.

Sykes, Rebecca. ''Digital Makes Peace with Intel.'' *InfoWorld.* November 3, 1997.

Williams, Molly, and Gary McWilliams. ''Compaq Will Switch to Intel Processors.'' *The Wall Street Journal.* June 26, 2001.

SEE ALSO: Compaq Computer Corp.; Hardware; IBM Inc.; Intel Corp.; Microprocessor; Microsoft Corp.; Sun Microsystems; UNIX

DIGITAL SIGNATURE

The legally binding electronic autographs known as digital signatures were among the key technologies that made the Internet a forum for commerce in the early 2000s. They not only verify an individual's identity, but also guarantee the validity of the information attached to the signature, be it a credit card number, an order form, or a written document. Once they are widely used and supported, digital signatures will significantly reduce the costs of conducting business over the Internet.

Digital signatures usually are transported in digital certificates—encrypted electronic packages sent as e-mail attachments and increasingly used with Web forms. Digital certificates are assured by trusted third parties called certificate authorities, which issue certificates and act as a guarantor of their validity. Digital certificates generally contain more comprehensive data than digital signatures, including company information, the certificate's expiration date, and so on.

Using techniques from the field of cryptography, digital signatures are generated by applying a mathematical formula, or algorithm, to scramble the information into a string of digits. This ensures that only those with the correct keys—those who will make use of the signature, either for signing or for verification—can unscramble them. Only the holder of the private key—the one whose signature it is—can actually sign a document with that digital signature, while anyone with the public key can verify that it came from that individual. Moreover, digital signatures are bound to the document to which they are applied, and cannot be illicitly copied and transferred to another document. Therefore, signatures not only help to ensure legal validity, but security as well. While digital signatures are not immune from criminal mischief, they certainly are more difficult to forge than handwritten signatures. Their use over a public-key encryption system greatly fortifies digital signatures from attack by malicious hackers.

Digital signatures didn't originate with e-commerce. The basic principle behind digital signatures—electronic validation of a user's identity over computer networks—has been used for years, most notably with automatic teller machines (ATMs) and other systems that utilize a personal identification number along with another piece of information, such as a magnetic identification card. In the early days of e-commerce, the phrase ''digital signature'' was loosely defined. It could, for instance, even refer to a handwritten signature that had been scanned into an electronic format. However, such methods, which were extremely prone to forgery, rarely were considered legally binding and failed to win widespread support as a safe and viable means of validating transactions.

On June 30, 2000, President Bill Clinton signed into law—using a digital signature—the Electronic Signatures in Global and National Commerce Act, or E-Sign. This act, which went into effect on October 1 of that year, officially conferred the same legal status on digital signatures as handwritten signatures. The United States government, meanwhile, mandated that all federal agencies accept digital signatures by October 2003.

Despite such efforts, it likely will be some time before digital signatures are as ubiquitous as some hope. Research firm Gartner Group estimated that less than 40 percent of the public would use digital signatures by the middle of the 2000s. Forrester Research predicted even slower penetration, with only 10 to 15 percent of the marketplace capable of using digital signatures doing so by 2003.

Holding the widespread use of digital signatures in check in the early 2000s were the disparate software programs used to validate digital certificates. Since various software programs exist, and often are tailored to different organizations, the technological infrastructure that allows for seamless, wide ranging transactions was far from complete. Moreover, certificate authorities each maintain their own rules of certificate issuance, validation, and revocation. Therefore, legal responsibility and authentication frequently was muddled outside of a small, contained network. According to a report by Meridien Research, e-signature technology was expected to take the most immediate hold in business-to-business transactions, primarily because it was in such arrangements that players could establish consistent implementation of compatible signature solutions.

FURTHER READING:

Ceniceros, Roberto. ''Digital Signatures Mean Better Security Online.'' *Business Insurance.* December 4, 2000.

''E-Signatures to Take Hold Slowly, Report Says.'' *Bank Systems & Technology.* February 2001.

Edfors, Patty. ''Your John Hancock Goes Digital.'' *Communications News.* December 2000.

Gelbord, Boaz. "Signing Your 011001010: The Problems of Digital Signatures." *Communications of the ACM.* December 2000.

Hallenborg, John C., and Orla O'Sullivan. "Not By Software Alone." *U.S. Banker.* February 2001.

Hammar, Sven. "PKI Enables Digital Signatures." *Network World.* October 30, 2000.

Stephens, David O. "Digital Signatures and Global e-Commerce: Part I—U.S. Initiatives." *Information Management Journal.* January 2001.

SEE ALSO: Cryptography, Public and Private Key; Digital Certificate; Digital Certificate Authority; Digital Signature Legislation; Encryption

DIGITAL SIGNATURE LEGISLATION

Legislators and business leaders long recognized that the passage of some kind of digital legislation was of central importance to the development of e-commerce. However, for several years Republicans and Democrats in the U.S. Congress haggled over what should be included in such a bill. In the meantime, several states passed their own legislation allowing some forms of digital signatures to be legally binding in certain situations. When a major piece of national legislation went into effect in 2000, it was heralded as a giant step toward the harmonization of interstate and international laws, and was expected to help propel e-commerce forward in the early 2000s.

The most sweeping digital signature legislation on the books in the early 2000s was the Electronic Signatures in Global and National Commerce Act, popularly known as the E-Sign Act. President Bill Clinton signed the act into law on June 30, 2000, and it became effective on October 1 of that year. Under E-Sign, digital signatures used in interstate and foreign commerce assumed the same legally binding status as old-fashioned, handwritten signatures. The act defined electronic signature broadly as any "electronic sound, symbol, or process attached to or logically associated with a contract or other record and executed or adopted by a person with the intent to sign the record." This flexibility allows the legislation to remain valid through the course of technological development. It was expected to open the way for a flood of financial transactions over the Internet, from securing loans to transferring money between accounts to closing home sales.

Significantly, no individual is required to use a digital signature in any situation, nor is any business compelled to accept them. However, once parties agree to make use of digital signatures, then all parties are bound to recognize the signatures as legally binding. In short, the act bars discrimination against a signature for the sole reason that it is electronic.

Prior to E-Sign, almost every state had at least one law on the books that validated electronic signatures in some situations, while 20 states had signed onto the Uniform Electronic Transactions Act (UETA), which recognized digital signatures as legally binding for contracts. However, in adopting UETA, several states made their own modifications that progressively eroded the uniformity of the law. Such state laws tended to veer into their own directions, creating disharmony that could hamper interstate commerce. In particular, they tended to reflect the more popular technologies of the day, thereby reducing the degree of flexibility e-commerce law may need to remain valid over time and across borders. For example, Utah's Digital Signature Act of 1995 tended to favor electronic signatures using digital certificates over public key encryption systems. Effectively, E-Sign facilitated the harmonization between such laws and took national what many states had already allowed.

In addition, E-Sign includes provisions for electronic record keeping. It allows electronically stored records to be considered legally valid, provided they accurately convey the information in the original record and are freely accessible to all involved parties in a form that can be accurately reproduced. As long as these conditions are met, the record keeper fulfills the legal obligation to retain records in their original form.

E-Sign is a self-executing law. Thus, it makes no provisions or requirements for a state or federal regulatory agency to adopt or enforce its measures. Regulatory actions that involve aspects of E-Sign are permissible only if the regulations remain consistent with E-Sign, do not issue any requirement that a record be in paper form, remain technology neutral, and confer no unreasonable costs on the use of electronic signatures.

E-Sign charges the secretary of commerce with promoting the use of digital signatures in international transactions and the harmonization of signature standards. For these efforts, the act refers to the Model Law on Electronic Commerce as its basis, which was adopted by the United Nations Commission on International Trade Law. By the time E-Sign went into effect, many European countries already recognized digital signatures. Japan, meanwhile, began officially recognizing them in April 2001. Therefore, with its heavy emphasis on international commerce, E-Sign placed the United States on the same playing field as the most developed countries.

E-sign's importance to e-commerce is difficult to estimate. It may take some time before digital signatures take hold on a widespread basis, particularly in business-to-consumer markets. However, their growing approval at the national and international levels translates to more current laws that reflect the sweeping changes the Internet and other technologies effected through the 1990s and early 2000s.

FURTHER READING:

Edfors, Patty. "Your John Hancock Goes Digital." *Communications News.* December 2000.

Glover, K. Daniel. "John Hancock Goes Digital." *Financial Executive.* March/April 2001.

Harrell, Ron. "Electronic Signatures Will Change Business Practices." *American Agent & Broker.* February 2001.

Kromer, John. "The ABCs of the E-Sign Act for Community Banks." *Community Banker.* January 2001.

McElligot, Tim. "Pen Pals." *Telephony.* January 1, 2001.

Montana, John C. "The Electronic Signatures in Global and National Commerce Act: A Sea Change in Electronic Records Law." *Information Management Journal.* January 2001.

Wright, Benjamin. "Technology File: Laws Guide Uniformity for e-Signatures." *Credit Union Executive Journal.* November/December 2000.

Zinkewicz, Phil. "Sign on the Dotted Line." *Rough Notes.* December 2000.

SEE ALSO: Cryptography, Public and Private Key; Digital Certificate; Digital Certificate Authority; Digital Signature; Encryption

DIGITAL WALLET TECHNOLOGY

Digital wallets are small electronic packages that automatically supply information such as credit card numbers and shipping addresses for use in conducting Internet transactions. Also known more broadly as Internet payment services, they provide a means by which customers may order products and services online without ever entering sensitive information and submitting it via e-mail or the World Wide Web, where it is vulnerable to theft by hackers and other cyber-criminals. Digital wallets thus allow consumers to make online purchases easily and securely, safeguarding the privacy of purchasing habits and financial information alike.

Traditionally, digital wallets were stored on the desktops of personal computers. By the early 2000s new digital wallets were compatible with wireless and other mobile devices, and were more often stored on a central server owned by a digital wallet vendor or Internet service provider (ISP). Among the technologies touted as a cornerstone for the growth of e-commerce, digital wallets had a history of promise interrupted by false starts. They evolved in stages, with a series of incarnations since first emerging in the mid-1990s.

Digital wallet vendors maintain relationships with online merchants in a manner similar to those between credit card companies and brick-and-mortar stores. The digital wallet vendor either charges a commission to the retailer on every purchase involving the vendor's wallet, or merchants pay the vendor a flat fee for accepting the vendor's wallet in their transactions. In turn, businesses and customers mutually agree to use the products, software, and services of a particular digital wallet vendor, which then acts as an intermediary for all transactions between the firm and its customers. In this way, customers needn't transmit credit card numbers for each transaction. Instead, they send the purchase order to the wallet vendor, which simply charges it to the customer's account.

USING DIGITAL WALLETS

Digital wallets were heralded as one of the technological innovations that would help fulfill the promise of ultimate shopping convenience afforded by e-commerce. While online shoppers needn't wait in long lines or sit in traffic to make their purchases, the long and often convoluted form-filling process required in order to make a purchase online using a credit card number kept e-commerce from achieving the prominence that e-merchants had counted on. In 1999 the research firm Jupiter Communications reported that 27 percent of all customers who began placing an order online actually abandoned the process, primarily due to the amount of time and confusion involved in completing an online order, not to mention the fears involved in transferring credit card information over the Internet. Therefore, digital wallets were positioned to take e-commerce to the next level of penetration by easing the entire process and making individuals comfortable about sending their purchase orders over the Internet.

With digital wallets, customers could forego the process of filling out lengthy order forms each time they made an online purchase. Rather, they could simply activate the wallet to automatically and securely fill out the required information fields, including the customer's name, credit card number and expiration date, and billing and shipping information. When an online shopper is ready to make his or her purchase, he or she simply clicks on the digital wallet, which automatically fills out the entire order form and transmits the information to the online merchant. The wallet is then updated to reflect the most recent purchase.

Thus, digital wallets don't actually store cash as real wallets do. In 1999 Forrester Research reported that, while 100 percent of U.S. Internet retail outlets accepted credit cards, only 14 percent accepted alternative payment methods, such as debit cards. Digital wallets came about to exploit that framework rather than try to usher in completely new forms of Internet-based payment systems (such as digital cash) with which customers may not have been familiar or comfortable. So rather than overhaul the entire payment system, digital wallet vendors worked only to try to make the existing dominant payment method more user-friendly. Primarily, they facilitate what is known as one-click shopping, saving customers from having to repeatedly enter in the same information for each purchase.

Typically, digital wallets also allow customers to store preferences for Web sites and purchases, thereby allowing the merchants that support the wallet to personalize their offerings and notify the customer of special sales and new products. Moreover, when the digital wallet enters the required information in its appropriate fields, it automatically encrypts the data. In this way, customers can rely on an encryption system maintained by a company whose technology they already are familiar with, rather than relying on the security of the encryption systems of many different merchants.

THE PUNCTUATED EVOLUTION OF DIGITAL WALLETS

Digital wallets first emerged in the mid-1990s with a great deal of hype, but to a lukewarm public reception. The earliest wallets required customers to download the digital wallet vendor's software and store it on their desktops. This method largely inhibited customers from warming to the technology. Downloads generally were viewed with some skepticism by analysts, since they tend to limit overall distribution. Slow connection speeds exacerbated the problem, since customers tend to grow frustrated and abort downloads if they take an excessively long time to complete. In addition, any time the vendor updated its digital wallet software, customers had to download all over again. Moreover, once the software was downloaded, the digital wallet was stored on the computer's hard drive, requiring the customer to make all purchases from that computer. This lack of flexibility became increasingly problematic as more Internet shoppers roamed from one place to another and used multiple computers for surfing and shopping.

Another impediment to digital wallet penetration was customer awareness. In 1999, according to the research firm Bizrate.com, only 58 percent of online purchasers were even familiar with digital wallets, while only one-fourth understood their capabilities. In addition, the sheer glut of digital wallet offerings in the late 1990s—issued by merchants, software vendors, credit card firms, banks, and other outfits—led to customer confusion, not to mention frustration

stemming from the lack of compatibility between all these wallet packages. With no standardized payment system, customers were reluctant to fill up their hard drives with mutually exclusive digital wallets, nor maintain contracts with various firms.

Several online retailers, including Amazon.com, created their own versions of digital wallets for use only on their sites to encourage repeat purchases. After the first purchase, when a customer fills out an entire order form, he or she only needs to click a button to repeat the entire order-filling process automatically. However, only a small number of very large firms had the clout to make such an investment worthwhile. To benefit from digital wallets, most companies needed a larger framework of mutually shared technology. Furthermore, only the very largest, most leveraged companies could afford to contract with a variety of vendors at the same time, putting them at a great competitive advantage but also limiting the overall penetration of digital wallets.

In 2000, Forrester Research released the results of a survey of online merchants. The merchants were asked why digital wallets had failed to attain prominence. Sixty-two percent of U.S. e-merchants felt there simply was too little customer demand, while 54 percent reported that digital wallets weren't a priority. Twenty-seven percent thought the market was too immature, another 27 percent couldn't see any benefits in adopting the technology, and 19 percent thought that digital wallets would result in the loss of customer relationships.

One of the biggest drawbacks, however, was compatibility. Since customers may have maintained digit wallet accounts with vendors other than the one a particular company may have used, the layers of software downloads necessitated to use digital wallets with all the different businesses made the process more cumbersome than the lightning-fast world of e-commerce had promised. Thus, by the end of the 1990s digital wallets were fairly antiquated and used mainly in very tightly confined networks.

To amend this problem, several interested parties—including MasterCard, Visa, American Express, IBM, Microsoft, Trintech, and CyberCash—teamed up in the late 1990s to begin working toward the establishment of a digital wallet standard. The Electronic Commerce Modeling Language (ECML) was conceived as a mechanism to clearly define a format for online order forms that could incorporate digital wallet technology from any vendor. To adopt ECML, merchants need only reorganize their existing online order forms so that the fields correspond to those set forth in the ECML standard. No licensing or usage fees apply, and ECML requires no additional software or hardware, according to *Catalog Age*. The first digital wallet to comply with ECML was IBM's Consumer Wallet 2.1, which was that company's second shot at digital wallet technology. Meanwhile, ECML standardized the format in which the various fields were stored in digital wallets.

Digital wallet vendors increasingly aligned with credit card issuers, whose massive marketing clout was expected to further the wallets' cause. The popular American Express Blue credit card was packaged with American Express's own digital wallet to facilitate use of Blue on the Internet. Meanwhile, Visa and MasterCard spent 1999 and 2000 in vigorous competition to align with wireless software and hardware vendors with an eye toward capitalizing on the expected boom in digital wallet use. Some of these systems involved ''fat'' wallet technology, in which the wallets were embedded in handheld devices or on a smart card, while others simply utilized a server-side system over a wireless medium.

By the early 2000s, digital wallets were undergoing a mild renaissance. The models developed at that time abandoned software downloads altogether, opting instead for digital wallet systems that worked directly with ISPs and other telecommunications firms. In other words they involved server-side (or ''thin''), rather than client-side (''fat''), technology. This eliminated the need to download any software or to conduct transactions from a certain computer. When a customer places an order with such a system, his or her identity is secured in the eyes of the merchant by attaching a digital certificate to the order message. In this way, merchants supporting digital wallets were afforded some protection from online fraud while also allowing for greater convenience and flexibility.

Moreover, the details of purchases weren't generally shared directly with the ISP or other intermediary—only the connection to use the digital wallet was routed through these agents. In this way, consumer fears of privacy invasion were somewhat eased, as the information was shared only with a company with whom they already entrusted the data. Meanwhile, in an effort to hang on to market share in an increasingly competitive market, ISPs often pitched their Internet payment services options to their customers as an added value of their offerings.

CHALLENGES FOR THE FUTURE

Despite the improvements and the heating competition, digital wallet technology still was largely a novelty by the early 2000s, and it remained to be seen how well vendors could turn such systems into a widespread force in the e-commerce world. Vendors were very conscious of their market's less-than-glorious history. Digital wallets were more often referred to as Internet or Web-based Payment Systems by the early 2000s, in large part to disassociate the

products from their rather unsuccessful predecessors in the mid- and late 1990s. One challenge was to adapt Internet Payment Systems to tap into the vibrant business-to-business market. By the early 2000s, most digital wallet systems were designed for the business-to-consumer market.

Customer awareness, or lack thereof, was an irritatingly persistent problem. According to BizRate.com, in 2001 only 38 percent of online shoppers understood how digital wallets worked, 25 percent knew about digital wallets but were unfamiliar with how they worked, and 37 percent of online buyers had never heard of digital wallets at all. Meanwhile, only 22 percent of online shoppers had actually used a digital wallet at least once, and a humbling five percent used them frequently. This last figure, in fact, was equal to the percentage of customers who had used digital wallets at least once and swore they would never use one again. Such results clearly were a concern to vendors and merchants alike.

Still, analysts expected digital wallets to begin taking a firmer hold of the e-commerce market in coming years. In anticipation of more widespread acceptance and use of digital wallets, developers were expanding the capabilities of the technology, allowing customers to use the systems as a mechanism for comparison shopping, product searches, and to check merchant ratings, among other value-added services. With penetration disappointingly slow through the early 2000s, digital-wallet vendors increasingly sought to add such capabilities in order to turn digital wallets into more valuable and holistic e-commerce facilitators.

FURTHER READING:

''The Answer to Internet Debit Payments?'' *Electronic Payments International.* February 29, 2000.

Austen, Ian. ''A Chilly Welcome for Digital Wallets.'' *New York Times.* November 4, 1999.

Brewin, Bob. ''MasterCard, Visa Vie for Wireless Victory.'' *Computerworld.* April 3, 2000.

Bryant Quinn, Jane. ''Opening Soon: The Digital Wallet.'' *Washington Post.* December 5, 1999.

Collett, Stacy. ''IBM Unveils 'Easier' Digital Wallet Tool.'' *Computerworld.* September 20, 1999.

Courter, Eileen. ''Wait & See.'' *Credit Union Management.* August 2000.

Ehrenman, Gayle. ''Internet Trivia: Folks May Be Shopping Online, but They're Sticking to Traditional Forms of Payment.'' *Internetweek.* February 5, 2001.

''Industry Proposes New 'Digital Wallet' Standard.'' *Graphic Arts Monthly.* August 1999.

Kiesnoski, Kenneth. ''MasterCard Eyeing Voice-Activated Wallet.'' *Bank Systems & Technology.* June 2000.

———; and Bob Curley. ''Digital Wallets: Card Issuers Seek to Ease Web Shopping.'' *Bank Systems & Technology.* October 1999.

Lavonne, Kuykendall. ''No Small Change.'' *Internet Retailer.* May 2000.

Oberndorf, Shannon. ''The Promise of Digital Wallets.'' *Catalog Age.* November 1999.

Schwartz, Jeffrey. ''e-Commerce Leaders Agree on Standard Checkout Spec.'' *Internetweek.* June 21, 1999.

Short, Sharon Gwyn. ''Beyond Digital Wallets: Internet Payment Services as e-Commerce Boom or Bust.'' *Econtent.* April/May 2000.

Taneja, Sunil. ''Digital Wallets Ease e-Business.'' *Chain Store Age.* September 1999.

Walker, Christy. ''Digital Wallets.'' *Computerworld.* July 5, 1999.

SEE ALSO: Digital Cash; Digital Certificate; Digital Certificate Authority; Electronic Payment; Internet Payment Provider; Micro-payments

DISCUSSION FORUMS

Online discussion forums, also known as World Wide Web forums, bulletin boards, or message boards, emerged in the mid-1990s and allowed Internet surfers to post and respond to messages on the Web. Since that time, discussion forums have become increasingly popular. They cover a wide variety of topics ranging from sports, health, and business, to current events, finance, and entertainment.

The idea for Web-based discussion forums stemmed from newsgroups that used the Usenet system. Developed in 1979, Usenet operated as a bulletin board system and was supported by UNIX machines. As technology advanced, discussion forums were developed to operate on the Web, rather than on a UNIX-based system. Along with newsgroups, discussion forums also were similar to Internet chat. Both discussion forum and chat technologies allowed Web surfers to communicate online. Discussion forums used asynchronous communication, however, which differed from chat in that it allowed its users to post and respond to messages from any computer at any time, rather than requiring all chatters to be logged on simultaneously.

Over time, discussion forums become increasingly user friendly. Forums typically arranged messages by thread—topic, date, and time—and allowed users to respond to a certain message or create a new message, or thread, of their own. In order to become part of a forum, many sites required Web surfers to register for a user ID and password. These forums also typically had a set of rules that discouraged malicious or inappropriate language and reserved the right to block any users that abused the forum. Certain discussion forums also had moderators, who viewed messages before they were posted in order to ensure they met the site's standards.

Discussion forums have been used by a wide variety of organizations, including businesses and educational institutions. For example, many college professors began utilizing these forums as a teaching tool in the late 1990s. Students were encouraged to use specific forums set up by the college or professor to discuss class topics. The largest group of discussion forum users, however, was made up of individuals seeking information. Countless discussion forums emerged for these users in the mid-1990s.

In 1996, Forum One Communications Corp., a consulting firm for online communities, began publishing its Online Community Index, a compiled list of thousands of Web forums. Available on the company's Web site, the index divided forums into topics such as entertainment or gardening and listed the recommended discussion forums for those topics. By 2001, more than 300,000 Web forums were listed by the index. Search engine Yahoo! also operated discussion forums on a wide variety of topics, allowing its users to post and respond to messages. In addition, many traditional businesses integrated discussion forums into their sites. For example, *BusinessWeek Online's* Web site included a forum section that enabled users to discuss investment issues, magazine topics, technology trends, and career issues.

As discussion forums continued to become increasingly popular, not only were Web surfers given the option of participating in an existing forum, they also were given the ability to create new forums of their own. For example, ezboard Inc. allowed its members to design a unique forum on the topic of their choice. The company, dedicated to promoting online forums to foster communication and commerce, had secured 10.9 million users across the globe and was rated as one of the top 100 Web sites by Internet traffic measurement firm netScore in April 2001. As the number of Internet users is predicted to continue rising, discussion forums likely will remain a popular avenue for Internet communication.

FURTHER READING:

''About the Online Community Index.'' Alexandria, VA: Forum One Communications Corp., 2001. Available www.forumone.com.

Cashel, Jim. ''Top Ten Trends for Online Communities.'' *Online Community Report.* July 2001. Available from www.onlinecommunityreport.com.

SEE ALSO: Community Model; Virtual Communities

DISINTERMEDIATION

In the business world, third parties like distributors traditionally served as links between the consumers and manufacturers or providers of goods and services. Such middlemen also played important roles in the business-to-business sector, connecting companies with various suppliers of parts, components, and raw materials. Disintermediation occurs when third parties are eliminated from the supply chain, allowing direct links between buyers and sellers.

DISINTERMEDIATION, PROS AND CONS

Disintermediation has several advantages. In addition to giving consumers simpler and more direct access to goods and services, it can also mean lower prices, because supply chains are streamlined and the fees charged by distributors and logistics providers are eliminated or sharply reduced. The advent of e-commerce made it possible for many companies to begin selling directly to consumers, some of whom had never done so before.

While the potential to sell directly via the Internet was appealing because of the potential for greater profits, it also had several drawbacks. First, disintermediation caused tension between many companies and their business partners, including salespeople, rep firms, distributors, dealers, and retailers. Because of this tension, industry trade associations like the National Automotive Dealers Association and the Wine Wholesalers Association took steps to preserve their roles. Their efforts made it impossible for wineries to sell wine online, or for automobile manufacturers like Ford and Chrysler to bypass local dealers and sell cars directly to consumers.

Another drawback to disintermediation was that some companies failed to identify the kind of infrastructure required for handling fulfillment online. Fulfillment, the act of filling and shipping orders received from customers, is different on the Internet because high volumes of smaller orders are often received. This stands in contrast to traditional fulfillment involving large shipments of product to distributors or retail chains. Successful online fulfillment requires responsive, integrated back-end processes in areas like accounting, customer service, marketing, and shipping. This makes it possible to offer customers real-time information about available products, shipping and order confirmations, problem notifications, and more. Having a fancy Web site to accept orders simply isn't enough, which many companies eventually discovered to their dismay.

EXAMPLES OF DISINTERMEDIATION AND ITS IMPACT

Disintermediation has had varying degrees of impact on different industries. One industry where the Internet has caused noteworthy disintermediation is healthcare. Before the World Wide Web, local healthcare providers often served as a primary resource for individuals with questions or concerns about health issues. Furthermore, a doctor's opinion was accepted with little or no question. The explosion in online information had a significant impact on consumers who were thirsty for healthcare information, spurring them to seek answers about healthcare from various Web sites instead of from local professionals.

The Internet also helped to render patients better informed. Just as automobile consumers, armed with information obtained through online research, went to local dealers armed with information about the price and reliability of vehicles, healthcare consumers began investigating health issues and possible treatments prior to visits with physicians. This was beneficial for patients in many cases. In addition to large numbers of articles, online communities and support groups made it possible for people suffering from diseases to share information and strategies about treating and coping with their conditions.

Disintermediation in the healthcare industry had downsides as well. Among the negative factors were the reliability and integrity of the sources from which the information was obtained. In some cases, information was old, outdated, or simply inaccurate. Objections also arose from many physicians who felt their professional skills and authority were being second-guessed. In *Health Management Technology,* Peter J. Plantes, M.D., explained: ''While disintermediation has fueled the growth of e-commerce in many industries, it can have negative consequences for health systems. Removing the local healthcare organization and their physicians from the healthcare equation decreases patients' identification, reliance and access to local resources and healthcare options that can best meet their needs. For healthcare organizations and their physicians, disintermediation erodes the local patient base and creates roadblocks to reaching physicians, and can be in opposition with outreach and integration strategies.''

By the early 2000s, disintermediation had infiltrated a wide array of industries. In the packaged goods and toy industries, companies like Nabisco and Mattel sold a percentage of their products directly. In the computer industry, Dell Computer sold directly on an exclusive basis. Because of the company's overwhelming success in the early 2000s, Dell is an excellent example of how disintermediation can work. The company, which climbed to the top of the overall world market in the first quarter of 2001, built computers on demand for both individual consumers and organizations. A large percentage of Dell's direct orders came via the World Wide Web.

The disintermediation caused by e-commerce has affected long-established business channels. Although some third parties have been eliminated altogether, many continue to survive because their services bring real value to the business world. Warehousing, inventory management, storage, and shipping, which collectively fall under the umbrella of logistics, are examples of valuable services offered by intermediaries. Rather than cutting them out of the picture, some manufacturers also have asked third-party business partners to change their focus and provide training or consulting services to customers, thereby becoming value-added services while leaving the selling processes to the companies themselves. Finally, some companies were able to successfully sell both directly and through traditional distributor channels. Herman Miller Inc., a manufacturer of office furniture, used this approach by selling directly to home office users (a market its dealers didn't target), and through dealers to larger corporate accounts. Part of the company's philosophy, which it communicated through regular meetings with dealers, was that home office users might eventually evolve into larger corporate accounts.

Although many predicted the Internet would eliminate most middlemen through disintermediation, e-commerce actually gave birth to many companies for whom acting as intermediaries is a primary focus. According to *InfoWorld,* ''Organizations such as eBay and eLoan, perfect intermediaries, have had such a huge impact on how people search for goods and information. The most successful intermediaries add value by creating more intimate relationships between the partners they serve. Companies quick and agile enough to detect opportunities in complex markets will prosper as intermediaries.'' Besides eBay and eLoan, NetZero was another example of a third party infomediary that was born during the Internet age. The company offered free Internet access to consumers in exchange for marketing information.

The use of direct sales channels between manufacturers and buyers was expected to significantly increase in the early 2000s, boding well for many companies. Peppers and Rogers Group of Stamford, Connecticut and the Menlo, California-based Institute for the Future conducted a study that revealed a healthy forecast for companies selling direct. The research predicted the number of consumers using the direct sales channel would triple between 1998 and 2010 from 11 percent to 33 percent, respectively. It also forecast consumer direct sales to grow from $190 billion to $1.1 trillion during the same timeframe.

FURTHER READING:

Berghel, Hal. ''Predatory Disintermediation.'' *Communications of the ACM,* May 2000.

''Consumer Direct Sales To Explode.'' *Web Trend Watch,* July 14, 1999. Available from www.mediainfo.com/ephome/news/newshtm/webnews.

Kador, John. ''New Economy Rules for Recruiting.'' *InfoWorld,* July 3, 2001.

Keenan, William Jr. ''E-commerce Impacts Channel Partners.'' *Industry Week,* July 19, 1999.

Plantes, Peter J. ''Disintermediation: The New Competitor.'' *Health Management Technology,* September 2000.

''Progressive Policy Institute: Middlemen Hampering Ecommerce.'' *Nua Internet Surveys,* February 1, 2001. Available from www.nua.ie/surveys/index.

Rodgers, Denise. ''Who's Afraid of Disintermediation?'' *Catalog Age,* August 2000.

SEE ALSO: Channel Conflict/Harmony; Fulfillment Problems; Order Fulfillment

DISPUTE RESOLUTION

As with any form of commerce, disputes between two parties engaged in e-commerce arise from time to time. As the number of online businesses grew throughout the 1990s, so did the need for online dispute resolution. As a result, several organizations began responding to this need, among them BBBOnline, ICANN, eResolution.com, and the Online Ombuds Office.

In some cases, a consumer may seek dispute resolution services regarding a complaint it has with an online business. One option for such an individual is BBBOnLine. The Council of Better Business Bureaus, an advocate for fair and ethical business practices, decided to broaden its scope to include e-commerce in the summer of 1996, when it founded BBBOnLine Inc. to operate as the Better Business Bureau of the World Wide Web. Along with offering information on specific companies and consumer guides, the site also allows visitors to seek help with dispute resolution by filing four types of complaints: general complaints about both BBB members and non-members, as well as both online and traditional businesses; complaints regarding new vehicles, which are handled by a program called BBB Auto Line; complaints about charitable groups, which are handled by the BBB Philanthropic Advisory Service; and complaints about the use of personal information, which are handled by the BBBOnline Privacy program.

Those seeking dispute resolution regarding Internet domain names, or site addresses, can turn to the

Internet Corporation for Assigned Names and Numbers (ICANN), a non-profit organization that oversees domain name distribution, as well as the assignation of other identifiers that differentiate one Web site from another. ICANN replaced IANA (Internet Assigned Numbers Authority), a government entity that had been created by the Internet Society and Federal Network Council to handle the assignment of domain names and other Internet protocol. The Clinton Administration had decided in July of 1997 that the increasing number of clashes surrounding domain name ownership warranted the creation of a standard international policy regarding domain name assignation and dispute resolution procedures. This led the U.S. Department of Commerce to facilitate the creation of ICANN, a private, non-profit association run by Dr. Jon Postel, in 1998.

In 2000, ICANN accredited eResolution.com as one of four official domain name dispute resolution services providers in the world. A leading online dispute resolution services provider, eResolution also offers three additional services: arbitration, which is legally binding; mediation, which is voluntary; and keyword dispute resolution, offered in conjunction with RealNames Corp., a provider of keywords (a relatively new alternative to traditional domain names).

The Online Ombuds Office serves both individuals and institutions seeking online assistance with dispute resolution. The site was created in June of 1996. When the Hewlett Foundation and the Department of Legal Studies at the University of Massachusetts decided to fund the creation of the Center for Information Technology and Dispute Resolution of the University of Massachusetts in June of 1997, the Online Ombuds Office began operating as the dispute resolution unit of the new center. The site offers both general resources and a dispute form, which can be completed and submitted by visitors wishing to handle dispute resolution procedures via the Internet. In early 1999, auction giant eBay.com asked the Online Ombuds Office to provide mediation services for its bidders and sellers. As a result, eBay created a link to the dispute resolution site in mid-March. Within two weeks, more than 150 requests for dispute resolution services were logged. Having verified the need for such a service, eBay hired SquareTrade, a San Francisco, California-based online dispute resolution services provider founded in 1999, via a two-year contract starting in August of 2000.

As methods for conducting business online continued to evolve, dispute resolution services for specific types of online endeavors also emerged. For example, a firm named WebMediate began offering online dispute resolution services to business-to-business marketplaces like GoTradeSeafood.com. The need for these types of specialized services will more than likely increase as e-commerce continues to grow and evolve.

FURTHER READING:

''About BBBOnLine.'' Arlington, VA: BBBOnLine Inc., 2001. Available from www.bbbonline.org.

''About ICANN.'' Marina del Rey, CA: Internet Corporation for Assigned Names and Numbers, 2001. Available from www.icann.org.

Enos, Lori. ''Consumer Watchdog Unveils Net Conduct Code.'' E-Commerce Times. October 25, 2000. Available from www.ecommercetimes.com.

''SquareTrade to Serve As eBay's Exclusive Provider of Online Dispute Resolution.'' Business Wire. August 2, 2000.

SEE ALSO: BBBOnline; ICANN (Internet Corp. for Assigned Names and Numbers)——

DISTRIBUTED SYSTEMS

The Internet consists of an enormous number of smaller computer networks which are linked together across the globe. No one central computer is responsible for the Internet's performance, or for the sea of available information that people obtain from it every day. Rather, this performance and information is distributed among and affected by millions of individual entities (individuals, companies, and organizations) and devices (routers, servers, workstations, desktop computers, and other pieces of the Internet's infrastructure). In this sense, the Internet is a distributed system.

This same principle applies to smaller computing environments used by companies and individuals who engage in e-commerce. For example, employees at a large company may use a software application to enter customer data into a database. Rather than being directly installed on each user's computer, this software application is more often installed on one server and shared among hundreds or thousands of users via a network. Applications used in such distributed environments often are object-oriented programs, and the parts (objects) they consist of can be located on one or more machines and accessed by many users as needed. Additionally, even though different parts of a program may be located on different machines, to users it appears as if the application were running right from their computer.

The general concept of distributed systems grew in popularity and prominence along with the evolution of computer technology. When companies began using computers for the first time, large mainframe systems, and later minicomputers, were used to solve complicated business problems and perform difficult computing tasks. Computers became tools for performing calculations and analyzing different combinations of variables that were virtually impossible, or which would be too time consuming, for humans to do. Since that time, such operations have become increasingly decentralized and networks of smaller distributed systems, working collectively, have been applied to modern day information processing challenges. As *Red Herring* explained: "Companies have begun using distributed computing to harness unused computing power to better solve problems. In the United States, there are already 100 million computers connected to the Internet. If you could put them all together, you'd have a computer 3,333 times more powerful than the most powerful computer on earth, IBM's ASCI White, which has the power of around 30,000 desktops."

The SETI Institute is one example of how an organization has used distributed computing in this way. SETI is "an institutional home for scientific and educational projects relevant to the nature, distribution, and prevalence of life in the universe." SETI scans radio frequencies from space in an attempt to discover communications from extraterrestrial life forms. Through the organization's SETI@home program, individuals with computers and Internet access were able to help SETI by loading a special screen saver onto their computers. The screen saver connected to SETI while computers were not being used, retrieved data from SETI, analyzed it for signs of life, and reported back to SETI. The alternative to this approach was for SETI to obtain an expensive supercomputer to perform analyses, which was beyond its financial means.

Distributed computing not only allows otherwise idle computing resources to be used, it also allows data to be distributed more efficiently. For example, companies that offer software or various forms of content downloads on the Internet can address potential traffic overload issues by distributing downloadable data at strategic Internet locations instead of forcing the world's users to download it from only one source. In the early 2000s, Digital Island was one company that specialized in making networks and content delivery faster and more reliable. Digital Island's Footprint network put content geographically closer to individual users on a network of special caches (devices which hold content and make it more readily available to users). In mid-2001 the company announced that it had teamed with Internet services software provider Novell Inc. to make content delivery faster across the Footprint network. This was partially in response to the habits of online users, who generally wait only a handful of seconds to obtain online content before looking elsewhere.

The future of distributed computing looked very bright in the early 2000s. At that time, IBM had obtained what *Technology Review* described as "an apparently broad patent on a way to broker large computing tasks." This approach was similar to what SETI was doing in that a special screen saver coordinated the use of otherwise idle computing resources at homes or at large companies from a central computer. However, unlike SETI's method, which was applied to a single task, IBM's approach could handle multiple computing tasks. In addition to scientific applications, IBM's approach held potential for business use, such as financial data analysis. Supporting this, *ZDNet* reported that analysts predicted distributed computing would take off in 2001 as companies realized its value as a way to affordably analyze large amounts of data, as opposed to buying large, expensive supercomputers.

FURTHER READING:

Berst, Jesse. "No Alien Idea: How Distributed Computing Will Change the Web." *ZDNet,* December 27, 2000. available from www.zdnet.com.

"Distributed Computing." *Red Herring,* November 1, 2000. Available from www.redherring.com.

"General Information." The SETI Institute. July 15, 2001. Available from www.seti-inst.edu/general/purpose.html.

Shankland, Stephen. "Buddy, Can You Spare Some Processing Time?" *CNET News.com,* September 1, 2000. Available from www.cnet.com.

Talbot, David. "Collective computing." *Technology Review,* May 2001.

DISTRIBUTION

The manner in which commercial goods are distributed has evolved throughout history. Long ago, consumers directly traded physical goods and services. Eventually, different forms of physical currency, such as coins and paper money, were added to the mix. Increasingly sophisticated methods of communication played an important role in the evolution of distribution. As *Purchasing* explained, "In the past, to communicate needs, buyers used couriers, which evolved to using water, rail, and air as each new transportation mode came into being. For critical needs, telegraph replaced the horse followed by phone, telex, fax, private networks and, finally, the Internet."

The Internet, and later the World Wide Web, gave birth to e-commerce. For the first time in history, it was possible for buyers and sellers to communicate instantly with one another, regardless of physical location, and make arrangements regarding the exchange of goods and services. While it was relatively simple to enable online payments, the part of the transaction involving the movement of goods was another matter. Physical goods still had to be transported in some manner. On the other hand, digital goods could be transported as quickly as online payments.

DIGITAL GOODS

Digital goods, also known as soft goods or virtual goods, exist in an electronic format. Digital goods normally include different varieties of information, including text documents, audio, and video. The vast majority of computers used by the public, and by those engaging in e-commerce, are digital devices. At their most basic level, digital computers understand and process information in a binary format of zeroes and ones (0, 1, 10, 11, 100, 111, and so on). The programming languages used to create software like Web browsers, databases, word processors, and spreadsheets are written in formats closely resembling human grammar that ultimately are converted to a computer's machine language of ones and zeroes.

One of the advantages of digital goods is their minimal storage requirements. Unlike videocassettes, record albums, compact discs, and paper books, large amounts of digital goods can be stored on magnetic media like a computer's hard drive. This requires less physical storage space for buyers and seller alike. Digital goods also are perpetual. This means that text documents, computer software, digital audio, and digital video can be preserved without fear of deterioration from environmental conditions that might affect physical goods over long periods of time. Additionally, digital goods can be duplicated infinitely with each copy retaining the exact properties of the original, without a loss in quality. While this is an advantage in one regard, it also is a weakness because digital goods can be easily pirated and distributed illegally.

In the early 2000s digital goods presented several different areas of opportunity for third party companies. For example, in November 2000 Virage Inc., a provider of Internet video production software and services, joined with digital commerce services provider Qpass to offer video content providers with an outsourced means of managing, selling, and distributing their content via the Web. Another leading area of opportunity was in the area of security.

SECURITY

Once a consumer pays for digital goods, which are normally received in the form of a downloadable file, it is possible for the recipient to make endless copies of the file and redistribute them for profit or for free. This obviously damages the original seller's profit potential. One area where this kind of fraud has cost manufacturers is software. Pirates are well known for duplicating software applications that cost many hundreds of dollars in stores and selling them at lower costs via online auctions or other means.

Obviously, law enforcement agencies prosecute pirates for copyright violations and online fraud. However, this problem presented a serious roadblock for companies looking to sell digital goods via e-commerce in the early 2000s. While companies like the *Wall Street Journal* were able to sell information with little concern over privacy (the information quickly becomes outdated), piracy was a more serious threat for companies selling digital goods like books or audio, which had much longer life spans.

In addition to permanent copyright notices called digital watermarks, which serve as means of identifying when illegal distribution has occurred, several measures were being developed to safeguard these kinds of goods during distribution. These involved limiting what people were able to do with digital content after a file was downloaded. One example were digital music files that only played on the computer to which they were downloaded. Another was a system that allowed digital goods to be transferred between media with the condition that they were removed from the system they were copied from, leaving only one copy. InterTrust Technologies Corp. was one company offering technology like this. It offered solutions in the area of digital rights management to content providers, service providers, application builders, and others. Its technology ensured that organizations could ''release digital information and profitably benefit from it throughout its full lifecycle by persistently protecting it, implementing a wide variety of business models, monitoring usage, and getting paid.''

THE FUTURE OF DISTRIBUTION

Digital goods likely will play more central roles in e-commerce as technology continues to evolve. According to the Association for Computing Machinery, desktop computers will be capable of storing approximately one terabyte of information by 2010, making the long-term storage and use of digital information increasingly practical. Besides scanning and storing items of importance or historical significance, consumers will be able to accept and store vast amounts of digital audio and video content as well, leading to new distribution patterns and preferences, and opportunities for companies supporting the distribution of electronic information.

FURTHER READING:

Bell, Gordon. "A Personal Digital Store." *Communications of the ACM,* January 2001.

Bulkelely, Michael. "Machines Talk to Machines." *Purchasing,* December 22, 2000.

"Digital and Analog Information." *The PC Guide,* May 9, 2001. Available from www.pcguide.com.

"Going Straight." *The Economist,* April 5, 2001.

Hane, Paula J. "Qpass Teams With Virage for Video-content Solution." *Information Today,* November 2000.

"The MetaTrust Utility." InterTrust Technologies Corp. May 13, 2001. Available from www.intertrust.com.

Schull, Jonathan. "Infonomics 101: A Map of the Information Economy." *Inform,* February 1999.

"What is Digital Rights Management?" InterTrust Technologies Corp. May 13, 2001. Available from www.intertrust.com.

SEE ALSO: Fulfillment Problems; Order Fulfillment; Shipping and Shipment Tracking

DOBBS, LOU

One of the leading cable television talk show hosts, Lou Dobbs also has been a front-runner in the dot-com world. An executive vice president with CNN, Dobbs founded CNN's Financial News (CNNfn) and its Web affiliate, CNNfn.com, the first programming services that were launched simultaneously on television and the Internet. Dobbs also anchored CNN's show *Moneyline News Hour.*

Dobbs was born in rural Idaho, far away from the nation's financial centers, and eventually won a scholarship to Harvard, where he graduated in economics. However, he pursued a journalism career, beginning as a financial news reporter on Seattle's KING-TV until Ted Turner hired him in 1980 as CNN's chief economics correspondent and as host of *Moneyline.* Dobbs became president of CNNfn in 1997. With Dobbs as anchor, *Moneyline* ranked among CNN's highest income-earning programs, though initially critics labeled its content as "boring."

Dobbs's first Internet endeavor was CNNfn.com, a Web site affiliated with the popular cable program. A fully searchable site, CNNfn.com featured financial news and hosted a financial information directory. Dobbs predicted the site would double its 2 billion hits after its first year in operation. Unlike many dot-com ventures, CNNfn.com turned a profit of approximately $25 million.

After 19 years with *Moneyline,* in July 1999 Dobbs resigned to launch another Internet venture, Space.com. The site provided news, information, entertainment, and educational content on outer space and was aimed at a wide online audience. The site was served by a news staff of 27 journalists operating from bureaus in Washington, D.C., Cape Canaveral, Houston, and Pasadena. It drew revenue from several sources, including online and television advertising, content syndication, a magazine, and retail licensing and merchandising. Dobbs also envisioned developing the site's business-to-business capability.

In early 2001, Dobbs announced that he intended to return to CNN and *Moneyline.* He also planned to help launch the network's new show *Money.* This financial program targeted average Americans, rather than the upper-income households attracted by *Moneyline.* Dobbs would resign as chief executive of Space.com, but remain chairman and keep his stake in the company. In 1999, Dobbs won the Horatio Alger Association award for Distinguished Americans.

FURTHER READING:

Bernstein, Roberta. "Space Cadet." *Adweek.* May 1, 2000.

Dogar, Rana. "Taking a Flier on the Web." *Newsweek.* September 20, 1999.

Greene, Kira. "TheGrassIsGreener.com." *Broadcasting & Cable.* April 17, 2000.

Grimes, Christoper. "Dobbs Plans Return to CNN." *Financial Times.* April 11, 2001.

Mardesich, Jodi. "What Alanis Morissette and Lou Dobbs Share." *Fortune.* December 20, 1999.

McAdams, Deborah. "No Gain, Just Pain at CNNfn." *Broadcasting & Cable.* August 30, 1999.

DOMAIN NAME

A domain name identifies an Internet Protocol (IP) address, or series of addresses, on the Internet. Each site on the Internet is assigned a series of 11 or 12 numbers, known as an IP address. Addresses are translated via a Domain Name System (DNS) server into domain names, which simply are the names assigned to the numbers. The main reason for the DNS is to make Internet addresses easier to remember. For example, 134.167.21.147 is the IP address for the domain name techcorps.org, the Internet site for an organization known as Tech Corps. The.org suffix is considered a top-level domain for organizations such as non-profit associations. Other common top-level domains include.edu for educational institutions,.gov for governmental bodies,.com for companies,.mil for military organizations, and.net for network administrators. Internet sites operating in countries other than the United States attach two-letter top-level domains, such as.ca for Canada and.jp for Japan, to the ends of their domain names. To secure a domain name, those wishing to create an Internet site simply must verify that the domain name they desire is not in use, via a firm such as Checkdomain.com, and then pay a fee to register that name.

In 1995, the number of top-level domain names registered totaled roughly 100,000. By the spring of 1999, more than 7 million domain names had been registered. That number jumped to 28.2 million by the end of 2000. As the level of domain name registration intensified through the mid- and late-1990s, issues such as the unapproved use of trademarked names arose, prompting calls for legislation dealing with domain name registration. In 1997, the Clinton administration started pushing for the creation of international policy standards regarding the assignment of domain names and the resolving of disputes over domain name rights. At the directive of the U.S. Department of Commerce, Dr. Jon Postel founded Internet Corporation for Assigned Names and Numbers (ICANN) in 1998. ICANN is a U.S.-based, private, non-profit association overseeing Internet infrastructure issues, including addressing protocol and dispute resolution. It replaced the government operated IANA (Internet Assigned Numbers Authority), a unit of the Internet Society and Federal Network Council that had been handling the assignment of domain names and other Internet protocol parameters.

DOMAIN NAME DISPUTE RESOLUTION

One of ICANN's first tasks was to begin developing an international dispute resolution policy for domain name disagreements. The resulting Uniform Domain Name Dispute Resolution Policy (UDRP) stipulated that entities using one of the three most common top-level domains—.com.,.net, and.org— must resolve any trademark-based domain name squabbles via litigation, arbitration, or formal agreement before a registered name could be transferred or canceled. In 1999, the organization approved two domain name dispute resolution service providers: World Intellectual Property Organization (WIPO) and National Arbitration Forum. The following year, ICANN selected two more dispute resolution services providers: eResolution and CPR Institute for Dispute Resolution. To have a case reviewed by these arbitrators typically costs $1,500.

In the late 1990s, pop singer Madonna was one of several celebrities to file a complaint over the use of a trademarked name in a domain name by an unauthorized agent. Madonna alleged that Dan Parisi used her name to attract viewers to his pornographic Web site at www.madonna.com. According to an October 2000 article in *E-Commerce Times,* Madonna was required to demonstrate that ''the domain name registered by Parisi was identical or confusingly similar to a trademark or service mark in which Madonna has rights; Parisi had no legitimate interests in respect of the domain name; and the domain name had been registered and used in bad faith.'' Because Parisi could not satisfactorily justify his use of the word ''Madonna'' in his domain name, a three-member panel of WIPO came to the conclusion that the defendant was using the trademarked name to lure Internet users into visiting his site in hopes of finding information related to Madonna. As a result, WIPO found in favor of Madonna in October of 2000, and ordered Parisi to transfer the domain name rights to the entertainer.

Large corporations also made use of UDRP. In 2000, the Esquire.com domain name was transferred to publishing house Hearst at the behest of WIPO, which also ordered several domain names using the Harry Potter trademark to be transferred to AOL Time Warner.

Offering additional legal options to U.S.-based trademark holders is the Anti-Cybersquatting Consumer Protection Act, a federal law passed by the U.S. Congress in 1999. Those found guilty of cybersquatting—attempting to use a trademark in a domain name to profit from it, either by capitalizing on name recognition or by selling the domain name to the trademark holder at an elevated price—can be fined up to $100,000 in damages. According to the April 2001 issue of the *San Diego Business Journal,* the act ''differs from the Uniform Dispute Resolution Process in that it is a court proceeding, rather than an administrative proceeding, and is U.S. law rather than internationally enforced policy.''

DOMAIN NAME DISTRIBUTION AND REGISTRATION

Along with developing dispute resolution policies, one of ICANN's primary roles is to oversee the distribution of Internet domain names and the assignment of IP addresses. The organization also is responsible for ending the domain name registration monopoly held by Herndon, Virginia-based Network Solutions Inc. (NSI) since it had agreed to take domain name assignation responsibilities from the U.S. government in 1993. Established in 1979, NSI was the first privately owned firm to offer domain name registration services. In 1995, NSI began charging a fee for domain name registration services. Each Internet site registering a domain name with NSI pays $70 for the first two years, and $35 per year thereafter.

Verisign bought NSI in March of 2000, taking over NSI's joint business of both selling domain names and controlling the registries, or master lists, of.com,.org, and.net addresses. Shortly after its formation, ICANN started accrediting new domain name registrars, such as Register.com, to compete with NSI. All registrars are required to adhere to the UDRP, and those who register for a domain name also must accept the terms of the UDRP. By signing a subscriber agreement, registrants declare that, as far as they know, their domain name, as well as the way in which it will be used, in no way violates trademark law. They also agree to participate in a dispute resolution proceeding in the event of a complaint.

NSI continues to control the three largest top-level domain registries. In mid-2001, ICANN announced its intent to introduce three new top-level domains over the next several months. The.biz domain will be operated by NeuLevel. Register.com will oversee the.pro domain, which will be split into three different domains:.med.pro for doctors;.law.pro for lawyers; and.cpa.acc.pro for accountants. The registrar of the third new top-level domain,.info, is yet unnamed. ICANN plans to launch four additional top-level domains by 2002.

FURTHER READING:

''Domain Monopoly's Days are Numbered.'' *Reuters.* April 12, 1999.

''Domain Name.'' In *Ecommerce Webopedia.* 2001. Available from e-comm.webopedia.com.

Hoisington, Michael J. ''A Perfect Domain Name Within a Business's Reach.'' *San Diego Business Journal.* April 2, 2001.

''ICANN.'' In *Ecommerce Webopedia.* Darien, CT: Internet.com, 2001. Available from e-comm.webopedia.com.

''ICANN.'' In *Techencyclopedia.* Point Pleasant, PA: Computer Language Co., 2001. Available from www.techweb.com/encyclopedia.

Mahoney, Michael. ''Madonna Wins Domain Name Dispute.'' *E-Commerce Times.* October 17, 2000. Available from www.ecommercetimes.com.

Posnock, Susan T. ''Conquering Cybersquatters.'' *Folio: the Magazine for Magazine Management.* April 2001.

''Scramble for New Internet Domains Begins.'' *United Press International.* June 22, 2001.

''Uniform Domain-Name Dispute-Resolution Policy.'' Marina del Rey, CA: ICANN, 2001. Available from www.icann.org.

SEE ALSO: Cybersquatting; Dispute Resolution; ICANN (Internet Corp. for Assigned Names and Numbers); URL (Uniform Resource Locator)

DOT-COM

At the most basic level, ''dot-com'' is simply a colloquial term born of the suffix appended to Uni-

form Resource Locators (URLs), as in www.companyname.com. But the term has come to stand for a variety of phenomena. By the early 2000s it stood for Internet-based businesses, the business craze born of the outlandish stock boom these companies enjoyed and exacerbated, a certain type of unorthodox business model, and even an era of contemporary economics.

The opening of the Internet to commerce in the 1990s unleashed a flurry of new business possibilities, and no one seemed to know just where it would all land. Still, a palpable sense of optimism was in the air. In many ways, dot-com companies were widely seen as being removed from the ''real world.'' On a literal level, this removal refers to their virtual presence in cyberspace, remote from the brick-and-mortar economy. Figuratively, dot-com firms were famously immune—until the tech-market stock bubble burst in spring 2000—from traditional forms of valuation and the importance of tried and true business fundamentals. However, in a way their wild-eyed success in the late 1990s fertilized the soil for the vicious backlash against the dot-com economy in the early 2000s.

The speed and extent of the dot-com boom in the late 1990s helped propel this seeming immunity of dot-com companies from such old economy staples as sound business strategies, plans for long-term value and profitability, and attention to macroeconomic warning signs. Dot-coms defied all market logic through the end of the decade, and the flow of cash into the Internet industry seemed nearly endless. The soaring stock prices seemed to lend weight to dot-com entrepreneurs' claims that this was, indeed, a new economy in which the old rules no longer applied.

Valuations were a consistent mystery, with companies registering market values in the hundreds of millions of dollars without ever turning profits. As *Business Week* pointed out, when Yahoo! Inc.'s market value came in at an astronomical $1 billion in 1997, sober investors might have been wise to disbelieve it. However, had they done so they would have missed out on a massive three-year run that would have generated a fortune.

The tech-market stock bust in early 2000 set off a massive dot-com shakeout, and the Web was littered with sunken Internet companies. Meanwhile, the cultural tone shifted away from dot-com euphoria and toward a more tempered attitude about e-commerce. At least 210 dot-coms closed their doors in 2000. Meanwhile, the dot-com bust had many holdouts sneering at broken dot-com investors, saying ''I told you so.''

FURTHER READING:

''Getting Over the Dot-Con.'' *Business Week.* December 11, 2000.

''Leaders: Is There Life in e-Commerce?'' *Economist.* February 3, 2001.

Mullaney, Timothy J. "Gone but Not Forgotten." *Business Week*. January 22, 2001.

Wilder, Clinton. "Success: Opiate of Dot-Com Elite." *Informationweek*. February 12, 2001.

SEE ALSO: Cyberculture: Society, Culture, and the Internet; New Economy; Shake-out, Dot-com

DOUBLECLICK INC.

DoubleClick Inc. is a pioneer in providing Internet advertising services, both to those seeking to advertise on the World Wide Web and to Web publishers who want to attract advertisers. Founded in January 1996 in New York City, DoubleClick created the first Internet advertising network, a group of Web sites that the firm represented to advertisers. It was a model that other Internet advertising agencies would emulate. Over the course of its first five years, DoubleClick expanded the network of Web sites it represented, segmented it to match the needs of Internet advertisers, and reorganized it to reflect changing market conditions. In March 2001 the company announced it would offer two distinct networks in the United States. One, the DoubleClick Brand Network, consisted of branded Web sites that had substantial brand recognition, a significant amount of traffic, and a marketable inventory of advertising opportunities. The other network was the DoubleClick Audience Network, which emphasized audience reach, targeting, and optimization in specific vertical categories. Outside of the United States, DoubleClick would continue to offer networks based on the local content of each country.

Another innovation credited to DoubleClick is its proprietary Dynamic Advertising Reporting and Tracking (DART) software technology, which enables the company to determine within 15 milliseconds which banner ad should be presented to the current user, based on pre-selected criteria. In order for DART to match ads to target audiences within milliseconds, it uses the controversial "cookie" technology that creates a user profile and monitors an Internet browser's movements through Web sites in DoubleClick's media network. Using this technology, DoubleClick created a database of user profiles that enabled it to better target banner ads to users who visited Web sites in the DoubleClick network.

DoubleClick's information-gathering practices put it at the center of Internet privacy concerns, and privacy advocates have closely monitored how DoubleClick obtains and uses information about Internet users. At issue is the fact that cookies obtain information about a user's hardware and software as well as their Internet connections without obtaining permission. Privacy advocates are most concerned that the technology could be used to obtain confidential information against the wishes of individual users. Another key issue involves combining online and offline information to create even more comprehensive user profiles that might include individual names, addresses, and telephone numbers. DoubleClick has maintained that it uses the information in aggregate form only, and does not reveal information on an individual basis. In March 2001 the Federal Trade Commission (FTC) ended its investigation into DoubleClick's privacy practices without saying that any violations had or had not occurred.

OFFERED REAL-TIME TARGETING

DoubleClick had its roots in the New York advertising firm Poppe Tyson, a subsidiary of Bozell, Jacobs, Kenyon & Eckhardt Inc. It was established by Poppe Tyson, Kevin O'Connor, and Dwight Merriman. O'Connor and Merriman had enjoyed success with Intercomputer Communications Corp., a software company that O'Connor sold for $25 million when they were in their early twenties. In 1995 Tyson's interactive unit was trying to find ways to place online advertising. The firm contacted O'Connor, who was in charge of the Internet Advertising Network at the time. He was in the process of developing software to position ads on the World Wide Web for maximum effect. O'Connor and Tyson then joined forces to create a network of Web sites that they could represent to potential advertisers.

DoubleClick launched its network in January 1996, representing about 30 Web sites. O'Connor and Merriman developed software for DoubleClick that could match online banner ads to a user's demographic and psychographic profile in a matter of milliseconds. This gave the firm a powerful tool to deliver targeted ads to highly segmented audiences. In its first year of operation DoubleClick quickly built a database of some 10 million user profiles. Among the first sites represented by the DoubleClick Network were Travelocity, excite.com, and AltaVista.

Investors were attracted to DoubleClick's business model. Initially, the company raised more than $2 million from Bozell, Jacobs, Kenyon & Eckhardt. In mid-1997 it raised another $40 million from six venture capital firms. At the end of 1997 the company filed for an initial public offering (IPO), which took place in February 1998 and raised $62.5 million. Its IPO filing revealed that DoubleClick had $30.6 million in revenue for the first nine months of 1997, 43 percent of which was accounted for by AltaVista. Advertisers accounted for about 30 percent of the company's revenue. DoubleClick also had begun to expand internationally, opening sales offices in the United Kingdom, Canada, and Australia. DoubleClick Japan was formed in September 1997 as a joint venture with three other Japanese firms.

Another innovation credited to DoubleClick was introduced in mid-1998. DoubleClick Local was a new service that allowed advertisers to target Internet users on a regional and local basis by tracking their IP addresses. The new service used the geographic targeting capabilities of DoubleClick's DART technology. DoubleClick had mapped out the individual points of presence for major national Internet service providers (ISPs), but not for America Online users.

Later in 1998, DoubleClick launched a new business unit, Closed-Loop Marketing Solutions, that offered three new services for advertisers. One service, DART for Advertisers, helped them to manage and traffic ads and easily change their creative content. DataBank was a reporting service that anonymously tracked shoppers' patterns and provided the information to advertisers. A third service called Boomerang gave advertisers the ability to create distinct lists of people on their site and what they did, and to continue the relationship after they left the site.

EXPANDED THROUGH ACQUISITIONS IN 1999

In an effort to expand its reach in January 1999, DoubleClick began representing the ad inventory of Web sites on a non-exclusive basis. Sites whose ads were sold only by DoubleClick became part of the DoubleClick Select group. While DoubleClick remained selective about which sites it would represent, the move to represent some sites on a non-exclusive basis gave the firm greater flexibility in meeting the needs of advertising buyers. In early 1999 DoubleClick claimed to have ads placed on 6,400 Internet sites worldwide. It delivered 5.6 billion ads in December 1998 and represented ad sales for about 60 Web sites on an exclusive basis. Internationally, DoubleClick had 27 sales offices in 17 countries.

In spite of losing $18 million on revenue of $80 million in 1998, DoubleClick was in a strong financial position to expand through acquisition. It renewed its contract with AltaVista for three years, which represented about 40 percent of DoubleClick's revenue. The company raised $95 million in December 1998 through a secondary stock offering, followed by another $250 million in March 1999. In the second half of 1999 DoubleClick made three significant acquisitions. In June the company announced it would acquire Abacus Direct Corp. in a transaction valued at $1 billion. Abacus Direct was an information and research provider for direct marketing and maintained databases of customer buying histories from catalogs and retailers. When announced, the acquisition alarmed privacy advocates, who envisioned DoubleClick would combine its online data with the offline data collected by Abacus Direct to create customer profiles with complete contact information, including home addresses and telephone numbers.

The second major acquisition of 1999 involved NetGravity Inc., which was DoubleClick's biggest competitor. DoubleClick acquired the firm for $530 million. As a result, DoubleClick pulled away from its competitors to assume leadership in the online advertising business. Before the year was over, rumors were flying that DoubleClick would acquire another leading competitor, 24/7 Media, but nothing came of it.

The third major acquisition of 1999 gave DoubleClick a better position in e-mail marketing. In December 1999 the company announced it would acquire Opt-In Email.com, an Internet provider of e-mail marketing, publishing, and list management. The acquisition coincided with DoubleClick's introduction of its suite of e-mail products, called DARTmail, with DARTmail for Publishers and DARTmail for Advertiser set to launch in the first half of 2000.

Late in 1999 DoubleClick reorganized its DoubleClick Network into six vertical divisions: automotive, business, travel, women and health, entertainment and youth, and technology. The company retrained its sales representatives to be experts dedicated to only one field. The DoubleClick Network consisted of premium branded sites. To be represented by the DoubleClick Network, a site had to have at least 1 million page views per month. In January 2000 DoubleClick established a second network, called Sonar, to serve smaller sites. The Sonar network initially was divided into 16 categories and was expected to expand to about 40 categories throughout 2000. Web sites generating as few as 100,000 page views per month were eligible to become part of the Sonar network.

PRIVACY CONCERNS DOMINATED 2000

Privacy concerns again took center stage for DoubleClick in 2000. In January 2000 a Marin County, California, woman filed a lawsuit against DoubleClick, claiming that the firm violated consumers' privacy by improperly using the information it collected about the Web sites they visited. Following the acquisition of Abacus Direct, with its huge database of information on millions of consumers, it became known that DoubleClick planned to link its own online data with the offline data in Abacus's database. The lawsuit asked DoubleClick to change its information-gathering policy so that it would have to ask for a consumer's explicit permission before collecting data on them. At the time, DoubleClick only had an "opt-out" policy in effect, whereby a consumer could visit the company's Web site and request that the company refrain from gathering information on them. Many critics claimed this placed an unfair burden on consumers.

Further action on privacy issues was taken by the Electronic Privacy Information Center (EPIC), which filed a complaint with the FTC. The complaint argued that it was illegal for DoubleClick to track Internet users' online activity and then combine that information with offline data to create a national marketing database. The complaint led to an FTC investigation into DoubleClick's practices. In March DoubleClick announced it would halt its plans to merge names with anonymous user activity until the Internet industry and the federal government established firm guidelines to protect the privacy of Internet users. Later in the year the company convened a privacy panel to study the issue and appointed a chief privacy officer.

CONTINUED TO EXPAND IN 2000

Although DoubleClick cut back on its acquisitions in 2000, it continued to expand. A strategic partnership with e-mail network Topica gave DoubleClick a stronger position in e-mail marketing. The firm's new DARTmail service would manage Topica's opt-in e-mail lists, which numbered some 5 million unique users. Topica also agreed to buy a half-billion impressions on DoubleClick's Sonar network to promote its opt-in lists. In October 2000 DoubleClick introduced the DoubleClick eMail Network, which aggregated e-mail newsletters into six content categories so that advertisers could run banner and text ads across multiple newsletters with a single media buy.

Internationally, DoubleClick was preparing for a roll-out in Asia, where it established offices in seven regional markets and hoped to break into China's on-line market. In October 2000 DoubleClick announced a partnership agreement to provide ad management services to China's top Web site, Sina.com. In the United Kingdom, DoubleClick acquired @plan.inc, a market research planning provider. The company's U.K. ad network was reorganized into five specific market sectors: technology, automotive, business, consumer, and leisure.

AD REVENUE EXPECTED TO DECLINE IN 2001

DoubleClick ended 2000 with total revenue of $505.6 million, up from $258.3 million in 1999. The company, which had not turned a profit in its five-year history, reported a net loss of $156 million for 2000, compared to a net loss of $55.8 million in 1999. Nevertheless, the company was optimistic about its financial position. It achieved its first-ever profitable quarter in the third quarter of 2000 and broke even in the fourth quarter. Its market capitalization was $1.75 billion in December 2000, and the company said it had close to $900 million in cash.

For 2001 DoubleClick projected that advertising revenue, which accounted for about half of the firm's revenue, would decline 25 to 30 percent in 2001. The firm lost its AltaVista account, and the Internet economy in general was expected to experience a downturn. DoubleClick's remaining revenue came from its data and technology divisions. As a cost-cutting measure, DoubleClick laid off about 200 workers, or 10 percent of its workforce, in March 2001. Meanwhile, the company was planning to invest heavily in e-mail marketing. In March 2001 DoubleClick announced it would acquire Toronto-based FloNetwork Inc., a rapidly growing e-mail marketing technology provider that delivered more than 540 million e-mail messages for 125 clients in the fourth quarter of 2000. The acquisition positioned DoubleClick to become a leader in e-mail marketing. Prior to the acquisition DARTmail had scaled to deliver more than 150 million e-mail messages a month.

FURTHER READING:

Blankenhorn, Dana. "DoubleClick Sharpens Customer Focus." *Advertising Age.* March 1, 1999.

Bray, Hiawatha. "DoubleClick Doubles Back on Plan to Track Internet Users Online." *Knight-Ridder/Tribune Business News.* March 2, 2000.

"Company Information." DoubleClick Inc. April 9, 2001. Available from www.doubleclick.net.

"EPIC Sues DoubleClick over Tracking Net Users." *Communications Today.* February 14, 2000.

Flamm, Matthew. "Advertiser in Top Spot." *Crain's New York Business.* November 27, 2000.

"FTC Clears DoubleClick." *Promo.* March 2001.

Owens, Jennifer. "DoubleClick Convenes Privacy Panel." *Brandweek.* June 26, 2000.

Sabatini, Joanna. "DoubleClick Creates New Network." *Mediaweek.* January 31, 2000.

Vonder Haar, Steve. "DoubleClick Opens Ad Network for Small Sites." *Inter@ctive Week.* January 31, 2000.

Wang, Nelson. "Wall St. Embraces DoublClick as a Leader among Web Advertising Firms." *Internet World.* May 10, 1999.

SEE ALSO: 24/7 Media; Advertising, Online; Electronic Privacy Information Center (EPIC); Privacy Issues

DOW JONES INTERNET INDEX

Since its inception in February of 1999, Dow Jones and Co.'s Dow Jones Internet Index has served as a benchmark for the stock performance of U.S.-based Internet companies. Companies listed on the index must use the Internet to garner at least 50 percent of their annual sales, must have operated as a public company for a minimum of three months, and must have a market capitalization (the full value, expressed in dollars, of all outstanding shares) averaging $100 million or more over three months. A company's stock also must average a closing price of roughly $10 per share, and it must be traded frequently enough to offer liquidity, which allows investors to buy and sell without major disturbance.

Dow Jones established the Dow Jones Internet Index in response to the intense trading of Internet stocks that took place in the late 1990s. The Internet stock craze began in the mid-1990s when a few upstarts found themselves boasting billion dollar market valuations soon after their initial public offerings (IPOs). For example, when Netscape conducted its IPO in 1995, its stock price jumped 108 percent in a single day. Less than a year old, Yahoo! was valued at almost $1 billion after it completed its IPO in 1996. The stock of online auction site eBay jumped more than 900 percent within three months of its 1998 IPO. The following year, an unprecedented 240 Internet-based firms went public. Dow Jones decided to create its Internet Index early in 1999 because, as stated by Dow Jones Indexes Managing Director Michael A. Petronella in *Information Today,* ''Internet stocks have rapidly become among the most volatile, popular sectors of the equities market. This has led to the need for an Internet benchmark that can be the standard Internet stock measurement tool for all investors.''

Dow Jones wasn't alone in identifying the need for a stock index for Internet companies. In fact, several competing indexes were in operation by the end of 1999. For example, the Business 2.0 Internet index included 20 stocks, while the USA Today Internet 100 indexed 100 stocks. TheStreet.com and Inter@ctive Week @Net also had launched Internet indexes, and Internet.com operated Isdex. Dow Jones believed its name recognition and concrete inclusion criteria would differentiate its index from those offered by rivals.

The firm divided its Internet Index, which consisted of 40 stocks, into two sub-indexes: the Services Index and the Internet Commerce Index. Companies originally listed on the Service Index included America Online Corp., Netscape Communications Corp., and other entities like Internet service providers and Internet access providers. America Online was later removed from the index when it merged with Time Warner, because the bulk of its revenues were attributed to the non-Internet operations of Time Warner. The Internet Commerce Index included companies engaged in some form of Internet-based e-commerce, such as book e-tailer Amazon.com Inc. and online stock trader E*Trade Group Inc.

By the end of 1999, the Dow Jones Internet Index had grown 167 percent since its inception. However, that meteoric rise was soon interrupted by what became known as the dot-com fallout. Between May of 1999 and May of 2000, the Internet Index grew only 3.1 percent. By October of 2000, more than 60 percent of Internet upstarts were trading below their initial IPO price. Companies that had once been listed on the Dow Jones Internet Index at a price-to-earnings ratio of more than 300—meaning that the firm could have been sold for 300 times what it secured in earnings—found their stock prices plummeting as investors, no longer willing to overlook poor earnings or a lack of profitability, began dumping shares. Many of the firms that had yet to earn a profit folded, and even those that had achieved profitability, such as Yahoo! Inc., saw stock prices nosedive. In fact, Yahoo!'s stock, which had reached a high of $237.50 per share in January of 2000, was hovering around $20 per share in early 2001.

At that time, along with Yahoo!, Amazon.com, and E*Trade, the Internet Commerce Index included Ameritrade Holding Corp.; CNET Networks Inc.; Ebay Inc.; FreeMarkets Inc.; MP3.com Inc.; Next Card Inc.; Priceline.com Inc.; Ticketmaster; VerticalNet Inc.; WedMD Corp.; and Webvan Group Inc. The Service Index included Akamai Technologies Inc.; Ariba Inc.; Art Technology Group Inc.; BEA Systems Inc.; Broadvision Inc.; CheckPoint Software Technologies Ltd.; CheckFree Corp.; CMGI Inc.; Commerce One Inc.; Covad Communications Group Inc.; Doubleclick Inc.; Earthlink Inc.; Excite@Home; Exodus Communications Inc.; I2 Technologies Inc.; Infospace Inc.; Inktomi Corp.; Internet Capital Group Inc.; Interwoven Inc.; Portal Software Inc.; PSINet Inc.; RealNetworks Inc.; TIBCO Software Inc.; VeriSign Inc.; and Vignette Corp.

FURTHER READING:

''AOL-Time Warner Merger Will Trigger Changes in Dow Jones Internet Indexes.'' *Business Wire.* January 2, 2001.

Colkin, Eillen. ''Net Stocks Tracked.'' *InformationWeek.* February 22, 1999.

''Dow Jones Indexes Launches Internet Index.'' *Information Today.* April 1999.

''Dow Jones Internet and Technology Sector Indexes Become Now Tradable Through New Exchange-Traded Funds; Total Assets Linked to Dow Jones Internet Indexes Top $240 Billion.'' *Business Wire.* May 18, 2000.

Futrelle, David. "The Internet Index Mania: There Are Many Benchmarks, but Few Measure Anything Meaningful." *Money.* November 1, 1999.

Henssler, Gene W. "Past Year a Great Lesson." *Georgia Trend.* February 2001.

Johnson, Patrice D. "On Internet Time." *Money.* December 1, 2000.

SEE ALSO: Shake-Out, Dot-com; TheStreet.com; Volatility

DUE DILIGENCE

In general business terms, due diligence refers to the scrutiny used by an individual or a group of individuals considering making a purchase of some sort. Those conducting due diligence do so to determine the degree of risk associated with a particular course of action, such as funding an initial public offering (IPO) or an investment. In the case of an acquisition or merger, the attorneys or accountants working for the purchasing party conduct due diligence when they examine the financial status, competitive position, and management practices of the business under consideration, as well as the legality of the deal. When upstarts and established companies seek funding, one of the main reasons they complete detailed business plans is to assist lenders in conducting due diligence. It is the responsibility of the lenders, however, to verify the data contained in such a document.

In the late 1990s, the dot.com bubble, which continued to grow as highly publicized predictions of astronomical growth in e-commerce began to saturate mainstream media outlets, prompted many venture capitalists considering an investment in a young Internet upstart to relax due diligence standards. The highly successful IPOs of firms like Netscape Communications Corp., Amazon.com, and eBay.com, fueled the investment community's desire to move dot.com upstarts towards IPOs as quickly as possible, despite the fact that obtaining profitability would, in all likelihood, take many years. Venture capitalists tended to overlook the fact that most of these new businesses were based on unproven business models. The examination of things such as the likelihood of long-term success, the experience of executives, and the integrity of financial forecasts became increasingly relaxed. According to an April 2001 issue of *Oregon Business,* "Many investors,

fearful of missing out, seemed to skip the traditional drawn-out due diligence and hardly paused before infusing startups with capital to get a piece of the dot.com action. The message was clear: strike now or taste dust." Formal business plans for dot.coms, if they were submitted at all, tended to be much shorter and less detailed than their traditional counterparts. In fact, a March 2000 study of 300 e-commerce businesses in California revealed that most launched operations with no business plan in place.

This lack of planning eventually caught up with many of the fledgling firms when shareholders began pressuring on some of them to achieve profitability. When dot.com stocks began tumbling in 2000, funding sources evaporated in a hurry. Many upstarts, which had relyied on the availability of additional capital for expansion, had no choice but to close their doors, a phenomenon which drove the stock prices of the remaining Internet players down even further. Recessionary economic conditions compounded the problem, and dot.com investors sustained major losses. As a result, venture capital funding by the middle of 2001 was less than half of what it had been during the first half of 2000. In the third quarter of 2001, only 540 companies had raised $6.7 billion in venture capital funds, compared to the 1,634 companies that raised $23.9 billion during the third quarter of 2000. Although investors willing to pour capital into Internet related ventures still exist, the level of scrutiny to which they subject their applicants has substantially increased. As stated by an October 2001 article in *Puget Sound Business Journal,* "The venture community is witnessing a return to stricter investment criteria, more thorough due diligence and tighter term sheets...venture capital funds can no longer rely upon abundant capital, frothy IPO markets, and a carnivorous mergers and acquisitions market to mitigate lax investment practices."

FURTHER READING:

"Back to Basics." *Oregon Business,* April 2001.

Blakey, Elizabeth. "Tech VC: Looking Back While Looking Ahead." *E-Commerce Times,* May 31, 2001. Available from www.ecommercetimes.com.

Simpson, Tom. "Investing Today Versus During the Dot-Com Boom." *Puget Sound Business Journal,* October 5, 2001.

Walsh, Mark. "Wary Angel Investors Answer Fewer Prayers; Due Diligence Replaces 'Just Do It'; Entrepreneurs Scramble for Funds." *Crain's New York Business,* June 18, 2001.

SEE ALSO: Initial Public Offering (IPO); New Economy; Shake-Out, Dot-com

E

As the second largest Internet Service Provider (ISP), behind America Online (AOL), Earthlink Inc. serves more than 4.8 million consumers and small businesses. The company offers its members dial-up services; broadband access such as digital subscriber line (DSL), cable, and wireless; domain registration; Web design; Web hosting; and various other services aimed at helping enterprises with their e-business efforts.

EARLY HISTORY

Earthlink Network was founded in 1994 by Sky Dayton. Dayton had developed the idea for Earthlink when he became frustrated with his ISP after unsuccessful attempts to log on to the Internet. In 1993, he set plans in motion to create an ISP whose major focus would be providing customer service. Dayton sought out investors Reed Slatkin and Kevin O'Donnell and secured $100,000 in funding for his new business. Offering technical support by phone, Dayton had secured his first customer by July 1994. Earthlink's first member logged on to the Internet using one of the start-up's 10 modems.

Earthlink became increasingly popular as use of the Internet by businesses and consumers grew quickly. In 1995, the firm teamed up with Netscape Communications Corp. in a deal that provided Earthlink members with Netscape's Navigator, an Internet browser. Dayton also launched Earthlink Software, an innovative package that set up computers for Internet access. In August of that year, Earthlink broadened its service area dramatically when it signed a deal with UUNET Technologies. The alliance allowed Earthlink to use UUNET dial-up access numbers to provide national service in 98 U.S. cities. The company also became the first ISP to offer unlimited dial-up access for a flat rate of $19.95 per month, allowing members to surf the Web without time constraints.

Earthlink continued its expansion and in July of 1996 partnered with PSINet to offer dial-up access across the United States and Canada. The firm also teamed up with industry giant Microsoft Corp. and began distributing its Internet Explorer browser to members. Earthlink, in turn, was included on Microsoft's Windows 95 operating system desktop. Along with capturing a large portion of individual accounts, the company also began to focus on providing services to businesses as well. In late 1996, it began to offer nationwide integrated services digital network (ISDN) and frame relay services, which provided higher-speed access to the Internet.

In January 1997, Earthlink went public with a membership of nearly 300,000 North American-based individuals and businesses. The firm launched its online mall later that year, promoting the e-business efforts of many e-tailers such as BarnesandNoble.com, NetGrocer, and Travelocity by offering links to their Web sites at the online mall. The company also kept pace with ever-changing Internet technologies and began offering 56K-flex modem lines, which were twice as fast as 28.8K modems. Earthlink and Charter Communications also initiated a partnership to provide high-speed Internet access through cable modems—an emerging technology at the time—to Charter's customers in California.

GROWTH VIA STRATEGIC ALLIANCES AND EXPANDED SERVICES

Working toward its goal of becoming the largest independent ISP, Earthlink forged several strategic alliances in 1998. In February, the firm teamed up with Sprint Corp. in a deal that combined the two companies' Internet services and gave Sprint a stake in Earthlink. It also positioned Earthlink as a major player in the Internet services market and gave the firm access to Sprint's large customer base. By April, Earthlink had signed on its 500,000th member. In another deal, Earthlink's Internet software became the default on Apple Computer's newly launched iMac computer. The alliance with Apple—one of the most successful in Earthlink's history—solidified the firm's commitment to expansion through original equipment manufacturer (OEM) channels. In similar deals, Packard Bell and NEC Ready Computers named Earthlink the default ISP on their computers in late 1998, just in time for the upcoming holiday season. The partnerships secured more member sign-ups than any other marketing promotion in Earthlink's history to date. Finally, an agreement with CompUSA, a major U.S. computer retailer, secured Earthlink as the chain's official ISP and also gave Earthlink access to CompUSA's customers and exposure in the store's promotional materials. By the end of the year, Earthlink's customer base had reached 1 million.

The ISP experienced continued growth into the following year. In March of 1999, Earthlink launched TotalCommerce, which offered small businesses the opportunity to set up online storefronts. It also continued to promote its Click-n-Build Web site creation tool that allowed members to build Web pages. Additionally, members had an opportunity to create a personal start page, which loaded automatically each time they logged on to their accounts. These pages could be personalized with links to various retail sites, investment information pages, and a variety of other online products and services.

Along with helping its members to create a presence on the Web, the company also began to offer high-speed access options. For example, utilizing Sprint's DSL network, Earthlink began offering its customers alternatives to basic dial-up access. It also teamed up with UUNET to offer nationwide DSL access to consumers—the first such offering in the industry. The firm continued to secure lucrative OEM partnerships as well, including being named the official ISP of Micron Millenna computers. Phoenix Technologies also added an Earthlink icon to its new computers.

Earthlink entered the new millennium with a mission of becoming the largest ISP in the world. To facilitate this, Earthlink merged with Mindspring En-terprises, an ISP formed in 1994 by Charles Brewer who, like Dayton, was frustrated with current ISP offerings. After the $1.3 billion deal was completed, Earthlink—which formally changed its name from Earthlink Network to Earthlink Inc.—served more than 3 million members and operated as the second-largest ISP in the United States. A few months later, Earthlink broadened its subscriber base once again with the purchase of OneMain.com, a leading ISP that served 762,000 dial-up, broadband, and Web hosting members in rural and suburban areas. Building upon that deal, Earthlink partnered with Hughes Network Systems in November 2000 to offer high-speed satellite broadband services to those in rural areas.

Believing broadband services were essential to remaining competitive in the ISP industry, Earthlink sought out rival AOL, looking to forge key technology partnerships. In December 2000, AOL agreed to allow Earthlink to use AOL and Time Warner cable lines to offer high-speed services to its members. Despite Earthlink's position as the second-largest ISP in the country, its membership base of 4.8 million was still far behind AOL's nearly 29 million users. Although revenues grew 32 percent in 2000 to reach $986.6 million, the firm had yet to record positive net income. Nevertheless, Earthlink management continued to focus its efforts on offering high-speed access and converting regular dial-up members to broadband services. The ISP industry, which had been experiencing considerable merger and acquisition activity for the past several years, continued to consolidate, prompting speculation concerning Earthlink's future. In a March 2001 *BusinessWeek Online* article, Earthlink CEO Garry Betty commented: ''I could speculate all day about who would buy a company like Earthlink. Our story is that we've been successful providing the basics better than the competition.'' While Earthlink's future remains uncertain, the company pledges to continue to develop shareholder value in the future while pursuing strategic alliances that fit in with company plans to remain a leader among ISPs.

FURTHER READING:

''Earthlink Beats Wall Street Q4 Forecasts.'' *Futures World News.* May 21, 2001.

''Earthlink, DirectPC in Two-Way Satellite Internet Deal.'' *Newsbytes.* November 18, 2000.

Earthlink Inc. ''Earthlink History.'' Atlanta, GA: Earthlink Inc., 2000. Available from www.earthlink.com.

Hillebrand, Mary. ''Earthlink Broadens Base, Buys One-Main.com.'' *E-Commerce Times.* June 9, 2000. Available from www.ecommercetimes.com.

Shook, David. ''Street Wise.'' *BusinessWeek Online.* March 26, 2001. Available from www.businessweek.com.

SEE ALSO: Bandwidth; Broadband Technology; Connectivity, Internet; Internet Access, Tracking growth of; Internet Service Providers (ISPs); UUnet.com

EBAY

eBay was founded in 1995 by Pierre Omidyar, who wanted to set up an auction site for sellers of obscure and collectible items. After the site proved popular, eBay was incorporated in May 1996. All of the inventory, ordering, shipping, and payments were handled by sellers and buyers who registered on the eBay site. The company's revenue came from commissions on items that were sold and from listing fees.

In 1998 Margaret C. "Meg" Whitman became eBay's CEO, joining the company after working at FTD Inc., Walt Disney Co., and Hasbro Inc. eBay was both popular and profitable, having transformed auctions into highly charged classified ads. Last minute bidding frenzies were common on the timed auctions. By providing feedback from buyers and sellers, eBay had succeeded in establishing an online community. Customer loyalty was a key factor that allowed the site to maintain a dominant position in the auction market. Tips and gossip were shared on chat boards, and many people came to earn their living by selling items on eBay.

After Whitman joined eBay, she revamped the site to make it easier for users to participate. She sought ways to make it safer for customers to purchase items. Whitman revamped the payment process by allowing customers to use credit cards instead of personal checks or money orders. She also began expanding eBay beyond its core model of collectibles. eBay acquired art auctioneer Butterfield & Butterfield in 1999 and used the Los Angeles area as a test market for local auctions of items that were difficult to ship, such as cars and furniture. As Whitman told *Newsweek* in 1999, "We are enabling a kind of commerce that didn't exist to any extent before, and that's person-to-person commerce."

BECAME PUBLIC COMPANY IN 1998

In September 1998 eBay went public with an initial public offering (IPO) that raised more than $60 million. Potential investors were attracted by the fact that eBay would not have any money invested in inventory. Items that were auctioned over eBay remained the property of the seller, who received payment directly from the buyer. At no point would eBay take possession of an item to be sold or payment

for an item. Sellers paid eBay a small commission for listing items, from $.25 to $2 per item. They could pay an additional $50 for additional promotion on the eBay site. When an item was sold, eBay received a percentage ranging from slightly more than one percent to five percent of the selling price.

According to the company's 1998 IPO prospectus, revenue for 1997 totaled $5.7 million. Net sales for the first half of 1998 were $14.9 million, with gross profits of $13.2 million. Earnings from operations for the first six months of 1998 were $2.8 million, and the company managed to earn net income of $348,000. During that period the number of registered users increased from 340,000 to more than 850,000. At the time of the IPO, founder and chairman Pierre Omidyar owned 42 percent of the company, and venture capital firm Benchmark Capital had a 21.5-percent interest after investing $5 million.

When eBay held its IPO in September 1998, investors quickly bid up the initial offering price of $18 to more than $54. After the stock settled down to around $47 a share, analysts noted that the valuation reflected consumer excitement over online auctions and investor awareness of the potential for profit. At the time, most Internet ventures were losing money.

Just before its IPO, eBay entered into a three-year agreement with America Online (AOL). In exchange for $12 million in payments to AOL, eBay became the exclusive online trading community for AOL. By October 1998 eBay's community had grown to more than 1 million registered users, and some 700,000 items were listed on eBay in more than 1,000 categories.

ENJOYED GROWTH AND EXPANSION, 1999-2000

Throughout 1999 and 2000 eBay grew by adding new categories, forming strategic partnerships, and making acquisitions. Following the acquisition of Kruse International in May 1999, eBay launched a new automotive category later in the year. Kruse was an Indiana-based automotive auction house that sold some 130,000 collectible cars each year through more than 40 events. In March 2000 eBay launched a co-branded automotive site with AutoTrader.com, called eBayMotors.com, that sold only used and collectible cars.

In May 1999 eBay also acquired Billpoint, a company that facilitated person-to-person credit card payments over the Internet. In March 2000 eBay formed a strategic partnership with Wells Fargo & Co. to develop an online person-to-person payment platform. The partnership involved Wells Fargo taking a 35-percent equity interest in Billpoint. Later in 2000 eBay and Wells Fargo launched Electronic Check, a new payment option for eBay buyers and sellers.

In 1999 eBay formed strategic partnerships with Warner Bros. and Juno Online Services, among others, and expanded its partnership with AOL. The agreement with Warner Brothers gave that company's online users a way to bid on entertainment merchandise featured on different areas of eBay. Links to Warner Brothers' online properties were added to eBay's site. eBay's agreement with Juno Online Services made eBay the exclusive provider of online trading services on JunoLand, Juno's online community site, and on Shop@Juno, the company's online shopping channel. eBay expanded its arrangement with AOL by launching four new co-branded sites on several AOL brands.

eBay's high-flying stock price enabled it to acquire the prestigious art and antiques auction house Butterfield & Butterfield in May 1999 for $260 million. The acquisition was designed to accelerate eBay's entry into higher-priced items and to enhance its position in middle-tier items priced from $500 to $5,000. During 1999, eBay also rolled out more than 30 regional Web sites in U.S. cities nationwide. While items on the regional Web sites were available internationally, the sites made it easier to buy and sell items that required a physical pick-up, or which were expensive to ship.

eBay introduced a new service in 1999 called Personal Shopper. Designed to retain shoppers in niche markets where items were not always for sale, Personal Shopper provided potential buyers with e-mail alerts when an item in a category they were interested in came up for auction. In November 1999 eBay, together with collectible and hobby publisher Krause Publications, launched *eBay Magazine.* Two books, *The Official eBay Guide* and *eBay for Dummies,* also were published in 1999.

Internationally, eBay purchased alando.de AG, Germany's largest online trading company in 1999. In early 2000 eBay Japan was launched, with NEC Corp. taking an equity stake and promoting the site. Unfortunately, eBay launched its Web site five months after Yahoo! opened Yahoo! Japan in September 1999. While eBay charged a commission for each transaction, Yahoo! did not. As a result, by mid-2001 Yahoo! held 95 percent of the online auction market in Japan, while eBay only had a three-percent share.

If eBay had any problems in 1999, the most persistent involved its servers going down. In mid-1999 the company experienced its worst outage to date when software problems and a lack of server redundancy put the company offline for more than a day. As a result, eBay lost more than $5 million and 20 percent of its market value. After expending capital to rebuild its information technology (IT) infrastructure, eBay reported strong financial results for the first quarter of 2000, beating analyst's expectations.

In the second quarter of 2000 eBay announced several wireless agreements as part of its eBay Anywhere strategy. The strategy was designed to make eBay accessible from any Internet-enabled mobile device. eBay partnered with 2Roam to format its content and deliver it to virtually any mobile device on any carrier network. Specific agreements also were announced with OracleMobile, a subsidiary of Oracle Corp., and with Sprint PCS.

A mid-2000 report from Nielsen/NetRatings found that eBay users spent an average of one hour and 42 minutes on the site and viewed 256 pages, making eBay the ''stickiest'' Web site on the Internet. At the time eBay had more than 12 million registered users. It also was in mid-2000 that eBay acquired Half.com for more than $300 million in stock. Half.com was a fixed-price, person-to-person trading marketplace. The addition of a fixed-price alternative expanded eBay's trading platform and increased its potential to attract a wider customer base. After the acquisition, Half.com and eBay continued to operate independently and to promote each other.

In November 2000 eBay announced that it would begin to license its auction technology to enable other firms to create their own applications. The eBay application program interface (API) initially was made available to selected licensed partners and developers. By February 2001 some 20 to 30 other sites and developers were enrolled in the program or had expressed an interest in joining. FairMarket, which hosted private label auctions for 70 companies including J.C. Penney, Dell Computer, and CompUSA. Using API, FairMarket linked its merchants, manufacturers, and distributors directly to eBay auctions. It took its customers' merchandise out of their inventory systems, prepared it for auction, massaged the bids, and got the information back to the fulfillment systems. FairMarket also would supply the back-office capabilities that eBay did not supply. Another licensee, GoTo Auctions, became the first application to be certified for eBay's API program. GoTo Auctions' ChannelFusion Network allowed users to sell items on six different auction sites, including eBay, Amazon.com, and Yahoo! Auctions. For 2000, eBay reported revenue of $431.4 million and net income of $48.3 million. The company was debt free and had no interest expense.

EBAY COULDN'T BE BEAT IN 2001

In January 2001 eBay launched eBay Premier, a new site for art, antiques, and rare collectibles available at www.ebaypremier.com. The site grew out of the previously existing eBay Great Collections site and was the result of the connections eBay had made in the art world. In March 2001 eBay Premier hosted an online auction of Marilyn Monroe memorabilia, including the famous "Red Velvet" nude photos from 1949, in conjunction with a live auction at Butterfield & Butterfield. Although bidding for the photos failed to reach the necessary minimum and they were not sold, other items were sold in the $15,000 to $20,000 range. eBay reported that close to 60 percent of the bids were placed through eBay Premier, as were about 20 percent of the items that sold.

In January 2001 eBay announced that it would acquire a majority interest in Korea's largest auction Web site, Internet Auction Co. Ltd., for about $120 million. The South Korean company had about 2.8 million registered users. About one-third of South Korea's citizens were online, making the country the sixth-largest Internet market in the world. At the time eBay was reported to be the number one online auctioneer in the United States, the United Kingdom, Germany, Canada, and Australia. It also operated sites in France and Japan.

At the end of January 2001 eBay raised its listing fees. The announcement came after Yahoo! Auctions began charging listing fees after being a free auction service since its inception. The fee increases on eBay were the company's first since December 1996. Analysts indicated that the fees could boost eBay's revenue by as much as five percent in 2001.

In early 2001 eBay attempted to address the problem of spamming that its registered users were experiencing. Through data mining, e-mail addresses were being harvested from the eBay system and used for unsolicited commercial mailings, or spam, by non-eBay sellers. For example, bidders on software subsequently received spam e-mail offering them pirated software. To help protect its users from spam, eBay changed its e-mail policy to gain more control over online contacts between eBay users. The company announced that any users not involved in a particular auction would only be able to contact each other by sending messages through the eBay system. Sellers would still be able to obtain the e-mail addresses of bidders on their auctions, and winning bidders were able to contact sellers directly. All other contact would be channeled through a new "Contact an eBay Member" feature. Critics of the new policy said it was designed to stop offline sales between members. In December 2000, eBay announced that it would begin enforcing its ban on offline sales between members.

eBay also provided its members with some protection against auction fraud. Some analysts believed that fraud and the threat of losing money online were the biggest inhibitors to the growth of e-commerce in the 21st century. eBay users were covered for up to $200 worth of losses through an automatic insurance plan. In addition, an escrow program was in place that enabled users to hold their money in a neutral account until their transaction was completed.

In March eBay's unique audience grew by nearly 4 million to a total of more than 22.1 million unique users for the month. It moved up in the Nielsen/NetRatings ranking from 15th to 11th in terms of unique visitors. While eBay's number of unique visitors was comparable with that of Amazon.com, eBay did better in terms of the number of pages viewed and the time each person spent on its site. eBay ranked second among all Internet sellers, capturing 14.5 percent of all Internet shoppers. Amazon.com led with 15.1 percent. Analysts noted that combining eBay's numbers with those of recently acquired Half.com would make eBay the top Internet e-tailer.

In March eBay announced an alliance with Microsoft that would integrate eBay's auction marketplace into selected Microsoft Web sites. Other new partnerships included an alliance with Artnet.com that made Artnet.com's fine art pricing database available to eBay Premier customers. An alliance with Eppraisals.com gave eBay users access to professional art and antiques appraisers. During the second quarter eBay expanded offerings on Half.com, adding millions of new items across four main categories: computers, consumer electronics, sporting goods, and trading cards. eBay's fixed-price formats, such as Buy it Now, also performed well. Buy it Now enabled buyers to instantly buy an auction item.

eBay's goal was to increase its annual revenue to $3 billion by 2005. The company had international operations in 18 countries. It completed its acquisition of the Paris-based online trading network iBazar S.A. in May 2001 for $112 million in stock. iBazar hosted online auction sites in eight European countries. In March eBay opened Web sites in Ireland, New Zealand, and Switzerland. The company's best performing international units were Germany and the United Kingdom.

Analysts were skeptical of eBay's $3 billion target, because it would require the company to grow 50 percent each year. For the first half of 2001 eBay again beat analyst expectations in both quarters. Quarterly net revenue was $147.4 million in the first quarter, a 90-percent increase from the same quarter in 2000, with quarterly net income of $21.1 million. In the second quarter revenue reached $180.9 million. As a result of its strong first-half financial performance, eBay raised its expectations for 2001 and projected that second-half revenue could reach $400 million.

In June 2001 eBay launched a two-week pilot test of eBay Stores. Some 18,000 merchants signed up to sell musical instruments, jewelry, electronics, and collectibles. President and CEO Meg Whitman called eBay Stores "the next step in eBay's evolution." The storefronts combined fixed-price retailing with eBay's auction system. eBay's entry into storefronts followed that of Amazon.com and Yahoo!, whose storefronts gave merchants that were too small to establish their own Web sites a way to sell goods online.

Other new initiatives included an agreement with luxury gift e-tailer Ashford.com to sell its leftover and closeout merchandise on eBay in both a fixed price and an auction format. eBay also formed a new alliance with Terra Lycos to integrate eBay auctions into the Lycos auction site and make eBay a featured advertiser on the Lycos network. The agreement gave eBay exposure to the 94 million unique visitors to Lycos sites each month.

In mid-2001 eBay launched a new service involving newspaper classified ads. The eBay Seller Classifieds program gave sellers the opportunity to market their items to a wider range of potential buyers. Sellers who had items listed on eBay for auction were given the option of advertising their items in a branded eBay section in local newspaper classifieds. The program was first offered in the Minneapolis-St. Paul area, with plans for expansion into Florida's *St. Petersburg Times*.

POSITIONED TO MAINTAIN LEADERSHIP POSITION

eBay was one of the first Internet companies to achieve profitability and figure out how to make online auctions work. It was first company to enter the online auction market, after which it experienced rapid growth. By mid-2001 eBay held a clear leadership position and its name was a household word. Little competition was to be seen on the horizon, although Amazon.com and Yahoo! were creating a niche in the online auction marketplace through new initiatives. With online auction sales increasing 149 percent in May 2001 to $556 million, eBay accounted for more than 65 percent, according to a study by Nielsen/NetRatings and Harris Interactive.

As of mid-2001 eBay's strategy was to expand its business into new markets and improve current services. The company's goal was to expand its platform as quickly as possible in order to have more business transacted. eBay's business model gave it almost unlimited capacity and advantages of scale over traditional auction houses. In auctions, the biggest market has a clear advantage over other competitors because sellers desire the liquidity that comes from having a bigger audience and more potential buyers. In addition to auctions, eBay has successfully expanded its platform to include fixed-price offerings, both through its acquisition of Half.com and through its eBay Stores program, as well as through its Buy it Now service.

FURTHER READING:

Ashman, Anastasia. ''Two Auction Players Launch eBay Infrastructure.'' *Internet World*. February 21, 2001.

''Auction Brawl.'' *Business Week*. June 4, 2001.

''Auction Nation.'' *Time*. December 27, 1999.

''eBay's Bid for Fixed Prices.'' *Business Week*. June 26, 2000.

Enos, Lori. ''Can Anyone Catch eBay?'' *E-Commerce Times*. June 19, 2001. Available from www.ecommercetimes.com.

Mahoney, Michael. ''eBay Beats Street, Raises 2001 Expectations.'' *E-Commerce Times*. July 20, 2001. Available from www.ecommercetimes.com.

Regan, Keith. ''eBay Storefronts Arrive.'' *E-Commerce Times*. June 11, 2001. Available from www.ecommercetimes.com.

Ressner, Jeffrey. ''Online Flea Markets.'' *Time*. October 5, 1998.

Saliba, Clare. ''eBay Jumps into Newspaper Classifieds.'' *E-Commerce Times*. May 4, 2001. Available from www.ecommercetimes.com.

Sausner, Rebecca. ''Report: Yahoo! Retains Online Ratings Crown.'' *E-Commerce Times*. May 1, 2001. Available from www.ecommercetimes.com.

Schwartz, Vira Mamchur. ''Bidding, Buying as Lifestyle.'' *Folio: The Magazine for Magazine Management*. December 1, 1999.

Virzi, Anna Maria. ''eBay Buys Major Auto Auction House.'' *Internet World*. May 24, 1999.

Wang, Nelson. ''Auction Site eBay Files to Go Public with $64M IPO.'' *Internet World*. July 27, 1998.

''We Have Lift-Off: Amazon, Yahoo! and eBay Grow Up.'' *The Economist (US)*. February 3, 2001.

''Wired for the Bottom Line.'' *Newsweek*. September 20, 1999.

SEE ALSO: Auction Sites; Business-to-Consumer (B2C) E-Commerce; FairMarket Auction Network; Omidyar, Pierre; Whitman, Margaret; Yahoo! Inc.

E-BOOKS

An electronic book, or e-book, is a book that is accessed electronically via a personal computer (PC), a specially designed e-book reader, or a handheld device like a Palm Pilot. In most cases, users download the text from an Internet site after paying with a credit card. Depending on the technology used, e-book purchasers quite often have the capability to highlight, bookmark, and annotate specific passages, as well as the ability to search an entire document. Despite many bold predictions in the late 1990s that e-books would soon render paper publications obsolete, e-book sales remained weak in both 2000 and 2001 as three main issues—incompatible formats, difficult-to-use reading devices, and uncertainty surrounding copyright laws—continued to plague the industry by undercutting both supply and demand.

ADVENT OF E-BOOK TECHNOLOGY

Although the concept of electronic publishing had existed for several decades, it wasn't until the summer of 1998 that specific devices for reading e-books, as well as e-books themselves, became available at the retail level. Both NuvoMedia Inc. and Softbook Press Inc. developed e-book readers at that time. Designed to offer users an experience as close to reading a print book as possible, the NuvoMedia Rocket eBook's screen was roughly the same size as a page in a traditional paperback book. Specific buttons allowed users to select either a landscape or portrait format, view the next or previous page, and pull down various menu options. The hardware appliance was designed to allow users to download texts from various online sites. While the Softbook reader offered many of the same features as the Rocket, its screen was nearly double in size, and the only way to import texts was to use a telephone line or Ethernet connection to link to a Softbook Press information center. In 1999, the two firms sold a total of roughly 10,000 e-book readers and offered less than 5,000 titles. Gemstar International Group Ltd. paid $400 million to buy both NuvoMedia and Softbook Press in January of 2000, planning to use advertising campaigns and licensing agreements to generate a higher demand for the e-book readers.

That same month, Barnesandnoble.com and Microsoft announced their intent to work together to develop an e-book reader for PCs. Another e-book hardware maker, Glassbook, revealed plans to do the same. Popular author Stephen King released a new novella as an e-book in March, in conjunction with publisher Simon & Schuster. Problems with security measures allowed Internet users who had paid for the book to download multiple unauthorized copies. Publishers continued experimenting with e-book technology despite such problems. In fact, Simon & Schuster also began publishing novels by Mary Higgins Clark as e-books in May. The first Spanish language e-book made its way online in June. Two months later, Stephen King circumvented traditional publishers by offering a new novel, *Ride the Bullet,* on the Internet for $1 per chapter. More than 40,000 readers downloaded the first chapter within 15 hours of its release. At roughly the same time, Adobe Systems Inc. acquired Glassbook, and in November Franklin launched its palm-sized reader known as eBookman.

SUPPLY AND DEMAND PROBLEMS

By the autumn of 2000, roughly 25,000 e-book reading devices had been sold, a number much lower than many analysts had predicted. Despite sluggish sales, several industry pundits cited the success of King's online novel as an indication that e-books were finally finding a mainstream audience. Andersen Consulting predicted that e-book sales would exceed $2.3 billion by 2005, compared to less than $5 million in 2000. However, skeptics pointed out that King's novel might not have generated such interest if a print version had been available as well.

Along with meager demand, the e-book industry also contended with limited supply. E-book availability was growing at a much slower pace than e-book reading device makers had anticipated. In March of 2001, the number of e-books compatible with the industry's leading platform—Gemstar's RocketBook—had only reached a few thousand. Afraid that e-book sales might undercut traditional sales—particularly on new blockbuster releases likely to make the best-seller lists—many publishers only offered electronic versions of classics like *Moby Dick, The Iliad,* and *Romeo and Juliet.*

Concerns regarding the impact e-book sales would have on traditional sales represented only a minor problem for the industry, however. Three others factors contributed more significantly to the supply and demand problems experienced within the e-book industry. One of the most pressing problems had to do with incompatible formats. By the end of the twentieth century, three main e-book players had emerged as industry leaders: Gemstar, Adobe, and Microsoft. According to a November 2000 article in *The Atlantic Online,* the fact that each firm was trying to position its format as the industry standard undercut the e-book industry as a whole. ''E-books are software, and the future of reading is presently being held hostage in a computer 'standards war' where competing companies try to ensure that their proprietary technology becomes the toll-taker at the gate. Most publishers and retailers now offer every e-book title in at least two incompatible formats, sometimes three, and it may not stop there.'' Uncertain as to which format would eventually dominate the industry and hesitant to commit to a format that might soon be rendered obsolete, many publishers entered the e-book industry more slowly than they otherwise might have. At the same time, and for similar reasons, consumers balked at the idea of paying hundreds of dollars for an e-book reading device that could read only one format.

Another reason e-book readers were not selling well as the twentieth century came to an end had to do with the technology itself. The e-book reading devices simply were unable to compete with the convenience of a print book. Readers used to stuffing a paperback into a beach bag or setting a novel on the edge of the tub were unwilling to do the same with an expensive electronic device. Also, many e-book readers were difficult to read in the bright sun, some had to be held at a certain angle for optimal viewing, and all ran on a battery that required recharging.

At the same time that book lovers proved reluctant to give up the convenience and familiarity of print books for the increased functionality offered by electronic readers, many publishers proved reluctant to make a significant investment in e-book technology due to concerns over copyright issues. While new laws like the Digital Millennium Copyright Act, which made it illegal to make or sell products designed to skirt copyright laws, had been put in place to help protect copyright holders, publishers remained uncertain as to how to best protect copyrighted material offered electronically. In addition, those unwilling to publish electronic versions of their copyrighted books also worked to prevent other companies from doing so. For example, when RosettaBooks secured permission from authors such as Kurt Vonnegut and Robert Parker to publish electronic versions of their books, Random House, copyright holder of the traditional print books written by those authors, filed suit. The litigation, formally launched in February of 2001, likely will have a significant impact on the e-book industry.

NEW TRENDS WITHIN THE E-BOOK INDUSTRY

Despite the industry's supply and demand problems, many leading publishers continue to develop new e-book ventures, believing that jockeying for position now might pay off in the long run. For example, Time Warner founded iPicturebooks.com in February of 2001, offering roughly 200 e-books to children between six months and 10 years of age. Random House and Simon & Schuster also launched e-book initiatives aimed at youngsters. According to a May 2001 article in *Inside.com,* ''The assumption—or hope— behind this foray into children's e-books is that today's computer-savvy kids will be more receptive to books on screen than adults are. To them, the thinking goes, it will be nothing to read a 200-page young adult novel or look at the illustrations in *Eency Weency Spider* in an electronic format.''

Some industry experts believe that the future of e-books is in other niche markets, such as text books and reference publications. According to *PC Magazine* writer Christina Wood, ''the Electronic Document Systems Foundation predicts that the likelihood of people reading novels or even magazines digitally in the future is low. The chance that they will read digital reference materials, professional journals, and reports, however, is good.'' While the direction the e-book industry will take in the future is unclear—as is the impact e-books will have on the traditional book industry—authors, publishers, and readers will likely continue to influence and be influenced by e-book technology.

FURTHER READING:

Chenoweth, Emily. ''Psst. Hey Little Girl, Wanna Try an E-Book?'' *Inside.com.* May 9, 2001. Available from www.thestandard.com.

Garber, Joseph R. ''Publish and Perish.'' *Forbes.* October 16, 2000.

Kafka, Peter. ''Horror Story.'' *Forbes.* August 21, 2000.

Lombreglia, Ralph. ''Exit Gutenberg?'' *The Atlantic Online.* November 16, 2000. Available from www.theatlantic.com.

Manes, Stephen. ''Electronic Page-Turners.'' *Forbes.* May 28, 2001.

Morgan, Eric L. ''Electronic Books and Related Technology.'' *Computers in Libraries.* December 1999.

Peek, Robin. ''Jump-Starting Electronic Books.'' *Information Today.* March 2000.

Pike, George H. ''A Book is a Book is E-Book.'' *Information Today.* July 2001.

Runne, Jen. ''Why eBooks are Sputtering.'' *eMarketer.* March 14, 2001. Available from www.emarketer.com.

Wood, Christina. ''The Myth of E-Books.'' *PC Magazine.* July 1, 2001.

SEE ALSO: Barnesandnoble.com; Electronic Publishing; Microsoft Corp.

E-BUSINESS SERVICE PROVIDER (EBSP)

E-business service providers (eBSPs) are companies that help other companies use e-business technology to improve operations. This might involve tasks like the design, construction, and operation of a company's Web site or the streamlining of procurement processes for a business. The original e-business service upstarts, including Scient Corp., emerged in the late 1990s, believing that companies, particularly smaller businesses unable or unwilling to hire their own technology specialists, would find e-business technology crucial to long-term survival. Many established technology giants, such as IBM Corp., also turned their focus to e-business services.

Initially, e-business service providers mainly were seen as firms that helped small businesses erect online storefronts. According to a September 2000 article in *Money,* ''Not only do eBSPs host your site and provide templates and tools to help do-it-yourselfers build engaging electronic storefronts, but many also offer merchant accounts to facilitate secure credit-card transactions.'' However, as more firms began to offer e-business services, the definition of an e-business service provider grew to include a wider range of e-business services than simply those related to storefront design, construction, and operation. The notion of what type of customer might seek e-business services also expanded to include more traditional, larger firms.

Scient Corp. was founded in late 1997 as a traditional e-business service provider. The firm's early marketing tactics centered around the slogan, "It takes courage to be legendary." Advertising campaigns aimed at potential clients stressed the advantages of being the first to utilize new e-business technology, as well as the disadvantages of being left behind. These efforts paid off as the firm landed several contracts not long after its creation. In addition to securing business from fledgling Internet ventures like Wineshopper.com, furniture e-tailer Living.com, PlanetRx Inc., and ePhysician, the firm also helped to launch sites such as Chase Online for Chase Manhattan Corp. By the end of 1999, Scient had built a total of 15 e-businesses from the ground up and provided e-business integration services to another 85 companies. Speed-to-market was the firm's major selling point.

Sales continued to climb in early 2000, and Scient achieved profitability for the first time. However, within a few months, as investors began to shy away from dot-com startups, e-business service providers like Scient watched their client base shrink. In August, rivals iXL Enterprises Inc., Viant, and Marchfirst Inc. announced layoffs. Scient's stock price plummeted to roughly $10 per share, where it had started trading at the firm's mid-1999 initial public offering. Several Web sites Scient had built, including environmental news hub Verde Media and jewelry e-tailer Miadora.com, closed down. Roughly half of Scient's revenues, the percentage for which dot-com startups had accounted, simply disappeared.

The dot-com meltdown allowed larger companies to regard smaller, more technologically savvy firms like Scient less fearfully. As a result, issues such as quality and added value replaced speed-to-market as a key focus. This opened the door to industry giants like IBM, which believed e-business services would prove a highly lucrative market. According to a July 2001 article in *The Financial Times,* "the small-scale Internet consultancies, which shot to prominence by building web sites during the dot-com bubble, are fighting for survival in the wake of the technology slowdown and resurgence of larger, more established consultancies, who have made up for lost time in the e-business market." Recognizing that it needed to strengthen its ability to secure larger accounts, particularly when faced with increased competition from such formidable rivals, Scient agreed to merge with rival iXL in July. The deal was scheduled for completion in early 2002.

IBM Corp., the largest maker of computer hardware in the world, also is the top computer services provider. The firm spent the latter half of the 1990s retooling itself as an e-business services provider. These efforts began in earnest in June of 1995, when

IBM acquired Lotus Development Corp. Management saw the purchase as an opportunity to bolster IBM's position in the computer software industry. IBM also planned to use the Lotus Notes messaging software to offer integrated e-mail, data processing, and Internet services to clients.

Within two years, services had become the most rapidly growing portion of IBM's operations. To increase its visibility as an e-business products and services provider, IBM upped its advertising budget by 21 percent in 1998. Highlighting its e-business servers, software, hardware, technology, and services, the firm targeted business managers expected to use the Internet to streamline processes, improve bottom lines, and increase visibility. In 1999, IBM upgraded its own Internet-based e-commerce operations. Early the following year, the firm established an e-Business Innovation Center in Santa Monica, California. The new operation had 16 employees.

At the core of IBM's e-business services was its WebSphere server software, which helped to power the e-commerce enterprises, including online stores, of IBM customers. The WebSphere Commerce Suite 4.1 package launched in 2000 included Web development tools, as well as technology that allowed businesses to classify customers in a variety of ways. This functionality allowed e-business to improve the results of future marketing campaigns. By December, employees at the first e-Business Innovation Center had increased to 135, and e-business accounted for $5.2 billion of IBM's revenues. Thanks to the previous year's upgrades, sales from IBM's Web site grew 65 percent to a record $9 billion.

Unlike many competing e-business service providers, IBM marketed its services to traditional businesses rather than targeting dot-com upstarts. Consequently, when the dot-com crash in 2000 left many e-business service providers contending with a sharp drop in orders, IBM saw demand for its e-business services continue to grow. Twenty-five e-Business Innovation Centers were either operating or being constructed by the start of 2001. As stated in the January 2001 issue of the *Los Angeles Business Journal,* IBM's goal was to "establish itself as the one-stop shopping source for customers seeking Web-related creative design, consulting and tech support." By then, services, both e-business and otherwise, accounted for more than one-third of IBM's annual revenues.

FURTHER READING:

Frook, John Evan. "Big Blue Boosts Ad Spending 21% to Spread E-business Message to the Web-Challenged." *Business Marketing.* December 1, 1999.

Garcia, Erica. "The Web Store Solution: Small Firms Turn to E-Business Service Providers to Help Build Internet Storefronts." *Money.* September 1, 2000.

Ibold, Hans. "IBM's Internet Arm Grows Despite Market Downturn." *Los Angeles Business Journal.* January 29, 2001.

Mand, Adrienne. "All About E: New IBM Site Targets E-Business Market." *Mediaweek.* February 15, 1999.

Moschella, David. "IBM: Your One-Stop E-Commerce Shop?" *Computerworld.* October 27, 1997.

Moules, Jonathan. "Internet Consultancies Scient and iXL to Merge." *The Financial Times.* July 31, 2001. Available from news.ft.com.

"Rebuilding the Garage." *The Economist.* July 15, 2000.

Songini, Mare. "IBM Rolling Out New E-Commerce Software." *Network World.* January 31, 2000.

Thackray, John. "IBM Act II: Can Lou Really Execute?" *Electronic Business.* July 1998.

SEE ALSO: E-Commerce Solutions; IBM Inc.; Scient

E-COMMERCE CONSULTANTS

Transforming a firm into a competitive e-business calls for meticulously planned and informed strategies. Understanding the e-marketplace and where one's firm can find its niche; implementing the right internal and external networks and acquiring the correct software and equipment; and developing an e-commerce strategy requires a holistic analysis of a business and its goals and practices. Increasingly, by the late 1990s and early 2000s, firms were turning to e-commerce consultants to help them make the transformation. In doing so, they sought services at the lowest possible cost which promised the greatest overall benefits.

Companies, ranging from old economy stalwarts to young hopefuls, often lack either the internal knowledge or internal resources necessary to devise and implement a successful e-business strategy. As the e-commerce shakeout in the early 2000s proved, a comprehensive and effective e-commerce strategy can make or break a company's online prospects. Moreover, the lightning pace of technological development typically was too fast for companies, concerned with their core business operations, to keep up with. Finally, with e-commerce still a largely haphazard industry in the early 2000s, companies often face a great deal of confusion over just where to take their online hopes.

Customers' perceptions of companies are increasingly influenced by their experiences on the Web. In other words, a consumer's opinion of a firm may sour if he or she encounters excessive delays in downloading pages or convoluted Web-purchasing procedures. Because of this, firms turn to consultancies for expertise in meeting consumers' online expectations. When a firm transitions to the Web, its internal business practices may be too specialized to understand the subtle nuances required to make a Web site customer-friendly and appropriate to their line of work. E-commerce consultancies not only try to eliminate those features of their clients' Web sites that detract from the customers' online experience, but try to integrate the feel of the Web site with that of the firms' call centers and storefronts. In short, consultants try to help companies shape how they relate to the world online, and integrate the image they project on the Internet with that of their bricks-and-mortar operations.

As a result, the market for e-commerce consulting was booming, despite some setbacks in the early 2000s. Framingham, Massachusetts-based research firm International Data Corp. forecast total revenues for Internet-related consulting services to skyrocket through the middle of the 2000s, from $16.1 billion in 1999 to $99.1 billion in 2004.

INDUSTRY ORGANIZATION

The nature of e-commerce consulting contracts can vary considerably. Some consultants are brought in merely for short-term planning. In this case, they simply may offer guidance or play devil's advocate en route to mapping out a broad direction for e-commerce strategies. Such consulting operations typically are conducted on an hourly basis and last a very short time, from several days to several months. Other contracts amount to more comprehensive partnerships in which a consultancy agrees to handle e-commerce strategies and concerns as they arise over the long term, meeting new challenges as they present themselves. In such contracts, firms essentially outsource an essential component of their business to a consultancy. These agreements can last for years, or indefinitely through the lifetime of the client company. International Data Corp. estimated that the average e-commerce consulting project lasted about eight months, where the first three months are spent devising an e-business strategy and the final five months are devoted to constructing the technological and organizational infrastructure for that strategy to be realized.

Consultants usually start by running several days of workshops with company leaders to map out where the firm currently stands and where it wants to go, and to get a feel for the challenges involved in getting the firm online in a competitive manner. In this way, consultants can pare down the project to keep it within the scope of the company's and the consultant's practical reach. According to *Fortune,* some major consultancies offer very short-term assessment and evaluation services. Big Five consultancy KPMG, for instance, launched a three-week program called Saved, which promised an assessment of companies' e-business systems and recommended improvements, while IBM's Global Services provided an online e-commerce evaluation program.

The myriad issues within the broad spectrum of e-commerce—from securing online transactions and customer data to implementing cutting-edge software and choosing a model for the Web site—add up to a ripe market for consulting firms, creating niche markets in which consultancies can distinguish themselves and begin to build market share. According to *Fortune,* specific areas of e-commerce consulting were more or less characterized as follows: technology implementation was the specialty of systems integrators and the Big Five consulting firms; e-commerce business strategies were the domain of management consultants; consultants known as ''interactive strategists'' focused on the marketing, customer service, and outreach aspects of e-commerce; and start-up consultancies known as ''i-builders'' worked to combine technology, strategy, and marketing consulting for quick overall development of an e-commerce presence. *Fortune* provided rough estimates of costs and project durations for each category, reporting that management consultants generally work for three to four months and cost between $400,000 and $800,000; interactive strategy consultants take six to eight weeks and charge $200,000 to $400,000; systems integrators and Big Five consultancies take projects for six months to three years and run between $1 million and $10 million; and i-builders' engagements last about four to six months and cost between $750,000 and $2 million.

E-COMMERCE CONSULTING TAKES OFF

Following the widespread fears surrounding the ''Y2K bug'' that generated so much business for technology consultants in the late 1990s, the most lucrative line of work for such consultants was the transformation of established businesses into e-commerce firms. Unfortunately, the Y2K issue was a vacuum for a lot of money devoted to companies' technology budgets. This was money that needed to be regenerated before it could be spent on e-commerce implementation, and thus kept the explosion of e-commerce consulting somewhat in check.

Nonetheless, the major consulting firms, including the Big Five, rapidly shifted focus to incorporate e-commerce services into their operations, sometimes launching entire new divisions devoted to large-scale or more focused e-business initiatives. However, according to many analysts the big consultancies,

steeped in traditional consulting activities, had to regroup extremely quickly to adjust to the e-commerce onslaught. In so doing, Big Five players such as KPMG, PricewaterhouseCoopers, and Ernst & Young wound up laying off significant portions of their workforces while they reorganized their business lines, later rebuilding their ranks with a greater focus on e-commerce. In addition, according to *Fortune,* major companies in various industries chose to augment their businesses with selective e-commerce consulting ventures. For example, Chase Manhattan Bank partnered with the Big Five consultancy Deloitte Consulting to create a consulting service for the development of online payment systems, and Microsoft teamed up with Deloitte rival Andersen Consulting to offer e-commerce services using Microsoft's Windows platform.

The dot-com explosion, while creating a boom period for consulting, also put a severe strain on established consultancies, which were forced to scramble to recruit top-notch talent. Traditionally, consultancies mined undergraduate colleges and business graduate schools for their talent pools, but dot-com startups in the late 1990s and early 2000s were quick to tap into these sources for their own ranks. According to *Consulting to Management,* dot-coms gobbled up more than half of Harvard Business School's 1999 MBA graduates. Sometimes this hurdle was surmounted as consultancies offered to partner with dot-coms during the initial development stages, whereby the consultants themselves, while working directly with the startup, were actually maintained by the consultancies.

By the late 1990s, many e-commerce consulting firms turned to the stock market to generate the funding needed to purchase other technology and consulting firms and grab a piece of the market. Thus, they were following their clientele and launching initial public offerings (IPOs) at a dizzying pace by the end of the 1990s. With the field both full of promise and devoid of clear leaders at that time, firms saw the opportunity to emerge as major players by acquiring the funding necessary to blossom into full e-business solutions providers and build the capabilities necessary to procure the larger, more prestigious, and more lucrative e-commerce consulting projects.

Since many consultancies also maintain a hand in the accounting business, they were tailor-made for another branch of e-commerce consulting, which involved integrating old office accounting systems with Web-based and information technology. Particularly as business-to-business e-commerce and market-to-market integration heats up, the digitization of accounting and inventory systems for easy data sharing across business, industry, and regional lines will call for greater involvement of e-commerce consultants to provide technological expertise.

However, this movement of traditional accounting firms, including the Big Five consultancies, into the field of e-commerce consulting was not without controversy. The most prominent concerns included the potential conflict of interest posed by accounting firms who audit and devise tax strategies for the firms they also consult and provide e-commerce solutions for. In late 2000 the U.S. Securities and Exchange Commission (SEC) proposed new rules to bolster its auditor independence standards, which would compel the Big Five firms to scale back their e-commerce consulting operations. Recognizing the potential losses they would accrue the Big Five, along with the American Institute of Certified Public Accountants (AICPA), mobilized opposition to the proposed SEC rules, insisting that the scope of consulting not be curtailed.

Under traditional rules, auditors were forbidden to maintain a financial stake in the firms they audited. Through the late 1980s and especially as the Internet economy opened up in the mid-1990s, the line between these interests grew increasingly clouded, particularly as accounting firms branched out into consulting and often took equity stakes in their Internet-based clients—clients that, as startups, had no source of revenue from which to pay for the consulting services. The SEC feared that such financial stakes in clients' performance could potentially compromise the integrity of their auditing and accounting practices.

After months of ugly fighting, the SEC and the Big Five reached a compromise. In its final ruling in November 2000 the SEC announced that, while it wouldn't ban the accounting firms from consulting or helping to install information technology systems, the burden of proof was on the consultancies to prove there was no conflict of interest between their accounting and auditing practices and their consulting businesses.

For their part, Big Five firms increasingly spun off their consulting units, e-commerce or otherwise, into separate, independent businesses to prevent any accusations of compromised independence. However, even in such cases the line between their tax accounting and auditing practices on the one hand and their consulting activities on the other was nebulous. According to many Big Five executives, the nature of the new economy made it impossible for them to completely separate their tax and audit advice from other consulting activities.

Unfortunately for the industry, when the bottom fell out of the dot-com market in early 2000, companies severely retrenched their e-business consulting budgets, culminating in massive layoffs at e-commerce consultancies. The larger, diversified consultancies were able to manage without too much difficulty, but the smaller firms devoted to e-commerce consulting found themselves without the experience necessary to shift into new areas, and many were forced to shut down. After the market began to regroup and firms continued with their e-commerce strategies—albeit without the enthusiasm that characterized the late 1990s dot-com craze—the field began to expand again. The industry as a whole, however, gravitated toward established *Fortune* 1000 companies and away from riskier dot-com startups. In fact, many dot-coms diversified their operations to include e-commerce consulting following the Internet shakeout in an effort to stay afloat. Recognizing that, while the market euphoria may have abated, e-commerce was hardly at an end, such firms hoped to generate a revenue stream by helping other companies build their online storefronts and e-commerce strategies.

FURTHER READING:

Fisher, Susan E. "E-Business Strategy Boom." *Upside.* October 1999.

Gallagher, Terry. "The War for E-Commerce Talent." *Consulting to Management.* May 2000.

Glater, Jonathan D. "A High-Tech Domino Effect: As Dot.com's Go, So Go the E-Commerce Consultants." *New York Times.* December 16, 2000.

Jastrow, David. "Ushering In the 'E' Millennium." *Computer Reseller News.* December 20/December 27, 1999.

Levinsohn, Alan. "SEC and Accountants Cut a Deal on Audit Rules." *Strategic Finance.* December 2000.

Mateyaschuk, Jennifer. "Consulting Firms Tap Stock Market." *InformationWeek.* October 18, 1999.

Noguchi, Yuki. "A Tough Time for Consultants: Cost-Cutting Dot.Coms Start to Shun Advice From Experts." *Washington Post.* December 4, 2000.

Rosa, Jerry; and Craig Zarley. "Big Five Feeling E-Business Pressure." *Computer Reseller News.* February 28, 2000.

Stimpson, Jeff. "Brave New E-World." *The Practical Accountant.* March 2000.

"Tell Me How." *Fortune.* Summer 2000.

Zarley, Craig. "Big Five See Writing on the Wall." *Computer Reseller News.* August 7, 2000.

———. "Under Scrutiny." *Computer Reseller News.* August 28, 2000.

SEE ALSO: Forrester Research; International Data Corp.; Startups; Y2K Bug

E-COMMERCE SOLUTIONS

E-commerce solutions are the products and services that help a company conduct business electronically. The range of available e-commerce solutions is vast, including those that allow traditional businesses to design, create, and operate World Wide Web sites. Some solutions focus on a specific problem. For example, a company selling its wares via a World Wide Web site might purchase a bandwidth management solution from a firm like Packeteer Inc. in an effort to allocate more resources to actual commerce transactions than to other applications. Similarly, an electronic merchant who wants to improve the online checkout process for its clients might turn to a specialized vendor like VirtualCart for a shopping cart solution.

As the needs of those engaged in e-commerce have grown more complex, however, the demand for more comprehensive solutions has intensified. As a result, many e-commerce solutions providers now focus on offering a suite of products and services designed to meet multiple needs and solve various problems. According to an October 2000 article in *InformationWeek.com*, "e-commerce isn't just about transactions anymore. Companies are increasingly carrying out all facets of their businesses online, from customer interactions to extended supply-chain management with trading partners." As a result, "businesses are demanding more than just online transaction support. They need full-fledged E-business, and that means providing a Web site that helps them build relationships with customers-be it in a business-to-business, business-to-consumer, or online marketplace model." Many of the e-commerce solutions upstarts that had emerged in the early 1990s began working to meet these changing e-commerce needs, as did many computer industry giants looking to position themselves as leading e-commerce players.

INDUSTRY GIANTS AS E-COMMERCE SOLUTION PROVIDERS

IBM CORP. Computer hardware and services giant IBM Corp. began working to recreate itself as an e-business services provider in the mid-1990s. The firm's push into e-business began as early as June of 1995, with the purchase of Lotus Development Corp. The acquisition was meant to bolster IBM's position in the computer software market, as well as allow IBM to offer integrated email, data processing, and Internet services to clients via Lotus Notes messaging software. Within two years, services had become the fastest growing operating unit at IBM, and the firm began working to sell itself as an e-business solutions provider. IBM increased its advertising budget by 21 percent in 1998, aggressively marketing its e-business servers, software, hardware, technology, and services to managers expected to use Internet technology to improve operations. Central to the firm's e-business

services was its WebSphere server software, which IBM used to support the e-commerce initiatives, including retail Web sites, of clients. The WebSphere Commerce Suite 4.1 package launched in 2000 included Web development tools and customer categorizing functions that allowed e-business to sharpen future marketing efforts. In 2001, IBM released WebSphere Commerce Suite Pro 5.1, a "Java-based, e-commerce solution," according to *InfoWorld* writer James R. Brock, that provides "an infrastructure for building, deploying, and administering e-commerce sites."

HEWLETT-PACKARD CO. Founded in 1938, Hewlett-Packard Co. (HP) is second only to IBM Corp. among the world's largest computer firms. Along with manufacturing and marketing computers and printers, HP also sells Web-based hardware, software, and services. In 1997, the firm released an Internet Solutions line, creating the Internet Applications Systems Division to oversee its new products. Two years later, the firm restructured its offerings into three divisions: information tools, infrastructure for these tools, and e-services. In late 1999, HP launched its 9000 N Class server, which was designed to offer Internet Service Providers (ISPs) a comprehensive suite of e-commerce tools, and the Commerce for the Millennium system. By mid-2000, the company had grouped its technology into various e-services solutions packages.

The HP 9000 Superdome server, which allowed different operating systems to run at the same time, was at the core of HP's quest to become the leading computer system supplier for Internet-based enterprises. The firm began marketing its new release to major dot-com businesses in September of 2000. HP's purchase of e-business tools maker Bluestone Software Inc. in January of 2001 allowed the firm to launch 25 software products the following month, including the Netaction e-services development and implementation suite and the OpenView e-services systems management suite. A few months later, HP added 19 Internet server appliances to its growing line of e-business solutions.

MICROSOFT CORP. The largest software firm on the globe, Microsoft Corp. spent the late 1990s developing its presence in the Internet arena. In February of 2000, the firm released Windows 2000, a version of Windows NT that had taken nearly five years to develop. Windows 2000 was designed to serve as the platform on which businesses, including e-commerce companies like BarnesandNoble.com and Buy.com, could operate. In an effort to compete with IBM's WebSphere server, Microsoft launched BizTalk in December of that year. According to *Network World* writer John Fontana, "BizTalk is one of the foundation pieces of Microsoft's attempt to recast its Windows operating system and applications as a platform for the Internet. The loosely defined effort is called.Net.''

ORACLE CORP. Microsoft's closest software rival is Oracle Corp., founded in 1977. The firm also competes with Microsoft in the e-commerce solutions arena. Oracle became a major e-commerce solutions provider in 1998 when it unveiled Oracle 8i, a version of its flagship database program that permits a company's database functions to be handled on the Web. The firm also started using other e-business products it had developed to streamline its own operations. For example, Oracle's order fulfillment and shipping networks were blended with its sales network to allow the firm to handle customer service from a single source. In addition, by using a Web-based expense reporting system, the accounts payable department was able to cut its staff by 25 percent and deposit paychecks into employee bank accounts more quickly. Oracle also consolidated the 97 servers and 120 databases running its e-mail system into just two servers and four databases.

In May of 2000, Oracle released its E-Business Suite. According to *Forbes* columnist Elizabeth Corcoran, ''Instead of selling separate packages for sales force automation, accounting, employee benefits and so on, Oracle ties together 70 'modules' in a package and juices them up with Internet technologies.'' The Oracle 9i software database management system, another product launched that year, included an application server that allowed users to run e-commerce applications related to their databases. In 2001, Oracle 9i helped more than 8,500 firms across the globe manage their data on a variety of operating systems.

UPSTARTS AS E-COMMERCE SOLUTIONS PROVIDERS

AMAZON.COM The upstart who has, perhaps, had the easiest time developing its e-commerce solutions is Amazon.com. The online retailing giant was simply able to license its already existing, highly successful e-commerce platform, complete with features like its patented one-click checkout, to other e-tailers struggling to move into e-commerce. Toyrrus.com was the first online merchant to use Amazon's technology to power its site when the two firms agreed to relaunch toysrus.com as a co-branded site in August of 2000. Amazon also agreed to take over inventory, customer service, and shipping services. According to the terms of the deal, Amazon receives a base fee, as well as a commission on each toy sold on the site, for allowing toysrus.com to use its software. The deal also proved lucrative for toyrus.com; with Amazon technology

underlying its infrastructure, the site saw its holiday sales grow more than threefold. In April of 2001, Borders Online Inc. reached a similar agreement with Amazon, as did United Kingdom-based specialty book vendor Waterstone a few months later. Some analysts believe Amazon's ability to market itself as a full-scale e-commerce solutions provider will be a key factor in whether or not the firm achieves profitability.

COMMERCEONE INC. Commerce One is an e-commerce solutions provider that got its start in 1994 as a maker of office automation software for banks. Within a few years, the firm had diversified into multimedia catalog development, and it eventually began selling products and services that facilitated business-to-business (B2B) e-commerce. CommerceOne constructs B2B procurement exchanges that allow companies to do business via the Web or some other electronic platform. These exchanges, or marketplaces, allow buyers, sellers, distributors, and suppliers to complete commerce transactions in a single place.

Based on the firm's Market Site Portal software, Commerce One exchanges include auction functionality, which allows clients to solicit offers for their merchandise to get the best prices they can. Along the same lines, reverse auctions allow businesses to collect and compare bid prices for products and services they wish to purchase. Commerce One also offers a procurement software suite known as BuySite, which creates private supply-chain sites for individual companies. BuySite allows purchasers to not only access supplier catalogs online, but it also facilitates the completion of electronic transactions.

To make money off of these exchanges, Commerce One licenses its software and charges service and network fees. It also typically retains a 50 percent stake in the exchanges it creates. Market Site Portals range in price from $500,000 to $2 million; the total cost is determined by the level of work involved in tasks like putting catalogs online, developing search engines, and educating employees. When the site becomes operational, the business or businesses operating the exchange charge the suppliers, distributors, sellers, and buyers who use the site a fee for each transaction completed. An agreed upon percentage of these fees goes to Commerce One.

FIRSTSOURCE CORP. Firstsource Corp. is an e-commerce solutions provider that started out as an Internet-based reseller of computers and related hardware systems to individuals and small and mid-sized companies. After its purchase by En Pointe Technologies in 1998, firstsource.com, which later changed its name to Firstsource Corp., began eyeing the B2B e-commerce services market. B2B markets were outpacing business-to-consumer (B2C) markets in the late 1990s, and analysts forecasted that B2B sales would eventually exceed $1 trillion. As a result, many Internet resellers like Firstsource began focusing on business clients, particularly those looking to move operations online. According to *Computer Reseller News* in June of 1999, Firstsource began "repositioning itself as an Internet portal for business-to-business transactions." The firm began offering e-commerce solutions, such as Web site configuration, marketing, staffing, and information technology services to small and medium-sized businesses.

To complement its new service offerings, Firstsource also beefed up its technology offerings in an effort to provide solutions able to meet all the B2B e-commerce needs of clients. Early in 2000, the firm launched its Firstsource Connect, which designs Web-based purchasing hubs connected to various product distributors for businesses looking to streamline their procurement processes. Eventually, the firm also began licensing inpowr, the platform that powers Firstsource Connect, to businesses wanting to conduct operations online.

BLUE MARTINI SOFTWARE, INC. Blue Martini Software is best known for its customer relationship management solutions (CRMs). Since its founding in 1998, the firm has carved out a niche in the e-commerce solutions market by offering a comprehensive suite of online merchandising, content management, customization, and transaction services. In 2001, the firm's Blue Martini 4 software won the Crossroads OSA A-List Award for Best Java-based E-Commerce Suite. As stated in a June 2001 article in *VARBusiness*, "Blue Martini's product vision focuses on online branding and personalization for e-business applications, not just e-commerce sites."

BROADVISION, INC. Another e-commerce solutions startup, BroadVision, Inc., was founded in 1993. The firm's One-to-One Enterprise platform helps its customers—including Bank of America, E*Trade, Circuit City, Toyota, and Boeing—conduct business over the Internet. The platform includes order processing, transaction management, reporting, and monitoring functions. B2C players can opt for the One-to-One Retail Commerce suite, which automates things like content selection based on compiled customer information. The One-to-One Business Commerce Suite, which is designed to serve B2B operations, automates order processing, contract administration, and customer service. Additional e-commerce solutions include the InfoExchange Portal, which assists with the creation of information portals for businesses; Amadeus Travel Commerce, which allows a Web site operator to offer personalized online travel booking services; MarketMaker, which assists with the cre-

ation of online exchanges for specific markets; and publishing, finance and billing tools.

FURTHER READING:

Brock, James R. "WebSphere Keeps the World of E-commerce Turning." *InfoWorld.* March 5, 2001.

Bull, Katherine. "Mark Hoffman: Changing the Face of the Digital Exchange Industry—Commerce One CEO Believes Digital Exchange Growth Depends on Supplying Both Software and Services." *InfoWorld.* July 3, 2000.

Conner, Deni. "Hewlett-Packard Unveils Bevy of Internet Appliances." *Network World.* April 23, 2001.

Corcoran, Elizabeth. "Oracle: Walking the Talk." *Forbes.* January 8, 2001.

Cox, John. "Oracle Eats Its Own E-business Dog Food." *Network World.* July 17, 2000.

"Firstsource Connect Customized Portals for the Web Marketplace." *PC World.* March 2001.

Fontana, John. "Microsoft Relies on BizTalk Server 2000." *Network World.* December 18, 2000.

Frook, John Evan "Big Blue Boosts Ad Spending 21 Percent to Spread e-Business Message to the Web-challenged." *Business Marketing.* December 1, 1999.

Gladwin, Lee C. "Borders Turns to Amazon for Outsourcing." *ComputerWorld.* April 16, 2001.

Greenmeier, Larry. "How HP Carves Out the Magic—Hewlett-Packard Wants to Expand Its Service Offerings into the Product-Agnostic World of E-Business." *InformationWeek.* November 13, 2000.

"Hewlett-Packard Buys Bluestone in E-Business Bid." *Newsbytes.* October 16, 2000.

Jastrow, David. "Internet Resellers Alter Web Strategies." *Computer Reseller News.* June 21, 1999.

Meister, Frank, Patel, Jeetu, and Fenner, Joe. "E-Commerce Platforms Mature." *InformationWeek.* October 23, 2000. Available from www.informationweek.com.

———. "Evolution of E-Commerce." *VAR Business.* June 11, 2001. Available from special.northernlight.com.

Moschella, David. "IBM: Your One-Stop E-Commerce Shop?" *Computerworld.* October 27, 1997.

SEE ALSO: E-business Service Provider (eBSP)

ECONOMIES OF SCALE

Economies of scale refer to the reduction of average production costs over the long term as a result of boosted output. As production increases, either within a firm or within an industry, a comparatively lower level of investment is required for each individual unit. The utility of the production process is thereby rendered more efficient as its application is spread over a wider range. The competitive attractiveness of building economies of scale lies in the fact that they allow firms to pass their cost savings on to customers, thereby lowering prices and undercutting competitors without damaging profit margins.

Scale economies also tend to heighten barriers to market entry, as smaller competitors find it increasingly difficult to cut costs to the levels possible for larger firms (made possible by their economies of scale). In this way, larger firms see economies of scale as an attractive business strategy, since it keeps new competitors from sapping their customer bases and profit margins. On the other hand, progressively cheaper technologies can pull against the advantages of economies of scale by lowering the barriers to entry and leveling the investment required to compete in a given industry.

Amazon.com is a prime example of a dot-com firm that created an economy of scale. Amazon used the strong revenues it generated as an online book merchant to escalate its size as quickly as possible. The company built large warehouses to stock its inventory and to enable it to purchase books directly from publishers, thereby bypassing its reliance on wholesalers and dramatically expanding its product line. While Amazon.com clearly built a scale economy, the strategy backfired in 2000 and 2001. The main reason for this was that the strategy banked on sustained growth in e-commerce, an assumption that proved faulty when the tech market stock bubble burst in March 2000.

As economists note, bigger doesn't always mean better. Business analysts coined the term ''diseconomies of scale'' to describe those conditions in which expanded production actually contributes to rising production costs and declining productivity. Usually, this is caused by excessive bureaucratization within an organization and the use of too many people in the production process, which entails more training to bring people up to speed and winds up using time and money inefficiently.

FURTHER READING:

''E-Commerce: Too Few Pennies from Heaven.'' *Economist.* July 1, 2000.

Gallaugher, John. ''Challenging the New Conventional Wisdom of Net Commerce Strategies.'' *Communications of the ACM.* July 1999.

Hof, Robert D. ''Amazon's Go-Go Growth? Gone.'' *Business Week.* February 12, 2001.

Pearce, David W., ed. *The MIT Dictionary of Modern Economics.* 4th ed. Cambridge, MA: The MIT Press, 1992.

SEE ALSO: Amazon.com; Economies of Time

ECONOMIES OF TIME

By enabling global connectivity, the Internet made it possible for companies to reduce the number of steps involved in many business processes, prevent duplication of effort, and in some cases eliminate the need for manual human tasks. Because the efforts of staff then could be focused on improvements and developments versus repetitious tasks, the resulting ''economies of time'' led to cost savings for many organizations, along with lower labor costs and increased productivity. Online business-to-business marketplaces, where companies are able to link their systems with those of suppliers, distributors, and manufacturers, are one example of how companies can increase efficiency and save time. For example, automated procurement systems replenish some of a company's supplies automatically from suppliers, thereby freeing staff to focus on more valuable tasks.

Under the right conditions the Internet can make companies more agile and responsive to the needs of customers and other business partners. According to the Boston Consulting Group's George Stalk, Jr., many companies have discovered that in addition to providing customers with the most value at the lowest cost, doing it quickly is an important part of the equation. Stalk explained: ''To improve its responsiveness a company needs to organize for economies of time and for visibility. To do so, many companies disassemble their functional organizations and reassemble them into permanent, multifunctional teams. The members of these teams focus on entire processes, products, projects, customers, and/or competitors. The teams include everyone who can slow or speed the process and are often in one location. Their performance measures are set to achieve goals rather than efficiency.''

The emphasis on time and speediness has received a great deal of attention as related to the Internet. In the early 2000s it was common to hear representatives from leading technology companies emphasize the importance of being first-to-market with developments on the World Wide Web. The term ''economies of time'' also is based partially on ideas like this. In addition to other benefits, pioneering companies often get to set the stage about what is standard, normal, or expected in their particular niche. However, it is important to note that while being first has its advantages in a networked world, it does not necessarily guarantee a company's success. Technology that is both flexible and scalable; a solid business model; strategic plans; and other factors were key variables that also contributed heavily to a company's success or failure.

FURTHER READING:

"Encyclopedia of the New Economy." Wired Digital Inc. June 13, 2001. Available from www.hotwired.lycos.com/special/ene/index.html.

Odlyzko, Andrew. "The Myth of 'Internet Time.'&edquo; *Technology Review,* April, 2001.

Stalk, George Jr. "The Time Paradigm." The Boston Consulting Group Inc. 1998. Available from www.bcg.com/publications.

SEE ALSO: Economies of Scale

EGGHEAD.COM CORP.

Formerly a chain of retail software shops, Egghead Corp. shuttered its brick-and-mortar stores in favor of the Internet in 1997. The Menlo Park, California-based online merchant, renamed Egghead.com Corp., sells computer hardware and software, consumer electronics, and office products. The firm also offers closeout products in its online clearance center and via online auctions. Although Egghead's bold decision to transform itself into an Internet retailer seemed promising at first, a slowdown in technology spending and general recessionary economic conditions in North America began to take a toll on performance in 2000. In August of 2001, the firm filed for Chapter 11 bankruptcy protection.

Egghead was founded in 1984 by Victor D. Alhadeff, whose financial backers included Paul Allen, a co-founder of Microsoft Corp. Alhadeff had noticed that computer salespeople quite often used technical jargon that left the average consumer bewildered. Believing that the process of purchasing computer software could be improved by more effective customer service, Alhadeff opened a store Bellevue, Washington. To make customers feel comfortable in his shop, the retailer used a cartoon character named Professor Egghead as the store mascot and called his employees software "eggsperts."

Within three years, nearly 60 Egghead stores had opened and total sales reached $77.5 million. The firm conducted its initial public offering in 1988. By then, more than 100 stores were in operation. Egghead's rapid expansion proved too aggressive when profits tumbled despite record sales of $350 million

in 1989. As a result, the firm closed 29 stores, tightened its inventory management practices, and made store managers responsible for the financial performance of their unit. A new management team refocused Egghead on direct sales to business clients, which accounted for more than half of total revenues. Restructuring paid off in 1990 as sales reached $519 million and earnings rebounded to $15.4 million.

Price wars in the software industry in the early 1990s prompted Egghead to launch an aggressive marketing campaign. The largest retailer of software for personal computers (PCs) in the United States, Egghead became the first retailer to join the Business Software Alliance, an organization formed to reduce software piracy, in 1995. Sales peaked that year at $862.5 million, with 200 stores in operation and roughly 2,500 workers employed. However, according to a June 1999 article in *InformationWeek,* "competition from the computer superstores that dominated the market by the mid-1990s was taking its toll." In addition, computer software sales were undercut by the fact that many PCs were sold to consumers with software already loaded onto the hard drive.

Egghead divested its direct sales units to Software Spectrum Inc. for $90 million in 1996. As a result, revenues were more than halved to $403.8 million. An ill-fated experiment with a new retail format boosted losses in 1997, prompting Egghead to close 70 struggling stores, shut down a distribution center, and lay off administrative staff. Sales fell to $360.7 million. That year, the firm merged with Surplus Direct Inc., a catalog and Internet reseller of computer hardware and software.

In 1998, Egghead made the drastic decision to exit traditional retailing and focus solely on Internet sales. The firm changed its name to Egghead.com Inc. and slashed nearly 80 percent of its workforce. E-commerce functionality was added to Egghead's already existing Web site. Wanting the ability to handle intense traffic surges without bandwidth problems, Egghead opted to use an Oracle platform for its e-commerce site rather than the Informix and Microsoft SQL server systems it had been using. To increase its visibility, Egghead began forging strategic alliances with firms like @Home Network, Netscape Communications Corp., Yahoo!, and Microsoft Corp. As a result, a link to the new e-tailer was featured on many leading Web sites, such as the Microsoft Network and Yahoo.com. An affiliate agreement with GeoCities allowed merchants selling wares on a GeoCities site to also sell Egghead products and earn a commission for each product sold. Sales that year totaled $293 million, and losses reached roughly $50 million.

Egghead began merger discussions with Internet auctioneer OnSale Inc. in July of 1999. Both firms were concerned with Amazon.com's decision to move into both software sales and auctioning, and they viewed a merger as a means of more effectively competing against the online retailing giant. OnSale and Egghead completed the deal in November, forming an online retailer and auctioneer of discounted computer software, hardware, and related technology. The newly merged entity retained the Egghead name. By mid-2000, Egghead.com was considered a leader in online software and consumer electronics sales. Because it relied heavily on small business and home office consumers, Egghead was less dependent on holiday shoppers than its rivals. However, despite growing sales, like many online merchants the firm struggled to achieve profitability. Stock prices began to tumble, and reduced spending in the technology sector undercut sales. Despite a $20 million loan from IBM Corp. and a series of layoffs that eventually reduced the firm's workforce by two-thirds, Egghead found itself unable to stay afloat. In August of 2001, the company filed for Chapter 11 bankruptcy protection and announced its intent to sell a portion of its assets to Fry's Electronics, a computer technology retailer based in Sunnyvale, California.

FURTHER READING:

"Egghead Files Chapter 11." *San Francisco Business Times.* August 17, 2001.

"Egghead.com Merger Complete." *InformationWeek.* November 29, 1999.

"Egghead.com Rated No. 1 Online Consumer Electronics Retailer by Nielsen/NetRatings; Top Rankings Also Awarded by PC Data Online and Gomez.com." *Business Wire.* March 29, 2000.

"Egghead.com Shows Signs of Cracking." *Chain Store Age Executive with Shopping Center Age.* May 2001.

Liebeskind, Ken. "Egghead Breaks Out of Its Shell." *Editor & Publisher.* May 8, 2000.

Mearian, Lucas. "IBM Throws Egghead.com a $20M Lifeline." *Computer World.* March 12, 2001.

Wilde, Candee. "Egghead's Net Bet Pays Dividends, Move to Internet-Only Operation Lets Vendor Cut Inventory Costs, Boost Sales." *InformationWeek.* June 7, 1999.

SEE ALSO: Allen, Paul; Amazon.com; Auction Sites; Business-to-Consumer (B2C) E-commerce

E-GOVERNMENT WEB PRIVACY COALITION

Following the budget restrictions imposed by preparations for the Y2K bug, state and local governments were finally able to invest in e-government systems. Constituencies increasingly demanded that basic governmental information and citizenship services be made available over the Internet, as they were at the federal level, and thus vendors flocked to the booming market for state and local government information technology. Local governments thus began reengineering and Web-enabling their systems to provide their constituents with portal-based integrated systems, alleviating the need for individuals to keep track of many different electronic contact points within government. But while citizens increasingly demanded electronic government services, there existed the fear—similar to that with online shopping—that with the convenience came a price of potentially compromised privacy and security. The financial stakes were significant. Gartner Group estimated that local, state, and federal governments would spend $6.2 billion on e-government in 2005. Obviously, governments were under intense pressure to make such hefty investments pay off. Because of this, ensuring security and privacy became very important.

To address this issue in collaborative fashion, in June 2000 representatives from state and local governments and private-sector technology companies—facilitated by the e-government technology leader NIC Technologies Inc. of Westlake Village, California—formed the e-Government Web Privacy Coalition to debate, discuss, and reach policies on issues of key importance to the development of electronic government. Among these issues were public-key infrastructure and other encryption schemes, digital signatures, and network and infrastructure security. The coalition's mission was to protect citizens and their sensitive data by constructing an environment in which electronic data could flow freely and securely between governments and citizens in a safe network. If e-government is to fulfill its potential, according to the coalition, citizens need to feel comfortable that their participation in an online democracy is accompanied by the requisite level of privacy and security.

The group maintained two stated goals. The first was to devise and disseminate methods and processes by which standards can be achieved to promote confidentiality, privacy, and "the preservation of the public trust." The second was to build itself into an independent organization leading the development and guidance of e-government via voluntary certification programs for e-government portals and other applications. Certification was marked with a privacy seal, awarded only to those e-government portals and applications that met the privacy standards and protocols enacted by the coalition.

While the coalition's policies primarily were driven by its public-sector representatives, the involvement of private companies was intended to facilitate a smooth, cooperative relationship between governments and the companies that would need to adopt the standards and protocols the coalition set. The original private-sector members were Cisco Systems Inc., Compaq Computer Corp., Digital Signature Trust Co., and Oracle Corp., all of which were invited by NIC Technologies based on their record of developing comprehensive privacy systems. In addition, the Progress & Freedom Foundation (PFF), a think tank devoted to the digital revolution and state and local e-government initiatives, acts as an advisor to the coalition.

FURTHER READING:

Keegan, Daniel. ''Technology and Gov Leaders to Debate e-Gov Privacy.'' *civic.com*. June 5, 2000. Available from www.fcw.com.

''Lining Up for e-Gov.'' *civic.com*. June 5, 2000. Available from www.fcw.com.

NIC Technologies Inc. ''Government and Technology Leaders Come Together to Form eGovernment Web Privacy Coalition.'' Westlake Village, CA: NIC Technologies Inc. May 31, 2000. Available from www.nicusa.com.

SEE ALSO: Biometrics; Cryptography, Public and Private Key; Digital Certificate; Digital Certificate Authority; Digital Signature; Encryption; Privacy: Issues, Policies, Statements; Safe Harbor Privacy Framework

ELECTRONIC COMMUNICATIONS NETWORKS (ECNS)

Electronic communications networks (ECNs), the headache of major stock exchanges in the late 1990s and early 2000s, are computerized trading systems through which buyers and sellers of stocks and other securities have their orders matched via instant digital transactions. Although electronic trading through ECNs takes a variety of forms, one thing they all have in common is that they undercut the major brokerage houses and New York Stock Exchange (NYSE) specialists, such as Merrill Lynch and Goldman Sachs. By eliminating these middlemen in securities trading, ECNs offer significantly lower transaction costs. Because of their speed and low costs, ECNs were widely used by online brokerages, some institutional investors, and day traders.

ECNs are most conspicuous on the NASDAQ exchange, where they got their start. The NYSE, with its layers of complex rules and regulations regarding the trading of large-capitalization securities, has been much more resistant to encroachment by ECNs. By early 2001, ECNs accounted for a hefty 35 percent of all NASDAQ trading volume, and research firm Cerulli Associates predicted that share would reach 50 percent in 2001. Celent Communications, however, didn't expect ECNs to capture that much of NASDAQ until 2003.

HOW ECNS WORK

In order to understand ECNs, one must understand the system they're up against. The chief competition to ECNs came from what are known as market makers on NASDAQ: the investment banks and brokerage houses that stampede to buy and sell stocks so as to fill open orders from clients, providing instant liquidity. While such firms carry a great deal of clout and tend to dominate the exchanges, they typically generate their margins by selling shares at higher prices than what they paid for them.

Meanwhile, ECNs simply create the networks traders use to find each other without relying on the market makers to facilitate transactions. To create a revenue stream, ECNs simply levy a small surcharge—usually no higher than a few cents per share, and often much less—on each trade. Buyers and sellers connect to ECNs, either personally or through a brokerage, and enter a bid. These orders are then listed anonymously on the ECN's notebook, or order book, while the computer searches the entire system for a match, or a corresponding bid that matches the buyer's or seller's listed price. Once the match is found, the ECN executes the transaction. Since ECNs don't earn money on the spreads between buy and sell orders, as traditional brokerages and investment banks do, they rely on the sheer volume of trading through their networks to generate revenue.

Traditionally, ECNs were open only to other users on the same system, meaning that an order would wait on the ECN's order book until a corresponding bid was placed on the same system. However, in the early 2000s the use of such closed systems was declining in popularity. ECNs like Archipelago began offering open trading systems in which unmatched orders were transferred to and listed on other trading systems. In this way, ECNs can offer the greatest amount of liquidity to investors, allowing them to complete their order as quickly as possible. To boost the level of liquidity, many ECNs began to pool their resources using inter-ECN links and powerful order routing and search engine technology to sift through many ECNs simultaneously, seeking out order matches. Since investors typically place a premium on liquidity, the pressure on ECNs to open their systems was likely to intensify.

In the face of heating competition, differentiation has come to drive competition in the ECN industry. Some, such as Instinet, sought to capture the institutional investment market for electronic trading. Other ECNs, like Island, settled on the day trading market, which, while humbled, was still vibrant in the early 2000s. Meanwhile, to hedge their bets some of the major brokerage houses threw their money and support behind ECNs. Merrill Lynch, J.P. Morgan Chase, and Goldman Sachs were a few of the major names with a stake in ECNs.

In March 2000, Island president Matthew Andersen testified before the U.S. Senate Banking Securities Subcommittee, praising ECNs with ushering in "a rapid and sweeping democratization of the markets." Many ECN enthusiasts sounded similar praises, insisting that ECNs brought to the common trader the kinds of benefits larger, institutional investors have always enjoyed.

THE DEVELOPMENT OF THE ECN INDUSTRY

The earliest precursor to the modern ECN was Instinet Corp., founded in 1969 by Reuters Group PLC as a venue for institutional investors to trade after regular trading hours. Thus, Instinet was more of a private system that catered to established investors, rather than to the more wide-open customer base served by modern ECNs.

On the heels of a NASDAQ trading scandal in the mid-1990s—in which market makers were accused of conspiracy to skim profits by refusing to carry out unprofitable orders and by filling orders at prices that didn't meet buyers' expectations—the Securities and Exchange Commission (SEC) issued new order handling rules in 1996, requiring all market makers to publish their orders on NASDAQ. Alternatively, the SEC allowed market makers to publish on an ECN that would subsequently list the order on the NASDAQ Level II quotation system. As a result of this ruling, the activities of the exclusive electronic trading networks like Instinet were forced into public view, and the modern ECN industry was born.

The emergence of major ECNs coincided, happily enough, with the day-trading phenomena of the late 1990s. This worked out perfectly for ECNs, since day traders typically were nontraditional investors with no solid roots in, or relationships with, the large brokerages. Instead, day traders were looking for quick and cheap ways to place a flurry of orders and reap a quick profit. Thus, the market conditions were ripe for new investment vehicles like ECNs to grab a piece of the action. One of the biggest ECNs, Island ECN Inc., was majority-owned by the online brokerage Datek Online Holdings Corp., which was deeply entrenched in day trading.

By late 2000, only a dozen or so ECNs were in operation. However, the floodgates were ready to open during the early 2000s, unleashing many new ECNs that sought to grab a piece of the market and carve out a distinct competitive niche. At the same time, however, analysts generally agreed that the field could not sustain such a glut of competitors over time, and the industry was expected to ripen for consolidation rather quickly. One factor driving the influx of new ECNs was the relatively low barrier to market entry. A viable system capable of handling heavy trading volume could be set up for less than $10 million, according to some estimates.

DUKING IT OUT WITH THE EXCHANGES

By the turn of the 21st century, ECNs were generating heavy enough trading volume to make the customary exchanges, such as NASDAQ and NYSE, extremely nervous. Indeed, several leading ECNs even filed with the SEC to acquire exchange status themselves, which set off a small war with the traditional exchanges. When ECN giant Archipelago Holdings LLC merged with the Pacific Stock Exchange to create the first ECN-exchange hybrid, it was able to simultaneously function as an exchange and trade stocks through NYSE. Island and NexTrade Holdings Inc. followed a similar path, and as they moved closer to regulatory approval the major exchanges, particularly NASDAQ, took arms in defense. Upon assuming exchange status, ECNs would enjoy direct access to the National Market System linking all stock exchanges, while having their quotations listed alongside those of other exchanges across the nation.

In 2001 NASDAQ attacked Archipelago's ambitions, going so far as to complain to the SEC that such moves were anticompetitive. At first blush, this complaint from a system that trafficked 2 billion shares per day against an ECN that moved 100 million daily shares looked incongruous, but it was in fact indicative of the exchanges' fear of ECNs' potential—particularly that of NASDAQ, which was the most immediately threatened.

The move toward exchange status had a pragmatic component as well. Following the tech market bust in 2000, day trading suffered a tremendous blow. While it hardly disappeared from the scene, a large portion of the natural customer base that ECNs enjoyed on their way to success was no longer a sure bet. Therefore, taking advantage of the benefits of exchange status would help to maintain them during the post-bull market. Exchange status also is the doorway to the extremely lucrative business of packaging and selling market data like stock prices. This is a coveted benefit, particularly since ECNs still suffer a competitive disadvantage when it comes to liquidity.

ECNs were given a break on the NYSE in 2000, courtesy of the SEC. The NYSE's Rule 390 prohibited ECNs from trading NYSE stocks that had been listed since before 1979. This added up to nearly one-third of total NYSE shares and half of the exchange's trading volume, including some of the biggest blue-chip stocks. This rule clearly restricted the range of business ECNs could conduct, and excluded them from some of the most widely demanded stocks on the NYSE. However, by 2000 the SEC strongly pressured the NYSE to repeal Rule 390, creating new opportunities for ECN growth.

One threat to ECNs was the looming possibility of a total overhaul of the NYSE and NASDAQ to create centralized systems that would effectively render ECNs superfluous by incorporating the major ECN functions. NASDAQ received approval in late 2000 to introduce its SuperMontage, a quote aggregation and execution system that will display the three best prices for a given stock and provide a vehicle by which customers' orders can be routed to any venue for completing the transaction. By combining the efficiencies and transparency of ECNs with the vastly greater liquidity of NASDAQ, SuperMontage posed a serious threat to ECNs, which registered their chagrin in the political arena. The ECN lobby caught the ear of House Commerce Committee Chairman Tom Bliley, who sent a letter to the SEC questioning the potentially unfair advantages SuperMontage would afford NASDAQ. Meanwhile, the NYSE began rolling out its own ECN, called Network NYSE.

ECNs also led the way in moving trading systems away from the antiquated practice of listing stock prices with fractions. Island ECN began the decimalization of its stock listings in July 2000, prompting other trading systems to follow suit. In this way, listed stock prices appeared in the form of dollars and cents. This practice also was competitively advantageous to ECNs in their struggle against the market makers. Market makers, earning margins by the spread between the buy and sell price, could use the fraction system to artificially pad those spreads. While this effectively adds up to less than seven cents a share—or one-sixteenth of a dollar, the smallest trading ''tick'' available in the fraction system—those pennies add up to astronomical sums over several million trades. And given that ECNs survive by the few pennies or less per share they charge for trades through their systems, switching to the more accurate decimal systems and pressuring the exchanges to do likewise closes off a major competitive rift between ECNs and market makers.

In the early 2000s, analysts were mixed in their predictions for the future of ECNs. Some felt they would drive securities trading while others insisted they would be phased out once the major exchanges co-opted their advantages. However, all agree that ECNs have been a major force in driving innovation in securities trading, and that the future of the markets will reflect the ECN influence.

FURTHER READING:

Awe, Susan. ''Electronic Privacy Information Center.'' *Library Journal*. October 1, 2000.

Barnett, Megan. ''The Exchange Revolution.'' *Industry Standard*. August 16, 1999.

''Cents and Sensibility.'' *Money*. September 2000.

Der Hovanesian, Mara; and Emily Thornton. ''Tough Times in Electronic Trading.'' *Business Week*. October 23, 2000.

''ECNs Poised to Take Off.'' *Wall Street & Technology*. July 2000.

Gogoi, Pallavi. ''Behind NASDAQ's Hissy Fit.'' *Business Week*. March 5, 2001.

Guerra, Anthony. ''NASDAQ Rolls Back the Curtain on Super-Montage.'' *Wall Street & Technology*. October 2000.

James, Sylvia. ''From Trading Floor to ECN.'' *Information World Review*. June 2000.

Jovin, Ellen. ''Fair Trades: Enthusiasts Say ECNs Level the Playing Field for Traders, but Many Others Remain Skeptical.'' *Financial Planning*. June 1, 2000.

Minkoff, Jerry. ''Market & Exchanges: ECNs Adapting to Rapidly Changing Environment.'' *Web Finance*. February 28, 2000.

Moskovitz, Eric. ''Matt Andersen vs. Wall Street.'' *Money*. July 2000.

Radcliff, Deborah. ''Trading Nets Give Exchanges a Run for Their Money.'' *Computerworld*. December 18, 2000.

Santini, Laura. ''A Rebel's Gamble: Island Wants to Join the System, but Will It Work?'' *Investment Dealers' Digest*. January 29, 2001.

Springsteel, Ian; and Michelle Celarier. ''The ECN Dilemma.'' *Investment Dealers' Digest*. March 2000.

Vinzant, Carol. ''Do We Need a Stock Exchange?'' *Fortune*. November 22, 1999.

Weinberg, Neil. ''The Big Board Comes Back From the Brink.'' *Forbes*. November 13, 2000.

SEE ALSO: Archipelago Holdings LLC; Datek Online Brokerage Services LLC; Day Trading; Instinet Group LLC; Island ECN Inc.; Nasdaq Stock Market

ELECTRONIC DATA INTERCHANGE (EDI)

Electronic data interchange (EDI) is the electronic exchange of business information—purchase orders, invoices, bills of lading, inventory data and various types of confirmations—between organizations or trading partners in standardized formats. EDI also is used within individual organizations to transfer data between different divisions or departments, including finance, purchasing and shipping. When the focus of EDI centers on payments, especially between banks and companies, the term financial EDI (FEDI) is sometimes used. Along with digital currency, electronic catalogs, intranets and extranets, EDI is a major cornerstone of e-commerce overall.

Two characteristics set EDI apart from other ways of exchanging information. First, EDI only involves business-to-business transactions; individual consumers do not directly use EDI to purchase goods or services. Secondly, EDI involves transactions between computers or databases, not individuals. Therefore, individuals sending e-mail messages or sharing files over a network does not constitute EDI.

While the concept of e-commerce did not receive widespread attention until the 1990s, large companies have been using EDI since the 1960s. The railroad industry was among the first to adopt EDI, followed by other players in the transportation industry. By the early 1980s, EDI was being used by companies in many different industry sectors. In the beginning, companies using EDI transferred information to one another on magnetic tape via mail or courier, which had many drawbacks including long lead times and the potential for a tape to be damaged in transit. During the 1980s, telecommunications emerged as the preferred vehicle for transferring information via EDI.

By the new millennium, EDI was used widely in many industries including manufacturing, finance, and retail. Some large retailers, among them Sears and Target, required suppliers to use EDI in order to engage in business transactions with them. Additionally, the Federal Acquisition Streamlining Act of 1994 (FASA) required all agencies within the United States government to use EDI.

ADVANTAGES OF EDI

Companies use EDI to exchange information for a variety of different reasons, mainly increased efficiency and cost savings. For example, EDI allows business transactions to occur in less time and with fewer errors than do traditional, paper-based means. It reduces the amount of inventory companies must invest in by closely tying manufacturing to actual demand, allowing for just-in-time delivery. By doing away with paper forms, EDI also reduces postage costs and the expenses and space considerations involved in paper-based record storage. Some companies have seen dramatic improvements in their business processes, such as the shortening of delivery times from days to hours. However, other EDI users have continued to experience snags. In *Planet IT*, Procter & Gamble, a leading packaged goods manufacturer, reported that it found errors in more than 30 percent of its electronic orders, although these were mainly due to human mistakes.

Although many companies don't view EDI as a strategic weapon, it certainly can be used as one. Having the capability to engage in EDI is a marketing tool, because it makes suppliers attractive to retailers and other companies who buy goods and services. In a situation where several suppliers offer similar products, being EDI-enabled can be an important differential. EDI also can be used to form alliances between companies that provide advantages over competitors in several ways, including the ability to offer the lowest market prices and the best customer service. Such alliances also can lead to newer or more innovative services.

HOW EDI WORKS

During EDI, information is sent from one participant's computer system and translated to a standard format with special translation software. It is then transmitted to another participant, translated back from the standard format into a format used by the receiver and entered into the receiver's computer system. Thus, EDI allows participants to transfer information between their respective computer systems, even if the systems utilize different, incompatible platforms.

Before using EDI, companies usually enter into specific agreements with their trading partners (called trading partner agreements or TPAs). These contracts often spell out the kinds of information they will exchange and how they will exchange it. Because entering into and terminating TPAs is expensive and time consuming, traditional EDI isn't always ideal for companies who change suppliers often, or for companies who frequently enter into temporary relationships with suppliers or other companies.

COMMUNICATION METHODS. After identifying trading partners, entering into TPAs with them and purchasing the necessary hardware and software, a means of communication must be chosen. EDI can occur point-to-point, where organizations communicate directly with one another over a private network; via the Internet (also known as open EDI); and most commonly, via value-added networks (VANs) provided by third-party value-added-network services.

VANs are networks dedicated exclusively to EDI. Not only do they function like telephone lines by allowing for the transfer of information, they also contain storage areas, similar to e-mail boxes, where data sent from one party can be held until it is scheduled to be delivered to the receiver. VANs are able to provide translation services to small organizations that find it too cost prohibitive to do in-house with their own software. Companies may need to join more than one VAN because their partners belong to more than one. However, by the early 2000s most VANS were able to communicate with one another.

In addition to translation, VANs offer a wide variety of other services including data backup, report generation, technical support, training, and the issuance of warnings if data is not properly transmitted between parties. Depending on need, all of the services offered by a VAN may not be required by a particular company. VANs vary in the way they charge companies. Some charge high implementation or setup fees followed by low monthly usage fees, or vice versa. Charges often are made based on the number of documents or characters involved in a given transmission. For example, one EDI provider charged its clients a monthly mailbox fee of $17.50, followed by a charge of 30 cents per 1,024 characters (per kilo character or k/char) transmitted. Additionally, charges can vary depending on participants' phone companies and the time of day when transactions are made. It can be less expensive for companies to make transactions during off-peak or evening hours.

In the early 2000s, although many companies still relied on VANs, the Internet was playing a larger role in EDI. It is possible for companies to translate EDI files and send them to another company's computer system over the Internet, via e-mail or file transfer protocol (FTP). Because it is an open network and access is not terribly expensive, using the Internet for EDI can be more cost effective for companies with limited means. It has the potential to provide them with access to large companies who continue to rely on large, traditional EDI systems. The low cost associated with open EDI also means that more companies are likely to participate. This is important because the level of value for participants often increases along with their number. However, this also presents a dilemma for large companies who have invested a considerable sum in traditional EDI systems. Furthermore, Internet service providers (ISPs) usually do not offer the kinds of EDI-specific services provided by VANs.

While the automotive and retail industries have experimented with open EDI for some time, the efforts didn't result in widespread adoption by small suppliers, usually due to cumbersome requirements like the installation of on-site software. Incorporating EDI into e-marketplaces was an approach that held more potential. In March 2000, an e-marketplace called the WorldWide Retail Exchange (WWRE) was established. It allowed suppliers and retails in various industry sectors—including retail, general merchandise, food and drugstores—to conduct transactions over the World Wide Web. After one year of operation, the WWRE had 53 retailer members with combined annual turnover of $722 billion. Leading retailers, among them Kmart, Rite Aid, Best Buy, and Target, planned to offer a Web-to-EDI translation service on WWRE so it would be easier for smaller suppliers to do business with them. In this arrangement, the retailers send purchase orders to a data center where they are translated to a language that can be read with a Web browser like Internet Explorer or Netscape Navigator. Suppliers are then notified about

the PO and allowed to respond. This is a break from true EDI, since orders are handled manually by suppliers.

In addition to the Internet, intranets (private internets) and extranets (links between intranets and the Internet) also showed potential for EDI. According to *The International Handbook of Electronic Commerce*, ''The Extranet makes it possible to connect several organizations behind virtual firewalls. For example, suppliers, distributors, contractors, customers, and trusted others outside the organization can benefit from establishing an Extranet. The Internet is used to provide access to the public; the Intranet serves the internal business; Extranets provide a critical link between these two extremes. Extranets are where the majority of business activity occurs. They enable commerce through the Web at a very low cost and allow companies to maintain one-to-one relationships with their customers, members staff and others.''

COMMUNICATION STANDARDS. As previously mentioned, when companies use EDI to exchange information, translation software is an important part of the process. During EDI, information is usually translated to and from one of several different standard languages, including ANSI X12 and EDIFACT. These languages are more flexible than custom standards developed by individual companies for their specific use.

Because of its reliability and flexibility, ANSI X12 was the most widely used North American standard in the early 2000s. Also called ASC X12, ANSI X12 was developed by the American National Standards Institute (ANSI), which administrates and coordinates voluntary industry standardization within the United States. In addition to its prevelance in North America, this standard also was used in Australia and New Zealand.

Created in 1987 with the cooperation of the United Nations, Electronic Data Interchange For Administration Commerce and Transport (EDIFACT) standards combine the best aspects of ANSI X12 and a standard known as United Nations Guidelines for Trade Data Interchange (UNTDI). Because it is so universal, EDIFACT is suited for use in international EDI. Although EDIFACT was becoming increasingly popular in the early 2000s, it lacked the comprehensiveness of ANSI X12.

In addition to ANSI X12 and EDIFACT, other EDI standards also exist, including Global EDI Guidelines for Retail (GEDI), used within North America for international trade; the grocery industry's Uniform Communication Standard (UCS); Voluntary Inter-Industry Commerce Standards (VISC), used by retailers of general merchandise; Warehouse Information Network Standard (WINS), used by public warehouses; TRADACOMS, created by the Article Numbering Association and used by retailers in the United Kingdom; and NACHA, developed by the National Automated Clearing House Association and used for transactions in the banking industry.

For companies using open EDI, a language called extensible markup language (XML), similar in some respects to hypertext markup language (HTML), allows users to share information in a universal, standard fashion without making the kinds of special arrangements EDI often requires and regardless of the software program in which it was originally created.

SECURITY ISSUES

The paper checks and balances that exist within the clerical world are not possible with EDI. While rare, the possibility that data will be intercepted and stolen or altered in transit does exist. Messages also may be deliberately or mistakenly duplicated. This can result in overcharges, wasted resources, and damaged relations between trading partners. For these and other reasons, companies take measures to ensure accuracy and security, including security policies that limit the authority to engage in transactions to certain individuals; means of verifying that messages sent were received intact (electronic "seals"); the use of proper encryption methods; digital signatures or biometrics (the use of human attributes like fingerprints or voice) to verify the identity of senders and receivers; audits that verify the accuracy of electronic records; efforts to ensure that translation software has been written correctly and not altered; and so on.

THE FUTURE OF EDI

EDI is expected to grow with business-to-business e-commerce overall, a sector that was growing quickly in the early 2000s. In 2000 alone, business-to-business sales were estimated to be $3.3 trillion, with forecasts predicting an increase to $5.2 trillion by 2004, according to *Corporate EFT Report*. The Gartner Group forecast sales in this sector to be even higher, reaching $7.29 trillion by 2004. The use of EDI also is expected to grow along with international trade agreements like the North American Free Trade Agreement (NAFTA).

According to *Corporate EFT Report,* in the early 2000s the lines between EDI and other Internet channels—including hybrid EDI/Internet electronic trading networks, Internet e-marketplaces, extranets, Internet company-to-company links, and private e-markets—were beginning to blur, and companies were relying on a variety of channels to conduct business with suppliers, depending on the nature of their business goals.

In a *Planet IT* article, David Yockelson provided a similar snapshot of EDI in the early 2000s, as well as a glimpse at the road ahead: "VANs haven't gone away, but the demands of businesses and their trading partners have changed dramatically. Internet-based transport, broader and more robust sets of information and real-time connectivity are just a few of the items that have been appended to the connectivity wish lists of most companies. Moreover, the basic language of data movement has suddenly become XML, despite the presence of decades-old EDI standards. VANs aren't dead. EDI isn't going away any time soon. And XML, while incredibly exciting as an application and data-neutralizing standard, is in its infancy."

FURTHER READING:

"E-Commerce Growth Prospects Remain Strong." *Corporate EFT Report,* January 17, 2001.

Karpinski, Richard. "The Future of EDI." *Planet IT,* March 3, 1999. Available from www.PlanetIT.com.

Kosiur, David. *Understanding Electronic Commerce,* Seattle: Microsoft Press. 1997.

Kumar, Ram, and Connie Crook. "Educating Senior Management on the Strategic Benefits of Electronic Data Interchange." *Journal of Systems Management,* March/April 1996.

Moozakis, Chuck. "No Longer E-Biz Misfits." *Planet IT,* March 3, 1999. Available from www.PlanetIT.com.

Shim, Jae K., Anique A. Qureshi, Joel G. Siegel, and Roberta M. Siegel. *The International Handbook of Electronic Commerce.* New York: AMACOM. 2000.

Tiernan, Bernadette. *E-tailing.* Chicago: Dearborn Financial Publishing Inc. 2000.

Yockelson, David. "Cross-Firm Transport Not Just For VANs." *Planet IT,* June 5, 2000. Available from www.PlanetIT.com.

SEE ALSO: Business-to-Business (B2B) E-commerce; Intranets and Extranets; UN/EDIFACT; Vortals; XML

ELECTRONIC DATA SYSTEMS CORP. (EDS)

Electronic Data Systems Corp. (EDS) is the largest information systems and business process services firm in the United States. Second only to IBM Corp. in the worldwide systems consulting market, EDS offers network operations, systems integration, data center administration, applications development, and management consulting. In the late 1990s, at the prompting of new CEO Dick Brown, EDS began overhauling its own internal operations with the e-business technology it had spent years selling to other clients. The restructuring paid off as annual sales in

2000 reached $19.22 billion, compared to $18.5 billion in 1999. More importantly, the Plano, Texas-based firm's earnings more than doubled, from $420.9 million to $1.1 billion, over the same time period.

EARLY HISTORY

EDS was created in 1962 by H. Ross Perot, a former IBM salesman. Recognizing that companies were struggling to recruit employees with the technical expertise needed to operate new equipment, Perot had come up with the idea that IBM should offer electronic data processing services along with selling computer equipment. When IBM discarded Perot's idea, he resigned to found EDS. The firm's first client, Collins Radio, bought computer time, which Perot had purchased on a wholesales basis, on an IBM 7070 machine at Dallas, Texas-based Southwestern Life Insurance. The following year, EDS began securing data processing contracts with firms like Mercantile Security Life and Frito Lay. To differentiate his firm from competitors who marketed two- and three-month contracts, Perot established five-year contracts with a predetermined price. EDS operated by putting in place a computer system and supplying staff qualified to run it. EDS employees were replaced by the client's workforce once they had learned to operate the machines.

EDS began establishing Medicare and Medicaid claims processing systems in 1965. Three years later, Medicare and Medicaid accounts were generating 25 percent of total sales. The Dallas Bank signed on as the first financial institution to use EDS, and later became a world leader in providing data processing services to banks and savings and loan institutions. The firm also secured its first $1 million contract and conducted its initial public offering at $16.50 per share. Sales in 1970 reached $47 million. After reaching a high of $160 per share in 1971, stock plummeted to $66 by the year's end. As a result, Perot hired Morton H. Meyerson and charged him with the task of preventing further stock drops. However, stock fell to $15 per share in 1973. The following year, eight credit unions signed up for EDS service, and sales reached the $100 million mark. EDSNET, an internal communications network, was launched.

In 1976, EDS faced litigation filed by F&M Schaefer Corp. for what F&M alleged was the firm's erroneous and defective data processing system. EDS contended that F&M was merely trying to wrangle its way out of paying its $1.2 million bill. Eventually, EDS agreed to pay F&M $200,000 to settle the case. The firm also made its first international foray, securing a $41 million contract to provide computer services to the Iranian government for three years. EDS landed a contract from King Abulaziz University in Saudi Arabia as well. In 1978, after waiting six months for payment from Iranian officials, EDS discontinued its operations in the country.

Morton Meyerson was named president in 1979, and was appointed CEO shortly thereafter. Perot retained the role of chairman. EDS diversified by securing contracts with hospitals, small banks, small businesses, and other organizations it had not targeted before. The firm also acquired Potomac Leasing, gaining access to its first government contract. In 1982, Meyerson was lauded by the *Wall Street Transcript* as "The Best CEO in the Computer Services Industry," an award he also won in 1983 and 1984. In the early 1980s, EDS signed a federal government contract that was the largest such deal ever assigned. The firm also landed a $656 million contract, known as Project Viable, to develop the U.S. Army's computerized administrative system over a period of 10 years. The system became known as Army Standard Information Management Systems (ASIMS). In June of 1984, General Motors Corp. paid $2.8 billion for EDS, completing the most costly purchase to date for a computer services company. As specified by the terms of the deal, EDS retained its corporate culture and most of its workforce. GM assigned a class E stock to EDS, tying its value to the new subsidiary's performance. Perot was named to the General Motors board of directors, and EDS took over management of General Motors' unwieldy data processing system and began whittling down the automaker's data processing expenditures, which totaled roughly $6 billion each year. Eventually, EDS connected the firm's suppliers and dealers in one of the first major electronic data interchanges.

GROWTH AS A UNIT OF GM

After its takeover by General Motors, EDS moved into Europe, setting up operations in the United Kingdom. The following year, in 1985, sales grew threefold to $3.4 billion. The firm's workforce also nearly tripled, reaching roughly 40,000. However, earnings fell by 5.5 percent. International expansion continued with the creation of units in Australia, Brazil, Canada, France, Germany, Mexico, New Zealand, and Venezuela. GM paid Perot more than $700 million for his remaining shares of EDS stock and dismissed him from the board. Eventually, Perot established a competitor to EDS, known as Perot Systems. Meyerson resigned, and Lester M. Alberthal was named as his successor. As this management shakeup was taking place, EDS diversified into factory automation and the telecommunications industry with the goal of growing its client base and reducing its reliance on the GM contract, which accounted for the majority of the firm's revenues. EDS also made its first foray into Asia by establishing a unit in Japan that housed two information processing centers and catered to automobile manufacturers, electronics firms, and financial institutions.

EDS forged two major deals in 1987. The Beijing Municipal Government's Commission for Science and Technology hired the firm to create the Beijing International Information Processing Co. It also secured a contract from Nippon Information Industry Corp. of Japan to develop Nippon EDS to offer computer and telecommunications services. International growth efforts resulted in the creation of an information processing center in Paris. The Health and Benefits Strategic Business Unit of EDS agreed to supply data processing services to the National Account Service Co., which was a joint venture established by five U.S. Blue Cross and Blue Shield plans. In 1988, *Fortune* magazine named EDS as the leading diversified services company in the United States. Also, Alberthal was named one of the top 10 executives of companies with more than $1 billion in revenues. Acquisitions that year included M&SD Corp.; the $347 million purchase of Mtech Corp.; General Data Systems Ltd.; VideoStar Connection Inc.; and a 50-percent stake in China Management Systems Corp., the top information services provider in Taiwan. Sales grew to $5.5 billion, and operations had expanded to 27 countries.

In March of 1989, EDS completed work on its 153,000-square-foot Information Management Center, a communications home base for the more than 7,000 EDS clients across the globe and the headquarters facility for 21 information processing centers, six of which were overseas. Hitachi Corp. agreed to develop Hitachi Data Systems Corp., a joint venture with EDS which marketed computer hardware made by Hitachi. In June, EDS began merging EDSNET with the communications network of General Motors to create the world's largest proprietary digital telecommunications network. The project, which took three years and 2,000 employees to complete, cost more than $1 billion. Systems management contracts secured during the year included a 10-year deal between EDS Hong Kong and Hong Kong's biggest bank, and an agreement between EDS Australia and Australia's leading private food producer. The firm also purchased BancSystems Association Inc. and the electronic fund transfer operations of Automatic Data Processing Inc.

Employees reached roughly 61,000 in 1990. The Army, Navy, and Defense Logistics Agency awarded EDS a $712 million contract. Efforts to increase its presence in the travel and transportation industry paid off when EDS secured major contracts with National Car Rental System, Continental Airlines/System One CRS, and Hospitality Franchise Systems Inc. In 1991,

Stratus Computer began working with EDS Personal Communications Corp. on developing a Home Location Register (HLR) system for the burgeoning cellular telephone industry. CAPSCO Software Canada Ltd. and EDS Canada began working together to target Canadian life insurance businesses. EDS also began providing data processing and communications network services to China's Ministry of Railways. The firm restructured operations around new Centers of Service, such as e-commerce, customer services technology, document processing, performance services, and technical products. Sales in 1992 grew to $8.5 billion, 40 percent of which were attributed to the GM account. GFI Informatique merged with EDS France to form one of the top information technology (IT) service providers in France.

Merger negotiations between EDS and long-distance telephone service provider Sprint Corp. dissolved in 1994. That year, EDS added to its international holdings with the purchase of French consultancy Eurosept and Brazilian consultancy F.C. Consultoria. In August of 1995, General Motors revealed its intent to spin off EDS as the largest independent computer services firm in the world. Valued at $25 billion, EDS was worth 10 times the amount General Motors had paid for it 11 before. In September, EDS bought A.T. Kearney for $628 million. When A.T. Kearney's 1,900 consultants had been integrated with the 1,600 consultants from EDS, the firm became one of the leading business consultancies in the world. In June of 1996, EDS stock was listed on the New York Stock Exchange after General Motors finalized its spin-off of the firm. EDS agreed to pay General Motors $500 million and provide computer services at a discount until 2006.

REORGANIZATION AFTER SPINOFF BY GM

BellSouth Telecommunications selected EDS for its $4 billion computer systems operation contract in 1997. The deal marked the first billion-dollar contract secured by EDS in more than a year and a half. In August of 1998, EDS was listed on the Standard and Poor's stock index. At that time, employees exceeded 90,000, and operations spanned more than 40 nations. Alberthal resigned as CEO and chairman, and was succeeded by Richard H. Brown in early 1999. According to William Schaff in an August 1998 *InformationWeek* article, Brown's challenge would be to maintain the firm's competitive edge as demand for IT outsourcing grew. ''Companies are outsourcing more IT functions, including their Web sites and E-commerce systems, as they focus on their core business. This puts EDS in a good position, but the booming market has also attracted strong competitors, including Computer Sciences Corp. and IBM Global Services, which have started winning some of the megacontracts that used to be EDS's private domain.'' Another issue facing EDS was that costs were growing as quickly as revenues, undercutting earnings growth.

One of Brown's first accomplishments was the purchase of Advanced Computing. He also oversaw the $12.4 billion, 10-year dual outsourcing agreement between EDS and MCI WorldCom, through which MCI WorldCom contracted EDS to handle a portion of its IT operations for $6.4 billion, and EDS contracted MCI WorldCom to oversee a chunk of its network operations for $6 billion. As part of the deal, EDS acquired MCI Systemhouse Corp., which designed, constructed, and operated systems that connected computers with data, voice, and Internet networks. It also offered e-commerce services such as call center management. Eventually, MCI Systemhouse was folded into a new Web-based electronic business unit called E-Business Solutions, which later became known as E.Solutions.

Decreased earnings in 1999, due in large part to increased competition and rising costs, prompted the firm to undertake a $1 billion reorganization effort which resulted in the layoff of 13,000 employees. Brown also combined the 48 business units of EDS into four divisions. In 2000, EDS purchased France's Captimark Corp., a customer service management systems provider. Rolls-Royce hired EDS to oversee its IT services; the contract was valued at $2.1 billion. The firm also secured a $6.9 billion IT systems contract from the U.S. Navy. At the dawn of the new millennium, EDS employees totaled roughly 115,000 and the firm operated more than 800 offices across the globe. Sales continued to grow, and profits more than doubled, reflecting the success of cost cutting measures launched by Brown in 1999. According to *InternetWeek,* when Brown took over, ''not only did EDS have aging systems, but it wasn't using the e-business technology it recommends and deploys for so many of the large enterprises that make up its clientele. Upon his arrival, Brown kicked off an extensive systems-modernization effort and insisted upon the implementation of e-business applications.'' For example, the firm began training its employees via online courses, which drastically cut training costs.

In early 2001, EDS bought the outsourcing operations of online travel agent Sabre for $670 million and Germany's IT systems provider Systemantics for $570 million. In June, EDS also agreed to acquire collaborative software manufacturer Structural Dynamics Research for $950 million to bolster a push into Web-based collaborative product design. The deal reflects the firm's continued efforts to broaden the reach of its e-business solutions operations.

FURTHER READING:

Boyd, Jade.'' EDS Helps Itself—Technology Services Firm Finally Gets Some E-Biz Religion as Major Systems.'' *InternetWeek.* March 12, 2001.

Deckmyn, Dominique. ''EDS/MCI $12.4 Billion Outsourcing Deal Nailed Down.'' *Network World.* November 1, 1999.

''Electronic Data Systems Corp.'' In *Notable Corporate Chronologies.* Farmington Hills, MI: Gale Group, 1999.

''Electronic Data Systems Corp.'' *Sacramento Business Journal.* March 16, 2001.

Forman, Preston P. ''With Global Focus, EDS Embraces Security Role.'' *Computer Reseller News.* May 24, 1999.

Goldstein, Alan. ''EDS Plans to Acquire Two Firms.'' *Dallas Morning News.* May 24, 2001.

''History.'' Plano, TX: EDS Corp., 2001. Available from www.eds.com.

Hunt, Ben. ''EDS Pushes into Germany with $570M Acquisition.'' *Financial Times.* April 2, 2001.

Schaff, William. ''The Problem with EDS—The Company's Growth Has Slowed Over the Past Few Years, and Margins Are Shrinking. Can New Management Turn Things Around?'' *InformationWeek.* August 17, 1998.

Schaff, William. ''Turnings Point for EDS?—After Several Years of Slow Growth, the Outsourcing Giant May Be on the Verge of Winning Back Investors.'' *InformationWeek.* March 1, 1999.

SEE ALSO: E-commerce Solutions; Information Management Systems; Information Technology; Perot Systems

ELECTRONIC FRONTIER FOUNDATION

The Electronic Frontier Foundation (EFF) is a non-profit organization that advocates the creation of legal and structural approaches in the computer and communications arenas in order to protect civil liberties such as privacy and freedom of expression. The foundation's goal is to advise policymakers and foster public understanding of the opportunities and challenges posed in the ever-changing computing and communications fields. Its efforts in the area of e-commerce include crafting policies that allow public and private information providers to distribute and sell their information products over the Internet.

Established in July 1990, the EFF initially was funded by private contributions from Mitchell D. Kapor and Apple Computer Inc. co-founder Steve Wozniak. Kapor founded the EFF with John Perry Barlow, and they raised contributions from a wide constituency. One of the first legal cases in which the foundation intervened involved a game manufacturer that was the target of the Secret Service's Operation

Sun Devil. Steve Jackson's company's computer equipment was seized by the government, and the EFF pressed for a full disclosure of that action. A second case had the EFF seeking ''friend of the court'' status for Craig Neidorf, a 20-year-old University of Missouri student who edited the electronic newsletter *Phrack World News*. Kapor discussed the foundation's interest in these cases in an EFF press release, explaining: ''It is becoming increasingly obvious that the rate of technology advancement in communications is far outpacing the establishment of appropriate cultural, legal, and political frameworks to handle the issues that are arising. And the Steve Jackson and Neidorf cases dramatically point to the timeliness of the Foundation's mission. We intend to be instrumental in helping shape a new framework that embraces these powerful new technologies for the public good.''

The expansive web of electronic media that links society is ushering in a new age of communications. New digital networks are the subject of significant debate, in terms of governance and jurisdiction. While generally a positive thing, pressing issues arise when information flows so freely. These problems include protecting children from sexually explicit materials, guarding intellectual property rights, and determining which country's laws have jurisdiction over a medium that is nowhere and everywhere at the same time. Ensuring that controversial speech is not stifled is another concern. The new electronic media is not so easily governed as its conventional counterpart, which is given structure and coherence through time-honored legal principles and cultural standards. The EFF's mission is to find ways to resolve these and other issues while protecting fundamental civil liberties.

Based in San Francisco, California, the EFF also has offices in Washington, D.C., and New York. The foundation dedicates itself to preserving free expression, protecting digital privacy, and defining online fair use. They work toward these goals through active involvement in legal cases, conducting educational programs, providing free hotlines, and encouraging access to new media by non-technical users.

FURTHER READING:

''About EFF.'' *Electronic Frontier Foundation Online*. May 1, 2001. Available from www.eff.org.

''New Foundation Established to Encourage Computer-Based Communications Policies.'' *Electronic Frontier Foundation Online*. May 1, 2001. Available from www.eff.org.

SEE ALSO: Cyberculture: Culture, Society, and the Internet; Kapor, Mitchell; Privacy: Issues, Policies, Statements; Wozniak, Stephen G.

ELECTRONIC INCOME-TAX FILING

Electronic filing of taxes enables professional tax preparers and most taxpayers to submit tax returns to the Internal Revenue Service (IRS) and some state agencies via computer modem. Taxpayers have various options for filing their taxes electronically. They can use special tax software to prepare their returns, and then transmit the completed forms electronically to an authorized intermediary who will forward them to the IRS. They also can take a completed paper form to an authorized intermediary for transmission, or have an authorized preparer complete their taxes and transmit them. As of 2001, taxpayers could not transmit their completed tax forms to the IRS directly via the Internet. A limited number of taxpayers also can file returns using a touchtone phone. In 2001, only taxpayers who were expecting a refund could e-file. However, that year the IRS announced that, under a pilot program in nine selected states, e-returns would be accepted from taxpayers who owed the government taxes.

In addition to filing electronically with the federal government, taxpayers can file state taxeselectronically in some states. Using an IRS program called Federal/State E-File, taxpayers transmit their state and federal returns together to the IRS. The agency then forwards the state return to the appropriate state's tax board. The service initially was available in 37 states and the District of Columbia.

The number of tax returns filed annually has paralleled the rise of the World Wide Web. In 1986 the IRS reported about 25,000 electronic tax returns. In 2001 more than 40 million federal income tax returns, of a total 130 million, were filed electronically. However, the IRS must find ways to inspire ever more taxpayers to e-file—a 1998 act of Congress required that 80 percent of all returns be made electronically by 2007.

HISTORY

By the time the IRS introduced electronic filing during the 1986 tax year, more and more taxpayers had begun preparing their returns on personal computers. The agency's main idea was to cut its own costs of processing returns. Every year thousands of temporary employees had to be hired to sift through mountains of tax returns, and then check and enter the data by hand into IRS computers. E-filing eliminated much of that human labor. In 2001, according to the agency, processing an e-return cost only 74 cents, compared to about $1.50 for a traditional paper return.

E-filing was tested in three cities in 1986 and proved so successful it was expanded to four more cities the following year. In 1988 the program included 14 states. From the beginning, e-filers did not submit returns directly to the IRS. They were transmitted to an IRS-authorized private agent, usually an established tax firm, which transmitted them to a regional IRS office. Intermediaries usually charged a fee, anywhere from $25 to $75, for e-filing returns. One attraction of the service for taxpayers was the promise of a refund check in as few as two weeks. To sweeten the deal, the tax firms sometimes offered, for another fee, ''refund anticipation loans''—a check for the expected refund issued as soon as the return was sent to Washington. Following the e-submission of a return, taxpayers affixed their signature to a paper form and mailed it to the IRS separately.

The rationale for using intermediaries to e-file at the time was partly that the modems and other necessities for e-transmission were still expensive and uncommon in most homes. Ironically, for the first few years the IRS did not have the technical capability to transmit returns electronically from regional offices to its headquarters in Washington. They had to be copied to magnetic tapes, which were then mailed to IRS headquarters.

In 1988 the lure of quick refunds drew 583,462 e-returns. In mid-March 1990, with still nearly a month to go until the filing deadline, the IRS had received 3.5 million returns. In 1992, 11 million e-returns were made. In 1993, the IRS approved commercial software for the 1040PC—a tax form that could be filled out on a PC, printed, and then mailed to the IRS. Even those helped trim IRS costs because of the higher accuracy compared to older methods.

Despite demands from some congressional members that taxpayers be allowed to transmit their tax forms directly to the agency rather than forcing them to pay an intermediary to do it, the original system has survived. However, by the end of the 1990s tax returns could be submitted to authorized businesses for further transmission using a software package approved by the IRS. In 1998, 500,000 individuals filed from home. The following year, that number mushroomed to 2.5 million. In 2001 the paper signature form was eliminated for those electronic filers and replaced by a five-digit number that the IRS issued to each e-filer. Together with specific information from the previous year's tax return, that number was used to identify each taxpayer.

ADVANTAGES AND DISADVANTAGES

E-filing provides many advantages to taxpayers. Quick processing means refunds are received much sooner, particularly if they are deposited directly into a bank account. Errors are reduced at both ends and e-tax preparation software can sometimes suggest de-

ductions, review returns for data that could lead to an audit, or even download W-2 and 1099 forms. Federal and state returns can sometimes be calculated together. However, e-filing has disadvantages as well. About one-fifth of e-filers had their e-signatures rejected for some reason in 2001. Between the cost of software and finding an authorized agent, e-filing can cost more than mailing a traditional paper return. About 40 forms were not available in e-versions as of 2001, according to the IRS, and some 10 percent of taxpayers were still not eligible to file electronically.

However, perhaps the most serious downside of e-filing for most taxpayers was the question of the security of their personal and tax data. These concerns were exacerbated by a 2001 General Accounting Office report that uncovered lax security in the IRS's computer systems. Although no evidence of hacking into the system was uncovered, GAO investigators were able to gain unauthorized access to computers containing taxpayer files. Following the report, the IRS took steps to improve its computer security. Additional security concerns were raised by a proposed IRS plan to increase the number of e-filers. In return for distributing free tax software to consumers, the IRS considered sharing taxpayer information with private firms. The plan eventually was scrapped. However, despite such concerns, the continuing expansion of personal computers and Internet access will make the growth of electronic tax returns inevitable.

FURTHER READING:

Abramson, E.M. ''IRS Flirts With Concept of Electronic Filing.'' *Washington Post.* August 18, 1986.

Barker, Jeff. ''IRS Urged to Make Filing Easier; Technology Could Aid Taxpayers, Deconcini Says,'' *Arizona Republic.* March 8, 1993.

Beaupre, Becky, ''Despite Kinks, Millions Will E-file 2000 Taxes.'' *Chicago Sun Times.* March 18, 2001.

Fogarty, Thomas A., ''Taxes: How e-filing Options Stack Up.'' *USA TODAY.* February 11, 2000.

Granelli, James S. ''Hitting the Return Key; Tax Filing By Computer Means You Can Get Your Refund Faster.'' *Los Angeles Times.* October 18, 1988.

Luther, Jim. ''IRS Expands Use of Computerized Tax Returns; Electronic Filing to Be Available Next Year to Professional Preparers in 14 States.'' *Washington Post.* June 10, 1987.

Meyer, Gene. ''E-Z Tax Filing; The Internet makes it cheaper, faster for Some to Fill Out Their Form 1040.'' *Kansas City Star.* February 6, 2000.

Reid, T.R. ''Form 1040 Would Never Be Missed; IRS Might Let Taxpayers File by Computer, Instead.'' *Washington Post.* April 14, 1985.

Waggoner, John. ''Electronic Filing is Perfect but Far From Popular; Agency's Low Tech Can't Keep Up.'' *USA TODAY.* March 26, 1990.

Weston, Liz Pulliam. ''IRS Considers Plan That Could Allow Marketing Pitches.'' *Los Angeles Times.* August 15, 2000.

————. "Lax Security Found in IRS Electronic Filing System." *Los Angeles Times.* March 15, 2001.

SEE ALSO: Digital Signature

ELECTRONIC PAYMENT

In the world of e-commerce, electronic payment most commonly refers to the use of a credit or debit card by a consumer to purchase a product or service online. For online merchants to accept credit or debit card numbers as payment, they must use online credit card processing technology that processes payments via online platforms such as the World Wide Web. To alleviate consumer concerns regarding the risk involved in using credit and debit cards online, most online sites use secure electronic transaction specifications that help to protect personal information like credit card numbers.

Like traditional merchants, online businesses also must work in conjunction with an acquiring bank in order to process transactions and obtain cash from credit card purchases. For example, once a consumer at a music e-tailer like CDNOW.com inputs his or her credit card information as payment, the online merchant uses real-time online processing software to send the information to the acquiring bank. Once the acquiring bank receives the request, it seeks credit card authorization from an acquiring processor, which handles credit card processing, billing, reporting, and settlement services. The acquiring processor transmits the request to the card-issuing bank—the bank that issued the credit card to the consumer—which either responds with an approval or denial code. The acquiring processor then sends the code to the merchant. Despite its complexity, this entire process typically is completed in less than 15 seconds.

During the late 1990s, a phenomenon known as electronic bill presentment and payment (EBPP) began to grow in popularity. EBPP is a process that allows businesses to bill clients and secure payment via the Internet. Invoices typically are transmitted by an e-mail message that includes a link to an online payment service provider's Web page, which houses more detailed billing information and allows payees to make an electronic payment with a single click. The most popular online payment service provider is CheckFree Corp., which makes money by charging transaction fees to the billing companies. International Data Corp. predicted that by 2004, EBPP will produce revenues in excess of $1 billion as consumers become more comfortable with security issues and as business-to-business enterprises increase their use of such technology.

FURTHER READING:

"EBPP." In *Ecommerce Webopedia.* Darien, CT: Internet.com, 2001. Available from e-comm.webopedia.com.

"EBPP." In *Techencyclopedia.* Point Pleasant, PA: Computer Language Co., 2001. Available from www.techweb.com/encyclopedia.

Greenberg, Paul A. "One Year Ago: CheckFree Acquires TransPoint for $1B+." *E-Commerce Times.* February 14, 2001. Available from www.ecommercetimes.com.

Hillebrand, Mary. "Report: Online Bill Payment to Reach $1B by 2004." *E-Commerce Times.* March 28, 2000. Available from www.ecommercetimes.com.

SEE ALSO: Acquiring Bank; Authorizaton and Authorization Code; Card-Issuing Bank; Charge-back; Interchange and Interchange Fee; Online Payment Options and Services; Recurring Payment Transactions; Secure Electronic Transactions (SEC)

ELECTRONIC PRIVACY INFORMATION CENTER

Founded in 1994, the Washington-based, nonprofit Electronic Privacy Information Center (EPIC) serves as a clearinghouse to disseminate information concerning the protection of Internet users' privacy. Its founder and executive director, Marc Rotenburg, created the organization to address perceived Internet privacy violations committed by both the government and businesses that operate Web sites.

EPIC's Web site includes Internet privacy news, the organization's newsletter, details on pending legislation, and an "Online Guide to Practical Privacy Tools." It identifies suppliers of secured e-mail, anonymous re-mailers for private e-mail, and computer programs that permit users to surf anonymously or to block cookies. The site also archives reports and articles concerning computer security, free speech, and cryptography. The site's privacy section includes information about securing online privacy in the workplace, eliminating spam and junk mail, and protecting one's social security number. Finally, the site furnishes an annotated listing of relevant organizations, print publications, national and international Web sites, privacy tools, and electronic newsgroups.

Early in 2001, EPIC joined with 16 other organizations in calling on President George W. Bush and Congress to implement national online privacy protection measures. Their request promoted the establishment of proposed fair information practices to mandate that online companies make the personal information they collect via their Web sites available to Internet users. The proposal also argued for the right of users to be able to modify incorrect data that has been captured online and to limit companies' use of such data. It promoted the creation of a special commission devoted to monitoring online surveillance technologies. Finally, it recommended that the laws regulating user privacy online be created at the state, rather than the national level since state legislation could be more stringent than federal legislation. Online trade groups countered that they either should be permitted to police themselves or that federal privacy legislation should be drafted.

EPIC makes frequent use of the Freedom of Information Act (FOIA) in its online privacy litigation. Among its targets, EPIC has criticized the FBI for failing to guarantee whether its Carnivore Internet surveillance system, which debuted in 1997 as Omnivore, unduly violates the public's online privacy. Omnivore was created ostensibly to monitor criminals' use of the Internet. However, EPIC alleged that the FBI also monitored the Internet communications of ordinary individuals, in what constituted an excessive breach of their privacy rights. In July 2000 it filed a FOIA suit against the FBI to obtain the data gathered by Carnivore. A U.S. District Court judge ordered the FBI to release records generated by Carnivore to EPIC every 45 days, after the Bureau delayed in responding to EPIC's initial request for material. When it did release records, the FBI withheld or censored about 600 pages of material. The FBI also refused to provide the Carnivore source code, according to EPIC. The group's original FOIA request sought all records and documents on Carnivore, including the FBI's legal analysis of the system's impact on privacy and the source code describing how data is gathered.

Another FOIA suit, begun by EPIC in 1999 against the National Security Agency, sought the release of internal NSA documents concerning the legality of the agency's intelligence activities. EPIC also brought suit against the Federal Trade Commission (FTC) concerning the commission's investigation of consumer privacy complaints, as a result of which EPIC successfully obtained the material. Other U.S. government agencies that have been the object of EPIC litigation include the Department of State, the Department of Commerce, and the National Security Council.

EPIC has used similar tactics against members of online industries. For example, it filed a federal complaint against the online marketer DoubleClick Inc. for planning to merge data about Internet users, such as their addresses and purchasing habits, with offline databases and then sell that information without notifying consumers. EPIC's complaint successfully impeded DoubleClick from acting. Other EPIC targets included the Clinton administration and Intel, whom it threatened to boycott if the company activated technology in Pentium III chips that would have facilitated the tracking of Internet surfing.

EPIC also issued a series of "Surfer Beware" reports. Its first report in 1997, entitled "Surfer Beware: Personal Privacy and the Internet," formed the foundation for the FTC's review of online privacy practices, the Fair Information Practices, which it outlined in 1998. EPIC released its most recent report, "Surfer Beware III: Privacy Policies Without Privacy Protection," in winter 2000. This report investigated the top 100 most popular online shopping sites for their compliance with the Fair Information Practices. Despite the companies' claims that they secure their data, the report concluded that 18 of the shopping sites failed to display a privacy policy, 35 included profile-based advertisers that gathered personal data from the sites, and 86 used cookies.

FURTHER READING:

Awe, Susan. "Electronic Privacy Information Center." *Library Journal*. October 1, 2000.

"Electronic Privacy Information Center." Washington, D.C.: Electronic Privacy Information Center, 2001. Available from www.epic.org.

Harrison, Ann. "Privacy Group Critical of Release of Carnivore Data." *Computerworld*. October 9, 2000.

————; and Kathleen Ohlson. "Advocates: Sites Still Don't Protect Privacy." *Computerworld*. January 3, 2000.

Stepanek, Marcia. "Marc Rotenberg." *Business Week*. May 15, 2000.

Weiss, Todd. "Bush Faces His First Privacy Challenge." *Computerworld*. January 22, 2001.

SEE ALSO: e-Government Web Privacy Coalition; Electronic Frontier Foundation; Privacy: Issues, Policies, Statements

ELECTRONIC PUBLISHING

Electronic publishing is much like traditional publishing, the main difference being the medium by which an author's work is delivered to readers. In place of the print sources typically used with traditional publishing, electronic publishing uses an online medium, most often the Internet, to present works to readers. In some cases, electronic publications—such as books, magazines, newspapers, or newsletters—are posted on Web sites. In other cases, they might be delivered to a reader's e-mail address. Despite many predictions in the late 1990s that electronic publishing would render print publishing obsolete, demand for electronic publications thus far has failed to meet expectations. In fact, by 2001 only a handful of publishers had figured out how to turn electronic publishing into a viable business.

ELECTRONIC BOOKS

Electronic books, also known as e-books, became available at the retail level in 1998. That year, e-book readers—the lightweight, paperback book-sized electronic devices used to display e-books—were released by NuvoMedia Inc. and Softbook Press Inc. Both readers allowed users to highlight, bookmark, and annotate specific passages, and to search an entire document. Many e-books also were accessible via a standard personal computer (PC). NuvoMedia and Softbook sold a total of roughly 10,000 e-book readers in 1999. At the time, less than 5,000 titles were available electronically. Hoping to use advertising campaigns and licensing agreements to generate more of an interest in e-book readers, Gemstar International Group Ltd. paid $400 million for both NuvoMedia and Softbook Press in January of 2000.

At roughly the same time, Barnesandnoble.com and Microsoft began working on their own e-book reader for PCs, and another e-book hardware manufacturer, Glassbook, disclosed similar plans. Via an agreement with publisher Simon & Schuster, celebrated author Stephen King released a new novella as an e-book that spring. Several security glitches allowed Internet users who had paid for the book to download multiple unauthorized copies. However, despite concerns over copyright infringement issues such as this, a few publishers persisted with various e-book trials. For example, Simon & Schuster released e-book versions of Mary Higgins Clark novels in May. The following month, the first Spanish language e-book was published. In July, Stephen King bypassed traditional publishers by selling chapters of his new novel, *Ride the Bullet,* on the Internet for $1 apiece. Within 15 hours of its release, more than 40,000 readers had downloaded the first chapter.

By the end of the year, only 25,000 e-book reading devices had been sold, and e-book sales were less than $5 million. Along with sluggish demand, the e-book industry was also forced to deal with limited supplies. E-book availability was growing at a much slower pace than e-book reading device makers had anticipated. In March of 2001, the number of e-books compatible with Gemstar's RocketBook—the industry's leading platform—had reached only a few thousand. Concerned that e-book sales might undermine print sales, particularly on new releases likely to make the bestseller lists, many publishers were only willing to offer electronic versions of classics like *Moby Dick* and *Romeo and Juliet.*

Incompatible formats posed another problem for the e-book industry. By the end of 2000, each of the three e-book industry leaders—Gemstar, Adobe, and Microsoft—was working to position its format as the industry standard. According to a November 2000 article in *The Atlantic Online,* "the future of reading is presently being held hostage in a computer 'standards war' where competing companies try to ensure that their proprietary technology becomes the toll-taker at the gate. Most publishers and retailers now offer every e-book title in at least two incompatible formats, sometimes three, and it may not stop there." This left many publishers leery about committing to any single format, and many decided to wait and see which format proved dominant before investing in the e-book industry. For the same reason, consumers resisted spending money on e-book reading devices, most of which could read only one format.

Copyright issues also proved daunting to many publishers. Despite legislation like the Digital Millennium Copyright Act—which made the manufacture or sale of products designed to dodge copyright laws illegal—many publishers were unsure how to go about protecting copyrighted books offered electronically. At the same time, publishers unwilling to release electronic versions of their copyrighted books also worked to prohibit other companies from doing so. For example, although authors like Kurt Vonnegut and Robert Parker granted RosettaBooks permission to publish electronic versions of their books, questions arose as to whether or not RosettaBooks needed to gain permission from Random House, the copyright holder of the traditional print books written by those authors. In February of 2001, Random House filed a copyright infringement lawsuit, the outcome of which is liable to have a considerable impact on the electronic publishing industry.

Although the e-book market has grown much more slowly than anticipated, some major publishers continue to pursue new e-book ventures. Many industry experts believe that the future of e-books is in niche markets, such as children's books, textbooks, and reference publications. According to a July 2001 article in *PC Magazine,* "the Electronic Document Systems Foundation predicts that the likelihood of people reading novels or even magazines digitally in the future is low. The chance that they will read digital reference materials, professional journals, and reports, however, is good."

ELECTRONIC NEWSLETTERS

Electronic newsletters, also known as online newsletters, gained in popularity during the late 1990s. As consumers began using the Internet regularly for things like gathering information and purchasing goods and services, many businesses began using online newsletters to provide information about their company and Web site, and to promote their products and services. Quite often, online newsletters serve the same purpose as their print counterparts. According to the February 2000 issue of *BusinessWeek Online,* "they remind customers you're there, spark repeat business, and help attract new clients."

While many companies make online newsletters available on their Web site, the most popular online newsletter delivery method is e-mail. Web surfers can sign up to receive newsletters, both free and fee-based, which are sent directly to their e-mail accounts. For example, CNET.com, a site covering the computer and technology industries, has more than 40 free online newsletters, all of which are sent to subscribers via e-mail. The Motley Fool, known for its witty investment advice, also offers members free newsletters including *FoolWatch Weekly* and *Investing Basics.* Both of these investment newsletters are sent to each subscriber's e-mail address on a weekly basis. In June of 2001, Japanese Prime Minister Junichiro Koizumi launched an online newsletter covering political and technological issues. Within two weeks, nearly 2 million readers had subscribed.

While some online newsletters are published simply to convey information, many are published to generate additional sales for the publisher. In fact, a 2001 study conducted by *Opt-in News* revealed that one out of three online newsletter publishers uses newsletters to generate advertising revenue. Advertising in online newsletters is growing in popularity, mainly because it is often more effective than placing a banner ad on a Web site. According to Forrester Research, ads in e-mailed newsletters had an average response rate of 18 percent in 2000, compared to a Web site banner ad response rate of less than one percent. As Internet use continues to rise, the number of online newsletters—including those offering information, as well as those containing advertising—will likely continue to grow. Forrester Research predicts that by 2002, businesses will transmit a total of 250 billion e-mail newsletters.

ELECTRONIC MAGAZINES AND NEWSPAPERS

Electronic magazines, or e-zines, are magazines published electronically, most often on the Web. Similarly, electronic newspapers, also known as online newspapers, are newspapers published on the Web. In addition to online content, most e-zines and online newspapers offer interactive features, such as the ability to search current and archived articles for a particular topic or keyword. Many also operate message boards, allowing readers to comment on articles. Some e-zines and online newspapers rely on advertising to make money, others charge subscription fees, and many rely on both revenues sources.

Online newspapers have been offered to readers in some form since the early 1990s. In 1994, the *News and Observer,* based in Raleigh, North Carolina, became the first daily newspaper to publish its full contents on the Internet. By 2000, the online versions of the *New York Times, USA Today,* the *Wall Street Journal,* and the *Washington Post* had established themselves as the online newspaper industry leaders.

The only publisher to actually make money from an online newspaper was WSJ.com, the online version of the *Wall Street Journal.* When online advertising revenues began their drastic downturn in 2000, WSJ.com was able to rely on its base of nearly 600,000 paying subscribers for revenue. In fact, by early 2001 subscription sales had begun to account for more than advertising revenues. A major contender to WSJ.com, the online version of the *New York Times* (NYTimes.com), dealt with the online advertising industry slump in a different manner. According to an August 2001 article in *Business Journal-Portland,* "Like WSJ.com, NYTimes.com is seeing significant declines in advertising revenue. However, the online edition of the paper is not moving to a subscription model like WSJ's. Like many online publications, NYTimes.com is leery of charging for what has already been offered for free. Instead, New York Times Digital is charging for 'premium content' such as archive searches, and some wireless delivery of content."

One of the earliest well-known e-zines, *Slate,* was first published by Microsoft Corp. in 1996. To run the news, politics, and culture e-zine, Microsoft hired Michael Kinsley, formerly a senior editor for the *New Republic* and a co-host of *Crossfire,* CNN's political commentary program. Initially, access to Slate cost $19.95 per month. A MySlate feature allowed readers to customize the site. A discussion forum, dubbed The Fray, permitted readers to comment on articles and interact with one another. In 1999, the e-zine's managers realized that they were spending more money trying to secure paying subscribers than they were actually generating in subscription fees. According to *Slate* publisher Scott Moore, as quoted in a September 2001 *EContent* article, "I projected what would happen to our audience if we made *Slate* free, given that we could take advantage of the distribution power of MSN. I modeled what that would do for our advertising potential, and it looked like there was a lot more upside with that strategy than continuing to slug along selling subscriptions, so that's what we did and it has paid off." By 2001, roughly 2.5 million unique readers logged on to *Slate* every month.

One of *Slate's* major rivals, *Salon* was created in 1995 to cover political and cultural issues. The e-zine's initial public offering in 1999 raised $35.6 million in capital. Access to the site was free, which meant *Salon* had to rely on advertising to generate revenues. Consequently, the site was particularly susceptible to the online advertising slowdown that started in 2000. That year, *Salon* lost roughly $19 million on only $8 million in revenue. To reduce its dependence on advertising, *Salon* began working on a fee-based site with expanded content and no advertising. Cost cutting measures included layoffs and a 15-percent pay cut in 2001. According to *BusinessWeek Online* writer Thane Peterson, *Salon's* reliance on advertising was not the only reason the firm found itself struggling; it also lacked the name recognition of industry giants like *Newsweek* and *Time.* "Established print magazines can constantly remind readers to log onto their Web sites, so, like *Slate,* they require far less marketing expense than an independent like *Salon.*"

Analysts disagree over which business model will prove the best choice for online books, newsletters, newsletters, and magazines. Advances in technology certainly will impact online publishing, as will new legislation. Business models not yet conceived may well emerge as online publishers continue working to attain profitability.

FURTHER READING:

Brady, Diane. "Six Parties a Night? It's a Living." *BusinessWeek Online.* April 3, 2000. Available from www.businessweek.com.

Chenoweth, Emily. "Psst. Hey Little Girl, Wanna Try an E-Book?" *Inside.com.* May 9, 2001. Available from www.thestandard.com.

Earnshaw, Aliza. "Making Money's the Big Challenge Online." *Business Journal-Portland.* August 3, 2001.

Garber, Joseph R. "Publish and Perish." *Forbes.* October 16, 2000.

Kafka, Peter. "Horror Story." *Forbes.* August 21, 2000.

Lindorff, Dave. "Draw More Business With an Online Newsletter." *BusinessWeek Online.* February 18, 2000. Available from www.businessweek.com.

Lombreglia, Ralph. "Exit Gutenberg?" *The Atlantic Online.* November 16, 2000. Available from www.theatlantic.com.

Luskin, Donald L. "Walk It Like You Talk It." *The Industry Standard.* June 14, 2001. Available from www.thestandard.com.

Manes, Stephen. "Electronic Page-Turners." *Forbes.* May 28, 2001.

Olsen, Stefanie. "Newsletter Authors Reap Banner Profits." *CNET News.* March 30, 2000. Available from news.cnet.com.

Owens, Jennifer. "Study: E-Newsletters Drive Site Traffic." *Adweek.* April 2, 2001. Available from www.adweek.com.

Peek, Robin. "Jump-Starting Electronic Books." *Information Today.* March 2000.

Peterson, Thane. "The Wolf at Salon's Door." *BusinessWeek Online.* August 7, 2001. Available from www.businessweek.com.

Pike, George H. "A Book Is a Book Is E-Book." *Information Today.* July 2001.

Runne, Jen. "Why eBooks are Sputtering." *eMarketer.* March 14, 2001. Available from www.emarketer.com.

Wimpsett, Kim. "Newsletter Know-How." *CNET News.* December 1, 2000. Available from news.cnet.com.

Wood, Christina. "The Myth of E-Books." *PC Magazine.* July 1, 2001.

SEE ALSO: Barnesandnoble.com; E-book; E-Zines

ELLISON, LAWRENCE J. (LARRY)

Lawrence J. (Larry) Ellison is founder and CEO of Oracle Corp., one of the world's largest software companies. Serving as CEO since the firm's inception in 1977, Ellison steered its initial growth as a database software maker and its eventual move into e-commerce in the late 1990s. The recipient of Harvard Business School's Entrepreneur of the Year award, Ellison is considered an information technology industry pioneer. He owns 24 percent of Oracle.

Ellison co-founded Oracle with fellow computer programmer Robert N. Miner in Belmont, California. The partners used their combined experience in specialized database program design to convince the Central Intelligence Agency (CIA) to hire them to build a $50,000 customized database program. It was while working for the CIA that Ellison recognized the potential profit in IBM's efforts to develop a relational database, using Structured Query Language (SQL), that would allow users to pull corporate data from various sources. Ellison and Miner beat IBM to the market by nearly two years when they launched Oracle RDBMS, the world's first relational database using SQL, in 1978.

When Ellison took Oracle public in 1986, the firm had become one of the fastest-growing software companies in the world, as well as the world's leading database management software maker. Ellison began to focus his firm on the Internet in 1998. According to *Business Week Online* columnist Sam Jaffe, "Back then, some experts argued that the database software market Oracle dominates would quickly erode as companies found cheaper and simpler ways of managing their data on the Web. Instead the opposite happened—after CEO Larry Ellison ordered an 'Internetization' of his company." Not only did Oracle begin manufacturing products that allowed users to manage data from the World Wide Web, it also began using this e-business technology to streamline its own operations. It was this shift in direction that allowed Oracle to outperform many of its competitors through the end of 2000, although the technology industry's downturn finally took its toll on the firm, when Ellison announced in March of 2001 that sales were slowing.

Along with running Oracle, Ellison also sits on Apple Computer's board of directors. In addition, he serves as chairman of New Internet Computer Co., an upstart he co-founded in January of 2000 to manufacture and sell New Internet Computers—inexpensive machines that offer e-mail capabilities and access to the Internet.

FURTHER READING:

Corcoran, Elizabeth. "Oracle: Walking the Talk." *Forbes.* January 8, 2001.

Cox, John. "Oracle Eats Its Own E-business Dog Food." *Network World.* July 17, 2000.

Doyle, T.C. "The Oracle Economy: Warning Lights are Flashing—The Company Must Outline What the Opportunity for Integrators Will Be." *VARbusiness.* April 2, 2001.

Jaffe, Sam. "Oracle: A B2B Rebirth That Few Foretold." *BusinessWeek Online.* April 6, 2000. Available from www.businessweek.com/technology.

"Larry Ellison's New Internet Computer Company Announces Second Generation Hardware of Its NIC Internet Appliance." *Business Wire.* March 21, 2001.

"Oracle Corp." In *Notable Corporate Chronologies.* Farmington Hills, MI: Gale Group, 1999.

Slywotzky, Adrian. "Four Lessons From Larry: Ellison Was Late in Reshaping Oracle for the Net. But When He Did It, He Did It Fast. Here's How." *Fortune.* March 5, 2001.

SEE ALSO: Database Management; Oracle Corp.

E-MAIL

Electronic messages sent over a network are known as e-mail. Users may send messages to a single recipient or to a group of several recipients anywhere in the world. In many cases, messages are transmitted along high-speed data communications networks in a matter of seconds or minutes. Once a message is received, a user may view it, save it, delete it, or forward it on to other recipients. E-mail programs consist of two main components: the store-and-forward messaging system and the send-and-receive interface, which is what a user sees when working with an e-mail program. The text itself usually is in ASCII format and sent via Simple Mail Transfer Protocol (SMTP). Advances in technology like Multipurpose Internet Mail Extensions (MIME) allow e-mail users to attach files—including graphics, audio files, word processing documents, spreadsheets, and even executable programs—to their messages for recipients to open on their machines.

The first e-mail message was sent by Ray Tomlinson in 1971. Tomlinson came up with the idea for e-mail when he was working for Bolt Beranek and Newman, a Cambridge, Massachusetts-based research and development outfit contracted in 1968 by the U.S. Department of Defense to construct ARPAnet, a network that would allow the government to have messaging capabilities in the event of nuclear war. To create his e-mail program, Tomlinson used a rudimentary file transfer protocol known as CYPNET along with SNDMSG, an electronic messaging system that allowed users of a single machine to leave messages for each other on that machine. He decided to use the @ (pronounced "at") symbol to identify messages that were going to be sent along the network to another machine. When Tomlinson sent his new e-mail program to other ARPAnet users, who loaded it onto their computers, e-mail essentially was born. However, it was not until years later that Tomlinson and his colleagues recognized just how widespread e-mail would become as a communications tool for educational, social, and commercial endeavors.

The Internet, which eventually replaced ARPAnet, had an immeasurable impact on e-mail technology. Although Internet-based e-mail programs emerged in the 1980s, most simply allowed local area network (LAN) users to communicate with one another. It wasn't until the 1990s, when the Internet began to function as a portal between incompatible online services like America Online and Prodigy, that e-mail truly began to evolve into the open communications system it is today. Although measuring the technology's use is difficult, it is clear that many millions of users send many billions of messages every year.

This method of quickly and easily communicating with large numbers of people is not without complications. One major issue for many e-mail users is the increasing amount of unsolicited advertisements, commonly known as spam, they receive. Many companies and individuals purchase huge mailing lists of e-mail addresses from various information sources and send unwanted advertisements to recipients. In some cases these advertisements are legal, and in other cases they are not, but the senders are quite often very difficult to trace. Many proprietary e-mail programs, such as those offered to workers by an employer, include filtering technology that helps to block spam. Users of freely available Internet-based mail services, such as Hotmail and Juno, are more likely to receive spam.

Another problem inherent in an open communication system like e-mail is the ease with which viruses can be spread via e-mail message attachments. Many virus programs are disguised as attached files from colleagues or friends. Once they are unwittingly opened by a recipient, the virus reads the recipient's address book and forwards the virus on to each user in that address book. Because the e-mail looks as though it was sent by the victim of the virus, the likelihood that future recipients will open the disguised virus is quite high.

As e-mail technology has extended its reach across the globe, individuals and businesses have begun to use it for increasingly diverse reasons. A multitude of Web sites now exist that allow individuals to create free personalized greeting cards they can e-mail to family members and friends. Students in online courses are able to e-mail their work to professors, who then offer feedback via e-mail. Online retailers quite often e-mail receipts to customers within seconds of a purchase. These same retailers also may e-mail customers to let them know when their goods are actually shipped, and if a customer has indicated they would like to receive information in the future, they may send e-mail messages regarding upcoming promotions or special deals. Some online travel companies e-mail discounted fares each week to a list of people who have subscribed to such a service. While there is no way to predict how e-mail might be used in the future, new ways in which the technology can be used for educational, social, and commercial endeavors are certain to develop.

FURTHER READING:

''A Brief History of Email.'' Kirkland, WA: Vicom Technology Ltd., 2001. Available from www.vicomsoft.com.

Campbell, Todd. ''The First E-mail Message.'' *PreText*. March 1998. Available from www.pretext.com.

''E-mail.'' In *Ecommerce Webopedia*. Darien, CT: Internet.com, 2001. Available from e-comm.webopedia.com.

''E-mail.'' In *Techencyclopedia*. Point Pleasant, PA: Computer Language Co., 2001. Available from www.techweb.com/encyclopedia.

''E-mail or Email.'' In *NetLingo*. NetLingo Inc., 2001. Available from www.netlingo.com.

SEE ALSO: ARPAnet; E-mail Marketing; History of the Internet and World Wide Web (WWW); Local Area Network (LAN); MIME and S/MIME

E-MAIL MARKETING

The term e-mail marketing covers a wide range of e-mail used to deliver commercial messages. It includes e-mail newsletters that deliver news, information, or content that people have specifically requested. These newsletters typically contain advertising messages targeted to the interests of the newsletters' readers. At the other end of the e-mail marketing spectrum is unsolicited bulk e-mail, often referred to as ''spam.''

When e-mail became a part of people's daily routine, using it as a marketing medium became an opportunity that marketers couldn't ignore. According to a mid-2001 Gallup Poll survey, 97 percent of Internet users agree that e-mail has made their lives better. According to the survey, e-mail is the most popular online activity, with e-mail users (96.6 million) outnumbering Web users (87.9 million) by 10 percent. In the United States alone, more than 1 billion e-mail messages are sent daily, according to *eMarketer*.

eMarketer also reported that e-mail message volume increased from 394.2 billion messages in 1999 to 536.3 billion in 2000. Volume was projected to reach 677.1 billion messages in 2001, 840.1 billion in 2002, and more than 1 trillion in 2003. In early 2001 Jupiter Media Metrix predicted that by 2005, the average online consumer in the United States could get as many as 950 e-mail messages every day.

E-MAIL MARKETING VS. TRADITIONAL DIRECT MAIL

Marketers have found that e-mail marketing is cheaper and more effective than traditional direct mail. A 1999 study by Jupiter Research (now Jupiter Media Metrix) estimated the cost per piece of e-mail to be $.25, compared to $2 per piece sent by regular U.S. mail. *eMarketer* estimated that in 2003 some $2.2 billion would be spent on e-mail marketing, compared to $40 billion on traditional direct mail. Jupiter Media Metrix estimated that companies would spend $1.3 billion in 2001 to send 43 billion commercial e-mail messages.

A 2001 study by Opt-In News found that direct e-mail was considered the most responsive marketing method worldwide by some 50 percent of media buyers, and e-zines or e-mail newsletters were ranked the most responsive by 23 percent. Only 11 percent of media buyers surveyed said that direct mail was the most responsive marketing method, while eight percent voted for TV and radio.

E-mail is more targeted, custom, and flexible than traditional direct mail—and it comes at a fraction of the cost. This is largely due to the use of marketing databases. During an e-mail campaign, available technology can capture and track individual responses, provide marketers with the information to learn more about customers from response and purchase behavior, and refine and update customer profiles for future communications. These types of services typically are available from messaging solution providers. The flexibility of e-mail marketing makes it possible to change an offer the next day if a special discount doesn't bring in enough traffic right away.

Marketers conducting e-mail marketing campaigns have access to packaged e-mail marketing software and outsourced e-mail marketing services. A company can use its own customer database to deliver personalized messages based on one or more database attributes and specific e-mailings can be targeted to customer groups based on past purchase and response behavior.

Opt-in e-mail campaigns, in which recipients have asked to receive information, are conducted to achieve different objectives. They can be used to prospect for new customers outside of a company's established customer base. The low cost of e-mail makes it possible to test market new products and services more quickly and inexpensively. E-mail marketing campaigns also are used to drive traffic to a company's Web site.

For existing customers, e-mail marketing can help to build relationships through more frequent contact. E-mails can be used to alert customers to new products or services, special promotions, or discounts. They also can be customized according to online and offline purchase patterns. Such messages help to build customer loyalty. Additionally, as surveys e-mails can be used to get feedback from customers. Such surveys typically include an incentive to get customers to participate.

Opt-in e-mail lists are available from list brokers and managers as well as from some online ad agencies. Online ad agency DoubleClick became the biggest e-mail marketing message distributor in early 2001 with the acquisition of Toronto-based FloNetworks. The acquisition enabled DoubleClick to expand its distribution capability from 150 million e-mails per month to more than 600 million. As of mid-2001 DoubleClick had 32 million e-mail names under exclusive management and brokered an additional 55 million names. Chicago-based Yesmail.com is a fast-growing company that specializes in e-mail marketing solutions. As of mid-2001 it had more than 25 million e-mail subscribers and was acquiring new names at the rate of more than 500,000 per month.

OPT-IN AND OPT-OUT METHODS

''Opt-in'' and ''opt-out'' are two kinds of privacy mechanisms that have been adapted to e-mail marketing. With the opt-in method, consumers must actively agree to receive commercial e-mail messages, usually by clicking a box or making some other type of positive response. Under this system, consumers only receive commercial e-mail messages after they have expressly given their permission. Therefore, opt-in e-mail lists consist only of e-mail addresses for individuals who have given their permission to receive commercial e-mail messages. Double opt-in means that, after giving their permission, consumers must also send in a confirming e-mail.

Under the opt-out method, consumers are given the option of not receiving any further promotional e-mails after they have already received one. Under this system, messages are sent to individuals until they ask to be removed from the mailing list. A similar system, known as passive consent or negative opt-in, allows marketers to add consumers to their lists if they do not click or unclick a checkbox on a Web page in order to avoid receiving commercial e-mail. The fairness of such systems has become a matter of debate in some circles, the argument being that the necessity to actively opt-out places an undue burden on consumers who may routinely visit numerous commercial Web sites, for example.

According to a 2001 study by Opt-in News and reported in *eMarketer,* opt-in was the most frequently used method to acquire customers. The study found that 54 percent of the companies surveyed used opt-in, while 32 percent used opt-out and 14 percent used double opt-in to prospect for new customers. One problem with using the opt-out method was that, in many cases, the unsolicited messages might be perceived as spam. In the absence of express permission to send e-mail, marketers are more likely to send irrelevant and intrusive e-mail that consumers will ignore.

ACCEPTABLE TO CONSUMERS

E-mail marketing appears to be more acceptable to consumers than banner advertising. A consumer survey conducted by Valentine Radford from September 2000 through March 2001 found that 75 percent of online consumers thought banner ads were annoying, and only 30 percent believed they provided essential information. More than half of the surveyed consumers felt that e-mail advertising was enjoyable, and more than 80 percent said they enjoyed receiving e-mail newsletters.

E-mail also appeared to be the preferred medium for consumers to receive discount offers and coupons. Some 55 percent of online shoppers preferred to receive coupons through e-mail, compared to 29 percent who preferred newspaper coupons, and 16 percent who preferred to receive them through regular mail. With respect to content, 72 percent of online shoppers said that they enjoy rich media, while 60 percent preferred HTML over text. A very large number of consumers (80 percent) would rather receive a link to rich media content in an e-mail message.

Although e-mail marketing was preferred by many, business-to-consumer (B2C) e-mail marketers must be careful because e-mail is a much more personal medium than banner ads. Marketers can avoid alienating existing and potential customers by making certain the e-mails they send are relevant. Consumers will perceive relevant offers as less intrusive than e-mails that are not relevant to their needs. E-mails that take too long to read may cause consumers to ignore future messages from the same source. Additionally, although consumers appreciate personalization in commercial e-mail messages, marketers must be careful not to appear to have too much knowledge about their lives.

BUSINESS-TO-BUSINESS E-MAIL MARKETING

E-mail is a cost-effective way to generate high-quality sales leads in business-to-business (B2B) marketing. Compared to B2C, B2B has a much smaller target audience, and one that generally is more sophisticated. The objective usually is for a company to generate qualified sales leads and then distribute them to its sales force. An integrated e-mail campaign includes planning, media choices for outbound messages and inbound responses, list acquisition, developing an offer, providing incentive options, and copywriting and design.

A key element of an integrated B2B e-mail marketing campaign is to obtain targeted opt-in e-mail lists. Selections are based on criteria such as title and annual budget. Enough e-mails must be sent to generate enough leads for the sales team to pursue. Testing also is part of an effective e-mail campaign—for lists, products, and creative elements. In order to test effectively, e-mails must drive traffic to a unique Web page that pitches the offer and any related incentives. Respondents can be qualified by asking them to provide basic information about their industry, annual revenue, and timeframe for needing a particular product or service. Leads can then be categorized and prioritized in terms of urgency.

According to *DM News,* click-through rates on e-mail lead generation campaigns for B2B commonly are five percent. Conversion rates indicate that 50 percent of those interested respondents who click through to the Web page will actually fill out response information, thus providing the sender with a desired lead.

A LOW-COST ALTERNATIVE FOR SMALL BUSINESSES

E-mail marketing isn't just for large companies. For small businesses, e-mail marketing offers a low-cost alternative to traditional direct marketing. At the local level, this marketing tool can be extremely targeted and highly personal. Ideally, e-mail direct marketing offers the opportunity to have a one-to-one conversation with each and every customer.

According to *eMarketer,* the number of U.S. small businesses adopting e-mail marketing will increase from 1.6 million in 2001 to 3.7 in 2003. The

amount they will spend on e-mail marketing was projected to increase from $398 million in 2001 to $1.3 billion in 2003, compared to $211 million spent in 2000. A 2001 study by The Kelsey Group found that 11 percent of small businesses used e-mail marketing in 2000. By the end of 2001, the study predicted that 16 percent of small businesses would be using e-mail marketing. The study also projected that by 2005, approximately 42 percent of all U.S. small businesses would use e-mail marketing.

DUPLICATE E-MAIL ADDRESSES AND OTHER PROBLEMS

When the use of e-mail for direct marketing began in 1994, the e-mail industry adopted the standard practice of having list owners retain possession of their customers' e-mail addresses. Marketers who rented the lists had to rely on the list owners to send out their messages. When marketers rented e-mail lists from multiple vendors, there was a likelihood of duplication, with some customers receiving duplicate e-mails. In addition, marketers could not eliminate existing customers from the mailings. Finally, there was no consistency in message format among the different list owners, so marketers had difficulty comparing the results from different lists.

As of 2001, list owners continued to refuse to release e-mail lists to mailers, and problems with duplicate mailings continued. Proposed solutions include shipping the e-mail files to a trusted third-party service bureau so that duplications and existing customers can be removed from the files to be mailed. Other solutions are being developed to merge and purge e-mail files in order to eliminate duplicates from multiple lists and suppress mailings to a marketer's existing customers.

Another problem plaguing e-mail marketers is the lack of a change-of-address system similar to the one in place for regular mail. According to *DM News,* only nine to 20 percent of consumers who change their e-mail addresses notify marketers and update their e-mail subscriptions to online newsletters, Web sites, and discussion lists. An early 2001 study conducted by NFO Research estimated that the annual rate of e-mail address changes was about 32 percent. Some 41 percent of consumers changed their e-mail addresses at least once during the past two years. To address this problem, Return Path Inc. was established in 1999 to provide an e-mail change-of-address service that optimized e-mail marketing lists and gave consumers an easy way to notify all of their personal, business, and commercial contacts of their new e-mail address.

REGULATING E-MAIL MARKETING

In June 2001, Washington's anti-spam law was upheld by that state's Supreme Court. The law had been challenged as placing an undue burden on interstate commerce. However, the state's high court ruled that the only burden the law placed on spammers was the requirement of truthfulness. Washington's law was designed to prevent e-mailers from using the Internet to distribute deceptive commercial messages. It bans unsolicited commercial e-mails from containing misleading information in the subject line, an invalid return address, and a disguised transmission path. The law allows for fines from $100 to $1,000 per e-mail.

As of mid-2001 spam was regulated by a patchwork of state laws, some of which were more effective than others. Bills to regulate spam were pending in both the U.S. House of Representatives and the U.S. Senate that would require unsolicited commercial e-mail messages to be clearly labeled as such, include a valid return e-mail address, and give consumers a way to opt-out of receiving future mailings. The proposed federal laws also would allow the Federal Trade Commission (FTC) to fine violators. State attorneys general would be allowed to take legal action against spammers on behalf of citizens.

The Coalition Against Unsolicited Commercial E-Mail (CAUCE), an organization that lobbies for federal anti-spam legislation, found that state laws generally were ineffective at stopping spam. CAUCE noted that states must avoid violating the interstate commerce clause of the U.S. Constitution, which prevents states from placing an undue burden on interstate commerce. Generally, the federal position on anti-spam legislation has been that state laws would put an undue burden on interstate commerce and thus be a violation of the U.S. Constitution. Marketers certainly would have difficulty complying with 50 different state laws, as compared to a single federal standard. According to *E-Commerce Times*, even the strongest anti-spam legislation would only require that e-mails be clearly marked and have opt-out information readily available.

The Direct Marketing Association (DMA) supports anti-spam laws that crack down on false and misleading commercial e-mail messages and e-mails that fail to give consumers a way to opt-out of future mailings. However, the DMA noted that legitimate e-mail marketers should not be categorized as spammers, especially when they provide consumers with a way to opt-out of future mailings. Other obstacles to effective anti-spam regulation included a lack of resources to sue spammers. Under the proposed federal legislation, individual consumers would not be able to sue spammers. Instead, they would have to rely on government agencies or Internet service providers (ISPs) to take legal action. That in turn would likely overload law enforcement agencies that did not have the resources to handle a large volume of anti-spam cases.

THE FUTURE: WIRELESS E-MAIL, STREAMING AUDIO AND VIDEO

According to *eMarketer's* 2001 eWireless Report, e-mail was by far the most popular Internet activity conducted over wireless devices. The report indicated that 69 percent of wireless Internet device owners in the United States used their devices for e-mail, compared to 32 percent for research, 26 percent for games, 25 percent for news, 24 percent for general entertainment, and 21 percent for shopping and buying. Other reported activities included obtaining sports scores, making travel arrangements, looking up stock quotes, and paying bills.

Wireless e-mail marketing has the potential to become the "killer application" for wireless devices. Special offers delivered by e-mail to wireless devices would enable a mobile user to purchase an item by clicking on a link within the e-mail message. Another potential wireless application would be to deliver commercial e-mail messages based on the mobile user's location. Among the technical issues that e-mail marketers must overcome to effectively market to mobile users is that e-mail delivered to a wireless device looks much different than e-mail delivered to a regular computer.

Future applications and features in commercial e-mail will include streaming audio and video. In May 2001, e-mail marketing firm Yesmail.com introduced software that would allow clients to add audio capabilities to their e-mail. As rich media content becomes more common in commercial e-mail messages, marketers can look forward to higher response rates and new ways to interact with customers and prospects.

FURTHER READING:

Berkowitz, David. "How Is Direct Marketing Faring? Survey Says. . . ." *eMarketer.* July 25, 2001. Available from www.emarketer.com.

Centeno, Cerelle. "eConsumers Prefer eMail Newsletters and Coupons." *eMarketer.* June 6, 2001. Available from www.emarketer.com.

Cruz, Wil. "Video E-Mail Test Leads to Alliance." *DM News.* May 7, 2001.

"Don't Follow the Leader—Be One." *Internet World.* January 15, 2001.

Enos, Lori. "Washington State's Highest Court Upholds Anti-Spam Law." *E-Commerce Times.* June 8, 2001. Available from www.ecommercetimes.com.

Hardigree, Steve. "Opt-In E-Mail as Prospecting Source." *DM News.* May 21, 2001.

Jackson, Jonathan. "All eMail Is Local." *eMarketer.* July 31, 2001. Available from www.emarketer.com.

———. "Disregard At Your Peril." *eMarketer.* May 7, 2001. Available from www.emarketer.com

———. "eMail Is Our Friend." *eMarketer.* May 28, 2001. Available from www.emarketer.com.

———. "eMail Mistakes." *eMarketer.* July 24, 2001. Available from www.emarketer.com.

———. "Killer eMail." *eMarketer.* May 21, 2001. Available from www.emarketer.com.

Joffe, Rodney. "Merge/Purge of E-Mail Addresses." *DM News.* February 5, 2001.

The Kelsey Group. "U.S. Small Businesses to Spend $2.2 Billion on E-Mail Marketing by 2005 According to The Kelsey Group." May 22, 2001. Available from www.kelseygroup.com.

Regan, Keith. "Walking the Line Between E-Mail and Spam." *E-Commerce Times.* April 17, 2001. Available from www.ecommercetimes.com.

Schwartz, John. "Marketers Turn to a Simple Tool: E-Mail." *The New York Times.* December 13, 2000.

SEE ALSO: Advertising Online; Business-to-Business (B2B) E-Commerce; Business-to-Consumer (B2C) E-Commerce; E-Mail

EN POINTE TECHNOLOGIES INC.

Los Angeles, California-based En Pointe Technologies Inc. resells computers and related equipment manufactured by the industry's leading players, including IBM Corp., Hewlett-Packard Co., and Compaq Computer Corp. The firm's electronic catalog, known as Access Pointe, lists more than 700,000 items, including information regarding cost and availability, allowing En Pointe customers to comparison shops for computer technology at a single site. En Pointe operates with a virtual inventory, avoiding the costs associated with traditional inventories, thanks to deals with distributors who ship products to En Pointe clients. The company owns 43.5 percent of Firstsource Corp., an e-commerce solutions provider that builds purchasing hubs linked to distributors for businesses wanting to handle procurement via the World Wide Web. It also owns 36.7 percent of SupplyAccess Inc., an Internet-based business-to-business provider of automated procurement services for businesses seeking products and services related to information technology MRO (materials, repair, and operation).

After managing a retail personal-computer chain for several years, Pakistan native Attiazaz Din founded En Pointe in 1993. Din financed his business by mortgaging his home and emptying his savings account. When that proved inadequate, Din began charging business expenses on his American Express card. According to a May 1998 article in *Success,* Din had recognized that "explosive demand and rapidly changing technology were creating havoc for corporate resellers, who traditionally bought hardware on spec from manufacturers and then paid to freight it to their own warehouses until they found customers." Because computer hardware prices were decreasing at a rate of up to 40 percent annually, warehouses were filled with inventory that continually dropped in value. Believing he could use e-business technology to operate as a much more efficient reseller, Din created a "risk-free virtual warehouse" system which allowed him to search for the best possible price once an order was placed. Rather than having the factory ship merchandise to him, Din had purchases shipped directly to customers.

By 1998, sales had reached $500 million and the firm was posting a profit of $5.8 million. En Pointe conducted its initial public offering. In April, First Source International Inc. sold its online reseller unit, named firstsource.com, to En Pointe. Firstsource.com resold computers and related hardware systems via the Internet to individuals and small and mid-sized companies. Later that year, En Pointe agreed to market the wearable computers manufactured by Xybernaut Corp. and the handheld computers made by DataRover Mobile Systems. Although sales in 1999 grew 18 percent to $668 million, the firm posted a $16.6 million loss. During the year, a jury had ruled against En Pointe in a lawsuit filed by NovaQuest Systems Inc. regarding a breach of contract. Damages were estimated at $1.7 million. Also, the firm's plans to sell its integration complex in Ontario, California—established in September of 1998—had fallen through, subjecting En Pointe to additional charges.

Recognizing that the computer reselling industry was slowing, particularly in comparison to the e-business services market, En Pointe shifted its focus in mid-2000 by establishing a professional services division. The firm's system consulting services included needs assessment, new system design and existing system customization, training, and systems integration. Two new contracts were secured that year: one with the state of Minnesota and another with Los Angeles World Airports. Sales in 2000 dropped to $494.4 million, and losses grew to $19.4 million. That year, the firm also created its SupplyAccess subsidiary, which targeted *Fortune* 1000 clients with automated procurement of MRO products and services. Within a few months, En Pointe had reduced its stake in SupplyAccess to a minority one, a move that prompted shareholders to file a class-action lawsuit against the firm. The litigation regarded allegations that En Pointe had made misleading statements regarding the potential success of SupplyAccess.

In February of 2001, En Pointe and Web Associates Inc. jointly launched an upgraded En Pointe

Web site that provided customers with a direct link to the purchasing system En Pointe uses to procure computers and related equipment. The firm posted a $1.1 million profit for the first quarter of 2001, its second consecutive quarterly profit. Some analysts point to the turnaround as an indication that En Pointe's mid-2000 restructuring was successful.

FURTHER READING:

Churcher, Sharon. "A Pointe Well Taken; He Charged Ahead When the Going Got Tough." *Success.* May 1998.

"En Pointe Taps Web Associates for Corporate Redesign." *Business Wire.* February 15, 2001.

"En Pointe Technologies Announces New Corporate Operational Plan." Los Angeles, CA: En Pointe Technologies Inc., 2001. Available from www.enpointe.com.

"En Pointe Technologies, Inc. Reports Net Income for the First Quarter of Fiscal Year 2001." *PR Newswire.* February 12, 2001.

Jastrow, David. "En Pointe Banks on Electronic Links—Virtual Distribution in Place with Four Compaq Distributors." *Computer Reseller News.* May 31, 1999.

Roberts, John. "Sizing Them Up—The Ten Most Overvalued/Undervalued Companies." *Computer Reseller News.* November 6, 2000.

Rosa, Jerry. "NovaQuest Wins $1.4M Suit Against En Pointe." *Computer Reseller News.* April 12, 1999.

SEE ALSO: Compaq Computer Corp.; Firstsource Corp.; Hewlett-Packard Co.; IBM Corp.; Supply Chain Management

ENCRYPTION

The Internet is an open and interconnected system that is both a boon and a hazard to businesses and consumers. On one hand, it makes the act of shopping, comparing, and purchasing extraordinarily quick and convenient. On the other hand, with so many people able to access information and potentially misuse it, there are justified fears of transferring sensitive information, such as credit card numbers and purchasing habits, over the Internet. To eliminate the hazards so that the benefits of e-commerce can be more widely enjoyed, encryption was developed. Encryption is the scrambling of sensitive information, such as credit card numbers, personal information, legal documents, confidential records, and even personal communications, in such a way that only authorized persons or organizations are able to decipher it.

Encryption is the fruit of cryptography, the study of codes and ciphers for the guarding of secret information. While crude (by contemporary standards) encryption methods have existed for centuries, modern encryption typically involves processing the concerned information with one or more mathematical algorithms using sophisticated computer technology, which allows for vastly more complex, and thus stronger, encryption schemes. However, while encryption technology has developed rapidly over the years, particularly in the 1990s and early 2000s, so have the skills of those who would seek to break encryption codes to steal, tamper with, or otherwise illicitly access sensitive data. As a result, the development of ever more impenetrable encryption methods amounts to an arms race between those aiming to protect information and those aiming to compromise it.

Encryption has a long and contentious history, pitting governments concerned with the security of unclassified domestic documents and information against technological libertarians, businesses, and privacy groups pushing for more open systems of encryption use and commerce, particularly in the international arena. By the 2000s, the latter groups were slowly emerging victorious in these debates, as the potentials of e-commerce gradually convinced governments to relax restrictions on the sale and export of encryption technologies. As a result, encryption was moving to its expected place as a key element in the development of e-commerce, finding increasing prominence in online transactions by way of digital certificates and digital signatures.

POPULAR ENCRYPTION TECHNOLOGIES

Countless encryption schemes were used throughout the world for commerce, communication, and other purposes. However, only a small handful achieved particular prominence through the 1990s for use over the Internet in general, and in conjunction with e-commerce in particular. At the top of the list was the RSA encryption system, developed by Ronald Rivest, Adi Shamir, and Leonard Aldeman in the late 1970s at the Massachusetts Institute of Technology. RSA went on to become one of the most widely used and best-known encryption systems, programmed into such major software packages as Windows, Quicken, and Netscape Navigator. The CEO of RSA Security, Joe Bidzos, who had long been one of the encryption industry's foremost proponents and a champion of the relaxation of export restrictions, went on to found the RSA spin-off VeriSign in 1995. VeriSign was the leading digital certificate authority through the late 1990s, highlighting the connection to e-commerce. Meanwhile, RSA's encryption software appeared on more than 450 million computers worldwide.

Security Sockets Layer (SSL), a public-key encryption scheme widely used in client-to-server applications, was developed by Netscape and was supported by both Netscape and Microsoft browsers. Identified in commercial software by the small gold lock symbol that appears upon loading a Web page secured by SSL, the scheme was employed for the transmission of personal identification numbers (PINs), credit card information, and passwords, among other things. However, SSL suffered from its complex computation system, which prolongs the time it takes to perform the encryption and decryption processes.

Another popular encryption technology was Pretty Good Privacy (PGP), developed by Phil Zimmerman and released in 1991. PGP was hailed for its easy-to-use format and strong encryption. PGP actually was targeted by government investigators on suspicion of violating export restrictions in the mid-1990s, though the government dropped its case in 1996. Shortly thereafter, PGP Inc. was launched to commercialize the software. After Network Associates purchased PGP, Zimmerman continued to develop the encryption scheme to more widely adapt it to emerging technologies and ripen it for e-commerce applications.

Over the years, a number of file encryption products became available on the market. Most were geared toward individual users seeking to protect information on their hard drives, rather than companies operating over a large network. These programs, such as Symantec Corp.'s Norton Your Eyes Only, encrypted individual files or hard disks and required personal passwords to access them. However, according to *Network Computing,* these were often seen as excessively cumbersome, particularly for the office setting, since in order to fulfill their function, they required users to remember to encrypt files each time they use them and avoid leaving unprotected copies elsewhere on their hard drives. Moreover, in an office, recovery of data following an employee's departure was crucial, and not always feasible with such programs since they usually lacked data-recovery features. By the 2000s, software programs such as Windows 2000 came equipped with automatic encryption schemes, in which users only needed to set a specific attribute to save encrypted data in a specified, central location on the computer's hard drive. Alternatively, such programs could encrypt data onto a company server and allow only those with authorized access to the files to decrypt them.

CUTTING-EDGE ENCRYPTION SCHEMES

Encryption system developers never gave up on the possibility of an entirely unbeatable encryption code. In 2001, Michael Rabin of Harvard introduced an outline of his "hyper encryption" program. Al-

though the feasibility of such a system was hotly contested, Rabin's notions were highly intriguing to cryptographers and policy analysts. Hyper encryption involves the generation, perhaps by satellite, of such a large quantity of random numbers that no storage system could possibly retain and interpret them. The involved communicators settle on a method of retrieving certain numbers, which are then used to decrypt the information. Immediately upon encrypting or decrypting, their computers then discard the numbers. In this way, in the event that a hacker is able to intercept a message and discover the method by which the random numbers were picked from the stream, he or she would still be without the crucial numbers themselves, and thus would be unable to decrypt the information. Also on the horizon was the development of quantum cryptography, which combined high-tech encryption technology with the latest developments in quantum physics for unbeatable encryption. However, by the early 2000s these were mere promises.

ENCRYPTION IN THE E-COMMERCE ARENA

In the 2000s, encryption was the preferred method of disguising and protecting information during Internet transactions. Encryption was at the heart of many of the key technological breakthroughs furthering e-commerce. In particular, it served as the cornerstone of digital certificates and digital signatures, which were increasingly used to authenticate, secure, and sign electronic documents on the Internet using public-key encryption. Public-key encryption refers to an open encryption system in which a number of individuals maintain a public key or code to encrypt documents, but where only one entity retains the private key that can decrypt them. In an e-commerce transaction, for instance, the online merchant maintains the private key while its customers use the public key.

In 2000, RSA's Bidzos won the praise of Ed Hart, the former deputy director of information security at the U.S. National Security Agency (NSA), for laying the foundation for the commercial encryption industry in the 1980s, and for having the prescience of the importance of encryption technologies for the development of electronic business. Lynn McNulty, a former official at the National Institute of Standards and Technology (NIST) told *Computer Reseller News* that Bidzos "almost single-handedly commercialized the use of public key encryption." Bidzos had long insisted, since his early days at RSA in the mid- and late 1980s, that the commercialization of and relaxed export controls for encryption technology was crucial for the commercialization of the Internet and the development of e-commerce, long before most businesses, let alone consumers, had even heard of the Internet.

THE DEVELOPMENT OF ENCRYPTION STANDARDS

The NIST adopted the Data Encryption Standard (DES) in 1977. DES was designed in the realization that individuals, including those outside of the spying racket, needed to protect their sensitive information, even though it wasn't classified. Over time the private sector came to adopt DES and, especially, its younger and stronger cousin, Triple DES. DES earned its share of critics over the years. A common complaint was that the relatively short 56-bit key wasn't as strong as it could have been. The most cynical of such critics, according to *Communications of the ACM,* even surmised that the National Security Agency may have purposely left the encryption standard fairly easy to decrypt so that it could view DES-encrypted documents.

For many years encryption technology was the jurisdiction of the NSA. The U.S. government was, in fact, one of the biggest foes of the spread of strong encryption technology, and cryptographers battled with the government for years to open up the playing field. The main focus of this battle was over the length of encryption keys. A 1992 agreement between the government and industry groups allowed encryption algorithms utilizing no more than 40 bits to be exported, which ruled out those algorithms conforming to DES. As a result, the allowable encryption technologies were generally weaker than those that had become commonplace within the United States, and weaker than what most industry experts felt was necessary at the time to adequately safeguard information.

Particularly after the opening of the Internet, the 56-bit DES began to show its age, culminating in its cracking, as part of a test of DES, in 1998 by a computer built especially for the task by the Electronic Frontier Foundation. Two years earlier, the National Research Council report on cryptography called for the relaxation of export restrictions, but no action had been taken. Moreover, as a sign of its time, DES was geared more specifically toward use with hardware. NSA scientists had not anticipated the proliferation and importance of software.

Realizing that the old standard had realized its value, the Clinton administration used the occasion of DES's cracking to announce that the United States would at last relax the restrictions on the export of encryption technologies. In 1997, seeing the writing on the wall, NIST began seeking out a new encryption algorithm that could replace DES as the official encryption standard for government computers. The private sector, both inside and outside the United States, was expected to adopt the new standard as well.

In October 2000, NIST finally settled on its choice for the Advanced Encryption Standard (AES).

The requirements for the AES competition, which involved dozens of contestants worldwide (a signal that the United States was committed to an open, international standard after years of protectionism under the NSA), demanded that the new standard incorporate 128-, 192-, and 256-bit encryption; demonstrate versatility and flexibility across platforms; consistently maintain high speeds of encryption and decryption; and exhibit an exceptionally high degree of impenetrability. The winning algorithm, called Rijndael, was designed by Belgian cryptographers Vincent Rijmen and Joan Daemen.

GOVERNMENTAL CONTROL: SECURITY VS. FREEDOM?

The ability to break codes and intercept secret information was a crucial element of security work for many countries, including the United States. For that reason, many governments were wary of allowing their domestic encryption products to be exported and proliferate throughout the world, where they conceivably could fall into enemy hands and make international eavesdropping especially cumbersome.

According to *Federal Communications Law Journal,* the Clinton administration, which was the first to deal with encryption policy in the age of e-commerce, initially ruffled the feathers of privacy advocates and industry proponents by proposing the ''Clipper Chip'' initiative in 1993. Developed by the National Security Administration, the Clipper Chip used an algorithm called ''Skipjack,'' a classified code that would have allowed the government to access classified information. The proposal failed, as did three subsequent Clipper Chip movements. All included measures to tightly restrict the export of encryption technologies.

By the 2000s, protection of encryption technology in the name of national security was falling out of favor among governments and especially businesses. This especially was the case in the United States. For one thing, technology had advanced to the point where encryption systems were common throughout the world, and governmental impediments to the export of encryption was thus seen as a fruitless policy. However, more important to many business leaders was that encryption had become a big business, one that played a key role in global e-commerce. Thus, in order to remain competitive in this burgeoning world market, businesses needed to be free to market their technologies across borders.

In 2000, the Washington, D.C.-based Electronic Privacy Information Center (EPIC) released a study entitled ''Cryptography and Liberty 2000: An International Survey of Encryption Policy.'' The study reported that governments around the world were slowly coming to perceive the commercial value of encryption technology and its importance in the growth of many industries, particularly in the broad field of e-commerce.

While many governments, such as those of Pakistan, China, and Russia, maintained some form of control over encryption use and exportation, the trend by the 2000s was certainly blowing in the other direction toward greater openness and proliferation of strong encryption schemes. In this movement, governments may have to adjust their security strategies to compensate for the inevitable loss of some information in the interests of enjoying the benefits of and staying competitive in e-commerce.

FURTHER READING:

Black, Tricia E. ''Taking Account of the World As It Will Be: The Shifting Course of U.S. Encryption Policy.'' *Federal Communications Law Journal,* March 2001, 289.

Dugan, Sean M. ''e-Business Innovators: Phil Zimmerman, Security.'' *InfoWorld,* October 9, 2000, 64.

''Electronic Security Technology Roadmap.'' *Power Engineering,* November 2000, 37.

Gingrich, Newt. ''Bush Faces Two Top IT Challenges.'' *Computerworld,* January 15, 2001.

Harrison, Ann. ''Feds Propose New Encryption Standard.'' *Computerworld,* October 9, 2000.

———. ''Web Outpaces Crypto Rules.'' *Computerworld,* April 10, 2000.

Landau, Susan. ''Designing Cryptography for the New Century.'' *Communications of the ACM,* May 2000.

Levy, Steven. ''An Unbreakable Code?'' *Newsweek,* March 5, 2001.

Messmer, Ellen. ''Crypto Proposal Faces Long Journey.'' *Network World,* October 16, 2000, 33.

O'Mara, Debora L. ''Encryption Stands Tough in PC Security.'' *Security,* December 2000.

Savage, Marcia. ''Jim Bidzos: The Security Warrior.'' *Computer Reseller News,* November 13, 2000.

Stijns, William, and Mark Gunton. ''Safe from Prying Eyes.'' *World Trade,* September 2000.

SEE ALSO: Advanced Encryption Standard (AES); Cryptography; Data Encryption Standard (DES); Digital Certificate; Digital Certificate Authority; Digital Signature; Digital Signature Legislation; Electronic Frontier Foundation; Electronic Privacy Information Center (EPIC); Privacy: Issues, Policies, Statements

ENTERPRISE APPLICATION INTEGRATION (EAI)

Enterprise application integration (EAI) is the process of allowing two or more enterprise systems to operate as one. Most EAI offerings include software, hardware, and services. Typically, EAI systems are used to integrate incompatible systems—such as an older system in which a major investment has already been made, commonly referred to as a legacy system, and a newer application, such as a customer resource management (CRM) system—within a single business. However, EAI systems are also used with increasing frequency to integrate the enterprise systems of various companies to allow business transactions between enterprises to take place electronically.

A highly complex process, EAI can take place at many levels within an enterprise system. For example, disparate databases can be linked to allow for information sharing between the databases. In addition, two or more applications can be integrated to allow for either data or business processes to be shared among the applications. In this case, an EAI package could link a World Wide Web site to a company's existing inventory management system to allow for real-time inventory updating. The most comprehensive form of EAI, a common virtual system, integrates all elements of an enterprise so that they operate as a single application.

The need for EAI arose in the 1980s as many companies that had already used information technology (IT) to automate various business processes began to recognize that the integration of these applications could, among other things, increase efficiency and improve accuracy within business processes. According to Internet portal ITtoolbox.com, ''many corporate IT staff members attempted to redesign already implemented applications to make them appear as if they were integrated. Examples include trying to perform operational transaction processing (associated with enterprise resource planning (ERP) system functionality) on systems designed for informational data processing.'' ERP systems, which integrated accounting, human resources, distribution, manufacturing, and other back-end processes—those business procedures that do not directly involve customers—grew in popularity throughout the early 1990s as most major corporations began upgrading their mainframe systems with the new client/server-based ERP systems developed by industry leaders like SAP AG, PeopleSoft Inc., and J.D. Edwards & Co. To make these systems compatible with their legacy systems, businesses turned to EAI vendors for integration solutions.

Another factor fueling the growth of the EAI industry was the growing popularity of e-commerce, which required the integration of front-end business processes—those which involve interaction with clients, such as CRM and online sales—with back-end functions like inventory management. Although many leading ERP vendors began working to incorporate these front-end processes into their systems, several new companies focused specifically on EAI emerged as well. For example, Vitria Technology, Inc. was founded in Sunnyvale, California, in 1994. Four years later, the firm shipped its blockbuster BusinessWare integration server, which linked the existing IT systems and applications of enterprises like Sprint Corp. and Deutsche Bank with the Internet. Firms could also use BusinessWare to link all sorts of disparate systems within their enterprise. For example, wireless receivers maker DMC Stratex Networks Inc. used Vitria's EAI solution to integrate its Oracle order management, financial, and manufacturing systems with its Siebel sales force automation system and its Nortel CRM system. In April of 2001, WinterGreen Research Inc. named Vitria the fastest growing application integration vendor.

Another growing EAI vendor, Fairfax, Virginia-based webMethods, Inc., was founded in 1996 to create a business-to-business (B2B) integration tool based on the Internet's extensible mark-up language (XML). The firm conducted its initial public offering (IPO) in early 2000; by then, its client base included the likes of SAP, Eastman Chemical, Lucent Technologies, and Dell Computer Corp. In November of 2001, electronics retailer Best Buy selected webMethod's integration platform to centralize communications with its top suppliers. Also founded in 1996 was CrossWorlds Software Inc., an integration tools and services provider based in Burlingame, California whose clients included Nortel Networks and Caterpillar. IBM Corp. paid $129 million for CrossWorlds in October of 2001 in an effort to add EAI functionality to its WebSphere application server suite.

The EAI leader, San Jose, California-based BEA Systems, Inc., was founded in 1995 by Bill Coleman, Ed Scott, and Alfred Chuang. In early 1996, the partners decided to acquire Tuxedo, a transaction processing application, from Novell, Inc. It was this purchase that formed the core of BEA's online transaction processing (OLTP) software, which would later fuel its rise to dominance in the EAI industry. ERP giant PeopleSoft agreed to bundle BEA Tuxedo with its major product releases later that year. BEA also released Jolt, its first Java-based program, which allowed users to move business applications to the Internet. The firm listed its shares publicly for the first time in April of 1997, in what turned out to be the third most lucrative IPO that year.

To gain access to an application server, BEA acquired WebLogic in 1998. In February of 1999, BEA eLink, which formed the EAI component of future releases of WebLogic, was shipped. The new EAI program included adapters for integration with SAP and PeopleSoft ERP systems, as well as older legacy systems. According to a June 2000 article in *Computer Reseller News*, what differentiated BEA "from the pack of fierce competitors in this fragmented and evolving market—such as New Era of Networks, Active Software, Vitria, Mercator, and others—is it supplies the application development platform and integration platform, as well as a formidable services organization." Essentially, the firm was able to support its EAI solution with the well known Tuxedo system.

Because EAI solutions can help companies integrate their existing systems, such as ERP and CRM, as well as allow businesses to integrate their systems with Web-based operations, the need for EAI solutions will likely continue to grow. In fact, International Data Corp. predicts that EAI industry sales will grow from $5 billion in 2000 to more than $20 billion by the year 2005.

FURTHER READING:

BEA Systems, Inc. "Company Milestones." San Jose, CA: BEA Systems, Inc., 2001. Available from www.bea.com.

"EAI Overview." Scottsdale, AZ: ITtoolbox.com, 2001. Available from eai.ittoolbox.com.

Gold-Bernstein, Beth. "EAI Market Segmentation." *EAI Journal*. July 1999. Available from www.eaijournal.com

Gonsalves, Antone. "Value of EAI Grows as Integration Needs Expand." *InformationWeek*. May 28, 2001, 60.

Liebmann, Lenny. "Enterprise Application Integration." *InternetWeek*. September 18, 2000.

Parkes, Clara. "Business Snapshot: EAI." *Enterprise Systems Journal*. November 2001.

SEE ALSO: Integration

ENTERPRISE RESOURCE PLANNING (ERP)

Relied upon by more than 90 percent of Fortune 100 companies, enterprise resource planning (ERP) systems integrate accounting, human resources distribution, manufacturing, and other back-end processes—those that do not directly involve customers—for businesses of all sizes. In recent years, they have also evolved to include front-end processes—those that involve customers—such as customer relationship management (CRM), supply chain management, and e-commerce. In the early 1990s, most major corporations began upgrading their mainframe systems with the new client/server-based ERP systems developed by industry leaders like SAP AG, PeopleSoft Inc., and J.D. Edwards & Co. As the World Wide Web began to replace client/server platforms later in the decade, ERP firms began working to enable their technology to operate via the Web. Although some analysts predicted that the rise of the Internet as a business platform would render the $20 billion ERP industry obsolete, others believed that ERP and e-commerce technology vendors would likely work together in the early years of the twenty-first century to create new e-business applications.

EARLY DEVELOPERS OF ERP SYSTEMS

SAP AG The world's largest provider of ERP software, Germany's SAP AG, was founded in 1972 by five German engineers working for a branch of IBM. SAP's first project was to develop integrated enterprise software applications that could run on a mainframe; the five engineers had been working on a similar project for IBM, and when IBM moved the enterprise software project to a different unit, the partners decided to form their own company and continue working on the software. Originally, SAP was an acronym for systems analysis and program development; however, the wording was later changed to systems, applications, and products in data processing.

Within six years, SAP had secured 40 corporate clients. The firm began working on a real-time, mainframe-based business software suite to integrate accounting, sales and distribution, and production processes for corporations. The new product, known as R/2, allowed users to unify financial and operational data into a single database; it also eliminated paperwork and streamlined data entry processes. R/2 was formally introduced in 1979, and SAP found itself attracting clients such as Dow Chemical and Bayer. In the early 1980s, many competitors to SAP's clients began purchasing the software in an effort to keep pace with their rivals. SAP expanded outside of Germany for the first time in 1985. Two years later, the firm formed an alliance with IBM Corp., agreeing to help IBM standardize all of its systems and platforms to increase the compatibility of SAP and IBM products. International expansion continued with a unit in Switzerland. In 1988, SAP moved into the U.S. for the first time, creating an office in Philadelphia, Pennsylvania. To fund future research and development efforts, the firm conducted its initial public offering (IPO) that year.

By the early 1990s, R/2 had become the European standard for integrated business software. SAP unveiled R/3, which had been a work in progress since the late 1980s, in 1992. An ERP for the burgeoning client/server market in which data was processed via a networked server linked to multiple clients, such as personal computers (PCs), R/3 operated on IBM's OS/2 platform; it utilized IBM's DB2 database program, as well as several application components manufactured by SAP. Many of the businesses looking to streamline operations in the recessionary economic conditions of the early 1990s turned to SAP for the R/3 system. In 1993, R/3 accounted for 80 percent of SAP's total revenues. Sales grew by 66 percent the following year, and Microsoft Corp. convinced SAP to manufacture a version of its software compatible with Windows NT, SQL Server, and other Microsoft products.

By 1995, SAP had installed R/3 for more than 1,100 billion-dollar companies; installations for small and mid-sized clients reached 1,300. Complex R/3 installations cost up to $30 million, although the cost for an average client, not including consultants' fees, was $1 million. North American sales garnered nearly one-third of total revenues by then. That year, Microsoft selected R/3 to integrate its global finance and accounting system. Sales grew 48 percent to $1.35 billion. SAP was considered the most valuable company in Germany in 1996. Its stock had grown roughly 1,000 percent in the eight years since its IPO. R/3 was offered in 14 different languages as international operations grew to include South Africa, Malaysia, Japan, the Czech Republic, Russia, mainland China, and Mexico.

PEOPLESOFT, INC. One of SAP's first true rivals in the ERP market emerged in 1987, when software developers Dave Duffield and Ken Morris left their posts at Integral Corp. to establish PeopleSoft, a maker of human resources software that could run on the increasingly popular client/server computer systems. The following year, the company introduced PeopleSoft HRMS, the market's first viable human resources software application for a client/server platform. Eastman Kodak became the first large client to purchase HRMS. Sales in 1989 reached $1.9 million as PeopleSoft products gained recognition for their ability to assist companies undergoing reorganization, as well as companies looking to cut costs by streamlining operations. Sales jumped to $6.1 million in 1990. Expansion into Canada helped boost revenues to $17 million in 1991, and earnings exceeded $1 million for the first time. With a 40 percent share of the human resources applications market, PeopleSoft began working on financial management programs in 1992. To generate funds for additional research and development efforts, the firm conducted its IPO that year, raising $36 million. International expansion efforts intensified in 1993 as PeopleSoft opened branches in Sydney and Melbourne, Australia. The firm also began selling its products in France, England, and South America. Earnings grew nearly twofold, to $8.4 million, on $320 million in revenues. In 1994, the firm launched PeopleSoft Distribution and PeopleSoft Financials products. Expansion into Mexico took place in 1995 with the establishment of a subsidiary there.

In 1996, PeopleSoft began to compete directly with SAP when it acquired Red Pepper Software Co., a maker of ERP software, which it folded into its new PeopleSoft Manufacturing unit. New product releases that year included PeopleSoft Human Resources for Federal Government.

J.D. EDWARDS & CO. An ERP systems provider targeting smaller clients than SAP and PeopleSoft, Denver, Colorado-based J.D. Edwards was founded in 1977 by Jack Thompson, Dan Gregory, and Edward McVaney. Originally a designer of software for small and mid-sized computers, J.D. Edwards evolved into a developer of ERP systems after it began focusing its efforts on software for IBM's System/38 machine in the early 1980s. The firm's flagship ERP product, WorldSoftware, eventually ran on IBM's AS/400 computer. The application was designed to integrate the back-end functions, including accounting and manufacturing, of businesses with $50 million to $1 billion in sales.

In 1996, after recognizing that its software's dependency on a single platform was limiting its reach, J.D. Edwards released OneWorld, a client-server-based suite of applications that could run on a variety of platforms, such as Unix and Windows NT. The firm completed its initial public offering (IPO) the following year. By then, customers exceeded 4,000.

IMPACT OF THE INTERNET ON ERP SYSTEMS

As early as 1994, SAP began working to upgrade its flagship R/3 product with Internet capabilities; the move reflected SAP's desire to compete with increasingly popular "intranets," the in-house data networks similar in structure and appearance to the Web that were adopted by many corporations. However, despite these early efforts toward integration with Internet technology, SAP found itself lagging behind rivals in the late 1990s. For example, PeopleSoft unveiled a series of self-service, Internet-based applications in 1997. Also, database giant Oracle Corp., which diversified into ERP software in the late 1980s, became the first ERP vendor to move its client/server applications to the Web that year. According to a July 2001 article in *BusinessWeek Online*, upon receiving the news in early 1999 of SAP's less than desirable position, CEO Hasso Plattner, "reacted like a man shot out of a cannon. In a matter of days, a series of frenetic brainstorming sessions yielded a brand new strategy, which he personally christened mySAP.com. SAP's array of software programs would be made Net-ready before the end of the year, and millions of

office workers from Berlin to Bangkok would tap into the Net and their own companies' networks on computer screens with SAP's logo on them." Plattner believed mySAP.com could become a major online gateway for businesses, reaching the business masses in the same way online services provider America Online (AOL) had reached consumer masses.

What SAP eventually realized, however, was that making its products compatible with the Web was not enough to reposition itself as a business systems leader in the rapidly evolving ERP market. The firm also needed to reconsider its tradition of developing all of its own software in-house and seek out partnerships as a means of gaining quick access to new technology. For example, the firm began using Commerce One Inc.'s business-to-business (B2B) software when it created a U.S. subsidiary, known as SAPMarkets, to build and operate e-marketplaces. SAP also forged an alliance with Siemens AG to offer mySAP.com via Siemens's mobile devices.

While SAP was undergoing its metamorphosis, competitor PeopleSoft also continued working to stay abreast of cutting edge technology. In 1999, PeopleSoft paid $600 million for Vantive Corp. to gain access to CRM technology for the first time. The firm also began licensing procurement software leader CommerceOne Inc.'s BuySite application. PeopleSoft released PeopleSoft 8, a suite of e-business applications that was designed to put all the back-end and front-end operations of a business on the Web, in 2000; by the end of the following year, roughly 1,500 clients had signed up for the new package.

J.D. Edwards also spent the late 1990s and early 2000s retooling itself. The firm made its first acquisition in 1999, paying $12 million for The Premisys Corp., a sales automation software provider. The firm also purchased supply chain software provider Numetrix, eventually adding supply chain functionality to its OneWorld suite. J.D. Edwards also pursued deals with Siebel Systems Inc. for access to its CRM applications and with Ariba Inc. for B2B e-commerce technology. Although the alliance with Siebel Systems eventually proved fairly fruitless, the firm did eventually acquire CRM technology via its September 2001 purchase of Youcentric Inc. Late in 2000, the firm unveiled OneWorld Xe, which used the Web's extended markup language (XML) technology to allow clients to electronically connect to business partners using other platforms and software applications.

According to an October 2000 article in *InternetWeek*, what companies like SAP, J.D. Edwards, and PeopleSoft were doing entailed "the Webification of enterprise resource planning software, a migration long promised but only recently realized. The core ERP applications, which until recently meant back-office functions such as accounting, human resources, payroll, and fulfillment among others, are expanding to embrace strategic functions such as e-business relationships (EBR), supply chain management (SCM) and e-commerce services.'' According to many industry experts, however, adding front-end applications and Web functionality to their products only scratches the surface of what ERP vendors must do to stay afloat in constantly shifting e-business landscape. Although many firms have moved toward developing a comprehensive end-to-end enterprise management system that fully integrates all business functions, several analysts argue that such a system has yet to be developed.

FURTHER READING:

Borck, James R. ''Enterprise Strategies: ERP Faces Rocky Road.'' *InfoWorld,* May 14, 2001.

Chiem, Phat X. ''ERP Vendors Make Move From Back Office to Front.'' *B to B,* February 19, 2001.

J.D. Edwards & Co. ''J.D. Edwards Corporate Backgrounder.'' Denver, CO: J.D. Edwards & Co., 2001.

Hamm, Steve. ''Meet the New Hasso Plattner.'' *BusinessWeek Online,* July 9, 2001. Available from www.businessweek.com

Mullin, Rick. ''ECM: Where ERP Meets the Web.'' *Chemical Week,* April 25, 2001.

Pender, Lee. ''J.D. Edwards Shifts Its Focus to Front Office.'' *PC Week,* March 1, 1999.

Schaff, William. ''J.D. Edwards Breaks Out.'' *Information-Week,* June 8, 1999.

Stein, Tom. ''Beyond ERP—New IT Agenda—A Second Wave of ERP Activity Promises to Increase Efficiency and Transform Ways of Doing Business.'' *InformationWeek,* November 30, 1998.

Stevens, Tim. ''ERP Explodes.'' *Industry Week,* July 1, 1996.

Sutton, Neil. ''JDE Buys Into CRM Space.'' *Computer Dealer News,* September 28, 2001.

Sweeney, Terry. ''ERP Takes On E-Business.'' *InternetWeek,* October 30, 2000.

SEE ALSO: Customer Relation Management (CRM); J.D. Edwards; PeopleSoft Corp.; Supply Chain Management

ENTERPRISE SERVER

As the number of businesses adopting e-business strategies continued rising into the new millennium, technology firms began offering a host of hardware and software options designed to meet enterprise needs. These offerings, enterprise servers among them, were developed to give companies a competitive edge by providing high performance infrastructures, as well as control over growing networks and Internet operations.

In a basic client/server relationship, the server acted as the host computer that stored information and was shared by clients within a network. The client, another computer or remote device, could retrieve information from the server. The term server also referred to the software that allowed the transfer of information to take place.

As technology advanced and businesses began using computers for a variety of tasks, different types of servers were developed to manage different types of resources. For instance, file servers were used to store files, printing servers were used to manage printers on a network, network servers evolved to handle traffic within a network, and database servers were developed to control information and process database queries. Application servers, most often used by enterprises with both intranet and Internet operations, performed data processing tasks that allowed up-to-date information to be delivered to clients. Application servers typically linked to Web servers, which enabled content to be transferred over the Internet. Web servers would receive a request from a Web browser, retrieve the stored Web page, and then process the request so the page could be viewed via the browser.

Enterprise servers emerged in the late 1990s as businesses began looking for solutions that could manage their e-business infrastructures and networks. As demand for these types of servers increased, technology firms began developing products that could manage growth; provide flexibility in selecting, creating, and utilizing applications; provide security; and insure reliable performance.

Designed to benefit the organization as a whole, enterprise servers were developed as enhanced servers involved in a multitude of tasks including Web development, content management, and data processing. Enterprise servers also could manage many aspects of a company's network, acting as file, printing, network, database, application, and Web servers. The sale of these servers was targeted toward businesses needing to become Web-enabled in order to begin conducting commerce on the Internet.

IT managers in search of enterprise servers had many options. By 2001, technology firms including IBM Corp., Compaq Computer Corp., Hewlett Packard Co. (HP), Microsoft Corp., and iPlanet E-Commerce Solutions all offered versions of enterprise servers. Netscape Communication Corp.'s Enterprise Web Server, which became the iPlanet Enterprise Web Server—iPlanet was formed in 1999 by an alliance between Sun Microsystems Inc., America Online Inc., and Netscape—was a leader in the enterprise market. It was voted the top enterprise server in 1998 by *PC Magazine* and was used to run Internet sites such as E*Trade, Charles Schwab, Digex, Excite, and

Lycos. Microsoft also offered enterprise servers under the name.NET Enterprise Servers. This server package was designed to integrate, manage, and prepare enterprises for doing business on the Web. IBM's zSeries was developed to manage data and transaction processing. The firm touted the product as the first "e-business" enterprise server for its performance and application management capabilities.

In 2000, the enterprise server industry slowed, due in part to the lagging economy. A study done by Cutter Consortium in 2001 showed that 27 percent of those polled cut spending related to e-business. The slowdown was not expected to last long, however, as most companies viewed e-business strategies as a key element to long-term business plans. Nevertheless, many technology firms felt the financial pains of weakening demand. In a 2000 *E-Commerce Times* article, e-business solution provider Unisys stated: "we are feeling the impact of the economic slowdown most heavily in our systems integration and enterprise server businesses. As customers look for ways to control costs and trim budgets, they are reducing their spending on leading-edge e-business solutions that require systems integration and consulting expertise." However, firms such as Sun Microsystems, IBM, Compaq, and HP did post positive revenue results from enterprise server sales in 2000. Whether posting gains or losses, firms in the server industry felt confident that the market would rebound as companies entering the e-business world would be compelled to purchase enterprise servers to gain the Internet infrastructure and applications necessary to succeed on the Web.

FURTHER READING:

"Best of 1998." *PC Magazine.* January 1999. Available from www.zdnet.com.

"The Enterprise-Strength Web Server." Mountain View, CA: Netscape Communications Corp., 2001. Available from home.netscape.com/enterprise.

"The Evolution of Enterprise Computing." *ServerWorld Magazine.* February 2000. Available from www.serverworldmagazine.com.

Macaluso, Nora. "Unisys Falls on Results, Outlook." *E-Commerce Times.* April 17, 2001. Available from www.ecommercetimes.com.

Wittman, Art. "The Yin and Yang of Enterprise Computing." *Network Computing.* September 1998. Available from www.networkcomputing.com.

SEE ALSO: Compaq Computer Corp.; E-commerce Solutions; Hewlett-Packard Co.; IBM Inc.; Microsoft Corp.; Sun Microsystems

E-PROCUREMENT

Procurement is the process whereby companies purchase goods and services from various suppliers. These include everything from indirect goods like light bulbs, uniforms, toilet paper, and office supplies, to the direct goods used for manufacturing products. Procurement also involves the purchase of temporary labor, energy, vehicle leases, and more. Companies negotiate discount contracts for some goods and services, and buy others on the spot. Procurement can be an important part of a company's overall strategy for reducing costs. Historically, the individuals or departments responsible for purchasing a company's goods and services relied on various methods for doing so. The most basic included placing orders via telephone, fax, or mail. Electronic procurement methods, generally referred to as e-procurement, potentially enable the procurement process to unfold in a faster, more efficient manner, and with fewer errors. These methods include electronic data interchange (EDI), online marketplaces or e-marketplaces, and various blends of the two.

In a January 2001 *Works Management* article, a report from e-Net revealed that 70 percent of companies in the finance and retail sectors used the Internet for some purchases. The adoption rate was much less among manufacturers, where only 17 percent used formal e-procurement systems. Besides varying from industry to industry, different companies use different blends of traditional and electronic procurement methods, and individual e-procurement systems themselves may incorporate traditional capabilities like telephone or fax.

PROCUREMENT METHODS

ELECTRONIC DATA INTERCHANGE. Since the 1960s, many large companies have relied on electronic data interchange (EDI) for the procurement of goods. EDI deals more with the way information is communicated during procurement than it does with the act of linking buyers and suppliers. By definition, EDI is the electronic exchange of business information— purchase orders, invoices, bills of lading, inventory data, and various types of confirmations—between organizations or trading partners in standardized formats. EDI also is used within individual organizations to transfer data between different divisions or departments, such as finance, purchasing, and shipping. Two characteristics set EDI apart from other ways of exchanging information. First, EDI only involves business-to-business transactions; individual consumers do not directly use EDI to purchase goods or services. Secondly, EDI involves transactions between computers or databases, not individuals. Therefore, individuals sending e-mail messages or sharing files over a network does not constitute EDI.

EDI can occur point-to-point, where organizations communicate directly with one another over a private network; via the Internet (also known as open EDI); and most commonly, via value-added networks (VANs), which function like telephone lines by allowing for the transfer of information. In the early 2000s, although many companies still relied on VANs, the Internet was playing a larger role in EDI. It is possible for companies to translate the files used during EDI and send them to another company's computer system over the Internet, via e-mail, or file transfer protocol (FTP). Because it is an open network and access is not terribly expensive, using the Internet for EDI can be more cost effective for companies with limited means. It has the potential to provide them with access to large companies who continue to rely on large, traditional EDI systems. The low cost associated with open EDI also means that more companies are likely to participate. This is important because the level of value for participants often increases along with their number.

While the automotive and retail industries have experimented with open EDI for some time, the efforts didn't result in widespread adoption by small suppliers, usually due to cumbersome requirements like the installation of on-site software. Incorporating EDI into e-marketplaces was an approach that held more potential. In March 2000, an e-marketplace called the WorldWide Retail Exchange (WWRE) was established. It allowed suppliers and retailers in various industry sectors—including retail, general merchandise, food, and drugstores—to conduct transactions over the World Wide Web. After one year of operation, the WWRE had 53 retailer members with combined annual turnover of $722 billion. Leading retailers, among them Kmart, Rite Aid, Best Buy, and Target, planned to offer a Web-to-EDI translation service on the WWRE so it would be easier for smaller suppliers to do business with them. In this arrangement, the retailers send purchase orders to a data center where they are translated to a language that can be read with a Web browser. Suppliers are then notified about the PO and allowed to respond. This is a break from true EDI, since orders are handled manually by suppliers.

For companies using open EDI, a language called extensible markup language (XML), similar in some respects to hypertext markup language (HTML), allows users to share information in a universal, standard way without making the kinds of special arrangements EDI often requires and regardless of the software program it was originally created in.

XML played an important role in the development of online marketplaces like WWRE.

ONLINE MARKETPLACES. Online marketplaces bring many buyers and sellers together in an online environment and function as intermediaries between the two parties. In the early 2000s, third-party companies like Commerce One Inc. and Ariba Inc. offered high-end e-procurement software and services that were used to operate different online marketplaces. Numerous other companies provided similar kinds of services and applications. Online marketplaces existed for many different industries, ranging from the food and beverage industries to consumer packaged goods and interior design. The costs for participating in an online marketplace varied. In some cases, participating companies (suppliers, purchasers, or both) were required to purchase special software from a third party. Third parties also levied different charges for making transactions, joining the network, and updating catalogs of available products.

In addition to connecting buyers and sellers, online marketplace providers add value to the procurement process by offering various services, ranging from inventory management and process improvement to tracking shipments and arranging financing. In addition to adding value, online marketplaces also can simplify the process of procurement. For example, some allowed suppliers to choose the manner in which they received orders from purchasers, such as XML, fax, e-mail, or EDI.

OTHER APPROACHES. In addition to EDI and online marketplaces, there are other approaches to e-procurement. One involves software applications that allow purchasing agents to establish systems for managing things like invoices, purchase orders, receipts, and requests for quotations (RFQs). These applications also enable companies to place orders for products from many different suppliers through one simple interface. Some companies relied on third-party organizations to use these systems via the Web. Acting like an outsourced purchasing department, the third party hosted the software instead of selling it to the user off-the-shelf. This approach was useful to companies without the resources to develop and maintain their own e-procurement systems. Some companies also purchased pre-packaged software products that performed many of the same functions.

Online auctions were another tool companies used to procure goods and services for both contract and spot buys. A number of factors were critical to the success of online auctions, including the kind of bidders involved, the number of bidders, and the length of the bidding periods. Although it's not directly part of the auction, online negotiation also can be a factor if the auction involves complicated elements like delivery and support.

PROS AND CONS

No matter what method is used, there are many advantages to using e-procurement systems as opposed to those involving paper-based forms or oral communications. The main benefits are increased efficiency and cost savings. For example, EDI allows business transactions to occur in less time and with fewer errors than do traditional, paper-based means. It reduces the amount of inventory companies must invest in by closely tying manufacturing to actual demand, allowing for just-in-time delivery. By doing away with paper forms, EDI also reduces postage costs and the expenses and space considerations surrounding paper-based record storage.

Online marketplaces provide similar benefits. As Commerce One explains, they "make the entire business-to-business marketplace more efficient by expanding the range of sellers and buyers and by making the entire market mechanism more transparent. They reduce procurement and sales costs and improve the efficiency of the process. For buyers, these e-marketplaces aggregate content so it's easier to find new sources and pricing. For sellers, the e-marketplaces break down geographic barriers and make product catalogs available to a wider market of buyers."

In some large organizations, purchasing responsibilities are distributed over several different areas of the company. E-procurement systems may enable a company to consolidate orders for similar items with one supplier, resulting in deeper volume discounts and cost savings. Additionally, e-procurement may allow a company to simplify purchasing by reducing the number of variables (available products) involved. Instead of having to sort through large volumes of paper or electronic catalogs, purchasing professionals are able to build custom catalogs that include only the items the company is interested in. Besides simplifying matters, this approach also drives up volumes of smaller numbers of items, which is another possible way of generating volume discounts.

Along with all of the positives, there also are disadvantages to e-procurement. Some EDI users have experienced snags. In *Planet IT,* Proctor & Gamble, a leading packaged goods manufacturer, reported that it found errors in more than 30 percent of its electronic orders, although they were mainly due to human error. Additionally, some companies have been disappointed by e-procurement software applications that don't meet their needs. *InformationWeek* revealed that two of the leading obstacles to successful e-procurement are enabling suppliers to support e-transactions and generating and maintaining electronic product information.

Additionally, *InformationWeek,* explains that numerous firms "sign on for E-procurement without an-ticipating the long road ahead. They dive into projects only to learn that E-procurement applications are limited in the types and scope of purchasing activity they address. Managing electronic catalogs with thousands of products, providing employees with the right mix of products and adequate information about them, and making it easy to search for items can also be tricky, requiring additional tools and threatening the efficiencies promised by moving purchasing to the Web."

FURTHER READING:

Banham, Russ. "Procurement Made Easy." *World Trade,* October 2000.

Copacino, William. "Auctions Expand E-procurement Menu." *Logistics Management & Distribution Report,* January 2001.

Dwyer, John. "Who's Afraid of the Big, Bad E?" *Works Management,* January 2001.

"E-Commerce Growth Prospects Remain Strong." *Corporate EFT Report,* January 17, 2001.

Gilbert, Alorie. "E-procurement for Smaller Users." *InformationWeek,* November 27, 2000.

———. "E-procurement: Problems Behind The Promise." *InformationWeek,* November 20, 2000. Available from www.informationweek.com.

Hartmann, Greg. "Pleasures and Pitfalls of E-procurement." *Lodging Hospitality,* November, 2000.

Kosiur, David. *Understanding Electronic Commerce.* Seattle: Microsoft Press. 1997.

Kumar, Ram and Connie Crook. "Educating Senior Management on the Strategic Benefits of Electronic Data Interchange." *Journal of Systems Management,* March/April 1996.

Moozakis, Chuck. "No Longer E-Biz Misfits." *Planet IT,* March 3, 1999. Available from www.PlanetIT.com.

Shim, Jae K., Anique A. Qureshi, Joel G. Siegel, and Roberta M. Siegel. *The International Handbook of Electronic Commerce.* New York: AMACOM. 2000.

Welty, Terry. "Beware The Pitfalls Of Internet Procurement." *Planet IT,* April 2, 2000

SEE ALSO: Auction Sites; Business-to-Business (B2B) E-commerce; Electronic Data Interchange (EDI); XML

E-TAILING

Electronic retailing, or e-tailing, refers to the practice of selling goods and services over an electronic medium like the Internet. Many traditional brick-and-mortar firms like Toys 'R' Us and Barnes and Noble also sell their wares via Web sites. Other companies, such as Amazon.com, rely solely on the Web to conduct business. While books, CDs, and computer software and hardware are the most common goods sold by e-tailers, clothes, cosmetics, perfume, plants, toys, and other types of merchandise also made their way to the Web in the late 1990s.

One of the first and most well-known e-tailers, Amazon.com got its start in July of 1995. Because the business-to-consumer (B2C) model was relatively new and unproven then, Amazon had to develop its own architecture and manage its own site. As online shopping grew in popularity—accounting for $3 billion in consumer spending in 1997 and $7.1 billion in 1998—technology vendors like IBM Corp. moved into e-commerce and began offering to build and even oversee sites for companies wanting to launch an e-tailing venture.

Several e-tailing blunders occurred during the 1999 holiday shopping season. For example, Toysrus.com found itself ill prepared to handle an unexpected surge in orders and failed to deliver shipments by Christmas day that year. Some analysts believed that the resulting dip in consumer confidence did not bode well for the future of online sales. However, as sites continued to address issues important to consumers, such as the security of online payment via credit card, an increasing number of consumers continued to make online purchases.

Although surveys conducted by Ernst & Young showed that in the year 2000 consumers were not fond of the shipping costs quite often associated with online purchases, they did like the convenience of being able to shop from their personal computer, as well as the wide selection available on the Web. More importantly, concerns about the security of online transactions were waning, perhaps because online shoppers could access watchdog sites like the Better Business Bureau's BBB Online and e-tailer rating service Bizrate.com. These served as resources for consumers to gather information about an e-tailer's track record prior to making a purchase. Many analysts believe the likelihood that consumers will continue to embrace e-tailing as a viable shopping method is high. They point out that although more online shopping takes place in the United States than in any other nation, only 34 percent of U.S. households access the Web, and only half of those make online purchases. While worldwide online spending may or may not reach $40 billion by the end of 2001, as predicted by research companies like Jupiter Communications and Boston Consulting, there certainly appears to be room for growth.

FURTHER READING:

Bonisteel, Steven. ''Online Retailing Only In 'Second Inning'—Global Report.'' *Newsbytes.* February 6, 2001.

Brookman, Faye. ''E-Sales Surge Despite Flaws.'' *Discount Store News.* January 25, 1999.

Donegan, Priscilla. ''The State of Cybershopping.'' *Grocery Headquarters.* May 2000.

Falla, Jane M. ''Business-to-Consumer E-Commerce: What Is(n't) the Problem?'' *e-Business Advisor.* August 2000.

Manes, Stephen. ''If You Buy It Online, Will It Come?'' *PC World.* March 2000.

Prince, C.J. ''Etail's Big Comeback.'' *Chief Executive.* July 2000.

SEE ALSO: BBBOnLine Inc.; Bizrate.com; Business-to-Consumer (B2C) E-commerce; Electronic Payment

ETOYS INC.

eToys was established in 1997 to provide a simplified shopping experience for toys and other children's merchandise—one that would eliminate annoyances like the long lines and loud kids found in typical toy stores. At eToys shoppers would not have to contend with packed parking lots and lack of sales support. The company's Web site, eToys.com, launched in October 1997 and let consumers browse for products based on age group and price range. Customers also could access detailed product descriptions, including lists of safety features, which were unavailable to shoppers at toy stores. As eToys founder Edward ''Toby'' Lenk, former vice president of corporate strategic planning at Walt Disney Co., told *Inc.,* ''We take two days of shopping and compress it into 15 minutes. That must be worth something.''

For four holiday shopping seasons eToys was indeed worth something. In the end, however, the company ran out of money and had to close its online doors. At the eleventh hour, however, KB Holdings acquired the eToys Web site at a bankruptcy auction in May 2001 for about $3.35 million. Later in that year the eToys Website went live as a unit of KB's subsidary, KBKids.com. Several factors contributed to its demise, especially the dot.com shakeout of 2000 that severely limited the company's access to capital. Hardly alone in its plummet, several other online toy retailers also went out of business in 2000. Perhaps the final nail in eToys's coffin came when Amazon.com and Toys 'R' Us teamed up to create the number one online Web site for toys, which cut into eToys' holiday revenue at a crucial time in 2000. Nonetheless, as the first online toy retailer, eToys was an important e-commerce player.

EMULATED AMAZON.COM'S ONLINE MODEL

eToys aimed to emulate Amazon.com, which was launched in 1995, by providing a Web site where customers could search among a large selection of items, order them online, pay by credit card, and receive delivery in a short period of time. In its first year eToys—which was headquartered in Santa Monica, California, and had a nearby warehouse—generated awareness for its site through marketing relationships with America Online and Yahoo!, among others. It established relationships with about 350 toy manufacturers, including all of the major ones, and offered some 8,000 products, some of which were stored in its warehouse. The company's initial financing included more than $10 million that Lenk raised from venture capital firms, former Disney colleagues, and other sources. In March 1998 the company acquired Toys.com, which was operated by Web Magic Inc.

In fall 1998 eToys launched its first national advertising campaign in anticipation of the all-important holiday shopping season. Although competitor Toys 'R' Us had launched its retail Web site in June 1998, analysts noted that Toys 'R' Us appeared to have difficulty developing an online strategy that worked with its traditional retail stores. For example, Toys 'R' Us neglected to establish any marketing partnerships with the major Internet portals, such as America Online and Yahoo!, and offered about half as many items online as eToys. According to Media Metrics, eToys had 3.4 million visitors during the 1998 holiday season, nearly three times that of Toys 'R' Us and the fifth-highest number of visitors for all online shopping destinations that December. As a result, eToys enjoyed fourth quarter revenues of $22.9 million. Sales for fiscal 1999 ending March 30th reached $34 million, third among all Internet retailers behind Amazon.com and barnesandnoble.com.

SPENT HEAVILY TO GAIN CUSTOMERS

At this point—and indeed throughout its four-year history—eToys was not concerned with turning a profit. The company had lost $2.3 million in its first fiscal year ending March 31, 1998, and another $15.3 million in the nine months ending December 31, 1998. Its goal was to acquire customers, and it spent heavily to do so. With venture capital running out, the company turned to the public equity markets and held its initial public offering (IPO) in May 1999. Eight percent of the company was offered to the public. Shares began trading on the NASDAQ on May 20, 1999 at $20 a share, raising $166 million for eToys. The stock rose as high as $85 on the first day of trading and ended the day around $76.50, giving eToys a market value of $7.8 billion, more than the $5.6 billion market value of Toys 'R' Us.

Around this time the company acquired Baby-Center Inc. (which it later sold off at the end of 1999), and outsourced its e-commerce order fulfillment to Fingerhut Companies Inc. Preparing for the 1999 holiday shopping season, eToys increased its stock to 15,000 items, not including children's books. It also carried music, videos, and video games. In July, eToys began selling children's books, offering some 80,000 titles, and its acquisition of BabyCenter expanded the company's demographic to infants and toddlers. Based on its 1998 performance, eToys had become the brand to beat in merchandise for children up to age 12. For 1999 it would face increased competition from Toys 'R' Us, which spun off its Web site as a separate company and planned to invest $80 million in it, as well as from Amazon.com., which added a toy section in July 1999. Other competitors included KB Toys, a subsidiary of Consolidated Stores Corp., and Wal-Mart Stores Inc., the largest U.S. toy seller, which had plans to overhaul its Web site in time for the 1999 holiday season.

eToys attempted to distinguish itself from its competitors in several ways. One was the depth of its product offerings—15,000 items compared to Toys 'R' Us' 10,000. The company also focused on offering services that its competitors could not match, such as putting personalized gift tags on each item and offering multiple wrappings, a gift registry that parents could protect with a password, a wish-list feature for kids, and a spare parts and repair service for toys. The company also had a compelling product bundling strategy, whereby no item was treated as a single entity. Rather, toys were bundled with books and videos, for example, and customers could select which items they wanted to include in their bundle.

In August 1999 eToys expanded its marketing relationship with America Online by committing to a three-year, $18 million agreement that made eToys the premier retailer of children's products on several AOL channels, including Shop@AOL, AOL Families Channel, AOL.com, Netscape Netcenter, and CompuServe. The company's national print and television advertising campaign, which launched in October, was expected to cost $20 million. eToys also expanded into the United Kingdom for the 1999 holiday season, opening a U.K. Web site in October and stocking some 5,000 items at a British warehouse.

WALL STREET NOT IMPRESSED WITH STRONG HOLIDAY SALES

In January 2000 *Business Week* reported, "eToys remains the player to beat in this fast-growing field." The company had more customers for the holiday quarter than in its previous two years combined and was the third-most-visited e-commerce site behind Amazon.com and eBay.com. Although eToys's holiday sales for the quarter ending December 31, 1999 more than quadrupled to $107 million, the company reported a quarterly loss of $62.5 million, compared to a loss of $8.2 million for the same quarter in 1998. Responding to the news, Wall Street sent eToys's stock down to around $17 a share at the end of January 2000. eToys attributed its losses to the high cost of fulfilling orders, due mainly to its outsourcing arrangement with Fingerhut. eToys planned to bring its order fulfillment in-house for 2000, opening a new warehouse in Virginia to service the eastern United States and expanding its southern California facility. During the 1999 holiday season eToys also declined to copy its competitors, many of whom offered free shipping, deep price discounts, and coupons worth as much as $10. As a result, eToys enjoyed a healthy gross profit margin of 19 percent. The company's customer service was also able to keep up with the heavy traffic, and eToys did not experience a high level of customer complaints like many other online retailers did that holiday season.

As Wall Street continued to punish tech and e-commerce stocks, eToys's stock price fell to around $6 a share in April 2000. Both *Fortune* and *Los Angeles Business Journal* reported that some analysts now thought eToys would have difficulty making it through the next e-Christmas. The company had about $220 million in cash and liquid assets, and in June it raised another $100 million through a direct placement of convertible preferred stock to private equity funds and a group of investors. Analysts felt that eToys needed to raise another $100 million to continue operating until it could turn a profit.

Meanwhile, the rest of the online toy industry was suffering. In May, Walt Disney Co. closed its Toysmart.com site after it was unable to raise additional capital. Other toy sites that closed included ToyTime and Red Rocket, which was backed by Viacom International through its subsidiary Nickelodeon. KBkids.com remained open but cancelled plans for its IPO in June. The early shakeout in the online toy industry was attributed in part to falling stock prices—especially on the Nasdaq, a technology-heavy stock market, distinct from the New York and American Stock Exchanges—and difficulty in raising new capital. Click-and-mortar operations that had both online and physical storefronts were coming into favor at the expense of ''pure play'' Internet companies. As a result, the largest toy sellers, Toys 'R' Us and Wal-Mart, appeared to be in the strongest market position for the coming holiday season.

HOLIDAY SALES SHORTFALL LED TO OPERATIONS CRISIS

With everything riding on its holiday sales, eToys faced an operations crisis even before December 25 rolled around, when it reported that its holiday sales would be around $120 million to $130 million, well below the projected $210 million to $240 million. That meant the company would run out of oper-

ating cash three months sooner than expected and would have to raise new capital by March 31, 2001. Wall Street sent the company's stock below one dollar a share for the first time, giving eToys a market value of just $37 million. The biggest factor affecting eToys's holiday performance was the online joint venture between Amazon.com and Toys 'R' Us, which dominated holiday sales with 123 million visitors during the holiday season, compared with 21.12 million visits to eToys.

From there it was all downhill for eToys, which could not raise capital under those market conditions. In January it shuttered its European operations, and laid off 700 workers the United States, or 70 percent of its workforce. The company also quit delivering to Canada, closed its two distribution centers, and finally announced that it had sent layoff notices to its remaining 293 employees. The company planned to file for Chapter 11 bankruptcy protection and cease operations by April 2001.

FURTHER READING:

Brinsley, John. ''eToys: Stock Went from Hot to Shot.'' *Los Angeles Business Journal.* April 10, 2000.

Enos, Lori. ''eToys to File for Bankruptcy.'' *E-Commerce Times.* February 27, 2001. Available from www.ecommercetimes.com.

''eToy Story.'' *Business Week.* January 10, 2000.

''eToys Files for IPO.'' *InformationWeek.* February 22, 1999.

''The Fortune Indexes: Street Sweep.'' *Fortune.* April 17, 2000.

Gorchov, Jolie. ''Pundits Point to eToys as Dot-Com Dud.'' *Los Angeles Business Journal.* April 24, 2000.

Guglielmo, Connie. ''Medium of Exchange: E-Com in Toyland.'' *Inter@ctive Week.* October 4, 1999.

———. ''Medium of Exchange: Toy Story 2000.'' *Inter@ctive Week.* October 9, 2000.

Macaluso, Nora. ''Amazon and Toys 'R' Us Take E-Holiday Prize.'' *E-Commerce Times.* January 2, 2001. Available from www.ecommercetimes.com.

———. ''eToys Site Back in Business.'' *E-Commerce Times.* October 18, 2001. Available from www.ecommercetimes.com.

Mahoney, Michael, and Jon Weisman. ''The Last Days of eToys.'' *E-Commerce Times.* March 7, 2001. Available from www.ecommercetimes.com.

Regan, Keith. ''eToys Fires Staff, Sets April Shutdown.'' *E-Commerce Times.* February 6, 2001. Available from www.ecommercetimes.com.

''This Toy War Is No Game.'' *Business Week.* August 9, 1999.

Trager, Louis. ''Toy Market's Batteries Die.'' *Inter@ctive Week.* June 26, 2000.

Walker, Leslie. ''Market Punishes eToys for Losses.'' *The Washington Post.* January 28, 2000.

Weisman, Jon, and Elizabeth Blakey. ''Embattled eToys Slashes 700 Jobs.'' *E-Commerce Times.* January 5, 2001. Available from www.ecommercetimes.com.

"With Early-Bird Web-Site and Portal Deals, Former Disney Executive Seeks to Preempt Toys 'R' Us." *Inc.* October 1998.

SEE ALSO: Amazon.com; Business-to-Consumer (B2C) E-Commerce

E*TRADE GROUP INC.

E*Trade Group Inc. provides a range of online personal and institutional financial services through its wholly-owned subsidiaries. Access to the company's offerings can be found at its primary Web site, which offers links to investment options, financial services, discussion groups, live events, and more. The company's principal subsidiaries include E*Trade Securities Inc., which provides online retail brokerage services to individual investors. Investment options offered through E*Trade Securities Inc. include stocks, options, initial public offerings (IPOs), mutual funds, bonds, and extended hours trading.

E*Trade Group also provides online banking services through E*Trade Bank and owns E*Trade Access, a national network of more than 9,600 automated teller machines (ATMs) located in 48 states and three countries. E*Trade Bank launched in April 2000 following the acquisition of Telebanc Financial Corp. and its Internet banking subsidiary, Telebank, which was the largest Internet bank. Through its Web site www.etradebank.com, E*Trade Bank allows customers to open accounts, view consolidated balance statements, transfer funds between accounts, pay bills, and compare rates. While nearly 90 percent of E*Trade Bank's customer contact comes over the Internet, the company maintains customer service call centers that are open 24 hours a day. E*Trade Access was formed in May 2000 following the acquisition of Card Capture Services Inc. E*Trade Access is in the process of developing financial services kiosks as a complement to its ATM network.

Internationally, E*Trade Group offers online retail brokerage services, as well as financial services to institutional investors. The company operates nine Web sites outside the United States, either through licensees or through wholly owned subsidiaries, which serve investors in the United Kingdom, Denmark, Norway, Sweden, South Africa, Germany, Australia and New Zealand, Canada, Denmark, Japan, and Korea. After terminating an agreement with a French licensee, the company is seeking to re-enter the French market. E*Trade's international strategy is to leverage its brand name, Web site design, and proprietary technology to create a fully electronic cross-border trading network. By linking financial markets globally, the company hopes to make trading in foreign securities an affordable reality for retail investors. The prototype for this vision is E*Trade Sweden, which launched during fiscal 2000 and allows Swedish customer to purchase U.S. equities online in real time.

E*Trade Group provides financial services to institutional investors internationally through TIR Holdings Ltd., which it acquired in 1999, and Versus Technologies Inc., which it acquired in 2000. The acquisition of TIR expanded E*Trade's business to include institutional investors. TIR provides global multi-currency securities execution and settlement services, along with independent research, to institutional investors. Versus is a Canadian-based provider of electronic trading services for both institutional and retail investors. The company was E*Trade's licensee in Canada prior to its acquisition. Following the acquisition of Versus, E*Trade incorporated Versus' proprietary electronic trading technology into its global product offerings.

E*Trade customers can buy and sell more than 5,000 mutual funds through the company's Mutual Fund Center, which was established in 1997. Included among the mutual fund offerings are eight proprietary mutual funds, four of which were launched in fiscal 2000. Other services and activities include corporate financial services relating to employee stock option and stock purchase plans and the operation of two venture capital funds.

ONE OF THE FIRST ALL-ELECTRONIC BROKERAGES

E*Trade Securities was founded in 1992 in Palo Alto, California, as a subsidiary of Trade*Plus, but its online trading technology was in use as early as 1983. Trade*Plus was a service bureau founded in 1982 by Bill Porter, a physicist and inventor with more than a dozen patents. The company provided online quote and trading services to Fidelity, Charles Schwab, and Quick & Reilly. When Porter asked himself why he had to pay a broker hundreds of dollars for stock transactions, he realized that someday everyone would have computers and use them to buy and sell stocks and other securities. It wasn't until 1992 that Porter launched E*Trade Securities, one of the first all-electronic brokerages. At first E*Trade offered online investing services through America Online and CompuServe. From 1993 to 1995 E*Trade made Trade*Plus the fastest-growing private company in Silicon Valley, according to a survey by *The Business Journal*. E*Trade's lowest trading fee was $19.95, and in 1994 sales from Trade*Plus and E*Trade reached $10.9 million. In 1996 E*Trade began Internet trading with the launch of www.etrade.com.

By 1996 E*Trade had evolved organizationally from an entrepreneurial type of company to one with a more well-defined corporate structure. In March 1996 Porter turned over his CEO duties to Christos Cotsakos while remaining as chairman. Cotsakos was a decorated Vietnam veteran with 19 years of experience with Federal Express and five years at A.C. Nielsen Co., where he was co-CEO, chief operating officer (COO), president, and a director. Under Cotsakos's leadership, E*Trade would become a public company and one of the leading online financial services companies. In April 1996 the company opened a second facility in Rancho Cordova, near Sacramento. Its goal was to duplicate operations there, so there would never be any lost connections with clients. In August the company went public as E*Trade Group Inc. with an initial public offering (IPO). By the end of December 1996 E*Trade had 112,800 customer accounts, up three times from the previous year.

In 1997 E*Trade raised additional capital through a secondary offering. During the year the company launched E*Trade Canada, its first international venture, as well as its Mutual Fund Center, which initially offered some 3,500 funds. Revenue for the year was $142.7 million, and the company was profitable with net income of $13.9 million. Perhaps the most challenging event of the year was the stock market "crash" of October 20, 1997, when on two consecutive days the Dow Jones Industrial Average and the NASDAQ Composite Index experienced the largest one-day point drops and the largest one-day point gains in the history of Wall Street. Trading volume reached never-before-experienced levels. On the Monday following "Black Friday," E*Trade processed 45,000 transactions.

By the end of calendar 1998 E*Trade had nearly 700,000 customer accounts and claimed to retain more than 95 percent of its accounts. The launch of a redesigned Web site, dubbed Destination E*Trade, in September 1998 helped the company gain industry recognition as the leading online brokerage service for the second half of the year. Heavy expenditures on the new Web site and related marketing costs resulted in an anticipated loss on annual revenue of $245 million. In December 1998 the company launched its E*Trade Bond Center, bringing the benefits of online brokerage and financial services to fixed-income investors. Other events for 1998 included two acquisitions: OptionsLinc, a Web- and telephone-based service for executing and managing employee stock option and purchase plans; and ShareData Inc., the leader in stock plan software for private and public companies. The two acquisitions gave E*Trade an entry into the large corporate marketplace. The company improved its capital position with a $400 million strategic investment from Softbank Corp., its Japanese partner and that country's leading software distributor. Internationally, E*Trade added two licensees in Japan and the United King-

dom, for a total of 11 master licensees serving more than 32 countries.

In 1999 E*Trade's brand-building expenditures and temporary moratorium on profits paid off. The company's revenue climbed to $621.4 million for fiscal 1999 ending September 30, with a reported net loss of $54.4 million. Much of the revenue was used to build one of the strongest brands in online financial services, and to fuel new product development and diversification. The launch of Destination E*Trade in September 1998 helped the company to gain 1 million net new active accounts in fiscal 1999. E*Trade was receiving an average of $52 million in deposits every business day, compared to an average of $20 million the previous year. Customer assets increased 154 percent to $28 billion. Market share, as measured by online trades per day, rose from 10 percent of the market to 15 percent, and Opinion Research Corp.'s Internet Brand Study ranked E*Trade as the fourth-most-recognized e-commerce brand, behind Amazon.com, eBay, and Priceline.com. In its fourth quarter of 1999 E*Trade had 4.69 million unique visitors, making it the most visited online investing site, according to Media Metrix. The company also expanded its Mutual Fund Center, offering more than 5,000 funds and introducing four E*Trade proprietary funds.

Internationally, E*Trade expanded in fiscal 1999 by opening Web sites in France, Japan, Sweden, and the United Kingdom. It completed three major acquisitions: ClearStation Inc., a financial media Web site that combined investment analysis with community discussion and opinion; TIR Holdings Ltd., discussed above; and Confluent Inc., whose main product was a calendar engine that E*Trade planned to use to create a personal financial manager.

DIVERSIFIED REVENUE STREAMS AIMED TO BALANCE GROWTH

E*Trade's revenue diversification strategy was designed to reduce the company's reliance on online trading volume as a primary source of revenue. Planned diversifications included Internet banking, the IPO market, stock plan management services for corporations, and venture capital funds. The company's pending acquisition of Telebanc Financial Corp., which operated the leading Internet bank, signaled E*Trade's entry into Internet banking. Announced in mid-1999, the acquisition of Telebanc closed in January 2000. E*Trade Bank was launched in April 2000, and wireless banking and brokerage services were first offered by E*Trade in October 2000. E*Trade's stock plan management services were organized under the company's E*Trade Business Solutions Group (BSG), and the company launched its first Strategic Venture Fund in fiscal 1999 to invest in technology and Internet companies.

E*Trade returned to profitability in fiscal 2000 ending September 30, 12 months ahead of plan. For the year the company had $1.4 billion in net revenue and net income of $19.2 million. The growth in revenue was attributed to the successful diversification of E*Trade's revenue stream. The company had $475 million in earnings before marketing expenses, a testament to the strength of its business model. Annual revenue per customer amounted to $547, compared to a customer acquisition cost of $263 per customer. During fiscal 2000 E*Trade doubled its customer base to more than 3 million customer accounts.

E*Trade's branding strategy contributed to a successful first year for its E*Trade Bank, which was signing up new customers at twice the rate of the old Telebank. During fiscal 2000 the bank's deposits surpassed $4.6 billion, and its total assets were $9 billion, making it the 19th-largest federally chartered savings bank in the United States. E*Trade Bank contributed 52 percent of the E*Trade Group's total interest income and 25 percent of its gross revenue. The company also benefited from cross-selling its online brokerage service to the bank's customers at an acquisition cost of only $60 per customer. The company believed that its new ATM network represented the next growth phase for E*Trade Bank.

Global growth also was strong in fiscal 2000, another testimonial to the company's brand recognition. E*Trade in the United Kingdom, Sweden, Canada, and Australia all recorded triple digit growth in accounts and assets. The company consolidated E*Trade Germany, gaining 100-percent ownership there as well as a banking license. E*Trade South Africa was launched during the year, and in September 2000 E*Trade Japan completed its IPO. E*Trade sold 20 percent of its equity stake in E*Trade Japan for $80 million, while retaining a 32-percent interest in the venture. For 2001 E*Trade planned to roll out its international trading platform, based on Versus Technologies, for more than 650 institutional customers worldwide.

Looking to the future, E*Trade planned to penetrate consumers' lives even more through the introduction of E*Trade Zones in retail outlets, starting with SuperTarget stores. E*Trade Zones would feature ATMs, customer service representatives, and full-service E*Trade financial kiosks offering brokerage and banking capabilities, electronic transfer of funds, streaming media, and more. In the corporate marketplace, E*Trade planned to launch E*Trade Virtual Credit Union to make the E*Trade brand part of corporate infrastructures throughout the United States. In addition, its Business Solutions Group was poised to reach 1.3 million employees of its corporate customers, representing more than $130 billion in unrealized assets in vested and unvested options. With such a diversity of potential revenue sources, E*Trade appeared to be in a strong position to weather the bear market of 2001 and the expected reduction in online trading volume.

FURTHER READING:

''Company Information.'' E*Trade Group Inc. March 17, 2001. Available from www.etrade.com.

Fernandes, Lorna. ''ETrade Seeking Security in Sacto.'' *The Business Journal.* April 8, 1996.

Gerlach, Douglas. ''Special Report.'' *PC World.* February 1999.

Gunn, Eileen. ''Huge Growth for E-Brokers.'' *Internet World.* May 3, 1999.

Kerr, Deborah. ''Number One: A Second-Thought Success.'' *The Business Journal.* October 23, 1995.

Schifrin, Matthew. ''E-warning.'' *Forbes.* February 22, 1999.

Schnitt, Paul. ''Rancho Cordova, Calif., Firm Rides the Electronic Investing Wave.'' *Knight-Ridder/Tribune Business News.* January 30, 1997.

Swett, Clint. ''California-Based ETrade Takes Huge Gamble with Online Stock Trading.'' *Knight-Ridder/Tribune Business News.* June 17, 1998.

Wasserman, Elizabeth. ''Online Trading Soars with Stock Market Decline.'' *Knight-Ridder/Tribune Business News.* October 28, 1997.

Weisul, Kimberly. ''Marketing Can Boost Brokers.'' *Inter@ctive Week.* January 24, 2000.

SEE ALSO: Ameritrade Holding Corp.; Charles Schwab & Co. Inc.; Datek Online Brokerage Services LLC; Day Trading; Volatility

EUROPEAN COMMISSION'S DIRECTIVE ON DATA PRIVACY

In October 1995, the European Commission issued a parliamentary directive on data protection (Directive 95/46/EC) that contained comprehensive guidelines for safeguarding the privacy of Internet issues. The guidelines addressed the collection, storage, retrieval, and dissemination of personal data that could be gathered and transferred over the Web. The directive is aimed at the European Union (EU) member states and constitutes one of the strongest statements regarding the protection of online users' privacy rights in the international Internet forum. By January 2000 about two-thirds of EU member states had adopted the directive.

The directive, which took effect in the fall of 1998, creates a standardized framework for online privacy rights for citizens of all EU member states. It sets out minimum standards that the Internet privacy legislation of each EU member nation must meet. For example, it prohibits the processing and collection of personal data unless the user consents to such an activity. In addition, data considered to be of a particularly sensitive nature—such as that concerning political or religious beliefs, racial or ethnic origin, or sexual preference—cannot be gathered at all, except in cases where the individual user has explicitly agreed, or where pressing medical or legal circumstances mandate it. Finally, the transferal of personal data outside of the EU can only occur if the recipient demonstrates it will provide an "adequate" level of protection for the individual's privacy consistent with the directive's standards. The acceptability of non-EU data recipients is gauged by the industry rules and security measures taken to be the standard in the recipient's country. Under the directive, individual EU citizens may sue for breach of privacy.

The United States lacks clear legal remedies for breaches of data privacy. For this reason, the EU does not consider the American approach to online privacy "adequate" enough to permit data transfers to American companies. This difficulty concerning data transfers affects intranets and e-mail, as well as data transportation on floppy disks and laptop computers.

Critics of the directive—prominent among them governmental officials and industries in the United States—feel that the it is too restrictive, and that by privileging user privacy it stifles both economic enterprise and free expression on the Web. In contrast to mandated legislation, American online marketers have argued for industry self-regulation. The United States worked to establish this through the Safe Harbor Privacy Program, which requires that participating organizations voluntarily provide proof to the U.S. Department of Commerce that they have "reasonable data protections" in place. In July 2000, the European Commission ruled that the American Safe Harbor Privacy Principles met the protection standards outlined by the commission directive. According to those standards, Safe Harbor certification can be earned by becoming a member of a self-regulatory program that follows Safe Harbor guidelines; by developing an internal privacy policy that meets those guidelines; or by submitting to an administrative, regulatory, or statutory body or law that provides an acceptable level of data protection.

If such practices satisfy the standards of the EU directive, compliant organizations are exempt from prosecution for violating the directive's guidelines when they transfer personal data into or out of any EU member country. Though a fledgling Safe Harbor program was put into place in 2000, U.S. companies were slow to embrace the terms of the agreement.

FURTHER READING:

Argen, Per-Olof. "Is Online Democracy in the EU for Professionals Only?" *Communications of the ACM*. January 2001.

Gillin, Donna. "Safe Harbor Principles for the European Privacy Directive Are Finalized." *Marketing Research*. Winter 2000.

Johnson, Mark. "As Seen from Europe: A Very Public War Over Privacy." *Global Finance*. January 2001.

Thibodeau, Patrick. "Big Companies Shy Away from Safe Harbor Accord." *Computerworld*. February 19, 2001.

White, Martin. "The Impact of Data Protection Legislation on Intranets." *Econtent*. August/September 2000.

SEE ALSO: Global e-commerce: Europe; Privacy: Issues, Policies, Statements; Safe Harbor Privacy Framework

EVANS, NANCY

Nancy Evans is co-founder and editor-in-chief of iVillage Inc., one of the Web's largest content sites and the leading online service for women. Visitors to the site total more than 5 million each month. iVillage targets women between the ages of 25 and 54 with 18 different channels: Astrology, Babies, Beauty, Books, Computing, Diet & Fitness, Food, Games, Health, Home & Garden, Lamaze, Money, News & Issues, Parenting, Pets, Relationships, Shopping, and Work. iVillage users can converse with online experts on a variety of subjects, participate in support and discussion groups, read frequently asked questions and answers on a wide range of topics, take quizzes, post links to their own Web sites, enroll in giveaways, and purchase goods and services. Membership in iVillage is free. The site garners its revenues via advertising and sponsorships and also from taking a percentage of the profits of products sold online at iVillage.

An English literature graduate from Skidmore College, Evans launched her publishing career as an editor for *Harper's Weekly*. She left that position to serve as contributing editor for *Glamour,* where she oversaw book reviews and featured editorials for the magazine. In 1985, Book-of-the-Month Club hired Evans as editor-in-chief and vice president. Two years later, she moved to Doubleday, serving as both president and publisher until 1991. With partner Jann Wenner, Evans founded and managed *Family Life* magazine in the early 1990s.

In June of 1995, Evans helped former Time Warner executive Candice Carpenter create iVillage.com. As president and editor-in-chief, Evans was responsible for developing the site's content, including that available on iVillage's first two networks, About Work and Parent Soup. Evans continued to oversee the addition of new content to the site throughout the late 1990s and early 2000s. For example, in November of 2000 iVillage launched Adoption Central, a clearinghouse of information on the adoption process for birth parents, adoptive parents, and adoptees. Evans continues to work to maintain editorial standards and develop content at iVillage.

FURTHER READING:

''Adoption Central Debuts on iVillage.com's Award-Winning Parenting Website, Parent Soup.'' *PR Newswire.* November 2, 2000.

''Corporate Profile.'' New York: iVillage Inc., 2000. Available from www.corporate-ir.net.

Flinn, John; and Laura Rich. ''Nancy Evans & Candice Carpenter: iVillage is Building Virtual Communities for Grown-Ups to Call Home on the Internet.'' *ADWEEK Eastern Edition.* September 23, 1996.

Post, Tom. ''It Takes More Than an Ivillage.'' *Forbes.* February 22, 1999.

SEE ALSO: Carpenter, Candice; iVillage.com

EXCITE@HOME

Excite@Home was formed in January 1999 when high-speed Internet access provider @Home acquired the Excite Network for $6.7 billion. At the time Excite had 20 million registered users for its Internet portal and search engine services. @Home had 330,000 subscribers signed up for its high-speed Internet access service. @Home also had cable distribution agreements in place reaching 60 million homes. However, since many of those systems had not yet been upgraded to offer high-speed Internet access, @Home was available to only about 13 million homes at the beginning of 1999.

The acquisition was fueled by several factors. Other portal consolidations were taking place, including the acquisition of Netscape Communications by America Online and Walt Disney Co.'s investment in Infoseek Corp. @Home was willing to pay a premium for access to Excite's customer base, valuing the company well above its market capitalization. The new combined company was to be called At Home, formerly the name of @Home Network's parent company and now Excite@Home's parent. It would have about 1,200 employees and projected revenue of $2 billion by 2002. CEO Thomas Jermoluk predicted operating margins in the range of 30 to 35 percent. George Bell, formerly CEO of Excite, became president of Excite@Home.

The acquisition enabled @Home to transmit across multiple platforms, including both dial-up and broadband. It also gave cable operators an incentive to upgrade their cable systems to handle two-way Internet traffic. Through Excite, @Home would be made available as a dial-up service in areas where cable modem service was not yet available.

At the time of the acquisition, AT&T was in the process of merging with Tele-Communications Inc. (TCI). Following that merger, AT&T became the largest shareholder with a 26-percent majority stake in Excite@Home and 58-percent voting control of the company. AT&T also was the preferred provider for Excite's dial-up service through AT&T WorldNet. WorldNet, which was AT&T's Internet service provider (ISP), had about 2.3 million customers in early 1999, 1.3 million of which were residential. Other major shareholders in Excite@Home included cable operators Cox Communications Inc. and Comcast Corp.

EXCITE, 1994-1998

Excite was one of the first Internet search engines. It began in 1994 as a project of some Stanford University graduate students who founded Architext Software and developed software to navigate large databases. As Internet use began to grow, Excite was used as a search engine for Usenet. After changing its name to Excite Inc., the company went public on April 4, 1996 with its initial public offering (IPO). The Tribune Co. bought an eight-percent interest in Excite for $7 million. George Bell, former senior vice president of Times Mirror Magazines, was hired as CEO.

Following the introduction of My Yahoo!, Excite introduced a makeover of its Web site in July 1996 that included a menu of defined-content categories on its opening page. The new Excite also included reviews and ratings of some 60,000 Web sites and claimed the largest database of all search engines with 50 million Web pages. The company also acquired The McKinley Group, creator of the Magellan On-Line Guide. At the time, Excite ranked fifth among Internet search engines.

Before the end of 1996 Excite had added a broad array of information and services to encourage Web users to make the site their default home page. Among these offerings were City.Net, an information service covering major U.S. and international cities, along with a variety of reviews, news, directories, and other references. In December 1996 Excite and America Online (AOL) announced that Excite would become AOL's exclusive Internet search engine, although AOL users could still navigate the Web with other search engines. At the time AOL had about 7 million subscribers and was in the process of introducing its fixed price plan at $19.95 per month. As part of the deal, AOL also sold its WebCrawler to Excite and doubled its ownership interest in Excite to 20 percent.

An article in *Fortune* noted that, of all the leading Internet search engines, Excite appeared to be in the most precarious financial position at the end of 1996. The company's stock had lost about two-thirds of its value since its IPO. Additionally, the firm had spent $30 million on acquisitions, partnerships, and advertising in 1996.

As Internet usage surged in 1997, Internet search engines earned higher advertising revenue. For the third quarter Yahoo! reported a $1.6 million profit on revenue of $17 million. However, Excite and Lycos continued to operate at a loss.

During 1998 Excite and other Internet search engines continued to redefine themselves as Internet portals, adding new services and content. In its review of 11 Web portals, *PC Magazine* rated Excite as ''the best portal on the Web.'' The magazine noted that Excite offered excellent personalization tools, a search feature that anticipated what you were looking for, and a sense of community. For example, Excite Communities—a service that combined e-mail, chat, calendar, and other online networking functions—was introduced in August 1998. For 1999, Excite's goal was to be among the top five Internet portals.

@HOME, 1995-1998

@Home was formed in 1995 as a national high-speed Internet service. Its principal backers were cable TV system operator TCI and investment banking firm Kleiner, Perkins, Caulfield & Byers. William Randolph Hearst III was the company's first CEO. The company planned to offer high-speed Internet access over cable TV systems by forming partnerships with cable multi-system operators (MSOs) such as Continental, Cox, and Comcast. At the time manufacturers such as Hewlett-Packard and Motorola were just beginning to consider making cable modems and were looking for ways to make them inexpensively. For @Home's vision of high-speed Internet access to succeed, its service needed wider availability, and the price of cable modems needed to come down.

In October 1995 @Home entered into an agreement with Netscape to license Netscape's software. Together, @Home and Netscape planned to develop a customized version of Netscape's Navigator software that would allow for local content, advertising, and e-commerce over a cable connection to the Internet. To stimulate the manufacture of low-cost cable modems, TCI sent out an RFP (request for proposal) to vendors such as Motorola, Zenith, Intel, Northern Telecom, and Hewlett-Packard for hundreds of thousands of units.

@Home expected to roll out to a limited number of homes in early 1996 but had to scale back its plans due to a lack of infrastructure. In June 1996 cable companies Comcast Corp. and Cox Communications Inc. agreed to invest in @Home and take equity stakes of 14 percent each. TCI's stake was reduced to 45 percent, and investment-banking firm Kleiner, Perkins, Caulfield & Byers's interest was also 14 percent. In August @Home named Tom Jermoluk as its chairman, president, and CEO. Jermoluk was formerly president and chief operating officer (COO) of Silicon Graphics Inc. (SGI). Founding CEO William Randolph Hearst III remained as vice chairman of @Home.

Late in 1996 @Home signed content agreements with the HotWired Network, *The New York Times,* and *USA Today* for multimedia services the company would introduce in early 1997. In February 1997 @Home signed charter advertisers for its high-speed service including General Motors Corp. and Conde Net. Some 100 companies that had agreed to provide content for @Home were allowed to run unpaid ads on the network.

In 1997 @Home began to establish its @Work division to provide high-speed Internet access to businesses and their employees. Through an agreement with competitive access provider Teleport Communications Group, @Home gained access to potential business customers in more than 55 major cities and other markets. The company continued to sign cable partners to carry its high-speed Internet service in 1997, including Marcus Cable in Fort Worth, Texas. It also entered the Canadian market through an agreement with Rogers Cablesystems and Shaw Communications, Canada's two largest MSOs, who took a joint five-percent interest in @Home. Later in the year @Home gained access to 5.5 million potential customers in the Northeast through an agreement with Cablevision Systems Corp.

@Home filed for an initial public offering in May 1997 and went public in July. Its stock more than doubled on the first day of trading, from its initial $10.50 price to a high of $25.50 before settling at $19. The IPO gave @Home proceeds of $94.5 million and a market capitalization of more than $2 billion. For 1997 @Home had revenue of $7.4 million, compared to $700,000 in 1996.

In 1998 @Home's market capitalization reached more than $23 billion as investors drove up the price of Internet stocks. @Home added more cable partners, including Jones Inter-cable Inc., Cogeco Cable Inc., and Garden State Cable TV. By mid-1998 @Home was close to reaching 60 million homes in North America through agreements with its cable partners. During 1998 AT&T acquired TCI and became the principal shareholder in @Home. That December, @Home acquired Narrative Communications Corp., an interactive advertisement software provider, for $90 million in stock.

Excite@Home planned to move forward on three fronts. First, the company planned to grow its narrowband Internet service, which had more than 28 million regular users. Second, it wanted to expand the @Home subscriber base, in part by targeting registered Excite users who lived in areas where @Home's cable partners already had upgraded their systems. Third, the company planned to develop new programming opportunities for the exclusive use of its @Home broadband customers.

As of mid-1999 Excite@Home had exclusive rights to provide high-speed data over cable to 67 million homes through 22 cable operator partners. The main problem facing the company was that its inventory of potential homes far exceeded the company's ability to install its service. In many cases consumer demand, fueled by the company's marketing efforts, exceeded the cable operators' ability to service that demand. Excite@Home principally was competing with telephone operators and America Online to build a critical mass of subscribers. In one promotion, Excite@Home offered three months of free service to convert AOL subscribers.

In June 1999 Excite introduced two new services, Excite Voicemail and Excite Voice Chat. With Excite Voicemail, which was free for up to 60 messages and 10 faxes per month, callers could leave voice messages or send a fax by calling a central toll-free phone number provided by Excite. Each user received a unique 10-digit extension number to be used with the toll-free number. To use Excite Voice Chat, which enabled voice conversations with other Excite chatters, users needed a personal computer, an Internet connection, a microphone, and speakers or a headset. Both services were ad-supported.

In July 1999 Excite acquired iMall for $425 million in stock. An e-commerce pioneer founded in 1994, iMall operated shopping portals and also offered e-commerce packages for businesses. The acquisition enhanced Excite@Home's shopping network by adding merchants and also built up its business-to-business e-commerce solutions. Additionally, the acquisition gave Excite@Home a new relationship with First Data Corp., an e-commerce transaction processor that owned 11 percent of iMall. Excite@Home and First Data teamed to offer merchants the ability to complete credit card transactions. iMall claimed that it could help merchants set up an Internet storefront in one day.

In October 1999 the company launched Work.com, a service for business professionals and their companies. It was the first step of the company's initiative to develop a business portal through its B2B division, @Work. Work.com also was available on Excite's recently introduced Business Channel, which carried company and product information on 36 industries. Work.com also included business applications, a directory of business resources, and links to other business-related areas on Excite. In December 1999 Excite@Home acquired electronic greeting site Blue Mountain Arts for $780 million and also launched a new consumer site, Excite Photo Center, where users could upload, download, store, edit, and print high-resolution photos.

At the beginning of 2000 Excite ranked third among Internet search engines in terms of unique visitors, behind Yahoo! and Lycos. In February Excite partnered with Dow Jones & Co. to produce Work.com, a Web site for small and medium-sized businesses. The new Work.com would include content from Dow Jones and Excite@Home's existing Work.com site.

In July 2000 Excite launched a new free online storefront service, called Freetailer. The service allowed small businesses to establish a presence on the Web at no cost. The company reported that more than 1,000 new businesses had signed up within the first 24 hours of the service being offered. Each e-tailer was given 25 megabytes of computer storage space and one gigabyte per month of bandwidth to accommodate site traffic. Excite Messenger, a new instant messaging application that replaced Excite Pal, was introduced in September 2000. Excite Messenger could be used in a text mode, as well as for voice chat if users' PCs were equipped with a microphone and speakers.

For 2000, Excite@Home lost $7.44 billion, compared to a $1.5 billion loss for 1999. Post-first quarter filings in 2001 by majority shareholder AT&T and by Excite@Home revealed the company's precarious financial position. AT&T said its investment in Excite@Home would reduce its first quarter income by $280 million to $320 million. Excite@Home reported that it needed to raise $75-$85 million by June 30 in order to maintain its operations and liquidity. Under a non-binding letter of agreement, AT&T agreed to provide the necessary cash in exchange for Excite@Home's fiber network. Excite@Home would then lease back the network on a monthly basis for 20 years. The company solved its cash problem by selling $100 million of notes.

Excite@Home's financial problems primarily were attributed to shrinking online advertising revenues. The downturn in Internet advertising resulted in Excite@Home closing its operations in France, Germany, and Spain in mid-2001. The company planned to focus its European strategy on the United Kingdom and Italy, where there were better prospects for growth.

As part of AT&T's acquisition of MediaOne, AT&T phased out MediaOne's high-speed Internet access service, Road Runner, and replaced it with Excite@Home. Although Excite@Home had increased its high-speed cable modem subscriber base from 330,000 in early 1999 to more than 3.7 million in August 2001, costly investments contributed to the firm's financial problems.

Quarterly losses of $832.6 million in the first quarter and $346.3 million in the second quarter left Excite@Home's future in doubt. A filing addendum to its annual report included an auditors' statement that expressed "substantial doubt about the company's ability to continue as a going concern." Comcast and Cox both terminated their exclusive high-speed Internet access agreement with the company and opened their systems to other high-speed providers. With its stock trading at a 52-week low of less than $1 a share, Excite@Home also faced the possibility of being de-listed from the NASDAQ. By the end of 2001 the company had declared bankruptcy.

FURTHER READING:

"@Home IPO Zooms." *Broadcasting & Cable.* July 14, 1997.

"AT&T Sings Broadband Blues.rdquo; *Communications Today.* April 23, 2001.

Brady, Mick. "Excite's Free Online Stores an Overnight Hit." *E-Commerce Times.* July 14, 2000. Available from www.ecommerctimes.com.

Centeno, Cerelle. "ExciteAtHome Bails Out of Key European Markets." *eMarketer.* June 23, 2001. Available from www.emarketer.com.

Conlin, Robert. "iMall Snapped Up by Excite@Home for $425 Million." *E-Commerce Times.* July 13, 1999. Available from www.ecommerctimes.com.

Fernandes, Lorna. "Internet Search Engines Are On a Roll." *The Business Journal.* November 17, 1997.

Ferranti, Marc and Mary Lisbeth D'Amico. "@Home Buys Excite for $6.7B." *Computerworld.* January 25, 1999.

"Internet Service Provider Excite@Home May Not Survive." *Knight-Ridder/Tribune Business News.* August 21, 2001.

Krantz, Michael. "Start Your Engines: Excite and Yahoo, the Two Leading Web-Search Sites, Race to Remake Themselves into 'Portals.'" *Time.* April 20, 1998.

Leger, Jill. "Excite." *PC Magazine.* September 1, 1998.

Mermigas, Diane. "High-Speed Slowdown: Excite@Home Growth Outpacing Cable's Capacity." *Electronic Media.* August 2, 1999.

Needle, David. "Fast Growth, Fast Friends." *PC Magazine.* September 22, 1998.

Spooner, John. "Excitable Boy." *Adweek Eastern Edition.* July 7, 1997.

Stapleton, Paul. "Excite@Home." *Boardwatch Magazine.* May 2000.

Tedesco, Richard. "Excite's New Engine Points at Yahoo's Pole Position." *Broadcasting & Cable.* July 29, 1996.

"Top Search Sites." *PC Magazine.* May 9, 2000.

Wang, Andy. "Excite@Home Goes to Work.com." *E-Commerce Times.* September 30, 1999. Available from www.ecommerctimes.com.

SEE ALSO: AT&T Corp.; Netscape Communications Corp.; Portals, Web

EXODUS COMMUNICATIONS INC.

Exodus Communications Inc. was founded in 1994 by K.B. Chandrasekhar and B.V. Jagadeesh. Just six years later, with annual sales reaching $818 million, Exodus had secured the leading position among Internet hosting and network management firms. The company serves more than 4,500 customers and provides Internet Data Center (IDC) facilities in North America, Europe, and the Asia Pacific region that allow clients to store their servers in secure locations. Along with server hosting, Exodus also offers equipment maintenance services and solutions for content distribution and caching, security, performance measuring and monitoring, managed Web hosting, and networking.

EARLY HISTORY

Fulfilling a lifelong dream of owning his own firm, Chandrasekhar formed network software design and development firm Fouress Inc. in 1992. Within two years, Fouress had become a profitable $1 million firm. Eyeing the growth potential of the Internet, Chandrasekhar teamed up with Jagadeesh to form Exodus, an Internet Service Provider (ISP). The firm began operations in 1994 with 15 employees. The following year, the Fouress business was merged into Exodus, and revenues reached $1.4 million.

By 1996, revenues had climbed to $3.1 million. That year, Exodus shifted its focus from operating as an ISP to offering IDC services. According to Exodus Marketing Vice President Mark Bonham in the 1997 issue of *The Business Journal,* the firm changed its focus because "customers began wanting their Internet equipment in a service center rather than in-house. If you are a company with a significant amount of business on the Internet, you don't want to rely on the skills of one or two in-house people to keep your network going." Also, demand had increased for IDC services—such as providing servers to run Internet-based businesses with network connections to those servers. Exodus opened its first IDC in Santa Clara, California, and soon followed with another in Jersey City, New Jersey.

To expand further, Exodus raised $10 million in capital in 1996 and secured additional financing in

1997 to open future IDCs in Washington, DC; Chicago, Illinois; Los Angeles, California; Seattle, Washington; Japan; and the United Kingdom. During 1997, the company's Santa Clara facility served Web-based customers including Blizzard Entertainment, Hotmail Corp., Inktomi Corp., I/PRO, Sierra On-Line, and Tibco Inc. Revenues for the year continued to climb, reaching $12.4 million.

MAJOR ACQUISITIONS

In March of 1998, Ellen Hancock, a former executive for Apple Computer Inc., IBM, and National Semiconductor Corp., was hired to take the lead of Exodus. That same month, the firm went public. Under the leadership of Hancock, Exodus made its first acquisition in October, with the purchase of Arca Systems Inc., a leading Internet security solutions provider. As concern for security in network systems continued to rise in the late 1990s, Exodus was able to tap into Arca's expertise in security solutions.

Exodus's second major acquisition was the January 1999 purchase of American Information Systems (AIS), a Chicago, Illinois-based provider of co-location, Web hosting, and various other Internet management services. The deal smoothed the firm's entry into the Midwest market and gave it access to handful of large customers including ABN Amro, Ameritech, *Crain's Chicago Business,* First Chicago Bank, and Motorola. Exodus opened its Chicago IDC shortly after the purchase. The firm also completed the $100 million purchase of Cohesive Technology Solutions Inc. in April. Cohesive's networking, Web applications, and technology solutions became part of Exodus' managed service offerings. As part of the deal, Exodus secured the leading position in the Web hosting provider market. Additional acquisitions included Service Metrics Inc., a performance analysis provider; and Global Online Japan Co. Ltd., a Japanese-based IDC provider that gave Exodus quick access to the Asian market.

Exodus entered the new millennium intent on continuing its buying spree. The firm beefed up its security offerings once again when it bought the Professional Services Division of Network-1 Security Solutions Inc., a security and network design consultancy. With the purchase of testing services provider KeyLabs Inc., Exodus was able to offer its customers services that tested e-commerce sites for performance problems or other issues before they went live.

In January 2001, Exodus acquired GlobalCenter Inc., a subsidiary of Global Crossing Ltd., for nearly $6.5 billion. The purchase positioned Exodus as the leader in the Internet hosting services market with more than 4,500 customers, including the likes of AC Nielsen Corp., Adidas, Ernst & Young LLC, Google,

Lycos Inc., *USA Today,* and Yahoo!. Upon completion of the deal, Exodus' strategic partners included Accenture, Cisco Systems Inc., Compaq Computer Corp., EMC Corp., Inktomi Corp., Microsoft Corp., Oracle Corp., StorageNetworks Inc., and Sun Microsystems Inc.

Although Exodus had grown significantly from its early days in 1994, the company was undermined by shifting industry demand in 2001. In April, the firm's chief financial officer, chief operating officer, and vice president of marketing left suddenly after substantial cash losses were reported. According to a May 2001 *Forbes* article, the firm's "simple brand of hosting is falling out of favor. In the Exodus model, customers rent floor space and Internet access, buy their own servers and manage them on their own. Today customers want 'managed hosting' with the Web hoster buying the iron and looking after it, selling computing power the way a utility sells electricity." In response to the changing demand, Exodus began its foray into managed services, an expensive shift that required restructuring among the firm. To cut costs, the company reduced its work force by 15 percent, but at the same time it also needed to hire and train additional engineers to oversee the move into managed services.

Another issue plaguing Exodus was the downturn of many dot-com companies. Exodus secured nearly 40 percent of sales from Web-based businesses, but the e-business firms that had experienced great success in the late 1990s were falling short of sales expectations and going out of business at a rapid pace. Exodus also faced increased competition as telecom and other tech firms joined the hosting services market, which was expected to continue growing into 2004. As Exodus battled these problems, management continued to focus on developing managed and professional services. The company also worked to expand its core business and emerge in new geographical areas in order to remain the leading U.S.-based hosting service provider.

FURTHER READING:

"Company Information." Santa Clara, CA: Exodus Communications Inc., 2001. Available from www.exodus.net.

Darrow, Barbara; and Lisa Picarille. "Hancock Becomes Exodus President." *Computer Reseller News.* March 23, 1998.

Elgin, Ben. "Making Her Own Luck." *BusinessWeek Online.* November 20, 2000. Available from www.businessweek.com.

"Exodus Acquires Cohesive for $100m, Revenues Keep Growing." *Computergram International.* April 22, 1999.

Holden, Daniel J. "Exodus Communications Inc." *The Business Journal.* October 27, 1997.

Koblentz, Evan. "Changes at Exodus Under Scrutiny." *eWeek.* May 7, 2001.

Lyons, Daniel. "Hostess With the Mostest Problems." *Forbes.* May 28, 2001.

Macaluso, Nora. "Exodus Down on Job Cuts." *E-Commerce Times.* May 9, 2001. Available from www.ecommercetimes.com.

Mulqueen, John T. "Exodus to Network Centers." *CommunicationsWeek.* April 12, 1997.

SEE ALSO: Internet Service Provider (ISP); Software Hosting

E-ZINES

E-zines are magazines published electronically, most often on the World Wide Web. The terms e-zine and Web zine typically refer to the same thing. Initially, a "zine" referred to a niche magazine targeting a small, unique market. However, as the number of mainstream publications that made their way to the Web grew throughout the late 1990s, the term e-zine grew to encompass both niche and mainstream magazines that were published via the Internet. In addition to online content, most e-zines offer interactive features, such as the ability to search current and archived articles for a particular topic or keyword. Many also house message boards, which allow readers to respond to articles. Some e-zines rely solely on advertising to make money, others charge subscription fees, and many rely on both revenue sources.

One of the most well-known e-zines, *Slate,* is published by Microsoft Corp. Roughly 2.5 million unique readers log on to *Slate*—which covers news, politics, and culture—each month. The e-zine was created in 1996 by Michael Kinsley, a former *New Republic* senior editor and co-host of CNN's political commentary program, Crossfire. Readers initially were charged a $19.95 monthly subscription fee. Eventually, the site grew to include MySlate, a site personalization feature, and a discussion forum known as the Fray. In 1999, *Slate's* managers realized that they were spending more money attempting to recruit paying subscribers than they were securing in subscription fees. According to *Slate* publisher Scott Moore, as quoted in a September 2001 issue of *Econtent,* "I projected what would happen to our audience if we made *Slate* free, given that we could take advantage of the distribution power of MSN. I modeled what that would do for our advertising potential, and it looked like there was a lot more upside with that strategy than continuing to slug along selling subscriptions, so that's what we did and it has paid off." Along with traditional banner bars, *Slate* also relies on larger advertisements and sponsorships agreements, whereby the e-zine posts links to other sites.

A major competitor to *Slate, Salon* is perhaps a more typical e-zine as it does not have access to the deep pockets and marketing reach of a firm like Microsoft. *Salon* was created in 1995 to cover political and cultural issues. Its writers included the likes of radio host Garrison Keillor and social activist Camille Paglia. An initial public offering in 1999 raised $35.6 million in capital and resulted in Adobe Systems holding a 15-percent stake in the site. Access to the e-zine was free, as *Salon* relied solely on advertising to generate revenues. Consequently, *Salon* was particularly vulnerable to the downturn in online advertising the e-content industry began to see in 2000. That year, the firm lost $19.2 million on sales of $8 million. In response, *Salon* began working in 2001 to develop and market a subscriber-based site with increased content and no advertising. The e-zine also began cutting costs by laying off marketing employees and implementing a 15-percent pay cut. According to *BusinessWeek Online* writer Thane Peterson, *Salon* also was at a disadvantage because it lacked the name recognition of online magazines published by industry giants like *The New York Times, Newsweek,* and *Time.* "Established print magazines can constantly remind readers to log onto their Web sites, so, like *Slate,* they require far less marketing expense than an independent like *Salon.*"

Another well-known e-zine, *TheStreet.com,* was created in response to predictions that the number of U.S. households trading stocks electronically, 1.5 million in 1996, would grow exponentially throughout the late 1990s. Hedge fund manager and *New York* magazine columnist James J. Cramer and *New Republic* Editor-in-Chief and Chairman Martin Peretz created *TheStreet.com* in November of 1996. Cramer and Peretz believed that many individual stock traders would be willing to pay for immediate market information, and they charged a monthly subscription fee of $12.95 for access to their financial e-zine, which included performance reports profiling Wall Street analysts, news and commentary on current trading activity, and other articles written by Cramer himself, as well as by Michael Lewis, a senior editor at *New Republic.*

Shortly after its inception, *TheStreet.com* began adding interactive features, such as the ability to track mutual fund and stock portfolios in real time. The 30 articles published each day were grouped into four sections: Fund Watch; Company Watch; Truth Serum; and Market Facts. Most articles totaled 800 to 1,000 words, compared to the 1,500 to 2,000 words typical of articles in most businesses publications, a fact which reflected the widespread belief that attention spans for online content were shorter than for print content. In 1998, subscriptions accounted for roughly 70 percent of total sales, while advertising from Charles Schwab, Ameritrade, Fidelity, and other brokerages accounted for the remaining 30 percent. When the firm conducted its IPO in 1999, the starting share price of $19 jumped to $75 during the first day of trading. The following year, *TheStreet.com* decided to make a general version of its site available for free in an effort to gain a mass market. To meet needs of more active investors, the company offered additional stock analysis content on a new site, RealMoney.com, which charged a monthly subscription fee of $20. A third site, TheStreetPros.com, was designed solely for industry professionals and charged a monthly subscription rate of $40.

Like most other e-zines attempting to reach a mass market, *TheStreet.com* found profitability elusive. Cost cutting efforts were launched in 2000, and the firm also began pursuing ventures not related to the Internet. Some analysts believe that the most successful online content providers will be those that use the Internet as one of many distribution vehicles. Other analysts believe that smaller, more specialized e-zines, particularly those that offer unique content, are more likely to remain viable contenders. According to an August 2001 article in *BusinessWeek Online,* ''While both *Salon* and *TheStreet* raised tens of millions of dollars in flashy IPOs, each has struggled to come close to breaking even. . .just about everybody is still struggling with the question of how to make any money off the business model. . .that's where the new crop of upstarts come in.''

Two niche e-zines that came close to profitability in 2001 were investigative news site *WorldNet Daily,* with roughly 20 employees and 450,000 visitors each month, and community-based spirituality site *Beliefnet,* with more than 950,000 monthly users. In fact, during the first half of 2001, while most other e-zines watched advertising revenues slow to a trickle, *Beliefnet* saw advertising sales grow 300 percent. Like most other e-commerce business models, the e-zine likely will continue to evolve as upstarts find new ways to succeed.

FURTHER READING:

Black, Jane. ''On the Web, Small and Focused Pays Off.'' *BusinessWeek Online.* August 28, 2001. Available from www.businessweek.com.

Luskin, Donald L. ''Walk It Like You Talk It.'' *The Industry Standard.* June 14, 2001. Available from www.thestandard.com.

Pack, Thomas. ''Slate's Moore Has Faith in Online Ads.'' *EContent.* September 2001.

Peterson, Thane. ''The Wolf at Salon's Door.'' *BusinessWeek Online.* August 7, 2001. Available from www.businessweek.com.

Stern, Gary M. ''TheStreet.com: Gaining the Competitive Edge.'' *Link-Up.* February 1998.

Taylor, Cathy. ''Takin' It to the Street.'' *Mediaweek.* November 18, 1996.

SEE ALSO: E-books; Electronic Publishing; TheStreet.com

F

FairMarket Inc. is a provider of e-business selling and marketing solutions through dynamic pricing. Its customers include retailers, distributors, and manufacturers, and its offerings include automatic markdown, auction, fixed-price, and merchandising tools. The company's main service offering, FairMarket Network, includes the development, hosting, and maintenance of private-label online auction sites. This consortium of Web sites allows companies to offer auction sites to their customers, increasing product exposure and allowing customers a wider selection. Without this type of service, companies would be forced to make steep investments in their own auction technology.

FairMarket Inc. was founded in early 1997 by Harvard Business School graduate Scott Randall in order to match buyers and sellers of computer products. The company gradually began to market software that supported person-to-person auctions, also called "community auctions," as well as business-to-person and business-to-business auctions, also known as "merchant auctions." Chairman Randall was quoted in *Knight-Ridder/Tribune Business News* as saying, "I came to the conclusion that auctions were going to be on everybody's site, and consumers were going to go where they were already going." FairMarket then started outsourcing auction services and eventually created its auction network in 1999. The company's first clients included Microsoft's MSN, Excite@Home, and Dell Computer.

In an effort to sell large quantities of seasonal goods and excess inventories, companies are implementing FairMarket's auction method. *InfoWorld* explained the trend: "Many chief financial officers like the technology because it is subject to the truest laws of supply and demand, eliminating much of the guesswork in creating pricing strategies." Another benefit is the generation of traffic that auction technology creates, and when consumers find good prices in such a market, they are likely to return to search out another deal. In general, the more traffic on a Web site, the higher the advertising price on that site becomes.

FairMarket Network appeals to companies by handling the entire auction business, charging a monthly fee plus a percentage of the transactions conducted on their Web sites. FairMarket's clients either choose to distribute their auction listings to all members of the network, or to a select group of FairMarket-hosted sites, allowing for a targeted, private audience. If a person wants to auction off a set of baseball cards, the item can be made available to possible buyers on every other site that has a FairMarket auction, greatly increasing the item's selling potential.

In February 2001, FairMarket Inc. entered into an agreement with online auction giant e-Bay, which allows FairMarket's auction customers to list their auctions simultaneously on the 20 million-plus members' Web site. Mark Sutton, FairMarket's product marketing manager, discussed the deal with *CNET News.com,* explaining: "FairMarket has been all about helping merchants get their products out in front of different buyers. This helps extend that notion. We're putting those products in front of buyers in the biggest marketplace online."

One of FairMarket's largest clients is retailer J.C. Penney. This retailer considers its e-commerce business to be one of three major components in its distribution strategy: stores, catalogs, and the Internet. J.C. Penney wanted to use its auction site to increase the speed with which it moved clearance merchandise and reduce the expenses associated with regional outlets. FairMarket worked to help J.C. Penney realize these goals by tying its clearance site directly into JCPenney.com, ensuring a seamless shopping experience for customers. J.C. Penney's e-commerce vice president reported the results on FairMarket.com, stating: ''Are we going to close all of our brick-and-mortar outlets this year? Absolutely not. But what we can do now—that we couldn't do before—is evaluate a new clearance model against the old. We've reached a scale that makes that kind of question possible. And that is a giant leap forward.''

FairMarket client SAM'S CLUB, a major warehouse club, began utilizing the auction service in 2001 to test merchandise for selling price and popularity. The system also allows SAM'S CLUB to automatically identify and transfer products from its inventory system to the auction area of samsclub.com. FairMarket President and CEO Eileen Rudden explained these benefits on FairMarket's Web site: ''Dynamic pricing adds both excitement and value to the SAM'S CLUB shopping experience. FairMarket enables SAM'S CLUB to maximize yield on a variety of merchandise while maintaining ownership of the consumer shopping experience.'' SAMS'S CLUB planned to expand its product offering to include overstocks and end-of-season merchandise.

Based in Woburn, Massachusetts, FairMarket Inc. has offices and offers online auction services in the United Kingdom, Australia, and Germany. Its e-commerce model provides a marketplace for vendors and a trading place for person-to-person sales. The network provides an extensive online audience to its clients and allows consumers to access auction resources through a single Web site.

FURTHER READING:

''About Us.'' *FairMarket, Inc. Online*. March 2, 2001. Available from www.fairmarket.com.

Bray, Hiawatha. ''Action Junkie Turns Woburn, Mass.-Based Firm into Serious Rival to eBay.'' *Knight-Ridder/Tribune Business News*. October 13, 1999.

———. ''Woburn, Mass., Online Auction Service Makes Deal with eBay.'' *Knight-Ridder/Tribune Business News*. February 21, 2001.

Briody, Dan. ''Web Auctions Making a Big Impact.'' *InfoWorld*. September 27, 1999.

''FairMarket CEO Eileen Rudden Named to Mass eComm 10; Organization Recognizes Rudden for Leadership in Development of e-Commerce.'' *Hoover's Online*. April 23, 2001. Available from hoovnews.hoovers.com.

''FairMarket, Inc.'' *Hoover's Online*. March 2, 2001. Available from hooversonline.com.

''FairMarket Opens for Business in Australia.'' *Asia Pulse*. July 10, 2000.

''J.C. Penney Wanted to Sell Clearance Merchandise in New Ways. FairMarket Delivered an Online Solution That Met the Retailer's Strict Criteria.'' *FairMarket, Inc.* April 2000. Available from www.fairmarket.com.

Metcalfe, Robert M. ''From the Ether: Auction Network Service to Give Internet First Mover a Serious Run for Its Money.'' *InfoWorld*. October 11, 1999.

''NNM:FAIM.'' *The IPO Reporter*. April 17, 2000.

''SAM'S CLUB to Offer Members a Variety of Merchandise Through New and Exciting Selling Methods.'' *FairMarket, Inc.* March 12, 2001. Available from www.fairmarket.com.

Stoughton, Stephanie. ''Tech Tumble No Hindrance to Woburn, Mass.-Based Web-Auction Firm.'' *Knight-Ridder/Tribune Business News*. March 14, 2000.

Wolverton, Troy. ''eBay Rival Does About-Face, Agrees to Partner.'' *CNET News.com*. February 20, 2001. Available from news.cnet.com.

———. ''FairMarket Moving into Online Outlet Centers.'' *CNET News.com*. February 26, 2001. Available from news.cnet.com.

SEE ALSO: Auction Sites; eBay Inc.

FEDEX CORP.

With a workforce of nearly 150,000, holding company FedEx Corp. operates FedEx Express, the largest express shipping company in the world, handling more than 3 million deliveries a day. Three other subsidiaries—FedEx Ground, FedEx Custom Critical, and FedEx Freight—round out the firm's delivery services. While FedEx boasted a 51-percent share of the overnight delivery market, it spent most of the late 1990s trying to strengthen its foothold in the faster growing ground shipping market, which was being fueled by the rise of online shopping. Although FedEx made several acquisitions to build up its home delivery network, rival United Parcel Service (UPS) handled roughly 70 percent of all U.S. ground shipping in 2001.

EARLY HISTORY

In 1971, Frederick W. Smith raised $91 million in venture capital. After adding $4 million of inherited money to his funding, Smith purchased a used aircraft company in Little Rock, Arkansas. He began using the aircraft to provide overnight delivery services for envelopes and small packages being shipped within the United States. Smith eventually named his business Federal Express. Operations at Memphis International Airport in Tennessee were established in 1973. By then, Federal Express owned a fleet of 14 Dassault Falcon airplanes and employed nearly 400 workers. Services included both overnight and two-day package and envelope delivery services, as well as Courier Pak. The firm began marketing itself as "a freight service company with 550-mile-per-hour delivery trucks." When Smith found himself struggling to pay expenses, including payroll, he approached venture capitalist General Dynamics for a loan. After his funding request was rejected, Smith flew to Las Vegas, Nevada, where he won $27,000 at the black jack tables.

Smith's tenacity paid off in 1976, when the firm achieved profitability for the first time. Federal express launched a direct mail advertising campaign to boost its visibility. With roughly 19,000 packages delivered every day, sales reached $3.6 million. In 1977, the firm benefited from a strike by employees of rival UPS and the bankruptcy of another competitor, REA Express. The U.S. government also loosened airline regulations, allowing Federal Express to use larger aircraft, such as Boeing 727s, and take advantage of more flexible flight schedules. Sales grew to $110 million, and earnings reached $8 million. In April of 1978, the firm conducted its initial public offering. The New York Stock Exchange began listing Federal Express shares that December. In 1979, FedEx began using a centralized computer system known as COSMOS to track packages, routes, weather, vehicles, and employees. Soon thereafter, a digitally assisted dispatch system (DADS) was put in place to allow clients to electronically request pickups.

By the 1980s, package delivery rates had reached 65,000 per day. The firm operated units in nearly 90 U.S. cities. Advertising agency Ally & Gargano developed the firm's first major television advertising campaign in 1981, with the tag line, "Federal Express: When it absolutely positively has to be there overnight." That year, the firm launched its FedEx Overnight Letter and began international service to Canada. By then, Federal Express had become the leading airfreight services provider in the United States. Sales reached $1 billion in 1983. The firm was the first in the nation to attain such high sales in less than a decade since its inception without making any mergers or acquisitions. A new facsimile delivery service, known as ZapMail, made its debut in 1984. It guaranteed delivery of five pages or less in less than two hours for $35. That year, the firm made its first acquisition, package courier Gelco Express. Other acquisitions soon followed, including businesses in Europe and the Middle East. International expansion continued in 1985 when Federal Express established a European headquarters in Brussels, Belgium. Sales grew to $2 billion.

The company's ZapMail service proved unprofitable. As a result, Federal Express discontinued it in 1986. To streamline operations and cut costs, the firm set up regional sorting facilities in New Jersey and California, which allowed for increased control of deliveries. Each region was evaluated via a new Service Quality Indicators program, which monitored overdue deliveries, lost shipments, packages sent to the wrong recipient, and other errors. Federal Express also began housing merchandise for its larger clients, making shipments upon request. Acquisitions in 1987 included Cansica and Island Courier Companies. The firm added to its international holdings in 1988, with the purchase of Italy's SAMIMA and three freight carriers based in Japan. Earnings grew to $188 million as sales neared the $4 billion mark. Federal Express also launched a new unit, called Business Logistics Services, which offered transportation and operations management to other businesses.

In its largest purchase to date, Federal Express paid roughly $885 million for Tiger International Inc. in 1989. Tiger operated an air cargo delivery service known as the Flying Tigers, which held runway rights in major metropolitan airports in Asia, Europe, and South America. The purchase allowed the firm to strengthen its airfreight services, particularly overseas, where sales nearly doubled. However, it also brought with it government safety regulation issues and additional debt. When the deal was completed, Federal Express was forced to contend with a debt load of more than $2 billion. As a result, the firm's international arm posted a loss of $194 million, despite the higher sales.

By the start of the 1990s, Federal Express held 43 percent of the express transportation market, compared to the 26-percent market share of its largest rival, UPS. The firm effectively brought a price war to its close when it upped its rates for the first time in seven years. The Malcolm Baldrige National Quality Award for service companies was bestowed up Federal Express in 1990. The following year, the company launched international cargo service EXPRESSfreighter and a new subsidiary known as FedEx Aeronautics Corp. The firm also decided to divest a 50-percent share of its operations in the United Kingdom. In May of 1992, Federal Express shuttered its domestic operations in Italy, Germany, France, and the United Kingdom, focusing instead on shipping freight to and from Europe, rather than from one destination to another within the nation. By the end of the year, sales had grown to $7.6 billion. The Business Logistics unit established a base office in Singapore and secured contracts from IBM Corp. for early morning parts deliveries, and from Laura Ashley, for inventory and transportation management.

Express packages delivered daily averaged 1.4 million in 1993. By then, Federal Express had grown into the largest overnight delivery service on the globe. During contract negotiations with Federal Express, the Airline Pilots Association began pushing for major raises, better benefits, and increased job security for Federal Express pilots. However, a tentative agreement was not reached until three years later. In 1994, Federal Express changed its name to FedEx. To compete with the same-day delivery and early morning delivery services offered by UPS, FedEx began offering similar services for both packages and letters in 1995. The firm also began making deliveries to eight countries located in the former USSR. In early 1996, a blizzard took a $20 million toll on FedEx. Targeting the rapidly growing small business and home office markets, FedEx convinced OfficeMax to let it place self-service drop boxes at OfficeMax stores nationwide. The firm also became the first U.S. cargo carrier allowed to fly in China. A 15-day strike at UPS allowed FedEx steal market share from its rival. By then, the firm's fleet had grown to 590 airplanes and 38,500 vehicles.

MOVE TO THE INTERNET

According to a November 1997 article in *Fortune,* FedEx had been engaged in e-commerce since the 1970s with its COSMOS and DADS systems. Its PC-based automated shipping system, known as FedEx PowerShip, had first been implemented in 1984. The company's handheld bar code scanner system, known as SuperTracker, had been in place since 1986. "Smith figured out two decades ago that FedEx was in the information business, so he stressed that knowledge about cargo's origin, present whereabouts, destination, estimated time of arrival, price, and cost of shipment was as important as its safe delivery. He has therefore insisted that a network of state-of-the-art information systems—a sophisticated melange of laser scanner, bar codes, software, and electronic connections—be erected alongside the air and vehicle networks." By the late 1990s, more than 60 percent of clients were using FedEx desktop terminals and software to create their own labels and send electronic messages to the firm when their shipments were ready for pickup. Eventually, FedEx was able to use this information technology to determine the profitability level of each customer and negotiate price increases with those who actually had been costing the firm money. The firm also began offering supply chain consulting services, helping clients to streamline order fulfillment processes electronically.

In 1994, FedEx launched its Web site, which allowed clients to track package shipments online. Software known as FedEx Ship permitted shipment processing via desktop terminals. It was two years later that FedEx made its first major move toward conducting operations on the Internet. The company released its first version of FedEx interNetShip, the first service that permitted clients to manage shipping via the Internet. interNetShip also allowed users— both shippers and recipients—to access shipping information via the Internet and print shipping documentation. FedEx began offering e-business tools related to FedEx shipping and tracking processes in 1997. One year later, the firm launched FedEx Logistics to oversee its growing supply chain services operations.

Despite the firm's early e-business savvy, most analysts believed that rival UPS had gotten the upper hand in Internet-based shipping. This partly was because it focused on deliveries to residences, which began dramatically increasing as businesses and consumers alike started to purchase everything from books and CDs to computers and software on the World Wide Web. Hoping to compete with UPS and its leading domestic ground delivery service, FedEx paid $2.4 billion for Caliber System, a trucking company with a fleet of 13,500 trucks, in January of 1999. The deal was designed to strengthen FedEx's small foothold on the business-to-business ground shipping market and also allow it to launch business-to-consumer delivery services. FedEx established FedEx Home Delivery to handle its new residential ground delivery operations. The firm also established the FDX Corp., a holding company under which was placed the FedEx air shipping operations, as well as Caliber and RPS, a former Caliber unit that was the single largest ground shipment rival of UPS. Online holiday shopping, which accounted for $650 million in 1997, grew to roughly $4 billion over the holiday season of 1999. At that time, FDX handled shipping for only 10 percent of all goods sold online, compared to the 55 percent handled by UPS, which had forged alliances with the likes of e-tailing giant Amazon.com. The FedEx Marketplace was designed that year as a hub for e-merchants using Federal Express shipping.

In early 2000, FDX diversified into customs brokerage with the purchase of Tower Group International, a unit that eventually formed the core of a new subsidiary, FedEx Trade Networks Inc. The trading unit also provided trade consulting and international transportation and logistics services. In April, FDX changed its name back to FedEx Corp., and the core Federal Express business shortened its name to FedEx Express. Ground delivery operations, including RPS, were renamed FedEx Ground. The firm forged a deal with Orbit Commerce Inc. to jointly offer e-commerce services to small businesses—those with less than 100 employees—via a new FexEx eCommerce Solutions unit which would provide site design, online catalog development, transaction processing, and shipping services. According to a June 2000 article in *B to B,* the new venture faced many challenges. ''For starters, FedEx is late to the party. Web portals such as Yahoo! have for some time offered store-building services, as does nearly every Internet service provider. Closer to home, competitor United Parcel Service of America has provided e-commerce services on its Web site since 1997, through vendors Harbinger Corp. and IBM Corp.'' FedEx began offering its eCommerce Builder Internet platform free to clients in July. Along with e-commerce services, it included hosting on the FedEx MarketPlace site, with 5MB of storage and 50MBps bandwidth, and four Web pages.

Also in 2000, in an alliance with Amazon.com, FedEx agreed to deliver 250,000 copies of a new Harry Potter release to residential customers. The firm upgraded its NetReturn system in November, realizing that e-tailers were seeking ways to avoid many of the problems encountered with merchandise returns made by online shoppers after the previous holiday season. The enhanced program allowed shoppers to print return labels from their own computers and provided maps to sites that accepted drop-offs for returns. FedEx also continued to offer its traditional NetReturn service, which involved actually retrieving the package from the online shopper and sending it to the location specified by the e-merchant. To expand its less-than-truckload freight operations, the firm paid $1.2 billion for American Freightways Corp. in December. FedEx merged American Freightways with former Caliber Systems unit Viking Freight into its FedEx Freight arm. As part of the deal, FedEx assumed $250 million in American Freightways' debt. This concerned some analysts, since FedEx already was spending billions of dollars each year to maintain its costly infrastructure. By the end of 2000, more than 20,000 client Web sites were linked to the FedEx MarketPlace, and the eCommerce Builder unit had secured roughly 2,000 customers. Earnings totaled $688 million on sales of $18 billion.

In February of 2001, the U.S. Postal Services agreed to put FedEx boxes in roughly 10,000 post offices across the nation. A month later, in conjunction with w-Technologies Inc., FedEx began making its FedEx.com site available on most wireless devices, like cell phones. FedEx also continued working on the expansion of its home delivery network, which it expected to complete by 2003. As the Internet continues to change the way businesses operate and consumers shop, major shipping and logistics firms like FedEx likely will continue to benefit. However, whether or not the firm's new ground shipping and home delivery operations will help FedEx steal market share from competitor UPS remains to be seen.

FURTHER READING:

Cruz, Mike. ''Integration is Key to Survival—FedEx Says Companies Must Unite in a Collaborative Supply Chain.'' *Computer Reseller News*. December 4, 2000.

''FedEx Assists Online Deployments.'' *InfoWorld*. July 31, 2000.

FedEx Corp. ''Corporate Timeline.'' Memphis, TN: FedEx Corp., 2001.

''FedEx Corp.'' In *Notable Corporate Chronologies*. Farmington Hills, MI: Gale Research, 1999.

''FedEx Moves Ahead with Wireless Plans.'' *eWeek*. April 2, 2001.

''FedEx Picks Up American Freightways.'' *Mergers & Acquisitions*. January 2001.

Fonseca, Brian. ''FedEx Readies Online Returns Program for the Holiday Rush.'' *InfoWorld*. October 16, 2000.

Frook, John Evans. ''FedEx, Orbit Offer E-Commerce Help; Late to the Party, Shipping Giant to Offer Web-Building Services for Small Businesses.'' *B to B*. June 19, 2000.

Grant, Linda. ''Why Fed-Ex Is Flying High.'' *Fortune*. November 10, 1997.

O'Reilly, Brian. ''They've Got Mail! The Growth of Internet Commerce Has Raised the Stakes in the Boxing Match Between UPS and FedEx.'' *Fortune*. February 7, 2000.

Robinson, Sean. ''E-Commerce Delivers Growth in Shipping Industry.'' *Puget Sound Business Journal*. May 12, 2000.

Rynecki, David. ''Net Effects: Why E-Commerce Makes UPS a Complete Package, But Not FDX.'' *Fortune*. February 7, 2000.

Tatge, Mark. ''Going Postal'' *Forbes*. February 5, 2001.

SEE ALSO: Fulfillment Problems; Order Fulfillment; Shipping and Shipment Tracking; United Parcel Service (UPS)

FIBER OPTICS

Fiber optics is the transmission of data via light waves passed through glass threads. Most major telephone companies have replaced, or are in the process of replacing, traditional copper telephone lines with fiber optic cables. Additionally, local-area networks often use fiber optic technology. Single-mode fiber is used in conjunction with laser light to transfer data more than five miles in distance. Multi-mode fiber is used with a lower frequency light-emitting diode (LED) for shorter transmissions.

Fiber optic cables can carry significantly more data at a much greater speed than metal cables. For this reason, companies across the globe became interested in the technology, starting as early as the 1970s. For example, several Japanese companies, including Furukawa Electric Company Ltd., worked cooperatively to develop fiber optic cables capable of transmitting more information faster and more reliably than conventional microwave cable. Furukawa's developments throughout the 1980s included the first single-mode fiber optic connector using high-heat fusion splicing methods; a stronger, more heat resistant fiber optic cable; and a flexible fiber optic scope for use in examining the inside of pipes.

Western Electric engineers started experimenting with fiber optics in 1979. In 1980, AT&T Corp. sought permission from the U.S. Federal Communications Commission to build a 611-mile fiber optic network connecting major cities in the Northeastern United States. By 1984, fiber cables in the United States had reached 250,000 miles. Other leading telecommunications players, such as Nippon Telegraph and Telephone Corp., also began to focus on fiber optic technologies in the early 1980s. To bolster its fiber optic efforts, MCI Communications Corp. bought 100,000 kilometers of fiber optic cable from Corning Inc., which invested $87 million on new fiber optic plant facilities in 1986. At roughly the same time, the Williams Companies created Williams Telecommunications, a telecommunications unit which developed a fiber optic cable network that could be run inside unused steel pipelines; AMP Inc. spent more than $100 million in the development of fiber optics technology; and NYNEX Corp. entered the international long distance business by forming a $400 million joint venture to lay a transatlantic fiber optic cable. In 1988, GTE Laboratories developed the first fiber optic amplifier, and Bell Laboratories sent light pulses over fiber optic cables for 2,480 miles, setting a distance record. That year, the first transatlantic fiber optic cable was completed. In 1989, AT&T and Kokusai Denshin Denwa brought the first transpacific fiber optic cable into use.

Advances in fiber optics continued into the next decade as an increasing number of telecommunications companies, as well as firms in other industries, began embracing the technology. MCI Communications Corp. and British Telecom began working together to lay a transatlantic fiber optic cable in 1990. Cable company Cox Enterprises Inc. acquired a 50-percent stake in fiber optics vendor Teleport Communications Group. In 1992, Nynex Corp. revealed its intent to lay a fiber optic cable connecting the eastern United States with Japan via England and the Middle East. LDDS Communications, the predecessor to WorldCom, gained access to its first nationwide fiber optic network in 1995 when it paid $2.5 billion for WilTel Network Services, a unit of the Williams Companies. Chevron Corp. pioneered the use of fiber optic cables to monitor oil field production in 1996. Simplex Technologies Inc. partnered with Tyco into 1997 to form Tyco Submarine Systems Ltd., an undersea fiber optic telecommunication cable system. The following year, ADC Telecommunications Inc. introduced the EtherRing switch, which allowed less expensive implementation of Ethernet technology over fiber optic networks. Furukawa began developing and marketing fiber optic products in North America in 1999 via its FITEL Technologies Inc. subsidiary.

Fiber optic developments continued to improve telecommunications in 2000 and 2001. To improve the speed and quality of their networks, many organizations began upgrading to optical Ethernet systems. Nortel Networks, for example, started converting its North American ATM systems to optical Ethernet networks. Canadian financial giant CICB also began using optical Ethernet networking in Toronto. According to an October 2001 article in *Business Communications Review,* "the rationale for these activities is straightforward: simpler, faster and more reliable networking opportunities for rethinking server and storage distribution, and increased knowledge-worker productivity. The reason these are taking place now is the maturing of Ethernet transmission and switching, and the increased investment in metropolitan optical networking." Many industry analysts believe that all communications eventually will use fiber optic technology in one form or another.

FURTHER READING:

"About Fiber Optics." Port Huron, MI: AboutFiberOptics.com, 2001. Available from www.aboutfiberoptics.com.

"Fiber Optics." In *Webopedia.* Darien, CT: Internet.com, 2001. Available from e-comm.webopedia.com.

"Fiber Optics to the Fore." Washington, DC: National Academy of Sciences, 2001. Available from www4.nas.edu.

Rybczynski, Tony. "Optical Ethernet—Preparing for the Transition." *Business Communications Review.* October 2001.

SEE ALSO: AT&T Corp.; Bandwidth; Connectivity, Internet; Internet Infrastructure; Photonics

FILO, DAVID

David Filo co-founded Yahoo! Inc. with fellow Stanford University doctoral student Jerry Yang in March of 1995. Initially a search tool for the World Wide Web, Yahoo! grew into the leading Internet portal with more than 100 million surfers using the site every month by the year 2000. Filo continues to oversee the technological development of Yahoo! and owns roughly eight percent of its stock.

Filo earned an undergraduate degree in computer engineering from Tulane University. After completing his master's degree in electrical engineering at Stanford University, Filo elected to stay at Stanford to begin working on a doctorate degree in electrical engineering. It was there that he and Yang became friends in 1989. After having difficulty keeping track of his growing list of favorite sites with the new Mosaic software that allowed users to browse the World Wide Web, Filo enlisted Yang's help to develop a program that would let him to group these pages together by subject. Filo and Yang then posted the organized list of sites, named "Jerry's Guide to the World Wide Web," on the Web. After receiving e-mail from Web users across the globe about the usefulness of the list, Filo and Yang decided to catalog the entire Web, using several layers of categories and subcategories.

As traffic on the site grew, Stanford began experiencing bottlenecks and eventually asked Filo and Yang to move the site to the commercial sector. After turning down buyout offers from the likes of Netscape and AOL, Filo and Yang decided to postpone their dissertations and co-found Yahoo!, an acronym for "Yet Another Hierarchical Officious Oracle." Recognizing their limitations, the pair hired Tim Koogle to run the business, focusing their efforts instead on developing the technology (Filo's area of expertise), and creating a household brand name (a task well suited to the outgoing Yang). When the company conducted its initial public offering in 1996, Filo and Yang both became millionaires. Their shares eventually were worth billions.

As the head of technology, Filo is largely responsible for creating many of Yahoo's innovations, including its main sources of revenue. The firm makes its money mainly from advertising, specifically the banner bars and button ads that appear along the edges of Web pages. Thanks to technology that allows the firm to monitor a browser's online activity, Yahoo! is able to push advertising closely related to each user's interests. That technology also allows the firm to keep track of how many surfers click on an advertisement, giving marketing firms valuable information about how many people they are reaching. Other revenue sources include operating e-stores for retailers and designing Web sites for corporate clients. Although declining advertising sales and tumbling stock prices prompted Yahoo! to announce in 2001 that its CEO, Timothy Koogle, would be stepping down to make room for a new leader, Filo and Yang both plan to retain their roles at Yahoo!.

FURTHER READING:

Mangalindan, Mylene; and Suein L. Hwang. "Yahoo!'s Isolation Plays into Downfall; The Coteries of Early Hires Made the Company a Hit, but an Insular Place." *Contra Costa Times.* March 11, 2001.

Schlender, Brent. "How a Virtuoso Plays the Web: Eclectic, Inquisitive, and Academic, Yahoo's Jerry Yang Reinvents the Role of the Entrepreneur." *Fortune.* March 6, 2000.

Stross, Randall E. "How Yahoo! Won the Search Wars." *Fortune.* March 2, 1998.

"Web Crawlers." *Forbes.* October 9, 2000.

SEE ALSO: Koogle, Timothy; Yahoo! Inc.; Yang, Jerry

FINANCING, SECURING

All new companies need financing of some sort to launch operations. In some cases, entrepreneurs are able to simply dip into their existing personal savings accounts. For example, Jerry Greenberg and Stuart Moore, who co-founded Sapient Corp. in 1991, used $40,000 of their own savings and charged nearly $70,000 on their credit cards rather than seek outside funding for their new information technology (IT) consultancy. In other cases, entrepreneurs will ask a friend or relative for funding, as Gateway, Inc. founder Ted Waitt did in 1985, when he secured a $10,000 loan from his grandmother to establish his mail order computer business. Most often, though, new businesses will turn to outside sources such as banks and venture capital firms for startup funding. Because venture capital firms actually purchase a portion of the company they are funding, quite often they help to steer the firm's strategic development.

Funding for firms which have not yet launched operations is known as seed money or seed investing, while funding for fledgling upstarts that have already opened for business is called early stage investing. Banks and venture capitalists also loan money to established businesses seeking additional growth; this process is known as expansion stage financing. Wealthy individuals who fund startups are sometimes called angel investors. To gain access to outside funding, entrepreneurs typically submit some sort of a business plan, which details exactly how a new or existing company will accomplish goals like launching operations, finding customers, making money, and expanding into new markets. Typically, the most successful business plans, at least in terms of securing funding, are those with a clearly defined target market. In many cases, once officials at a bank or other funding institution determine that a business plan warrants further consideration, they expect the individuals requesting the funding to pitch their ideas in person as well. Many investors also favor startups with experienced management, a diverse and qualified board of directors, and an exit strategy, such as a planned initial public offering (IPO), which allows investors to cash out in three to five years, if desired.

In the U.S., securing financing proved an easier task than ever before for Internet-related startups in the mid-1990s as predictions of astronomical growth in e-commerce fueled what became commonly known as dot.com mania. In fact, many venture capital firms began to focus solely on Internet markets. For example, Internet Capital Group, founded in 1996, invested specifically in business-to-business (B2B) ventures, such as Internet Commerce Systems and VerticalNet. Dot.com incubators—firms that allowed startups to grow in-house before venturing out on their own—also began to emerge. One such operation, idealab!, eventually launched both eToys and eve.com. According to Coopers & Lybrand, venture capital firms invested roughly $6 billion in technology firms, including PointCast, Yahoo!, and Amazon.com, in 1996. This proved to be only the tip of the iceberg, however. According to *BusinessWeek Online* writer Peter Elstrom in an April 2001 article, ''For years, venture capitalists declared their mission was to build rock-solid, sustainable businesses. They would seed startups with millions of dollars, betting that two out of ten would hit it big, and they would be richly rewarded. When Net mania hit, they abandoned that approach and began rushing companies onto the public market with the ink barely dry on the business plans.'' Through the late 1990s and early 2000s, three of the most active dot.com financiers proved to be Tokyo-based Softbank Corp.; Menlo Park, California-based Benchmark Capital; and Andover, Massachusetts-based CMGI, Inc., which created @Ventures to handle its venture capital operations.

@VENTURES

One of the first Internet-only based venture capital firms, @Ventures was founded by holding company CMGI in 1995. CMGI had made its first investment in an Internet-based firm the previous year with its $900,000 round of funding for Book Link Technologies, one of the first commercial World Wide Web browsers, which also allowed users to search for and purchase textbooks. Book Link was later sold to America Online (AOL) for $30 million in stock, and it was with the proceeds from the Book Link sale that CMGI formed @Ventures. Initially, @Ventures provided funding to companies building Web communities, those providing Web tools for online advertisers and direct marketers, and those offering e-commerce, infrastructure, and content-related services.

In 1995, @Ventures invested in Lycos, Inc., a fledgling Internet hub founded that year. Less than a year later, Lycos conducted its IPO; in October 2000, it merged with Spain's Terra Networks to form Terra Lycos. @Ventures also provided financing to Web-based community developer GeoCities Inc. in January of 1996. GeoCities went on to complete its IPO in 1998 and was acquired by Yahoo! Inc. the following year. Early stage financing was also provided to Silknet Software, Inc., a customer relationship management (CRM) system developer that merged with Kana Communications in February 2000 and Half.com, a fixed-price online marketplace operator acquired by eBay, in July of that year. CMGI secured its own investments from Intel Corp. and Microsoft, which allowed the holding company to continue pumping funds into @Ventures. Other Internet startups financed by @Ventures included CarParts Technologies, Critical Path, ONElist (later named eGroups), Ikonic, KOZ.com, MotherNature.com, PlanetAll, Reel.com, Softway Systems, Speech Machines, Chemdex (later named Ventro Corp.), and Vicinity.

The aggressive growth strategy of @Ventures ground to a halt in the second half of 2000 when holding company CMGI began to flounder. In an effort to improve its performance, CMGI restructured its 17 operating companies into six different business units: search and portals, infrastructure and enabling technologies, Internet professional services, e-business and fulfillment, interactive marketing, and venture capital. CMGI also announced that @Ventures would limit new investments in 2001.

Standard initial investments by @Ventures range from $2 million to $10 million, and the firm most often acts as the lead investor when it participates in a round of financing. Typically, @Ventures takes a seat on the board of each firm to which it provides financing, and it also offers incubation services to businesses seeking such an arrangement.

SOFTBANK CORP.

The largest information service firm in Japan in the early 1990s, Softbank Corp. made its first major investment in the U.S. Internet market in 1995, when it invested in the upstart World Wide Web searching tool Yahoo! Inc. Over the next three years, Softbank paid a mere $374 million for a 31 percent stake in what became the world's largest Internet portal. Another major Internet investment by Softbank Corp. came in 1999 when BlueLight.com was established as part of Kmart Corp.'s efforts to develop an Internet presence. In May 1998, Kmart had launched Kmart.com, which neither improved the firm's faltering image nor increased revenues. Run by an inexperienced in-house staff, the site was a far cry from what Kmart executives envisioned. Consequently, Kmart sought out Softbank to secure the funding it needed to develop a new site, which essentially operated as a separate company. Although it was concerned about Kmart's battered brand image, Softbank was impressed with the retailer's customer reach. Roughly 85 percent of the U.S. population lived within 15 minutes of a Kmart store, four million people visited a Kmart store each day, and over 70 million Kmart advertising circulars were mailed out each week. Believing Kmart's existing customer base offered a significant advantage over rival Internet service providers (ISPs), Softbank agreed to fund the floundering retailer's Internet venture. Bluelight.com—which was majority owned by Kmart and funded by Softbank, Martha Stewart Living Omnimedia, and Yahoo!—

originally operated solely as an ISP. In just two years, however, BlueLight had not only grown into a leading ISP with nearly seven million subscribers; it also evolved into an online discount shopping destination. In August 2000, BlueLight secured a second round of financing-roughly $80 million—from Kmart and Softbank for expansion efforts.

Along with providing financing to startups like Yahoo! and Bluelight.com, Softbank also funded more established firms. For example, the first the firm invested in three-year-old e-commerce site-rating service Gomez Inc. in October 2000, after Gomez announced that it was postponing its upcoming IPO. Blaming weak market conditions for the delay, Gomez instead secured private financing from Softbank and other investors to continue developing new marketing and product initiatives designed to cater to both consumers and businesses. By 2001, Softbank had invested in more than 600 Internet-related companies, including Buy.com, E*Trade, Key3Media, E-Loan, Inc., Viacore, Inc., ZDNet, ADIR Technologies, Critical Path, Inc., Net2Phone, Inc., Reelplay.com, Verisign, Inc., 1-800-FLOWERS.com, Toysrus.com, and WebMD.

BENCHMARK CAPITAL

Founded in 1995, Benchmark Capital is best known for its $5 million investment in online auctioneer eBay in 1997. eBay's founder, Pierre Omidyar, realized that he needed help managing what was becoming one of the most highly trafficked sites on the World Wide Web. As part of the financing deal, Benchmark obtained a 22 percent stake in eBay, which was eventually worth more than $3 billion. Also that year, Benchmark, along with Sequoia Capital and Stanford University, contributed $20.5 million in capital to Internet and e-commerce consultancy upstart Scient. In 1999, Benchmark, again working in tandem with Sequoia and other venture capitalists, provided $122 million to Louis Borders, the founder of the Borders bookstore chain, to create Webvan, an online grocery delivery service. Benchmark also invested in firms like online mortgage vendor E-loan Inc. and B2B technology upstart Ariba Inc., typically offering an initial round of financing worth $3 to $5 million. In some cases, the firm spent upwards of $15 million over the life of a company.

IMPACT OF THE DOT.COM FALLOUT ON VENTURE CAPITAL

When dot.com upstarts—many of them funded by venture capital firms like Benchmark, Softbank, and @Ventures—saw their stock prices tumble in 2000, funding sources began to run dry. This posed a major problem for the dot.coms, most of which had been counting on additional capital for expansion. Many were forced to shutter operations, which drove the stock prices of the remaining Internet players down even further. Recessionary economic conditions compounded the problem, making venture capital firms increasingly leery of investing in new Internet ventures. As a result, venture capital funding by the middle of 2001 was less than half of what it had been during the first half of 2000. In the third quarter of 2001, only 540 companies had raised $6.7 billion in venture capital funds, compared to the 1,634 companies that raised $23.9 billion during the third period of 2000.

One group of e-commerce players who continued to secure funding after the dot.com meltdown were the online merchants peddling luxury items. According to a September 2001 article in *E-Commerce Times,* "venture capitalists are willing to bet that the upper class is still going to spend online for the things they want." For example, Blue Nile.com was able to secure a total of $7 million in funding from Bessemer Venture Partners, Kleiner Perkins Caulfield & Byers, and other venture capitalists in 2001. The jewelry e-tailer targeted professional men likely to purchase a diamond engagement ring or to make some other major jewelry purchase; working in the firm's favor was the low cost of shipping for objects as small as rings. Winetasting.com also secured financing in 2001, obtaining a $5 million round of funding from William Hambrecht in September. The site's narrow focus—specialty wines not easily found elsewhere—was credited for keeping the firm afloat while rivals like Wine.com went bankrupt.

Many analysts predict that even if the North American economy rebounds in the early and mid-2000s lenders will likely scrutinize the business plans of Internet-related ventures requesting financing far more closely than they did the dot.com business plans of the past. As stated in a November 2001 *BusinessWeek Online* article, "So here's how it works these days: The right company with the right technology and management in a potentially hot market is going to get a reasonable amount of money—but probably not much more than it needs to achieve liftoff. That's venture capital today—the way it was before the Internet bubble began to inflate."

FURTHER READING:

Berst, Jesse. "Financing Your Digital Dream: Where and How to Get All the Venture Capital You Need." *ZDNet,* March 21, 1997. Available from www.zdnet.com.

Blakey, Elizabeth. "Venture Capital Oasis: Luxury E-Tailers." *E-Commerce Times,* September 27, 2001. Available from www.ecommercetimes.com.

Cawley, Rusty. "Angel Investors Look for More Than a Business Plan." *Dallas Business Journal,* December 10, 1999.

Elstrom, Peter. "The Great Internet Money Game." *BusinessWeek Online,* April 16, 2001. Available from www.businessweek.com.

Forsman, Theresa. "The New VC Style: Deep Pockets, Short Arms." *BusinessWeek Online,* October 15, 2001. Available from www.businessweek.com.

Himselstein, Linda. "Robert C. Kagle." *BusinessWeek Online,* September 27, 1999. Available from www.businessweek.com.

National Venture Capital Association. "What is Venture Capital?" 2001. Available from www.nvca.org.

Macaluso, Nora. "Raising Capital: Dos and Don'ts for Small E-Businesses." *E-Commerce Times,* November 20, 2001. Available from www.ecommercetimes.com.

————. "Report: U.S. Venture Capital Investment Falls 60 Percent." *E-Commerce Times,* October 1, 2001. Available from www.ecommercetimes.com.

Shook, David. "VCs Go Back to the Future." *BusinessWeek Online,* November 14, 2001. Available from www.businessweek.com.

@Ventures. "Success Stories." Andover, MA: @Ventures, 2001. Available from www.ventures.com.

SEE ALSO: Angel Investors; Business Plan; CMGI Inc.; Dot-com; Due Diligence; Shakeout, Dot-com

FIRSTSOURCE CORP.

Firstsource Corp. is an e-commerce solutions provider. Its Firstsource Connect unit designs purchasing hubs, connected to various product distributors, for businesses looking to use the World Wide Web to streamline their procurement processes. The firm also licenses access to its FSP platform, which it uses to power Firstsource Connect, to businesses wanting to conduct operations online. En Pointe Technologies Inc. owns 43.5 percent of the firm.

En Pointe Technologies acquired First Source International Inc.'s online reseller unit, known as firstsource.com, in April of 1998. At the time, firstsource.com's primary activity was reselling computer and related hardware systems via the Internet to individuals and small and mid-sized companies. It was as a subsidiary of En Pointe Technologies that firstsource.com first began focusing on business-to-business (B2B) services. With B2B Internet sales outstripping business-to-consumer (B2C) Internet sales in the late 1990s, and many analysts predicting that online B2B sales eventually would exceed $1 trillion, many Internet resellers began focusing on business markets, particularly the services that those businesses would likely need to move operations online. According to a 1999 *Computer Reseller News* article, firstsource.com began preparing for this growth "by repositioning itself as an Internet portal for business-to-business transactions." Branching out from its initial focus of reselling information technology (IT) products at low prices to consumers and businesses, the firm began offering configuration, marketing, staffing, and IT services to small and medium-sized businesses, hoping to develop long-term relationships with clients.

Although IT products no longer formed the core of firstsource.com's strategy, the firm didn't abandon them. Rather, it began beefing those up, along with its new service offerings, in an effort to become a one-stop e-business shopping site. By the end of 1999, firstsource.com had added office equipment, office supplies, and telecom equipment stores to the site's computer hardware and computer software stores. A 24-hour live customer service staff also had been put in place to field questions from purchasers. The site allowed users to search for specific products, or types of products and services; make comparisons to similar products or services; complete a purchase; and monitor shipping. Lists of top sellers and weekly sale items also were offered. To facilitate the searching, buying, and shipping of products, firstsource.com used the EPIC virtual warehousing platform. EPIC allowed users to peruse, in real time, a variety of products from the firm's multi-distributor inventory. The technology also handled price quoting and purchase ordering, shipment tracking, and returns.

Early in 2000, firstsource.com changed its name to Firstsource Corp. A few months later, the firstsource.com site added a business resources section to its service-based offerings, which already included technology support services and financial services. The business resources store offered Web hosting and site design, business administration services, URL (universal resource locator) registration, business e-mail, company intranet development, and Web conferencing. The firm also launched its Firstsource Connect service. One of the first Firstsource Connect clients, TheBancorp.com, used the e-procurement service to research the pricing and availability of various products, develop billing reports, create budgets, and electronically approve or decline the purchase requests submitted by employees. In 2001, Firstsource allowed Solutions4Sure.com, a unit of Computers4Sure, to become the exclusive online seller of the nearly 300,000 products—including software, hardware, office equipment and supplies, and telecommunications equipment—it had been selling on firstsource.com.

FURTHER READING:

"En Pointe Acquires Online Reseller Division of First Source International." Los Angeles, CA: En Pointe Technologies Inc., 1998. Available from www.enpointe.com.

"En Pointe Technologies Devotes New Resources to Technology Initiatives at firstsource.com." Los Angeles, CA: En Pointe

Technologies Inc., 1999. Available from www.enpointe.com/news.

Ferguson, Renee B. "Bulking Up E-Biz Platforms." *eWeek.* March 19, 2001.

"Firstsource Connect Customized Portals for the Web Marketplace." *PC World.* March 2001.

"Firstsource.com Adds 10th Internet Storefront." *Business Wire.* April 13, 2000.

"Firstsource.com Expands Online to Provide One-Stop Shopping for All Business Needs." *PR Newswire.* October 25, 1999.

Jastrow, David. "Internet Resellers Alter Web Strategies." *Computer Reseller News.* June 21, 1999.

———. "Plugging In—Firstsource Uses Multiple Sources to Its Advantage." *Computer Reseller News.* April 17, 2000.

SEE ALSO: E-commerce Solutions; En Pointe Technologies, Inc.

FISCHER, ADDISON

Addison Fischer is considered by many to be a trailblazer in the computer security industry. He has founded and made major investments in several firms that specialize in authentication and encryption software. Up until 1996, Fischer served as a board member for RSA Data Security Inc., maker of the world's leading data encryption software. His current board seats include Surety Technologies and Xcert International. Fischer also is chairman of SmartDisk Corp., which he spun off in 1998 from Fischer International Systems Corp., a firm he founded in 1982. He continues to service as chairman of Fischer International.

After graduating from West Virginia University with both a B.S. and an M.S. in mathematics, Fischer began working on his Ph.D. As a college student, he worked for the university's computer center, where he gained his first experience with the development of mainframe computer security systems. Hooked by the seemingly limitless possibilities computer technology afforded to nearly all business sectors, Addison postponed his doctoral studies to work on an electronic stock predictor for the financial industry, which he completed in 1980. That year, he also was named partner at Duquesne Capital Management. Two years later, when Fischer founded Fischer International, his goal was to create security software for data housed on personal computers, as well as for a technology that was just beginning to grow in popularity: e-mail. Tao, one of the new firm's first products, used IBM mainframes as a platform for electronic messaging.

One of Fischer's most well known developments is Smarty, a hardware device that allows personal computers to decipher smart cards—small cards with computer chips that allow the holder to access data such as financial records, gain access to restricted areas, and purchase goods and services. In 1998, Fischer spun Smarty off into SmartDisk Corp. He initially retained a 60-percent stake in SmartDisk, but later reduced his holding to 38 percent.

The National Institute of Standards and Technology (NIST) and the U.S. Department of Defense's National Computer Security Center both formally recognized Fischer for his government report entitled, "Electronic Document Authorization" in the early 1990s. In 1996, Fischer became the major investor in public key encryption technology vendor Xcert and one of the original investors in Certco, an electronic certification software provider spun off by Bankers Trust Corp. The chief investor in RSA Data Security in the late-1980s, Fischer also contributed capital when RSA spun off its digital authentication technology holdings into publicly held VeriSign Inc. in 1998. Along with his many business commitments, Fischer also serves on various computer security committees established by the U.S. government to address issues related to electronic commerce, and has made presentations on such topics as digital signature methodology and digital telephony to the U.S. Congress.

FURTHER READING:

"Company Profile." Fischer International Systems Corp. Naples, FL: Fischer International Systems Corp., 2001. Available from www.fisc.com.

"Director Biography." Naples, FL: SmartDisk Corp., 2001. Available from investor.smartdisk.com.

Souccar, Miriam K. "Smart Cards: 'Building the Future' Drives E-commerce Pioneer." *American Banker.* February 24, 1999.

SEE ALSO: Computer Security; Cryptography, Public and Private Key; Digital Certificate Authority; Encryption; RSA Data Security Inc.

FLASHCOM INC.

Founded in 1998, Huntington Beach, California-based Flashcom Inc. was one of the first companies to offer digital subscriber line (DSL) service to small businesses and individuals. DSL technology makes use of the copper telephone lines already running from telephone companies into most homes and businesses, allowing recipients continual Internet access at speeds 50 times faster than traditional dial-up modems. DSL also facilitates connections to local area networks (LANs) such as corporate intranets. Unlike dial-up connections, DSL does not interfere with telephone activity. Rather, via the same dedicated line, users can make and receive phone calls and faxes despite the fact that they are always online.

The growth of bandwidth intensive applications, such as Web hosting, video conferencing, and online selling, sparked a demand for faster connections like DSL in the late 1990s. In fact, some analysts predicted that roughly 1.5 million companies would move to DSL connections by 2002. Ironically, the promise of this technology—what prompted Flashcom's founders to create the business—ultimately led to the upstart's demise. Like many other DSL service providers, Flashcom found itself unable to keep pace with the crush of orders it received. In December of 2000, the two-year-old firm filed bankruptcy.

When Flashcom was first established, it began offering DSL services to medium and small businesses in Southern California. The firm's SoloSurfer software was designed for a single workstation, while its MultiSurfer application used a single phone line to offer DSL services to all of those who were connected to a LAN. Touting itself as a full-scale digital solutions provider, Flashcom also sold long-distance services, firewall and other security applications, virtual private networks, and Web site development and hosting. One of the company's first major moves was to allow Internet Service Providers (ISPs) to resell Flashcom's DSL services to their customers. Many smaller ISPs had been unable to offer DSL services, mainly because the equipment to put the technology in place was so costly. Flashcom sought to make its DSL services attractive to the smaller players by having the technology already in place for an ISP to connect directly to its network.

Within months of its founding, Flashcom had expanded its services to major markets in Massachusetts and New York. Its monthly service fee—which included all equipment, e-mail, and round-the-clock Internet access—ranged from $59.95 to $375, depending on connection speed. In December of 1998, Crosspoint Venture Partners agreed to fund a portion of Flashcom's expansion. By then, service also was offered in New Jersey; Connecticut; Illinois; Washington, D.C.; and the Carolinas. A June 1999 agreement with Bell Atlantic allowed the firm to expand further into the Northeast, including major metropolitan markets in Pennsylvania and Maryland. Basic monthly fees were dropped to $49.95, and eventually to $39.95 in some areas. By the end of 1999 Flashcom was servicing more than 25,000 clients in 21 states.

ISP Sonicport.com, operator of the Seeyaonline.com Web portal, began offering Flashcom's DSL services to its clients in January of 2000. Despite difficulties fulfilling customer requests for DSL, Flashcom continued to expand into new markets, where it advertised its services heavily. In February of 2000, a *BusinessWeek Online* article stated, ''underneath the marketing push lie serious customer service problems. . . .very few of those pushing lots of ads come out well—especially Flashcom, which has become something of a flash point of subscriber anger.'' In fact, although Flashcom was providing DSL service to roughly 15,000 clients, another 15,000 orders had been backlogged. Some pundits likened the dilemma faced by Flashcom and other DSL service providers to the problems American Online encountered in 1997 when demand outstripped the online service provider's technology and customer support capabilities. To counter the negative publicity about its inability to provide service quickly, Flashcom brought in new management and spent millions of dollars overhauling its support infrastructure by increasing customer service staff and improving technical support.

Flashcom raised an additional $84 million from investors such as BancBoston Ventures, Behrman Capital, Capital Research and Management, the Carlyle Group, and Kohlberg Kravis Roberts & Co. in April of 2000. According to Flashcom President and CEO Richard Rasmus, as quoted in *Business Wire,* the fresh capital would be used for ''enhancing our back-office system, upgrading and expanding our network and operating facilities, and recruiting the talent needed to deliver a superior and constantly improving customer experience.'' In spite of its troubles, Flashcom expanded into Wisconsin and inked a technology sharing agreement with Texas Instruments Inc. in June. A month later, the firm acquired managed network services provider Worldwide Axcelerant Group. In October, Flashcom began using Norton Internet Security products to enhance its security capabilities, and Viasource Communications Inc. agreed to handle installation services for a portion of Flashcom's waiting customers. A major layoff took place in November. However, despite these efforts to improve bottom line performance, the firm continued to struggle. Not only had Flashcom's inability to fulfill requests for service quickly alienated a growing base of potential clients, it also had prevented Flashcom from securing potential revenue. In December, Flashcom sold its DSL lines to NorthPoint Communications and filed for bankruptcy.

FURTHER READING:

''ADSL: Flashcom Receives Funding to Accelerate Nationwide Deployment.'' *EDGE, On & About AT&T.* December 7, 1998.

April, Carolyn A. ''Acquisition: Flashcom Buys Managed Network Service Provider.'' *InfoWorld.* July 17, 2000.

Carlson, Caron. ''DSL Providers Scramble for Survival.'' *eWeek.* December 18, 2000.

''Flashcom and Texas Instruments Join Forces to Simplify Nationwide Delivery of DSL Services.'' *Cambridge Telecom Report.* June 5, 2000.

"Flashcom Teams with Bell Atlantic to Broaden High-Speed Internet Access Service Areas in Northeast." *Business Wire.* June 21, 1999.

"Major Residential Broadband Service Provider Turns to Symantec for Security." *Business Wire.* October 4, 2000.

Rendleman, John. "DSL Deployments Hitting Snags." *PC Week.* February 14, 2000.

"Viasource Forms Strategic Relationship with Flashcom for Retail Distribution of Digital Subscriber Line (DSL) Services." *PR Newswire.* October 16, 2000.

"Wholesale vs. Retail: Who Sells What in High-Speed DSL." *BusinessWeek Online.* February 17, 2000. Available from www.businessweek.com/smallbiz.

SEE ALSO: Bandwidth; Broadband Technology; Connectivity, Internet; Internet Service Providers (ISPs); Local Area Network (LAN)

FLOW

For some people, surfing the Web brings on a light, trance-like state of mind that stems from being totally focused on viewing information online. Known as flow, this state of mind can make one oblivious to surroundings, and to the amount of time that passes while they are online. This is similar to what happens when one becomes completely absorbed in a book or article. The concept of flow has been around for some time. Mihaly Csikszentmihalyi, a University of Chicago psychologist whose interests include creativity and socialization, began using the term during the 1970s when he conducted research in the field. In 1990, Csikszentmihalyi wrote a book entitled *Flow: The Psychology of Optimal Experience.*

Although flow has been studied in a number of areas, including sports, games, and work, it has especially powerful implications for companies engaging in e-commerce. Vanderbilt University Professors Donna Hoffman and Thomas Novak have conducted research on the concept of flow as it relates to the Internet. In the *Los Angeles Times,* Hoffman explained: "The implications of flow go beyond advertising and are even broader for online transactions and purchases. If the online experience isn't compelling, people aren't going to stay very long on the Web in general, and your site in particular. A consequence of flow is the reinforcement of a good feeling, so much so that it may be important for encouraging repeat visits or repeat purchase behavior."

In their research, Novak, Hoffman, and Yiu-Fai Yung of the SAS Institute indicated that flow was of importance to Web site designers and online marketing professionals. Creating Web sites that provide ample excitement for a wide audience was a major challenge for designers. If users find a site uninteresting, boredom can break a pattern of flow and they'll move on to another site or an offline task. This defeats one of the central marketing tactics of e-commerce, to keep consumers on a company's site as long as possible, increasing the chance they will purchase goods or services or view online advertising.

FURTHER READING:

"The Creative Flow of Change Makers." *Futurist,* May/June 1997.

Geirland, John and Eva Sonesh-Kedar. "Cyberculture Q&A. What Is This Thing Called Flow? Think Nirvana on the Web." *Los Angeles Times,* July 6, 1998.

"Internet Users Go with the 'Flow.'" *USA Today,* April 29, 1996. Available from www.usatoday.com.

Novak, Thomas P., Donna L. Hoffman, and Yiu-Fai Yung. "Measuring the Customer Experience in Online Environments: A Structural Modeling Approach." *eLab,* October 7, 1999. Available from www2000.ogsm.vanderbilt.edu/flow.

SEE ALSO: Attention Economy

FORECASTING, BUSINESS

Business forecasting has always been one component of running an enterprise. However, forecasting traditionally was based less on concrete and comprehensive data than on face-to-face meetings and common sense. In recent years, business forecasting has developed into a much more scientific endeavor, with a host of theories, methods, and techniques designed for forecasting certain types of data. The development of information technologies and the Internet propelled this development into overdrive, as companies not only adopted such technologies into their business practices, but into forecasting schemes as well. In the 2000s, projecting the optimal levels of goods to buy or products to produce involved sophisticated software and electronic networks that incorporate mounds of data and advanced mathematical algorithms tailored to a company's particular market conditions and line of business.

Business forecasting involves a wide range of tools, including simple electronic spreadsheets, enterprise resource planning (ERP) and electronic data interchange (EDI) networks, advanced supply chain management systems, and other Web-enabled technologies. The practice attempts to pinpoint key factors in business production and extrapolate from given data sets to produce accurate projections for future costs, revenues, and opportunities. This normally is done with an eye toward adjusting current and near-future business practices to take maximum advantage of expectations.

In the Internet age, the field of business forecasting was propelled by three interrelated phenomena. First, the Internet provided a new series of tools to aid the science of business forecasting. Second, business forecasting had to take the Internet itself into account in trying to construct viable models and make predictions. Finally, the Internet fostered vastly accelerated transformations in all areas of business that made the job of business forecasters that much more exacting. By the 2000s, as the Internet and its myriad functions highlighted the central importance of information in economic activity, more and more companies came to recognize the value, and often the necessity, of business forecasting techniques and systems.

Business forecasting is indeed big business, with companies investing tremendous resources in systems, time, and employees aimed at bringing useful projections into the planning process. According to a survey by the Hudson, Ohio-based AnswerThink Consulting Group, which specializes in studies of business planning, the average U.S. company spends more than 25,000 person-days on business forecasting and related activities for every billion dollars of revenue.

Companies have a vast array of business forecasting systems and software from which to choose, but choosing the correct one for their particular needs requires a good deal of investigation. According to the *Journal of Business Forecasting Methods & Systems,* any forecasting system needs to be able to facilitate data-sharing partnerships between businesses, accept input from several different data sources and platforms, operate on an open architecture, and feature an array of analysis techniques and approaches.

Forecasting systems draw on several sources for their forecasting input, including databases, e-mails, documents, and Web sites. After processing data from various sources, sophisticated forecasting systems integrate all the necessary data into a single spreadsheet, which the company can then manipulate by entering in various projections—such as different estimates of future sales—that the system will incorporate into a new readout.

A flexible and sound architecture is crucial, particularly in the fast-paced, rapidly developing Internet economy. If a system's base is rigid or inadequate, it can be impossible to reconfigure to adjust to changing market conditions. Along the same lines, according to the *Journal of Business Forecasting Methods & Systems,* it's important to invest in systems that will remain useful over the long term, weathering alterations in the business climate.

One of the distinguishing characteristics of forecasting systems is the mathematical algorithms they use to take various factors into account. For example, most forecasting systems arrange relevant data into hierarchies, such as a consumer hierarchy, a supply hierarchy, a geography hierarchy, and so on. To return a useful forecast, the system can't simply allocate down each hierarchy separately, but must account for the ways in which those dimensions interact with each other. Moreover, the degree of this interaction varies according to the type of business in which a company is engaged. Thus, businesses need to fine-tune their allocation algorithms in order to receive useful forecasts.

According to the *Journal of Business Forecasting Methods & Systems,* there are three models of business forecasting systems. In the time-series model, data simply is projected forward based on an established method—of which there are several, including the moving average, the simple average, exponential smoothing, decomposition, and Box-Jenkins. Each of these methods applies various formulas to the same basic premise: data patterns from the recent past will continue more or less unabated into the future. To conduct a forecast using the time-series model, one need only plug available historical data into the formulas established by one or more of the above methods. Obviously, the time-series model is the most useful means for forecasting when the relevant historical data reveals smooth and stable patterns. Where jumps and anomalies do occur, the time-series model may still be useful, providing those jumps can be accounted for.

The second forecasting model is cause-and-effect. In this model, one assumes a cause, or driver of activity, that determines an outcome. For instance, a company may assume that, for a particular data set, the cause is an investment in information technology, and the effect is sales. This model requires the historical data not only of the factor with which one is concerned (in this case, sales), but also of that factor's determined cause (here, information technology expenditures). It is assumed, of course, that the cause-and-effect relationship is relatively stable and easily quantifiable.

The third primary forecasting model is known as the judgmental model. In this case, one attempts to produce a forecast where there is no useful historical data. A company might choose to use the judgmental model when it attempts to project sales for a brand new product, or when market conditions have qualitatively changed, rendering previous data obsolete. In addition, according to the *Journal of Business Forecasting Methods & Systems,* this model is useful when the bulk of sales derives only from a relative handful of customers. To proceed in the absence of historical data, alternative data is collected by way of experts in the field, prospective customers, trade groups, business partners, or any other relevant source of information.

Business forecasting systems often work hand-in-hand with supply chain management systems. In such systems, all partners in the supply chain can electronically oversee all movement of components within that supply chain and gear the chain toward maximum efficiency. The Internet has proven to be a panacea in this field, and business forecasting systems allow partners to project the optimal flow of components into the future so that companies can try to meet optimal levels rather than continually catch up to them.

In integrated supply chain networks, for instance, a single company in the supply chain can enter slight changes in their own production or purchasing schedules for all parties to see, and the forecasting system immediately processes the effects of those changes through the entire supply chain, allowing each company to adjust their own schedules accordingly. With business relationships and supply chains growing increasingly complex—particularly in the world of e-commerce, with heavy reliance on logistics outsourcing and just-in-time delivery—such forecasting systems become crucial for companies and networks to remain efficient.

FURTHER READING:

Allen, David. "Looking Forwards." *Management Accounting.* March 2000.

Culberston, Scott; Jim Burruss; and Lee Buddess. "Control System Approach to E-commerce Fulfillment." *Journal of Business Forecasting Methods & Systems.* Winter 2000/2001.

Jain, Chaman L. "Which Forecasting Model Should We Use?" *Journal of Business Forecasting Methods & Systems.* Fall 2000.

Lapide, Larry. "New Developments in Business Forecasting: The Internet Does Not Eliminate the Need to Forecast." *Journal of Business Forecasting Methods & Systems.* Fall 2000.

McKeefry, Hailey Lynne. "Adding More Science to the Art of Forecasting." *Ebn.* March 5, 2001.

Safavi, Alex. "Choosing the Right Forecasting Software and System." *Journal of Business Forecasting Methods & Systems.* Fall 2000.

"Squeeze the Process." *CMA Management.* Oct 1999.

SEE ALSO: Data Mining; Electronic Data Interchange (EDI); Enterprise Resource Planning (ERP); Forecasting, Technological; Scenario Planning; Simulation Software; Supply Chain Management

FORECASTING, TECHNOLOGICAL

In order to effectively prepare business strategies in the technologically fast-paced worlds of e-commerce, information technology, and the global economy, it has become important for companies and policy makers to look into the future with sophisticated models and techniques to determine the course of technological change. The field of technological forecasting, more commonly referred to as foresight studies, emerged as an energetic and vibrant area of study and practice in the 1960s. Although its methods and, more importantly, its purposes have shifted, it has continued to develop into the 21st century. By the early 2000s, the United States—and indeed much of the global economy—was entirely dependent on rapidly developing information technology and other sophisticated technologies, operating in the context of increased organizational complexity. Thus, technology was not only increasingly important and influential, but its pace of development was accelerating, rendering the task of foresight studies all the more significant and challenging.

While the 1960s witnessed the coalescence of various practices and techniques into a coherent and systematic field of study, the roots of technological forecasting reach back even further. According to *Technological Forecasting and Social Change,* perhaps the first organized and systematic attempt at comprehensive technological forecasting was the study—conducted under the auspices of President Franklin D. Roosevelt's National Resource Commission in 1935—of the likely future of 13 major inventions for the purpose of assessing their possible social and economic impacts. However, it was in the 1960s, when post-World War II economic development produced rapid and influential technological innovations, that researchers began to systematically organize the field and devise a number of standard observations and techniques.

The S-Shaped Logistic Curve is a technique that highlights an S-shaped technological development curve divided into three stages: the relatively lackluster period of initial growth, in which the emergent technology struggles to distinguish and assert itself as a viable force against its competitors; the subsequent period of accelerated growth once the technology has proven superior and proceeds to edge out existing technologies; and the maturation stage, characterized by a leveling off of growth patterns as the technology reaches an equilibrium with its economy. To take maximum advantage of the S-shaped curve, businesses employ sophisticated mathematical models. These pinpoint the most advantageous strategy of exploiting the technology's natural growth.

Envelope curves involve a series of S-curves based on the development of successive generations of particular technologies. In this scenario, each generation improves upon its predecessor, creating an overall envelope curve of the generations' individual S-shaped curves. In this way, analysts can study the development of technologies over time and devise methods for the extrapolation of knowledge into the future.

At the heart of foresight studies was the Delphi Method, which takes its name from the prophetic oracle of Greek antiquity. First developed by the Rand Corporation, the Delphi Method assumes that the best source of predictive information for any given technological field is the technical experts in that field. Thus, building a technological forecast begins with simply querying a committee of experts as to where they believe the technology is headed. To avoid the biases of or pressure from dominant players in the field, the Delphi Method insists that experts participate in such a committee anonymously. Once panel members are assembled—by virtue of peer selection, honors and awards, involvement and rank in a professional society, or other qualifications—the director of the Delphi procedure queries members individually on the course of development for that particular technology. For instance, the director may ask an expert his or her opinions as to the likely timing and impact of certain technological breakthroughs. After each round of questioning, the directors analyze the information derived from that round and organize it for panel members to consider in the next round. Panel members analyze the reasoning behind other members' predictions and reconsider their own views; through an iterative process, members come to reach a viable consensus in their predictions. After a satisfactory consensus is achieved, the director organizes the findings into a final report, upon which a company bases its own technological forecast and accordant strategies.

Technological forecasting covers a wide swath of analytical activities. In addition to the effort by businesses to map out commercially viable roadmaps for technological development, the field includes more social and diffuse measurements as well. For example, governments use national foresight studies to assess the course and impact of technological change for the purposes of effecting public policy. This includes what is known as technology assessment (TA) or social impact analysis, which examines the likely long-term effects of technological development as its impact spreads throughout society. Meanwhile, the uses of technological forecasting are influenced by the attitudes of companies, governments, and individuals about the nature and course of economic competition, the involvement of government in technological development, and so on.

For years, the thrust of technological forecasting was on assessing the likely development and characteristics of useful inventions, and forecasts were measured by the extent to which predictions proved accurate. According to *Technological Forecasting and Social Change,* the difficulties of forecasting amidst great uncertainty were partly responsible for the decline in foresight studies' popularity in the later 20th century. However, the needs of forecasters also shifted as the century drew to a close, with an increasing emphasis on the potential for market exploitation as the thrust of technological forecasts. Thus, the focus of technological forecasts in the 1990s and early 2000s extended beyond mere technical aspects to include more comprehensive views of particular market conditions and the effects of technological development thereon. In the economic environment of the early 2000s, driven as it was by the development of information technology, the criteria for evaluation of technological forecasts shifted to whether such forecasts gave executives useful information upon which to base their strategies. Technology forecasting is now likely to examine, first and foremost, how a company can most effectively make use of technology to respond to market dynamics and enhance profit margins. Foresight studies also can help companies to establish their priorities in light of long-term assessment of technological and market conditions.

Foresight studies not only encompass methods and techniques for technological predictions, but also the focus on strategic research and the benefits and potential disadvantages or ill effects of specific technologies. Foresight studies will try to incorporate all available information in order to devise a series of possible futures rather than one set course of development. In doing so, any successful foresight study will avoid too much certainty in its prediction of various influential conditions. In other words, studies need to account for a degree of uncertainty in their variables. Other factors foresight studies need to take into account include the independent development of technologies in other industries that could affect the market dynamics of one's own technological field. Most crucially, technological forecasts should take into consideration the possible development of technologies from other fields that could spill over and affect the course of development in the field directly studied.

Propelled in no small part by growing concerns over the environmental effects of technological developments, recent years have witnessed an expansion in the range of individuals consulted for useful forecasting information. Going beyond technical experts, this includes a sample of the individuals or groups that are likely to be affected by particular courses of development. For instance, a government undertaking a social impact analysis as an element of a national foresight study might consult with environmental and consumer groups to gauge the likely effect of development on their interests, behavior, and attitudes. Meanwhile, a corporation may choose to bring in customers and academics to balance the opinions of the fields' scientific experts.

FURTHER READING:

Coates, Vary, Farooque, Mahmud, et al. "On the Future of Technological Forecasting." *Technological Forecasting and Social Change.* May 2001.

du Preez, Gert T. and Carl W. I. Pistorius. "Technological Threat and Opportunity Assessment." *Technological Forecasting and Social Change.* July 1999.

Martin, Michael J.C. "Technological Forecasting." in Marilyn Helms, ed. *Encyclopedia of Management.* Farmington Hills, MI: The Gale Group, 2000.

Tegart, Greg. "The Current State of Foresight Studies Around the World." *ATSE Focus.* The Australian Academy of Technological Sciences and Engineering. November/December 2000. Available from www.atse.org.au.

SEE ALSO: Forecasting, Business; Moore's Law; Scenario Planning; Simulation Software

FORRESTER RESEARCH INC.

With roughly 2,500 business clients, nearly 745 employees, and sales of $157.1 million in 2000, Cambridge, Massachusetts-based Forrester Research Inc. is one of the leading market research firms covering the Internet and related technology. Its early focus on Internet technology, which began in 1995, helped to bolster the firm's image as an Internet industry expert capable of predicting future trends in technology, business practices, and customer behavior. Unlike its rivals, the firm's projections are based on surveys of major corporations rather than statistical data analysis. Forrester gears its services, which cost anywhere from $5,000 to $10,000, toward senior managers, marketing and technology executives, and business strategists at major corporations.

Forrester offers a wide variety of services and products, including two types of strategy research: Market Focus and Core Skills. Clients who opt for the Market Focus package receive reports and briefs that analyze the trends and industries related to a particular topic, as well as forecasts based on that information. Core Skills customers receive reports and briefs regarding the issues inherent in operating an e-business. Forrester also offers Technographics Data. To obtain its Consumer Technographics, the firm queries more than 400,000 households in North America and Europe to gain insight into how consumers are using technology for entertainment, shopping, and money management. Business Technographics data is obtained via interviews with executives at more than 2,500 corporations with annual sales exceeding $1 billion. Interview questions relate to technology procurement.

The Advisory Services component of Forrester's offerings includes four programs: Web & Commerce Site Review, Web Site Review Boot Camp, Research Inquiry, and the Partners Program, which assigns a team of analysts to work with a business to develop and monitor some aspect of its corporate strategy. Level One clients participate in a kickoff meeting, two advisory days, four advisory calls or meetings, and two strategy workshops, while Level Two clients receive one less advisory day, one less advisory call or meeting, and one less workshop. Finally, Forrester's eBusiness TechRankings assessment tool evaluates emerging technologies for clients.

Forrester got its start in 1983 when, after a five-year stint at rival Yankee Group conducting telecommunications and office automation market research, Harvard University graduate George Forrester Colony decided to open his own market research firm. The new company, operated out of Colony's basement, first focused on telecommunications market research. Forrester eventually moved into the PC and networking markets. According to an October 1996 article in *Marketing Computers,* "Colony, credited with coining the term 'client/server' practically defined the course of network technology in the late '80s and '90s, and led many through its dark alleyways as the technology developed." The need for market research grew as new technology continued to emerge, and by the mid-1990s Forrester had evolved into a "leading prognosticator on Internet computing, having recognized early the effects that the Internet would have on business." Employees Mary Modahl and Bill Bluestein recognized the Internet's importance in 1993. Within two years, they convinced Colony to create the New Media Research Group to devote resources to analyzing Web site operations, new Internet-based technologies, and the demographics of Web surfers.

In 1996 Forrester was focused on three markets: strategic management; corporate information technology (IT); and new media research, which included the Internet. Sales grew 71 percent to roughly $25 million, and clients exceeded the 1,000 mark. By then, the firm had expanded domestically into both the Midwest and the West Coast. Internationally, it served both the United Kingdom and Australia. Worldwide employees totaled 135. *Business Week* ranked Forrester 13th on its "Hot Growth" list.

Forrester set itself apart from competitors by making bold predictions about emerging technologies. For example, the firm accurately predicted the integral role intranets would come to play for corporations. That willingness to make proclamations about the future of technology was not without risk, however. For example, Forrester incorrectly favored IBM Corp.'s OS/2 operating system over Windows NT, which later emerged as the clear winner in the networking industry. In the early 1990s, Forrester also forecasted the success of the System 10 database developed by Sybase Inc., which turned out to fare poorly. After much speculation about whether or not the firm would succeed if it were required to answer to shareholders, who might want to tone down predictions in the interest of profits, Forrester conducted its initial public offering in November of 1996.

Earnings in 1998 grew to $7.5 million on sales of $61.6 million. Forrester launched its PowerRankings service, which listed the best e-commerce sites among different categories of online retailers, the following year. To compile its list, Forrester surveyed nearly 20,000 online customers and also conducted its own anonymous shopping tests at the busiest Web sites in the following categories: airline; apparel; books, music, and video; brokerage; computer hardware and software; educational; general merchandise; healthcare; flowers; and toys and games. The e-tailers were evaluated for six different criteria: cost, customer service, delivery, features, transacting, and usability. Forrester eventually listed these rankings, as well as information about each category it surveyed, on a separate Web site. However, this site was later discontinued. In November, to bolster its international operations, Forrester acquired London, England-based Fletcher Research, a two-year-old market analysis firm covering Internet usage in the United Kingdom.

Forrester teamed up with Information Resources Inc. in June of 2000 to create Netquity, a brand marketing research service targeting brand managers selling products on the Internet. A few months later, BuyerZone.com and Forrester began offering market analysis reports to small and medium-sized businesses. In November, the firm began working with the National Association of Purchasing Management to monitor the utilization of Internet-based procurement by various businesses. Also that year, Forrester developed its eBusiness TechRankings. Sales grew from $87.3 million to $157.1 million, and net income nearly doubled from $11 million to $21.6 million. European research centers were located in London, England; Frankfurt, Germany; and Amsterdam, the Netherlands.

Despite the widespread downturn among Internet-related ventures at the end of the century, Forrester continued to grow. In the first quarter of 2001, both sales and earnings grew nearly 40 percent. The firm's latest service, Business Technographics, analyzed the purchasing behaviors of major corporations. According to CEO George Colony, the product was particularly helpful to firms undergoing cost cutting. "It helps our vendors focus their limited marketing and sales resources on the right places," he explained. It was during the second quarter of the year, when sales growth slowed to 21 percent, that Forrester started to feel the effects of the economic slowdown. As a result, the firm eliminated 111 jobs in July, which amounted to roughly 15 percent of its workforce. Forrester also divested Internet AdWatch, the online marketing tracking tool it had acquired via its purchase of Fletcher Research.

FURTHER READING:

"BuyerZone.com and Forrester Research Form Channel Partnership." *PR Newswire.* October 3, 2000.

Fattah, Hassan. "Would Wall Street Muzzle George Colony?" *Marketing Computers.* October 1996.

"Forrester Research and the National Association of Purchasing Management Collaborate to Generate a Quarterly Report on eBusiness." *Business Wire.* November 6, 2000.

"Forrester Research's Creative Thinker." *InformationWeek.* November 15, 1999.

Judge, Paul C. "Forrester Research: Sassy, Quirky, and Rich." *BusinessWeek Online.* May 26, 1997. Available from www.businessweek.com.

Konicki, Steve. "Economic Slowdown Hits Hard at Analyst Firms." *InformationWeek.* September 10, 2001.

Violino, Bob; and Rich Levin. "Analyzing the Analysts." *InformationWeek.* November 17, 1997.

SEE ALSO: E-Commerce Consultants; International Data Corp. (IDC); Internet Access, Tracking Growth of; Jupiter Media Metrix

FORTRAN

FORTRAN (FORmula TRANslating) is a programming language historically used in math, science, and engineering programs. It is recognized as the first high-level programming language. High-level programming languages are much closer to human language than machine language, through which computer hardware accepts commands. High-level languages eventually get translated to a primary, numeric machine language consisting of zeros and ones.

FORTRAN was developed by John Backus at IBM's world headquarters in 1954, and was released in 1957 after three years of development. IBM was trying to make computers more user-friendly to in-crease sales. FORTRAN achieved this goal because it was easy to learn in a short period of time and re-quired no previous computer knowledge. It eliminat-ed the need for engineers, scientists, and other users to rely on assembly programmers in order to commu-nicate with computers. Assembly code is a form of programming language that is closer to, and more complicated than, high-level languages.

FORTRAN's strength lies in its ability to per-form numeric computations. However, in *Computer Languages,* Backus explained that most people incor-rectly assumed FORTRAN's main contribution was that it allowed programmers to replace machine code with algebraic formulas, while in reality the lan-guage's main benefit was that it mechanized the orga-nization of loops within programs, a device that became critical to many scientific applications.

After its initial release, FORTRAN evolved through several different versions. FORTRAN II was introduced about one year after the original, followed by FORTRAN III in 1958 and FORTRAN IV in 1962. To avoid confusion, the American National Standards Institute (ANSI) issued a standardized ver-sion of FORTRAN in 1966. Because this version had some limitations, Canada's University of Waterloo developed a version for students called WATFOR (WATerloo FORtran), followed by an enhanced ver-sion known as WATFIV. ANSI later introduced FORTRAN 77 around 1977, which cleared up some of the uncertainties surrounding its 1966 version and improved its compatibility as well as its ability to ma-nipulate nonnumeric data and process files stored on removable disk and magnetic tape. In the early 1990s, ISO and ANSI developed FORTRAN-90.

Although FORTRAN is often referred to as being somewhat of a relic, computer science students were still taught the language in the early 2000s for historical reasons, and because FORTRAN code still exists in some applications. According to Computer-Literacy.com, in 1999 Fortran was still widely used in the aerospace and automotive industries, as well as government and research institutions, utilities and en-ergy companies, and within various scientific com-munities.

FURTHER READING:

Appleman, Daniel. *How Computer Programming Works.* Berkeley: Apress. 2000.

Computer Languages. Alexandria, Virginia: Time-Life Books. 1986.

''ComputerLiteracy.com Inks E-Commerce Pacts.'' *BizReport,* March 9, 1999. Available from www.bizreport.com/news/1999.

''FORTRAN.'' *Ecommerce Webopedia,* March 26, 2001. Available from e-comm.webopedia.com.

''FORTRAN.'' *Techencyclopedia,* March 7, 2001. Available from www.techweb.com/encyclopedia.

Leff, Lawrence F., and Arlene Podos. *Computer Programming In FORTRAN The Easy Way.* Woobury, New York: Barron's Educational Series Inc. 1985.

SEE   Programming Language
ALSO:

FRAUD, INTERNET

According to the U.S. National Consumers League, Internet-related fraud cost individuals and businesses $3.2 billion at the turn of the 21st century. The U.S. Federal Trade Commission (FTC) identified 18,660 instances of potential Internet fraud in 1999, with fully 25 percent of all consumer fraud com-plaints concerning the Internet, up from three percent in 1997. The Securities and Exchange Commission (SEC) received about 2,000 e-mails each day con-cerning possible online scams.

In many ways, the Internet seems tailor-made for engaging in fraudulent activity. A single individual can perpetrate elaborate, low-cost schemes while en-joying anonymity and a platform from which to reach potential victims all over the world. Among the crimes the Internet facilitates are identity theft and the generation of false, but valid, credit card numbers. Cyberspace also provides a new home for more tradi-tional forms of fraud that can be more easily, and often more damagingly, committed online than in the physical world.

The true impact of Internet fraud is difficult to measure. Gartner Group reported that a survey of 166 retailers revealed an online credit card fraud rate that was 18 times higher than overall credit card fraud, while the U.S. Secret Service states that online and of-fline fraud rates are roughly the same. Part of this variation is caused by reluctance on the part of con-sumers and merchants to report fraud. Since there are no national reporting standards for credit card fraud, and claimed losses due to alleged fraud often are tal-lied in with all disputed claims, accurate measures are difficult to come by.

VARIETIES OF ONLINE FRAUD

Internet scams come in a wide range of guises. The most common online fraud concerns the compro-mise of shoppers' personal financial information when it is released to complete a sale on the Internet. Even well known retailers seem prone to security breaches and hacking. A variety of sensitive personal information is revealed in such transactions, including a person's name, address, e-mail account, phone and social security numbers, passwords, and credit card data.

Online auction sites present prime breeding grounds for online fraud. The FTC reported that Internet fraud complaints rose from a mere 100 in 1997 to about 11,000 in 2000. The most common auction-related problem was that buyers failed to receive the items that they had paid for. The courts generally have refused to hold auction sites liable for any fraudulent activities perpetrated by sellers who use their sites. Potential customers are left to investigate the reliability of vendors through independent avenues. Some sites will post the names of fraudulent buyers who have been caught in scams designed to artificially inflate the highest price bid or in other ways fix the outcome of a sale. Auction site eBay draws roughly 16 million users each month. Nearly 87 percent of all online fraud cases in 2000 were believed to involve online auctions, with an average victim losing $600 per order. In addition to auctions, stock scams also are popular, especially the so-called ''pump and dump'' schemes in which con artists posing as investment experts fraudulently promote stocks via the Internet and then quickly sell their shares of those stocks in order to realize large profits.

Fraud perpetrators frequently utilize computer viruses, such as Trojan horse programs that arrive as e-mail attachments or JPEG images that, once opened, can steal passwords or grant hackers access to a user's PC. Dialer programs—applications that can terminate an ISP and dial another telephone number—also are involved. They often are presented as porn site downloads. Another online scam involves dot-coms whose sites closely mimic those of respected online companies. Web con artists use such sites to collect credit card information from inattentive online shoppers.

Identity theft constitutes a particular subset of online fraud. Hackers break into poorly protected servers, set up clone sites that resemble legitimate sites, and then use them to gather personal information. With merely a name, thieves can access Web directories or dossier services to acquire addresses and phone numbers.

Though most notorious online scams were perpetrated by teenagers in highly publicized cases of stock fraud, authorities actually are far more concerned about the international online fraud rings that have cropped up. The Gartner Group predicted that the most vigorous growth in online fraud in the early 2000s would involve petty larcenies committed by individuals operating from economically depressed countries, particularly Russia. The FBI indicates that stolen credit card data frequently is sold to Eastern European organized crime operations.

Among recent innovations in cyber fraud is domain name extortion, in which individuals receive faxes from phony domain name monitoring firms indicating that a third party is trying to register a dot-net version of a dot-com domain name that the individual owns. Then the firm offers to register the dot-net name for that individual, upon payment of a fee for the service. The U.S. Securities & Exchange Commission also launched an investigation of online frauds that attempt to sell investments in nonexistent nations, including New Utopia, the Kingdom of EnenKio, and the Dominion of Melchizedek.

Wireless subscription fraud also is emerging, since Internet security systems can't easily be transferred to a wireless environment. Merchants involved in fraudulent transactions conducted over the wireless Net that are completed with stolen credit card numbers are liable for the cost of the item, while wireless carriers are exempt from responsibility. In a wired environment, security is maintained by SSL protocol, digital certificates, and user name/password verification; in wireless environments, SSL is translated to wireless transparent LAIN service. This translation permits information transferred from a wireless device to become decrypted, at which point credit card numbers and passwords can be stolen.

At the end of 2000, consumer protection agencies identified a ''top 10'' list of ''dot-cons'' as part of a multi-national effort to combat Internet fraud. The list was compiled from complaints lodged at Consumer Sentinel, a consumer fraud database. The list included, in decreasing order of prevalence: Internet auction fraud; Internet access services that lure consumers into unknowingly entering long-term access contracts; credit card fraud; offers of free access to porn sites when a viewer or dialer is downloaded; ''Web cramming,'' or offers of a free 30-day trial use of a custom-designed Web site, which is later invoiced even if the recipient does not agree to continue use of the site; and finally, traditional ''real world'' scams transported to the Internet, such as pyramid schemes, vacation frauds, get-rich-quick offers, and miracle healthcare products.

PROTECTION AGAINST E-FRAUD

Most industry-standard encryption technologies only protect customer data during its actual transmission. An equally vulnerable point—the Web site's storage of personal data after the transaction occurs—often remains unprotected. Many hackers break into the servers that store customer data collected from past e-commerce transactions. Third-party sites that process credit card information also may furnish weak links. Thus, most online merchants rely on secure sockets layer (SSL) encryption technology to protect e-commerce data while in transit. However, it does nothing to safeguard information before or after it arrives on the server. Ideally, sites should possess a complex combination of firewalls, digital certificates, intrusion detection, access control, passwords, anti-virus software, and even biometrics systems to verify customers' identities. Retailers also can require the three-digit card verification value (CVV or CVV2), which is printed above the signature on the back of credit cards, to prevent unauthorized use of credit card numbers that have been obtained over the Web. Finally, transaction-risk scoring software exists that can spot deviations from customers' usual shopping patterns. One of the latest developments was a smart card payment option, which became popular in Europe.

Federal legislation concerning online fraud includes the Computer Fraud and Abuse Act of 1986, which authorizes both criminal remedies and civil remedies for such offenses. The Electronic Signatures in Global and National Commerce Act (''E-Signature Act'') of October 1, 2000 guaranteed that electronic signatures on legal agreements or commercial transactions enjoy the same legal status and protection as written signatures.

The Federal Trade Commission and the Internet Fraud Complaint Center (a joint initiative of the FBI and the National White Collar Crime Center) host Web sites where victims of online schemes can post complaints. In May 2000, the FBI teamed up with the National White Collar Crime Center to create the Internet Fraud Center, whose 161 full-time employees will conduct preliminary investigative work into complaints and then forward their findings to field agents. The FTC manages the world's biggest database on Internet fraud, though it cannot lodge criminal charges in cases.

Some electronic payment processors were developing special digital certificate codes that identify consumers as rightful credit-card holders. Also in the works were virtual, single-use credit cards. Ultimately, many firms hope that biometric identification systems, which read unique voice or retinal patterns, will provide higher e-commerce security.

The federal Fair Credit Billing Act limits consumer liability for all incidents of credit card fraud to only $50 of any unauthorized charges. Thus, online merchants often stand to lose the most from online fraud. Beyond the expenses of charge-backs and bank fees (which are higher than those paid by their traditional retail counterparts), companies that gain reputations as vulnerable to online fraud often lose customer confidence and business. The CSI/FBI Computer Crime and Security Survey for 2000 indicated that 44 percent of all companies interviewed revealed that they failed to report incidents, while 20 percent notified their legal counsel, and only 25 percent went to law enforcement agencies. More than half stated that they wanted to avoid negative publicity or would prefer to handle the situation themselves.

THE EXTENT OF E-FRAUD

A survey of 140 members of the Worldwide eCommerce Fraud Prevention Network indicated that many international firms consider online fraud is a serious but manageable problem. However, despite their assertion, only 10 percent of those firms surveyed spent more than three percent of their total revenue on fraud protection, while 60 percent spent less than one percent. Of the varieties of online fraud, one-third found the difficulty in prosecuting Web-based fraud to pose the greatest threat to their online businesses.

The Internet Fraud Complaint Center received more than 20,000 complaints during its first six months of operation, according to the FBI and the National White Collar Crime Center. Computer users made more than 37.5 million visits to the Web site. Auction fraud was the most reported Internet fraud, comprising 64.1 percent of all referred complaints. Several of the complaints involved monetary losses of $100,000 or more, including one involving more than $366,000. Internet-related fraud complaints to the Federal Trade Commission were up from 8,000 in 1998 to 23,000 in 2000 (not including identity theft).

FURTHER READING:

Atanasov, Maria. ''The Truth about Internet Fraud.'' *Ziff Davis Smart Business for the New Economy.* April 2001.

Beliakov, Victor; and Thomas Barnwell. ''Investigative Investing.'' *Asian Business.* April 2000.

''By the Numbers.'' *Internet World.* May 15, 2001.

Carbonara, Peter. ''The Kid and the Con Man.'' *Money.* March 2001.

Davis, Jessica. ''Watch Out for Top 10 'Dot-Cons' Named by Consumer Protection Agencies.'' *InfoWorld.* November 6, 2000.

Feldman, Amy. ''A Classic Scam Takes to the Internet.'' *Money.* July 2001.

Foster, Ed. ''Phony Lotteries, Domain Name Extortion May Be the Latest Internet Con.'' *InfoWorld.* January 8, 2001.

Haney, Clare. ''Auction Sites Hit Hard by Electronic Crime.'' *InfoWorld.* January 15, 2001.

Kandra, Ann. ''The Myth of Secure E-Shopping.'' *PC World.* July 2001.

McNamee, Mike. ''Invest in Freedonia!'' *Business Week.* December 11, 2000.

Radcliff, Deborah. ''Think Like a Crook.'' *Computerworld.* April 9, 2001.

Smith, Hilary. ''Internet Opens New Avenues for Wireless Fraud.'' *RCR Wireless News.* November 20, 2000.

Wallerstein, Lisa. ''Fraud in the 'New Economy.''' *Business Credit.* November/December 2000.

''www.Going-Going-Gone!'' *Consumer Reports.* May 2001.

SEE   Biometrics; Computer Crime; Computer Fraud and
ALSO: Abuse Act of 1986; Computer Security; Hacking; Mis-
       information Online

FUCHS, IRA

Ira Fuchs is credited with co-founding Because It's Time Network (BITNET), the world's first computer messaging network for liberal arts professors, in 1981. His work played a crucial role in the early development of the Internet and e-mail technology, and he continues to pioneer information technology projects in the academic world.

As an undergraduate student majoring in physics at Columbia University, where he later earned a master's degree in computer science, Fuchs was approached by Kenneth King, director of the Thomas Watson computer laboratory, which had been funded by IBM Corp. Fuchs agreed to take on some systems programming work, and when King accepted a position with the City University of New York (CUNY), he took Fuchs with him. At the age of 24, Fuchs became director of CUNY's computing center. It was there that Fuchs began to see a need among liberal arts scholars for messaging capabilities similar to those offered to math and physics researchers on ARPAnet, a messaging network established by the U.S. Department of Defense in 1969.

Fuchs began discussing his idea with Yale scholar Greydon Freeman. Recognizing that most campuses already were equipped with the remote spooling communications system (RSCS) built into IBM computers, Fuchs and Freeman began researching ways to use RSCS in conjunction with a mainframe system, a modem, and a phone line to allow messages and files to pass back and forth between universities. Hoping to generate additional support for their ideas, Fuchs and Freeman headed up a consortium of technology representatives from several universities in the Northeast that would soon serve, under Fuchs' guidance, as the executive committee to BITNET.

CUNY and Yale were linked on May 5, 1981, marking the birth of BITNET. By 1984, BITNET had connected more than 150 campuses. Interested in the potential of such a network, IBM began working with Fuchs and agreed to fund BITNET's expansion into Europe, Asia, and the Middle East, and also to pay for the establishment of a headquarters facility. In 1986, Eric Thomas created LISTSERV, mailing list software specifically designed to work with BITNET. As a result, BITNET users were able to send e-mail messages to a special LISTSERV address and then see their message automatically forwarded to multiple people whose names were on the list. While BITNET is no longer used today, except for a version called BITNET II that transfers BITNET data via the Internet, LISTSERV evolved into a popular commercial mailing list software program.

In the mid-1990s it became apparent to Fuchs and the rest of BITNET's managerial board—by then known as the Corporation for Research and Educational Networking (CREN)—that BITNET, in its original form, had been rendered virtually obsolete by the Internet. However, despite his network's short life, Fuchs' impact on messaging technology has been profound. According to Internet researcher Paul Gilster, as quoted by Barbara Fox in a *U.S. 1 Newspaper* article, "Fuchs and Freeman were the ones who took networking out of the technical and made it available as a practical daily tool."

Fuchs left City College in 1986 for Princeton University, where he accepted the position of vice president for computing and information technology. After spearheading the development of the university's Web site, he began working on getting the entire campus, including students living in dormitories, hooked up to the Internet. While working for Princeton, Fuchs also became the chief scientist for Journal Storage (JSTOR), a program funded by the Andrew W. Mellon Foundation that catalogs out-of-print academic journals and makes articles accessible online. In July of 2000, Fuchs accepted the post of vice president for research in information technology at the Mellon Foundation, where he began working on a project to compile images of fine art works and make them accessible to online researchers.

FURTHER READING:

Fox, Barbara. "Making the Internet Work for Princeton." *U.S. 1 Newspaper.* November 27, 1996. Available from www.princeton.edu.

Grier, David Alan; and Mary Campbell. "A Social History of Bitnet and Listserv, 1985-1991." In *IEEE Annals of the History of Computing.* Washington: Institute of Electrical and Electronic Engineers, 2000. Available from www.computer.org.

Indiana University Knowledge Base. "What Was BITNET and What Happened to It?" Bloomington, IN: Indiana University, 1998. Available from kb.indiana.edu.

"Ira Fuchs." Philadelphia, PA: University of Pennsylvania, 1997. Available from www.upenn.edu.

Olsen, Florence. "Mellon Foundation Hires Princeton's Ira Fuchs for a New Technology Post." *The Chronicle of Higher Education.* April 17, 2000. Available at chronicle.com.

SEE   ARPAnet; BITNET; History of the Internet and World
ALSO: Wide Web (WWW)

FULFILLMENT PROBLEMS

Online fulfillment is a cornerstone of e-commerce, encompassing all of the steps involved in purchasing and receiving a product, from order placement and billing to packaging, shipping, and beyond. Fulfillment problems arise when a breakdown or bottleneck occurs at some point in the process. Before the advent and wide use of the Internet, companies could often hide inefficient fulfillment systems, but with e-commerce this is not possible. Online fulfillment differs considerably from fulfillment models used for "brick-and-mortar" stores. Rather than shipping relatively small numbers of large orders to retail chains or distributors, high volumes of smaller orders for individual consumers must be processed. This presents a new set of requirements for retailers, especially in the areas of speed, connectivity, and customer service.

KINDS OF FULFILLMENT PROBLEMS

Most fulfillment problems stem from companies not being able to make good on promises of product availability and fast shipping as made in their advertisements. While accepting orders is quite simple, filling them quickly and efficiently is another matter. Among the factors that cause problems are a lack of real-time connectivity and integration, poor planning or forecasting, and trouble with warehouse operations.

Lack of real-time connectivity—either between businesses and consumers or businesses and other businesses—is a primary cause of fulfillment problems. Generally speaking, e-commerce happens very quickly. The amount of time that elapses between the sales transaction process and when a product is actually shipped can literally be a matter of minutes. To achieve this high rate of speed, a company's Web site must be integrated with its other back-end systems, such as accounting or inventory, and the information must be made available to all trading partners. This creates confidence in the fulfillment system and allows potential problems to be identified before they develop into actual ones.

Providing shipping and order confirmations, notices about problems, and up-to-the-minute details in real-time is critical to an e-tailer's success. As explained in *World Trade,*—Today's customers want to know a lot about their order: whether it's in stock, when it was shipped, where it is, and how soon they'll get it. Statistics say that Internet customers typically check on their order seven times before they receive it.

When a company's Web site isn't integrated with its other systems, orders may come in via the World Wide Web and sit for days or weeks until they are manually re-entered by someone into another system. Not only does this cause fulfillment to move at a very slow pace, it also makes it difficult for companies to monitor the status of their operations and introduces the opportunity for human error. Product codes, prices, shipping addresses and more can be accidentally altered during manual re-entry.

Whether fulfillment occurs between businesses and individual consumers or businesses and other businesses, effective fulfillment systems are built from the inside out, instead of from the outside in. What this means is that they need to be flexible enough to work with and accept data in various formats from computer systems at other organizations. In the world of e-commerce, companies frequently change relationships with other manufacturers, suppliers, and distributors. Having a fulfillment system that can accommodate different trading partners, no matter what system they use, is attractive because it reduces the need for making special arrangements.

Poor forecasting and planning also creates problems in the fulfillment process. Forecasting involves using information from a variety of different sources to predict business fluctuations, sometimes with the use of special software programs. When this isn't done, companies lose their ability to deliver goods or services on-time due to embarrassing inventory shortages, inadequate warehouse staffing, and so on. Besides forecasting consumer demand for their own products and services, companies also may need to consider production forecasts from suppliers they rely on during the manufacturing process.

Finally, because of the need for constant, real-time information about the status of products and shipments, modern warehouses are a requirement for successful e-tailers. When warehouses are operated under manual systems, inefficiencies and mistakes often occur, such as shipping items to the wrong address and long delays. In the early 2000s, companies relied on warehouse management software (WMS), overhead scanners, conveyor belt systems, wireless computer networks, wearable computers, hand-held bar code scanners and portable printers to streamline operations and automate the movement of goods through their warehouses. The way such technologies were used was complex and varied depending on the warehouse or distribution center. However, in general they eliminated the need for human involvement for tasks like checking incoming shipments against paper purchase orders and figuring out where incoming shipments need to go in a warehouse (to inventory or to another dock for immediate delivery).

EXAMPLES OF FULFILLMENT PROBLEMS

Although many e-tailers had fine-tuned fulfillment systems by the early 2000s, this wasn't always the case. The 1999 holiday season in particular was characterized by a bevy of fulfillment problems. That year, many companies beefed up their physical infrastructures, buying additional servers to make sure no consumer's order went unprocessed. They also spent large sums on advertising their Web sites. However, in the end many consumers did not receive the goods they ordered online by Christmas. Some orders arrived late, some were wrong, and others never arrived at all.

As *Planet IT* explained, ''Many starry-eyed e-tailers and dot-coms neglected the basics by not keeping a tight rein on inventory and inaccurately forecasting the heightened customer demand, analysts say. And when some e-tailers became buried in orders, they added fuel to the fire by promising unrealistic delivery times and capabilities.'' In addition to dissatisfied consumers, the mishaps led the Federal Trade Commission (FTC) to levy large fines on leading retailers for violating its Mail and Telephone Order Rule, which according to the FTC requires retailers to ship goods by the promised date, or within 30 days if no date is promised. Companies that are unable to do this must notify buyers with a revised shipping date and give them an opportunity to cancel their order if they desire. Toysrus.com, The Original Honey Baked Ham Company of Georgia, Macys.com, KBKids.com, CDNow, Minidiscnow.com, and Patriot Computer all received fines ranging from $45,000 to $300,000. The e-tailers eventually settled in July 2000 by paying $1.5 million in civil penalties for making promises they couldn't keep.

After the 1999 season, the FTC continued to scrutinize e-tailers who promised fast delivery. Macys.com, which in 1999 updated inventory on its site once per day to once per week, changed its practices in 2000 so that real-time data was available to consumers. In *Forbes,* Kent Anderson, president of Macys.com, explained the retailer rebuilt its entire order management process and developed a more timely, effective e-mail management system for communicating with customers.

Along with Macys.com, other retailers made enhancements and improvements to their fulfillment systems. However, according to *Warehousing Management,* Accenture's annual U.S. E-fulfillment study revealed that the 2000 holiday season was fraught with many of the same mishaps. The study, which included Web sites run by mail-order catalog companies, retailers with both brick-and-mortar stores and Web sites, and pure-plays (retailers who do business exclusively on the Web), found that 12 percent of deliveries were not delivered in time for Christmas, and 67 percent were not received as ordered.

FURTHER READING:

Cruz, Mike and David Jastrow. ''Christmas Fulfillment.'' *Planet IT.* December 15, 2000. Available from www.planetit.com.

Johnson, John R. ''Fulfilling Web Expectations.'' *Warehousing Management.* March, 2001.

Kontzer, Tony. ''Ignoring Your Fulfillment Systems? Bad Move.'' *Planet IT.* July 28, 2000. Available from www.planetit.com.

Leon, Mark. ''Online Retail Success Lies Behind the Scenes.'' *InfoWorld.* June 12, 2000.

Patsuris, Penelope. ''FTC Demands Dot-com Christmas Delivery.'' *Forbes.* September 29, 2000.

Rosen, Anita. *The E-Commerce Question and Answer Book.* New York: AMACOM, 2000.

Scheraga, Dan. ''The Nightmare Before Christmas.'' *Chain Store Age.* March, 2000.

Schindler, Esther. ''Interview: The Path To E-Fulfillment.'' *Planet IT.* December 8, 2000. Available from www. planetit.com.

''Seven Internet Retailers Settle FTC Charges Over Shipping Delays During 1999 Holiday Season.'' Federal Trade Commission. July 26, 2000. Available from www.ftc.gov/temp/toolate.htm.

Terreri, April. ''Bar Code Gold.'' *Warehousing Management.* March 2001.

Tiernan, Bernadette. *e-Tailing.* Chicago: Dearborn Financial Publishing, Inc., 2000.

Verton, Dan. ''Tis the Season to Build Long-term Loyalty Online.'' *Computerworld.* October 30, 2000.

SEE ALSO: Order Fulfillment; Shipping and Shipment Tracking

G

With roughly 800 consultants, Gartner Inc. is one of the largest information technology (IT) consulting firms in the United States. Its client base includes nearly 10,000 businesses, institutions, and other organizations which prefer to let outside experts advise them on decisions regarding computer hardware and software, communications devices, and other technology-related topics. In 2000, sales neared the $1 billion mark, and operations spanned 80 countries.

Gartner was established in 1979 by partners Gideon Gartner and David Stein to offer research and analysis regarding the information technology (IT) industry to buyers and sellers of computers and related devices. Six years later, the firm founded Gartner Group Securities, a unit serving the investment community with IT recommendations and information. Sales reached $40 million in 1988, and earnings exceeded $2 million. Britain's Saatchi & Saatchi paid $90 million for Gartner Group that year. However, Saatchi & Saatchi found itself struggling with cash flow problems, and less than a year later it announced plans to divest Gartner Group. Gideon Gartner revealed his intent to buy the company himself, and threatened to resign if anyone else purchased the firm. Gartner Group's managers conducted a leveraged buyout in 1990 with the help of Dun & Bradstreet. The firm was placed under ownership of a new company called Information Partners Capital Fund L.P., and Manny Fernandez was named president and CEO. A few years later, Gideon Gartner sold his stake in Gartner, breaking all ties with the company he had founded.

In 1993, sales reached $123 million and net income neared the $7 million mark. By then, operations spanned 20 countries. Gartner Group conducted its initial public offering, listing its shares on NASDAQ. The firm then used its fresh capital to begin making acquisitions, including IT system evaluator Real Decisions and IT research and analysis provider New Science. Profits more than doubled in 1994 to $15 million, and sales grew to $170 million. In 1995, Gartner Group bought IT market researcher Dataquest Inc. and MZ Projekte, an IT research and recommendation firm serving Germany, Switzerland, and Austria. International expansion continued with the creation of Gartner Group Japan, K.K.

In 1996, Gartner paid $2.5 million for project management software consultant Productivity Management Group Inc. The $4.3 million acquisition of healthcare industry technology consultant C.J. Singer & Co. marked Gartner's first foray into the healthcare industry. Gartner also purchased a 40-percent stake in Web content provider EC Cubed. The Parana Institute of Technology (Tecpar) and the Secretary for Science, Technology and University Instruction worked with Gartner Group in 1997 to establish a research center in Brazil that would work to modify Gartner products and services to meet the need of the Brazilian market. That year, the company acquired a 32-percent stake in Jupiter Communications LLC, a consumer online and interactive industry researcher that would grow to be one of Gartner's largest competitors. Additional acquisitions included Swedish management consultant Informatics MCAB, Singapore-based IT product and vendor database compiler Datapro Information Services, and French IT information publisher Bouhot and Le Gendre. Earnings grew to $73 million on revenues of $511 million.

The firm's aggressive acquisition spree continued in 1998. International purchases included the National Institute of Management Technology, an IT consultant based in Cork, Ireland; AICC Consultores and Technology, an IT and management consultant serving Argentina and Chile; Norbert Miconnet Information Technology Advisors, an IT assessment firm serving the financial services industry in France; and Wentworth Research, an IT consultant serving executives in the United Kingdom and Hong Kong. Domestically, Gartner strengthened its position as a leading IT consultant by acquiring market researcher Griggs-Anderson Research; financial services IT assessment firm Mentis Corp.; online security services provider International Security Association Inc.; and IT cost measurement and analysis software vendor Interpose Inc. Gartner also established an information technology training program in five post-secondary institutions. Both instructors and students were granted access to Gartner Group research.

Several events took place in 1999 that undercut Gartner's performance. The firm's largest shareholder, IMS Health Inc., sold its 47-percent stake in Gartner. CEO William Clifford also resigned to join a fledgling dot-com firm. Perhaps most damaging was the perception that Gartner had lost ground to competitors by not paying enough attention to the emerging e-business industry. As a result, new President and CEO Michael Fleisher announced the firm's intention to invest millions of dollars in developing Gartner's e-business services. To this end, Gartner acquired INTECO Corp., a research firm focused on Internet and e-commerce technology. The company also bought a 70-percent stake in cPulse LLC, which had developed an e-business application that tracked the satisfaction level of online customers.

Gartner hired 441 new employees, including 24 e-business consultants, in the first half of 2000 as part of a $10 million employee recruitment and retention program. Silver Lake Partners L.P. paid $300 million for a 20-percent stake in Gartner. In March, Gartner paid $80 million for TechRepublic Inc., a Web site for IT professionals. Four months later, the firm launched its eMetrix service, a real-time e-business monitor that cautioned IT managers and other executives if a major supply chain problem appeared imminent.

Gartner's Web site upgrade in January of 2001 drew criticism from both industry analysts and clients when several glitches remained unresolved for months. In June, Gartner released Gartner G2, a research service designed to assist non-technology executives utilize the technology they have to grow their business. This new service marked the first attempt by Gartner to target non-technology professionals. While Gartner continued to expand into new areas, it was the firm's core research and analysis that helped it to weather both the dot-com fallout and economic downtown at the turn of the century better than its rivals did.

FURTHER READING:

Ferranti, Mark. "Gartner, Align Thyself." *CIO,* November 15, 2001.

"Company Information." December 2001. Available from www.gartner.com.

SEE ALSO: E-commerce Consultants; Forrester Research; International Data Corp. (IDC); Jupiter Media Metrix

GATES, WILLIAM H. (BILL)

William H. (Bill) Gates is the founder, chief software architect, and chairman of Microsoft Corp., the world's leading software company. In 2000, revenues at Microsoft reached roughly $23 billion, and employees totaled more than 39,000. Gates's firm is best known for its two landmark products: the Windows operating system, which holds a 92-percent share of the global personal computer (PC) market, and the Microsoft Office suite, which secures $9 billion in sales each year, making it the firm's best-selling product. In 2000, Gates handed managerial control of the firm over to president Steve Ballmer, opting instead to focus on technology development, which is centered around the firm's new.Net strategy. Due in large part to his 14-percent share of Microsoft, Gates is one of the wealthiest men on the planet.

FOUNDING A NEW COMPANY

A native of Seattle, Washington, Gates became interested in computer programming when he was in high school. In 1973, he began his undergraduate studies at Harvard, where he lived in the same dormitory as Steve Ballmer. In February of 1975, at the age of 19, Gates and Honeywell employee Paul Allen, a childhood friend of Gates, began tinkering with a computer language known as BASIC (Beginner's All-Purpose Symbolic Instruction Code). The partners soon developed a version of BASIC for Albuquerque, New Mexico-based MITS, manufacturer of Altair, the world's first personal computer (PC). Because the creators of BASIC, two mathematics professors at Dartmouth College, had never copyrighted or patented the language, programmers throughout the world had customized BASIC to meet their needs. Gates and Allen used variations of BASIC as the basis for their new company, Microsoft, formally founded on April 4, 1975. Eventually, Gates also created DiskBASIC, a disk management program. Other variations of BASIC eventually formed the core of many of Microsoft's most successful products. For example, Visual BASIC was created in the early 1990s to serve an object-oriented language for Microsoft Windows applications. QBASIC was developed to serve an interpreter between BASIC and Microsoft's DOS and Windows platforms; it superseded GW-BASIC, the interpreter designed specifically for DOS.

In 1976, Gates dropped out of Harvard in order to devote more time to his new business. He moved the headquarters to Albuquerque, New Mexico and hired four new computer software programmers. Aside from his innovations with BASIC, Gates's first major impact on the computer industry came in the form of a legal contract. Gates devised an agreement which allowed hardware developers to use and sell variations of proprietary software languages. This contract eventually served as a model for future software licensing deals.

In the late 1970s, Gates oversaw the development and release of software products based on versions of Fortran and COBOL-80. He also inked deals to license BASIC software to Radio Shack and Apple Computer. Sales reached $1 million, and Microsoft became the leading microcomputer language distributor in the United States, due in large part to the deal Gates struck with firms like Sirius, Zenith Electronics, Sharp, and Texas Instruments, who started using Microsoft software on a rudimentary operating system known as CP/M. Believing that international markets were just as important as North American ones, Gates launched operations in Japan. He also moved headquarters to Bellevue, Washington.

Microsoft sold its one millionth copy of BASIC in 1980. By then, employees totaled 25, and sales had reached $2.5 million. In November of that year, Gates forged an alliance with IBM Corp. that would help to position Microsoft at the core of the PC industry. Microsoft became the exclusive developer of not only several programming languages, but also the operating system for IBM's first PCs. To allow BASIC to operate on Apple II machines, Microsoft introduced technology known as Softcard.

When Gates and Allen incorporated their company on June 25, 1981, Gates took over as president and chairman of the board, while Allen adopted the role of executive vice president. Two months later, Microsoft completed its MS-DOS operating system, allowing IBM to begin selling its new PCs. More than 50 microcomputer manufacturers had signed MS-DOS licensing agreements with Microsoft by the end of the year. Gates pushed into Europe in 1982, with the establishment of a unit in Great Britain. Microsoft's major product release that year, the Multiplan Electronic Worksheet, was named software product of the year by *InfoWorld* magazine.

STEERING MICROSOFT'S GROWTH AS A SOFTWARE MANUFACTURER

Gates oversaw the release of several flagship products in 1983. Along with the Microsoft Mouse—a device that enabled users to manipulate a cursor by ''pointing and clicking'' rather than using various keys on a keyboard—the firm shipped its first version of Microsoft Word, a word processing program that eventually would compete with Novell Inc.'s popular WordPerfect program. Although Word initially received a lukewarm reception in North America, sales in European markets were brisk. In November, Gates unveiled his firm's new Windows operating system, the success of which would be key in Microsoft's eventual dominance of the PC industry. Although it was based on the MS-DOS operating system, Windows looked nothing like the text-based platform. Rather, Windows employed a graphical user interface (GUI), much like the one used by Apple Computers on its Macintosh computers. More than 500,000 copies of Windows were sold within a month of its release. Also that year, Gates fostered European growth by creating subsidiaries in France and Germany, and total sales grew to $70 million.

In 1984, as U.S. computer users became more receptive to Word, Microsoft began selling roughly 20,000 copies of the word processor per month. The firm also created a version of Word for Macintosh machines. Windows continued to grow in popularity as well, with more than 200 computer makers holding MS-DOS licenses. Gates established Microsoft's first overseas manufacturing facility, in Ireland, in 1985. That year, Gates also began allowing the distribution of Windows to retailers. He began talking with Compaq, Digital Equipment, Hewlett-Packard, Texas Instruments, and other major IBM competitors, hoping to loosen IBM's hold on PC standards development. In response, IBM began forging alliances with Microsoft's competitors. Despite the deteriorating relations between Microsoft and IBM, Gates persuaded IBM to use an upgraded version of the Windows platform, which he promised would resolve several complaints users had about the system, on its next line of PCs.

Gates moved his growing firm to Redmond, Washington, in February of 1986. He completed Microsoft's initial public offering one month later, selling shares for $21 apiece and raising $61 million in fresh capital. In less than one year, when shares began selling for more than $84 each, Gates found himself a billionaire at the age of 31. Product releases in the late 1980s included Microsoft Word 3.0, which quickly became the top seller at Microsoft, and a Windows-based spreadsheet program called Excel. In 1988, Apple Computers brought charges against Microsoft, asserting that Gates and his cohorts had cribbed the ''look and feel'' of the Macintosh operating system when developing Windows. Apple demanded that Microsoft either pull Windows off the shelves or pay royalties of some sort. Gates, who had grown Microsoft into the top manufacturer of PC software in North America, with more than 4,000 employees, had no intention of meeting either request. By then, more than 2 million copies of Windows 3.0 had been sold worldwide, and annual sales had reached almost $800 million.

Revenues at Microsoft reached the $1 billion mark in 1990, and roughly 90 percent of worldwide PCs used either MS-DOS or Windows as a platform. As Gates's relationship with IBM worsened, IBM began looking to develop ties with other PC industry leaders. For example, IBM inked a deal with Apple to jointly develop a more user-friendly operating system that would increase compatibility between IBM and Apple computers. IBM also began to market Novell's Netware. Gates initiated his firm's foray into desktop publishing software in 1992, the same year Microsoft released its first televised commercial. The legal dispute with Apple was resolved in Microsoft's favor, despite Windows' similarity to Macintosh. Apple filed an immediate appeal, which eventually made its way to the U.S. Supreme Court, which rejected the case.

Gates's dominance of the PC industry continued to grow, and Microsoft's market valuation reached a whopping $25 billion by 1993. Multimedia efforts paid off when Microsoft's Encarta CD-ROM earned the distinction of consumer disc product of the year. Gates also oversaw his firm's diversification into network servers, which culminated in the launch of Windows NT, a platform for the network servers increasingly used by large enterprises. Gates had been working on Windows NT since 1990. According to David Kirkpatrick in a May 1997 issue of *Fortune,* the development of NT was part of a long-term goal of Gates, Allen, and other technology gurus: ''shunting the world's biggest computing tasks from mainframes to cheaper, smaller machines.'' This move began during 1970s, when minicomputers began handling tasks previously completed by mainframe machines. The development of UNIX by AT&T Corp.'s Bell Labs spawned the client/server era, during which time UNIX-based networks began handling database applications. In the early 1980s, Gates was unsuccessful in his attempts to forge an alliance with Bell Labs to work together on the development and standardization of UNIX. By the end of the decade, Gates had decided that Microsoft would develop its own network server platform, one that would closely resemble Windows and have the ability to run Windows applications. Like most of Microsoft's earliest versions of its products, the first release of NT needed quite a bit of tweaking. In fact, it wasn't until the launch of Windows 2000 that NT had evolved into the system Gates had envisioned.

While Gates's decision to push Microsoft into as many new PC-related industries as possible had allowed his company's brand to become one of the most recognized in the world by the mid-1990s, it also compounded the firm's legal troubles. Several competitors filed complaints against Microsoft, alleging that the firm repeatedly used anticompetitive tactics to gain market share. As a result, the U.S. Department of Justice began scrutinizing Microsoft. Hoping to bring the investigation to an end once and for all, Microsoft offered to alter its marketing practices in 1994. Although the Justice Department accepted the firm's offer, those who had raised the original complaints insisted that the settlement ignored several of Microsoft's monopolistic activities. U.S. District Judge Stanley Sporkin began reviewing the settlement, eventually finding that the Justice Department's settlement with Microsoft was incomplete. Microsoft and the Justice Department both filed appeals, which resulted in the restoration of the initial settlement by the U.S. Court of Appeals.

Work began in the mid-1990s on Windows 95, an upgrade to Microsoft's operating system that would completely alter the look of most desktop machines. In September of 1994, upstart Netscape Communications Corp.'s Web browser, which served as a GUI for the Internet much in the same way Windows served as a GUI for PCs, caught Gates's attention. As a result, he licensed technology from Spyglass and ordered the quick development of a product that would compete with Netscape's Navigator. Gates also unveiled Microsoft's BackOffice, a Windows NT suite that combined various server applications. In early 1995, Gates saw his plans to acquire Intuit Inc. for $2.1 billion quashed by the Justice Department, which raised various antitrust concerns regarding the deal.

REFOCUSING MICROSOFT ON INTERNET TECHNOLOGY

As work on Windows 95 was winding down, Gates began to realize that his firm was lagging behind rivals like Sun Microsystems, America Online, and Netscape in the burgeoning Internet arena. With the long awaited Windows 95 operating system near completion, Gates changed Microsoft's focus from PC operating systems to Internet technology. When the company launched Windows 95 in August, in one of technology industry's most highly anticipated product releases, it included the Internet Explorer browser, a direct competitor to Netscape's Navigator, which had secured 80 percent of the Internet browser market. The new operating system also included the Microsoft Network, an online service competing with America Online, Compuserve, and other Internet service providers.

In November of 1995, Gates published *The Road Ahead,* which went on to become a *New York Times* bestseller. He also recruited Michael Kinsley to create *Slate,* an online magazine first published the following June. Microsoft introduced Internet Explorer 2.0 to compete with the second version of Netscape's Navigator, and what became known as the ''browser wars'' began in earnest. Gates also began working with NBC on the online news source that eventually became known as MSNBC.

To aggressively market the Microsoft Network, Gates enlisted the help of MCI Communications Corp., the telecommunications industry's most intense marketer, in January of 1996. Although the Microsoft Network signed on its one millionth customer less two months later, it continued to lag behind industry leader America Online. To further facilitate Microsoft's shift to Internet technology, Gates reorganized the firm's four platform groups into three divisions. He appointed Brad Silverberg head of the new Internet Platform and Tools Division. In a major coup against rival Netscape, Gates convinced America Online to license the Internet Explorer browser, rather than Navigator. When sales of Windows NT, which competed with the UNIX-based servers on which corporate networks operated, surged 86 percent in 1996, Gates began paying closer attention to network servers. This was a sector of the technology industry that was being stoked by the Internet revolution, as an increasing number of enterprises began to take their operations online, some via corporate intranets and others via Web-based e-commerce endeavors. According to a May 1997 article in *Fortune,* ''Forget Internet browsers, forget MSNBC, forget multimedia, Slate, and the Microsoft Network. Gates's strategy is to extend Microsoft's hegemony from the desktop into the windowless rooms housing the servers, minicomputers, and mainframes that are still central to business data processing. If he succeeds, Microsoft could dominate information technology well into the next decade.''

While Gates did dump considerable resources into Windows NT, and its related BackOffice suite, he also preserved the firm's other Internet initiatives. For example, the firm released Internet Explorer 4.0 in mid-1997. By that time, Microsoft had reduced Netscape's browser market share to roughly 40 percent. Complaints regarding Microsoft's bundling of its Internet Explorer with Windows 95 to allegedly undermine Netscape's ability to compete led to yet another Justice Department investigation. It was at this time that reports began to emerge about alleged threats by Gates and his higher-ups to cancel the Windows licenses of PC makers not willing to install Explorer on their machines in place of Netscape's Navigator. The litigation resulted in a U.S. District Court ruling that Microsoft must sell a version of Windows 95 unbundled from Internet Explorer. Gates initially resisted the decree, insisting that his pro-

grammers would be unable to separate the programs without damaging the operating system. However, to avoid contempt of court charges, Gates eventually decided to allow computer manufactures sell Windows 95 without Internet Explorer.

Early in 1998, Microsoft bought Hotmail, a free Web-based e-mail system which soon became the leading such service. Sales that year surged by 30 percent to $14.5 billion. Valued at $466 billion, Microsoft was the world's largest company. However, Internet-based technology accounted for a mere $548 million of total revenues, despite the firm's success with several Web sites, such as Carpoint, Home Advisor, the Sidewalk city guides, the Expedia virtual travel agency, Microsoft Investor, and online bill payment service MSFDC. Although the firm had trounced Netscape in the browser wars, the fact remained that many of Gates's Internet endeavors had simply fallen short of expectations, leaving Microsoft reliant on the nearly saturated PC operating system and PC applications suite industries. As a result, growth at Gates's software behemoth began to decelerate in the late 1990s. Adding to the downturn were delays in the release of Windows NT 5.0, a product Gates needed to pursue his plan to storm the network server market. By many accounts the most complex program ever developed by the company, the newest version of Windows NT was simply taking much longer to develop than expected. Recognizing that a major overhaul was in order, Gates named longtime Microsoft employee Steven Ballmer president in 1998.

Early in 1999, Ballmer and Gates launched a major client-focused reorganization at Microsoft. For the first time in its history, Microsoft dumped its product-based arrangement and organized itself around five customer-based divisions: corporate systems clients; knowledge workers; ordinary Windows customers; programmers; and consumers interested in digitized content, entertainment, and shopping. Both Ballmer and Gates recognized that to lure the large corporate accounts it aimed to target with Windows NT, Microsoft needed to be more in tune with its clients. Larger enterprises typically demanded from their technology providers a high level of service, something that even Microsoft admitted wasn't its strong suit. That year, Gates published his second best-selling book, *Business @ the Speed of Thought.*

In January of 2000, Gates appointed Ballmer CEO, retaining his role as chairman and taking on the additional role of chief software architect. In a letter to employees detailing the management changes, Gates pointed to Microsoft's success in altering the way individuals interacted with computers as a metaphor for his firm's new focus. ''Today we must make a similar bet on using software to improve the way people experience the Internet—an even more important revolution than the GUI.'' One month later, the firm shipped its long awaited new version of Windows NT, renamed Windows 2000, which was designed to serve as the operating platform for large enterprises, including leading e-commerce players like Buy.com and BarnesandNoble.com.

The lengthy antitrust investigation of Microsoft climaxed in April of 2000, when trial judge Thomas Penfield Jackson ruled that the firm had aggressively monopolized the PC operating systems industry. Along with 17 states, the Justice Department proposed that Gates separate Microsoft into two companies, one overseeing the firm's Office software applications, and the other handling its Windows-based operating systems. As predicted, Microsoft's lawyers appealed the judgment, which several industry pundits believed an appeals court would overturn.

Ironically, it was during these potentially devastating legal conflicts that Microsoft seemed to grow stronger. The firm completed its largest acquisition ever, paying $1.1 billion for Great Plains Corp., an enterprise management software maker serving small and mid-sized businesses. The firm also developed and launched bCentral, an e-business hosting service for small companies. With Gates at the helm of new technology developments, the firm unveiled Office XP, the latest version of the Office suite, in June of 2001. Microsoft also announced its intent to launch Windows XP, its biggest new product in five years, in October. According to *USA Today* writer Byron Acohido, the latest version of Microsoft's operating system will be more that just another upgrade. ''Microsoft has fashioned XP into its weapon of choice for subjugating the Internet, just as it conquered desktop PCs.'' The new operating system is at the core of Microsoft's new strategy, known as.Net, which Gates and his cohorts envision as ''a framework of software programs and services connecting every computing device to the Internet and to each other. With Windows XP as the dominant operating system, Microsoft could touch virtually every transaction.'' With Gates free to concentrate solely on software architecture efforts at Microsoft, this bold prediction may well prove accurate.

FURTHER READING:

Acohido, Byron. ''Microsoft Aims to Conquer Net.'' *USA Today.* June 6, 2001. Available from www.usetoday.com.

''At War with Microsoft.'' *The Economist.* May 23, 1998.

Baker, Sharon M. ''Microsoft Pushing Ahead on Many Fronts.'' *Puget Sound Business Journal.* March 12, 1999.

''Bill's Big Roll-Out.'' *The Economist.* September 18, 1999.

Kirkpatrick, David. ''He Wants All of Your Business—and He's Starting to Get It.'' *Fortune.* May 26, 1997.

———. ''Microsoft: Is Your Company Its Next Meal?'' *Fortune.* April 27, 1998.

———. ''The New Face of Microsoft: The Management Change is Just the First Step.'' *Fortune.* February 7, 2000.

''Microsoft: The Beast Is Back.'' *Fortune.* June 11, 2001.

''Microsoft Corp.'' In *Notable Corporate Chronologies.* Farmington Hills, MI: Gale Group, 1999.

Mitchell, Russ. ''Microsoft's Midlife Crisis.'' *U.S. News & World Report.* October 19, 1998.

Nocera, Joseph. ''The Men Who Would Be King: Case Has Content. Gates Has Software. The Internet Will Be Their Battleground.'' *Fortune.* February 7, 2000.

''William H. Gates.'' Redmond, WA: Microsoft Corp., 2001. Available from www.microsoft.com.

SEE ALSO: Allen, Paul; Ballmer, Steve; IBM Inc.; Microsoft Corp.; Microsoft Network (MSN); Microsoft Windows; Netscape Communications Corp.

GATEWAY, INC.

Gateway, Inc. is a leading personal computer (PC) maker in the U.S. with a 15 percent share of the market as of 2001. The firm sells its machines by phone and via the Internet. Operations include 15 call centers, five manufacturing plants, and 275 Country Store showrooms. Declining prices and market saturation in the PC industry prompted the firm to diversify into Internet access services and other Web-based ventures in the late 1990s.

EARLY HISTORY

Gateway was founded in 1985 when partners Ted Waitt, who dropped out of the business management program at the University of Iowa, and Mike Hammond launched TIPC Network, a computer mail-order business, in the Waitt family farmhouse in Sioux City, Iowa. The upstart was funded by a $10,000 loan from Waitt's grandmother. Initially, customers were charged a $20 membership fee to gain access to TIPC's mail order inventory, which included peripheral hardware and software for Texas Instruments computers. Within four months, TIPC generated $100,000 in sales. In 1986, the company began assembling its own computers; however, sales of these machines accounted for only a small percentage of annual revenues, which reached $1 million.

In 1987, Gateway developed an IBM-compatible personal computer (PC) using components from other PC makers. Although Gateway's PC was similar to one sold by Texas Instruments, with two floppy disk drive and a color monitor, it cost only $1,995, roughly half the price of Texas Instruments' machine. The firm changed its name to Gateway 2000 in 1988, which proved to be a pivotal year for the direct-sales PC upstart as its low-cost machines, powered with 286 processors, began to garner attention. Increased growth prompted Gateway to move headquarters from the Waitt ranch to a 5,000-square-foot building. The firm also launched its first major advertising campaign, running a full-page ad in which a photo of the Waitt family cattle herd appeared above a caption reading, ''Computers from Iowa?'' In addition, Waitt launched a performance incentive program for his staff, rewarding hourly employees with monthly cash bonuses that were tied to profits. Efforts paid off as sales skyrocketed from $1.5 million to $12 million in less than 12 months.

Sales grew nearly sixfold in 1989, exceeding $70 million. In 1990, Gateway relocated to South Dakota, a state with no income taxes. The firm also launched several light-hearted advertisements that poked fun at its rural location and portrayed a Holstein cow as Gateway's mascot. Continued growth prompted Waitt to bolster his management team with six executives from large PC firms. Sales jumped to $275 million that year as the firm shipped roughly 225 PCs per day. Employees totaled 185. Gateway was named the fastest-growing private company in America by *Inc.* magazine in 1991. To house its expanding operations, Gateway built a new 44,000 square-foot headquarters building. The firm also began targeting corporate markets for the first time. Sales continued to soar, reaching $626 million.

In 1992, Gateway unveiled its first notebook computer, The HandBook, which weighed less than three pounds. The Handbook proved to be one of the few Gateway products that sold poorly in the early 1990s. Although the recession at that time had taken a toll on other PC makers, Gateway found its sales exploding as those in the market for a new PC began seeking out less expensive models. As a result, revenues exceeded $1 billion for the first time. Earnings of $1.1 million boosted Gateway into the first-place spot among mail-order computer companies. Because demand for its products was so high, Gateway found itself unable to fill orders. When clients began complaining about lengthy delays, as well as flaws with the computers that did finally arrive, the firm hired 200 new workers.

International growth took place for the first time in 1993, when Gateway opened a complex in Dublin, Ireland. That year, the firm completed its initial public offering (IPO), selling nearly 11 million shares for $150 million. Upon completion of the IPO, the Waitt family owned 85 percent of Gateway. The firm used the fresh capital to diversify into software as well as peripheral equipment, such as printers, fax modems, and networking devices. In an effort to improve ser-

vice to its business customers, Gateway increased its support staff more than twofold, hired additional technicians, and added a separate phone line dedicated to providing support services to companies using Gateway machines. Although many rivals had begun to levy fees for technical support, Gateway continued to offer its services for free. The firm created a sales and customer support unit in Kansas City, Missouri, in 1994. International expansion continued with the creation of showrooms—which allowed potential customers to examine Gateway merchandise prior to making a purchase—in France, Germany, Japan, and the United Kingdom. Sales reached $2.7 billion that year.

Gateway made its first foray into the Pacific Rim in 1995, creating a manufacturing plant in Malaysia to make PCs. The firm also moved into Australia with the purchase of Osborne Computer, based in Sydney. Steady demand prompted the firm to create a third U.S. manufacturing plant, located in Hampton, Virginia, in 1996. To gain a foothold in Greece, the firm forged a distribution alliance with Dakos S.A. In a similar move, Gateway also inked a distribution deal with Al Yousuf Computers, based in the United Arab Emirates. Growth in Europe was bolstered with a new showroom in Sweden. New product developments included a large-screen PC and television set combo known as Destination; it was the first Gateway product to be marketed by traditional retailers. It was in the mid-1990s that Gateway also established its Country Stores Inc. subsidiary. Gateway's 8,000-square-foot Country Stores, similar to the firm's European showrooms, gave customers the chance to examine Gateway merchandise before purchasing it via mail or telephone. The first Country Stores were based in Connecticut and North Carolina.

MOVE TO THE INTERNET

In 1996, Gateway was spending roughly $90 million on advertising annually to continue bolstering its name recognition. By then, the firm had become the world's tenth-largest computer company with earnings of $250 million on sales of $5 billion. It was second only to Dell Computer Corp. among direct sellers of PCs. According to a March 1997 issue of *Success,* the firm achieved that success because Waitt had made ''a number of critical calls that put Gateway ahead of its industry. In 1988 it was the first to make EGA color monitors standard on all its systems. In 1990 it was the first to make Windows standard on all systems. In 1994, before anyone else, it made the Pentium chip standard. That same year Gateway was first to make CD-ROM drives standard on all its systems. And in July 1996 it became the first computer maker to allow customers to custom-order and pay for a new computer over the World Wide Web.'' Clients could order customized PCs via the firm's World Wide Web site using a process similar to the one used by clients who placed telephone orders, which were typically filled in less than five days. Initially, some of the site's visitors would simply check prices and compare models before calling Gateway to formally place an order. Eventually, however, Web surfers became more comfortable with the idea of actually making the purchase online. Internet sales grew from $300 million to $700 million in 1997, as total annual revenues climbed to $6.3 billion.

The firm also began targeting business markets that year by launching its E-Series line of PCs for larger corporations. Designed to serve networked environments, each of the PCs offered in the E-Series line included Ethernet networking capabilities. To gain access to the server technology it needed to serve the networking needs of large enterprises, Gateway paid roughly $194 million in stock for Advanced Logic Research. The firm also diversified into Internet access with the launch of gateway.net, a service it developed in conjunction with UUNet Technologies, the predecessor to WorldCom. For a flat fee of $12.95 per month, purchasers of new Gateway PCs were able to use gateway.net software, which came bundled with the PC, to surf the Internet for up to 30 hours. These new activities reflected the firm's recognition that it needed to reduce its reliance on the PC market, which was nearing saturation. Price cuts by rivals like Dell and Compaq Computer Corp. forced Gateway to lower its prices by 12 percent.

With the millennium approaching, Gateway 2000 Inc. shortened its name to Gateway, Inc. in 1998. By mid-year, roughly 58 Country Stores spanning 26 states were in operation. A new pricing option, dubbed ''Your:)Ware,'' allowed customers to pay a monthly fee for a PC, Internet access, and other options, as well as a guarantee that Gateway would repurchase the machine when a client was ready to upgrade to a newer model. Falling PC prices continued to hammer away at the firm's bottom line, prompting its relocation to San Diego, California, where it could access a larger pool of technological and managerial talent. In a major overhaul of operations, Waitt replaced 10 of 15 top executives.

In 1999, to attract new customers, Gateway began offering one year of free Internet access, with a limit of 150 hours per month, to those who purchased a Gateway machine costing more than $1,000. The firm also extended its e-commerce operations via an alliance with NECX Office and Personal Technology Center, one of the largest computer products e-tailers. According to the terms of the agreement, NECX and Gateway jointly operated SpotShop.com, which offered Gateway merchandise as well as peripheral equipment and software from other computer industry leaders. A deal with Yahoo! allowed gateway.net users to customize their home pages via a new Gateway My Yahoo! application that operated as a news and shopping portal. In October, America Online (AOL) invested $800 million in Gateway to operate Gateway.net, the company's Internet service provider (ISP), which boasted 600,000 subscribers. Despite these efforts to diversify, PCs continued to account for 85 percent of earnings. However, Gateway made successful inroads into the corporate, education, and government sectors, as nearly half of total sales in 1999 came from these non-consumer markets. By year's end, 200 Country Stores were operating in the U.S., and Waitt had been succeeded as CEO by Gateway president Jeff Weitzen. Together, in the months prior to Waitt's resignation, Weitzen and Waitt reshuffled Gateway's increasingly diverse operations into six segments: systems, software and peripherals, service and training, Internet access, portals and content, and financing. Waitt remained chairman and charged Weitzen with the task of developing Gateway's peripheral, or ''beyond-the-box,'' efforts.

Falling prices and near saturation in the PC industry forced Gateway to begin selling its PCs via traditional retail outlets in 2000. For example, the OfficeMax chain began carrying Gateway products that year. In an effort to cut costs, Gateway reached an agreement with rivals Compaq Computer Corp. and Hewlett-Packard Co. to create an independent Internet-based procurement operation for PC parts and supplies; each firm contributed $5 million to the new venture. Profits that year tumbled 26 percent to $316 million on revenues of roughly $10 billion; sales growth was just seven percent, compared to an average of 20 percent over the previous five years.

Unhappy with the company's performance, Waitt resumed his role as CEO, ousting Weitzen in January of 2001. In an effort to return Gateway to its core PC business, Waitt fired six of eight top executives and rehired several executives who had resigned during Weitzen's short tenure. He also closed 27 Country Stores and laid off 3,000 workers. While the firm continued to develop ''beyond-the-box'' products and services, PC sales once again became Gateway's key focus. Competition intensified when rival Dell Computer slashed its prices by roughly 20 percent, forcing Gateway to once again reduce its prices. Losses in the first half of the year reached $523.7 million on sales of $3.5 billion. Believing drastic action was in order, Waitt slashed Gateway's staff by one-fourth in September 2001, releasing 2,200 international workers and 2,500 domestic employees. The cuts, estimated to save $300 annually, were an effort to offset the negative effects of the firm's lowered prices. However, Gateway also shuttered several international operations, which reduced revenues another 14 percent. After reducing its size, Gateway also began to look to its Country Stores, which offered services like online bill payment and small business technical support, as potential growth areas.

FURTHER READING:

Allen, Mike. ''Gateway's 'Retrenching' Continues.'' *San Diego Business Journal,* September 3, 2001.

Brooker, Katrina. ''I Built This Company, I Can Save It: Retired Gateway CEO Ted Waitt Shocked the Computer World When He Ousted His Successor and Seized Control.'' *Fortune,* April 30, 2001.

Conlin, Michelle. ''For Whom the Dell Tolls.'' *Forbes,* August 10, 1998.

Gordon, Joanne. ''Green Pastures for Gateway.'' *Chain Store Age Executive,* November 1997.

Holstein, William J. ''Gateway Gets Citified.'' *U.S. News & World Report,* May 3, 1999.

''Internet Access: Gateway Breaks Ground with Internet Strategy.'' *EDGE: Work-Group Computing Report,* March 1, 1999.

Kirkpatrick, David. ''New Home. New Ceo. Gateway Is Moo and Improved.'' *Fortune,* December 20, 1999.

Loro, Laura. ''Gateway Raking In Online PC Orders.'' *Business Marketing,* October 1997.

''New PCs: Gateway 2000 Launches E-Series PCs Designed for the Corporate Market.'' *EDGE: Work-Group Computing Report,* May 26, 1997.

Popovich, Ken. ''Gateway Moves to Stem Wounds—But High Inventory and Weak Consumer Demand Dog Faltering PC Maker.'' *eWeek,* February 5, 2001.

Warshaw, Michael. ''Guts and Glory: From Farm Boy to Billionaire: Ted Waitt's Inspiring Story of Incredible Growth.'' *Success,* March 1997.

Weintraub, Arlene. ''Can Gateway Survive in a Smaller Pasture?'' *BusinessWeek Online,* September 10, 2001. Available from www.businessweek.com.

SEE ALSO: Dell Computer Corp.; Hardware; Waitt, Ted

GENERAL USAGE FOR INTERNATIONAL DIGITALLY ENSURED COMMERCE (GUIDEC)

E-commerce is powerful because it enables companies and individuals from across the globe to engage in business transactions. However, this same advantage also can be a roadblock. Business standards that are deemed acceptable in one part of the world may be viewed quite differently in another region. Furthermore, when business transactions occur between parties on opposite sides of the globe, matters of security become major concerns. Determining the honesty and integrity of a business partner be-

comes more difficult. It was for reasons such as these that the International Chamber of Commerce (ICC) developed General Usage for Digitally Ensured Commerce (GUIDEC)—specific guidelines for ensuring the trustworthiness of digital transactions done via the Internet.

Encryption techniques are essential to e-commerce. They allow information to be scrambled before it is sent over a network like the Internet, and then de-scrambled by the person or company receiving the information. Keys are numeric sequences that make this possible. Often, the sender has a public key and the receiver has a private key. Digital signatures are another critical component of e-commerce. They allow senders of messages to electronically prove their legitimacy. Digital signatures or certificates are normally issued by third party authorities who do background checks before issuing them.

According to the ICC, GUIDEC ''governs the use of public key cryptography for digital signatures and the role of a trusted third party—called a certifier—in establishing that holders of public keys are who they purport to be.'' Based in Paris, the ICC is a global business organization that represents companies and associations from more than 130 countries. It is involved in establishing guidelines and rules that companies voluntarily abide by when conducting international business transactions, and acts as an arbitrator to settle international commercial disputes.

Developed by experts in the legal, software, commercial banking, and certification authority fields, GUIDEC was first drafted in 1995, when it was called Uniform International Authentication and Certifications Practices (UIACP). Two years later, in November 1997, GUIDEC was unveiled to the world at the ICC's international conference, The World Business Agenda for Electronic Commerce. It was created as a living document, meaning that it can be modified as the world of e-commerce changes. The document takes different legal systems across the globe (both civil and common law) into consideration as related to e-commerce, and provides a glossary of core concepts and different best-practice examples companies can look to for clarification.

FURTHER READING:

''E.commerce: GUIDEC.'' *Hong Kong Telecommunications Users Group Newsletter,* February, 1998. Available from www.hkbu.edu.

''GUIDEC.'' International Chamber of Commerce. February 27, 2001. Available from www.iccwbo.org/home/guidec.

Essick, Kristi. ''Internet & I-Commerce: ICC Offers Guidelines to Standardize I-commerce Usage.'' *InfoWorld,.* November 17, 1997.

''Making Rules for Electronic Commerce.'' International Chamber of Commerce. November 14, 1997. Available from www.iccwbo.org.

Tiernan, Bernadette. *e-tailing*. Chicago: Dearborn Financial Publishing Inc. 2000.

SEE ALSO: Cryptography, Public and Private Key; Digital Certificate; Digital Certificate Authority; Digital Signature; Digital Signature Legislation; Encryption; Global E-commerce Regulation

GLASER, ROBERT

Once an employee at Microsoft Corp., Robert Glaser is the founder of Seattle-based RealNetworks. He turned himself and his company into a major competitor and bitter rival of Microsoft by the end of the 20th century, while simultaneously pioneering the market for streaming media, the technology that allows Internet surfers to download, listen to, or watch media clips online.

Glaser, a Yale graduate with degrees in computer science and economics, joined Microsoft in 1983 at the age of 21. He rose to the rank of vice president of multimedia and consumer systems within a decade, while also helping to develop popular Microsoft programs such as Excel and Word. However, as Microsoft grew into a commercial behemoth and its employee ranks grew from 250 to 15,000, Glaser grew restless, missing the excitement of a startup company and the thrill of taking on established giants.

In 1993, Glaser decided to leave Microsoft and form his own company, originally called Progressive Networks to highlight its ostensible mission of spreading progressive political ideas over the Internet. The company quickly invented the technology of streaming media. Following the release of its first product, RealAudio, the company changed its name to RealNetworks to more accurately reflect its line of work.

At one point, there seemed to be a harmonious relationship between RealNetworks and Microsoft, which purchased 10 percent of RealNetworks as an investment to improve its own Media Player and work toward greater interoperability between the two streaming media packages. However, as the U.S. government's case against Microsoft heated up in 1998, Glaser testified before the U.S. Senate that the current Media Player deliberately shut out RealPlayer music files, thus bolstering the government's anti-trust case against Microsoft. Microsoft, meanwhile, withdrew its investment from RealNetworks.

Despite such hitches, Glaser and RealNetworks continued to flourish. By summer 2001, RealNetworks maintained a registry of more than 170 million users, and radio stations, online record stores, and even major record labels all made their products available for download using the company's products. Glaser also served as the chairman and interim CEO of MusicNet, a subscription-based music delivery service that in 2001 was created by RealNetworks and three major record companies—Bertelsmann, EMI Group, and AOL Time Warner—to stream music packages over the Internet. This was a continuation of Glaser's fight against Napster, the free music-exchange network that panicked the record industry in the late 1990s and early 2000s.

Through the 1990s and early 2000s, RealNetworks, with its line of streaming audio products such as RealAudio and RealJukebox, dominated the streaming media market, which had grown into a $900 million industry, earning Glaser a sizable fortune. In 1999, *Forbes* placed him on its list of the richest individuals, with an estimated net worth of $2.4 billion.

FURTHER READING:

Bozza, Anthony, et. al. ''Major Labels Go Online.'' *Rolling Stone*. May 19, 2001.

Careless, James. ''Almost a Single Standard.'' *Broadcasting & Cable*. January 31, 2001.

Essex, Andrew. ''Robert Glaser: The Real Deal.'' *Rolling Stone*. October 12, 2000.

Kover, Amy. ''Is Robert Glaser For Real?'' *Fortune*. September 4, 2000.

Lenatti, Chuck. ''Multimedia Gets Real.'' *Upside*. August 1999.

Newcomb, Peter. ''The Forbes 400: Microsoft Money.'' *Forbes*. October 11, 1999.

Walker, Rob. ''Between Rock and a Hard Drive.'' *New York Times Magazine*. April 23, 2000.

SEE ALSO: Microsoft Corp.; Napster; RealNetworks; Streaming Media

GLOBAL E-COMMERCE: AFRICA

While businesses coveted the relatively untapped African e-commerce market and saw tremendous opportunity there, Africa faced a number of troubling obstacles to the development of e-commerce at the start of the 21st century. These problems ranged from the technical to the social to the political. For instance, the continent was characterized by inadequate telecommunications and business infrastructure, structural inequality, a number of severe armed conflicts, political upheaval, massive public debt, and enormous health problems including the world's gravest AIDS epidemic. Lastly, in both Internet advancement and overall economic activity, Africa was marked by severe internal economic inequality both within and between nations. South Africa was the clear standout in terms of national economic performance and e-commerce, while a few Northern African nations were performing respectably. However, the bulk of sub-Saharan Africa languished in dire poverty, and it faced a number of severe obstacles on the path to prosperity.

Still, businesses, investors, and policy makers generally weren't sour on the prospects for African e-commerce. Rather, the debate centered on which issues needed to be addressed first so that African e-commerce could prove profitable and sustainable over the long term. Should the technical shortcomings be addressed so as to give later e-commerce programs a leg to stand on? Did the root lay in international financial tinkering so as to spur investment that would support e-commerce? Was it incumbent upon African and international leaders to first focus their attention on relieving some of the dire social maladies faced by the African people, or was the development of e-commerce a means toward that end? By the early 2000s, there were no definitive answers to these questions, but various interests were pushing forward in all these areas.

INTERNET PENETRATION

Despite the continent's lackluster performance in overall Internet connectivity, African countries vastly improved their levels of Internet access in the late 1990s. Only 11 African nations were even connected to the Internet at the close of 1996. However, by 2000 all 54 countries maintained a permanent connection. Still, for the most part reliable Internet connectivity was limited to the national capitals and other major cities. Rural areas, where about 75 percent of the continent's population resides, enjoyed little or no connectivity at all. By early 2000 there were some 450 public Internet service providers (ISPs) throughout Africa, excluding South Africa. According to *Communications International,* seven countries—Egypt, Kenya, Morocco, Nigeria, South Africa, Tanzania and Zimbabwe—boasted 10 or more ISPs, but 20 countries had only one.

Worldwide, an average of one out of every 35 individuals is an Internet user, but in Africa that ratio drops to about one in 250. Personal Internet accounts were a luxury beyond the reach of most Africans in the early 2000s. *Communications International* reported that there were roughly 1 million dial-up Internet accounts throughout Africa, with 650,000 of those in South Africa alone, although precise counts were hard to come by. Another 200,000 accounts were

based in the North African Arabic-speaking nations. The end result of this count is a paltry 150,000 personal accounts spread among the remaining 50 countries. Internet connection through much of Africa, in fact, was only the tip of the iceberg, given that in many countries less than one person per 100 enjoyed access to a telephone. A few smaller countries with less geographical ground to cover, such as Cote d'Ivoire and Mauritius, could claim teledensities reaching 25 percent (or one telephone for every four persons). However, even well-developed South Africa maintained a teledensity of only 12 percent.

One strategy to combat the digital divide between the capital and major cities and rural areas and small towns was to provide special area codes for local areas that charge for service at local tariff levels. In this way, national telecommunications providers can significantly cut the cost of delivering service to such isolated areas. A handful of countries, including Ethiopia, Mali, Morocco, Senegal, Tunisia, and Zimbabwe, have adopted this strategy.

By 2001 the number of Internet hosts in all of Africa was roughly equivalent to that of the small, Eastern European country of Latvia, according to *Communications International.* In another comparison, there were as many ISPs in Tokyo as existed in all of Africa. The continent's largest commercial ISP, Nairobi, Kenya-based AfricaOnline, boasted 600,000 dial-up accounts in nine countries in 2001. Each of those accounts averaged seven individual users. South Africa, the largest Internet market, was dominated by two major ISPs that commanded 90 percent of the market between them, while more than 40 tiny companies specializing in local service shared the rest of that country's market. The market leader, Mweb, boasted 145,000 subscribers in early 2001, while its rival Yebo Net claimed some 100,000 subscribers.

TELECOMMUNICATIONS AND INFORMATION INFRASTRUCTURE

In telecommunications infrastructure, South Africa, Nigeria, Egypt, and Tunisia, were clear standouts on the continent, but Africa faced a massive degree of internal inequality in this area. Most sub-Saharan countries, which counted among them some of the poorest nations in the world, had little reliable telecommunications infrastructure to speak of, particularly in rural areas.

On the other hand, many analysts noted that Africa's infrastructure problems pose some key advantages as well. Most notably, the relative lack of telecommunications systems in Africa may allow developers to bypass the less efficient first- and second-generation networks and systems adopted by Europe and North America. This could potentially enable the implementation of more sophisticated setups under development in the early 2000s, featuring, for instance, widespread convergence between fixed-line and mobile networks. In fact, mobile technology was expected to be a primary means of escalating Internet penetration in Africa.

Some countries, such as South Africa and Botswana, already were successful in laying down sophisticated fiber-optic and mobile networks that reached substantial portions of their populations. In South Africa, the number of mobile Internet users surpassed that of fixed-line users in August 2000. Several other major investment schemes in the late 1990s and early 2000s aimed at placing fiber-optic networks in various African sub-regions, according to *African Business*. For example, AT&T launched Africa One, an initiative to line the entire continent with a fiber-optic backbone, while Telkom of South Africa implemented a project known as SAFE to set up fiber optics between South Africa and Malaysia. The United States government also has been directly involved in lending a hand to the development of the African Internet. In 1995, the U.S. Agency for International Development launched the Leland Initiative, which allocated $15 million to bring Internet access to the whole continent.

The late 1990s and early 2000s were characterized by the deregulation and privatization of telecommunications sectors in many African countries, in the hope that less stringent barriers would invite greater influxes of foreign investment. While most countries—Ethiopia and Mauritius are the exceptions—have abandoned government monopolies for ISPs as an element of official state policy, many governments still retained such control in practice.

In an effort to stimulate the Internet sector, open its telecommunications industry to outside investment, and reduce its public debt, in 2001 the South African government decided to take its telecommunications monopoly, Telkom, public. Beginning in 1997, Telkom Malaysia and SBC Communications owned 30 percent of the firm, while the remaining 70 percent belonged to the government. The government planned to sell up to 30 percent of its share. With a monopoly as the sole fixed-line operator in South Africa, and with a majority interest in the country's leading cellular phone operator, Telkom was highly coveted as an entry into this highly prized African e-commerce market.

African governments took the lead at the International Telecommunications Union's Telecom '98 conference in Johannesburg, South Africa, where they produced a policy document called African Connection. The thrust of the paper was to build a common agenda that the entire African business community could rally behind to establish an information-technology backbone for the whole continent. Before devising technical solutions, however, the African Connection working groups were first devoted to creating the institutional foundation that would be able to coordinate and provide for future development of Internet and e-commerce sectors. This work enjoyed support from major governments and institutions around the world, including the World Bank, the European Union, the United Nations Economic Commission on Africa, and the African Development Bank.

SOCIAL AND POLITICAL CONCERNS

The United Nations viewed the building of telecommunications infrastructure and tapping into the economic, educational, and communicative power of the Internet as key components for the economic development of poorer countries, including Africa. In fact, the UN saw the Internet as a tool for speeding development, skipping over many of the stages that characterized the development of countries in earlier years. UN Secretary-General Kofi Annan championed the building of what he called "digital bridges" to less developed countries. Especially in Africa, infrastructure problems are particularly pronounced—postal systems, roads, power supplies, and telephone systems are in extremely poor condition—and the effects on business are drastic. Without access to reliable information, the prices of ordinary consumer goods such as food go out of equilibrium. The UN and other concerned parties hoped that the Internet would provide the ability to access such information and result in tremendous incidental cost savings by, for instance, substituting e-mail for faxes and regular mail.

Meanwhile, business and government leaders generally agreed that failure to develop Internet capabilities and launch an e-business sector could push African development even further behind more developed regions. With international trade escalating and markets and economies integrating, to fail to get online is to risk cutting oneself off from the main avenue of economic and social development in the 21st century. Indeed, the international financial community positioned the Internet as a centerpiece of its development programs for the African continent. In 2000, the World Bank allocated $500 million to the International Finance Corp. for an initiative, in conjunction with the Japanese Internet group Softbank, to spur Internet technology and access in approximately 100 developing countries, including most of the African nations. The goal of the program, according to World Bank President James Wolfensohn, was to close the digital divide and "accelerate the inclusion of the developing countries in the information revolution. It will transfer technology from the rich countries to the developing world, fostering sustainable new local businesses which will promote prosperity and reduce poverty.'' African leaders remain cognizant of the gap between rich and poor countries in the world, and the general consensus holds that setting up a viable e-commerce infrastructure will at least assist in keeping that gap from widening at the expense of African nations. However, given the enormous structural difficulties facing African governments—in the form of severe international debt burdens, political instability, and other grave hardships—the bulk of the investment in Internet technology was expected to come from the private sector.

Delegates at the African Development Forum in 2000 debated the issue of technology, particularly Internet technology, in light of broader development schemes. While Internet development was a goal for all the continent's leaders, some were wary of placing too much emphasis on investment into information technology and telecommunications relative to other basic development needs, such as anti-poverty programs. Short-term realities, in other words, were a key caveat to the more ambitious schemes proposed by African and non-African developers. As Mali's president, Alpha Oumar Konare intoned, ''[a]s an African, I am keeping a cool head—a computer can cost eight years' salary or send 20 children to school. If we don't have our own clear vision on information and communication technology, we will be disappointed.''

The forum, however, spawned several major initiatives designed to utilize the Internet to tackle issues of specific concern to the African community. For instance, the Schoolnet Africa program, according to *African Business,* devised a working group devoted to wiring African schools for Internet access with the specific intention of communicating information centered on the prevention of HIV/AIDS, preserving cultural traditions, and fostering peace on the continent.

More basic consumer problems linger as well. Literacy, general education, and computer skill levels remain relatively low throughout Africa. Moreover, Africans on the whole are significantly less likely to use a credit card in transactions than are those in most developed regions. Since e-commerce basically eliminates cash transactions, the low credit card penetration is another inhibiting factor for African e-commerce, since it renders the building of a clientele that much more problematic. Thus, a major focus of foreign investment was on the wiring of medium and large businesses, as well as the more affluent sectors of consumer society, for Internet access. Not only would this create a foundation for new Internet-based business, it also would create a vibrant vehicle for international trade.

BRIGHT LIGHTS OF AFRICAN E-COMMERCE

By the turn of the 21st century African e-commerce already had registered some clear successes. According to *African Business,* one business sector in which e-commerce gained a foothold in Africa was tourism. With the ability to set up a Web site and distribute tour information for minimal cost anywhere in the world, African tourism companies were able to promote themselves on a par with tourist packages globally. Tourism firms, now able to accept reservations directly via e-mail, are decreasingly dependent on foreign travel agencies, thereby significantly lowering the cost of business by eliminating the agents' fees.

Some of the economic news bode well for Africa as it entered the Internet age. Through the mid- and late 1990s, even while much of Asia and Latin America found themselves in severe economic crisis, Africa enjoyed steady economic growth. Moreover, while Africa's share of global trade didn't change significantly in the mid- and late 1990s, the volume of African exports was generally keeping pace with the expansion in international trade. Building as it was on two decades of economic decline, however, these successes were particularly fragile. For instance, according to a 1999 article in *Law and Policy in International Business,* the growth levels achieved in the 1990s, while certainly a positive trend, weren't great enough to overcome the massive poverty levels that plague the continent.

Despite persistent problems, African countries made tremendous gains in the late 1990s and early 2000s in establishing their presence on the Internet. As late as 1997, e-mail itself was extremely rare on the continent, particularly outside South Africa, while general Internet access was almost unheard of. By the turn of the 21st century, however, Internet cafes had sprouted in most towns that had a vital business or cultural community.

ONGOING DEBATE

Everyone didn't agreed that e-commerce was the key to sustainable and democratic development in Africa. Some critics even insisted that the electronically driven globalization was akin to the patterns of colonialism that subjugated and exploited Africa throughout the late 19th and 20th centuries. According to such arguments, the nature of many African economies renders them largely dependent on raw export commodities, and the instant availability of rival commodity supplies from other parts of the world subjects the industries to excessively low prices—too low to meet the needs of the industries and the economies they support. In this way, critics claim, the prices of exports such as coffee, wheat, tea, timber, and other goods are removed from the process of negotiation based on quality and supply and into the hands of international financiers, who, treating these items as mere commodities, take no account of such factors.

In response, e-commerce proponents insist that trade and economic growth could flourish only if African governments gave up protectionist measures and point to successes like the tourism industry, where the opening of e-markets has produced positive results. For instance, many governments charge high international tariffs discouraging international ISPs from setting up efficient networks. There was growing international pressure on African governments to dismantle their telecommunications monopolies and open their doors to greater competition in the ISP sector.

Ultimately, of course, e-commerce is only part of the equation. African countries aren't likely to achieve sustainable, long-term democratic development only on the commercial possibilities of e-commerce. Rather, analysts insist that the adoption of Internet technologies must proceed in an integrated fashion, addressing the specific needs of the particular populations and utilizing the technology to further educational policies and open the channels of communication so opinions can flow freely within and between countries.

FURTHER READING:

Banfield, Jessie. "Naidoo Message Spans Africa." *African Business.* June 1999.

Commey, Pusch. "Let the Telkom Games Begin!" *African Business.* April 2001.

Esterhuysen, Anriette. "The Comms Industry in Africa." *Communications International.* September 1999.

"International: Tapping into Africa." *Economist.* September 9, 2000.

Mbogo, Steve. "Can Africa Exploit the Internet?" *Review of African Political Economy.* March 2000.

Moors De Giorgio, Emmanuelle. "The African Internet Revolution." *African Business.* April 2000.

Nevin, Tom. "IT As the Saviour?" *African Business.* January 2000.

O'Kane, Gerry. "World Bank to Boost Internet in Africa." *African Business.* March 2000.

Vesely, Milan. "E-commerce Bonanza for African Firms." *African Business.* October 1999.

———. "A U.S. Perspective on Globalisation." *African Business.* October 2000.

Williamson, Irving; and Stephen D'Alessandro. "New Prospects for Private Sector Led Trade, Investment, and Economic Development in Sub-Saharan Africa." *Law and Policy in International Business.* Summer 1999.

Wilson, David. "Somewhere Over the Rainbow." *Communications International.* March 2001.

SEE ALSO: Digital Divide; Global Presence, Becoming a; International Telecommunications Union

GLOBAL E-COMMERCE: ASIA

With a tremendous population, several highly developed countries, and a rapidly escalating Internet penetration, Asia is among the most promising regions for e-commerce development. In March 2000, about 69 million people had access to the Internet in Asia, compared with 83 million in Europe. Still, internal disparities and a series of logistical difficulties hampered some of the most optimistic expectations for online commerce in the region. James Wang, an Internet analyst in Taiwan, told *Far Eastern Economic Review* in late 2000 that, when it comes to e-commerce, "Asia is where the U.S. was two to three years ago. Once consumers feel more comfortable buying on-line, it'll start to pick up." The challenge for both Asian and non-Asian entrepreneurs was to generate that level of comfort and provide the infrastructure to take advantage of it.

ASIAN E-COMMERCE STUCK AT THE GATES

Despite the emerging possibilities, Asian businesses were slow to fully integrate e-commerce strategies into their overall business plans, according to *Far Eastern Economic Review.* They also were slow to overhaul the physical and network infrastructures necessary for Internet-based business. Though Asia was bursting with firms of all sizes using all manner of e-commerce software, only a tiny minority of Asian firms had radically transformed their internal and external operation to reflect a serious concern with, and involvement in, e-commerce.

Meanwhile, without substantial investment in an online presence, the average Asian business that had set up an online outlet didn't establish an infrastructure capable of actually making sales over the Internet. Rather, Asian business Web sites tended to be little more than electronic brochures where the company and its products were introduced and explained, but without the kind of interactivity that allowed for sales, customer service, and so on.

In Hong Kong, one of the most technologically developed centers in all of Asia, only 40 percent of the local firms conducted business over the Internet, according to Systems Union, a financial systems company based in the United Kingdom. The Boston Consulting Group, meanwhile, conducted a far broader survey of 500 executives in markets throughout Asia and reported that Asian companies were, for the most part, taking their initial steps toward setting up shop online in 2000. As of the early 2000s, only a few markets, including Singapore, South Korea, and Hong Kong had the reliable and advanced telecommunications infrastructure necessary for widespread Internet access. According to International Data Corp., less than one percent of all Asian-Pacific Internet surfers (outside of Japan) engaged in at least one e-commerce transaction in 1998, a figure that was expected to reach 2.6 percent in 2002. In Japan, the most advanced nation in the region when it came to e-commerce, 8.7 percent of Web users shopped online in 1998, and fully 60.8 percent were expected to do so in 2002.

However, Asian business-to-business e-commerce enjoyed a significant boom, beginning with the recovery from the Asian economic crisis of the late-1990s and continuing into the early 2000s. According to New York-based eMarketer Inc., this field of online business in Asia and the Pacific Rim reached $36.2 billion in 2000, exceeding the business-to-business market in Europe by some $10 billion. eMarketer expected the boom to continue through 2002, when it predicted the figure would hit $121.2 billion. By way of comparison, the firm pinned North American business-to-business e-commerce at $159.2 billion in 2000, and expected it to reach $563.9 billion in 2002. Stanford, Connecticut-based research firm Gartner Group was even more optimistic for the Asian business-to-business future, expecting total sales in this sector to reach $995.8 billion by 2004, equal to 13.6 percent of the $1.3 trillion global business-to-business market. One segment of the business-to-business market that was exceptionally healthy in Asia in the early 2000s was the digital marketplace—central Web locations that brought buyers and sellers of supplies together to haggle over prices and build new company relationships.

Despite the lower penetration of dot-coms on the Asian landscape than in the United States, the technology market meltdown of spring 2000 washed up on Asian shores as well, littering the market with dead or dying Internet businesses. Like the United States, this shock was felt most severely by business-to-consumer models and content sites, while business-to-business online firms, although hardly emerging unscathed, were nonetheless able to stay afloat with relative ease. Still, by 2001 many dot-coms that seemed doomed were hanging on and seeking out new models to breathe life into their businesses. Many firms tried to build a constant revenue stream by offering e-business strategies and solutions to firms looking to get their storefronts online.

E-COMMERCE HURDLES IN ASIA

Unfortunately, the explosion of e-commerce in the west, particularly in the United States, coincided fairly closely with the Asian economic crisis, which began in 1997 and continued for about two years. When one country after another saw its currency plummet and other economic cracks widened into gaping holes, foreign investors divested from the region in a hurry. In turn, this accelerated the economic hardships. As a result, during e-commerce's developmental stage, most of the Asian region was too busy trying to hold existing economies together than to take the time or money to open up whole new business and technological strategies.

Timing was a factor in slowing Asia's e-commerce acceptance in another way as well. With the pace of e-commerce in the region trailing that of the United States, the dramatic stock market letdowns that affected the U.S. Internet market in 2000 and 2001 hit Asian e-commerce when the latter was in a far more precarious state of development. By the 2000s, e-commerce was a more or less established shopping medium in the United States. However, Asian companies and governments were only beginning to seriously dive in and reorganize business and technological infrastructures to accommodate e-commerce. When the boom in funding was pulled out from under the dot-com market, the Asian Internet economy couldn't recover as easily, and many Asian investors thought it was wise to pull back on their e-commerce ambitions, at least for the time being. In this way, the tech market bust was more devastating to the nascent ''Asian New Economy'' than it was to the more advanced Internet economy of the United States.

Similarly, Asia suffered from a shortage of venture capitalists—the lifeblood of the dot-com boom—compared with North America and Europe. According to *The Economist,* high-tech startups have never enjoyed strong financial support throughout Asia. However, this problem was meeting some remediation among Asian tigers such as Hong Kong, Malaysia, and Singapore, where businesses and governments were coordinating efforts to pool funds and expertise in order to help innovative Internet companies get on their feet.

Asia was relatively susceptible to trends in the international economy, particularly in the United States. With severe financial shocks rocking the country in the late 1990s, largely due to unstable currencies and international investment, Asian businesses kept a close eye on the economic health of the most developed nations, from which international investment is most vibrant. In the early 2000s, when many Asian businesses were dusting themselves off from the economic crisis and seriously considered adopting e-business strategies, the slowing U.S. economy gave pause to many business leaders. With declining U.S. investment in Asia and diminishing demand for Asian manufactured goods by U.S. consumers, the prospects for e-commerce were held in check.

There were also cultural barriers to the mass proliferation of e-business, according to *Far Eastern Economic Review.* Throughout many regions of Asia, established, personal relationships confer a value of their own, something that is simply not accounted for in the purely cost- and efficiency-driven world of e-business. Meanwhile, credit card use in Asia remains relatively light, and those who do use plastic to shop were largely uncomfortable using it online, much as many U.S. consumers were. Additionally, many consumers didn't see the utility in shopping on the Internet, particularly in regions of bustling economic activity in which everything shoppers needed was available in a nearby store. Compounded with lingering security fears, such apprehension among consumers severely hindered the growth of e-commerce in the region.

Within Asia, the borderless world of the Internet didn't translate well into the real world, where physical products still had to be shipped. With complex and rapidly fluctuating currency conversions, exorbitant shipping costs, and excessive delays in delivery, the added costs of shopping online at international business sites tended to be prohibitive. As a result, the majority of Internet businesses in Asia trafficked only within their own countries.

Retaining quality high-tech and information-technology (IT) professionals was an additional problem for the development of sound IT infrastructures in many Asian countries. *Far Eastern Economic Review* indicated that many of the leaders in these fields, particularly in countries such as China and India, leave their home countries for positions in Silicon Valley. However, this didn't always culminate in the negative effects associated with a brain drain. Particularly in the late 1990s, many of these individuals capitalized on the skyrocketing venture capital industry in Silicon Valley to start their own businesses and pour investment back into their home countries. Still, in the aftermath of the dot-com shakeout that began in early 2000 when the market for technology stocks went bust, the level of venture capital spending tailed off.

International Data Corp. (IDC) concluded that a key to bringing Asia into competitive parity with Europe and North America was the harmonization of interregional legal and technological standards. However, IDC remarked that varying cultural patterns and conflicting legal frameworks likely would impede progress toward such harmonization. Moreover, the lack of pan-regionalism often made it difficult for Asian firms to compete with larger firms, such as Am-azon.com, in established e-commerce market sectors. With its tremendous reach and economy of scale, Amazon.com was among the major international e-commerce outfits to strike a resonant chord with Asian consumers, and had begun to build a significant brand name and customer loyalty in the region. In this light, Amazon.com's expansion past its original bookstore foundation and into a more comprehensive online superstore posed a danger to Asian e-commerce firms. This was something they would need to address in order to capture market share when the business-to-consumer market in Asia finally explodes, as it was expected to.

GROWTH ON THE WAY

Despite the obstacles, analysts were optimistic for the future of Asian e-commerce. IDC felt 2001 was the breakthrough year for online business in the region, with forecasted sales of $10.7 billion. In the interest of pushing global competitive strengths, the pressure to put business online in Asia was expected to accelerate rapidly. More than half of Asia's products were sold to North America and Europe, which represented the greatest amount of Internet connectivity, the most advanced infrastructure, and the strongest consumer taste for e-commerce. Thus, market pressures were bound to force Asian companies to scramble to avoid being left out of the international trading system by more Internet-savvy competitors.

U.S. businesses looking to invest in Asia faced a number of tempting opportunities tempered by serious obstacles. On one hand, the market potential was enormous and growing all the time, particularly in light of closer trading ties with China. That country's economy was growing rapidly in the early 2000s and was largely untouched by the Asian economic crisis. On the other hand, the number of high-tech employees available for employment by U.S. firms in Asia was rather thin, and navigating the nuances of the region's IT infrastructure, regulations, and cultural patterns entailed a significant investment in its own right. According to *World Trade,* outsourcing work to local Asian firms can help alleviate the costs and headaches of learning the ropes and nuances of conducting business in Asian countries. On the World Wide Web, the business Web sites need to reflect the U.S. business model translated to the languages and cultural needs of the Asian countries in which they hope to do business.

The Chinese market was relatively warm to e-commerce. Approximately 60 million individuals were expected to be online in China by 2005. However, credit card penetration was exceptionally slight in the Chinese market, and most online transactions were paid for by regular checks or wire transfers.

Moreover, China's markets were still under the tight control of governmental regulation, despite opening up considerably in recent years, and there were many technological shortcomings.

Far Eastern Economic Review explained that the Chinese government was very aware that business-to-business digital marketplaces were an extremely positive development for the generation of sales to alleviate the excess capacity in many of the nation's state-owned enterprises and industries. Still, from the standpoint of international commerce, the relatively large degree of governmental control over the economy was a hindrance to regional e-commerce. With tight control over a range of key technologies—including the crucial encryption technologies upon which many e-commerce transactions rely—and even Internet content itself, it was still tricky for international firms, both inside and outside Asia, to fully tap into the potential offered by China's large—and growing—Internet user base and strengthening economic foundation.

Korea benefited from a healthy infrastructure for, and widespread use of, broadband technology. This facilitated high-speed Internet access, which is a key component of online shopping. By 2002, broadband Internet access was expected to reach approximately 2 million subscribers in Korea, mostly in South Korea. This translated into a dramatically higher proportion of the population with high-speed access than existed in the United States.

In South Korea, giant, diversified conglomerates called chaebols maintain the lion's share of control over economic output. The Internet was seen as a force for loosening this control and spurring renewed economic vigor. While the chaebols were fierce international competitors, their size, according to analysts, allowed them to become slow and unresponsive to domestic market forces. This provided just the opening that startup companies needed. Meanwhile, major conglomerates like Samsung reacted by spinning off large chunks of their Internet-based business. The country famously welcomed the Internet with open arms and incorporated e-commerce more quickly and readily than any other Asian nation. Its total e-commerce market was second only to Japan's. However, according to Boston Consulting group, South Korea's per capita online spending was significantly greater than that of Japan. By the early 2000s, small Internet startups were all the rage in South Korea and were attracting a steady flow of venture capital. Through 2005, Salomon Smith Barney noted that South Korea would boast the largest Asian e-commerce market outside of Japan and account for more than one-fourth of all Asian e-commerce revenues outside Japan.

Business leaders within Asia remained confident, predicting that Asia would emerge as a pivotal region, and eventually a leading region, in the new economy. At the World Economic Forum's Asia Pacific Economic Summit in Melbourne, Australia in fall 2000, several speakers proposed that, despite the region's slow acceptance of e-commerce, its economic strengths and emerging trends portended a bright e-commerce future. The firms, both Asian and otherwise, that supply the infrastructure, such as telecommunications firms and those trafficking in data networks, were pouring money into the region. The relaxed telecommunications regulatory structures through much of Asia, allowing for greater competition, were expected to continue to spur greater investment in that area. Meanwhile, with many of the world's leading manufacturers of IT hardware based in Asia shifting their business strategies to capitalize on software and other knowledge-based products and services, a new paradigm was emerging in the region. According to *The Futurist,* this would coincide with developing IT infrastructure to push Asia to the forefront of the e-commerce world.

FURTHER READING:

"Asia Online: The Tiger and the Tech." *Economist.* February 5, 2000.

Bickers, Charles. "Back to Basics." *Far Eastern Economic Review.* August 24, 2000.

———. "Going Dotty Over dot.coms." *Far Eastern Economic Review.* December 23, 1999.

Biers, Dan. "Asian Economic Forecast: United States—California's Bad Dream." *Far Eastern Economic Review.* February 1, 2001.

———. "Trading Up." *Far Eastern Economic Review.* August 10, 2000.

Burns, Simon. "e-Business Special Report: A Look at the Data." *Far Eastern Economic Review.* November 23, 2000.

———. "e-Business Special Report: The Winners." *Far Eastern Economic Review.* November 23, 2000.

Clark, Philip B. "Asia-Pacific Rim Surpasses Europe in e-Transactions." *B to B.* February 5, 2001.

De Kruif, Bill. "Outsourcing May Be the Ticket for Taking Your e-Business into Asia." *World Trade.* January 2001.

Goad, G. Pierre. "Riding the Net." *Far Eastern Economic Review.* March 23, 2000.

Lewis, Steven. "Asia Embraces B2B e-Commerce." *Asian Business.* April, 2000.

McKinsey, Kitty. "Asians Miss the e-Biz Mark." *Far Eastern Economic Review.* March 15, 2000.

———. "Shoppers Lost in Cyberspace." *Far Eastern Economic Review.* February 22, 2001.

Messmer, Ellen. "Lessons from an Asian B2B Exchange." *Network World.* May 1, 2000.

Mi-Young, Ahn. "Asia Awakes to e-Commerce." *Industry Week.* May 1, 2000.

Wilhelm, Kathy. "Ground Zero for a Data Explosion." *Far Eastern Economic Review.* November 16, 2000.

Zabala, Hector. "Time to Play Catch-Up." *Asian Business.* June 2000.

SEE ALSO: Digital Divide; Global Presence, Becoming a

GLOBAL E-COMMERCE: AUSTRALIA

The development of e-commerce throughout the world ranges from the widely adopted use of the Internet as a medium for both business-to-consumer (B2C) and business-to-business (B2B) commerce transactions in North America, to the relatively embryonic stages of basic telecommunications service in many Third World countries. E-commerce development in most other areas, including Australia, tends to fall somewhere in between these two extremes, depending on factors such as existing technological infrastructure; the technological expertise of residents; the available of qualified employees; funding available for e-commerce ventures from governmental, commercial, and individual sources; and national, regional and local commerce regulations. Fueling the North American e-commerce boom was an unprecedented level of venture capital available from a variety of sources, as well as access to the world's largest base of technical experts, many of whom had obtained the skills to not only work for other e-commerce businesses, but also to establish their own ventures. Although both funding and technical expertise were available in Australia, they existed on a much smaller scale. Australians also tended to be skeptical about the potential of e-commerce ventures, which meant that many existing businesses were in no rush to build Web sites. In addition, Australia's technological infrastructure had developed more slowly than that in North America. As a result e-commerce there grew at a slower pace. However, the growing number of Australians with Internet access—an estimated 7.4 million, or 55 percent of residents, in early 2001—does position Australia as a potential e-commerce leader in the Asia/Pacific region.

EARLY HISTORY OF INTERNET USAGE

The Australian Overseas Telecommunications Commission created an international dial-up service in the mid-1970s that allowed a few Australians to connect to ARPANet, a U.S. Department of Defense network that proved to be the predecessor of the Internet. At roughly the same time, the Australian Computer Science Network (ACSNet), a modem-based network using the Unix-to-Unix Copy Protocol (UUCP), was developed by computer science professors at the University of Melbourne and the University of Sydney. It was in the early 1980s that Australia put in place a permanent e-mail connection to ARPANet. A few years later, an e-mail gateway was added to ACSNet. ACSNet's storing, forwarding, and transferring features allowed Australia's computer scientists to engage in many of the same technologies, such as e-mail and file transfer protocol (FTP), that had recently been embraced by their colleagues around the world. Ironically, it was the success of this early network that many industry analysts blamed "for Australian computer scientists gaining access to the Internet about 5 years later than they should have," wrote Roger Clarke in May of 2001.

Efforts to expand network access to non-computer science areas of academia resulted in the creation of the South Pacific Education and Research Network (SPEARNet) by the Australian Vice-Chancellor's Committee (AVCC). In the late 1980s, work began on the creation of a national network for data, voice, and fax services. Eventually, this project evolved into what became known as the Australian Academic & Research Network (AARNet), which was officially launched in 1990 as an Internet protocol (IP) network without voice or fax capabilities. Like SPEARNet, AARNet was operated by AVCC. Melbourne University helped to oversee the development of Pegasus Networks, an early Internet Service Provider (ISP) that granted international Internet access via a connection to AARNet, in 1991. Within a year, several thousand Australians signed up for the service. Also in 1992, the Australian Public Access Network Association was created to offer hosting services to a growing number of bulletin boards and newsgroups; it eventually evolved into a noncommercial Internet access provider. The Asia-Pacific Network Information Centre, which was created in 1993, began to oversee IP address registration in the Asia-Pacific region shortly after its formation. That year, ARPANet decreed that acceptable use of the Internet could be expanded beyond research-oriented endeavors; this decision proved to be a major milestone in the transformation of the Internet into a commercial medium.

The advent of the World Wide Web sparked increased demand for Internet access across the globe. To better facilitate the growth of the Internet market in Australia, AARNet decided to implement a Value Added Reseller (VAR) program, through which it would allow ISPs to connect to its Internet backbone for a fee based on usage. In May of 1994, connect.com.au became the first ISP to sign up for the VAR program. That year, iinet Technologies, based in Perth, also began offering dial-up connections to the Internet. Australia's public telephone company, Telstra, launched its own ISP the following year. According to Clarke, "In mid-1995, AVCC transferred its commercial customers, associated assets, and the management of interstate and international links to Telstra. Telstra thereby acquired the whole of the infrastructure that at that stage constituted 'the Internet in Australia.'" Many analysts, including Clarke, believe that Telstra's sluggishness in responding to the demands of Internet growth worked to hinder the development of an Internet infrastructure, and thus e-commerce, on the continent. "During 1994-97, the international linkage represented a serious bottleneck, but gradually Telstra started releasing additional capacity at something closer to the rate at which demand was growing."

GROWING E-COMMERCE EFFORTS

It was in the mid-1990s that e-commerce efforts in Australia began in earnest. One of Australia's first CD e-tailers, SiteZero, emerged in 1996. That year, Melbourne IT secured a license to oversee administration of the com.au domain name registry. The firm began charging roughly $125 for domain name registration, prompting a surge in requests for net.au names, which were still free. Unable to keep up with demand, net.au registrar Connect.com began charging fees comparable to those of Melbourne IT. In 1997, Microsoft Corp. made its way into Australia with the creation of ninemsn.com. A joint venture with Australian media giant PBL, the new site was able to pull content from Nine Network television programming and ACP magazines. It also allowed its users to access a variety of free Microsoft services, such as e-mail service Hotmail, MSN search, and Messenger. By 2001, more than five million visitors every month were visiting ninemsn.com, which had grown into Australia's leading Web site. Other top Web sites by then included Yahoo!, eBay Australia, Excite Australia, and Telstra.com.

Depsite the launch of successful sites like dstore, which grew into Australia's leading online department store, Australians proved hesitant to embrace e-commerce. A mere 2.7 percent of Australian adults made online purchases in 1998; in 1999, that percentage grew to only six percent. A February 2000 study conducted by Australian law firm Freehill, Hollingdale & Page surmised that privacy issues were at least partly to blame. Although 80 percent of the online companies surveyed in the study adhered to some sort of a privacy protection standard, only 12 percent bothered to publish a privacy statement, which is a brief description of what it is a Web site does to protect the private information—such as credit card numbers and e-mail addresses—of its visitors. In addition, roughly 25 percent of the firms were unable to provide an on-line method of payment that was encrypted. However, despite their impact on e-commerce, security concerns certainly did not prevent Australians from getting online; during 2000, nearly 1.9 million new users, many of them residents of more rural areas, signed up for Internet access.

By then, the world's largest online services provider, America Online Inc. (AOL), had made its way into Australia via a joint venture with German publishing giant Bertelsmann AG. In March of 2000, AOL forged an alliance with AAPT Ltd., the third largest telecommunications provider in Australia. The joint venture, dubbed AOL Australia, took the place of the previous joint venture with Bertelsmann. The deal between AOL and AAPT called for the continuing development of content and e-commerce options on the AOL Australia Web site, as well the creation of wireless Internet access services for the continent.

According to a November 2000 press release by Jupiter Research Inc., "Despite Australia's current 40 percent online penetration rate—one of the highest in the world—revenue opportunities for both advertising and commerce have yet to materialize." According to a study conducted by Jupiter, online advertising in 2000 garnered $35 million, roughly 0.5 percent of total ad expenditures on the continent, compared to the 1.7 percent of total ad spending that online ads accounted for in Canada, a country with a 42 percent online penetration rate. Although the percentage of Web surfers in Australia making online purchases doubled that year from six to 12 percent, e-commerce rates continued to lag behind those in North America, where nearly 25 percent of Canadian Internet users and 40 percent of U.S. Internet users completed online purchases. The study cited a lack of e-commerce players in Australia as one culprit; a survey of 100 retailers revealed that less than 40 percent had made an effort to launch Internet operations, and many of those not conducting Internet-related business had no plans to do so in the near future. By the end of the year, e-commerce activity in Australia reached $2.9 billion; although sales were well below those of both Europe and North America, they did position Australia as one of the e-commerce leaders of the Asia-Pacific region.

Australia's two largest telecommunications firms, Telstra and Cable & Wireless Optus Ltd., began to make substantial advances in connectivity options in 2000. Although the copper wire infrastructure of the continent sorely needed updating, high-speed DSL connections were available to many residents. In addition, faster dial-up connections were also made more accessible to a wider range of Australians. In 1998, only 30 percent of rural Internet users had access to modem connections of 28.8 kbps or faster; by 2000, this percentage had doubled. In metropolitan areas, 73 percent of Australians could access the Internet at speeds faster than 28.8 kpbs. This compared to 80 percent of U.S. Internet users, 93 percent of British users, and nearly 100 percent of Canadian users.

Unlike North America, where a multitude of dot.com upstarts saturated the e-commerce arena well before many traditional firms made their way online, most Australian e-tailers in 2000 were the online outlets of brick-and-mortar firms. According to a January 2001 article in *E-Commerce Times,* "Australian e-tailing is dominated by the traditional retailers who have entered the e-commerce realm. Currently, 50 percent of online stores in Australia are the e-tailing arms of traditional retailers. The next 35 percent of Australian e-commerce sites are online-only merchants, while the remaining 15 percent are wholesalers who use the Internet to sell directly to customers."

Early in 2001, in an effort to foster increased levels of e-commerce, the Australian government passed the Commonwealth Government Privacy Act, a series of privacy stipulations that all online businesses were required to follow by the year's end. The requirements included publishing a privacy policy and making its location obvious to Web surfers. Other e-commerce efforts by Australia's government included continued deregulation of the telecommunications industry, a move designed to increase competition and thus drive down prices and foster the release of innovative products and services. In July, the government set aside $6.64 million in funding for B2B projects through 2006. Projects that secured grants from this program, dubbed Information Technology Online, included MarketBoomers, an online marketplace for the hotel and hospitality industry of Queensland, and Pharmaceutical Electronic Commerce and Communication, an online marketplace for health care products manufacturers.

E-commerce continued its steady pace of growth in Australia throughout 2001. Although only 5.4 percent of Australians used high-speed Internet connections that year, many analysts believed the DSL market would grow as telecommunication firms continued to make those services available to rural areas. Several market researchers also predicted that improved privacy measures on Australian e-commerce sites would entice more Australians to make online purchases. According to Ernst & Young, e-commerce in Australia will grow to $39 billion by 2004, as the number of online shoppers jumps from 2.2 million in 2000 to 5.84 million.

FURTHER READING:

"AAPT and America Online Announce New AOL Australia Joint Venture." *Business Wire,* March 29, 2000.

"Aging Infrastructure Holding Back Australia." *Newsbytes,* July 25, 2001. Available from www.nua.com.

"Australian Users Turn Slowly to Broadband." *Newsbytes Asia,* September 21, 2001.Available from www.nua.com.

Clarke, Roger. "A Brief History of the Internet in Australia." May 2001. Available from www.anu.edu.au.

Enos, Lori. "Australian Government Funds B2B E-Commerce." *E-Commerce Times,* July 11, 2001. Available from www.ecommercetimes.com.

————. "Report: E-Commerce Surging Down Under." *E-Commerce Times,* January 18, 2001. Available from www.ecommercetimes.com.

Freehill, Hollindale & Page. "E-Commerce Suffering Down Under." February 28, 2000. Available from www.nua.com.

Jupiter Research Inc. "Australian Online Population Reaches 40 Percent Penetration, But Ventures Slow to Capture Internet Revenue, Say Jupiter Research." November 2000. Available from www.jup.com.

Nicholas, Katrina. "Survey Finds Cavalier Approach to Privacy." *Sydney Morning Herald,* April 10, 2001.

"Statistics—E-Commerce in Australia Nov 1999." *AsiaPulse News,* March 1, 2000.

SEE ALSO: Digital Divide; Global Presence, Becoming a

GLOBAL E-COMMERCE: CENTRAL AND SOUTH AMERICA

In the early 2000s, the development of e-commerce in Central and South America was several years behind similar development in North America and Europe. However, the region still represented a market with great promise. With a large and increasingly connected population, and markets that were ever more linked to those in the north, particularly those in the United States, business leaders both in the region and around the world were anxious to see the development of Central and South American e-commerce. Despite such hopes, however, only the growth of business-to-business e-commerce was assured in the short term, while the consumer market faced more serious challenges. A number of social, political, technological, and economic factors kept the most ambitious dreams somewhat in check. Perhaps most troublesome, much of the region is beset by political instability, which in turn can lead to fluctuating currencies and precarious economies. In addition, civil unrest, particularly in Colombia, increasingly encroached upon borders in the early 2000s, threatening to lead to more widespread instability.

Complicating matters is the fact that there is little in the way of a defined "Latin American market." Rather, Central and South America are highly fragmented and every country—and often regions within countries—has to be considered on its own terms. This concept poses a great challenge to both outside investors and domestic entrepreneurs. On one hand, those seeking to reap great financial rewards in Central and South America might want to push forward to develop a pan-regional market in which they could emerge as the standard bearer. On the other hand, an individual or company that is too aggressive risks losing sight of the nuances of the varying markets and thereby overextending its resources for diminishing returns.

CHALLENGES

REGULATORY AND TAX ISSUES. The legal framework for e-commerce in South and Central America was fairly underdeveloped in the very early 2000s, thus inhibiting the possibilities for growth. In this vein, Latin American countries had done little, by and large, to address e-commerce taxation issues, as they were still struggling with the basic establishment of an Internet infrastructure. Central and South American governments derive their greatest share of revenue from value-added taxes, which are those levied on the sale of imported goods. When the various players involved in a transaction are all located in different countries, which often is the case with e-commerce, the assessment of a value-added tax becomes increasingly difficult.

For the most part, e-commerce taxation throughout the region is tied to the existing rules for physical-world taxation. However, the difficulty in enforcing such taxation and the resulting decline in tax revenues is expected to spur the region's governments into action to coordinate with governments elsewhere, particularly in Europe, to implement taxation schemes geared specifically toward e-commerce. A few countries that have negotiated tax treaties with the Organization for Economic Cooperation and Development (OECD) include Argentina, Brazil, Chile, and Venezuela. Additionally, several countries were working toward harmonizing some elements of their tax policies with their North American neighbors in 2001.

Many of the region's countries also retained relatively protectionist economic policies that aimed to cradle their own developing industries from foreign competition. Some countries, such as Brazil and Argentina, took large strides in opening up their markets to a more liberalized trade policy. This was attractive to foreign investors, including major North American and European Internet and telecommunications firms. According to many analysts, in a borderless Internet environment at least some degree of liberalization is necessary to attract such investment and to compete in the e-commerce world.

U.S. Federal Communications Commission (FCC) Chairman William E. Kennard, speaking in Lima, Peru, in spring 2000, insisted that it was the function of regulators in Latin America to check the influence of the powerful Internet carriers and level the playing field so that all people could enjoy and benefit from the Internet. Kennard announced the launching of a development initiative aimed at fostering telecommunications and information technology infrastructure throughout Latin America. The aim of the initiative was to bring more people in the region online and enable them to benefit from e-commerce. It was primarily based around the exchange of information and ideas, but signaled the U.S. government's interest in expanding e-commerce among its southern neighbors.

SOCIAL AND ECONOMIC INEQUITY. A great deal of social and economic disparity, both within and between countries, plagued much of Central and South America, inhibiting the spread of e-commerce. Because Internet access throughout the region was so expensive and presented so many technical problems, Internet penetration hovered at around three percent in the early 2000s. Jupiter Communications placed the entire online population in Latin America at 11 million in 1999, while the most optimistic estimates for the year 2000 placed the total at 30 million users. However, Jupiter expected the total to skyrocket to 67 million by 2005, making Latin America the fastest-growing Internet population in the world. As a result, in the eyes of many e-merchants, the time was ripe to jump into the Central and South American market in order to capture the eyes of those users as they come online, thereby building early customer loyalty. According to Jupiter, one critical consideration for e-commerce was that its estimated number of Internet users referred to individuals versus households. Latin Americans were far more likely than North Americans to surf the Web at kiosks or other locations outside of the home, because PC penetration throughout the region was markedly low. As a result, those accessing the Internet were far less likely than those to the north to engage in e-commerce, since they didn't enjoy access in the privacy of their own homes.

For the most part, computer ownership in Latin America is a hobby for elites, and therefore business-to-consumer e-commerce has been fairly limited in its possibilities. This trend showed few signs of letting up in the early 2000s. However, as technologies become cheaper and information technology and telecommunications infrastructure grow more sophisticated and widespread, entrepreneurs remain hopeful that the consumer Internet market in Central and South America will ripen.

According to *Euromoney,* optimists hoped that the Internet could serve a social function in Latin America, one that eventually would filter down to generate benefits for e-commerce. By opening the information infrastructure, the Internet held the potential to serve as a democratizing force and break down what many saw as the region's rampant political and economic corruption. Such hopes, *Euromoney* reported, were fueling valuations of companies trying to stake a claim to Latin American e-commerce markets. Indeed, *Business Week* reporters Katz and Malkin noted that the Internet already was responsible for helping to reduce some of the corruption involved in the granting of both public- and private-sector contracts.

INADEQUATE INFRASTRUCTURE. The biggest obstacle to Central and South American e-commerce in the late 1990s and early 2000s was the lack of a comprehensive telecommunications infrastructure throughout the region. This problem was beginning to be addressed, largely by outside investors eyeing the region's explosive potential, by way of new phone lines, computers, information technology, Internet service providers (ISPs), and wireless technology.

Katz and Malkin noted that the structural difficulties in the region, as of 1999, were deeply rooted. For instance, only about 10 percent of the population was connected to a phone line, while the average gross domestic product per capita was less than $4,000—hardly conditions that bring joy to the hearts of e-commerce merchants. The phone line penetration was expected to rise—to a still-miniscule two per every 10 people—by the middle of the 2000s, while PC sales trends were moving in the right direction to eliminate some of the extreme disparity within the region.

However, developing regions such as Central and South America had a key advantage over the more developed regions. North America and Western Europe pioneered the Internet infrastructure and e-commerce. However, the less developed regions benefit from the hindsight those leaders provided, and can avoid the same mistakes in the nascent stages. Moreover, the telecommunications infrastructure largely will move straight to the more sophisticated models, such as broadband, rather than try to adapt the Internet to a scarcely existing infrastructure. Indeed, Microsoft in 1999 pumped $126 million into the Globo Cabo, a leading Brazilian television and cable company, to develop a broadband infrastructure, and other U.S. and European companies followed suit with their own deals throughout the region.

E-merchants throughout Central and South America needed to come up with alternative models to facilitate shopping and purchasing rather than simply mimicking the U.S. model. Credit card ownership was exceptionally limited, as low as 10 percent in some areas, according to Jupiter Research. To dramatize the problem, Jupiter studied one of the most upscale neighborhoods in the region's most economically developed nation, Brazil, and found that even there

half of the households did not own a credit card. Thus, the overwhelmingly preferred payment method for e-merchants in North America and Europe was not feasible in Central and South America. Some solutions that have been furthered in the region were the development of alternative currencies specifically for use in Web-based transactions.

Even where users did have credit cards, they were relatively unlikely to use them over the Internet in Central and South America, where merchants generally assume little responsibility for their products—''where 'caveat emptor' is the conventional wisdom,'' as *Brandweek* put it. Security fears, big enough problems in the United States, were greatly magnified in Latin America and highlighted another challenge for e-commerce in the region: overcoming consumers' reluctance to shop online in the first place. These fears were faced in North America and Europe, and have been largely dealt with through implementation of improved encryption technologies to safeguard credit card numbers, along with the establishment of formal government-sponsored frameworks designed to address such issues. However, in Latin America the problems are far more deeply rooted, and may not be remedied by simple technological solutions.

BUSINESS-TO-BUSINESS E-COMMERCE SET TO TAKE OFF

In early 2001, *World Trade* pointed toward Latin America as the next great market for business-to-business e-commerce, claiming that the first few years of the new century would see the rise of a range of new B2B exchanges and startups, while the leading firms for the long term would take root. Unlike most North American firms, much of Latin American business, according to *World Trade,* still relied on manual, paper-based accounting, procurement, and inventory management systems. Because of this, the switch to B2B market exchanges should add significantly more than incremental benefits to companies in Central and South America, promising to dramatically streamline their value chains. Forrester Research predicted that, in the early 2000s, business-to-business transactions would account for 93 percent of all Latin American e-commerce activity. By 2004, Forrester indicated that B2B e-commerce in Latin America, including Mexico, would total $76 billion.

Business-to-business development in Central and South America also was aided by the fact that, compared to North American firms, industries in that region were heavily fragmented and relatively inefficient. Therefore, they stood to benefit from the ability to trade goods and supplies online rather than using the established infrastructure. *World Trade* insisted that successful business-to-business ventures in South and Central America would be those that catered to industries with high fragmentation among both buyers and sellers, company and industry-wide inefficiency, little to lose in overhauling existing technological infrastructures to incorporate B2B e-commerce, and large size.

Among the large markets that were most likely to embrace business-to-business e-commerce in South America are Brazil, Chile, and Argentina. Not only are these countries home to the region's strongest economies overall, their technological infrastructures are the most advanced. Because B2B frameworks are most effective in large marketplaces where liquidity is relatively assured, these countries were the most ideal.

THE OVERALL MARKET: BRIGHT SPOTS AND FUTURE OUTLOOK

Total e-commerce volume for the region, as predicted by Forrester Research, will reach $82 billion by 2004. While this represents strong growth and an encouraging trend for Latin America, that figure still amounts to a relatively small share of the global e-commerce market. By way of comparison, Forrester estimated that by 2004 the total e-commerce traffic in the United States would reach $3.2 trillion, while the Asia-Pacific region would total $1.6 trillion, and Western Europe would amount to $1.5 trillion. Trailing the Latin American region would be Eastern Europe, Africa, and the Middle East, which would reach a combined total of $68.6 billion.

Some analysts were especially optimistic about the prospects for e-commerce in particular countries, such as Brazil. With about half the region's population and the eighth-largest economy in the world, Brazil was the nation most coveted by e-commerce players for growth in the short term, and was the most common invading ground for U.S. Internet companies seeking to make inroads into the South and Central American markets. Jupiter Communications predicted compound annual growth rates for Internet penetration of 19 percent between 1998 and 2003; by 2003, some 20 million Brazilians will be online. Brazil clearly is the largest e-commerce player in the region, with total e-commerce sales expected to reach $64 billion by 2004, according to Forrester Research. The Northbrook, Illinois-based consulting firm Core Strategies predicted that "e-commerce will experience an explosion in Brazil no place else in the world will equal." Core sited characteristics of the Brazilian market that make it so favorable. Among them are the fact that 40 percent of the Brazilian population lives more than 20 miles from a retail center, with transportation sporadically available. Such demographic fea-

tures, Core suggested, will encourage the spread of e-commerce. Also, the Internet infrastructure is in place in Brazil as it is in no other Central or South American country, with about half, or $17 billion, of the Latin American information technology market centered in Brazil.

Brazil also harbored the highest percentage of South or Central American Internet shoppers. Fully 31 percent of Brazilian Internet users reported making an online purchase in 1999, a proportion nearly as high as that in the United States. And, while still paltry, credit card use was rising more quickly in Brazil than in any other country in the region. As might be expected, Brazil also had the most online merchants, according to *Business Week.* Brazil, in fact, faced a glut of ISPs in the early 2000s, with more than 500 providers. Internet analysts insisted that a shakeout was on the way.

According to the report "Web Sellers Best Practices 2000: Chile and Latin America," compiled by the Chilean Chamber of Commerce and International Data Corp. (IDC) Chile, e-commerce in Latin America's six-largest economies, including Mexico, grew 117 percent in 2000 to reach $1.1 billion, representing 4.3 percent of all retail sales in those countries. The report noted that Brazil led the region with 27 percent of all online retail sales, while Argentina claimed 21 percent, Chile 15.4 percent, Venezuela 9.3 percent, and Colombia 6.2 percent. Argentina, another regional powerhouse, would rack up $10 billion in e-commerce sales by 2004, according to Forrester Research.

With the growing population of Spanish-speaking individuals in the United States, which has close geographical proximity to Central and South America, many U.S. Internet businesses were shifting to capture a Spanish-speaking market. A growing flow of money was going south, and U.S. firms were realizing extraordinary benefits from trading with businesses in Central and South America. Indeed, the region constituted an extremely contentious field among international players in the late 1990s and early 2000s, as a few United States-based Web portals spent that period battling for position in the Central and South American markets. Yahoo!, StarMedia Networks, and Microsoft squared off against Brazil's own Universo Online, Argentina's El Sitio, and a handful of others to stake a claim as the region's preeminent Web portal. The leading force in the Internet service provider (ISP) field, meanwhile, was Telefonica of Spain, which operated major ISPs in Chile, Peru, and Brazil, building on its ownership of several leading telephone companies.

The Latin American market, therefore, offered savvy investors—who may have missed out on the dot-com explosion in the more developed regions—

another chance, and with the benefit of hindsight as well. Estimates variously place the Central and South American Internet markets three of four years behind that of the United States—a prospect that greatly delighted entrepreneurs and venture capitalists in the early 2000s.

FURTHER READING:

Cleaver, Joanne. "Online Explosion." *Marketing News.* June 21, 1999.

Disabatino, Jennifer. "U.S., Latin America Blending e-Commerce." *Computerworld.* May 29, 2000.

Ebenkamp, Becky. "Manana's Opportunities." *Brandweek.* February 28, 2000.

Fattah, Hassan. "Latin Crowd." *MC Technology Marketing Intelligence.* August 2000.

Gross, Jorge A.; Nicasio del Castillo; Manuel Solano; and Eduardo Pupo German Jimenez. "Latin America Explores Cyberspace." *International Tax Review.* December 2000/January 2001.

"Hypergrowth for e-Commerce?" *Futurist.* September/October 2000.

Katz, Ian; and Elisabeth Malkin. "Battle for the Latin American Net." *Business Week.* November 1, 1999.

Kennard, William E. "Connecting the Globe: The Latin American Initiative." *Presidents and Prime Ministers.* March/April 2000.

Patino, Martha. "Focus on Latin America." *World Trade.* February 2001.

Pereiera, Pedro. "e-Business Washes into Latin America." *Computer Reseller News.* December 13, 1999.

Piper, Mark. "Dot Coms Discover Another Eden." *Euromoney.* July 2000.

Saba, Jennifer. "O Brazil!" *MC Technology Marketing Intelligence.* November 1999.

SEE ALSO: Digital Divide; Global Presence, Becoming a

GLOBAL E-COMMERCE: EUROPE

The development of e-commerce across the globe varies widely depending on factors such as an area's technological infrastructure; the technological expertise of residents, which is related to both the ability of e-commerce companies to find qualified workers and the ability of citizens to engage in Internet-related transactions; funding available for e-commerce ventures; and national, regional, and local commerce regulations. In the late 1990s, e-commerce grew most quickly in North America, particularly in the U.S., due to the increasing number of Internet savvy shoppers there, as well as the world's largest base of technical experts, who not only were available to work for e-commerce ventures, but also launched their own firms in many cases. Also fueling the U.S. e-commerce boom was the unprecedented level of venture capital available from a variety of sources.

E-commerce grew more slowly in Europe for a variety of reasons. In general, Europeans proved more skeptical regarding the potential of e-commerce ventures, which meant funding was more difficult for up-starts to obtain. E-commerce players also faced many more regulatory hurdles than in the U.S. as online commerce laws varied widely across the different countries within Europe, a fact that not only dissuaded some traditional European firms from engaging in e-commerce, but also slowed the European expansion of some worldwide e-commerce giants. In addition, interactive information services, such as teletext television, also enjoyed more prominence in Europe, which undermined the novelty of the Internet for many Europeans. Perhaps one of the largest obstacles to Internet use in Europe was the cost of local phone access, which was billed by most major telecommunications firms there on a per-minute basis. Since local telephone lines provided the most common form of access to the Internet, users were forced to pay not only monthly fees to their Internet services provider (ISP), but also per-minute fees for the call as well.

However, Internet access across the continent did begin to increase in 1999, due in large part to the free Internet access offered by firms such as United Kingdom-based Freeserve, launched by European electronic retailing giant Dixons Group in September of 1998. While Internet users were still required to pay the local telephone call charges incurred while using the Internet, Freeserve did not charge any sort of premium or monthly subscription fee. The roughly $20 per month these free ISPs saved most European Internet surfers was enough to entice hordes of new users to sign up for service. In fact, roughly 16 million Europeans began using the Internet for the first time in 1999. As a result, the percentage of Europeans with Internet access grew to 13 percent. Venture capital became increasingly available that year as well. For example, French venture capitalist Bernard Amault established Europ@web, an online startup fund worth 500 million euros. French conglomerate Vivendi partnered with the Internet investment unit of Softbank, a Japanese publishing group, to form @Viso; the new venture received $100 million to expand CarPoint, Onsale, and the other U.S.-based online operations owned by Softbank into Europe. In addition, established funding firms such as 3i, Atlas Ventures, and Net Partners also began investing in European dot.coms.

In 1999, the number of European businesses using the Internet for sales, marketing, and other business-to-consumer (B2C) efforts grew from 53 percent to 72 percent, while the number of European firms using the Internet to conduct business-to-business (B2B) transactions, such as procurement, reached 47 percent. Despite this growth, however, e-commerce sales in Europe, which totaled $18 billion, lagged far behind the $507 billion in e-commerce sales transacted in the U.S. Europe held only a 14 percent stake of the worldwide B2B e-commerce market, compared to the 67 percent stake held by the U.S., and a only 14 percent stake of the worldwide B2C market, compared to 76 percent in the U.S.

Internet usage rates among Europeans continued climbing in 2000, as the number of European homes with Internet access jumped by 55 percent between March and October. In fact, the number of Internet users in Europe exceeded the number of U.S. Internet users for the first time. Fueling this growth was the deregulation of the European telecommunications industry, which finally forced some local phone monopolies to give local phone line access to ISPs wanting to offer unlimited Internet access for a set monthly fee, as was the norm in the U.S. For example, Freeserve was able to offer unmetered Internet access for the first time in April of 2000.

In early 2001, despite their increased Internet usage, less than five percent of European Web surfers were making regular online purchases. Regardless of these disappointing numbers, however, some industry analysts believed Europe faced a better e-commerce future than the U.S. According to *E-Commerce Times* writer Michael Mahoney, ''It may be taking Europeans longer than Americans to gravitate toward online shopping, but the numbers also mean that European dot-coms have not had so far to tumble. With European e-commerce averaging some 18 months or so behind that in the States, the U.S. dot-com shakeout has served as a highly visible business lesson for European e-tailers—helping to prevent them from making the same mistakes.'' In fact, a Pricewaterhouse-Coopers study released in September of 2001 revealed that 90 percent of the 400 European Internet companies it surveyed in July of 2000 were still afloat one year later, despite many predictions otherwise. Many of the firms even achieved profitability due, in part, to cost cutting efforts and the ability to alter business models based on market conditions.

E-COMMERCE EFFORTS IN THE UNITED KINGDOM

The United Kingdom proved to be a leading European e-commerce arena. By November of 1999, 25 percent of adult citizens there accessed the Internet regularly. A key component in the country's online development was Freeserve, the Internet access service launched by Dixons Group in late 1998, which offered U.K. residents Internet access for free. To sign up, customers simply had to stop by a Dixons, Curry's, PC World, or Link store to pick up the necessary software. Within five months of its inception, Freeserve had signed on more than 1 million customers.

When the upstart conducted its initial public offering (IPO) in August of 1999, listing its shares on both the London Stock Exchange and NASDAQ, it had secured roughly 30 percent of the Internet market in the U.K. In early 2000, Freeserve reorganized its online content into the following channels: business, careers, entertainment, learning, life, money, motoring, news and weather, shopping, sport, travel, and women. Eventually, property and health channels were added to the site's offerings. Like free ISPs in North America, Freeserve soon realized that although the free ISP model was highly effective for securing a large base of subscribers quickly, monthly service fees were necessary for the sake of profitability. As a result, the firm introduced several fee-based subscription options in April. The least expensive service, Freeserve HomeTime, allowed subscribers to access the Internet between 6 p.m. and 8 a.m. during the week and all day and night during the weekend. For a slightly increased rate, clients could opt for Freeserve AnyTime to gain unrestricted access to the Internet. Those who used the Internet less frequently could opt for Freeserve No-Ties, which billed clients based on the amount of time they used the Interet.

Freeserve began offering a high-speed broadband Internet service—the first of its kind in the U.K.—in September of 2000. Three months later, the leading online services provider in France, Wanadoo Group, offered to purchase Freeserve from Dixons. The deal was completed in the first quarter of 2001. By then, Freeserve had seen its subscriber base grow to 2.1 million, one-quarter of which had signed on for a fee-based subscription.

Late in 2000, the U.K. government took an active role in promoting e-commerce by publishing the U.K. Online Strategy. Among other things, the new plan called for increased assistance for small businesses going online; the creation of learn-direct centers, which offered various online courses and telephone help lines; and the creation of 6,000 online centers to allow for Internet access and training in various communities. In addition, the government launched its own Web site and began delivering a variety of government services online.

In addition to the e-commerce efforts coming from within the U.K., many leading U.S. e-commerce players had also began to move into the country. For example, America Online (AOL) Europe, a direct competitor to Freeserve that arrived in the U.K. in 1996, secured a base of 1 million customers there by 2001. In March of that year, AOL was able to offer unlimited online access to U.K. residents for $20 per month. Leading women's Internet portal iVillage.com created iVillage.co.uk in conjunction with leading U.K. retailer Tesco in December of 2000. Internet auction leader eBay moved into the U.K. even earlier, launching a site there in 1999.

E-COMMERCE EFFORTS IN GERMANY

According to an April 2001 article in *Campaign*, ''Germany is one of the biggest Internet markets in Europe. With 11.99 million home Internet visitors in January 2001 and a total online ad spend of 204 million euros last year (source: Jupiter MMXI), it vies with the UK as the region's largest online economy. Currently, the UK has 12.84 million home users and a market value of about 224 million euros. Between them, these two territories account for 45 percent of Europe's 943 million euro online ad market.'' The country's leading ISP is T-Online, a subsidiary of Deutsche Telekom, which also happens to be the largest ISP in Europe, with operations in Austria, France, Portugal, Spain, and Switzerland. T-Online boasted 6.53 million German subscribers and 7.94 million total subscribers at the end of 2000. Although sales that year grew 86 percent to 797.2 million euros, the firm posted a loss of 125 million euros. A flat-rate unlimited use package, which T-Online first implemented that year, had contributed the loss, a fact which prompted the firm to eliminate flat-rate pricing in 2001.

Germany's leading e-commerce player is Bertelsmann AG. Although Bertelsmann dabbled in various online ventures in the mid-1990s, it wasn't until a few years later that the publishing powerhouse devised a concrete e-commerce plan. In 1998, the firm acquired a 50 percent stake in BarnesandNobel.com for roughly $200 million to strengthen its position in the U.S. online book industry. More importantly, Bertelsmann also launched its own retail book site, BOL.com, to compete with Amazon.com in Europe. By 2000, Bertelsmann had funneled more than $13 billion into its Internet operations. In May of that year, the firm played a role in the creation of Terra Lycos, formed when Spain's Terra Networks paid $12.5 billion for Lycos, one of the largest U.S.-based World Wide Web gateways. Bertelsmann agreed to spend roughly $1 billion on advertising and other Internet services from Terra Lycos over the next five years in exchange for access to the 50 million customers already using either Terra Networks or Lycos. The next month, Bertelsmann merged its increasingly diverse e-commerce operations into a single entity known as Bertelsmann

eCommerce Group. Adding to its growing e-commerce holdings, Bertelsmann also bought online music retailer CDNOW. In a move that demonstrated its determination to emerge as a worldwide leader in e-commerce, the firm joined forces with music indexing site Napster in October of 2000, despite widespread controversy over alleged copyright infringement regarding the technology that allows Napster users to exchange songs for free.

E-COMMERCE EFFORTS IN FRANCE

When Socialist party candidate Francois Mitterand took control of France in the early 1980s, the country embarked on its first real online effort. The government-owned France Telecom distributed a set-top appliance, known as the Minitel, which first operated as an electronic directory connected to a government network, to every household. According to a December 2000 article in *DSN Retailing Today*, ''As France's networking needs evolved, the Minitel soon became Europe's first e-commerce channel, offering travel packages, concert tickets, hotel reservations and messageries, the precursor to the present-day chat room.'' Although France made early use of online technology, its widespread adoption of the Minitel was seen by many as a long-term liability that prevented the nation from embracing newer e-commerce technology. ''By distributing the Minitel to virtually all of France, France Telecom had created a market standard within the country—and a limited one at that—which for better or worse was in large part responsible for the late arrival of the World Wide Web in that country.''

France Telecom launched Wanadoo, an ISP, in 1996, the same year that AOL first began offering online services to residents of France. Five years later, in an effort to become one of the top three ISPs in Europe, Wanadoo acquired the leading U.K.-based ISP, Freeserve; the purchase boosted Wanadoo's subscriber base to nearly five million. Other leading e-commerce ventures in France included FNAC.com, the online version of the 50-store bricks and mortar chain selling book, music, and electronics throughout France. eBay moved into France in 2001 when it paid $112 million for iBazar S.A., a French auction site with 2.4 million users and operations in Belgium, Brazil, France, Italy, the Netherlands, Portugal, Spain, and Sweden. Online efforts by major French companies such as Louis Vuitton S.A. also continued to bolster e-commerce throughout the nation.

E-COMMERCE EFFORTS IN IRELAND

Ireland has also emerged as an e-commerce leader in Europe. In 1999, wanting to foster competition and growth in the emerging Internet-based markets, the Irish government deregulated its telecommunications industry and privatized its state-owned telecommunication monopoly, Eircom. The government also forged an alliance with Global Crossing to construct an underwater fiberoptic cable that would enhance the speed and capacity of the country's existing telecommunications infrastructure. These efforts attracted the attention of several high-tech firms, including Hewlett-Packard Co., which opened a European Outsourcing Center in Dublin in December of 1999. At roughly the same time, Novell Inc. transformed Novell Software Ireland Ltd., based in Dublin, into the home base for its European, Middle Eastern, and African e-commerce activities. In addition, Dublin also gained a new Oracle Corp. e-business center; an AOL development center, the only such center outside of the U.S.; and the Massachusetts Institute of Technology MediaLab Europe, the first international arm of the world renowned technology-based research lab.

The Irish government passed an e-commerce bill, covering such issues as electronic signatures and online contracting, in July of 2000. A few months later, Sun Microsystems, Oracle, Cisco, and Wolfe Group joined forced to create business-incubator.com, a small business service designed to help Internet-based startups in Ireland for significantly reduced consulting fees. eBay made its way into Ireland in March of 2001. That year, the Irish government earmarked 75 million euros for broadband network developments throughout the country.

THE FUTURE OF EUROPEAN E-COMMERCE

A major concern for businesses engaged in European e-commerce is pending legislation, called Rome II, that would grant legal authority for resolving cross-border e-commerce disputes to the country in which a consumer lives. According to a July 2001 *E-Commerce Times* article, "Rome II, if enacted as is, has the potential to stunt the growth of international e-commerce. We are talking about stunting the growth in a way unlike any other issue from tax debates to security glitches." Critics of the legislation believe it would dissuade many companies from expanding into Europe, due to the costs and complexity associated with understanding and complying with such a diverse group of regulations. The outcome of this proposal, expected to be subject to a vote by the European Commission by the beginning of 2002, along with the continued rate of telecommunications deregulation within European countries, will factor significantly in the future of European e-commerce.

FURTHER READING:

Addison, Dominick. "Free Web Access Business Model is Unsustainable in the Long Term." *Marketing,* August 9, 2001.

Dembeck, Chet. "Internet Gold Rush Grips Europe." *E-Commerce Times,* August 17, 1999. Available from www.ecommercetimes.com.

"E-Commerce Growth Quickens." *Europe,* October 1999.

Freeserve.com. "Our History." London: Dixons Group plc, 2001. Available from www.aboutfreeserve.com.

Fry, Andy. "Online Shockwaves." *Campaign,* April 13, 2001.

Greenberg, Paul A. "Blurring the Borders of E-Commerce."*E-Commerce Times,* July 3, 2001. Available from www.ecommercetimes.com.

———. "Europe Struggles to Standardize E-Commerce Laws."*E-Commerce Times,* November 1, 1999. Available from www.ecommercetimes.com.

Gwin, Peter. "AOL's European Expansion." *Europe,* June 2001.

Hewitt, Patricia, and Andrew Pinder. "Online Strategy is Back on Schedule." *Computer Weekly,* March 29, 2001.

"Ireland Becoming Europe's E-Commerce Hub." *PR Newswire,* December 17, 1999.

Mahoney, Michael. "Europe Learns Its E-Commerce Dos and Don'ts."*E-Commerce Times,* April 20, 2001. Available from www.ecommercetimes.com.

Milmo, Sean. "E-Commerce Gains Speed as Europe Evolves." *Chemical Market Reporter,* October 25, 1999.

Perera, Rick. "Most European Dot-Coms Still Afloat." *The Standard,* September 19, 2001. Available from www.thestandard.com.

Spiegel, Rob. "Europe Closing E-Commerce Gap with U.S." *E-Commerce Times,* December 21, 1999. Available from www.ecommercetimes.com.

Yates, Karen. "Dixons Provides Free Internet Access to Gain Retail Foothold." *Campaign,* October 30, 1998.

SEE ALSO: General Usage for International Digitally Ensured Commerce (GUIDEC); Global E-commerce Regulation; Global Trading Web Association; Safe Harbor Privacy Framework

GLOBAL E-COMMERCE: NORTH AMERICA

The development of e-commerce varies widely in different regions across the globe. Factors that impact e-commerce include the technological expertise of residents, which affects both the ability of e-commerce companies to find qualified workers and the ability of citizens to engage in Internet-related transactions; funding available for e-commerce ventures; and the technological infrastructure of an area. In the late 1990s, e-commerce grew most quickly in North America, particularly in the U.S., due to the increasing number of Internet savvy shoppers there, as well as the world's largest base of technical experts, who not only were available to work for e-commerce ventures, but who also, in many cases, launched their own firms. Also fueling the North American e-commerce boom was the unprecedented level of funding available from a variety of sources. Moreover, many analysts believed that the time savings afforded by shopping online appealed to U.S. residents, who were considered more time conscious than individuals in other parts of the world, such as Europe or Asia.

EARLY HISTORY

The rise of e-commerce in North America has at its roots the founding of several key companies, including online services provider America Online Inc. (AOL), online retailing giant Amazon.com, online auction powerhouse eBay, Internet portal Yahoo!, and World Wide Web browser developer Netscape Communications Corp. The success of each of these firms played a pivotal role in the North American Internet revolution and the subsequent growth of e-commerce across the continent.

The first of these firms was founded in May of 1985, when 26-year-old Steven Case partnered with Jim Kimsey to establish the predecessor to AOL, Quantum Computer Services, in conjunction with Commodore International, Ltd. At first, Quantum offered Q-Link, its modem-based online service, to Commodore personal computer (PC) users only. Owners of PCs made by Tandy Corp. and other companies were able to link in to the service starting in 1987, and owners of IBM-compatible PCs, as well as Macintosh machines, were granted access shortly thereafter. Believing that a mass market for interactive online services and content existed, Case put together a nationwide online network for PC owners called America Online in 1989, and eventually changed Quantum's name to America Online, Inc. The new AOL service included games, e-mail, and real-time chat capabilities.

Case spent the early 1990s honing AOL's focus to IBM-compatible and Macintosh computer markets and growing its subscribers by doing things like giving AOL software away for free. To expand its content, AOL began seeking partnerships with media firms. The firm completed its initial public offering (IPO) in 1992, and rejected a buyout offer from Microsoft Corp. the following year. Deals with media firms like Knight-Ridder and CNN further expanded AOL's content. When Microsoft's Windows platform began to grow in popularity, AOL developed a Windows-based version of its online service, and when analysts began forecasting that the fledgling World Wide Web would render proprietary online services like AOL obsolete, the firm created a gateway, known as AOL.com, to offer subscribers a link to the Internet. AOL members exceeded one million for the first time in 1994.

AOL became available in Canada in 1996. That year, Microsoft agreed to include AOL software on its Windows 95 platform in exchange for AOL's inclusion of Microsoft's Internet Explorer Web browser in its software. Determined to position his firm as the leader in online services, Case reached similar cross marketing deals with AT&T, Apple, Sun Microsystems, Hewlett-Packard, and Netscape Communications. In October of 1996, Robert Pittman was hired as president and chief operating officer and charged with the task of developing AOL's e-commerce strategy. Shortly thereafter, Pittman began forging alliances with online retailing giants like Amazon.com, which agreed to sell its merchandise on AOL. Revenues exceeded $1 billion in 1997, and membership grew to more than ten million subscribers. Despite highly publicized technical problems surrounding the firm's inability to handle traffic surges resulting from a new $19.95 per month unlimited access program launched in 1997, the flat fee pushed AOL's subscriber base even higher. By then, AOL had solidified its position as a leading Internet player. According to *BusinessWeek Online* writer Catherine Yang, ''more than any other leader in e-business, the 41-year-old chairman of America Online Inc. is responsible for bringing the Internet revolution to the masses.''

At roughly the same time as AOL was developing its portal to the Web, Silicon Graphics co-founder Jim Clark partnered with 22-year-old Marc Andreessen, one of the developers of the Mosaic graphic user interface (GUI) program for the Web, to create Mosaic Corp. Officially established in April of 1994, the predecessor to Netscape was funded with $3 million of Clark's personal savings and additional venture capital from investor John Doerr. In October, Clark and Andreessen offered Jim Barksdale, an executive for AT&T Corp., a seat on Netscape's board; three months later, they convinced him to leave his post at AT&T to take the helm at Netscape. Although the firm wasn't yet profitable, Clark convinced Andreessen and Barksdale to conduct Netscape's initial public offering (IPO) in 1995. The IPO turned out to be one of the most lucrative in the technology industry's history, setting the stage for the multitude of upstarts, also not yet profitable, that conducted IPOs later in the decade. Clark and Andreessen's launch of Netscape's free Web browser, Navigator, is viewed by many industry analysts as a key reason for the advent of the Internet revolution. According to Charlotte Dunlap in *Computer Reseller News,* ''Clark helped launch the Internet craze by commercializing the government-based network's first GUI.'' Less than a year after Netscape's IPO, Navigator had secured roughly 80 percent of the Web browser market. This success attracted the attention of Microsoft Corp., which decided to include a version of its own browser, Internet

Explorer, with its Windows 95 platform. By giving this software away for free, both Netscape and Microsoft made Internet access even easier for PC users to obtain.

Less than a year after Netscape's inception, Stanford University doctoral students David Filo and Jerry Yang co-founded Yahoo! Inc. In the early 1990s, the two began using Mosaic to browse the Web. After having difficulty keeping track of his growing list of favorite sites, Filo sought Yang's help to develop a program that would allow him to group Web sites into subject categories. The partners named the resulting list of sites ''Jerry's Guide to the World Wide Web'' and posted it on the Web. When Web surfers across the globe e-mailed positive feedback regarding Jerry's Guide, Yang and Filo decided to begin indexing all Web sites. They set a goal of cataloging 1,000 sites per day; when subject categories became unwieldy, they added layers of subcategories to improve organization. The site's popularity grew rapidly, and Stanford's server began struggling under the increased traffic load. As a result, the university asked Yang and Filo to find another organization to host what they renamed Yahoo!, an acronym for ''Yet Another Hierarchical Officious Oracle.'' Buyout offers emerged from executives at Netscape, AOL, and what would become other leading Internet firms, but Yang and Filo turned them down. Instead, they agreed to take a leave of absence from their studies to co-found Yahoo Inc. in March of 1995. After securing financial backing from Sequoia Capital, Yang and Filo hired Tim Koogle to run their business. When the company went public in 1996, Yang and Filo became overnight millionaires.

Within months of Yahoo!'s official launch, Amazon.com appeared on the Web. Amazon's founder, 30-year-old Jeff Bezos, resigned as a Wall Street executive in 1994 to pursue his dream of creating an Internet retailer. After deciding to focus on the book market, he hired four employees and began working in the garage of his new home in Seattle, Washington, to build the retail site. Bezos chose the Amazon, believing the title of the largest river in the world expressed his site's ability to reach vast numbers of customers. When Amazon.com went online in July of 1995, the site allowed visitors to search for books by author or title, as well as subject or keyword. Book prices, considerably lower than those of traditional book retailers, coupled with free shipping, attracted many users to the site. In fact, in just three months Amazon achieved its first 100-order day.

During Amazon's second year of operation, Bezos began focusing on increasing the firm's growth. One of his most lauded moves, the creation of the ''associates'' program in July 1996, allowed individual Web site owners and operators to offer links to Amazon from their site. The associate then received a commission any time a visitor clicked on that link and bought a book. Bezos also forged alliances with America Online Inc. and Yahoo Inc., securing Amazon's promotion on those high-traffic sites. Although it had not yet earned a profit, Amazon conducted its IPO in May of 1997. In October of that year, Amazon became the Internet's first retail operation with one million customers. Amazon's success left traditional book retailers scrambling to retain customers. Many chains began staying open later, offering entertainment, hosting book clubs, selling coffee and pastries, and even opening up their own retail Web sites, which Barnes & Noble did in May of 1997. According to a September 1997 *Chain Store Age Executive* article, Amazon.com permanently altered book retailing. ''Bezos redefined book and information merchandising and distribution. He has changed the way some customers shop and purchase books, and continues to challenge the definition of the traditional book store.''Amazon also helped fuel the e-commerce boom in North America by prompting many Web surfers to make their first online purchase.

eBay.com also emerged on the Web scene in 1995 when Pierre Omidyar's girlfriend, a Pez candy dispenser collector, began looking to contact other nearby collectors. Omidyar—a Tufts University computer science graduate who worked for communications software maker General Magic Inc.—realized that the Internet could help make this possible. He created Auction Web, an online auction site that let sellers post items for sale by describing the merchandise, setting a minimum bid, and choosing the length of the auction, which could range anywhere from three to ten days. Buyers could then bid on an object, and the highest bidder at the end of the auction was able to purchase the object for the bid price. Payment and delivery were handled by the buyer and seller. Site traffic grew well beyond Omidyar's expectations in 1996, prompting his resignation from General Magic. Seeing the potential to make money, Omidyar decided that Auction Web—renamed eBay in September 1997—would start charging a small fee, including a commission based on the final price, for each item listed for sale. Because the entire auctioning process was automated, overhead costs remained minimal; as a result, Omidyar's business became profitable very quickly, setting it apart from other Internet ventures and validating the Internet as a viable business medium.

EXPLOSIVE GROWTH

As the number of North American Internet users began to climb and e-commerce sales continued to grow, the stock prices of Internet-based firms began to soar. Amazon's shares, which originally listed on

NASDAQ for $18 apiece, rose in value to nearly $100 in less than a year, leaving founder Bezos near billionaire status. Yahoo's stock prices also skyrocketed in the late 1990s, and both Yang and Filo also became billionaires. In September of 1997, eBay conducted its IPO; eBay stock jumped from $18 to $50 in a matter of minutes, and within two months, share prices reached $100.

eBay's registered users reached 1.2 million by the end of 1998, and sales soared 724 percent to $47.4 million. In December of that year, more than one million new customers shopped online at Amazon for holiday gifts. Total customers exceeded 6.2 million, securing Amazon's position as the number three U.S. bookseller, behind Barnes & Noble and Borders. In addition, Yahoo! became one of the few Web-based ventures to make money via online advertising. In fact, the only one of the five major Internet pioneer firms facing difficulty was Netscape, which struggled to hang onto its browser market share in the face of stiff competition from Microsoft. In November of 1998, Netscape agreed to be purchased by American Online for roughly $4.2 billion. Stock prices soared on news of the deal, and by the buyout's completion in March of 1999, the price tag exceeded $10 billion. These success stories prompted venture capital firms to fund hordes of e-commerce startups, including business-to-consumer B2C ventures like Pets.com and X.com, as well as business-to-business (B2B) ventures like Internet consultancy Scient. At the end of 1999, despite significant e-commerce growth across both Europe and Asia, North America accounted for 67 percent of the worldwide B2B e-commerce market and 76 percent of the worldwide B2C market.

DOT.COM FALLOUT

Total North American online consumer sales in 2000, according to eMarketer, reached an unprecedented $38.3 billion. However, concerns regarding the performance of many Internet-based firms, including leaders like Amazon, caused stock prices to plummet during the second half of the year. In June, Lehman Brothers analyst Ravi Suria publicly criticized Amazon's financial status, prompting a share price drop of 19 percent. Suria pointed out that although Amazon had experienced incredible sales growth in the late 1990s, its $2 billion debt was costing about $125 million in interest each year and competition was heating up from the likes of Wal-Mart and other major retailers who were opening their own online stores. In fact, Amazon lost $720 million on sales of $1.6 billion in 1999. By August 2000, Amazon's stock prices plummeted to $28 per share.

Dot.com funding started to dry up when stock prices began to fall, leaving many upstarts short of cash. When dot.coms like Pets.com and X.com began closing their doors, Yahoo! found itself scrambling to find advertising customers to take their place. As a result, Yahoo!'s stock also took a drastic nosedive. By the end of 2000, it was clear to even the most bullish analysts that the North American "Net craze" had come to an abrupt halt. As stated in an April 2001 article in *BusinessWeek Online,* "Of the 367 Internet outfits taken public since 1997 that are still trading, the stocks of 316 are below their offering prices, according to Thomson Financial. Only 55 companies, or 15 percent, have made money for public investors. And a staggering 224 have tumbled 75 percent or more since their IPOs. A total of $2.5 trillion has disappeared from Net company market caps since the peak last year."

The dot.com debacle was further exacerbated by recessionary economic conditions in North America. Despite the downturn, however, companies like AOL and eBay continued to thrive. And although the rate of e-commerce growth slowed, many analysts predicted that North American e-commerce sales in the early and mid-2000s, both B2C and B2B, would outpace 2000 figures. With an estimated 180.68 million Internet users in 2001—compared to 154.63 million users in Europe and 143.99 million users in Asia—North America remained the e-commerce leader of the world.

FURTHER READING:

"At the Epicenter of the Revolution." *BusinessWeek Online,* September 16, 1999. Available from www.businessweek.com.

Dunlap, Charlotte. "5 Biggest Investors: Jim Clark—The Man With the Midas Touch—Integral to the Launch of Three Billion-Dollar Start-up Companies." *Computer Reseller News,* September 20, 1999.

Eads, Stephani. "Will Jeff Bezos Be the Next Tim Koogle?" *BusinessWeek Online,* March 12, 2001. Available from www.businessweek.com.

Elstrom, Peter. "The Great Internet Money Game." *BusinessWeek Online,* April 16, 2001. Available from www.businessweek.com.

Hazleton, Lesley. "Jeff Bezos: How He Built a Billion-Dollar Net Worth Before His Company Even Turned a Profit." *Success,* July 1998.

Heun, Christopher T. "Online Retailers Stick to the Basics." *InformationWeek,* October 29, 2001.

Jaffe, Sam. "Online Extra: eBay: From Pez to Profits." *BusinessWeek Online,* May 14, 2001. Available from www.businessweek.com.

Lee, Jeanne. "Why eBay is Flying." *Fortune,* December 7, 1998.

Mahoney, Michael. "Report: Global E-Commerce to Hit $550B in 2001." *E-Commerce Times,* March 21, 2001. Available from www.ecommercetimes.com.

———. "Report: North American E-Commerce to Grow 46 Percent in 2001." *E-Commerce Times,* May 3, 2001. Available from www.ecommercetimes.com.

Vogelstein, Fred. "The Talented Mr. Case." *U.S. News & World Report,* January 24, 2000.

Yang, Catherine. "Stephen M. Case." *BusinessWeek Online,* September 27, 1999. Available from www.businessweek.com.

SEE
ALSO: Amazon.com; AOL Time Warner Inc.; eBay Inc.; Global Presence, Becoming a; Netscape Communications Corp.; Safe Harbor Privacy Framework; Shake-Out, Dot-com; Yahoo Inc.

GLOBAL E-COMMERCE REGULATION

In the early days, when the Internet was mainly a tool for government, military, and academic personnel, regulation was barely an issue, outside of the basic requirements for and restrictions on access. Once the World Wide Web came along and the Internet was opened to commercial activity, however, cyberspace became tied to the conflict-ridden world of national and international economic policies and regulations, to the chagrin of many interested parties, among them businesses, industry groups, legislators, governments, and issue advocates.

Regulating the Internet was a contentious issue, coming at a time when the trend throughout much of the world was toward deregulating markets. While many civil libertarians viewed the Internet as a distinctly new medium that should remain free of the hands of government, the reality, according to *The Economist,* was that "the Internet is neither as different nor as 'naturally' free as wired utopians claim." Along with the Internet's possibilities for democratization and the unleashing of creative and empowering forces came new opportunities for mischief, such as the invasion of privacy and theft, not to mention legal concerns relating to contracts, transactions, and trade. In these areas there were increasing calls for regulation to sort out the various considerations and, in a sense, free the Internet from ambiguity.

JURISDICTION

Many Internet pioneers hoped to keep the medium more or less free from government controls. Tim Berners-Lee, inventor of the World Wide Web, and the World Wide Web Consortium (W3C) that he heads, were committed to keeping the Web as open as possible, allowing for the widest range of input and choices. The standards and protocols they sponsored had a tremendous impact toward this end, but the group was a private nonprofit organization, not a government regulatory body. The W3C worked with business leaders, citizen groups, and others to reach a wide consensus, and drew praise for this laid-back and cooperative approach.

As the Internet proliferated further around the globe, many saw a need for a single body that could act as a global regulator of one sort or another. The nature of such a regulatory body, however, was much disputed. Questions abounded over how much power it should or could have, how it should enforce regulations, and how it would be structured. Some proposed that either the W3C or the Internet Corporation for Assigned Names and Numbers (ICANN) take on a broader regulatory function, but as of the early 2000s it seemed unlikely that either organization could or would assume such a role. Other likely prospects included more established government forums such as the Organization for Economic Cooperation and Development (OECD) and the World Trade Organization (WTO), but critics warned that these bodies lacked the kind of openness, accountability, and consensus-based decision-making that would be required to negotiate competing global interests.

SELF-REGULATION

At the same time, calls were growing for the creation of an international e-commerce regulating body, not to impose new regulations from above, but to see to it that the increasing number of national regulations didn't wind up impeding global e-commerce. These sentiments were shared by industry groups and others who felt that the best way to foster e-commerce was to impose as little regulation from above as possible, and to allow industries to meet their own specific challenges and coordinate with other industries to achieve a common end.

The Software and Information Industry Association (SIIA) was one industry group to strongly promote and implement self-regulatory measures rather than rely on governmental bodies to impose regulations from the outside. The group created comprehensive membership guidelines requiring member companies to abide by clear standards of behavior to protect consumer privacy, and conducted industry-wide educational and policy forums to address issues important to members.

The Clinton administration, the U.S. presidency that oversaw the opening of the Internet to e-commerce, was fairly hands-off, particularly compared with its European counterparts, tending to favor self-regulation rather than promote and enforce laws that might have hampered its development. While business leaders applauded this approach, it left many problems unresolved, which regulators in the 2000s were expected to deal with.

REGULATING A CYBERSPACE WITHOUT BORDERS

A regulatory problem of mounting concern was how to implement national regulations in a borderless

Internet world. Most regulations of the Internet largely applied existing, physical-world rules to cyberspace, and didn't address the possibility that essential parts of an electronic transaction might lie outside national borders. The Internet increasingly made borders superfluous, and the full potential of the Internet, particularly for commerce, was based on this characteristic. This fueled the growing calls for international regulatory bodies to oversee developments in cyberspace.

For instance, according to the U.S. Federal Trade Commission's e-commerce regulation report *Consumer Protection in the Global Electronic Marketplace: Looking Ahead,* released in September 2000, online shoppers may be vulnerable to compromised security of their financial information when shopping at foreign Web sites due to the uneven nature of international privacy and security measures. The FTC encouraged the U.S. government to be proactive in working with other countries toward harmonization and stronger enforcement of international consumer-protection laws.

While the FTC report advocated a degree of uniformity in global e-commerce rules, it stopped short of advocating any particular organization to set or enforce such regulations. Rather, it envisioned a future Internet world in which private industry groups and governments established an alternative dispute resolution procedure and came to internationally accepted standards of fair marketing practices. It also saw a prominent role for self-regulation born of "private sector initiatives," in which industry groups agreed to standard business practices that would address the industry's specific needs.

Countries with more closed economic systems, such as China, were mixed in their reactions to and regulation of e-commerce. While the Chinese government encouraged e-commerce and was investing in the infrastructure to make China competitive in the online marketplace, it continued to maintain tight controls on the development of Chinese e-commerce, strictly implementing a legal framework for e-commerce to reflect the nation's interest. After linking to the Internet in 1994, China gradually implemented new laws regulating Internet access and the registration of domain names. By the late 1990s and early 2000s, however, new legislation was abundant. China was unusual, for instance, in maintaining strict controls over domestic encryption technology via state-controlled encryption authorization. Most countries, concerned with the security of their domestic networks, protected their encryption systems via export controls, but allowed encryption to circulate more or less freely domestically.

In December 1999, the Chinese Ministry of Information Industry (MII) unveiled its guidelines for the development of Chinese e-commerce, which broadly sought to sketch out a legal framework in which China could become competitive in international e-commerce, but also which "fits the global scheme of things," according to MII Deputy Minister Lu Xinkuei. This caveat was read by many analysts as a signal that China intended to continue its tight grip on the reins of e-commerce and Internet use in China. The guidelines themselves seemed to bear this out, as they stipulated that the Chinese government would manage e-commerce development and implement laws and launch businesses with an eye toward maintaining Chinese national security.

In some cases, the regulation of global e-commerce gets caught up in broader international trade politics. As *America's Network* reported, the Association of Petroleum Exporting Countries (APEC) was leading a charge to create equitable cost systems for connecting to international Internet circuits. Telecommunications operators and Internet service providers (ISPs) from the countries of the Pacific Rim, in particular, had long argued that, even though U.S. ISPs use them, they must bear the entire cost of connecting to international circuits in the region. The U.S. generally favored leaving these issues for the market to decide. While it was unclear just who should regulate such fees, the United States and Canada, according to *America's Network,* were increasingly isolated in their calls to keep governmental regulation out of such decisions. APEC proposed placing authority with the World Trade Organization or even the International Telecommunication Union to settle disputes over the matter.

International dispute resolution, whether between different companies or between companies and consumers, drew greater attention from regulators in the early 2000s, particularly in Europe, where the Brussels Convention and Rome Convention began carving out the space for dispute resolution and enforcement of fair international e-commerce practices. The Brussels Convention allowed consumers involved in a disputed transaction to sue in either their own country or the country in which the business resides as long as there was a specific advertisement or invitation to the consumer that prompted the purchase. The Rome Convention, meanwhile, aimed to coordinate the laws of different countries so those who sue couldn't choose the courts in one country over another for any particular advantage.

The European Union, particularly its governing body the European Commission, has been more aggressive than the United States in playing an active role in e-commerce regulation. In large part, this proactive approach came about because the European Union was already in the midst of a much wider economic integration, for which precise rules, structures, and commercial complications still needed to be ironed out. In this case, leaving the e-commerce framework more open to self-regulation, according to EU administrators and analysts, would only create more confusion and possibly impede the development of e-commerce in Europe. This in turn could diminish the EU's global competitiveness just at the moment it was getting on its feet. In 2000, the European Council and the European Commission devised the eEurope Action Plan, which, as part of its broader goals to stimulate wider use of the Internet and e-commerce, called for a creating a comprehensive legal environment to legislate and enforce guidelines for European e-commerce.

TAXATION

Taxation is a crucial issue for e-commerce regulators both within the United States and across the globe. In particular, customers and companies engaging in international e-commerce transactions have to negotiate a web of tax laws in countries where they do business—including national tax laws with special provisions for foreign transactions or for e-commerce—as well as their domestic tax regulations. Beyond that, most countries have been sorting out specific tax measures for Internet purchases, creating separate categories of regulations. These issues highlight again the tension between nation-based legal structures and the borderless Internet.

The countries of the European Union, for instance, taxed Internet transactions via value-added taxes, which act as consumption taxes and can reach as high as 20 percent, while the United States maintained a moratorium on e-commerce taxes through the Internet Tax Freedom Act. In 2000, this disparity sparked fierce debate between the two regions after the European Commission proposed requiring companies that sell certain electronic services, including software, in the European Union to collect value-added taxes from those EU customers. U.S. companies balked at the notion of collecting taxes for European governments, according to *Upside,* and various EU leaders came up with alternative proposals, each of which ruffled some feathers on both sides of the Atlantic.

The European members of the G7 group of advanced industrial nations, furthermore, were far more enthusiastic than the United States to establish a system requiring e-businesses to register with national tax authorities in the countries where they wish to sell digital products for downloading, such as music files and software. Aside from the greater aversion among U.S. policy makers to establishing regulatory schemes for the Internet, U.S. resistance to such proposals had a practical element as well, since it was U.S. mer-

chants that clearly dominated the market for digital transactions, and thus would be most affected by such regulations. For its part, in the late 1990s, the World Trade Organization placed its own moratorium on e-commerce taxation.

PRIVACY

Elsewhere, the United States and the European Union clashed over the EU Commission's stringent Data Privacy Directive, which the EU initially wanted to impose on U.S. businesses as well. In the end, however, a compromise was reached when U.S. businesses agreed to regulate themselves and stand accountable to the U.S. Federal Trade Commission (FTC), which pledged to punish any lapses in protecting and securing the personal and financial information of EU consumers.

This form of regulation was still voluntary, though businesses that failed to sign on could suffer consequences in the market. Consumers might lack confidence in those companies' ability or willingness to safeguard their private information, and such lack of confidence was, in turn, one of the largest impediments to consumer e-commerce. Participating companies agreed to abide by the U.S. Department of Commerce's Safe Harbor Privacy Framework, which called for firms to notify customers of the reasons they are collecting consumer data; allow customers the option of withdrawing their information should it be disclosed to a third party; allow customers to access their own data stored in companies' records; and make serious efforts to protect that information from unauthorized access and use.

COMPETITION

National or regional governments have also played a strong role in antitrust enforcement concerning Internet-related markets, as the U.S. case against Microsoft and the European Union's ruling against the proposed merger between Sprint and WorldCom demonstrated. The FTC also closely eyed the development of Web-based business-to-business trade exchanges, in which companies came to a central electronic market to trade supplies and finished goods. The FTC was concerned that such exchanges harbored the potential for the establishment of price-fixing schemes and illegal market barriers to outside competitors. The FTC supported the concept behind the exchanges, acknowledging their potential for lowering the costs of transactions, but worried that the potential for antitrust violations would impede fair competition.

CONTENT CONTROL

Content was another area in which the regulation debate was exceptionally heated. While most of the world's major players extolled the Internet as a great leveler and democratizing force and a tool for the free exchange of information, there were numerous efforts by regulators all over the world to restrict certain kinds of access, and sometimes these efforts spiraled into international controversies. Regulators in the United States and elsewhere have been vigilant in trying to stamp out, or at least restrict access to, generally offensive materials such as child pornography on the Web, but sometimes these actions veered too close to the abridgement of free speech and free flow of information for civil libertarians to stomach. One highly publicized case occurred in the early 2000s when the French government worked to restrict French Web surfers' access to sites containing Nazi content and paraphernalia, a move that many international observers decried as excessively restrictive and a dangerous precedent. Critics pointed out that not only should anyone have the right to express beliefs, particularly political beliefs, on the Internet, but Web surfers should have the right to visit such sites, and that their visits, moreover, couldn't be construed automatically as endorsement of the views expressed.

In other parts of the world, such as China, government suspicions of potentially subversive foreign materials led them to restrict access to Web content stemming from outside the government's own network. Such cases highlighted the tensions born of the Internet's dissolving borders, which some viewed as the dissolution of national sovereignty.

Other content that continually wrought tension between and among regulators, consumers, and businesses included sites depicting violence or providing information about weaponry, online gambling sites, and various shades of online pornography. In all these cases, approaches differed as to the degree and nature of regulatory involvement.

In general, the European Union opted for the self-regulation of online content. The EU's plan to combat illegal and harmful content encouraged companies, industries, and Internet users to devise and enforce their own safety provisions, implement content filtering systems, generate awareness about responsible Web surfing and online content, and facilitate harmony in international standards. In that spirit, a coalition of European companies launched the Internet Content Rating for Europe (INCORE) initiative.

AN EMERGING CONSENSUS?

Business leaders were by no means universally opposed to regulations. In fact, regulation in some areas was often strongly encouraged by businesses and industry groups as a way of clarifying rules and processes and removing ambivalence about the path of e-commerce. One of the overriding concerns driving regulatory efforts was the need to level all playing fields in order to allow for the greatest and fairest proliferation of e-commerce. The players driving e-commerce also took into consideration that a completely unregulated commercial cyberspace environment would erode consumer confidence and damage the development of e-commerce. By the early 2000s, most business leaders, governments, and other policy makers recognized the economic importance and opportunities of e-commerce, and were not willing to risk damaging its prospects, thus opting for a pragmatic regulatory environment. Nonetheless, the tension was far from resolved.

FURTHER READING:

Allan, Alex. "The e-Business of the House." *Director,* September 2000.

Banham, Russ, and Charles Wesley Orton. "A Taxing Problem." *World Trade,* June 2000.

Jarvis, Steve. "FTC Report is Net Security 'Wish List.'" *Marketing News,* November 20, 2000.

Kennedy, Gabriela. "China Rushes to Catch Up With the Internet." *International Financial Law Review,* July 2000.

———. "e-Commerce: The Taming of the Internet in China." *China Business Review,* July/August 2000.

L'Hoest, Raphael. "The European Dimension of the Digital Economy." *Intereconomics,* January/February 2001.

Litan, Robert E. "The Internet Economy." *Foreign Policy,* March/April 2001.

"Leaders: Regulating the Internet." *Economist,* June 10, 2000, 18.

McGraw, Harold III. "Monetizing Digital Content." *Executive Speeches,* February/March 2001, 26.

Patel, Ajay, and Allison Lindley. "Resolving Online Disputes: Not Worth the Bother?" *Consumer Policy Review,* January/February 2001.

Lynch, Grahame. "Nationalizing the 'Net." *America's Network,* July 1, 2000.

Piazza, Peter. "Companies Steer Toward a Safe Harbor." *Security Management,* February 2001.

Prem, Richard, Ned Maguire, and Jeff Clegg. "United States." *International Tax Review,* September 1999.

Sinrod, Eric J. "Looking for a Cyberlaw Legacy." *Computerworld,* March 5, 2001.

Thompson, Bill. "Meet the Regulators." *New Statesman,* July 10, 2000.

SEE ALSO: Computer Crime; Dispute Resolution; European Commission's Directive on Data Privacy; ICANN; Internet Society (ISOC); Internet Tax Freedom Act; Legal Issues, Overview of; Privacy: Issues, Policies, Statements; Safe Harbor Privacy Framework; Taxation and the Internet; World Intellectual Property Organization (WIPO); World Wide Web Consortium (W3C)

GLOBAL PRESENCE, BECOMING A

With the world's disparate economies increasingly integrating into one global economy, and with the Internet affording more companies the ability to extend their reach overseas, the competitive pressures to establish a global presence—and the opportunities that abound therein—have taken on great importance. While a truly integrated and seamless economy was still a long way off in the early 2000s, the Internet was propelling the business climate in that direction, and companies were eager to stake a claim to this new economic environment. The boom in e-commerce coincided with the dissolving of international borders in the business world, thereby heating competition both domestically and internationally. Companies operating in markets with global reach have the option of trying to build a global presence, being acquired by a company doing the same, finding a localized niche, or being driven out of business.

While the United States was by far the largest e-commerce market in the late 1990s and early 2000s, analysts estimated that the proportion of online shoppers based in countries other than the United States would expand dramatically through the 2000s. For example, according to International Data Corporation, approximately two-thirds of the world's 31 million online shoppers would be based outside the United States by 2003. This attractive market potential, combined with the dramatically enhanced reach of individual companies with the aid of the Internet, sent companies on a course to extend their reach across the globe seeking to take advantage of the lowered costs and barriers to entry of foreign markets via e-commerce.

The proliferation of trade agreements and cross-border corporate cooperation and interaction are at the heart of the drive to become a global presence. The economy of the 21st century, according to nearly all economists, will be characterized by a continued blurring of national boundaries and the advancement of business models that are distributed electronically, thus offering vastly expanded flexibility and far greater reach than traditional business models of the past.

This development, however, is far from a panacea for corporations. With consumers able to purchase goods and services from companies situated anywhere in the world, the competitive pressures on individual businesses mount considerably. In addition, as products and services circulate in global markets, there is a tendency for them to become commoditized—that is, the sheer proliferation of such items forces prices downward and blurs qualitative distinctions between them, forcing customers to make their purchasing decisions based almost solely on price. As a result of the process of commoditization, companies are compelled to innovate not only their products but also their business practices and strategies to take advantage of the opportunities afforded by information technology and the global economy. In so doing, firms need to reconsider several of their traditional business practices in light of the new economic environment. Companies establishing a global presence devise strategies related to

- language

- cultural awareness and sensitivity

- global distribution schemes

- foreign and international legal, political, and economic environments

- local technical considerations

- and their own information-technology infrastructure

COOPERATIVE EFFORTS

To facilitate global e-commerce and to ease the trepidation many companies may have toward negotiating the various obstacles to establishing a global e-commerce presence, several standards organizations from around the world, including the American National Standards Institute (ANSI) and the International Standard Organization's Committee on Consumer Policy (COPOLCO), are working toward the creation and implementation of international e-commerce standards. The main thrust of these standardization efforts is the goal to protect consumers, whose fears over the compromise of financial data and invasion of their privacy, many analysts conclude, have hampered the growth of e-commerce, and could limit its future potential if not remedied.

Such proposed standards measures include the implementation of various certification schemes, including trust marks and logos, for those firms that meet various international securities benchmarks. COPOLCO and others proposed the implementation of consensus-based codes of conduct, appropriate to the particular markets in which firms operate, detailing the kinds of behavior and commitments to consumers that certified companies would be obligated to maintain. COPOLCO also proposed the establishment of an e-commerce solutions forum at which concerns over e-commerce standards could be debated and enhanced in accordance with consumers' concerns. Such measures would give businesses clear goals and guidelines in the development of their global e-commerce strategies.

LANGUAGE AND CULTURE

While English has indeed been the dominant language on the Web, that lopsided balance is not expected to continue as countries upgrade their online access and telecommunications infrastructure. As a result of this trend, and to take advantage of key foreign markets, globalizing companies increasingly design their Web sites to facilitate all the major languages for those countries in which they do business. The easiest way to establish a multilingual Web site is to outsource translation work to a third party, although machine-based translation services continue to emerge.

Perhaps the most crucial element of utilizing local languages for a successful international business strategy was the mastering of contextual issues. The subtleties of linguistic variations that are so easily overlooked can offend cultural sensibilities and potentially reap tremendous damage to a company's international efforts. Therefore, simple understanding of the grammar and vocabulary isn't enough—firms need to maintain staff or partner with specialists who boast an intimate understanding of the cultural nuances of the client countries.

Thus, for companies trying to succeed in a global marketplace, diplomacy is key on a variety of fronts. First, diplomacy builds contacts, trust, and opportunities between the company and the foreign business it seeks to engage. Firms increasingly hire cultural representatives specializing in the languages and cultures of particular countries to act as liaisons between themselves and those countries. This type of first-hand knowledge, where affordable, can be significantly more valuable than indirect studies, since it actively builds new and potentially valuable relationships. Secondly, diplomacy allows companies to learn and manage the subtle- and not-so-subtle-cultural and linguistic variations that are so crucial—and potentially devastating—to an international business operation. By building bridges with local players, companies acquire on-the-ground details about what sorts of practices are likely to succeed or fail, to ingratiate or offend.

ECONOMIC AND LEGAL ENVIRONMENTS

While the information revolution has produced software and systems for managing and moving goods on a global scale, the headaches of adjusting local practices to respective national laws, taxes, and tariffs remain—although moves toward regional common markets were alleviating such difficulties somewhat. Firms in the early 2000s operated in the context of national political jurisdictions, each with their own tax and legal structures. A challenge for companies establishing a global presence was to negotiate these jurisdictions across their operations. More than simply coming to terms with these various legal environments, there were clear-cut strategies for optimizing a firm's interaction with them. For instance, while the propensity to conduct business in one country or another is subject to traditional cost-benefit analysis that includes the legal and tax codes of those countries, there were methods for transforming those red-tape headaches into added value, most particularly in trying to limit overall tax liability based on where certain business operations are based. Clearly, companies will, within the context of their overall business strategies, attempt to locate particular operations where they are least costly in overall terms, including where taxes on those operations will be most limited. Finessing the banking systems and acting diplomatically to create influential contacts and networks in foreign countries was often an expensive and daunting undertaking, but could pay off substantially in the long run.

The nuances of global e-commerce opportunities from region to region are staggering. For instance, some regions, particularly Africa, were beset by a relative dearth of Internet access; others, like Western Europe, boasted widespread access but still struggled with a clear and coherent e-commerce tax structure; China, meanwhile, remained committed to centralized economic planning but was aggressively pursuing e-commerce.

Technical considerations are another factor in global business decision-making. Different countries and regions have vastly different information-technology and telecommunications infrastructures, and this consideration factors greatly into how, when, —and even if— particular companies decide to enter certain markets. For instance, in countries with a higher relative rate of mobile Internet connectivity, companies need to adjust their e-commerce strategies to those technological factors. Elsewhere, regions with relatively low Internet access or with little tradition of credit-card use could be prohibitive, or alternatively could provide opportunities for novel approaches that rival firms may be reluctant to employ. In addition to localized Web content, Web pages geared toward specific countries and cultures also need to account for local telecommunication capacities. For instance, in areas where capacity is limited or expensive, Web sites with sophisticated graphics or otherwise intensive downloads may serve to alienate rather than attract customers.

Along the same lines, consumers in different countries have different propensities to, and reservations about, making purchases online. While in the United States both consumers and companies have relatively clear guidelines about the responsibilities of all parties in a transaction, such codes are far from universal. For instance, consumers in Latin America tend to be reluctant to use a credit card with a business with whom a relationship of trust has not been established. In Germany, moreover, the most common form of e-commerce payment is not via credit card but via electronic debit. Other countries prefer traditional cash-on-delivery payment schemes. Companies need to be aware of often-intangible characteristics such as these if they are to embark on successful marketing strategies.

The currency in which companies opt to bill their customers is another major consideration. With rapid and often dramatic currency fluctuations marking the global economy, companies need to carefully consider the comparative advantages and disadvantages of billing customers in their local currencies versus billing in U.S. dollars. By billing in U.S. dollars, companies may be shifting the risks of currency fluctuations to their customers; alternatively, firms that bill in local currencies assume the currency risks themselves. Understanding the international banking and financial environment in light of currency fluctuations thus becomes an added pressure for globalizing businesses.

TECHNOLOGY AND BUSINESS ARCHITECTURE

In order to truly harness the potential of information technology and the Internet for a global business strategy, companies need to find a way to implement decentralized flexibility into their centralized corporate structures. The Internet itself was pushing things in this direction already, with greater emphasis on distributed networks, but when such networks include cross-border enterprises, each with their own particular considerations, such an architecture was ever more important. Thus, becoming a global presence involved something of a balancing act—affording the flexibility to local outlets and networks to adapt to the local culture and logistical situations on the one hand, while on the other hand leveraging brand loyalty and technological investments to take advantage of economies of scale and prevent the separate local chapters from diverging into different directions of development, thereby hampering the overall vision of the firm.

As a result, a company's Web architecture, for instance, needs to remain—to the extent possible—culturally neutral, capable of seamlessly adapting user and employee interfaces to different languages, cultures, laws, business customs, and so on. Thus, companies require systems for updating several layers of content simultaneously. It is not enough to maintain a central Web site serving a firm's entire global operations; they must be able to support localized content that reflects cultural flavors and characteristics indigenous to the region.

Supply chain management applications and methods provide companies with the tools to monitor

and optimize their global supply chains for optimal efficiency, saving costs at several turns: by cutting down inventory, by speeding deliveries to customers, and by coordinating all supply movements in line with overall business expectations, for instance. With the complications of global logistics and delivery, efficient supply chain management—in which demand, rather than supply, drives production and distribution—becomes a paramount concern.

LOGISTICS

After taking advantage of the Web's global reach, companies face the challenge of getting their products to their destinations. International logistics operations can be extraordinarily tricky to implement, particularly at the level of speed and efficiency that the Internet promises. Companies must weigh the cost of maintaining inventory against the cost of shipping for their various markets. A number of information-technology vendors created software and other products to aid companies in cross-country logistics, including applications designed to tie together various business processes into a simple, integrated enterprise system. Other applications merge operations with databases designed to help firms navigate various tax laws and shipping concerns.

Perhaps the greatest obstacle to establishing efficient logistics operations was the red tape involved in getting goods into different countries. According to analysis firm Benchmarking Partners, the average company maintains about 25 percent of its internationally sourced inventory at distribution warehouses, which adds significant costs. In addition, according to *InformationWeek,* the duties and other costs levied on companies that don't efficiently negotiate a country's trading environments can make or break a company trying to achieve a global presence.

FURTHER READING:

Asmus, Carl W. ''Revamping the Supply Chain for a Global Economy.'' *World Trade,* November 2000.

Baker, Sunny. ''Global E-commerce, Local Problems.'' *Journal of Business Strategy,* July/August 1999.

''Business Poses New Challenges For IT Architectures.'' *InformationWeek,* February 7, 2000.

DePalma, Donald. ''Think Globally, Act Consistently.'' *e-Business Advisor,* June 2001.

Hohenstein, Peter C. ''Crossing E-commerce Borders Like a Diplomat.'' *Afp Exchange,* Fall 2000.

Portnoy, Sandy. ''Language is No Barrier.'' *Crn,* March 12, 2001.

Sweat, Jeff. ''Ship It.'' *InformationWeek,* January 22, 2001.

Tellez, Sonia. ''Think Globally When Designing a PM Solution.'' *Computing Canada,* December 10, 1999.

Winder, Davey. "Tapping Into a New Customer Base is Simply a Case of Minding Your Language." *Network News,* October 25, 2001.

Zuckerman, Amy. "Hot Global Standards and Testing Trends." *World Trade,* October 2000.

SEE ALSO: Business Plan; Change, Managing; Commoditization; Global E-commerce: Africa; Global E-commerce: Asia; Global E-commerce: Australia; Global E-commerce: Central and South America; Global E-commerce: Europe; Global E-commerce: North America; Global E-commerce Regulations; Supply Chain Management; Time and Time Zones

GLOBAL TRADING WEB ASSOCIATION

Based in Delaware and founded in Zurich, Switzerland in 2000, the Global Trading Web Association was the world's first commercial, international organization devoted to the development of worldwide business-to-business (B2B) e-commerce. The voluntary, non-profit organization was established by 23 major international corporations representing 15 nations, including India, Switzerland, Singapore, Australia, Spain, Canada, Mexico, Japan, and the United States. In addition to Commerce One, several leading international firms were among the association's signature members, including Deutsche Telekom; NTT Communications Corp.; Banco Nacional de Mexico; PricewaterhouseCoopers; Australia's Cable & Wireless Optus Ltd.; India's Gate2Biz.com; Hong Kong's Asia2B; and Covisint, the major B2B portal established by the auto giants General Motors, Ford, and DaimlerChrysler. Individual members each claim one seat on the association's board. The organization was chartered to promote e-commerce alternatives to traditional B2B exchanges, and to lower trade barriers among nations, thereby facilitating the global online purchase and sale of goods and services.

The Internet procurement firm Commerce One launched the Global Trading Web as on online community for international B2B e-commerce in 1999, establishing industry-based trading portals to streamline transaction processes across industry lines and foster economies of scale for international businesses. Thus, any company that logs on to the Global Trading Web can connect with any e-marketplace under its umbrella anywhere in the world, allowing them entry into any connected market. The Global Trading Web Association aimed to capitalize on these portals and use them as a springboard for the development of international standards and technical harmony for B2B e-commerce.

The Global Trading Web Association's most distinguishing characteristic is that, unlike the myriad online business-to-business exchanges, it isn't restricted to one industry or region. Instead, it brings together companies representing several industries and remains open to expansion into new territories. Because of this, it has helped to facilitate international B2B e-commerce. The main ingredient that pushed the Global Trading Web a step above the existing electronic data interchange (EDI) networks was Extensible Markup Language (XML). XML is a hypertext meta-language allowing businesses to define types of data and employ a graphical interface. It also allows them to communicate effectively with each other across an array of networks and technology platforms.

The Global Trading Web culminated the efforts of Jay Tenenbaum, a former researcher in artificial intelligence, who in 1994 created CommerceNet, a non-profit organization devoted to building e-commerce by encouraging companies to exchange data and collaborate on research. Tenenbaum's chief priority soon became discovering a way to expand on EDI networks, which exchanged online purchase orders within a particular industry. Tenenbaum sought to transcend industry barriers and facilitate all types of global B2B trading. His earlier efforts in this area included founding Enterprise Integration Technologies in 1989, which later diverged into Internet security. In 1992 Tenenbaum linked up with Tim Berners-Lee, who created the World Wide Web, as well as Marc Andreessen, who founded Netscape. In 1996 he met Bob Glushko, who later served as director of advanced technologies at Commerce One, and who told Tenenbaum about XML. Commerce One, which was already established as a major player in facilitating B2B e-commerce through its BuySite system, recognized that XML was quickly emerging as the B2B standard and found Tenenbaum's ideas appealing enough to bring him aboard in early 1999. This led to the opening of the Global Trading Web a few months later.

Whereas EDI networks are closed systems that are limited to certain kinds of data exchange, the Global Trading Web is promoted as a forum in which businesses across industry lines and national borders can not only engage in transactions, but also post price quotations for easy comparison shopping, and upload catalogs and other company documents. This created an international, cross-industry virtual community that acts as an umbrella for existing industry-based and regional communities. Additionally, the Global Trading Web is a portal to industry-specific and pan-industry regulatory and legal information.

FURTHER READING:

Baldwin, Howard. "First Things First." *Line56.com.* April 15, 2001. Available from http://www.line56.com.

Grande, Carlos. "Wrapping Trades and Services on to the Web." *Financial Times.* August 4, 2000.

Hirst, Clayton and Jason Nisse. ''World's Top Firms Set to Launch Online Exchange.'' *The Independent.* July 30, 2000.

McCarthy, Jack. ''Commerce One Unveils Global Trading Net.'' *Network World.* November 1, 1999.

Nairn, Geoffrey. ''Pushing Towards A 'Global Trading Web.''' *Financial Times.* October 20, 1999.

SEE ALSO: Andreessen, Marc; Berners-Lee, Tim; Business-to-Business (B2B) E-commerce; Electronic Data Interchange (EDI); Global Presence, Becoming a; Taxation and the Internet; XML

GOMEZ INC.

Gomez Inc., formerly Gomez Advisors, was founded in 1997 by Julio Gomez, John Robb, and Alexander Stein. Just four years later, Gomez had secured the leading position among Internet research firms that served both consumers and e-business firms. The company evaluated over 6,000 e-commerce sites using its ''Internet Scorecard,'' which ranked the performance and quality of World Wide Web sites in various industries such as finance and banking, travel, airline, and other retail-based sites. The firm also developed GomezPro, a subscription-based Web site that catered to businesses, and GomezNetworks, a division that offered real-time Web site and transaction performance measurement and diagnostic services. Through its Internet Quality Measurement (IQM) Program, the company helped its customers evaluate and compare its offerings, measure and monitor its performance against others in its industry, and develop online strategies.

DEVELOPMENT OF THE INTERNET SCORECARD

In 1997, Gomez, Robb, and Stein created Gomez Advisors as part of The Ashton Technology Group. Operating as a subsidiary of the group, Gomez was first focused on evaluating the online services provided by brokers. With a goal of improving the online experience for consumers, the company established its Internet Scorecard in June 1997 and began rating various Web sites. Gomez ratings—rankings based on various criteria—soon became quite popular in the brokerage industry. Receiving top accolades from Gomez was considered a coup among industry players. A 1999 *BusinessWeek Online* article claimed that ''for online brokers, getting a top rating from Gomez Advisors Inc. is like winning an Oscar.''

The Internet Scorecard ranking consisted of roughly 150 different criteria points. Gomez collected data on those points by visiting Web sites, conducting business and using customer service on those Web sites, and monitoring performance. The online sites were then ranked by Scorecard categories, which included ease of use, customer confidence, on-site resources, relationship services, and overall cost. Ease of use, for example, used between 30 and 50 criteria points such as functionality, simplicity of opening an account or making a purchase, and ease of Web-site navigation. Customer confidence used criteria such as the availability and depth of customer service options, and the ability to resolve customer service issues. The On-site resources category was rated based on criteria such as product availability, and Relationship services were based on criteria such as online help, advice, frequent buyer incentives, and personalized data. The Overall Cost category was ranked using criteria such as average cost for typical services and additional fees related to shipping and handling.

The Scorecards were then listed on the Gomez Web site. For example, a consumer who wanted to find information on different full service broker Web sites could go to the Gomez site and peruse the broker Internet Scorecards that the firm had listed. The consumer could view the ranking listed by overall score, or view the ranking by individual category such as Ease of Use. A profile of each company was listed as well and offered information on the pros and cons of the site and how the company performed in each category.

EXPANSION

In April of 1999, Gomez sold 1.1 million shares as part of a private placement effort; Ashton kept a 28 percent interest in the firm. Using the $5.5 million it raised, Gomez began to broaden its marketing efforts and also started to develop new products. During that year, Gomez expanded into rating the online efforts of companies in other industries. Touting itself as ''The E-Commerce Authority,'' the company launched scorecards for airlines, apparel retailers, consumer electronics and computers retailers, drug stores, furniture stores, grocery delivery services, hotels, loan and insurance providers, pet stores, sporting goods retailers, and toy stores.

In late 1999, Gomez also formed several key partnerships as part of its brand recognition effort and in order to gain an increased presence on the Web. In October, it teamed up with Hoovers Online, a provider of business news and company information. As part of the deal, the Gomez Advisors Internet Broker Scorecard became part of the Hoovers Stock Web site. It also partnered with Marketwatch.com, the operator of the CBS.Marketwatch.com Web site, and America Online. As a result, Gomez's financial-related scorecards became available on both sites.

As Gomez entered the new millennium, it began to focus on providing services to businesses as well as consumers. In March 2000, the firm launched GomezPro.com, a business-to-business site created to help companies in their e-commerce efforts. Through its IQM Program, the site offered e-commerce tools, quarterly Internet Scorecard reports, custom advisory services, and market research studies. That same month, Gomez also developed a Merchant Certification program designed to reward the efforts of online merchants in over 25 different industries, as well as foster consumer confidence among online shoppers. Merchants that met eight different criteria, such as having customer support access and published privacy policies, received a Gomez PASS seal. If the merchant met more advanced criteria, it received a PASS PLUS seal. By May 2000, over 2,000 online merchants were part of the program.

Gomez also continued to form alliances as part of its growth effort. The firm joined with InfoSpace, a provider of information and commerce infrastructure services, to provide InfoSpace customers access to Gomez certified merchant information. The firm also teamed up with Yahoo! Inc. to provide its Internet Banker Scorecards on the Yahoo! Finance banking center Web site. CNET.com, an online technology information site, also began using the Gomez Merchant Certification program on CNET Shopper.com.

In order to strengthen its foothold in the business services market, Gomez announced the formation of GomezNetworks in September 2000. This new division was developed to provide real-time Internet site and transaction performance measurement and diagnostic services. The firm hoped to use the network division in conjunction with GomezPro to capture increased business from online firms looking to compare their e-business initiatives against others in their industry.

The following month, Gomez announced that it was pulling the plug on its upcoming initial public offering. Citing weakening market conditions as the cause, Gomez instead secured private financing from Softbank Ventures Inc. and various other investors. The firm utilized the funds for continued development of new marketing and product initiatives designed to cater to both consumers and businesses. While a September 2000 *Washington Post* article reported that Gomez had become ''a top spot for comparing the cost and quality of Internet brokerages, banks, and other e-commerce services,'' the firm also continued to promote the services offered on GomezPro and GomezNetworks to businesses. By securing customers such as Charles Schwab, Lycos, JP Morgan, Intel, America West Airlines, and Dollar Rent-a-Car, Gomez appeared poised for future growth.

FURTHER READING:

Gomez Inc. ''About Gomez.'' Waltham, MA: Gomez Inc., 2001. Available from www.gomezadvisors.com.

''Gomez Launches GomezNetworks.'' *Business Wire*. September 29, 2000.

Haley, Colin C. ''Gomez Advisors to Make National Push.'' *InternetNews*. February 21, 2000. Available from www.internetnews.com/ec-news.

Smith, Geoffrey. ''How Good Are the Gomez Ratings.'' *BusinessWeek Online*. October 25, 1999. Available from www.businessweek.com.

Young, Vicki M. ''IPOS Stunted in Harsh Climate.'' *WWD*. November 17, 2000.

SEE ALSO: CNET Networks Inc.; E-commerce Consultants; Yahoo! Inc.

GREENBERG, JERRY

Jerry Greenberg is the co-founder and co-CEO of Sapient Corp., a firm that provides Internet integration services to organizations like the U.S. Marine Corps, as well as businesses like iwon.com, Janus, Nabisco, Staples, United Airlines, and WalMart. Greenberg handles sales, marketing, and public relations for Sapient, while Stuart Moore, the firm's other co-founder and co-CEO, oversees the more internal operations of the firm. In 1999, both men were included among those listed as the 40 wealthiest Americans under the age of 40 by *Fortune*. The following year, with sales exceeding $500 million, Sapient became the first company focused solely on Internet integration services to join the Standard & Poor's 500-stock index. Greenberg and Moore each retain an 18 percent stake in the firm.

A native of rural New Jersey, Greenberg studied philosophy at Harvard University before switching his major to economics. After graduation, he began working for various information technology consulting firms, eventually ending up at Cambridge Technology Partners, where he met Moore. In 1991, 25-year-old Greenberg and 29-year-old Moore co-founded their own business, called Sapient Corp., in Cambridge, Massachusetts. Rather than seek outside funding, the partners used $40,000 of their own savings and charged nearly $70,000 on their credit cards. Initially, Sapient focused on offering client-server integration services. Greenberg and Moore set out to differentiate their firm from its many competitors not only by helping customers figure out how technology could eliminate difficulties or enhance operations, but also by creating, executing, and supporting whatever applications they decided to use. Also unlike many other consultancies, Greenberg and Moore offered predetermined prices and deadlines, and linked employee pay, including their own, to client satisfaction.

Employees grew from 95 in 1994 to 213 in 1995, and sales and profits both more than doubled. By then, offices had been opened in San Francisco and New York. Sapient was listed publicly in April of 1996, raising $33 million that was earmarked for expansion efforts. Initially, Greenberg and Moore each retained roughly 36 percent of the firm's stock. Recognizing that many of Sapient's clients were growing increasingly interested in e-commerce, Greenberg began repositioning the firm to offer e-business integration services. He oversaw four small acquisitions— including Adjacency and Studio Archetype, two World Wide Web design firms—that enhanced Sapient's technology and services without overwhelming the firm. Eventually, Sapient was able to offer a full range of e-commerce services that included the planning and creation of online stores. Unlike many CEOs of e-business service firms, Greenberg also kept a tight rein on advertising spending and promotional hype, careful not to make promises his firm could not keep. Greenberg's efforts translated into something that eluded so many e-commerce players in the late 1990s: profits. In 1998, Sapient earned $9.4 million on sales of $165 million. Those numbers were upped to $30.3 million in profits and $277 million in sales in 1999. According to a November 2000 article in *Computer Reseller News,* ''In an industry screaming with hype and larger-than-life personalities, Sapient co-CEO Jerry A. Greenberg stands out quietly.'' The article credits Greenberg and Moore for transforming ''a nine-year-old consulting and integration company grounded in client/server computing into one of the foremost Web integrators on the scene.''

By the end of 2000, the firm had 2,600 employees working in 18 offices around the world. However, despite the strength of Sapient's position, the North American economic slowdown, particularly in the e-commerce sector, did undercut Sapient's profits in the first quarter of 2001. As a result, Greenberg and Moore announced that the workforce would be reduced by 20 percent, the office in Sydney, Australia, closed, and U.S. operations consolidated.

FURTHER READING:

Mulqueen, John T. ''Young Company Flourishes.'' *CommunicationsWeek.* June 17, 1996.

Rosa, Jerry. ''Eleven—Jerry Greenberg—The Stalwart.'' *Computer Reseller News.* November 13, 2000, 145.

''Sapient Corp.'' *Advertising Age.* June 19, 2000.

Sapient Corp. ''Jerry A. Greenberg.'' Cambridge, MA: Sapient Corp., 2001.

Whitford, David. ''The Two-Headed Manager: Sapient Co-CEOs Jerry Greenberg and Stuart Moore Have (Almost) Nothing in Common. That Helps Explain Why Their Relationship Works.'' *Fortune.* January 24, 2000.

''U.S. Business Brief: Sapient Cuts 720 Jobs, Warns of Losses.'' *Futures World News.* May 7, 2001.

SEE ALSO: Sapient Corp.

GREENLIGHT.COM

Greenlight.com was an online buying service for automobiles that launched in January 2000. The service was initially available in four Southern cities, then expanded to 31 states by mid-2000. The company was backed by a combination of venture capital firms, large automobile dealers, and Amazon.com. As the bear market took its toll on Internet stocks in 2000, the company laid off 25 percent of its workforce in December 2000. In February 2001, just over a year after it began, Greenlight.com was acquired by CarsDirect.com, a competing service.

HOW GREENLIGHT.COM WORKED

Like CarsDirect.com, which launched in May 1999, Greenlight.com bought cars from dealers for resale to online customers at a fixed price, but Greenlight.com claimed that it would be more dealer-friendly than other online buying services. Greenlight.com gave dealers direct contact with customers, and customers took delivery of their vehicle from a dealer that would handle most of the post-sale customer service.

The first step in buying a car through Greenlight.com was for a customer to describe the vehicle they wanted and the state in which they wanted to take delivery. Greenlight.com then provided a guaranteed, no-haggle price. If the price was right, the customer would then fill out an online order form. Greenlight.com promised that a dealer would reply to the customer within 24 hours with a confirmed delivery time. The customer then took delivery of the car from the dealer.

Dealers were granted exclusive territories from Greenlight.com, but they had to respond within 24 hours or Greenlight.com would send the customer to another dealer. If the selected dealer did not have the car in stock, Greenlight.com would help arrange a dealer trade. Greenlight.com did not charge fees to the dealers; rather, it made money on each vehicle's markup. Dealers who were part of Greenlight.com's network were free to continue their relationships with other online buying services and to receive leads from their own stand-alone Web sites.

ATTRACTED THE INTEREST OF LARGE DEALERS

Greenlight.com was formed in 1999 and launched in January 2000 by Asbury Automotive Group, based in Conshohocken, Pennsylvania, and the venture capital firm Kleiner Perkins Caulfield & Byers with about $15 million in venture capital. Kleiner Perkins Caulfield & Byers had participated in the launch of such Internet giants as Amazon.com and Netscape Communications. With more than 70 dealerships in 10 states and some $4 billion in annual revenue, Asbury Automotive Group was the largest privately held dealership chain in the United States. For the Greenlight.com service, which had its headquarters in San Mateo, California, the company was seeking to sign up more dealers that had multifranchise coverage in major markets and that were comfortable using the Internet for business.

In its first month of business Greenlight.com struck a deal with Amazon.com. For an undisclosed amount, Amazon.com took a five-percent interest in Greenlight.com. Under a marketing agreement between the two companies, Amazon.com would receive $82.5 million over five years for promoting Greenlight.com to its customers. At the time Amazon.com had about 16 million customers.

Greenlight.com gained important credibility among automobile dealers when Joel Manby, former CEO of Saab Cars USA Inc., joined the firm as its president in April 2000. Manby's immediate goals were to build a committed network of dealers and to gain the support of the major automakers. Dealers were offered the opportunity to take an equity stake in Greenlight.com. One of the first dealer groups Manby signed up was Sonic Automotive Inc. of Charlotte, North Carolina, which operated 110 dealerships and had a large presence in the Southeast, California, and Las Vegas. It would take about six months for all of the Sonic dealerships to be set up for Greenlight.com referrals. Meanwhile, the large automakers—including Ford Motor Co.'s Ford Division and Lincoln Mercury—were opposing services like Greenlight.com's by threatening their dealers with severe penalties if they sold new vehicles to Internet brokers for resale.

ADDED DEALERS IN 31 STATES

In July 2000 Greenlight.com added 10 dealer groups to its service. The largest was the Hendrick Automotive Group of Charlotte, North Carolina. With annual sales of more than $2.5 billion, Hendrick was ranked sixth by *Automotive News* among the top 100 dealer groups. Hendrick had 48 dealers with 61 franchises in nine states and the District of Columbia. Altogether, the 10 new dealer groups represented 130

dealers with 150 franchises in 14 states and D.C., bringing Greenlight.com's total to 1,500 affiliated dealers in 31 states. None of the new dealers made any cash investments in Greenlight.com. However, they were made equity partners, which gave them the opportunity to earn equity shares in Greenlight.com based on their performance and the performance of Greenlight.com. Of Greenlight.com's more than 1,500 affiliated dealers, nearly 900 had a ''platinum'' arrangement whereby they could earn stock in Greenlight.com.

Manby predicted that Greenlight.com would have affiliated dealers in every state by the end of 2000. He claimed that Greenlight.com was reaching 75 percent of all e-commerce customers and about 45 percent of the total population. The company recently signed deals with e-loan.com and AutoTrader.com, both of which agreed to use Greenlight.com as their new-car partner; they provided links on their Web sites to Greenlight.com. In August 2000 Amazon.com announced it would begin selling cars on its Web site with a new link to Greenlight.com. The link, which would present automobile information in the familiar Amazon.com format, was part of Amazon's new ventures section. It gave Greenlight.com access to Amazon's growing customer base of 23 million Internet purchasers.

It was around this time that Greenlight.com received an additional $39 million in financing from investors, including Amazon.com, Techno-Venture Co., original investors Kleiner Perkins Caulfield & Byers and the Asbury Automotive Group, and others. The terms of Greenlight.com's agreement with Amazon.com were changed. Instead of paying Amazon.com $82.5 million over five years, Greenlight.com agreed to pay $15.25 million over two years in exchange for being the exclusive new-car buying service on Amazon.com. The new terms were made in part because of the difficulty Internet firms were having in raising capital in 2000. The company's top management also changed, with CEO and cofounder Todd Collins becoming the firm's chief strategy officer. Manby replaced Collins as CEO, and Mark O'Neil, former division president of CarMax Inc., was hired as president and chief operating officer (COO). Greenlight.com also moved its headquarters from San Mateo to Livermore, California.

CUTBACKS FOLLOWED BY SALE TO CARSDIRECT.COM

In the second half of 2000 Greenlight.com was faced with a tightening capital market and increased competition from other online car buying services. The major automakers were opposed to their dealers selling to Internet brokers and were looking for an appropriate Internet model that would satisfy their dealer networks. In December 2000 the company laid off 25 percent of its staff as a cost-cutting measure. In February 2001 Greenlight.com agreed to be acquired by CarsDirect.com for an undisclosed amount. Visitors to the Greenlight.com site were referred to CarsDirect.com, and the combined companies claimed to offer access to more than 400,000 vehicles. The acquisition gave CarsDirect a base of more than 3,000 affiliated dealers.

Analysts noted that while more Americans were using the Web to research their vehicle purchases, fewer were actually buying cars over the Internet. *E-Commerce Times* reported that a recent study by the Gartner Group found that while 45 percent of U.S. households used the Web as part of their car-buying process, only 3 percent actually bought their cars online. Another study by Forrester Research projected that 28 percent of all new-car buyers would visit an online auto service by 2003, three times the current level, and technology research firm IDC predicted that new car sales over the Internet would climb from 15,000 in 1999 to more than 500,000 by 2003.

FURTHER READING:

''Amazon in New E-Tail Deals.'' *Puget Sound Business Journal.* January 28, 2000.

Avalos, George. ''Livermore, Calif.-Based Greenlight.com Bought by CarsDirect.'' *Knight-Ridder/Tribune Business News.* February 2, 2001.

''Cars.'' *Forbes.* September 11, 2000.

Harris, Donna. ''Asbury Group Launches Online Buying Service.'' *Automotive News.* January 17, 2000.

Harris, Donna. ''Greenlight.com CEO Steps Down.'' *Automotive News.* August 14, 2000.

''Internet Used Car Sales Seen Reaching $164 Billion.'' *Providence Business News.* October 16, 2000.

Kisiel, Ralph. ''Greenlight.com Extends Reach to 31 States.'' *Automotive News.* July 17, 2000.

Metinko, Chris. ''San Mateo, Calif.-Based Online Car Dealer Makes Deal with Amazon.com.'' *Knight-Ridder/Tribune Business News.* August 25, 2000.

Regan, Keith. ''CarsDirect to Buy Amazon-Backed Greenlight.'' *E-Commerce Times.* February 1, 2001. Available from www.ecommercetimes.com.

Rice, Melinda. ''Amazon Rolls into Online Auto Sales.'' *E-Commerce Times.* August 23, 2000. Available from www.ecommercetimes.com

Sawyers, Arlena. ''Greenlight.com Extends Its Reach with Amazon Deal.'' *Automotive News.* August 28, 2000.

SEE ALSO: CarsDirect.com

GROSSMAN'S PARADOX

Information has long been a cornerstone of business strategy. Firms need to know where they fit into the broader market, what the competitive openings are, what their customers' tastes and needs are, and how to manipulate all this information to their advantage. In the Information Age, particularly with the proliferation of the Internet, data moves at hyperspeed and is ever more critical as businesses try to seek out exclusive information before their competitors. As information gathering, processing, and application accelerates, it steadily bears out an interesting theory of market efficiency known as Grossman's paradox.

Under traditional market theory, it is assumed that markets function best when market players have full and complete knowledge of all information relevant to the market. In this way, actors can predict the consequences of their behavior—and that of their competitors—and adjust their strategies accordingly, leading to the greatest overall efficiency for the market. Sanford Grossman, an economist at the University of Pennsylvania's Wharton School, pointed out an inherent flaw in such market assumptions. Perfectly efficient markets would provide no incentive to seek out new information. In other words, no profit could be gained by such activity. But if there's no profit, no business would gather information, and no one could possibly be perfectly informed, thus undoing the market equilibrium. This is to say, firms that have ceased gathering new information about the market couldn't possibly make informed decisions about prices or allocation of resources, and the market's efficiency would be destroyed. Grossman suggests that perfect information, or anything close to it, is purely fiction and is a contradiction in the efficient market theory. As a result, according to Grossman, no player in a market could ever be perfectly informed, and thus the drive to obtain more information than the next competitor will always be a component of market economics.

FURTHER READING:

''The Devil's Derivatives Dictionary.'' *The Derivatives Zine,* July 2000. Available from www.derivativeszine.com.

Wired Digital Inc. *Encyclopedia of the New Economy.* Waltham, MA: Wired Digital Inc., 2001. Available from hotwired.lycos.com.

SEE ALSO: Data Mining

GROVE, ANDREW (ANDY) S.

Andrew S. Grove is the chairman of Intel Corp. He served the firm as president from 1979 to 1987, when he replaced Gordon Moore as CEO. During Grove's eleven-year tenure at the helm of Intel, he orchestrated the firm's pivotal shift from memory chips to microprocessors and grew Intel into the world's leading microprocessor maker, as well as one of the most profitable manufacturers on the globe. In May of 1998, Grove was succeeded as CEO by Craig Barrett. As chairman, Grove continues to work at Intel on a regular basis and remains an active participant in the firm's shift from central processing units (CPUs) to networking technology, including flash memory chips and cell phone processors, and Internet services, such as World Wide Web hosting.

A native of Budapest, Hungary, Grove earned his undergraduate degree in chemical engineering from City College of New York and his doctorate degree from the University of California at Berkeley. In 1967, Grove took a position as an assistant director in the research and development laboratory of Fairchild Semiconductor. The following year, when Robert Noyce and Gordon Moore established NM Electronics—later renamed Intel, from the first syllables of ''integrated electronics''—Grove helped the partners secure an office and set up manufacturing facilities. His official title was vice president of operations. Although Grove was not technically a founder of the firm, he was an instrumental player from the start, according to *Fortune* writer Brent Schlender. ''It was he who masterminded Intel's pivotal 11th-hour marketing victory of Motorola to get the contract to supply microprocessors for IBM's landmark PC in 1979. Six years later, he was the one who made the gutsy and prescient decision to pull Intel out of the memory chip business, firing 6,000 employees in the process, and to focus the company on more lucrative microprocessors.''

While driving Intel's growth as a CPU manufacturer, Grove also continued to teach at Stanford and published several books, including *Physics and Technology of Semiconductor Devices,* a textbook used by many university professors after it was published in 1967; *High Output Management,* first published in 1983; *One-on-One with Andy Grove,* first published in 1987; and *Only the Paranoid Survive,* published in 1996. Grove also wrote several articles for *Fortune, The New York Times*, and *The Wall Street Journal. Time* magazine named him ''Man of the Year'' in 1997; that year, he also earned *Industry Week*'s ''Technology Leader of the Year'' award and *CEO* magazine's ''CEO of the Year'' distinction. By then, more than 80 percent of all personal computers (PCs) housed Intel CPUs, which were the fastest on the market.

Grove stepped aside for Craig Barrett just as personal computer growth began to slow. Although the Internet revolution played a major role in fueling Intel's success as growing numbers of consumers purchased PCs to access the Internet, it also eventually sparked technological developments that offered consumers alternative means of accessing the Internet. As a result, Intel began to reposition itself as a networking technology and Internet services provider. Although it was his successor who oversaw nearly $8.5 billion in acquisitions of communications and networking enterprises and the launch of World Wide Web hosting services, Grove continued to help steer the firm he is credited for parlaying into an industry powerhouse.

FURTHER READING:

Intel Corp. ''Andrew S. Grove, Intel Corporation.'' Santa Clara, CA: Intel Corp., 2001. Available from www.andygrove.com/intel/people.

Roth, Daniel. ''Craig Barrett Inside.'' *Fortune,* December 18, 2000.

Schlender, Brent. ''The Incredible, Profitable Career of Andy Grove.'' *Fortune,* April 27, 1998.

———. ''Their Reign Is Over.'' *Fortune,* October 16, 2000.

SEE ALSO: Intel Corp.

H

HACKING

During the late 1990s and into the new millennium, hacking became a popular term for the act of breaking in, tampering with, or maliciously destroying private information contained in computer networks. The FBI's Computer Emergency Response Team (CERT) reported 17,672 hacking incidents in 2000, a 79 percent increase over 1999 figures.

EARLY HISTORY

During the 1960s, the word ''hacker'' grew to prominence describing a person with strong computer skills, an extensive understanding of how computer programs worked, and a driving curiosity about computer systems. Hacking, however, soon became nearly synonymous with illegal activity. While the first incidents of hacking dealt with breaking into phone systems, hackers also began diving into computer systems as technology advanced.

Hacking became increasingly problematic during the 1980s. As a result, the Computer Fraud and Abuse Act was created, imposing more severe punishments for those caught abusing computer systems. In the early 1980s, the Federal Bureau of Investigation (FBI) made one of its first arrests related to hacking. A Milwaukee-based group known as the 414s were accused of breaking into 60 different computer systems including the Memorial Sloan-Kettering Cancer Center and the Los Alamos National Laboratory. Later that decade, the infamous Kevin Mitnick was arrested and sentenced to one year in jail for damag-ing computers and stealing software. He was arrested again in 1995 for computer fraud and put in jail for hacking Motorola Inc., Sun Microsystems Inc., NEC Corp., and Novell Inc. to steal software, product plans, and data. Mitnick eventually cost the firms a total of roughly $80 million.

As negative publicity surrounding hackers continued to grow, those who considered themselves true hackers—computer programming enthusiasts who pushed computer systems to their limits without malicious intent and followed a hacker code of ethics—grew weary of the media's depiction of hackers. As a result, several hacker groups coined the term 'cracker' in 1985 to define a person who broke into computer systems and ignored hacker ethics; however, the media continued to use the word hacker despite the fact that although most early hackers believed technical information should be freely available to any person, they abided by a code of ethics that looked down upon destroying, moving, or altering information in a way could cause injury or expense.

AT&T Corp., Griffith Air Force Base, NASA, and the Korean Atomic Research Institute all fell prey to hackers in the early 1990s. Federal World Wide Web sites, including those of the U.S. Department of Justice, the U.S. Air Force, and the CIA, were also attacked by hackers and defaced. During 1995 alone, U.S. Defense Department computers dealt with 250,000 hacker attacks. As technology advanced and business transactions conducted over the Internet increased, malicious hackers became even more destructive. Popular Web sites such as Yahoo!, America Online, eBay, and Amazon.com were hacked, costing millions and leaving online shoppers doubtful about security on these sites; a 16-year-old Canadian boy operating under the name Mafiaboy was arrested for these attacks, as well as for breaking into both Harvard's and Yale's university computer systems. Under the terms of his parole, Mafiaboy was not allowed to use the Internet or go into stores that sold computers, and his computer use was limited to that which was supervised by a teacher at school.

DIFFERENT TYPES OF HACKING ACTIVITY

As the cost of hacking attacks continues to rise, businesses have been forced to increase spending on network security. However, hackers have also developed new skills that allow them to break into more complex systems. Hacking typically involves compromising the security of networks, breaking the security of application software, or creating malicious programs such as viruses.

The most popular forms of network hacking are denial of service (DoS) attacks and mail bombs. DoS attacks are designed to swamp a computer network, causing it to crash. Mail bombs act in a similar fashion, but attack the network's mail servers. When eBay was attacked in February 2000, its Web server was bombarded with fake requests for Web pages, which overloaded the site and caused it to crash. Network hackers also try to break into secure areas to find sensitive data. Once a network is hacked, files can be removed, stolen, or erased. A group of teens in Wichita, Kansas, for example, hacked into AOL and stole credit card numbers that they then used to buy video games.

Application hackers break security on application software—software including word processing and graphics programs—in order to get it for free. One way they gain access to software that requires a serial number for installation is by setting up a serial number generator that will try millions of different combinations until a match is found. Application hackers also sometimes attack the program itself in an attempt to remove certain security features.

Hackers that create viruses, logic bombs, worms, and Trojan horses are involved in perhaps the most malicious hacking activities. A virus is a program that has the potential to attack and corrupt computer files by attaching itself to a file to replicate itself. It can also cause a computer to crash by utilizing all of the computer's resources. For example, e-mail systems were inundated with the ''ILOVEYOU'' and the ''Love Bug'' viruses in May of 2000, and the damage to individuals, businesses, and institutions was estimated at roughly $10 billion. Similar to viruses, logic bombs are designed to attack when triggered by a certain event like a change in date. Worms attack networks in order to replicate and spread. In July of 2001, a worm entitled ''Code Red'' began attacking Microsoft Internet Information Server (IIS) systems. The worm infected servers running Windows NT 4, Windows 2000, Windows XP, and IIS 4.0 and defaced Web sites, leaving the phrase ''Welcome to www.worm.com! Hacked by Chinese!'' Finally, a Trojan horse is a program that appears to do one thing, but really does something else. While a computer system might recognize a Trojan horse as a safe program, upon execution, it can release a virus, worm, or logic bomb.

PREVENTING HACKING ACTIVITY

While preventing all hacking activity is deemed nearly impossible by many computer experts, businesses spend billions on protecting computer networks. According to research group Datamonitor, spending related to network security will increase from $10.6 billion in 2001 to $22.3 billion in 2004.

The most popular method of protection against hacking among personal home computer users is anti-virus software. Companies including McAfee.com Corp. provide anti-virus software that scans a computer's hard drive for infected material, alerting customers when bad files are found. Firewalls, typically used for computer networks, have also become popular with home users, particularly those who use continual online connections such as cable modems and digital subscriber lines. Firewalls act as a deterrent to hacking by protecting private networks from the public, thus keeping most outsiders from tampering with computer systems.

Other software options—mainly used to protect larger computer systems—include Intrusion Detection Systems (IDS), content filtering software, sandboxing software, and behavior analysis software. IDS is considered one of the best protection methods for large networks. With an IDS in place, system administrators can monitor network requests and detect large-scale malicious attacks. Content filtering software is advanced antivirus software that reads compressed files and allows IT managers to set specific filtering parameters to block threatening email. Sandboxing software protects against malicious codes. The software creates a protected space within a computer where suspicious code can run, before it has a chance to interact with the main operating system. Still in its infancy in 2001, behavior analysis software protects computer systems by monitoring entire networks and checking every command of all operations.

Unfortunately, many malicious hackers eye security systems not as a deterrent but as a mere obstacle to overcome. However, as long as hacking attacks persist, both individuals and businesses will continue to invest in programs and software designed to protect systems from unwanted visitors.

FURTHER READING:

Blakey, Elizabeth. ''Commit a Cybercrime? You're Hired!'' *E-Commerce Times,* July 17, 2000. Available from www.ecommercetimes.com.

Costello, Same. '''Code Red' Raises Disclosure Flags.'' *Info-World,* July 20, 2001.

Enos, Lori. '''Mafiaboy' Denies New Hacking Charges.'' *E-Commerce Times,* August 4, 2000. Available from www.ecommercetimes.com.

Mandeville, David. ''Hackers, Crackers, and Trojan Horses.'' *CNN In-Depth Reports,* March 29, 1999. Available from www.cnn.com/TECH/specials/hackers/primer.

Morgan, Lisa. ''Intrusion Detection Systems.'' *InternetWeek,* January 8, 2001. Available from www.internetweek.com.

Radcliff, Deborah. ''At Black Hat, Ties Seen Tightening Between Hackers, Legal Officials.'' *ComputerWorld,* July 13, 2001. Available from www.computerworld.com.

Trigaux, Robert. ''A History of Hacking.'' *St. Petersburg Times,* 2000. Available from www.sptimes.com/Hackers/history.hacking.html.

Vamosi, Robert. ''Alternative Protection Against Malicious Code.'' *ZDNet,* May 21, 2001. Available from www.zdnet.com.

SEE ALSO: Computer Crime; Computer Ethics; Computer Security; Denial of Service Attack; Fraud, Internet; Viruses

HARDWARE

The term hardware most often refers to computer machinery and equipment one can see and touch, such as central processing units (CPUs), disk drives, modems, memory chips, monitors, speakers, and printers. Memory and disk devices send data and instructions to the CPU. The type of hardware housed inside a computer determines how quickly the CPU can process these instructions. The software applications that reside on a computer—such as Windows or Unix operating systems, word processors, spreadsheets, databases, e-mail programs, and World Wide Web browsers—make the hardware useful to computer users in the same way that television programming makes televisions and remote controls useful to viewers.

Major hardware companies include Compaq Computer Corp., Intel Corp., and Dell Computer Corp. In the late 1990s, as prices for personal computers (PCs) began plummeting, many of these firms sought both diversification as a means of growing sales and consolidation as a means of cutting costs. For example, Compaq paid $3 billion for Tandem Computers Inc. in 1997. The deal, which marked the computer hardware industry's largest transaction that year, doubled Compaq's sales force and allowed the company to begin offering clients more fully integrated products. Roughly one year later, Compaq bought Digital Equipment Corp for $9 billion—the industry's largest acquisition to date—to become the worldwide leader in multi-user storage systems.

In the late 1990s, the growth of the Internet forced many hardware companies to move into networking technology and World Wide Web services. For example, although the popularity of the Web helped fuel Intel's success when hordes of consumers bought PCs to gain access to the Internet from their homes, it also eventually sparked the development of hardware devices like cell phones and inexpensive Internet terminals that offered consumers alternative means of accessing the Internet. As a result, Intel began to restructure itself as a networking technology and Internet services provider. In 1998, the firm launched an $8.5 billion purchasing spree that included the acquisition of communications and networking firms and the development of Web hosting services. In 2000, it developed the e-Commerce Directory, which enhances the speed of online purchases, and Traffic Director, which helps to balance loads on e-commerce servers. In May of 2001, one of the largest players in the computer hardware industry, IBM Corp., launched Web Services, which allows the applications used by one online business to communicate with the applications used by other businesses to better facilitate electronic business-to-business transactions.

FURTHER READING:

Abreu, Elinor. ''Big Blue Joins Web Service Fray.'' *The Standard.* May 14, 2001. Available from www.thestandard.com.

''Hardware.'' In *Ecommerce Webopedia.* Darien, CT: Internet.com, 2001. Available from e-comm.webopedia.com.

''Hardware.'' In *Techencyclopedia.* Point Pleasant, PA: Computer Language Co., 2001. Available from www.techweb.com.

McDougall, Paul. ''Intel Products Aim at Speeding E-Commerce Transactions—Netstructure Line Designed to Keep Consumers From Giving Up on Online Orders.'' *InformationWeek.* February 21, 2000.

SEE ALSO: Compaq Computer Corp.; Digital Equipment Corp.; IBM Inc.; Intel; Microprocessor

HARVARD CONFERENCE ON INTERNET AND SOCIETY

The Harvard Conference on Internet and Society is a high-profile event held every few years at Harvard University that brings together leading thinkers, policy-makers, technologists, businesses, and innovators involved with the Internet. At the conference, these individuals discuss and debate major topics relative to the development of the Internet, its impact on the economy and society, and its future direction. Moreover, the conference serves as an open forum where representatives from industry, government, academia, science, and interest groups can do a number of things. These include discussing the direction of the Internet as it pertains to continued industrial development and global competitiveness; working toward a consensus in the creation of innovative and complementary e-business infrastructures and strategies; negotiating concerns and goals for U.S. and international Internet policies regarding trade, regulation, taxation, and technological development; and speculating on the many ways in which the Internet could positively and negatively influence human life.

The first meeting took place in May 1996, at the dawn of the e-commerce age and before the economic boom fueled largely by the Internet and its related technologies. As a result, the general tenor of the conference centered on the novelty and promise of the Internet, including great speculation about the direction it would take and its place in history. Harvard University President Neil Rudenstine chimed in with a talk comparing the development of the Internet and its potential for research and information sharing with the modern university library infrastructure that emerged at the end of the 1800s.

By contrast, the 1998 gathering took place right in the middle of the dot-com boom. Companies and policy-makers alike were focused on the way to most vigorously embrace the Internet and turn it into a competitive tool. U.S. President Bill Clinton's Internet policy adviser, Ira Magaziner, issued a broad outline of the president's strategy for the Internet and information technology, noting that the boom in IT innovation was largely responsible for much of the country's mid- and late 1990s economic prosperity and charging the private sector with taking the lead in the development of the digital economy. Magaziner outlined that the general tendency of U.S. government was toward self-regulation of the Internet by the private sector, rather than the top-down regulation favored by many European countries.

At the same meeting, top executives from IBM, Oracle, Sun Microsystems, Microsoft, and other major industry players contributed their thoughts on how the Internet and related information technologies not only were opening up new business channels via the emergence of e-commerce, but were also transforming the ways in which old and new businesses alike operate. Esther Dyson, one of the noted public intellectuals of the digital age, weighed in with her notion that small companies were going to be the primary engines of innovation in the Internet era.

While optimism and the drive for new business opportunities were the thrust of the 1998 conference, it wasn't short on negativity. The most obvious target was the Microsoft Corp. At the time, Microsoft was at the outset of its investigation by the U.S. Justice Department for alleged antitrust violations. Heads of rival companies in the Internet business took turns taking Microsoft to task for what they saw as heavy-handed business tactics.

When the year 2000 conference rolled around, it lacked the feeling of boundless optimism, particularly related to the possibilities of e-commerce, that characterized earlier meetings. Scheduled just after the precipitous decline of the NASDAQ stock market and in the midst of the massive e-commerce shakeout, the meeting took place during a time of relative uncertainty for Internet companies. So instead of a focus on business opportunities and speeches from leading Internet players, the 2000 conference was geared more heavily toward issues of public policy, social uses of the Internet, and politics; odes to the financial goldmines waiting to be discovered on the Internet were barely visible. The conference primarily concentrated on how the Internet transforms human social life via alterations in business practices, policy, law, technology, and education. The ability of the Internet to allow political parties to quickly disseminate personalized information during campaigns was widely discussed, as was the Internet's utility as a campaign fundraising vehicle. Keynote speaker and Internet pioneer Mitch Kapor, the founder of Lotus Development Corp., took the opportunity to decry the excessive commercialization of the Web and its attendant "strip mall" feel. In place of an online shopping medium, Kapor called for enhanced emphasis on the Internet's original purpose: to facilitate greater communication, networking, and understanding throughout the world.

The Harvard Conference also served other, less lofty purposes as well. Companies used the conference as a platform for public relations and marketing by showcasing new products and hyping innovative new business models. Individuals and firms sometimes took to settling personal scores through thinly veiled jabs, underscoring some of the political overtones of the event. But the common, recognized purpose of the Harvard Conference on Internet and Society was to seek out a positive development scheme for the Internet. Such contentious social issues as the digital divide and the commercialization of the Internet were assessed, argued, and theorized, with an eye toward forming a general policy framework in which the Internet could develop for the greatest overall benefit to society, consistent with the various interlocking interests the attendees represent.

FURTHER READING:

Bradner, Scott. "The Web as Luther, the Net as Widener." *Network World.* June 10, 1996.

Kaplan, Karen. "Harvard Conference on Internet and Society: At Highbrow Event, Low Blows for Microsoft." *Los Angeles Times,* June 1, 1998.

Katz, Frances. "Internet Access, Microsoft Top Harvard Agenda." *Atlanta Journal and Constitution.* May 31, 1998.

———. "The Party's Over." *Atlanta Journal and Constitution.* June 25, 2000.

Machlis, Sharon. "Crystal Balls Focus on Internet and on E-Commerce at Harvard Confab." *Computer World.* June 1, 1998.

O'Reilly Associates, eds. *The Harvard Conference on the Internet & Society.* Cambridge, MA: Harvard University Press, 1997.

Weil, Nancy. "Group to Manage Domain Names." *InfoWorld.* June 8, 1998.

"Welcome to Harvard Third Annual Internet & Society Conference Web Site." Cambridge, MA: Harvard University, 2000. Available from www.is2k.harvard.edu.

SEE ALSO: Cyberculture; Digital Divide; Global E-Commerce Regulation; Microsoft Corp.; Shakeout, Dot-com

HEWLETT, WILLIAM R.

William R. Hewlett is the co-founder of Hewlett-Packard Co. (HP), the second largest computer company in the world, behind IBM Corp. Along with partner David Packard, Hewlett was instrumental in growing the California-based firm from a small manufacturer of measurement instruments into a personal computer and printer powerhouse that reached $49 billion in sales in 2000. Lauded for their innovative management style, which fostered creativity and open communications between employees and managers, Hewlett and Packard are considered two of the fathers of Silicon Valley.

A native of Ann Arbor, Michigan, Hewlett earned his undergraduate degree from Stanford University, where he first met Packard, in 1934. After completing his Master's degree in electrical engineering at the Massachusetts Institute of Technology, Hewlett returned to California, earning an additional engineering degree from Stanford in 1939. The previous year, he and Packard started a business in the garage of a home Packard was renting in Palo Alto. The partners launched operations with just $538 in capital. Their first major product was a resistance capacity audio oscillator (HP 200A), essentially a sound equipment testing device, that Hewlett devised as a graduate student. Hewlett's advisor at Stanford, Frederick Terman, encouraged the partners to market the oscil-

lator, and this advice proved well heeded when Walt Disney ordered eight of the new oscillators for the production of *Fantasia.* Hewlett and Packard officially established their firm in January of 1939 as Hewlett-Packard Co. Hewlett's name was positioned first because he won a coin toss that he and Packard agreed would decide the issue.

When Hewlett returned to Palo Alto after serving in World War II, he was named vice president of HP. It was at this time that he and Packard began setting in motion the innovative management policies that would later earn them accolades. For example, HP's Open Door Policy was designed to help all employees feel comfortable enough to communicate their ideas and concerns to management. To this end, Hewlett placed employees in open cubicles and created offices without doors for executives. He also oversaw HP's decision to become one of the first firms to add profit sharing to the compensation package it offered employees. After working as executive vice president from 1957 to 1964, Hewlett took over as president. By then, Hewlett and Packard's management style had become known as the "HP Way." According to Jeff Bliss, writer for *Computer Reseller News,* it was the HP Way that fueled the growth of Silicon Valley, because it was the HP Way that began attracting East Coast technology experts to California. "The best talent at Eastern institutions such as the Massachusetts Institute of Technology and Bell Labs took notice, and the Western migration of the country's technological brain trust began. The environment awaiting these scientists, teachers, and engineers could not have been more conducive to encouraging technology."

Hewlett added CEO to his list of titles in 1969, when Packard left the firm to serve as Secretary of Defense for the Nixon administration. One of Hewlett's first decisions at the helm of HP was to further decentralize the firm. The divisions had been operating fairly autonomously since the late 1950s. Each department oversaw its own research and development, manufacturing, and marketing operations. Wanting to preserve the company's entrepreneurial spirit, Hewlett and Packard also decided that each time a group reached 1,500 employees, it would be split in two. To decentralize this structure even further, Hewlett pushed decision-making authority down the executive chain, granting the control previously held by executive vice presidents to the general managers who supervised divisions with associated product lines.

With Hewlett at the reigns, HP unveiled its first blockbuster product, the world's first handheld scientific calculator, known as the HP 35, in 1972. He also oversaw HP's move into the business computer market with the launch of the HP 3000 minicomputer and the decision to eliminate time clocks and offer flexible work hours to employees. Hewlett served as both president and CEO until 1977 and as CEO only until 1978; between 1978 and 1983, Hewlett acted as chairman. HP created its first personal computer, the HP-85, in 1980, and its first desktop mainframe machine, the HP 9000, in 1982.

Hewlett reduced his activity in the firm in 1983, when he took on the role of vice chairman. The following year, HP launched its LaserJet printer, which became its most successful product ever. While Hewlett was no longer in charge of day-to-day operations when the printer was unveiled, he certainly played a role in fostering the environment out of which such a product was conceived. For his contributions to science and technology, Hewlett was awarded the National Medal of Science by Ronald Reagan in 1985. In 1987, he was named chairman emeritus, a role he retained until his death in January of 2001.

FURTHER READING:

Akin, David. ''Hewlett Helped Define Silicon Valley Success.'' *National Post,* January 13, 2001, D6.

Bliss, Jeff. ''William Hewlett.'' *Computer Reseller News,* November 16, 1997, 45.

Hewlett-Packard Co. ''History and Facts.'' Palo Alto, CA: Hewlett-Packard Co., 2001 Available from www.hp.com/hpinfo/abouthp/histnfacts.htm.

Hewlett-Packard Co. ''William R. Hewlett.'' Palo Alto, CA: Hewlett-Packard Co., 2001 Available from www.hp.com/hpinfo/execteam/bios/hewlett.htm.

''Hewlett-Packard Co.'' In *Notable Corporate Chronologies.* Farmington Hills, MI: Gale Research, 1999.

SEE ALSO: Hewlett-Packard Co.; Packard, David

HEWLETT-PACKARD CO.

Hewlett-Packard Co. (HP) is second only to IBM Corp. among the world's largest computer firms. Along with manufacturing and marketing its top selling computers and printers, the firm also sells hardware, software, and services for World Wide Web-based operations. Under CEO Carly Fiorina, at the helm since July of 1999, HP has set it sights on becoming a premier e-business technology and services provider.

EARLY HISTORY

In 1938, Stanford University electrical engineering graduates William Hewlett and David Packard started their own company in the garage of a home Packard was renting in Palo Alto, California. With a mere $538 in capital, the partners began marketing a resistance capacity audio oscillator (HP 200A), which was essentially a sound-equipment testing device that Hewlett created as a graduate student. The company's first break came when Walt Disney ordered eight of the new oscillators for the production of *Fantasia.* In January of 1939, Hewlett and Packard named their new electronics manufacturing partnership Hewlett-Packard Co., after flipping of a coin to decide upon the order of their names in the company's moniker.

Throughout the late 1940s, Hewlett and Packard devised and implemented management policies that would later lead to their recognition as pioneers in corporate management and employee relations. For example, they created an Open Door Policy, believing that all employees should feel empowered to approach management about issues and concerns. To facilitate this policy, employees worked in open cubicles, and managers worked in offices with no doors.

HP released the HP 524A, a device that lessened the time needed to measure high-speed frequencies from about 10 minutes to one or two seconds, in 1951. Radio stations began using the HP 524A to ensure accurate broadcast frequencies, especially on the fledgling FM band. By that time, sales exceeded $5 million. HP completed its initial public offering in November of 1957. It was then that Packard created objectives for HP, believing that concrete goals would help to facilitate consistent choices by the firm's management team. The following year, HP completed its first acquisition when it purchased graphics recorder manufacturer F.L. Moseley. International expansion began in 1959 when a manufacturing plant was constructed in Germany, and an office was established in Geneva, Switzerland, to serve as a headquarters for European operations. That year, HP became one of the first firms to add profit sharing to the compensation package it offered employees.

By the end of the 1960s, sales at HP exceeded $165 million, HP Laboratories was created to serve as the main research hub for the firm, and the firm invented the first scientific desktop calculator in the world, the HP 9100. Hewlett, who had recently replaced Packard as CEO, decided to decentralize operations. Although divisions had been operating fairly independently since the late 1950s—with each department handling its own research and development, manufacturing, and marketing activities—this new structure granted the decision-making authority previously held by executive vice presidents to general managers, who oversaw divisions with similar product lines.

TRANSITION TO COMPUTER MANUFACTURING

After spending nearly three decades manufacturing various instruments for analysis and measurement, HP diversified into computers by developing the HP 2116A, a machine designed to control HP's test and measurement instruments; although the HP 2116A was not intended for the commercial computer market, it eventually helped to facilitate HP's move in that direction. Even more instrumental in HP's shift to computers was its 1972 launch of the HP 35, the first scientific handheld calculator. The product is viewed by many industry analysts as a major stepping stone in the growth of the personal computing industry because it rendered obsolete the engineer's slide rule. HP also moved into the business computer market—dominated by IBM Corp. and Digital Equipment Corp.—when it introduced the HP 3000 minicomputer. Innovations in employee relations continued throughout the mid-1970s as flexible work hours were offered to employees, and as time clocks were eliminated.

In 1977, John Young took over as president; the following year, he was also named CEO. HP unveiled its first personal computer, the HP-85, in 1980. Sales exceeded $3 billion that year. In 1982, the firm introduced its first desktop mainframe machine, the HP 9000. In 1984, HP launched the ThinkJet printer and its most successful product to date, the LaserJet printer. That year, sales topped $6.5 billion as earnings reached a record $500 million. To handle its growing number of operating groups—each time a group reached 1,500 employees, it was split into two separate groups—HP created four broad sectors to oversee these units.

HP developed a line of computer systems using Reduced-Instruction-Set Computing (RISC), in place of Complex Instruction-Set Computing (CISC), in 1986. The group of machines, dubbed HP Precision Architecture, was able to execute programs two to three times faster than normal by excluding many routine instructions. Though RISC chips were denounced for their inflexibility, other computer firms soon began developing their own versions of the technology. The DeskJet printer, an inkjet printer for the mass market, was launched in 1988. Although HP had succeeded in positioning itself as a leading computer maker by the late 1980s, each of its major computer lines, created for a specific purpose, was incompatible with the others. Recognizing that this strategy had resulted in redundant research and development efforts and limited expansion capabilities for consumers, HP began working to enhance the compatibility levels of its machines. As a result, all computer operations were placed in the same operating sector. Based on revenues of $9.8 billion, HP ranked 49th among *Fortune* 500 firms in 1988.

HP bought Apollo Computers, an engineering workstations vendor, for $500 million in 1989. The next year, after profits tumbled roughly 11 percent, Packard became more actively involved in managing HP, which laid off 3,000 employees. In 1991, sales reached $14.4 billion, and earnings rebounded to $755 million. HP developed the 95LX, a personal computer weighing just eleven ounces, and laid off another 2,000 employees. Young was replaced by Lewis E. Platt in 1992. Two years later, HP and Intel Corp. agreed to work together to create a computer chip able to run more than one operating system by the end of the decade. HP also moved into the home PC market with the launch of the HP Pavilion.

The mid-1990s were marked by price cuts for Hewlett-Packard as competition in the PC market intensified. In 1995, Hewlett-Packard reduced prices on its commercial PCs by up to 16 percent. The firm also launched its CopyJet color copier and printer, pricing it at roughly one-tenth the price of conventional color copiers. In an effort to enhance its share of the PC market in Europe, HP reduced prices there roughly ten percent in 1996. Two years later, HP introduced the Pavilion home PC line, pricing the base model, the Pavilion 3260, at an unprecedented $800. By then, HP was the second largest computer manufacturer in the world, with annual sales of more than $42 billion. Although *Fortune* named HP one of the most admired companies in the U.S., profits dipped by six percent, due mainly to increased competition and price slashing in the personal computer market. After deciding to hone its focus to personal computers, printers, workstations, and servers, HP spun off its non-computer related operations as Agilent Technologies in 1999.

MOVE TO THE INTERNET

One of the first major firms to engage in telecommuting, in 1994 HP developed a set of guidelines for employees who wished to work from home or at other offices. The firm's intranet, considered one of the largest in the world, allowed employees from all over the world to communicate with one another. Despite the firm's timeliness in this regard, however, it actually began a whole-hearted embrace of the Internet much later that its competitors. The reason for this, ironically, was that the decentralized structure that had worked so well for HP since its inception had "become a recipe for inward focus and bureaucratic paralysis," according to *The Economist*. By the 1990s, "the company had become a collection of 130 independent product groups that tried harder to meet their own financial targets than to find any common thread. It was no surprise, then, that HP was late to the Internet party—even though it had the technology in its labs. While Sun Microsystems and IBM were busy marketing themselves as dot.com revolutionaries, HP was still focusing on hardware.'' CEO Platt, in an effort to jumpstart HP's slowing growth, oversaw the release of an Internet Solutions line in 1997 and put in place an Internet Applications Systems Division to oversee the new products. However, it wasn't until Carly Fiorina took over in mid-1999 that the firm truly turned its focus to the Internet.

Fiorina launched a full-scale restructuring of HP, overhauling not only its internal organization by reshuffling operations into four major groupings—computer products, imaging products, consumer sales, and corporate sales—but also the firm's marketing strategies and corporate vision. She narrowed HP's focus to providing information tools, infrastructure for these tools, and e-services. By the end of the year, HP had unveiled two new products: the Commerce for the Millennium system and the 9000 N Class server, which was designed to offer Internet Service Providers (ISPs) a comprehensive suite of online commerce tools. Her efforts were rewarded just a short while later, in mid-2000, when Internet retailing titan Amazon.com selected HP to provide roughly 90 percent of its Internet infrastructure, including Internet servers, storage devices, and PCs linked to the Internet. By then, HP had integrated its technology into various e-services solutions packages.

To bolster its position in the server market, in September 2000 HP introduced the HP 9000 Superdome server, which allows different operating systems to run at the same time. The new machine, a key component in HP's quest to become the leading computer system supplier for Internet-based enterprises, was marketed to major dot.com businesses. In January 2001, HP bought Bluestone Software Inc., a maker of e-business tools. Rapid integration of the acquisition allowed HP to release 25 software products the following month, including the Netaction e-services development and implementation suite, and the OpenView e-services systems management suite. In April, HP balanced out its new software releases with several new hardware products, namely 19 Internet server appliances.

Foirina's efforts to retool HP received mixed reviews in 2001. While some analysts saw the many changes at HP as overdue, others expressed concern that HP was attempting to make too many changes at once, particularly as the slowing North American economy started to undercut the performance of most players in the information technology industry.

FURTHER READING:

Burrows, Peter. ''The Radical: Carly Fiorina's Bold Management Experiment at HP.'' *BusinessWeek Online,* February 19, 2001. Available from www.businessweek.com.

Conner, Deni. ''Hewlett-Packard Unveils Bevy of Internet Appliances.'' *Network World,* April 23, 2001, 14.

Greenmeier, Larry. ''How HP Carves Out the Magic—Hewlett-Packard Wants to Expand Its Service Offerings into the Product-Agnostic World of E-Business.'' *InformationWeek,* November 13, 2000, 64.

''Hewlett-Packard Buys Bluestone in E-Business Bid.'' *Newsbytes,* October 16, 2000.

Hewlett-Packard Co. ''History and Facts.'' Palo Alto, CA: Hewlett-Packard Co., 2001 Available from www.hp.com/hpinfo/abouthp/histnfacts.htm.

''Hewlett-Packard Co.'' In *Notable Corporate Chronologies.* Farmington Hills, MI: Gale Research, 1999.

''Hewlett-Packard Debuts Super Server.'' *Xinhua News Agency,* September 13, 2000.

Levine, Daniel S. ''Hewlett-Packard Leaps Into Software Market.'' *San Francisco Business Times,* February 16, 2001, 8.

Neel, Dan. ''Amazon.com Becomes a Hewlett-Packard Shop.'' *Network World,* June 5, 2000.

''Rebuilding the Garage.'' *The Economist,* July 15, 2000, 59.

SEE ALSO: Hewlett, William R.; Packard, David

HIGHER EDUCATION, E-COMMERCE AND

Since its inception, university and college faculty have used the Internet as a powerful research tool and a vehicle for the dissemination of information. By the mid-1990s, many instructors communicated with students and colleagues via e-mail and incorporated Web-based materials into their courses. As the 21st century began, educators and administrators positioned the Internet as a central component of learning. Both private corporations and educational institutions expected the expanding commercial Internet to revolutionize higher education and open a lucrative source of revenue. International Data Corp. (IDC) projected a 33-percent growth in the U.S. e-learning market—to about $12 billion—from 1999 to 2004. However, the economic downturn of the early 2000s led to a shakeout in the online education industry and many e-learning endeavors shut down completely.

The U.S. spends $600 billion on education annually, making it the second largest industry after healthcare. Web-affiliated and online learning (also called e-education or e-learning) constituted one of higher education's fastest-growing trends. In 2000, about 75 percent of America's 4,000 colleges and universities offered online courses, up from 48 percent in 1998, according to Market Retrieval Service.

With a growing emphasis on an information-driven global economy, higher education was viewed as increasingly essential for the world's population.

E-education's proponents insist that its geographically unlimited nature provides an efficient and cost-effective medium for supplying education to anyone with online access. Proponents perceive e-learning as an alternative to traditional, face-to-face classroom education and hail it as the great democratizer of higher education.

In contrast, critics cautioned that a wholesale drive to digitize course content and teaching raises serious questions about intellectual property rights, academic freedom, and the very goals of higher education. They cautioned that cyber-education threatened to abolish the need for human educators and to reduce higher education to "Webucation" purveyed by "McUniversities."

The Internet's impact has been felt in many arenas of higher education. It facilitates communication and research. It has spawned courseware and college portal companies that provide streamlined university services to faculty, administrators, and students. It increasingly has become the school itself, as more cyber-colleges and fully online universities emerge, offering everything from technical certificates to full-blown advanced graduate and professional degrees.

About 2.2 million students are expected to enroll in online courses by 2002, up from 710,000 in 1998, according to IDC. Additionally, the U.S. Department of Education Statistics indicated that about half of all post-secondary students consisted of adults 25 years or older. This group in particular stands to benefit from the flexibility and availability of Web-affiliated higher education courses.

HISTORY

During the 1950s and 1960s, computers on campuses were employed primarily for scientific research. By the late 1960s, computer technology was adopted for instructional and administrative purposes. Most research universities built centralized computer centers with powerful and expensive machines, usually to serve the physical sciences. With the personal computer revolution of the 1980s, more departments provided individual computers for faculty, and computing resources became increasingly integrated into humanities and arts teaching and research. The Internet caused an explosion in the range and kinds of information available to even remote, small campuses. Institutional libraries in particular became early converts to the possibilities offered by this technology, which permitted the automation of nearly all steps involved in the acquisition and cataloging of library materials. Electronic catalogs generated the ability to search other institutions' holdings online, which caused a quantum leap in library users' research capabilities.

Courses delivered over the Web represented a new development in distance learning. They continued an educational trend dating back to the 19th century, when mail correspondence courses first offered access to higher education for much of America's widely scattered population. In the 20th century, distance education harnessed new communication technologies. The first educational radio station received its license in 1921, and the first such television station in 1945.

The World Wide Web's dramatic expansion in the 1990s led to the growth of online education. The first schools to adopt it as a teaching vehicle frequently designed and generated their own software platforms for course delivery, since user-ready products weren't commercially available. By 2000, many software products appeared that allowed instructors to tailor online courses to their individual needs. These applications also featured electronic grade delivery and course assessment options.

Colleges and universities experimented with various forms of online education. Some institutions required even residential students to complete a portion of their coursework online. Others formed consortia of several schools, making their pooled course offerings available via online portals. UCLA was the first university to mandate that all of its arts and sciences classes develop Web sites.

The United States lacks a centralized accrediting agency for higher education, and only a portion of existing accreditation agencies are recognized by the U.S. Department of Education (DOE) or the Council on Higher Education Accreditation (CHEA). In 2000, the DOE authorized the Distance Education Demonstration Program as a part of the Higher Education Act. The program was instituted to determine ways to adapt financial aid requirements to accommodate distance and online students. A pilot, two-year assessment of 15 schools was set up to discover whether e-learning curricula were rigorous enough to qualify for aid. Reliable statistics concerning student retention and completion rates for e-learning weren't compiled by late 2001, but they generally are thought to be lower than for traditional learning methods.

TYPES OF VIRTUAL HIGHER-ED INSTITUTIONS

A wide variety of higher-education institutions have implemented e-learning programs. Large public university systems often turned to e-learning as a cost-effective means of expansion. They also looked at it as a way to accommodate a projected 20-percent increase in applications by 2008, when Generation Y graduates from high school. In general, online courses became more attractive in an era of shrinking state education budgets. Community colleges embraced e-learning to serve rising numbers of returning and first-time adult students; by 2000, nearly half of all college students were more than 21 years of age.

Elite, private institutions also began testing cyber-education as a revenue-generating endeavor. Their early experiments frequently involved online engineering or business programs targeted at professionals seeking additional training. Fearful of jeopardizing their academic reputations, many schools spun off independent, for-profit online units offering only non-credit courses. Collaborations among private Internet companies, museums, publishers, and universities also appeared, such as UNext.com, which counted Stanford, the University of Chicago, and the London School of Economics among its contributors. Faculty from those institutions developed the online courses and delivered lectures via streaming media. However, part-time instructors handled the actual grading and student communication via e-mail. By 2001, the profitability of such ventures was still unproven. Some of these collaborations provided scholarly articles and lectures for free, hoping to convince online visitors to enroll in affiliated cyber-courses. They also featured online bookshops. At least one prestigious university, MIT, decided to place all of its courses online; anyone can access the classes, though only those paying to enroll will be granted any credit for them.

The most controversial entrants into the e-education arena were for-profit, degree- and certificate-granting institutions, which exist entirely online. One such school, the University of Phoenix, had become the largest private higher-education provider in the United States by 2000. Another, Jones University, was the first exclusively online university to gain accreditation in 1999. Most such ventures offer standardized online courses taught by adjunct instructors.

Two educational areas particularly well served by e-learning were corporate and U.S. Military training. American businesses spend approximately $60 billion annually on employee education, and online courses well suit the scheduling needs of working adult students. Such students often possess a more focused, disciplined approach to education than traditional college-age students, and thus can handle the less-structured learning environment of cyber-education. The U.S. military adopted online instruction to help retain enlistees. In 2000 the Army proposed creating an educational portal that would permit active-duty personnel to continue their education online from any location in which they were serving, with the military footing the bill.

Beyond cyber-classes, the Internet also has affected traditional, face-to-face classroom education. A majority of campus personnel utilize e-mail for transmitting feedback on assignments and conducting teacher-student meetings. Educational software, or "courseware," initially consisted of student-generated, course-affiliated Web sites and professors'

lecture notes posted online. However, these delivery platforms have become increasingly elaborate. Many were developed as collaborations between e-learning companies and high-profile professors from famous institutions; the online course content is licensed from the faculty or institutional developers. Some courseware provides templates that permit instructors to set up online chat rooms and course bulletin boards, post syllabi, and provide links to course-relevant sites. Software also features online grading and diagnostic components to monitor and assess student learning. With "smart classrooms," teachers can incorporate online audio and visual resources into their lectures, or students can attend real-time "guest lectures" given by professors located anywhere in the world.

Some observers predict that "benchmark" versions of the most popular general-education courses required by nearly all higher-education institutions will soon replace lectures written by individual instructors at each institution. These courses, usually introductory surveys in psychology, American history, English composition, calculus, and biology, generate roughly half of all credit enrollment in the United States. Preparatory courses for standardized admission tests also have gone digital.

College portals also have emerged. These allow students to apply to multiple schools online, fill out financial aid applications, as well as register for classes, pay tuition, and order textbooks. Other portals were intended for college faculty and administrators who can use the Web to track enrollments, submit grades, and so on. Many of these services initially came free of charge to interested colleges and universities, provided that the institutions allowed advertising and e-commercial applications to be supplied alongside campus-oriented information. Most also used cookies to trace users' Web habits.

THE DEBATE OVER E-LEARNING

The increasing presence of the Internet and e-commerce in higher education sparked heated disagreement over its appropriateness and effectiveness. Given a dearth of rigorous studies of the trend, few definitive conclusions have been reached and policy recommendations have been difficult for governmental agencies and educators to formulate.

Proponents argue that Internet technology facilitates expanded communication among faculty, students, and administrators. They state that in-class lectures are enhanced by the incorporation of online graphics, audio, and visual displays. Furthermore, students gain instant access to lecture notes, readings, and links to relevant external sites without even entering a library or classroom. The Internet also provides sophisticated interactive learning and assessment tools for teachers and students.

The flexibility and accessibility of online learning appeal to many students, particularly working adults pursuing additional professional education. Studies based on students' perceptions of the value of e-learning indicate that many felt they experienced more interaction with teachers than in face-to-face classes. Students who were intimidated in regular classrooms contributed more freely to online discussions.

E-learning supporters characterize cyber-learning as a democratizer of higher education because geography no longer prevents learners from enrolling in courses offered by premier institutions. E-learning can also accommodate the myriad students who desire continuing education, but are unable to take advantage of it because of job or family responsibilities, as e-learning tends to occur at the student's convenience.

Supporters also applaud the Internet's role in increasing the commercialization of higher education. They argue that traditional institutions remain bastions of privilege and financial inefficiency, with under-worked, tenured professors drawing large salaries for little effort in the classroom. They also decry the waste of costly campus buildings and equipment. As they point out, online institutions offer benchmark products tailored to the needs and desires of educational consumers and delivered with very little investment in labor or physical plants. In 1998, Washington Governor Gary Locke pronounced that online courses eventually could replace all public university faculty.

In contrast, critics fear that as online education expands, administrators gain much greater control over faculty performance and course content, endangering academic freedom. Opponents question e-learning's unproven track record. Students must be disciplined and motivated, because virtual classrooms lack the supervision, interaction, and encouragement that physically present instructors and classmates supply. The quality of online offerings varies greatly and program retention rates range from 20 to 97 percent. The lack of accredited programs may indicate that many online institutions are little more than "degree mills." One of the most prominent concerns voiced by skeptics of e-learning is the lack of information regarding acceptable educational standards for online education. The American Federation of Teachers (AFT) proposed that a set of quality standards for college-based distance education programs be developed.

In response to arguments that the Internet equalizes access to higher education, critics cite a College Board study entitled "The Virtual University and Educational Opportunity," which indicated that the increasing digitization of education actually can intensify the problems of unequal educational opportunities since lower-income students often lack computer skills and Web access. Additionally, accredited online institutions often charge slightly more than traditional colleges and universities, putting their offerings further out of poorer students' reach.

Critics also worry about the effects of the virtual education trend on academic freedom and on faculty. Whether professors own the intellectual property rights to their online courses, and whether their institutions or private companies can dictate what and how they teach, remain unsettled issues. Existing legal standards regarding "fair use" exceptions to copyright protection for scholarly and educational purposes may not hold up in cyberspace. The licensing arrangements that govern the purchase and use of online courseware also are indeterminate. Finally, libraries' right of "first sale," which permits them to purchase items and then lend them to borrowers, may be imperiled. An American Federation of Teachers survey of distance instructors revealed that one-half said they received no monetary compensation or release time in exchange for the extra time required to develop online courses, which 90 percent said required more preparation time than traditional classroom courses. This places adjunct part-timers in a particularly vulnerable position. State administrators see a switch to online education as a means of cutting costs while expanding the reach of their educational systems. Finally, critics state that the e-learning trend has been promoted by administrators, courseware vendors, and e-learning corporations, with little or no involvement of faculty and students.

E-LEARNING WORLDWIDE

E-learning's presence has been felt around the globe, particularly in developing nations whose educational infrastructures often could not satisfy the existing demand. For decades these countries relied on distance education delivered via radio or TV, and many sought to tap online learning to bring courses from high-prestige, western universities to their citizens. If underdeveloped nations are to become competitive in the global marketplace, they too will require highly educated work forces conversant with the latest information technology. Therefore, the demand for ongoing education and skill development can be expected to remain constant.

However, throughout many parts of Asia, Africa, and South America, a fundamental obstacle to expanding online education was the lack of an even rudimentary infrastructure, particularly in rural areas. Such areas also face shortages of computer-literate teachers. Many of the same concerns about the virtualization of higher education voiced by industrialized nations also affected the developing world, such as issues of the quality and effectiveness of online learning and confusion about intellectual property rights. However, additional problems emerged in underdeveloped areas of the globe. For example, if local e-learning programs succeed, some fear that they will face foreign competitors seeking to penetrate emerging markets. Some countries, such as Argentina and Chile, require all distance education offered in their countries to come under the purview of their national accreditation agencies. All foreign universities seeking to offer courses in India must register with the government. Brazil's education ministry refuses to recognize any degree earned from programs sponsored by foreign institutions.

In 2001, the European Commission adopted a $3.3 billion "eLearning Action Plan" to promote online education in European universities. The plan advocated improving information technology infrastructures, providing teacher instruction, and linking all EU higher-education institutions in a single network.

E-learning's greatest potential impact may eventually be felt in the developing world. With burgeoning populations and a lack of skilled workers, these nations experienced a pressing need to expand access to higher education quickly and affordably. The United Nations Educational, Scientific, and Cultural Organization (UNESCO) estimated that only three percent of young people in sub-Saharan Africa and seven percent in Asia received some post-secondary education, compared with 58 percent in industrialized countries overall and 81 percent in the United States. Many developing countries are experimenting with national, virtual universities to be financed primarily by the World Bank.

THE FUTURE OF CYBER-EDUCATION

Many fundamental questions remain unanswered. Among these are: Who owns the rights to courseware and other online educational materials? What conditions should govern employment of instructors in virtual universities? What limitations should be placed on Internet use by educational institutions and for-profit endeavors? How should privacy be protected in the e-learning environment? And what guidelines should govern research conducted online? But while the precise nature of e-learning remains fiercely contested, the rush of universities to set up infrastructure on the Internet continues unabated.

FURTHER READING:

Barker, Jacquelyn. "Sophisticated Technology Offers Higher Education Options." *Technological Horizons In Education Journal.* November 2000.

Birchard, Karen. "European Nations Promote Online Education." *Chronicle of Higher Education.* April 27, 2001. Available from chronicle.com.

Blumenstyk, Goldie. "Colleges Get Free Web Pages, but with a Catch: Advertising." *Chronicle of Higher Education.* September 3, 1999.

Bollag, Burton. "Developing Countries Turn to Distance Education." *Chronicle of Higher Education.* June 15, 2001.

Carnevale, Dan and Jeffrey Young. "Who Owns On-Line Courses? Colleges and Professors Start to Sort It Out." *Chronicle of Higher Education.* December 17, 1999.

Carr, Sarah. "With National e-University, Britain Gets in the Online-Education Game." *Chronicle of Higher Education.* August 17, 2001.

Charp, Sylvia. "E-Learning." *Technological Horizons in Education Journal.* April 2001.

Clayton, Mark. "Click 'n Learn." *Christian Science Monitor.* August 15, 2000.

Cohen, David. "In Cyberuniversities, a Place for South Korea's Women." *Chronicle of Higher Education.* April 6, 2001. Available from chronicle.com.

Dunn, Samuel. "The Virtualizing of Education." *The Futurist.* March/April 2000.

Farrington, Gregory; and Stephen Bronack. "Higher Education Online: How Do We Know What Works—And What Doesn't?" *Technological Horizons in Education Journal.* May 2001.

Green, Joshua. "The Online Education Bubble." *American Prospect.* October 23, 2000.

Grossman, Wendy. "On-Line U." *Scientific American.* July 1999. Available from www.sciam.com.

Johnston, Chris. "The Information Age Draws Nearer." *The Times Educational Supplement.* January 5, 2001.

Katz, Stanley. "In Information Technology, Don't Mistake a Tool for a Goal." *Chronicle of Higher Education.* June 15, 2001.

Kleiner, Carolyn. "Degrees of Separation." *U.S. News & World Report.* 2001. Available from www.usnews.com.

Marcus, David. "A Scholastic Gold Mine." *U.S. News & World Report.* January 24, 2000. Available from www.usnews.com.

Michaels, James W.; and Dirk Smillie. "Webucation." *Forbes.* May 15, 2000. Available from www.forbes.com.

Morris, Kathleen. "Wiring the Ivory Tower." *Business Week.* August 9, 1999.

Nobel, David. "Digital Diploma Mills: The Automation of Higher Education." *First Monday.* January 5, 1998. Available from www.firstmonday.dk.

Stross, Randall. "The New Mailbox U: Discarding Standards in Pursuit of a Buck." *U.S. News & World Report.* January 15, 2001. Available from www.usnews.com.

Weiss, Stefanie. "Virtual Education 101." *Washington Post.* April 9, 2000.

SEE ALSO: Digital Divide; Intellectual Property; Legal Issues

HISTORY OF THE INTERNET AND WORLD WIDE WEB (WWW)

In its short history, the Internet has had a revolutionizing effect, not only on communications and computing, but also on broader areas of life such as economics, culture, language, and social relations. In that same time, however, the Internet and, subsequently, the World Wide Web have undergone a number of permutations, and the intentions of its developers have not always coincided with the ways in which the technology has been realized. As the technology and its influence spread, of course, the designs of the original planners were diluted. From its origins as a military-based, Pentagon-funded networking architecture for experimental communications, the Internet flowered into perhaps the most sweeping revolution in the history of communications technology. The World Wide Web, meanwhile, grew from a vehicle designed to universalize the Internet and democratize electronically based information to a commercial juggernaut that transformed the way business is conducted.

THE PREHISTORY OF THE INTERNET

Although in the popular imagination the Internet is a feature of the 1990s, the earliest inklings of the possibilities of networked computers can be traced to the early 1960s. In 1962, J.C.R. Licklider at the Massachusetts Institute of Technology (MIT) first elucidated his dream of a ''Galactic Network'' connecting computers across the globe for the distribution and access of data and programs. Licklider went on to become the first director of the Defense Advanced Research Projects Agency (DARPA), an arm of the U.S. Department of Defense and the body that funded and coordinated the original research into what became the Internet.

Licklider's MIT colleagues Leonard Kleinrock and Lawrence G. Roberts performed the groundbreaking work toward the development of the Internet's architecture. First, Kleinrock published a revolutionary paper touting the plausibility of using packet switching rather than circuits for communications, thereby paving the way for the necessary computer networking. Roberts built on Kleinrock's theories to devise the first wide-area computing network, using a regular, circuit-based telephone line to allow computers in Massachusetts and California to communicate directly. While the computers were indeed able to run programs and exchange data, Roberts was convinced that Roberts's insistence on the superiority of packet switching was correct.

Having joined DARPA, Roberts in 1967 presented a paper outlining his vision for the original version of the Internet, known as ARPANET, the specifications of which were set by the following fall. Roberts's main position was that the network DARPA was building could be expanded and put to greater use once it was completed. Kleinrock relocated to UCLA just in time for DARPA to send a proposal for the further development of his packet switching ideas for the network DARPA was constructing. Keleinrock and a handful of other interested scholars at UCLA established the Network Measurement Center for the ARPANET project.

ARPANET's first host computer was set up at Kleinrock's Network Measurement Center at the University of California-Los Angeles (UCLA) in 1969, and other nodes, at Stanford Research Institute (SRI), UC Santa Barbara (UCSB), and the University of Utah in Salt Lake City, were connected shortly afterward. As computers were added to ARPENET, the Network Working Group worked to devise a communication protocol that would enable different networks to talk to each other, resulting in the host-to-host Network Control Protocol (NCP), which was rolled out in 1970. Thus the Internet as we know it today began to bloom.

OPENING THE INTERNET

Still, for the first few years of its existence, ARPANET was largely unknown outside of the relatively esoteric group of technologists that was developing it. That changed in 1972, Robert Kahn of Bolt Beranek and Newman (BBN), one of the chief figures in the development of the ARPANET architecture, organized a conference at the International Computer Communication Conference (ICCC) where ARPANET was first demonstrated publicly. That same year, the first major Internet application, called electronic mail, or e-mail, was introduced. Over the next decade, e-mail was the most widely used network application in existence.

The early years of ARPANET saw the network grow slowly, as nodes were gradually added and the vast array of computers plugged into it demanded software and interface hardware so as to adequately interact with ARPANET. As ARPANET expanded into what is now referred to as the Internet, it was grounded on what is known as an open architecture network. In such an environment, other networks could connect to and interact with the Internet and all other networks to which it is connected, but the technology used to build each network could be decided by that network's provider and needn't be dictated by any particular architecture. Packet switching, pioneered by Kleinrock, allowed for such architectural freedom to connect networks on a peer, rather than hierarchical, basis. In fact, open-architecture networking was originally referred to as ''Internetting'' when it was introduced to DARPA in 1972.

While this greatly expanded the uses of the Internet in its limited environment of the day, enabling network designers to tailor their architectures to the specific needs of their users while still linking it to the overall Internet, it resulted in the lack of a common user interface on the Internet. In fact, most of the early networks connected to the Internet were designed for a closed community of researchers and scholars, so the issue of cross-network capacity was a very low priority. For academics, military officials, and scientists, this was satisfactory on the whole as the Internet was geared toward very specialized users. It limited the overall availability of the Internet, however, in a manner that wouldn't be remedied until the 1990s and the introduction of the World Wide Web.

For several years, the bulk of the research involving Internet communications, including work on the various networking and transmission logistical concerns, was funded primarily by the United States Department of Defense, and thus was primarily designed around and translated into military concerns. For instance, the first demonstration of an Internet transmission linking three different kinds of gateways, including a mobile packet radio in California, the Atlantic Packet Satellite Network (SATNET), and several ground-level ARPANET systems through the eastern United States and Europe, were designed to mimic military scenarios the depended on linking mobile units to central command stations across an intercontinental network.

Network Control Protocol, however, proved limited in an open-architecture environment since it was dependent on the ARPANET network design for end-to-end reliability, and any transmission packets that were compromised could bring the protocol to an abrupt stop. To get multiple packet networks to communicate with each other regardless of the underlying networking technology, a common communication protocol was needed. The first efforts toward this end were the work on the Transmission Control Protocol (TCP) by Vinton Cerf at the Stanford Research Institute and Robert Kahn at BBN. TCP was designed specifically to sidestep any centralized global control at the level of internetworking operations using the communications protocol. The design called for gateways, or routers, to connect networks to the Internet without calling for any network reconfiguration. After several years of research and design, the first TCP specification was published in December 1974. Just a few months later, DARPA transferred ARPANET as a fully operational Internet to the Defense Communications Agency (later renamed the Defense Information Systems Agency).

By the late 1970s, the U.S. military became interested in Internet technology not just as an experimental and theoretical tool, but as an actually existing military communications system. As a result, the military began to use Internet communications protocols in packet radio systems and various ground-satellite stations in Europe. The transfer of voice messages highlighted complications in these radio-based networks and led to the development of a complementary Internet Protocol (IP), which was combined with TCP to produce the TCP/IP protocol suite. TCP/IP quickly emerged as the standard for all military Internet systems, and, by extension, the Internet itself.

Through the early 1980s, Internet products consolidated into the TCP/IP protocol, setting the stage for the opening of commercial applications. Sure enough, according to Vinton Cerf, in the mid-1980s a substantial market for Internet-based products began to flower. In large part this was due to the NSFNet initiative. This program, which was born of a network designed to link supercomputers together based on software designed by David Mills of the University of Delaware, and which was led by Dennis Jennings at the National Science Foundation (NSF), quickly generated supporting software and systems by IBM, MCI, and Merit to accommodate the quickly escalating networking demand. Thanks to the outgrowth of technologies stemming from NSFNet, the number of computers connected to the Internet jumped from only several hundred in 1983 to over 1.3 million in 1993, while the number of networks leapt from a tiny handful to over 10,000. By 1990, the NSFNet, in fact, had generated such a profound transformation in the Internet's backbone and reach that ARPANET itself was decommissioned. Soon commercial e-mail carriers, already devising systems and software for use in intranets, began exploiting the possibilities of Internet-based e-mail; commercial Internet service providers came along in their wake, sprouting up from the original handful of networks brought to life under NSFNet. For several years, however, these services were still primarily geared toward researchers and businesses-those few groups that already had a need for and access to the Internet. The Internet as a household resource was still largely unheard of.

The rapid expansion of the Internet in the 1980s necessitated new methods of management such as the Domain Name System (DNS). In its earliest incarnations, users had to memorize numerical addresses to access the fairly limited number of host networks, but that became unfeasible as the number of connected networks took off. With the proliferation of local area networks (LANs), Internet managers designed the DNS to create easily identifiable hierarchies of hosts to facilitate easy Internet navigation.

In the late 1980s and early 1990s, a series of policy initiatives, including a forum at the Harvard Kennedy School of Government on ''The Commercialization and Privatization of the Internet'' and a National Research Council committee report titled "Towards a National Research Network," paved the way for the next steps of Internet evolution, including the sponsorship by the U.S. government of high-speed computer networks that would serve as the backbone for the explosion of the information superhighway and e-commerce in the 1990s.

THE WORLD WIDE WEB

Perhaps the invention that most facilitated the growth of the Internet as a global information-sharing system is the World Wide Web. Unlike the Internet, however, the early design and development of the World Wide Web was primarily the doing of just one person: Tim Berners-Lee. Working as a contract programmer at the Geneva, Switzerland-based Centre Europen de Recherche Nucleaire (European Laboratory for Particle Physics, or CERN), Berners-Lee repeatedly proposed to develop a global interactive interface for use on the Internet so as to turn the fragmented and relatively exclusive Internet into a popular and seamless whole. After several rejections, Berners-Lee simply developed a prototype using the laboratory's phone-book entries in 1989. Called Enquire Within Upon Everything, the prototype was designed to link and connect elements much in the way that the brain makes random connections and associations. Unlike the average database system, according to Berners-Lee, the Web was to be designed to make random associations between arbitrary objects in the files.

Just as the Internet evolved to ensure the greatest possible flexibility and interoperability, so the Web's original architectural design specifically minimized the degree of specification so as to minimize constraints on the user. In this way, the design could be modified and updated while leaving the basic architecture undisturbed. Thus, for instance, users could enter the existing File Transfer Protocol (FTP) in the address space and it would be as workable as the new Hypertext Transfer Protocol (HTTP). HTTP was the communications protocol that allowed the Web to transfer data to and from any computer connected to the Internet, and was designed as an improvement on the FTP standard in that it took advantage of the Web's capacity to read and translate intricate features. The intermixing of these protocols and file formats was the key, for Berners-Lee, to ensuring not only the widest proliferation but also the greatest durability of his creation. Not only would the Web in this way be able to evolve with changing systems and protocols, but the early adoption would be made smoother in that users could adopt the Web from whatever systems they were currently using as a parallel or supplementary system. Shortly after the successful demonstration of the phonebook prototype, the Internet community, still relatively esoteric, began experimenting with browser platforms for viewing the Web. One of the early successes was the Mosaic program written by Marc Andreessen, later the founder of Netscape.

Taking advantage of the Internet's gateways and bypassing centralized registries, Berners-Lee devised the universal resource locators (URLs) that are the basis for Web addresses under the DNS. URLs were built to highlight the central power of the Web: that any link can connect to any other document or resource anywhere on the Internet, or in the "universe of information," as Berners-Lee puts it. URLs are structured to identify the kind of space that is being accessed (for instance, by the prefixes "http:" or "ftp:") followed by the specific address within that information space.

The last piece of the WWW puzzle was the medium's lingua franca: Hypertext Markup Language (HTML), a language of codes, built on hypermedia principles dating back to the 1940s, that informs the browser how to interpret the files for the Web. By 1991, all the elements were in place, and the World Wide Web was released from Berners-Lee's laboratory to the public free of any charge.

Perhaps the biggest story in the development of the Web through the early and mid-1990s was the fight to stave off the fragmentation of Web standards that could potentially undermine the ability of the Web to fulfill its original function-namely, to create a seamless universe of information. The World Wide Web Consortium (W3C), of which Berners-Lee was the founder, was born in 1994 just as the Web was beginning to hit critical mass. The organization, though not a governing body, was founded to guide and oversee the Web's development and minimize proprietary battles over standards and protocols in an effort to keep the Web nonproprietary and freely accessible. Based at MIT, the W3C is a neutral organization that brings together technicians, researchers, policy advocates, software vendors, and business interests to compromise on technical standards and specifications to ensure that the Web remains undivided.

COMMERCIALIZATION

Beginning in the mid-1990s, the World Wide Web helped propel the Internet to a new stage of mass consumption, and in the process both were radically transformed, as was the society that used them. The Internet and World Wide Web opened new fields of debate over social and cultural concerns, including the right to privacy, the protection of children from harmful or inappropriate materials, freedom of speech as it pertains to electronic networks, intellectual property, issues of social equality, the security of financial and personal data online, and a host of other issues.

As businesses grew increasingly interested in the Internet and the Web for their own strategies, the race to take advantage of the emerging e-commerce markets highlighted the needs of commercial interests in the Internet architecture, in Web- and e-mail-based security measures, and in business models structured on Internet communications and technology. In turn, businesses used these technologies as tools to enter and take advantage of new markets throughout the world, in the process furthering the proliferation of the Internet and the globalization of the world's economies. In the process, the range of social and cultural concerns connected to the Web and the Internet were intensified.

It is clear that, far from the special provenance of technicians, computer scientists, and scholarly researchers, the Internet and the World Wide Web by the mid-1990s had evolved into critical components of the national—and increasingly the international—infrastructure, components with which the rest of economic and social life were increasingly intertwined. As a result, the spate of questions, concerns, cautions, and enthusiasm about these technologies required careful negotiation to ensure that these forces served the good of everyone they affected. Several organizations sprouted up for just that purpose, including the W3C and the Internet Society, which brought together diverse interests to attempt to oversee the development of these technologies within the context of the overall common good. While these debates remained contentious as competing groups wrangled to assert their positions, and consensus over the future direction of these technologies was far from realization, there was little doubt that the Internet and the World Wide Web were thoroughly enough integrated into the fabric of society that they would both affect and be affected by the social forces that attempt to guide them.

FURTHER READING:

Berners-Lee, Tim, and Mark Fischetti. *Weaving the Web: The Original Design and Ultimate Destiny of the World Wide Web by its Inventor.* San Francisco, CA: HarperCollins, 1999.

————. ''The World Wide Web: Past, Present, and Future.'' Cambridge, MA: World Wide Web Consortium, August 1996. Available from www.w3.org/People/Berners-Lee.

Cerf, Vinton. ''How the Internet Came to Be,'' in Bernard Aboba, *The Online User's Encyclopedia.* Boston, MA: Addison-Wesley, 1993.

Internet Society (ISOC). ''All About the Internet: History of the Internet.'' Reston, VA: Internet Society, May 2001. Available from www.isoc.org.

SEE ALSO: ARPAnet; Berners-Lee, Tim; BITNET; Communications Protocol; Internet; Internet Society (ISOC); Local Area Network (LAN); Three Protocols, The; URL (Uniform Resource Locator); World Wide Web (WWW); World Wide Web Consortium (W3C)

HOME NETWORKING

Home networking is the connection of several electronic devices, such as personal computers (PCs) and printers, to a single network, which is known as a home-area network (HAN). Although proponents of the technology claim future home networks will allow homeowners to link all sorts of appliances, like microwaves, stereos, and televisions, most of the HANs in existence in 2001 comprised desktop computers, laptop computers, modems, and printers. This type of technology allows home computer users with more than one PC to do things like share files between multiple machines, use a single Internet connection, and send documents from various PCs to a single printer. In the late 1990s, many research firms predicted that home networking would become a billion dollar market within a couple of years. For example, Dataquest Inc. forecasted $2 billion in U.S. home networking sales by 2002 and $4 billion in sales by 2004. However, the technology caught on less quickly than anticipated and sales only had reached $290 million by 2000. Projections for 2001 were scaled back to less than $600 million.

Several leading technology firms—including Nortel Networks Corp., Intel Corp., IBM Corp., and Compaq Computer Corp.—had begun investing in home networking technology by 1998. Anticipating an increase in demand for this type of network, Microsoft Corp. included an application known as Internet Connection Sharing (ICS) in its Windows 98 platform. The new technology allowed users to share an Internet connection—via modem, digital subscriber line (DSL), ISDN, or cable—with other networked machines running Windows 98. Problems with the first version of ICS prompted Microsoft to offer an upgraded version of ICS, along with a tutorial program dubbed ICS Wizard, in both Windows 98 Second Edition and Windows ME.

In 1999, Lucent Technologies began working on communication chips for the home networking market. Cisco Systems Inc. began offering At Home Networks to explain the benefits of home networking to consumers, hoping to boost interest in its home networking products. Broadcom Corp. also diversified into home networking by developing products that connected in-home appliances via existing telephone lines. In fact, Broadcom, Compaq, IBM, Lucent, Intel, Hewlett-Packard, 3Com, AT&T Wireless, AMD and others formed an organization known as HomePNA to create compatible home networking appliances for use on existing telephone wires. These companies were betting on market research reports, many of which indicated that the number of networked homes—roughly 15,000 in early 1999—would reach 5 million or 6 million by 2002.

Along with telephone lines, home telephone networks also can be created using power lines, with Ethernet connections as the speediest option, and wireless connections, such as Wi-Fi, a wireless standard officially known as 802.11b. Wireless home networking products began to garner more recognition in 2001. That year, EarthLink, a leading Internet Service Provider (ISP), began selling 2Wire home networking products, known as residential gateways, which allow multiple PCs in a single home to share a DSL Internet connection. 2Wire's HomePortal 1000 allows customers to create a home network using the Wi-Fi wireless standard.

Microsoft's highly marketed Windows XP—released in late 2001—also contains technology to support Wi-Fi. According to a September 2001 article in *CNET News.com,* ''Microsoft's promotion of Wi-Fi in XP could educate consumers and spur interest in the hyped but still emerging market for home networking.'' With more than 20 million households using multiple computers at the turn of the century, home networking technology developers continued to work on new applications that will simplify for homeowners the process of connecting their machines via a network.

FURTHER READING:

''Cisco's Plan to Pop Up in Your Home.'' *Fortune.* February 1, 1999.

Costello, Sam. ''Earthlink Offers Home Networking to DSL Users.'' *Network World.* April 2, 2001.

''Home Networking: Broadcom Enters Home Networking Market; Broadcom Announces MediaShare Technology Providing More than 10 Times the Performance of Existing HomePNA Solutions.'' *EDGE: Work-Group Computing Report.* February 15, 1999.

''Household Networking Takes Up Residence.'' *Computer Dealer News.* January 15, 1999.

Tyson, Jeff. ''How Home Networking Works.'' 2001. Available from www.howstuffworks.com.

SEE ALSO: Connectivity, Internet

HOOVER'S ONLINE

Hoover's Online is a business information resource and portal that is operated by Hoover's Inc., a publicly traded company headquartered in Austin, Texas, with fiscal 2001 revenue of $30.8 million and more than 300 employees. A subsidiary, Hoover's Media Technologies, Inc., is a content aggregator and application services developer that was formed when Hoover's acquired Powerize.com, Inc. in August 2000. Hoover's Inc. also licenses its content and publishes books, reports, and CD-ROMs. For fiscal 2001 ending March 31, about 49 percent of Hoover's overall revenue was derived from online subscriptions, 37 percent from advertising and e-commerce, 10 percent from licensing, and 4 percent from print products and CD-ROMs.

Hoover's Online offers a wide range of business information, some of which is available for free and some to paid subscribers only. The site includes proprietary information developed by Hoover's as well as content from third-party providers. Hoover's proprietary database of business information covers more than 17,000 public and private enterprises worldwide and more than 300 industries. Through alliances and partnerships with other information providers, Hoover's Online contains content and links from sources such as Dun & Bradstreet, Harris InfoSource, InfoUSA.com, Market Location, Media General Financial Services, Mergent FIS, and NewsEdge.

The Hoover's Online site is organized into the following channels: Companies and Industries, Money, Career Development, News Center, Business Travel, and Purchasing Center. The site also features an easy-to-use site search where users can search for company names, ticker symbols, personal names, and more. Additional links are provided at the home page for such services as IPO Central, e-mail news alerts, portfolio tool, free newsletters, business links, small business, Hoover's wireless, and Hoover's European sites.

Hoover's core asset is its database of information on public and private companies and industry segments. Much of this information can be accessed for free through a site search or through the Companies and Industries channel. For specific companies and industries, non-subscribers have access to company capsules, which include basic contact information, a descriptive paragraph or two, a list of the top three competitors, the most recent year's sales and net income, a link to stock quotes, number of employees, and profiles of the company's top three executives. Subscribers have additional access to a more detailed company profile and history, in-depth financial information, a more comprehensive list of competitors, and information on the competitive landscape, as well as access to advanced search features. As of 2001, Hoover's offered individual subscriptions for $29.95 per month or $199.95 per year and annual enterprise subscriptions ranging from $1,750 for five seats to $45,000 for 1,000 seats. Larger enterprise subscriptions were negotiated on an individual basis, based on the number of seats. Hoover's Online had about 285,000 paying subscribers as of March 31, 2001.

Hoover's other channels organize links and information targeted at the other interests of individuals and companies looking for business-related information. The Money channel includes investment-related links to mutual funds, emerging markets, foreign markets, bonds, IPO news, insider trading, stock buybacks, and earnings and forecasts. Available links and content at the Career Development channel include a job bank, a salary wizard, and information on trade shows. The Business Travel channel organizes links to facilitate flight bookings, car rentals, and hotel reservations. Informational links are furnished for more than 100 city guides; a flight tracker; travel tools such as maps, a currency converter, and even information on traffic delays; and weather information. Hoover's Purchasing Center channel is where users can buy industry and topical reports written by Hoover's and other sources, including Dun & Bradstreet, Factiva, ICON Group, eMarketer, and others. Hoover's also offers four free e-mail newsletters: *IPO Update,* a weekly roundup of IPO activity; *Hoover's Online: Week at a Glance,* which includes news summaries, a brief description of a new company, and tips for finding business information; *Hoover's Industry News Digests,* twice-weekly news summaries available for the advertising, healthcare, Internet, and telecommunications industries; and *Hoover's Online Europe Weekly.*

HOOVER'S GOES ONLINE

The company that became Hoover's Inc. was established in 1990 as the Reference Press by entrepreneur Gary Hoover and former University of Chicago classmates Alta Campbell and Patrick Spain. The company's flagship publication was a reference directory called *Hoover's Handbook.* First published in 1991, the book contained profiles of more than 500 major corporations. It was aimed at general readers as well as professionals and was available in bookstores. When Gary Hoover left the company in 1992 to start a chain of travel superstores, Patrick Spain became CEO.

From the start the company was interested in exploring the electronic delivery of its informational database. Through a partnership with Sony, information from the *Hoover's Handbook* was made available in electronic form. In 1993 the company began licensing information from its database to America Online. In 1994 Time Warner, through its subsidiary Warner Books, took a significant minority position in the Reference Press and assumed responsibility for bookstore distribution of its titles. In 1995 the Reference Press launched Hoover's Online, a Web-based business ref-

erence service. By the end of 1996 the company had more than 20 online services and was on *Inc.* magazine's list of the 500 fastest-growing private companies. In August 1996 the Reference Press changed its name to Hoover's Inc., in recognition of the strong brand it had created. In November 1996 the company published *Cyberstocks: An Investor's Guide to Internet Companies* and launched a companion Web site that contained the full text of the book at no charge, along with other financial information and interactive services, including daily updates of the 100 stocks profiled in the book.

CONSTRUCTING AN ONLINE BUSINESS INFORMATION PORTAL, 1996-2001

Over the next several years Hoover's would evolve from a traditional reference book publisher to a provider of business information and electronic commerce across different media. By 1997 Hoover's database contained information on more than 10,000 public and private companies. During 1997 the company gained two equity investors, Internet search engine InfoSeek and Media General, Inc., a provider of news, information, and entertainment services. Both companies gained seats on Hoover's board of directors.

In 1998 Hoover's Online redesigned its site to create a portal that provided visitors with a variety of free, subscription, and personalized online services and databases. The focus of Hoover's portal was information about companies. By March 1998 the company's subscriber base reached 15,000, more than doubling over a six-month period. During 1998 the company partnered with Amazon.com to launch the Store at Hoover's, where visitors to Hoover's Online could purchase books, magazines, and CDs.

Hoover's Inc. went public on July 21, 1999, with an initial public offering that netted $42 million for the company. For its fiscal year ending March 31, 1999, Hoover's reported revenue of $9.2 million and a net loss of $2.2 million. During the coming year Hoover's losses would mount as the company spent more on sales and marketing and product development. During the year Hoover's formed new strategic partnerships and alliances and expanded existing ones. It signed an agreement with AltaVista Search Service to include its company capsules and profiles on AltaVista's investment area. An agreement with Reuters news service gave Hoover's access to additional information for new company profiles, while Reuters users could access Hoover's company capsules and industry snapshots. Hoover's also agreed to license some of its company information to CNBC.com and began co-producing exclusive editorial content for use at CNBC.com and on-air at

CNBC. CNBC parent NBC purchased a minority interest in Hoover's, as did Knowledge Net Holdings and Nextera Enterprises. Hoover's also gained access to additional content through agreements with Media General Financial Services, Dow Jones & Co., and News Alert, Inc.

In September 1999 Hoover's launched a $10 million advertising campaign that included print ads in national business publications as well as the *New York Times* and *USA Today*. The campaign, which featured the tagline ''Know Thy Stuff,'' also appeared in 15-second television spots on CBS, CNN, CNBC, ESPN, and MSNBC. At the time the campaign was launched, Hoover's was generating about 20 million page views per month and boasted more than 100,000 paying subscribers. The campaign was intended to introduce the newly designed Hoover's Online: The Business Network—developed through partnerships with Monster.com, Internet Travel Network, and Knowledge Universe—which offered a wider range of business-oriented services, including career information and business travel services. The site also featured a News and Analysis section, where users could find news items about specific companies and industries.

During 2000 Hoover's continued to enter into strategic alliances to gain additional content and wider distribution of its information. Through an agreement with Vault.com, Hoover's users could access Vault.com's Employer Reports, which provided inside information about companies that was useful to job seekers. An agreement with Gomez Advisors gave Hoover's users access to rankings of Internet brokers and a link to Gomez.com. Other new content added to Hoover's during the year included Salary Wizard, made available for free from Salary.com, and interactive financial ''tombstone'' advertisements that announced the sale of new securities. During the year Hoover's invested in Intellifact.com and agreed to provide data to Intellifact's vertical Web sites. Hoover's also acquired Powerize.com for $17.1 million. Powerize.com was a content aggregator, and its Web site carried a wide range of business research and analysis.

Hoover's maintained an established presence in the United Kingdom through its London-based subsidiary, Hoover's Online Europe. At the beginning of 2001 Hoover's expanded its European presence by opening localized Web sites in France, Germany, Italy, and Spain. However, 2001 was a difficult year financially for Hoover's. It posted losses of $21.6 million in the quarter ending March 31 and of $2.8 million in the following quarter. In September 2001 the company announced it would close its London office and pursue international sales through its Austin, Texas, and New York offices as well as through sales agencies overseas. The company also said it would re-

duce its workforce by about 20 percent. During the year Jeffery Tarr, formerly CEO of now-defunct All.com, became Hoover's president and CEO, while Patrick Spain moved to his new position as executive chairman of the board for a time before he resigned to serve as chairman in a non-executive capacity effective. In a company news release, Tarr said that by sharpening its focus, streamlining its product offering, reducing its cost structure, and shifting the responsibilities of several key management positions, Hoover's expected to return to net income profitability by the quarter ending March 31, 2002.

FURTHER READING:

''Austin, Texas, Online Business Information Company to Take New CEO.'' *Knight-Ridder/Tribune Business News,* May 4, 2001.

Dzinkowski, Ramona. ''Creating New Revenue Streams at Hoover's Online.'' *Strategic Finance,* January 2001.

''Hoover's Expands Presence with New Sites in Europe.'' *Austin Business Journal,* October 20, 2000.

''Hoover's Focuses on Subscriptions.'' *PR Newswire,* September 25, 2001. Available from biz.yahoo.com/prnews

Hoover's Online. ''Home Page.'' Austin, TX: Hoover's Inc., October 11, 2001. Available from www.hoovers.com .

Martin, Nicole. ''Capitalizing on Content.'' *EContent,* May 2001.

Milliot, Jim. ''Hoover's Has New Investor, Will Boost Online.'' *Publishers Weekly,* September 22, 1997.

Rivkin, Jacqueline. ''Reaching the Business Book Buyer Via the Mass Market.'' *Publishers Weekly,* January 11, 1991.

Tudor, Jan Davis. ''Hoover's Online: Data Worth Paying For.'' *EContent,* December 1999.

Vonder Haar, Steven. ''Web Portals Give Users the Business.'' *Inter@ctive Week,* September 13, 1999.

SEE ALSO: Business-to-Business (B2B) E-commerce; Content Provider

HTML (HYPERTEXT MARKUP LANGUAGE)

Hypertext markup language (HTML) is an authoring or presentation language (not a programming language) used for creating pages on the World Wide Web. The language consists of special codes or tags that determine a page's visible appearance when read by a Web browser. In addition to defining the overall structure and layout of a Web page, HTML also is used to denote links to other Web pages, the placement of graphics or pictures on a page and the appearance of text, including bold or italicized type and different fonts.

According to The National Center for Supercomputing Applications (NCSA), Tim Berners-Lee invented HTML at CERN, the European Laboratory for Particle Physics in Geneva. Because of Berners-Lee, it became possible for entrepreneurs, small businesses, and large corporations to post information about their products and services onto the Internet in a visual format.

HTML is closely related to another language called Standard Generalized Markup Language (SGML). In the early 2000s a subset of SGML known as Extensible Markup Language (XML) led to the development of XHTML, a hybrid language that combines HTML with XML. XHTML has powerful implications for e-commerce because the language's XML component allows users to share information in a universal, standard format without making the kinds of special arrangements required by Electronic Data Interchange (EDI), the protocol in which many large companies exchange electronic data with suppliers and other entities. According to *ABA Banking Journal,* "XML is a set of simple rules for converting the meaning of a document written in any software into a globally standardized format that any other software can understand." According to the journal, online banking pioneer Wells Fargo was among the very first financial institutions to use XML.

According to *American Demographics,* in the early 2000s companies like Jive Records, Hewlett-Packard, and Office.com began to use HTML for more than just Web pages. The companies found that by integrating HTML into e-mail, marketing messages could be delivered in a richer, more meaningful way. In this scenario, rather than sending out plain text messages to current or potential customers to promote products, services, or entertainment offerings, companies incorporate streaming-video clips, pictures, and sound directly into e-mail. Although this approach wasn't widely used and some consumers were opposed to receiving large e-mail messages requiring lengthy download times, the overall use of media-rich e-mails was expected to increase as more people connect to the Internet through high-speed connections.

FURTHER READING:

"The ABC's of HTML." The National Center for Supercomputing Applications. February 11, 2001. Available from www.ncsa.uiuc.edu/General/Training/HTMLIntro.

"A Beginner's Guide to HTML." The National Center for Supercomputing Applications. February 11, 2001. Available from www.ncsa.uiuc.edu/General/Internet/WWW/HTMLPrimerAll.

Blank, Christine. "Beating the Banner Ad." *American Demographics,* June 2000.

"HTML." *Ecommerce Webopedia.* February 10, 2001. Available from e-comm.webopedia.com.

"HTML." *Tech Encyclopedia.* February 10, 2001. Available from www.techweb.com/encyclopedia.

Schwartz, Matthew. "Spreading the Word on XHTML." *Computerworld,* June 19, 2000.

SEE ALSO: Berners-Lee, Tim; Electronic Data Interchange (EDI); XML

I

IBM CORP.

IBM Corp. is the world's leading maker of computer hardware—including mainframes, notebooks, personal computers, and servers—as well as the number one computer-related services provider. The firm is also second only to Microsoft Corp. in the computer software industry. While its position as a mainframe system powerhouse allowed it to experience stellar growth in the 1970s and 1980s, IBM spent most of the 1990s working to reinvent itself as an e-business services provider. By 2001, services—both e-business and otherwise—accounted for more than one-third of annual revenues.

EARLY HISTORY

In 1911, Charles F. Trust oversaw the formation of Computing-Tabulating-Recording Co. (C-T-R) by merging three companies: Hollerith's Tabulating Machine Co.; the Computing Scale Co. of America, established in 1901; and International Time Recording Co., founded in 1990. A manufacturer of industrial time recorders, scales, tabulating machines and more, C-T-R formed the core of what would become International Business Machines (IBM). Clients included railroads, chemical companies, utilities, and life insurance companies. Based in New York, the new firm employed 1,300 workers.

Flint hired National Cash Register Co. executive Thomas J. Watson, Sr. to run C-T-R as general manager in 1914. He laid the groundwork for what would become a key factor in IBM's long-term success—excellent customer service. Watson also focused on fostering employee loyalty by putting in place programs that offered rewards for meeting sales goals and by hosting various events for the families of employees. He was appointed president in 1915. That year, at the firm's first sales convention, Watson began to recognize that C-T-R's tabulating machines were its most promising products. He shifted focus from clocks and scales to tabulators and other basic office gadgets. In 1917, C-T-R launched its first international venture when it established a subsidiary named International Business Machines Co. in Canada. A unit also opened in Brazil. By then, employees totaled 3,000.

International expansion continued two years later when C-T-R moved into Europe for the first time. The firm launched an electric synchronized time clock system, which was quickly followed by the release of a printing tabulator and an electric accounting machine in 1920. C-T-R bought Chicago, Illinois-based Ticketograph Co. in 1921. In February 1924, C-T-R changed its name to International Business Machines Corp. New product releases included the Carroll Rotary Press, which produced punched cards at a high rate of speed; a self-regulating time clock system; and a horizontal sorting machine. Offices opened in Asia, Latin America, and the Philippines, and in 1925, the firm's accounting machines were launched in Japan. That year, shareholders received their first stock dividend.

Stock split three-for-one in 1926. Several IBM products were awarded first prize at the Sesquicentennial Exposition in Philadelphia, Pennsylvania. By most accounts, the firm was considered exceptionally profitable by the late 1920s, when earningss exceeded

$5 million on sales of nearly $20 million. By then, IBM had become a leading player in office technology. The firm's punched cards could hold 80 columns, nearly double their previous capacity. In 1928, IBM unveiled an accounting machine able to perform subtraction. Although the stock market crash of 1929 left many businesses floundering, IBM was able to pay a five percent stock dividend. In fact, throughout the Great Depression, IBM hired new employees and continued growing operations and building inventory. In 1931, the firm launched its 400 series alphabetical accounting machines and 600 series calculating machines.

The firm faced its first legal battle in 1932 when the U.S. Justice Deptartment filed an antitrust suit against IBM after finding that its cross-licensing agreement with rival Remington Rand—a deal that was put in place in the 1910s—was anti-competitive. The suit also addressed IBM's exclusive punch card agreements, which prevented clients from using the cards with non-IBM machines. Four years later, after determining that IBM held 85 percent of the U.S. keypunch, tabulating, and accounting equipment markets, the Supreme Court ordered IBM to nullify its restrictive agreements. However, the ruling's impact on IBM was minimal as sales of its machines continued to grow.

In 1933, IBM built a new research and development laboratory in Endicott, New York. The firm also constructed the IBM Schoolhouse, a training facility for employees. After acquiring Electromatic Typewriters, Inc., based in Rochester, New York, IBM established a new electric writing division. The firm divested a portion of its scale manufacturing operations to Hobart Manufacturing in 1934. That year, the firm launched the 405 Alphabetical Accounting Machine and began offering a group life insurance plan to employees; survivor benefits were added to compensation packages shortly thereafter. The Social Security Act of 1935 offered an unprecedented opportunity to IBM as the government needed calculating machines that could maintain employment records for more than 26 million citizens. Because IBM had bolstered its inventory throughout the Depression, it was able to fulfill the landmark contract for more than 400 accounting machines and 1,200 keypunchers. The firm continued making new product releases, including its first successful electric typewriter and a proof machine to clear bank checks.

In 1936, IBM became one of the first U.S. companies to offer employees paid holidays and vacations. That year, the firm released a collator and a test-scoring machine. Employees exceeded more than 10,000. By the start of World War II, IBM was posting earnings in excess of $9 million, or roughly one-quarter of sales. With revenues nearing the $50 million mark, IBM had become the leading office machine maker in the U.S. Analysts pointed to three major practices that enhanced IBM's performance: its policy of leasing its machines to clients; its focus on large-scale, customized systems; and its cross-licensing deals with rivals.

MOVE TO COMPUTING

IBM operations were focused on the war effort beginning in 1941, and the firm manufactured fire control instruments for ships and planes, automatic rifles, and bomb sighting devices. It was during the war years that IBM made its first move toward computing. In 1944, in conjunction with Harvard University, IBM created the Automatic Sequence Controlled Calculator, the first large-scale device that could process lengthy calculations. Over eight feet tall, the five-ton machine, known as Mark I, housed nearly 500 miles of wire and 765,000 parts. Some industry experts consider Mark I the world's first computer.

IBM established the Watson Scientific Computing Laboratory at Columbia University in 1945. Sickness, accident, and retirement plans were offered to employees that year, and special programs were put in place for handicapped workers. IBM also became the first company to grant money to the United Negro College Fund. In 1946, IBM introduced its first small, electronic calculator, known as the 603 Multiplier, and pocket-sized braille writing devices. Stock split five-for-four. Watson continued building the firm's non-cash employee compensation package, adding a hospitalization plan. He also began hosting dinners for employees and their spouses. By then, the firm's workforce totaled roughly 22,500. A vested rights pension plan, along with total and permanent disability income plans, were added to the benefits package in 1947. The following year, IBM introduced its Selective Sequence Electronic Calculator, its first large-scale digitized calculator. Other innovations included the 604 Electronic Calculating Punch. The Card-Programmed Electronic Calculator, unveiled in 1949, was the firm's first product built exclusively for computing centers. The 407 Accounting Machine and the IBM Model A "Executive" Electric Typewriter were also shipped that year.

IBM moved into Israel and the United Kingdom in the early 1950s. When competitor Remington Rand began marketing the UNIVAC computer and gained a significant share of the new computer market, IBM opted to monitor demand before delving deeper into computers. Thomas Watson, Jr. took over as president in 1952. Believing IBM should, in fact, focus its efforts on computers, Watson launched a large-scale research program with the goal of bypassing Remington Rand. According to IBM's Corporate History, "Just as his father saw the company's future in tabulators rather than scales and clocks, Thomas J. Watson, Jr. foresaw the role computers would play in business, and he led IBM's transformation from a medium-sized maker of tabulating equipment and typewriters into a computer industry leader.'' The U.S. Justice Deptartment filed its second antitrust suit against IBM that year; the litigation eventually resulted in a consent decree between IBM and the government. Shortly thereafter, the firm launched a computer designed for scientific calculations, the IBM 701. The vacuum tubes used in the 701 were smaller and easier to replace than the switches used in earlier machines. Product introductions in 1953 included the IBM 702, the 650, and the Model A Toll Biller. That year, IBM created a formal equal opportunity hiring policy, vowing not to discriminate on the basis of race, color, or creed. IBM constructed the Naval Ordnance Research Calculator for the U.S. Navy in 1954; it was considered the fastest and most powerful electronic computer to date.

IBM created two new divisions for its electric typewriter and military product operations in 1955. The IBM 705 machine, launched that year, was the firm's first general purpose business computer; its success help to oust Remington Rand from its first place spot in the new computer market. In fact, the majority of businesses already using IBM office machines—roughly 85 percent of the market—eventually switched to IBM computers. IBM reorganized into six autonomous divisions in 1956. Employees totaled 72,500. To fund additional growth, the firm offered 1.05 million shares of stock. IBM also established Service Bureau Corp. as a wholly owned subsidiary; created the first computer disk storage system, known as RAMAC (Random Access Method of Accounting and Control); and introduced the FORTRAN computer language. In 1958, Control Data and Sperry Rand launched computers using new transistor technology in place of vacuum tubes. As a result, IBM began working on the IBM 7090, a transistor-based machine that could perform nearly 230,000 calculations per second. IBM also divested its time equipment operations. The following year, IBM created its Advanced Systems Development unit to experiment in emerging markets.

Thomas J. Watson, Jr. took over as chairman of the board in 1961, and Albert L. Williams was appointed president. That year, IBM established its components division. Three new divisions—industrial products; real estate and construction; and research—were created in 1963. In April of 1964, IBM introduced the System/360, which used software and peripheral equipment compatible with each of the five models in the line of computers. This interchangeability was a new concept in the computer industry, and it proved to be one of IBM's most important moves. The firm also acquired Science Research Associates, Inc. and created a field engineering division. The electric typewriter division was renamed the office products division. Gaining its largest space-based contract to date, IBM's federal systems division landed a contract to build a component for the Saturn launch vehicles. In 1965, the firm used a computer-based communications network to connect its U.S. and European engineering, manufacturing, and administrative facilities to coordinate work on System/360. IBM also shipped the 2361—the largest computer memory in history—to NASA space center in Houston, Texas. Orders for System/360 continued to grow. T. Vincent Learson succeeded Albert Williams as president in 1966, and employees neared the 200,000 mark. Thomas J. Watson, Jr. was named ''Businessman of the Year'' in *Saturday Review*. The firm found itself facing a third lawsuit in 1968 when Control Data Corp. brought charges against IBM for allegedly selling its clients ''phantom'' computers to prevent them from ordering Control Data machines. The following year, the U.S. Justice Department filed its own suit against the firm, finding merit with Control Data's complaints, as well as concerns regarding other anti-competitive activities.

Product releases in the 1970s began with the System/370, IBM's most powerful computer ever, and a photocopy machine. The firm also introduced an electronic supermarket checkout station; a consumer banking transaction facility that proved to be the precursor to Automated Teller Machines (ATMs); the 5100 Portable Computer, which was discontinued early in the next decade; the 5110 Computing System; and the 5520 Administrative System. Thomas Watson, Jr. resigned as CEO in 1971, and Learson took the reigns of IBM. In 1973, a federal district court dismissed Control Data's case against IBM after IBM agreed to sell its Service Bureau Corp. to CDC. Frank T. Cary took over as CEO that year. He reorganized the firm's overseas operations into two groups: IBM World Trade Europe/Middle East/Africa Corp. and IBM World Trade Americas/Far East Corp. The Justice Department's antitrust suit against IBM went to trial in 1975. Throughout the 1970s, the firm successfully defended itself against antitrust cases by Xerox Corp., Memorex, Transamerica, and others. In 1979, the field engineering division began offering 24-hour telephone assistance for customers with software problems. The first IBM retail shops, called IBM Product Centers, opened in London and Buenos Aires.

The first IBM Product Centers in the U.S. opened in 1980. A fledgling IBM subsidiary, known as IBM Instruments, Inc., launched a line of analytical instruments. IBM also began shipping the 5120 Computer System—the least expensive IBM machine to date—and its Displaywriter word processing system. In

1981, IBM changed its marketing practices to allow marketing teams to sell and distribute an entire product line to clients. John R. Opel took over as CEO. The firm introduced its landmark IBM Personal Computer (PC), which helped to launch the PC revolution, in August of that year. The machine was the firm's smallest and least expensive computer system to date. It used a processor chip from Intel Corp. and the DOS operating System of Microsoft Corp.

To sell its PCs, IBM began authorizing retailers like Sears, Roebuck & Co. and Computerland. The firm also expanded its sales channels to include manufacturers who integrated IBM products into their systems. In 1982, the U.S. Justice Department finally dropped its 13-year antitrust suit against IBM. The firm developed independent business units to explore new high-growth markets, such as telecommunications. IBM also acquired a minority stake in Intel Corp. Research, development, and engineering costs totaled $3 billion for the year. In 1984, IBM, acquired ROLM Corp. Dealer outlets across the globe totaled 10,000. Sales reached $46 billion, with net income growing to $6.6 billion.

John F. Akers took over as CEO in 1985. After several decades of considerable growth, the firm faced a slowdown in both earnings and sales, and stock prices begin a long, gradual decline. One factor in the firm's plateau was stiff competition from rivals like Compaq Computer Corp., which was able to developed its own IBM-compatible PC. In fact, makers of these IBM "clones" were able to outsell IBM in the retail PC market. In 1985, IBM developed the token-ring local area network (LAN), which allowed employees working at desktop PCs to share files and peripheral equipment like printers with other desktop PC users. Ironically, the PC revolution that IBM had played a major role in sparking also eventually forced the computing giant to reinvent itself. Used to selling large-scale systems to businesses, IBM was ill prepared to target the fastest growing segment of the burgeoning PC market: individual consumers. By the end of the decade, IBM had made plans to cut thousands of jobs through attrition and take a $2.3 billion charge against earnings for restructuring.

Although the firm spent the early part of the 1990s pursuing new markets and forging joint product development agreements with other firms, it continued to flounder. The accelerating rate of technological advancements in the data processing industry had eroded IBM's dominant position, which depended on businesses using very large and expensive mainframes designed essentially for number crunching. As increasingly powerful semiconductor chips allowed for smaller computers able to handle a broader range of functions, minicomputers, microcomputers, and work stations had undercut the value of huge mainframes. Believing that IBM needed a major overhaul to best respond to these market changes, Akers announced his intention to divide IBM into nine semi-autonomous divisions, each accountable for its own corporate decisions and performance. In 1992, IBM launched its first laptop computer. Losses reached $8 billion the following year.

SHIFT TO E-BUSINESS SERVICES

RJR Holdings executive Louis V. Gerstner, Jr. was hired to take over as CEO and chairman on April 1, 1993. He canceled Akers' plan to divide IBM into separate entities, believing that the firm's ability to offer comprehensive business solutions to clients would prove beneficial in the long run. He also began reigning in IBM's research and development spending, which had reached $6 billion by 1992. In June of 1995, IBM bought Lotus Development Corp., hoping to strengthen its foothold in the computer software market and use the Lotus Notes messaging software to offer integrated email, data processing, and Internet services to clients. The firm also folded its software operations into a single unit to simplify purchasing and support services for customers. Sales that year totaled $71 billion. In 1996, IBM added network software maker Tivoli Systems Inc. to its holdings.

By mid-1997, services had become the fastest growing segment of IBM's operations. The firm began touting itself as an e-business products and services provider. Earnings reached $6 billion on sales of $78.5 billion. IBM divested its Global Network operations to AT&T Corp. for approximately $5 billion. In 1998, the company acquired wireless communications chip maker CommQuest Technologies. That year, IBM increased its advertising budget by 21 percent, pushing its e-business servers, software, hardware, technology, and services in an effort to target business managers expected to use the Internet to streamline processes, improve bottom lines, increase visibility, and so on. The firm bought Denmark-based corporate resources planning software maker Management and Applications Support in 1999. It also updated the e-business portion of its own World Wide Web site. Sales climbed to $88.4 billion.

IBM's first e-Business Innovation Center was launched in Santa Monica, California, in January of 2000 with 16 employees. Central to the firm's e-business services was its WebSphere server software, which IBM used to support the e-commerce initiatives, including retail Web sites, of clients. The WebSphere Commerce Suite 4.1 package launched that year included Web development tools and customer classification functions that allowed e-business to hone future marketing efforts. By December, employees at the center had grown to 135, and e-business services had increased more than 70 percent to $5.2 billion. IBM's own Web site realized a 65 percent increase in sales, reaching $9 billion.

Rather than targeting dot.com upstarts, as many e-business service providers had done, IBM peddled its services to traditional businesses. As a result, when the dot.com fallout in 2000 left many in the e-business services industry floundering, IBM continued to grow. By 2001, 25 e-Business Innovation Centers were either operating or being constructed. According to a January 2001 article in the *Los Angeles Business Journal,* "IBM wants to establish itself as the one-stop shopping source for customers seeking Web-related creative design, consulting and tech support."

FURTHER READING:

Bartholomew, Doug. "Can It Weather the Storm?" *Industry Week,* March 19, 2001.

Foley, Mary Jo. "Second Chance for IBM?" *Datamation,* July 1996.

Frook, John Evan. "Big Blue Boosts Ad Spending 21% to Spread e-Business Message to the Web-challenged." *Business Marketing,* December 1, 1999.

———. "IBM Pushes Product Into Whole New Sphere." *B to B,* February 5, 2001.

IBM Corp. "Corporate History." Armonk, New York: IBM Corp., 2001. Available from www-1.ibm.com/ibm/history.

Ibold, Hans. "IBM's Internet Arm Grows Despite Market Downturn." *Los Angeles Business Journal,* January 29, 2001.

"International Business Machines Corp." In *Notable Corporate Chronologies.* Farmington Hills, MI: Gale Group, 1999.

Mand, Adrienne. "All About E: New IBM Site Targets E-Business Market." *MEDIAWEEK,* February 15, 1999.

Moschella, David. "IBM: Your One-Stop E-Commerce Shop?" *Computerworld,* October 27, 1997.

Songini, Mare. "IBM Rolling Out New E-Commerce Software." *Network World,* January 31, 2000.

Thackray, John. "IBM Act II: Can Lou Really Execute?" *Electronic Business,* July 1998.

SEE ALSO: e-Business Service Provider (eBSP); E-commerce Solutions; History of the Internet and World Wide Web (WWW)

ICANN (INTERNET CORPORATION FOR ASSIGNED NAMES AND NUMBERS)

ICANN (Internet Corporation for Assigned Names and Numbers) oversees the distribution of Internet domain names, or site addresses, and other identifiers that distinguish one Internet site from another. The non-profit entity handles the assignment of IP addresses, which identify computers that are connected to a TCP/IP network; port numbers, which identify the type of port being used to ensure that data is connected to the proper service; and other protocol parameters that allow the Internet to operate as it does.

As mandated by the U.S. Department of Commerce, ICANN was founded in 1998 by Dr. Jon Postel as a private, non-profit association to handle Internet addressing policies and procedures. The growing number of Web sites, particularly those engaged in commerce, had resulted in a number of skirmishes between domain name holders. Incorporated in the U.S., ICANN was the end result of an effort launched in July of 1997 by the Clinton administration to facilitate the formulation of standard international policy regarding domain name assignation and dispute resolution procedures. ICANN supplanted the governmentally operated IANA (Internet Assigned Numbers Authority), which was established by the Internet Society and Federal Network Council to handle the assignment of domain names and other Internet protocol parameters.

ICANN was also established to eliminate the monopoly on domain name registration held by Network Solutions Inc. (NSI), the first private organization to register domain names. Founded in 1979, NSI began charging a fee for the service in 1995. Verisign bought NSI in March of 2000, and took over NSI's joint business of both selling domain names and controlling the registries, or master lists, of.com,.org, and.net addresses. While the advent of ICANN spawned the growth of several upstarts selling.com addresses on a retail level, the organization has yet to address the monopoly NSI holds on the registries themselves, which make money by charging address seekers a fee to join each registry. Several industry experts believe ICANN needs to put in place registries of new suffixes, or top-level domains—such as.biz,.store, and.shop—to offer more choices to new Internet site operators seeking domain names. While ICANN continued to research the matter, upstart competitor New.net began selling top-level domains such as.kids and.sport. in March 2001.

FURTHER READING:

"Domain Strain; Internet Governance; ICANN's Unwelcome Rival." *The Economist,* March 10, 2001.

"ICANN." In *Ecommerce Webopedia,* Darien, CT: Internet.com, 2001. Available from e-comm.webopedia.com.

"ICANN." In *Techencyclopedia,* Point Pleasant, PA: Computer Language Co., 2001. Available from www.techweb.com/encyclopedia.

"Icann's Latest Gaffe." *Computer Weekly,* April 5, 2001.

Internet Corporation for Assigned Names an Numbers. "About ICANN." Marina del Rey, CA: ICANN, 2001. Available from www.icann.org.

SEE ALSO: Cybersquatting; Domain Name; Internet Society (ISOC); URL (Uniform Resource Locator)

INCUBATORS, E-COMMERCE

An extremely hot phenomenon at the height of the dot-com craze in the late 1990s, incubators are the nurseries in which Internet startups can develop their business plans, products, services, and infrastructures, secured with plenty of financial capital, physical space, and on-hand expertise. In short, incubators are companies in business to support and bring to life new companies, particularly dot-coms.

HOW INCUBATORS WORK

Even before startup entrepreneurs are ready to seek out a first round of venture capital, they need the time and resources to develop their businesses into models that venture capitalists will find attractive. This is especially true for companies seeking to attain venture capital from the leading VC funds, which typically gravitate toward larger projects and have less time for seed investment for the initial development stage. Incubators thus saw a market niche in the business development market to provide an economy of scale unavailable to early-stage companies. Business acceleration is their line of work, in that they take a concept under their wings and nurture it through its early growth period and turn it into a living company. They exchange their initial capital investment and expertise for equity in the startup company.

Incubators are full-service company accelerators, offering everything from finance capital and management expertise to marketing analysis and legal advice. They tend to provide their e-commerce companies with office space, ample facilities and infrastructure, and recruitment services so as to attract executives capable of making the business stand on its own. Typically, incubator firms maintain their own staff to comb over the companies' business plans and implement Web sites and technological infrastructure, while at the same time seeking out venture capital funding and creating equity pools for each client. Once the companies are prepared to stand on their own, they are turned loose to generate their own later-stage venture capital and move toward an initial public offering (IPO). Incubators generate their own profits primarily by reaping returns on their initial investment, as the formerly incubating firm grows and its stock price soars, the value of the incubator's original stake grows as well.

Incubators vary considerably in the degree of control they exercise over their incubating companies.

Some incubators concentrate primarily on sheer volume, and therefore have less time and resources to devote to the development of their firms. Others, however, exercise extensive authority over the direction of the companies' development, since the incubator's success depends on the eventual success of their companies and because brining startups to life is, after all, the incubator's area of expertise. In general, this is the main feature distinguishing incubators from venture capitalists. While some VC firms take an active role in guiding a company's development, incubators' activities often border on co-founding firms, and even the most hands-off incubators have more direct participation in the company's early gestation and growth than do venture capitalists.

Successful incubators require more than just a thick wallet and high-powered connections, a fact many incubators in the early 2000s discovered to their dismay. In addition to ample capital, for an incubator to truly generate a sustainable business model, it must be able to provide the kind of hands-on support that will be able to generate excitement about the product or service the business is offering. It also must be able to put the firm directly into contact with its potential customer base. Most importantly, the business must have a long-term plan for profitability and a route toward repaying its benefactor's initial investments. This seemingly obvious rule was often lost during the height of dot-com mania, which had some enthusiasts insisting that the laws of business were forever changed by the new economy. Incubators in the 2000s were likely to be much more sober-minded in their expectations, analysis, and in the practical guidance they offered to incubating firms.

INCUBATORS' RAPID RISE AND FALL, AND BEYOND

The incubator concept was largely popularized, according to *Fortune,* in 1996 when Bill Gross founded the incubator firm Idealab, which went on to become one of the leading incubators through the dot-com craze. Idealab claimed Internet firms like eToys, NetZero, and GoTo.com as alumnae of its incubation. Another incubator called CMGI quickly emerged as Idealab's major rival, and between them those two companies defined the basic incubator paradigm that others adopted. For a while, in the thick of the excitement over the new economy, and Internet startups in particular, the incubator concept was hailed by many dot-com enthusiasts as a central innovation for company creation in the Internet age. The result was an extremely rapid pace of company development at incubators such as Idealab, where ideas were transformed into viable startups at a remarkable pace, and in great quantity.

Through the Internet market heyday of the late 1990s, incubators were all the rage, and new ones cropped up at an astonishing rate. Even major venture capital firms, such as Benchmark Capital and Kleiner Perkins Caufield & Byersor, set up their own incubator operations or partnered with existing incubators, recognizing that many of the dot-com startups they wished to back required a good deal more hand holding than they were used to providing. Other businesses outside of the traditional equity-funding field also took advantage of the emerging field to spin off incubator outfits. These organizations included the likes of Andersen Consulting, Dell Computer, Hewlett-Packard, Panasonic, IBM, and even a number of business schools at universities such as the University of North Carolina and the University of California-Berkeley.

After the dot-com boom fizzled in the early 2000s, many skeptics eyed incubators suspiciously, seeing them as among the more garish excesses of the dot-com craze. Indeed, following the bust of the technology stock market beginning in March 2000, incubators rapidly disappeared as investors rushed to liquidate their capital investments. Thus, by 2001 the incubator model had largely fallen out of favor, with few investors ready to sink money into risky startups following the drudging many took at the tail end of the dot-com craze, and with the U.S. economy slowing considerably.

The sudden crash of the incubator sector in the early 2000s partly mirrored, and was directly related to, many of the features that led to the abrupt shift in fortune for the Internet industry in general. With investors pouring money into Internet stocks and valuations soaring through the roof, many incubators became convinced that their time was at hand, and that just about any Internet idea could generate enormous returns. As a result, they tended to go overboard by financing shaky ideas and accumulating far too many startup hopefuls under their umbrellas. Once the tech market began to falter, incubators suddenly found themselves with far too many companies to incubate, and realized that they had invested a great deal of money that would never be seen again. These realities scared investors away from the incubators themselves. Ultimately, once the Internet industry fell to earth, there were too few good ideas to sustain the incubators and their bloated portfolios.

Like the Internet market in general, the success enjoyed by many incubators in the late 1990s encouraged hordes of imitators to join the field. Not only were these imitators ill-equipped for the business, they also contributed to a market glut that demanded a shakeout. As Nicole Weber, an analyst of incubators at Framingham, Massachusetts-based International Data Corp., bluntly told *InfoWorld,* "people who had no business becoming an incubator got involved." In October 2000, *Business Week* reported that less than

one-third of all incubators had managed to turn out even one company, while just under half nursed a company that had proved attractive enough to generate financing from outside the incubator itself.

By fall 2000, just before the industry shakeout really took hold, there were some 350 incubators growing at least 10 businesses under their shell, according to a study by Harvard Business School. The primary survival method for the bulk of these firms was to attempt to merge their struggling companies—especially those in which they had invested substantial resources—with already successful companies. Another strategy was to shut down less promising startups and concentrate their portfolios on those companies with the most thoroughly developed and viable business plans. Co-author and Harvard professor Nitin Nohria told *Business Week* that less than a third of those were expected to survive into the mid-2000s, while the National Business Incubation Association predicted that about 50 incubators might survive if things go well.

However, this didn't mean that incubators were creatures of the exuberant 1990s, on their way to extinction. Many investors with a more sober-minded analysis of the potential of Internet-based companies, and typically with more thoroughly devised business plans, still clung to the idea of providing breathing room for companies at the seed stage as a valuable and profitable venture. With dramatically thinned ranks due to the massive incubator shakeout, those firms that ultimately survived were likely to perform strongly, as the Internet market recovers from setbacks in the early 2000s and the incubator concept continues to diversify into new areas of business.

FURTHER READING:

Christopher, Alistair. "Incubators Lose Favor, Some Still See Potential." *Venture Capital Journal.* May 1, 2001.

Guglielmo, Connie. "Bringing Up Baby." *Upside.* October 2000.

Kolle, Claudine. "Wanted: Fresh Ideas." *Asian Business.* January 2001.

Nicolle, Lindsay. "Nurtural Selection." *Director.* November 2000.

Nocera, Joseph. "Bill Gross Blew Through $800 Million in 8 Months (and He's Got Nothing to Show for It). Why is He Still Smiling?" *Fortune.* March 5, 2001.

Sanborn, Stephanie. "Incubators Endure." *InfoWorld.* December 18, 2000.

Vizard, Michael and Eugene Grygo. "Start-up Incubator Firms Pulling the Plug." *InfoWorld.* October 30, 2000.

Weisul, Kimberly. "Incubators Lay an Egg." *Business Week.* October 9, 2000.

SEE ALSO: Angel Investors; CMGI Inc.; Dot-com; Financing, Securing; Shake-out, Dot-com; Startups

INDEPENDENT SALES ORGANIZATION (ISO)

Since the overwhelming majority of e-commerce transactions involve credit cards, the ability to accept credit cards as a form of payment was essential for e-commerce proprietors (also known as merchants) in the early 2000s. In order to obtain this capability, merchants had to apply for special merchant accounts with acquiring banks. After such an account was established, acquiring banks accepted funds from card-holding consumers on behalf of the merchant. Although a number of different steps and variables were involved in this process, this essentially involved monies being transferred (from the bank that issued the credit card to the consumer) to the acquiring bank, and ultimately to the merchant.

For good reason, acquiring banks are selective about the businesses to which they provide merchant accounts. Some kinds of businesses—such as online wagering or adult entertainment sites and those that are small, home-based, or not yet established—are more prone to risk and credit-card fraud than others. For these kinds of businesses, obtaining merchant accounts directly from acquiring banks can be difficult. Independent sales organizations (ISOs) are third-party organizations that partner with acquiring banks to find, open, and manage merchant accounts on behalf of such businesses in exchange for a higher fee, or for a percentage of the merchant's sales. ISOs also are called merchant service providers (MSPs) when they offer financial transaction processing services. ISOs are able to offer merchant accounts to riskier merchants, and charge higher fees, because they do not fall under the same laws and regulations that actual banks do. Along with the acquiring banks they work with, ISOs also assume much of the liability and risk that comes with this service.

AuctionWatch explained that in the early 2000s, merchant account industry sources indicated ISOs and MSPs were responsible for opening roughly 80 percent of all merchant accounts, with banks accounting for the remainder. Although the exact number of ISOs and MSPs was hard to come by due to lack of regulation within the merchant account industry, *Auction-Watch* placed the figure between 700 on the low end to as many as several thousand, with fewer than 200 representing legitimate operations. This latter point indicated a cause for concern and caution on the part of merchants. It was not uncommon for businesses to file complaints against malicious ISOs that advertised low rates to get their business and then levied additional excessive fees or inflated charges for credit-card processing equipment. Although it generally cost merchants more to obtain merchant accounts through ISOs, the fees and other costs involved varied considerably, which caused confusion. Additionally, according to Workz.com, "To confuse matters further, ISOs often refer to themselves as merchant account providers even though they do not provide the account. This is a matter of semantics which has not been clarified or enforced by any governing body."

FURTHER READING:

Buscher, Ranae. "Merchant Account Provider Types Defined." Pinnacle WebWorkz Inc. November 29, 2000. Available from www.workz.com.

Neville, Kate. "Qualifying for a Merchant Account—Do You Meet the Criteria?" Pinnacle WebWorkz Inc. November 29, 2000. Available from www.workz.com.

Roe, Andy. "Merchant Beware." *AuctionWatch,* February 18, 2000. Available from www.auctionwatch.com.

SEE ALSO: Acquiring Bank

INFOMEDIARY MODEL

In order to understand the definition of an infomediary model, it is helpful to first understand the concept of a basic business model.

WHAT IS A BUSINESS MODEL?

Whether a company sells products or services to consumers, other businesses, or both, there are many different ways to approach the marketplace and make a profit. Business models are used to describe how companies go about this process. They spell out the main ways in which companies make profits by identifying a company's role during commerce and describing how products, information, and other important elements are structured. Just as there are many different industries and types of companies, there are many different kinds of business models. While some are simple, others are very complex. Even within the same industry, companies may rely on business models that are very different from one another, and some companies may use a combination of several different models.

General business models by themselves do not necessarily map out a company's specific strategy for success. Strategic marketing plans, which are a specialized type of business model, are used for that purpose. They identify the specific situation in which a company finds itself in a particular marketplace, the differentials that set a company apart from its competitors, the marketing tactics used to accomplish strategic objectives, and so on.

Business models involve different levels in what are known as supply/value chains. Value chains outline the activities involved in creating value from the supply side of economics, where raw materials are used to manufacture a product, to the demand side when finished products or components are marketed and shipped to re-sellers or end-users. Companies review and analyze different steps in value chains to create optimal and effective business models.

Some long-established business models used in the physical world have been adopted on the Internet with varying degrees of success. Among these are mail-order models, advertising models, free-trial models, subscription models, and direct-marketing models. Other business models are native to the Internet and e-commerce and focus heavily on the movement of electronic information. These include digital-delivery models, information-barter models, and freeware models.

Every business model has its own inherent strengths and weaknesses. Just as is the case in the physical world, online business models vary in their suitability for different enterprises. Business models themselves are not enough to guarantee success in the physical or online worlds. As Jeffrey F. Rayport explains, ''Every e-commerce business is either viable or not viable. They hardly qualify for the paint-by-number prescriptions that business people seem to expect. Business models themselves do not offer solutions; rather, how each business is run determines its success. So the success of e-commerce businesses will hinge largely on the art of management even as it is enabled by the science of technology.''

THE INFOMEDIARY MODEL

A major Internet business model, the infomediary model is characterized by the capture and/or sharing of information. The simplest form of an infomediary model is the registration model. In this scenario, companies require users to register before gaining access to information on their Web sites, even if the information itself is provided at no charge. One possible scenario for this example involves companies that offer white papers, or expert articles containing valuable advice, to Web site visitors. These white papers usually are written by the company's experts, who are available as consultants. Registration is a condition for viewing or downloading the articles so the company can capture contact information and

other data from the interested party and use it to make sales calls and potentially acquire new clients for its consultants.

Companies using an infomediary model also may be third parties that provide products like free computers or services like free Internet access to consumers in exchange for information about themselves. This information is then sold to other companies who use it to develop more sophisticated, successful marketing campaigns. The information collected commonly includes things like product and service preferences; buying habits; and demographic details like age, sex, and income level.

In the early 2000s, NetZero was one example of a third-party infomediary. The company offered 40 hours of monthly Internet access to more than 8 million consumers in exchange for their marketing information. As part of the deal, consumers were required to allow a special browser called the ZeroPort to remain on their screen while online. The ZeroPort displayed ads that, based on the marketing information they provided to NetZero, were likely to interest them. It also served as a Web navigation tool and displayed customized information like sports, e-mail, news, and stock prices. Using technology from marketing software manufacturer Amazing Media, NetZero also allowed small businesses to reach local or regional consumers through the ZeroPort and view the daily results of their online ad campaigns.

In addition to its free service, NetZero customers were able to pay a low monthly fee for Internet access without banner ads. This was attractive to Compaq, which partnered with NetZero to offer its services via affinity programs. According to NetZero, these programs ''are an emerging distribution channel where computing hardware products and Internet services are bundled and customized for a particular market segment such as financial companies, healthcare providers, telephone companies, and education institutions. These companies then engage with their consumer customer base, their employees, or members of their organization via the Internet by offering a bundled access device and integrated ISP as the means for providing the connectivity.''

Companies using an infomediary model also might provide unbiased information to consumers about different businesses on the Internet, helping them to choose the right ones. Gomez Inc. is an example of this kind of company. It provides users with three different services. Gomez.com offered Internet scorecards and consumer reviews for different categories of online products and services including shopping, travel, and personal finance. According to the company, its rankings used at least 120 criteria to ''capture the quality of the Internet delivery of goods and services for a given sector.'' Gomez.com also certified more than 6,000 merchants in more than 75 different industries. GomezPro was a subscription-based market research service the company offered to businesses.

Finally, some companies use an infomediary approach by functioning as third-party communication channels where positive and negative feedback about other businesses can be exchanged or shared with the businesses themselves. Epinions is one example of this kind of infomediary. According the company, personalized recommendations, unbiased advice, and comparative shopping are at the heart of its Web-based offerings. These elements help consumers make purchasing decisions and let others know about their experiences. PlanetFeedback.com and BizRate were two other examples of companies that rely on customer feedback and word-of-mouth. These companies sell software to companies that want to glean instant feedback from their customers after an online order has been placed, rather than relying solely on focus groups and customer service surveys to find out what consumers think.

FURTHER READING:

"About Gomez." Gomez Inc. April 22, 2001. Available from www.gomez.com.

Bambury, Paul. "A Taxonomy of Internet Commerce." *First-Monday,* 1998. Available from www.firstmonday.dk.

"Biz—QuickStudy." *Computerworld,* November 1, 1999.

McDowell, Dagen. "Dear Dagen: Business Models Explained." *TheStreet.com,* September 13, 1999. Available from www.thestreet.com/funds.

"Most Viral Companies, Industries Emerge as Consumers Share Opinions With Others." *PRNewswire,* March 29, 2001. Available from hoovnews.hoovers.com.

Rappa, Michael. "Business Models On The Web." April 9, 2001. Available from www.academic.uofs.edu.htm.

Rayport, Jeffrey F. "The Truth About Internet Business Models." *Strategy & Business,* Third Quarter, 1999. Available from www.strategy-business.com.

Sviokla, John. "Listen Up!" *CIO Magazine,* April 15, 2001. Available from www2.cio.com/archive.

Timmers, Paul. "Business Models for Electronic Markets." *Electronic Markets.,* April, 1998. Available from www.electronicmarkets.org/netacademy/publications.

SEE ALSO: Business Models

INFORMATION ARCHITECTURE

Before the widespread adoption of computers, individuals were limited to some degree by the physi-cal space needed to store paper-based information. With digital information, this is not the case, and the volumes of information to which users have access can be enormous. Furthermore, people have many different options when it comes to the ways in which they access information, ranging from closed private systems to open Web-based systems to wireless networks. As diverse as these many different systems are the interfaces individuals use to select and retrieve data.

Information architecture (IA) is an emerging field in an increasingly information-based age. At the core of IA is the concept of creating information systems (including applications, databases, and complex Web sites) based on the unique needs of those who use them. Therefore, effective information architecture involves professionals—who may or may not officially carry the title of information architect—focusing on the needs of customers or users first, and then on the information used to create an application or system. This allows for the development of systems that are logical and useful.

Although IA pertains to Web sites used during e-commerce, it also applies to other valuable systems including intranets (private areas of the Internet), digital libraries, and knowledge management systems. Because of its broad scope, information architects often bring varying degrees of different skills to the table, and no one job title (like Web designer) adequately covers all of the responsibilities these elements require. According to Louis Rosenfeld, who at one time operated a leading IA consulting firm, the field of IA draws on the skills and abilities of a wide variety of different fields including design, anthropology, computer science, library science, information retrieval, human-computer interface engineering, interface and interaction design, markup and data modeling, and technical communications. In addition to skills in one or more of these areas, common sense, logical thinking, and good communication skills are critical for information architects.

One example of the issues information architects face is exemplified in a report issued by Forrester Research called *The End of Commerce Servers.* The report predicted the demise of the servers (computers used to host Web sites) being used for e-commerce in the late 1990s. It described "scenario servers," capable of delivering more interactive and personalized experiences than existing technology was delivering at that time. The new kind of server also would integrate more fully with companies' back-end systems (such as accounting, shipping, and customer service) to deliver more seamless experiences. Information architects could play key roles in making such technology a reality.

FURTHER READING:

Dillon, Andrew. ''Practice Makes Perfect: IA at the End of the Beginning?'' *Bulletin of the American Society for Information Science,* April/May 2001.

Peek, Robin. ''Defining Information Architecture.'' *Information Today,* June 2000.

Wiggins, Richard W. ''Argus Associates, Inc. Closes Shop.'' *Information Today,* May 2001.

SEE ALSO: Auction Sites; Business-to-Business (B2B) E-commerce; Electronic Data Interchange (EDI); XML (Extensible Markup Language)

INFORMATION MANAGEMENT SYSTEMS

If businesspeople from the early 1900s had been able to look ahead and foresee the 21st century corporate landscape, it's likely they would have been amazed by the role information plays in today's economy. Not only does the world rely more heavily on information than ever before, the speed at which it must travel and the ways in which it must be organized and accessed are critical. This stands in stark contrast to the days before e-mail, database systems, and fax machines, when it was acceptable to wait weeks for a letter to travel between business partners in different cities.

As information began to take center stage in the business world, systems were required to manage its many uses. Information management systems evolved for this purpose. These systems involve the collection, identification, analysis, storage, presentation, and distribution of information. They play central roles in many business processes, including transactions and communication within organizations, and between companies and their many business partners (suppliers, manufacturers, distributors, vendors, and customers).

According to the Association for Information and Image Management (AIIM), ''the center of an effective business infrastructure in the digital age is the ability to capture, create, customize, deliver, and manage enterprise content to support business processes.'' AIIM identified several information management technologies that play key roles in the success and development of e-business, including: content and document management, enterprise portals, business process management, image and knowledge management, data mining, and data warehousing.

In addition to facilitating many different processes, information management systems are often used for specific global uses or applications. For example, organizations use human resource information systems (HRIS) to manage important employee data such as job classifications, pay ranges, salaries, income tax withholdings, benefit information, and so on. In the healthcare industry, physician practices, hospitals, healthcare systems, and insurance companies use these systems to manage information about patients, including medical records and data that can be used to tailor communications with them based on medical conditions or interest areas. In the realm of e-commerce, information management systems are used to organize and process complex arrays of data regarding products and customers. Information about a company's inventory of available items might be stored in an information management system, along with specific data regarding customer orders.

In the early 2000s, Borders Books and Music relied on database technology from Oracle to align the marketing efforts of its physical retail stores with its Web initiatives. It did this by providing in-store kiosks that featured Title Sleuth, the search tool found at Borders.com, so that customers could easily search for in-stock titles. If a specific title was not found, Title Sleuth suggested related books on the store's shelves and gave customers an option to order by credit card for home delivery. The kiosks also provided added information like book reviews and author interviews. Borders also used a separate customer relationship management (CRM) system to centralize and manage customer data for targeted marketing campaigns.

FURTHER READING:

Agnew, Marion. ''CRM Plus Lots of Data Equals More Sales for Borders.'' *InformationWeek,* May 7, 2001.

Waltz, Mitzi. ''Oracle E-business Suite Draws Cautious Interest.'' *InformationWeek,* October 16, 2000.

SEE ALSO: Data Mining; Data Warehousing; Database Management; Knowledge Management

INFORMATION REVOLUTION VS. INDUSTRIAL REVOLUTION

As e-commerce became all the rage in the late 1990s and as the Internet, World Wide Web, and other information technologies rapidly transformed the economic and social environment, many analysts, journalists, and scholars took the time to reflect upon the current transformations and breakthroughs and situate them in a broad, historical context. The fruit of these labors was the conception of the current era as the Information Revolution, akin in its historical importance and impact to previous economic revolutions, particularly the Industrial Revolution.

The attempts to theorize a new economic and social era—particularly one whose effects have yet to be fully realized—inevitably generated widely disparate definitions and characteristics of the Information Revolution, not to mention predictions, prescriptions, and levels of enthusiasm. Several key questions arise: Does the Information Revolution in fact constitute a historical epoch on a par with previous revolutionary transitions? What are the comparative features and effects of the Information Revolution and the Industrial Revolution? How did the Industrial Revolution alter previously existing conceptions of economics, social organization, the nature of work, cultural patterns, and so on? What needs to be done to either take advantage of the benefits of the Information Revolution, or—if one is of a different theoretical persuasion—what steps must be taken to mitigate its worst effects?

Since even the most enthusiastic proponents of the Information Revolution agreed that, in the early 21st century, the new era was still in its infancy, it remained to be seen whether the Information Revolution would truly revolutionize society on a scale comparable with the Industrial Revolution, which produced greater change in just two centuries than occurred in the rest of human history combined.

LOCATING REVOLUTIONS

The initial step in attempting to compare social epochs is to locate them historically and sketch a broad outline of what they entailed. At the most basic level, the Industrial Revolution calls to mind a succession of breakthrough inventions: the steam engine, the cotton gin, railroads, and so on. More broadly, the Industrial Revolution refers to an epoch that saw economic production shift from small-scale, relatively localized production based on individual skills and craftsmanship by artisans to large-scale, centralized production incorporating heavy, mechanized machinery and mass numbers of wage workers. In addition, the Industrial Revolution shifted the center of economic activity from agriculture to industry and manufacturing. Thus, the Industrial Revolution was marked by a series of sweeping social and economic transformations that upended existing paradigms.

As economies grew and became more integrated, the Industrial Revolution was generally marked by successive leading economic sectors. Viewed broadly, the Industrial Revolution can be broken into three major phases. The first phase, in the late 18th and early 19th centuries, saw the development of textiles, coal, and iron into modern industries. The second occurred in the mid-19th century, with the opening of new territories to economic development and the overhauling of transportation via the large-scale implementation of railroad systems, aided by develop-

ments such as the steam engine. The third epoch came in the early 20th century, when the development of the mass-factory and industrial machinery transformed the industrial and social landscape. Through the first half of the 20th century, the economic center was dominated by science-based technologies, particularly those related to steel, chemicals, the internal combustion engine, and electricity, such as automotive technologies and petroleum-based industries.

While each of these epochs ushered in sweeping changes and innovations, they also produced profound social disruptions, as individuals and groups readjusted their places in society, often resulting in great upheaval. Relatedly, each of these phases was marked by booming economic growth followed by periods of sharp decline as these technologies and processes took root in society, as the social dislocations played themselves out, and as the growth opportunities inherent in the new technologies exhausted themselves.

Like the Industrial Revolution and most historical periods, the Information Revolution wasn't as abrupt a cataclysm as the name might suggest. Rather, what became known as the Information Revolution, although largely associated with the closing decades of the 20th century, had direct roots in the thick of the Industrial Age. The most direct forebears to the Information Revolution appeared around World War II in the 1940s. This period was marked by heavy government investment in new technologies, particularly those of use by the military for the war effort. Among these technologies were electronics and computers, which shortly after the war began to be applied more broadly in the business world. By the late 20th century, the leading economic sectors, particularly in the United States, were those involving electronics, computers, high technology, telecommunications, and related service sectors. In the process, these technologies ushered in the information economy, centered on knowledge-based industries.

TECHNOLOGY

Like previous economic revolutions, the Information Revolution is marked most noticeably by a series of technological breakthroughs. In this case, the developments in electronics and computer technologies, along with dramatic changes in telecommunications, provided the basis for economic change. One of the central dates for the Information Revolution was 1959, when two scientists working separately—Jack Kilby at Texas Instruments and Robert Noyce at Fairchild Semiconductor—arrived almost simultaneously at the invention of the silicon chip, the device that inscribes electronic information in a microscopic space, allowing for the mass production—and mass dissemination—of computers. With the vastly enhanced powers of memory, calculation, and control placed in a microscopic chip, computers were poised to assume a central role in economic life. Following this breakthrough, computers came to constitute the central infrastructure of everything from office telephone networks to transportation control systems to industrial production facilities, setting the stage for further information-breakthroughs once the vastly enhanced communication powers of the Internet were unleashed.

Of course, one of the preeminent—and least expected—hallmarks of the Information Revolution is electronic commerce. E-commerce, in theory, takes the potential of the information economy to its logical conclusion by propelling commercial activity into the borderless world of hyperspace, where transactions for everything from groceries to industrial equipment take place with little regard for geography and with nearly instantaneous satisfaction of commercial wants. Of course, as of the early 2000s e-commerce still had a long way to go before turning this theory into a smooth reality; e-commerce models were still in the gestation process, and no clear paradigm had emerged to set the stage for the explosive e-commerce growth most analysts expected was on the way. But even in its crude earliest versions, e-commerce already altered conceptions of business strategy and relationships, and on the consumer side e-commerce overhauled customer expectations of speed and convenience, pushing the field of business competition to new grounds.

ECONOMICS

Throughout the Industrial Revolution, there was a common expectation of more or less continued economic growth, a concept largely foreign to previous epochs in which subsistence and extremely modest growth were the norm. Average annual growth rates throughout the industrial world during this period, particularly in the United States, rose from virtually nonexistent to about 2 percent—leading to a doubling of the average standard of living every 36 years.

The engine of this rapid growth was technological innovation. New technologies provided new avenues for investment and growth; capital flowed heavily from one technology to another, and often from one location to another in accordance with technological developments. Innovations—be they new products, industrial processes, communications, or transportations—generally proved a boon to certain economic sectors into which investment capital flowed. Over time, the applications and effects of those innovations and investments proliferated and spread throughout the economy, but with inevitably

diminishing returns for the capital investment; eventually, capital must seek out new technologies and new avenues for investment.

By virtue of annual growth rates, if one were to locate the true onset of the Information Revolution immediately following the Cold War with the dissemination of the Internet to critical mass, one would find similar characteristics. For example, the economic boom of the 1990s saw annual growth rates in the United States leap above 3 percent for the first time in decades, simultaneously keeping inflation in check and generating healthy profits for continued investment. The slowdown in the U.S. economy of the early 2000s gave pause to some commentators, but it remained to be seen how much of a setback that downturn would prove to be; while some skeptics argued that the slowdown proved that the 1990s boom was an anomaly based on speculative bubbles, others argued that the recession was a mere market adjustment amidst a profoundly new economic era.

The Information Revolution also features a new era of economic globalization as geography gradually disappears as a barrier to economic activity. The world economy has undergone enormous globalization processes before, particularly in the late 19th and early 20th centuries, but the process was continually ebbing and flowing with the winds of political and social change. The level of globalization fostered by the Information Revolution, however, is altogether unprecedented in human history, as the speed with which information, transactions, and capital can travel virtually anywhere in the world render distance almost obsolete, at least in certain key economic sectors.

SOCIAL RELATIONS, WORK, AND DEMOGRAPHICS

The Industrial Revolution changed where and how we live. For instance, while the early stages of the Industrial Revolution gave birth to the modern metropolis—huge cities acting as economic and social centers—the later stages of the Industrial Revolution, such as that involving the development of the internal combustion engine, gave rise to suburbs, highways, and dramatically increased personal mobility. Thus, that revolution completely overhauled both the geography of the industrial countries and the way social life was organized. Whole communities were destroyed and built as a direct result of these economic breakthroughs—often in just a matter of decades.

It was unclear just what the overall effects of the Information Revolution would be in changing social relationships and geography. The creation of the information superhighway, for instance, could conceivably have effects on demographics as dramatic as—

but very different in character from—those caused by the Industrial Revolution. For instance, with geographic location diminishing in importance to the production process, people may be freer to live in remote locations; at the least, people may be less bound by their work lives to certain locations, potentially leading to vastly new kinds of communities and other social organizations.

In terms of social relationships and relationships to the production process, the Information Revolution has indeed led to radical transformations. The mass-scale, centralized-factory paradigm of the Industrial Revolution featured a production process in which individual workers were relatively "de-skilled" compared to their predecessors, and had only to perform minute functions requiring little training and with little overall understanding of the production process as a whole. As a result, companies were able to produce at vastly accelerated rates while keeping costs down, leading to tremendous profits that, in boom times, afforded them the option of paying higher wages in order to quell labor unrest. On the one hand, this created an economic environment in which centralized, hierarchical managerial bureaucracies were essential to organize production and maintain control over the production process. On the other hand, the centralized factory created an atmosphere in which it was relatively easy for workers to organize themselves for greater remuneration for their labors.

In comparison, the Information Revolution presents something of a paradox. With computers, information technology, and high-tech communication systems dominating the business environment, production can be scattered across diverse locations and coordinated at high speed with great precision. This allows businesses to concentrate their particular production facilities where they are optimally efficient—for example, where labor costs and regulatory red tape are minimal—leading to greater profit margins. Moreover, the movement toward computer controls creates a less egalitarian environment for wage workers than the mass assembly-line model, since it creates a hierarchical advantage for those highly educated workers with technical skills, and thus decision-making could potentially be decentralized and located at the various production facilities. At the same time, however, despite the geographical dispersion of production and the more nuanced worker relationships, information systems give top management greater direct control over the production process. By systematizing facilities via computers that provide reliable information across wide networks, top executives have a diminished need for middle-level managers, leading to the wave of downsizing and restructuring that characterized the 1980s and 1990s.

Moreover, the geographical dispersal of production facilities and the enhanced means of computer controls overhauled the relationships between workers and the nature of work itself. In the information economy, work is much more flexible, favoring more fluid schedules and multitasking, in which workers are expected to perform several jobs more or less simultaneously and respond to immediate demands as they arise rather than coordinate their work solely by the clock. This radical restructuring of work in the late 20th and early 21st centuries had a profound impact on the role of organized labor in society. Flexible schedules and dispersed production facilities render the traditional models of labor organizing extremely difficult, and by the early 21st century no dominant model of labor organization had emerged to suit the information economy.

The transformation of work was potentially even more dramatic than that produced by the Industrial Revolution, given that, in the information economy, nearly every profession was likely to undergo radical alteration as computer systems and the Internet infiltrate the farthest reaches of the economy. In the Industrial Revolution, many knowledge-based occupations, such as accounting, were relatively unaffected qualitatively by the sweeping changes produced by industrial development. The Information Revolution was unlikely to leave many layers of work untouched, as everyone from knowledge-intensive workers to manual laborers to government officials would likely see the routines they came to know swept aside in favor of more computer-intensive processes.

Industrial parts producers, for example, are accustomed to working an assembly line in more or less consistent fashion, building products destined for distribution via long-established logistics partners. With information technology leading to supply chain management, just-in-time manufacturing, and mass customization, production processes were being retooled to facilitate greater flexibility in production scheduling, while distribution and transactions were increasingly channeled through handfuls of industry-specific Internet-based marketplaces. As a result, hiring, training, scheduling, production organization, sales, and marketing were unlikely to closely resemble their traditional Industrial Revolution models.

CONTINUING DEBATES

At the theoretical level, there were still radically divergent takes on the Information Revolution and what it means. Enthusiasts, such as Francis Fukuyama, proclaim that we have entered a radical new age full of sweeping transformations and profound economic, social, and political possibilities. Fukuyama argued that the wealth of information at consumers' fingertips—combined with the ability to seek out and shop for exactly what they want without regard to borders and other restrictions—would lead to a market-led democratization that went far beyond the possibilities of the welfare-state democracies of the Industrial Revolution. Fukuyama pursues this argument to its conclusion, insisting that private companies would increasingly assume many of the duties previously performed by governments. He argues that corporations powered by information technology and responding to the speed of the market are much less cumbersome and can more easily and flexibly respond to demand than can governments. Moreover, while Fukuyama sees the Industrial Revolution as massively disruptive of the traditional family unit, he argues that the Information Revolution holds possibilities of reconstructing the nuclear family as a central social network.

One of the best-known theorists of the Information Revolution was Manuel Castells, professor of sociology and planning at the University of California at Berkeley. Castells presented a more nuanced interpretation of the sweeping changes wrought by information technology than either the hyper-enthusiasts or the alarmists. While Castells argues against critics' claims that the Information Revolution was producing a numbing glut of information, he points out that information technology was not the panacea for global ills that it was sometimes painted to be. For instance, according to Castells, proponents looking to information technologies as the preeminent tool for development and democratization around the world misjudge both the severity of current poverty and disenfranchisement and the likely effects that rapid IT-led globalization would have on those peoples.

Castells argued that as powerful new information technologies are grafted onto and reshape the existing economic order, their development will produce not only vast new concentrations of wealth, but rising inequality, social exclusion, and psychological bewilderment on a global scale. Castells sees the technology-centered vision, in which social ills are fixed via technological means, as fundamentally flawed. While maintaining great faith in the powers of Enlightenment values of reason and science to propel humankind to a better world, he cautioned that, "there is an extraordinary gap between our technological overdevelopment and our social underdevelopment."

For instance, Castells argues that the social benefits inherent in these new technologies will not automatically spread to those peoples most in need. On the contrary, Castells sees the trajectory of the technology and their effects as largely dependent on the nature of the societies and institutions implementing them. Authoritarian, exclusionary, inegalitarian societies, according to Castells, will likely use information age technologies as tools to consolidate power, expand social divisions and inequality, and increase the level of exclusion. More egalitarian societies, on the other hand, were more likely to use information technologies for democratic, egalitarian purposes. In other words, information technologies aren't inherently positive or negative; rather they are more or less neutral tools, the effects of which depend on those in a position to establish a framework for their application.

FURTHER READING:

Castells, Manuel. *The Information Age: Economy, Society and Culture,* Blackwell, 1996.

Cote, Marcel. "Reinventing Our Jobs." *CA Magazine,* April 2000.

Drucker, Peter. "Knowledge Work." *Executive Excellence,* April 2000.

Fukuyama, Francis. *The Great Disruption: Human Nature and the Reconstitution of Social Order.* New York: The Free Press, 1999.

Gerstner, John. "The Other Side of Cyberspace." *Communication World,* March 1999.

Krauss, Michael. "Visionaries Don't Take Technology for Granted." *Marketing News,* June 19, 2000.

Matthews, Jessica T. "The Information Revolution." *Foreign Policy,* Summer 2000.

Taylor, Timothy. "Thinking About a 'New Economy.'" *Public Interest,* Spring 2001.

Watson, Max. "Golden Age of Customers and IT." *InformationWeek,* April 24, 2000.

SEE ALSO: Cyberculture: Society, Culture, and the Internet; Digital Divide; Internet and WWW, History of the; Knowledge Worker; Mass Customization; New Economy

INFORMATION TECHNOLOGY (IT)

Information technology (IT) broadly describes the processing and management of data in computer systems. Within IT's wide parameters are the hardware (including hard drives, modems, monitors, servers, mainframe systems, and routers) and software (word processing and spreadsheet programs, Web browsers, and databases) that make the movement, manipulation, and storage of information possible. Thus, IT also gives life to the Internet, the World Wide Web, and e-commerce. A 1999 *Computer Weekly* poll identified the World Wide Web (1989); the first IBM PC (1981); and COBOL, a high-level programming language created in 1959 and used for writing business software as the top three IT developments of all time. E-mail (1971); Visicalc (1979), the first spreadsheet program; MS-DOS (1980); and the Apple Macintosh computer (1984); were among the top 10.

From the early 1970s onward, computers and electronic information were increasingly critical elements of the corporate landscape. Large companies devoted entire departments to information technology. These IT departments went by a variety of names, including information systems (IS) and management information systems (MIS). E-commerce created additional demand for IT workers. Although there were many layoffs in the technical industry during the early 2000s due to poor market conditions and failing Internet companies, overall demand remained strong in mid-2001, according to *InternetWeek*. This was especially true for workers with e-commerce and Web development experience. *InfoWorld* identified plenty of opportunity for IT workers, especially those with the ability to use programming languages like Java and C++.

When the Internet and e-commerce exploded in popularity, many companies spent hefty sums on IT in an effort to keep up with or exceed the competition. According to *Fortune,* the amount spent on software and equipment increased from four percent annually in the last quarter of 1999 to 21 percent in the first quarter of 2000. However, due partly to worsening economic conditions, this had changed by March 2001. At that time, a survey by Merril Lynch found that chief information officers in the United States and Europe were planning to scale back IT spending on things like mainframe computers, printers, consulting, and outsourcing. Conversely, spending on Internet-related technologies, including servers, wireless products, and storage, was expected to remain strong. Information from International Data Corp. (IDC) forecast stronger growth in IT spending throughout the rest of the world, with the strongest potential in Australia, Western Europe, and developing markets like Latin America, the Middle East, Africa, Eastern Europe, and Asia.

The term IT includes a mind boggling number of different brands, variations, and kinds of computer systems, platforms, devices, applications, and products. As consumers and businesses purchase these products over time, issues of integration and compatibility frequently arise. Because of issues like this, companies rely on relationships with the vendors from whom they purchase products for technical advice and support. In addition to hiring IT professionals of their own, organizations also rely heavily on consultants to improve the functionality of systems and processes.

Although consultants often provide strategic value to companies, such is not always the case. Like other business practices, there are advantages and drawbacks to using consultants. As explained in *Computerworld,* "IT has always depended on strategic relationships with vendors and its heavy use of consultants to a degree that's unmatched in any other field of business. That's because no company can go it alone. The best consultants either provide special skills, handle the ever-growing IT workload and provide development and integration capabilities or take on the management of large-scale projects. The worst consultants believe their companies are smarter than their IT clients, instead of recognizing that they're extensions of their clients' resources.''

Advances in IT and the widespread adoption of the Internet allowed e-commerce to develop and evolve. Some professionals held that by eliminating human involvement from business transactions, companies would achieve greater profits. While this may be true to a degree, the human element still was very important to a company's success in the early 2000s. Some leading organizations found customer service delivered by human employees to be an important differential in a competitive market where all players had access to similar technology. Thus, the human touch was still important for developing and maintaining customer relationships, problem solving, helping customers to understand and accept technology used for e-commerce, and more. As e-commerce evolves, so will IT. Each is a critical piece of a larger whole.

FURTHER READING:

Bernasek, Anna. "Buried in Tech." *Fortune,* April 16, 2001.

"Corporations to Cut IT Budgets." Nua Internet Surveys. March 7, 2001. Available from www.nua.ie/surveys.

"Information Technology." *Techencyclopedia,* May 7, 2001. Available from www.techweb.com/encyclopedia.

"IT." *Ecommerce Webopedia,* May 7, 2001. Available from e-comm.webopedia.com

"IT 'Classics' Beaten by the Web in Reader Poll." *Computer Weekly,* November 25, 1999.

Joachim, David. "Report: IT Workers Still In Short Supply." *InternetWeek,*. April 30, 2001.

Keen, Peter G. "Consultant, anyone?" *Computerworld,* March 12, 2001.

Prencipe, Loretta W. "Management Briefing—The Job Market: Are IT Professionals Working in a Time of Feast or Famine?" *InfoWorld,* April 9, 2001. Available from e-comm.webopedia.com.

"U.S. IT Spending to Slow, but Global Outlook Positive." Nua Internet Surveys. March 23, 2001. Available from www.nua.ie/surveys.

Whiteley, Philip, and Max McKeown. "The Human Face of IT." *Computer Weekly,* April 12, 2001.

SEE ALSO: Database Management; Knowledge Management

INFORMATION THEORY

Information theory posits that information is simply data that reduces the level of uncertainty on a given subject or problem, and can be quantified by the extent to which uncertainty is diminished. More importantly for the practical uses of information theory, however, is that it fits the concept of information and communication into mathematical theory. All content, no matter what its form-music, text, video-can be reduced to a simple string of ones and zeros, thereby allowing tremendous flexibility in the mode of interpretation of that information. The application of information theory has had a tremendous impact on telecommunications and information technology and, by implication, the Internet, since it deals expressly with information-carrying capacities.

CLAUDE SHANNON

Information theory is the product of the renowned scientist Claude Shannon, widely acknowledged as one of the most innovative thinkers of his day. Born in 1916 in Petoskey, Michigan, Shannon grew up in an era when telecommunications were primarily limited to the telegraph and the telephone. From an early age, Shannon displayed an affinity for electronic equipment and radios and a penchant for devising his own inventions, much in the spirit of his hero and distant relative Thomas Edison.

Shannon attended the University of Michigan and later the Massachusetts Institute of Technology (MIT), studying electrical engineering and mathematics, in which he excelled. After college, he went to work for Bell Telephone Laboratories, where he worked on cryptographic systems using early computers. In 1948, on the strength of his work and research, Shannon published his ''A Mathematical Theory of Communication,'' a breakthrough paper that for the first time demonstrated that all information exchanges could be expressed digitally in terms of ones and zeros, based on mathematical reductions.

Shannon redefined the traditional concept of entropy to mean, in the realm of information theory, the amount of uncertainty in a given system. Information was simply anything that reduced the level of uncertainty, and hence the degree of entropy. To measure the amount of information, Shannon devised a mathematical theory in which capacities could be expressed in terms of bits per second. In fact, many historians of science insist Shannon was the first to employ the term ''bit,'' which is shorthand for ''binary digit.'' All information, Shannon claimed, could ultimately be understood as a string of bits, and could therefore be stored and transmitted as such. Shannon also developed theories on the practical transmission of digital information. He surmised that when information is sent over ''noisy'' or compromised channels, simply adding redundant bits to the message can smooth out and correct the corruption in the information.

INFORMATION THEORY TODAY

As the foundation upon which modern telecommunications systems, technologies, and theories are built, information theory was of central importance to the Internet era; it was ultimately responsible for most of the revolutionary breakthroughs in digital communication and information storage. Compact discs and digital television, not to mention the Internet, are everyday items that owe their existence to information theory. Information theory holds that all channels of information transmission and storage can also be expressed and analyzed in terms of bits, thereby providing the link that allowed for perfecting physical methods of information transmission, including how to send highly encoded Internet signals over simple telephone wires.

In the Internet world, information theory proved tremendously important not only for the basics of Internet telecommunications but also for cryptography, another field in which Shannon worked. Cryptography, in the contemporary sense, refers to protecting electronic information from compromise by applying mathematical algorithms consisting of a series of bits that scrambles the information and later decodes it when necessary. Cryptography was a key component of the development of e-commerce, since it lay at the heart of privacy and transaction protection.

Shannon's theory proved one of the great intellectual breakthroughs of the 20th century, as it gave scientists a new way to consider information and provided the basic framework within which all digital communications technology would take shape. In addition to its role as the bedrock of modern telecommunications, information theory also washed over fields as disparate as biology, ecology, medicine, mathematics, psychology, linguistics, and even investment theory.

FURTHER READING:

''Claude Shannon.'' *The Times* (London), March 12, 2001.

Golomb, Solomon W. ''Retrospective: Claude E. Shannon (1916-2001).'' *Science,* April 20, 2001.

Robinson Pierce, John. *An Introduction to Information Theory: Symbols, Signals and Noise.* 2nd ed. Mineola, NY: Dover Publications, 1980.

SEE ALSO: Cryptography; Encryption

INITIAL PUBLIC OFFERING (IPO)

An initial public offering (IPO) takes place when a privately held company goes public and makes its first offering of shares to the public. It is a significant stage in the growth of a business. It provides the business with access to capital, not only through the IPO, but also through subsequent secondary stock offerings. For the company's founders and venture capital backers, an IPO can provide the opportunity to realize a substantial cash return on their early investments. IPOs also tend to generate a lot of publicity and create more interest in a company. Once a company has gone public, it can use its stock in acquisitions and mergers. Stock can also be offered to key employees and used to attract new talent.

Investors were attracted to the IPOs of high-tech and e-commerce companies in the last half of the 1990s. Many of those companies had yet to turn a profit, yet their IPOs were successful beyond all expectations. Investors appeared more interested in a firm's potential for success in the online world, as indicated by its market position or market share, and seemed willing to overlook its losses. This displacement of profitability by market potential in the eyes of investors was one phenomenon that led observers to develop the concept of the New Economy.

Although America Online went public in 1992, it was the hugely successful IPO of Netscape Communications in August 1995 that was credited with starting the investor craze for Internet start-ups that lasted until the end of the decade. Netscape's stock was first offered at $28 a share; it was worth $75 after one day of trading, and it peaked at $171 on December 5, 1995. The company's first-day market capitalization was $2.2 billion.

In 1996 it was the IPOs of Internet search engines that attracted the interest of investors. Yahoo!, Lycos, and Excite all went public in April 1996. Yahoo! sold 2.6 million shares at $13 per share on the NASDAQ. By the end of the first week shares more than doubled to nearly $33. Following its IPO Yahoo! had a market capitalization of more than $1 billion. Lycos raised $40 million with its IPO. Following their successful IPOs, other Internet companies announced plans to go public.

From mid-1996 through mid-1997 investors began to view electronic commerce companies more realistically, and relatively few high-tech or e-commerce IPOs were executed. Weak first quarter earnings in 1997 from established firms made investors more selective about buying new technology stocks.

MORE E-COMMERCE COMPANIES GO PUBLIC, 1997-1999

More well-known e-commerce companies began to go public in 1997. Online bookseller Amazon.com held its IPO in May 1997. The company sold 8 million shares at $18 a share after the market closed. The next day the stock opened at $27 a share and rose to $80 before closing at $25.50.

High-speed Internet access provider @Home filed for an initial public offering in May 1997 and went public in July. Its stock more than doubled on the first day of trading, from its initial $10.50 price to a high of $25.50 before settling at $19. The IPO gave @Home proceeds of $94.5 million and a market capitalization of more than $2 billion.

The success of Amazon.com's and @Home's IPOs created an air of exuberance around high-tech and Internet IPOs that lasted for a couple of years. Neither Amazon.com nor @Home had shown any profits at the time of their IPOs, yet their stock increased in value following their IPOs. At the end of 1997 Internet advertising network DoubleClick filed for an IPO that took place in February 1998 and raised $62.5 million.

Online auction site eBay went public in September 1998 with an IPO that raised more than $60 million. When eBay held its IPO, investors quickly bid up the initial offering price of $18 to more than $54. After the stock settled down to around $47 a share, analysts noted that the valuation reflected consumer excitement over online auctions and investor awareness of the potential for profit. At the time most Internet ventures were losing money, but eBay managed to show a positive net income of $348,000 for the first six months of 1998.

The IPO market for Internet companies that had yet to turn a profit remained strong in 1999. With its venture capital running out, online retailer eToys turned to the public equity markets and held its IPO in May 1999. Eight percent of the company was offered to the public. Shares began trading on the NASDAQ on May 20, 1999, at $20 a share, raising $166 million for eToys. The stock rose as high as $85 on the first day of trading and ended the day around $76.50, giving eToys a market value of $7.8 billion, more than the $5.6 billion market value of established retailer Toys 'R' Us.

Priceline.com's IPO on March 30, 1999, was one of the hottest Internet IPO's of the year. Interest in the IPO was so strong that Priceline.com was able to raise its IPO price twice before the offering, first from the original $7-$9 range to $12-$14, then to the final offering price of $16. The company raised about $115 million from the initial sale of shares at $16 each. By April 18 the stock reached nearly $60 a share. When the company announced on April 26 that more than 1 million customers had tried Priceline.com in its first year, the stock rose to $121 a share. *Forbes* noted that founder Jay Walker's initial $25 million investment in the company was now worth $4.3 billion.

In the area of online publishing and bookselling, BarnesandNoble.com and Hoover's Inc. both enjoyed successful IPOs in 1999. BarnesandNoble.com raised more than $430 million with its IPO in May 1999, selling more than 24 million shares at $18 a share. At the end of its first day of trading, BarnesandNoble.com had a market capitalization of $2.52 billion. Hoover's, a business information service, went public on July 21, 1999, with an initial public offering that netted $42 million for the company. For its fiscal year ending March 31, 1999, Hoover's reported revenue of $9.2 million and a net loss of $2.2 million.

Online research firm Media Metrix went public in May 1999 with an initial public offering that raised $51 million. In July 1999, 64 companies held their IPOs, making it the busiest month for IPOs since November 1997. The strong market for IPOs helped Internet companies such as Drugstore.com and MP3 more than double their stock prices on the first day of trading.

Among technology companies, the successful IPO of Red Hat, a seller of Linux software, in August 1999 helped to generate interest in Linux. The stock opened at $14 a share and climbed to more than $50 on the first day. The volatile stock later rose as high as $123 in September.

IPO SLOWDOWN BEGAN IN 2000

The IPO market remained strong in the first quarter of 2000. According to figures cited in *Business Week,* 33 Internet firms went public in January and February, with average first-day gains of 160 percent in January and 144 percent in February. IPO.com projected there would be more than 500 high-tech IPOs in the coming year, compared to 387 in 1999. The research firm did not know that conditions for high-tech and e-commerce IPOs would change dramatically during the year.

Buy.com's IPO took place in February 2000. The company sold 14 million shares at $13 per share, raising approximately $182 million. Investors quickly bid the price up to $35 on the first day of trading before closing at $25.12 a share. Investor interest appeared to be unaffected by Buy.com's failure to turn a profit. Although revenue for 1999 increased nearly fourfold to $296.8 million, the company's loss for the year was $130.2 million, compared to a loss of $17.8 million in 1998.

New companies in the business-to-business sector also attracted investor interest. WebMethods Inc., whose B2B software suite was based on XML, saw its shares increase 508 percent from $35 to over $212 on its first day of trading in February 2000. A month later the stock was trading at $240 a share. While the company's XML software generated a lot of interest, investors may have also been attracted by WebMethods' level of sales, clear cost savings for customers, and a demonstrable path to profitability.

While the IPO market remained strong through the first quarter of 2000, it finally cooled off in the second quarter of the year. Buy.com and other Internet companies that had gone public saw their stock prices fall to their IPO levels and below. Investors were becoming more concerned about the cash-flow problems and high cash-burn rates of online retailers. For the rest of 2000, a shakeout of dot.com companies took place, with many going out of business for a lack of funding. In November 2000, approximately 27 companies withdrew their IPO filings because of the weak market for IPOs, including PetSmart.com and CarsDirect.com.

Conditions for high-tech IPOs had not improved much when Loudcloud, an e-commerce solutions company started by Netscape co-founder Marc Andreessen, held its initial public offering on March 9, 2001. The unfavorable investment climate for Internet-based companies forced the company to lower its initial offering price. Instead of selling 10 million shares at $10 to $12 a share, Loudcloud had to sell 25 million shares at an offering price of $6 in order to raise the $150 million it needed.

As of mid-May 2001, only six technology-related IPOs had been executed in 2001, and none for e-commerce companies. In fact, no e-commerce company had held an IPO since 1999, according to VentureOne. One of the strongest technology offerings in 2001 was Instinet, which rose 22 percent on opening day. However, technology companies in general appeared to be waiting to launch their IPOs. According to IPO.com, only 11 companies went public in July and August 2001, and none in September. The drought in IPOs was attributed to several factors, including a general economic slowdown and market uncertainty.

FURTHER READING:

Clancy, Heather. "Linux Lovefest on Wall Street." *Computer Reseller News,* August 16, 1999.

Dembeck, Chet. "Has the IPO Bubble Burst?" *E-Commerce Times,* August 6, 1999. Available from www.ecommercetimes.com

"E-Investors Embrace Business-to-Business." *Business Week,* March 6, 2000.

Hersch, Warren S. "IPO Market Shows Robust Performance." *Computer Reseller News,* July 28, 1997.

Macaluso, Nora. "E-Commerce IPO Market Falls to Earth." *E-Commerce Times,* April 7, 2000. Available from www.ecommercetimes.com

Marjanovic, Steven. "Internet Commerce Stocks Seen Headed for a Hard Landing." *American Banker,* May 18, 1998.

Regan, Keith. "PayPal to End IPO Drought." *E-Commerce Times,* October 1, 2001. Available from www.ecommercetimes.com

———. "Tech Stock Rally Raises Hopes for IPO Revival." *E-Commerce Times,* May 21, 2001. Available from www.ecommercetimes.com

Sloan, Allan. "Step Right Up." *Newsweek,* April 29, 1996.

———. "Trains You Can Miss." *Newsweek,* June 2, 1997.

Tracey, Brian. "Wall St. Throws Cold Water on Internet Commerce." *American Banker,* March 18, 1997.

SEE ALSO: New Economy; Shakeout, Dot-com; Volatility

INKTOMI CORP.

Inktomi Corp. was founded in 1996 by Eric A. Brewer and Paul Gauthier. Just six years later, with annual sales reaching $223.5 million, Inktomi had secured a leading position among search engine technology providers. By 2001, the firm's partner and customer base included the likes of America Online Inc. (AOL), Ameritech, Cisco Systems, Compaq Computer Corp., Intel Corp., Microsoft Corp., Sun Microsystems Inc., Nextel Communications, and Yahoo! Inc. Along with its search engine software, Inktomi developed its Traffic Server—software using caching, or storing, technology to speed up the delivery of content on the Web—and also offered various other content networking and wireless solutions that catered to both enterprises and service providers.

EARLY HISTORY

Brewer, a University of California at Berkeley professor, and Gauthier, a graduate student there, established Inktomi in 1996 while working on Brewer's Ph.D. dissertation. The pair set out to prove that a cluster of desktop computers could be wired together to be as powerful and have the same data-processing capabilities as more expensive supercomputers. To test the theory, they developed search engine software that could sort through Web pages to retrieve information. Eyeing the research project as a lucrative business opportunity, Brewer and Gauthier exited the academic world.

In 1996, the pair sought out David Peterschmidt, CEO of data specialist firm Sybase, to manage the search engine startup. With six employees, Inktomi—named after a Native American word meaning cun-

ning spider—secured its first customer in May, when it began providing the search engine technology for the HotBot Web site. Under the leadership of Peterschmidt, the company also began to develop caching technology that would allow Internet Services Providers (ISPs) to speed up content delivery over the Web by storing frequently requested Web pages locally on their computers. In 1997, Inktomi began testing the software under the name Traffic Server.

By the time the firm went public in June 1998, it had partnered with some of the industry's largest players and expanded into Europe and Asia. Inktomi's Traffic Server began running on Intel Corp.'s systems in a deal that included Intel's purchase of a small stake in the firm. AOL also tapped into Traffic Server to manage data flow throughout its network. Yahoo! teamed up with Inktomi and began using the firm's search technology on its site in July of that year, replacing AltaVista as the default search engine.

EXPANSION

The firm focused on expansion after the IPO. In September of 1998, Inktomi purchased C2B Technologies, a producer of online shopping comparison software. The acquisition added a third product line to Inktomi's arsenal—Inktomi Shopping Engine—and marked the company's entrance in the growing e-commerce industry. Inktomi also secured lucrative customer contracts with high-speed ISP @Home Networks and Microsoft-owned MSN Network.

Furthering the growth of its new Shopping Engine, Inktomi purchased online merchandising software developer Impulse! Buy Network Inc. in April 1999. By this time, the Shopping Engine had been improved to allow consumers to research products, compare prices, and purchase items. It also powered sites like Go Network, CNET, Snap, and Time Inc.'s New Media. At the same time, Inktomi also created its Directory Engine, which enabled portals like Yahoo! to create and maintain Web directories.

By 1999, with revenues of $71.2 million, Inktomi emerged as the leading search technology provider. A September 1999 *BusinessWeek Online* article attributed the firm's success to Peterschmidt's foresight. "Search companies like Excite and Lycos decided to mimic Yahoo and become Web directories and, ultimately, gateways to the Web. But rather than turn Inktomi into yet another Yahoo copycat, Peterschmidt positioned it as a behind-the-scenes provider of essential technology that all of the major Web sites needed. By not competing with its potential customers, the company has avoided conflicts, enabling it to sell its products to the fiercest of rivals, like Yahoo and AOL."

While its search engine segment thrived—by August of 1999, the Inktomi Search Engine powered over 50 portals and destination sites—the company's Traffic Server business accounted for the largest portion of revenue, securing $40.3 million in 1999. As a result, the firm continued to focus heavily on that division. In September, Inktomi announced plans to purchase WebSpective Software Inc., a content distribution management firm. Upon completion of the deal, the company began offering the Inktomi Content Delivery Suite, the first integrated content delivery, distribution, and management solution package available in the industry.

Inktomi continued expansion efforts into the new millennium. It purchased FastForward Networks, an online streaming media provider, as well as Ultraseek Corp., a subsidiary of Internet portal GO.com. The company also teamed up with Adero Inc., a network services provider, and AOL to form Content Bridge, an alliance of technology-based firms working together to improve content delivery over the Internet. In 2000, revenues tripled for the third year in a row; network products accounted for nearly 70 percent of the total. The company operated in the black for the first time. By then, the firm's product line consisted of Content Networking Solutions, Inktomi Search Solutions, and Wireless Solutions, a new segment that included Inktomi Wireless Data Accelerator software that was designed to boost network capacity. As part of the firm's effort to focus on its Content Networking offerings, it sold the Inktomi Commerce engine to e-centives Inc. in March 2001.

While many firms in the information technology sector began feeling the effects of the economic slowdown and increased competition in the late 1990s, Inktomi remained virtually unscathed until 2001. In April of that year, the firm announced job cuts and stated in an *E-Commerce Times* article that ''economic conditions in the United States and Europe have declined more quickly than we had initially anticipated, forcing us to take strong cost-cutting measures for the continued health of our business.'' Inktomi stock was trading at $5.45 in March, down from a 2000 high of nearly $240 per share.

Believing the Content Networking Solutions segment would continue to be a major growth area, Inktomi focused on research and development in that area. By offering both service providers and enterprises control over network content, Inktomi aimed to gain a strong foothold in the increasingly competitive e-business market. Despite weakening economic conditions, Inktomi was determined to remain a leader in providing Internet infrastructure solutions.

FURTHER READING:

Balderston, Jim. ''Inktomi Revs Up Hotbot Web Search Engine.'' *InfoWorld,* May 20, 1996.

Eddy, Andy. ''Inktomi: Show Me the Money.'' *Network World,* June 29, 1998.

Harbrecht, Douglas. ''Inktomi Scours the Net for Profits.'' *BusinessWeek Online,* April 4, 2001. Available from www.businessweek.com.

''Inktomi Acquires WebSpective as Content Distribution Grows.'' *Computergram International,* September 17, 1999.

LaPolla, Stephanie. ''Inktomi Traffic Servers Ease Web Jams.'' *PC Week,* April 28, 1997.

Macaluso, Nora. ''Inktomi Falls on Warnings, Layoffs.'' *E-Commerce Times,* April 3, 2001. Available from www.ecommercetimes.com.

Moeller, Michael. ''A Hidden Goldmine Called Inktomi.'' *BusinessWeek Online,* September 27, 1999. Available from www.businessweek.com.

Quinton, Brian. ''Inktomi Buys Into E-Commerce.'' *Telephony,* September 21, 1998.

Uimonen, Terho. ''Inktomi, Partners Launch Content Delivery Alliance.'' *Network World,* August 28, 2000.

Wang, Andy. ''Inktomi Makes Impulse Buy.'' *E-Commerce Times,* April 23, 1999. Available from www.ecommercetimes.com.

Woods, Bob. ''Competition Between Alta Vista, Yahoo Leads to Inktomi Corp. Deal.'' *Computer Dealer News,* June 8, 1998.

SEE ALSO: Search Engine Strategy

INNOVATION

As a relatively new way of conducting business, e-commerce itself is a technological innovation. Within the e-commerce industry are also multiple and varied examples of businesses using innovative ideas to attract new customers and increase sales. For example, the decision by Lands' End Inc. to add to its World Wide Web site ''Your Personal Model,'' an application that allows users to create a 3-D model of their body shape and then suggests appropriate clothing, was an innovation that attracted new customers. In many cases, the simple act of creating an Internet-based company—such as eBay, Amazon.com, or Yahoo!—is also an innovation.

The world's largest online retailer, Amazon.com, is the result of an innovative idea aggressively pursued by 30-year-old founder Jeff Bezos. In 1994, Bezos moved to Seattle, Washington, to take advantage of the anticipated surge in Internet use many analysts were predicting for the mid-1990s. Bezos perused roughly 20 different products, including magazines, CDs, and computer software, that he deemed appropriate for sale on the Internet. Eventually, Bezos decided to pursue books, believing that the electronic searching and organizing capabilities of an online site could help to organized the industry's sizable and varied offerings. At the same time, the small size of most books would simplify distribution efforts. Bezos also believed that customers would be more likely to make their first online purchase if the risk was minimal; an inexpensive object like a book might prove less intimidating than something more costly, like computer equipment.

After building one of the first viable online retail operations, Bezos continued to use innovative ideas to build his customer base. His "associates" program, established in July 1996, permitted individual Web site owners and operators to offer links to Amazon from their site. In return, the associate earned a commission any time a user clicked on the link to Amazon and purchased a book. Within two years, this associates program secured 30,000 members. Another major innovation was the one-click shopping technology developed by Amazon in 1997. According to *Electronic Business* writer Marc Brown, Amazon.com developed the technology in an effort to reduce the number of sales lost to customers frustrated with online checkout processes that included completing lengthy personal information forms. "Amazon.com captures the buying impulse immediately by storing this information in a database, assigning the customer a unique I.D., and storing the I.D. in a cookie on the customer's computer. The next time the customer visits, the I.D. is automatically read and used to locate the customer's record." Thanks to the one-click innovation, for which Amazon secured a patent in October of 1999, any returning Amazon.com customer is able to make a purchase simply by clicking on the "Buy Now" icon located next to each product.

Another key e-commerce innovator is Pierre Omidyar, founder of eBay.com. When Omidyar's girlfriend, a Pez candy dispenser aficionado, expressed her desire to interact with other nearby collectors, the 31-year-old Omidyar created Auction Web, a basic online auction site that permitted sellers to post items for sale by describing the object, setting a minimum bid, and selecting the auction's length, which could extend from three to ten days. Buyers were able to bid on an object at any time during the auction, and the highest bidder won the right to purchase the object for the bid price. Omidyar stipulated that payment and delivery were to be handled by the buyer and seller. Despite the fact that the site offered no search engine, no guarantees of any type regarding the merchandise sold, and no dispute resolution services, it attracted an immediate following. Eventually, Auction Web evolved into eBay, which became the world's largest online auction site, with more than 22 million registered users and roughly 8,000 product categories.

Leading Internet portal Yahoo! also has at its roots a single, innovative idea. After finding it diffi-cult to keep track of his growing list of favorite sites with the new Mosaic software that allowed users to browse the fledgling World Wide Web, David Filo sought the help of his friend, Jerry Yang. Together, Yang and Filo created a program that would allow sites to be grouped together by subject. The partners then posted their categorized site list, dubbed "Jerry's Guide to the World Wide Web," on the Web. After receiving email from Web users across the globe about the usefulness of the list, Filo and Yang decided to catalog the entire Web, using several layers of categories and subcategories. What was initially an organizational tool for Web site classification eventually grew into a top Internet destination, with more than 100 million monthly visitors, by the year 2000.

FURTHER READING:

"An Amazonian Survival Strategy: The E-Tailer is Long on Web Savvy, Short on Profits. The World is Full of Companies with the Opposite Problem. Will the Two Tango?" *Newsweek*, April 9, 2001.

Brown, Marc E. "'One-Click Shopping' Still Risky to Implement." *Electronic Business*, May 2001.

Govidarajan, Vijay. "Strategic Innovation: A Conceptual Roadmap." *Business Horizons*, July 2001.

Hazleton, Lesley. "Jeff Bezos: How He Built a Billion-Dollar Net Worth Before His Company Even Turned a Profit." *Success*, July 1998.

Jaffe, Sam. "Online Extra: eBay: From Pez to Profits." *BusinessWeek Online*, May 14, 2001. Available from www.businessweek.com.

Schlender, Brent. "How A Virtuoso Plays the Web: Eclectic, Inquisitive, and Academic, Yahoo's Jerry Yang Reinvents the Role of the Entrepreneur." *Fortune*. March 6, 2000, F-79.

SEE ALSO: Affiliate Model; Amazon.com; Bezos, Jeff; eBay Inc.; Filo, David; Omidyar, PierreYahoo!; Yang, Jerry

INSTILL CORP.

Instill Corp. offers e-commerce technology and services that streamline the supply chain processes—including procurement, tracking and analysis, and demand forecasting—used by businesses of the $376 billion food service industry. Clients in the early 2000s included Applebee's Neighborhood Bar & Grill, Bon Appetit, Delaware North Companies, Fine Host Corp., Five Star, Harrah's, Hilton, Marie Callender's, Marriott, Subway, and Tricon.

Instill was established in Redwood City, California, by Mack Tilling, the former operations director of California-based brewery restaurant chain Gordon

Biersch Brewing Co., and his partner, Ted Daley, in 1993. Tilling came up with the idea for his business after recognizing that the supply chain used by restaurant operators, food service distributors, and food product manufacturers, was highly inefficient. After securing capital from several investors, including Altos Ventures, Aspen Ventures, Charles River Ventures, Deutsche Bank, Applebee's International, and Intel Corp., Tilling and Daley began working on developing a universal product code system for merchandise offered by various food service distributors.

In 1995, Instill began offering an automated procurement solution and landed its first major account: Marriott. According to *InternetWeek* writer John Evan Frook, Instill was able to streamline the food service industry's supply chain by acting as an "on-line middleman whose service performs the mundane function of automating the ordering of food and supplies, such as aprons and dishwashing detergent, from suppliers and distributors by customers in the food service industry." Rather than manually ordering merchandise from several suppliers and processing the resulting pile of paperwork, restaurant operators like Marriott could simply send purchase orders to Instill, which charged a monthly fee to route these orders to various distributors. The data Instill compiled while handling procurement for its clients eventually allowed the firm to begin offering additional services, such as purchase and order fulfillment tracking, market analysis, and demand forecasting. In October 1997, Instill began offering its procurement services via the World Wide Web through a service known as Instill Purchase Web. By the beginning of the following year, Instill boasted 1,000 customers. Branch offices operated in Atlanta, Georgia; Chicago, Illinois; New York, New York; and Washington, D.C.

Instill launched an Internet-based purchase analysis service in 1999, called Instill Purchase Insight, marketing it to clients as a subscription ranging in price from $2,000 to $50,000 each month, depending on the number of purchases a client typically completed. The new product reviewed past purchases and indicated where clients might be spending more money than necessary. In May of 2000, Instill worked in conjunction with the National Restaurant Association, *Nation's Restaurant News,* Hewlett Packard, and other partners to create Foodscape.com, a Web portal serving independent restaurants. By then, employees totaled roughly 180.

In early 2001, the firm laid off 36 employees, roughly 17 percent of its work force, as it discontinued its market analysis services, which were known as Instill Market Intelligence. Instill refocused its efforts on its core supply chain management operations, and via a joint venture with Manugistics Group Inc., added demand forecasting technology to its suite of products and services. Refocusing efforts continued in 2001, when Instill shut down the Foodscape.com operations. By mid-2001, the firm's offerings centered around three major solutions. Instill Purchase Web allowed purchasers to access all suppliers, including those not on the Web, from a single site. Services included automated invoicing approval and payment and delivery tracking. Instill Purchase Insight consolidated the purchase order and invoice data into a single system that allowed for purchasing pattern analysis. Collaborative planning services included demand forecasting and automated replenishment, tools which allowed businesses to reduce inventory and increase their ability to stock the items their customers wanted. A direct sales force marketed Instill's products and services to clients; those who signed up were assigned a project manager who oversaw implementation.

In April of 2001, Instill secured the purchasing arm of Tricon Global Restaurants—the second-largest restaurant chain operator in the U.S.—as a client. As a result, more than 18,000 restaurants, including KEG, Pizza Hut, and Taco Bell, began using Instill Purchase Insight to scrutinize their major purchases. Having secured four of the 15 largest accounts in the food service industry, Instill continued to focus on acquiring other leading accounts, as well as on achieving profitability by the end of 2002.

FURTHER READING:

"Corporate Profile for Instill Corporation." *Business Wire,* June 9, 2000.

Frook, John Evan. "Taking Orders Off E-Commerce Menu." *InternetWeek,* January 19, 1998.

Instill Corp. "Corporate and Market Backgrounder." Redwood City, CA: Instill Corp., 2001. Available from www.instill.com.

"Instill Cuts Itself a Slice of Tracking Software Pie." *San Francisco Business Times,* April 6, 2001.

"Instill Launches Purchase Analysis Software." *Nation's Restaurant News,* June 7, 1999.

"Instill Redefines Business Strategy to Focus on Supply Chain Management Services." *Business Wire,* January 5, 2001.

Karpinski, Richard. "No Hunger for Instill's Market Research." *B to B,* January 22, 2001.

SEE ALSO: Supply Chain Management

INSTINET GROUP LLC

Instinet Group is the oldest and largest of the electronic communication networks (ECNs), privately owned systems that post the buy and sell prices of stock. Unlike traditional institutional stock brokers, Instinet uses an Internet-based electronic platform to match stock buyers and sellers and to process transactions instantaneously. Rather than purchasing large chunks of stocks and holding on to them until it can sell them at a better price, a practice known in the industry as seeking a favorable spread, Instinet makes its money by charging a fee for each trade it completes. The firm also levies charges for displaying public stock order prices on its terminals, a practice that helps NASDAQ meet order handling requirements put in place by the SEC in 1997. In 2000, parent company Reuters Group PLC announced its intent to spin off Instinet as a publicly traded company. This set the ECN apart from competitors like Island and Archipelago, who were petitioning the SEC for permission to operate as exchanges. Another distinguishing component of Instinet's service is its ability to keep confidential the name of the company buying or selling the stock, which allows a firm to place orders without impacting the market. The firm also has the furthest international reach of the ECNs, with membership in several exchanges in Europe and the Pacific Rim, as well as in the U.S. and Canada.

Instinet was founded in 1969 as Institutional Networks Corp. by Jerome Pustilnik, once a director of research at Spingarn Heine. It was purchased in the early 1980s by Bill Lupien who continued to develop the computer-based trading system that served large institutions. By conducting transactions electronically, the firm was able to offer its clients, mainly large institutions, anonymity in their stock purchases and sales. However, it wasn't until Reuters acquired it for $120 million, or $8.50 per share, after the stock market crash in 1987 that Instinet began to attract widespread attention. According to *Forbes* writer Paul Pedrosky, "Institutions, weaned on a decade of spectacular market growth, started looking for ways to cut costs and improve performance. Enter Instinet." The firm's technology, which eliminated the need for a team of in-house brokers, allowed it to charge lower transaction fees and stay open 24 hours a day, seven days a week. Even more important, however, was Instinet's ability to offer anonymity. Because traditional traders would quite often have to deal with several other brokers before closing a deal, the potential for information leaks was high; as a result, using Instinet as a trading vehicle was seen by many large companies, particularly other traders like mutual fund companies, as a way to avoid unwanted publicity—quite often a cause of major market fluctuations—regarding the purchase and sale of large chunks of stock.

Another factor in Instinet's success was its ability to link up to multiple international stock exchanges. The firm's international initiative was given a boost in 1995, when a London Stock Exchange regulation was loosened, granting the ECN access to that market. That same year, despite years of vehement protests from Canadian traders, the Ontario Securities Commission allowed Instinet to install terminals in organizations there for the first time. Eventually, Instinet gained entrance to nearly 20 different exchanges in Asia, Europe, and North America.

In 1997, the U.S. Securities and Exchange Commission (SEC) made changes to the order handling rules for stockbrokers, opening the door for new competition to Instinet, by then the largest electronic broker in the world. The revisions grew out of a price-fixing investigation conducted by the SEC regarding measures taken by certain Wall Street companies and NASDAQ dealers to ensure specific spreads between buy and sell stock prices. The defendants settled the resulting class-action suit for roughly $1 billion, but the SEC felt changes to trading practices in general were in order to prevent future abuses of the system. The new rules "opened the door to ECNs by requiring limit orders be displayed on the NASDAQ system and that the best prices be matched by market makers," said Ian Celarier in an *Investment Dealers' Digest* article. Consequently, newer ECNs like Island and Archipelago, who were approved by the SEC to display quotes on NASDAQ terminals, gained access to the NASDAQ market they would not have otherwise enjoyed. Along with displaying quotes, these ECNs were able to list their own prices, which were sometimes better than the NASDAQ quotes.

The increasing growth of ECNs brought with it intensified scrutiny of the burgeoning ECN industry. Concerned that the lines between brokers and actual exchanges were becoming a bit too blurred, and leery about the unregulated exchange activity conducted by ECNs, the SEC decided in April 1999 to allow ECNs to apply for permission to operate as official stock exchanges. Although Island and Archipelago both submitted applications, Instinet opted for another route: an initial public offering (IPO). Along with preparing for its IPO, the firm sought other ways to distinguish itself as much as possible from the upstart ECNs by continuing to diversify into things like bond trading and expanding its solid international foothold with the purchase of a stake in Belgium's Tradeware S.A. Plans to set up an online retail brokerage site were delayed late in 2000 due to a downturn in the industry.

Instinet faces competition from more traditional operations as well. Determined to compete in the new landscape carved out by ECNs, NASDAQ and the New York Stock Exchange (NYSE) both began considering public offerings of their own. In addition, NASDAQ—which saw in 2000 more than one-third of its transactions being processed by ECNs, roughly 16 percent of which was handled by Instinet—began working on the Super Montage, an ECN that would display stock buy and sell prices on a single system. Despite charges by Instinet and other ECNs that the Super Montage would eliminate competition, the SEC approved NASDAQ's plans to build the new system in January 2001.

Wall Street brokerages, who found themselves having to expand their hours and cut their prices to compete with ECNs like Instinet, also waged their own war against the ECNs beginning in the late 1999s. By arguing that the growing number of ECNs resulted in the stock market's fragmentation, which can make it more difficult for smaller investors to get the best price, Wall Street convinced the SEC to launch a one-year investigation of the impact ECNs have had on the industry. The ECNs contend that the Wall Street firms are simply trying to eliminate competition. These battles for control of the stock trading industry will likely continue to play out during the early years of the 21st century, and as the Internet-based platform that prompted the market's transformation continues to evolve, new conflicts will likely emerge.

FURTHER READING:

Dwyer, Paula. "Rethinking Wall Street." *BusinessWeek Online,* October 11, 1999. Available from www.businessweek.com/1999

Celarier, Ian S. "The ECN Dilemma: Blasting Fragmentation, Wall Street Calls for a Centralized Market Structure That Threatens the Upstarts." *Investment Dealers Digest,* March 6, 2000.

Ceron, Gaston F. "Tales of the Tape: ECNs Face a Fork in the Road." *Dow Jones News Service,* March 8, 2001.

Horowitz, Jed. "Nasdaq Dealers Push for ECN Status Under New Rules." *Investment Dealers Digest,* March 31, 1997.

Instinet Group LLC. "Corporate Information: History." New York: Instinet Group LLC, 2001. Available from www.instinet.com

Labate, John. "Companies & Finance International: Instinet Puts Off Plan." *Financial Times,* December 21, 2000. Available from globalarchive.ft.com.

Lacey, Stephen. "Instinet Instigates ECN IPO Battle." *Red Herring,* February 12, 2001.

McNamee, Mike. "Still King of the E-Bourses?" *Business Week,* June 21, 1999.

Pedrosky, Paul. "Big Brother Vs. Big Broker." *Forbes,* August 26, 1996.

Weinberg, Neil. "Darwinism On Wall Street." *Forbes,* November 13, 2000.

SEE ALSO: Archipelago Holdings LLC; Island ECN, Inc.; Nasdaq Stock Market; Day Trading; Electronic Communications Networks (ECNs); Investing, Online

INTANGIBLE ASSETS

In the corporate world, companies possess many different tangible assets with real marketplace value. Real estate, office equipment, office furniture, computers, cash, and accounts receivable are assets that, if necessary, can be exchanged in trade or used to pay off debts. Assets like these normally carry established market values, which vary depending on different economic and geographic factors. These kinds of assets are relatively easy to quantify and include on financial reports.

However, tangible assets are only part of the total picture. Companies also possess vast arrays of intangible assets. Intangible assets have real vale and are very important to a company's success, but are much harder to measure and quantify than their tangible counterparts. These kinds of assets can be customer-, technology-, or market-based. Examples of intangible assets include organizational ability, research and development, brand equity, customer databases, exclusivity within a particular market or geographic area, software, drawings, special expertise, customer satisfaction, the speed at which companies are able to bring new products and services to market, and more. Such assets usually involve information and are knowledge-based, focusing on products, services, and organizational systems. Knowledge-based, intangible assets are sometimes referred to as intellectual capital.

Although they may not be visible to the naked eye the same way tangible assets are, it is important for companies to take stock of the intangible assets they have and find ways to capture and preserve them. In the early 2000s, there were different ways of doing this. One approach was to keep employees with special knowledge, skills, and abilities happy so that they did not leave and seek employment with competing organizations. Another approach to retaining intangible assets involved storing them in computerized "expert systems." Based on artificial intelligence technology, expert systems are databanks of human knowledge that users can query in order to receive answers to common problems or challenges. Such systems have been used in the finance and insurance fields, where information is key, as well as in retail settings. There also are other ways companies store and share their collective knowledge. Home Depot, which operates a chain of home improvement stores, posts information on its intranet (a private Internet site for employees) containing quick answers to a variety of home improvement and repair questions. This allows employees to consistently provide customers with more value at the store level.

As information and knowledge play increasingly prominent roles in the business world, identifying and managing intangible assets become issues that physical retailers like Home Depot must deal with, as must companies doing business exclusively online. According to *Investor Relations Business,* Wayne Upton of the Financial Accounting Standards Board indicated this was a challenge for all companies, regardless of size. ''The issue of intangible assets is just as important for a company like Pfizer Corp. as it is for a start-up, although Pfizer may do a better job,'' he explained.

One of the reasons intangible assets are so important is because they can be converted to tangible assets, ultimately generating revenue. Books, software products, equipment, patents, and inventions are prime examples. Intangible assets also are of considerable interest to investors. In the past, a company's book value often was closely associated with its market value. However, by the early 2000s market values often exceeded book values, and the difference was often attributable to the value of a company's intangible assets. The dollar value of such assets is considerable. *Futurist* cited information from the editors of the Harvard Business School's newsletter, *Harvard Management Update,* indicating intangible assets were worth ''an average of three times more than the physical assets a company may possess, such as equipment and buildings.''

Despite the importance of intangible assets to both companies and their investors, they remained difficult to define, recognize, and measure in the early 2000s, and uniform standards for doing so did not exist. The fact that such information was not being disclosed to investors and analysts along with other, more easily quantifiable assets, presented serious problems. After all, it made it more difficult for investors to make sound decisions in the absence of such information. Because of these concerns, professionals in the fields of academia and accounting were seeking to alter the ways companies measured performance and value. By proposing new methods, they acted as change agents, challenging established principles that no longer met the information needs of the business community.

FURTHER READING:

Boulton, Richard E.S., Barry D. Libert, and Steve M. Samek. ''A Business Model for the New Economy.'' *Journal of Business Strategy,* July/August 2000.

Stewart, Thomas A. ''Accounting Gets Radical.'' *Fortune,* April 16, 2001.

Wagner, Cynthia G. ''Making Intangible Assets More Tangible.'' *Futurist,* May/June 2001.

''You're Not Special, FASB Tells Dotcoms.'' *Investor Relations Business,* April 30, 2001.

SEE ALSO: Intellectual Capital; Intellectual Property

INTEGRATION

Connectivity is a main element of e-commerce. It is a requirement for engaging in electronic transactions between two or more parties, be they businesses or consumers. However, companies that excel at e-commerce do more than simply connect with customers, suppliers, and other business partners; they find ways to integrate the many different computer systems and databases that are part of their operations with each other (internal integration), or with parties on the outside (external integration) so they function together seamlessly.

EXTERNAL INTEGRATION

External integration is especially important in the realm of business-to-business e-commerce, where companies can realize significant cost savings and increased efficiencies by integrating their systems. Companies and business partners may integrate systems at different points in a supply chain, which encompasses all of the different levels involved in manufacturing products. Supply chains include everything from raw materials to finished products, which can be used by other companies in their manufacturing processes or purchased by consumers. For example, an automotive manufacturer might integrate certain systems that contain information about production forecasts with a tire manufacturer's systems. With this information, the tire manufacturer is able to tie its production levels closely with the automotive manufacturer's demand. This allows for better production control, satisfactory shipment times, and more manageable inventory levels.

In the early 2000s, business-to-business transactions happened mainly through both traditional and Web-based electronic data interchange (EDI) and online marketplaces or exchanges. It was in these environments that issues concerning external integration became important. EDI involves exchanging electronic business information like bills of lading, confirmations, purchase orders, and inventory information between organizations or trading partners in agreed upon, standard formats. Through EDI, computers and databases communicate directly with one another over value-added networks (VANs), private networks, and the Internet (open EDI).

The Internet was fast becoming an important means of engaging in EDI during the early 2000s, especially for smaller companies that previously could not afford the high costs associated with traditional EDI. Extensible markup language (XML), a computer language similar in many ways to hypertext markup language (HTML), which is used to create Web pages, was playing an important role in this arena. It enabled external integration by allowing companies to share information in universal ways, no matter what kinds of software systems they used. XML also played an important role in developing online marketplaces or exchanges, which are Web-based environments where buyers and sellers are able to come together and engage in trading. These marketplaces were operated by third parties who charged buyers and sellers to engage in electronic transactions that might not otherwise have been possible due to system incompatibilities.

The need for external integration was growing rapidly in the early 2000s along with the business-to-business sector. According to *Corporate EFT Report,* business-to-business sales were estimated to be $3.3 trillion in 2000 and were projected to reach $5.2 trillion by 2004. The Gartner Group forecast more optimistic business-to-business sales for 2004, placing the figure at $7.29 trillion.

INTERNAL INTEGRATION

Successful e-commerce companies also make sure the many different systems they use within their enterprises are integrated. Known as internal integration, this allows many different pieces of relevant information about transactions and other business activities to be shared with appropriate divisions or departments. For example, in business-to-consumer commerce, when a customer orders a product online via an order form on a company's Web site, data about the order is instantly sent to the accounting department for billing and financial reporting purposes; to the warehouse for packing and shipping purposes; and to customer service in the event of questions or concerns regarding the status of the order.

When e-commerce exploded in popularity, many companies rushed into the game by putting up Web sites and accepting online orders. However, these front-end elements represented only half of the equation. Many organizations failed to think through processes and systems on the back end, namely how they would connect systems together. When companies take this approach, bottlenecks arise in what otherwise would be a seamless process. Orders that come in via the Web might be billed quickly to a customer's credit card, but are then printed out on paper and held for days or weeks in the warehouse before being filled. Practices like these hinder what e-commerce is all about.

As explained in *InfoWorld,* ''Retail success hinges on what happens behind that fabulous Web site: logistics and fulfillment, payment systems, systems and policies to handle returns, customer service, and, running through it all, integration. Without these the site won't scale, and customers who once loved the Web store will quickly turn fickle and point their browsers elsewhere.''

SOLVING INTEGRATION PROBLEMS

Integration-related problems, both internal and external, usually arise from incompatible computer systems. According to *eCompany Now,* a Forrester Research survey revealed that although most big companies (72 percent) understand the importance of external integration, less than 25 percent had integrated their systems externally. The publication explained: ''There are a lot of businesses out there that have spent millions of dollars and thousands of hours automating every aspect of their operation, only to discover that their wondrous new systems stopped cold whenever their business touched their customers, suppliers, and partners.'' Information in *Computerworld* also indicated that a large number of businesses were not prepared to reap the many benefits the Internet and e-commerce had to offer, explaining that the IT infrastructures of most enterprises were fragmented collections of different programs, devices, and networks without the ability to communicate seamlessly.

Complicating matters further is the fact that some of these systems are custom, and represent significant investments both in development and user training. While starting from scratch with new systems is one possible solution, for this reason it usually isn't a practical or feasible one for many companies. After a large number of e-commerce companies failed in the early 2000s, many executives also were skeptical about investing millions of dollars in information technology that might not result in an immediate return-on-investment.

In the early 2000s, application-integration software was a potential solution for companies needing to integrate their systems internally (enterprise application integration) or externally (inter-enterprise integration). Application-integration solutions normally fall into the category of middleware—software residing between applications that functions as a translation layer. There are a variety of different kinds of middleware. Certain kinds pertain to database programs, some enable programs to connect with each other, and others exchange messages between programs and systems on different networks.

webMethods Inc. was one company offering integration solutions to leading companies in the early 2000s. Its customers included Ford Motor Co., Motorola, Starbucks, Dell, Citibank, and Eastman Chemical. The company's EDI Adaptor version 4.0 helped companies to bridge a strategic gap by supporting their existing EDI systems while they transitioned to newer Internet technologies like XML. According to the company, "While most people agree that 'XML over the Internet' is the strategy of the future, the migration path to XML is not yet clearly defined for many companies. Many of these companies have spent years building their EDI systems and want to leverage their investment. By allowing trading partners to utilize their existing EDI infrastructure, implementation time and cost are reduced."

In 2000, webMethods helped Airborne Express—a leading transportation company that also provides order fulfillment and distribution services for its customers—to win the business of a major retailer that was unveiling a new online business. It did this by giving Airborne the ability to communicate and exchange files in XML format, thereby enabling external integration. The capability allowed Airborne to process 10,000 orders daily during the Christmas holiday that year. It also enabled the shipper to improve the level of customer service it provided, because the XML code was easy to review, correct, and change if needed.

TIBCO Software Inc. also provided middleware integration solutions to companies in the early 2000s, including Bell South, Hitachi Semiconductor, Saturn, Ameritrade, Chevron, TNT Logistics North America, 3COM, Netscape, and Philips Medical Systems. Philips Medical Systems provides diagnostic imaging products (including machines used for X-rays, MRIs, and CAT scans) and related services to healthcare providers throughout the world. It used TIBCO's ActiveEnterprise software as an internal integration solution. In order to quickly meet the needs of its customers, Philips needed to connect orders it received from them with its factories in real-time. Prior to adopting TIBCO's system, Philips had a patchwork of different computer systems responsible for different functions like sales, manufacturing, and distribution. The company estimated that more than 2,000 different interfaces were needed to connect these systems, which included various business functions, computer applications, and mainframe systems. Not only was this expensive for Philips, it was slow and cumbersome for people trying to do business with them. TIBCO's solution allowed Philips' different systems to interface with one another in real time, providing enormous benefits for the company and the healthcare providers it served.

FURTHER READING:

Baum, David. "Middleware." *InfoWorld,* November 30, 1992.

———. "Middleware to the Rescue." *Computerworld,* May 10, 1993.

Borck, James R. "Web Commerce From the Ground Up." *InfoWorld,* August 2, 1999.

Caulfield, Brian. "Systems That Talk Together, Kick Butt Together." *eCompany Now,* January 2001. Available from www.ecompanynow.com.

Champy, Jim. "New Infrastructure." *Computerworld,* February 26, 2001.

Grygo, Eugene. "Bringing Web Exchanges Into the Back End—Companies consider connecting digital exchange transactions with internal apps." *InfoWorld,* March 27, 2000.

Leon, Mark. "Online Retail Success Lies Behind the Scenes." *InfoWorld,* June 12, 2000.

Meehan, Michael. "Vendors Try to Make Middleware More User-Friendly." *Computerworld,* May 15, 2000.

"Middleware." *Tech Encyclopedia,* February 23, 2001. Available from www.techweb.com/encyclopedia.

Ryan, Vincent. "WebMethods Links Companies with Trading Partners." *Upside,* March 2000.

SEE ALSO: Enterprise Application Integration (EAI)

INTEL CORP.

The world's largest maker of microprocessors, Santa Clara, California-based Intel Corp. also is one of the five most profitable manufacturing companies of any business sector. In 2000, the firm posted earnings of $10.5 billion on revenues of $33.7 billion. Although Intel spent considerable effort attempting to move into new markets—such as communications and networking equipment and Internet hosting services in the late 1990s—it essentially remained a PC chip maker, with an 80-percent share of the market in 2001.

EARLY HISTORY

In the late 1960s, the co-founders of Fairchild Semiconductor, Gordon E. Moore and Dr. Robert Noyce, became dissatisfied with the level of financial support they were receiving from their owners. Despite the firm's status as the largest semiconductor company in the world, Moore and Noyce left Fairchild in 1968 to found NM Electronics, which was based on a one-page business plan developed by Noyce. NM Electronics was later renamed Intel, from the first syllables of "integrated electronics." Early products included a new high-speed RAM device, LSI semiconductor memories, and a metal oxide semiconductor chip. In 1972, Intel released an eight-bit microprocessor known as the 8008. Two years later, it introduced the 8088, the world's first general purpose microprocessor, which quickly became an industry standard. By 1975, sales had reached $135 million.

SHIFT FROM MEMORY CHIPS TO MICROPROCESSORS

In August of 1981, IBM selected the 8088 chip for its new personal computer line, which helped to launch the PC revolution when it was shipped. The following year, IBM acquired a 12-percent stake in Intel for $250 million. However, these shares were later sold. By the mid-1980s, Intel had become the tenth-largest maker of semiconductors. It was then that Intel's management decided to shift gears, reducing the company's focus on memory chip operations in favor of the more profitable microprocessor market. Part of this restructuring involved the layoff of 6,000 employees. Intel introduced its revolutionary 80486 microprocessor in 1989. By the end of the decade, Intel had moved its way up to third place among the world's leading semiconductor makers.

Intel's aggressive advertising campaign, centered around the ''Intel Inside'' logo, proved successful as the company's earnings exceeded $1 billion for the first time in 1992. The following year, Intel released its Pentium processor, which could execute more than 100 million instructions per second and was five times more powerful than its latest 486 microprocessor. In 1994, when the Pentium microprocessor was discovered to make calculation errors under certain conditions, Intel discounted the problem as minor. However, increasingly negative public relations prompted the firm to replace the chips with new ones at no additional cost to customers. As a result, the firm took a $475 million pretax charge. Despite the setback, sales that year grew 31 percent to $11.5 billion. By then, roughly 80 percent of the world's PCs ran on Intel's processors. In 1996, the firm unveiled 150-megahertz and 166-megahertz Pentium models, which were significantly faster than the 133-megahertz model. Revenues soared to $25 billion in 1997. Making its most expensive acquisition to date, Intel paid $40 million for competitor Chips and Technologies Inc. in 1998.

ATTEMPTED SHIFT FROM MICROPROCESSORS TO NETWORKING AND INTERNET TECHNOLOGY

According to a March 2000 article in *Business Week,* ''After 10 years of 30 percent-plus compound annual growth, Intel hit a milewide pothole in 1998. Earlier attempts to expand into new businesses such as modems and video conferencing had gone nowhere. Then falling PC prices, computer industry consolidation, and increased competition piled on top of one another, causing Intel's revenue growth to slow to 5 percent, while earnings declined for the first time in a decade.'' A major blow to Intel had come in February of 1997, when Compaq Computer Corp. re-leased a PC powered with a Cyrix Corp. microprocessor for less than $1000. Soon thereafter, other PC manufacturers began manufacturing their own lines of inexpensive PCs, leaving room for rivals like Cyrix and Advanced Micro Devices (AMD) to market their less expensive microprocessors.

Eventually, Intel decided to develop its own series of microprocessors for inexpensive PCs. Intel named the line Celeron. Chips for more costly servers and workstations were grouped together under the name Xeon. The firm also realized that it could no longer rely on the PC industry as its sole source of profits. As a result, it began diversifying beyond central processing units into things like flash memory chips—those used in digital cameras, handheld computers, and cell phones—and other networking and communications devices. In January of 1999, Intel began offering Internet services such as Web hosting.

A multi-billion dollar acquisition spree included the purchase of Dialogic Corp., IPivot Inc., and Parity Software Development Corp. The firm also paid $1.6 billion for wireless technology maker DSP Communications Inc. and $2.2 billion for broadband device chipmaker Level One Communications Inc. That year, Intel released a series of chips for networking and communications devices that help to power the Internet. At the time, the market for such devices was growing roughly 30 percent faster than the PC market. In an effort to gain access to emerging technology, Intel began investing in upstart software and Internet firms. By 2000, the company's Intel Capital arm had poured roughly $1.2 billion into ventures such as eToys and Inktomi.

Along with efforts to diversify, Intel also continued developing faster microprocessors, such as the Pentium III, a 1 gigahertz (GHz) processor introduced in early 2000. Rival AMD unseated Intel as the maker of the world's fastest chip with its less expensive 1.2 GHz Athlon processor, unveiled in February of that year. Intel's efforts to regain its title with a slightly faster chip failed when the firm was forced to recall that chip in August. However, in November Intel released the Pentium IV, a 1.5 GHz chip.

Growth via acquisition continued as the firm paid $1.25 billion for Denmark-based GIGA A/S and $450 million for Basis Communications Corp. Intel also bought computer telephony solutions provider Picazo Communications Inc. In addition, the firm announced its intent to begin selling appliances such as set-top boxes for televisions via Internet Service Providers (ISPs), screened telephones via telephone companies, and network servers for Web applications.

Despite Intel's bold plans to reinvent itself as a networking and communications technology provider, in 2001 revenues declined for the first time in approximately 10 years. One reason for the lower revenues was a price war initiated by Intel. In September, in an effort to wrest lost market share back from rival AMD, Intel unveiled its 2 GHz Pentium IV processor at a price much lower than normal for a new release by the firm. It also reduced prices on its other Pentium products by an unprecedented 40 percent. While the price cuts helped to bolster market share, they also reduced revenues. Another problem, according to *BusinessWeek Online* columnist Cliff Edwards, was that Intel's diversification efforts had not begun to pay off. "Intel's new businesses—everything from Web hosting to processors for phones—have reaped zilch in profits, with losses doubling every year since 1998." Although some analysts recommended that Intel abandon many of its diversification efforts—particularly in the Web hosting industry, which saw major players like Exodus Communications bail out in the wake of the dot-com shakedown—the firm decided to forge ahead, hoping to be well positioned for the industry's eventual rebound.

FURTHER READING:

Edwards, Cliff. "Can Craig Barrett Reverse Intel's Slide?" *BusinessWeek Online.* October 4, 2001. Available from www.businessweek.com.

"Intel—Chipzilla Takes a Beating." *The Economist.* November 11, 2000.

"Intel Corp." In *Notable Corporate Chronologies.* Farmington Hills, MI: Gale Group, 1999.

"The New Intel." *Business Week.* March 13, 2000.

Roth, Daniel. "Craig Barrett Inside: Can This Nature-Loving Onetime Professor Lead Intel out of the Woods? One Thing's For Sure: He's Got Awfully Big Hiking Boots to Fill." *Fortune.* December 18, 2000.

Schlender, Brent. "Intel Unleashes Its Inner Attila." *Fortune.* October 15, 2001.

SEE ALSO: Compaq Computer Corp.; IBM Inc.; Microprocessor; Moore, Gordon; Noyce, Robert

INTELLECTUAL CAPITAL

The term intellectual capital defines a range of intangible assets that a company possesses alongside its physical and financial assets but which can't be quantified in the same manner. Among these are the intellectual property and patents claimed by the firm; its employees' and managers' collective knowledge about their products and services and about the way the firm and its market function; and the internal information infrastructure, systems, and software that enable the dissemination, sharing, manipulation, and optimization of that knowledge. The Organization for Economic Cooperation and Development (OECD) defines intellectual capital simply as "the economic value of two categories of intangible assets of a company: (a) organizational (structural) capital; and (b) human capital." Structural capital, according to *Financial Management,* covers supply chains, distribution networks, and proprietary software systems. While these features of businesses are not native to the New Economy, the importance they have assumed in the Information Age, in terms of the workings of the firm and its perceived value, is altogether unprecedented and rapidly escalating.

In part, the concept of intellectual capital grew out of a growing dissatisfaction among many academics, accountants, and—perhaps especially—investors with standard accounting methods, which did a poor job of assessing the actual value of firms, particularly firms operating in or around the fields of information technology (IT) or other knowledge-intensive sectors. In order to accurately assess the value and prospects of such firms, these critics contended, it was necessary to somehow quantify and account for the collective knowledge and the organization of that knowledge within a firm.

The major factors contributing to the growth and importance of intellectual capital were economic globalization, which greatly intensified global competition and trade; the trend, especially in the United States but in much of the rest of the world as well, toward the deregulation of markets, particularly in such IT-heavy sectors as telecommunications that had previously largely worked outside of the competitive market system; and, of course, the tremendous technological innovation in knowledge-related fields, particularly the growth in IT and computers, which placed information at the center of firms' operations. All these changes forced a shift in corporate organization toward a less centralized and vertical model of corporate organization, greater outsourcing of operations, and more fluid channels of interaction within and between firms, all of which enhanced the importance of intellectual capital.

FIRMS TAKE STOCK OF THEIR INTELLECTUAL CAPITAL

Intellectual capital was a lively topic in the business literature of the early 1990s, but the idea fizzled, according to *Information Today,* largely on the inability of researchers to devise a satisfactory method of measuring it. Without an adequate means of quantification, the idea essentially had no way of being practically integrated into accounting methods. As a result, the issue faded into the background for several years before reemerging in the late 1990s when the Internet and information technology proved among the primary engines of the fantastic boom in the U.S. economy. While quantification techniques continued to be debated and compared, intellectual capital, an increasingly recognized asset, became a field ripe for management concerns, as companies, determined to maintain their competitiveness in an information-centered economy, required an accurate assessment of the intellectual value harbored in their ranks.

To organize and capitalize on intellectual capital, an entire field of knowledge management was born, including theoretical techniques and extensive and sophisticated knowledge management software programs that companies increasingly integrated into their infrastructure to facilitate the transfer, support, and optimal use of knowledge within the firm.

As intellectual capital grew increasingly central to a firm's operations and value, managers were compelled to take ever-greater steps to protect their intellectual capital from compromise. The task of keeping knowledge, including knowledge inside employees' heads, within the purview of the firm at all times was a growing concern in the 1990s and early 2000s. One mark of this trend was the increasing number of confidentiality agreements devised by companies for their employees to sign, thereby guaranteeing that while they work at the firm and even after they leave, they will not divulge information and company secrets to other parties.

Quantification of intellectual capital involves consistent performance measurements and knowledge assessments that must then be publicized in a manner that investors and accountants can recognize. One leading authority on intellectual capital, New York University's Leonard N. Stern School of Business Professor Baruch Lev, defined intellectual capital in terms of an asset: a claim to a benefit a company expects to reap in the future but which, unlike a piece of machinery or commercial property, doesn't have a physical or financial embodiment. Intellectual property, such as patents or copyrights, is thus one branch of intellectual capital, the one that was in fact legally recognized and secured. The fact that the field of patenting has expanded to include not only physical inventions but also business processes and practices also greatly boosted the centrality of intellectual capital.

ASSESSING VALUE IN THE INFORMATION AGE

According to *Computer World,* the growing difference between a company's book value share price and its market value share price is often, and increasingly, chalked up to intellectual capital. As Arthur Levitt, former chairman of the Securities and Exchange Commission (SEC) told the Economic Club of New York, ''As intangible assets grow in size and scope, more and more people are questioning whether the true value—and the drivers of that value—are being reflected in a timely manner in publicly available disclosure.''

Indeed, *Fortune* reported the results of a long-term study by Arthur Andersen consultants Richard Burton, Barry Libert, and Steve Samek, who for two decades monitored the gap between the book value and the market value of 3,500 U.S. companies. The results strongly favor those who insist that intellectual capital is being unduly, and potentially dangerously, ignored. In 1978, according to the study, book value for all the companies averaged 95 percent of market value. By the end of the 1990s, book value amounted to just 28 percent of market value. While the precipitous decline in technology stocks and the attendant slowing of the U.S. economy in the early 2000s showed some of this discrepancy to be the result of a stock-market bubble, analysts were in general agreement that no small amount of the difference could indeed be chalked up to unquantified intellectual capital. In other words, investors increasingly saw value in companies that traditional accounting methods were simply incapable of quantifying. Federal Reserve Board Chairman Alan Greenspan warned that such a gap between hard accounting data and the perceptions and confidence of investors was bound to breed tremendous problems in the future if left uncorrected.

FURTHER READING:

Bernhut, Stephen. ''Measuring the Value of Intellectual Capital.'' *Ivey Business Journal,* March/April, 2001.

Duffy, Jan. ''Managing Intellectual Capital.'' *Information Management Journal,* April, 2001.

Guthrie, James. ''Measuring Up to Change.'' *Financial Management,* December, 2000.

Koenig, Michael. ''The Resurgence of Intellectual Capital.'' *Information Today,* September, 2000.

Stewart, Thomas A. ''Accounting Gets Radical.'' *Fortune,* April 16, 2001.

Taylor, Christie. ''Intellectual Capital.'' *Computer World,* March 12, 2001.

SEE ALSO: Data Mining; Intellectual Property; Knowledge Management

INTELLECTUAL PROPERTY

Few fields of law faced more rapid transformation from the effects of Internet and e-commerce than the realm of intellectual property. Intellectual property (IP) is considered to be the intangible result of intellectual work, such as inventions, literary and artistic works, and commercial symbols, names, images, and designs. Advances in communication and information technology have dramatically affected intellectual property rights.

Intellectual property laws concern the rights and protections pertaining to copyright, patents, trademarks, and trade secrets. Copyright and patent law debates often bring society's desire for free access to information into conflict with creators' and inventors' wishes to profit from and protect their creations. Businesses have intellectual property interests in safeguarding their identities and competitiveness through trademark and trade-secret protections.

The resolution of intellectual property questions was generating large-scale transformations in many Internet-related industries, as well as in fundamental legal issues such as privacy and freedom of information and expression. Since many online transactions transcend national borders, some observers predict that the challenges created by the Internet will result in the wholesale revision of both U.S. and international intellectual property laws.

COPYRIGHTS

Copyright protects a creator's or copyright owner's rights to control the publication, performance, duplication, and profitability of created works. Such works include literature, musical compositions, choreography, graphic and fine arts, motion pictures, and sound recordings. U.S. copyright protects the expression of ideas, rather than ideas themselves; it arises automatically when a creative work is expressed (or "fixed") in a tangible medium. Though registration for copyright is optional, creators cannot file suit for infringement without having registered. Copyright owners can sue for damages and courts can issue injunctions to prevent further infringement.

Limitations on copyright protection include the unauthorized "fair use" of a work by others for non-commercial purposes such as criticism, comment, news reporting, teaching, or research. Under the "first sale doctrine," libraries and archives may generate one copy of a work for archival conservation and the owner of a copy of a work may sell, lend, or dispose of that copy. Finally, all works in the public domain may be freely duplicated, performed, and distributed.

U.S. copyright laws must maintain the difficult balance between protecting creators' rights to control and derive compensation for their works and society's right to free access and spread of information. That the Internet enables users anywhere to produce essentially identical copies of any digital content and disseminate them throughout the world at virtually no cost has significantly raised the stakes of copyright protection.

The Copyright Clause of the U.S. Constitution provides that: "Congress shall have power... to promote the progress of science and useful arts, by securing for limited times to authors and inventors the exclusive right to their respective writings and discoveries." Even unintentional or accidental violation of these rights may be prosecuted.

The basic provisions of American copyright law are set forth in the Copyright Act of 1976. In addition to traditionally recognized creative works, the Act also protects online text, image, and sound files. Copyright holders may bring civil suits or the federal government may prosecute the intentional infringement of copyright committed for commercial advantage or financial gain. Besides direct infringement, contributory infringement and vicarious liability, through which one person aids another in carrying out copyright infringement, can constitute criminal liability.

Several subsequent copyright laws affect copyright in cyberspace. In 1992, the Copyright Felony Act targeted computer software piracy; earlier, only unauthorized copying of sound recordings, motion pictures, or audiovisual works constituted federal copyright felonies. The Digital Performance Right Act of 1996 required that anyone wishing to use non-original music for public digital performance on a Web site obtain license from the copyright owner.

In 1997, the No Electronic Theft (NET) Act abandoned the requirement that intentional infringement be committed for financial gain in order to be prosecutable. This criminalized even infringement carried out simply to harm another. Some commentators suggested that henceforth, since online browsing involves copying in the statutory sense, anyone who browses copyrighted content without permission could be guilty of actionable copyright infringement.

Congress enacted the Digital Millennium Copyright Act (DMCA) of 1998 to further amend U.S. copyright law in light of Internet-related concerns. The Act aligned U.S. legislation more closely with international copyright legislation as embodied in the World Intellectual Property Organization's (WIPO) Copyright Treaty. In addition, it prohibited anyone from circumventing technology intended to block unauthorized access to copyrighted material on the Web, such as decrypting protected content. The DMCA does permit authorized institutions to make up to three digital copies for preservation and to electronically "loan" those copies to other institutions.

At the state level, the Uniform Computer Information Transactions Act (UCITA) has been under consideration by state legislatures since 1999. It limits fair use rights of copyrighted digital materials, and classifies software and software-related products as "licensed information." UCITA faced stiff opposition from many state Attorneys General, the American Intellectual Property Association, and advocacy groups representing consumers, publishers, newspapers, libraries, retail, and law professors, who warn that UCITA's insistence on widespread digital-content licensing could severely erode legitimate fair use exceptions of online content, since licenses can contain clauses regulating the manner and time period for which the content can be accessed, and limit who can use it.

Still, the law on the Internet and copyright remains unclear. Several areas of particular confusion are:

- Whether a specific online work is original enough to merit copyright protection—articles, essays, and many graphic or sound works usually are, but factual content and databases may not be.

- Which specific Internet-related activities constitute copyright violations. Does uploading hard copies to the Internet, forwarding online content to a listserv, or linking to another Web site constitute infringement or fair use?

- Does an author's consent to having his or her creation put onto the Web imply tacit agreement to users browsing, downloading, and forwarding copies of their work?

- What is the liability of internet service providers (ISPs) and bulletin board operators for possible copyright infringements committed by their subscribers? Can they be sued for unintentional, vicarious liability?

Intellectual property rights in higher education was an area of particular concern, raising questions about who owns rights to online course content, lectures, and e-publications. In cyberspace, traditional fair-use exceptions regarding copyrighted materials may not protect free access to online materials for academic purposes. Libraries may not enjoy the right of "first sale"—which traditionally permits them to purchase works and then lend them to borrowers—when it comes to e-materials.

The Clinton administration's Information Infrastructure Task Force Working Group on Intellectual Property Rights encapsulated a series of sweeping policy recommendations in a 1995 report, "Intellectual Property and the National Information Infrastructure." The report detailed emerging trends and proved highly influential in shaping U.S. domestic and foreign intellectual property initiatives. Among its conclusions, the report argued that browsing and distributing content without the creator's explicit permission violates the Copyright Act. It also called for the creation of copyright holders' exclusive rights to control the transmission of their copyrighted digital content. The report spurred controversy, with opponents claiming that these copyright extensions harmed the public interest in the free flow of information. Proponents, however, noted that creators and copyright holders have much more precarious control over their works in cyberspace than they do in the real world.

TRADEMARKS

A trademark protects a company's name and logos and distinguishes them from competing products or services sold by others. Registering trademarks permits the owner to enjoy exclusive use of the trademarks in the U.S. or a state, and to sue others for infringement in federal or state court. Registration is not granted if the mark is identical to an existing mark or resembles one closely enough to cause "confusion" or "to deceive."

Trademark law affects Internet-related issues in two particular areas. Domain names can function almost like trademarks and help to identify a business online. Trademarks and domain names have become the targets of cyber-squatters, who illegally register them in the hopes of later reselling them to the original owner for a profit. A particularly noted form of domain-name dispute involved Hollywood celebrities who pursued arbitration via WIPO's Uniform Dispute Resolution Policy channels to combat cyber-squatters for "bad faith" registration of domain names similar to their own. The other major problem concerns how trademark law is implicated in the use of URLs in hyperlinks.

PATENTS AND TRADE SECRETS

The federal Patent and Trademark Office (PTO) can issue patents to anyone who invents or discovers a process, machine, or method of manufacture that is "novel," "useful," and "nonobvious." The patent grants exclusive rights to control the production, use, and sale of the invention within all U.S. jurisdictions. The patent holder can sue even for inadvertent infringement.

A trade secret is any information used in the operation of a business that provides the business an advantage, including scientific, technical, or commercial information, and even customer lists. The owner must protect the trade secret from becoming widely known. Wrongful disclosure or use of a trade secret may be enforced in court against anyone who has a duty to maintain secrecy.

Among recent legislation was the Economic Espionage Act (EEA) of 1996, which made the theft of trade secrets a federal crime. It broadened the definition of property to include the phrase, "tangible or intangible, and whether or how stored," which facilitates prosecution for trade secrets taken in electronic form.

INTERNATIONAL IP

Economic globalization and international e-commerce have had profound effects on the status of intellectual property in the global arena. Complications are acute for copyright, and encompass problems of legal jurisdiction, difficulties of enforcement, and countries with widely divergent levels of intellectual property protection. The most widely reported international IP infringement was piracy. Many observers remark that globalization will force the increasing standardization and convergence of intellectual property laws internationally.

Numerous bilateral and multilateral treaties govern international copyright. The fundamental treaty for copyright protection remains the Berne Convention for the Protection of Literary and Artistic Works. Dating from 1886, the Convention grants authors exclusive rights to control the reproduction, public performance, broadcast, and adaptation of their works. The U.S. did not join the Berne Convention until 1988.

Many European countries extend stronger copyright protection than does the U.S. These include the recognition of authors' "moral rights" in a work, which are separate from economic rights. Moral rights include the rights to be recognized as a work's creator, to shield a work from distortion, to retract or amend content, and to decide whether a work should be published at all.

The leading international authority on intellectual property law is the World Intellectual Property Organization (WIPO), which administers relevant international treaties and helps settle international disputes. WIPO unveiled two major intellectual property treaties in 1996: the Performances and Phonograms Treaty and, more importantly, the Copyright Treaty. The latter extended Berne Convention protection to digital works, classifying computer programs as literary works. It expanded the basic notion of copyright to embrace the "right of communication," including online transmission. It also contained the earliest regulations prohibiting the circumvention of measures designed to protect copyrighted works, such as encryption and digital-rights management systems.

The most wide-ranging international legislation was the 1994 Agreement on Trade-Related Aspects of Intellectual Property Rights (TRIPs) Agreement. It sets forth comprehensive, minimum standards of international intellectual property protection that largely favor protection over the free flow of information. TRIPs contains mandatory enforcement procedures and sanctions for the failure to implement them. TRIPs prohibits preferential measures for developing countries, which were held to full compliance after a five-year transitional period. Critics argue that such provisions will place developing countries, which often lack even rudimentary intellectual property protection regimes, at an even greater disadvantage in the global e-commerce arena.

FURTHER READING:

"Digital Rights and Wrongs." *Economist,* July 17, 1999.

Dinwoodie, Graeme. "A New Copyright Order: Why National Courts Should Create Global Norms." *University of Pennsylvania Law Review,* December, 2000.

Ellis, Davis. "Cyberlaw and Computer Technology: A Primer on the Law of Intellectual Property Protection." *Florida Bar Journal,* January, 1998.

Gladney, Henry. "Digital Intellectual Property: Controversial and International Aspects." *Columbia-VLA Journal of Law & the Arts,* Fall, 2000.

Hsieh, Lilli, McCarthy, Jennifer, and Elizabeth Monkus. "Intellectual Property Crimes." *American Criminal Law Review,* Spring 1998.

Mutchler, John. &lquo;Will the Digital Millennium Copyright Act Stunt Global Electronic Commerce?'' *Intellectual Property Today,* October, 2000.

Panchak, Patricia. "Old Rules for the New Economy." *Industry Week,* March 5, 2001.

Reichman, J.H. "The TRIPs Agreement Comes of Age: Conflict or Cooperation with the Developing Countries?" *Case Western Reserve Journal of International Law,* Summer, 2000.

Samuelson, Pamela. "The Digital Rights War." *Wilson Quarterly,* Autumn, 1998.

Tennant, Roy. "Copyright and Intellectual Property Rights." *Library Journal,* August, 1999.

SEE ALSO: Cybersquatting; Higher Education and the Internet; Intellectual Capital; Legal Issues; World Intellectual Property Organization (WIPO)

INTELLIGENT AGENTS

Intelligent agents are a member of the bot family—software programs that operate unattended, usually on the Internet. Therefore, agents are sometimes referred to as bots. Individuals or organizations use intelligent agents to perform functions or tasks that otherwise would involve human interaction or repetition. Operating independently on behalf of their users, some intelligent agents mimic human behavior and thought processes and are able to make decisions, learn, and interact with other intelligent agents. Intelligent agents come in stationary and mobile varieties, meaning that they can either reside on individual computer systems or travel from server to server across the Internet to carry out different tasks.

According to *Online,* there is agreement among many authors in the field of artificial intelligence that a true intelligent agent must be social, adaptable, proactive and autonomous. In the early 2000s, intelligent agent technology was still evolving and a single agent with all four of these traits had not been created. Multi-agent systems, or groups of intelligent agents in which each exhibits one or several of the four behaviors, were in development. Nevertheless, many evolving forms of intelligent agents existed in everything from search engines to computer help systems.

In the world of e-commerce, intelligent agents known as shopping bots are used by consumers to search for product and pricing information on the Web. Each shopping bot operates differently, depending on the business model used by its operator. In one scenario, shopping bots direct users to retailers who, by subscribing for a fee, are part of a closed system. Shopping.Yahoo and Shop@AOL are examples of this model. Open systems are a more common arrangement and involve agents that include the entire Web in their searches.

Shopping bots have become very popular with consumers. In *Time,* International Data Corp. revealed that about 4 million shoppers took advantage of the technology in October 2000 alone. However, they weren't popular with some companies because of their ability to initiate bidding wars and eat away profits in the process.

In addition to searching for durable goods, electronics and other items, consumers also were expected to use intelligent agents more frequently in the area of personal finance. In *Bank Systems & Technology,* a report from Andersen Consulting stated that personal financial bots (PFBs) would reshape this industry by becoming "virtual financial intermediaries" that carry out transactions and searches for financial products via ATMs, wireless phones, and televisions. While this concept had not been widely adopted in the early 2000s, it posed a possible threat to the umbrella model used by many traditional banks, in which several products and services—including loans, credit cards and insurance—were offered to customers by one provider.

Intelligent agents also provide varying levels of customer service on the Web. In addition to providing direct answers to common questions, they can save companies money by helping customers narrow down their problem before speaking to a live customer service rep. One emerging intelligent agent was able to anticipate what customers might want based on the Web pages they looked at. Created by Denver-based Finali, the netSage also was able to mimic human emotions, including disappointment if it was unable to answer a customer's question. In addition to reducing customer service costs, intelligent agents are useful for converting potential customers, many of whom abandon online "shopping carts" without making purchases, to actual customers.

Although they have been used more frequently in the consumer arena, intelligent agents also have potential applications in the area of business-to-business e-commerce. For example, a manufacturer requiring many different parts to create one product could use an intelligent agent to not only find the best prices from different suppliers, but to consider many other variables that impact the total manufacturing cost, such as shipping, cost and quality. Theoretically, the intelligent agent could do this more quickly and efficiently than a human. Ultimately, this could result in significant cost savings for companies.

By maximizing efficiency and convenience, intelligent agents will likely play increasingly important roles in the world of e-commerce. In *Computer Reseller News,* the Gartner Group estimated that bots would account for as much as four percent of all IT spending by 2002. The following statement from IBM, printed in *Computerworld,* is further indication of the key role this technology will play in the near future: "We envision the Internet some years hence as a seething milieu in which billions of economically motivated software agents find and process information... Agents will naturally evolve from facilitators into decision-makers."

As IBM's vision becomes reality, security will become a concern for buyers and sellers alike. When consumers send agents out with strategic objectives and the ability to negotiate terms and conditions and make purchases on their behalf, they will need assurances that the agents can't be manipulated or compromised by other agents. Likewise, companies will need to watch for agents that are used for malicious purposes.

FURTHER READING:

Allen, Maryellen Mott. "The Myth of Intelligent Agents." *Online,* November/December 2000.

Baumohl, Bernard. "Can You Really Trust Those Bots?" *Time,* December 11, 2000.

Clancy, Heather. "Bots on Parade for ISVs." *Computer Reseller News,* November 20, 2000.

Gove, Alex. "Bot and Sold." *Red Herring Magazine,* August 1999. Available from www.redherring.com.

Mandry, Torsten; Pernul, Gunther; and Alexander W. Rohm. ''Mobile Agents in Electronic Markets: Opportunities, Risks, Agent Protection.'' *International Journal of Electronic Commerce,* Winter 2000-2001.

Pallmann, David. *Programming Bots, Spiders, and Intelligent Agents in Microsoft Visual C++.* Redmond, Washington: Microsoft Press. 1999.

Schwartz, Ephraim. ''Web Bots Enhance Self-Service Experience.'' *InfoWorld,* February 7, 2000.

Schneider, Ivan. ''R2-D2 Meets 401(k).'' *Bank Systems & Technology,* November 2000.

''Special Issue: Intelligent Agents for Electronic Commerce.'' *International Journal of Electronic Commerce,* Spring 2000.

Trott, Bob. ''Online Agents Evolve for Customer Service.'' *InfoWorld,* December 11, 2000.

Ulfelder, Steve. ''Undercover Agents.'' *Computerworld,* June 5, 2000.

SEE ALSO: Shopping bots

INTERCHANGE AND INTERCHANGE FEE

The vast majority of financial transactions that happen during e-commerce involve credit cards, especially those between consumers and companies that sell goods and services. The credit cards that consumers use are issued by one of many different card-issuing banks throughout the world, to which one must apply and be approved before receiving a card. In general, when credit cards are used to make purchases several different parties are usually involved. These include the cardholder, card-issuing bank, merchant, and the acquiring bank that handles credit card transactions for the merchant.

Interchange is the process by which a card-issuing bank transfers monies to a merchant's acquiring bank in order to cover a cardholder's purchase. During interchange, the card-issuing bank deducts an interchange fee for every transaction. The interchange fee eventually is passed along to the merchant, along with other ''discount fees'' that make it possible for acquiring banks to profit from the transactions. The income that card-issuing banks received by charging interchange fees was growing in the early 2000s, partly because interest income was decreasing. According to *Credit Card Management,* interchange income increased 28 percent during 1999, at which time it represented 14 percent of card issuers' revenues.

Interchange fees have been a source of controversy, especially in the area of anti-trust violations. *Antitrust Bulletin* argued that ''interchange fees for modern payment card systems are part of a long historical line of vertical price restrictions that have reflected the exercise of market power. When new payment systems require the cooperation of large segments of the banking industry, it naturally gives rise to the concern that those banks will enact systems and rules that are not necessary to the success of the payment system, but that result in a significant reduction in the benefits that will flow to the public from the new technology.''

In October 2000 the European Commission opened an investigation after receiving complaints about Visa's interchange fees from Eurotrade, a European retail industry association. The commission charged that Visa was acting like a cartel because of the way it determined and set fees. Visa denied the charges, arguing that interchange fees benefit both consumers and competition.

FURTHER READING:

Britt, Phil. ''Credit & Debit Cards: Can Community Banks Compete?'' *Community Banker,* June 2000.

Chang, Howard H. and David S. Evans. ''The Competitive Effects of the Collective Setting of Interchange Fees by Payment Card Systems.'' *Antitrust Bulletin,* Fall 2000.

Daly, James J. ''Many Happy Returns.'' *Credit Card Management,* May 2000.

''Visa Hits Rough Waters Abroad.'' *Credit Card Management,* December 2000.

SEE ALSO: Acquiring Bank; Card-Issuing Bank; Transaction Issues

INTERNATIONAL CHAMBER OF COMMERCE (ICC)

The International Chamber of Commerce (ICC), also known as the world business organization, was founded in 1919 to promote peace among countries through trade and prosperity. The ICC grew throughout the century to become the leading body of representation for enterprises around the globe. Its rules and guidelines, while being voluntary, govern international business actions and have become a standard used by ICC members, which include businesses and associations in over 130 countries involved in international trade. The ICC was given the highest level of consultative status with the United Nations shortly after its formation.

The ICC is involved in business related issues such as trade and investment policy, financial services, information technologies, telecommunications, marketing ethics, the environment, transportation, competition law, and intellectual property. As an increasing number of business transactions began taking place on the World Wide Web throughout the 1990s, the ICC began focusing on Internet-related issues and formed the Commission on Telecommunications and Information Technologies. The commission was founded to ''formulate policy on issues such as electronic business, information security, telecommunications, and competition,'' according to the ICC. Upon its formation, its agenda included advising governments on competition in the telecommunications industry and pushing for the implementation and increased development of the World Trade Organization telecommunications agreement, along with aiding developing countries in meeting telecommunications objectives.

Along with the development of the Commission, the ICC also created the Electronic Commerce Project (ECP). The ECP consisted of experts from various other ICC commissions including Banking Technique and Practice, Telecommunications and Information Technologies, Financial Services and Insurance, Transport, and International Commercial Practice. According to the ICC, the ECP was developed ''to create global trust in electronic trade transactions by defining best business practices for the digital age.'' In 2001, the project was divided into three major areas including the General Usage for Internationally Digitally Ensured Commerce (GUIDEC), the Electronic Trade Practices Working Group, and E-terms service.

GUIDEC, a set of international rules, definitions, and guidelines for the use of electronic authentication techniques, was the first ECP initiative. It became available on the ICC Web site in November 1997 and was considered to be one of the first sets of global regulations for electronic commerce. GUIDEC was created to promote a global understanding of techniques used in electronic commerce and business transactions on the Internet, and to ''establish a general framework for the ensuring and certification of digital messages, based upon existing law and practice in different legal systems.''

The Electronic Trade Practices Working Group (ETP) was also developed to establish a set of rules regarding electronic trade and settlement. The ETP was formed to make trade more efficient on the Internet by setting guidelines for buyers and sellers who negotiate; make contracts; and arrange for financing, transport, and insurance on the Web. The ETP has worked to integrate international trade regulations that typically related to transactions in the physical world with those taking place with more frequency on the Web.

The third component of the ECP, E-terms service, was in its developmental stage in 2001. Designed to serve small businesses needing legal expertise, E-terms service provided the information needed to write online contracts and conduct business transactions on the Web.

The ICC, while working on its own e-commerce projects, also worked with many other international organizations to aid in the development of global e-commerce. In 2000, the ICC teamed up with the Business and Industry Advisory Committee to the Organization for Economic Co-Operation and Development, and over 72 companies that make up The Global Business Dialogue on Electronic Commerce (GBDe). Together, the organizations formed agreements to work together to identify ''best practices'' for electronic commerce and develop guidelines for Internet property rights and cybersecurity.

The ICC was also a founding member of the Alliance for Global Business (AGB), a group of major international trade associations that was created to provide information and leadership on e-commerce related issues. The ICC also played a large role in formation of the Global Action Plan for Electronic Commerce released by the Global Information Infrastructure Commission (GIIC) in October 1999. The plan was developed to boost consumer confidence in e-business by providing guidelines for self-regulation among businesses that provide products and services on the Web. Through its Telecommunications and Information Technologies Commission, the ICC also provided a forum for discussions on telecommunications and information technologies for intergovernmental organizations such as the International Telecommunications Union (ITU), World Bank, United Nations Committee on Trade and Development (UNCTAD), and the International Standards Organization (ISO).

In February 2001, Talal Abu-Ghazaleh was elected chairman of the Commission on Telecommunications and Information Technology and pledged that the ICC would continue its efforts relating to global e-commerce. In a 2001 ICC press release, Abu-Ghazaleh stated, ''the Internet may have transformed the way people live and work in the developed world, but for a vast proportion of the world's population, it remains an inaccessible pipe dream. ICC will work through its countless member companies in the developing world and in tandem with other international organizations to ensure the vast potential of the Internet to generate prosperity in all corners of the globe is realized.''

FURTHER READING:

International Chamber of Commerce. ''GUIDEC.'' Paris: International Chamber of Commerce, 2001. Available from www.iccwbo.org/home/guidec.

International Chamber of Commerce. ''ICC's New Business Chief to Focus on Developing World.'' Paris: International Chamber of Commerce, February 15, 2001. Available from www.iccwbo.org.

International Chamber of Commerce. "The ICC Electronic Commerce Project." Paris: International Chamber of Commerce, 2001. Available from www.iccwbo.org.

Mahoney, Michael. "Europeans Crack Down on $3.9B Internet Banking Scam." *E-Commerce Times,* April 12, 2001. Available from www.ecommercetimes.com.

SEE ALSO: BBB OnLine Inc.; General Usage for Internationally Digitally Ensured Commerce (GUIDEC); Global Trading Web Association

INTERNATIONAL DATA CORP. (IDC)

With more than 45 offices worldwide, roughly 800 employees, and sales of approximately $150 million, International Data Corp. (IDC) is an information technology (IT) market research, analysis, and consulting leader. The firm's wide ranging research covers all aspects of the IT industry, including operating systems, PCs, peripheral equipment, semiconductors, software, services, telecommunications products, distribution channels, and the Internet. IDC's 3,900 clients—mainly IT professionals, IT suppliers, e-business executives, service suppliers, investment professionals, and corporate managers—have access to various information services, conferences, and research documents, many of which are available for purchase at IDC's online store. Those who opt for customized consulting appointments with IDC analysts may seek assistance with business strategy development, product development, assessment of competition, creation and achievement of marketing goals, and evaluation of potential alliances and purchases. Based in Framingham, Massachusetts, IDC operates as a subsidiary of International Data Group, the largest technology publisher in the world with sales of more than $3 billion and 12,000 employees.

IDC was founded in 1964 by Patrick J. McGovern, a biophysics graduate from the Massachusetts Institute of Technology (MIT), to offer IT statistics to the fledgling computer industry. While earning his degree at MIT, McGovern had worked as the associate editor for *Computers and Automation,* the first computer magazine published in the United States. When he graduated in 1959, McGovern had been promoted to associate publisher, a position he held for the next five years.

In 1967, IDC began publishing *Computerworld,* a weekly newspaper covering the computer industry. Eventually, publishing became the firm's main focus. By 1970, McGovern had moved his publishing activities—which eventually would include industry giants like *PC World, MacWorld, Network World,* and *CIO*—into a new entity called International Data Group (IDG). It was under this parent that IDC began to operate as a subsidiary.

The firm conducted its first industry briefing session in 1968. IDC expanded internationally for the first time in 1969, when it established an office in the United Kingdom. Six years later, the firm moved into both Germany and Japan. IDC bought Link Resources Corp. in 1980. Within three years, 13 offices were in operation, including units in Spain, France, Italy, Sweden, and Norway. IDC created IDC China Ltd. in 1986. By the end of the decade, the firm also had moved into Canada, Korea, and Latin America.

Kirk Campbell was named IDC president and CEO in 1990. IDC held its first European IT Forum in Venice, Italy, in 1991; roughly 200 industry professionals attended. International expansion continued the following year with the establishment of new offices in Greece, Nigeria, Turkey, South Africa, and Egypt. The firm conducted its Global New Media survey for the first time in 1995. Participants from 13 different countries were queried. That year, IDC created a subsidiary in Brazil. Aggressive growth efforts persisted in 1996 with the creation of a market research office in Moscow, Russia, and a Latin American research center in Miami, Florida. Sales that year reached roughly $100 million. By then, the firm was operating offices in 400 countries, employing 300 market researchers, and generating more than 2,000 IT market surveys each year.

Wanting to grant clients 24-hour access to its information, IDC launched its Internet-based IDCNet service in 1997. The firm conducted its first forum for Internet executives the following year. Sales in 1999 grew another 22 percent, and the firm's workforce grew by 17 percent to nearly 600. IDC began offering free IT industry newsletters, including *e-Business Trends* and *xSP Advisor,* via e-mail in 2000. Archived newsletter articles also were made available on IDC's Web site. The firm's rapid growth finally came to a halt that year as the dot-com meltdown undercut the need for e-commerce market research, prompting IDC to lay off numerous e-commerce analysts in 2001.

FURTHER READING:

"Company Information." Framingham, MA: International Data Corp., 2001. Available from www.idc.com.

Konicki, Steve. "Economic Slowdown Hits Hard at Analyst Firms." *InformationWeek.* September 10, 2001.

Violino, Bob; and Rich Levin. "Analyzing the Analysts." *InformationWeek.* November 17, 1997.

SEE ALSO: Information Technology; Internet Access, Tracking Growth of

INTERNATIONAL TELECOMMUNICATIONS UNION (ITU)

The International Telecommunications Union dates back to 1865, when 20 countries jointly signed the framework agreement at the International Telegraph Convention, establishing common rules and standard equipment for transmitting telegraph messages across international lines. The International Telegraph Union was launched to provide a forum to turn this agreement into a living framework through the evolution of international communications technologies, facilitating dialogue and enabling amendments to the initial agreement. Within a matter of years, the International Telegraph Union was busily devising legislation aimed at developing international standards for telephony and radio communications, further solidifying its role as the primary body governing and promoting international communications.

In 1932, the Telegraph Union merged the 1865 International Telegraph Convention and the 1906 International Radiotelegraph Convention into one agreement called the International Telecommunications Convention, and in 1934 changed its name to the International Telecommunications Union (ITU), assuming responsibility for promoting and standardizing all international communications. The ITU moved under the auspices of the United Nations in 1947 under an agreement aimed at modernizing the union.

In 1989, at a Plenipotentiary Conference held in Nice, France, the ITU took responsibility for spearheading technical telecommunications assistance to developing countries, placing such activities on a par with their traditional standardization and coordination activities. Through the Telecommunications Development Bureau, established the following year, technological developments in telecommunications are met with new initiatives from the ITU aimed at integrating these innovations into the infrastructures of developing countries, thereby connecting them to a broader world network. Its most ambitious development on this front at the start of the 2000s was its leadership in the development of a Global Information Infrastructure (GII), an international network aimed at providing universal access to modern telecommunications and information technologies so as to level the playing field between nations and help integrate and further the global economy.

In this way, the ITU was busily working to bridge the digital divide, a contemporary situation within what the ITU refers to, more broadly, as the "telecommunications gap." The ITU saw telecommunications infrastructure as the principal problem underlying the digital divide, and promoted itself not so much as a regulator but as a facilitator for different policymakers from across the world to hammer out compromises, insisting that its regulatory scope was limited to ensuring open access to telecommunications.

In the United States, however, the ITU generated its share of criticism, most particularly because the body increasingly served as a forum for countries registering complaints against the United States. For instance, in the late 1990s and early 2000s countries complained to the ITU that U.S. Internet users and carriers were the largest users of their international circuits but didn't pay for them, urging the ITU to compel U.S. carriers to shoulder some of the costs through a global charging mechanism. The U.S. is only one vote out of 189 countries at ITU, and thus lacks the power within the body that it exercises throughout the world economy, making it less capable of shaping the agenda. As a result, many U.S. policy makers and business leaders were extremely skeptical of the ITU. Partly as a result of this resistance from the U.S. and partly due to the largely self-regulated nature of the Internet, the ITU, while overseeing the broader telecommunications development schemes, had little voice in setting standards for the Internet itself.

FURTHER READING:

International Telecommunications Union. "Welcome to the International Telecommunications Union." Geneva, Switzerland: International Telecommunications Union, 2001. Available from www.itu.int.

Lynch, Grahame. "The World vs. America." *America's Network,* January 1, 2001.

Malim, George. "E-Commerce a Priority." *Telecommunications,* August 1999.

Yarbrough, Tanya L. "Connecting the World: The Development of the Global Information Infrastructure." *Federal Communications Law Journal,* March 2001

SEE ALSO: Digital Divide

INTERNET

An online network linking million of computers throughout the world, the Internet is used by millions of people for things like research, communication, and commerce transactions. Via technology that spawned the "information age," the Internet has become a tool millions of individuals employ every day for professional, educational, and personal exchanges. As the Internet's popularity has increased, so have the opportunities for making money online. The skyrocketing stock prices of Internet-based companies like Web browser firm Netscape, book retailer Amazon.com, and auction site ebay.com in the mid-1990s reflected common perceptions about the Internet's potential as a commerce tool. Although investors began shunning these stocks later in the decade as analysts started to examine the business models of Internet-based businesses more closely, the Internet already had been firmly established as a viable means of conducting commerce.

The precursor of the Internet, ARPAnet, was created in 1969 by the Advanced Research Projects Agency (ARPA) at the directive of U.S. Department of Defense, which sought a means for governmental communication in the event of nuclear war. To create what would become the world's largest wide area network (WAN), ARPA chose Interface Message Processors (IMPs) to connect host computers via telephone lines. To create the underlying network needed to connect the IMPs, ARPA hired Bolt Beranek and Newman, a Cambridge, Massachusetts-based research and development firm. The last component needed was a protocol, or a set of standards, that would facilitate communication between the host sites. This was developed internally by the Network Working Group. ARPAnet's Network Control Protocol allowed users to access computers and printers in remote locations and exchange files between computers. This protocol eventually was replaced by the more sophisticated Transmission Control Protocol/Internet Protocol (TCP/IP), which allowed ARPAnet to be connected with a several other networks that had been launched by various institutions. It was this group of networks that eventually formed the core of what later became known as the Internet. No longer useful, ARPAnet was shut down in 1990.

A National Science Foundation decree that prevented commercial use of the Internet was dissolved in 1991, the same year the World Wide Web came into existence. By then, personal computer use by businesses, institutions, and individuals had spiraled. When the graphics-based Web browsing program known as Mosaic was released in 1993, the Internet's growth exploded. Firms like Netscape and Yahoo! were founded soon after, making access to the Internet even easier. By 1996, an estimated 40 million individuals were accessing the Internet, and by 1999, that number had grown to 200 million.

FURTHER READING:

"Internet." In *Ecommerce Webopedia*. Darien, CT: Internet.com, 2001. Available from e-comm.webopedia.com.

"Internet." In *Techencyclopedia*. Point Pleasant, PA: Computer Language Co., 2001. Available from www.techweb.com/encyclopediat.

"An Internet Time Line." *PC Week*. November 18, 1996.

National Museum of American History. "Birth of the Internet: ARPANET: General Overview." Washington, D.C.: Smithso-

nian Institution. Available from smithsonian.yahoo.com/arpanet2.

PBS Online. "PBS Life on the Internet: Timeline." Alexandria, VA: PBS Online, 2001.

SEE ALSO: ARPAnet; Berners-Lee, Timothy; Communications Protocol; History of the Internet and World Wide Web (WWW); Internet Infrastructure; MIT and the Galactic Network

INTERNET ACCESS, TRACKING GROWTH OF

Tracking the growth of Internet access has become increasingly popular as the Web continues to evolve into a tool for gathering information, communication, marketing, and commerce. According to NUA Internet Surveys, the number of people online increased to 513.41 million in August 2001. Africa accounted for 4.15 million online users. The Asia/Pacific region had 143.99 million Web surfers. There were 154.63 million people with access in Europe, 4.65 million in the Middle East, 180.68 million in Canada and the U.S., and 25.33 million in Latin America. Tracking both access and usage patterns has begun to play an important role in e-business strategies as enterprises see Web surfers and advertisers as potential revenue generators.

Beginning in the mid-1990s, surveys were used as a tool for measuring Internet access. Michigan State University professors Mark I. Wilson and Hairong Li described these surveys in a paper entitled "Measuring Internet Access and Use: Conceptual and Methodological Issues" when they presented at the 1999 International Conference on the Measurement of Electronic Commerce in Singapore. "Surveys can be used in a number of ways to assess the state of the Internet, providing information about both access levels and user characteristics," the pair claimed. Surveys that continue to be used to guage Internet access include general population surveys, online surveys, and random surveys.

In general population surveys, a sample of the general population is taken to compare those that have Internet access with those who do not. Online surveys, on the other hand, are used to discover certain characteristics of those who already use the Internet. Two popular types of online surveys include "one-step" and "two-step" surveys. In a one-step survey, Web surfers are able to participate by simply answering a series of questions found on the Web site of the firm conducting the survey. In 1994, the Graphics, Visualization, and Usability Center (GVU) of Georgia Tech University began using these types of surveys to study Internet access. The GVU would post a survey on its Web site and then solicit participation by advertising in newsgroups, sending email, and by using banner ads on search engine sites. Unlike a one-step survey, a two-step survey involves securing a pool of Internet users who are willing to act as survey participants. Polling companies, including Harris Interactive Inc., select participants from their pools to participate in various surveys. A random survey is conducted via the telephone or through personal interviews. Companies including MediaMark Research Inc. and IntelliQuest Inc. began random surveys in the mid-1990s to gather information about Internet usage.

Along with surveys, Internet access is also recorded through tracking. Two forms of tracking became popular in the 1990s: site-centric and user-centric. According to the aforementioned paper, in a site-centric approach ''server log files are analyzed to generate statistics on the numbers of times a Web page was requested and number of users who visited a page or site.'' The user-centric method, however, tracks Internet access by installing a device on a willing participant's computer that monitors his or her Web and e-mail use.

While there were many organizations that tracked and researched Internet access and usage patterns in the new millennium, keeping tabs on the growth of Internet access was not an exact science. Several factors continue to hinder the accuracy of Web measurement. First of all, the rapid growth of the Internet makes gathering information about its size extremely difficult. While the percentage of growth has slowed since the late 1990s, the number of people accessing the Internet continues to rise each year causing information regarding Internet access to become obsolete in a short period of time. Second, the Web has no spatial or geographic boundaries. Third, tracking Internet access is a relatively new concept, and as such, there is much debate on how to measure the growth of the Web. Lastly, concern exists over standards and the impartiality of those measuring access and usage.

MAJOR INTERNET TRACKING FIRMS

NETRATINGS, INC. NetRatings was created in July 1997 to provide accurate and timely Internet audience information and to monitor and track Internet audience exposure and interaction with Web-based advertising. The company was established through a partnership with Hitachi Ltd. In October 1998, NetRatings teamed up with Nielsen Media Research to develop and market Internet measurement and tracking services under the Nielsen/NetRatings name. By 1999, the firm had launched its audience measurement service and secured over 100 customers in its first month of operation. Later that year, NetRatings

debuted its Internet Investment Strategies service, which catered to the online investment industry by providing information on Internet use and trends in that market. The firm also launched its E-commerce Strategies service, which tracked user activity on commerce-based Web sites.

In September 1999, NetRatings partnered with ACNielsen and eRatings.com to provide global measurement services in countries including Europe, Asia, the Middle East, and Africa. By then, operations spanned the 29 countries that accounted for 91 percent of the Internet population. By the time the firm went public in December, it had launched its Internet Media Strategies service, which offered information on streaming media and Internet connectivity speeds, as well as local market data for businesses seeking demographic information. NetRatings continued its international expansion in 2000, entering the French and Latin American markets. It also forged alliances with the likes of Spectra Inc., Claritas Inc., and Yahoo! Inc. to further develop its Internet usage and measurement services. During that year, the firm released its first report on Internet access and usage in Europe, Asia Pacific, and North America.

In 2001, Netratings joined with Harris Interactive to create eCommercePulse, a service that tracked online consumer spending and behavior. By then, the firm had become a leading provider of audience measurement and tracking tools with over 225,000 tracking meters installed on computers in both work and home situations in 29 countries across the globe. Its customers included traditional brick-and-mortar and consumer packaged goods firms using online marketing and advertising, companies involved in Web-based commerce, advertising firms, media and content Web sites, and investment firms. Through its Global Internet Trends service, it provided its clients with information on worldwide Internet access and usage trends, as well as information concerning Web access in the United States. For example, according to an October 2001 NetRatings report, the Internet population in the U.S. increased by 15 percent in 2001, to 115.2 million Web surfers, and the number of Americans with Internet access increased to 62 percent, up from 57 percent in 2000.

JUPITER MEDIA METRIX Jupiter Media Metrix is another popular Internet tracking firm. Formed from the merger of Jupiter Communications LLC and Media Metrix in September 2000, the company has over 1,800 clients—including advertisers, media companies, e-commerce and technology-based firms, and financial institutions—that utilize its site measurement and audience measurement services.

Jupiter Communications was formed in 1986 by Josh Harris, who started out writing industry reports relating to the entrance of telephone companies into the information technology industry. By 1989, these reports were quite popular and Harris was hosting annual conferences related to his research. The following year, Gene DeRose joined Harris; soon thereafter, the pair began to shift the company's focus to tracking developments related to the Internet. As the Web evolved into a marketing and selling venue, Jupiter focused on providing research that detailed consumer behavior on the Internet. By 1997, the firm was publishing seven monthly newsletters, dozens of industry reports, and hosting eight annual conferences.

Media Metrix had its beginnings as a product research and development division of market research firm NPD Group Inc. In March of 1996, NPD established PC Meter L.P. to develop and market Internet audience measurement services. The following year, PC Meter changed its name to Media Metrix. Eventually, NPD spun off Media Metrix via an initial public offering, and the newly public firm grew in the late 1990s through a series of acquisitions including RelevantKnowledge Inc. and AdRelevance.

By mid-2000, both Jupiter and Media Metrix were struggling, as many businesses began to cut budgets related to their e-business strategies. As a result, Jupiter agreed to be purchased by Media Metrix in a $414 million deal. The newly formed company, Jupiter Media Metrix, hoped to attract new clients by combining Jupiter's site measurement services along with Media Metrix's Digital Media Audience Ratings service. Site measurement services included visitor statistics, which tracked the frequency of a customer's visit, how much time a customer spent at the site, and how the customer got to the site. The audience-ratings service used real-time meters placed on over 100,000 computers across the globe. The information gathered from these meters provided information on the demographics, behavior, and usage patterns of Web surfers.

While NetRatings and Jupiter Media Metrix provided similar services, both companies measured Internet access based on their own proprietary systems. Because tracking Internet access remained an inexact science, the two company's findings did not always match, a fact which created some controversy. For example, in October 2001, both companies released reports that rated the top Web sites based on number of visits by both at-home and at-work Web surfers. NetRatings' results ranked Microsoft Corp.'s MSN network number three behind AOL Time Warner and Yahoo! Inc., while Jupiter's results ranked MSN number two, ahead of Yahoo!. While both MSN and Yahoo! could claim a top spot over their competitor based on the different reports, those utilizing the rankings as a basis for advertising decisions were left confused, not knowing which site was truly the leader.

In October 2001, NetRatings announced its intent to acquire Jupiter for over $70 million. The merger was scheduled for completion in 2002, and upon conclusion of the deal, both companies hoped to set one standard for Internet tracking. While the outcome of the deal remains to be seen, tracking Internet access and usage patterns will, no doubt, remain an important part of e-business strategy as Web-based commerce and marketing continue to grow.

FURTHER READING:

Jaffe, Sam. ''Why Jupiter Could Juice Up Media Metrix.'' *BusinessWeek Online,* July 17, 2000. Available from www.businessweek.com.

Jupiter Media Metrix Inc. ''Corporate Fact Sheet.'' New York: Jupiter Media Metrix Inc., 2001. Available from www.jmm.com.

Li, Hairong, and Mark I. Wilson. ''Measuring Internet Access and Use: Conceptual and Methodological Issues.'' Paper presented at the International Conference on the Measurement of Electronic Commerce, December 1999.

Messina, Judith. ''Web-gazing Pays for Research Firm.'' *Crain's New York Business,* August 11, 1997, 19.

Mullins, Robert. ''Internet Ratings Merger Expected to Bring New Measurement.'' *San Jose Business Journal,* November 2, 2001, 19.

NetRatings Inc. ''Company Overview.'' Milpitas, CA: NetRatings Inc., 2001. Available from www.neilsen-netratings.com.

NUA Internet Surveys. ''How Many Online?'' Dublin, Ireland: Scope Communications Group, 2001. Available from www.nua.ie.

SEE ALSO: Digital Divide; International Data Corp. (IDC); Jupiter Media Metrix; Market Research

INTERNET INFRASTRUCTURE

Generally speaking, infrastructures are the frameworks or architectures that systems are made of. For example, a nation's transportation infrastructure consists of roadways, railroads, airports, ocean ports, and rivers. Although not as visible to the naked eye, the Internet also has an infrastructure consisting of many different elements, each of which plays a critical role in the delivery of information from one point to another.

EVOLUTION OF THE INTERNET INFRASTRUCTURE

Simply defined, the Internet is a very large network of many other computer networks. The United States Government played an important role in creating what eventually became the Internet during the

1960s. The Department of Defense Advanced Research Projects Agency (DARPA) funded early research into packet switching technology, which computer systems use to communicate. This approach differed from the way telephone systems transmitted data. Packet switching technology led to the development of ARPANET, the Internet's predecessor.

DARPA, the Defense Communications Agency, and Stanford University supported the development of important communication protocols—called Transmission Control Protocol and Internet Protocol (TCP/IP)—that define the way information is transmitted on the Internet. TCP/IP became the standard communication protocol used on ARPANET in January of 1983. Generally speaking, communication protocols like TCP/IP are the means by which devices understand and agree upon how and when they will share information with one another.

In 1990, ARPANET was succeeded by NS-FNET, which the National Science Foundation created in 1987 to link university computer science departments across the United States. The NSF established regional networks that aggregated traffic from the universities and accordingly fed it into the ''backbone'' of NSFNET. The universities that connected to the NFSNET backbone further connected other networks of colleges and individuals.

In 1995, the NSF did away with its backbone and turned what had been NSFNET over to the commercial sector. It created network access points (NAPs) that made it possible for telecommunication companies like MCI and Sprint to establish Internet backbones of their own, to which national or regional Internet Service Providers (ISPs) could connect. Organizations or individuals seeking Internet access then had to obtain it directly from a NAP, or subscribe to ISPs like America Online (AOL) with NAP access.

ELEMENTS OF THE INTERNET INFRASTRUCTURE

At the most rudimentary level of the Internet infrastructure are endless miles of telephone lines and fiber optic cable. These cables connect millions of individual users and businesses to other parties, transmitting data at varying speeds, depending on the types of cabling used. Another factor that affects the speed and quality of a user's connection is the means of connection, which include telephone modems; high-speed connection methods like cable modems, ISDN, DSL, and T1 lines; and company networks. According to the Strategis Group, high-speed residential Internet service was expected to surpass telephone dial-up methods in the United States by 2005, at which time Strategis predicted there would be 36 million broadband subscribers.

It's easier to understanding how pieces of the Internet infrastructure work if one visualizes them transmitting data. The first step involved in sending or receiving data involves ISPs, which maintain racks upon racks of modems. Users connect to these modems in order to gain access to the ISP's network, which can vary in reach depending on the ISP's size. In the early 2000s, there were more than 7,000 ISPs throughout the world. The top 10 accounted for only 25 percent of total Internet access traffic. Once connected to an ISP, users then attempt to communicate by sending e-mail messages to other Internet users or by requesting Web pages or downloadable files from any number of servers located across the world. Servers are the computers used by individuals, companies, and other organizations to host Web sites, e-mail systems, or files that can be downloaded.

The process used to send and receive information across the world is more or less hidden to the user, and occurs in just seconds. In order for this to happen, a user on one ISP's network must be able to connect to users on another ISP's network, which may be located across the nation or across the globe. An exception to this would be if two users were located on the same ISP's network. ISPs connect to one another at NAPs, also called Internet exchanges (IX), which are major pieces of the Internet's backbone.

When the NSF opened the Internet to commercial enterprises in 1995, the first NAPs were located in Chicago; Pennsauken, New Jersey; Washington, D.C.; and San Francisco. These were operated by Ameritech, Sprint, Pac Bell, and MFS (a predecessor of MCI WorldCom). MFS later created two coastal access points called metropolitan area exchanges (MAE). By the early 2000s, there were more than 10 major access points throughout the United States. Sometimes ISPs make arrangements to establish direct connections between their networks. Known as private peering, this eliminates the need for relying on one of the major NAPs and helps to reduce congestion on the Internet.

Devices known as routers make sure that the packets of data sent from a computer on one ISP's network are sent to the intended machine on another local or wide-area network via the quickest, most efficient route, in accordance with communication protocols like TCP/IP. Just as the post office needs to know a street address before it can deliver a letter, routers need to know the address of the device to which information is being sent via the Internet. All devices communicating on the Internet, including servers used to host Web sites, have unique Internet Protocol (IP) addresses, which are four sets of numbers separated by decimals. Corresponding to numeric IP addresses are domain names, which are easier for humans to remember than long sequences of numbers. In the Web site address www.yahoo.com,.COM (like.ORG or.NET) is called the top-level domain and the word

Yahoo is called the second-level domain. As the Internet evolved, a distributed database called the Domain Name System was created which contains all of the domain names and IP addresses associated with registered entities. Domain name servers located across the Internet are responsible for finding registered domain names and converting them to IP addresses so a connection can occur.

INSTITUTIONS OVERSEEING INTERNET INFRASTRUCTURE

In addition to the technical pieces of the Internet infrastructure, there are several organizations that regulate different aspects of it, or that seek to improve its stability and functionality. The Internet Society is a professional society that ''provides leadership in addressing issues that confront the future of the Internet, and is the organization home for the groups responsible for Internet infrastructure standards, including the Internet Engineering Task Force (IETF) and the Internet Architecture Board (IAB).'' The society's mission is ''to assure the open development, evolution, and use of the Internet for the benefit of all people throughout the world.''

According to the IAB, that organization is a technical advisory group whose responsibilities include providing ''oversight of the architecture for the protocols and procedures used by the Internet.'' It ''acts as a source of advice and guidance to the Board of Trustees and Officers of the Internet Society concerning technical, architectural, procedural, and (where appropriate) policy matters pertaining to the Internet and its enabling technologies.'' The IETF is ''a large open international community of network designers, operators, vendors, and researchers concerned with the evolution of the Internet architecture and the smooth operation of the Internet.''

Several other organizations were involved in overseeing the Internet in the early 2000s. The American Registry for Internet Numbers (ARIN) was a non-profit organization that administered and registered IP numbers for North America, South America, the Caribbean, and sub-Saharan Africa. Two other regional Internet registries, Reseaux IP Europeens Network Coordination Centre (RIPE NCC), and the Asia Pacific Network Information Centre (APNIC) were responsible for administration and registration for the rest of the world.

The Internet Corporation for Assigned Names and Numbers (ICANN) was a non-profit corporation ''formed to assume responsibility for the IP address space allocation, protocol parameter assignment, domain name system management, and root server system management functions previously performed under U.S. Government contract by IANA and other

entities.'' Domain names were assigned to people or organizations through a registration process performed by a number of different registrars accredited by ICANN. A company called Network Solutions was responsible for keeping track of registered domain names to avoid duplication.

Finally, the World Wide Web Consortium was an organization responsible for developing ''interoperable technologies (specifications, guidelines, software, and tools) to lead the Web to its full potential as a forum for information, commerce, communication, and collective understanding,'' and the Cooperative Association for Internet Data Analysis (CAIDA) collected, monitored, and analyzed information about Internet traffic patterns and performance that was useful to researchers, educators, and policy makers in a variety of fields.

INFRASTRUCTURE ADEQUACY

By the early 2000s, the size of and traffic on the Internet had grown significantly. Research from Telcordia revealed that the number of Internet hosts, which includes things like routers, mail servers, workstations, and Web servers, increased 45 percent during 2000, reaching 100 million. At that time, the global population of Internet users was estimated to be 350 million. Furthermore, the kinds of services, including e-commerce, being performed on the Internet were growing in sophistication and complexity. Corresponding to this were increasing demands in the areas of network quality and performance.

Concerns existed regarding the ability of the Internet, and the communication protocols it relied on, to support the world's users. This was complicated by the Internet's large size and the fact that no one entity controlled it. Therefore, the quality, integrity, and performance of different areas of the network varied, and control was distributed to many different entities throughout the world.

One infrastructure concern that existed in the early 2000s concerned the ability of routers to handle the skyrocketing number of entries to the Internet backbone's routing table, which stores information about all of the existing network destinations on the Internet. According to *Network World,* this was leading to instability in the Internet's backbone routing infrastructure. Part of the problem involved large companies that engaged in multi-homing, a practice of connecting to two ISPs at once in case service with one failed. Although this helped to ensure a more consistent Internet connection (which is critical for e-commerce companies), the practice required a separate listing in the routing table for each ISP used.

Another concern involved the burgeoning number of international users in developing nations without the sophisticated infrastructure found in Europe and the United States. In March of 2001, *Information-Week* reported that although 100 million computers were connected to the Internet, that figure represented less than two percent of the world's population. It also explained that 88 percent of Internet users lived in industrialized nations.

This placed increased demands on limited resources in developing nations. Telecordia's research found that while the ratio of Internet users to hosts was 2.4 to one in the United States, the number was as high as 100 to one in countries like India where, according to *eMarketer,* less than one percent of the adult population has Internet access. In India, 2.2 phone lines exist per 100 people, and many of those are substandard for connecting to the Internet at appropriate speeds. Inadequate infrastructures in areas like India and Latin America have strong implications for e-commerce. Forrester Research predicted that by 2004, 85 percent of online trade will occur in only 12 countries, led by the United States and Western Europe. Although wireless and satellite connections were one solution for nations where ground-based network infrastructures were virtually non-existent, the Internet's TCP/IP protocol didn't work consistently well via satellite, requiring special software to remedy the problem.

FURTHER READING:

''About Arin.'' American Registry for Internet Numbers. May 19, 2001. Available from www.arin.net.

''About ICANN.'' Internet Corporation for Assigned Names and Numbers. May 19, 2001. Available from www.icann.org.

''All About the Internet Society.'' The Internet Society. May 17, 2001. Available from www.isoc.org.

Botsford, Charles C. ''The Internet: Infrastructure and Technologies.'' *HowtoSubnet.com,* 1999. Available from www.learntosubnet.com/Internet_Infrastructure.htm.

Cerf, Vinton G. ''Computer Networking: Global Infrastructure for the 21st Century.'' 1997. Computing Research Association. Available from www.cs.washington.edu.

''eMarketer: The Net in India: a Luxury Few Can Afford.'' *Nua Internet Surveys,* January 8, 2001. Available from www.nua.net/surveys.

Marsan, Carolyn Duffy. ''Faster 'Net Growth Rate Raises Fears About Routers.'' *Network World,* April 2, 2001.

''Regional Registries System.'' Reseaux IP Europeens Network Coordination Centre. May 19, 2001. Available from www.ripe.net.

''Strategis Group: Broadband in U.S. to Peak in 2005.'' *Nua Internet Surveys,* January 24, 2001. Available from www.nua.net/surveys.

''Telcordia: Number of Internet Hosts Reaches 100 Million.'' *Nua Internet Surveys,* January 24, 2001. Available from www.nua.net/surveys.

Thareja, Ashok K. ''Enabling a Faster Global Internet Via Satellite.'' *Telecommunications,* February, 2001.

Thyfault, Mary E. ''Developing Nations Schooled in Quality, Reliability, Speed.'' *InformationWeek,* March 26, 2001.

Tyson, Jeff. ''How Internet Infrastructure Works.'' *How Stuff Works,* May 15, 2001. Available from www.howstuffworks.com.

Weinberg, Neal. ''Here's a Quiz: Can You Name the Top Five ISPs?'' *Network World,* April 16, 2001.

SEE ALSO: ARPAnet; Connectivity, Internet; Digital Divide; History of the Internet and World Wide Web (WWW); ICANN (Internet Corp. for Assigned Names and Numbers); Internet Access, Tracking growth of; Internet Society (ISOC); Optical Switching; Photonics; World Wide Web Consortium (W3C)

INTERNET METRICS

In general, Internet metrics encompass a wide variety of measurements or assessments made on the Internet. These can be very broad measurements, applying to the traffic patterns and usage of the Internet as a whole; or they can apply specifically to an organization's Internet infrastructure, which might include the network connections, cables, workstation computers, servers (computers used to host Web sites, shared software applications, and e-mail systems), and e-commerce software.

On the broader scale, Internet metrics refers to any number of Internet aspects that can be measured or presented in a statistical format, including online advertising industry revenue reports and projections, trends about the preferences of Web site users, or other statistics about the Internet economy. Global Internet metrics also apply to different technical aspects of the Internet's infrastructure, including the miles of cable that connect the world's computers, routers (computers that relay information between devices on the Internet and different Internet Service providers).

In the early 2000s, the Cooperative Association for Internet Data Analysis (CAIDA) was one organization devoted to Internet metrics on a large scale. CAIDA collected, monitored, analyzed, and visualized data about the Internet in four broad areas. Topology measurements helped to reveal global characteristics about the Internet, describing the ways in which the many networks that constitute the Internet are joined together, and revealing information about the size and constituency of the Internet's core. Workload measurements monitored the distribution and flow of Internet traffic. Performance measurements provided a means for ''isolating global problems within the infrastructure, as well as assessing service quality by country or other granularity of interest.'' Finally, routing data provided details about ''relationships between individual Autonomous Systems at a given point in time.''

Internet metrics also play critical roles at the organizational level. Just as companies use Internet metrics to measure, monitor, and report on their financial performance, successful ones also take steps to measure the electronic elements of their business efforts. This involves monitoring performance and statistics at the user (client) level, on the back end (different computer systems and databases that may be used during the company's e-commerce activities), and at a level in between these that includes things like network performance and servers.

To obtain metrics related specifically to Web sites, companies rely on software applications designed to provide details on a wide variety of factors, including everything from the number of hits, page views, and unique visitors a site registers within a specific time frame to click-through rates on banner advertising and information about the most-requested pages on a site. In the early 2000s, NetIQ's WebTrends software was among the leading applications in this area, and was used by 55,000 customers worldwide, including many *Fortune* 500 companies. Pharmacia & Upjohn, a leading pharmaceutical company, used WebTrends to determine who was using its corporate intranet and what information was being viewed. The intranet was launched in 1996 to provide a means of communicating with more than 30,000 employees worldwide. The software helped Pharmacia & Upjohn improve the design of the intranet and to improve its performance based on usage patterns.

Metrics related to Web site traffic can be used to lure potential advertisers to a company's site, to understand how customers use a Web site, and to improve or streamline processes that make a Web site experience better. However, as with any statistic, the meaning of Internet metrics varies depending on how they are calculated, the context in which they are used, and the value or weight users assigned to them. Additionally, different metrics mean different things to different parties. At a large magazine, for example, the publication's marketers may rely on one set of figures for e-commerce purposes, while the editorial department and potential advertisers review other numbers.

FURTHER READING:

Claffy, KC. "Tracking a Metamorphic Infrastructure." Cooperative Association for Internet Data Analysis (CAIDA), April 13, 2001. Available from www.caida.org.

Levine, Shira. "Tracking the Packets." *America's Network,* March 1, 2000.

NetIQ Corp. "Company Information." NetIQ Corp., July 8, 2001. Available from www.webtrends.com.

"Sizing up Internet Benchmarking Tools." *Folio,* Winter 2000/2001.

SEE ALSO: Internet Access Tracking, Growth of

INTERNET PAYMENT PROVIDER

Because they are widely used to pay for goods and services online, credit cards are an important part of e-commerce. According to Electronic Transfer Inc., analysts in the credit-card industry estimate that out of every four card holders, three use credit cards to place orders online. Just as consumers must apply to a card-issuing bank before they can receive and use a credit card, companies wishing to accept them as a means of payment must set up merchant accounts with banks. Although companies can establish merchant accounts directly with banks, it also is possible for this service to be handled by Internet payment providers. In addition to setting up merchant accounts, Internet payment providers also provide additional services that fill companies' needs related to the processing of financial transactions.

CyberCash Inc. was one leading Internet payment provider during the early 2000s. According to the company, it offered electronic payment software and services to more than 25,000 Internet merchants. Besides offering merchant accounts to companies so they could accept credit card payments from consumers, CyberCash provided solutions in the area of business-to-business transactions. These transactions extended beyond credit cards to include electronic fund transfer (EFT) and purchasing cards. The company also provided services in the area of fraud detection and risk management via FraudPatrol, its product that worked "by combining the advanced technology used by nine out of the top ten U.S. credit card issuers with comprehensive historical transaction data."

VeriFone was another leading Internet payment provider in the early 2000s. A division of Hewlett-Packard, the company provided payment solutions to consumers, merchants, and banks throughout the world. Its products included the point-of-sale terminals used at physical retail locations to process credit-card transactions, as well as software that accomplished the same for companies doing business on the Internet. VeriFone also provided installation, repair, and consulting services. According to the company, VeriFone has "shipped more than nine million electronic-payment systems, which are used in more than 100 countries."

Besides VeriFone and CyberCash, there were many other Internet Payment Providers in the early 2000s. Some catered to small- and medium-sized companies that experienced difficulty obtaining merchant accounts directly from banks. Others specialized in servicing companies in industry segments like adult entertainment or online wagering, which are considered to carry a higher-than-average risk for fraud or disputes. Many banks were leery to offer merchant accounts to e-commerce companies because of concerns over fraud and high charge-back rates, especially those in high-risk categories.

FURTHER READING:

"About CyberCash, Inc." CyberCash Inc. June 13, 2001. Available from www.cybercash.com/company.

"Delivering E-payment Solutions to the World." VeriFone. June 13, 2001. Available from www.hp.com/solutions1/verifone.

Hisey, Pete. "At War Over Merchant Risk." *Credit Card Management,* July 2000.

Messmer, Ellen. "Credit Crunch for E-comm Wannabes." *Network World,* May 31, 1999.

Sisk, Michael. "Enabling On-line Credit Card Use in Minutes, Not Weeks." *US Banker,* April 2000.

SEE ALSO: Acquiring Bank; Card-Issuing Bank; Charge-back; Interchange and Interchange Fee

INTERNET SERVICE PROVIDER (ISP)

Internet service providers (ISPs) provide access to the Internet through telephone dial-up connections as well as through permanent or "always-on" connections. As of 2001, businesses and consumers could choose from among an estimated 7,000 national, regional, or local ISPs.

HISTORY AND DEVELOPMENT

Prior to ISPs, access to the Internet required an account at a university or government agency and a working knowledge of Unix. The Internet began accepting commercial traffic in the early 1990s, but commercial users had to honor the peering protocol of swapping data free of charge. The National Science Foundation commissioned four private companies in 1994 to build public Internet access points, and in 1995 the federal government closed its own Internet backbone. Those four public access points—located in Washington, D.C., San Francisco, New Jersey, and Chicago—came under the control of WorldCom, Pacific Bell, Sprint, and Ameritech. As Internet traffic increased, those public access points became clogged, and the major telecommunications companies began building their own faster, private access points and

building out the Internet backbone. For a while the larger backbone providers established peering agreements with smaller ISPs, whereby they would swap Internet traffic for free. In 1997 UUNET, Sprint, and AT&T stopped peering with smaller ISPs and required them to pay fees to gain access to their networks.

At the beginning of 1995 there were approximately 160 commercial Internet access providers in the United States. According to *PC Magazine,* average monthly fees were about $17.50, with connect time billed at $3 per hour. Some ISPs could only be reached through a long-distance telephone call. ISPs offered Internet access through three basic types of accounts. Shell or terminal-emulation accounts connected the user to a Unix system with either a command-line interface or a proprietary GUI (graphical user interface). SLIP or PPP dial-up accounts used a modem to make a temporary direct Internet connection and required TCP/IP software. Permanent direct connections for LANs over leased lines were provided primarily for business customers. At the time America Online, CompuServe, and other online services offered limited Internet access. IBM and Microsoft were in the process of building Internet software into new versions of Windows and OS/2.

During 1995 the ISP market became more competitive. The dominant ISPs in 1995 were UUNET Technologies (annual revenue of $94 million), Netcom Online Communications Services ($52 million), and PSINet ($39 million). UUNET was focused on business and corporate customers, while Netcom pioneered flat-rate pricing for the consumer market. In addition to these national and international ISPs, the ISP market included large interexchange carriers, such as AT&T and MCI Communications Corp., and regional ISPs, which numbered in the thousands and were growing daily by mid-1996. Netcom began providing Internet service in 1995 and had 400,000 subscribers after one year in business. AT&T also entered the ISP market in 1995 and claimed it signed up 200,000 subscribers in the first few weeks. Both AT&T and MCI offered unlimited Internet access to consumers for a flat rate of $20 per month, while Netcom charged a flat fee of $20 for 400 hours per month. Sprint Corp. followed with a plan similar to its long-distance competitors, AT&T and MCI. UUNET, on the other hand, charged businesses an average of $1,000 a month for Internet service. Consumers were more interested in low-cost access, while reliability and speed were priorities for corporate customers.

At this stage the Internet was growing rapidly, and ISPs were challenged to build out their infrastructure, improve their router technology, and increase their access points. By 1996 regional Bell operating companies (RBOCs) and long-distance carriers were forming new subsidiaries to provide Internet service. After AT&T rolled out its WorldNet service in 1995, the RBOCs saw Internet service as a way to leverage their large networks. Pacific Bell, through its newly formed subsidiary Pacific Bell Internet, began offering Internet access in April 1996 to 75 percent of its residential customers in the San Francisco Bay area, Los Angeles, Sacramento, and San Diego, as well as dedicated frame relay access for businesses. Bell Atlantic's Internet Solutions began offering dedicated Internet service to businesses and flat-rate dial-up services to residential users in mid-1996.

PROLIFERATION AND CONSOLIDATION

According to *Boardwatch,* the number of ISPs increased from about 1,400 in early 1996 to 3,000 at the beginning of 1997. By mid-1997 there were an estimated 4,000 ISPs in the United States and Canada. Many of them were small operations that served consumers and small businesses in local markets by leasing and reselling the Internet services of larger ISPs. To stay in business smaller ISPs merged with the telephone companies to provide customers with a single source for a range of telecommunications services. Earthlink Network Inc. emerged as one of the largest national ISPs serving consumers, with 320,000 customers. Its strategy was to acquire smaller ISPs and make them part of the Earthlink network while letting them retain their local identities. Earthlink provided the smaller ISPs with Earthlink startup CDs, then handled the billing and services and paid the ISPs for the new customers.

Consolidation among ISPs and telephone companies began in earnest in 1997. Long-distance carrier WorldCom Inc. acquired UUNET's parent company MFS Communications Co. for $12 billion, giving WorldCom the second-largest Internet backbone in the United States. GTE Corp., the largest U.S. provider of regional telephone service, acquired Internet backbone operator BBN Corp. for $616 million. Digex Inc., an early ISP, was acquired by another ISP, Intermedia Communications, for $150 million.

ISPs also formed alliances to network and share their customers with other ISPs, so that users who traveled abroad could save on long-distance connect charges. Peering arrangements were established between ISPs who agreed to carry each other's traffic. By 1998 it was more common for bandwidth wholesalers who operated their own networks, such as UUNET and PSINet, to sell access to their shared-use modem pools and other equipment to local ISPs. That made it easier for start-up ISPs to go into business without investing in equipment, while fast-growing ISPs could lease infrastructure from a larger provider.

UUNET and other providers also offered turnkey ISP services to smaller telecommunications companies and others interested in entering the ISP market.

MAJOR PROVIDERS FOR CONSUMERS AND BUSINESSES

As electronic commerce became more widespread in 1999, corporate customers favored ISPs that could provide audience reach. According to a mid-1999 survey by *Data Communications,* UUNET serviced 178 of the 500 largest domains, followed by Exodus Communications Inc. and Cable & Wireless Inc. UUNET also handled a large number of dial-up users on behalf of major consumer ISPs such as America Online, GTE, and Earthlink. Another 1999 survey of ISPs by *Inter@ctive Week* found that BellSouth.net, UUNET, IBM Global Network, MindSpring Enterprises, and AT&T WorldNet were leading ISPs for business customers. According to the survey, key factors in selecting an ISP for business users were reliability, network performance, cost-effectiveness, customer service responsiveness, network capacity, and technical support.

According to a 2000 survey by *Inter@ctive Week* that measured customer satisfaction among business users, the top four national ISPs were MindSpring, EarthLink, PSINet, and UUNET. Regional ISPs as a group ranked fifth. While weak in network reach and brand awareness, regional ISPs scored well in getting their customers' service up and running, customer service responsiveness, value for price, and network reliability. Value for price and network reliability were the two most important factors in choosing an ISP, according to the survey. A 2001 survey of ISPs for corporate customers by *Network Magazine* ranked Cable & Wireless, AT&T, and UUNET as the top three national ISPs.

Inter@ctive Week ranked the following ISPs as the top five among consumers in mid-2001: EarthLink, Excite@Home, The Microsoft Network, Prodigy Communications, and America Online. At the time the survey was conducted, America Online was the largest ISP for consumers with 23.2 million subscribers. EarthLink had 4.7 million subscribers. By 2001 EarthLink was pursuing a broadband strategy; the company was under contract with Time Warner Cable to deliver Internet access over cable into 20 million homes. From 2000 to 2001, EarthLink experienced a 760 percent increase in the number of DSL customers and a 0.2 percent drop in dial-up customers.

In the early 2000s, the Microsoft Network boasted nearly 5 million U.S. subscribers and was expanding globally, while Excite@Home had 3 million home subscribers. Much smaller in terms of revenue and subscribers, Prodigy Communications was accessible to more than 90 percent of the United States. Prodigy had strategic partnerships in place with Covad Communications and SBC Communications to boost its DSL resale business. The company claimed to be the largest DSL retailer with 600,000 customers.

By 2001 ISPs providing free Internet access were having difficulty surviving. While offering free Internet access could succeed in gaining new customers, anticipated revenue from advertising, electronic commerce, and connect fees proved disappointing. A report from Jupiter Media Metrix stated that the free ISP business model was not sustainable. Toward the end of 2000 several portals terminated their free ISP services, including Alta Vista and Terra Lycos. In mid-2001 NetZero, the last pure-play free ISP, announced it would merge with Juno Online Services to form a new company, United Online, which would continue to offer free Internet access under the NetZero brand. Later NetZero announced it would reduce the number of free Internet hours from 40 hours per month to 10 hours per month. The company also reduced its staff by 26 percent.

Kmart's BlueLight.com managed to purchase the assets of the infrastructure provider for its free Internet access service in order to keep its customers online in 2000. After introducing a two-tier model of 100 hours of online access for $9.95 per month or 12 hours of access per month for free, BlueLight.com discontinued its free Internet access service in July 2001. Instead, the company offered unlimited access for $8.95 per month and gave customers the opportunity to get free Internet service in return for buying products at the BlueLight.com Web site.

COMPETITION BETWEEN LARGE AND SMALL PROVIDERS

While no one owns the Internet, by 2000 it was clear that much of the infrastructure on which the Internet ran was controlled by a handful of very large corporations. With access to 300,000 miles of fiber and cable, UUNET owned an estimated 30 percent of the Internet's infrastructure. Other major U.S.-based players included AT&T, GTE, Global Crossing, Qwest Communications International, and PSINet. Control of the Internet infrastructure gave companies the power to charge smaller ISPs for peering arrangements and to charge fees for operating network access points (NAPs) where ISPs traded packets with each other. Large national ISPs, such as America Online, were able to negotiate better deals than smaller ISPs from infrastructure providers. According to some analysts, the result has been less competition in the ISP market, higher barriers to entering the ISP market, and more consolidations and mergers. The end result, they say, is fewer choices for users.

Smaller ISPs can be frustrated by a lack of connectivity to high-speed network hubs owned and operated by large ISPs such as UUNET or Qwest. An estimated 30 percent of Internet traffic traveled over UUNET's network. UUNET, Sprint, Cable & Wireless, AT&T, and GTE together controlled about 80 percent of long-distance Internet traffic. When a local or regional ISP cannot connect to a high-speed hub, its Internet traffic is much slower. While smaller ISPs have to pay a fee to access the larger backbone operated by the major ISPs, the backbone owners generally swap traffic among themselves at no charge under peering arrangements.

Smaller regional and local ISPs have been able to compete with national ISPs by offering better service. What they lack in network reach and brand awareness, smaller ISPs make up for by offering a range of value-added services, including Web design and e-commerce services.

Although the ISP market experienced consolidation and was dominated to some extent by large national providers, businesses and consumers could choose from an estimated 7,000 ISPs in 2001. While millions of consumers gained Internet access from well-known portals such as America Online and the Microsoft Network, there was enough demand to support countless smaller local and regional ISPs. Businesses appeared to prefer large national ISPs, some of which operated their own Internet backbone and could thus guarantee a wide reach and high-speed Internet access.

FURTHER READING:

Addison, Dominick. ''Free Web Access Business Model Is Unsustainable in the Long Term.'' *Marketing,* August 9, 2001.

Dunlap, Charlotte. ''Internet Service Providers.'' *Computer Reseller News,* June 3, 1996.

Freeman, Paul. ''How to Choose the Right Internet Service Provider.'' *Washington Business Journal,* June 15, 2001.

Gerber, Cheryl. ''Where David and Goliath Clash.'' *Telephony,* November 18, 1996.

Gonzalez, Sean. ''Routes to the Net.'' *PC Magazine,* February 21, 1995.

''Internet Service Providers.'' *Inter@ctive Week,* June 4, 2001.

Kopf, David. ''So You Want to Be an ISP?'' *America's Network,* May 15, 1996.

McDonald, Tim. ''ISP Survey: Bigger Is Not Necessarily Better.'' *E-Commerce Times,* August 9, 2001. Available from www.ecommercetimes.com.

Rhine, Jon. ''Not Easy Being Free.'' *San Francisco Business Times,* December 15, 2000.

Weil, Nancy. ''Owning the Net.'' *InfoWorld,* March 20, 2000.

Weinberg, Neil. ''Backbone Bullies.'' *Forbes,* June 12, 2000.

Wetzel, Rebecca. ''ISP Customers Tell It Like It Is.'' *Inter@ctive Week,* December 13, 1999.

———. "Regional ISPs Score Big." *Inter@ctive Week,* September 25, 2000.

Williams, David. "Top 25 ISPs." *Data Communications,* June 7, 1999.

SEE ALSO: AOL Time Warner; AT&T; EarthLink; Excite@Home; Exodus Communications; Juno Online Services; MSN; Qwest Communications International; UUNET

INTERNET SOCIETY (ISOC)

By the 2000s, there were countless societies, taskforces, initiatives, and organizations ostensibly in place to guide or regulate myriad facets of e-commerce and the Internet. One of the most prolific and respected was the Internet Society (ISOC), a nonprofit corporation based in Reston, Virginia, whose broad goal was to facilitate global cooperation and coordination for the Internet by helping to devise new regulatory and technical standards to keep the Internet open, vibrant, and competitive.

A holistically oriented body, the ISOC addresses the broader framework of how the Internet fits into and serves society and how to best shape it. It sees the proliferation and development of the Internet as an end in itself, as well as a mechanism by which companies, individuals, and governments around the world can cooperate in and enhance their respective fields of interest.

Thus, the ISOC specifically addresses several diverse areas of concern.

- It helps to devise and implement technical standards for the Internet and its internetworking technologies and applications.

- It harmonizes policies and developments at the international level.

- It devises and contributes to administrative policies and processes.

- It leads educational and research efforts to promote better understanding of and dialogue about the Internet.

- It collects and stores data for archiving and disseminating the history of the Internet.

- It performs hands-on work in helping developing countries to implement a viable Internet infrastructure.

The proposed formation of the Internet Society was formally announced at an international networking conference in Copenhagen in June 1991, and officially launched in January of the following year. By the early 2000s, its professional membership consisted of more than 150 organizational and 6,000 individual members from more than 100 countries around the world including government agencies, nonprofit organizations, leading corporations, and startup entrepreneurs. Its guiding principles call for an Internet that is free of direct or indirect censorship (such as restrictive governmental or private control of Internet technology), absent of discrimination in any form, and free of the misuse of personal information. Its principles also call for self-regulation and the cooperative development of technical standards, as well as greater networking between individuals and organizations.

One of the ISOC's greatest concerns at the start of the 2000s was the management of the global Domain Name System (DNS). Its most ambitious proposals, generated under its Council of Registrars (CORE), would have transformed the International Corporation for Assigned Names and Numbers (ICANN) into a governing body with the power to set—and the teeth to enforce—its own rules governing domain name accreditation. The ISOC also worked to promote the commercial potential of the Internet, and its input helped to shape the U.S. White House strategy paper on global e-commerce.

The ISOC channeled funding and support to the other organizations under its umbrella, including the Internet Advisory Board (IAB) and the Internet Engineering Task Force (IETF). The IAB's primary functions included guiding the architecture for protocols and procedures devised for the Internet; representing the Internet Society's interests in relationships with other concerned organizations; and administrative duties, such as overseeing the process by which standards are created to ensure that they are committed to open participation and fair practice. The IETF serves a more explicitly technical role. It is comprised of technology experts—including software and technical designers, vendors, operators, and researchers—joined in the development and promotion of design standards for the harmonious operation and evolution of the Internet.

FURTHER READING:

Gittlen, Sandra. "Recycled Domain Naming Plan Still Misses the Mark." *Network World.* March 8, 1999.

"The IETF Home Page." Reston, VA: Internet Engineering Task Force, 2000. Available from www.ietf.org/.

"Internet Architecture Board Home Page." Reston, VA: Internet Architecture Board, December 2000. Available from www.iab.org/iab/.

"Internet Society (ISOC)." Reston, VA: Internet Society, 2001. Available from www.isoc.org/.

Rudich, Joe. "Private Standards for Public Web." *Computer User.* March 2000.

SEE ALSO: Global e-Commerce Regulation; Internet Infrastructure; World Wide Web Consortium (W3C)

INTERNET TAX FREEDOM ACT

The U.S. Congress addressed the controversial issue of taxation and e-commerce with the passage of the Internet Tax Freedom Act (ITFA), which took effect in October 1998. ITFA prohibited the imposition of new e-commerce taxation from October 1, 1998 to October 21, 2001. According to the legislation's sponsors, ITFA was enacted to create a tax-free period that would allow for the unfettered growth of Internet commerce during its formative stages. At the same time, a clear and efficient national e-commerce tax policy could be developed.

Interest in the burgeoning world of e-commerce boomed as the financial stakes involved became more apparent. Some estimates projected that e-commerce transactions will top $300 billion by 2002, representing a huge potential source of sales, and possibly tax, revenues. As of 2001, 45 states and the District of Columbia levied sales taxes on commercial transactions that occurred within their borders. They also imposed use taxes on goods and services that customers bought out-of-state but consumed in their home state. Under the Commerce and Due Process Clauses, states or localities traditionally could only claim tax jurisdiction if they could demonstrate that a "substantial nexus" existed between vendor and purchaser, which generally was understood to mean that the seller had a physical presence, such as a store or warehouse, in the state in which the item was purchased. Part of the dilemma concerning the taxing of e-commerce transactions is that in many cases such a substantial nexus does not exist, because an online customer can buy items over the Internet regardless of where he or she and the seller are physically located.

The question was further complicated by the fact that sales taxes can be more easily applied to transactions involving the transfer of tangible goods. However, many of the items sold online are intangible, such as downloaded songs, information services, and other goods that traditionally have been exempt from sales taxes. Finally, the United States contains more than 30,000 independent state and local tax jurisdictions. Thus, the duty of the seller to collect and remit sales and use taxes is vastly more challenging if they must be able to calculate the appropriate tax rates for each jurisdiction, rather than only that of the state and locality in which they are located.

Among ITFA's major provisions was a three-year moratorium placed on several types of e-commerce taxes. First, it prohibited the taxation of Internet service providers (ISPs) such as AOL; states could not require that ISPs charge state taxes in addition to their monthly service fees. However, ITFA did incorporate a grandfather clause that permitted the continuation of any taxes that had been "generally imposed and actually enforced prior to October 1, 1998." Such taxes existed in the District of Columbia and eleven states.

ITFA instituted another three-year ban on any new state or local taxes considered to be "multiple and discriminatory"—that is, those that would subject buyers to e-sales taxation in more than one state. This provision followed the taxation guidelines set down for interstate mail-order sales by the U.S. Supreme Court's 1992 decision in Quill Corp. v. North Dakota, in which the court ruled that the Commerce Clause exempted mail order houses from a duty to collect sales taxes unless they possessed a "substantial nexus" (understood to be a physical presence) with the taxing jurisdiction. ITFA also shielded from taxation all goods and services sold exclusively online for the duration of the moratorium.

Under ITFA, for a state or locality to tax e-commerce transactions, the conditions surrounding the imposition of the tax and the taxation rate must match those that pertain to traditional, "bricks-and-mortar" sales transactions. In such cases, the e-tailer would be responsible for collecting and remitting the amount of that tax, just like traditional commercial retailers.

Finally, ITFA urged the president to collaborate with the European Union and the World Trade Organization to guarantee that all e-commerce continued to be exempt from tariffs and other international taxes. In addition, ITFA established a national Advisory Commission on Electronic Commerce to study the issues surrounding e-commerce taxation and to submit a final report of its findings and recommendations to Congress by April 2001. The commission's 19 members—federal, state, and local governmental officials, as well as representatives from taxpayer and business groups—represented all viewpoints in the e-commerce taxation debate.

However, the commission did not submit a comprehensive final report for Congress by the scheduled deadline, since it failed to gather the two-thirds majority necessary to issue an official statement. Instead, the situation remained unresolved, with the commission agreeing to extend the moratorium on Internet taxes until 2006 and to conduct further discussions. Among its "non-official" recommendations, the commission advocated the repeal of the three-percent federal excise tax on telecommunications services, the permanent banning of state and local taxation on Internet access fees, the simplification of state sales and use taxes, and a ban on all international tariffs on e-commerce transactions.

FURTHER READING:

Cox, Christopher. "Internet Tax Freedom at One: No Net Taxes, More Sales Tax Revenue." Washington, D.C.: Office of U.S. Representative Christopher Cox, 1998. Available from cox.house.gov/.

———. "'Plain English' Summary of the Internet Tax Freedom Act (P.L. 105-277)." Washington, D.C.: Office of U.S. Representative Christopher Cox, 1998. Available from cox.house.gov/nettax.

Fallaw, Timothy. "The Internet Tax Freedom Act: Necessary Protection or Deferral of the Problem?" *Journal of Intellectual Property Law.* Fall 1999.

Huddleson, Joe. "Internet Taxation Issues Remain Unanswered." *The Tax Adviser.* February 2001.

McLaughlin, Matthew. "The Internet Tax Freedom Act: Congress Takes a Byte Out Of the Net." *Catholic University Law Review.* Fall 1998.

SEE ALSO: Digital Divide; Taxation and the Internet

INTRANETS AND EXTRANETS

INTRANETS

Intranets combine all the features of the Internet, including e-mail, Web sites, interactivity, and cross-network uploading and downloading, but are specifically for use inside a particular organization, such as a business, research facility, or school. In other words, an intranet is a sort of bordered, limited-access Internet that allows for more comprehensive and efficient passageways to company information. They find their most prolific use in the business world, where they help to streamline company operations by providing access to corporate data—everything from meeting schedules to sales projections to product-development reports—to those inside the firm. Many companies even build portals on their intranets to provide a central point of access and navigation scheme for company information and news.

Typically, intranets grow out of the need to address specific problems within a firm or department that requires data to be readily available to a number of separate users. From these initial steps, the network grows to incorporate more company information and provide access to more and more members of the firm. Corporate applications and software also are geared toward integration with the internal network. The intranet really begins to pay off, however, when it graduates from a massive information storage device to a tool for knowledge creation.

By the 2000s, companies were looking to their intranets not just as a forum for data storage and transfer, but also as a mechanism for exponentially enhancing the creation of corporate intellectual capital. By providing the tools for mining through the mass of data stored in company files and extracting relevant information in a meaningful and useful fashion, intranets are a mechanism for the creation of company knowledge and a cutting-edge vehicle for competitive strategy.

EXTRANETS

Extranets operate on the same general principle as intranets, but link an enterprise's internal networks to those of strategic business partners. That is, extranets link two or more businesses in an exclusive network open only to those parties. Extranets include everything from simple intra-firm electronic ordering systems to more complex and comprehensive information-sharing networks. Extranets were increasingly common as the move to digitally integrate data pertinent to sales and joint development blossomed. Business-to-business e-commerce pushed extranets to the forefront of business planning in the early 2000s.

Often referred to as business-to-business Webs, extranets typically evolve from intranets when the latter are opened up to suppliers and trading partners to eliminate inefficiencies in their business channels. By opening up the company's internal network to suppliers, for instance, corporate databases are rendered transparent so as to ensure adequate inventory control and optimal delivery schedules.

However, this arrangement is not without its complications. While businesses enjoy clear advantages by integrating portions of their networks with those of partnering firms, that integration can cause sticky problems between businesses that partner in some lines of business but compete in others. There is always the worry that the other firm may try to gain a bit more information and advantage from the arrangement. As a result, companies increasingly institute internal safeguards, in the form of security checks and network firewalls, to keep partnering firms confined to only those areas of the network that are pertinent to the partnership. To avoid the appearance of acting in bad faith, the establishment of security measures, proper use guidelines, and clear access limits is increasingly a part of the initial negotiating process when establishing an extranet partnership. The owners of data typically maintain control over, and set policies regarding, the level of protection their information requires.

By integrating suppliers, partners, and even customers into a cohesive network, extranets allow for quicker and more efficient responses to subtle or rapid shifts in market opportunities and phenomena. Extranets ideally put all parties into seamless contact with each other, regardless of their respective locations. More contentiously, extranets connect partners to such an extent that middlemen, such as wholesalers, are often cut out of the transaction process altogether, resulting in significant cost savings. Alternatively, extranets force such intermediaries to broaden their focus and offer value-added services in order to keep their businesses worthwhile to clients.

In addition to the growth of business-to-business e-commerce, the wave of business outsourcing in the 1990s was another impetus toward the development of extranets. Businesses increasingly located their primary areas of competence and then outsourced the rest of their operations in order to maximize efficiency and minimize costs to remain competitive. The continuing contacts between the original firm and its outsourcing partners called for an adaptation of Internet technologies specifically for business-to-business purposes, broadening the intranet concept to include partners whose borders were increasingly blurry. As Karl Wierzbicki explained in *Computing Canada,* ''[t]he real benefit of an extranet will be its ability to bring together all of the extended enterprise, serving no longer as just an authorized conglomeration of corporate fact, but as the neural centre of corporate intelligence.''

According to *Telephony,* extranets combine salespersons, catalogs, call centers, and technicians into a single, round-the-clock system through which full business services and deals can be conducted without regard to time or physical location. As a result of the advantages involved in developing extranets, companies were scrambling to build their own extranets as a value-added service, fearing that failure to take advantage of the possibilities of such electronic communications would leave them at a strategic disadvantage.

THE CLIMATE FOR INTRANETS AND EXTRANETS

In an economy increasingly based on digital information, intranets and extranets are becoming central tools in the effort by businesses and other organizations to streamline their operations and maximize their available resources, both physical and intellectual. Increasingly, intranets were a given for large companies. According to *The Journal of Business Strategy,* between 1997 and 2001, 90 percent of major corporations implemented an intranet strategy. In the early 2000s, extranets also were rapidly becoming an expectation rather than a bonus.

InformationWeek reported that IT managers generally had high expectations for their intranets and ex-

tranets, noting that 80 to 90 percent of all IT managers expected a positive return on their investments in such network systems. The lowered costs of doing business with other firms was the most obvious and immediate advantage posed by the implementation of intranets and extranets, though the efficiencies of data flow throughout and between firms was an important subsidiary advantage.

Security, of course, was a primary concern with intranets and extranets, since their purpose was to invite some but exclude others. Access can be secured by a variety of techniques, including traditional identification and passwords, or by other methods such as digital certificates or IP address recognition. A favored method of managing the access of internal data systems by outside parties is to employ enterprise directories. Enterprise directories are a relatively easy way to manage outside access because their hierarchical structures can serve to provide layers of authentication, determining what kinds of information can be made available to what kinds of partners. Because the layers of access restrictions for extranets can be complex—for instance, a company may choose to provide open access to all partners for product testing information, but to only certain partners for confidential sales information—extranet security is labor intensive and requires skilled IT managers and security experts.

In addition to basic information sharing capabilities, intranets and extranets play a prominent role in corporate communications, both inside and outside the firm. With advanced audio and video technologies wired for Internet capabilities, intranets and extranets can facilitate secure real-time conferencing, seminars, and other discussions. This enables executives and workers to communicate directly and immediately, and allows them to transfer information on a moment's notice, thereby making such meetings much more efficient.

Intranets and extranets also favor the model of corporate organizing that was on the rise in the Internet age of the 1990s and early 2000s. Instead of relying heavily or exclusively on top-down communications structures—whereby instructions and ideas are announced by executives to lower-level workers—companies can utilize intranets and extranets to encourage creativity and decision-making among their lower-level employees. This facilitates cross-departmental collaboration and results in a constant dialogue among all members of an organization, thereby maximizing the knowledge at the firm's disposal.

FURTHER READING:

Baker, Sunny. ''Getting the Most from Your Intranet and Extranet Strategies.'' *The Journal of Business Strategy.* July/August 2000.

Krill, Paul. ''Portals Play Key Role as Intranets and Extranets Evolve.'' *InfoWorld.* May 7, 2001.

Moch, Chrissy. "Everything You Always Wanted to Know About Extranets, but Were Afraid to Ask." *Telephony.* September 13, 1999.

Schwarzwalder, Robert. "The Extraordinary Extranet." *Econtent.* December 1999.

Wierzbicki, Karl. "Extended Intranets Add to Your Business' Reach." *Computing Canada.* October 29, 1999.

Yasin, Rutrell. "Tools, Policies Make Good Security Mix—Companies Aim to Build Safer Internet." *InternetWeek.* October 30, 2000.

SEE ALSO: Business-to-Business (B2B) E-commerce; Channel Conflict/Harmony; Channel Transparency; Data Mining; Digital Certificates; Intellectual Capital; Knowledge Management

INVESTING, ONLINE

As the Internet opened to the mass public in the 1990s, it didn't take long for investors to see the potential for buying and selling securities online. While forms of online investing existed before the Internet became popular, the proliferation of Internet access and the coinciding stock market boom ushered in a vast industry catering to all kinds of investors. The Internet had something to offer for individual bidders, those who worked through brokers, and both aggressive and defensive investors. Between late 1998 and late 2000, the number of stock-owning households that supplemented their investments with online trading more than doubled from 10 percent to 21 percent, amounting to about 10 million households, according to Jupiter Communications.

Online investing generally is well within the reach of any Internet user with enough cash to risk in the market. Meanwhile, mountains of information about investing and up-to-the-minute updates about worldwide markets turned investing into a populist sport in the 1990s. In addition, entering buy and sell orders to online brokers typically carries lighter commissions, thereby allowing the investor to hold on to more of what he or she earns in the market. As a result of these potential benefits, the Internet was inundated with Web sites catering to all manner of investors, from neophytes to professionals, from fund managers to day traders. Supplementing these sites were countless forums, mailing lists, and discussion groups where users could discuss stock market wisdom, trade tips, perpetuate or dispel rumors, and compare investing war stories.

THE ACTORS

INDIVIDUALS. One of the most widely proclaimed glories of online investing was its potential to democratize the securities markets and spread the wealth among broader segments of the population. The convenience, low barriers to entry, and technical ease of trading over the Internet thus spurred a massive influx of individuals taking control over their own financial investment schemes. Forrester Research expected the number of online investors to rise from 1.1 million in early 2000 to 7.2 million in 2003, and reported that about 26 percent of all Americans connected to the Internet to regularly check their stocks. This nearly was as high a percentage as those who regularly read the news online. By putting such a fantastic wealth of financial information only a mouse-click away, the Internet fosters the idea that becoming an investor is well within reach of the average Internet user. In addition to keen market insight, experienced online investors boast sophisticated software for charting and technical and fundamental analysis. A number of Web sites offered free real-time stock quotes.

The reach of online investing even extended to children. According to *Business Week,* nearly one in five students in grades eight through 12 owned stocks or bonds in 2000, up from 10 percent in 1993, while some 2 million actively traded and picked their own stocks. Able to bypass their parents by connecting to the Web at home or even in school, students increasingly sought to reap their own fortunes and a measure of financial independence via online investing. And many succeeded; the bull market of the late 1990s produced scores of teenage success stories in which young students amassed fortunes on par with or exceeding many successful adults. Juveniles typically require parental approval to open accounts; parents usually maintain custodial accounts for their children. However, as long as children know the account's password they can trade freely of their own accord.

The online investing boom launched its own breed of individual investor: the day trader. Day traders generally were non-traditional investors, often fancying themselves as rebels in the investment world, with few or no ties to large brokerages or market makers. Day trading and electronic trading were a perfect match, with the latter pitched as a vehicle by which the market was democratized and wrested from the exclusive hands of traditional market players. Day traders work by sheer volume and speed, purchasing a flurry of securities early in the day and unloading them all by the time the markets closed, with the goal of profiting from the incremental price movements of those securities throughout the day. While on average these fluctuations were miniscule for individual securities, by purchasing mountains of securities day traders hoped that the tiny gains would combine to reap tremendous rewards.

Inevitably, this unorthodox investment practice turned out to be controversial. Analysts chalked up no small amount of the market volatility in the late 1990s to the day traders, who critics claimed undermined the ability of public companies to maintain steady projections of cash flow and thus effectively plan for the future. In addition, employers feared that day trading was eating into their employees' work hours, prompting many businesses to install software designed to block employees out of day-trading sites.

The backlash against day trading reached its zenith after a distraught Atlanta day trader went on a shooting rampage, killing 11 individuals and himself. Day traders were roundly accused of typifying the over-exuberance of investors in the late 1990s. Professionals likened day trading to gambling by amateur investors rather than reasoned investing strategies. Repeated research concludes that the more traditional buy-and-hold strategy, despite the dramatic success stories of the late-1990s bull market, are much more profitable than quick in-and-out investment behavior. To illustrate this point, analysts pointed out that go-it-alone investors were the hardest hit by the poor performance of the stock markets, particularly the NASDAQ, in the early 2000s. Still, the effects of day trading were profound, altering perceptions of risk exposure and boosting the degree of market volatility, which both made and lost vast fortunes.

BROKERAGES, OLD AND NEW. At first, major traditional brokerages such as Merrill Lynch, Morgan Stanley Dean Witter, and Salomon Smith Barney were slow to adopt online trading as part of their services. However, after watching the explosive growth of electronic communications networks and individual online investing, they too jumped online to catch up to the upstarts. Gomez Advisors reported that the number of online brokerages jumped from 12 in 1994—the year the first brokerages went online—to more than 140 by the end of the 2000, though by then a shakeout was imminent. Meanwhile, Forrester Research projected online brokerage accounts for stocks and funds would reach $1.5 trillion by 2003.

While most online brokerages simply set up a Web site through which they conduct transactions, some—including CyberCorp (which was purchased by Charles Schwabb), myTrack, and TradeCast—eschew Web browsers altogether and allow their clients to link directly to the brokerage trading desk using proprietary software. This method tends to call for greater bandwidth and was thus inconvenient for many Internet users. However, the software, which users normally downloaded from CDs, usually carried vastly more—and more sophisticated—features than were available on most Web sites.

Having received an order, electronic brokers have a variety of procedures for processing the transaction. For instance, the brokerage may pass the order through an approval process verifying that the client is authorized to trade in particular securities. Then, once approval is met, brokerages transfer the order to either an electronic trading system such as NASDAQ, or to their own agents located on the floors of exchanges like the New York Stock Exchange, depending on where the particular security is listed. Alternatively, online brokerages may choose not to go directly to the trading centers themselves, but opt instead to channel orders through market makers. Third-party market insiders, market makers enjoy the financial backing of major investment banks and brokerage houses. They rush to fill open buy and sell orders for their clients, thereby providing them with instant liquidity.

Online brokers generate revenues primarily from two sources: the commissions charged to the investor for processing his or her order, and from a percentage of the market maker's spread—the difference between the buy and sell price that constitutes the market maker's profit.

Leading online brokers such as E*Trade, Ameritrade, and Datek ascended to prominence almost under the noses of the established powerhouse brokerages. By the end of the 1990s it was the stalwarts who were humbled and playing catch-up. The perpetually rising bull market encouraged increasing trading volume through these channels. However, after the market went bust in early 2000, many analysts realized that all too many online investors and online brokerages were confusing the bull market with individual market savvy and know-how. The early 2000s were characterized by layoffs and losses among online brokerages.

No brokerage made it through the sour turn in the market unscathed. However, traditional brokerages, with greater diversity and economies of scale, were able to weather the storm much better. In the meantime, such brokerages sought to purchase or drive out much of their upstart competition, realizing that while the bull market may well be in hibernation, the trend of online investing was here to stay. In their defense, the largest online brokers sought out partners with deep pockets to help them diversify their offerings and float them through the tough times. As a sign of trends to come, E*Trade partnered with Ernst & Young in 1999. Most analysts expected that the line between traditional brokerages and online brokerages would blur and eventually dissolve altogether in an industry that seamlessly integrates both varieties.

According to *Business Week,* online brokers bore some of the responsibility for feeding investors false promises. Many brokerages advertised to customers by ensuring that millions could be earned by investing, based solely on information derived from the Web. While the ultimate responsibility for investments lies with the investors themselves, analysts point out that if the online investment industry were to continue to grow and go mainstream, a more responsible atmosphere would need to take hold.

ELECTRONIC COMMUNICATIONS NETWORKS. Electronic communications networks (ECNs) are digital trading systems where investors post their buy and sell orders, which are then matched to other bids electronically, bypassing market makers and other middlemen altogether for significant cost savings and high speed. ECN clients include online brokerages, institutional investors, and individual investors. In the late 1990s, the bread and butter for ECNs was the day trading phenomenon, which brought in the overwhelming bulk of their business. Since trading volume was the path to riches for ECNs and day traders alike, their models fit perfectly in the 1990s bull market.

ECNs emerged as a significant threat to major exchanges—particularly NASDAQ—by the early 2000s. This prompted such exchanges to vastly overhaul their trading systems and technological infrastructure and practices, often adopting architectures similar to that of ECNs. By 2001, ECNs accounted for more than one-third of the total trading volume on NASDAQ. While ECNs directly challenged both exchanges and market makers in the late 1990s, the early 2000s saw major brokerages such as Merrill Lynch and Goldman Sachs increasingly investing in ECNs, perhaps recognizing that the model of investment they offer has produced an undeniable shift in investors' expectations.

Either individually or through a brokerage, investors enter their bids. These are then listed anonymously in the ECN's electronic order book while the system searches out the book for a corresponding bid—for instance, a buy price that matches the proposed sell price. Increasingly, ECNs eschewed a closed system—in which buy and sell orders are only matched within that system—in favor of a model that linked various trading systems together in an open network, thereby facilitating greater liquidity and faster transactions.

Unlike brokerages, ECNs don't actually process orders for investors. Rather, they simply provide networking space where investors can find each other and have their buy and sell bids met. ECNs earn revenue by applying a miniscule surcharge—usually less than a few cents per share—to the transactions that take place on their network. Thus, ECNs rely on the sheer volume of trading to stay afloat, rather than on the spreads between buy and sell prices.

THE ONLINE INVESTING PHENOMENON

Electronic trading had its genesis in the desire by institutional investors to be able to trade after hours.

In 1969 Reuters Group PLC founded Instinet Corp. for just this purpose. Thus, while online trading eventually would come to prominence as a populist practice, its origins lay in the demands of a relatively exclusive club of established investors.

The three primary advantages attributed to online investing are the lower commissions levied on trades, around-the-clock portfolio access, and greatly enhanced access to and control over the investment process. However, simply giving individuals greater access and control means that those same individuals, to truly take advantage, must familiarize themselves with the wealth of global market information available on the Internet. They also must become familiar with the subtle techniques—and enormous potential risks—involved in playing the securities markets.

Much of the online investing climate in the late 1990s was advertised as rugged individualist and even anti-establishment. However, effective stock research, trade execution, and portfolio management were all highly sophisticated and knowledge-heavy endeavors, particularly in times, like the early 2000s, when the bull market turned bearish. Before the online investing craze took hold, these practices usually were the purview of professional brokers. But the democratization that the Internet promised spurred a demand for greater individual control, and the bull market reaped enough reward to make this widely applicable.

The availability of the Internet as a convenient and relatively democratic investment vehicle helped to transform the nature of financial markets by stimulating vastly greater movement of securities prices and resultant market fluctuations. For instance, analysts frequently noted the decline of the buy-and-hold mentality among the investor pool, whereby investors purchased stocks with the intention of holding onto them for some length of time, thereby providing longer-term financial streams to the companies. Instead, online investors were more likely to purchase stocks and unload them in a relatively short period of time, simultaneously contributing to and hoping to profit from rapid market fluctuations. This certainly was true of day traders, who operate under this logic by definition. However, other online investors also helped to shrink the average period of time that an individual investor holds on to a particular security.

In 1999, University of California at Davis professors Brad Barber and Terrance Odean released the results of their study of about 1,600 investors between 1992 and 1996—just before the thrust of the online investing boom—who abandoned telephone-based, broker-mediated trading in favor of online investing. On average, these investors were active traders, with about 75-percent annual portfolio turnover. Before their switch, they bested major market indexes—a composite of the New York Stock Exchange, NAS-DAQ, and the American Stock Exchange—by a healthy 2.4 percent.

After turning to online trading, their trading activity increased substantially, with annual portfolio turnover reaching 96 percent. However, their performance fell to 3.6 percent behind the indexes. Barber and Odean concluded that the convenience of online trading was accompanied by a combination of over-confidence and over-exuberance, with traders more and more itchy to trade and capitalize on presumed knowledge based on past successes. Thus, despite the lower commissions spent on online trades, the investors actually incurred higher transaction costs due to their more active and speculative trading.

Odean and Barber explained that online trading fostered an illusion of greater control through the use of computers to make trades. This was because information was at one's fingertips. They also explained that, in general, for all but the most experienced investment professionals, highly active trading is not as beneficial as the buy-and-hold model.

Finally, online investing reached its zenith alongside the euphoria surrounding the dot-com market and the great fanfare over the new economy. According to critics, as these factors coalesced, an environment was established whereby investors grew convinced that the market could do no wrong, that the laws of economics and securities trading had fundamentally changed, and that to fail to take advantage of can't-miss opportunities was to risk missing out on a financial windfall. Supported by enough success stories, this mythology floated both the online investing boom and the new economy for awhile. However, when the high-tech and dot-com sectors plummeted in the early 2000s and the new economy turned sour, analysts turned sour on online investing, particularly in the form of day trading. While the excesses of online investing fell into disrepute, there was little doubt that the transformations of financial markets and the trading industries were here to stay, and that online investing would continue as a major sector of the trading world.

FURTHER READING:

Beliakov, Victor; and Thomas Barnwell. "Investigative Investing." *Asian Business*. April 2000.

Carey, Theresa W. "The Electronic Investor: Direct Connections." *Barron's*. April 17, 2000.

Crockett, Roger O., "Netting Those Investors." *Business Week*. September 18, 2000.

Konana, Prabhudev, Nirup M. Menon, and Sridhar Balasubramanian. "The Implications of Online Investing." *Communications of the ACM*. January 2000.

Koretz, Gene. "Shootout at the Online Corral." *Business Week*. May 15, 2000.

"Online Investors Deserve Better." *Business Week*. May 22, 2000.

Rafalaf, Andrew. "Full-Service Brokerages Begin to Embrace the Internet. . .Finally." *Wall Street & Technology*. August 1999.

Smith, Geoffrey and Anne Tergesen. "Your Guide to Online Investing." *Business Week*. May 24, 1999.

Tergesen, Anne. "Readin', Writin', and Stockpickin'." *Business Week*. September 25, 2000.

Thornton, Emily. "Why e-Brokers Are Broker and Broker." *Business Week*. January 22, 2001.

SEE ALSO: Ameritrade Holding Corp,; Day Trading; Dot.com; Electronic Communications Networks (ECNs); E*Trade Group Inc.; Island ECN; Nasdaq Stock Market; New Economy

ISLAND ECN

Island ECN has played a key role in redefining how stocks and other securities are traded. Island is an electronic marketplace that enables market professionals to display limit orders for stocks and other securities, directly matching buyers and sellers, and in doing so eliminating many of the traditional stock market middlemen and their fees. Thousands of market participants enter over 2 billion shares into Island every trading day, averaging over 400 million shares traded on a daily basis.

As an Electronic Communication Network (ECN), Island is part of the NASDAQ. The NASDAQ functions as a collection of marketplaces, offering a quotation service, whch lists the best price for the stocks traded, and connectivity services that enable participants to interact with each other. The NAS-DAQ, however, does not offer trading services. Therefore market professionals must ensure that their orders for NASDAQ securities are posted in a marketplace that offers best liquidity, that is, the best chances of getting an execution quickly at low-cost. Island ECN proved that it could meet all these needs. In 2001 Island was the second largest ECN, after Instinet Inc.

HOW ISLAND WORKS

Suppose an investor decides to sell 100 shares of a particular stock for $20.00 a share. Island's system is scanned instantaneously for unfilled orders for that stock at $20.00. If a match is found, the order is executed immediately. If there is no match, the order is displayed on Island's order book until a matching order to buy is entered or the original order is cancelled. Island accepts orders from market makers, agency brokers, retail brokers, day-trading firms, proprietary trading firms, and institutional firms. Trades on Island can only flow through one of its seven hundred-plus client brokers; individual investors cannot use Island's services directly. During the 1990s, Island concentrated on serving retail investors; in 2001 it began to refocus its efforts on business-to-business trading.

Virtually all orders can be viewed, in real-time and without charge, on Island's Web site through the BookViewer, an online representation of Island's limit order book. The best-priced order on Island for a NASDAQ security is also represented on the NASDAQ Level II screen, where the best bids and offers of all market participants are posted. If an order on Island is the best price from among all the different market participants, it will also be featured on the NBBO, the National Best Bid/Offer display. Island was the first marketplace to make its order information available on such a scale. The BookViewer does not track the activity of the entire NASDAQ by any means. However, because Island accounts for such a high percentage of NASDAQ trading—about 16 percent in 2001—its online order book can offer a fairly accurate picture of NASDAQ activity. Island also provides investors with an online toolbox that includes a list of the 20 most active issues on Island; a time and sales report generator that shows what time trades took place, and at what price; and an instant alert feature that notifies investors when a stock hits a predefined price or level of volume.

Island sees tremendous activity every trading day—during the first two quarters of 2001 trading activity on Island accounted for approximately one in every 6 trades on NASDAQ. Trading at Island ECN grew by leaps and bounds in the 2000s. Between 1999 and 2000 volume doubled to 53.7 billion shares; it increased by 80 percent in 2001. Its base of client subscribers also grew rapidly, from about 150 in late 1998, to 400 at the beginning of 2001. By the end of that year the number had passed 700.

THE EMERGENCE OF ISLAND

The groundwork for Island ECN was laid by Joshua Levine, who in the mid-1990s wrote the software that would become the basis for its electronic trading system. Levine's system grew out of NASDAQ's SOES—small order execution system—which was introduced after the 1987 stock market crash. SOES automatically matched trades of 1,000 shares or less, making it possible for investors to deal with one another directly, without the intervention of the traditional middlemen.

Island was founded in 1997 by Jeff Citron and Levine with funding from Datek Online Holdings

Corporation. Island was an immediate hit, its popularity driven in part by the day trading fad of the late 1990s. The effects were felt throughout the stock world. Competing ECNs were soon opening their virtual doors, and NYSE and NASDAQ were compelled to look for ways to simplify their business in order to meet the challenge. Levine himself fueled the competition with his outspoken criticisms of NYSE and NASDAQ as anticompetitive monopolies. Thanks to Levine's efforts, the NYSE eventually repealed its rule prohibiting its members from trading substantial amounts of NYSE-listed stock off the trading floor. The repeal made it possible for Island to begin trading in stock listed on the New York Stock Exchange.

Levine stepped aside in 1998 and was replaced as Island's President and CEO by Matthew Andresen, who was also fired by a passion to change the way securities were traded. Under Andresen, in June 1999 Island applied to the SEC to become the nation's first for-profit exchange, enabling it compete head-to-head with NYSE and NASDAQ for orders. Some critics speculated market status would impose on Island the crippling costs of instituting and enforcing a complex set of SEC rules. Island maintained that its electronic form and the high degree of transparency that form entailed—providing, for example, an easy-to-follow audit trail for every order—would make enforcement far easier than in traditional securities markets. It would also provide Island with the opportunity to make millions of dollars in earnings every year from the sale of its market data.

After being fined for several trading violations, Island's parent Datek sold a 90 percent interest in Island to a group comprised of Bain Capital, TA Associates, and Silver Lake Partners. The sale was seen by some as an attempt to distance Island from Datek's problems while its exchange application was being considered. As of October 2001 the SEC had not handed down a decision on the application.

MEASURING UP TO COMPETITION

Island ECN offers investors a variety of advantages. It provides the flexibility of the longest trading session available. Island begins matching orders at 7:00 am, before the market opens, and continues until 8:00 pm, hours after the market has closed. It is able to do business much faster than traditional markets, with a speed as fast as 3/100ths of a second, compared to several seconds for traditional markets. That speed can be the difference between executing or failing to execute an order. Finally ECNs such as Island have cut the cost of trading significantly, charging fractions of a cent per share instead of five to six cents charged by traditional middlemen.

Island ECN has also shown itself to be more reliable than traditional markets. Between 1997 and the end of 2001, its system did not experience a single shutdown as a result of intensive volume. It accomplished this through a unique computer system designed to sustain heavy trading volumes. Rather than relying on a single mainframe computer, Island's system distributes work among hundreds of linked personal computers. Each PC in the system performs a single function, for example receiving orders, matching orders, or canceling orders. At the same time, the PCs back each other up. If one fails, another one running the same function takes over. Island's systems are required to comply with SEC standards governing security, capacity and reliability.

The system twice succeeded when NASDAQ's own system failed. First on January 3, 2001, and again on April 18, 2001, when announcements of interest-rate cuts by the Federal Reserve led to sudden, high-volume in trading, NASDAQ computers experienced delays in delivering execution messages. While the NASDAQ delays were occurring on January 3, Island continued to handle more than 10,000 orders a minute without a slowdown. Island had its highest volume day to date on October 4th, 2001, executing more than 550 million shares. Island's systems have been also internally benchmarked at handling well over 1,000 executions per second.

FURTHER READING:

Andresen, Matthew, ''Don't CLOBber ECNs.'' *Wall Street Journal,* March 27, 2000.

''Island ECN Calls on Congress to Revamp National National Market System, Eliminating ITS.'' *Daily Report fot Executives,* April 18, 2001.

''Island Won't Strand Traders.'' *Active Trader,* October 2001.

Kolbert, Elizabeth, ''The Last Floor Show.'' *New Yorker,* March 20, 2000.

Pegg, Jonathan, ''Driving Harder in a Bear Market to Pump Up Volume.'' *Fortune Banker,* April 2001.

Ponczak, Jeff, ''Super, or Just So(es)-so?'' *Active Trader,* October 2001.

Santini, Laura, ''A Rebel's Gamble.'' *Investment Dealers' Digest,* January 29, 2001.

SEE
ALSO: Archipelago Holdings LLC; Day Trading; Electronic Communications Networks (ECNs); Instinet Corp.; Investing, Online; Nasdaq Stock Market

IVILLAGE

iVillage was the first site on the Web devoted to the concerns and interests of women in the prime of their lives. But during the first six years of its exis-

tence, iVillage also came to epitomize the quicksilver nature of the Internet economy. By late 2001, the firm had experienced the entire dot.com boom-and-bust cycle. It launched one of the most wildly successful public stock offering in history, swallowed its main competitor, and was recognized as the leading site for women 18 and older on the World Wide Web. But after the dot.com crash of late 2000, it was teetering on the edge of bankruptcy.

Besides the Web site iVillage.com, the iVillage media organization included Business Women's Network, Lamaze Publishing, The Newborn Channel, Astrology.com, and iVillage Solutions. The Web site offered members email, message boards, chat rooms and access to some twenty content areas, including Astrology, Babies, Beauty, Books, Diet & Fitness, Entertainment, Food, Games, Health, Home & Garden, Lamaze, Money, News & Issues, Parenting, Pets, Pregnancy, Relationships, Relaxation, and Work.

With well over one million registered members, and nearly seven million unique visitors in 2000, iVillage was well-positioned to deliver an audience—and advertisers appreciated it; by 2001 more than 90 percent of iVillage's revenues were derived from advertising and sponsorship deals. Nonetheless, more than six years after its founding, the company's future remained a question mark. The firm had not enjoyed a single profitable year in its entire existence, though it promised its investors to show a profit in fall 2001. From 1995 until 2001, it flitted through a series of business concepts and problems retaining employees. The departure—resignation or dismissal—of iVillage's visionary founder in early 2001 only put the company's ultimate survival more deeply in doubt.

Candice Carpenter conceived of iVillage in 1995. A graduate of Stanford and Harvard, Carpenter was hired as a consultant by the fledgling America Online (AOL). She knew next to nothing about computers or the developing Web culture, but she was immediately impressed by the various online communities she found lurking under the surface at AOL: a community for gays, one for pet-owners, another for quilters, and so on. Carpenter's insight was that such communities would be a determining factor for the Internet's future; her genius was to take that realization and create a business brand around it.

With New York media veterans Nancy Evans and Robert Levitan, Carpenter sketched out her ideas about Web community. In September 1995 they planned out three online comunities centered on health, family, and careers. They took the name iVillage because ''i'' as in ''Internet'' was the online prefix of choice at the time. iVillage's first incarnation was not aimed at women surfers in particular. However, it was soon apparent that Carpetner, Evans, and Levitan had found the bait to lure an elusive audience—women in the prime of their lives made up about 80 percent of iVillage traffic. AOL was interested in those numbers; so were the Tribune Company and Kleiner, Perkins, a venture capital firm. All put up money for iVillage. AOL's backing represented its first investment in an independent company.

Parent Soup, iVillage's first interactive community, went online on AOL in January 1996. The site's content included articles and polls on a broad spectrum of parenting topics, as well as chat rooms where parents could exchange advice or consult experts. At the same time, the company began forging deals with product manufacturers, like KidSoft, a maker of software for parents and children. Products were featured on the Web site and could be purchased at iVillage's Parent Soup General Store. A second community, At Work, devoted to career and work issues, debuted later in 1996, followed by Better Health & Medical, and a general community for women, Life Soup. Life Soup was designed as a site where women could exchange ideas on a broad range of interesting topics, including finance, fitness, food, sex, and relationships.

By fall 1997 iVillage boasted an average of 51 million page views per month. It represented, according to iVillage, a bloc of women more than twice as big as any other on the Web. With experts at the time predicting that 34 million women were about to begin using the Web, iVillage's prospects looked bright indeed. Soon it was attracting established advertisers, such as Polaroid, Compaq Computer, and Astra-Merck. Other companies wanted to partner with iVillage. In May 1998 it was the beneficiary of a $32.5 million infusion from one group of companies. AT&T partnered with iVillage in November 1998 to launch an Internet service provider targeted specifically at women. Shortly thereafter, NBC was given a stake in iVillage in return for promotion on its regular and cable networks. By the end of 1998, iVillage had 14 channels online, one million registered users, and was reporting nearly three million visitors every month. It was by far the most popular site for women on the Internet and the stage was set for one of the most spectacular stock offerings in modern financial history.

Nonetheless, there were skeptics when iVillage announced in March 1999 that it would go public. Some said the company was not well known enough to generate interest among investors; others said its business was not sufficiently rooted in the ''real world,'' of the traditional economy; that is, it was seen as too heavily tied to the virtual New Economy. At first shares were to be offered for about $13 a piece. Then, just before the offering, iVillage's underwriter upped the price to $23. That would have given the company a market value of about $556 million. Against most expectations, though, the stock opened at a blockbusting $95.875 a share. At the end of the first day of trading, iVillage was worth over $2 *billion* and its share price would continue to climb, eventually topping off at $130 a share.

It was a bubble waiting to burst. By mid-1999 the company had yet to earn a penny of profit. By design or default, iVillage had begun shifting its focus away from its original business plan. No longer was it a pure community—nearly 30 percent of its revenue was coming from e-commerce, mainly its online shops. On other fronts, it was sued by ex-employees who charged, among other things, that they had been bilked out of promised stock options. Worst of all, from an investor's point of view, was the fact that iVillage was still hemorrhaging cash. It lost $86.7 million in the first nine months of 1999 alone. By the end of the year, iVillage's share price had plunged to $9.50.

In April 2000, in an attempt to stabilize the company's fortunes, Doug McCormick, a member of the iVillage board, was named president. Three months later McCormick replaced founder Candice Carpenter as CEO. Shortly after, Carpenter resigned her board position—or was pushed out—and left iVillage altogether. Various reasons were put forward for Carpenter's surprising and rapid departure. Some blamed her abrasive management style, which some said was responsible for the high turnover among iVillage staff. iVillage's five CFOs in just four years time, coupled with charges that Carpenter fired one CFO after she had questioned Carpenter about irregularities in the company's books, gave rise to questions about Carpenter's handling of company finances. The most important factor, however, was undoubtedly iVillage's poor showing on Wall Street, a downturn Carpenter was unable to turn around. By spring 2001 the firm's shares were hovering around the $1 mark and were threatened with delisting by NASDAQ.

McCormick's appointment raised questions of its own, most prominently about the wisdom of installing a man as the head and public face of a Web site aimed at women. However, McCormick made changes right away. He signaled a move away from e-commerce by selling off iBaby, iVillage's online baby shop. In early 2001, he oversaw iVillage's purchase of its main competitor, Women.com, for $25 million in cash. Publicly it was referred as a merger because the Hearst Corporation, Women.com's primary shareholder, made a $20 million investment in iVillage. The move created a mega-women's site and made iVillage the default choice of advertisers looking to reach women through the Web. As of fall 2001, iVillage had still not had a single profitable quarter.

FURTHER READING:

Barlas, Pete. ''Investors Find Way To 'Women's' Web.'' *Investor's Business Daily,* August 5, 1998.

———. ''It Takes NBC To Build Ivillage.'' *Investor's Business Daily,* November 30, 1998.

''iVillage.'' *IPO Reporter,* March 15, 1999.

''iVillage and AT&T to Launch First Women's Internet.'' *Business Wire,* November 18, 1998.

''iVillage Announces Online Network for Women.'' *PR Newswire,* September 8, 1997.

Kaufman, Joanne. ''iVillage: Learning the Hard Way.'' *Fortune Small Business,* March 2001.

Scheier, Rachel. ''Working On a Cure for iVillage's Ills.'' *Daily News,* July 17, 2000.

Seo, Diane. ''Rivals Battle To Be New Online Force.'' *Los Angeles Times,* July 23, 1999.

Siwolop, Sana. ''A Shifting Landscape At the iVillage Offering.'' *New York Times,* March 21, 1999.

SEE ALSO: Carpenter, Candice; Community Model; Evans, Nancy; Virtual Communities; Women and the Internet